TOPICS IN KOREAN LANGUAGE AND LINGUISTICS

KLEAR-RILI Studies in Korean Language and Linguistics

TOPICS IN KOREAN LANGUAGE AND LINGUISTICS

Ho-min Sohn

고려대학교출판부
KOREA UNIVERSITY PRESS

Korea University Press
82-2-3290-4230 (Tel.) 82-2-923-6311 (Fax)
http://www.kupress.com kupress@korea.ac.kr
145, Anam-Ro, Seongbuk-Gu, Seoul, 136-701 Korea

Published October 2013

ISBN 978-89-7641-832-6 93710

KRW 40,000

In memory of my dear mother

CONTENTS

PART I
LINGUISTIC AND PEDAGOGICAL OVERVIEW

PART II
STRUCTURAL DYNAMISM

PART III
SOCIOLINGUISTIC AND PRAGMATIC ISSUES

PART IV
TEACHING KOREAN AS A FOREIGN LANGUAGE

PREFACE

Topics in Korean Language and Linguistics is an anthology of selected papers on Korean language and linguistics that I have written for academic conferences, journals, and/or chapters in edited books during the past twenty odd years.

The idea of publishing my widely dispersed papers in a single monograph for easy access was often suggested by my graduate students and colleagues. Dr. Seok Hoon You of Korea University pushed this idea forward and gratefully made arrangements with the Korea University Press to publish this monograph.

A total of thirty-four papers were selected to encompass topics on diverse aspects of Korean language and linguistics. These papers are topically classified into four major categories: (a) linguistic and pedagogical overview, (b) structural dynamism, (c) sociolinguistic and pragmatic issues, and (d) teaching Korean as a foreign language.

I retained the contents of original papers intact, even though inevitably there are partial repetitions of contents across some chapters, with the exception of unifying notations, correcting typos, and making minor clarifications. I did not unify the two Romanization systems that I had used to transcribe Korean expressions: the Yale system and the McCune-Reischauer system. I had used the former in papers addressed to linguists and the latter in the papers addressed to general readers. In this volume, only the use of the latter system is so indicated in the first-page footnote (*) of relevant chapters, otherwise the Yale system is used.

I have taken the liberty of reprinting my papers and chapters from various journals, edited books, and proceedings. I extend my utmost gratitude to the relevant journal editors, monograph editors, publishers, and conference organizers. I indicated the sources of the papers with due acknowledgements in the first-page footnote (*) of each chapter.

I take this opportunity to express many thanks to my teachers, colleagues, and former and current graduate students for providing me with continued encouragement, support, and love. I extend my heartfelt thanks to Seok Hoon You and the Korea University Press for enabling this volume to see the light.

Ho-min Sohn
Honolulu, August 2013

ABBREVIATIONS

ABL	ablative particle
AC	accusative particle
AD	adverbializer ender
ADC	adverbial clause
AH	addressee honorific suffix
AP	apperceptive ender
CAS	causative suffix
CK	contemporary Korean
CLS	classifier
CM	comitative particle
CN	connective particle
COM	complementizer
COP	copula
DC	declarative sentence ender
DR	directional particle
DS	disjunctive particle
DT	dative particle
DF	definitive suffix
EMK	Early Middle Korean
EMP	emphasis
EP	explicit performative
EXC	exclamatory
FC	focal clause
FML	familiar-level ender
GL	goal particle
GN	genitive particle
HLOC	honorific locative particle
HSM	honorific subject marker
HT	honorific title
IM, IMP	imperative sentence ender
IN	indicative mood suffix
INF	infinitive suffix
INT	intimate ender
IO	indirect object particle
ISA	indirect speech act
LC, LOC	locative/goal particle
LMK	Late Middle Korean
MK	Middle Korean
MOD	modal suffix
MOK	Modern Korean
NM	nominative particle
NOM	nominalizer
OH	object honorific suffix
PAS	passive suffix
POL	polite ender
PR	propositive sentence ender
PRM	promissive ender
PRS	prospective relativizer suffix
PST	past tense suffix
Q	question (interrogative) sentence ender
QT	quotative particle
RL	relativizer suffix
RT	retrospective mood suffix
SC	supporting or subordinate clause
SH	subject honorific suffix
SK	Sino-Korean
SR	source particle
SS	speaker-subject suffix
SUF	suffix
SUG/SUP	suggestive/suppositive suffix
TC	topic particle
VOC	vocative particle

TABLE OF ROMANIZATION SYSTEMS

The following table shows correspondences among the hankul letters, the Yale Romanization system (Yale), the McCune-Reischauer (M-R) system, and the current Korean government system (ROK).

• *Consonants*

Hankul	Yale	McCune-Reischauer	ROK
ㄱ	*k*	*k, g*	*g, k*
ㄲ	*kk*	*kk, k*	*kk, k*
ㄴ	*n*	*n*	*n*
ㄷ	*t*	*t, d*	*d, t*
ㄸ	*tt*	*tt*	*tt*
ㄹ	*l*	*l, r*	*r, l*
ㅁ	*m*	*m*	*m*
ㅂ	*p*	*p, b*	*b, p*
ㅃ	*pp*	*pp*	*pp*
ㅅ	*s*	*s, t*	*s, t*
ㅆ	*ss*	*ss*	*ss, t*
ㅇ*	*ng*	*ng*	*ng*
ㅈ	*c*	*ch, j, t*	*j, t*
ㅉ	*cc*	*tch*	*jj*
ㅊ	*ch*	*ch'*	*ch, t*
ㅋ	*kh*	*k'*	*k*
ㅌ	*th*	*t'*	*t*
ㅍ	*ph*	*p'*	*p*
ㅎ	*h*	*h*	*h, t*

* This letter occurs in both initial and final position of a syllable block, as in 아 *a*, 강 *kang*, and 앙 *ang*. The sound *ng* is associated with only the final ㅇ, while the initial ㅇ has a null sound value.

• *Vowels and diphthongs*

Hankul	Yale	McCune-Reischauer	ROK
ㅏ	*a*	*a*	*a*
ㅐ	*ay*	*ae*	*ae*
ㅑ	*ya*	*ya*	*ya*
ㅒ	*yay*	*yae*	*yae*
ㅓ	*e*	*ŏ*	*eo*
ㅔ	*ey*	*e*	*e*
ㅕ	*ye*	*yŏ*	*yeo*
ㅖ	*yey*	*ye*	*ye*
ㅗ	*o*	*o*	*o*
ㅘ	*wa*	*wa*	*wa*
ㅙ	*way*	*wae*	*wae*
ㅚ	*oy*	*oe*	*oe*
ㅛ	*yo*	*yo*	*yo*
ㅜ	*wu**	*u*	*u*
ㅝ	*we*	*wŏ*	*wo*
ㅞ	*wey*	*we*	*we*
ㅟ	*wi*	*wi*	*wi*
ㅠ	*yu*	*yu*	*yu*
ㅡ	*u*	*ŭ*	*eu*
ㅢ	*uy*	*ŭi*	*ui*
ㅣ	*i*	*i*	*i*

* Romanized as *u* after *p, pp, ph,* and *y.*

• ***Spelling examples***

Hankul	Yale	McCune-Reischauer	ROK
한국 'Korea'	*Hankwuk*	*Han'guk*	*Han-guk*
한글 'Korean alphabet'	*hankul*	*han'gŭl*	*han-geul*
조선 '조선 dynasty'	*Cosen*	*Chosŏn*	*Joseon*
대전 '대전 city'	*Taycen*	*Taejŏn*	*Daejeon*
풀 'grass'	*phul*	*p'ul*	*pul*

• ***Middle Korean hankul letters***

The Middle Korean *hankul* letters that represented the sounds which are no longer used in contemporary Korean are Romanized as follows in this volume.

ㅸ	*β*
ㅿ	z
ㆆ	*ʔ*
ㆍ	*ó*
ㅇ	*ɦ*

Part I

LINGUISTIC AND PEDAGOGICAL OVERVIEW

1 Salient Features of Korean*

1. Introduction

Korean is the only native language spoken on the Korean peninsula and is spoken overseas as a second or foreign language. In terms of the number of speakers, Korean is rated as the eleventh or twelveth among as many as six thousand languages existing on the globe. The current population of South Korea is approximately 50 million and that of North Korea around 24.5 million. Some 6 million Koreans (8 percent of the total Korean population) reside outside of the Korean peninsula, the major countries with a large Korean population being China (2 million), the United States (2.1 million), Japan (700,000), and the former Soviet Union (500,000). Due to constant immigration and natural population increase, Koreans in the United States have become the fastest-growing segment of the worldwide overseas Korean population.

As a foreign language, Korean was first taught at St. Petersburg University in Russia in 1897 and was subsequently taught in many countries in Europe, America, Asia, and the Pacific. It was hardly popular among non-Koreans, however, until quite recently. Interest has boomed since the latter half of the 1970s, when Korea began to gain visibility mainly due to its rapid economic growth, the massive overseas emigration of its people, and the South Korean government's deep concern with and commitment to globalizing Korean language and culture. Korean is now being learned by an ever-increasing number of non-Koreans worldwide, as well as by ethnic Koreans overseas.

Salient features of Korean are examined through a brief survey of its genetic affiliation, historical development, dialectal variations, vocabulary, the Korean alphabet *han'gŭl*, speech sounds, word structure, sentence structure, and linguistic etiquette (politeness and honorifics).[1]

---

* This paper was originally written for a chapter in an aborted collaborative book project titled *Korea: Its Tradition, Culture and Society*. A slightly shortened version appeared as chapter 7 in Sohn, H., S. Cheon, and H. Jeong (eds.), *Essentials of Korean Culture* (Korea University Press, 2013). The McCune-Reischauer system of Romanization is followed in transcribing Korean expressions in this chapter.

2. Genetic affiliation

Little authentic documentation is available on the origin of the Korean language. Earlier forms of the language are not readily accessible because written historical data are scarce and cannot be traced far back. Some old language fragments are available only in the literature dating from the eleventh century, such as *Kyunyŏjŏn* (Life of the Great Master Kyunyŏ, 1075) by Hyŏngnyŏn Chŏng, *Kyerim yusa* (*Things on Korea*, 1103–4) by Chinese Sung-dynasty scholar Sun Mu, *Samguk sagi* (*Historical Record of the Three Kingdoms*, 1145) by Kim Pusik, and *Samguk yusa* (*Memorabilia of the Three Kingdoms*, 1285) by Monk Iryŏn, all of which are written in Chinese characters. Moreover, much of the earlier vocabulary has been either irretrievably lost or obscured by succeeding waves of language contacts, including a massive influx of Chinese loan words.

Numerous linguists, however, have proposed that Korean and Japanese are genetically related with each other and these two languages are related to Altaic languages. Some attempts have also been made to relate Korean and Japanese to Austronesian and Dravidian languages.[2] While an Austronesian stratum is quite dense in Japanese, however, any hypothesis associating Korean to Austronesian is premature. The Dravidian hypothesis deserves further investigation in view of many lexical look-alikes and interesting grammatical similarities (cf. Sohn 1999). In the following, only the linkage between Korean and Japanese and the Altaic hypothesis will be briefly touched on.

2.1 Genetic linkage between Korean and Japanese

Available lexical, phonological, and grammatical evidence indicates that Korean and Japanese are each other's closest sister language, although they are not mutually intelligible and their relationship is much more distant than that between, say, English and French. The common origin of Korean and Japanese was proposed as early as 1717 by Arai Hakuseki, a Tokugawa Confucian, and again in 1781 by Fujii Teikan, a pioneer of modern archaeology in Japan.[3] The most significant breakthrough, however, was the work of Martin (1966: 185-251), who systematically compared 320 sets of word pairs, reconstructed their hypothetical original forms. Let us observe below some of the word pairs that Martin presented.[4]

---

1 For an extensive discussion of the sections in this chapter, see Sohn (1999/2001). Further useful references are Martin (1992), I. Lee and Ramsey (2000), and K. Lee and Ramsey (2011).

2 Hulbert (1905); Ohno (1970; 1981); Murayama (1976: 413–36); and Clippinger (1984: 1–57).

3 Miller (1967: 61–62).

Korean	Japanese	gloss
pŏl	*pati*	'bee'
pul-	*púk-*	'blow'
pŏl	*pára*	'plain'
pyŏl	*posi*	'star'
mal	*masú*	'measure'
kom	*kumá*	'bear'
kut-	*kata-*	'hard'
kŏt	*kotó*	'thing'
talk	*tori*	'chicken'
tat-	*tód(i)-*	'close it'
tal	*tukí*	'moon'
sŏm	*sima*	'island'

The grammatical similarities between Korean and Japanese are conspicuous. Both are typical subject-object-verb (SOV) order languages. Thus, all predicates (verbs and adjectives) come at the end of a sentence or a clause. All modifiers (adjectives, adverbs, numerals, possessive phrases, relative clauses, etc.) precede their modified elements; and all particles follow their associated nominals as postpositions. Both languages are agglutinative in word formation, in that numerous particles and suffixes may be agglutinated to roots or stems in fixed order. Both are pitch-accent languages although in Korean only two of seven dialects (Kyŏngsang and Hamgyŏng) remain so. Both are honorific languages in that intricate human relationships are encoded in the linguistic structure in terms of speech levels and honorifics.[5]

2.2 Altaic hypothesis

Many scholars also claim that Korean and Japanese belong to the Altaic language family in that they display numerous Altaic features.[6] This Altaic hypothesis assigns Korean and Japanese to the Altaic family, which is composed mainly of Turkic, Mongolian, and Manchu-Tungus groups that range widely in the regions west and north of China. Original (or proto) Altaic is thought to be

4 The Japanese pitch accents are marked on the vowels concerned. Whitman (1985) also analyzed Korean-Japanese correspondences in vowels, consonants, and accents, presenting 352 lexical correspondence sets, many of which are shared with Martin's. Recently, Vovin (2009) claims that most of the word pairs that Martin and Whitman regard as cognates are in fact borrowings.

5 Kuno (1973); Shibatani (1990); and Sohn (1999/2001).

6 K. Lee (1976); B. Sung (1997).

a linguistic unity spoken sometime during the Neolithic period, and its original homeland is assumed to be somewhere in northern or north-central Eurasia. According to the Altaic hypothesis, original Koreans and Japanese were Altaic people who migrated to Korea and Japan, bringing with them the basic elements of their languages.

Shiratori Kurakichi (1914–6) was the first scholar to claim the Korean–Altaic relationship, based on his 595-entry vocabulary comparing Korean and other Altaic languages.[7] Finnish linguist G. J. Ramstedt (e.g. 1949), however, was the first to assign Korean to the Altaic family in a systematic way. For instance, Ramstedt and others found that the original Altaic word-initial consonant *p* had the following development: *p* > *f* > *h* > *ZERO*. Thus, for example, 'to pray' is Korean *pil-*, Manchu *firu-*, Evenki *hiruge-*, Middle Mongolian *hirwige-*, Mongolian *irwige-*; 'village, plain' are Manchu *falga*, Mongolian *ail*, Turkish *al*, Korean *pŏl*; and 'to blow' is Korean *pul-*, Manchu *fulgiye*, Lamut *hu-*, Middle Mongolian *hulie-*, Mongolian *uliye-*. Japanese may be included in the above set in view of its having *h* in such words as *hara* 'plain', *huk-* 'to blow', and *haru* 'spring'.

Korean and Altaic languages share many grammatical features. As in Korean and Japanese, the basic word-order of Altaic languages is SOV; all modifiers (words and clauses) precede the elements they modify, while postpositions occur in place of prepositions; no affix exists in adjectives to express the comparative or superlative degree; the endings indicating sentence-types such as declarative, interrogative, propositive, and imperative are placed at the end of the sentence; and sentences may consist only of a predicate, with the contextually understood subject and other understood elements omitted.

Another shared feature is that the internal structure of words common to Korean, Japanese, and Altaic languages is agglutinative, in that words are formed by adding one or more semantically clear-cut suffixes or particles to an unchanging stem. Furthermore, existence of vowel harmony (e.g. Korean bright/dark (Yang/Yin) vowel harmony as in *kkobak-kkobak* vs. *kkupŏk-kkubŏk* 'noddingly') and the lack of liquid sounds (*r* and *l*) in the initial position of native (not Sino-Korean) words are features shared by Altaic, Japanese, and Korean. In short, the Altaic origin of Korean and Japanese is a generally accepted hypothesis, although the hypothesis must be further refined and verified.

3. Historical development

3.1 Old Korean period (prehistory to tenth century)

Due to the dearth of reliable data, the nature of the Korean language prior to the period of the Koguryŏ kingdom in the north and the Samhan states (Mahan, Chinhan, and Pyŏnhan) in the south of the Korean peninsula is difficult to access. The few fragmentary records in *Wei Chih* (*Records of Wei*, written by Chen Shou in the third century), *Houhan Shu* (*History of Later Chinese Han*, written by Fan Yeh in the latter half of the fifth century), and *Chou Shu* (*History of Chou*, compiled at the beginning of the seventh century) lead us to believe that the Koguryŏ language was Tungusic, along with the languages of Puyŏ, Okchŏ, and Yemaek; that the languages of the Samhan states were merely dialects of each other; and that Koguryŏ and other northern languages, on the one hand, and the Samhan languages, on the other, were considerably different.

Regarding linguistic data of the three Old Korean kingdoms—Silla (57 B.C.–A.D. 935), Paekche (18 B.C.–A.D. 660), and Koguryŏ (37 B.C.–A.D. 668), only some reflexes have been observed in some existing records written in the Idu (Clerk Reading) script of Chinese characters, such as the proper nouns in *Samguk sagi* (1145), fourteen vernacular poems in *Samguk yusa* (1285), and eleven poems in *Kyunyŏjŏn* (1075). Old Korean forms have been reconstructed from these linguistic fragments written in Idu. While very little is known about Koguryŏ and Paekche, information about the Silla language is relatively abundant. The languages of Silla and Paekche, which absorbed Samhan, are regarded as much more similar to each other than they are to the Koguryŏ language.

Distinctly Altaic, the Koguryŏ language is the only one of the northern languages with some extant linguistic data, limited to a vocabulary of about eighty words, which appears mainly in the *Samguk sagi*. While showing a similarity to Tungus languages (e.g. Koguryŏ *nuami* vs. Tungus *namu* 'sea', Koguryŏ *nanŏn* vs. Tungus *nadan* 'seven'), Koguryŏ also reveals a certain likeness to Japanese and to the Silla language. The Paekche language was a Samhan dialect. Although the ruling class came from Koguryŏ, evidence does not indicate an extensive influence of the northern group. For instance, according to a record in *Chou Shu,* the word for 'king' was *woraka* in the language of the ruling class and *kiji* in the language of the commoners. The latter appears to correspond to the Silla word *kyesye* or *kese* 'king'.[7] Some data in *Samguk sagi* reveal that the Paekche language was similar to the Silla language and Middle Korean (MK), as shown by *turak* 'stone' (MK *tolh*), *sa* 'new' (MK *say*), and *pŭri* 'fire' (MK *pŭl*). [8]A glimpse of the Silla language leads us to regard contemporary Korean as the descendant of the language of Unified Silla and the succeeding dynasties. The language of Unified Silla is assumed to have been composed mainly of the Samhan dialects with very little influence from the northern languages.

7 B. Kim (1984: 104–05).

8 I. Lee, S. Lee, and Chae (1997: 289).

The period of Old Korean was the initial stage of the influx of Chinese character words. In the sixth century, the titles of the kings were changed from pure Korean to Sino-Korean terms, using the term *wang* 'king'. In the middle of the eighth century, i.e. during the Unified Silla period, native place names were altered and modeled after the Chinese tradition, so that they consisted of two Chinese characters as they do now.

3.2 Middle Korean period (tenth century to sixteenth century)

With the founding of the Koryŏ dynasty (918–1392) in the early tenth century, the capital was moved from Kyŏngju (in Kyŏngsang province) to Kaegyŏng (present Kaesŏng in North Korea), which became the new political and cultural center. Early Middle Korean data in the Koryŏ period were recorded in Chinese characters, whereas Late Middle Korean data in the Chosŏn period were recorded in *han'gŭl*, the Korean alphabet. The creation of *han'gŭl* made extensive and exact transcriptions of the Korean language possible for the first time.

The Middle Korean period may be characterized by, among other things, the influx of a huge number of Chinese words into the Korean vocabulary. Before this period, Chinese words were limited, in general, to the names of places, people, and government ranks. But starting with the Koryŏ dynasty, Chinese words pervaded the spoken language alongside their exclusive use in writing. Due to the massive importation of words from this prestigious non-Altaic language, Korean has undergone a wide range of changes, not only in its vocabulary but also to a lesser degree in the sound system and word structure. Major properties of Middle Korean are summarized below.

The fifteenth century Korean (Middle Korean) contained some sounds, such as fricative *p/b* (represented as ㅸ), *z* (ㅿ), fricative *k/g* (ㆁ), *hh* (ㆅ), and *á* (sound between *a* and *o* represented by •), which are not used in Contemporary Korean. The system lacked the two current vowels *e* (ㅔ) and *ae* (ㅐ). Also, it had consonant clusters, each consisting of two or three consonants, which, unlike in Contemporary Korean, occurred in word-initial positions, as in *ptŭt* 'intention', *psi* 'seed', *pchak* 'pair', *pskul* 'honey', and *pstay* 'time' [contemporary forms are *ttŭs* (뜻), *ssi* (씨), *tchak* (짝), *kkul* (꿀), and *ttae* (때), respectively)].

Middle Korean was a tonal language. There were three tones: high tone (indicated by one dot to the left of the *han'gŭl* syllable block), rising tone (by two dots to the left), and low tone (by the absence of dots). Tones ceased to exist in the sixteenth century, however, except in the Kyŏngsang and Hamgyŏng dialects.

Fifteenth-century Korean (MK) had more rigid vowel harmony than Contemporary Korean (K). Yang (bright) vowels *o, a, á* occurred only with Yang or neutral (*i*) vowels, and Yin (dark) vowels *u, ŭ, ŏ* occurred only with Yin or neutral vowels, as in MK *namo* : K *namu* 'tree' and MK *sarám ál* : K *saram ŭl* 'person' (object). Notice that contemporary counterparts do not necessarily manifest vowel harmony.

There were more complex honorific patterns than in Contemporary Korean. Middle Korean also developed a host of other linguistic characteristics that remain the same in Modern and Contemporary Korean. As for the lexicon, there were already a large number of Chinese loan words.

3.3 Modern and Contemporary Korean

Modern Korean (seventeenth to nineteenth century) is sharply different from Middle Korean as a result of the accumulated changes that occurred during the Middle Korean period. Modern Korean underwent even further changes, probably expedited by the social and political disorder in the wake of the seven-year Japanese invasion that started in 1592, the popularization of vernacular literature, contact with foreign languages, and the importation of Western civilization. Since the latter half of Modern Korean is much the same as Contemporary Korean, only the changes that happened primarily in its early half will be taken into account here.

Word-initial consonant clusters such as *pt-*, *ps-*, and *pch-* were reduced to tensed consonants, as already indicated (e.g. *psi* > *ssi* 'seed'). The consonant *z* disappeared in the early part of the seventeenth century. This sound was deleted in most dialects, as in *ŏbŏzi* > *ŏbŏi* 'parents'. There are exceptions in the southern dialects (Chŏlla, Kyŏngsang, and Cheju), where in many words it has become *s*, as in *chizŭmyŏn* > *chisŭmyŏn* (southern dialects), *chiŭmyŏn* (elsewhere) 'if (he) builds'.

The vowel *á* became extinct in the latter part of the eighteenth century. It became *ŭ*, *o*, or *a*, as in *modán* > *modŭn* 'all' and *stál* > *ttal* 'daughter'. Vowel harmony started to break down due partly to these changes because *á* is a bright vowel and *ŭ* is a dark vowel. The other major cause was the influx of Chinese words, where no vowel harmony was observed.

A number of new grammatical suffixes and particles have developed from existing elements, such as the past tense suffix *-at/-ŏt* (< *-a/ŏ* 'and' + *it* 'exist'), the particle *choch'a* 'even' (< *choch'* 'follow' + *-a* 'and') the particle *put'ŏ* 'from' (< *put'* 'stick to' + *-ŏ* 'and'), the particle *hago* 'and, with' (< *ha* 'do' + *-go* 'and'), and the particle *pakke* 'except' (< *pakk* 'outside' + *e* 'at').

Many native words went out of use due to the continuous influx of Chinese words and new words formed with Chinese characters. For instance, native words like *moe* (< *moy*) 'mountain' and *karam* 'river' were replaced by Sino-

Korean words *san* and *kang,* respectively. This happened throughout the Middle and Modern Korean periods. On the other hand, new Western cultural words began to be introduced into the Korean vocabulary in the Modern Korean period, largely due to the importation of books on science and religion as well as other cultural items and through contacts with foreigners in Korea.

Contemporary Korean has undergone an unprecedentedly complex history: the entry of missionaries, the collision between foreign powers in Korea, Japanese domination of Korea for thirty-five years, liberation from Japanese rule, division into North and South Korea, wide international contacts, the Korean War, rapid economic and technological growth, and social transformation in recent decades. All these events have had various effects on the language.

4. Dialectal variations

4.1 Dialectal division

The Korean language is relatively homogeneous, with good mutual intelligibility among the speakers from different areas. There are, however, minor but rather distinct geographically based dialectal differences. The Korean peninsula, including both North and South Korea, may be divided into seven dialectal zones, which correspond by and large to administrative districts as described below.[9]

a. Hamgyŏng Zone: North and Hamgyŏng Provinces extending to the north of Ch'ŏngp'yŏng, and Huch'ang in North P'yŏngan Province
b. P'yŏngan Zone: North and South P'yŏngan Provinces (excluding Huch'ang)
c. Central Zone: Kyŏnggi Province, Kangwŏn Province, Hwanghae Province, and South Hamgyŏng Province extending to Yŏnghŭng to the north
d. Ch'ungch'ŏng Zone: North and South Ch'ungch'ŏng Provinces and Kŭmsan and Muju in North Chŏlla Province
e. Kyŏngsang Zone: North and South Kyŏngsang Provinces
f. Chŏlla Zone: North and South Chŏlla Provinces (other than Kŭmsan and Muju)
g. Cheju Zone: Cheju Province (the island of Cheju)

The seven dialectal zones and administrative districts are roughly indicated in the following map.

9 As H. Kim (1982) indicates, although Seoul is a separate administrative unit, it is regarded as part of Kyŏnggi Province, in view of its being surrounded by the province.

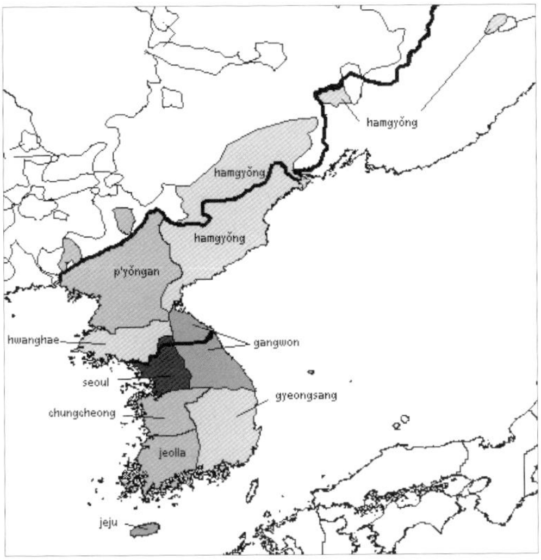

The dialect used by the Korean community in the Yanbian Autonomous Prefecture of China in Manchuria can be included in the Hamgyŏng Zone because it has evolved as part of the Hamgyŏng dialect due to the early immigration of Hamgyŏng people to that area and their subsequent linguistic contacts. The dialects spoken by Koreans in the other areas of China and other countries around the globe also reflect the seven dialectal zones, depending on the areas from which the speakers and their ancestors originally migrated.

The major cause of the formation of the dialectal zones has been geographic, but historical and political factors have also played important roles. For instance, the characteristics of the Cheju dialect have been formed largely due to its isolation from the mainland. Also, the two neighboring areas, Kyŏngsang and Chŏlla, manifest great differences since, in the past, there was no major transportation network connecting the two zones. Historically, too, these two zones were under two different dynasties, Kyŏngsang being the Silla kingdom and Chŏlla, the Paekche kingdom. Another historical factor explains the demarcation between the Hamgyŏng dialect and the Central dialect, where there is no natural barrier. During the Koryŏ (918–1392) and Chosŏn (1392–1910) dynasties, the area between Chŏngp'yŏng in the Hamgyŏng Zone and Yŏnghŭng in the Central Zone was a place of constant battle between the Manchu tribes called Yŏjin (Jurchen or Nuchen) in the north and the Koreans in the south. After the Manchu tribes were driven away to the north during the Chosŏn dynasty, P'yŏngan Province was inhabited by people from the neighboring Hwanghae Province, and Hamgyŏng Province was settled mainly by people from

Kyŏngsang Province in the south. This is the reason for the similarity between the P'yŏngan dialect and the Central dialect, on one hand, and between the Hamgyŏng dialect and the Kyŏngsang dialect on the other. While influencing each other, the two northern dialects have constantly been influenced by foreign languages such as Chinese, Tungus, Yŏjin, and Russian, a fact responsible for the maturation of the P'yŏngan and Hamgyŏng dialects.

4.2 Dialectal features

Different linguistic features distinguish Korean dialects. Of particular interest are the following sound patterns.

While Middle Korean was a tonal language with low, high, and rising tones, tones have since disappeared in the Central (standard) and other dialects, except in the Kyŏngsang and Hamgyŏng dialects (e.g. *mal* (L) 'horse', *mal* (H) 'measuring unit', *mal* (R) 'word'). Instead, the Central and other dialects retain vowel length in the places where a rising tone occurred, except in the Cheju and some other dialects, where neither tones nor vowel length occurs.

The Middle Korean vowel *á* is reflected in four different shapes in Contemporary Korean: *a, ŭ, o*, and *á*. As discussed earlier, the first three shapes exist in all dialectal zones, but the Cheju dialect retains the unchanged form (e.g. Cheju *tál* vs. standard *tal* 'moon'; Cheju *hák* vs. standard *hŭk* 'soil'). While Middle Korean word-initial *á* is generally reflected as *a,* it has become *o* after a bilabial consonant only in Kyŏngsang and Chŏlla Provinces and the Yukchin area in Hamgyŏng Province, e.g. *mol* vs. standard *mal* (from Middle Korean *mál*) 'horse'; *p'ori* vs. standard *p'ari* (from Middle Korean *p'ári*) 'house fly'. There is no distinction between *ŏ* and *ŭ* in the Kyŏngsang dialect, both sounding like *ŏ*.

The Middle Korean consonant *z* has been completely deleted in all words in the Central and P'yŏngan zones, whereas it remains as *s* in many dialects, as in *muu* (< MK *muzu*) 'turnip' (South Ch'ungch'ŏng, Kangwŏn, Kyŏnggi, Hwanghae, P'yŏngan, South Hamgyŏng), *musu* (Chŏlla, Ch'ungch'ŏng, Kangwŏn, South Hamgyŏng), *musi* (Chŏlla, Kyŏngsang), *mui* (Kangwŏn, Hwanghae), and *muyu* (Kyŏnggi, Hwanghae).

The Middle Korean "fricative" *β* has changed to *w* in the Central and many other dialects and to *b* in Kyŏngsang and Hamgyŏng Provinces and some areas of Chŏlla and Ch'ungch'ŏng Provinces. For instance, Middle Korean *saβi* 'shrimp' is reflected variously as *saeu* (Central, Hwanghae, Kyŏnggi, Kangwŏn, South and North P'yŏngan), *saeo, saebi/syaebi* (South and North Hamgyŏng, South and North Chŏlla, South and North Kyŏngsang), and *saebaengi* (South and North Ch'ungch'ŏng, southern Kyŏnggi).

Northern dialectal zones including the provinces of P'yŏngan and Hamgyŏng retain the pronunciation of initial *r* in Sino-Korean words, whereas the rest of the dialectal zones have either lost it (before *i* or *y*) or replaced it with *n* (elsewhere). This *r* is often replaced with *n* before *i* or *y* in the P'yŏngan zone, as in *ribal/nibal* (standard *ibal*) 'haircut', *ryŏksa/nŏksa* (standard *yŏksa*) 'history', and *rodong* (standard *nodong*) 'labor'. The P'yŏngan Zone and the Yukchin dialect of North Hamgyŏng Province also retain the pronunciation of initial *n* before *i* or *y*, whereas the other dialects have lost it, as in *nyŏja/nŏja* (standard *yŏja*) 'female', *nima* (standard *ima*) 'forehead', *nilgup* (standard *ilgop*) 'seven', and *nu-wŏl* (standard *yu-wŏl*) 'June'.

There are three dialectal groups in regard to palatalization (change to a palatal sound): (a) dialects with no palatalization, as in *tŏl* (standard *chŏl*) 'Buddhist temple' and *tŏmsim* (*chŏmsim*) 'lunch' (P'yŏngan, Yukchin in North Hamgyŏng), (b) dialects with change from *t/d/t'* to palatal *ch/j/ch'* before a suffix beginning with *i* and *y*, as in *kat'* + *i* > *kach'i* 'in the same way' (all dialects except (a)), and (c) dialects with change from *t/d/t'* and *k/g/k'* to palatal *ch/j/ch'* before *i* and *y*, as in *chirŭm* (standard *kirŭm*) 'oil', *chil* (standard *kil*) 'road', and *chŏt* (*kyŏt*) 'side' (Kyŏngsang, Chŏlla, Hamgyŏng, Ch'ungch'ŏng, Cheju, Kangwŏn).

Many characteristics are quite unique either to each dialectal zone or to only a few zones. The general intonation patterns, utterance tempo, and sound qualities are quite different from one dialect to another. Vocabulary, word structure, and sentence structure are all slightly dissimilar.[10]

4.3 Linguistic divergence in South and North Korea

In addition to the geographically based dialectal differences discussed thus far, there is a superordinate politico-social dialectal bifurcation between North and South Korea. Linguistic divergence between the two Koreas since 1945 has been accelerated mainly by three interrelated factors: (a) complete physical insulation for more than fifty years, (b) polarized political, ideological, and social distinctions (with socialism in the North and capitalism in the South), and (c) the different language policies implemented by the two governments, culminating in North Korea's institution of the P'yŏngyang-based 'Cultured Language' (*munhwaŏ*) as their standard speech as against the traditional Seoul-based 'Standard Language' of South Korea (*p'yojun-mal*). Linguistic divergence appears, to varying degrees, in the lexicon, sound patterns, grammar, usage, and orthography, with the lexicon being affected most. The brief survey below covers the different language policies involved and the range of linguistic divergence ef-

10 Sohn (1999/2001).

fected.

As soon as Korea was liberated from Japan in 1945, use of the Korean language and *han'gŭl* was restored. The two separated Koreas independently launched extensive crusades against illiteracy based on *han'gŭl*. Thus, language-purification movements have been continuing in both Koreas, with essentially the same spirit but with considerably different results.

Noteworthy is the evolution of language policies toward the use of Chinese characters in the two Koreas. In South Korea, due to the Korean Language Society's forceful movement to eliminate Chinese characters altogether in , the National Assembly passed a law to enforce the exclusive use of *han'gŭl* in 1948. While schools observed the law, society did not. Presidential decrees for the exclusive use of *han'gŭl* in 1956 and 1957 achieved only limited success, such as the *han'gŭl*-only practice in government documents and in street signboards, but the general public and newspapers kept using characters. Thus, in 1964 the Ministry of Education (MOE) agreed to allow the teaching of 1,300 common Chinese characters in elementary (600), intermediate (400), and high (300) schools. At the urging of *han'gŭl* scholars, however, the MOE again enforced a *han'gŭl*-only policy in January 1970, allowing no characters in documents and textbooks in elementary and secondary schools. The ensuing situation in which even high school graduates would be unable to read newspapers led the MOE in 1972 to reinstate character education, choosing 1,800 basic characters to be taught in secondary schools, but not in elementary schools. As a result, from 1975, secondary school textbooks were revised to include Chinese characters side by side with *han'gŭl*. This practice still obtains at present, although the 1,800 characters do not have a binding force on South Korean society. Pros and cons for the exclusive use of *han'gŭl* and the mixed use of *han'gŭl* and hantcha are a perrenial issue involving the academia, socio-political and business circles, the press, and the general public.

In North Korea, on the other hand, the language policies from 1945 to the early 1960s were aimed at eradicating illiteracy by eliminating the use of Chinese characters and promoting intensive Korean language education, thereby facilitating to popularize the doctrine of socialism. Through his 1964 and 1966 Teachings (via dialogues with linguists), however, Jim Il Song revived character education for reading purposes only, so that the people could read South Korean publications as well as the books and records of the past. Thus, a total of 3,000 Chinese characters are currently taught from the fifth grade of elementary schools to college (2,000 characters before college and 1,000 characters in college).[11]

---

11 M. Kim (1999).

Significant linguistic divergence between the two Koreas has been caused by North Korea's initiation of the Pyongyang-based Cultured Language as their standard speech as against the traditional Seoul-based Standard Language of Korea. The Cultured Language policies have also been implemented according to Kim Il Song's above-mentioned two sets of Teachings (1964 and 1966). Kim directed the linguists to preserve and develop the national characteristics of the Korean language (*chuch'e*-oriented Korean) based on the speech of Pyongyang, denouncing Seoul-based Standard Language as having lost its legitimacy as a national language because "it is deprived of national characteristics and popular elements and has become the speech of bourgeoisie, a jumble filled with Western, Japanese, and Chinese elements." His directives include, among others, that coinage of new words and recovery of old words be based on native elements; introduce fine dialectal words into the Cultured Speech lexicon; use of loan words be limited and change new loan words to native words, except technical terms; and unnecessary Sino-Korean words be removed from dictionaries, while preserving native-like Sino-Korean words. Despite the unprecedented language reform that has taken place to implement Kim's Teachings, it has turned out that Cultured Language is, in fact, based much more on Standard Language than on the speech of Pyongyang in great many respects. For instance, unlike the Pyongyang words *abaji* 'father', *omani* 'mother', *konaengi* 'cat', *kau* 'scissors', and *tangch'u* 'red pepper', both Cultured and Standard words are *apŏji, ŏmŏni, koyangi, kawi,* and *koch'u,* respectively.

Although pronunciations and spellings in the two Koreas also manifest noticeable differences,[12] the most significant linguistic divergence is in the lexicon, in that independent refinement movements based on divergent language policies have targteted lexical items primarily and most extensively. The targets are mainly Sino-Korean words and loan words.

In South Korea, for instance, in 1992 the Korean Government's Department of General Affairs published a list of 8,673 refined legal and administrative terms. In 1996, the Department of Culture and Sports issued a collection of 5,575 words refined from Japanese loans, Japanese-style Sino-Korean words, and English and other loanwords in areas such as construction, arts, sewing, daily life, politics, diatary, newspaper, forestry, and computer.[13]

In North Korea, lexical purification movement (*mal tadŭmki undong*) started from 1946 with the goals of making words easy, simple, concise, clear, and accurate, eliminating Japanese loans and Japanese-style Sino-Korean words,

12 Chon and Choy (1989: 258–70). Also see Sohn (1997: 193–217); MOE (1988); KLAC (1988).

13 S. Lee, et al. (1999); Y. Park (2001).

and refine wrong or undesirable expressions.[14] The movements have involved refining existing words, activating dialectal and obsolete native elements, and coining new words based on native elements as much as possible. In particular, since the 1960s, North Korea has carried out an all-out *mal tadŭmki* campaign as part of the Cultured Language movement in accordance with Kim Il Song's avobe-mentioned Teachings. As a result, in 1986, North Korea established approximately 25,000 refined words as standard.[15]

Although statistics indicates that some 63,000 North Korean words are different from the corresponding South Korean words, a major portion of the lexical differences is in spellings and pronunciations (e.g. South *iron* vs. North *riron* 'theory'; S. *nae.il* vs. N. *rae.il* 'tomorrow') and high-frequency daily words in the two Koreas manifest a high level of homogeneity, thus rarely hampering communication between the two Koreas.[16] Major lexical divergence is due to the use of an enormous quantity of English loanwords in South Korea and the great disparity in the use of technical terms in the two Koreas. While North Korea has refined the existing loan words and suppressed incoming foreign words as much as possible, changing them into appropriate native or common Sino-Korean words, South Korea, despite purification efforts, has been unable to block the massive, forceful, ever-increasing infiltration of English words into all areas of Korean life since the 1960s. The extent to which younger generation South Koreans use and abuse English loanwords is great indeed. T. Kim states that North Korean residents are totally unaware of 8,284 loanwords commonly used in South Korea, including such simple terms as *nyusŭ* 'news'.[17] The second distinct and treacherous area of lexical divergence is related to all kinds of technical terms, such as political, military, economic, legal, medical, mass media, and information technology terms. These terms are mostly related to loanwords and Sino-Korean words.

5. Korean vocabulary

Due to its long and frequent historical contacts with China and Japan and rapid modernization in all walks of life, Korea has come to have a rich vocabulary. Some 450,000 lexical items are entered in *Urimal K'ŭn Sajŏn* (A Great Dictionary of the Korean Language).[18] The contemporary Korean lexicon consists of approximately 30 percent native, 65 percent Sino-Korean (hereafter, SK) and 5

14 Chon and Choy (1989: 45); Y. Park (2001: 138).
15 Kwak (2001).
16 Chon and Choy (1989).
17 T. Kim (2001).
18 KLS (1991).

percent loan elements.

Native elements include not only the vocabulary essential to the maintenance of basic human life but also other items that are unique to the time-honored culture of traditional Korea. Thus, body parts, natural objects, flora and fauna, basic kinship and color terms, personal pronouns, low-level numerals, basic actions, physical and psychological states, items relating to essential food, clothing, and shelter, terms for agriculture and fishery, honorific expressions, onomatopoeia, and basic grammatical relations are all symbolized by native words, although many of the content words coexist with SK counterparts. [19]

Native terms for numbers go up to ninety-nine in Contemporary Korean. The higher numbers being taken over by either SK numerals (e.g. *paek il* '101') or SK-native compounds (e.g. *paek hana* '101'). Native numeral counters (e.g. *charu* for pencils, brooms, etc.; *k'yŏlle* 'pairs' for shoes, socks, gloves; *mari* for animals), are well developed, while there are also a number of SK (e.g. *kwŏn* 'volume', *tae* 'machine', *kae* 'item') and a small number of loan counters (e.g. *k'iro* 'kilogram, kilometer', *p'ŭro* 'per cent', *t'asŭ* 'dozen').

The Korean lexicon is characterized by the proliferation of several thousands of sound symbolic or ideophonic words, most of which belong to the native stock. Such words have delicate connotational nuances and not only give vividness, expressiveness, and vitality to daily human interactions but are widely employed for their effect in literary works of all genres. Many ideophonic words appear in two or more shapes, associated with different connotational variants of the same words, as in *p'adak* vs. *p'ŏdŏk* 'flapping, flopping, splashing', *norat'a* vs. *nurŏt'a* 'be yellow', *pantchak* vs. *pŏntchŏk* 'glittering', and *challang* vs. *ch'allang* vs. *tchallang* 'jingling'. As observed in these examples, sound symbolism is reflected in both vowels and consonants. As for vowels, "bright" (Yang) vowels *a, ae, o* tend to connote brightness, sharpness, lightness, smallness, thinness, and quickness, whereas "dark" (Ying) vowels *e*, *u*, *ŏ* indicate darkness, heaviness, dullness, slowness, deepness, and thickness. As for consonants, sound symbolic words show differences among plain, aspirated, and tensed consonants. A plain consonant tends to connote slowness, gentleness, heaviness, and bigness, an aspirated consonant flexibility, elasticity, crispness, and swiftness, and a tensed consonant compactness, tightness, hardness, smallness, and extra swiftness. For instance, *chul-jul, ch'ul-ch'ul*, and *tchul-tchul* 'trickling, flowing persistently' denote, among other things, an increasingly smaller quantity of liquid but faster action

Most of the native words have been either inherited or coined on the basis of the native stock. Some SK words were borrowed from written Chinese in

19 Sohn (1999/2001: 87–120).

ancient times and have undergone radical change either in form alone or in both form and meaning. In addition, a small number of words were introduced from spoken Chinese and have undergone formal and/or semantic change. Examples of these sorts are *paech'u* 'Chinese cabbage' (SK *paek-ch'ae* 'white vegetable'), *si-wŏl* (SK *sip-wŏl*) 'October'; *(l)yu-wŏl* (SK *(l)yuk-wŏl*) 'June'; *ka* 'edge' (SK *kye* 'edge', Ancient Chinese *kai*); *kage* 'store' (SK *ka-ga* 'false house'); *sarang* 'love' (SK *sa-ryang* 'consideration'); *sanyang* 'hunting' (SK *san-haeng* 'mountain going'); *ssŏlmae* 'sled' (SK *sŏl-ma* 'snow horse'); and *ssŭ* 'write' (SK *sŏ* 'write', Ancient Chinese *siwo*). All these forms are generally treated as native.[20]

Traditional borrowing was mainly from China. Although borrowings from Chinese ceased long ago, Chinese characters and the concepts they represent have been used expediently and productively to coin thousands of new words as needs arose. All Koreanized words based on Chinese-characters, whether they are ancient borrowings directly from China, reborrowings indirectly from Sino-Japanese, or coinages in Korea, are called Sino-Korean words, or *hanchaŏ* 'Chinese character words'. The SK origin of more than half of the total Korean vocabulary can be attributed to two facts: (a) that Chinese culture and learning permeated deeply all facets of Korean life in the past, as historically Korea long subordinated herself to the political and cultural influence of China, and (b) that, due to the ideographic and monosyllabic nature of the characters, SK forms facilitate new word formation, much more efficiently than native forms, to represent the new concepts and products that continuously appear as civilization progresses. Thus, nearly all terms in academic fields, politics, occupations, economy, law, society, and other cultural aspects, as well as personal, place, and institutional names, are SK words. Numerals, months, days of the week, color terms, and a large number of kinship terms and numeral counter nouns are also in SK. The majority of these terms were coined in Japan as Sino-Japanese and then introduced to Korea, as well as to China, since Japan, during the Meiji Restoration period, was the first nation in the East to import Western civilization and culture. The difference between Sino-Japanese and SK words is primarily in pronunciation.

The question of when Chinese and Chinese characters were first introduced into Korea remains unanswered due to the lack of historical data. The only deduction we can make, however, is that Chinese words and characters must have been used in Korea as early as the first century B.C., when Han China colonized the western and northern parts of the Korean peninsula and established its four commanderies there. A historical record shows that a Paekchean named Wang In went to Japan with many Chinese books around A.D. 400, suggesting that Chi-

20 Shim (1983); C. Kim (1993).

nese culture and characters had achieved considerable popularity in the Korea of the Three Kingdoms period. With the unification of the Korean peninsula by the Silla dynasty in 677, the use of Chinese characters gained more popularity in Korea in that Silla's unification was achieved with Tang China's military support and subsequently contact between the two countries became very frequent. Earlier, the name of the country and the title of the king were changed from native terms to SK terms in the fourth year of King Chijŭng (503) of Silla. In the second year of King Sinmun (682) of the unified Silla, Kukhak (lit. 'national studies'), a government organization in charge of national education, was established and many Chinese classics began to be taught. In the sixteenth year of King Kyŏngdŏk (757), native place names were changed to two-character SK, and in his eighteenth year, all official titles were also Sino-Koreanized. Personal names of upper-class people also began to be Sino-Koreanized during the Silla period.

Native words began to be overwhelmed by SK words in the Koryŏ dynasty. This was particularly the case after King Kwangjo adopted, in 958, the Chinese system of civil service examinations based on the Chinese classics. The Chosŏn dynasty observed the all-out infiltration of Chinese characters into every facet of Korean culture and society, chiefly because of the dynasty's adoption of Confucianism as a national religion and, as a result, the popular admiration of everything Chinese.

Scholars do not agree on the details of the origin of SK sounds. It is generally assumed, however, that the pronunciations of Chinese characters used in the northern part of China during the Su and Tang dynasties around the seventh and eighth centuries constituted the basis of SK sounds. This was during the Unified Silla period when massive written materials on Chinese civilization were imported from China. Thus, pronunciations of contemporary Chinese-character words in Korean are similar to those of Middle Chinese, although some independent vowel and consonant changes as well as the loss of tones have occurred in Korea.

There are three layers of SK words: (a) SK words from Chinese (e.g. *ch'ŏn-ji* 'heaven and earth', *chil-mun* 'question', *hak-saeng* 'student', *pu-mo* 'parents'); (b) SK words from Sino-Japanese (e.g. *ip-ku* 'entrance', *kwa-hak* 'science', *su-sok* 'procedure', *yak-sok* 'promise'; and (c) SK words coined in Korea (e.g. *ch'ong-gak* (all-horn) 'bachelor', *oe-sang* (outside-uperside) 'on credit', *p'yŏn-ji* (comfortable paper) 'letter', *sa-ju* (four-pillar) 'one's destiny' ('4 pillars: year, month, day, and hour of a person's birth'), *sik-ku* (eating-mouth) 'family member'). The first of the three layers has the largest number of members. The SK words in this layer were introduced mainly through Confucian classics, history and literary books, and Chinese works written in the colloquial Chinese. Sino-

Japanese coinages also abound in Korean. Many Sino-Japanese words are used in Chinese too. Words like *pi-haeng-gi* (fly-go-machine) 'airplane', *yŏng-hwa* (shine-picture) 'movie', *kong-jang* (work-place) 'factory', *ch'uk-ku* (kick-ball) 'football', *pul* [shape of $] 'dollar', and many other words coined by Japanese are used only in Japan and Korea, not in China.

The modern borrowing has been predominantly from scientifically and technologically advanced America and Europe. These non–Sino-Korean borrowings are called loan words or *oeraeŏ* 'words from abroad'. Up until 1945, when Korea was liberated from thirty-five years of Japanese domination, loan words were introduced into Korean exclusively through Japanese, with necessary spelling and pronunciation adjustments in accordance with Korean sound patterns. Only since 1945 has direct importation from English been prevalent. A large number of English words have been introduced as new loan words and many existing loan words from other languages have been replaced by English loans. As a result, the total number of current loan words is estimated at more than 20,000, of which English occupies more than 90 percent. In fact, most borrowings in South Korea since 1945 are words from English that range over all aspects of life, including clothing, food and drink, electricity and electronics, automobiles, sports, arts, social activities, politics, and economy. Random examples are *aisŭ-k'ŭrim* 'ice-cream', *allibai* 'alibi', *heding* 'heading (in soccer)', *hint'ŭ* 'hint', *k'alla* 'collar', *k'aemp'ŏsŭ* 'campus', *k'ŭredit k'adŭ* 'credit card', *kolp'ŭ* 'golf', *nyusŭ* 'news', *pija* 'visa', *pijŏn* 'vision', *sŏbisŭ* 'service', *seil* 'sale', *syop'ing* 'shopping', and *s(y)up'ŏ* 'supermarket'.

Both SK and loan words are an integral part of the Korean vocabulary. The impact of such non-native words on the Korean language is great. One effect is the proliferation of a large number of synonymous expressions, as illustrated below.

Native	Sino-Korean	Loan	
—	*an-ma*	*masaji*	'massage'
—	*chŏng-gu*	*t'enisŭ*	'tennis'
—	*chu-ch'a*	*p'ak'ing*	'parking'
—	*sa-jin-gi*	*k'amera*	'camera'
tanch'u	—	*pŏt'ŭn*	'button'
t'wigim	—	*hurai*	'frying (food)'
tosirak	—	*pentto*	'lunch box'
almom	*nach'e*	*nudŭ*	'nude'
ch'um	*mu-yong*	*taensŭ*	'dance'
kit	*e-ri*	*k'alla*	'collar'

Frequently, synonymous words are associated with different shades of meaning and stylistic or social values, thus enriching the Korean vocabulary. When synonyms exist, native words usually represent rather unsophisticated traditional culture, both mental and physical, whereas SK words, conveying more formality, tend to denote higher quality objects and more formal, abstract, and sometimes more socially prestigious concepts than their native counterparts do. Loan words are, in general, associated with modern and stylish objects and concepts. For instance, the native word *karak* for 'rhythm' is usually used with reference to traditional Korean folk songs, the SK word *un-yul* (rime-law) in formal or academic situations, and the loan word *ridŭm* for some sort of Western flavor. The triplet *ch'um* (native), *mu-yong* (SK dance-leap), and *taensŭ* (loan) for 'dance' have similar connotational differences. The native word *chip* is used when referring to one's own house or a house of a social inferior, but the SK word *taek* is used when referring to a social superior adult's house.

Many native words have been lost in the battle with SK and loan words and, as a result, disappeared from usage long ago, frequently irrecoverably. While Chinese characters in Japanese are read in both Sino-Japanese pronunciation and the pronunciation of corresponding native words, thereby contributing to the maintenance of native words, Chinese characters in Korea have been read only in Sino-Korean pronunciation, which has contributed to the disuse of native words. For instance, SK *san* 'mountain', *kang* 'river', *paek* '100', and *ch'ŏn* '1,000' have completely replaced the native *moe*, *karam*, *on*, and *chŭmŭn*, respectively.

6. The Korean alphabet, *han'gŭl*

At present, the Korean alphabet called *han'gŭl* (lit. 'great script') is the main writing system used by all Koreans to represent native, Sino-Korean, and loan words, while Chinese characters are optionally used to represent only Sino-Korean words.

Before the nineteenth century, when Western cultures began to permeate East Asia, China had long been the center of East Asian civilization. Chinese civilization was propagated to neighboring countries mainly through written Chinese based on Chinese characters. Thus, the Chinese script has long been an integral part of the writing systems of Koreans and was the only system before the creation of *han'gŭl* in 1446. Before *han'gŭl*, since Chinese characters were used mostly by upper-class people, commoners were devoid of any means of written communication. Members of the ruling class of Korea devoted their entire lives to the study of Classical Chinese written in characters, because it was the main goal of education, the official means of government affairs, and the medium of the civil service examinations.

In an effort to improve this predicament, early scholars devised writing systems using Chinese characters for the pronunciation and transcription of native Korean affixes, words, and sentences. A few varieties of this writing were subsumed under the term Idu (lit. Clerk Reading), and were used during all three ancient kingdoms (Silla, Paekche, and Koguryŏ) and also later during the Koryŏ and Chosŏn dynasties. The Idu script was used to record Korean expressions by means of (a) Chinese characters borrowed in their Chinese meaning but read as the corresponding Korean sounds (glossograms) or (b) Chinese characters borrowed in their Chinese sounds only (phonograms). Thus, for instance, in 加于 *tŏuk* (current SK pronunciation: *kau*) 'all the more', the first character is a glossogram meaning *tŏ* 'more' and the second one is a phonogram pronounced as *uk*. This script allowed people to record personal names, place names, and vernacular songs and poems. This writing was also used to clarify government documents and other books written in Chinese. The stele for King Kwanggaet'o of Koguryŏ contains many phonetic transcriptions written in the Idu script, as do early Silla inscriptions. Also, a number of Chinese characters used in the Idu script are found in *Samguk sagi* and *Samguk yusa*. However, this writing was extremely inadequate as a means of written communication as well as being difficult to learn. It was under these circumstances that *han'gŭl* was created, a phonetic writing system that was completely disengaged from the Chinese script.

This indigenous phonetic alphabet is one of the most remarkable writing systems ever devised in the world.[21] For the design of the *han'gŭl* alphabet, Sejong (1397–1450), the fourth king of the Chosŏn dynasty, and the scholars of the royal academy called Chiphyŏnjŏn (lit. 'Hall of Assembled Sages') studied the rich Chinese linguistic tradition, such as the concepts of consonants, syllables, and tones, as well as their underlying philosophical background. The orthographical design of *han'gŭl*, which was based on a rigorous analysis of Korean and Sino-Korean sound patterns, was completed in 1443. To test the new writing system, the king ordered his subjects (Kwŏn Che, et al.) to write the voluminous *Yongbi ŏch'ŏnga* (Songs of Flying Dragons, published in 1447) in *han'gŭl* with translations in Chinese characters. Songs is a eulogy cycle in 125 cantos comprising 248 poems, composed to celebrate the founding of the Chosŏn dynasty and praise the achievements of Sejong's predecessors.

King Sejong promulgated *han'gŭl* to the public on October 9, 1446, in the name of *Hunmin jŏngŭm* 'The Correct Sounds to Educate People'. *Hunmin*

21 This alphabet was named *han'gŭl* by Chu Sigyŏng (1876–1914), a pioneer linguist of Korean. Before, it was popularly called *ŏnmŭn* 'vernacular writing, vulgar script'. Works (in English) on the study of *han'gŭl* includes: Ledyard (1966); C. Lee (1972), Kim-Renaud (1997); and Kim-Cho (2000).

jŏngŭm (written by Sejong himself) was accompanied by *Hunmin jŏngŭm haerye* (Explanations and Examples of the *Hunmin jŏngŭm*), compiled by a group of scholars (headed by Chŏng Inji) commissioned by Sejong. These two documents were published as a single book.

The text of *Hunmin jŏngŭm* consists of three parts: preface, pronunciation of the twenty-eight letters, and rules regarding the use of the letters. The preface briefly summarizes Sejong's motives for inventing *han'gŭl* as follows in English translation.

The speech sounds of Korea are distinct from those of China and thus are not communicable with Chinese characters. Hence, many people having something to put into words are unable to express their feelings. To overcome such distressing circumstances, I have newly devised twenty-eight letters that everyone can learn with ease and use with convenience in daily life.

In the second part, the sounds of the newly devised twenty-eight (seventeen consonant and eleven vowel) letters are explained in Chinese characters. These letters and corresponding sound values are: ㄱ *k/g*, ㅋ *k'*, ㆁ *ng*, ㄷ *t*, ㅌ *t'*, ㄴ *n*, ㅂ *p/b*, ㅍ *p'*, ㅁ *m*, ㅈ *ch/j*, ㅊ *ch'*, ㅅ *s*, ㆆ(glottal stop sound), ㅎ *h*, ㅇ(glottal fricative sound), ㄹ *l/r*, ㅿ *z*, •(*á* — sound between *a* and *o*), ㅡ *ŭ*, ㅣ *i*, ㅗ *o*, ㅏ *a*, ㅜ *u*, ㅓ *ŏ*, ㅛ *yo*, ㅑ *ya*, ㅠ *yu*, and ㅕ *yŏ*.[22] The third part of *Hunmin jŏngŭm* presents rules regarding the use of *han'gŭl* letters and other symbols in syllable blocks. For instance, it is stipulated that single or cluster consonant letters are used for both syllable-initial and syllable final positions and that a high tone is represented by one dot added to the left of a syllable, a rising tone by two dots, and a level (low) tone by the absence of a dot.

Hunmin jŏngŭm haerye explains and illustrates the contents of *Hunmin jŏngŭm* in detail. It consists of seven parts: design of the letters, syllable-initial sounds, syllable-medial sounds, syllable-final sounds, combination of letters, examples of the use of the letters, and a brief postface by Chŏng Inji. Some important points are summarized below.

(a) The universe is governed by the principle of Yin 'dark' and Yang 'bright' and the rotation of the Five Elements—water, wood, fire, metal, and earth. Human speech sounds are also based on the same cosmological principles, that is, the patterns of Yin–Yang and the Five Elements. So are the speech sounds of Korean.

(b) The seventeen consonant letters were designed to depict the shapes of the speech organs. The symbol ㄱ *k* depicts the shape of the root of the tongue blocking the throat; ㄴ *n*, the shape of the tongue touching the alveo-dental area; ㅁ *m*,

22 South Koreans celebrate October 9 as *Han'gŭl* Day, which is the day *han'gŭl* was promulgated by King Sejong in 1446.

the shape of the mouth (i.e. lips); ㅅ *s*, the shape of an incisor; and ㅇ (glottal fricative), the shape of the throat. Other consonants were made by adding strokes to the above basic symbols. For instance, ㅋ *k'* is pronounced using the same oral position (soft palate) as ㄱ *k*, but it has an added stroke because its articulation is more 'severe' or aspirated than that of ㄱ *k*. The sounds represented by ㄴ *n*, ㄷ *t*, ㅌ *t'*, and ㄹ *l/r* are all pronounced using the same oral place (the alveo-dental area), but compared with ㄴ *n*, ㄷ *t* has an added stroke, symbolizing the blockage of the passage leading to the nasal cavity, whereas ㅌ *t'* has one more stroke by virtue of its aspiration, and ㄹ *l/r* one more by virtue its sound quality of trill or flap. Similarly, ㅂ *p/b*, ㅍ *p'*, and ㅁ *m* are all bilabial sounds, but the first two have some added strokes in view of their manners of pronunciation. The sounds ㅿ *z*, ㅈ *ch/j*, and ㅊ *ch'* are written parallel to ㅅ *s*, and ㆁ *ng*, ㆆ (glottal stop), and ㅎ *h* are modeled after ㅇ (glottal fricative).

(c) The speech organs are related to the Five Elements. The throat is water because it is deep and moist; the molar is wood because it is uneven and extended; the tongue is fire because it is pointed and moving; the incisor is metal because it is hard and cutting; and the lips are earth because they are squarish and yet joined. Just as water is the source of life and fire is the operation that perfects things, so are the throat and the tongue sounds primary, in that the throat is the articulator and the tongue the differentiator of speech sounds.

(d) Eleven vowel letters make up the syllable-medial sounds: three cardinal • (sound between *a* and *o*), ㅡ *ŭ*, and ㅣ *i*; four derived ㅗ *o*, ㅏ *a*, ㅜ *u*, and ㅓ *ŏ*; and four yodized ㅛ *yo*, ㅑ *ya*, ㅠ *yu*, and ㅕ *yŏ*. For •, the tongue retracts and its sound is deep; the roundness of its shape is a depiction of Heaven. For ㅡ, the tongue retracts a little, and its sound is neither deep nor shallow; the flatness of its shape is a depiction of Earth. For ㅣ, the tongue does not retract, and its sound is shallow; the uprightness of its shape is a depiction of Man. Thus, the cardinal vowel letters symbolize the trinity of Heaven, Earth, and Man. The other vowel and diphthong letters are combinations of these cardinal letters.

(e) In ㅗ *o*, ㅏ *a*, ㅑ *ya*, and ㅛ *yo*, the round dot (Heaven), i.e. a short stroke in the contemporary alphabet, is located above and on the outside, hence they are called Yang 'bright' sounds. In ㅜ *u*, ㅓ *ŏ*, ㅠ *yu*, and ㅕ *yŏ*, the round dot is located below and on the inside, hence they are called Yin 'dark' sounds.

Although the current rules of building syllable blocks are essentially the same as those stated in *Hunmin jŏngŭm haerye*, the *han'gŭl* letters and spelling conventions have undergone considerable modifications, due partly to the sound changes that have since taken place in Korean and partly to the research conducted by many *han'gŭl* scholars. The following changes are noteworthy.

(a) The consonant letters ㅿ *z*, ㆅ *hh*, and ㆆ (glottal stop) have been abolished because the first two sounds disappeared from the Korean language and the third sound turned out to be insignificant in distinguishing the meanings of words.

(b) The consonant letter ㆁ, which formerly represented the nasal sound *ng* is no longer in use. Instead, ㅇ, which has lost the original throat sound quality (voiced glottal friction) and turned out to be silent, takes dual functions, assuming null sound quality in the syllable-initial position and *ng* quality in the syllable-final position, as in 앙 *ang*.

(c) The vowel sound that the basic letter • represented has since disappeared from the language. Thus, the letter is no longer used to represent an independent vowel, but is used only in combination with another vowel letter to represent other vowel or semivowel sounds. The letter has been changed to a short vertical or horizontal stroke, as in ㅏ *a* and ㅗ *o*.

(d) Tone has disappeared from the language in most areas. Accordingly, tone markers have been completely abolished.

(e) When *han'gŭl* was created, the letters were combined into blocks consisting essentially of spoken syllables. The current practice, since Korean linguists' enactment of the Unified Spelling System in 1933, is binding letters into meaning-based syllables. For instance, the previous spelling 기픈 *ki.p'ŭn* 'deep' is now changed to 깊은 *kip'.ŭn* to represent the meanings of 'to be deep' (깊) and its suffix (은).

Since its creation, *han'gŭl* has undergone several major ordeals in the course of its diffusion in the face of the long tradition of the use of Chinese characters by the nobility and government officials during the Chosŏn dynasty period. Although King Sejong's invention of *han'gŭl* was the greatest cultural achievement, a group of scholar-officials led by Ch'oe Malli, then associate academician of Chiphyŏnjŏn, vehemently opposed the king's promulgation of *han'gŭl* to the public. They presented an anti-*han'gŭl* appeal to the throne in 1444. Their main argument was that Korea had long emulated Chinese ideas and institutions and that adoption of Korea's own writing system would make it impossible to identify Korean civilization with that of China but rather identify Korea with "barbarians" such as Mongolians, Tanguts, Jurchen, Japanese, and Tibetans, who had their own scripts. This appeal had little effect on Sejong's determination.

After the death of Sejong, the opposition to *han'gŭl* was resumed and continued until Sejo, the seventh king of the Chosŏn dynasty, propagated *han'gŭl* with Buddhism. Still, Classical Chinese and Idu were predominant while *han'gŭl* served as an aid for the study of Classical Chinese and was used mostly by women. Not until the Kabo Reform was implemented by the government as a modernization movement in 1894 did *han'gŭl* come to be used in official documents. King Kojong's royal decree issued on 21 November 1894 stipulated that all regulations and royal decrees be written in *han'gŭl*. However, exclusive use of *han'gŭl* in government documents was rather exceptional, and a host of government regulations were written in *han'gŭl* mixed with Chinese characters. Mixed use of the two scripts became a common practice among the general public.

During the Japanese occupation of Korea (1910–45), the use of Korean, including *han'gŭl*, was suppressed, and the Korean people were forced to use Japanese. When Korea was liberated from Japan in 1945, use of the Korean language and *han'gŭl* was restored in both South and North Korea and became a symbol of liberation, independence, and the reawakening of national consciousness.[25]

7. Speech sounds

Korean speech sounds consist of consonants, vowels, and semivowels. Some dialectal zones lack a few of these consonants and vowels. The consonants and corresponding *han'gŭl* letters can be arranged as follows, according where and how the sounds are pronounced.

			Where in speech organs				
How			lips	tooth-gum	palate	velum	Glottis
Stop	lax	voiceless or voiced	*p/b* ㅂ	*t/d* ㄷ	*ch/j* ㅈ	*k/g* ㄱ	
	aspirated	voiceless	*p'* ㅍ	*t'* ㅌ	*ch'* ㅊ	*k'* ㅋ	
	tense	voiceless	*pp* ㅃ	*tt* ㄸ	*tch* ㅉ	*kk* ㄲ	
Fricative	aspirated	voiceless		*s* ㅅ			*h* ㅎ
	tense	voiceless		*ss* ㅆ			
Nasal		voiced	*m* ㅁ	*n* ㄴ		*ng* ㅇ	
Liquid	lateral or flap	Voiced		*l/r* ㄹ			

The sounds *p*, *t*, *ch*, and *k* are basically voiceless, with only a minor degree of aspiration and no tenseness. They become lightly voiced (*b*, *d*, *j*, and *g*) between voiced sounds, as in *pabo* 'fool', *toduk* 'thief', *panji* 'ring', and *kogi* 'meat'. The sounds *p'*, *t'*, *ch'*, *k'* are always pronounced with a strong puff of air, while *pp*, *tt*, *tch*, *kk* are not. Compare *pul* 'fire', *p'ul* 'grass', *ppul* 'horn' and *kŭn* 'a pound', *k'ŭn* 'big', *kkŭn* 'string'.[23] The lax *s* sounds somewhat like *s* in English *strong*, whereas *ss* does not contain any aspiration, sounding like *s* in *sun*.

The liquid ㄹ has two sounds *l* and *r*. The "lateral" *l* sounds like *l* in English *lips*, *look*, etc., appearing in the syllable-final position, as in *kul* 'tunnel' and *pal-mok* 'ankle'. The sound *r* is a flap sound like the Japanese and Spanish *r*, appearing after a pause or between two vowels, as in *radio* 'radio' and *mŏri* 'head'.

Korean has ten vowels which may be arranged in terms of the oral place of pronunciation (front, back), lip shape (round, unround), and tongue height (high, mid, low) as shown below.

Place	front		back	
Lips	unround	Round	unround	Round
High tongue	*i* ㅣ	*wi* ㅟ	*ŭ* ㅡ	*u* ㅜ
Mid tongue	*e* ㅔ	*oe* ㅚ	*ŏ* ㅓ	*o* ㅗ
Low tongue	*ae* ㅐ		*a* ㅏ	

Korean has two semivowel sounds *w* and *y*, which have sound qualities similar to English *w* and *y*. Examples are *kwak* 'box', *wang* 'king', *pyŏk* 'wall', and *yang* 'sheep'.

In Korean, there is a difference between written and spoken syllables, in that the former allow consonant clusters in the syllable-final position (e.g. *kaps* 'price') while the latter do not allow more than one consonant in that position (e.g. *kap* 'price'). Korean spoken syllables have a simple structure. One vowel must be present as the nucleus. It may be preceded by a consonant, a semivowel, or both, and may be followed by a consonant, as in *i* 'this', *na* 'I', *hyŏ* tongue', *ip* 'mouth', *yŏl* 'ten', *pŏl* 'bee', and *kyul* tangerine'.

8. Agglutinative word structure

Korean is called an 'agglutinative' language, in that one or more affixes with constant form and meaning may be attached to various stems. In *po-i-si-ŏt-kes-sŭm-ni-da* '(a respectable person) may have been seen', for instance, the passive verb stem *po-i* 'be seen' consists of the verb stem *po* 'see' and the passive suffix *-i*. The suffixes following the passive *-i* indicate various grammatical functions of the stem *po-i*. That is, *-si* (respect to subject person), *-ŏt* (past), *-kes* 'may', *-sŭm* (respect to addressee), and *-da* (statement) occur in that order. Numerous

23 While the sounds of the lax stops are not shared by English, the aspirated stops are similar to English voiceless stressed stops occurring in word-initial position, as in *pill*, *till*, *chilly* and *kill*. The tensed quality is comparable to that of the English voiceless stops that occur after *s*, as in *speak*, *strong* and *ski*, and that of *j* in such an utterance as 'Please sit, John'. The sound of the Korean *pp* is very close to *pp* in English *happy*.

Korean suffixes either do not have any counterparts or correspond to independent words in many non-agglutinative languages such as English and Chinese. For instance, many English conjunctive words are equivalent to Korean inflectional suffixes, as in *ka-go* 'go and' and *ka-myŏn* 'if (one) goes' where *-ko* 'and' and *-myŏn* 'if' are suffixes.

Numerous words are formed by compounding and affixation. For instance, the greeting expression *annyŏnghaseyo* 'How are you?' is an adjective word, consisting of SK root *an* 'peace', SK root *nyŏng* 'safety', native adjective *ha* 'be', the subject honorific suffix *–se*, and polite suffix *–yo*. The two roots *an* and *nyŏng* constitute a compound noun which in turn goes into compounding with *ha*. Of all types of compounds, compound nouns are the most numerous and varied. The forms and meanings of the component elements may be fused, as in *harabŏji* 'grandfather' (< *han-abi* 'big father'), *haenggil* 'main street' (< *han-gil* 'big-road'), and *karangbi* 'drizzle' (< *karu-bi* 'powder rain'). Change may occur only in meanings, as in *mok-sum* (neck-breath) 'life', *sin-bal* (shoe-foot) 'shoes', *son-wi* (hand-upper) 'senior (in terms of age)', *son-mok* (hand-neck) 'wrist', *ch'am-girŭm* (true-oil) 'sesame oil', *cha-dong-ch'a* (self-move-vehicle) 'car', *paeng-mirŏ* (back-mirror) 'rear-view mirror', *o-l hae* (come-will year) 'this year', *chŏn-mŏg-i* (milk-eat-er) 'baby'.

Examples of compound verbs are *pit-nada* (light-come out) 'shine', *sum-jida* (breath-fall) 'die', *am-mot-poda* (front-unable-see) 'be blind', *maŭm-mŏkta* (mind-eat) 'intend, plan', *sarang-hada* (love-do) 'love', *son-boda* (hand-see) 'fix', *ar-a tutta* (know-hear) 'understand', *hon-naeda* (soul-take out) 'give a good scolding,' and *temo-hada* (demonstration-do) 'demonstrate'. Examples of compound adjectives are *nun-mŏlda* (eye-far) 'be blind', *haengbok-hada* (happiness-be) 'be happy', *yŏlsim-ida* (diligence-be) 'be diligent', and *sŭmat'u-hada* (smart-be) 'be smart'.

Numerous words are formed through affixation (prefixing and suffixing). Affixes are from both the native and SK stocks. There are hardly any loan affixes. In general, a native affix occurs with a native root or stem, and rarely with an SK root or stem, and vice versa. There are several hundreds of derivational affixes (bold-faced below) in Korean, which occur predominantly in nouns, verbs and adjectives. Examples of derived nouns are ***maen**-bal* (bare-foot) 'barefoot', ***mad**-adŭl* (first-son) 'the eldest son', ***si**-ŏmŏni* (husband's family-mother) 'mother-in-law', ***pi**-gongsik* (non-formal) 'informality', *kang-**aji*** (dog-baby) 'puppy', *naksi-**jil*** (fishhook-activity) 'fishing', *kwahak-**cha*** (science-person) 'scientist', *nor-**i*** (play-act) 'game', *nal-**gae*** (fly-tool) 'wing', *ch'u-**m*** (dance-fact) 'dance', and *k'-**i*** (< *k'ŭ-**i*** 'big-quality') 'height'. Derived verbs include ***cit**-papta* (randomly-step on) 'overrun', ***pi**-utta* (twisted-laugh) 'scorn', ***pin**-nagada* (aslant-go out) 'go astray', *sum-**jida*** (breath-fall) 'die', *chungŏl-**daeda*** (mutter-repeatedly) 'mutter repeatedly', *paeda* (*pae* 'belly') 'conceive', and *sinta* (*sin* 'shoes') 'wear shoes'. Derived verbs also include words with causative or passive suffixes such as ***-i, -hi, -ki, -li,*** as in *po-**ida*** (see-cause/be) 'show, be seen', *chop-**hi**da* (narrow-cause) 'make narrow', *mut-**hi**da* (bury-be) 'be buried', *ut-**ki**da* (laugh-cause) 'make (him) laugh', and *mul-**li**da* (bite-cause/be) 'cause someone to bite, be bitten'. Examples of derived adjectives are ***sae**-kkamat'a/**si**-kkŏmŏt'a* (vivid-black) 'be deep black', *nop-**tarat**'a* (high-rather) 'rather high', *hyanggi-**rop**ta* (aroma-characterized by) 'be fragrant', *sarang-**sŭrŏp**ta* (love-seeming) 'be adorable', and *sanae-**dap**ta* (man-worthy of) 'be manly'.

Korean is characterized by the boundness of predicates, another agglutinative nature. While most nouns are free, all verbs and adjectives are bound and unable to function without a clause- or sentence-ending suffix. For this reason, the dummy suffix *-ta/-da* is attached to a stem for citation or dictionary entry, as is done in this chapter. For instance, the verb stem *po* 'see' and the adjective stem *choh* 'be good' are entered in the dictionary as *poda* and *chot'a,* respectively.

9. Sentence structure

Korean sentences are predicate-final (often called a Subject-Object-Verb or SOV order language), sharing the grammatical properties of other predicate-final languages such as Japanese, Altaic, and Dravidian languages, and are very different from sentences of English, French, Chinese, Austronesian, etc. In normal speech, the predicate (verb or adjective) comes at the end of a sentence or a clause, while all other elements, including the subject and object, must appear before the predicate, as illustrated below.

Kim-sŏnsaengnim	*i*	*han.gungmar*	*ŭl*	*karŭch'i-se-yo.*
Kim-teacher	NM	Korean	AC	teach-SH-POL

'The person we met teaches Korean.'

Notice that the verb *karŭch'ida* occurs at the end of the sentence.

In Korean, all modifiers, whether they are adjectives, adverbs, numerals, relative clauses, subordinate or coordinate clauses, pre-nouns, or genitive constructions, must precede the element they modify. In the following sentence, *Pusan-kkaji* and *aju ppalli* modify their head verb *tallida*; *aju* modifies its head *ppalli*, and the whole relative clause *Pusan-kkaji aju ppall talli-nŭn* modifies its head *kich'a*. Further notice that the relativizer *nŭn* functions like an English relative pronoun.

Pusan	*kkaji*	*aju*	*ppalli*	*talli-nŭn*	*kich'a*
Pusan	to	very	fast	run-ning	train

'the train which runs very fast to Pusan'

As observed in the above examples, particles are postpositional, occurring after a nominal, as in *Kim-sŏnsaengnim-i*, *hangungmar-ŭl*, and *Pusan-kkaji*. Titles follow names (e.g. *Kim-sŏnsaengnim*). As already observed, elements (suffixes) indicating various grammatical functions occur as suffixes attached to predicate stems. Also, there is no inversion of any element in question sentences, as in the following example where the question word *ŏnje* 'when' follows the subject.

Kim-sŏnsaengnim	*i*	*ŏnje*	*o-se-yo?*
Kim-professor	NM	when	come-SH-POL

'When does Professor Kim come?'

The comparative expression takes the order: standard + comparative particle + degree adverb + adjective as shown below, where *Mia* is a standard, *boda* is a comparative particle, *tŏ* is a degree adverb, and *yeppŭ* is an adjective stem followed by the declarative (statement) sentence suffix -*da*.

Yumi	*nŭn*	*Mia*	*boda*	*tŏ*	*yeppŭ-da*
Yumi	TC	Mia	than	more	pretty-DC

'Yumi is prettier than Mia.'

Although the subject tends to appear first in a sentence, it and the other nominal elements can be scrambled rather freely for emphatic or other figurative purposes.

a.	*na*	*nŭn*	*ŏje*	*pada*	*e*	*ka-ss-ŏyo.*
	I	TC	yesterday	beach	to	go-PST-POL

'I went to beach yesterday.'

b. *ŏje na nŭn pada e ka-ss-ŏyo.*
c. *na nŭn pada e ŏje ka-ss-ŏyo.*
d. *pada e ŏje na nŭn ka-ss-ŏyo.*

Korean is often called a situation- or discourse-oriented language, in that contextually or situationally understood elements (including subject and object) are left unexpressed more frequently than not. Thus, for instance, in *ŏdi ka-se-yo?* (where-go?) 'Where are you going?', the subject 'you' does not appear.

Using a word denoting 'you' in the above expressions would sound awkward in normal contexts, unless 'you' is emphasized or contrasted with someone else, as in 'as for you'.

Korean is also a 'macro-to-micro' language, in that the universe is represented in the order of a set (macro) and then its members (micro). Thus, for instance, Koreans say or write the family name first and then the given name followed by a title; say or write an address in the order of country, province, city, street, house number, and personal name; and refer to time with year first and seconds last. Macro-micro relation also obtains in productive double subject constructions, as in *Mia-nŭn nun-i yepp-ŏyo* 'Mia has pretty eyes' (lit. 'Mia, her eyes are pretty').

There are four major sentence types that are characterized by sentence-ending suffixes: declarative (statement), interrogative (question), propositive (proposal), and imperative (command). These four types are interwoven with six speech levels, as we will see shortly in the following section.

10. Politeness expressions and honorifics

Language has two important functions: the function of transmitting information and knowledge (transactional or referential function) and the function of maintaining human relationships (interactional or affective function). It is the interactional or affective function that is relevant to linguistic politeness. Although linguistic expressions of politeness are ubiquitous across all languages, their forms and functions are different from language to language, being conditioned by respective linguistic structures and usage, and patterns of underlying socio-cultural values of the speakers. The socio-cultural values that are relevant to linguistic politeness are related to not only power variables such as age, kinship, gender, social status, and occupational rank, and solidarity (or familiarity) variables such as the in- and outgroupness scale, the intimacy–distance scale, and the formality scale, but also different degrees of face threat associated with various speech acts.

There are two types of politeness, normative and strategic. The function of normative politeness is social indexing, while that of strategic politeness is face-saving. In general, expression of normative politeness is bound by cultural norms of a society, while expression of strategic politeness is controlled by interlocutors in interactive situations in performing their communicative goals. Thus, while the former is largely culture-bound, the latter is universal to a great extent. Both types of politeness expressions normally occur together in the same discourse.

By and large, normative politeness in Korean is expressed by time-honored grammatical forms of politeness, which are popularly called honorifics, whereas strategic politeness is expressed by various assertion-softening or assertion-reinforcing measures, such as phatic expressions, conversational formulae, hedges, intonation, direct and indirect speech acts, and silence, as well as praises, approval, sympathy, seeking agreement, and giving options to the addressee.

Honorifics are a set of linguistic forms in which interpersonal relationships are systematically encoded. Unlike English, Korean is a language with an elaborate system of honorifics.[24] Sentences cannot be uttered without the speaker's approximate knowledge of his social relationship with the addressee and/or referent in terms of age category (adult, adolescent, or child), social status, kinship, and/or in- and outgroupness. For instance, compare English and Korean in expressing 'Good night' by son and father.

English	Son:	*Good night, Dad.*
	Father:	*Good night, John.*
Korean	Son:	*Abŏji, annyŏnghi chumu-se-yo.* father peacefully sleep
	Father:	*nŏ do chal cha-ra.* you also well sleep

Notice in English that son and father use the same expression except for the address terms, a kinship term by the son and a given name by the father. In Korean, on the other hand, they use entirely different utterances. Not a single element is shared. Under no circumstances can the son use any part of his father's utterance in expressing 'Good night' to his father, and vice versa. Both the son's and the father's utterances are appropriate and polite. They must always be used in that way. Use of them is by no means strategic, but is socially and culturally normative.

The patterns of Korean honorifics include the structure and use of speech levels, personal pronouns, address-reference terms, some content words and particles, and subject- and addressee-honorific suffixes.

10.1 Speech levels

Korean has six speech levels (or 'styles') represented by sentence-ending suffixes. These six speech levels are interwoven with four sentence types, as il-

24 The honorific system of Korean is one of the most systematic among all known languages, along with Japanese and Javanese. In this respect, Korean may be called an honorific language.

lustrated below with the verb *poda* 'see'. Different speech levels are used by the speaker based on whom he is talking to.

	Declarative	**Interrogative**	**Imperative**	**Propositive**
plain	*po-n-da*	*po-ni?*	*po-ala*	*po-ja*
intimate	*po-a*	*po-a?*	*po-a*	*po-a*
familiar	*po-ne*	*po-na?*	*po-ge*	*po-se*
blunt	*po-o*	*po-o?*	*po-o*	*po-p-si-da*
polite	*po-ayo*	*po-ayo?*	*po-ayo*	*po-ayo*
deferential	*po-m-ni-da*	*po-m-ni-kka?*	*po-si-p-si-o*	*po-si-p-si-da*

The plain level is used by any speaker to any child, to one's own siblings, children, or grandchildren regardless of age, to one's daughter-in-law, or between intimate adult friends whose friendship started in childhood, etc. The intimate level (polite-level form minus *-yo*), also called a half-talk style, is used by an adult to an adult junior such as a student, by a child of pre-school age to his or her family members including parents, or between close friends whose friendship began in childhood or adolescence. This level is frequently intermixed with the plain or familiar level in the same discourse with the same person. The familiar level is typically used by a male adult to an adult inferior or adolescent such as a high school or college student or to one's son-in-law or to an old friend. The blunt level, sometimes used by a boss to his subordinates, tends to disappear from daily usage probably due to its blunt connotation. Most young speakers use only the plain, intimate, polite, and deferential levels.

The most popular level towards an adult is the polite one, which is an informal counterpart of the deferential level. This level is widely used by both males and females in casual conversations. While females predominantly use this level in all conversations, males use both the polite and deferential levels to address an equal or superior adult. Even in a formal conversational situation, the deferential and polite levels are mixed by the same interlocutors in the same discourse. In formal situations such as news reports and public lectures, only the deferential style is used.

10.2 Personal pronouns

While English personal pronouns distinguish person, number, and gender as in *I, you, he, she, it, we,* and *they*, Korean ones have person, number, and speech level distinctions.

		Singular	Plural
First person:	Plain	*na*	*uri(-tŭl)*
	Humble	*chŏ*	*chŏ-hŭi(-dŭl)*
second person:	Plain	*nŏ*	*nŏ-hui(-dŭl)*
	Familiar	*chane*	*chane-dŭl*
	Intimate	*chagi*	*chagi-dŭl*
	Blunt	*tangsin*	*tangsin-dŭl*
		taek	*taek-tŭl*

Third person: (*D* stands for a demonstrative)

	Singular	Plural
Thing	*D-kŏt*	*D-kŏt-tŭl*
Child	*D-ae*	*D-ay-dŭl*
Adult-familiar	*D-saram*	*D-saram-dŭl*
Adult-blunt	*D-i*	*D-i-dŭl*
Adult-polite	*D-bun*	*D-bun-dŭl*

Reflexive pronouns: 'self'

	Singular	Plural
Plain	*chŏ(-jasin)*	*chŏ(-jasin)-dŭl*
Neutral	*chagi(-jasin)*	*chagi(-jasin)-dŭl*
Deferential	*tangsin(-jasin)*	*tangsin(-jasin)-dŭl*

In general, the first person plain form *na* is used when talking to a child or a younger adult, the humble form *chŏ* is used when talking to a senior or an adult equal. The second person plain form *nŏ* is used to address or refer to a child or equivalent (e.g. one's own child or grandchild). The familiar form *chane* is used by a superior to a much younger adult or adolescent inferior (e.g. one's adult student), or by a parent-in-law to a son-in-law, etc. Use of the reflexive pronoun *chagi* as a second person 'you' is a recent innovation that is used to one's spouse or boyfriend or girlfriend. The blunt form *tangsin* is used to refer to an adult inferior, e.g. by a boss to his subordinate. It is also used between husband and wife in which case the form carries an affectionate connotation. The form *taek* (lit. '(your) honorable house') is used to refer to an adult stranger and cannot be used to an ingroup member or a social superior. Thus, even though there are many second person pronouns, Korean does not have a pronoun to refer to a socially superior person. Consequently, Koreans make an extensive use of nouns for pronominal substitution, as in *sŏnsaeng-nim* 'you' (lit. 'esteemed teacher') and *sajang-nim* 'you' (lit. 'esteemed company president').

For third person pronouns, demonstrative compounds are used, which consist of nouns *kŏt* 'thing', *ai*/*ae* 'child', *saram* 'person', *i* 'person', and *bun* 'esteemed person'. Between *i* and *saram*, the former is considered relatively higher.[14] Reflexive pronouns are also of three kinds which are sensitive to speech levels. The form *chŏ* is used to refer to a child or a lower person, *chagi* is used for children and equal adults, and *tangsin* is used to refer to a respected person.

10.3 Address-reference terms

The pattern of English address-reference terms is relatively simple, as shown below.

title sequence	*Mr. President, Mr. Chairman*
title alone	*Professor, Sir, Doctor, General, Madam*
title + last name	*Professor Smith, Mr. Haig, Dr. Ing*
full given name	*James, Christine, Samuel*
nickname	*Jim, Chris, Sam*
affectionate nickname	*Jimmy, Chrissy, Sammy*

The first three kinds of terms indicate professional roles. They are used when no solidarity is involved. The second three kinds are essentially based on different degrees of solidarity. Thus, a title and last name can easily be changed to a nickname when the interlocutors become closer.

Compared to the relatively simple English pattern, an extensive set of highly stratified address-reference terms are used in Korean, as illustrated below roughly in decreasing deference and/or distance.

abŏ-nim	'hon. father'[25]
Kim-baksa-nim	'hon. Dr. Kim'
abŏji	'father'
misisŭ Kim	'Mrs. Kim'
Kim-gwajang	'Division Chief Kim'
Kim-baksa	'Dr. Kim'
takt'ŏ Kim	'Dr. Kim'
Kim Mia-ssi	'Ms. Mia Kim'
misŭt'ŏ Kim	'Mr. Kim'
misŭ Kim	'Miss Kim'
Mia-ssi	'Miss Mia'
Kim-ssi	'Mr. Kim'

25 Noteworthy is the fact that a married woman uses *abŏ-nim* 'father' and *ŏmŏ-nim* 'mother' to address or refer to her parents-in-law and *abŏji* and *ŏmŏni* or *appa* and *ŏmma* for her own parents.

Kim (Minho)-gun	'Mr. (Minho) Kim'
Kim (Mia)-yang	'Miss (Mia) Kim'
Minho!; Kihan i!	'Minho; Kihan!'
Mia ya!	'Mia!'

While English honorific titles such as *Mr., Mrs., Miss,* and *Ms.* are used primarily to indicate gender roles and marital status and are not hierarchical, Korean honorific titles are definitely hierarchical. For instance, *-nim* is widely used for one's superiors or distant adult equals, *-ssi* for colleagues or subordinates, and *-gun/-yang* for much younger inferiors or subordinates.

The most frequently used form for a social superior or a distant adult equal is title + honorific suffix *-nim*. All kinds of professional titles (including section chief, company president, nurse, and taxi or bus driver) plus *-nim* are used, as in *kwajang-nim* 'Section Chief'*, kanhosa-nim* (lit. 'Ms. nurse'), and *kisa-nim* (lit. 'Mr./Ms. driver'). This indicates that unlike Americans, Koreans are very status conscious in all walks of life. When *-nim* is removed, no deference is shown. Thus, terms without *-nim* are used to address or refer to a close colleague or an adult social inferior.

Sino-Korean title suffixes *-ssi*, *-gun*, *-yang* and loan *misŭt'ŏ*, *misisŭ*, *misŭ*, *takt'ŏ* do not convey deference. Unlike in English, the loan titles *Dr.* and *Mrs.* are used to an adult equal or junior adult, and never to a senior person. *Mr.* and *Miss* are usually used to a junior adult. A family name + *-ssi* is used by an adult to an adult male whose occupation is socially low, such as an adult janitor or a delivery person, as in *Kim-ssi*. This may be because a family name without a given name does not carry any solidarity and *-ssi* does not carry deference. Thus, a preferred recent practice is to add *ajŏssi* (lit. 'uncle') or *ajumŏni/ajuma* (lit. 'aunt') after *-ssi* as in *Kim-ssi ajŏssi* and *Kim-ssi ajuma.* A similar case is that *hyŏng* 'older brother' is used to address or refer to one's (usually male's) male senior but family name + *hyŏng* (e.g. *Kim hyŏng*) is used for one's equal or junior.

Given names with the vocative particle (*i*) are used to address one's intimate adult friends or one's adult or adolescent students, as in *Kihan-i* 'Kihan!' and *Yongho* 'Yongho!' Given names or other nouns with the particle *(y)a* are for addressing children, as in *Yongho-ya* 'Yongho!' Homin-a '*Homin!'*, and *pabo-ya* 'You fool!' Sometimes, *(y)a* is used to family members as a diminutive marker without lowering the honorific level, as in *abŏm-a* '(child's) Dad!' (addressing one's adult son), *ŏnni-ya* 'Sis!' (female speaker), and *nuna-ya* 'Sis!' (male speaker).

In English, the difference between a title and family name like *Mr. Smith* and first name like *John* are dependent not so much on the power dimension as on the solidarity dimension. In Korean, on the other hand, solidarity functions little in the use of address-reference terms in a power-laden relationship such as between a professor and a student. No matter how close a person is to his senior in the workplace, he cannot use an address term without a professional title and the honorific title *-nim*. Thus, he must use *Kim (Minho) kwajang-nim* or *kwajang-nim,* but never *Kim (Minho) kwajang* or *kwajang,* let alone *Kim Minho, Minho* or *Minho-ya.*

Unlike in English, kinship terms used as address-reference terms are highly diversified in Korean, including terms for older siblings such as *oppa, hyŏng, nuna,* and *ŏnni.* Furthermore, kinship terms are extensively used to non-kin for strategic politeness. Among ingroup members, terms like *hyŏng* and *ŏnni* are commonly used.

10.4 Content words and particles

English distinguishes between "like" and "care for", between "eat" and "dine", between "Hi" and "Good Morning", etc. Again, this distinction does not imply social hierarchism. Korean has a limited set of nouns and predicates to refer to a superior or distant adult's family member, possession and action, as well as some humble predicates to refer to one's own or an inferior person's action in reference to a superior person. Humble predicates are transitive, and their direct or indirect object is a superior person. In addition, two particles, nominative and dative-locative-goal, have both neutral and honorific forms. While the neutral particles are used for both children and adults, the honorific ones are used only for adults to indicate special deference.

	Honorific	**Plain**	**Gloss**
noun	*puin/samo-nim*	*chŏ/anae/manura*	'wife'
	taek	*chip*	'house'
	adŭ-nim	*adŭl*	'son'
	chinji	*pap*	'meal'
	sŏngham	*irŭm*	'name'
	yŏnse	*nai*	'age'
predicate	*kyesida*	*itta*	'stay'
	chapsusida	*mŏkta*	'eat'
	chumusida	*chada*	'sleep'
	toragasida	*chukta*	'die'
	annyŏnghasida	*chal itta*	'be well'

	Humble	**Plain**	**Gloss**
predicate	*tŭrida*	*chuda*	'give'
	mosida	*terida*	'accompany'
	poepta	*poda*	'see'
	yŏtchuda	*mutta*	'ask'

	Honorific	**Neutral**	**Case**
particle	*kkesŏ*	*ka/i*	subject
	kke	*ege/hant'e*	dative/locative/goal

10.5 Subject- and addressee-honorific suffixes

Unlike English, Korean has a productive suffixal device for subject honorification, employing the inflectional suffix *-(ŭ)si/-(ŭ)se* immediately after a predicate stem when the subject referent deserves the speaker's deference, as in *kyosu-nim i ka-si-nda* 'The professor is going.'

Korean also has the addressee honorific suffix *-(sŭ)p* (*-sŭp* after a consonant; *-p/-m* after a vowel). This suffix appears only with the deferential speech level, as in *i kŭrim ŭn chot-**sŭm**-ni-da* 'This picture is good' and *chŏ-nŭn ka-**m**-nida* 'I am going.' In *Kim sŏnsaeng-nim ŭn ka-**si**-ŏs-**sŭm**-nikka?* 'Did Professor Kim go?', both the subject referent and the addressee are honorified.[26]

10.6 Strategic politeness expressions

In addition to the use of honorifics, politeness is expressed in many strategic ways both in Korean and English. If a speech act is performed for the benefit of the addressee, the utterance is usually direct, often utilizing the imperative sentence type, as strong assertion is frequently needed for politeness. Examples are *ŏsŏ o-sipsio* 'Welcome' (lit. 'Come quickly') and *annyŏnghi chumu-seyo* 'Good night' (lit. 'Sleep peacefully').

If a speech act is not for the benefit of the addressee but for the speaker or somebody else, indirect speech acts are felicitous because direct speech acts are often 'face-threatening' to the addressee's positive self-esteem or to his freedom from imposition. Indirect utterances are used especially when the addressee is a senior or a distant equal or the utterances in question are made for the benefit

26 The distinction between the perspectives of speaker–addressee and speaker–referent is structurally so tenacious that even when the addressee is coreferential to the subject referent, the two are grammatically differentiated, as in ***sŏnsaeng-nim kkesŏ*** *ŏnje ttŏna-**si**-kess-**sŭp**-ni-kka?* 'When are you going to leave, Professor?', where both the subject honorific suffix and addressee honorific suffix occur.

of the speaker. Observe in the following the decreasing degrees of indirectness which in turn denote decreasing degrees of politeness in both Korean and English. English translations are approximate.

a. *sillyeha-mnida man, mun chom yŏr-ŏ chu-si-gess-ŏyo?*
'Excuse me, but would you please open the door for me?'
b. *mun chom yŏr-ŏ chu-si-gess-ŏyo?*
'Would you please open the door for me?'
c. *mun yŏr-ŏ chu-si-gess-ŏyo?*
'Would you open the door for me?'
d. *mun chom yŏr-ŏ chu-se-yo.*
'Please open the door for me.'
e. *mun yŏr-ŏ chu-se-yo.*
'Open the door for me.'
f. *mun yŏ-se-yo.*
'Open the door.'

All these sentences are in the polite speech level, and thus may be uttered to an adult. However, (f) is a sheer command in both Korean and English and thus impolite unless the act of opening the door is for the sake of the addressee. In general, the longer a sentence is, the more indirect and therefore the more polite it is, since more hedges are included. In (a), several hedging devices are involved: the request-introducing formula *sillyeha-mnida man* 'excuse me but'; the diminutive *chom* 'just, a little, please'; the benefactive auxiliary verb *chuda* 'do for'; the suffix *-ket* 'would'; and the interrogative sentence type with rising intonation. Use of interrogative sentences for requests has become quite popular recently.

Use of "indirect" sentence-ending suffixes is a productive mechanism to express strategic politeness. Using this strategy, the speaker can give the addressee the option of making the final decision, as illustrated below.

pi ka o-nŭn-de-yo. 'It's raining. (What shall we do?)'
pi ka o-gŏdŭn-yo. 'It's raining, you know.'

There are many indirect speech acts which are idiomatized. One such case is to pose a question to a social superior about his or her name, age, and other things. The formula is *ŏttŏ-k'e toe-seyo?* 'What is . . . ?' (lit. 'How does it become?'), as illustrated below.

a. *nai ka myŏch'-i-ci?* (to a child)
'How old are you?'

b. *yŏnse ka etto-ŏk'e toe-seyo?* (to a senior or distant adult)
'May I ask your age?' (lit. 'How does your age become?')

A noticeable fact is the productive use of the phrase ~ *kŏt kat'-ayo* 'it seems that . . .' in daily conversational interactions, as in *chŏ nŭn mot kal kŏt kat'-ayo* 'I may not be able to go' instead of the intended expression *chŏ nŭn mot ka-yo* 'I am unable to go.' This is a politeness strategy to tone down the assertion on the part of the speaker.

Thus far, sketchy observations of the linguistic expressions of normative and strategic politeness in Korean have been made in brief comparison to English. One major difference between Korean and English politeness expressions is the presence in Korean and the absence in English of an extensive system of honorifics. As has been observed, Korean honorifics are essentially hierarchical, from plain at the bottom to deferential at the top, and their uses are generally normative. In contemporary Korea, the primary socio-cultural variable in using honorifics appears to be the addressee's age categories such as adult, adolescent, and child. Then come such other variables as in-/out-groupness, occupational rank, kinship, and formality. In English, on the other hand, the system of honorifics is negligible. At most, English has several kinds of address-reference terms. Unlike in Korean, however, these terms carry little hierarchical connotation. Rather, their uses are governed by professional roles and the degree of solidarity.

These differences between Korean and English can be ascribed to different underlying socio-cultural values. Despite the recent trend towards democratization in all walks of life, Koreans still value traditional hierarchism to a considerable extent in interpersonal interactions, whereas English-speaking people generally hold egalitarian value orientations. In addition, as alluded to here and there in the above, use of Korean honorifics and politeness strategies is also governed by the collectivistic value of Koreans. Extensive use of kinship terms to non-kin is an example. In short, the structure and use of politeness expressions in Korean cannot be properly grasped without understanding Korean people's deep-rooted hierarchical and collectivistic consciousness as against English-speaking people's egalitarian and individualistic consciousness.

REFERENCES: Chapter 1

Aston, W.G. 1879. A comparative study of the Japanese and Korean languages. *Journal of the Royal Asiatic Society of Great Britain and Ireland.* New Series 11.3.

Brown, P. and S.C. Levinson. 1987. *Politeness: Some Universals in Language Usage*. Cambridge, UK: Cambridge University Press.

Chang, Suk-Jin. 1996. *Korean*. Amsterdam/Philadelphia: John Benjamins.

Cho, Choon-Hak. 1982. *A Study of Korean Pragmatics: Deixis and Politeness*. Seoul: Hanshin.

Chon, Su-Tae and Hochol Choy. 1989. *Nambuk'an ŏnŏ pigyo* (A Linguistic Comparison between South and North Korea). Seoul: Nokcin.

Clippinger, M.E. 1984. Korean and Dravidian: Lexical evidence for an old theory. *Korean Studies* 8: 1–57.

Hulbert, H.B. 1905. *A Comparative Grammar of the Korean Language and the Dravidian Languages of India.* Seoul: Methodist Publishing House.

Hwang, Juck-Ryoon. 1975. Role of sociolinguistics in foreign language education with reference to Korean and English: terms of address and levels of deference. Ph.D. dissertation. University of Texas at Austin.

Jeon, Jae-Ho. 1992. *Kugŏ Ŏhwisa Yŏngu* (A Study of the History of the Korean Lexicon). Taykwu, Korea: Kyongbuk University Press.

Kawamoto, Takao. 1974. Agreements and disagreements in morphology between Japanese and Austronesian (chiefly Melanesian) languages. *Minzokugaku Kenkyu* 39.2: 113–29.

Kim, Bang-Han. 1984. *Hangugŏ ŭi kyet'ong* (Genealogy of Korean). Seoul: Min.umsa.

Kim, Chong-Taek. 1993. *Kugŏ ŏhwiron* (Korean Lexicology). Seoul: Tower.

Kim, Hyong-Kyu. 1972. *Kugŏhak kaeron* (An Introduction to Korean Linguistics). Seoul: Ilcokak.

Kim, Hyong-Kyu. 1982. *Hanguk pangŏn yŏngu* (A Study of Korean Dialects), I and II. Seoul: Ilchogak

Kim, T'aesik. 2001. ŏllon ŭi nambukhan ŏnŏ tongjilsŏng hoebok pangan (A proposal to recover the homogeneous mass media language in the South and North). *Sae Kugŏ Saenghwal* 11.1.

Kim-Cho, Sek Yen. 2000. *The Korean Alphabet of 1446: the Orthophonic Alphabet for the Instruction of the People.* ms. State University of New York at Buffalo.

Kim-Renaud, Young-Key (ed.). 1997. *The Korean Alphabet: a Unique Invention*. Honolulu: University of Hawaii Press.

Kiyose, Gisaburo. 1986. Tunguz and other elements in the languages of the Three Kingdoms. *Korean Linguistics* 4: 17–26.

KLAC (Kugŏ Sajŏng Wiwŏnhoe: Korean Language Assessment Committee). 1988. *Kaejŏnghan chosŏnmal kyubŏm-jip* (A Revised Collection of Korean Language Norms). P'yŏngyang: Sahoy Kwahak Chwulphansa.

KLS (Korean Language Society) 1991. *Urimal K'ŭn Sajŏn* (A Great Dictionary of the Korean Language). Seoul: ŏmungak.

Koo, Jasook. 1995. Politeness theory: universality and specificity. Ph.D. dissertation. Harvard University.

Ledyard, G.K. 1966. The Korean language reform of 1446: the origin, background, and early history of the Korean alphabet. Ph.D. dissertation. University of California at Berkeley.

Lee, Cheong-Ho. 1972. *Haesŏl yŏkchu Hunmin Chŏngŭm* (Annotated and Translated *Hwunmin Cengum*). Seoul: Korean Library Science Research Institute.

Lee, Hyun Bok. 1989. *Korean Grammar*. Oxford: Oxford University Press.

Lee, Iksop and S. Robert Ramsey. 2000. *The Korean Language*. Albany: State University of New York Press

Lee, Iksop, Sang-Oak Lee, and Wan Chae. 1997. *Hanguk ŭi Ŏnŏ* (The Language of Korea). Seoul: Singwu Munhwasa.

Lee, Ki-moon. 1958. A comparative study of Manchu and Korean. *Ural–Altaische Jahrbucher* 30: 104–20.

Lee, Ki-moon. 1976. *Kaejŏng kugŏsa kaesŏl* (A Revised Introduction to the History of Korean). Seoul: Minjung Sogwan.

Lee, Ki-moon and S. Robert Ramsey. 2011. *A History of the Korean Language*. Cambridge, UK: Cambridge University Press.

Lee, Won-Kyu. 1991. Honorifics and politeness in Korean. Ph.D. dissertation. University of Wisconsin at Madison.

Martin, S. E. 1966. Lexical evidence relating Korean to Japanese. *Language* 42: 185–251.

Martin, S. E. 1992. *A Reference Grammar of Korean*. Rutland, Vermont and Tokyo: Charles E. Tuttle.

Martin, S. E. 1995. On the prehistory of Korean grammar: verb forms. *Korean Studies* 19: 139–50.

Miller, R. A. 1967. *The Japanese Language*. Chicago: University of Chicago Press.

Miller, R. A. 1976. The relevance of historical linguistics for Japanese studies. *Journal of Japanese Studies* 2.2: 335–88.

MOE (Ministry of Education). 1988. *Han'gŭl match'umpŏp* (*Han'gŭl* Spelling Conventions). Seoul.

Mun, Mae-Ran Park. 1991. Social variation and change in honorific usage among Korean adults in an urban setting. Ph.D. dissertation. University of Illinois at Urbana-Champaign.

Murayama, Shichiro. 1976. The Malayo–Polynesian component in the Japanese language. *The Journal of Japanese Studies* 2.2: 413–36.

Ohno, Susumu. 1970. *The Origin of the Japanese Language*. Tokyo: Kokusai Bunka Shinkokai.

Ohno, Susumu. 1981. *Nihongo to Tamirugo* (Japanese and Tamil). Tokyo: Shinchosha.

Park, Young-soon, 2001. *Han'gugŏ ŭi Sahoe-ŏnŏhak* (Sociolinguistics of Korean). Seoul: Han'guk Munhwasa.

Polivanov, E.D. 1927. K voprosu o rodstvennyx otnosenijax korejskogo i 'altajskix' jazykov (On the issue of the genetic relationship of Korean and Altaic languages). *Izvestja Akademia Nauk*, SSSR, Ser. VI, XXI. 15–17: 1195–204. Moscow.

Ramstedt, G.J. 1949. *Studies in Korean Etymology*. Helsinki: Suomalais-Ugrilainen Seura.

Shim, Jaegi. 1983. *Kugŏ ŏhwiron* (Korean Lexicology). Seoul: Chimmundang.

Shiratori, Kurakichi. 1914–6. Chosengo to Ural-Altai-go to no hikaku kenkyu (A comparative study of Korean and Ural-Altaic languages).

Sohn, Ho-Min. 1986. *Linguistic Expeditions*. Seoul: Hanshin.

Sohn, Ho-Min. 1997. Orthographic divergence in South and North Korea: toward a unified spelling system. In Kim-Renaud, Y.K. (1997, 193–217).

Sohn, Ho-Min. 1999/2001. *The Korean Language*. Cambridge, UK: Cambridge University Press.

Suh, Cheong-Soo. 1996. *Kugŏ munpŏp* (A Korean Grammar). Seoul: Hanyang University Press.

Sung, Baeg-in. 1997. The present state and problems of genealogical studies of Korean. *Korea Journal* 37.3:166–225.

Sung, Kychul. 1985. *Hyŏndae kugŏ taeupŏp yŏngu* (A Study of Korean Honorifics). Seoul: Kaemunsa.

Vovin, A. 2009. *Koreo-Japonica: A Re-Evaluation of a Common Genetic Origin*. Honolulu: University of Hawaii Press.

Wang, Hahn-Sok. 1984. *Honorific Speech Behavior in a Rural Korean Village: Structure and Use*. Ph.D. dissertation. University of California at Los Angeles.

Whitman, J. B. 1985. *The Phonological Basis for the Comparison of Japanese and Korean*. Ph.D. dissertation. Harvard University.

Yun, Sung-Kyu. 1993. *Honorific Agreement*. Ph.D. dissertation. University of Hawaii.

2 Middle Korean*

1. Introduction

1.1 Historical background

Middle Korean (MK) is usually viewed as covering the period from the tenth to the sixteenth century (e.g. K. Lee 1976, Y. Choy 1987, K. Kang and K. Hwang 2003. Y. Ko 2007). That is, MK ranges over the Kolye dynasty period (918–1392) and the first 200 years of the Cosen dynasty.[1]

It is further divided into Early Middle Korean (EMK) and Late Middle Korean (LMK). EMK lasted from the beginning of Kolye until the creation of the Korean alphabet *hankul* in the early Cosen dynasty. LMK was the language represented in the *hankul* texts in the fifteenth and sixteenth centuries, specifically from King Seycong's promulgation of the *hwunmin cengum* (later termed *hankul*) in 1446 to the Japanese invasion in 1592 and the subsequent seven-year Imcin Wars.

Of all the stages of Korean language development, MK, especially LMK, is linguistically the most important, in that with the invention of the Korean alphabet in the fifteenth century detailed aspects of the Korean language were revealed for the first time. EMK data in the Kolye period were recorded in Chinese characters, whereas LMK data in the Cosen period were recorded in *hankul*. The creation of *hankul* made extensive and exact transcriptions of the Korean language possible.

With the founding of the Kolye dynasty (from which the national title *Korea* came) in the early tenth century, the capital was moved from Kyengcwu (in the Kyengsang province) to Kaykyeng (present Kayseng in the southern part of North Korea) which became the new political and cultural center until the capi-

* This chapter is a reprint (with minor notational changes) of chapter 4 (Middle Korean) of N. Tranter (ed.), *The Languages of Japan and Korean* (Routledge 2012).

1 P. Nam (2009) claims that Old Korean extend to the middle of the 13th century. His argument is based on the marked difference he observed between the grammar of *sektok kwukyel* available until the middle of the 13th c. and the grammar of *swuntok kwukyek* used thereafter.

tal moved to current Seoul (then called Hanyang) in 1392 with the establishment of the Cosen dynasty. Thus, unlike Old Korean with Silla language data as the backbone, available MK data are assumed to heavily reflect the language of the central area (Kaykyeng and Seoul). Even so, it is safe to say that MK is the direct descendant of the language of unified Silla, of which Kaykyeng and Seoul were a part.

1.2 Early Middle Korean

Although the situation is slightly better than for Old Korean, EMK is still observed in fragmentary reflexes in existing records written in Chinese characters used as phonograms. Thus, our knowledge of EMK is limited, since linguistic facts can essentially be understood only from Chinese characters by way of internal reconstruction. Such scanty written texts include 11 vernacular poems (*hyangka*) in *Kyunye-cen* (*Stories about Abbot Kyunye,* by Hyeklyen Ceng, 1075), *Kyeylim yusa* (*Things on Korea*, by Chinese Song dynasty scholar Sun Mu, 1103-4), *Samkwuk saki* (*Historical Record of the Three Kingdoms,* by Kim Pusik, 1145), *Hyangyak kwukuppang* (Herbal Medicine Emergency Treatments, c. 1250), 14 *hyangka* poems in *Samkwuk yusa* (Memorabilia of the Three Kingdoms, by Monk Ilyen, 1285), *Taymyengyul cikhay* (Translation of the Chinese Ming dynasty penal code *Ta Ming Lü,* 1395), and *Cosenkwan yeke* (A Korean-Chinese Translated Lexicon, 1408). In addition to these books, there are a number of *kwukyel* ('oral formulae') texts, including Buddhist sutras, annotated in the Kolye period. Such texts contain extensive information about the use of grammatical endings.

Of these, *Kyeylim yusa*, *Hyangyak kwukuppang*, and *Cosenkwan yeke* are considered the most important and valuable materials for EMK. *Kyeylim yusa* is a vocabulary list of about 360 Kolye words and phrases written with a total of 385 Chinese characters.[2] The *Hyangyak kwukuppang* is a pharmacological work from 1250 that lists the names of some 180 plants, animals, and minerals used in Korean herbal medicine. *Cosenkwan yeke* is a list of 596 words covering 19 areas including astronomy, geography, time, and flora and fauna. *Kyelim yusa* is the most representative of these to overview the general linguistic profile of EMK.[3]

---

2 Scholars are not in agreement as to the exact number of vocabulary items in *Kyeylim Yusa*: 353 (*à la* B. An 1985: 25 and others' counts), 355 (S. Kang 1980, J. Shim 1993), 356 (Kwuklip Kwuke Yenkwuwen 1999), 359 (T. Chin 1974), and 361 (T. Kim 2002 and T. Chin 2003).

3 A number of studies on the Kolye dialect (EMK) written in *Kyeylim Yusa* are available, including monographs such as T. Chin (1974), S. Kang (1980), and B. An (1985). A recent grammatical summary is found in J. Chung (2004).

Most of the basic Kolye words appearing in *Kyeylim yusa*, which are written with Chinese characters used as phonograms, are reflected in Middle and Contemporary Korean. In the following illustrations, reconstructions of Kolye words from the Chinese phonograms (e.g. *mól* 'horse' from the Chinese character 末 *mal*; *onal* 'today' from Chinese characters 烏捺 *o-nal*; *hanól* 'sky' from 漢捺 *han-nal*; *kelim* 'picture' from 乞林 *kel-lim*; *pólam* 'wind' from 孛纜 *pól-lam*) are approximate, based on S. Kang (1980), B. An (1985), J. Chung (2004), p.Nam (2009), and others. The fifteenth-century words are from Nam's (1982) MK dictionary, omitting tone marking. MK is transcribed with the Yale Romanization system.[4]

(1)

Kyeylim Yusa	**15C MK**	**CK**	
pal	*pal*	**pal**	foot
iup	*ip*	**ip**	mouth
ni	*ni*	**i**	tooth
son	*son*	**son**	hand
kwui	*kwuj*	**kwi**	ear
pói	*pój*	**pay**	belly
mwun	*mom*	**mom**	body
hanapi	*hanapi*	**halapeci**	grandfather
nach	*nóch*	**nach**	face
caapi	*api*	**api**, **apeci**	father
ami	*emi*	**emi**, **emeni**	mother
p(o)tal	*stól*	**ttal**	daughter
atal	*atól*	**atul**	son
aca	*aó*	**awu**	younger brother
kelim	*kulim*	**kulim**	picture
nwun	*nwun*	**nwun**	snow
hanól	*hanól*	**hanul**	sky
tol	*tolh*	**tol**	stone
kwulim	*kwulwum*	**kwulum**	clouds
psal	*psól*	**ssal**	husked rice
pólam	*pólóm*	**palam**	wind

4 There are several sounds in MK which are not shared in CK. For these sounds, new symbols are introduced in addition to the Yale system: *β* (ㅸ), *z* (ㅿ), *ɦ* (ㅇ), *ʔ* (ㆆ), *ó* (•), and *j*. The semivowel *j* is used here in MK instead of CK *y*, because the MK semivowel functioned as both on-glide and off-glide, whereas the CK counterpart functions only as on-glide and the original off-glide has merged with the preceding vowel, together generating a separate vowel phoneme: e.g. MK *saj* [saj] vs. CK *say* [sɛ] 'bird'.

pól	*pul*	**pwul**	fire
mój	*moj*	**moy** (archaic)	mountain
sjwupól	*swupul*	**swul**	wine
kahi	*kahi*	**kay**	dog
koki	*koki*	**koki**	fish, meat
hoal	*hwal*	**hwal**	bow
mól	*mól*	**mal**	horse
sjo	*sjo*	**so**	cow, ox
mil	*mil*	**mil**	wheat
kot	*koc*	**kkoch**	flower
omol	*wumul*	**wumwul**	water well
mol	*mul*	**mwul**	water
namk	*namk-, namo*	**namwu**	tree
sam	*sam*	**sam**	hemp
nipul	*nipul*	**ipwul**	blanket, cover
kachuki	*kachi*	**kkachi**	magpie
pittari	*pitólki, pitwuli*	**pitwulki**	pigeon
jangci	*jangci*	**yangchi**	tooth cleaning
onal	*onól*	**onul**	today
mosipaj	*mosipoj*	**mosipey**	ramie cloth
moloj	*moloj*	**molay**	day after tomorrow

Some numerals appearing in *Kyeylim yusa* include the following. SK stands for Sino-Korean.

(2)	*haton*	*hónah*	**hana**	one
	topal	*twulh*	**twul**	two
	taswut	*tasós*	**tases**	five
	iswut	*jesus*	**yeses**	six
	ilkup	*nilkwup*	**ilkop**	seven
	itap	*jetulp*	**yetelp**	eight
	aho	*ahop*	**ahop**	nine
	iol/iel	*jel*	**yel**	ten
	swumol	*sumul*	**sumwul**	twenty
	silhan	*sjelhun*	**selhun**	thirty
	siwun	*sujn*	**swin**	fifty
	on	*on*	[**payk**] (SK)	100

Kyeylim yusa also reveals EMK morpho-syntax, which is essentially the same as that of LMK and Contemporary Korean, for example, nominative marking (3a), relative clause formation (3b), negation (3c), imperative constructions (3d), vocatives (3e), collocations (3f), conjunctives (3g), and questions (3h) are shared by EMK and Contemporary Korean.

(3)	*Kyeylim Yusa*	**Contemporary Korean**	**Glosses**
a.	*hólk-i*	**hulk i**	soil (nominative)
	kach-i	**kacwuk/kecwuk i**	skin (nominative)
	namk-i	**namwu ka**	tree (nominative)
	nó-j	**na**, **nay** 'I, me'	I (nominative)
	nach-i tjoh-ón	**nach i coh-un**	good-looking ('face good')
b.	*noph-ón*	**noph-un**	high
	hój-n	**huy-n**	white
	isi-l	**iss-ul**	to exist
	noló-n soj	**nola-n soy**	gold ('yellow metal')
	sik-un mol	**sik-un mwul**	cold water
	nik-un mol	[tew-un] **mwul**	hot water
c.	*nach i mot tjoh-ón*	**nach i an coh-un**	bad-looking ('face not good')
	ani masj-a	**an masy-e**	not drinking
	paj cha ani	**pay cha-[ci] an**	not full (of one's stomach)
d.	*aci-kala*	**anc-kela**	Sit!
	tó-la	**tal-la**	Give!
	o-la	**o-la**, **w-ala**	Come!
	sal-la	**sal-la**, **sal-ala**	Live!
	o-swusej	**o-sose**	Please come! (super-polite)
	pili-swusej	**pilli-sose**	Borrow!, Lend!
e.	*ak-a*	**ak-a**	Child!
f.	*kel po-*	**kul po-**	read books ('see writing')
	pal chi-kola	**pal chi-kela**	hang a bamboo-blind!
g.	*son sis-ja*	**son ssis-e**	wash hands and so
	sjwupól masj-a	**swul masy-e**	drink wine and so
h.	*nwu-ko*	**nwu-kko** (Kyengsang dialect)	who is it?
	mjech isj-e	**myech i iss-e**	how many are there?

As observed in (3a) and (3f), case particles are frequently omitted. In particular, no examples of the accusative particle are given in *Kyeylim yusa,* although *itwu, hyangka,* and *kwukyel* data of the EMK period show abundant examples of case particles including nominative, accusative, and locative.

Even with the above *Kyeylim yusa* data alone, it is apparent that the sounds, as well as structures, of EMK were not particularly different from those of LMK. Other records also show striking similarities between Early and Late Middle Korean. For instance, in *Samkwuk saki* (1145), 'horn' was recorded with two Chinese characters, which would be pronounced as *spul*, exactly the same pronounciation in *hankul* during the LMK period. It is thus safe to assume that fifteenth and sixteenth-century Korean (LMK) of which abundant *hankul* texts are available for the first time is representative of overall MK.

There are possibilities to internally reconstruct a more comprehensive system of EMK language phenomena based on fifteenth- and sixteenth-century *hankul*-based written records, *itwu* and *hyangchal* transcriptions, and the traditional readings of Chinese characters, which were standardized in the Silla period (as was attempted for example in P. An 1977, 1992; P. Nam 1999, 2009; Y. Chang 2002; T. Pae 2002). Yet, the majority of Korean historical linguists have preferred to work on the abundant written data of fifteenth-century MK. Following this scholarly trend, the survey of MK in this chapter will be based largely on fifteenth- and sixteenth-century data.[5]

1.3 Late Middle Korean texts

The *hankul* texts that appeared during the fifteenth and sixteenth centuries are impressive in terms of quantity, quality, and variability. In terms of number, Korean translations of Buddhist sutras and works of Buddhist literature are predominant. Representative texts that are frequently quoted for linguistic description include the following. Abbreviations are given in brackets.

Hwunmin cengum haylyey (Explanations and Examples of Hwunmin Cengum, by Ceng Inci, et al., 1446) [Cengum Haylyey]
Yongpi echenka (Songs of the Dragons Flying to Heaven, by King Seycong's royal subjects, 1447) [Yongka]
Sekpo sangcel (Detailed Articles on the Record of Sakyamuni, by Prince Swuyang, 1447) [Sekpo]
Tongkwuk cengwun (Correct Rhymes of the Eastern Country, 1447) [Tongk-

5 For detailed studies of overall MK structure, see P. An & K. Lee (1990); B. Choy (1990); Y. Choy (1987); W. Huh (1992, 1975); K. Kang & Hwang (2003); D. Kim (2003); M. Kim (1957); Y. Ko (2007); Y. Ko & K. Nam (1999; J. Kwon (1998); H. Lee (1994); K. Lee (1976); L. Lyu, et al. (2005); and B. Pak (1989), among other works. For studies on MK phonology, see N. Chang (1982); S. Kang (1990); W. Kim (1971); K. Lee (1972), and Y. Moon (1974), among other studies.

wuk]

Welin chenkang ci kok (Songs of the Moon's Imprint on a Thousand Rivers, by King Seycong, 1449) [Welin]

Welin sekpo (combination of the preceding two volumes, by King Seyco [= Swuyang], 1459) [Welsek]

Hwunmin cengum enhay (Korean translation of Hwunmin Cengum, included in Welin sekpo, 1459) [Cengum Enhay]

Nungemkyeng enhay (Korean translation of Nungem Sutra, 1462) [Nungem]

Pephwakyeng enhay (Korean translation of Pephwa Sutra, 1463) [Pephwa]

Kumkangkyeng enhay (Korean translation of Kumkang Sutra, 1464) [Kumkang]

Kumkangkyeng samkahay (Korean translation of Three Authorities in Kumkang Sutra) [Kumkang Samka]

Wenkakkyeng enhay (Korean traslation of Wenkak Sutra, 1465) [Wenkak]

Kwukuppang enhay (Korean translation of Emergency Treatments, 1466) [Kwukuppang]

Mongsan pepe enhay (Korean translation of Mongsan's Buddhist Teachings, 1467) [Mongsan]

Samkang nayhwun (Teaching for Females, 1475) [Nayhwun]

Twusi enhay (Korean interpretation of Du Fu's Poems, 1481) [Twusi]

Kwanumkyeng enhay (Korean translation of Kwanum Sutra, 1485) [Kwanum]

Akhak kweypem (Music Codes, 1493) [Akhak]

Akcang kasa (Movement Lyrics, sometime during 1506~1567) [Akcang]

Pakthongsa enhay (Korean translation of Interpreter Pak, by Choy Seycin, before 1517) [Pakthongsa]

Nokeltay enhay (Korean translation of the Old Cathayan, by Choy Seycin, before 1957) [Nokeltay]

Hwunmong cahoy (Chinese-Korean Glossary, by Choy Seycin, 1527) [Hwunmong]

Samkang hayngsilto (Depictions of Confucious Role Models, 1581) [Samkang]

Sekpong chencamun (Sekpong's 1,000 Characters, 1583) [Sekpong]

Sohak enhay (Korean translation of Primary Learning, 1588) [Sohak]

Tayhak enhay (Korean translation of Advanced Learning, 1590) [Tayhak]

In addition, there are many Kolye ballads that are written in *hankul* in the fifteenth and sixteenth centuries (Y. Choy 1987; K. Kang & Hwang 2003; Ko 2007).

2. Phonology

2.1 Background

MK succeeded the Silla language (Old Korean). K. Lee (1976:93–9) assumes that the following phonological developments occurred in EMK: (a) addition of the voiced fricative *z* to the consonant system, as in *kózól* 'autumn', *azó* 'younger brother', and *mózóm* 'mind'; (b) addition of the voiced bilabial fricative *β*, as in *nwuβi* 'younger sister', *swuβel* 'liquor', and *twuβul* 'two'; and (c) development of the tensed consonant series (*pp, tt, cc, kk, ss, hh*), as observed in *ppul (< spul < sepul*) 'horn', *ttal (< ptól < potól)* 'daughter', and *ssal (< psól < posól)* 'rice'.

B. An (1985: 47) identifies thirteen consonants, six vowels, and a number of diphthongs in EMK based on his phonological analysis of the words that appear in *Kyeylim yusa*. The 13 consonants are: stops *p, t, c, k, ʔ, ch*; fricatives *z, s, h*; nasals *m, n, ng*: and liquid *l*. The six vowels are: *i, u, wu, o, a, ó*. An's system shows that the tense consonant series had not developped yet and even the aspirated consonant series was not fully established. The later mid-central vowel *e* has not been identified, which makes the vowel system asymmetrical. An's system is considerably different from what K. Lee assumed above. It appears that Lee's assumption of the tensed consonant series in Early MK is somewhat weak because the series was not firmly established even in Late MK, as seen shortly. On the other hand, as An's reconstructions are based only on words in *Kyeylim yusa*, which are transcribed with approximate Chinese characters, his assumed system cannot be said complete. This is particularly the case when we compare the system with that of LMK.

T. Kim (2002) compares seven sets of EMK consonant systems proposed by seven different linguists, from a nine-consonant system to a 15-consonant system. For instance, the 15-consonant system includes: stops *p, t, c, k, ph, th, ch, kh*; fricatives *s, h*; nasals *m, n, ng*; and liquids *l, r* (e.g. B. Choy 1990). None of these systems include *z* nor *ɦ*. Only one includes *ʔ*.

Based essentially on Kang's (1980) study on *Kyeylim yusa* and his own analysis, P. Nam (2012:64) presents EMK (his Late Old Korean) consonant system, consisiting of *p, t, c, k, ph, th, ch, kh, s, h, z, m, n, ng, l, r*. He notes that MK *β* still did not exist and that *k, n, r, l, m, p, ng* were used as syllable codas. He assumes that EMK had a seven-vowel system as in LMK: *i, u, wu, e, o, ó, a*.

The later period of MK (from the fifteenth century) observed a flood of literature written in *hankul*, most of which reflected the language used in the capital, the Kaykyeng dialect. The phonemic system of fifteenth-century Korean consisted of 22 (*à la* W. Huh 1983; Y. Choy 1987, and others) or 23 (*à la* K. Lee 1972 and others) consonants, seven vowels, and two semivowels. Unlike Huh (ibid.) and others, K. Lee (ibid.:15-26), Y. Ko (2007:29), and a few earlier Korean linguists include *ɦ* in the MK consonant system. K. Lee assumes that contemporary standard words like **kasay** (or **kawi**) 'scissors' and **molay** 'sand' derived from fifteenth-century words like **kózɦaj* and **molɦaj*, respectively, in view of the existence of forms like *kasi**k**ay* 'scissors' and *mol**k**ay* 'sand' in southern and other dialects.

2.2 Consonants

The 23 consonant phonemes are given in Table 1. Examples with these phonemes are given in (4).

Table 1. Late Middle Korean Consonants

		Bilabial	Dental	Palatal	Velar	Glottal
Stop:	Lax	p ㅂ	t ㄷ	c ㅈ	k ㄱ	
	Aspirated	ph ㅍ	th ㅌ	ch ㅊ	kh ㅋ	
	Tensed	pp ㅃ	tt ㄸ	cc ㅉ	kk ㄲ	
Fricative:	Lax-voiced	β ㅸ	z ㅿ			(ɦ) ㅇ
	Lax-voiceless		s ㅅ		h ㅎ	
	Tensed		ss ㅆ		hh ㆅ	
Nasal:		m ㅁ	n ㄴ	ng ㆁ		
Lateral:			l ㄹ			

(4)

pul 'fire'	*twul* 'two'	*cohój* 'paper'	*koc* 'flower'	
phól 'house fly'	*kothi* 'cocoon'	*chej* 'sieve'	*khong* 'soybean'	
ppwul(< *spwul*) 'horn'	*tta* (< *sta*) 'earth'	*ccek* 'time'	*-kka* (question)	
nwuβ- 'lie down'	*kezuj* 'almost'			*mol(ɦ)aj* 'sand'
	sjem 'island'		*him* 'power'	
	sso- 'shoot'		*tolóhhi-* 'return'	
skwum 'dream'	*nap* 'monkey'	*cjwung* 'monk'		
	nolaj 'song'			

In fifteenth-century Korean, words with a tensed stop written *pp, tt, cc, kk* were rare. Rather, tensed sounds resulted from sandhi with a preceding 'tensifying' sound such as *l* or a stop as in CK, e.g. *hol* ***kk**es* 'single thing' and *coch* ***cc**ap-* 'follow and catch'. The tensed series was developing as an innovation in the system, especially from clusters as discussed shortly.

King Seycong's *Hwunmin Cengum* includes a *hankul* symbol (ㆆ) representing the glottal stop [ʔ]. However, most historical linguists of Korean agree that it was not a phoneme. *Hwunmin Cengum Hyeylyey* itself indicates that word-initial *ʔ* + vowel is similar to the same vowel without *ʔ*. Furthermore, the book does not provide any examples illustrating the sound.

The *hankul* symbol ㆆ occurred rather rarely in fifteenth-century *hankul* texts, e.g. *hanólʔptut* 'heaven's will' < *hanól* 'heaven' + *ptut* 'will'.

As indicated by Y. Ko (2007:23-4, 28), *ʔ* was recorded in fifteenth-century Korean only after *l*, or after the final vowel of the first noun in a noun-noun compound, and other letters such as *s, z, k, t,* and *p* occur in the same role: *pój**s** koc* 'pear flower', *nimkum**z** mal* 'king's words', *myes kan.**t** cip* 'house of how many rooms', *phjeng.sajng.**k** ptut* 'life-time wish', and *salóm**p** ptut* 'people's wish'. It is thus clear that the function of *ʔ*, as well as the other epenthetic consonants, was to indicate tensification of the following lax consonant across word boundaries. Only the so-called epenthetic **s** continues in this function.

Y. Choy (1987:21) indicates that the Chinese 日 'day' was transcribed as *ziʔ* in *Hongmwu Cengwun* and as *zilʔ* in *Hwunmin Cengum Enhay.* The current Korean form is **il**, while the current Japanese form is *nichi* or *niQ-* (as in *niQpon* 'Japan') reflecting Middle Chinese *-t*. In view of all this, the sound must have been a glottal stop or catch not having a full-fledged phonemic status but had the function of keeping the meanings apart as the epenthetic **s** in CK does.

Due to their limited distribution and low functional load, the voiced fricative consonants *β, hh,* and *ɦ* disappeared between the mid-fifteenth and early sixteenth century. *β,* which generally occurred between voiced sounds and did not occur word-initially, changed primarily to *w,* as in *teβi* > **tewi** 'heat' and *kulβal* > **kulwal** 'sentence, letter', but also merged with *p* in some dialects as in the Kyengsang dialect *tepi* 'heat' and the Cenla/Kyengsang dialect *saypi* 'shrimp' from MK *saβi* (= **saywu**). The tensed *hh* occurred only in a small number of words, such as *hhje-* 'pull' and *chihhje-* 'raise' and later changed generally to **kh**: **khye-** and **chikhi-**. *ɦ* has either dropped or remained as *k,* as in *kózɦaj* 'scissors' > **kawi**, *kasay* or *kasikay* (Cenla, Kyengsang, etc.); *molɦaj* 'sand' > **molay**, *molkay* (Kyengsang); *pelɦej* 'bug' > **pelley**, *pel(k)eci* (Cenla, Kyengsang, etc.); *melɦwuj* 'wild grapes' > **melwu**, *melkwu* (Cenla, Kyengsang, etc.); and *silɦej* 'shelf, rack' > **sileng** (standard CK), *silkeng* (Cenla, Kyengsang, etc.).

z generally occurred between voiced sounds, as in *mózóm* 'heart', *kózól* 'autumn', *kjezul* 'winter', *mózól* 'village', *nójzil* 'tomorrow', *niz-e* 'connect-INF', *hanzum* 'sigh', *sózi* 'space'. It persisted until the end of the sixteenth century and thereafter either (rarely) merged with *s* (especially some words in southern and other dialects) or (more frequently) disappeared completely: **maum**, **kaul**,

kyewul, **maul**, **nayil**, **i-e**, **hanswum**, **sai**. Forms in other dialects are generally the same, except that 'connect-INF is *is-e* in Cenla, Kyengsang, and some other dialects, where 'autumn', 'winter', and 'village' are reflected in two forms: *kaul* and *kasil*, *kyewul* (new form) and *cesil* (old form), *maul* and *masil*. The two forms **kasil** and **masil** acquired specialized meanings: *kasil* meaning 'autumn harvest' and *masil* used only in *masil ka-* 'goof around (in the village)'.

c and *ch* were alveo-dental [ts] and [ts^h], respectively. When followed by *j*, they became palatal. Thus, there were contrasts between *cang* 'cupboard' and *cjang* 'soy sauce' (both **cang**) and between *cho* 'vinegar' and *chjo* 'candle' (both **cho**). *s* was pronounced as it is today, but, in many words, was followed by a *j* that has since been lost: *sjem* 'island' > **sem**, *sjo* 'cow, ox' > **so**.

t and *th* could occur before *i* or *j*, since palatalized to **c** and **ch**: *thjenti* 'heaven and earth' (**chenci**), *tjotha* 'good' (**cohta**), *tje* 'that over there' (**ce**), *tina* 'elapsing' (**cina**), *thita* 'strike' (**chita**). Palatalization of *t* and *th* before *i* or *j* occurred around the seventeenth or eighteenth century. MK also allowed *n* word initially before *i* or *j*: *ni* 'tooth' (**i**), *niph* 'leaf' (**iph**), *njelum* 'summer' (**yelum**). Most other sound alternations such as the epenthetic *s* phenomena, tensification of lax stops after the prospective relativizer *-(u)l,* and nasalization of non-nasal sounds before a nasal sound were, by and large, similar to parallel CK phenomena. Also as in CK, *l*-ending predicates lost their final *l* before a homorganic sound in a suffix, as in *mójngkó-noni* 'make and so', where *mójngkól* 'make' lost its final *l*.

There was a set of consonant clusters (5), illustrated in (6).

(5) Sequence of two consonants:	*pt*	*pth*	*ps*	*pc*
	sp	*st*	*sn*	*sk*
Sequence of three consonants:	*pst*	*psk*		

(6) *ptul* 'yard'	*pthuj-* 'jump'	*psi* 'seed'	*pcak* 'pair'
spje 'bone'	*sto* 'again'	*snóhój* 'boy'	*skoli* 'tail'
pstaj 'time'	*pskum* 'gap'		

The values of orthographic *sp*, *st*, *sk*, *ps*, *pst*, *psk*, *pt, pc* are still disputed: were they pronounced as written or were they simply allographs of tensed *pp*, *tt*, *kk*, *ss*, *tt*, *kk*, *tt, cc*? Certainly they correspond to modern tensed consonants: *ptut* (**ttus**) 'meaning, intention', *psi* (**ssi**) 'seed', *psu* (**ssu**) 'use', *skwum* 'dream' (**kkwum**), *spul* 'horn' (**ppwul**), *pcak* (**ccak**) 'pair', and *pskwul* (**kkwul**) 'honey'. Most Korean historical linguists agree that they were pronounced as written. For instance, standard **ttek** 'rice cake' and **ttong** 'dung' are still pronounced as *sitekwu* in some northern dialects and *sitong* (in the sense 'manure') in some southern (e.g. Cenla) dialects. The reduction processes involved are assumed to have been **sitekwu* > MK *stek(wu)* > **ttek** and **sitong* > MK *stong* > **ttong**. Similarly, MK *psól* 'hulled rice' is currently **ssal**. However, **p** is retained in such compounds as **copssal** (**co** 'millet' + /p/ + **ssal**) 'hulled millet', **haypssal** (**hay**/**say** 'new' + /p/ + **ssal**) 'new hulled rice', and **chapssal** (**chal** 'sticky' + /p/ + **ssal**) 'glutinous rice', where the syllable boundary falls between **cop**/**hayp**/**chap** and **ssal**. MK *pstaj* 'time' is now *ttay*, but the initial *p* remains in **cepttay** (**ce** 'that' + /p/ + **ttay**) 'the other day'. MK *snóhój* 'boy' is **sanai;** it seems that, unable to be tensified, *sn* instead acquired an epenthetic vowel.

MK observed implosivization (unrelease) of syllable-final consonants, except *s* which was, unlike in CK, not neutralized to *t* but spelled *s,* suggesting it was pronounced [s], as in *mos* [mos] 'pond' versus *mot* [mot] 'unable'. Thus, all bilabial consonants were neutralized to *p,* all dental, palatal, and glottal consonants to *t,* and all velar consonants to *k* syllable-finally, as in CK. As a result, only *p*, *t*, *k*, *m*, *n*, *ng*, *l*, *s* were actually pronounced syllable-finally.[1]

2.3 Vowels and semivowels

The fifteenth-century seven vowels and two semivowels are as follows. The semivowels did not have their unique *hankul* symbols, but were written, in the case of *j,* by adding an additional dot or short stroke (horizontal or vertical) to a vowel symbol, as in ㅛ /jo/ or ㅑ/ja/; and, in the case of *w,* by combining two vowels in a syllable block, as in ㅜ /u/ + ㅏ /a/ = /wa/.

(7) a. Vowels

	Front	Central	Back
High	*i* /i/ ㅣ	*u* /ɨ/ㅡ	*wu* /u/ㅜ
Mid		*e* /ə/ ㅓ	*o* /o/ㅗ
Low		*a* /a/ ㅏ	*ó* /ʌ/ •

b. Semivowels *j* *w*

The vowel system was asymmetrical with only one front vowel. King Seycong and his linguists classified vowels into three groups: the bright or *yang* vowels *a, ó, o,* the dark or *yin* vowels *e, u, wu,* and the neutral vowel *i*. This classification explained vowel harmony patterns.

MK had rigid vowel harmony: *yang* vowels *o, a, ó* occurred only with *yang* or neutral (*i*) vowels, and *yin* vowels *e, u, wu* occurred only with *yin* or neutral vowels. *Yang* vowels are characterized as having more sonority than other vowels in that they are pronounced with retracted tongue root. Vowel harmony in MK was observed within a word (8a), across nominal and particle (8b), and across predicate stem and suffix (8c). Current Korean often no longer retains this vowel harmony.

(8)				
	a.	*namo*	**namwu**	'tree'
		kamakoj	**kamakwi**	'crow'
		taló-	**talu-**	'different'
		kwulwum	**kwulum**	'clouds'
		nilkwup	**ilkop**	'seven'
		halmi	**halmi**	'old woman'
	b.	*son-ólo*	**son-ulo**	'with a hand'
		mal-ól	**mal-ul**	'horse-ACC'
		skwum-ul	**kkwum-ul**	'dream-ACC'
		son-ój	**son-uj**	'hand-GEN'
		cip-uj	**cip-uj**	'house-GEN'
	c.	*mak-óni*	**mak-uni**	'as one blocks'
		mek-uni	**mek-uni**	'as one eats'
		nól-kaj	**nalkay**	'wing'
		tep-kej	**tepkay**	'cover'

The vowel *ó* is believed to have been a sound between *a* and *o,* primarily because Ceycwu dialect still retains it. It was lost in all other dialects, becoming *a* word-initially syllable and *u* elsewhere, e.g. *mózóm* 'heart' > **maum**.

With *j* and *w*, 18 diphthongs and triphthongs were formed, given in (9) and illustrated in (10). Unlike in CK, MK *j* occurred as an off-glide as well. There were no *w* off-glides.

(9)							
Diphthongs							
	On-glides:	*ja*	*je*	*jo*	*jwu*		
		wa	*we*				
	Off-glides:	*aj*	*ej*	*oj*	*wuj*	*uj*	*ój*
Triphthongs							
	On-off glides:	*jaj*	*jej*	*joj*	*jwuj*		
		waj	*wej*				

(10)				
	On-glides:	*pójam* 'snake'	*nje-* 'go'	*tjoh-* 'good'
		sjwulwup 'umbrella'	*cwasi-* 'eat-*hon*'	*pwuhwengi* 'owl'
	Off-glides:	*haj* 'a lot'	*sejs* 'three'	*moj* 'mountain'

	swujβ- 'easy'	*pkuj* 'meal'	*hój* 'sun'
On-off glides:	*cókjaj* 'nacre'	*njej* 'old times'	*sjojkoki* 'beef'
	chjwujhó- 'drunk'	*tasswaj* '5 days'	*kwej* 'chest'

2.4 Suprasegmentals

MK was a tonal language. Early *hankul* used a simple way to mark tones. There were three tonemes: high pitch or "going tone" (indicated by one dot to the left of the *hankul* syllable block), rising pitch or "rising tone" (two dots to the left), and low pitch or "even tone" (absence of dots):

(11)	a.	*·kil* 'road'	*·son* 'hand'	*·pal* 'foot'
		ka·ci 'variety'	*·kaci* 'branch'	*·mal* 'a unit of measure'
	b.	*:saj* 'bird'	*:pal* 'the blinds'	*:mal* 'word'
	c.	*cip* 'house'	*son* 'guest'	*mal* 'horse'
	d.	*pwulhwuj* 'root' + *·i* (SUBJ) → *pwul:hwuj*		
		tóli 'bridge' + *·i* (SUBJ) → *tó:li*		

Tones ceased to exist from the middle of the sixteenth century on, except in parts of the Kyengsang and Hamkyeng dialects. All vowels that had a rising tone became (and still are) long, whereas vowels with a high or low tone remained short.[6]

3. Script

Chinese character script has long been an integral part of the writing systems of Koreans and was the only system before the creation of *hankul* in 1446, and literacy was restricted to male members of the ruling class, who devoted their entire lives to the study of Classical Chinese written in characters, because it was the main goal of education, the official means of government affairs, and the medium of civil service examinations.

In an effort to improve this predicament, *itwu* script (including *hyangchal* and *kwukyel* transcriptions) was used to record Korean by means of (a) Chinese characters borrowed for their Chinese meaning but read as the corresponding semantically equivalent Korean word (semantograms) or (b) Chinese characters borrowed for their Chinese pronunciation only (phonograms).

Itwu script allowed people to record personal names, place names, and ver-

---

6 For some studies on MK tones, see Y. Jeong 1971, 1972; W. Huh 1972; W.J. Kim 1973; S.O. Lee 1979; Martin 1992:60-86; and Ramsey 1978, among other works.

nacular songs and poems. It was also used to clarify government documents and other books written in Chinese. However, it was extremely inadequate as a means of written communication as well as being difficult to learn. It was under these circumstances that *hankul* was created, a phonetic writing system completely disengaged from the Chinese script.

The indigenous phonetic alphabet now called *hankul* is one of the most remarkable writing systems ever devised.[7] For the design of the *hankul* alphabet, Seycong (1397–1450), the fourth king of the Cosen dynasty, and the scholars of the royal academy called Ciphyencen (lit. 'Hall of Assembled Sages') studied the rich Chinese linguistic tradition, such as the concepts of consonants, syllables, and tones, as well as their underlying philosophical background. The orthographical design of *hankul*, which was based on a rigorous analysis of Korean and SK sound patterns, was completed in 1443. To test the new writing system, the king ordered subjects (Kwen Cey, et al.) to write the voluminous *Yongpi Echenka* (Songs of Flying Dragons, 1447) in *hankul* with translations in Chinese characters, a eulogy cycle in 125 cantos comprising 248 poems, composed to celebrate the founding of the Cosen dynasty and the achievements of Seycong's predecessors.

King Seycong promulgated *hankul* on October 9, 1446, as *hwunmin cengum* 'the correct sounds to educate people'. *Hwunmin Cengum* (written by Seycong himself) was accompanied by *Hwunmin Cengum Haylyey* (Explanations and Examples of the *Hwunmin Cengum*), compiled by a group of scholars (headed by Ceng Inci). These two documents were published as a single book.

The text of *Hwunmin Cengum* consists of three parts: preface, pronunciation, and usage rules. The preface briefly summarizes Seycong's motives for inventing *hankul* as (12) in English translation.

(12) The speech sounds of Korea are distinct from those of China and thus are not communicable with Chinese characters. Hence, many people having something to put into words are unable to express their feelings. To overcome such distressing circumstances, I have newly devised 28 letters that everyone can learn with ease and use with convenience in daily life.

In the second part, the sounds of the newly devised 17 consonant (ㄱ ㅋ ㆁ ㄷ

7 This alphabet was named *hankul* (meaning 'Great Writing') by Cwu Sikyeng (1876–1914), a pioneer linguist of Korean. Before, it was popularly called *enmwun* 'vernacular writing, vulgar script'. Works in English on the study of *hankul* include: Ledyard (1966); C. Lee (1972), Kim-Cho (2000); and Kim-Renaud (1997). South Koreans celebrate October 9 as Hankul Day, which is the day Hankul was promulgated by King Seycong in 1446; North Koreans erase Seycong and celebrate January 15.

ㅌ ㄴ ㅂ ㅍ ㅁ ㅈ ㅊ ㅅ ㆆ ㅎ ㅇ ㄹ ㅿ) and 11 vowel (ㆍ ㅡ ㅣ ㅗ ㅏ ㅜ ㅓ ㅛ ㅑ ㅠ ㅕ) letters are explained in Chinese. It is also indicated that when ㄱ ㄷ ㅂ ㅈ ㅅ ㅎ are doubled, they are pronounced tense: ㄲ *kk*, ㄸ *tt*, ㅃ *pp*, ㅉ *cc*, ㅆ *ss*, ㆅ *hh*.

The third part of *Hwunmin Cengum* presents rules regarding the use of *hankul* letters and other symbols in syllable blocks. For instance, when ㅇ is placed under a bilabial sound, a bilabial fricative sound results (e.g. the bilabial fricative sound β is represented by placing ㅇ under ㅂ as in ㅸ). It also stipulates use of tone dots.

Hwunmin Cengum Haylyey consists of seven parts: design of the letters, syllable-initial sounds, syllable-medial sounds, syllable-final sounds, combination of letters, examples of use, and a brief postface by Ceng Inci.

Since its creation, *hankul* has undergone several major ordeals in the course of its diffusion in the face of the long tradition of Chinese character use by the nobility and government officials during the Cosen dynasty. Although King Seycong's invention of *hankul* was the greatest cultural achievement, a group of scholar-officials led by Choy Manli, then associate academician of Ciphyencen, vehemently opposed the king's promulgation of *hankul* to the public. They presented an anti-*hankul* appeal to the throne in 1444. Their main argument was that Korea had long emulated Chinese ideas and institutions and that adoption of Korea's own writing system would make it impossible to identify Korean civilization with that of China but rather identify Korea with "barbarians" such as Mongolians, Tanguts, Jurchen, Japanese, and Tibetans, who had their own scripts. This appeal had little effect on Seycong's determination.

After the death of Seycong, opposition to *hankul* resumed and continued until Seyco, the seventh Cosen king, propagated *hankul* with Buddhism. Classical Chinese and Itwu remained predominant while *hankul* served as an aid for the study of Classical Chinese and was used mostly by women.

4. Morphology

The *hankul* literature of the fifteenth century is the oldest data to show the comprehensive grammatical system of Korean. Overall, the basic morphological structure of MK such as word formation and inflection patterns is similar to that of CK, although there are conspicuous differences in detail.

Nine word classes are recognized in MK: Noun, Pronoun, Numeral, Verb, Adjective, Copula, Determiner, Adverb, and Particle. Noun, Verb, Adjective, and Adverb are open classes. Noun, Pronoun, and Numeral function as heads of noun phrases, whereas Verb, Adjective, and Copula function as heads of predicates, inflecting in tense, aspect, modality, mood, and sentence/clause type ender. Determiner (demonstratives and specifiers) modifies nominal arguments, while Adverb modifies predicates, noun phrases, clauses, and sentences. Particle marks a wide variety of syntactic and semantic functions, including case, delimiter, conjunctive, and complementizer functions. In addition, various derivational affixes contributed to generating new words, while inflectional affixes (mostly suffixes) mark grammatical categories, relations, and functions. For initial approximation and illustration of uses of different word classes and inflectional suffixes, observe some excerpts from the Yongpi Echenka (1447) in (13a), Hwunmin Cengum Enhay (1450) in (13b), and Welin Sekpo (1459) in (13c).

(13) a. *pwulhwuj kiph-un namk*[8] *ón pólóm aj ani mwuj-lssój*
root deep-RL tree TC wind by not move-so
koc tjo-kho jelum ha-nó-ni
flower good-and fruit much-IN-DC
'Deep-rooted trees do not move by wind. So, flowers are good and fruits are plentiful.'

b. *na j i lól wujhój-a ejespi nekj-e*
I NM this AC serve-for pitifully think-s
sajlo sumul.jetulp ca lól mójngkó-noni
newly 28 letter AC make-as
'I felt sorry for this and newly made twenty eight letters. And thus [...]'

c. *salóm ój mokswum i mwusanghó-n kes i-la*
person GN life NM uncertain-RL thing be-DC
'People's life is something uncertain.'

The above sentences can be analyzed as in (14) in terms of word classes and inflectional suffixes.

(14) Nouns: *pwulhwuj* 'root', *namk* 'tree', *pólóm* 'wind', *koc* 'flower', *jelum* 'fruit', *ca* 'letter', *salóm* 'person', *mokswum* 'life', *kes* 'thing, fact'
Pronouns: *na* 'I', *i* 'this fact/thing'
Numerals: *sumul jetulp* '28'
Verbs: *mwuj-* 'move', *mójngkól-* 'make', *wujhój-* '(do) for', *neki-* 'think'

8 A small number of nouns that end in a vowel in their citation form replace this vowel with an original *k* before vowel-initial particles, e.g. *namo* (<*namok) vs. *namk ón*.

Adjectives: *kiph-* 'deep', *tjoh-* 'good', *ha-* 'many, much', *ejespu-* 'pitiful', *mwusanghó-* 'uncertain'
Copulas: *i-* (in *i-la*) 'be'
Adverbs: *ani* 'not', *sajlo* (*saj* 'newness' + *lo* 'with, in') 'newly', *ejespi* (*ejespu* 'pitiful' + *-i* '-ly') 'pitifully'
Determiners: *i* 'this' (when it occurs before a nominal)
Particles: *ón* 'as for' (topic), *aj* 'at, on, in, to' (locative/goal), *lól* (object or accusative), *j, i* (subject or nominative), *ój* (genitive)
Inflectional suffixes: *-(u)n* relativizer, *-lssój* 'as, so, because', *-ko* 'and', *-nó* indicative mood, *-ni* neutral declarative sentence ender, *-noni* 'as, since', *-a/-e* 'and, so', *-la* declarative sentence ender after a copula

4.1 Nouns and particles

4.1.1 Nouns

Due to the allout influx of Chinese words into MK, the lexicon was rich with many native and SK doublets with some connotational differences. Most Chinese words were imported as nouns, regardless of their original nominal or predicative status in Chinese. Thus, there were and still are a large number of SK verbal nouns and adjectival nouns derived from verbs or adjectives in Chinese. Proper nouns were generally written in Chinese characters in MK texts.

Bound nouns

In MK most nouns were free and independent, but there were also a considerable number of bound nouns, which cannot stand alone without a preceding determiner or relative clause. Most carry abstract or general meanings, which become more specific with a preceding determiner or a relative clause:

(15)	Semantic class	Bound noun	Gloss
	Person	*pwun*	'person' (honorific)
		i	'person' (adult)
	Thing/fact	*kes*	'thing, fact'
		pa	'thing, fact, what'
		i	'thing'
		cwul	'way, assumed fact'
		tó	'assumed fact'
	Place	*tó(j), taj*	'place'
		njek	'direction, region'

Time, chance	*cek*	'time'
	tet	'during, interval'
	cej	'time'
Limit	*spwun*	'only'
	stólóm	'alone'
	man	'only, extent'
Cause	*tas*	'blame, cause'
	ach	'reason, cause'
State, condition	*jang*	'state'
	tós	'seeming, appearance'
	cahi	'intact, just as it is'
Quantity, volume	*pól*	'the span of both arms'
	móli	(counter for animals)
	nat	'piece, unit'

Compounding

New nouns in MK derived most productively from compounding. Examples of co-compounds are *achóm-naco* (morning-evening) 'morning and evening', *ezi-atól* (parents-son) 'parents and children', *mó-sjo* (horse-cow) 'horses and cows', *cwuk-sal-i* (die-live-nom) 'life and death', and *anh-pask* (inside-outside) 'inside and outside'. Examples of sub-compounds are *amh-thalk* (*amh* 'female' + *talk* 'hen, cock') 'hen', *hwa-sal* (*hwal* 'bow' + *sal* 'arrow') 'arrow', *petu-namo* (*petul* 'willow' + *namo* 'tree') 'willow tree', *muls-kóz* (*mul* 'water' + epenthetic *s* + kóz 'edge') 'waterside', *muls-kjel* (*mul* 'water' + epenthetic *s* + *kjel* 'texture') 'wave', *sjoj-koki* (*sjo* 'cow' + genitive *j* + *koki* 'meat') 'beef', *nól? -cjwung-sójng* (*nól* 'fly' + epenthetic *?* + *cjwungsójng* 'animal') 'winged animal', *hanapi* (*ha* 'big' + relativiser *–n* + *api* 'father') 'grandfather', and *kan-pam* (*ka* 'go' + relativizer *–n* + *pam* 'night') 'last night'.

Affixation

Noun formation via affixation used prefixation and suffixation. Prefixation was not able to change word classes (–WCC), while suffixation includes those which changed word classes (+WCC), e.g. noun from verb or adjective, and those that could not (–WCC).

(16)		MK affixes	MK examples
	Prefixes	*ni-* 'unglutinous'	*ni-psól* 'unglutinous rice'
	–WCC	*tul-* 'wild'	*tul-pskaj* 'Perilla japonica'

	achón- 'small'	*achón-atól* 'nephew' *achón-stól* 'niece'
Suffixes +WCC	*-i* 'activity, state, thing'	*hój-tot-i* (sune-rise-) 'sunrise' *wuzum-wuz-i* 'laughing'
	-ój/-uj 'state'	*noph-ój* 'height'[9] *nep-uj* 'width'
	-(u)m 'activity, state, thing'	*kel-um* 'walking, stepping' *kuli-m* 'picture' *el-um* (freeze-) 'ice'
	-kaj/-kej 'instrument'	*pje-kaj* (rest.head-) 'pillow'
	-aj/-ej after *l*	*nól-aj* (fly-) 'wing' *nol-aj* (play-) 'song' *wul-ej* (cry-) 'thunder'
	-ki 'activity, state'	*mól-po-ki* (horse-see-) 'easing nature'
Suffixes –WCC	*-pal* 'lines, streaks'	*pis-pal* (rain-) 'streaks of rain' *hós-pal* (sun-) 'streaks of sun'
	-nim (honorific)	*acóma-nim* 'aunt'(hon.) *apa-nim* 'father' (hon.) *mótató-nim* 'oldest son' (hon.)
	-math 'side'	*meli-math* (head-) 'bedside'
	-cil 'activity'	*pwulmwu-cil* (bellows-) 'blowing with the bellows'
	-aci 'young'	*mó-j-aci* (horse-gen-) 'foal' *móng-aci* (horse-) 'foal' *sjo-j-aci* (cow-gen-) 'calf' *sjong-aci* (cow-) 'calf'
	-i 'animate, thing'	*kongcak-i* 'peacock'

4.1.2 Particles

Particles, along with inflectional suffixes, perform important grammatical and semantic functions in MK. While inflectional suffixes occur after predicates, particles occur most frequently after nouns. They also follow pronouns, numerals, nominalized clauses, complement clauses, and conjunctive clauses. Observe the following MK sentence, where particles are bold-face while inflectional suffixes are in roman letters.

9 Note that this word was distinguished from the adverb *noph-i* 'highly' in MK. The two words have merged as homonyms in CK.

(17) *sejcon* ***i*** *sangtwusan* ***aj*** *ka*-sj-a *ljong* ***kwa*** *kwujsin* ***kwa***
Sakya NM Mt.Sangtwu to go-SH-and dragon and ghost and
wujhój-a *selpephó*-te-si-ta
serve-for lecture-RT-SH-EC
'I saw Sakya going to Mt. Sangtwu and giving a Buddhist lecture for dragons and ghosts.' (Sekpo 6:1)

Case particles

Case particles occur after nominals such as nouns, pronouns, and numerals. In most cases, vowel harmony was strictly observed. In table 2, *U* stands for *u* after a dark-vowel syllable and *ó* after a bright-vowel syllable.

Table 2. Late Middle Korean Case Particles

Function	MK forms	
Nominative	*i/j*	
Genitive 'of, 's'	*s* (after honorific animate or inanimate nominal)	
	Uj (after nonhonorific animate nominal)	
Accusative	*lUl* (after open syllable)	
	Ul (after closed syllable)	
Goal/dative/static locative 'to, at, in'	Animate:	*skej/skuj* (honorific)
		Ujkej/jkej (neutral)
	Inanimate:	*ej* (after closed dark-vowel syllable)
		jej (after open dark-vowel syllable)
		aj (after bright-vowel syllable)
Source/dynamic locative 'from, at, in'	Animate:	*skejsje/skujsje* (honorific)
		Ujkejsje (neutral)
		sontój (neutral)
	Inanimate:	*ejsje* (after closed dark-vowel syllable)
		jejsje (after open dark-vowel syllable)
		ajsje (after bright-vowel syllable)
Instrument/directional	*Ulo* (after closed syllable)	
	lo (after open syllable)	
Comitative 'with'	*kwa* (after closed syllable)	
	wa (after open syllable and after *l*)	
Connective 'and'	*kwa* (after closed syllable)	
	wa (after open syllable and after *l*)	
	imje (after closed syllable)	

	mje (after open syllable)
	hóko
	ilang (after closed syllable)
	lang (after open syllable)
Comparative 'than'	*lawa*
	twukon, twukwun, tokon
Ablative 'from'	*puthe*
	Ulosje (after closed syllable)
	losje (after open syllable)
Vocative	*ha* (honorific)
	a (plain; after closed syllable)
	ja (plain, after open syllable)
	ije (exclamatory; after closed syllable)
	je (exclamatory; after open syllable)

The nominative *i,* typically marking a subject, was reduced to *j* after a vowel, as in *sjo* ***j*** 'cow' (*sjo* 'cow' + nominative *j*). When a nominal stem ends in *i* or *j,* the nominative particle is omitted. Thus, the subject forms of *tóli* 'bridge', *pwul-hwuj* 'root', and *saj* 'bird' are the same as the nominal stems. The nominative particle was often used like a comitative, as in *sajngpwul* ***i*** *kóthó-si-mje* (Buddha SUBJ same-SH-and) 'is the same as a living Buddha and'.

The genitive particle *uj/ój* was reduced to *i* or *j* after a vowel, as in *sinha* ***i*** *mal* (royal.subject GN words) 'royal subject's words', *sjo* ***j*** *meli* (cow GN head) 'cow's head', and *na* ***j*** *mom* (I GN body) 'my body'. Genitive particles were often used to mark a subject or a static locative, as in *jelaj* ***s*** *niló-sja-n senpep* (enlightened.one GN say-SH-RL good.law) 'the good Buddhist laws that the enlightend one mentioned', *sajpjel i nacó* ***j*** *tot-oni* (morning.star NM evening GN rise-as) 'as the morning star rises in the evening', and *thongcwu* ***i*** *tatól-a* (Thoncwu GN arrive-and) 'after arriving at Thongcwu'. A genitive particle as a static locative marker + the inceptive particle *–sje* together behaved like the dynamic locative particle *(j)ejsje.*

(18) *chwuksajng ón salóm i cip* ***uj.sje*** *chi-nón cjwungsójng i-la*
livestock TC people NM home at raise-RL animal be-DC
'Livestock are animals raised at home.' (Welsek 1:46)

The accusative particle, typically marking an object, was frequently reduced to *l* after an open (vowel-final) syllable, as in *pójam i kachi* ***l*** *mul-e* (snake NM magpie AC bite-and; Yongka 7) 'A snake bit a magpie and'.

The locative/goal particle was often used to mark a comitative, as in *nala s malssóm i tjwungkwujk* ***ej*** *tal-a* (country GN language NM China LOC different-and.so) 'the national language is different from (that of) China, so'.

MK dative honorific *skej/skuj* was sometimes used to mark a comitative, as in *estjej sejcon skuj kót-cóo-lio* (how Sakya DAT same-OH-PRS) 'How could (he) be the same as Sakya?'.

All MK source or dynamic locative particles except *sontój* 'from' derived from goal/static locative particles with the suffixation of the inceptive particle *–sje.*

(19) a.

Namcong-ljwuk-co	***skujsje***	*na-lssój*	*namin*	*i-la*	*hó-ni-la*
namcong's-6-ancestors	from	born-as	*namin*	be-DC	call-DF-DC

'As (he) was born from Namcong's six ancestors, he was titled Namin.' (Wenkak se 7)

b.

*sjo-**jkejsje***	*cjes*	*na-ko*	*cjec*	***ejsje***	*lak*	*na-ko*
cow-from	milk	come.out-and	milk	from	dairy.food	come.out-and

'From cows comes milk, and from milk comes dairy food, and [...]' (Pephwa 5:155)

(20)

motón	*acómój*	***sontój***	*tul-o-ni*
all	aunt	from	hear-SS-as

'As (I) hear from all aunts [...]' (Nayhwun 2:27)

The instrument/directional particle often replaced the accusative or comitative particle. Thus, in *nolaj* ***lo*** *pulu-zóp-nónila* (song with sing-OH-DC) 'sang a song' (Welsek 2:17), the instrument particle *lo* was used instead of the accusative *lól,* and in *kumkang* ***ólo*** *kacólpi-si-ko* (diamond with compare-SH-and) 'compared with diamond' (Kumkang se 7), *ólo* was used instead of the comitative *(k)wa.*

The MK comitative/connective *kwa* was reduced to *wa* after vowels and *l*. It was generally attached to the last connected nominal as well.

(21)

hój	***wa***	*tól*	***wa***	*pjel*	***wa**-j*	*ta*	*pólk-ti*	*ani*	*hó-ja*
sun	and	moon	and	star	and-NM	all	bright-NOM	not	be-so

'The sun, the moon, and stars were not bright, so [...]' (Welsek 2:15)

Comparative particles *lawa* 'than' and *twukon/tokon* 'than' [< *twu-ko nun* (place-and TOP)] are illustrated in (22).

(22) b. *sekun* *sjenpój* ***lawa*** *nu-to-ta*
rotten scholar than better-EXC-DC
'(He) is better than a rotten scholar.' (Twusi 6:40)

c. *etwum* ***tokon*** *na-uli-la*
darkness than better-PRS-DC
'(It) will be better than darkness.' (Nokeltay sang 39)

puthe 'from' developed from *puth-* 'stick to, depend on' + the verbal connective suffix *-e* 'and'. It appears right after a nominal, as in *chezem puthe* 'from the beginning', after an accusative particle, as in *mózóm ól puthe* 'from one's heart', or after a directional particle, as in *hwuin ulo puthe* 'from the empress', or after the inceptive suffix *–s(j)e,* as in *elje-se puthe* 'from childhood'.

The compound particle *ulo-sje* (directional-inceptive) was used to denote source 'from', as in *wangsaseng ulosje* 'from Wangsa castle'.

A new pseudo-case particle, *tólje* 'to (a person)' developed from *tóli* 'accompany' + the verbal connective suffix *-e*. In *posal tólje niló-sja-tój* (Buddhist. saint to say-SH-that; Welsek 21.139) 'said to a Buddhist saint that', *tólj-e* lost its original meaning and obtained a pseudo-case meaning.

Case particles occurred in sequence, as in *(k)wa j* (connective + nominative/subject), *ulo puthe* (directional + ablative), and *lul puthe* (accusative/object + ablative); similarly a case particle with a delimiter, as in *ej-sje* (locative + inceptive), *uj-sje* (genitive + inceptive), *ulo-sje* (directional + inceptive), and *ej to* (locative + 'also').

(23) *saks* *kwa* *saks* ***kwa*** ***j*** *psi* ***lól*** ***puthe*** *na-ko*
bud and bud and NM seed AC from come.out-and
'Buds come out from seeds and [...]' (Wenkak sang 1.2:14)

Delimiter particles

Some delimiter particles were used after nominals and predicates, while others were used only with nominals. The former set was much more productive. Some frequently used ones are presented below.

a. Topic (TC) particle *nón* (after an open bright-vowel syllable), *nun* (after an open dark-vowel syllable), *ón* (after a closed bright-vowel syllable), *un* (after a closed dark-vowel syllable). The first two were optionally reduced to *n.* The topic particle occurred after a nominal (24a), after a conjunctive suffix (24b), and after another non-topic particle.

(24) a. *na* ***nón*** *icej* *silum* *i* *kiph-e*
I TC now worry NM deep-and
'I am full of worries now, and [...]' (Welsek 2.5)

b. *meli* *isj-e* ***n*** *po-zóp-ko* *kaskai* *w-a* ***n*** *mot*
far stay-by TC see-OH-and near come-by TC unable
po-zóβ-óli-le-la
see-OH-PRS-RT-DC
'(We) can see (him) by staying far but are unable to see (him) by coming close.' (Welsek 7.55)

b. The 'toleration' delimiter *(i)za/(i)sa* (derived from copula *i*/zero + verbal suffix *–za/–sa* 'only if') 'only if it be, only for': *iza/isa* occurs after a consonant and *za/sa* after a vowel. It occurred after a nominal as in *mokswum iza* 'as for only one's life'. After a predicate stem, the form *-aza/-esa* occurred, where *–a/-e* is an infinitive (connective) suffix, as in *ka-sj-asa* (go-SH-INF.*sa*) 'if only (he) goes'.

c. The 'inceptive' particle *sje* occurred after an overt or omitted case particle to give it an inceptive or dynamic meaning, as in *kózól tól alaj (aj)sje* (autumn moon bottom at) 'under the autumnal moon'. Preceded by an infinitive suffix *-a/-e,* it functions as a predicate conjunctive suffix denoting cause or temporal sequence 'as, so, and then', as in *tajtongkang nepu-n ti moll-a.sje* (Taytong. River wide-RL fact unaware-so) 'as (one) does not know how wide the Taytong River is' (Akcang).

d. The particle *(k)om* 'each': Its use after a nominal is illustrated in *un-ton hón nat kom* (silver-money one unit each) 'each one of silver coin', *hón atól om* 'one son each', and *hón pen kom* (one time each) 'each one time'. After an adverbial, it indicated emphasis, as in *noph-i kom* (high-ly EMP) 'highly' and *salóm ólo hój-e kom* (person with cause-by EMP) 'causing people (to do)'.

e. The 'limitation' particles *pós* 'only' and *(k)os* 'only':

(25) a. *skwum* ***pós*** *ani-mjen* *enu* *kilh* *ej* *tasi* *po-zóβ-li*
dream only not-if some road on again see-OH-PRS
'If it is not a dream, (we) will meet again on some road.'
(Welsek 8.82)

b. *ocik* *mawang* ***kos*** *ce* *j* *cwa* *aj* *phjenanhi* *mot* *anc-wa*
solely Satan only he GN seat at comfortably cannot sit-and
'Only the Satan could not comfortably sit in his seat, and [...]'
(Welsek 2.42)

c. *puthje* ***os*** *cwuksali* *l* *jehuj-sj-a*
Buddha only life.death AC lose-SH-and
'Only Buddha lost life and death, and [...]' (Welsek 1.21)

f. The 'inclusion' particle *to* 'also', 'alternative' particle *(i)na* 'or (something), rather', and 'focus/transferentive' particle *taka* 'while; and then' ('focus' after the goal particle *ej* as in *ejtaka*; 'transferentive' after a predicate as in *noni-taka* 'after strolling') were all used after a nominal and a predicate in the same way as in CK.

The following delimiter particles are examples that were used only after a nominal.

g. The particles *(u)lan* 'as for' and *(u)llan* 'and so on' were used in the following contexts.

(26) a. *tjohón* *il* *lan* *na* *jkej* *ponaj-o*
good thing as.for me to send-IM
'As for good things, send them to me.' (Kumkang 21)

b. *ing* *mwut-un* *cangku* *llang* *kaci-ko*
moss stick-RL plough etc. carry-and
'carrying a moss-covered plough and so on, and [...]'
(Chengsan Pyelkok)

h. Delimiter particles like *cocha* 'even, as well', as in *pulhwuj cocha psu-ni-la* (root even use-DF-DC) 'Even the roots are used' (Kumkang Samka 2:50), *man* 'only', and *mata* 'every, each', *kócang/skócang* 'until, up to, even, to the extent of, to the utmost of' (derived from *kócang* 'extremity, edge'):

(27) a. *stut* ***skócang*** *kólómh* *hanól* *hjanghó-no-la*
mind/will up.to river sky face-IN-DC
'Even (up to) the mind is looking out on the rivers and the sky.'
(Twusi 10.13)

b. *mózóm* **skócang** *kongjangh-kej* *hó-si-ni*
mind up.to offer.food.to.Buddha-to cause-SH-DC
'(He) was caused to offer food to Buddha to his utmost.'
(Pwulceng ha 9)

4.2 Predicates

MK predicates comprised verbs, adjectives, and the copula, which shared many morphological properties, more so in MK than in CK. Some morphological factors that distinguish adjectives from verbs in CK were not as strict in MK, as seen in 4.3.2.2.

4.2.1 Verbs

MK verbs can be subclassified into (a) transitive and intransitive, (b) independent and auxiliary, and (c) active, passive, and causative. (c) will be dealt with in 4.5.8.

Transitive verbs take an object, implicit or explicit. Examples are *pota* 'see', *makta* 'block', *kitulita* 'wait', *kilita* 'praise', *kojta* 'love', *kólóchita* 'teach, point to', *katota* 'collect', *muskta* 'tie', *mechwuta* 'stop', *alta* 'know', *molóta* 'do not know', *mastita* 'deposit, give (a thing) to (a person's) keeping', *ilpezta* 'steal', *kacólpita* 'compare', *keskta* 'break, snap', *kucihata* 'limit', *kujcihóta* 'promise', *paskota* 'exchange', *salanghóta* 'think', *sjejta* 'erect', *kwucjonghóta* 'scold', *hójta* 'cause, order', and *cwasita* 'eat' (honorific).

(28) a. *pjengma* *lól* ***mechwu****-esi-ni*
military.horse AC stop-SH-DC
'(He) stopped arms and horses.' (Yongka 54)

b. *na* *nón* *kutój* *lól* ***al****-enul*
I TC you (hon.) AC know-now.that
'Now that I know you, [...]' (Pen sohak10:5)

Verbs unable to take an implicit or explicit object are intransitive verbs. Examples are *kata, njeta* 'go', *nazakata* 'proceed', *ancta* 'sit', *motta* 'come together, swarm', *mólóta* 'dry up', *kaskolta* 'fall head first', *kuchuta* 'stop', *nathota* 'appear', *njelumcista* 'do farming', *niluta* 'say', *tóojta, tóβójta* 'become', *tólita* 'run', *sulhta* 'feel sad', *pajta* 'go to ruin', *sjeta* 'stand', *sólota, sólpta* 'tell, inform' (to a senior), *cehta* 'be scared', *ptetita* 'fall', and *thóta* 'burn'.

(29) a. *kómól* *aj* *ani* ***kuchu**-lssój*
drought by not stop-as
'(It) won't stop by draught.' (Yongka 2)

b. *nulk-un* *hanapi* ***tóoj**-jejs-to-ta*
old-RL grandpa become-PST-EXC-DC
'(He) became an old grandfather.' (Twusi 21:31)

A small number of verbs are both transitive and intransitive, for instance, *kólita* 'be sorted out; sort out' (vs CK **kalita** 'sort out'), as in *seng i kólita* 'sexes are distinguished' and *li lól kalita* 'sort out reasons'. Similarly, *tuliwuta* 'hang down; hang something down' (**tuliwuta** 'hang something down'), and *tita* 'fall down; cause to fall down' (**cita** 'fall down').

There were a relatively small number of auxiliary verbs. Most auxiliary verbs derived from independent verbs, e.g. auxiliary *pota* 'try, experience' < independent *pota* 'see, look at'. Independent and auxiliary uses coexisted in most cases, as they do in CK. Auxiliary verbs appeared after an independent verb, with or without an intervening connective suffix such as an infinitive suffix (*-a/-e/-ja/-je*) or a nominalizer suffix *–ti/-ke*.

(30) *pota* 'try, experience': *hjej-je pota* 'try to think over', *ka pota* 'try going'.
pólita 'finish up, completely': *nic-je pelita* 'completely forgot'.
kjesita 'stay, have' (hon.): *wang i tóoj-ja kjesita* 'became a king', cf. *jetulp wangca lól twu kjesita* 'has eight princes'.
nata 'come out': *pes-e nata* 'get out of, escape'.
najta 'take out': *ciz-e najta* 'make out, produce'.
tita 'get to, become': *sul-e tita* 'disappear'.
cita 'wish': *kwukjenghó-ja cita* 'wish to watch', *ni-ke cita* 'wish to go'.
isita 'stay, have': *nóm ój son ój cuj-je isita* 'be dominated by others', *hón mal to mot hó-ja is-tesita* 'stayed without saying anything'.
twuta 'keep, for later use': *móngkól-a twuta* 'make for later use'.
kata 'continue, gradually': *hój ti-je kata* 'the sun is setting'.
malta 'stop': *i ptut ul nis-ti mal-ósjosje* 'don't forget this intent'.
ani-hóta 'be/do not': *tini-ti ani-hóta* 'do not carry'.

New verbs were formed through compounding or affixation. Compounds included *cwuk-salta* (die-live) 'live and die', *cwuk-pajta* (die-perish) 'die and perish', *oló-nólita* (rise-descend) 'go up and down, rise and fall, fluctuate', *kams-tolta* (wind-turn) 'circle around', *nje-kata* (go-go) 'drop in', *tik-mekta* (dip-eat) 'dip and eat', *pte-tita* (crack-become) 'burst', *nil-e-sjeta* (rise-INF-stand) 'stand up', *tjangka-tulta* (wife's.house-enter) 'marry, take a wife', *alph-sjeta* (front-stand) 'go before', and *tat-najta* (separately-put.out) 'separate'. Affixation was not very productive, some examples being *pi-wusta* 'laugh scornfully', *es-makta* (aslant-block) 'block askew', *nep-nolta* (wide-play) 'stroll around', and *naj-thita* 'throw away'. Zero derivation from nouns includes *kómólta* 'be arid' from *kómól* 'drought', *kutta* 'cut' from *kut* 'end', *nechwulta* 'dangle down' from *nechwul* 'vine', *stujta* 'wear a belt' from *stuj* 'belt', and *pójta* 'conceive' from *pój* 'belly'.

4.2.2 Adjectives and the copula

Examples of adjectives are *kapójjaβta* 'light', *kantaβta* 'simple', *kóskós(hó) ta* 'clean', *koj.ojhóta* 'quiet', *kakókta* 'urgent', *tes-kwucta* 'worse', *ojta* 'wrong', *cephuta* 'scared', *kazómjeta* 'well-off', *cjeta* 'small (size, quantity)', *spospo-hóta* 'pointed', *phelehóta* 'blue, green', *wuzβuta* 'funny', and *ejkwutta* 'very bad'. Some words had meanings different from corresponding CK ones, as in MK *ejesputa* 'pitiful' > **yeypputa** 'pretty'.

In CK, the surest morphological criterion to distinguish adjectives and verbs is to see their non-past indicative form. Verbs have the indicative suffix **–n** or **–nun**, as in **ka-n-ta** 'goes' and **mek-nun-ta** 'eats', whereas adjectives have zero, as in **coh-ta** 'is good' and **huj-ta** 'is white'. MK adjectives were more like verbs than CK adjectives are in that many (not all) MK adjectives inflected exactly the same way as verbs in their indicative forms. Thus, many adjectives were followed by the indicative suffix *–nó* like verbs:

(31) a. *koc* *tjoh-ko* *jelum* *ha-**nó**-ni*
flower good-and fruit much-IN-DC
'Flowers are good and fruits are prentiful.' (Yongka 2)

b. *pólóm* *to* *ep-**nó**-ni-la*
wind also not.exist-IN-DF-DC
'There was even no wind.' (Welsek 1:50)

c. *kwulwum* *i* *etwup-**nó**-ta*
cloud NM dark-IN-DC
'Clouds are dark.' (Nungem 4:44)

Unlike in standard CK, some adjectives had the same indicative relative suffix as that of verbs, as in (32a). This practice is still observed in contemporary

Kyengsang dialect. Also, unlike in standard CK, the indicative relative suffix of the existential adjective *epsta* 'not exist' was *–un,* as in (32b; see also 31b).

(32) a. *etuketukhó*-***nón*** *naco* *ój*
dusky-RL evening in
'in a dusky evening' (Twusi 1:28)

b. *kuci* *eps*-***un*** *mimjohó-n* *ptut*
end lack-RL subtle-RL meaning
'endless subtle meanings' (Welsek Pre 8)

Another feature is that causativization of MK adjectives into transitive verbs by means of causative suffixes *–i, -hi, -ki, -o, -wu,* etc., was much more productive than in CK. Thus, while causativized adjectives like *pólk**i**ta* 'brighten' (**palkhita**), *nuch**i**ta* 'delay' (**nucchwuta**), *kwut**hi**ta* 'harden' (**kwuthita**), and *eps**iwu**ta* 'eliminate' (**epsayta**) have been inherited to CK, words like *njeth**o**ta* 'make it shallow', *kip**hi**ta* 'deepen', *kis**ki**ta* 'make happy', and *ce**hi**ta* 'terrify' are expressed only with periphrasic causative constructions in CK.

The copula root was *i-*. It always took *–la* as its declarative ender in MK. It reduced to *j-* or zero after a vowel (33b,c). The copula was frequently omitted before the question ender *–ko* (question word question) or *–ka* (polar question) (34).

(33) a. *kujk* *ón* *nalah* ***i****-la*
country TC country is-DC
'*Kujk* is (means) a country.' (Cengum Enhay)

b. *swujko* *nón* *sajng* *kwa* *lo* *wa* *pjeng* *kwa* *sa*
suffering TC life and oldness and sickness and death
*wa-**j**-la*
and-be-DC
'*Swujko* is (means) living, being old, being sick, and death.' (Sekpo 6:4)

c. *chi* *nón* *ni* *la*
tooth TC tooth be.DC
'*Chi* is (means) a tooth.' (Cengum Enhay)

(34) a. *hjenljang* *ón* *sto* *mjes* *salóm* *ko*
wise.person TC also how.many person Q
'Also, how many wise people were there?' (Twusi 19:10)

b.

ku	*nil-on*	*kes*	*un*	*musu*	*ko*
that	arise-RL	thing	TC	what	Q

'What was that which happened?' (Wenkak se 12)

c.

i	*twu*	*salóm*	*i*	*cinsillo*	*ne*	*j*	*hangkes*	*ka*
this	two	person	NM	truly	you	GN	master	Q

'Are these two persons truly your masters?' (Welsek 8:94)

The verb *tóojta* 'become' took both the subject and complement in the nominative case.

(35)

ku	*o-pajk*	*salóm*	*i*	*cejca*	*j*	***tóoj**-aci-ngi-ta*
that	500	people	NM	disciple	NM	become-wish-AH-DC

'Those five hundred people wished to become his disciples.' (Welsek 1:9)

4.2.3 Inflection

Verbs, adjectives, and the copula function as sentential or clausal predicates. All predicates inflected with suffixes, which consist of prefinal suffixes that denote tense, aspect, modality, and honorific (subject, object, addressee) suffixes, and final suffixes that denote clause- or sentence-type. While prefinal suffixes are optional in occurrence, clause- or sentence-type suffixes, which occur at the end of a clause or sentence and are thus termed enders, are obligatory. As in CK, sentence enders were of four major types: declarative, interrogative, imperative, and propositive. In addition, promissive, exclamatory, and desiderative enders were also available. Clause enders are subclassified into conjunctive, relative (or adnominal), complement (or adverbal), nominalized, and quotative. Let us briefly observe only tense, aspect, and modality elements and the declarative enders below just for illustration of the complexities involved, relegating detailed discussions of these and other inflectional elements to appropriate sections in syntax.

Tense, aspect, and modality (mood and modal) were not always clearly demarcated in form but often portmanteaued in the same forms. Thus, linguists do not always agree with each other in categorizing these suffixes, naming, for example, the suffix *–nó* a present tense marker or an indicative mood marker (e.g. Huh 1983; Kang & Hwang 2003; Ko 2007). The following classification is made in this chapter. The tense category consisted of past and non-past. The past tense was marked by *–ais/-eis, -jajs/-jejs, -ajs/-ejs*. As these forms had diverged and grammaticalized from the resultative compound *–a/-e isi* (infinitive + 'exist'), they retained resultative or perfective aspect meaning as well. Past time was also indicated by the confirmative modal *–ke/-kwa/-ka*. Non-past, indicating present and future time, was unmarked as in CK.

The mood category, which often indicates tense function as well, consisted of (a) indicative (often referring to present events) *–nó/-ni/-nón/-no* (*-no* = *–nó* + speaker subject *–o*; *-n* changed to *–l* after prospective *–li*), (b) retrospective (referring to the speaker's past observation or experience) *–tó/-ta/-le/-la,* (c) prospective (frequently referring to future events) *-(u)li/-(u)lh*, and (d) prospective-retrospective *–(u)li-le.* Modal suffixes, which appeared immediately before the sentence ender, include the definitive (DF) *–n(i)* (as in *–nila*), exclamatory *–(t) o(s)* (as in *–tota*), confirmative *–ke/-kwa/-ka,* and speaker subject marker *–o/-wu* (Huh 1983: 436-7).

The declarative enders were: (a) *-ta/-la* and (b) *–ni-la* (DF *-ni* + DC *-la*). Compared to *-ta/-la, -ni-la* was used in a more definitive, authoritative, and conservative manner. In addition, there were neutral-level declarative and interrogative enders *–ni* (< subordinator *–ni* (?)) and *–li* (< prospective *–li* (?)). These enders were used either as they were or preceded by other prefinal suffixes such as the indicative, retrospective, prospective, past, confirmative, and speaker-subject marker. For instance, the predicate *hóta* 'do, be' inflected as *hó-ta*, *hó-nó-ta*, *hó-te-la*, *hó-li-la*, *hó-jajs-ta, hó-ke-ta*, and *hó-la*. Notice that *-ta* changed to *-la* after *-te*, *-li*, and *-o*. Similarly, the definitive declarative ender *–ni-la* was used right after a predicate root or preceded by a prefinal suffix, as in *hó-ni-la, hó-nó-ni-la*, *hó-te-ni-la*, and *hó-li-ni-la*.

4.3 Numerals

There were two numeral systems in MK: the native system and the SK system. Numerals in the native system were available up to 1,000. Above that number, SK numerals were used. As SK numerals were similar to those in CK, suffice it to overview native ones. MK native cardinal numbers are as follows: *hónah* '1', *twulh (< twuβwulh)* '2', *sejh* '3', *nejh* '4', *tasós* '5', *jesus* '6', *nilkwup* '7', *jetulp* '8', *ahop* '9', *jelh* '10', *sumulh* '20', *sjelhun* '30', *mazón* '40', *sujn* '50', *jesjwujn* '60', *nilhun* '70', *jetun* '80', *ahón* '90', *on* '100', *cumun* '1,000', *jeleh* 'many'. *hónah* '1', *twulh* '2', *sejh* '3', and *nejh* '4' as determiners were reduced to *hón*, *twu, se(j)/sek,* and *ne(j)/nek*, respectively: *hón sal* 'one year old', *twu kulwel* 'two sentences', *sej sal* 'three years old', *se mal* 'three *mals* (unit of measure)', *sek tól* 'three months', *nej salóm* 'four persons', *ne mal* 'four *mals*', and *nek tól* 'four months'.

(36) a. *sajlo* **sumul-jetulp** *ca* *lól* *mójngkó-noni*
newly 28 letter AC make-as
'As (I) have made newly twenty eight letters, [...]'
(Cengum Enhay)

b. *tól* *i* **cumun** *kólóm* *aj* *pichujjom* *i* *kóth-ónila*
moon nm 1000 river at shining NM same-DC
'The moon seems to be shining in 1000 rivers.' (Welsek 1.1)

Approximate numbers were expressed by compounding neighboring numerals. Examples of numbers up to ten are: *hón-twu* 'one or two', *twu-ze* 'two or three', *se-ne* 'three or four', *ta-jes* 'five or six', *jej-nilkwup* 'six or seven', *nil-jetulp* 'seven or eight', and *twu-e-jel* 'scores'. Ten or more approximate numbers were expressed by suffixing the phrase *namón* (< *nam-* 'remain' + relativizer *–ón*), as in *je-namón* 'about ten', *sumu-namón* 'about twenty', *sjelhu-namón* 'about thirty', *mazó-namón* 'about forty', and *swuj-namón* 'about fifty'. Also used were multiplied compound numerals, as in *twu-nej* '8', *twu-jesus* '12', *twu-nilkwup*'14', *nej-nilkwup* '28'.

Ordinal numbers consisted of a cardinal number + *chahi* (also, *chaj, cha, cahi, caj, ca,* etc.): *hóna-chahi* '1st', *twul-chahi* '2nd', *sej-chahi* '3rd', *jel-chahi* '10th', *sumul hóna chahi* '21st', and *mazón-chahi* '40th'.

5. Syntax

MK syntax was largely the same as CK syntax. It had a predicate-final, postpositional, and head-final structure. Sentence and clause types were essentially the same in MK as in CK. Some quantative differences are: (a) in MK, determiners were not well developed; (b) nominal constructions were used much more extensively in MK. Thus, many predicative constructions including interrogatives consisted of nominalized forms; (c) compound or complex sentences were much more extensively used in MK; (d) in direct and indirect quotations, quotative particles (CK **ko** or **lako**) were not used in MK.

5.1 Noun phrase structure

Noun phrases (NPs) functioned as major (subject or object) or minor (oblique cases and adjuncts) nominal arguments of sentences and clauses. As such, they took a wide variety of particles that indicated the grammatical and semantic relations of the NPs vis-à-vis other parts of the sentences or clauses. NPs were of the structure:

(37) (Relative Clause) (Genitive NP) (Determiner) Head (Plural) (Particles)

The head, the only obligatory element, is occupied by a simple or compound nominal (a noun, a pronoun, a numeral, or a nominalized word). A relative clause, a genitive NP, and a determiner are all optional and their order may be scrambled for stylistic or pragmatic purposes if they cooccur.

As indicated in 4.4.1.2, two different particles, *ój/uj* and *s,* were used to mark the genitive. *ój* (after a bright vowel) or *uj* (after a dark vowel) was used with nonhonorific animate nouns as in (38a,b). The particle *-s* followed honorific nouns (39a) or inanimate nouns (39b) (cf. Lee and Ramsey 2000: 290–1). The bracketed constructions are NPs, in which bold faced parts are genitive constructions. A genitive could be modified by another genitive recursively (40).

(38) a. [***salóm*** ***ój*** *ptut* *ul*] 'people's wishes' (object)
person GN wish AC

b. [***kepwup*** ***uj*** *theli* *wa*] 'turtle's hair and'
turtle GN hair and

(39) a. [***sejcon*** ***s*** *sinljek* *ulo*] 'with Sakymuni's divine power'
Sakya GN divine.power with

b. [***nala*** ***s*** *malssóm* *i*] 'the country's language' (subject)
country GN language NM

(40) *ku* *tocók* *i* [*posal* ***s*** *cen-sejsajng* ***s*** *wenswu*]
that thief NM Buddhist.saint GN former-life GN enemy
-j-le-la
be-RT-DC
'That thief was the Buddhist saint's former life's enemy.' (Welsek 1:6)

Determiners were the least developed word class in MK. CK pure determiners were still generally nouns, pronouns, relativized verbs or adjectives in MK, which *also* syntactically functioned like determiners. For example, CK demonstrative determiners were demonstrative *pronouns* in MK and were also used like determiners, e.g. *i kes* 'this thing' and *ce kes* 'that thing over there'. *saj* was an independent noun 'new thing', yet functioned like a determiner 'new' in *saj kwusul* 'new beads'. Indefinite *enu* was a pronoun 'which one' and took case particles. It was used like a determiner in constructions like *enu nala* 'which country'. The determiners *oón* 'all the' (*oón nala* 'all the country'), *motón* 'every' (*motón hakca* 'every scholar'), and *ojn* 'wrong' (*ojn jak* 'wrong medicine') were relativized forms of the adjective *oólta* 'be all', the verb *motta* 'gather', and the adjective *ojta* 'be wrong', respectively. Thus, only a handful of fossilized determiners included *cjokomas* 'a small bit' (**cokoman**), *njenamón* 'some ten odd' (**jenamun**), and *ptón* 'different' (**ttan**). All numerals also functioned like determiners when they preceded nouns, as they are today.

Plain (non-honorific) nouns and pronouns were optionally followed by the plural suffix *-tólh,* as in *i salóm-tólh* 'these people', *cwungsajng-tólh* 'human beings', *wuli-tólh* 'we', and *nehuj-tólh* 'you all'. Honorific nouns and pronouns were pluralized by the plural suffix *-naj* (CK -**nay** means 'the family of'), as in *emanim-naj* 'mothers', *nwujnim-naj* 'sisters', *kutuj-naj* 'you all' (hon.), *cókjas-naj* 'they' (hon.), *pwuin-naj* 'ladies'.

5.2 Pronouns and anaphora

MK pronouns are classified into personal, demonstrative, indefinite-interrogative, and reflexive pronouns. Among personal pronouns, unlike in CK, there was no separate humble form for the first person. Thus, *na* covered both CK **na** 'I' (plain) and **ce** 'I' (humble) as in (41), where *na* is used even to the king.

(41) *tajwang* *ha* *estjej* *na* *lól* *moló-si-nó-ngi-sko*
Great.King VOC why me AC not.know-SH-IN-AH-Q
'Oh the Great King, why don't you know me?' (Welsek 8:92)

The second person had plain *ne* and honorific *kuti/kutuj* 'you', also used to an adult equal. The third person had plain *tje/ce* 'he, she', also used as a demonstrative pronoun ('that over there'), and honorific *cókja*, also used as a reflexive pronoun 'self'. This honorific form developed from Chinese 自家 'self's house', but degraded to the plain level after the sixteenth century (cf. Kang & Hwang 2003: 69) and then disappeared. The third person *ce* was also used as a reflexive pronoun. Plural forms were *wuli(-tólh)* 'we', *njehuj(-tólh)* 'you (pl.)', and *tje-tólh* 'they'.

Demonstrative pronouns were as follows:

Table 3. Late Middle Korean Demonstrative Pronouns

	Proximate to speaker	Proximate to hearer	Distal
	i 'this'	*ku* 'that near you; that we know'	*tje* 'that over there'

Thing (dem + bound noun *kes* 'thing')	*i-kes*	*ku-kes*	*tje-kes*
Place (dem + noun *ekuj* 'place')[10]	*i-ngekuj* (> **yeki**)	*ku-ngekuj* (> **keki**)	*tje-ngekuj* (> **ceki**)
Time (dem + bound noun *cjej* 'time')	*i-cjej* 'now'	*ku-cjej* 'that time'	*tje-cjej* 'that time'

Demonstratives were both deictic and anaphoric, with *ku* and *ku* compounds used most frequently as anaphors (42).

(42) a. *na j* ***i*** *lól wujhój-a ejespi nekj-e*
I NM this AC for-INF pitifully think-and
'As I felt pitiful about this, [...]' (Cengum Enhay 2)

b. ***ku*** *nón kócang swuj.wu-ni-la*
that TC most easy-DF-DC
'That is the easiest.' (Pakthongsa sang 48)

Indefinite-interrogative pronouns covered persons, things, qualtity, place, and time (Table 4 and (43)). Unlike *mjes* 'how many, several', which was used as both a pronoun and a determiner, *hjen* was used only as a determiner (44). *enu* (and its allomorphs) were used not only as a determiner (45a) but also as an adverb in the sense of 'how' (45b)

Table 4. Late Middle Korean Indefinite-Interrogative Pronouns

Referents	Forms
Persons	*nwu/nwuko/nwukwu* 'who, someone', *amo* 'any'
Things	*musus/muzus/musu/musuk/musum* 'what, some', *amo* 'any', *enu/enwu/enó* 'which, certain'
Quantity	*mjes* 'how many, several', *hjen* 'how many, several', *enma* 'how much, some amount'
Places	*etuj* 'where, somewhere', *etumej* 'where, somewhere', *etule* 'to where, to somewhere'
Time	*enu-cjej* 'when, some time'

10 Notice that *ekuj* was nasalized after a demonstrative. Similarly, the locative *ej* 'at, in' became nasalized after a demonstrative, as in *i-ngej, ku-ngej,* and *tje-ngej.*

(43) a. *sa* *i* *mwul-otój* *pwuthje* *j* ***nwu**-ko*
teacher NM ask-that Buddha NM who-Q
'The teacher asked, "Who is Buddha?"' (Welsek 21:195)

b. ***myes*** *kan-t* *cip* *uj* *saló-si-li-ngi-sko*
how.many room-GN house in live-SH-PRS-AH-Q
'A house of how many rooms would you live in?' (Yongka 110)

c. ***enma**-s* *pok* *ól* *tukhó-li-ngi-sko*
how.much-GN blessing AC get-PRS-AH-Q
'How much blessing is (he) going to get?' (Welsek 17:44)

d. *i* *póli-ko* ***etuj*** *puth-uli-o*
this abandon-and where stick-PRS-Q
'Where is (he) going to stick to, while abandoning this?'
(Welsek se 15)

e. *et-non* *yak* *i* ***musu*** *kes-ko*
get-RL medicine NM what thing-Q
'What medicine are you getting?' (Welsek 21:215)

f. ***musus*** *il* *ól* *kjes-ko* *o-lje* *hó-nón-ko*
what thing AC experience-and come-to do-IN-Q
'What kind of things are you going to do and come back?'
(Sekpo 6:27)

g. ***musuk*** *i* *eljeß-ulj-o*
what NM difficult-PRS-Q
'What would be difficult?' (Sekpo 11:19)

h. ***musum*** *liik* *isi-li-o*
what advantage exist-PRS-Q
'What kind of advantage will there be?' (Kumkang 64)

(44) a. *sa-co* *j* *phjenanhi* *mot* *kje-sj-a* ***hjen***
4-ancestor NM peacefully unable stay-SH-and how.many
kot *ól* *olma-si-njo*
place AC move-SH-Q
'How many places did the four ancestors move around without staying peacefully?' (Yongka 110)

b. ***hjen*** *pen* *pthuj-wun-tól* *nóm* *i* *oló-li-ngi-ska*
several time jump-RL-even.if others NM climb-PRS-AH-Q
'Would others go up even if they jump several times?' (Yongka 48)

(45) a. ***enó*** *nal* *aj* *pi* *kaj-ja*
certain day on rain clear-so
'As the rain was over one day, [...]' (Twusi 12:34)

b. *kujkin-s* *ptut* *ul* **enu** *ta* *sólβ-óli*
people-GN wish AC how all say-PRS.Q
'How can (I) say all the wishes of the people!' (Yongka 118)

5.3 Quantification

Quantification was expressed by numerals, native or SK. First, numerals directly precede countable nominals as determiners: *sek ca* 'three inches', *nej salóm* 'four persons', *nek tól* 'four months', *sumul jetulp ca* 'twenty eight letters', *nilhun sal* 'seventy years old', *sjelhu-namón hój* 'three odd years', *cumun kólóm* '1,000 rivers', *o-pajk sólóm* '500 people', and *il-chen nalah* '1,000 countries'. Nominals were also quantified by means of a construction numeral + classifier + nominal as in [*se mal swul*] *ul mek-ko* 'drinking three *mals* of liquid' (Twusi 15:40) or nominal + numeral + classifier as in [*swul se mal*] 'three *mals* of liquid'. Various quantifiers were used as determiners to quantify the following nominals, as in *motón hakca* 'all scholars', *oón nalah* 'all the country'. Interrogative-indefinite quantifiers such as *mjes* 'how many, several', *enma* 'how much, how many', *hjen* 'how many, several', were used as determiners, as in *mjes kan-t cip* 'house of how many rooms', *enma-s pok* 'how much blessing', *hjen pen* 'how many times'. The particle *mata* suffixed to a countable nominal indicates each and every member of the set denoted by the nominal.

(46) *nip* *alaj* ***mata*** *hanól* *s* *tongnam* *i* *is-nó-ngi-ta*
leaf under every heaven GN baby.boy NM exist-IN-AH-DC
'Under every leaf is a heavenly baby boy.' (Sekpo 11:32)

Finally, days are counted by special native forms: *hóló* '1 day', *ithul* '2 days', *saól* '3 days', *naól* '4 days', *tassswaj* '5 days', *jessswaj* '6 days', *nilwej* '7 days', *jetólaj* '8 days', *ahólaj* '9 days', *jólhul* '10 days'.

5.4 Sentence word order

All MK sentences are canonically predicate-final. Thus, all other sentential constituents are pre-predicate. The typical order is subject-initial. The subject may be followed by one or more nominals indicating various cases, copular complement, or adjuncts. Time and place nominals frequently precede subjects. Adverbials may be appropriately inserted before or after these nominal elements. Word order was not affected by sentence types such as interrogatives.

(47) a. [subject + copular complement]

i	*nón*	*wuli*	*hemul*	*i-la*
this	TC	our	fault	be-DC

'This is our fault.' (Pephwa 2:5)

b. [subject + object]

na	*j*	*thajca*	*lól*	*sjemki-zóβó-tój*
I	NM	prince	AC	serve-OH-but

'Although I serve for the prince, [...]' (Sekpo 6:4)

c. [subject + indirect object + direct object]

na	*j*	*hóma*	*cjwungsajng*	*ójkungej*	*culkeβ-un*	*kes*	*ul*	*phosiho-tój*
I	NM	already	public	to	happy-RL	thing	AC	disseminate-as

'I already disseminated happy things to the general public, such as [...]' (Sekpo 19:3)

d. [time + subject + object]

hwu	*ej*	*pólóm*	*i*	*mul*	*wuh*	*ul*	*pwul-e*
later	at	wind	NM	water	top	AC	blow

'At a later time, the wind blew the water surface, and [...]' (Welsek 1:39)

e. [instrument + object] (interrogative)

musu	*kes*	*ulo*	*to*	*lól*	*sam-alj-o*
what	thing	with	doctrine	AC	make-PRS-Q

'With what can we make doctrines?' (Welsek 9:22)

The typical order of these major nominal elements is scrambled rather freely for stylistic or focusing or topicalizing purposes.

(48) a. [object + subject]

pwuthje	*s*	*kujpjel*	*ul*	*cisin*	*i*	*nil-enul*
Buddha	GN	news	AC	Earth.God	NM	tell-now.that

'Now that the Earth God is telling the news about Buddha, […]' (Welin ki 82)

b. [direct object + indirect/dative object]

tjohón	*il*	*lan*	*na*	*jkej*	*ponaj-o*
good	thing	as.for	me	to	send-IM

'As for good things, send them to me.' (Kumkang 21)

Sentential elements are freely omitted when recoverable from sentential or situational contexts. Thus, a great many sentential utterances are without a subject, object, or other major argument. Moreover, if no ambiguity ensues, nominal particles are also omitted extensively, leaving the coocurring arguments alone.

As in CK, double or multiple subject constructions extensively occur in MK, where a higher subject and a lower subject appear in that sequence.

(49) a.

mól	*i*	*pjeng*	*i*	*kiph-e*
horse	NM	sickness	NM	deep-so

'As the horse is seriously ill, […]' (Yongka 109)

b.

salóm	*i*	*sa-hajng*	*i*	*kong*	*i*	*ilu-si-mjen*
person	NM	four-deeds	NM	merit	NM	achieved-SH-if

'If the merit of the people is achieved in four moral deeds, […]' (Pephwa 5:22)

5.5 Sentence types

There are four major sentence types: declarative, interrogative, imperative, and propositive. In addition, some less canonical sentence types such as promisive, exclamatory, and desiderative occur. All these sentence types are marked by respective sentence enders.

5.5.1 Declarative sentences

Declarative sentence enders are: (a) *-ta/-la* and (b) *–ni-la* (definitve). As indicated in 4.4.2.3, these enders are used either as they are or preceded by other prefinal suffixes such as the indicative *-nó,* retrospective *-te,* prospective *-li,* past *–jajs/-jejs,* confirmative *-ke/-kwa/-ka,* speaker-subject marker *-o,* addressee honorific *-ngi*, etc. Observe the declarative sentence examples in (50), which are uttered in interactive situations.

(50) a. *nilkwup hój nemwu ola-**ta***
seven year too long-DC
'Seven years is too long.' (Welsek 7:2)

b. *na j icej ne j em(i) uj ka-n stah ól*
I NM now you GN mom GN go-RL place AC
*poi-o-li-**la***
show-SS-PRS-DC
'Now I will show you the place your mom went to.' (Welsek 21:21)

c. *pulhwuj cocha psu-ni-**la***
root even use-DF-DC
'Even the roots are used.' (Kumkang Samka 2:50)

d. *na j kulen ptut ul moll-a hó-te-jng-**ta***
I NM such meaning AC not.know-INF do-RT-AH-DC
'I did not know such a meaning.' (Sekpo 24:32)

e. *nip alaj mata hanól s tongnam i is-nó-ngi-**ta***
leaf under every heaven GN baby.boy NM exist-IN-AH-DC
'Under every leaf is a heavenly baby boy.' (Sekpo 11:32)

f. *sengca j na-sj-a cengkak ilwu-si-li*
holy.son NM born-SH-and enlightenment achieve-SH-PRS
'A holy son will appear and achieve enlightenment.' (Welin ki 15)

Sentences (50a, b, c) are of the plain level, (50d) is a low-polite level, (50e) is a deferential level, and (50f) is a half talk style without a declarative ender.

5.5.2 Interrogative sentences

Interrogative sentence enders are: (a) *-ko* (*-sko* after the addressee honorific suffix *-ngi*), (b) *-ka* (*-ska* after the addressee honorific suffix *-ngi*), and (c) *-ta*. *-(s)ko* occurs in question-word question sentences (51), and *-(s)ka* in yes-no (polar) questions (52).

(51) a. *ezi atól ipjel i este-n-ko*
parent son separation AC how-IN-Q
'How is the parting of parents and children from each other?' (Welin 144)

b. *sejcon i hóló mjes li lól nje-si-nóni-ngi-sko*
Sakya NM a.day how.many ri AC go-SH-IN-AH-Q
'How many *ri*'s does Sakya go a day?' (Sekpo 1:39)

(52) a. *pil-on pap ól estjej cwa-si-nón-ka*
beg-RL rice AC how eat-SH-IN-Q
'How can you eat the rice you begged?' (Welin 122)

b. *hanapi l mit-uni-ngi-ska*
grandfather AC believe-IN-AH-Q
'Do you believe the grandfather?' (Yongka 125)

Both *-ko* and *-ka* are also attached directly to a copula complement, in which case the enders may be considered particles rather than suffixes. In this case, both the copula and its mood suffix are omitted. Sometimes *-ko* and *-ka* are reduced to *-o* and *-a*, respectively, especially after a vowel or *l*.

(53) a. *hjenljang ón sto mjes salóm ko*
wise.person TC also how.many person Q
'Also, how many wise people were there?' (Twusi 19:10)

b. *i twu salóm i cinsillo nej hangkes ka*
this two person NM truly your master Q
'Are these two persons truly your masters?' (Welsek 8:94)

c. *i nón sang ka pel a*
this TC prize Q punishment Q
'Is this a prize or a punishment?' (Mongsan 53)

After the mood suffixes *-ni* (indicative) and *-li* (prospective), the enders *-ko* and *-ka* lost the consonant *k*, and became new question enders *-nio/-njo* and *-nia/-nja/-nje* on the one hand and *-lio/-ljo* and *-lia/-lja/-lje* on the other.

(54) a. *nuj hóollo sulh-e hó-nó-**nio***
who alone sad-INF do-IN-Q
'Who alone feels sad?' (Twusi 19:40)

b. *sto* *eljep-ti* *ani* *hó-**nia***
again difficult-NOM not be-Q
'Isn't it difficult again?' (Twusi 10:42)

c. *i* *tajsicwu* *uj* *tukhó-n* *kongtek* *i* *ha-**nje*** *cjek-**unje***
this great.offerer GN obtain-RL merit NM big-Q small-Q
'Is the Buddhist merit that this great offerer has achieved big or small?' (Welsek 17:48)

d. *hemwul* *eps-uni* *etuli* *najthi-**ljo***
flaw lack-because where.to desert-Q
'As (he) is flawless, where can (you) desert (him)?' (Welsek 2:6)

e. *toj* *uj* *mokswum* *i* *ku* *nunghi* *ola-**lia***
barbarian GN life NM that possibly long-Q
'Would the barbarian's life be possibly long?' (Twusi 1:8)

The question ender *ta* is frequently used in a sentence whose overt or understood subject is a second person. Before *ta,* a relativizer suffix may appear as if *ta* were a bound noun, hence the space before it in (55). From this respect, it is distinguished from the declarative ender *-ta.* An emphatic counterpart of this ender is *són.ta* (87b).

(55) a. *sjang* *i* *niló-sj-atój* *towen-kwun* *ani* ***ta***
king NM tell-SH-that Towen-prince not be.Q
'The king asked, "Aren't you Prince Towen?' (Kumkang sasil 3)

b. *kutuj* *nón* *enu* *cek-uj* *tolao-l* ***ta***
you TC which time-at return-PRS Q
'When will you return?' (Twusi 22:30)

c. *ne* *j* *esti* *amh* *ól* *naj-ja* *cwu-ti* *ani*
you NM why female AC take.out-INF give-NOM not
hó-nó-n ***ta***
do-IN-RL Q
'Why don't you give out the woman?' (Welsek 7.17)

The lower-polite level examples, in which the addressee honorific suffix is *-ni*, are few. The two examples in (56) show that there is no distinction between the question word and the yes-no question enders, both appearing as *-ska* (Ko

2007: 339-40).

(56) a. *cwuin i musum chapan ól sonzo tótnj-e*
owner NM what food AC in.person go-and
*móngkó-nó-ni-s**ka***
make-IN-AH-Q
'As owner, what food are you making yourself by moving around?' (Sekpo 6:16)

b. *kutuj s apenim i is-nó-ni-s**ka***
you GN father NM exist-IN-AH-Q
'Do you have father?' (Sekpo 6:14)

The half talk (neutral) style occurs extensively in writing. This style does not have a question ender.

(57) a. *nimkum s malssóm i ku j ani olh-ósi-ni*
king GN words NM it NM not right-SH-IN.Q
'Are the king's words not right?' (Yongka 39)

b. *icej estjej wenswu lól nic-ósi-nó-ni*
now how enemy AC forget-SH-IN-AH.Q
'Now how can you forget the enemy?' (Sekpo 11:34)

c. *sengin sinljek ul enó ta sólβó-li*
saint divine.power AC which.one all narrate-PRS.Q
'Which divine powers can (we) narrate all?' (Yongka 87)

5.5.3 Imperative sentences

Imperative sentence enders are *-(a/e)la* (plain-level), *-(a/e)ssje* (low-polite level), *-(ó/u)sjosje* (deferential level), and *-kola/-kolje* (half-talk style) (58).

(58) a. *wu-nón sengnje ije sulh-e mal-**la***
cry-RL saintess VOC sad-INF stop-IM
'Oh you crying saintess! Don't be sad!' (Welsek 21:21)

b. *ne j wen-tahi hój-**ala***
you GN wish-as do-IM
'Do as you wish.' (Sekpo 24:14)

c. *"na j po-acje hó-nó-ta" sólβ-**assje***
I NM see-PR do-IN-DC tell-IM
'Please tell (him) that I would like to see (him).' (Sekpo 6:14)

d. *nimkum ha al-**ósjosje***
king VOC know-IM
'Oh King, please be aware of this!' (Yongka 125)

e. *sajngsajng aj na j wen ul ilh-ti ani-h-kej*
life in I GN wish AC forget-NOM not-do-to
*hó-**kola***
do-IM
'Be sure not to forget my wishes in your life.' (Welsek 1:13)

f. *na j aki wujhój-a et-e po-**kolje***
I GN child for-INF get-INF try-IM
'Try to obtain (it) for my child.' (Sekpo 6:13)

5.5.4 Propositive sentences

Not many data on propositive sentences exist. Ko (2007:344-6) lists about a dozen examples. Only plain and deferential sentences are found. The plain ender is *–cje* (59a,b). If this ender is preceded by the suffix *a* (usually called a 'confirmative' suffix) as in *-acje*, its meaning is strengthened with the sense of 'certainly, surely' (59c). The deferential propositive ender is *-sangita* (60).

(59) a. *i kep ilhwum ulan hjenkep i-la hó-**cje***
this eternity name TC wisdom-eternity be-DC call-PR
'As for the name of this eternity, let us call it "wisdom-eternity.'
(Welsek 1:40)

b. *twuj-s najh aj mól siski-la ka-**cje***
back river to horse wash-to go-PR
'Let's go to the back river to wash the horse.'
(Pakthongsa sang:21)

c. *"na j po-**acje** hó-nó-ta" sólβ-assje*
I AC see-PR do-IN-DC tell-IM
'Please tell (him) that I would surely like to see (him).'
(Sekpo 6:14)

(60) a. *cajngkethjen i thajca skuj sólβ-utój "ka-**sangita**"*
(name) NM prince to tell-that, go-PR
'Cajngkethjen told the prince, "Let's go."' (Sekpo 3:26)

b. *cajngtho aj hóntój ka na-**sangita***
clean.land to together go go.out-PR
'Let's go out to a clean land together.' (Welsek 8:100)

5.5.5 Minor sentence types

There are several minor sentence types. The promisive is expressed by the ender *–oma* (61a), "oughtness" by *-(u)l?-ti-ni-la* (61b), and "exclamation" by *-(ó/u)lssje, -tota/-twuta/-lota/-lwuta*, etc. (61c, d).

(61) a. *na j ne tólje kólóchj-**oma***
I NM you to teach-PRM
'I promise to teach you.' (Pakthingsa sang:10)

b. *sto pantóki casejhi mózóm ól psu-**l?-ti-ni-la***
again surely in.detail mind AC use-PRS-NOM-DF-DC
'Again you should pay close attention (to it).' (Mongsan 39)

c. *tajwang i chanthanhó-sja-tój tjoh-**ólssje** tjoh-**ólssje***
great.king NM admire-SH-that good-EXC good-EXC
'The Great King admired exclaiming, "Good! Good!" (Sekpo 11:27)

d. *cinsillo sulphu-**to-ta***
truly sad-EXC-DC
'I am truly sad!' (Kumkang hwuse 11)

5.6 Negation

There are several ways to express negation. First, the generic negative adverb *ani* 'not' + *hóta* is used after a clause that ends in the nominalizer ender *–ti*.

(62) *sejcon ha, estjej posal i [poktek swuh-**ti**] **ani***
Buddha VOC why saint NM blessing receive-NOM not
ho-m i-ni-ngi-sko
do-NOM be-IN-AH-Q
'Oh Buddha! Why is the Buddist saint not willing to receive the blessing?'

(Kumkang 142)

Secondly, the 'inability' negative adverb *mot* + *hóta* is used after a clause that ends in *–ti.*

(63) [*cjokomas pój thó-kocje s ptut ul nis-**ti***] ***mot***
small ship ride-intending GN wish AC forget-NOM cannot
hó-li-lota
do-PRS-EXC
'(He) will not be able to forget the wish to ride a small boat.' (Twusi 15:55)

Both *ani* and *mos* appear in both a short form in pre-predicate position (64a) and a long form in post-predicate position (64b).

(64) a. *nwu j **ani** sólanghó-zóβ-óli*
who NM not think-AH-PRS
'Who won't think about it?' (Yongka 78)

b. *nwu j hójjati-**ti ani** hó-nó-njo*
who NM wear.out-NOM not do-IN-Q
'Who is free from (his/her things) being worn out?' (Nungem 4:80)

A third type of negation is the use of the prohibitive verb *malta* 'stop doing'. This verb is preceded by the infinitive suffix *–a/-e* (after an adjective) or by the nominalizer *–ti* (after a verb).

(65) a. *wu-nón sengnje ije sulh-**e** **mal**-la*
cry-RL saintess VOC sad-INF stop-IM
'Oh, you, crying saintess! Don't be sad!' (Welsek 21:21)

b. *kwucwung ej tulu-sj-a thajphjeng ul nwuli-si-l cej*
palace to enter-SH-and peace AC enjoy-SH-PRS time
*i ptut ul nis-**ti** **mal**-ósjosje*
this idea AC forget-NOM stop-IM
'When you enter the palace to enjoy a peaceful reign, please don't forget this idea.' (Yongka 110)

5.7 Topic, focus and emphasis

The typical MK topic particle is *(n)ón* or its allomoph *(n)un*. Nominals with this suffix are usually placed sentence-initially (66). Topic is also expressed by *lan* 'as for, if it be' (67).

(66) a. *i* ***nón*** *wuli* *hemul* *i-la*
this TC our fault be-DC
'This is our fault.' (Pephwa 2:5)

b. *ok* ***ón*** *salóm* *kato-nón* *stah* *i-la*
jail TC people confine-RL place be-DC
'A jail is the place where people are confined.' (Sekpo 9:8)

c. *i* *tongsan* ***ón*** *namk* *i* *tjoh-ólssój* *noni-non* *stah* *i-la*
this hill TC tree NM good-so loiter-RL place be-DC
'As for this hill, there are good trees and thus it is a place to walk around.' (Sekpo 6:24)

(67) *tjoh-ón* *il* ***lan*** *na* *jkej* *ponaj-o*
good-RL thing as.for me to send-and
'As for good things, send them to me, and [...]' (Kumkang 21)

It appears that there is no specific morphological marker to uniquely indicate focus or emphasis, except perhaps for prosodic means of 'stress' and insertion of an epenthetic *s*. One syntactic means is scrambling of sentential constituents. Placing a constituent in sentence-initial position is often related to the speaker's or writer's intension to give focus or emphasis to that initial constituent. For instance, in (68), the object is fronted apparently for focus.

(68) ***pwutje*** ***s*** ***kujpjel*** ***ul*** *cisin* *i* *nil-enul*
Buddha GN news AC Earth.God NM tell-now.that
'Now that the Earth God is telling the news about Buddha [...],' (Welin ki 82)

5.8 Causative and passive

Causativization with a suffix is more productive in MK than in CK. Intransitive and transitive verbs and adjectives are made into causative verbs by means of a causative suffix. Thus, intransitive verbs and adjectives become transitive verbs and transitive verbs become ditransitive verbs. There are allomorphic variants in the suffix: *-hi, –i, -ki, -o/-wu, -ho/-hwu, -ó, -iwu.* Occurrence of some of these variants is phonologically conditioned, and occurrence of others is lexically conditioned and thus unpredictable.

The three variants *-hi, -i,* and *-ki* are most productive. The suffix *-hi* occurs after *t, p, c,* and *k,* as in *mwutta* 'be stained' (Vi) vs. *mwuthita* 'stain'; *ancta* 'sit' (Vi) vs. *anchita* 'make sit, place'; *macta* 'match' (Vi) vs. *machita* 'hit'; *nepta* 'wide' (ADJ) vs. *nephita* 'widen'; *patta* 'receive' (Vt) vs. *pathita* 'give, offer'; *nipta* (Vt) 'put on' vs. *niphita* 'clothe, cause to put on'. The suffix *–i* (or *j*) occurs after a vowel, after an aspirated consonant, and after *k* or *l(u/ó),* as in *nata* 'come out' (Vi) vs. *najta* 'take out, put out'; *sjeta* 'stand' (Vi) vs. *sjejta* 'stand'; *nokta* 'melt' (Vi) vs. *nokita* 'melt (something)'; *nikta* 'ripe' (Vi) vs. *nikita* 'get used to'; *salta* 'live' (Vi) vs. *salita* 'bring to life'; *olóta* 'climb' (Vi) vs. *olita* 'raise, lift up'; *kuchuta* 'stop' (Vi) vs. *kuchita* 'stop, cut (something)'; *kiphta* 'deep' (ADJ) vs. *kiphita* 'deepen'; *telepta* 'dirty' (ADJ) vs. *teleβita* 'make dirty, blemish'; *etwupta* 'dark' (ADJ) vs. *etwuita* 'darken'; *mólkta* 'clean' (ADJ) vs. *mólkita* 'make clean, purify'; *mekta* 'eat' (Vt) vs. *mekita* 'feed'; *malta* 'stop doing' (Vt) vs. *malita* 'make stop, dissuade'. The suffix *–li* (instead of *–i*) occurs after *l*, as in huluta 'flow' (Vi) vs. *hullita* 'shed, make flow'. The suffix *–ki* occurs after *s, m,* as in *swumta* 'hide' (Vi) vs. *swumkita* 'hide (something)'; *olmta* 'move (to)' (Vi) vs. *olmkita* 'move (something)'; *sista* 'wash' (Vt) vs. *siskita* 'make wash'; *pasta* 'take off' (Vt) vs. *paskita* 'unclothe, strip'.

The suffixes *-o/-wu, -ho/-hwu, -ó* are by and large vowel harmony sensitive. Examples include *totta* 'rise' (Vi) vs. *tototo* 'make higher'; *motta* 'gather' (Vi) vs. *mototo* 'collect'; *oólta* 'sound, sincere (of mind)' (ADJ) vs. *oólota* 'make (mind) sound/sincere'; *ilta* 'rise up' (Vi) vs. *ilwuta* 'accomplish'; *mwujta* 'move' (Vi) vs. *mwujwuta* 'move (something)'; *elta* 'be frozen' (Vi) vs. *elwuta* 'freeze'; *njethta* 'shallow' (ADJ) vs. *njethota* (instead of *njethwuta*) 'make shallow'; *kócta* 'be equipped' (Vi) vs. *kóchota* 'have, prepare'; *mecta* 'stop' (Vi) vs. *mechwuta* 'stop (something)'; *tolta* 'turn around' (Vi) vs. *tolóta* 'turn (something) around'. The compound suffix *-iwu/-jwu* occurs in words like *psuta* 'use' (Vt) vs. *psuj.wuta* 'make use'; *ptuta* 'float' (Vi) vs. *ptuj.wuta* 'set (a ship) afloat', as in CK.

(69) a. *mom* *aj* *moncój* ***mwuthi**-si-ko*
body to dust stain-SH-and
'(He) covered his body with dust, and [...]' (Welsek 21:219)

b. *sekpjek* *ej* *mól* ***oli**-sj-a*
rock.wall at horse lift.up-SH-and
'(He) had the horse crimb up the rock wall, and [...]' (Yongka 48)

c. *na j icej ne j em(i) uj ka-n stah ól* ***poi****-o-li-la*
I NM now you GN mom GN go-RL place ACshow-SS-PRS-DC
'Now I will show you the place your mom went to.'(Welsek 21:21)

d. *mólk-ón mos aj kahi pój lól* ***ptuj.w****-e nol-li-lo-la*
clear-RL pond in easily boat AC float-INF play-PRS-IN-DC
'(We) will easily set a boat afloat in a clear pond and enjoy ourselves.' (Twusi 1: 14)

Periphrastic causative constructions with the sequence *-kuj/-kej hó-* (so.that do/make) 'cause' are also extensively used. In general, while suffixal causatives express more direct causation, periphrastic causative constructions tend to express indirect causation.

(70) a. *sjwuko lól ta pesena-****kuj*** ***ho****-li-la*
suffering AC all escape-so.that do-PRS-DC
'(We) will have (them) escape from all suffering.' (Welsek 9:15)

b. *sajngsajng aj na j wen ul ilh-ti ani-h-****kej*** ***hó****-kola*
life in I GN wish AC forget-NOM not-do-so.that do-IM
'Be sure not to forget my wishes in your life.' (Welsek 1:13)

MK passives are expressed by attaching a passive suffix to transitive verbs. In terms of forms, passive suffixes are a subset of causative suffixes, in that only the same three productive forms *-hi, -i,* and *-ki* are used. This fact, together with the functional relatedness between causative and passive, supports a hypothesis that passive suffixes developed from causative suffixes by way of functional shift before the MK period.

The passive suffix *-hi* appears in words like *tatta* 'close' vs. *tathita* 'be closed'; *mekta* 'eat' vs. *mekhita* 'be eaten'; *capta* 'grasp' vs. *caphita* 'be grasped'; and *jencta* 'put on' vs. *jenchita* 'be put on'. Examples of the occurrence of the suffix *-i* are: *cochta* 'follow, chase' vs. *cochita* 'be chased'; *twuphta* 'cover' vs. *twuphita* 'be covered'; *jelta* 'open' vs. *jelita* 'be opened'; *asta* 'take away' vs. *asita* 'be taken away'; and *katota* 'collect' vs. *katoita* 'be collected'. The suffix *-ki* occurs in transitive verbs like *tamta* 'put in' vs. *tamkita* 'be put in'; *cómta* 'soak (something)' vs. *cómkita* 'be soaked'; and *sólmta* 'boil' vs. *sólmkita* 'be boiled'.

(71) a. *tongmwun i tolo* ***tathi****-ko*
East.Gate NM again closed-and
'The East Gate was shut again, and [...]' (Welsek 23: 80)

b. *hón* *pwuchej* *lul* *tat-óni* *han* *pwuchej* ***yeli**-kom* *hó-lssój*
one fan AC close-as one fan opened-each do-as
'As each time (someone) closed one fan, another fan was opened, and so […]' (Welsek 7: 9)

5.9 Speech levels and honorifics

A. Address-reference terms: In MK, unlike in CK, professional titles are used without any honorific title. Professional titles alone are sufficient for honorification: e.g. *sensajng* 'teacher', *nimkum* 'king', *wang* 'king', *pwuthje* 'Buddha', *miluk* 'Maitreya', *posal* 'Buddhist saint', and *zjelaj* 'Enlightened One'. The honorific title *-nim* (from the noun *nim* 'lord, king; beloved') was attached to kinship terms: *apanim* 'father', *emanim* 'mother', *acópanim* 'uncle', *acómanim* 'aunt', *atónim* '(other's) son', and *hjeng-nim* 'older brother'. No other suffixal title is attested.

B. Pronouns: See 5.2.

C. Content words: Most CK honorific words have their origins in MK, while many MK honorific words are obsolete in CK. Some MK examples are *cinci* (**cinci**) 'meal', *pwun* (**pwun**) 'person', *moj* (—) 'rice', *macóβój* (—) 'oldest child', and *sulha* (—) 'king's meal'. Honorific predicates include *cwasita* (**capswusita**) 'eat', *tukjesita* (—) 'place (something)', *kólota* (—) 'say', *kjesita* (**kyeysita**) 'stay, exist', *mojsita* (**mosita**) 'accompany', *pojta* (**poypta**) 'see (a superior)', *cehta* (—) 'fear', and *jetcópta* (**yeccwuta**) 'ask (a superior)', *sólpta/sólota* (**aloyta**) 'talk (to a superior)', and *tulita* (**tulita**) 'give (to a superior)'.

D. Case Particles: The MK and CK case particles relevant to the honorific system are summarized in (72) and discussed in 4.4.1.2 and 4.5.1.

(72)

	MK	CK	
Genitive	Honorific	*s*	—
	Neutral	*ój/uj*	**uy**
Dative/locative	Honorific	*skej/skuj*	**kkey**
	Neutral	*ejkej*	**eykey**
	Inanimate	*ngej*	**ey**
Vocative	Honorific	*ha, (i)je*	—
	Plain	*a*	**(i), (y)a**
Subject	Honorific	—	**kkeyse**
	Neutral	*i*	**i/ka**

Textual evidence and earlier analyses indicate that the dative/locative three-way distinction was innovated in the MK period. The following processes took place for the derivation of the honorific *skej/kkej* and the neutral *ejkej.* In MK, to indicate the dative/locative of an animate noun, the noun was followed by the anaphoric demonstrative pronoun *ku* 'that' + dative/locative particle *ngej.*

(73) a. MK honorific genitive *s + ku + ngej > skej/skuj > kkej >* **kkey**
b. MK neutral genitive *ój/uj + ku + ngej > ujkej >* **eykey**

Thus, for example, *puthje s ku ngej* 'to the Buddha' developed to *puthje skej* and both forms are attested. Similarly, *kjecip uj ku ngej* 'to the girl' developed to *kjecip ujkej.*

Three particles are used to mark the vocative case in MK: *ha, (i)je,* and *a.* The particle *ha* is to call a superior, as in *sejcon ha* 'O Shakyamuni!' The particle *(i) je* (defunct copula *i + je*; *ije* after a consonant and *je* after a vowel) is used with an exclamatory effect (Lee and Ramsey 2000: 292). The particle *a* is to call an equal or someone lower in rank. While *ha* is no longer used in CK, *(i)je* is still used only as a poetic or specialized form, as in *cwu ye* 'O Lord!' or *im iye!* 'O my beloved!' The MK plain vocative *a* corresponds to CK *(y)a,* which is used only to children. In CK, *(i)* is used to adolescents, as in *Hankon i* 'Hankon!' and *Yongho* 'Yongho!'

E. Subject honorific (SH) suffix: MK has three prefinal honorific suffixes: subject honorific, object honorific, and addressee honorific. The suffix *-(u)si* (contracted to *-(u)sj* or *-(u)sja*) marks the subject honorific.

(74) a.

hajtong	*ljwuk-ljong*	*i*	*nóló-**sj**-a*
Korea	six-dragon	NM	fly-SH-and

'Six dragons flew in Korea and [...]' (Yongka 1)

b.

na	*nón*	*puthje*	*s*	*sólanghó-**si**-non*	*az*	*i-la*
I	TC	Buddha	GN	love-SH-RL	brother	be-DC

'I am the younger brother whom Buddha loves.'

c.

puthje	*s*	*mokswum*	*i*	*kuc*	*i*	*eps-**usja**-m*	*ul*
Buddha	GN	life	NM	end	NM	lack-SH-NOM	AC

'the fact that Buddha's life is endless' (Y. Choy 1987: 191)

F. Addressee honorific (AH) suffix: The prefinal suffix *-ngi* marks addressee honorification. This suffix indicates the highest deferential level, as in (75a). Its contracted forms *-ng* and zero form are used, respectively, in the declarative and interrogative of the next higher speech level (see H). Historically, the suffix *-ngi* was gradually reduced to *-i* in all positions by the early CK period as illustrated in (75b). Then, the suffix *-i* was simply absorbed by the indicative mood suffix *-ni* when the addressee honorific function was taken over by **-sup** during the early CK period, as in (75c) (see G).

(75) a. MK: *kilu-sóβ-ósi-ni-**ngi**-ta*
raise-OH-SH-IN-AH-DC
'(X) is raising (Y).' (Welin 10:19; Huh 1972: 34)

b. early CK: *kilu-si-**op**-na-**i**-ta*
raise-SH-AH-IN-AH-DC

c. CK: ***kilu-si-**p**-ni-ta***
raise-SH-AH-IN-DC

Notice that MK *-sóβ* precedes the subject honorific *-ósi*, but occurs after the subject honorific suffix in early CK and CK. This is because the MK object honorific suffix underwent a functional shift to the addressee honorific in early CK, driving out *-ngi* (cf. H. Sohn 1998).

G. Object honorific (OH) suffix: Unlike in CK, MK (and OK) marks object (direct and indirect) honorification by way of the prefinal inflectional suffix *-sóp*.[11] This suffix is used as productively as the subject honorific suffix. It functions to express the subject referent's (and speaker's) respect to the higher person affected by the action of the inferior subject referent (76).

(76) a. *pilok zjelaj s sengsilhón mal ól tut-**cóβ**-óto*
Though Enlightened.One GN sincere word AC hear-OH-but
'Though we hear the sincere words of the Enlightened One, [...]'
(Welsek 21:15)

b. *na nón cungca skuj tut-**cóp**-ko cungca nón pwuca skuj*
I TC Cungca from hear-OH-and Cungca TC Puca from
*tut-**cóo-si**-ni*
hear-OH-SH-DC

11 It has a number of phonologically conditioned allomorphic shapes. Its initial consonant *s* changes to *z* (e.g. *-zóp*) after a voiced sound and to *c* after *t*, *c*, or *ch* (e.g. *-cóp*). Its final consonant *p* changes to *β* before a vowel (e.g. *-sóβ*, *-zóβ*, *-cóβ*).

'I heard it from Cungca and Cungca heard it from Pwuca.' (Sohak 4:18)

In (76a), the respected person, the Enlightened One, is the possessor of the object referent ('name'). The speaker/writer is the understood subject. In (76b), the subject (the speaker/writer) uses *-cóp* in the first clause to show respect to Cungca, and used *-cóp* in the second clause to indicate the subject referent Cungca's humility to his mentor Pwuca. The use of the subject honorific *-si* in the second clause denotes the speaker/writer's respect to the subject (Cungca).

H. Speech-level enders: Sentence-type enders interact with speech levels in MK. Korean linguists establish three or four speech levels for MK, but they are far from agreeing with one another in terms of the number, kind, and interpretations of suffixes in some categories such as interrogative sentences. Table 5 is based on the four-level system (e.g. Y. Ko 2007: 303–7).

Table 5. Late Middle Korean Speech-Level Sentence Enders

Speech level	Declarative	Interrogative	Imperative	Propositive
Plain	*-ta/-la*	*-nje/-njo, -nta*	*-((k)e)la*	*-ce* (rarely *-cela*)
Neutral	*-ni/-noj*	*-ni*	*-kola/-kolje*	(not attested)
Moderate respect	*-ng-ta*	*-nó-ni-ska/sko*	*-esje/-asje*	(not attested)
Deferential	*-ngi-ta*	*-nó/ni-ngi-ska/sko*	*-sjosje*	*-sa-ngi-ta*

Texts published after the fifteenth century show some other sentence enders. For example, sixteenth-century data contain the imperative ender *-so* or *-(z)o*, which was used between adult equals or to one's older brother (Y.O. Kim 1995: 118). This new imperative form is assumed to have developed from the deferential level *-sjosje* with the final syllable deletion.

5.10 Adverbs

Adverbs, constituting a relatively open word class, modify predicates or entire clauses. MK adverbs mark, variously, time, place, degree, manner, negation, m odal, conjunction, and discourse. There is a relatively small set of inherent (monomorphemic) adverbs, while the majority of adverbs have derived from other words (mostly predicates and some nouns) by means of the productive adverbial suffix *-i/-j* and some other idiosyncratic suffixes such as *-o, -aj,* and *-cahi* and particles such as *naj* and *zo*. Examples include *khi* 'greatly' (from *khu-* 'big' + *-i*), *niki* 'well, thoroughly' (from *nik-* 'ripe' + *-i*), *haj* 'a lot' (from *ha-* 'big'

+ *-j*), *nunghi* 'ably' (from *nungha-* 'able' + *-i*), *kojojhi* 'quietly' (from *kojojha-* 'quiet' + *-i*), *oj.o* 'wrongly' (from *oj-* 'wrong' + *-o*), *itaj* 'nicely' (from *it-* 'good' + *-aj*), *cukcahi* 'immediately' (from *cuk* 'immediacy' + *-cahi*), *móchómnaj* 'finally' (from *móchóm* 'end' + *-naj*), and *sonzo* 'in person' (from *son* 'hand' + *zo*).

Some verb and adjective roots were also used as adverbs without any suffix, e.g. the verb *sómósta* 'to go through, communicate' vs. the adverb *sómós* 'thoroughly', the adjective *palóta* 'be right, straight' vs. the adverb *paló* 'rightly, straightly', the adjective *iluta* 'be early' vs. the adverb *il* 'early', and the adjective *hata* 'be much, big' vs. the adverb *ha* 'much, a lot'. Frequently used adverbs are: (a.) Time: *mencje* 'before, first of all'; *pólsje* 'already, yet'; *hóma* 'already'; *sjangnjej* 'always'; *nójil* 'tomorrow'; *moloj* 'the day after tomorrow'; *eceskuj* 'yesterday'. (b.) Place: *ili* 'this way'; *kuli* 'that way'; *tjeli* 'that way over there'; *ingekuj* 'here'; *kungekuj* 'there'. (c.) Degree: *kócang* 'most'; *keuj* 'almost'; *mós* 'most'; *kós* 'barely'; *cjekomato* '(not) at all'; *elwu* 'nearly, almost, approximately'. (d.) Manner: *phele* 'in deep blue/green'; *zel-zel* 'gently'; *kwumul-kwumul* 'wigglingly'; *kót* 'like'; *selu* 'each other'; *kulu* 'wrongly'; *tamós* 'together with'; *ptólo* 'separately'; *tetuj* 'slowly, late, behind the time'; *nankjes* 'hurriedly'; *ilikom* 'like this'; *kantajlo* 'at random'. (e.) Negative: *ani* 'not'; *mot* 'unable, cannot'. (f.) Modal: *hótaka* 'if'; *sihok* 'by any change'; *hómólmje* 'still more, not to speak of'; *amato* 'perhaps'; *sóncój* 'rather'; *motój* 'surely'; *pantóki* 'surely'; *molomaj* 'surely, certainly'; *etuli, estjej, maj, enu* 'how, why'. (g.) Conjunctive: *kulena* 'but'; *kulemjen* 'then'; *kulelssój* 'therefore'; *sto* 'also'. (h.) Discoursal: *ój* 'oh'; *ejng* 'yes'; *aso* 'Good gracious!'. Some sentence examples with adverbs are given in (77).

(77) a. *nilkwup* *hój* ***nemwu*** *ola-ta*
seven year too long-DC
'Seven years is too long.' (Welsek 7:2)

b. *i* *twu* *salóm* *i* ***cinsillo*** *ne* *j* *hangkes-ka*
this two person NM truly you GN master-Q
'Are these two persons truly your masters?' (Welsek 8:94)

c. *nwu* *j* ***hóollo*** *sulh-e* *hó-nó-nio*
who NM alone sad-INF do-IN-Q
'Who alone feel sad?' (Twusi 19:40)

d. *hanca* *lo* ***mencje*** *kul* *ul* *móngkól-**o***
Chinese.character with first writing AC make-and
'made the writing with Chinese characters first, and [...]' (Sekpo se 5)

e. *cajngtho* *aj* ***hóntój*** *ka* *na-sangita*
clean.land to together go out.go-PR
'Let's go out to a clean land together.' (Welsek 8:100)

f. ***sto*** ***pantóki*** ***casejhi*** *mózóm* *ól* *psu-l?-ti-ni-la*
again surely in.detail mind AC use-PRS-NOM-DF-DC
'Again you should pay close attention (to it).' (Mongsanpepe Enhay 39)

5.11 Subordinate clauses

Subordinate clauses are of five types: (a) relative clauses, (b) predicative complement clauses, (c) nominalized clauses, (d) conjunctive clauses, and (e) quotative clauses. All these different clause types are so marked by pertinent inflectional clause enders. Frequently, several of these clause types occur together in a long sentence, as illustrated in (78).

(78) *salóm* *mata* ***hój**-e*](d) *swuβi* ***nikj**-e*](d) *nallo* ***pswu**-m*](c) *ej*
person each cause-and easily learn-and daily use-NOM for
***phjenanh**-kuj*](b) ***hó**-kocje*](b) ***hó**-l*](a) *stólóm* ***i**-ni-la*
comfortable-so.that make-wishing do-PRS only be-DF-DC
'My only wish is to have every person learn and use it easily and conveniently on the daily basis.' (Cengum Enhay)

5.11.1 Relative clauses

A relative clause modifies a following head nominal by means of a relativizer ender. Typical relativizers denote tense and aspect, in addition to the connective function.

Table 6. Late Middle Korean Relativiser Enders

Relativizers	MK
Non-past	*-nón, -non* (after verb)
	-(U)n (after adjective/copula)
Past/perfective	*-(Uu)n*
Prospective	*-(U)l*

Relative constructions consist of a relative clause followed by its head, as in [*hó-**nón***] ***il*** (do-RL work) 'the work (one) does', [*noph-**ón***] ***moj*** (high-RL mountain) 'high mountain', [*i cip uj sa-**nón***] ***elwun*** (this house at live-RL adult) 'the adult person who lives in this house', [*pwuin i nah-ósi-**l***] ***tól*** (lady NM deliver (baby)-SH-RL month) 'the month when the lady will give birth to a baby', where the bracketed parts are relative clauses and the bold parts are their respective relativisers and head nouns. More sentence examples with a relative construction are given in (79).

(79) a.

[*wu-**nón***]	***sengnje***	*ije*	*sulh-e*	*mal-la*
cry-RL	saintess	VOC	feel.sad-INF	stop-IM

'You crying saintess! Don't be sad!' (Welsek 21: 21)

b.

[*pwulhuj*	*kiph-**un***]	***namk***	*ón*	*pólóm*	*aj*	*ani*	*mwuj-lssój*
root	deep-RL	tree	TC	wind	by	not	move-as

'As trees whose roots are deept will not move by wind,'(Yongka 2)

c.

en	*un*	[*nilu-l*]	***ssi***	*-la*
en	TC	say-PRS	word	be.DC

'*En* is a word meaning "to say".' (Cengum Enhay 2)

d.

[*eli-**n***]	***pójksjeng***	*i*	[*nilu-kocje*	*hó-**l***]	***pa***	*j*
poor-RL	people	NM	report-wishing	do-PRS	thing	NM

isj-eto
have-though
'Even though simple people have things to report (to the government), [...]' (Cengum Enhay)

One MK pattern which is not shared with CK is the genitive particle *s* 'of' used as a special kind of (quotative) relativizer, which is attached to a complete sentence. Notice in (80) that the bracketed relative clause is a complete sentence followed by the genitive particle as a relativizer.

(80) a.

[*nepi*	*kwangmjeng*	*i*	*pichwuj-ta*	*s*]	***ptut***	*i-o*
widely	light	NM	shine-DC	GN	meaning	be-DC

'(It) is the meaning that the light shines widely.' (Welsek 2:9)

b.

[*nunghi*	*ta*	*mot*	*hó-li-la*	*s*]	***ptut***	*ul*	*kjelhó-ja*
possibly	all	unable	do-PRS-DC	GN	mind	AC	make-and

natho-si-ni-la
appear-SH-DF-DC
'(He) will appear with the decision that he cannot possibly do it all.' (Pephwa 3:47)

c. [*tinake-n mwuljangkep ej swuhajng i nik-usilssój mot*
past-RL eternity in discipline NM ripe-since cannot
ilwu-olʔ-ka *s*] ***ujsim*** *i eps-usi-na*
achieve-PRS-Q GN doubt NM lack-SH-but
'As (he) has been eternally disciplined in the past, there is no doubt that (he) would not succeed, but' (Welin ki 53)

5.11.2 Predicative complement clauses

This construction consists of a complement clause and a complement ender, which is followed immediately by its head predicate. The predicate and the preceding ender form a semantic unit (bold-faced in (81)) expressing desiderative, (periphrasitic) causative, habitual, and so on, as in CK. Complement enders are the same as conjunctive enders in form, the difference being that the former are semantically merged with the head predicates, which was not the case with the latter. Frequently used enders include *-kocje/-acje* 'wishing to, intending to', *-kej/-kuj* 'so that', and *-tós* 'as if'. The most frequently used head predicate following these complement enders is *hóta* 'do'.

(81) a. *eli-n pójksjeng i* [*nilu-**kocje***] ***hó**-l pa j*
simple people NM report-wishing do-RL thing NM
isj-eto
have-though
'Even though simple people have things that they wish to report, [...]' (Cengum Enhay)

b. [*na j po-**acje***] ***hó**-nó-ta sóβ-assje*
I NM see-intending do-IN-DC tell-IM
'Please tell (him) that I would like to see (him).' (Sekpo 6:14)

c. [*umsik ólo pój pulu-**kuj***] ***hó**-koza*
food with stomach full-so.that make-in.order.to
'in order to make (people) have a hearty meal with food' (Welsek 9:25)

d. [*pep i nepi phje-a ka-m i swulwujpti kuwu-**tós***]
law NM widely spread-INF go-NOM NM wheel roll-like
***hó**-lssój*
do-as
'As the way the laws were spreading was as if a wheal rolls, [...]' (Sekpo 13:4)

A subtype of predicative complement clauses is that of auxiliary or serial predicate constructions. In (82a), the auxiliary verb *pota* 'try' has the preceding clause as its complement. In (82b), the main verb *kjesita* 'stay' (honorific) has the preceding clause as its complement.

(82) a.

[*na*	*j*	*aki*	*wujhój-a*	***et-e***]	***po****-kolje*
I	GN	child	serve-INF	get-INF	try-IM

'Try to obtain (it) for my child!' (Sekpo 6:13)

b.

[*kos*	*nilkwup*	*cwulki*	*lól*	*kacj-**e***]	***kjesj****-atój*
flower	seven	stalk	AC	hold-INF	stay-and

'(She) was holding seven stalks of flowers, and [...]' (Welsek 1:9)

5.11.3 Nominalized clauses

A nominalized clause is composed of a clause followed by a nominalizer ender: *-(o)m, -ki,* or *-ti.* The most productive nominalizer suffix is *-(o)m,* which has allomorphs *-jom* and *-wum.*

(83) a.

[*tjoh-ón pep*	*task-**om***]	*ól*	*mot*	*hó-ja*
good-RLlaw	polish-NOM	AC	unable	do-so

'Being unable to polish up good laws, [...]' (Sekpo 9:14)

b.

[*hó-non*	*il*	*eps-**wum***]	*i*	*pilok*	*pwuj-na*
do-RL	work	lack-NOM	NM	though	vacant-but

'Although doing nothing is boring, [...]' (Welsek 8:31)

c.

sejcon	*ha,*	*estjej*	*posal*	*i*	[*poktek*	*swuh-ti*
Buddha	VOC	why	saint	NM	blessing	receive-NOM

ani	*ho-**m***]*i-ni-ngi-sko*
not	do-NOM be-IN-AH-Q

'Oh Buddha! Why is the Buddist saint not willing to receive the blessing?' (Kumkang 142)

-ti and *-ki* are less productively used. *-ti* corresponds to CK positive **-ki** and negative **-ci**. The nominalizer *-ki*, which is assumed to have developed from *-ti*, is also used, as in CK.

(84) a.

[*tewujcap-**ti***]	*eljep-tota*
grasp-NOM	difficult-EXC

'It is hard to hold on to it.' (Kumkang Samka 2:48)

b. *mózólh* *i* *mel-mjen* [*kelsikhó-**ti***] *eljep-ko*
village NM far-if beg.for.food-NOM difficult-and
'If the village is far, it is difficult to beg for food, [...]' (Sekpo 6: 23)

c. *estjej* *posal* *i* [*poktek* *swuh-**ti***] ***ani*** *ho-m*
why saint NM blessing receive-NOM not do-NOM
i-ni-ngi-sko
be-IN-AH-Q
'Why is the Buddist saint not willing to receive the blessing?' (Kumkang 142)

d. *longtamhó-ja* [*namcin* *elu-**ki***] *lól* *hó-mje*
joke-and male play.with-NOM AC do-and
'(She) did playing with males by making jokes, and [...]'
(Welsek 1:44)

5.11.4 Conjunctive clauses

Conjunctive clauses, which precede their main clauses, are marked by a conjunctive clause ender. There are scores of conjunctive enders in MK, as in CK, such as: (a.) Combination: *-ko, -o, -kok* (for emphasis) 'and'; *-mje* 'and'; *-taka* 'and then'; *-tój, -tójn* (for emphasis) 'and that'; *-keniwa* 'as well as'; *-tiβi* 'and, though, but'; *-esje/-asje* 'and then, and so'; *-e/-a/-ja/-je* 'and'; *-ntój, ntójn* (for emphasis) 'given that'. (b.) Opposition: *-na* 'but'; *-(ke)nmalón* 'though, despite'; *-ato/-eto* 'but, yet'; *-sje* 'and (then, so)'. (c.) Sequentiality: *-n tamata* 'as soon as'; *-ni* 'as, when'. (d.) Cause, reason: *-ssój* 'as, since'; *-(k)enul/-(k)enól* 'now that, since, as'; *-ketun* 'as, because'; *-kwantój* 'so ~ that, such ~ that'; *-ntaj, -ntajn* (for emphasis) 'since, because'; *-i-la* 'as/because it is'; *-m-aj* 'as, since'. (e.) Intention, goal: *-la* 'in order to'; *-kocje, -kejsko, kujsko* 'in order to, wishing to'; *-kwatje, -kwatja* 'in order to, wishing to'; *-lje, -lja* 'in order to'. (f.) Conditional: *-mjen* 'if'; *-tun* 'if'; *-lantój* 'if, in case, provided that'. (g.) Concessional: *-lmantjeng* 'even though, nevetheless, but'; *-lsjentjeng* 'rather, sooner than'; *-lspwuntjeng* 'rather, sooner than'; *-ntól* 'even if'. (h.) Manner, degree: *-kej, -kuj* 'so that'; *-tolok* 'so that, to the extent that'; *-tios* 'the more ~ the more'; *-tós(i)* 'like, as if'; *-i* (adverbial '*-ly*'). Some sentence examples with some of the above conjunctive enders are given in (85).

(85) a. *hanca lo mencje kul ul móngkól-**o***
Chinese.character with first writing AC make-and
'Made the writing with Chinese characters first, and […]'
(Sekpo se 5)

b. *ing mwut-un cangku llang kaci-**ko***
moss stick-RL plough etc. carry-and
'carrying a moss-covered plough and so on […]' (Chengsan Pyelkok)

c. *pójam i kachi l mul-e cumkejs kac(i) aj jencó-**ni***
snake NM magpie AC bite-INF big.tree branch on put-as
'As the snake bit a magpie and put it on a branch of a big tree, […]'
(Yongka 7)

d. [*i tongsan ón namk i tjoh-**ólssój***] *noni-non stah i-la*
this hill TC tree NM good-so loiter-RL place be-DC
'As for this hill, there are good trees and thus it is a place to walk around.' (Sekpo 6:24)

e. [[*cwuk-un-**tósi***] *ca-**taka***] [*hen kas os twuph-**esje***]
die-RL-as.if sleep-then old leather clothes cover-and
noll-a o-la
play-to come-IM
'Sleep as if you are dead, and then cover yourself with an old leather clothes and come to play.' (Twusi 22:1)

f. [*na j thajca lól sjemki-zóβ-**ótój***]
I NM prince AC serve-OH-but
'Although I serve for the prince, […]' (Sekpo 6:4)

g. *iwuscip pul un* [*pam i kip-**tólok***] *pólk-ajs-tota*
neighbor light TC night NM deep-until brighten-PST-EXC
'The neighbor's light was brightened until the night got deep.'
(Twusi 7:6)

5.11.5 Quotative clauses

The CK quotative particles **ko** and **lako**/**hako** had not developped in MK. The typical quotative construction was made of two clauses in sequence. Three types are observed. The first of them is the quoted sentence first and the saying verb second, as in CK, but without any quotative morpheme. This type appears to have functioned as indirect quotation. In (86a), for example, *-(a)cje* is a propositive ender, which is directly followed by the verb *hó* 'do, say' and furthermore the whole clause up to the declarative ender *-ta* is directly followed by the the saying verb *sólβ-*. The sentence is equivalent to CK **nay ka po-ca ko ha-n-ta ko malssumtuli-sio**.

(86) a. [[*na* *j* *po-acje*] *hó-nó-ta*] *sólβ-assje*
I NM see-PR say-IN-DC tell-IM
'Please tell (him that) I would like to see (him).' (Sekpo 6:14)

b. *zjelaj* *sangnjej* *wuli* *lól* [*atól* *i-la*] *niló-si-ni-ngi-ta*
Buddha always us AC son be-DC say-SH-IN-AH-DC
'Buddha always calls us his sons.' (Welsek 13:32)

The second, more productive type is that the first clause is a 'saying' clause with the conjunctive suffix *-atój/-otój/-ótój* 'that, but' and the directly quoted sentence comes next. The quoted sentence is not followed by any marker, except occasionally by a verb of saying such as *hóta* 'say, do'. This type appears to have functioned as direct quotation.

(87) a. *wang* *i* *hwangtanghi* *neki-sj-a* *nilu-sj-**atój*** [*i* *esten*
king NM fabulously think-SH-and say-SH-that this what
kwangmjeng-ko]
light-Q
'The king thought it fabulous and said that, "What kind of light is this!" (Welsek 10:7)

b. *tocók* *i* *mwul-**otój*** [*nehuj-tólh* *i* *musuk ul po-nó-són.ta*]
thief NM ask-that you-PL NM what AC see-IN-Q
'The thief asked, "What are you guys seeing?"' (Welsek 10:28)

The third type is using the genitive *s* as a quotative relativizer (4.5.11.1).

(88) a. [*cjokomas* *pój* *thó-ko cje* **s**] ***ptut*** *ul* *nis-ti*
small ship ride-to wish GN wish AC forget-NOM
mot *hó-li-lota*
cannot do-PRS-EXC
'(He) will not be able to forget the wish to ride a small boat.'
(Twusi 15:55)

b. [*tjwungsajng* *cejtohó-no-la* **s**] ***mózóm*** *i* *isi-mjen*
people control-IN-DC GN mind NM exist-if
'If (he) has the intention to control the general people, [...]' (Kumkang 2:13)

In (88a) that the form *–ko cje* was used not as a desiderative conjunctive ender *-kocje* 'wishing' but as a predicate complex equivalent to CK **-ko siph-eyo** 'wish to do'.

6. Lexicon

The MK period may be characterized by, among other things, the influx of a huge number of Chinese words into Korean. Before this period, Chinese words were limited, in general, to the names of places, people, and government ranks. But starting with the Kolye dynasty, Chinese words pervaded the spoken language.

When Chinese words and Chinese characters were first introduced into Korea remains obscure. The only deduction we can make is that they must have been used in Korea as early as the first century B.C., when Han China colonized the western and northern parts of the Korean peninsula and established its four commanderies there. Two Japanese sources show that a Paykcheyan named Wang In (written in *Nihon shoki* as 王仁, in *Kojiki* as 和邇, OJ *wani*) went to Japan with many Chinese books around AD 400, suggesting that Chinese culture and characters had achieved considerable popularity in the Korea of the Three Kingdoms period. Earlier, the name of the country and the title of the king were changed from native terms to SK terms in the fourth year of King Cicung (503) of Silla. With the unification of the Korean peninsula by the Silla dynasty in 677, the use of Chinese characters gained more popularity in Korea in that Silla's unification was achieved with Tang China's military support and subsequently contact between the two countries became very frequent. In the second year of King Sinmwun (682) of unified Silla, Kwukhak (lit. 'national studies'), a government organization in charge of national education, was established and many Chinese classics began to be taught. In the sixteenth year of King Kyengtek (757), native place names were changed to two-character SK, and in his eighteenth year, all official titles were also Sino-Koreanized. Personal names of upper-class people also began to be Sino-Koreanized during the Silla period.

Native words began to be overwhelmed by SK words in the Kolye dynasty. This was particularly the case after King Kwangco adopted, in 958, the Chinese system of civil service examinations based on the Chinese classics. The Chosen dynasty observed all-out infiltration of Chinese words and characters into every facet of Korean culture and society, chiefly because of the dynasty's adoption of Confucianism as a national religion and, as a result, the popular admiration of everything Chinese.

Due to the massive importation of words from this prestigious language during the MK period, Korean subsequently underwent a wide range of changes, not only in its vocabulary but also to a lesser degree in the sound system and word structure. There are several consequences of the all-out importation of Chinese words. First of all, Korean vocabulary was enormously enriched with various cultural words and abstract terms from Chinese. Thus, MK texts are full of content words written in Chinese characters, as illustrated in (89) where SK words are underlined.

(89) *sinkun*(信根) *i* *ljek*(力) *ul* *tuk*(得)hó-*mjen* *iltjeng*(一定)hi
trust.root NM power AC get-if surely
tinj-e *ujsim*(疑心) *ani* *hó-ko*
carry-so doubt not do-and
'If one's root of trust gets power, one constantly carries it and does not doubt, and [...]'(Welsek 7:45)

Due to the inundation of SK words, many native Korean words, even basic vocabulary items, have gradually been wiped out as a result of the battle for survival in doublet situations. Many of those native words which existed during the MK period have subsequently given in to SK, e.g. (36b), where native words *cumun* '1000' and *kólóm* 'river, lake' are no longer used in CK, replaced by SK equivalents **chen** (千) and **kang** (江). Examples of such extinct nouns include *kasi* 'wife', *kuze* 'shelter', *kuwuj* 'government office', *kilóma* 'saddle', *kip* 'silk', *naco* 'evening', *naks* 'taxes', *nap* 'monkey', *njenu* 'other person', *nuc* 'symptoms', *tiwuj* 'border', *moj* 'mountain', *mwulwuj* 'hail', *mecun mal* 'curse', *mójh* 'field', *pijwuk* 'chick', *sjaong* 'husband', *swulis nal* 'Tano Day', *swum thón kes* 'living thing', *sjwulwup* 'unbrella', *sjeks* 'reins', *cas* 'castle', *cjenchó* 'reason', *cjwuljen* 'female's towel, hankerchief', *cumkej* 'trees and shrubs', *cumkej* 'limit, end', *chól* 'source, origin', *hungcjeng-pachi* 'merchant', *azóm* 'kindred, relative', *achón atól* 'nephew, niece', *jak* 'a kin of turtle', *ezi* 'parents', and *ezi atól* 'parents and children'. On a smaller scale, verbs, adjectives, adverbs, and other word classes have also lost native words in favor of SK counterparts. Furthermore, many SK words have been nativized with radical sound changes to the extent that general native speakers in CK no longer recognized them as derived from SK (e.g. Shim 1983). Examples include *salang* 'love' (from SK *saljang* 'think'), *kakey* (from SK *kaka* 'temporary house'), *kimchi* (from SK *chimchaj* 'soaked vegetable'), and *paychwu* (from SK *pajkchaj* 'white vegetable').

REFERENCES: Chapter 2

An, Byongho. 1985. *Kyeylim Yusa wa Kolye Siki Cosene* (*Kyeylim Yusa* and the Korean Language in the Kolye Period). China: Huklyongkang Cosen Mincok Chwulphansa.

An, Pyonghui. 1977. *Cwunsey Kwuke Kwukyel uy Yenkwu* (A Study of Middle Korean *Kwukyel*). Seoul: Ilcisa.

An, Pyonghui. 1992. *Kwukesa Yenkwu* (A Study of Korean Linguistic History). Seoul: Mwunhak kwa Cisengsa.

An, Pyonghui & Lee, Kwangho. 1990. *Cwungsey Kwuke Mwunpeplon* (A Grammar of Middle Korean). Seoul: Hakkwusa.

Chang, Namgui. 1982. *Phonological Variation in 15th Century Korean.* Monograph 1. *Journal of Chinese Linguistics.*

Chang, Yunhui. 2002. *Cwungsey Kwuke Congkyelemi Yenkwu.* (A Study of Middle Korean Sentence Enders). Seoul: Thayhaksa.

Chin, Taeha. 1974. *Kyeylim Yusa Yenkwu* (A Study on *Kyeylim Yusa*). Seoul: Thap Chwulphansa.

Chin, Taeha. 2003. Kolyesitay wulimal yenkwu (A study on Kolye Korean). *Hankul Hanca Mwunhwa,* 14-6.

Choy, Beomhun. 1990. *Hankwuke Paltalsa* (A Developmental History of the Korean Language). Seoul: Kyengwun Chwulphansa.

Choy, Yunkap. 1987. *Cwungsey Cosene Mwunpep* (A Middle Korean Grammar). Yanji, China: Yenpyen University Press.

Chung, Jaeyoung. 2004. *Kyeylim Yusa* ey nathanan mwunpep hyengthay ey tayhan yenkwu (A study of grammatical forms in *Kyeylim Yusa*). *Kwukyel Yenkwu* 12: 99-132. Seoul: Kwukyel Hakhoy.

Han, Jaeyoung. 1996. *16 Seyki Kwuke Kwumwun Yenkwu* (A Study of the 16th Century Korean). Seoul: Sinkwumwunhwasa.

Huh, Woong. 1972. *Cwungsey Kwuke Yenkwu* (A Study on Middle Korean). Seoul: Cengumsa.

Huh, Woong. 1975. *Wuli Yeys Malpon* (A Historical Grammar of Korean). Seoul: Saym Mwunhwasa.

Huh, Woong. 1983. *Kwukehak* (*Korean Linguistics*). Seoul: Saym Mwunhwasa.

Huh, Woong. 1992. *15·16 Seyki Wuli Yeys Malpon uy Yeksa* (History of 15th and 16th Korean). Seoul: Thap Chwulphansa.

Jeong, Yeonchan. 1971. Cwungsey sengco wa kyengsangto pangen sengco uy pikyo (A comparison between Middle Korean and Kyengsang tones). *Hankul Hakhoy 50th Anniversary Anthology,* 29-46. Seoul: Korean Language Society.

Jeong, Yeonchan. 1972. Cwungsey kwuke sengco uy pyentong kwa kiponhyeng (Variations in Middle Korean tones and their basic forms). *Han-geul* 150.

Kang, Kyuseon & Hwang, Kyeongsu. 2003. *Cwungsey Kwuke Mwunpeplon* (Middle Korean Grammar). Seoul: Chengwun.

Kang, Sinhang. 1980. *Kyeylim Yusa Kolye Pangen Yenkwu.* (A Study of Kolye Dialect in *Kyeylim Yusa*). Seoul: Sungkyunkwa University Press.

Kang, Sinhang. 1990. *Hwunmin Cengum Yenkwu* (A Study of *Hwunmin Cengum*). Seoul: Sungkyunkwan University Press.

Kang, Sinhang. 1995. *Cosenkwan Yeke Yenkwu* (A Study on *Cosenkwan Yeke* 'Korean-Chinese Translated Lexicon'). Seoul: Sungkyunkwan University Press.

Kim-Cho, Sek Yen. 2000. *The Korean Alphabet of 1446: The Orthophonic Alphabet for the Instruction of the People*. Amherst, NY: Humanities Books.

Kim, Dongso. 2003. *Cwungsey Hankwuke Kaysel* (An Introduction to Middle Korean). Seoul: Hankwuk Munhwasa.

Kim, Minsu. 1957. *Cwuhay Hwunmin Cengum* (Annotated *Hwunmincengum*). Seoul: Thongmwunkwan.

Kim, Taewan. 2002. Kolye-e uy "kyey, thwu, pang"mo pwunsek ul thonghan *Kyeylim Yusa* yukium kochal (A study of aspirates in *Kyeylim Yusa* through an analysis of "kyey, thwu, pang" sounds). *Cwunge Cwungmwunhak* 30: 55-68.

Kim, Wanjin. 1971. *Kwuke Umwun Cheykyey uy Yenkwu* (A Study of Korean Phonological System). Seoul: Ilcokak.

Kim, Wanjin. 1973. *Cwubgsey Kwuke Sengco Yenkwu* (A Study of Middle Korean Tones). Seoul: Thap Chwulphansa.

Kim, Young-Uk. 1995. *Mwunpep Hyengthay uy Yeksacek Yenkwu* (A Historical Study of Grammatical Forms). Seoul: Pakiceng.

Kim-Renaud, Young-Key (ed.). 1997. *The Korean Alphabet.* Honolulu: University of Hawaii Press.

Ko, Young-geun. 1998. *Cwungsey Kwuke uy Sisang kwa Sepep* (Tense, Aspect and Modality in Middle Korean). Seoul: Thap Chwulphansa.

Ko, Young-geun. 2007. Phycwun Cwungsey Kwuke Mwunpeplon, Katcengphan (Standard Middle Korean Grammar–revised edition). Seoul: Cipmwuntang.

Ko, Young-geun & Nam, Kishim (eds.). 1999. *Cwungsey.e Calyo Kanghay* (Annotations of Middle Korean Data). Seoul: Cipmwuntang.

Kwon, Jaeil. 1998. *Hankwuke Mwunpepsa* (A Grammatical History of Korean). Seoul: Pakiceng.

Kwu, Pongwan. 1998. *15 Seyki Kwuke Phasayngpep ey tayhan Yenkwu* (A Study of Middle Korean Derivational Morphology) Seoul: Thayhaksa.

Kwuklip Kwuke Yenkwuwen (KKY). 1999. *Phyocwun Kwuke Taysacen* (A Standard Dictionary of Korean). Seoul: KKY.

Ledyard, G.K. 1966. *The Korean Language Reform of 1446: the Origin, Background, and Early History of the Korean Alphabet.* Ph.D. dissertation. University of California at Berkeley.

Lee, Chongho. 1972. *Haysel Yekcwu Hwunmin Cengum* (Annotated and translated *Hwunmin Cengum*). Seoul: Korean Library Science Research Institute.

Lee, Hyonhi. 1994. *Cwungsey Kwuke Kwumwun Yenkwu* (A Study of Middle Korean Constructions). Seoul: Sinkwu Munhwasa.

Lee, Iksop and S. Robert Ramsey. 2000. *The Korean Language*. Albany: State University of New York Press.

Lee, Ki-Moon. 1972. *Kwuke Umwunsa Yenkwu* (A Study of Korean Phonological History). Seoul: Thap Chwulphansa.

Lee, Ki-Moon. 1976. *Kayceng Kwukesa Kaysel* (*A Revised Introduction to the History of Korean*). Seoul: Mincwung Sekwan.

Lee, Sang-Oak. 1979. *Middle Korean Tonology*. Seoul: Hansin.

Lyu, Lyol, et al. 2005. *Cosenehakcense 4: Cosenmal Lyeksa* (A History of Korean) Vols 1, *2*, and *3*. Pyongyang: Sahoykwahak Chwulphansa.

Martin, S.E. 1992. *A Reference Grammar of Korean.* Rutland, Vermont and Tokyo: Charles E. Tuttle.

Moon, Yangsoo. 1974. *A Phonological History of Korean.* Ph.D. dissertation. University of Texas at Austin.

Nam, Kwangu. 1982. *Pocung Ko-e Sacen* (A Revised Dictionary of Old Korean Words). Seoul: Ilcokak.

Nam, Punghyon. 1999. *Kwukesa lul wihan Kwukyel Yenkwu* (*Kwukyel* Studies for Korean Language History). Seoul: Thayhaksa.

Nam, Punghyon. 2009. *Kotay Hankwuke Yenkwu* (A Study of Old Korean). Seoul: Sikan uy Mulley.

Nam, Punghyon. 2012. Old Korean. In Tranter, N. (ed.), *The Language of Japan and Korea*, 41-72.

Pae, Taeon. 2002. *Itwu Mwunpepso uy Thongsicek Yenkwu.* (A Diachronic Study of Grammatical Elements in *Itwu*). Masan: Kyengsang University Press.

Pak, Byongchae. 1989. *Hankwuke Paltalsa* (History of Korean Language Development). Seoul: Seyyengsa.

Ramsey, S.R. 1978. *Accent and Morphology in Korean Dialects: A Descriptive and Historical Study.* Seoul: Thap Chwulphansa.

Shim, Jaegi. 1983. *Kwuke Ehwilon* (Korean Lexicology). Seoul: Cipmwuntang.

Shim, Jaegi. 1993. Kolye sitay ene, mwunca ey kwanhan yenkwu (A study of the language and writing of the Kolye period). *Inmwun Nonchong* (Seoul: Seoul National University).

Sohn, Ho-min. 1998. Evolution of addressee honorifics in Korean. In Lee, S.O. and D.S. Park (eds.), *Perspectives on Korea*, 480-90. Sydney: Wild Peony.

Sohn, Ho-min. 2001. *The Korean Language.* Cambridge, UK: Cambridge University Press.

3 Modern Korean*

1. Introduction

Modern Korean (MOK) is viewed as the language used during approximately 300 years from the beginning of the 17th century and the end of the 19th century. MOK began in the wake of the Japanese Wars (1592-1598) and lasted until the Cosen Dynasty's Kapo Reformation (1894-1895). Compared to the enormous amount of studies available for Middle Korean (MK), MOK has not attracted as much scholarly interest, probably because it is simply relegated as a transitional language connecting MK to Contemporary Korean (CK).[1] Only recently have some Korean linguists begun to recognize the need and importance of exploring MOK in order to not only fill in the scholarly gap between MK and CK but also to better understand and explicate CK. Language texts useful for the study of Modern Korean include: *Chephay sine* (捷解新語, 1618), *Pakthongsa enhay* (朴通事諺解, 1676), *Nokeltay enhay* (老乞大諺解, 1677), *Yeke yuhay* (譯語類解, 1690), *Oy.e yuhay* (倭語類解, 1709), *Tongmwun yuhay* (同文類解, 1748), *Yeke yuhay pophyen* (譯語類解補編, 1755), *Chenge nokeltay sinsek* (淸語老乞大新釋, 1965), *Cwungkan samyek chonghay* (重刊三譯總解, 1774), *Phalsey.a* (八歲兒, 1774), *Soalon* (小兒論, 1774), *Hancheng mwunkam* (漢淸文鑑, 1774), *Pangen cipsek* (方言集釋, 1778), *Kayswu chephay sine* (改修捷解新語, 1781), and *Samhak yeke* (三學譯語, 1789), as well as creative literary works that appeared during Modern Korean period (e.g. J. Shim 1983: 18; Lee and Ramsey 2011: 242-52).

MOK is sharply different from MK, especially in phonology and morphology, as a result of the accumulated variations and changes that occurred during the post-*hankul* MK period. The influx of Sino-Korean words continued during this period as well. Distinct as it might be in many aspects, the first half of MOK naturally reflected and shared many phonological, lexical, and grammatical fea-

* A shorter version of this chapter is a part of my paper titled "Middle and Modern Korean", which is to appear in Brown, Lucien and Jaehoon Yeon (eds.), *The Handbook of Korean Linguistics* (Wiley-Blackwell, forthcoming).

1 For extensive surveys of MK and CK, see, for example, Sohn (2012, 1999).

tures with LMK and its second half with CK. This is a natural phenomenon, as normal linguistic evolution is gradual and continuous.

During the 300 years of the MOK period, language changes must have been expedited by the social and political disorder in the wake of the Japanese Wars, the Practical Learning movement, the popularization of vernacular literature, continued influx of Chinese words, contact with other foreign languages, and the importation of Western civilization.

The remainder of this chapter is devoted to summarizing the major characteristics of MOK as distinct from MK in vocabulary, phonology, morphology, and syntax. Extensive reference is made to some of the representative studies, notably Huh 1984; J. Hong 1998a,b; I.H. Lee 2005; D. Kim 2007, and K. Lee and Ramsey 2011.

2. Vocabulary

MOK was characterized by an unprecedentedly enriched vocabulary with many new native and Sino-Korean words (usually written in Chinese characters). The native stock was enriched with abundant new words, compounds, and derivatives. Publication of a large number of novels, translated books, poems, and songs introduced many new native words which had not been found in earlier periods (cf. D. Kim 2007: 318-21).

Some examples of new native words and compounds that appeared during the MOK period are *ka.jam* (*kay.am* in CK) 'hazelnut', *kacami* 'sole, flatfish', *kalthi* 'hairtail', *kapcel* 'double', *kas* 'mustard cabbage', *keóci* 'beggar', *kekceng* 'worry', *kotoli* 'mackerel', *kotómeli* 'bald head', *kwulejnalwus* 'beard', *kwungtwungi* 'buttocks', *chjemha* 'eaves', *chjansjwu* 'side dishes', *kkeksoj* 'clamp', *mwukpath* 'fallow field', *maknai* 'baby', *neptektali* 'thigh', *nwunchuj* 'sense, tact', *kapnota* 'expensive', *khultheota* 'bold', *kómphólóta* 'dark blue', *kancikhóta* 'keep', *kalójta* 'harass', *kamsamta* 'make by winding', *kescapta* 'roll up and hold', *nólpstwita* 'act violently', *tosjeta* 'turn around', *husnólta* 'scatter, blown away', *kottutta* 'take another's words as truth', and *kjelej* 'immediately'. Compounding a native noun with the native predicate *hóta* 'be, do' was productive, as illustrated in *kwumkwumhóta* 'anxious', *pantóshóta* 'certain, sure', *sjwukwullihóta* 'poor, hard', and *stumcilhóta* 'apply a heat treatment'. Attaching *-e/a-hóta* 'show the sign of' to an adjective to make it a verb (usually a transitive verb) is another productive compounding, as in *mwusew-ehóta* 'fear', *mujw-ehóta* 'hate', and *eljew-ehóta* 'feel constrained'.

A large number of native words derived through affixation. Productive derivational suffixes were the nominalizer *–i* and *–ki* as was the case in MK. Examples of the words derived this way include *kjeusali* 'passing the winter', *mitati* 'sliding door', *jetati* 'hinged door', *tungkulki* 'back scratcher', *pommaci* 'welcoming the spring', *kiphi* (<*kiphuj*) 'depth', *nophi* (< *nophuj*) 'height', *kwupi* (< *kwupuj*) 'turn, curve'*kejoki* 'vomiting', and *omkiki* 'moving'. New nouns derived from verbs with the suffixation of the 'instrument' suffix *–kaj, -kej, -aj,* or *–ej*, as in *skwumikay* 'ornament', *tolikaj* 'frail', *nissjwusikaj* 'tooth-pick', *cikej* 'A-frame', *panólkelej* 'pincushion', and *khostolaj* 'nose ornament'.

In addition, a countless number of native-Sino-Korean compounds and derivatives were newly generated during the MOK period as is the case in MK, most productively by affixing the native *hóta* 'be, do' to Sino-Korean verbal and adjectival nouns to derive the corresponding verbs and adjectives. Examples are *kanghóta* (强-) 'strong', *kangakhóta* (强惡-) 'vicious', *kujwuhóta* (忌憂-) 'worry', *kjektonghóta* (激動-) 'shake violently', *kjelpakhóta* (結縛-) 'bind, tie', and *pjengcakhóta* (竝作-) 'sharecrop'. Other compounds include *kanmaki* (間-) 'partition, screen', and *mjociki* (墓-) 'guardian of a grave'. The native adjectival suffixes *–low, –toj,* and *–sulew-* combined with Sino-Korean nouns in MOK, as in *phjey**lop**ti* (弊-) 'bothersome', *haj**lop**ti* (害-) 'harmful', *hjoto**low**um* (孝道-) 'filiality', *chon**suleon*** (村-) 'like a hick', *cjengsjeng**toj**ko* (精誠-) 'sincere and', and *wensjwu**suleun*** (怨讐-) 'like an enemy'. The nominalizer suffix *–i* and adverbializer suffix *–i* combined with Sino-Korean nouns, as in *tiljongi* (地龍-) 'earthworm' > *cilengi* 'earthworm' and *chin-i* (親-) 'in person'.

Many earlier native words underwent semantic change in MOK. Lee and Ramsay (ibid.: 283) and J. Shim (1983: 116) provide some examples. MK native adjectives *e.jespu-* 'pitiable', *eli-* 'foolish', and *cjem-* 'young (infant or small child)' came to mean 'pretty', 'small, young', and 'youthful', respectively, in MOK, as they do in CK. Similarly, MK native noun *pit* meant both 'price, value' and 'debt', but it came to refer to only 'debt' in MOK and CK. The native noun *him* meant 'sinew, muscle' in MK but it came to refer to 'strength' in MOK and CK.

The MOK vocabulary observed a sharp increase in the use of Sino-Korean words in both written and spoken Korean, greatly enriching the MOK vocabulary. This is evidenced in the word frequency counts, quoted in I.H. Lee (2005 Vol. 3: 245), of some representative texts published in the MK and MOK periods, as shown in (1).

(1)	Books	Native words	Sino-Korean words
	Dictionaries:		
	Hunmongcahoy (1527)	2713 (82.3%)	585 (17.7%)
	Way.e yuhae (18th c.)	1475 (45.2%)	1790 (54.8%)

Literary works:		
Yongpi echenka (1447)	615 (54%)	524 (46%)
Songkang kasa (18th c.)	482 (28.7%)	1199 (71.3%)
Texts in colloquial Korean:		
Nokeltay sang (early 16th c.)	664 (81.4%)	152 (18.6%)
Nokeltay enhay sang (1670)	579 (74.9%)	194 (25.1%)
Pakthongsa sang (early 16th c.)	822 (73.3%)	303 (26.7%)
Pakthongsa enhay sang (1677)	619 (54%)	528 (46%)

Notice the increased percentages of the use of Sino-Korean words in texts of the 17th ~ 18th centuries compared to the texts of the 15th ~ 16th centuries. In the three kinds of texts given above, the average increase of Sino-Korean usage in MOK vis-à-vis MK is 22.3%. The most prolific use of Sino-Korean words took place during the 18th and early 19th centuries.

New coinages and expansion in usage of Sino-Korean words were extensive and ranged over all walks of life not only for need of new words but also to maintain prestige associated with non-native words. In addition to ordinary words of daily use, a wide variety items and concepts of Chinese and Western civilization were imported into Korea along with their Sino-Korean names. Western items and concepts, including natural sciences and religion, were translated into Chinese in China, which were fast imported into Korea. Newly introduced Sino-Korean words included *kancung* (干證) 'testimony', *njangchek* (兩隻) 'plaintiff and defendant', *cungin* (證人) 'witness', *wencjeng* (原情) 'petition, appeal', *incjeng* (人情) 'bribe', *pangsong* (放送) 'set free', *haok* (下獄) 'imprison', *tungtój* (等待) 'waiting', and *palmjeng* (發明) 'pretext', *mjencil* (面質) 'confrontation', *cómjengcong* (自鳴鐘) 'alarm clock' and *chjenlikjeng* (千里鏡) 'telescopes', *cinamchel* (指南鐵) 'magnet', *hwajak* (火藥) 'gunpowder', *hwapho* (火砲) 'cannon', *sengkjeng* (聖經) 'bible', *sinjak* (新約), 'New Testament', *sinpwu* (神父) 'Catholic father', *cento* (傳道) 'propagation of religion', *cwukjo* (主教) 'bishop', *chentang* (天堂) 'heaven' (D. Kim 2007: 322). Many frequently used Sino-Korean words in all kinds of texts, including textbooks and novels, were popularized among Koreans in spoken Korean. Many Sino-Korean words were used in meanings quite different from their original meanings (Lee and Ramsey 2011: 284; J. Shim 1983: 116).

Furthermore, some Sino-Korean words were derived from Chinese loans, i.e. borrowings from spoken (not written) Chinese. Such words include *tangcik* (當直) 'in service' from *tangci* (當直), *tahong* (茶紅) 'deep red, crimson' from *tehjwung* (大紅), *cacwu* (紫朱) 'purple' from *cati* (紫的), and *pitan* (緋緞) 'silk' from *pitan* (匹段) (e.g. Lee and Ramsey ibid.: 285).

As a result, due to the extensive influx and use of Sino-Korean words resulted, first of all, dual lexical systems of the native stock and Sino-Korean stock were solidly established in MOK, with a large number of doublets, some of which are illustrated in (2).

(2)	Native words	Sino-Korean equivalents	
	stas-nimca	*cicwu* (地主)	'landlord'
	nakunaj	*kajkin* (客人)	'traveler, stranger'
	polmo	*tjentang* (典當)	'hostage, pawn'
	mekwi	*otong* (梧桐)	'paulownia'
	kokom	*hakcil* (瘧疾)	'malaria'
	kewul	*chjekjeng* (體鏡)	'mirror'
	onun-nal	*kumil* (今日)	'today'
	epei	*pwumo* (父母)	'parents'
	ceptongsaj	*twukjen* (杜鵑)	'cuckoo'

Even some proverbs or idioms were used as doublets. Examples include *soj kwi ey kjeng nik-ta* and *wu-i-song-kjeng* (牛耳誦經) 'reading a sutra to a cow's ears', *nó-masi-n kojjangi* and *hup-jen-mjo* (吸煙猫) 'a cat that breathed smoke', *sokjeng uj tancheng kwukjeng* and *majng-wan-tancheng* (盲玩丹靑) 'a blind person sightsees red and blue scenes', *kemtong kój mokjok kam-ta* and *hukkwu mokjok* (黑狗沐浴) 'a black dog takes a bath', and *na pulu-l nolój satonnój puló-ta* and *aka-sachang* (我歌査唱) 'my in-law sings the song I was going to sing'.

Second, in the long synonymic battle between the native and Sino-Korean stocks, that latter usually won out due mainly to the popular psychology that Sino-Korean is more prestigious than native Korean. Thus, many Sino-Korean words ousted and replaced native counterparts in doublet situations, even in words of daily use. Koreans in all social classes, especially the upper-class people, must have absorbed Sino-Korean words willingly for both needs and prestige, as everything Chinese was admired at that time. Native words that were replaced by Chinese words in the MOK period are illustrated in (3).

(3)	Lost native words	Sino-Korean replacements	
	cas	*seng* (城)	castle
	azóm	*chinchek* (親戚)	relative
	cumun	*chen* (千)	thousand
	hótaka	*manil* (萬一)	if
	kólóm	*kang* (江), *hoswu* (湖水)	river, lake
	moj	*san* (山)	mountain

on	*pajk* (百)	hundred
olaj	*mwun* (門)	gate
patólap-	*withaj-hó-* (危殆- *hó-*)	dangerous
sjulwup	*wusan* (雨傘)	umbrella
hujn-soj	*un* (銀)	silver
pas-nala	*ojkwuk* (外國)	foreign country
tjhón-soj	*kangchel* (鋼鐵)	steal
cjekun-chjangcó	*socang* (小腸)	small intestine
han-mul	*hongswu* (洪水)	flood
nómósaj[2]	*chajso* (菜蔬)	vegetables
sontowule	*cojek* (助役)	assistant
niken-hój	*wangnjen* (往年)	former years
toz-	*sóljang(-hó-)* (思量)	to love
kilóma	*ancang* (鞍裝)	saddle
cjwuljen	*swuken* (手巾)	female's handkerchief
azóm	*chinchek* (親戚)	kindred, relative'
kip	*pitan* (緋緞)	silk
kuwuj	*kwancheng* (官廳)	government office
mwulwuj	*wupak* (雨雹)	hail
swulis nal	*tano* (端午)	*Tano* Day

Many native kinship terms were even replaced by Sino-Korean counterparts since the 18th century. Thus, except for several native terms of the direct family line, which also had Sino-Korean counterparts, most of the native terms, were replaced by Sino-Korean kinship terms. For example, *apuj-nwui* was replaced by *komo* (姑母) 'aunt (father's sister)', *apuj-tongsóng* by *samchon* (三寸) 'uncle (father's younger brother')', *nwuuj-namcin* by *maypwu* (妹夫) '(male's) sister's husband' and *tasóm-emi* by *kjjemo* (繼母) 'step mother'. In this way, Sino-Korean *sachon-majpwu* (四寸妹夫) 'brother-in-law in first cousin', *komo-pwu* (姑母夫) 'uncle (father's sister's husbsnd)', *imo* (姨母) 'aunt (mother's sister)', *imo-pwu* (姨母夫) 'uncle (mother's sister's husband)', *oj-samchon* (外三寸) 'maternal uncle (mother's brother)', *hjengswu* (兄嫂) 'older brother's wife', *chehjeng* (妻兄) 'sister-in-law (wife's older sister)' and other kinship terms came to be exclusively used as both referent and address terms from the 18th century on (cf. I.H. Lee 2005 Vol. 3: 247).

Third, many earlier Sino-Korean words underwent formal and/or semantic changes. Formal changes were usually made towards native-like pronunciation.

2 This word was recovered as *namsaj* after the liberation of Korea from the Japanese rule in 1945.

Thus, due to their formal change from usual Sino-Korean pronunciations, these pseudo-native forms are often considered "native" by contemporary Koreans. The MK Sino-Korean *sóljang(-hó)* (思量) 'think of' and its MOK form *sólang(-hó)* came to mean 'love' as well as 'think of' in MK, making the native words *tóz-* 'love' and *koj-* 'esteem, favor' obsolete. It only meant 'love' in MOK as it is in CK. Similarly, *kakej* 'store' developed from Sino-Korean *kaka* 'temporary house', *kimchi* from *chimchaj* 'soaked vegetable', and *pajchwu* 'Chinese cabbage' from *pajkchaj* 'white vegetable'. I.H. Lee (ibid.: 251-3) provides developmental processes of pseudo-nativization of some Sino-Korean words, based on available historical texts, as in (4).

(4) *najcjong* (乃終) 'subsequently, soon, at last' > *nacjong* > *nacwjung* > *nacwung* 'later'
tiljongi (地龍이) 'earthworm' > *ciljongi* > *ciljengi* > *cilengi* 'earthworm'
amo (阿某) 'someone' > *amwu* 'anyone'
sanhójng (山行) 'going to the mountain' > *sanójng* > *san.jang* > *sanjang* 'hunting'
mangsek (網席) 'woven mat' > *mengsek* 'straw mat'
hjenpan (懸盤) 'suspension shelf' > *senpan* 'shelf'
kannan (艱難) 'difficulty' > *kanan* 'poverty'
chojchok (催促) 'urge' > *cójchjok* 'urge' (*cajchok* in CK)
cjwungsóng (衆生) 'living things' > *cumsóng* > *cumsung* > *cimsung* 'animal'
kwanhjek (貫革) 'target made of leather' > *kwanjek* 'target, mark'
selma (雪馬) 'sled (lit. snow horse)' > *sselmaj* 'sled'
kacó (茄子) 'eggplant' > *kaci* 'egg-plant'

Pseudo-nativization also occurred with (spoken) Chinese loan words, as in *mwumjeng* 'cotton' from *mwumjeng* (木綿), *phwun* 'penny, cent' from *phwun* (分) 'cent', and *thwungso* 'bamboo clarinet' from *thwungsjo* (洞簫).

Finally, MOK borrowed a small number of words from Manchu (e.g. *homuj* 'weeding hoe', *sjwusjwu* 'Indian millet', *kamthwu* 'cap of horse hair') and Mongolian (e.g. *celta-mól* 'red horse', *songkol* 'peregrine'). Hardly any words were borrowed from Western languages during the MOK period. One well-known word is *tampój* from *tobacco*, which appeared first in early 17th century as *tampako*. In short, the MOK vocabulary was characterized as a solid dual lexical system consisting of two competing and complementing stocks—native and Sino-Korean.

3. The writing system

As observed by Lee and Ramsey (2011: 253-6) and other linguists, the earlier orthographic standardization was gradually loosened in the 16th century and broken down to a great extent in the wake of the Imjin Japanese Wars. Thus, *hankul* orthography tradition underwent several major changes, as summarized below.

(a) Tone marks (side dots) completely disappeared.

(b) The letter used to write [ng], i.e. ㆁ with a large tick on top, and the syllable initial zero symbol, i.e. ㅇ without a tick, merged into the latter. Thus, ㅇ represented the syllable initial zero vowel and [ng] in the syllable final position *patchim*, as in 앙 [ang]. The letter Δ, used to write [z], completely disappeared.

(c) The orthographic distinctions between three series of initial consonant clusters (a. *sk-, st-, ss-, sp-*; b. *pt-, ps-, pth-*; c. *psk-, pst-*) broke down in the 17th and 18th centuries. Use of *psk-* and *pst-* became inconsistent. A new orthographic cluster, *pk-,* and *sk-* were used as an alternative way of writing *psk-*, as in *psketje* 'collapsing' and *sketinila, pketinila* 'collapsed'. Similarly, *pt-* was used as an alternative way of writing *pst-*, as in *pstaj, ptaj* 'time'. Furthermore, *pt-* was confused with *st-*, and *ps-* was confused with *ss-*, as in *ptut, stut* 'meaning' and *pswul, sswuk* 'mugwort'. The MK *hh-* was spelled as *sh-* in the 17th century, as in *shje* 'drawing, pulling'. In addition, the geminate spellings *pp-, tt-, kk-, cc-* reemerged in the MOK period as another alternative for consonant clusters, as in *spólli, ppólli* 'quickly'. In the 19th century, all the above complex initial consonants began to be usually written as *s*-clusters: *sk-, st-, sp-,* and *sc-,* with the exception of *ss-,* which was sometimes written as *ps-* (Lee and Ramsey ibid.: 254).

(d) Transcription of the syllable final consonants *–s* and *–t* became confused, as in *mas, mat* 'taste' and *mot, mos* 'pond'. In the 18th century, the final *-t* gradually was replaced in all cases by *–s.*

(e) The earlier syllable medial spelling *–ll-* became to be used interchangeably with *–ln-*, as in *cinsillo, cinsilno* 'truly', *pulle, pulne* 'calling', and *hulle, hulne* 'flowing'.

4. Phonology

The MOK phonology is quite different from that of MK, but in fact many changes were gradual ones beginning in the LMK period. Changes occurred in both consonants, vowels, and prosody.

4.1 Consonants

The phonemic inventory of consonants in the 17th century is different from that of the 15th century in that (a) it lacks a series of voiced fricatives, *β, ɦ, z,* represented respectively by ㅸ, ㅇ, and ㅿ, and (b) the series of reinforced consonants fully developed, including *cc*, from word-initial consonant clusters such as *pt-*, *ps-*, and *pc-*. The voiced fricatives *β* and *ɦ* disappeared completely by the end of the MK period, while the consonant *z* disappeared in the early part of the seventeenth century. This sound was deleted in most dialects, as in *epezi* > *epei* 'parents'. In the southern dialects (Cenla, Kyengsang, Ceycwu), it usually became *s*, as in *ciz-umjen* > *ci-umjen* (standard), *ci-sumjen* (southern dialects) 'if (he) builds'.

The development of initial clusters into reinforced (tensed) consonants began in the LMK period and is understood to have reached completion sometime in the middle of the 17th century (Lee and Ramsey ibid.: 257). Appearance of *sc-* (ㅾ-) in the early 18th century as in *scól* 'salty' and *scak* 'one of a pair', as well as the appearance of *cc-*, as in *ccóm* 'interval', in the 17th century, is construed as the existence of the tensed consonant *cc-*.

Other significant consonantal changes made in the MOK period include the following.

Palatalization. The most conspicuous phonological change in the MOK period was palatalization, which caused the dental consonants, *t, th, tt,* to change into the spirants, *c, ch, cc* when followed by *i* and *y*. In the southern dialects, even the velar consonants, *k, kh, kk,* underwent palatalization as well. These changes began quite early in the southern dialects and spread north from there. In Seoul, only the dental series palatalized very late, whereas, in the Phyengan dialects, the consonants have still remained unaffected by palatalization.

The earliest attestations of palatalization were found in the early 18th century texts, as in *chi-* 'hit' (< MK *thi-*), *stih-* 'pound' (< MK *stih*), and *cisaj* 'tile' (< MK *tisaj*) (Lee and Ramsey ibid.: 259). As a result of palatalization, the consonant-vowel combinations *ti, tja, tje, tjo, tjwu* and *thi, thja, thje, thjo, thjwu* disappeared from the Korean phonological system. However, in the early 19th century, *tuj, thuj, ttuj* monophthogized to *ti, thi* and *tti*, respectively, as in *kjenti-* 'endure' (< *kjentuj*) and *tti* 'belt' (< *ttuj*). Furthermore, palatalization affected other consonants such as *s* and *n,* so that these consonants had allophones like [ɲ] and [ʃ], as is the case with CK.

Word-initial n-deletion. The consonant *n-* is deleted in word-initial position before *i* and *y,* apparently beginning in the latter half of the 18th century, as in *imkum* 'king' (< *nimkum*) and *iluhi* 'until arriving' (< *niluhi*).

4.2 Vowels

The MOK observed some significant vowel changes as well. The following are major ones.

The loss of ó. The vowel *ó* became extinct in the phonemic system in the latter half of the 18th century. The loss began in non-initial syllables by merging with other vowels (usually *u*), as in *modón* > *modun* 'all', in the 16th century and was completed as *ó* merged with *a* in initial syllables, as in *stól* > *ttal* 'daughter', in the latter half of the 18th century.

Monophthongization. Following the merge of the syllable-initial *ó* with *a*, another major change occurred—monophthongization of the diphthongs *aj* [aj] and *ej* [əj] to [ɛ] and [e], respectively, as is the case with CK. This process is assumed to have taken place around the turn of the 19th century. There were some occurrences of *wuj* to *uj* in the 17th century, as in *pwulhuj* 'root' (< *pwulhwuj*) and *puj* 'empty' (< *pwuj*). Somewhat later, *uj* was reduced to *i* in some words, as in *mujp-* 'hateful' > *mip* and *pwulhuj* 'root' > *ppwuli.* The off-glide *j* was somewhat persistent after vowels other than *a* and *e*, as observed even in CK *kwi* [kü, kuj] 'ear', *oy* [øː, oi] 'cucumber', and *uy* [uj, u] (genitive particle).

The breakdown of vowel harmony. Another major change in MOK was loosening of vowel harmony. The merge of the *yang* vowel *ó* with the *yin* vowel *u* in non-initial syllables had a great effect on the MK vowel harmony system, as the *yang-yin* contrast became neutralized in non–initial syllables, making *u* a neutral vowel in such positions. MOK texts showed the raising (weakening) of the *yang* vowel *o* to the *yin* vowel *wu,* which contributed to eroding vowel harmony between stems and endings. A sharp increase and extensive use of Sino-Korean words, which are not sensitive to vowel harmony, further contributed to the breakdown of the formerly rigid vowel harmony system.

Labialization. The vowel *u* labialized after a labial consonant such as *m, p, ph,* or *pp,* making the *u-wu* contrast lost in that position. Thus, the former contrast between *mul* 'water' and *mwul* 'group' was no longer a minimal pair since the end of the 17th century. Other examples include *pwul* 'fire', *pwuthita* 'stick on', *spwul* 'horn', *phwul* 'grass', *nómwul* 'herbs', and *pwulkta* 'red'.

4.3 Prosody

MOK was not a tone (or pitch) language, as tones were lost in the 16th century. However, syllables that had been marked as rising tones consisted of two moras, and the length of the syllable persisted even after the loss of its pitch. As a result, the vowel length became distinctive.

4.4 The phonemic system

As a result of the loss of the voiced fricative series and *hh*, the MOK consonant system was simplified. Furthermore, the shaky MK tensed series was firmly established.

(5)

		Bilabial	Dental	Palatal	Velar
Stop:	Lax	ㅂ *p*	ㄷ *t*	ㅈ *c*	ㄱ *k*
	Aspirated	ㅍ *ph*	ㅌ *th*	ㅊ *ch*	ㅋ *kh*
	Tensed	ㅃ *pp*	ㄸ *tt*	ㅉ *cc*	ㄲ *kk*
Fricative:	voiceless		ㅅ *s*		ㅎ *h*
	Tensed		ㅆ *ss*		
Nasal:		ㅁ *m*	ㄴ *n*		ㅇ *ng*
Lateral:			ㄹ *l*		

Due to the loss of *ó* and monophthongization, the MOK vowel system became quite different from that of MK and identical to that of CK, as in (6).

(6)

Tongue height	*Tongue position*		
High	ㅣ *i* [i]	ㅡ *u* [ɨ]	ㅜ *wu* [u]
Mid	ㅔ *ej* [e]	ㅓ *e* [ə]	ㅗ *o* [o]
Low	ㅐ *aj* [ɛ]	ㅏ *a* [a]	
Semivowels	*j*[3]		*w*

5. Morphology

MOK was considerably different from MK in morphological structure due to gradual variations and changes, in many cases toward structural simplification plus some innovations. Representative changes and innovations in derivational and inflectional suffixes or particles are summarized below (Huh 1984: 448-60; J. Hong 1998: 20-26; Lee and Ramsey 2011: 268-81).

5.1 Derivation

Ordinalizer. The new word *ches-cay* 'first' in the 18th century. This suffix –

3 The semivowel *j* had the same sound value as the CK *y* except that it occurred as an off-glide as well in Middle Korean and the first half of MOK. The CK *y* occurs only as an on-glide, while, in the syllable-final position, it is monophthongized with the coocurring vowel, forming a separate vowel phoneme, as in *ay* [ɛ] and *ey* [e].

cay came to be used as the standard ordinalizer, as in *twul-cay* 'second', *seys-cay* 'third'.

Nominalizers. While the most common suffix used to derive nominal from predicate stems was still *–(o/u)m,* the nominalizer suffix *–i* became completely unproductive. Only some fossilized MK forms appeared in MOK: *mascwoi* 'welcoming' and *noli* 'playing'. The nominalizer suffix *–(o/u)j* that had derived nouns from adjectives monophthongized to *i* (as indicated above), as in *khi* 'size' (< *khuj*), *nophi* 'height' (< *nophuj*), and *kili* 'length' (< *kiluj*). As a result, these nominals became homophonous with the adverbs *khi* 'in a big way', *nophi* 'highly', and *kili* 'for a long time'.

Pluralizers. There were two plural suffixes, *-tulh* and *–nej*, which had developed from MK-*tólh* 'and others' and *–naj* 'and other esteemed persons' with much the same meaning and usage. The only difference was that the MOK *–nej* was no longer used as an honorific marker.

Causative suffixes: The suffixes *–hi* and *–wu* (MK *-βó*) were used to derive causative stems. The MK causative verb *hói-* of the verb *hó-* 'do' passed down into the 17th century, as in *pjesól hóita* 'place in a government post'. The form *hói-* was replaced by *siki-* in the latter part of the MOK period, as in *il sikita* 'give (someone) work to do'.

Passive suffixes: The MK passive suffix *–i* was replaced by *–hi* in some predicate stems in MOK. For example, the MK passive of *pólβ-* was *pol**i**-* (< *polβi-*) 'be stepped on'. In MOK, this passive stem became *pólp**hi**-*.

Transtivizers: A complex suffix that began appearing in MK and was firmly established in MOK was *–e/-a hó-* (infinitive suffix + 'do' verb) 'show the signs of'. This complex suffix derived a verb (frequently a transitive verb) out of an emotive adjective, *kisk-**e hó**ta* 'feel happy' and *mujj**e hó**ta* 'hate' (D.S. Kim 2007: 231).

Adjectivizers: The MK adjectivizer suffix *–loβ/-loβoj* and *-tóβ/-tóβoj* used to derive adjectives from nouns continued to be used in MOK in changed forms as *–low* and *–toj*, as in *haj**lop**ti* 'harmful' and *kulus**tojn*** 'mistaken'. In the 18th century, the suffix *–sulew* 'like' made its appearance, as *elwun**sulew**on* 'like an adult'. The MK adjectivizer suffix *-βó/-βu* that converted verb stems into adjective stems was no longer productive in MOK.

5.2 Inflection

Many case and delimiter particles underwent change either in form or function or both. Representative changes follow.

Nominative ka. Appearance of the nominative case particle *ka* (in addition to the long established *i*) was an innovation in MOK. It made its fleeting appearance in the 16th century, but it was firmly in place in 17th century texts and thereafter, as illustrated in *pój ka ol kesini* 'since the ship is coming' (1676 *Chephay sine*). Initially in the 17th century, *ka* attached to the nouns ending in *–y* (e.g. *pój* 'ship', *thuj* 'particles', *cój* 'sediment'), but its use spread to the positions following nouns ending in vowels, as it is in CK. From the 18th century, it also functioned to mark a complement (before the copula and the inchoative verb *toj* 'become').

Honorific subject particle. This particle was formed by combining the honorific dative particle *skej* with the source particle *sje* 'from, at' with, as shown in *cungco skejsje nasimjen* 'if the great-grandparents go out' (1632 *Kaley enhay* 2.2). It had allomorphs such as *kejsje, kjeosje,* and *kyeosje* in different texts.

Genitive particles. The MK particle *s* ceased to be productive as a genitive marker by the MOK period, leaving *uj* as the only functioning genitive. The form *s* was now used mainly to tense an initial lax consonant of the second member of compound nouns, as it does in CK.

Dative particles. The allomorphs of the dative particle for animates was unified as *ujkej,* as in *Coco ujkej* 'to (the Chinese general) Caocao', those of the honorific dative particle as *skej*, as in *kalo skej* 'to the family elders', and those for inanimates as *ej*.

Comitative particle. This particle, meaning 'with, and', became phonologically fixed as *wa* after a vowel and *kwa* after a consonant, as in CK.

Honorific vocative particle. The MK honorific vocative particle *ha* ceased to be used at all in MOK.

Comparative particle. The MK *twuko, twukon* (< *twu-ko(nón)* 'place and') 'than, compared to' continued to be used as *tokon*, as in *amu il tokon* 'compared to anything at all' in the early MOK period. In the 18th century, a new comparative particle *potaka* (< *po-taka* 'while looking at') appeared and gradually replaced *tokon,* and by the 19th century it was the only particle used to express comparisons (its current form is *pota*). An example quoted by Lee and Ramsey (ibid.: 273) is "… *pjeng tun kes potaka tewuk kinkup hóni* '… is more urgent than becoming sick' (1783 *Cahyul cenchik* 2).

Emphatic particles. Various MK emphatic particles disappeared, except *ja* and *kos*. The particle *ja* replaced the 15th century emphatic particle *za* around the end of the 16th century. The particle *kwos* came to be used mostly with negatives in MOK, as in *twu pwun kwos animjen* 'if it isn't just those two people'.

Major innovations and changes in inflectional suffixes occurred during the MOK period, including both prefinal ones and clause/sentence endings. Saliet prefinal suffixes include the following.

Honorific suffixes: The three honorific suffixes, subject honorific *–(ó/u)si-* (< *-sja*), third-person honorific *-zóβ*, and the addressee honorific *–ngi,* were gradually reduced to the two-dimensional system in the 17th century: subject honorific and addressee honorific). The suffix *-zóβ* shifted its MK function of honorifying a third-person referent to that of reinforcing the addressee honorification along with the MK address honorific suffix *–ngi.* On the other hand, *-ngi* was gradually weakened in both form and function to *–i.* Thus, in 17th century texts, addressee honorification was marked variously as *-ópnóngi-, -ópnóji-, ópnói-* (< MK *zóp-nó-ngita* where *nó* is an indicative mood marker) or *–sóp-* alone (cf. H. Sohn 1988 for grammaticalization processes involved). The CK addressee honorific suffix *–(u)pni-* is a result of these developments.

Speaker volitive suffix: The speaker subject suffix *–o/-wu,* which indicated the speaker's volition, was no longer productive and completely disappeared in the 17th century.

Indicative mood suffix: The suffix *-nó* diverged into two allomorphs in the 17th century, *-n* after a stem ending in a vowel, as in *ka-n-ta* 'goes', and *–nun/-nón* after a stem ending in a consonant, as in *nos-nón-ta* 'puts, places'.

Past suffix: The new past suffix, *-as/-es,* developed during the MOK period, as evidenced in *mullichjesta* 'defeated' and *ponajjesta* 'sent' (1704 *Samyek chenghay*). This suffix derived, through grammaticalization, from the resultative construction consisting of the infinitive *–a/-e* and the existential predicate *is(i)-*.

Modal/future suffix: Another MOK innovation was the suffix *–keys,* which denoted the speaker's volition/conjecture and prospective (future). Evidence shows that this suffix was created, via grammaticalization, from the construction *–kej hój-es* 'caused to do' (Huh 1984: 458-9). Derivation of*–kejss* from the past causative is justified by the semantic content of the future-oriented ender *–kej* and the pragmatic inference. That is, the speaker's 'having caused someone to do something' implies the speaker's pragmatic inference that 'someone will/may do something'. This pragmatic inferencing became semanticized, as frequently the case in the process of grammaticalization. The semantic shift was facilitated by the deletion of the 'do' verb *hó-* causing the orphaned past suffix to become defunct.

There were changes in clause or sentence endings. Major ones are presented below.

Relativizer: The MK relativizer ending *–(ó/u)n* combined with various prefinal endings, as in *nó-n, te-n, ke-n,* and *li-n.* Only *-nó-n* and *-te-n* survived into MOK.

Nominalizer: The MK nominalizer ending *–(ó/u)m* had been preceded by the prefinal speaker volitive suffix *–o/-wu.* As the volitive suffix fell into disuse in MOK, *-(ó/u)m* alone was used to nominalize a predicate or a clause. In nominalizations of predicate stems ending in *–l,* the epenthetic vowel no longer occurred between the stems and the following nominalizer, as in *kólm* 'replacement' and *tulm* 'entrance'. In MOK, the use of the nominalizer ending *-ki* became extremely productive.

Conjunctive endings: The MK coordinate conjunctive endings *–ko, -(ó/u) mje,* and *–a/-e* combined with many particles as in *ko-n, ko-k, ko-m, -(ó/u)mje-sje, -a-k,* and *–am.* All of these complex endings disappeared in MOK, except *-(ó/u)mje-sje*, which developed into *-(u)mjense* in the latter part of the MOK period. The MK conjunctive ending *–(o/wu)toj* 'but, even though' became *–toj.* The MK concessive ending *–kenmalón* although' became *–kenmanón.* The rare MK desiderative *kwatja* became *–kwacja* (*-koca* in CK). The rare MK incremental ending *–(ó/u)lq sólok* 'the more ... the more' replaced the more common MK counterpart *-tiños* in MOK.

Sentence endings: See the syntax section below.

6. Syntax

The overall MOK syntactic structure was not different from that of LMK. A comprehensive survey of MOK morpho-syntax may be observed in J. Hong (1998b) and studies of MOK causative/passive, tense and mood, negation, honorifics, and auxiliary constructions are included in J. Hong (1998a). Several salient morpho-syntactic changes made during the MOK period are as follows.

Use of predicates: One noticeable syntactic difference between MK and MOK is that predicate stems could appear in isolation in MK, but that was no longer possible in MOK. Lee and Ramsey (ibid.: 267) cites a passage in the 1446 *Yongpi echenka* where the adjective *kót* is used adverbially without any suffix: *hanóls pjel i nwun* ***kót*** *tiningita* 'the stars in heaven fall **like** snow'. This type of construction was no longer possible in MOK, as predicates were required to have a sentential or phrasal ending to be functional in sentences.

Subject and complement: Appearance of the particle *ka* was an innovation in MOK. It was productively used as a subject marker from the 17th century. Since the 18th century on, it has also functioned to mark a nominal complement as well (before the copula and the verb *toj* 'become').

Honorifcation: The three honorific suffixes, subject honorific *–(ó/u)si* (< *-sja*), third-person honorific *–sóp* (and its allomorphs), and the addressee honorific *–ngi,* were gradually reduced to the two-dimensional system in the 17th century: subject honorification and addressee honorification. The suffix *-sóp* shifted its function to reinforce the addressee honorification along with *–ngi,* which was gradually weakened in both form and function to *–i.* Thus, in 17th century texts, addressee honorification was marked variously as *-ópnóngi, -ópnóji, -ópnói* (< MK *zóp-nó-ngi-ta* where *nó* is an indicative mood marker) or *–sóp* alone (cf. Sohn 1988 for grammaticalization processes involved).

Pronouns: The CK *nay ka* 'I-subject' and *ney ka* 'you-subject' first appeared in texts of the end of the 18th century. The MK pronoun *na* 'I' and *ne* 'you' and the subject (nominative) particle *y* were monophthongized as *nay* [nɛ] and *ney* [ne] in MOK to which a newly innovated subject particle *ka* was attached. Similarly, the MK interrogative pronoun *nwu* 'who' and the question ending –*ko* fused together in MOK as the interrogative pronoun *nwuko* or *nwukwu*, to which the question ending was attached, as in *i pes un nwuko-ko?* 'who is this friend' (1670 *Nokeltay enhay* 2.5). The two forms *mues* and *muses,* both meaning 'what', were unified as *mwues* in the 18th century. The MK interrogative *enu* 'which' functioned as a pronoun in MK and took case particles. In MOK, it was grammaticalized as a pre-nominal determiner.

Question: The morphological distinction between the question-word question –*ko* and yes-no-question –*ka* broke down in favor of –*ka* in both questions.

Changes of order in inflectional suffixes: First, the LMK order of past –*es/-as* + subject honorific -*usi* became reversed as it is today. Second, due to its functional shift, the suffix -*sóp* that had preceded the subject honorific –*ósi* in MK gradually shifted its position after the subject honorific suffix by the early CK period. The CK subject-addressee honorific ending –*(u)si-p-nita* is a result of these developments.

Periphrastic constructions: Use of long-form negation and periphrastic causative and passive constructions became much more productive, as in CK.

Sentence endings: The MOK sentence endings, which reflected sentence types and speech levels, became considerably diversified. K. Ko (1998) presents the ending sets of the 17th, 18th, and 19th centuries, the last of which is given below, using contemporary terms (cf. Sohn 1999). Notice the similarities between the 19th century MOK and CK.

(7)

<table>
<tr><td rowspan="2"></td><td colspan="4">Formal styles</td><td colspan="2">Informal styles</td></tr>
<tr><td>Plain</td><td>Familiar</td><td>Blunt</td><td>Deferential</td><td>Intimate</td><td>Polite</td></tr>
<tr><td>Declarative</td><td>-ta/-la
-eta,
-ma</td><td>-ney
-lsjej
-msjej</td><td>-(s)o</td><td>-ita, -olsita
-(s)iota/oyta
-pnójta/
-pnita</td><td>-ci</td><td>-(j)o</td></tr>
<tr><td rowspan="2">Interrogative</td><td rowspan="2">-nja/
-njo
-lja</td><td></td><td>-o</td><td rowspan="2">-iska
-pnójka/
-pnika</td><td rowspan="2"></td><td rowspan="2"></td></tr>
<tr><td colspan="2">-nka/-nko, -lka</td></tr>
<tr><td>Imperative</td><td>-la
-ala/
-ela</td><td>-kej</td><td>-o
-kwulje</td><td>-sjosje
-psio</td><td>-a</td><td></td></tr>
</table>

Propositive	*-ca*	*-sej*		*-saita, -psita*		
Excla-matory	*-tota/-lota* *-la,* *-kwuna*					

The 19th century MOK was much the same as early CK. During the 20th century until today, however, CK has undergone an unprecedentedly complex history: massive entry of missionaries, collision between foreign powers in Korea, Japanese domination of Korea for thirty-five years, massive importation of Sino-Japanese words and English loan words, liberation from Japanese rule, ideological, political, and physical division between North and South Korea, wide international contacts, the Korean War, rapid economic and technological growth, enormous development of mass media and coinages of new words and expressions, and social transformation in recent decades. All these events have had various effects on CK. However, a survey of CK is out of the concern of this chapter.

REFERENCES: Chapter 3

Hong, Jongsun. 1998a (ed.). *Kuntay kwuke Mwunpep uy Ihay* (Understanding of Modern Korean Grammar). Seoul: Pakiceng.

Hong, Jongsun. 1998b. Kuntay kwuke uy hyengthay wa thongsa (Morphology and syntax of Modern Korean). In Hong, J. (1998a, 13-78).

Huh, Woong. 1984. *Kwukehak* (*Korean Linguistics*). Seoul: Saym Mwunhwasa.

Kim, Dongso. 2007. *Hankwuke uy Yeksa* (History of Korean). Daegu: Cenglimsa.

Ko, Kyongdae. 1998. Kuntay kwuke uy emal emi (Sentence endings in Modern Korean). In Hong, J. (1998a, 177-213).

Lee, In Ho. 2005. *Cosenmal Yeksa* 3 (A History of Korean 3). Pyongyang: Sahoykwahak chwulphansa.

Lee, Ki-Moon and S. R. Ramsey. 2011. *A History of the Korean Language.* Cambridge, UK: Cambridge University Press.

Shim, Jaegi. 1983. *Kwuke Ehwilon* (Korean Lexicology). Seoul: Cipmwuntang.

Sohn, Ho-min. 1998. Evolution of addressee honorifics in Korean. In Lee, S.O. and D.S. Park (eds.), *Perspectives on Korea.* Sydney: Wild Peony.

Sohn, Ho-min. 1999. *The Korean Language.* Cambridge, UK: Cambridge University Press.

Sohn, Ho-min. 2012. Middle Korean. In Tranter, N. (ed.), *The Languages of Japan and Korea,* 73-122. London, UK: Routledge.

4 미국에서의 한국어 교육의 역사와 미래 조망*

1. 머리말

외국어로서의 한국어 교육(이하 한국어 교육)은 양적으로나 질적으로 단시일 내에 빠른 속도로 발전해 왔다. 한국에서나 해외에서 학생 수가 대폭 증가했고 진지한 학회가 해마다 더욱 다양하고 빈번하게 개최되며 학회마다 다수의 열성적인 교수, 교사, 대학원생으로 성황을 이루고 있다. 한국어 습득, 교과과정 개발, 교수법, 교재개발, 평가, 컴퓨터를 통한 교육 등 한국어 교육 전반에 관한 논문이 대량 발표, 출판되고 있으며 새로운 이론과 실제를 바탕으로 한 새로운 교재도 다양하게 개발되고 교사 훈련도 다각도로 시도, 추진되고 있다. 또 최근 한국에서는 한국어를 세계화하려는 일련의 노력과 행사가 정부와 학계의 주도하에 진행되고 있고, 한국어 능력 시험을 개발, 실시하고 있으며, 여러 대학에 한국어 교수법의 학위과정도 생겼다. 이러한 고무적인 현실은 한국 국민, 해외 교포, 한국어 교육자 모두가 크게 자축해야 할 일이다.이 글의 첫 번째 목표는 어떤 역사적 과정을 거쳐서 한국어 교육이 여기까지 이르렀는가를 미국을 중심으로 간단히 살펴보는 일이다.[1]

한국어 교육의 지나온 발자취를 살펴보는 것 못지않게 앞으로의 전망을 살펴보는 것도 극히 중요하다. 미래 조망에서 무엇보다도 시급한 과제는 첨예한 국제 경쟁시대에 즈음하여 주어진 제반 여건 아래에서 앞으로 한국어 교육을 어떻게 더욱 발전시켜 나가느냐 하는 것이다. 당면한 문제는 어떤 것들이 있으며 그 해결책은 무엇인가를 미국을 중심으로 조망해 보는 것이 이 글의 두 번째 목적이다.

2. 미국에서의 한국어 교육의 역사

2.1 초기 이민의 한국어, 한국문화 교육

미국에서의 한국어 교육의 역사는 100년쯤 된다. 한국어 교육의 역사가 한국인 이민

---

* 이 논문은 『외국어로서의 한국어교육』(연세대학교 언어연구교육원) 25.26: 79-135(2001)에 실려 있음.

1 이 글의 논제는 이 학술지 기획팀의 요청에 따른 것임.

역사와 맥을 같이한다고 할 수 있기 때문이다. 미국의 한인사회는 1903년부터 1905년 사이에 하와이 군도의 사탕수수 농장에 이주한 7,200여 명(남자 6,048, 부녀자 637, 아동 547)의 노동 이민에 의해 비롯되었다(윤병석 1990: 234-41 참조). 그 후 1910-1924년 사이에 약 1,000명의 사진부인과 일제시대에 유학 온 소수의 한인 학생들도 초기 이민에 속한다(유의영 1991 참조).[2]

한인이 가는 곳에는 교회가 서고, 교회가 서면 학교가 선다는 말이 있듯이 1903년 11월 호놀룰루에서 한인 그리스도 연합감리교회의 창립예배를 보았고, 그후 각 농장마다 속속 한인 교회가 생겼다. 초기 하와이 이민사회에서의 교회의 역할은 선교와 문화교육과 민족운동이었다(유동식 1988 참조).[3]

이민 당초부터 교회마다 야간 국어학교를 경영하면서 이민들과 그 자녀들에게 한글, 한국어, 한국문화를 가르쳤다. 교회는 또 자녀들을 위해서 미국 정부가 인가한 초등, 중등과정의 주간학교를 시작했는데 그 대표적인 것이 그리스도 연합감리교회가 1906년에 호놀룰루에 설립한 한인기숙학교(후에 한인중앙학원, 대동한인학교 등으로 개명)였다. 초대 교장은 감리사 부인 Mrs.J.W.Wadman이었고 1913년부터 1915년까지는 이승만 박사가 교장직을 맡아 크게 발전시켜 학생 수가 158명에 이르렀다. 이 박사는 또 1915년에는 57명의 여학생으로 한인여자학원을 설립 운영했는데 1918년에 이를 한인기독학원으로 개명했다. 이 외에도 각 농장에 소규모 한인 학교가 11개가 있었다. 1910년부터 한국이 일본 식민통치하에 놓이게 되었는데, 하와이 한인들은 자녀들에게 한국어와 전통문화를 교육시켜서 한국인으로서의 민족적 동질성과 독립심을 갖도록 하고자 했고 이 목적을 위해 한인학교를 유지하는 일에 정성을 기울였다.

그러나 초기 이민으로부터 한 세대가 지난 1930년대를 기하여 2세, 3세의 영어 세대가 "한국인계 미국인"(Korean Americans) 사회로 형성되었는데, 이들의 교육수준, 문화의식, 사고방식, 가치관, 생활양식은 이민 1세의 그것과는 판이했다. 1939년도의 하와이 대학 한국인계 졸업생이 17명, 재학생이 87명이었고, 고등학교 졸업생 수가 123명이나 되었다(유동식 1988 참조). 그리고 상당수의 2, 3세는 미국 본토로 진출하였다. 미국의 현실주의 사회에서 이들 새 세대에게는 이미 일본의 식민지가 되어 버린 가난하고 힘없는 조국의 언어와 전통문화를 배워야 한다는 동기가 있었을 리 만무하다. 이리하여 한국어와 한국문화를 가르치고 배우려던 이민 1세의 열의는 빛을 잃고 1940년대에 들어서면서부터는 교포를 대상으로 한 민족언어, 민족문화 교육은 아예 중단되지 않을 수 없었다.[4]

2 현재 하와이를 중심으로 미국 한국인 교포들은 2003년의 이민 백주년 기념 행사를 위한 대대적인 준비를 하고 있다.

3 현재의 교회의 역할은 주로 선교 활동과 문화교육 활동과 이민봉사 활동이다.

4 1945년 제2차 세계대전이 끝날 무렵의 재미 한국인 수는 약 10,000명이었고 그중 7,000여 명은 하와이에 거주하였는데 이중 반수가 2, 3세 Korean-American이었다(뉴욕 한인회 1986 참조).

2.2 한글학교의 민족 언어, 문화 교육

1950년 6.25 동란 이후로 서서히 미국으로 밀려온 한국인 이민 물결에 힘입어 한국 교민사회의 민족언어, 민족문화 교육은 근 30년간의 공백기를 마감하고 1969년 하와이 한인사회학교의 개교를 기하여 다시 눈을 떴다. 흔히 한글학교라고 불리는 주말 한인학교 수가 처음은 극히 서서히 그러나 나중에는 기하급수적으로 불어나기 시작했다. 재미 한인학교 협의회의 14차(1996년) 학술대회 프로그램에 의하면 1976년 현재 미국에는 다음과 같은 7개의 한인학교가 있었다.

개교연도	학교명
1969년	하와이 한인 사회학교(Korean Community School of Hawaii)
1971년	인디애나폴리스 한글학교(Korean School of Indianapolis)
1972년	몬트레이 한국학교(Monterey Korean School)
1974년	미네소타 한국학교(Korean Institute of Minnesota)
1975년	베드포드파크 장로교회 한국학교 (Bedford Park Korean School of Presbyterian Church)
1976년	무궁화 한국학교(Moo Gung Hwa Korean School)[5]
1976년	롱아일랜드 연합 한국학교(Korean School of Long Island)

주말 한글학교는 1970년대 말부터 갑자기 불어나서 1987년에는 406개교(김영기 1988 참조), 1995년에는 834개교(이상오 1995), 그리고 2001년 현재 미국에 크고 작은 한글학교가 총 1,000개교가량이 있다. 놀라운 양적 증가라 아니할 수 없다.[6]

이러한 급격한 증가는 미국 전역에 기하급수적으로 늘어나는 한인 인구, 한인 교회의 수와 비례한다. 한글학교는 한국인이 모여 사는 전국 도처에 산재해 있는데 그중에서도 한국인과 한국인 교회가 가장 많은 로스앤젤레스, 뉴욕, 시카고, 샌프란시스코, 애틀랜타, 필라델피아, 시애틀, 하와이 등지에 집중되어 있다. 한글학교의 90% 이상은 수천 개에 이르는 한국인 교회에 부설되어 있다.

한글학교는 교육의 양과 질 면에서 큰 차이를 보이고 있다. 학생 10여 명에 불과한 학교가 있는가 하면 500명 이상의 학교가 있고, 언어능력 수준이 크게 다른 학생들을 모두 한 반에서 가르치는 학교가 있는가 하면 학생의 나이 또는 학년과 한국어 능력별로 반을 세분하여 가르치는 학교가 있다. 교사의 경험이나 영어 구사 능력도 천차만별이다. 이러한 다양성에도 불구하고 몇 가지 중요한 공통점이 있다.

---

5 유의영(1991: 876-7)에 의하면 무궁화 학원은 1972년에 20명 학생으로 시작하였는데 1991년에만 해도 15개의 분교로 자라서 200명가량의 교사가 2,650명의 아동을 가르쳤다고 한다.

6 뿐만 아니라 로스앤젤레스, 뉴욕, 시카고 등 한국계 인구가 많은 도시에는 많은 한국어 사설 학원이 있고 주 정부에서 운영하는 야간 성인 한국어 반이 있다.

① 교육목표는 한인계 후세 아동들에게 민족언어, 민족문화를 전수하는 뿌리교육이다.
② 교과과정이 대체로 동일하다. 대부분의 한글학교가 토요일 오전에만 3시간 수업을 하고 그중 처음 두 교시는 한국어 수업이고 삼 교시는 한국 문화에 관련되는 특별 활동이다. 특별 활동에는 미술, 서예, 음악, 고전무용, 현대무용, 태권도, 글짓기, 한문, 주산, 역사책 읽기, 영화 감상, 생활실습 등이 포함되는데 학교에 따라 다양하게 반을 나눈다. 한국어 수업을 1시간 또는 3시간 하는 학교도 예외적으로 있다.
③ 한국어 반은 대체로 기초반, 초급반, 중급반, 고급반으로 분류되나 학교에 따라 기초반과 초급반, 또는 중급반과 고급반이 통합된다.
④ 대체로 1년에 2학기 또는 4학기(봄, 여름, 가을, 겨울)가 있고 2학기의 경우에는 학기 당 20주(60시간)이고 4학기의 경우는 학기당 12주(36시간)로 구성되어 있다. 따라서 학생이 일 년을 계속할 경우 1년간 총 수업 시간은 120시간 내지 144시간이고 그중 한국어 수업 시간은 80시간 내지 96시간이 된다.
⑤ 학생 구성은 유치원생으로부터 12학년(고3)생까지 다양하고 대부분이 한인교포 2세이다. 학생 중 초등학생(유치원생 포함)이 70% 내지 80%를 차지하고 그 나머지가 중, 고등학생(7-12)과 극소수의 성인이다. 즉 한글학교를 다니는 학생들은 대부분 초등학교 과정으로 끝낸다. 최근 들어 고등학생의 경우는 상급반에서 SAT II-Korean의 시험 준비를 하는 것이 가장 큰 목적이다.[7]
⑥ 교사진은 한국 유학생(주로 대학원생), 해당 교회의 교인, 한국에서 교사 경험이 있는 일반인 등으로 구성된다. 교사에 대한 대우는 시간당 15달러-30달러 정도인데, 자원봉사 교사도 있다.
⑦ 교재는 주로 전국 한인학교 협의회에서 개발한 교과서와, 남가주 한국학교 연합회가 개발한 교과서 또는 한국 교육부의 국제교육 진흥원에서 발간하여 영사관을 통하여 매년 무상으로 배포하는 재외 교포용 교과서가 사용된다. 학교에 따라서는 자체 개발한 교재나 기타의 교과서를 쓰기도 한다.
⑧ 대다수 학생의 학습 동기는 부모의 권유 때문이다. 이영태(1997)의 설문 통계에 의하면 300명의 초·중등학생 응답자 중 213명(70.9%)이 부모의 결정에 의하여 한글학교에 다니며, 36명(18%)이 부모의 생각과 본인의 생각이 합쳐 다닌다고 한다. 친구 때문에 다니는 경우는 28명이고 본인이 다니고 싶어서 다니는 경우는 23명(주로 중학생)에 불과하다. 이렇게 볼 때, 한국인의 뿌리 교육은 절대적으로 부모의 결정에 달려 있다고 할 수 있다.

예를 들면, 한인계 인구 약 5만이 살고 있는 하와이 주에는 현재 약 20개의 한글학교가

7 1996년도의 한국 교육부 통계에 의하면, 교원 수 5,601명에 학생 수가 50,434명이고, 학생들은 유치원생 12,799명, 초등학생 22,336명, 중학생 8,869명, 고등학생 5,158명, 성인 1,272명으로 나타나 있다.

있는데 대부분 한인 교회에 부설되어 있고, 일부 한인 성당과 절에도 부설되어 있다. 가장 큰 학교는 호놀룰루 한인 감리교회 부설의 한인사회학교와 아이에아 한인 감리교회 부설의 한인문화학교인데 학생이 현재 각각 약 130명이다. 그 외의 학교는 학생 수가 평균 30명 정도이다. 미국의 한글학교의 효시가 된 한인 감리교회 부설 한인사회학교의 운영 내용에 대해서는 손호민(1999)에 제시한 바 있다.

1981년에 재미 한인학교 협의회(National Association for Korean Schools 또는 NAKS)가 설립되었는데 매년 증가하고 있는 한글학교의 상호 유대를 강화하고, 체계적이고 통합적인 한국어, 한국문화 교육을 개발 육성하고, 학생들의 한국인으로서의 긍지를 함양하고, 한국과 미국정부의 교육정책에 대한 건의와 협조를 할 것 등을 주목적으로 하고 있다. 비슷한 사업목적으로 남가주에는 따로 남가주 한국학교 연합회가 있다. 이들 두 단체는 직접, 간접으로 한글학교 활동을 돕고 있는데, 한글학교 교육과정 모델 개발(한국어, 역사, 문화, 전통 예술 등), 학술대회 개최, 교사연수회 개최, 교육과정 개발, 교재 개발 및 보급, 회지 발행, 각종 교육행사 주최, 한글학교 운영 및 2세 교육을 위한 재정 지원 등을 사업목표로 추진하고 있다.

이상과 같은 양적 팽창에도 불구하고 많은 한글학교의 뿌리교육은 아직 수업시간의 제한, 일부 교사들의 영어능력 부족과 미국문화에 대한 미숙, 교사에 대한 체계적 훈련의 부족, 교사의 대우 문제, 학생과 학부모의 한국어 교육에 대한 열의와 인식의 부족, 시청각 교재의 부족, 시설 미비 등으로 힘겨워하고 있다. 교육의 질적 향상을 위하여 앞으로 각계 각층의 많은 지원과 협조와 노력이 요구된다.

2.3 정규 초·중·고등학교의 한국어, 한국문화 교육

종교단체에 부속된 한글학교에서의 민족언어, 민족문화 교육과는 달리 미국 정규 초·중·고등학교에서의 한국어 교육은 외국어로서의 한국어 교육이다. 앞에서 기술한 바와 같이 하와이의 그리스도 연합감리교회가 1906년에 호놀룰루에 설립한 한인기숙학교, 1915년에 이승만 박사가 하와이에 설립한 한인여자학원 등이 한인 자녀들을 위한 정규 초, 중등 교육의 효시라 할 수 있다. 그러나 전술한 바와 같이 근 30년간 한국언어, 문화 교육이 중단되었다가 다음과 같은 일련의 역사적 변화와 더불어 여러 가지 형태로 서서히 부활되고 있다.

1968년 이중언어 교육법이 제정된 이래 정규 초, 중, 고등학교의 한국어 교육이 실시되었는데 이는 대체로 영어가 부족한 한국이민 학생들에게 영어가 익숙해질 때까지 과도기적으로 한국어로 수업을 받는 소위 과도적 이중언어 교육이었다. 지금도 많은 초등학교에서는 새로 이민 온 한국 학생들에게 필요에 따라 이러한 과도적 이중언어 교육을 실시하고 있는데, 그로 인해서 한국어 능력이 유지 또는 향상된다는 점에서는 일종의 한국어 교육이라고 할 수 있다.

영어를 잘 모르는 한국 학생들이 미국에 이민 오게 되면 지역이나 학교에 따라 다르기는 하지만 (ㄱ) 완전히 영어로만 수업을 듣는 경우(English immersion programs), (ㄴ) 주로 영어로 듣되 알아듣기 어려운 것만 한국어에 능숙한 이중언어 보조교사로부터 구두로 도움을 받는 경우(modified bilingual programs), (ㄷ) 과도적 이중언어 교육, 즉 영어가 익숙해질 때까지만 한국어로 수업을 받는 경우, 그리고 드물게는 (ㄹ) 말하기, 듣기, 읽기, 쓰기 모든 면에서 한국어, 영어 두 언어로 수업을 듣는 경우(Korean/English dual language programs 또는 two-way immersion programs)가 있다.[8]

대부분의 학부모는 (ㄴ)이나 (ㄷ)의 교육을 선호한다. (ㄹ)의 경우에는 한국어 사용 학생과 영어 사용 학생이 전 학년에 걸쳐 같은 반에서 전 과목을 한국어와 영어로 수업 받는다. 이 프로그램의 목적은 두 부류의 학생들 모두에게 말하기, 듣기, 읽기, 쓰기에서 한국어, 영어의 이중언어 사용자가 되도록 하는 것이다. 1992년에 로스앤젤레스 통합교육구에 있는 3개 초등학교의 유치원반 학생 32명을 대상으로 (ㄹ)의 교육이 실시되기 시작했다. 이 학생들은 학년이 올라가면서도 계속 이 프로그램에서 한국어와 영어로 학과목을 수강했다. 이 프로그램은 그후 더욱 확장되어 2000년 현재 5개 학교에서 실시되어, 초등학교 유치원반 포함)에서 8학년까지 총 600명 이상이 참여하고 있다(Merrill 2000). 이 프로그램의 특징은 희망자들로 반이 편성된다는 점과, 한국인 1.5세, 2세뿐 아니라 영어를 모국어로 하는 미국 학생들이 상당수 참여한다는 점과, 또 언어 중심의 교육이 아니라 내용 중심의 교육이라는 점 등을 들 수 있다.[9] 이 프로그램은 그 중요성을 감안하여 2.4항에서 재론하기로 한다.

미국에서 한인들이 운영하는 정규 학교로는 남가주 한국학원 재단에서 1985년 2월에 설립한 로스앤젤레스 한국 아카데미(Los Angeles Hankook Academy)가 있다(유의영 1991: 882). 처음에는 초등학생 12명, 교사 2명, 교장 1명으로 시작했는데 1991년에는 학생 수가 6학년까지 200명 정도 되었다고 한다. 남가주 한국학원은 현재 중, 고등학교도 운영하고 있는데, 초, 중, 고 모든 학교의 교과과정에 외국어로서의 한국어 과목이 들어 있다.[10]

정규 중, 고등학교의 한국어 교육의 실정을 보면, 초기에 과도적 이중언어 교육을 실시하던 소수의 공립 중, 고등학교의 경우는 차차 위에서 언급한 한-영 양방향 이중언어 교육과 비슷한 형태로 기능적인 변화가 일어났다. 즉 영어가 능숙하고 한국어 능력이 부족한 학생들까지도 영어가 부족한 갓 이민 온 한국 학생들과 함께 이중언어 반에서 한국어를 배우는 추세가 생겼다. 예컨대 뉴욕시의 경우, 시 교육구의 이중언어 교육 정책에 의거 1979년에 Newtown High School에서 처음으로 한국 이민 학생들에게 영어가 익숙해

8 한국어만으로 수업을 실시하는 학교로는, 한국 정부에서 재외국민의 교육을 위하여 로스앤젤레스에 설립한 정규 한국학교가 있는데 학생 수는 240명가량이라고 한다(박영순 2001: 233-5).

9 최근 로스앤젤레스에서 위에 든 (ㄱ), (ㄴ), (ㄹ) 방법을 사용하는 초등학교 중 각각 두 학교씩 선정하여 4학년생들의 유치원 때부터의 학습성과를 비교 연구한 결과가 발표되었다(S. Sohn, et al. 1999). 이 보고에 의하면, 방법 (ㄹ)이 다른 두 방법보다 학생의 한국어 능력은 물론이고 영어 발달과 다른 과목에서도 더 우월했다.

10 남가주 한국학원은 로스앤젤레스 여러 곳에 17개의 주말 한글학교도 운영하고 있다.

질 때까지 한국어로 수업을 했고, 이어 Bryant, Flushing, Bayside, Francis Lewis 등 중, 고등학교에서도 과도기적으로 한국어를 이용한 교육을 실시했다(Kwon 1999). 그러나 미국의 한국 인구가 급격히 늘어나고 한국의 경제가 급성장해 감에 따라 점차 한국어를 더 배우려는 1.5세나 2세 한국계 미국 학생들이 참여하게 되었고 최근에는 한국어가 대학 입학을 위한 SAT II 과목으로 채택되어 한국계 학생들의 중, 고등학교에서의 한국어 습득이 더 절실해졌다. 따라서 이러한 소수의 초기 중, 고등학교들은 이제는 차차 과도적 이중언어 교육이라기보다는 한국에 관한 여러 과목을 한국어로 가르치는 정규 한국어 교육이 되어 가고 있다(Kwon 1999).

한편, 최근 수 년 사이에 한국어프로그램을 시작한 중, 고등 학교에서는 처음부터 순수한 외국어로서의 한국어 교육을 지향하는 교과 과정으로 출발하고 있다. 그리하여 현재 30개 내외의 미국 중, 고등학교의 한국어 교육은 대체로 높은 수준의 한국어와 한국문화 교육을 그 목적으로 하고 있다.

과거에는 한인 학부모들이 자녀들의 미국 주류 사회로의 조속한 동화와 영어 능력의 향상을 위하여 한국어 교육에 대해 부정적인 태도를 보였었으나 이제는 SAT II-Korean의 좋은 성적으로 자녀들이 보다 우수한 대학에 입학할 수 있으리라는 기대 때문에 한국어 교육에 대한 긍정적인 인식이 점차 팽배해 가고 있다. 한인들이 많이 살고 있는 지역의 중, 고등학교에서 한국어 과목이 신설되고 많은 학생들이 수강하고 있다는 것이 이 사실을 단적으로 나타내고 있다. 로스앤젤레스 지역의 Sunny Hills High School, LA High School, Torrance High School, Valley High School 등이 그 예이다. 예컨대, 부유층 한인들이 많이 거주하는 오렌지 카운티 플러튼시 소재의 Sunny Hills High School 한국어 프로그램의 경우를 보면 한국 학부모들의 탄원 덕택으로 1989년에 한국어반이 개설되었는데, 현재 한국어 정교사 자격증을 소지한 전임 교사가 1급부터 5급까지 총 160명가량의 학생들에게 매일 한 시간씩 한국어를 가르치고 있다(손성옥 제보).[11]

사립학교와 대학에서는 특별히 교사 자격증을 요구하지 않으나 공립 초, 중, 고등학교에서 한국어를 가르치려면 우선 한국어 교사 자격증이 필요하다. 초, 중, 고등학교의 한국어 교육의 발전을 위하여서는 가급적 많은 인력이 사범대학에서 소정의 과정을 이수하고 주 정부에서 발급하는 정식 한국어교사 자격증을 취득하여야 한다(Blank 1999; 손호민 1999 참조).

중, 고등학교의 한국어 교육의 질을 높이기 위하여서는 교사 자격증의 문제뿐 아니라, 교재 문제도 심각하다. 실제로 시청각 등 부교재는 고사하고 미국 중, 고등학생에게 어울리는 마땅한 본 교과서조차 없는 실정이다.

11 이 학교는 전체 학생 2천여 명 중 한인계 학생이 4분의 1을 차지하고 있다.

2.4. 한-영 양방향 집중교육

1992년부터 로스앤젤레스에서 실시해온 조기 한-영 양방향 내용중심 집중교육은 전형적인 한국어 교육의 모든 약점을 보강한 가장 확실하고 바람직한 이중언어 교육 방법이라고 믿는다. 여러 면에서 일석다조의 방법이라 할 수 있다. 아래에서 이 양방향 교육을 좀 더 자세히 살펴보고자 한다.

1) 왜 조기(early)교육인가?

이중언어 교육을 언제부터 실시할 것인가? 두말할 것 없이 외국어는 학생이 어릴 때부터 배울수록 더 효과적이다. 많은 연구의 결과가 이를 입증한다. 가장 자연스럽고 신속한 언어습득이 대강 2살부터 12살 사이에 이루어지는데, critical period라고 하는 이 시기에 언어를 흡수하는 뇌가 가장 유연하게 많이 열려 있기 때문이라고 한다(예컨대 Lenneberg 1967, Johnson & Newport 1991 등 참조). 인간은 보편적 언어 능력, 즉 보편 문법을 가지고 태어나는데 어린이에게 특정 언어를 입력하여 주면 이것을 듣고 뇌에 있는 언어 습득 장치를 동원하여 보편 문법을 개별 문법으로 구체화하여 이를 이해하게 된다는 학설이 널리 받아들여지고 있다. 이러한 작동은 어린이에게는 빠르고 쉽게 진행되지만 12세가 넘으면 비례적으로 점점 더 힘들어진다는 것이다.

한국어는 영어와 전혀 다른 언어 구조나 글 체계나 사회언어학적 특징 때문에 성인 영어 화자에게는 가장 배우기 어려운 언어이다. 일본어, 중국어, 아랍어와 더불어 소위 category 4언어로서 미국인이 스페인어, 프랑스어, 독일어 등 전통 외국어를 배우는 것보다, 같은 수준에 도달하는 데는 세 배 정도의 시간이 걸린다는 것이 통계적 연구로 밝혀져 있다(H. Sohn 1995 참조). 아이들은 어른과 달리 언어를 부분적인 어휘와 문법을 이용하여 습득하는 것이 아니고, 뛰어난 기억력을 가지고 주어진 상황 속에서 문장이나 담화 전체를 한꺼번에 듣고 말하면서 자연스럽게 또 빨리 배우기 때문에 어른 습득자에게는 무척 어렵고 복잡한 언어구조나 사회언어학적 특징도 아이들은 아무런 특별한 노력 없이 쉽게 배운다. 한국어의 조기 교육은 궁극적으로 높은 수준의 언어 능력을 신속히 성취할 수 있는 것이다. 어린이들의 조기 외국어 습득은 Dulay & Burt(1974)의 실험에서도 밝혀졌듯이 모국어 배우는 것이나 마찬가지로 외국어의 언어적 간섭이 거의 없다. 그렇다면, 한-영 언어구조의 차이나 사회언어적 차이, 문화적 차이는 어린이들의 외국어 교육에서는 대체로 무시된다는 결론을 얻을 수 있다.

그 외에도 조기 교육은 수많은 이득이 있다. 참고로, 미국 상원의원 Thad Cockran(R-MS)은 2001년 3월 15일, technology와 기타 혁신적 교수법의 도입으로 외국어 교육을 더 효율적으로 실시하자는 법안 Foreign Language Acquisition and Proficiency Improvement Act of 2001을 의회에 상정하였다. 이 법안에는 조기교육에 관한 다음과 같은 글이 있다:

> According to the Center for Applied Linguistics, the early study of a second language offers many benefits for students including academic achievement, positive attitudes toward diversity, flexibility in thinking and a sensitivity to language. The evidence shows that children who learn foreign languages score higher in all academic subjects than those who speak only English. The evidence of need is great, and yet there is a lack of sufficient foreign language training at the K-12 level. I hope that we will give greater attention to this program when we make funding decisions.

2) 왜 집중(immersion)교육인가?

집중 교육은 소위 감가적 이중언어 사용(subtractive bilingualism)의 초래를 방지하는 한편 학생들로 하여금 높은 수준의 부가적 이중언어인(additive bilinguals)이 되게 하는 것이다. 예컨대 미국에서 사는 한국계 이민 가정의 아동은 부모에게서 한국어를 제1언어로 습득하다가 학교에 다니기 시작하면서 공용어인 영어를 제2언어로 습득하는데 공용어인 영어는 점차 우세해져서 흔히 한국어를 완전히 대치하게 된다. 이런 경우 한국어 사용 능력을 잃게 되므로 이것은 감가적이다. 한국어를 완전히 잊어버리지 않는 경우에도 아동들은 한국어를 이해할 수는 있지만 스스로 사용하지는 않는 수동적 화자가 되기 쉽고, 보통 5살의 수준에서 고정(stabilize, fossilize)된다(언어의 고정현상에 대해서는 Swain 1978, 1991; H. Kim 2001 등 참조). 한편 한국어를 유지하고 발전시키면서 영어를 습득하는 것이나 영어 사용 학생이 한국어 구사능력을 습득하는 것은 부가적이다. 한-영 집중 교육을 통해서 높은 수준의 균형있는 부가적 한-영 이중언어인을 길러 낼 수 있다.

가정에서 사용한 부모의 언어는 일상 생활에 필요한 극히 제한된 범위의 표현에 불과하고 그것도 주로 듣기에 국한되기 때문에 가정에서 쓰지 않는 어휘나 표현은 전혀 습득하지 못한다. 마찬가지로 한글학교는 주로 토요일에만 겨우 2시간 학습하는 데 지나지 않는다. 언어교육은 계속성이 있어야 하는데 일주일에 한번 모여서는 아무리 아동들의 뇌가 열려 있다 해도 보통의 경우 별 큰 성과를 기대하기 어렵다. 중, 고등학교나 대학의 경우도 다른 분야의 많은 과목과 더불어 외국어로서 일주일에 3시간 내지 5시간을 배우기 때문에 많은 경우 소기의 목적을 달성하기 힘들다. 집중교육의 중요성은 바로 여기에 있다.

아동들의 언어습득의 뇌가 충분히 열려 있을 때 집중교육을 통해서 아동들의 인지발달 수준에 맞는 다양한 내용의 언어를 가급적 많이 계속적으로 반복해서 넣어 줌으로써 아동들로 하여금 정확한 발음과 정확한 글뿐 아니라, 많은 어휘, 복잡한 문법구조, 사회와 상황과 문화에 부응하는 언어 표현을 풍부하게 습득하도록 하는 것이다.

외국어 습득/학습 방법에 대한 이론과 주장은 부지기수이다. 최근 거의 모든 학자들이 동의하는 바는 언어란 학습 대상 언어로 뜻을 듣고 읽고 말하고 쓰고 또 대화하고 교제할 때 배워진다는 것이다. 또 최근 가장 유력한 외국어 교수법인 의사소통을 위한 언어교수에서 가장 기본적인 전제는 언어는 사용함으로써 배운다는 것이다.

3) 왜 내용중심의 교육인가?

내용중심(content-based/content-driven) 언어교육이 기능중심(skill-based/language-driven) 언어교육 방법보다 우월하다는 점은 학자들의 실험을 통하여 증명되었다(Snow 1998 참조). 학생들은 각 학문분야에서 지능발달에 적합한 많은 분량의 새로운 정보와 지식을 직접적으로 흡수하게 되고 그 과정에서 수많은 어휘와 복잡한 표현 등 엄청난 양의 언어를 접하고 매일 활용하게 된다. 다양한 과목의 내용을 흡수해야 하고 각 학과목의 성적을 올려야 한다는 강한 학습 동기 때문에 학생들은 단순한 언어 기능의 습득만을 목적으로 하는 외국어 교육보다 더 적극적이고 능동적인 학습 태도로 임하게 될 것은 당연하고 따라서 언어 능력도 급속히 향상된다.

가정에서만 사용되는 언어는 유창성은 높아진다 해도 일상적으로 자주 쓰이는 어휘나 구문을 넘어서 더 이상 발달하지 못하고, 전술한 바와 같이 학교에 들어가기 전의 언어수준에 머무는 것이 보통이다. 통상적인 외국어 교육과는 달리 내용중심의 교육은 이러한 언어 발달상의 문제를 해소해서 학생의 언어능력을 교육받은 모국어 화자의 수준으로 끌어올릴 수 있다.[12]

참고로 Minnesota대학에서 출판된 CARLA UPDATE, Spring 2001호에는 내용중심 교육의 중요성에 관한 다음과 같은 기사가 있다.

> Far from being just a current fad in language teaching, content-based instruction is grounded in the common underlying principle that successful language learning occurs when students are presented with target language materials in a meaningful, contextualized form with the primary focus on acquiring information and knowledge. In content-based instruction (CBI), content becomes the organizing principle; the content itself influences the selection and sequence of language items (structures, functions, vocabulary). This contextualizes language learning for students, focuses the learners attention primarily on meaning, and gives a clear purpose for communication. In 1989, Brinton et al. wrote that CBI approaches encourage the teachers and learners to view the target language largely as the vehicle through which subject matter content is learned rather than as the immediate object of study. Imagining the language as a vehicle for content expands the thinking and possibilities of the daily occurrences in classrooms. More and more teachers around the country are looking for ways to use a content-based approach to teaching . . . .

---

12 캐나다의 프랑스어 집중교육의 성공적인 내용중심 집중교육에서 학생들은 듣기나 읽기에서 모국어 화자와 다름없는 유창성을 신속히 터득한 반면 말하기, 쓰기 등 능동적인 언어행위에서는 문법적 정확성이 결여되었다는 보고들이 있다. Swain (1991)과 여러 다른 학자들에 의하면 캐나다의 이런 현상은 교사들의 부주의로 학생들에게 반에서 능동적 언어사용의 기회를 충분히 주지 않았을 뿐 아니라 적절한 문법 교정을 하지 못했기 때문이었다고 한다.

4) 왜 양방향 교육인가?

양방향(two-way/dual) 교육은 동시적 이중언어 교육을 통하여 학생들로 하여금 균형 있는 이중언어인이 되게 한다. 이 교육의 특징은 내용 중심이므로 그 주요 목표가 아동들의 학문적 성장이고 언어 자체를 가르치는 것이 아니다. 그러나 이 교육을 통하여 아동들은 부수적으로 두 개의 언어에 통달하게 되는 것이다. 즉 모든 아동들은 모든 학과목에서 성적도 올리고 두 개 언어에 능통하게 되는 것이다. 모든 학문 분야에 걸쳐 두 언어를 사용함으로 동등한 양의 언어를 주게 되어 아동들을 균형 있는 이중언어인으로 양성할 수 있게 된다. 아동들은 주위 환경에서 가장 많이 쓰이는 언어를 더 빨리 습득하기 때문에 성공적인 이중언어인이 되기 위해서는 많은 언어 경험을 두 언어로 균등하게 접해야 함은 물론이다.

양방향 교육 방법의 중요성이나 장점과 실효성에 대하여는 이미 전문가들이 밝힌 바 있으므로 여기서는 생략한다(박영순 1997: 119-26의 인용 참조). 특히 지금 진행 중인 한-영 양방향 교육의 실효에 대해서는 S. Sohn, et al.(1999)과 Merrill(2000)을 참조하기 바란다.

한두 가지 점만 언급하자면, 이 방법의 실효성이 영어 화자에게는 한국어 화자만큼은 크지 않을 것이라는 주장이 있을 수 있다. 일단 학교에서 나오면 다시 영어만이 공용어로 사용되기 때문이다. 그러나 한-영 집중교육의 경우에는 영어 화자의 대부분이 초기 이민들의 후예이거나 한국에 대한 특별한 관심을 갖는 비한국계이기 때문에 한국어 습득의 동기가 유난히 강하고 한국 가정에서나 한국인 사회에서 한국어를 계속 사용할 수 있기 때문에 거의 같은 실효를 거둘 수 있다. 한국어가 약한 초기이민 학생과 영어에 아직 능숙하지 못한 후기이민 학생의 결합은 심리적으로 동족이라는 점에서 더 호의적인 상호보완과 상호협조가 이루어질 것이다. 양방향 교육을 통하여 모두가 공평하게 미국이 필요로 하는 완벽한 이중언어인이 될 것으로 기대된다.

현재 미국의 한국어 교육의 큰 난관은 UCLA 등 극소수의 대학 이외에는 한국계 학생과 비한국계 학생이 같은 반에서 학습하는 것이다(S. Sohn 1997 참조). 양쪽 학생들은 모두 원하는 수준의 한국어를 습득하기 어렵다. 대체로 이미 집에서 오랫동안 한국어를 듣고 이해하는 교포 학생들은 원하는 것을 충분히 배우지 못하게 되고 비교포 학생들은 너무 많은 것을 너무 빨리 가르치기 때문에 잘 배우지 못한다(H. Kim 2001 참조). 설상가상으로 교포 학생들의 한국어 수준은 매우 다양한 차이를 나타내고 있다. 일반적으로 한국어가 익숙하면 영어가 비례적으로 서투르고 한국어가 서투르면 비례적으로 영어가 유창하다. 내용 중심의 양방향 교육은 이들 다채로운 언어배경을 가지고 있는 학생들에게 가장 공정하고 평등한 언어교육을 부여한다. 아무도 불이익을 당하지 않고 모두가 같은 양의 이익을 얻기 때문이다.

2.5. 대학의 한국어 교육

미국 대학의 한국어 교육의 역사는 1930년대부터 극소수의 대학에서 극히 단편적으로 기초 한국어 과목을 가르친 것으로부터 시작되었다. 예를 들면 컬럼비아 대학은 1934년에 처음 윤응팔 감리교 목사가 한국어를 임시로 가르친 적이 있으나 한국어가 정식으로 교수된 것은 1962년 한국학 전임교수직이 생겨서 처음 두 명의 학생을 놓고 가르치기 시작하면서부터라고 한다(Carol Schulz 제보; Columbia대학 인터넷 사이트). 하와이 대학은 1946년부터 1950년까지 건축가 박관두 씨가 한국어를 시간강사로 가르치기 시작했고 그후에도 다른 분들이 계속 시간으로 가르치다가 1962년 문학 전임 교수직과 곧 이어 어학의 전임 자리가 생기면서 점차 체계화되었다. Harvard대학은 1952년부터 Korean Studies Institute에서 한국어를 개설하였다. 1960년대에는 UC Berkeley, Washington, Indiana대학 등에서도 한국어와 관련과목들이 개설되었고 1970년대에는 SUNY Stoney Brook, Kansas, Pennsylvania, Brigham Young, Southern California대학 등에서, 1980년대에는 UCLA, Georgetown, George Washington, Illinois, Ohio State, Stanford, Tufts, Maryland, Alaska, Brown, Duke, William and Mary, Chicago, Cornell대학 등에서 한국어, 한국학 과목들이 속속 개설되었다. 초기의 한국어 프로그램은 학생 수의 부족으로 허덕였으나 1970년 말경부터 학생 수가 급격히 증가하기 시작했다. 급속도로 불어나는 한국인 이민의 자녀들 때문임은 물론이다. 1987년에 한국어를 개설한 UCLA는 현재 일반 대학으로는 가장 많은 학생들이 한국어를 수강하는데 학기당 350명가량이라고 한다(손성옥 제보).

1980년대 말까지 30개가량의 대학에서 한국어가 교수되었는데 1990년도에는 그 수가 대폭 증가하여 2001년 현재 120개가량의 크고 작은 미국 대학에서 매 학기 5,000명 내외의 학생에게 한국어가 교수되고 있다. 그러나 학생 수, 교과과정, 교수진, 교수법, 평가방법, 사용 교과서와 부교재, 학교 당국의 지원 등 모든 면에서 학교마다 극히 다양하다. 한국계 학생이 많지 않은 비교적 작은 대학은 소수의 학생들에게 초급반만을 가르치거나 중급까지만 가르치고, 한국계 학생이 많은 대학에서는 초, 중, 상급, 최상급 한국어가 개설되는 경향이 있다. 한국학을 전공하는 대학원 학생이나 한국어문학을 전공하는 극소수의 학생을 제외하면, 한국어 수강 학생들의 대부분은 여러 다양한 학과에 소속되어 있으며 한국어를 선택과목이나 외국어 필수과목으로 수강한다. 현재 미국 대학 중 80% 이상에서 외국어를 1년 내지 2년간 필수적으로 배우도록 되어 있기 때문에 한국어가 개설되어 있는 경우, 다수의 한국계 학생들뿐 아니라 한국, 한국인, 한국어에 관심 있는 소수의 비한국계 학생들도 한국어를 택한다.

많은 대학에서 한국계 학생들과 비한국계 학생이 같은 반에서 한국어를 배우는데 이에 따른 적지 않은 문제가 있다. 이미 한글학교나 중, 고등학교에서 많은 단어와 읽기, 쓰기까지 배운 학생들은 중급이나 상급반에 배치될 수 있으나, 부모한테서 겨우 기본적인 말하기, 듣기만 익힌 한국계 학생들은 보통 초급 후반이나 중급 초반에 비한국계 학생들과 함께 배치된다. 이 때 말하기, 듣기 위주의 교재는 비한국계에게는 극히 유용하나 한국계에게는 시간 낭비이다. 또한 말하기, 듣기에 익숙한 한국계는 비한국계에게 적지 않은 위협이 된다. 이러한 교육상의 불균형과 불합리성을 시정하기 위하여 극소수의 큰 대학(UCLA, UC Berkeley, Columbia 등)에서는 몇 년 전부터 중급까지 반을 한국계-비한국계의 두 계열로 나누어 가르치는데 큰 효과를 거두고 있다(S. Sohn 1997). 그러나 대다수 대학은 한국어 프로그램이 비교적 작기 때문에 두 계열 제도 도입에는 예산상의 문제가 따른다.

대학의 한국어 수업은 대체로 초급과 중급은 매일 한 시간씩 실시하고 상급 이상은 일주일에 3시간 한다. 그 외에 어학 실습을 일주일에 학교에 따라 2시간 내지 5시간 실시한다. 초급, 중급의 교수 방법은 두 가지가 있는데 대부분의 대학은 한 강사가 한 반을 전담해서 가르치지만, 소수의 대학(Harvard, UCLA 등)에서는 교수가 일 주일에 2시간을 내용, 문법, 문화 등에 대하여 강의하고 나머지 3시간은 10여명씩 작은 반으로 나누어 조교들이 따로 연습시킨다. 이 후자는 소위 fact와 act를 구별하여 가르치는 방법이다.

다음은 교과 과정과 학위 과정이 비교적 잘 되어 있는 하와이 대학의 경우를 소개한다. 하와이대학 한국어문학은 중국어문학, 일본어문학과 더불어 동아시아 어문학과에 속해 있다. 교수진이 47명인 일본 프로그램과 교수진 19명의 중국 프로그램에 비하면 한국어문학은 규모가 작다. 2001년도 한국어문학 교수진은 3명의 영구직 교수(그중 2명은 어학, 1명은 문학), 4명의 조교, 2명의 시간강사로 구성되어 있다. 매 학기 140여 명의 학생들에게 각급 한국어를 교수하는 한편, 한국어문학의 학사(1995년부터), 석사(1987년부터), 박사(1987년부터) 전공학생들을 양성한다. 학사 과정은 어학과 문학의 구분이 없으나 석사, 박사 과정은 그 구분이 있다. 어학 분야는 학위 논문에서 다시 한국 언어학, 한국 사회언어학, 한국어 교수법으로 분류된다. 현재, 학사 과정에 2명, 석사 과정에 5명(전원 어학), 박사 과정에 10명(어학 8명, 문학 2명)이 있다. 그 외에 2001년부터 한국어 부전공 제도와 과정수료증 제도(certificate program)도 도입했다. 교과과정은 아래와 같다.[13] 아래에서 KOR은 Korean, EALL은 East Asian Languages & Literatures, 괄호 안 숫자는 학기당 학점, V는 유동학점을 나타낸다.[14]

학부 과정:

KOR 101-102 Elementary Korean (4-4)
KOR 111-112 Elementary Conversational Korean (3-3)
KOR 201-202 Intermediate Korean (4-4)

---

13 박영순(2001: 119)에 인용된 하와이 대학의 교과과정이 정확하지 않기 때문에 여기에서 비교적 상세히 기술한다.

14 하와이대학의 학부와 대학원의 교과 과정과 학위 과정을 설정하기까지는 아시아, 태평양학을 강조하는 대학의 정책적 배려도 있었지만, 중국어문학, 일본어문학에 질적으로 뒤지지 않으려는 한국어문학 담당 교수들의 끊임없는 노력이 있었다.

KOR 301-302 Third-Level Korean (3-3)
KOR 399 Directed Third-Level Reading (V)
KOR 401-402 Fourth-Level Korean (3-3)
KOR 420 Korean Composition (3)
KOR 451-452 Structure of Korean (3-3)
KOR 463 Introduction to Traditional Korean Literature (3)
KOR 464 Introduction to Modern Korean Literature (3)
KOR 470 Language and Culture of Korea (3)
KOR 481 Selected Readings in Korean (3) Repeatable once.
KOR 499 Directed Fourth-Level Reading (V)
EALL 281 Korean Literature in Translation: Traditional (3)
EALL 282 Korean Literature in Translation: Modern (3)
EALL 360 Literary Traditions of East Asia (3)
EALL 491 Senior Colloquium in East Asian Literature (3)

대학원 과정:
KOR 613 (Alpha) Korean Verse (3)
KOR 614 (Alpha) Korean Narrative (3)
KOR 615 (Alpha) Korean Drama (3)
KOR 631 History and Dialects of Korean Language (3)
KOR 632 Korean Phonology and Morphology (3)
KOR 633 Korean Syntax and Semantics (3)
KOR 634 Korean Sociolinguistics (3)
KOR 635 Teaching Korean as a Second Language (3)
KOR 640 Literary Translation of Korean (3) Repeatable.
KOR 699 Directed Research (V)
KOR 711 Korean Historical Sources (3)
KOR 720 Research Seminar in Korean Literature (3)
KOR 730 Research Seminar in Korean Language (3)
EALL 601 Method of Teaching East Asian Languages (3)
EALL 603 (Alpha) Bibliographical and Research Methods (3)
EALL 699 Directed Research (V)
EALL 700 Thesis Research (V)
EALL 735 Seminar in Comparative East Asian Literature (3)
EALL 750 Seminar in Comparison of East Asian Languages (3)
EALL 800 Dissertation Research (1)

한국어학 학위과정의 학생들은 본인의 전공에 따라 일본어학, 중국어학 프로그램에서나 자매학과인 언어학과, 제2언어 교수법 학과에서 필요한 과목을 광범위하게 택한다. 뿐만 아니라 논문 심사에도 이들 다른 학과의 교수를 참여시키고 있다.

Indiana, Hawaii, Columbia, SUNY계와 UC계 등의 대학에서는 여름 학기에 정규적으로 한국어 과목을 개설하고 있다. 미네소타 주에 있는 Concordia College에서는 여름 학기 외국어 프로그램인 Concordia Language Villages에 "숲속의 호수"라는 한국어 마을을 설치하여 고등학생과 대학생의 한국어, 전통 한국문화 교육을 실시하고 있다(www.ConcordiaLanguageVillages.org).

미국 대학의 한국어 교재 문제는 해외 한국어 교육의 중요한 현안이었지만 최근에 크게 호전되고 있다. 대학 초, 중급 교과서는 무척 많다. Myongdo's Korean, S. Martin/이영숙의 Beginning Korean, F. Lukoff의 An Introductory Course in Korean, 박용득의 Beginning Korean, UC Berkeley 교수진의 College Korean, 장남규/김용철의 Functional Korean, 이상억 외의 Korean Through English, 지영해의 Intensive Korean, KLEAR의 Integrated Korean, 고려대의 『한국어』와 『한국어 회화』, 연세대의 『한국어』와 『한국어 독본』, 서울대의 『한국어』, 이화대의 『말이 트이는 한국어』 등 다수의 기존 교과서가 있고 이들 기존 교과서에 만족하지 못한 교사들은 개별적으로 개발하여 사용하고 있다. 반면, 상급과 최상급 교과서는 많지 않다. 미국에서 출판된 것은 없고 상술한 고대, 연대 등 한국에서 나온 것을 쓰고 있는데, 필요한 영어 설명이 전혀 없거나 부족하기 때문에 학생과 교사 쌍방이 어려움을 겪는다. 그리고 미국 학생들의 수준에 맞추기가 힘들고 학생들의 관심과 요구 사항이 적절하게 반영되어 있지 않은 내용이 허다하다. 한편 작문, 한자, 고급독본, 문학교본 등 미국 학생들에게 적당한 부교재도 없는 실정이다(유영미 2001 참조).

이러한 상황에서, 한국 국제교류재단의 지원으로 하와이 대학 소재의 Korean Language Education & Research Center(KLEAR)에서 필자의 주도하에 1994년 중순부터 총 21권에 이르는 대대적이고 종합적인 영어권 교과서 개발 공동 사업을 추진해 오고 있다. 초, 중1, 중2, 상1, 상2급을 위한 총 16권의 기본 교과서(2권의 교사용 지침서 포함)의 각 권마다 여러 명이 공동으로 개발하는데, 최신 교수법의 제반 원리와 실제를 광범하게 도입하고, 기술한 미국의 외국어 교육의 목표와 기준에 준거하고, 영어권 학생들의 요구를 반영하고, 복잡한 언어 체계와 문화 체계를 비교 언어적, 비교 문화적 관점에서 설명하고 있다. 기본 교재 이외의 교과서로는 한자교본, 작문교본, 현대문학교본, 고급독본, 언어와 문화 등 5권이 있다. 이들 이외에 문법 용례사전도 개발하고 있다. 21권의 교과서는 하와이대학 출판부에서 2000년부터 출판되고 있다. 2001년 12월 현재 Integrated Korean 8권이 출판되었고, 8권은 출판 중이며, 나머지 5권은 집필 중이다. 이들 모든 교재가 출판되면 영어권 대학의 한국어 교육에 미증유의 공헌이 되리라 믿는다.

2.6. 미국 정부기관의 한국어 교육

미국의 한국어 교육에서 빼놓을 수 없는 것이 정부 요원에 대한 정부 직속 기관의 집중적 한국어 교육이다. Foreign Service Institute(FSI), Central Intelligence Agency(CIA), National Security Agency(NSA), Defense Language Institute(DLI)가 그것이다. 특히 미국 국방 외국어대학이라고 흔히 불리는 DLI는 1941년에 2차 대전 발발을 기하여 일본계 미국인들에 대한 일본어 교육을 위하여 설립되었고 종전 후 1947년부터 냉전에 대비하여 30개 이상의 언어를 군인들에게 교육시켰는데 그 당시 러시아어가 가장 규모가 컸고 그 다음으로 중국어, 한국어, 독일어의 순서였다. 2001년 현재는 총 약 3,000명 중 한국어가 가장 큰 규모인데 매번 600명 이상의 군인들이 하루에 6시간씩 1년 2개월간의 한국어 교육을 받고 있다. DLI 소속의 일곱 개의 대학 중 한국어만으로 대학 하나(Asian II 대학)를 이루고 있는데 그 대학 안에 여섯 개의 한국어 학과(Korean A-F)가 들어 있다. 현재 24개 언어와 수 개의 방언을 교육시키고 있는 DLI의 총 교직원 680명 중 140명가량이 한국어 전임 교직원(교수와 전임강사)이다.

DLI를 특히 언급하는 것은 일반 대학과 다른 점이 많기 때문이다. 첫째, 한국어 수강생 수가 어느 대학과도 비교할 수 없이 대규모이고, 둘째, 일반대학이 1주에 3 내지 5시간의 교육임에 비해 하루에 6시간씩의 집중 교육이며, 셋째, 학생들 거의가 비한국계이고, 넷째, 첨단 외국어 교육시설, 연구팀, 교재, 교수법으로 철저히 통제된 교육제도이다. 이러한 철저한 교육을 받은 군인들은 비교적 높은 한국어 능력과 한국문화의 지식을 보유하게 되어 현역 중이거나 제대 후이거나 한국인, 한국사회와 정신적으로나 실질적으로 친밀해질 수밖에 없다. 또 이들은 어렵게 배운 지식과 능력으로 제대 후 대학이나 대학원에서 한국학을 전공할 수 있는 계기가 되기도 한다. 한국어를 배우는 비한국계 미국인이 많아질수록 한국어는 단순히 한국계 미국인의 민족언어가 아니라 하나의 국제어로 승화되고 한국의 세계화에 기여할 것이다.

3. 한국어 교육의 발전 요인

위에서 살펴 본 바와 같이 미국에서의 한국어 교육은 질적으로나 양적으로 발 빠르게 발전해 왔다. 그러나 한국어 교육이 이처럼 급격하게 발전한 것은 우연이 아니다. 이민 문호 개방, 다민족 사회의 지향, 국제경쟁력 신장을 위한 외국어 습득의 강조 등 미국정부의 일련의 중요한 정책 변화가 있었고, 한국인의 대량 이민, 한국 경제의 급성장, 한국 정부의 한국어, 한국문화의 세계화 정책이 있었다. 특히 재미한인 인구의 급증과 한국의 국력 신장은 미국의 한국어, 한국문화를 떠받는 두 기둥이라 할 수 있다. 이미 1903년 사탕수수 이민에서 보았듯이 초기 한국어 교육의 성행은 일세 이민의 민족적 주체성, 독립정신의 덕택으로 유지되어 왔으나, 2, 3세에 이르러 한국어 교육이 완전히 문을 닫게 된 것은 한국 국력의 부재에 큰 이유가 있었다고 할 수 있다. 한국어 교육의 부활 발전 요인은 대강 다음과 같은 일련의 연쇄반응의 결과라고 할 수 있다.

① 1900년대 초반의 제1차 하와이 이민에 이어 제 2차의 이민 물결은 1950년 6.25 동란 발발 직후부터이다. 1964년까지 총 약 15,000명(전쟁부인 6,423, 입양고아 5,348, 유학 등으로 왔다가 영주한 3,278)이 미국 전역에 이민해 온 것이다. 그러나 그후 한국인의 대대적인 이민은 1960년대 후반에 일어난 미국의 이민 정책 변화가 가장 기본적인 도화선이 되었다. 이민의 나라 미국은 모든 사회적 정치적 요청으로 1964년에 인권법을 제정하여 인종과 출신국으로 인한 여하한 차별도 불법화하였다. 이리하여 모든 소수 민족이 백인 사회에 녹아 들어갔던 melting pot의 사회가 법으로 종식되어 각 민족의 주체성이 법으로 보장받는 다문화 사회로 확립된 것이다. 이어 1968년 개정 이민법 시행으로 동양인의 대량 이민이 허용되었다. 이로 인하여 한국인의 대폭적인 이민이 시작되었다. 이 제3차의 이민의 물결은 대대적이고 극히 빠른 속도로 미국 방방곡곡에 스며들었고 지금도 계속되고 있다. 통계마다 조금씩 다르지만, 1945년 이후 인구 증가와 한국어 교육의 양적 증가의 상관관계를 대충 요약해 보면 다음과 같다(H. Sohn 1990 참조).

연도	한인인구	한글학교	초등학교	중 · 고등학교	대학(교)
1945년	1만 내외	0	0	0	0
1975년	10만 내외	7	0	0	10 내외
1990년	110만 내외	500 내외	0	0	30 내외
2001년	210만 내외	1,000 내외	5	30 내외	120 내외

현재의 재미 한인 인구는 백 년 전 초기 이민 7,200명의 300배에 가까운 숫자이다. 한국인 인구의 급증으로 인하여 한국계 자녀 학생들이 한국어 습득의 필요성을 느끼게 되고 한국, 한국인, 한국어, 한국 문화가 미국 대중에게 가시화되어 비한국계 학생들 간에도 한국어를 배우려는 호기심이 일어났다고 할 수 있다.

② 1970년대 후반부터의 한국 국력의 급신장은 미국에서의 한국어 교육 발전의 또 하나의 중요한 요인이다. 한국의 기적적인 경제 발전으로 한국이 국제 사회에서 응분의 대접을 받게 되고 1988년 올림픽의 성공적인 개최나 한미간의 무역, 경제, 문화, 정치, 학문 등의 활발한 교류 등으로 인하여 한국어를 배우려는 실리적, 학문적, 교양적 동기가 유발되었다. 또한 해외 한국인의 급증(현재 600만으로 세계 전채의 한인 인구의 7.5%)과 한국의 국력 신장으로 인하여, 한국 정부 각 기관(예컨대 외교 통상부, 교육부, 문화 관광부와 그 산하기관)이 해외 한국인에 대해 각별한 관심을 갖게 되고 동시에 한국문화와 한국어의 세계화 정책을 추진해 오고 있다. 이 정책에 따른 각종 지원으로 미국의 여러 대학에 한국학 교수직과 한국학 프로그램이 생기게 되고 많은 한국어 과목이 개설되게 되었다.

③ 미국의 소수민족 언어정책과 외국어 교육 정책의 변화도 한국어 교육에 적지 않게 공헌했다. 미국은 오랫동안 백인 사회로의 동화 정책을 실시하고 학생들에게 표준영어 사

용을 요구한 한편 외국어(특히 소수민족 언어) 습득을 등한시하고 외국인들에게 "필요하면 영어를 배우라"는 태도를 견지해 왔다. 급기야 미국 국민과 정부는 이러한 영어 일변도의 획일주의가 대내적으로는 소수민족 아동의 중퇴 현상을 빚는 등 여러 가지 심각한 교육적, 사회적, 정치적, 인종적 문제를 야기하게 되고, 대외적으로는 외국어 문맹, 외국문화 무식으로 인하여 미국의 국제 경쟁력이 크게 저하되었다는 것을 실감하게 되었다. 그 결과 소수민족 학생을 위한 1968년의 이중언어 교육법, 1974년의 교육기회균등법 등의 제정으로 소수 민족의 언어가 존중되고 이중언어 교육이 합법화되었다. 이리하여 1968년부터는 소수민족 아동에게 우선 모국어(흑인영어 등 사회적 방언 포함)로 공부할 수 있게 하고 표준영어는 하나의 과목으로 배우기 시작하면서 학년이 올라갈수록 표준영어로 하는 과목 수를 늘리고, 모국어는 모국어대로 보존하게 하여 이중어어인이 되도록 하였다. 아동들은 이중언어인으로 자기의 정체성을 학교에서 인정받는 것이므로 자신감과 자긍심을 가지게 되고 학습의욕도 높아지며 학업성취도도 향상되었다.

한편 1970년대 말 카터 행정부 이래 미국 정부는 계속 강력한 외국어 교육 정책을 추진하고 이 목적을 위하여 막대한 예산을 배정해 왔다. 이러한 정책을 계기로 부진했던 미국의 외국어 교육은 상당히 활기를 띠게 되어, 각급 학교의 외국어 과목의 신설 내지 기존 프로그램의 확충, 외국어 습득의 필수화, 외국어 교육 시설의 개선과 교재 개발, 외국어 습득과 교수법에 관한 활발한 연구, 각종 외국어 관련 단체 및 학회의 신설 내지 활성화, 정부 및 여러 재단의 학술 지원 등 외국어 교육 전반에 걸쳐 많은 질적 양적 성장을 이룩하였다.

이와 같은 미국의 강력한 외국어 정책으로 인하여 한국어도 다른 인기 있는 외국어처럼 미국의 정규 교육 과정의 일환으로 자랄 수 있는 기본 여건이 마련되었다. 그러나 미국에서 교수되고 있는 크고 작은 수백 개에 이르는 외국어와 경쟁하여야 한다는 힘겨운 부담을 안아야 한다.

④ 미국과 한국 간의 긴밀한 우호관계와 경제적, 정치적, 외교적, 군사적 이해관계도 한국어 교육 발전에 크게 공헌하였다. 예컨대, 주미 대사관에서 출판한 Korea Update 2001.4(111.3호)에 실린 주미 대사의 말에 의하면 "Korea is the United States' seventh largest trading partner. The United States is Korea's number one trading partner and largest investor"라고 한다. 특히 북한과의 대치로 인한 한국의 전략적 중요성 때문에 미국 정부의 교육기관(DLI, CIA, FSI, NSA 등)에서 많은 정부 요원에게 한국어를 교육시킨다. 기술한 바와 같이 DLI에서는 매년 6백 명 이상의 비한국계 군인들에게 2,000시간의 한국어 교육을 집중적으로 실시하고 있다. 이들은 군 복무 중이나 제대 후나 소중한 한국어 사용자로 기능한다.

⑤ 한국의 수학능력시험에 해당하는 SAT II의 과목으로 (일본어, 중국어에 이어 아홉 번째 외국어로) 한국어가 1997년부터 채택되었다. SAT의 높은 성적으로 좋은 대학에 입학한다는 것은 모든 학생과 학부모의 간절한 소원이기 때문에 고등학교 졸업 전에 한국어 능력을 향상시켜야 한다는 열망이 일고 있다. 최근 갑자기 중, 고등학교에서 한국어 강좌

가 개설되고 한글학교의 상급반이 SAT II-Korean 준비 과정이 되고 있는 실정을 볼 때 SAT II-Korean의 채택은 학생들과 학부모에게 가장 실질적이고 직접적인 동기를 부여한다. 1997년에 2,447명의 고등학생이 이 시험에 응시했고(800점 만점 중 평균 649점), 1998년에 2,472명이 응시했으며(평균 751점), 1999년에는 2,548명, 2000년에는 2,766명이 응시했다(Ree 1999; 박영순 2001).

⑥ 여러 대학에서 학문적 목적으로 한국어 강좌를 개설하고 있는 사실도 간과할 수 없다. 많은 대학이 1900년대 초반부터 동아시아 3국 중 중국어, 중국학과 일본어, 일본학만을 교과 과정에 포함시켜 왔다. 그러나 두 나라 문화의 교량인 한국어, 한국학을 포함시켜 학문상의 불균형과 공백을 없애려는 노력이 팽배하게 된 것이다. 따라서 이제는 일본학, 중국학, 한국학을 포함한 아시아학의 일환으로 한국어 강좌를 개설하고 한국어 전임강사나 한국학 전문교수를 채용하는 대학이 늘고 있다. 교수직만 보더라도 1960년대에 겨우 몇몇 대학에 각 1명 정도의 한국학 교수직이 있었는데, 후술하는 바와 같이 현재 약 30개 대학에 각각 적게는 1명에서 많게는 (하와이 대학에서처럼) 15명에 이르는 한국학 관련 교수가 재직하고 있다. 이러한 추세는 계속될 전망이다.

4. 한국어 교육의 미래

4.1 한국어 교육의 현 실정

전술한 바와 같이 미국의 한국어 교육은 과거 30년간 괄목할 만한 양적 발전을 이룩하여, 학생 수로는 한글학교는 매 학기 총 약 50,000명의 초, 중, 고등학생들이 배우고 있고, 정규 초, 중, 고등학교에서는 매 학기 총 2,000명 정도가, 그리고 대학에서는 매 학기 총 5,000명 정도가 한국어를 습득하고 있다.[15]

이와 같이 한국어 수강생이 급속히 늘고 있지만 한국어는 국방외국어 대학의 경우를 제외하면 다른 인기 있는 외국어에 비하여 아직도 극히 열세임에 틀림없다.

한국어를 외국어 과정으로 가르치는 초등학교는 양방향 이중언어 프로그램이 있는 5개교와 남가주 한국학원의 초등학교를 제외하면 거의 없는 상태이다. 현재, 미국 초등학교에서는 극소수의 인기 있는 언어들(예를 들면 스페인어, 프랑스어, 독일어, 이탈리아

15 많은 한국계 학생들은 1세 가정에서 어릴 때부터 한국어를 매일 부모나 조부모한테서 듣고 배운다. 가정에서 이렇듯 장기간 자연스럽게 한국말을 배울 경우, 한국계 학생들은 한국어의 가장 중요한 기초인 일상 한국말을 구사할 수 있거나, 적어도 들을 수 있게 된다. 그래서 중, 고등학교나 대학에 가면 중급반이나 상급반에 배치되게 된다. 실로 한국어 사용을 통한 가정 교육은 각별한 중요성을 갖는다(이미선 2000 참조). 로스앤젤레스 지역의 초, 중, 고등학생과 부모들을 대상으로 실시한 이영태(1997)의 설문 조사에 의하면, 300명의 응답자 중 거의 모두가 한국말로 대화할 수 있는 상대자는 부모(67.6%)와 조부모(21%)라고 대답했다. 즉 한국어 전수의 주도자는 일차로 부모인 것이다. 한편, 한국인이 많이 사는 대도시에는 각종 사설 학원이 생겨서 아동들의 한글 읽기와 쓰기, 중, 고등학생들의 SAT II-Korean 시험 준비, 성인들의 실용 한국어 습득 등 극히 다양한 목적과 다양한 교과 과정을 가지고 상업적으로 실시되고 있다.

어, 일본어, 러시아어 등)만을 가르치고 있다.

정규 초, 중, 고등학교 한국어교육도 아직은 별로 보잘 것 없다. 겨우 30개교 내외에 불과하기 때문이다. Draper & Hicks(1996)에 의하면, 1994-95학년도에 미국의 중, 고등학교의 총 학생 수의 33.04%(6백만 이상의 학생)가 외국어를 배웠는데 스페인어가 64.5%, 프랑스어가 22.3%, 독일어가 6.1%를 차지하고 있어서 전통 외국어라고 일컫는 이들 세 언어가 외국어를 배우는 총 학생 수의 93%를 차지하고 있다. 당시 한국어는 17위로 0.01%(638명)에 그친다. 5년 전의 이 통계에 비하여, 중, 고등학교 한국어 교육은 최근 상당히 성장하여, 기술한 바와 같이 현재 30개 내외의 중, 고등학교(총 92개 반)에서 총 약 2,000명에게 실시하고 있다(Ree 1999).

한편, 미국 Modern Language Association의 대학 외국어교육 실태에 대한 1995년도의 조사에 의하면, 당시 한국어를 배우는 학생 수가 3,343명으로 14위를 기록했고, 한국어가 가장 빨리 성장하는 외국어로 나타났다(만다린 중국어가 두 번째로 빠름). 학생수는 스페인어(606,283), 프랑스어(205,351), 독일어(96,236), 일본어(44,723), 만다린 중국어(26,471) 등에 비하면 너무도 열세이다.

현재 대부분 대학의 한국어 교육은 여러 학문 분야의 학생들에게 한국어 구사 능력을 향상시켜주는 서비스교육에 국한하고 있다. 따라서 많은 경우 그런 대학에서는 가르치는 선생님들에게 교수직을 주지 않고 박사학위가 있더라도 전임강사직을 주는 것이 관례이다. 언어기능만을 가르치고 학문적인 내용은 교수하지 않기 때문이다. 예외적으로 언어만을 교수하는 DLI는 최근 교수제를 도입하여 교수 경험이 많거나 박사학위 소지자에게는 교수직을 부여하고 있다.

한편, 다음과 같은 30여 개의 일반 대학에서는 학교 자체로나 일부 한국국제교류재단의 도움을 얻어 한국어나 한국문학이나 한국학에 필요한 교수직을 설치하였는데 이들 대학 중 일부 소수 대학에서는 한국어학이나 한국문학이나 한국학의 학사, 석사, 박사학위를 수여한다.

> Arizona State University; Brigham Young University; Brown University; Claremont McKenna College; Columbia University; Cornell University; Duke University; Florida State University; Harvard University; George Washington University; Indiana University; Ohio State University; Rutgers University; Stanford University; State University of New York, Albany; State University of New York, Binghamton; State University of New York, Buffalo; University of California, Berkeley; University of California, Irvine; University of California, Los Angeles; University of California, San Diego; University of Chicago; University of Georgia; University of Hawaii at Manoa; University of Illinois at Urbana; University of Maryland at College Park; University of Michigan; University of Southern California; University of Washington

한국어반 학생의 분포를 보면, 수강생의 대다수는 한국계 학생이다. 이것은 미국의 대부분의 소수민족 언어에 공통된 현상이다. 특히 한글학교는 학생들의 대부분이 한국계 자녀이다. 이들 한글학교 중 90% 이상이 한인 교회에 부설되어 있기 때문에 한국인 자녀 이외의 학생들이 참여한다는 것은 그리 쉬운 일이 아니다. 정규 초, 중, 고등학교의 경우도 마찬가지 실정이다. 이중언어 교육을 받는 학생이건 한국어를 외국어로 배우는 학생이건 거의가 다 한국계 학생이다. 대학의 경우에는 보통 80%가량이 한국계라고들 한다. 대학에 따라서 차이가 있지만 일반적으로 초급반의 경우에는 비한국계가 상당수(20%~30% 정도)를 차지하지만 중급, 고급으로 올라갈수록 한국계가 압도적으로 많아진다. 예외적인 학교로는 모르몬교 선교에 역점을 둔 유타 주의 Brigham Young 대학과 DLI이다. 이들 대학의 한국어 반에는 한국계 학생이 거의 없거나 극소수이다.

4.2 미래 조명

미래를 점친다는 것은 그리 쉬운 일이 아니다. 그러나, 미국에서의 한국어 교육의 미래는 대체로 밝다고 말할 수 있다. 3항(한국어 교육의 발전 요인)에서 언급한 바와 같이 미국의 한국어 교육을 무에서 현재의 수준으로 끌어올렸던 제반 기반(즉 재미 한인 인구 증가, 한국의 국력 신장, 미국의 외국어 정책, 한국의 경제적 전략적 중요성, SAT-Korean의 등장, 한국학의 중요성 등)이 건재하고 계속 더 튼튼해지리라고 믿기 때문이다. 특히 이들 기반의 가장 중요한 두 지주는 전술한 바와 같이 첫째는 현재 2백만이 넘었고 앞으로도 계속 대폭 증가할 것으로 예상되는 재미 한국인 인구요, 둘째는 계속 발전하는 한국의 국력 특히 국제경쟁에서 세계 10위 권에 가까운 경제력이다. 이 외에도 다음과 같은 사정은 미래 미국의 한국어 교육 발전에 더욱 공헌하리라 확신된다.

1) 이중언어에 대한 태도 변화

미국을 위시하여 외국어 또는 이중언어 사용에 대한 세계인의 태도가 급속히 달라져 가고 있다. 즉 종전에는 소수민족의 언어는 사회의 문제거리로 여겨졌던 것이, 세계가 좁아지고 국제 경쟁이 치열해지고 소수민족의 인권이 존중되면서, 이제는 개인의 특권이요, 중요한 국가적, 교육적 자원이라는 인식이 확산되게 되었다. 종전의 획일주의나 차별주의는 구시대의 유물이 되어 가고 현재의 세계는 다원주의나 다양성의 개념에 높은 가치를 두게 되었다(McKay & Hornberger 1996). 더 부연하면 미국은 막대한 예산을 들여 이중언어교육을 실시하고 있는데 국민의 이중언어의 사용이 그만큼 중요하고 절실하기 때문이다.

① 국제적인 차원에서 볼 때, 외국어 구사는 극히 중요하다. 이제 지구촌은 교통 통신 수단의 전자화로 일일 생활권이 되어 수천만 세계 인구는 시간과 장소를 초월하여 즉각적인 국제교류에 임하고 있다. 세계가 단일 언어를 사용하고 단일 문화를 갖지 않는 한, 이

러한 현대의 필수적 생존 조건은 외국어 사용이다. 제2의 언어, 제2의 문화를 습득함으로서 서적, 다매체, 인간교류를 통하여 새로운 지식과 경험과 세계관을 넓히고 다른 나라와 국민을 잘 이해하고 국제간의 문화적 차이와 문화적 가치에 대한 인식을 높일 뿐 아니라 제1언어와 제1 문화를 더 객관적으로 그리고 비교적인 관점에서 이해할 수 있게 된다. 즉 21세기의 지구촌 사회의 일원으로서의 자질을 갖추는 것이다.

② 국가적인 차원에서 볼 때, 이중언어의 구사는 필수이다. 현재나 미래의 세계는 강한 나라이건 약한 나라이건 간에 상호의존 없이는 존속할 수 없다. 각국의 정치, 경제, 사회, 문화, 교역의 질서는 상호 유대의 방향으로 급격히 변화 발전하고 있고 나라마다 자국의 국제경쟁력을 강화시키려고 온갖 노력을 다하고 있다. 이 목적을 위하여 미국에서는 이중언어 정책 내지 강도 높은 외국어 교육 정책을 채택 실시하고 있다. 이중 언어인은 외국어를 자유자재로 구사하면서 외국의 정치, 경제, 무역, 재정, 사회, 문화, 군사, 외교 등 모든 분야를 실제적으로나 학문적으로 속속들이 파고들어 자국의 국제경쟁력을 크게 강화시키게 되기 때문이다.

③ 사회적인 차원에서 볼 때, 이중언어 사용은 여러 가지 사회문제의 해결과 평등 사회 구현에 크게 공헌한다. 따라서 미국과 같은 전형적인 다민족, 다문화 사회에서는 이중언어 사용이 필수적이다. 즉 미국의 경우, 최소한 보편언어인 영어와 각자의 민족언어의 구사이다. 재미 한국인에게는, 한국어는 민족언어로서 가족 친지 내지 2백만이 넘는 재미 한국인, 6천만의 남북한 한국인과 4백만의 미국 이외 세계 도처에 산재하는 한국인과의 의사소통을 위한 언어이다. 한국의 많은 신문, 방송, TV, Internet을 통하여 매일 매일의 소식과 각종 지식을 터득할 수 있는 언어이다.

소수민족들은 이중언어 사용과 이중언어 교육을 통하여 자민족의 존재와 중요성과 단합된 힘을 과시할 수 있고 그 결과로 그 민족의 사회적, 정치적 지위가 향상된다. 한국민족이 이중언어 교육을 통하여 한-영 이중언어인이 된다는 것은 미국 사회에서 한국민족의 지위를 향상시키는 원동력이 된다.

④ 민족적인 차원에서 볼 때, 이중언어 사용은 소수민족 아동들의 민족적 동질성 갈등 문제를 해소해 준다. 한국 아동의 경우, 민족언어인 한국어를 사용할 수 있고 한국문화에 익숙해 있으면 어렸을 때부터 한국 민족임을 알게 되기 때문에 동질성 갈등 문제가 일어나지 않고 민족적 주체성, 동질성, 자부심을 유지할 수 있다. Glew(2001)는 미국의 복합 다민족문화가 극도로 다양한 민족문화들로 형성된 점을 감안하면 많은 미국인들이 자기 부모와 조부모의 언어를 습득하려고 하는 것은 당연한 추세라고 하였고 필자도 그렇게 생각한다.

⑤ 개인적인 차원에서 볼 때도 이중언어 사용은 개인의 실리에 크게 기여한다. 단일언어 사용자에 비해 개인의 직업영역과 생활영역과 활동범위가 훨씬 넓어질 뿐 아니라, 외국에 자유롭게 진출할 수 있고 외국인을 상대할 수 있는 각종 사업을 운영할 수 있으며 각종 기업과 전문직에 종사할 수 있는 능력을 확보할 수 있다. 한국어의 경우, 미국, 한국 양국에서 자유롭게 살 수 있고 한국, 한국인과 관계되는 직업을 가질 수 있다. 한국의 경제,

교역, 정치, 사회, 문화, 학술 전반의 급격한 발전으로 한-영 이중언어 구사자를 대거 필요로 하고 있다는 것은 잘 알려진 사실이다.

실로 이중언어사용은 많은 단일 언어 사용자의 동경의 대상인 것은 우리 주위에서 자주 느끼고 경험하는 바이다. 이중언어의 능력은 국제적, 국가적, 상징적, 언어적, 문화적, 정치적, 경제적, 지능적 부의 일부라고 할 수 있기 때문이다. 영어 일변도만 믿어왔던 재미 한국인 학부모들과 학생들도 이러한 국제적인 흐름을 서서히 깨닫게 되어 점차 한-영 이중언어, 한-미 이중문화의 중요성을 인정하기 시작하고 있다(Choi 1999; H. Kim 2001 참조).

2) 미국의 외국어 정책 강화

미국 정부에서는 21세기에 대비한 초, 중, 고등학교의 외국어 교육의 발전을 위하여 1996년에 "21세기에 대비한 외국어 습득의 기준"(Standards for Foreign Language Learning: Preparing for the 21st Century)을 발표하였다(NSFLEP 1966; Lafayette 1996). 이 기준을 담은 109쪽의 지침서는 각 주정부의 정책 지침으로도 채택되었고 미국 전역 42개의 외국어교육 협회가 인준하였다.[16]

최근 이 지침은 대학의 외국어 교육에까지 적용되고 있다. 외국어의 습득과 민족어의 보존, 개발을 필수화시키고 있는 이 지침서에는 외국어 교육의 기본 원리와 교과 과정의 목표와 목표 달성을 위한 학습내용의 기준이 명시되고 구체적으로 해설되어 있다. 기본 원리는 몇 가지 중요한 원칙을 내포하고 있는데 첫째는 모든 학생으로 하여금 최상급의 외국어 능력과 외국 문화 지식을 장기간 필수적으로 습득하여야 한다는 것이고, 둘째는 외국어 필수 교과 과정을 각급 학교가 마련하여야 한다는 것이고, 셋째는 비영어권에서 온 학생들에게는 자기 모국어 능력을 유지, 발전시킬 수 있는 기회를 부여하여야 한다는 것이다. 이 기본 원리를 효율적으로 집행하기 위한 교과과정의 목표를 5C의 성취라고 규정하였는데 5C란 Communication(외국어를 통한 의사소통 능력의 습득), Cultures(외국 문화의 습득), Connections(외국어를 통한 여러 다른 학과목의 습득), Comparisons(모국어와 학습어 간의 언어적, 문화적 비교 능력의 습득), Communities(외국어를 통한 다문화 사회에의 참여)를 말한다. 각 C를 달성하기 위하여 학습내용의 단계적 성취 기준도 마련하였다. 예컨대, 의사 소통 목표의 경우, 대인 관계에서의 원활한 교신, 다양한 주제에 대한 청취 능력과 독해 능력, 다양한 주제에 대하여 말과 글로 청중이나 독자에게 의사를 발표할 수 있는 능력 등을 성취하기 위한 단계적 학습기준을 설정하고 있다. 문화학습의 목표의 경우는 외국의 정신문화, 행동문화, 물질문화의 습득과 이들 여러 가지 문화의 체계적인 상호관계의 습득을 위한 단계별 학습기준

---

16 예컨대, 하와이 주의 경우 연방 정부의 기준에 입각한 주 정부의 기준이 1999년 8월에 주 교육감으로부터 전 초, 중, 고등학교에 시달되었다(DOE of Hawaii 1999).

을 설정하였다.

이러한 새로운 외국어 교육 방침은 앞으로의 한국어 교육의 목표와 방향을 제시하고 있기 때문에 한국어 발전의 길잡이가 될 것이다. 각급 학생들이 각 교과과정 목표(5 C's)의 단계적 학습 내용을 성공적으로 성취하도록 앞으로 각급 학교의 한국어 교과 과정, 교재, 교수법 등을 대폭 수정 보완하고 향상시키게 될 것이고 한국어 교육의 질적 양적 발전이 있을 것이다.

또한 미국정부와 각급 학교에서는 아시아 언어에 대하여 특별히 강조하고 있다. 한국어, 일본어, 중국어 등 아시아 언어는 태평양 시대의 불가결한 언어일 뿐 아니라 미국에 거주하고 있는 수많은 우수한 아시아인의 언어이기 때문이다. 더욱이, 이들 아시아 언어는 미국 사람들이 언어구조상으로나 문화적으로나 그리 쉽게 배울 수 있는 성질의 언어가 아니기 때문에 보다 많은 정책적, 실제적, 교육적 노력이 요구된다(Brecht & Walton 1997). 아시아 언어에 많은 역점을 둔 결과로, 미국의 각급 학교와 정부 기관이 아시아 언어 교과 과정을 현저하게 확충하고 있다. Glew(2001)는 2001년 4월의 미국 교육부 장관 Richard Reley의 강연을 인용, 아시아 인구는 세계 인구의 압도적 다수인 30억이고 아시아는 세계 부의 80%를 차지하고 있고 미국에서 아시아 인구가 폭발적으로 증가하고 있는데도 현재 외국어를 습득하고 있는 미국학생들의 9%만이 아시아 언어를 공부하고 있음을 통탄하면서 아시아 언어습득을 강조한다.

3) 한인 사회의 민족언어, 민족문화 활동

최근 교포 2세의 한국어와 한국문화 교육의 양과 질을 높이기 위한 각종 활동(NAKS와 그 지부들, 교민단체들의 활동, 세계 한민족 협의회 추진)과 행사(웅변대회, 작문대회, 학예회, 운동 경기, 그림 그리기 대회, 연날리기 대회 등)가 미국 교포사회를 중심으로 행해지고 있다. 이러한 활동과 행사는 고삐를 늦추지 않고 계속될 전망이다. 또한, 한국어 교육자들은 한국과 미국 쌍방에서 학술 발표, 교사 훈련, 다양한 교재 개발 및 출판, 교과과정 향상, 평가 도구 개발, 컴퓨터를 통한 학습자료 개발 등 한국어 교육의 질적 향상을 위한 미증유의 학술적, 실제적 노력을 경주하고 있는데 이러한 노력은 계속될 것이며, 그러한 노력의 효과가 서서히 나타나기 시작하고 있다.

비교적 큰 도시를 중심으로 한국신문, TV, 라디오의 보급도 한국어 습득의 동기를 부여한다. 예컨대 하와이에서는 현재 하루 12시간의 한국 TV(KBS, MBC, SBS 등) 방송이 있고 한국일보, 중앙일보 등 주요 일간 신문이 광범하게 구독된다. 특히 한국의 다양한 TV 드라마는 영어자막의 도움으로 많은 비한국계 미국인이 시청하고 있다. 뿐만 아니라 인터넷의 수많은 한국사이트의 이용은 한국 교민들의 일상 생활이 되어 있다. 이러한 일련의 다매체의 등장은 한국, 한국인, 한국어, 한국문화를 미국사회에 현저하게 가시화시키고 아울러 한국어 습득의 필요성을 증진시킬 것이다.

이상과 같은 여러 적극적인 여건에 힘입어, 앞으로 더 많은 한글학교에서 질 높은 민족언어, 민족문화 교육이 실시될 것이고 한국인들이 집중적으로 살고 있는 대도시(로스앤젤레스, 뉴욕, 시카고 등지)를 중심으로 정규 초, 중, 고등학교에 외국어로서의 한국어 프로그램이 차차 더 많이 개설될 것이며 지금 로스앤젤레스에서 실시되고 있는 한-영 양방향 교육은 더욱 확장될 것으로 기대된다. 그에 발맞추어 대학 프로그램도 더 확충될 것으로 기대된다.

4.3 앞으로의 과제

전항에서 언급한 비교적 밝은 전망은 한국어 교육의 귀중한 고객인 학생 인구의 증가를 전제로 한다. 아무리 좋은 교과과정, 교원, 교재를 마련해 놓아도 배울 학생의 수가 줄면 한국어 교육의 장래는 밝다고 할 수 없고 한국어의 세계화는 공염불이 될 것이다. 위에서 열거한 여러 여건으로 미루어 보아 가까운 장래에 학생 수가 감소되리라고는 생각되지 않지만, 현상유지 수준에 머무를 위험성은 항상 있다. 그러므로 가장 시급한 과제는 어떻게 하여 더 많은 학생들로 하여금 한국어를 배우려는 의욕과 동기를 가지고 한국어 교실로 오도록 장려하고 이들에게 어떻게 해서 만족스러운 교육을 제공할 것인가 하는 것이다.

주지하는 바와 같이 미국의 교육도 다른 분야에서나 마찬가지로 여론에 기초한 민주주의 원리와 자유경쟁에 입각한 시장경제의 원리에 따르고 있다. 일반 교육기관에서 한국어 교육이 발전하려면 학부모들과 학생들의 강력한 요구가 있어야 하고 또 다른 수많은 다수, 소수 민족의 언어들과 부단히 경쟁해야 한다.

그러면 앞으로의 한국어교육의 발전을 위하여 무엇을 어떻게 할 것인가? 이하 사견을 피력하면, 우리의 당면 과제는 크게 두 가지라고 볼 수 있다. 첫째는 한국어 교육의 기반을 더욱 공고히 다지는 일이고, 둘째는 학생들의 한국어에 대한 적극적 태도와 한국어를 배우려는 동기를 유발시키고 학생들로 하여금 만족스러운 한-영 이중언어인이 되도록 교육시키는 일이다. 이들 과제는 상호의존적이고 보완적이기 때문에 동시에 추진시키는 것이 가장 효율적임은 물론이다.

1) 한국어 교육 기반 강화

미국에서의 한국어 교육의 질과 양을 높이기 위하여 교육의 기반구조를 더욱 공고히 다져야 하는데, 이 목적을 위하여 다음 아홉 가지의 방안을 제의한다(손호민 1999; 박영순 2001; Hadley 2001 등 참조).

① 각급 학교의 한국어 교육의 목표와 학습기준은 기술한 미국 정부의 "21세기에 대비한 외국어 습득의 기준"에 바탕을 둔다. 학생들로 하여금 장기간의 학습을 통하여 최상급 수준의 5C를 성취하도록 하는 것은 미국의 외국어 교육 정책이며 한국어 교육에 전적으로 부합된다. 그리고 한국인 교포 자녀에게 한국어 교육을 철저히 시키는 것도 미국 정책이 요구하는 바이다. 각급 학교의 학생들이 한국어 능력을 높이고 한국에 관한 지식을 광

범하게 터득히도록 한국어문학 과목과 문화 과목은 물론 여러 다른 학문 분야에 걸친 광범한 내용중심의 한국어 교육이 이루어져야 한다. 그리고 한국어 특유의 단계별 학습 성취 기준도 (예컨대 Swender & Duncan(1998)의 모델을 참조하여) 마련되어야 한다.

② 한국어의 교육방법은 계속 발전하는 일반 외국어 교육 이론과 실제에 따른다. 5C의 학습을 목표로 한 교과과정의 설계, 실러버스 작성, 교재 개발, 학습 지도, 평가 등 한국어 교육 전반에 걸쳐 현행 외국어 습득 이론, 교수법 이론, 평가방법 이론, 교과과정 및 교재개발 이론 등을 참조하여야 한다. 예컨대 최근 미국에서 외국어 교육방법으로 가장 강조되고 있는 소위 수행 중심(performance-based) 교육의 다음과 같은 일련의 원칙을 익혀서 한국어 교육의 여러 분야에 적절히 활용하여야 할 것이다(세부 설명은 H. Sohn 1995 참조):

learner-centeredness (학습자 위주의 교육)
personalization (개개인의 언어능력에 따른 교육)
contextualization (실제 상황에 기초한 교육)
authenticity (자연스러운 실제 언어의 사용)
task-basis (과제수행적 교육)
goal oriendedness (학습목표 설정)
sequencing (언어능력의 단계별 교육)
accuracy concerns (정확성 교육: 어휘, 문법, 발음, 사회언어, 화용, 유창성)
language-culture integration (언어-문화의 통합 교육)
four-skill integration (4기능의 통합 교육)
fact-act balancing (언어지식과 언어활용의 균형적 교육)

③ 각급 학교 간의 상호 교류를 증진시키고 한글학교로부터 대학까지의 교과 과정을 효율적으로 연결(articulation)시킨다.[17] 현재의 상황은 각급 학교 간(예컨대 한글학교 상호간, 초, 중, 고등학교 상호간, 대학 상호간)의 횡적 교류는 학회 등을 통해 극히 제한된 범위에서 이루어지고 있지만, 한글학교, 초, 중, 고등학교, 대학의 한국어교육은 전혀 종적인 연결고리 없이 독자적으로 실시되고 있다. 교과 과정, 교수 내용, 사용되는 교과서나 기타 보조 교재, 교수법이나 평가 방법 등 전혀 서로가 모르는 실정이다. 각급 학교의 전문가들이 한 군데에 모여 의견을 교환하고 공동 연구를 통하여 통합된 한국어 교육 지침서를 제정하기를 바란다. 그러한 지침에 의거하여 각급 학교의 교과 과정 설정, 교재 개발, 또는 현존 교재의 질적 향상, 교수법 개발 등 일련의 새로운 활동이 실시되어야 할 것이다. 이러한 사업에는 전문적인 지도자들이 자발적으로 그리고 헌신적으로 앞장서야 하고, 그에 따른 재정적 지원이 따라야 할 것이다.

한국어 교육이 한글학교, 초, 중, 고등학교, 대학은 물론이고 한국에서의 현지 교육까

17 Articulation의 중요성에 대해서는 예를 들면 Lange(1982)를 참조하기 바란다. Articulation의 정의는 'seamless transition from one level to the next'이다.

지 체계적으로 통합되어 연결된다면 한국계 학생들을 포함한 많은 학생들이 대학 졸업까지 지금보다도 훨씬 더 높은 수준의 한국어 구사 능력을 성취할 수 있을 것이다. 이미 초, 중, 고등학교에서 하위 수준의 한국어 능력을 체계적으로 성취하게 된 학생들은 대학에서는 상급반에 배치될 것이기 때문이다. 단계적이어야 할 교육 과정이 지금처럼 단절되어 있으면 언어 습득 과정을 심각하게 약화시키고 말게 된다.[18]

한국어 교육의 상호 유대의 일환으로 광범한 컴퓨터 정보망 구축의 필요성이 절실하다. 최근 사정이 상당히 호전되기는 했지만, 아직도 전국에 산재해 있는 한국어 교사들, 전문가들, 학생들의 상호 교류나 정보 교환의 부족 때문에 쓸데없는 노력의 중복으로 그렇지 않아도 제한된 시간, 자금, 인력의 낭비가 심한 편이다. 그러므로 각급 학교의 한국어 교육자들과 한국어 학습자들이 전국적으로 교류할 수 있는 정보망이 설치되어 모든 유용한 교과 과정, 인력 자원, 교수법, 교육 자료에 대한 정보가 체계적으로 입력되고 광범위하게 활용되어야 한다.

④ 다양한 학생들의 요구를 충족시킬 수 있는 다양한 교재의 개발이다. 초등학생이나 대학생도 그렇지만 특히 5C와 그 학습 기준에 따른 효율적인 초, 중, 고등학생용 교재의 개발이 더욱 시급하다. 현재 한글학교의 한국어 교육이 일부 훈련을 받지 못한 한국인 교사들이나 대학원 학생들에 의해서 실시되고 있고 또 독학으로 한국어를 배우는 사람들도 있기 때문에 훌륭한 교과서와 부교재가 더욱 필요하다. 전통적인 형태의 교과서 뿐 아니라 각자의 개별적인 필요를 충족시킬 수 있는 다채로운 학습교재, 다양한 시청각 교재, 컴퓨터화된 다매체 교재도 개발해야한다. 그리고 학생의 자습을 위하여 인터넷을 이용한 한국어 교육 코스도 광범하게 개발하여야 한다(Nielsen & Hoffman 1996; Hadley 2001 참조).

⑤ 각급 학교의 교사의 질을 높이기 위하여 체계적인 교사훈련을 계속한다. 신규 교사나 예비 교사 뿐 아니라 경험 있는 교사도 자주 교사 훈련 워크샵에 참여하여야 한다.[19] 가르칠 언어 내용과 언어구조, 교과과정 작성, 교수법, 평가법 등에 대하여 체계적인 연수가 필요하다. 외국어 교수법에 관해서는 최근 여러 가지 이론과 응용방법에 대한 연구가 나오고 있다. 이러한 연구 결과가 교사 연수를 통하여 일선 교사와 교수들에게 전수되어야 한다. 학술대회와 교사연수, 워크샵, 그리고 각종 미니 발표회와 학회지의 탐독을 통하여 교사와 교수는 꾸준히 자기 발전을 도모해야 한다. 각급 학교와 한국, 미국의 지원기관에서는 이러한 목적을 위하여 최대한의 투자를 아끼지 않기를 바란다.

⑥ 한국어 교육을 미국의 정규 초, 중, 고등학교 교과 과정으로 추진시킨다. 한글학교의 한국어 교육은 아직 한국 이민의 언어로만 인식되고 미국의 정규 교과 과정으로 인정받

---

18 현재 다른 여러 외국어들 측에서는 이러한 articulation작업에 전념하고 있다. 예컨대 일본어 교육자들은 유치원에서 대학까지를 연결시키는 교과 과정 마련에 부심하고 있다.

19 중, 고등학교 교사와 대학 강사에 대한 교사연수는 미국한국어교육자 협회(AATK: American Association of Teachers of Korean)의 연례 학술대회의 일환으로 매년 한국국제교류재단의 지원 하에 실시되고 있다.

지 않고 있는 한편, 정규 초, 중, 고등학교에는 외국어로서의 한국어 교육이 아직 극히 열악한 실정이다. 이러한 상황에서 많은 미국의 일반 학교에서 한국어를 정규 과목으로 개설하도록 추진하여야 한다. 로스앤젤레스에서 실시되는 한-영 양방향 이중언어 프로그램은 최선의 교육으로 여겨진다. 재미 일본계 인구가 겨우 80만 정도인데도 수백에 달하는 정규 초, 중, 고등학교에서 광범하게 일본어 교육이 실시되고 있는 점을 감안하면 200만이 넘는 재미 한국계 인구에 비추어 볼 때 초, 중, 고등학교 한국어 교육의 현 실태는 실로 통탄할 일이 아닐 수 없다. 한인 인구 4만밖에 안 되는 호주에서는 이미 55개의 초, 중, 고등학교와 9개의 대학에서 한국어 과목을 개설하고 있는 점을 상기할 때 미국의 한국어 교육에는 엄청난 공백이 있음을 알 수 있다. 기술한 바와 같이 SAT II-Korean이 채택되고 한국어 교사의 자격증 문제가 서서히 해결되고 있기 때문에 초, 중, 고등학교의 한국어 도입 문제는 이제 학부모를 중심으로 한 교민들과 한국어 교육자들의 노력에 달려 있다.

⑦ 한글학교 교육의 내실을 도모하여 정규학교의 한국어 교육을 대신케 한다. 미국의 전통 외국어나 다른 인기 있는 외국어의 실정과 비교해 볼 때, 한국어를 미국 전역에서 초, 중, 고등학교에 광범하게 도입한다는 것은 쉬운 일이 아니며 많은 시간과 노력이 소요될 사항이다. 학습 동기 등 여러 가지 이유도 있고 한국계 학생이 집결되어 있는 초, 중, 고등학교가 많지 않다는 것도 그 중요한 이유이다. 따라서, 일부 주(캘리포니아, 하와이 등)에서 부분적으로 시도하고 있듯이 전국의 각 교육구와 협의하여, 모든 한글학교의 한국어 과목을 정규 교과 과정으로 인정받는 방안이 마련되어야 한다. 일반 초, 중, 고등학교에서 할 수 없는 일을 한글학교에서 대신해 주기 때문이다. 그러기 위해서는 한글학교의 교육 내용과 시간 수에 있어서, 일반 학교의 교과 과정에 맞도록 개선되어야 하고 (현재 정규 초등학교는 대체로 주당 3시간이고 중, 고등학교는 5시간임) 교사들의 질과 대우도 향상되어야 한다. 그렇게 되면 한글학교 교육에 가일층 큰 동기를 부여하게 되고, SAT II와 더불어 한글학교 교육을 강력히 뒷받침하게 될 것이다. 그러므로 현 시점에서 미국 전역 1,000개 내외의 한글학교의 사명은 실로 막중하다.

⑧ 대학의 한국어 교육은 학문으로 발전시킨다. 미국 교육계에 한국어의 뿌리를 깊이 내리기 위하여서는, 대학의 한국어 교육을 다른 분야 학생들을 위한 서비스과목의 역할만으로 만족할 것이 아니라, 앞으로 더 많은 대학에서 한국어를 하나의 탄탄한 학문 분야로 발전시켜야 한다. 그러기 위하여서는 학생 수가 대폭 늘어나야 하고 교수직이 지금보다도 훨씬 더 많아져야 하고 임용된 교수들 개개인의 헌신적 봉사가 요구되며 전술한 하와이대학의 경우처럼 교과 과정이 대폭 개선되어야 한다. 비교적 큰 규모의 한국어 프로그램에서는 한국어문학의 학위 과정이 개설되기를 바란다. 교민, 한국 정부와 한국어 교육자들의 부단의 노력이 요구된다.

⑨ 효과적인 한국어 교육을 위한 꾸준한 연구가 요구되며, 더 많은 한국어 교육 전문가가 배출되어야 한다. 효율적인 교재와 부교재 개발, 교사 양성, 교과 과정 설정, 교수법과 평가방법의 개발, 한국계와 비한국계 학생의 교육 문제 특히 교포학생들의 교육문제 등 여

러 중요한 현안에 관해서 계속적인 연구가 요구된다. 이 분야의 전문적인 지식과 연구와 풍부한 경험의 소유자들이 대량 배출되어 한국어 교육에 앞장서야 한다. 한국어 교육의 전문가란 언어학적, 사회 문화적 지식과 연구 경험은 물론, 외국어 습득, 교과 과정, 평가 등의 이론적, 실천적, 방법론적 지식, 경험과 연구 업적을 풍부히 갖추고 있어서 이를 실제 상황에 적절히 응용할 수 있는 지도자들을 말한다. 이러한 전문가 없이는 효과적인 한국어 프로그램을 기대할 수 없다. 이러한 전문가는 많을수록 좋은데 불행히도 아직 한국어 교육 분야에서는 이론언어학자는 지극히 많지만 한국어 교육 전문가는 소수에 불과하다.

2) 학습동기의 유발

상기한 한국어 교육 기반 강화에 못지않게 중시해야 할 과제는 어떻게 해서 한국어 교육의 고객이 되는 학생들에게 한국, 한국어, 한국문화에 대해 적극적인 태도를 가지고 한국어 교실을 찾게 하느냐 하는 것이다. 학생들이 한국어를 배우는 데는 많은 이유가 있다. 단순히 한국어가 부모의 언어이기 때문인 경우, 한국인과 관계되는 직업을 추구할 경우, 한국을 방문했거나 방문할 계획이 있는 경우, 공적(군사적 포함), 사적 목적으로 한국에 거주했거나 거주할 예정인 경우, 한국인과 부부로 살고 있거나 결혼할 계획인 경우, 가까운 한국친구가 있는 경우, 한국 TV, 한국 영화, 한국 음식, 태권도 등을 좋아하는 경우, SAT-Korean 시험 준비를 하는 경우, 대학의 필수언어로 한국어를 택하는 경우, 학문으로 한국학을 연구하는 경우, 단순히 한국이나 한국인에 대한 호기심이 있는 경우 등 극히 다양한 동기로 한국어를 배운다. DLI에서처럼 국가정책에 따라 많은 군인들이 본인들의 의사와는 관계없이 의무적으로 한국어를 배우는 경우도 있다. 이렇게 해서 한번 배우기 시작한 후 수업이 효율적이고 재미있고 많은 새로운 정보와 지식을 얻게 되면 더 강한 동기가 생겨서 공부를 계속하게 된다.

그러나 위와 같이 학생들이 나름대로의 동기를 가지고 자발적으로 한국어 교실을 찾도록 방관하기에는 언어마다 학생 유치 경쟁이 너무도 치열할 뿐 아니라 자칫 학생들 특히 교포 학생들이 한국어 습득 기회를 놓치고 크게 후회할 수 있다. 그러므로 학부형들과 각급 학교 학생들에게 한국어와 한국 문화의 중요성을 강력히 인식시켜서 그들을 한국어 교실로 유치하는 일은 극히 시급한 당면 과제이다.

외국어 학습동기에 대해서는 과거 30년간 여러 학자들이 연구해 왔다(예컨대 Gardner & Lambert 1972, Gardner 1985, Baker 1992, Oxford 1996, McGroarty 1996, Dornyei & Schmidt 2001). Gardner(1985)에 따르면, 특정 언어에 대한 적극적, 우호적 태도는 그 언어의 학습 동기를 유발한다고 한다. 동기란 어떤 목적을 달성하려는 욕망이다. Gardner & Lambert(1972)는 언어습득 동기를 융화적 동기(integrative motivation)와 수단적 동기(instrumental motivation)로 구분하고, 전자는 목표 언어 화자들과 융화, 교류하는 것을 목적으로 언어를 배우려 하는 욕망이며 후자는 학문적 또는 직업적 성공 같은 다른 목적을 위한 수단으로 언어를 습득하려는 욕망을 말한다. 한국어

학습자들은 대체로 양쪽 동기를 다 가지고 있다.

전술한 바와 같이, 비한국계 학생이 대부분인 DLI 등 정부기관과 모르몬 선교와 관계되는 Brigham Young대학을 제외하면 각급 학교의 한국어 교실은 80% 이상이 한국계 교포학생이다. 그러나 현재 재미 한국계 학생들의 11% 정도만이 한국어를 배우고 있는데 이들은 한글학교의 학생이 대부분(90%가량)이다. 그리고 이들 한글학교 학생은 대체로 자발적인 동기에서 한국어를 습득하는 것이 아니고 학부모의 권유로 한글학교에 나간다. 그러므로 한국어 교육자뿐 아니라 재미 한국인 모두가 당면한 가장 심각한 과제는 모든 교포 학생들에게 어떠한 동기를 부여하여 한-영 이중 언어인이 되도록 하느냐 하는 것이다. 즉 한국어를 배워야만 한다는 강한 사회 심리적인 동기를 학부모와 2세, 3세들에게 어떻게 유발시키느냐 하는 문제이다. 2세의 한국어가 약하면 3세의 한국어는 더 약해지고 3세 보다는 4세가 더 약해지는 것을 우리는 역사를 통하여 알고 있다. 한국어 교육을 유지, 보존, 발전시키려면 비한국계의 계속적인 유치 노력과 더불어 교민 학생들의 한국어 습득의 동기부여에 범민족적인 노력이 요구된다.

이미 언급한 바와 같이, 교민 학생들의 한국어 습득의 중요성은 지대하다. 어려서부터 한국어를 배워서 한-영 이중언어인이 되어야 한다는 데에는 여러 가지 본질적인 이유가 있기 때문에 교민 학부모, 자녀 학생들, 교민 전반을 대상으로 개몽운동을 하여야 한다. 점점 수가 줄고 있기는 하지만 아직도 상당히 많은 한국 학부모들은 이중언어 능력에 대한 이해가 부족하여 한국어 교육이 후세들의 영어교육과 학교 수업에 지장을 초래한다고 잘못 생각하고 한국어 교육을 기피하는 경향이 있다(이동재 외 2000 참조). 그러나 학부모들의 자녀교육에 대한 이러한 염려가 쓸데없는 기우에 지나지 않고, 오히려 이중언어 능력이 자녀교육과 장래 출세에 얼마나 강한 장점이 되는가를 다음 여러 가지 점을 들어 확실하게 주지시켜야 한다.

① 민족적 정체성(ethnic identity)의 문제이다. 전술한 바와 같이, 이민의 나라 미국은 이미 백인 우월 주의의 사회가 아니고 모든 민족이 동등하게 대접받는 다민족, 다문화 사회이다. 모든 국민이 필연적으로 미국시민인 동시에 특정 (단수 또는 복수) 민족에 속한다. 한국 교민은 미국시민인 동시에 한국 민족이다. 이러한 시민-민족의 이중적 주체성이 어려서부터 확고히 인식되어야만 정체성 갈등이 일어나지 않는다. 이러한 정체성은 물론 한-영 이중언어를 통하여 가장 잘 인식되고 유지된다.

② 미국정부의 21세기의 확고한 교육정책상 모든 학생이 최소한 하나의 외국어를 필수적으로 배워야 하는데 부모의 언어인 민족어를 비교적 쉽게 배움으로써 상술한 민족적 동질성, 정체성 문제 해소는 물론, 부모, 친척, 다른 한국인과의 자유로운 의사소통 등 온갖 이득이 있다. 한국어는 세계의 6천여 개 언어 중 12위 내지 14위 안에 드는 많은 화자를 가지는 중요한 언어이다. 남한의 5천만, 북한의 2천4백만, 미국의 2백십 만, 중국의 2백만, 일본의 7십만, 구소련의 5십만 등 세계 도처에 있는 한국인들의 고유 언어이다. 한국계 학생들이 한국어를 배우는 것은 미국의 "21세기에 대비한 외국어 습득 기준"의 기

본 원리에도 전적으로 부합된다.

③ 이중언어인이 단일 언어인보다 지능적으로나 학술적으로 더 우수하다는 것은 그 동안 많은 실험과 연구에서 밝혀진 사실이다. 제2언어의 습득은 습득자의 분석적인 능력을 길러 주는 것이므로 한 언어만 아는 아동보다 이중언어 사용 아동이 언어 간의 차이를 더 잘 인식하고 각 언어의 문법적 특성에 잘 주목하여 문법 규칙을 더 정교하게 이해할 수 있다는 것이며 새로운 언어를 더 잘 배운다고 한다. 그뿐만 아니라, 언어 조작에 민감하여 훨씬 더 성공적인 의사소통을 한다고 한다. 또한 많은 최근 연구에 의하면 이중언어 화자가 인지능력적인 면에서 더 발달하여 더 다양하고, 유동적이고 창의적인 사고 능력을 가지며 학업 성적도 일반적으로 더 우월하다는 것이다(이미선 2000; 박영순 2001: 333-43 참조).

④ 양방향 교육과 관련하여 이미 지적하였듯이, 외국어 교육은 학생이 어릴 때 배울수록 더 효과적이다. 가장 자연스럽고 신속한 언어습득이 2살부터 12살 사이에 이루어지기 때문이다. 한국어는 성인 영어화자에게는 가장 어려운 언어이다. 한국어의 조기 교육은 성인이 겪는 어려움 없이 모국어처럼 자연스럽고 쉽게 배우기 때문에 궁극적으로 높은 수준의 언어 능력을 성취하는 데 크게 도움이 된다. 가정과 학교에서 자연스럽게 그리고 아주 빠르고 쉽게 배울 수 있는 조기 한국어 교육의 시기를 놓치게 되면 점점 한국어를 배우기가 힘들어진다. 시기를 놓친 뒤에 부모와 자녀가 크게 후회하는 예는 주위에서 흔히 본다.

⑤ 예외는 있지만, 원칙상, 한국계만이 완전한 한-영 이중언어인 이중문화인이 될 수 있다. 가정에서 어려서부터 이중언어를 구사하면서 자라고 한글학교를 다닐 수 있기 때문이다. 이들이야말로 미국이 갈구하는 완벽한 이중언어 국민이 될 수 있고 미국의 정치, 경제, 문화, 교역 등 모든 국제 관계에서 견인차 노릇을 할 필요 불가결한 인재들이다. 이들이야말로 모든 분야에서 미국과 한국을 직접적으로 연결시키는 교량적 역할을 하는 주역들이다. 한국어는 워낙 어려운 말이므로 미국에서 자란 비한국계가 배워서 이중언어인이 된다는 것은 불가능하지는 않더라도 극히 어려운 일이다.[20]

⑥ 한국의 경제 성장으로 미국에서나 한국에서 무한정하게 많은 한-영 이중 언어인이 필요하나 현재 극히 제한된 수의 불완전한 이중 언어인이 있을 따름이다.[21]

⑦ 상위권에 속하는 대학에서 입학 요건으로 2년 이상의 외국어 학습을 요구하고 있는데 어려서 한국말에 접한 아동들은 이것을 손쉽게 충족시킬 수 있다. 미국대학 중 80%가량이 졸업 요건으로 1년 또는 2년의 외국어 학습을 하고 있는데 이중언어인은 이것이 면제된

20 참고로, 막대한 국가 예산으로 하루 6시간씩 1년 2개월을 배운 DLI의 비한국계 군인의 언어능력 수준은 겨우 중상급 내지 상급초에 해당하는데, 이는 통상 전혀 학교에서 한국어를 배우지 않은 많은 교포학생들의 실력에도 못 미친다.

21 참고로, 미국 상원위원 Thad Cochran의 최근 법안 The Foreign Language Acquisition and Proficiency Improvement Act of 2001에는 다음과 같은 글이 있다: “In addition to the need for foreign language skills in the arena of national security, a *USA Today* survey found that top executives cited foreign language skills twice as great as any other skill in demand.”

다. 또한 SAT II 한국어 시험에서 좋은 점수를 얻어 우수 대학에 입학할 수 있다. 대학에 가서 다양한 고급 한국어 과목을 택할 수 있고 한국어와 한국 문화에 관계되는 분야에서 석사 내지 박사학위를 큰 어려움 없이 취득할 수 있다. 한국 신문 방송을 자유로이 읽고 들어서 평생 한국에 대한 정보와 지식을 무한정 넓힐 수 있고, 따라서 삶의 질을 높일 수 있다.

⑧ 이중언어 사용이야말로 소수민족의 존재 의의와 가치는 물론이고 사회적, 정치적, 문화적 역량을 과시하고 유창한 외국어 사용자로서의 능력과 자부심을 유지할 수 있는 무기이다. 이중언어 교육의 제도적 추진과 선양은 미국이 다민족, 다문화 사회임을 계속 미국 시민에게 확고하게 인식시키고 소수민족의 격을 높이는 원동력이 되므로 강력하고 지속적인 한-영 이중언어 교육을 추진시켜서 평등사회로의 의식 변동을 촉진시켜야 한다. 그것이 자손 만대에 다른 소수민족은 물론이고 현재 주류 사회를 이루고 있는 다수 백인 민족과 명실공히 완전히 대등한 바탕 위에서 선의의 경쟁을 할 수 있다.

⑨ 지금 세계인의 관심은 울타리 없는 지구촌을 만들되 각 민족 고유의 것을 널리 알려서 세계 속에서 유지 발전시키려고 노력하고 있다. 한민족 공동체의 민족적 과업은 특히 한국어와 글을 세계에 보급하여 8,000만 민족의 언어로서뿐 아니라 세계인들이 널리 사용하는 언어가 되도록 노력하는 일이다.

⑩ 그러므로 교포 학부모는 집에서 의도적으로 한국어만을 써서 자녀에게 귀중한 문화재인 한국어를 전수하여야 하고 한글학교와 일반 학교에서 계속 한국어를 배우도록 권장해야 한다. 아이들은 어차피 표준영어를 학교와 사회에서 자연스럽게 배우게 되므로 집에서는 의도적으로 한국어만을 쓰면 아이들은 이중언어인으로 발돋움하게 된다. 입학한 후에도 한국어를 유지하고 발전시키도록 영어를 모르는 조부모, 친지와 자주 접촉하게 하고, 한국에 있는 친척, 친지를 자주 방문케 하고 한국어를 사용하는 각종 행사와 특별활동에 참여할 기회를 만들어 주어야 한다. 또한 저녁에 시간을 정해서 규칙적으로 한국어로 된 아동 문학 등 지능 발달과 언어 수준에 맞는 책을 읽어 주거나 카세트 테이프를 들려주거나 한국어 영화를 보여 한국어 입력을 보충하여야 한다. 한가지 주목할 점은 통계적으로 보아 어려서 한글학교에 다녔던 학생은 대학에 입학해서 다시 한국어를 배우려고 하는 것이 보통이다.

그러면 한국계 학부모와 학생들에게 이상의 사실을 어떤 방법으로 주지시킬 것인가? 한가지 중요한 방법은 한국인 사회에 체계적인 홍보 활동을 실시하는 것이다. 한국어를 자유로이 구사함으로써 얻는 각종 이득과 한국어를 몰라서 어려움을 당하는 각종 재미있고 생생한 일화나 사례를 들어 신문, 책자, 라디오, TV방송, 강연, 워크샵, 종교단체 등을 통하여 학부모, 각급 학생들, 일반 교포를 대상으로 체계적이고 지속적인 홍보가 필요하다. 이러한 홍보를 통하여 위에 열거한 한국어 교육의 중요성을 강조하여야 한다. 특히 초등학교 아동들의 경우는 부모들의 인식이 절대적인 중요성을 갖기 때문에 부모들이 자녀의 이중언어 구사의 중대성을 충분히 납득하여서 자녀의 장래를 위하여 자발적으로 협조하여야 하고 언어 습득의 최적기인 2-12살을 놓치게 되면 그만큼 더 힘들어진다는 것을 부모들이 깊이 명심하여야 한다.

각급 학교 한국어 선생님들도 위에 열거한 이중언어의 중요성을 깊이 명심하고, 학생들에게 능률적으로 교수하는 한편, 학생들이 한국어 공부를 계속하도록 여러 가지 동기를 부여하여야 한다. 즉,

① 한국어 학습활동이 효율적이어야 한다. 여기에는 몇 가지 조건이 있다. 첫째는 학습활동이 즐겁고 유쾌하고 재미있어야 한다. 둘째는 새로운 내용과 언어 구조를 큰 어려움 없이 단계적으로 배울 수 있어야 한다(Krashen 1982 참조). 셋째는 학생이 배운 한국어의 실용성을 강하게 느껴야 한다. 즉 교실 밖에서 부모나 다른 한국인들과 의사소통을 할 수 있고 상급반 학생의 경우는 한국의 인터넷이나 신문이나 텔레비를 볼 수 있도록 배워야 한다. 넷째는 한국어를 배우는 것이 학생의 현재와 장래에 얼마나 중요한 일인가를 직접 간접으로 인식토록 배워야 한다.[22]
② 한국 학생들의 동아리 활동, 한국에 관한 각종 흥미로운 강연 또는 영화, 음악, 체육 등의 행사에 학생들을 참여하도록 한다.
③ 한국 방문을 장려한다. 여름이나 정규 학기에 한국으로 유학하도록 권유한다. 많은 교포 학생들이 한국에 단기 또는 장기로 한국어나 다른 분야를 공부하면서 자기의 정체성을 강하게 깨닫고 돌아왔다는 것을 증언한다. 과거에는 자기자신을 "American"으로 인식하고 살던 학생도 한국을 다녀온 뒤에는 자신을 "Korean American"으로 재발견하였다고 한다(최근의 KBS 뉴스).
④ 학생들에게 이중 언어인으로서 그리고 한국인으로서의 자부심을 심어 준다. 한국어 교사들은 미국이 이민의 나라로서 복수 민족 사회임을 강조하고, 모든 민족과 그들의 문화와 언어는 동등하게 존경받아야 함을 강조한다. 그리고 각자가 자기 민족어를 구사할 줄 모르면 심히 부끄러운 일일 뿐 아니라 장래 처신에 크게 손해를 입는다는 점을 직접 간접으로 인식시켜야 한다.
⑤ 외국어 교육의 원리와 방법에 익숙하여 한다. 특히 전술한 21세기 미국의 외국어 교육의 다섯 가지 목표와 그 목표를 달성하기 위한 여러 기준에 통달하여야 하고(손호민 1999 참조), 교육 방법으로는, 전술한 수행중심 교육의 일반 원칙 등을 익혀서 교과 과정 설계, 교수 요목 작성, 교재 개발, 학습 지도, 평가 등에 적절히 활용하여야 한다.
⑥ 대학의 경우, 한 학생이라도 더 각급 한국어 반에 들어오도록 많은 새롭고 매력 있는 혁신적 과목을 창설하여 선전하는 등 온갖 노력을 경주해야 한다. 예컨대 하와이대학에서는 현재 40개가량의 외국어가 개설되어 있는데, 학기 등록이 시작될 무렵부터 각종 언어의 다양한 과목이 선전된다. 참고로 일본어와 중국어의 경우만 보면, 2001년 12월 현재 하와이대학 동아시아어문학과의 입구와 여러 광고판과 엘리베이터에는 2002년 봄 학기를 겨냥하여 새로운 과목을 선전하는 다음과 같은 광고가 나붙어 있다. 이들 광고의 디자인은 학생들의 눈길을 끌도록 그림 등을 넣어서 독창적이고 재미있게 꾸며져 있다.

22 참고로 김혜영(2000)은 아동들의 효과적인 한국어 교육을 위하여 여러 가지 다양한 구체적 수업 방법을 제안하고 있으며 이미선(2000)은 가정에서의 효율적인 이중언어 교육에 대하여 논하고 있다.

광고 문구 일부만을 소개한다.

ㄱ) **Chinese 140 Introduction to Chinese Language and Culture**

◆ What is Chinese culture?

◆ What do Chinese do?

◆ What's good in Chinese food?

◆ What is Chinese opera?

◆ What is Chinese singing and dancing?

◆ Interested in Mandarin but don't know how and where to start.

Want to find out the answers? Come and join us Spring 2002. Many other interesting topics related to Chinese culture will also be introduced.

ㄴ) **Chinese 491 Oral Fluency through Chinese Films.** Spring 2002

◆ Interested In Chinese Movies?

◆Have been studying the Chinese Language for a long time but still lack of speaking fluency? Imagine how great it is to be able to understand Chinese movies and get fluency in speaking in just one semester!!! Register today!

ㄷ) **Japanese Online Course JPN 399 Advanced Japanese Reading & Writing** "Anywhere Anytime Japanese", Spring 2002.

Have you completed JPN301, but do not have time to continue studing Japanese, or your schedule does not work out with the regular Japanese course? Try JPN399 'Japanese on the Web', the very first online advanced Japanese course. If you are not familiar with computer work in Japanese, don't worry; we can train you at the beginning of the semester. All reading materials are authentic. Looking forward to meeting you online! (일본어로 "언제나 어디서나 日本語", "파자마로 日本語", "인터넷의 日本語", "그럼 배워야지!" 등의 어구가 곁들어 있다.)

ㄹ) **Japanese 490: Advanced Language Study-Japanese**

Will focus on current topical issues in Japan. Students will focus on one area of personal interest--social, legal, political, business, or economic . . . Students will primarily gather information from the Internet and from Japanese newspapers and converse on daily topics and read Japanese authentic materials in their field . . .

ㅁ) **Japanese 407B: Reading Japanese Newspapers and Magazines**

Nail it! Stop struggling with the same old problems. You can finally read those newspaper, magazine, and Internet artices that always

> seemed so beyond your reach. You'll learn the ropes in this class, and finally feel that all that hard work was worth it! AND: Specific training in Web resources!

이렇듯 학생들의 호기심과 실리에 호소하여 그들을 자기네 외국어 교실로 유치하려고 온갖 노력을 경주하고 있다. 즉 미국의 외국어 교육에서도 국제경쟁의 시대가 열린 것이다. 그러므로 우리의 과제는 다양한 한국어 과목을 개설하고 최대한 많은 학생을 한국어 교실로 유치하여 효율적으로 교육시키는 일이다. 동시에 학생들의 마음속에 한국어를 꼭 배워야 한다는 강한 동기를 심어 주어야 할 것이다.

5. 결론

지금까지 미국에서의 한국어 교육의 역사, 현황, 미래 조망, 앞으로의 과제 등을 사견을 토대로 두루 짚어 보았다. 특히 한국계를 위시한 각급 학교 학생들로 하여금 최고급 수준의 한-영 이중언어인이 되도록 하여야 한다는 데 각별한 역점을 두었다. 현재 미국의 전형적인 한국어 교육의 여건과 방법은 아직 학생들을 완전한 이중언어 사용인으로 만들어 내기 어렵다는 것은 일선 한국어 교육자라면 대부분 시인할 것이다. 한국어의 어려운 어휘와 문법, 미국과는 대조적인 문화, 미비한 교과 내용, 턱없이 짧은 학습 시간, 부족한 언어실습, 불충분한 교재, 열악한 교수법과 평가제도, 학생들의 위약한 동기 또는 한국어 학습에 대한 무관심, 초등학교에서 대학까지의 교과과정 연계의 부재 등을 감안할 때 학생들을 최상급 수준에 올리기에는 역부족이라고 말할 수 있다. 이 문제를 해결하기 위하여서는 한 편으로는 한국어 교육의 질적 향상을 도모하고, 또 한편으로는 학부모와 학생들에게 강한 한국어 학습동기를 유발하여 장기간의 한국어 습득을 장려하는 일이다. 비교적 완전한 이중언어인이 되려면, 한국인 가정에서 살면서 배우는 방법, 양방향 집중교육을 받는 방법, 방학 때나 정규학기를 이용해서 한국에서 현지교육을 받는 방법 등을 위시한 다면적 방법이 전형적 학교교육에 추가되어야 한다. 이 어느 것이나 언어습득은 어릴 때일수록 더 효율적인 것은 물론이다.

미국과 한국의 각급 학교에 종사하는 한국어 교육자들, 학자들, 교민 단체, 학부모들, 한국어 관련 각종 협회와 단체들, 한국의 지원 단체들이 혼연일체가 되어 지금까지 보다 더 적극적이고 조직적이며 강도 높은 노력을 아끼지 않아야 한다. 속수무책으로 자연적 상황만에 의존한다면 한국어 교육은 질적으로나 양적으로 지지부진하거나 최악의 경우 자칫 수렁에 빠져들 위험성조차 없지 않다. 비한국계는 물론이고 한국계 학생마저 배우기 쉽고 유력한 전통 외국어(스페인어, 프랑스어, 독일어 등)나 다른 인기 있는 아시아언어(일본어, 중국어 등)에 끌려가거나 아예 외국어 습득을 기피할 가능성이 있기 때문이다. 한국어를 하나의 민족언어로서가 아니라 자타가 공인하는 국제어로 승화시키고 발전시키기 위하여 우리는 하여야 할 일이 너무도 많다.

우리는 일류 역사를 통하여 한 나라의 운명이 지도자가 어떤 사람인가에 따라 좌우되는 것을 무수히 보아 왔다. 한 국가의 흥망도 단 한 사람 또는 소수의 사람이 결정할 수 있을진대 하물며 한국어 교육이야말로 수많은 헌신적인 한국어 교육자들의 힘이라면 얼마든지 발전시킬 수 있다고 믿는다. 한 사람 한 사람이 헌신적으로 최선을 다하는 한편 상호 긴밀히 협조한다면 놀라운 효과를 볼 것이다.

참고 문헌: Chapter 4

김영기. 1988.「미국에서의 한국어 교육 현황 및 연구와 그의 적용」.『한글』201/202.

김혜영. 2000.「학습의역을 높이기 위한 한국어 수업 방법의 다양화」. In Lee, D.J. et al. (2000).

뉴욕 한인회 편. 1986.『미국 속의 한인 사회』. 뉴욕.

박영순 1997.『이중/다중언어 교육론』. 서울: 한신 문화사.

박영순 2001.『외국어로서의 한국어 교육론』. 서울: 도서출판 월인.

새국어생활 1권 2호. 1991.『외국인의 한국어 학습』. 서울: 국립국어 연구원.

손호민. 1999.「미국에서의 한국어 교육방법」. 서울대학교 국어교육 연구소 주최 제1회 한국어교육 국제학술회의(1999. 12. 9-11) 발표 논문.

유동식. 1988.『하와이의 한인과 교회』호놀루루: 그리스도 연합감리교회.

유영미. 2001.「미국에서의 한국어 교재 개발 현황 및 방향」. 한국어 세계화 제2차 국제 학술대회 발표 논문. 서울 세종문화회관, 11월.

유의영. 1991.「재미 한인의 후세교육: 현황과 전망」. 世界속의 韓國文化. 870-887. 서울: 한국 정신문화 연구원.

윤병석 1990.『國外 韓人社會와 民族運動』서울: 일조각.

이동재 외 (편). 2000.『한인학교의 한국어교육 연구』. Honolulu: University of Hawaii, Second Language Teaching & Curriculum Center.

이미선. 2000.「이중언어 사용 개론」. In Lee, D.J. et al. (2000).

이상오. 1995.「세계화 시대의 한민족 공동체 구성과 해외 교민 2세를 위한 민족 교육」. *Korean Language in America* 1.

이영태. 1997.「미주지역 동포의 한국어 교육」. 한국 문화체육부 및 국제한국교육학회 주최 세종 탄신 600돌 기념 국제학술회의 발표 논문. 서울 세종문화회관, 9월 8일-10일.

Baker, C. 1992. *Attitude and Language*. Clevedon, UK: Multilingual Matters.

Baker, C. 1996. *Foundations of Bilingual Education and Bilingualism*. Philadelphia: Multilingual Matters.

Blank, Lenore Kim. 1999. Teaching Korean to diverse ethnic & cultural students in the 21st century. Presented at the 4th International Conference of Korean Studies (sponsored by the Foundation for SAT II Korean). Yonsei University. Seoul. June 28-30.

Brecht, R.D. & A.R. Walton 1997. National language needs and capacities: a recommendation for action. Presented at a UCLA Conference on Title VI Project. January.

Choi, Hyaeweol. 1999. Incorporating identity into language pedagogy: the case of Korean heritage students. *Proceedings of the Third International Conference on Korean Studies*. Los Angeles: Academia Koreana of Keimyung University. 403-15.

DOE (Department of Education) of Hawaii. 1999. *World Languages: Content Standards*. Department of Education, State of Hawaii.

Dornyei, Z. & R. Schmidt (eds.). 2001. *Motivation and Second Language Aquisition*. Technical Report #23. Honolulu: University of Hawaii, Second Language Teaching & Curriculum Center.

Draper, J.P.& J.H. Hicks. 1996. *Foreign Language Enrollments in Public Secondary Schools, Fall 1994*. American Council on the Teaching of Foreign Languages.

Dulay, H. & Burt, M. 1974. Errors and strategies in child second language acquisition. *TESOL Quarterly* 8: 129-38.

Gardner, R.C. 1985. *Social Psychology and Second Language Learning: The Role of Attitudes and Motivation*. London: Edward Arnold.

Gardner, R.C. & Lambert, W. 1972. *Attitudes and Motivation in Second Language Learning*. Rowley, MA: New House.

Glew, M. 2001. Why offer instruction in the less commonly taught languages? *CLEAR News* 5.2. Michigan State University.

Hadley, A.O. 2001. *Teaching Language in Context, Third Edition*. Boston, MA: Heinle & Heinle.

Johnson, J. & E. Newport. 1991. Critical period effects on universal properties of language. *Cognition* 39: 215-58.

Kim, Hi-Sun Helen. 2001. Language background, motivation, and attitude of heritage learners in KFL classes at the University of Hawaii at Manoa. Ms. University of Hawaii at Manoa.

Krashen, S. 1982. Principles and practice in second language acquisition. New York: Pergamon Press.

Kwon, Hyunjoo. 1999. Overview of the Korean native language arts program for bilingual Korean students in New York City public high schools. *Korean Language in America* 3: 319-27.

Lafayette, R.C. (ed.). 1996. *National Standards--A Catalyst for Reform. Lincolnwood*, ILL: National Textbook Company.

Lnage, D.L. 1982. The problem of articulation. In Higgs, T.V. (ed.), Curriculum, Competence, and the Foreign Language Teacher. Skoike, ILL: National Textbook Company.

Lenneberg, E. 1967. *Biological Foundations of Language*. New York: Wiley.

McGroarty, M. 1996. Language attitudes, motivation, and standards. In McKay, S.L. & N.H. Horberger (1996, 3-46).

McKay, S.L. & N.H. Hornberger (eds.). 1996. *Soviolinguistics and Language Teaching*. Cambridge, UK: Cambridge University Press.

Merrill, C.C. 2000. Articulation K-8 (elementary and middle school): the Korean/English dual language program. *Korean Language in America* 5: 17-24.

Nielsen, M. & E. Hoffman. 1996. Technology, reform, and foreign language standards: a vision of change. In R.C. Lafayette (1996, 119-37).

NSFLEP (National Standards in a Foreign Language Education Project). 1996. *Standards for Foreign Language Learning: Preparing for the Twenty-First Century*. Lawrence, KS: Allen Press, Inc.

Oxford, R.L. (ed.) 1996. *Language Learning Motivation.* Technical Report #11. Honolulu: University of Hawaii, Second Language Teaching & Curriculum Center.

Ree, Joe J. 1999. An overview of the SAT II Korean test. Presented at the 4th International Conference of Korean Studies (sponsored by the Foundation for SAT II Korean). Yonsei University. Seoul. June 28-30.

Snow, M.A. 1998. Trends and issues in content-based instruction. *Annual Review of Applied Linguistics* 18: 243-67.

Sohn, Ho-min. 1990. Korean language education in the United States. *Bilingual Education for the Overseas Koreans* 6: 19-79.

Sohn, Ho-min. 1995. Performance-based principles and proficiency criteria for KFL textbook development. *Korean Language Education* 6: 67-98.

Sohn, Sung-Ock. 1997. Issues and concerns in teaching multi-level classes: syllabus design for heritage and non-heritage learners. *Korean Language in America* 2: 131-8.

Sohn, Sung-Ock, et al. 1999. Research report on the Korean/English dual language program. Presented at the AATK Annual Conference. Columbus, Ohio. August.

Swain, M. 1978. Home-school language switching. In Rickards, J. (ed.), *Understanding Second Language Learning: Issues and Approaches,* 238-51. Rowley: Newbury House.

Swain, M. 1991. French immersion and its offshoots: getting two for one. In Freed, B.F. (ed.), *Foreign Language Acquisition Research and the Classroom*, 91-103. Lexington: D.C. Heath.

Swender, E. & G. Duncan. 1998. ACTFL performance guidelines for K-12 learners. *Foreign Language Annals* 31.4: 479-91.

5 재외동포 한국어 교육의 현황과 미래*

1. 서론

세계 150여 개국에 거주하는 600만명의 재외동포는, 7천만 남북한 인구의 근 9%에 해당한다. 한국동포가 많은 나라는 미국 212만, 중국 189만, 일본 64만, 구소련연방인 독립국가연합 52만, 캐나다 14만, 중남미 11만, 유럽 7.3만, 호주-뉴질랜드 6.5만 등이다.[1] 이들 동포는 남북한의 한국인과 더불어 세계 한민족 공동체의 번영과 발전에 크게 기여하고 있다. 한국어는 한민족의 사고와 생활의 근원이며 한국 문화의 거울이다. 따라서 한국어는 한민족 정체성의 본질이며 세계 한민족을 결속시키는 원동력이다. 실로 한국어는 재외동포에게는 가장 소중한 민족문화의 유산인 것이다.

더욱이, 한국어는 한국의 세계화 추진의 수단이자 목적의 하나이다. 미국을 포함한 외국의 입장에서 보면, 한국어는 한국인들과의 정치적, 사회적, 경제적, 문화적, 군사적, 학문적 유대와 교류의 윤활유이자 촉매제, 촉진제이고 한국, 한국인, 한국 문화의 이해와 연구의 필수적인 도구이기도 하다. 그러므로 재외 동포와 외국인을 위한 한국어 교육은 조금도 방심해서는 안 될 중대한 과제이다. 특히 동포의 경우, 한국어 습득 문제는 해외 동포 문제의 가장 중요하고 시급한 근본 문제이다. 여기서 우리 해외 한국어 교육자들의 사명이 무엇인지 실감하게 된다.

그러면, 한민족의 상징인 한국어에 대한 재외동포들의 교육은 어떤 실태인가? 그리고 동포 자녀의 한국어 교육 발전을 위한 우리의 미래의 과제 즉 한국어 교육의 극대화 방안은 무엇인가? 이 두가지 극히 방대하고 극히 중요한 질문에 대한 대답을 부분적으로나마 시도해 보는 것이 오늘 본인에게 주어진 과제이다.

2. 재외동포의 한국어 교육 개관

과거 20여 년 동안 세계 여러 나라의 한국어 교육은 괄목할만한 속도로 양적 성장을

---

* 미주한국학교연합회 제5차 한국어교사 학술대회(Los Angeles, August 28, 2004) 주제강의논문 (Proceedings, pp. 10-22).

1 박영순(2001: 229-30); 박갑수(2003: 24) 등의 통계 참조.

거듭해 왔다. 한국어 교육의 이러한 급진적 발전을 가능하게 했던 것은 물론 많은 인적, 물적 요소의 복합적인 상승 작용 때문이다. 해외 한국 동포의 급진적 증가, 한국의 경제 사회 문화의 눈부신 발전, 한국 위정자와 행정가들의 한국어 교육의 중요성 인식과 적극적인 태도, 해외 동포와 국내외 교육자들의 높은 교육열, 한국어 교육 학자들의 지대한 관심과 연구와 실천, 한국 정부와 지원기관들의 지원, 21세기의 아시아 시대를 맞아 세계 여러 선진국들의 국제경쟁력 증진을 위한 한국어 교육 장려 등이 그것이다. 언어학적으로 볼 때, 한국어는 세계의 6,000여 언어 중 사용 인구 수로 보아 12위 내외의 위치를 차지하는 세계 유수의 언어이고 언어의 형태적 구조적 사회언어적 특징과 문자적 특징 때문에 언어학적 각광을 받고 있기도 하다.

재외동포의 한국어 교육은 현지 국가의 언어 정책이나 정치, 경제, 사회 상황 등 여러 가지 요인에 따라 다르다. 그러나 동포들이 민족어로서 한국어를 배운다는 점에서는 같다. 우선 재외동포의 한국어 배움터로는 주로 다음과 같다. 통계 숫자는 출처마다 조금씩 다르기 때문에 평균치 또는 근사치를 사용했다. 출처로는 박영순(2001), 한국 국제교류재단(2002), 박갑수(2003), 황유복(2003); 김준시(2003) 등을 참고로 했다.

첫째, 동포 가정 특히 부모와 조부모가 가장 중요한 일차적인 배움터이다. 세계에 산재하는 600만 동포는, 중국, 일본, 독립국가연합 등의 경우이외에는, 대다수가 비교적 최근에 이민한 1세이거나 어려서 부모를 따라 이민한 1.5세이다. 어려서부터 가정에서 한국어로 생활할 때, 가장 자연스러운 한국어와 한국문화를 손쉽게 익히게 된다.

둘째, 학생 또는 성인을 대상으로 영리를 목적으로 하는 각종 한국어 사설 강습소나 지방 정부기관 등에서 실시하는 한국어 성인 교육반 등이 있다. 학생들이 일반 정규 학교에 한국어 반이 없을 경우에 이용하거나 일반 대중들이 흔히 수강한다.

셋째, 소규모이기는 하지만, 한국정부에서 재외동포의 교육을 위해 외국에 설립한 전일제 정규 학교 즉 한국학교가 있다. 일본 4, 중국 3, 사우디 3, 미국 2, 대만 2, 러시아 1 등 총 16개 국에 26개 교이고 학생은 약 6,000명, 교원은 약 750명이다.

넷째, 역시 소수이기는 하지만, 한국정부에서 파견되어 나가서 현지의 한국어 교육을 지원해 주는 한국어교육원이 있다. 일본 14, 미국 6, 러시아 3, 독일 1, 영국 1 등 총 13개국, 34개 교이고 총 파견 교원은 45명이다.

다섯째, 주로 종교단체나 동포단체와 관계되어 있는 소위 주말 한글학교다. 미국 1,027, 카자흐스탄 173, 우즈베키스탄 123, 일본 117, 러시아 113, 캐나다 86, 호주 39, 독일 36, 키르키즈스탄 36, 브라질 34, 중국 16, 영국 16, 우크라이나 13 등 총 94개 국에 1,810개 교이고 학생 총수는 약 106,000명이다.

여섯째, 중국과 일본 등의 경우, 수많은 각급 정규 민족학교가 있는데 여기서는 한국어와 거주국 언어로 강의한다. 중국의 경우, 중국 정부에서 규정하는 교과 과정과 교재를 사용하고 정규 자격을 가진 교사가 교육을 담당한다. 초등학교에서는 주로 민족어 교육을 시키고 중등학교에서는 한어 교육을 강조함으로써 이중언어 교육을 실시하고 있다. 1997년도 통계에 의하면, 중국의 정규 조선족 초등학교는 984개(학생 156,864명; 교원

16,078명), 중등학교는 211개(학생 88,304명; 교원 9,734명)이다.

일본의 경우, 북한과 관련된 총련계 학교는 초등학교 80, 중학교 57, 고등학교 12이고, 남한과 관련된 민단계 학교는 초등학교 3, 중학교 4, 고등학교 4(그리고 상술한 한글학교 117)이다.

일곱째, 거주국의 정규 초, 중, 고교에 외국어로서의 한국어 과목이 설치되어 있는 경우이다. 예를 들면, 미국에는 한국어를 개설하고 있는 정규 초등학교는 극소수이지만, 약 50개의 중고교에서 한국어를 강의하는 것으로 알려져 있다. 국제교류재단(2002)에 의하면, 2002년도 일본에서 한국어 교육을 실시하고 있는 정규 고등학교는 180개이고, 호주의 경우는 26개의 초등학교와 37개의 중고등학교에서 한국어를 강의하고 있는데 초, 중, 고의 학생 총수는 2,000명이상이다. 독립국가 연합에도 한국인이 많이 사는 지역 10개 정규 학교에서 한국어 교육을 실시하고 있다.

여덟째, 1992년부터 LA에서 실시해 온 조기 한-영 양방향 내용중심 집중교육 과정이다(S.O. Sohn, et al. 1999; Merrill 2000). 현재 6개 초, 중학교에서 모든 학과목을 한-영 두 언어로 실시하는 이중언어 교육 프로그램이다. 뉴욕 몇몇 고등학교에서 실시하는 이중언어 교육도 이런 형태의 교육 프로그램이라 할 수 있다(Kwon 1999; Yow 2001 참조).

아홉째, 많은 나라에 대학 수준에서 외국어로서의 한국어교육 과정이 있다. 한국학의 일부로 한국어를 강의하는 곳도 있고 한국어만을 강의하는 곳도 있는데 어느 대학에서나 우리 동포 학생과 외국 학생들이 공히 수강한다. 미국의 경우를 보면, 현재 미국 전역에 산재한 132개 대학에 크고 작은 한국어 프로그램이 있다. 학교에 따라 다르지만 평균해서 한국어 수강 학생의 80% 정도는 동포 학생이고 20% 정도는 비동포 학생으로 추산된다. 그리고 몬트레이의 국방 외국어대학에서는 매번 600명가량의 군인에게 200명가량의 한국인 교수가 한국어 강의를 집중적으로 실시하고 있는데 학생 대다수가 비동포이나 소수의 동포 군인도 있다. 미국의 대학 전체로 보면, 매학기 총 6,000명가량이 한국어를 수강한다.

일본에는 한국어과가 있는 대학은 동경외대, 오사카외대, 규슈대학, 텐리대학 등 7개교이나, 과는 없지만 한국어 강좌를 개설하고 있는 대학은 250개 정도로 알려져 있고 매학기 25,000명의 대학생이 한국어를 수강하고 있다고 한다. 중국은 1992년의 한중 수교 이전에는 연변대학, 북경대학 등 5개 대학에만 한국어과가 있었으나 수교 이후 팽창 일로로 현재는 약 35개 대학에 한국어과가 생기고 수십개의 연구소가 설치되어 있다(국제교류재단 2002). 과는 없지만 한국어 강좌를 개설하고 있는 대학도 상당히 많다.

대학에 한국어과목이 있는 그외의 나라는 러시아(20여 교), 몽골(8교), 호주(7교), 영국(5교), 캐나다(5교), 프랑스(4교), 독일(4교), 뉴질랜드(4교), 카자흐스탄-우즈벡(4교), 대만(4교), 말레이시아(4교), 인도네시아(4교), 인도(3교), 태국(3교), 필리핀(2교), 아르헨티나(2교), 이탈리아(1교), 브라질(1교), 이스라엘(1교), 터키(1교), 화란(1교), 베트남 (1교), 포르투갈(1교), 체코(1교), 헝가리(1교), 불가리아(1교), 덴마크(1교), 스웨덴(1교), 핀란드(1교) 등을 들 수 있다.

열째, 한국에서의 현지 교육이다. 재외동포 초, 중, 고생이 단기, 중기, 장기로 한국에 가서 국제교육진흥원 등에 다니면서 한국어를 배운다. 각국에서 온 많은 대학생들은 서울대, 연세대, 고려대, 이화대, 서강대, 경희대, 한양대, 선문대 등 15여 개 한국 대학에 있는 한국어 연수 프로그램에서 학습한다.[2]

재외동포는 이상과 같이 동포 가정과 주재국의 각종, 각급 교육 기관과 한국의 교육 기관에서 한국어를 습득하고 있는데, 대학의 경우에는 중국의 연변대학 같은 민족대학이 있기는 하지만, 대체로 어느 나라에서나 외국어로서의 한국어 교육을 실시하고 있다. 이에 반하여, 초, 중, 고학생 한국어 교육은 동포의 주재국에 따라 교육제도, 교과과정, 교재, 교육 방식 등이 상당히 다르다. 예컨대 미국 등 많은 나라에서는 한글학교가 이들 학생들의 교육을 가장 많이 담당하고 중국에서는 공립 민족학교에서 전담하다시피 하며 일본에서는 민족 학교인 각종 학교와 한글학교에서 담당하고, 호주 등지에서는 한글학교에서 민족어로서, 그리고 정규 학교에서는 외국어로서 학습한다.

3. 지역별 한국어 교육의 실정

정규 고등교육 기관인 대학의 경우에도 여러 가지 외적 내적 상황에 따라 한국어 교육을 성공적으로 수행하는 학교가 있는가 하면 크고 작은 문제와 애로점에 시달리는 학교도 있다. 그러나 여기서는 동포 교육의 기반이 되는 초등교육, 중등교육만을 중심으로 미국, 중국, 일본, 독립국가연합, 유럽 등의 경우를 살펴본다.

3.1 재미동포 한국어 교육

자유의 나라 미국은, 주지하는 바와 같이, 민족의 주체성이 법으로 보장받는 다문화 사회가 확립되었고 이로 인하여 소수 민족의 언어가 존중받고 있다.[3] 그리고 미국 정부에서는 국민의 외국어 능력은 국가 경쟁력 그 자체이며 국가 자원이고 자산이라는 인식하에 국가 정책 으로 외국어 교육을 강력히 추진하고 있다. 이러한 정부 정책은 1996년 정부와 미국외국어교육협회(American Council of Teaching Foreign Languages, ACTFL)가 제정, 공표하고 주정부를 통하여 현재 추진 중인 "21세기를 대비한 초중고생의 외국어 습득의 기준(Standards for Foreign Language Learning: Preparing for the 21st Century: K－12)"에 잘 반영되어 있다(Standards 1996). 이 기준의 기본원리(Philosphy)는 세 가지를 규정하고 있는바, 첫째는 모든 미국의 초, 중, 고 학생은 영어 외에 최소한 하나의 외국어에 능통할 것, 둘째는 각급 학교는 모든 학생이 외국어와 외국 문화를 습득하도록 하

2 한국 학생들이 영어나 중국어나 일어 등을 배우기 위해 해외 연수를 하듯이, 재외 동포와 외국 학생들은 한국어를 배우기 위하여 한국에 간다.

3 1964년에는 인권법이 제정되고 1968년에는 이중언어 교육법이, 1974년 에는 교육기회 균등법이 제정된 결과이다.

는 교과 과정을 마련할 것, 셋째는 비영어권에서 온 학생들은 자기 모국어 능력을 개발할 수 있는 기회가 주어져야 한다는 것이 그것이다.

한편, 동포 이세의 한국어, 한국 문화 교육을 위해서, 미국의 여러 한인 종교단체, 사회단체가 여러 가지 노력을 아끼지 않고 있으며, 한국 정부나 학술 지원 기관 등도 지원을 위해 노력하고 있다. 또한 미국의 한글학교를 발전시키려는 일념으로 두 거대한 연합인 미주 한국학교 연합회와 전국 한인학교 협의회가 교재 개발, 학술 대회, 교사 연수 등 다양한 활동과 지도력을 발휘하고 있는 것은 우리가 잘 아는 사실이다. 미국의 한글학교 교육과 운영에 대해서는 그동안 여러 논문에서 이미 발표하였기 때문에 여기서는 생략한다 (손호민 1997, 2000, 2001 등 참조).

각계 각층의 많은 노력에도 불구하고 수업 시간의 제한, 교사의 훈련 부족, 교사의 대우 문제, 학생과 학부모의 한국어 교육에 대한 열의 부족, 교재의 다양성 미비, 시청각 교재의 부족 등 아직 대체로 교육 환경이 열악함을 면치 못하다는 것이 많은 학교 관계자들의 공통된 의견이다. 그리고 연방정부나 주정부나 외국어 교육협회 등은 정규 초, 중, 고교만 관여하고 한글학교는 돌보지 않는 점, 한국어를 외국어로 채택한 정규 초등학교가 없다는 점, 소수의 중고등학교만이 한국어를 가르치고 있다는 점 등도 한국어 교육의 열악성을 드러내고 있다. 참고로 하와이 한글학교들의 실정을 알아보기 위하여 이달 초 미국 한글학교의 효시인 하와이 한인사회학교 김수아 교감(하와이대학교 캄피올라니 대학 한국어 조교수)과 대담한 바 있다. 그 결과, 다음과 같은 교무상, 운영상의 미비점 내지 문제점이 지적되었다.

(1) 보다 더 체계적이고 효율적인 교과 과정이 요구됨.
(2) 교과서가 질적으로나 양적으로 만족스럽지 못함.
(3) 많은 한글학교가 교회에 소속해 있고 운영 체계가 교회 관계자들로 구성되기 때문에 학교 운영이 부득이 교회의 이익에 맞아야 할뿐더러 비전문적인 의견에 좌우되는 경향이 있음. 예컨대, 한국말을 하는 사람이면 누구나 가르칠 수 있다는 인식이 팽배함.
(4) 시설이 미비하고 교육 환경이 만족스럽지 못함(예: 교실에 에어콘이 없음).
(5) 학부모들의 한글 교육의 중요성에 대한 인식 부족.
(6) 한국 정부의 체계적인 재정적 원조가 없고 매해의 행사로 그치고 있음.
(7) 문화를 가르칠 수 있는 비디오 등의 자료 부족. 문화 공보부처 등에서 만든 홍보용으로는 실효가 없음.
(8) 한글 학교의 난립과 협의회의가 한국어 교육의 발전에 별로 기여하지 못하고 있음.
(9) 한글 학교의 재정 문제 – 교사들에게 자원 봉사를 요구하여, 일에 대한 정당한 보수를 줄 수가 없으므로, 교과서, 배치 고사, 확습 활동 자료의 개발 등 교육에 직접적인 영향을 미치는 일련의 노력을 기울일 수가 없음. 따라서 학교가 세워진 33년 전이나 지금이나 크게 달라진 것이 없음.

(10) 비전문성인 교사들이기 때문에 수업 운영이 힘듦. 학생과 교사가 함께 고전하고 있음.
(11) 학교에 여러 가지 규칙이 있지만 현실적으로 시행하기 힘든 경우가 많음.

한국어 교육에 대해 지식과 경험이 많은 실무자의 지적인 만큼 위의 여러 가지 문제점을 명심할 필요가 있다. 학교에 따라 천차만별이겠지만, 많은 학교는 유사한 문제를 안고 있다고 생각된다.

3.2 중국동포의 한국어 교육

중국의 한국동포는 재외동포 중 가장 모범적인 민족교육 학습자로 여겨져 왔다. 56개 민족으로 구성된 중국은, 소수민족 우대, 자치지방 인정, 민족어 중시 등 정책을 헌법으로 규정하여, 이런 일련의 정책이 재중동포의 한국어 보존에 크게 기여하였다. 조선족 학교는 중국의 정규 학교이므로 시설, 교과 과정, 교재, 교사 자격 등에 있어서는 특별히 문제되는 바가 없다. 교사의 경우도, 중등학교 교사는 연변대학에서 양성되고 소학교 교사는 연변, 요녕성 등의 조선족 사범학교에서 양성된다(오상순 1998).

그러나 1992년 한중 수교와 중국의 개혁, 개방으로 조선족 농민들의 도시 진출과 한국 진출이 극심해졌고 그 직접적인 결과는 조선족 마을의 공동화 현상이다(황규복 2003: 84). 민족교육의 현장이었던 조선 족 마을들이 와해되면서 가장 직접적인 영향을 받고 있는 것이 바로 민족교육이다. 인구 분산으로 중국에 동화되는 속도가 빨라지고, 유능한 교사가 점점 유실되고 민족어를 상실한 학생 수가 증가하여 수십 년간 안정되었던 초, 중등학교들이 심각한 타격을 받고 있다. 연변자치주의 경우, 조선족 초등학교는 1985년까지만 해도 419교였는데 1995년에는 177교로 줄었고 조선족 중학교도 118교에서 49교로 줄어 들었다. 이런 상황은 계속되고 있으며 조선족 산재 지역의 상황은 그보다 더 심각하다.

3.3 독립국가연합 동포의 한국어 교육

구 소련의 민족정책은 "러시아화"의 추진이었기 때문에 재소 고려인의 대부분은 민족어인 한국어를 상실하였으나 1986년 페레스트로이카 이후 소련이 해체되고 독립국가연합이 탄생되어 민족어 교육도 부활되기 시작했다. 2002년 현재 이들 독립국가들에는 한국정부 파견의 한국교육원이 7개소(교사 84명; 학생 3,518명), 한글학교 총 480개 교(교사 706명; 학생 21,445명)가 있다(김중섭 외 2001). 교재는 한국 국제교육진흥원의 "한국어", 연세대 교재, 자체 개발 교과서 등을 사용하고 있다. 러시아 한국어교육자 협의회 회장 이발렌친(2003)에 의하면 러시아의 한국동포 청년들이 한국어 습득에 관심이 대단하다고 하며, 세인트 피터스버그 국립 151학교 교감 이나탈리아(2003)에 의하면, 그가 사적으로 경영하는 한글학교 즉 "한민족한글학교"에서는 10명의 무보수 교사가 60명(초, 중, 고 12명, 성인 46명)의 학생을 초급, 중급, 고급으로 나누어 매일 저녁과 토요일과 일요일에 걸쳐 지도한다고 한다. 교과 과정에는 한국어 구조, 한국어 연습, 한자, 한국역사, 고려인 역사, 기타 한국 문화, 풍물, 무용, 민요 등이 포함된다. 이나탈리아가 제시한 애로점은 열악한 교실 상태, 재정적인 어려움, 한국어 전문가의 부재, 참고도서 부족 등이다. 박갑수(2003: 39)도 독립국가연합 전체에서 교사의 자질과 부족한 교사가 문제가 되고 있다고 하며 능력 있는 교사가 극소수이고 대부분의 교사가 보조교사 수준에 불과하다고 한다.

러시아에는 정규 중등학교 열 군데에서 한국어와 한국문화 과목을 개설하고 있다. 대표적인 학교는 모스크바 제1086 한민족학교인데, 여기에는 한국어교사가 9명, 학생이 약 800명인데 이들 학생의 45%가 한국동포라고 한다. 이 학교는 기숙학교의 방식으로 운영하여 한국어 교육을 강화하고 친교를 통해 학습 효과를 올리도록 하고 있다. 이들 학교의 교재는 국제교육진흥원의 "한국어"(전4권), 한국의 초등학교 "국어" 등을 사용하고 있고 교사는 주로 고려인 3, 4세인데 이들의 모국어 수준은 극히 낮은 것으로 알려져 있다(박갑수 2003: 40).

3.4 재일동포의 한국어 교육

현재, 재일동포 중 한국 국적을 가진 동포와 북한 국적을 가진 동포의 비율은 4 : 1이라고 한다. 일본의 재일동포에 대한 정책은 동화 정책이고 교육도 마찬가지다. 그결과 대부분 동포 자녀(86%)가 일본 학교로 진학하여 동화 교육을 받고 있으며 일부는 귀화, 결혼 등에 의해 점점 일본에 동화되어 가고 있다. 한편 기술한 바와 같이, 재일동포의 꾸준한 민족교육 운동으로 160개가량의 민족학교와 120개가량의 한글학교가 운영되고 있다. 특히, 민족학교들은 각종학교라는 법적 인가를 받게 되었는데, 한-일 이중언어로 정규 학과목 교육을 실시하고 한국어 교육에 특히 많은 시간을 배정하고 있다. 그리고 1970년 이래 오사카, 교토 등 한국인이 많이 살고 있는 지역의 정규 공립학교인 초, 중, 고교에 "민족학급"이라는 것이 과외 시간으로 설치되어 "한국어, 한국 역사, 한국 문학, 한국 문화"를 가르치고 있다. 일본의 한국 및 한국어에 대한 태도가 점차 긍정적이고 관심이 커짐에 따라 2002년부터는 한국어가 영어, 독일어, 프랑스어, 중국어에 이어, 일본의 대학입학 시험에 외국어 과목으로 신설되어 앞으로 한국어 교육에 더욱 긍정적 영향을 미칠 것으로 기대된다(국제교류재단 2002).

재일동포의 교육에서도 문제가 되는 것은 교재와 교사이다. 민단계 학교에서는 본국 교과서와 국제교육진흥원에서 발행한 일본지역 재외국민용 "한국어"를 사용한다. 본국 교과서는 일시 체류인에게 국내 연계 교육을 위해서는 필요하나 영주자에게는 어울리지 않는다. 일본 현실에 맞는 교재를 개발해야 한다. 그리고 교사는 모국어와 일본어를 능숙하게 구사할 수 있는 자격증 소지자를 구하기가 용이하지 않다. 특히 민족학교의 경우 이 두 문제가 심각하다. 1999년부터는 일본 당국은 일본 국적이 없는 사람도 국가 교사 자격 시험을 볼 수 있게 하였다.

총련계 학교는 민단계와 달리 한국어 교육을 국어교육으로 실시하고 있다. 또한 민단계가 한국의 언어 규범을 따르는데 반하여, 총련계는 북한의 언어 규범을 따르고 있다. 따라서 일본에서는 두 가지 다른 한국어 능력 시험을 실시하고 있다.

3.5 재유럽동포 교육 현황

유럽 22개국에 총 85개의 한글학교, 교원은 총 588명, 학생은 일시거주자 1,867명, 영주권자 2,381명이다(김준시 2003). 이중 한글학교가 비교적 많은 나라는 독일이 36개 교, 영국이 16개 교, 프랑스가 6개 교이다. 교실은, 일반 정규 학교를 주말만 임대해서 쓰는 경우가 많고 재정은 수업료, 정부 지원금, 찬조금 등으로 이루어지고 수업료는 15-50 유로, 교사 봉급은 150-250유로, 정부 지원금은 벨린의 경우 1,100유로이다. 교재는 한국의 검정교과서, 국제교육진흥원의 "한국어", 한국 대학의 외국인을 위한 한국어 교재들을 각 학교 특성에 맞게 교사들이 재구성하여 사용한다. 교사는 주로 유학생이다.

애로사항은 (1) 학교의 산재로 인한 적은 수의 학생으로 운영이 어렵고; (2) 학생들의 한국어 실력이 천차만별이고, 연령(학년) 차이도 다양하기 때문에 제한된 예산 내에서 반 편성이 극히 어렵고; (3) 학부모들의 열의와 적극성이 부족하며; (4) 학생 자신들이 한국어 습득의 필요성을 느끼지 못하고; (5) 다수의 교사가 전문성 부족으로 학부모와 학생의 욕구를 충족시켜 주지 못하며; (6) 필요한 교재가 부족하고 한국에서 공급받는 교재나 기타 현존하는 교재는 현지 실정에 맞지 않은 경우가 많아 보충교재 내지 기존교재의 재편집이 불가피하며; (7) 학교의 각종 문화 행사가 예산 부족으로 무산된다는 것등이다(김준시 2003 참조).

4. 재외동포 한국어 교육의 미래

재외동포의 한국어 교육의 미래는, 나라에 따라 다소 기복은 있지만, 대체로 밝다고 말할 수 있다. 한국어 교육을 촉진시켜 온 여러 여건 즉 재외동포 인구의 증가, 한국의 국력 신장, 재외동포의 민족교육에 대한 열의, 강대국들의 외국어 정책, 한국의 경제적, 문화적, 전략적 중요성, 한국정부와 지원기관의 적극적 지원 등이 존속 내지 강화될 것으로 예상되기 때문이다. 특히 재외동포 인구의 계속적인 증가와 세계 10위권에 다가선 한국의 경제 발전과 각종 문화적 가시화는 한국어의 위상을 계속 높여 주게 되고 동포 학부모와 학생들은 한국어 습득의 실리적인 필요성을 점차 강하게 느끼게 될 것이다.

더욱이 소수민족의 언어에 대한 세계인의 태도가 급속히 달라져 가고 있다. 종전에는 소수민족의 언어는 사회의 애물단지처럼 여겨졌던 것이, 세계가 좁어지고 국제경쟁이 치열해지고 소수민족의 인권이 존중되면서, 이제는 개인의 특권이고 재산이요, 중요한 국가적, 교육적 자원이라는 인식이 확산되고 있다. 미국과 같은 강대국이 막대한 예산을 들여 외국어 교육을 실시하고 있는데 국민의 이중언어의 사용이 그만큼 중요하고 절실하기 때문이다(손호민 2001참조).

이러한 여러 여건 속에서 재외동포 한국어 교육은 세계 도처에서 그동안 이모저모로 많은 발전을 이룩하였다. 그러나 이미 보았듯이 아직도 여러 심각한 문제를 안고 있다. 학부모와 학생들의 한국어 교육에 대한 인식과 열의 부족, 학습 자료와 교육 자료의 부족 또는 미비, 특히 다매체 자료의 결여, 교사의 자질 부족, 교사의 대우 문제, 시설 미비, 자금 부족 등이 그것이다. 이런 여러 문제를 해결하기 위하여 우리 재외동포와 한국어 교육자, 한국의 정책 결정자, 지원기관들이 합심, 협조해서 거족적으로 수행해야 할 과제가 무한히 많다.

미래를 향한 재외동포의 한국어 교육의 목표는 모든 제외동포의 자녀를 한국어와 한국문화 그리고 거주국 언어와 문화에 능통한 이중 언어인, 이중 문화인으로 길러내는 것이다. 즉 전자는 한국 민족으로서, 그리고 후자는 거주국 시민으로서 21세기에 당연히 갖추어야 할 국제인의 자격 요건인 것이다. 그러기 위해서는 언어습득 능력이 가장 뛰어난 어린 시절부터 한국어를 쉽고 자연스럽게 습득하도록 모든 조치를 취해야 한다. 동포 자녀의 한국어 습득이야 말로 소홀히하거나 주저하거나 늦추어서는 안 되는 민족적 과업이다.

한국어 교육의 성공은 학습 동기가 강한 학습자와 잘 개발된 교과 과정과 그에 따른 효과적인 교육 자료와 유능한 교사가 일체가 되어 효율적으로 작용할 때 이루어짐은 물론이다.[4] 그런데 지역, 학교, 개인 등에 따라 다소 차이는 있지만, 교과 과정, 학습자, 교재, 교사 이 모든 분야에서 아직 여러모로 미비한 점이 들어나 있다. 우리의 과제는 이러한 문제의 해결책을 강구하고 실천에 옮기는 일이다. 이는 언어권에 따라 나라에 따라 지역이나 학교에 따라 구체적인 해결책이 다소 다르겠지만 대체적으로 다음과 같은 방향으로 문제를 해결했으면 한다.

4.1 학습동기 유발 문제

동포 학부모들과 한글학교 학생들의 한국어 학습 동기가 대체로 부족하다는 것은 여러 현지 교사들과 교육자들이 지적하는 바이다. 우선 학부모들의 동기 부족은 자녀들의 한국어 능력의 중요성을 과소평가하는 데서 나온다. 한국어 습득이 자녀들의 거주국 언어의 발달에나 학업에 지장을 초래할까 염려하는 학부모가 많다. 그러나 이러한 염려가 쓸데없는 기우에 지나지 않고, 오히려 이중언어 능력이 자녀 교육과 장래 출세에 얼마나

4 물론 교재나 교사 없이도 한국어를 배울 수는 있다. 한국에서 장기간 생활할 경우, 한국인의 직장에 근무할 경우, 해외 1세의 한국 부모에게서 배울 경우 등이 그것이다. 그러나 그렇게 배울 수 있는 사람에게조차도 교재와 교사는 정확하고 보다 높은 수준의 언어 구사를 가능하게 한다. 교재 없이 배운 외국어는 보통 일상 생활 언어 수준(survival level)에 머므르게 되기 때문이다.

강한 장점이 되는 가를 다음 여러 가지 점을 들어 확실하게 인식시켜야 한다. 교회, 강연, 워크숍, 매스컴 등을 이용하여 학부모들에게 널리 주지시켜야 할 것이다.

(1) **한국어 습득은 가족의 화합에 기여하고 한국인 사회에 참여하게 한다.** 자녀가 한국어를 배움으로서 동시에 한국 문화도 익히게 되고, 이민 1세 부모, 조부모, 친지, 기타 한국인들과 의사소통이 가능하게 되어 부드러운 인간 관계가 형성되고, 한국인 사회에서 소외되지 않는다. 한국 신문, 드라마, 영화, 뉴스 등을 볼 수 있어서 인생이 그만큼 풍부해지고 즐거워진다.

(2) **정체성(ethnic identity) 갈등의 문제가 해결된다.** 모든 동포는 필연적으로 거주국 시민인 동시에 한국 민족이다. 이러한 시민-민족의 이중적 정체성이 어려서부터 확고히 인식되어야만 정체성 갈등이 일어나지 않는다. 이러한 이중적 정체성은 물론 어려서부터 한국어 습득을 통하여 가장 자연스럽게 잘 인식되고 유지된다. 왜냐하면 언어란 문화의 거울이고 사고와 생활의 수단이므로 한편으로는 거주국언어를 사용하여 거주국 시민의 정체성을 유지하고 다른 한편으로는 한국어를 사용하여 한국민족의 정체성을 확보할 수 있기 때문이다.

(3) **동포 자녀의 한국어 능력은 21세기 국제인으로서의 필수 자질이다.** 세계는 이미 지구촌이 되어, 강한 나라이건 약한 나라이건 상호 의존 없이는 존속할 수 없다. 각국의 정치, 경제, 사회, 문화, 교역의 질서는 상호 유대의 방향으로 급격히 변화 발전하고 있고 나라마다 자국의 경쟁력을 강화시키려고 온갖 노력을 다하고 있다. 국가 간의 교류가 일일 생활권화되고 인터넷 전자메일을 통한 시간 공간을 초월한 국제 교신이 일과가 되었다. 지금은 단일 언어인이 할 수 있는 기능은 제한되어 있다. 이러한 현대의 필수적 생존 조건은 외국어 사용이다. 미국과 같은 선진국을 위시한 세계 각국은 자국의 경쟁력을 높이고 국가 안보 유지를 위하여 이해관계가 있는 상대국의 언어를 능숙하게 구사하는 인적 자원을 최대한 확보하려고 한다. 한국어는 미국, 일본, 중국, 호주 등을 위시한 세계 주요국가에서 가장 배우고 싶어하는 언어의 하나 이다. 한국어에 능통하면 경제강국으로 급부상하는 한국의 모든 분야를 실제적으로나 학문적으로 속속들이 파고들어 자국의 경쟁력을 크게 강화시키게 되기 때문이다.

(4) **이중언어인이 단일 언어인보다 지능적으로나 학술적으로 더 우수하다.** 이것은 그동안 많은 실험과 연구에서 밝혀진 사실이다. 제2언어의 습득은 습득자의 분석적인 능력을 길러 주는 것이므로 한 언어만 아는 아동보다 이중언어 사용 아동이 언어간의 차이를 더 잘 인식하고 각 언어의 문법적 특성에 잘 주목하여 모국어와 외국어를 더 정확히 배운다. 그뿐만 아니라, 언어 조작에 민감하여 훨씬 더 성공적인 의사소통을 한다. 또한 많은 최근 연구에 의하면 이중언어 화자가 인지능력적인 면에서 더 발달하여 더 다양하고, 유동적이고 창의적인 사고 능력을 가지며 학업 성적도 일반적으로 더 우월하다는 것이다(S.O. Sohn, et al. 1999; 이미선2000; 박영순 2001: 333-43 참조).

(5) **외국어 교육은 학생이 어릴 때 배울 수록 더 효과적이다.** 가장 자연스럽고 신속한

언어습득이 두 살부터 열두 살 사이에 이루어진다. 한국어는 언어구조상, 어휘상, 존대법 등 사회언어적 특성상 성인 특히 서양인에게는 가장 어려운 언어이다. 한국어의 조기 교육은 성인이 겪는 어려움이 전혀 없이 모국어나 마찬가지로 자연스럽고 쉽게 배울 수 있다. 언어는 열두 살 이후에는 비례적으로 배우기 힘들어진다. 어려서부터 배우기 때문에 궁극적으로 높은 수준의 언어 능력을 성취하는 데 크게 도움이 된다. 가정과 학교에서 자연스럽게 그리고 아주 빠르고 쉽게 배울 수 있는 조기 한국어 교육의 시기를 놓친 뒤에 부모와 자녀가 크게 후회하는 예를 흔히 본다. 아이들의 한시적 천부의 재능을 최대한 활용해야 한다는 것이다.

(6) **원칙상, 동포만이 완전한 한국어를 배울 수 있다.** 가정에서 어려서부터 이중언어를 구사하면서 자라고 한글학교를 다닐 수 있기 때문이다. 이들이야말로 거주국이 갈구하는 완벽한 이중언어 국민이 될 수 있고 모든 국제 관계에서 견인차 노릇을 할 필요불가결한 인재들이며 모든 분야에서 거주국과 한국을 직접적으로 연결시키는 교량적 역할을 하는 주역들이다. 한국어는 워낙 어려운 말이므로 비한국계가 성인으로 배워서 이중언어인이 된다는 것은 극히 어려운 일이다.

(7) **취업 영역, 성공 범위를 넓힌다.** 각종 전문 직종에 많은 한국어 화자가 필요하다. 한국어를 구사하는 전문직 종사자는 한국의 전문직들과의 교제뿐 아니라 한국어만을 사용하는 고객을 자유로 상대할 수 있다. 그리고 한국 신문 방송을 자유로이 읽고 들어서 한국에 대한 중요한 정보와 지식을 신속히 직접 얻을 수 있다. 한국어의 구사 능력은 그만큼 생활 범위, 활동 범위, 취업영역, 성공 범위를 넓혀 준다.

(8) **대학 진학과 학문 연구에 극히 유리하다.** 많은 대학에서 입학 요건으로 2년 이상의 외국어 학습을 요구하고 있는데 어려서 한국말에 접한 아동들은 이것을 손쉽게 충족시킬 수 있다. 또한 미국 대학의 경우 80%가량의 대학에서 졸업 요건으로 1년 또는 2년의 외국어 학습을 하고 있는데 이중언어인은 이것이 면제된다. 또한 미국의 SAT II 한국어 시험이나 일본, 호주, 중국 등의 대학 입시의 한국어 시험에서 좋은 점수를 얻어 우수대학에 입학할 수 있다. 대학에 가서 다양한 고급 한국어 과목을 택할 수 있고 한국어와 한국 문화에 관계되는 분야에서 석사 내지 박사학위를 큰 어려움 없이 취득할 수도 있다.

그러므로 학부모는 집에서 의도적으로 한국어만을 써서 어릴 때부터 동포 자녀에게 귀중한 문화재인 한국어를 전수하고 한글학교와 일반 학교에서 계속 한국어를 배우도록 권장해야 한다. 거주국 언어는 학교와 사회에서 자연스럽게 배우게 되므로 집에서는 의도적으로 한국어만을 써서 아이들이 이중언어인으로 발돋움하게 한다. 입학한 후에도 한국어를 유지하고 발전시키도록 조부모, 친지와 자주 접촉하게 하고, 한국에 있는 친척, 친지를 자주 방문케 하고 한국어를 사용하는 각종 문화 행사와 특별 활동에 참여할 기회를 만들어 주어야 한다. 또한 저녁에 시간을 정해서 규칙적으로 한국어로 된 재미있는 아동문학과 한국의 역사 등 지능 발달과 언어 수준에 맞는 책을 읽어 주거나 보게 하고 비데오를 보여주거나 카세트 테이프를 들려주고 한국어 영화를 보여 한국어 입력을 보충하여야 한다. 자녀는 보통 커가면서 부모에게도 거주국 언어만을 쓰게 되는데 그래도 부모는 계속 한국어만을 써야 한다. 자연스러운 한국어를 계속 듣고 이해한다 는 것은 한국어를 이미 반은 배운 것이 되기 때문이다. 그리고 계속 한국어를 써 주면 한글학교를 포함한 학교 교육에서 한국어를 배우 고자 하는 동기를 가지게 된다. 통계적으로 보아 어려서 한글학교에 다녔던 학생은 대학에 입학해서 다시 한국어를 배우려고 하는 것이 보통이다. 부모로서 자녀에게 한 푼의 비용도 들이지 않고 전수할 수 있는 귀중한 문화유산을 적기에 가장 효과적으로 전수하자는 것이다.

한편, 어린 학생들이 한글학교 등교를 기피하는 경우가 많은데, 그것은 당장 한국어의 필요성을 실감하지 못한 것, 교육 자료가 고루하여 흥미를 주지 못하고, 학습 내용이 실생활과 별로 관계되지 않고 교사들이 언어 문제, 문화 차이, 경험 부족, 교사 훈련 부족 등으로 만족스러운 교실학습 활동을 제시하지 못하는 등 여러 가지 이유 때문이다. 다음 항에서 이러한 학생들의 동기 부여 문제를 포함한 한국어 교육 전반에 걸친 다른 문제들을 극복하기 위한 방안들을 제안해 보고자 한다.

4.2 미래 한국어 교육 향상를 위한 방안

재외동포의 학습동기를 증진시키고 초, 중, 고생의 한국어 교육의 질과 양을 높이기 위하여 교육의 기반 구조를 더욱 공고히 다져야 한다. 이 목적을 위하여 다음 8개 항의 방안을 제의한다(손호민 1999, 2001; 박영순 2001; Hadley 2001 등 참조).

(1) **재외동포의 한국어 교육의 목표를 정체성 확립, 한국어를 통한 의사소통 능력의 배양, 한국 문화의 습득, 비교언어적-비교문화적 접근, 한국인 사회에의 참여에 둔다.** 이것은 미국 정부와 교육계의 "21세기에 대비한 외국어 습득의 기준"에 제시된 학습 목표와도 일부 상응한다. 특히 정체성 확립과 관련하여, 교사는 학생들에게 이중 언어인으로서 그리고 한국인으로서의 자부심을 심어 준다. 거주국이 복수 민족 사회임을 강조하고, 모든 민족과 그들의 문화와 언어는 동등하게 존경받아야 함을 강조한다. 그리고 각자가 자기 민족어를 구사할 줄 모르면 심히 부끄러운 일일 뿐 아니라 장래 처신에 크게 손해를 입는다는 점을 직접 간접으로 인식시켜야 한다. 한국 학생들의 동아리 활동, 한국에 관한 각종 흥미로운 강연 또는 영화, 음악, 체육 등의 행사에 학생들을 참여하도록 장려하고 한국 방문 또는 유학을 장려한다. 교포 학생들이 흔히 한국에서 공부하면서 정체성을 강하게 깨닫고 돌아왔다는 것을 증언한다. 미국의 경우, 과거에는 자기자신을 "American"으로 인식하고 살던 학생도 한국을 다녀온 뒤에는 자신을 "Korean American"으로 재발견하였다고 한다.

(2) **한국어의 교육 방법은 계속 발전하는 일반 외국어 교육 이론과 실제를 활용한다.** 교과 과정의 설계, 실러버스 작성, 교재 개발, 학습 지도, 학습 평가 등 한국어 교육 전반에 걸쳐 현행 대표적인 외국어 습득과 교육의 이론과 방법을 참조하고 적용하여야 한다. 예

컨대 최근 미국에서 외국어 교육방법으로 가장 강조되고 있는 소위 의사소통중심 교육(communicative approach)의 다음과 같은 일련의 원칙을 익혀서 한국어 교육의 여러 분야에 적절히 활용하여야 할 것이다: 학습자 위주의 교육; 개개인의 언어능력에 따른 교육; 실제 상황에 기초한 교육; 자연스러운 실제 언어의 사용; 내용중심의 교육; 과제수행적 교육; 언어능력의 단계별 교육; 정확성 교육: 어휘, 문법, 발음, 사회언어, 화용, 유창성; 언어-문화의 통합 교육; 듣기, 말하기, 읽기, 쓰기의 통합 교육;언어지식 습득과 언어활용의 균형적 교육(Sohn 1995 참조).

(3) **언어권별로 각급 학교간의 상호 교류를 증진시키고 한글학교로부터 대학까지의 교과 과정을 효율적으로 연결(articulation)시킨다.** 현재의 상황은 각급 학교간(예컨대 한글학교 상호간, 초, 중, 고등학교 상호간, 대학 상호간)의 횡적 교류는 학회 등을 통해 극히 제한된 범위에서 이루어지고 있지만, 한글학교, 초, 중, 고등학교, 대학의 한국어 교육은 전혀 종적인 연결고리 없이 독자적으로 실시되고 있다. 교과 과정, 교수 내용, 사용되는 교과서나 기타 보조 교재, 교수법이나 평가 방법 등 전혀 서로가 모르는 실정이다. 각급 학교의 전문가들이 email을 통하거나 한 군데에 모여 의견을 교환하고 공동 연구를 통하여 통합된 한국어 교육 지침서를 제정하기를 바란다. 그러한 지침에 의거하여 각급 학교의 교과 과정 설정, 교재 개발, 또는 현존 교재의 질적 향상, 교수법 개발 등 일련의 새로운 활동이 실시되어야 할 것이다. 이러한 사업에는 전문적인 지도자들이 자발적으로 그리고 헌신적으로 앞장서야 하고, 그에 대한 재정적 지원이 따라야 할 것이다. 한국어 교육이 한글학교, 초, 중, 고등학교, 대학은 물론이고 한국에서의 현지 교육까지 체계적으로 통합되어 연결된다면 학생들이 대학 졸업까지 지금보다도 훨씬 더 높은 수준의 한국어 구사 능력을 성취할 수 있을 것이다. 이미 초, 중, 고등학교에서 하위 수준의 한국어 능력을 체계적 으로 성취하게 된 학생들은 대학에서는 상급반에 배치될 것이기 때문이다. 단계적이어야 할 교육 과정이 지금처럼 단절되어 있으면 언어 습득 과정을 심각하게 약화시키고 말게 된다.[5] 즉 자칫하면 대학에서도 초급이나 중급 수준의 한국어에서 맴돌게 된다.

한국어 교육의 상호 유대의 일환으로 각급 학교의 한국어 교육자들과 학습자들이 전국적으로 교류할 수 있는 정보망의 설치가 필요하다. 모든 유용한 교과 과정, 인력 자원, 교수법, 교육 자료에 대한 정보가 체계적으로 입력되고 광범위하게 활용되어야 한다.

(4) **다양한 학생들의 요구를 충족시킬 수 있는 다양한 교재의 개발이다.** 한국어 교육용 교과서는 대학의 경우에는 비교적 다양하게 잘 개발되어 있다. 대학의 교재와는 달리 아동이나 청소년을 대상으로 한 교재는 국제교육진흥원 교재이외에는 대체로 별로 개발되어 있지 않다. 미국처럼 자체개발의 교재가 있다 해도 다양성이 결핍되어 있다. 기존 한글학교와 중고등학교 한국어 교육 자료를 철저히 검토하여 대폭 수정 보완함과 동시에, 거주국 언어로 된 현지 실정에 맞는 교재가 다양하게 개발되어야 한다. 현재 한글학교의

5 현재 다른 여러 외국어들 측에서는 이러한 articulation작업에 전념하고 있다. 예컨대 일본어 교육자들은 유치원에서 대학까지를 연결시키는 교과 과정 마련에 부심하고 있다.

교육이 훈련을 충분히 받지 못한 교사들이나 유학생들에 의해서 실시되고 있고 또 독학으로 한국어를 배우는 경우도 있기 때문에 훌륭한 교과서와 부교재가 더욱 필요하다. 전통적인 형태의 교과서뿐 아니라 각자의 개별적인 필요를 충족시킬 수 있는 다채로운 학습 교재, 다양한 시청각 교재, 컴퓨터화 된 다매체 교재, 특히 원거리 학습용 자료를 광범하게 개발해야 한다. 학생들이 시간과 장소에 구애받지 않고 아무 때나 어디서나 로그인해서 학습할 수 있기 때문이다. 한국어를 학습할 수 있는 학교가 주위에 없는 경우에는 더욱이 정적인 교과서만에 의존하는 것보다 생동하는 전자 기술매체를 사용한 학습은 학습효과를 대폭 증진시킬 것임은 물론이다. 전자기술 매체를 이용한 원거리학습 자료의 개발은 앞으로의 결정적인 새로운 방향이 될 것이다. 이것은 학습자 중심 교육의 관점에서 볼 때 여러모로 너무도 당연한 방향이고 미국을 위시한 선진국들이 소수민족언어 교육을 위해 활발히 추구하는 대세이기도 하다.

(5) **각급 학교의 교사의 질을 높이기 위하여 체계적인 교사 훈련을 계속하고 교사 자격증 제도를 창설 내지 강화한다.** 교사의 자질이 교육의 성패를 좌우한다는 것은 잘 알려진 사실이다. 그런데 현재 그 많은 한글학교에는 유능한 교사가 부족하다는 말을 자주 듣는다. 교사가 열악한 환경에서 자원봉사로 또는 낮은 대우로 학생을 지도한다는 탓도 있겠지만, 한국어 교육의 경험이나 훈련이 전혀 없이 한국인이라는 이유 하나로 교단에 설 경우, 서틀은 학생 지도 때문에 이런 비난을 면치 못하게 된다. 또 설사 한국에서 많은 교육 경험이 있었다 해도 너무도 다른 생소한 언어권, 문화권에 갑작이 들게 되면 학생 지도에 많은 지장을 초래하고 학생이 수업에 흥미를 잃게 되며 등교를 기피하게 된다.

신규 교사나 예비 교사뿐 아니라 경험 있는 교사도 자주 교사 훈련 워크숍에 참여하여야 한다.[6] 가르칠 언어 내용과 언어구조, 교과과정 작성, 교수법, 평가법 등에 대하여 체계적인 연수가 필요하다. 외국어 교수법에 관한 최근 여러 가지 이론과 응용 방법이 교사 연수를 통하여 일선 교사에게 전수되어야 한다. 한국 또는 거주국 대학 등 교사훈련 전문기관, 학술대회의 교사연수 워크숍, 그리고 각종 미니 발표회와 학회지의 탐독을 통하여 교사와 교수는 꾸준히 지기 발전을 도모해야 한다. 신규 교사는 자격시험을 보아 선발되어야 하고 교사 자격증 제도가 없는 나라에서는 새로이 도입되어야 한다. 또한, 교사는 학생들의 학습 동기를 강화하도록 백방으로 노력해야 한다. 교사가 유념해야 할 점은, 첫째는 학습 활동이 즐겁고 유쾌하고 재미있어야 한다. 둘째는 지능 수준에 맞는 새로운 내용을 어려움 없이 배울 수 있어야 한다. 셋째는 학생이 한국어의 실용성을 강하게 느껴야 한다. 즉 교실 밖에서 부모나 다른 한국인들과 의사소통을 할 수 있고 상급반 학생의 경우는 한국의 인터넷이나 신문이나 텔레비전을 볼 수 있도록 배워야 한다. 넷째는 한국어를 배우는 것이, 기술한 바와 같이, 학생의 현재와 장래에 얼마나 중요한 일인가를 직접 간접으로 인식토록 배워야 한다.

6 중, 고등학교 교사와 대학 강사에 대한 교사 연수는 전 미국 한국어 교육자 협회(American Association of Teachers of Korean)의 연례 학술대회의 일환으로 매년 한국 국제교류재단의 지원하에 실시되고 있다.

(6) **한국어 교육을 거주국의 정규 초, 중, 고등학교 교과 과정으로 추진시킨다.** 중국, 호주, 일본 같은 예외는 있지만 많은 나라에서 한국어는 아직 한국 이민의 언어로만 인식되고 거주국의 정규 학교 교과 과정으로 흡수되지 않고 있다. 미국도 정규 초, 중, 고등학교에는 외국어로서의 한국어 교육이 아직 극히 열악한 실정이다. 미국의 경우를 보면, 재미 일본계 인구가 겨우 80만 정도인데도 수백에 달하는 정규 초, 중, 고등학교에서 광범하게 일본어 교육이 실시되고 있는 점을 감안하면 200만이 넘는 재미 한국계 인구에 비추어 볼 때 초, 중, 고등학교 한국어 교육의 현 실태는 실로 통탄 할 일이다. 한인 인구 4만밖에 안 되는 호주에서는 이미 63개의 초, 중, 고등학교에 한국어 과목이 개설되어 있는 점을 상기할 때 미국의 한국어 교육에는 엄청난 공백이 있음을 알 수 있다. SAT II-Korean이 채택되고 한국어 교사의 자격증 문제가 서서히 해결되고 있기 때문에 초, 중, 고등학교의 한국어 도입 문제는 이제 학부모를 중심으로 한 교민들과 한국어 교육자들의 노력에 달려있다.

(7) **한글학교 교육의 내실을 도모하여 정규 학교의 한국어 교육을 대신케 한다.** 미국을 위시한 많은 나라에서 한국어를 초, 중, 고등 학교에 광범하게 도입한다는 것은 쉬운 일이 아니며 많은 시간과 노력이 소요될 사항이다. 학습 동기 등 여러 가지 이유도 있고 동포 학생이 집결되어 있는 초, 중, 고등학교가 많지 않다는 것도 그 중요한 이유이다. 따라서, 한글학교의 한국어 과목을 정규 교과 과정으로 인정받는 방안이 마련되어야 한다. 일반 초, 중, 고등학교에서 할 수 없는 일을 한글학교에서 대신 해 주기 때문이다. 그러기 위해서는 한글학교의 교육 내용과 시간 수에 있어서, 일반 학교의 교과 과정에 맞도록 개선되어야 하고 (현재 미국에서는, 정규 초등학교는 대체로 주당 3시간이고 중, 고등학교는 5시간임) 교사들의 자격증 제도가 확립되고 대우도 향상되어야 한다. 그렇게 되면 한글학교 교육에 가일층 큰 동기를 부여하게 되고, 한글학교 교육이 다방면으로 강력한 지지를 받게 될 것이다.

(8) **한국 정부, 동포사회, 거주국 정부 등 각계각층의 더 많은 지원이 필요하다**. 한국어 교육 발전을 위해 위에 제시한 여러 제안이 기획되고 실천되려면 광범한 재원이 필요하다. 한국정부, 동포사회, 그리고 거주국 정부의 적극적인 지원이 절실하다. 한국정부의 재외동포의 교육정책은 [1] 한국학교 및 한국교육원의 설치 운영 지원, [2] 한글학교 운영 지원, [3] 민족교육 담당교사 파견, [4] 민족학교 교사의 자질 향상을 위한 연수 실시 및 지원, [5] 민족교육 프로그램 개발 제공, [6] 교과서 및 교재개발, 공급, [7] 재외동포 학생 모국 수학 및 장학사업 등의 지원 등이다(박갑수 2003: 26). 그러나 이미 언급한 바와 같이 많은 경우 현재 한글학교 운영 지원이 대체로 유명무실하고 교재 개발, 교사 연수, 교과 과정 개발 등에 있어서도 현지 교육 전문가의 input이 없기 때문에 현지 실정에 맞지 않은 경우가 많다. 한국어 교육의 중대성을 감안하면 정부의 예산을 대폭 늘려야 할 뿐 아니라, 현지 사정을 고려하고 현지 교육자를 적극 참여시킨 더 집중적이고 체계적 이고 합목적적인 사업을 추진해야 한다.

한편, 동포 자녀의 백년대계의 교육인 만큼 동포사회의 적극적인 후원과 협조가 필요하다. 특히 열악한 한글학교들이 건전하게 자립할 수 있을 때까지 한국정부, 한인사회의 헌신적인 지원이 요구된다. 그리고 거주국 정부는 한글학교를 강건너 불구경하듯 하지 말고 다방면으로 육성, 지원하는 방향으로 나아가야 한다. 한국어 교육의 중요성 때문만이 아니라 정규학교에서 하지 못하는 교육을 대신해 주기 때문이다. 그리고 재외 동포가 한국어를 능숙하게 사용할 수 있다면 그 혜택은 동포 자신들뿐 아니라, 한국과 거주국과 한인사회가 두루 다 같이 받게 되기 때문이다.

참고 문헌: Chapter 5

국제교류재단. 2002.「해외 여러 대학의 인터넷 자료」. 국제교류재단 웹사이트.

김준시. 2003.「재 유럽 동포교육 현황(한글학교)」.『재외동포의 정체성 확립과 교육의 방향』. 2003년 국제학술대회 자료집. 재외동포교육 진흥재단.

김중섭 외. 2001.「러시아 및 중국지역 한국어교육 실태조사와 지원방안 연구」. 교육인적자원부.

박갑수. 2003.「한국어교육의 과제와 개선방향—재외동포교육을 중심 으로」.『재외동포의 정체성 확립과 교육의 방향』. 2003년 국제학술 대회 자료집. 재외동포교육진흥재단.

박영순. 2001.『외국어로서의 한국어 교육론』. 서울. 도서출판 월인.

손호민. 1997.「미국에서의 한국어 연구와 한국어 교육」.『교육한글』 제10호. 한글학회.

손호민. 1999.「미국에서의 한국어 교육 방법」. 서울대학교 국어교육 연구소 주최 제1회 국제한국어교육 학술회의 자료집.

손호민. 2000a.「미국에서의 한국어 교육」. In Lee, D.J. et al. (2000).

손호민. 2000b.「한국어 교재 개발의 현황과 발전 방향의 모색」.『21세기 한국어 교육의 발전 방향과 과제』. 국제한국어교육학회 제10차 국제 학술회의 자료집.

손호민. 2001.「미국에서의 한국어 교육의 역사와 미래 조망」.『외국어 로서의 한국어교육(연세대학교 언어연구교육원)』25, 26집: 79-135. Also, in this volume,

손호민. 2002.「외국어로서의 한국어 교수법의 미래」. 국제한국어 교육학회 제12차 대회 자료집.

오상순. 1998.「중국의 한글학교 교육현황, 해외한민족과 차세대」. 아카데미아 코리아나. 계명대학교 출판.

이나탈리아. 2003.「세인트 피터스버그 한민족 교육현황」.『재외동포의 정체성확립과 교육의 방향』. 2003년 국제학술대회 자료집. 재외동포 교육 진흥재단.

이미선. 2000.「이중언어 사용 개론」. In Lee, D.J. et al. (2000).

이발렌친. 2003.「로시아에서의 한국어 학습」.『재외동포의 정체성 확립과 교육의 방향』. 2003년 국제학술대회 자료집. 재외동포교육 진흥재단.

황유복. 2003.「중국의 조선족 동포 교육 현황」.『재외동포의 정체성 확립과 교육의 방향』. 2003년 국제학술대회 자료집. 재외동포교육 진흥재단.

Hadley, A.O. 2001. *Teaching Language in Context.* Boston: Heinle & Heinle.

Kwon, Hyunjoo. 1999. Overview of the Korean native language arts program for bilingual Korean students in New York City public high schools. *Korean Language in America* 3: 319–27.

Lee, Dong Jae et al. (eds.). 2000. *Studies on Korean in Community Schools.* SLTCC Technical Report #22. University of Hawaii at Manoa.

Merrill, C.C. 2000. Articulation K-8 (elementary and middle school): the Korean/English dual language program. *Korean Language in America* 5:17–24.

Sohn, Ho-min. 1995. Performance-based principles and proficiency criteria for KFL textbook development. *Korean Language Education* 6: 67-98. Also, in this volume.

Sohn, Sung-Ock, et al. 1999. Research report on the Korean/English dual language program. Presented at the AATK Annual Conference, Ohio. August.

Standards (National Standards in Foreign Language Education Project). 1996. *Stadards for Foreign Language Learning: Preparing for the 21st Century,* Lawrence, KS: Allen Press, Inc.

Yow, Bongsoon. 2001. Korean language education in New York City public schools. In Ree, J. (ed.), *The Korean Language in America* 6.

6 해외대학의 한국어교육과 한국학의 현안*

1. 배경

이 발표의 골자는 필자의 경험과 관찰에 토대를 두었다.[1] 필자가 과거 40년 동안 하와이대학 교수로 재직하면서, 그리고 9년간의 동아시아 어문학과 학과장, 6년간의 한국학연구소 소장, 현재까지 4년간의 한국어플래그십센터 소장직을 맡으면서, 보고 듣고 참여하고 기획하고 실천해 온 바를 보고하고자 한다.

필자의 세대가 가장 많은 격변을 겪으면서 살아남은 세대인 듯하다. 일본 식민지시대에 태어나서 어린 시절을 어렵게 살면서, 일본 본토(내지)와 한국(조선)은 한 몸이라는 "내선 일체"의 일본식민지 기치 아래 초등학교에서는 일어전용이 강요되어 한국어-일어 이중언어로 살아야 했다. 2차 세계대전 동안 우리 초등학생들은 거머리에 물리면서 모를 심고, 햇볕 아래서 벼를 베고, 일본전투기나 군함의 기름원료로 소나무뿌리를 캐러 다녔다. 전쟁이 끝나고 지긋지긋했던 일본식민통치를 벗어나니, 남북분단과 대치, 여순반란사건, 6.25 동란이 뒤따랐고, 임시수도 부산의 천막대학생활, 판잣집의 자취생활, 서울 수복과 정치사회의 혼란 등 우리 세대는 젊음을 이렇게 보냈다.

1970년대 후반부터 한국이 눈에 띄게 달라지기 시작했다. 초고속의 경제 발전, 88올림픽 개최, 세계를 상대로 한 첨단 과학기술산업의 발전이 잇따랐다. 한국인의 유례없는 자유민주주의화, 무서운 교육열에 힘입어 우수인력의 속출로, 한국은 국제정치, 외교, 무역, 학문, 문화, 체육활동 등 많은 분야에서 세계적인 두각을 나타내기 시작했다. 한국의 대중문화 한류는 젊은이, 노인 할 것 없이 세계인의 정서를 사로잡았다. 한편, 북미주, 대양주 등 영어권을 위시해서 많은 한국인이 세계 도처에 이주하여 성공하고, 건전한 지역사회를 형성했다. 여행이나 사업상 세계를 누비고 도처에 한국인의 빈번한 출입과 고급 한국제품의 진열로 이제 한국인은 외국인에게 부자 이웃이 되었다.

이렇게 최하수준의 빈곤에서 최고수준의 풍요로움으로 전환하는 한국의 격동적인 변화는 세계인의 한국, 한국인, 한국문화에 대한 인식에 급변화를 이르켰다. 일본식민지,

---

* 이 글은 한국학중앙연구원이 주관하여 2011년 8월 19일, 20일에 개최한 First International Conference on Korean Studies의 기조강연 논문이다. 동 대회의 자료집 Korean Studies Education for Intercultural Communication, pp.11-52, 에 국문과 영문으로 게재되어 있다.

1 이 논문의 제목은 대회 주최 측의 요청에 따른 것이다.

가난한 나라, 전쟁의 나라라는 부정적 이미지는 완전히 사라지고 1980년대부터는 자유 민주주의의, 고속 성장의, 첨단 기술산업의 성공한 나라라는 긍정적 이미지로 빠르게 격상되었다. 한국어에 대한 국제적인 위상도 따라서 격상되었다. 흔히 언어는 사회의 거울이라는 말을 쓴다(e.g. Chaika 1882). 또 많은 사회언어학자들이 주장하듯이, 한 언어의 힘, 경쟁력, 브랜드 또는 시장가치는 그 언어의 사용자들의 국력과 실력에 비례한다(e.g. Wardhaugh 2010). 우리 해외 한국어 교육자가 체험해 온 해외 한국어교육의 발전상이 세계인의 한국 인식의 변화와 한국어의 경쟁력 상승을 단적으로 입증한다. 한국에 대한 외국인의 부정적 이미지가 팽배했을 때, 별 필요없는, 힘없는 한국어를 누가 얼마나 배우려 했겠는가? 지금은 사태가 급전했다. 많은 세계인은 한국과 한국인 그리고 한국어를 알고 배우려 한다. 어떤 원인이나 이유로든지 필요해졌기 때문이다. 그 필요성이 깊고 넓어진 것이다. 한 예를 들면, 미국 정부는 한국어를 중국어, 아랍어, 러시아어 등 8개 외국어와 더불어 미국의 국책 외국어(critical language)로 지정했다. 미국의 경쟁력과 안보의 증진, 한국과의 원활한 국제교류의 필요성 때문이다. 미국은 국책언어인 한국어교육에 막대한 예산을 쓰고 있다. 국가정책으로 한국전문가를 양성하기 위해서이다. 한국어의 필요성에 대한 또 하나의 소박한 예를 보자. 담당 선생님으로부터 들은 이야기인데, 이번 하와이대학 여름학기에 기초한국어를 택하는 학생들에게 "한국어를 왜 배우려하는가?"라는 설문에서, 학급 학생 반수 이상이 "K-Pop"이라고 적어냈다고 한다. 한국의 젊은 가수들이 부르는 노래의 가사를 이해하고 싶어서 한국어를 배우겠다는 단순한 동기였다. 이제는 한국어도 힘있는 언어가 된 것이다.

2. 한국학에 대한 새로운 인식

세계인의 한국에 대한 인식의 변화와 더불어, 한국연구의 지역학인 한국학에 대해서도 해외학자들의 관심과 태도가 많이 변했다. 학자들의 인식변화의 한 예로, 1960~1965년대와 40년 뒤인1996년의 동아시아에 대한 권위 있는 저서를 비교해 볼 수 있다.

과거 미국에 동아시아를 소개하는 가장 권위 있는 저서로 알려진 것은 당시 Havard 대학 교수 Edwin Reischauer와 John Fairbanks 공저의 *East Asia: The Great Tradition*(1960년)과 그 자매편 E. Reischauer, J. Fairbanks, Albert Craig 공저의 *East Asia: The Modern Transformation*(1965년)이었다. 이 두 권에서 한국에 관한 기술은 피상적이었고 책 전체의 9% 정도를 할애해서 한국을 중국문화 패턴의 변종(variant)으로 다루었다. 그후 40년이 지나서 비슷한 제목의 또 하나의 권위있는 저서가 발간되었는데, Patricia B. Ebrey, Anne Walthall, James B. Palais 교수 공저의 *East Asia: A Cultural, Social, and Political History*(2006년)가 그것이다. 이 책에서는 중국을 50%, 일본을 30%, 한국을 20% 할애하고 한국을 독자적인 발전과정으로 기술하고 있다. 또 2009년 국제교류재단의 웹통계에 의하면 한국학을 전문으로 하는 미국과 캐나다 학자는 621명(미국 557; 캐나다 64), 일본학자는 228명, 중국학자는 1,043명이라고 한다. 이들 자료는 서양이나 이웃 나라 학자들에게 이제는 한국학이 일본학이나 중국학에 예속될 수 없는 학문이고, 중국학과 일본학의 교량역할까지 겸하는 독자적인 학문으로 자리를 굳혔음을 보여 준다. 동아시아학을 논할 때 한국학을 제외하면 심각한 학문적 공백이 초래되기 때문에, 한국학은 동아시아학의 필수 불가결한 구성성분이 되었다.

3. 한국어교육과 한국학

이 발표의 목적은 해외대학, 특히 미국대학의 한국어교육, 한국학의 발전상과 현황을 살피고 앞으로 해결해야 할 현안문제가 어떤 것이 있는지를 거론하는 것이다. 중국, 일본 등의 대학도 다소 언급하겠지만, 필자가 몸을 담고 있는 하와이대학 한국어프로그램을 중심으로 논의하겠다. 그리고 다른 나라의 현황에 대해서는 현지에서 오신 여러 교수님의 말씀을 경청하고자 한다.

논의에 앞서, 우선, 한국어교육과 한국학의 관계를 잠깐 보기로 한다. 한마디로, 이들의 관계는 상호보완적이며 밀접한 관계이다. 한국어는 모든 한국학 분야의 연구를 가능케 하는 도구언어이기 때문에 한국어교육은 한국학교육과 연구의 기본조건이다. 또한, 한국어는 그 언어구조와 사용방식에 한국인 고유의 문화와 사상과 가치관과 사고방식이 녹아 있기 때문에, 한국어를 모르고 한국학을 하는 데는 심각한 한계가 있다. 한국어의 능력을 통하여 소기의 한국학연구가 가능하고 원숙한 한국학 학자로 발전할 수 있다. 그리고, 한국어 자체가 연구대상이 되어 그 역사, 방언, 어휘, 어형, 구조, 기능 내지 사회적, 담화적 사용 등이 연구될 때, 한국어학이라는 한국학의 중요한 하위 분야를 이룬다.

한국어 교육이 보다 실효를 거두기 위해서는 학생들에게 한국의 문화의 본질 즉 전통, 역사, 언어구조, 문학, 사회, 정치 등 한국학의 여러 분야의 내용을 습득하게 하여야 한다. 언어의 유창성과 숙달도는 높더라도, 한국에 대한 학술적 지식기반이 없으면, 한국어를 통한 교양 있는 대화나 학술적 담화를 이해할 수 없고 대화나 담화를 지속할 수 없다. 즉 최상급 수준의 한국어능력에 이르지 못한다. 한국의 교육환경에서 초-중-고의 교육을 받지 않았기 때문이다. 최상급수준의 언어능력을 달성하려면, 내용에 대한 지식기반을 갖추어야 한다는 것은 외국어 습득이론의 정설로 되어 있다. 따라서 한국어 전공 학생에게는 한국학 배경지식, 특히 역사, 문학, 어학등 한국학의 기본 지식이 필수요건이다.

한국학 과목을 한국어자료를 가지고 한국어로 강의할 때 한국어 교육 쪽에서 보면 그것은 당연히 내용중심의 한국어교육이다. 그러나 한국학 쪽에서 보면 이것은 당연히 한국학교육과 연구분야이다. 한국어 교육과 한국학 교육이 겹치는 양면성(interface)이다. 그리고 위의 한국 국제교류재단 통계에서 엿볼 수 있듯이, 흔히 해외 한국학 분야의 공식통계에는 순수 한국어교육자도 한국학 전문인원으로 간주한다. 한국어교육을 한국학의 하위범주로 간주할 수 있는 것은 이러한 양면성 때문이라고 생각한다. 교육현장의 이러한 부분적인 양면성에도 불구하고, 개념, 교수목표, 교수내용, 교수방법 등에서는 구분되기 때문에 한국어 교육과 한국학교육-연구를 구분해서 살펴 보려고 한다. 필자의 분야가 한국어교육과 한국어학이고 또 해외의 한국어교육과 한국어학이 다른 인문사회 한국학의 교육과 연구분야에 비하여 훨씬 규모가 크기 때문에 한국어교육과 한국어학을 더 많은 지면을 할애하여 논의하려고 한다.

4. 해외 한국어 교육의 현황

위에서 언급한 대로, 외국인들의 한국, 한국인, 한국문화, 한국어에 대한 인식의 변화는 우리가 헌신하는 해외한국어교육에 현저히 반영되고 있다. 물론, 한국과의 교류나 이해관계의 정도에 따라, 해당 국가나 대학의 재정상태나 교육정책에 따라, 학생들의 필요와 요구에 따라, 교육자의 자질과 능력과 노력에 따라, 나라마다 지역마다 대학마다 한국어교육의 변화와 발전의 정도와 속도에 많은 격차가 있다. 그러나 세계인의 인식변화는 한국어의 힘과 경쟁력을 키웠고 시장가치를 빠른 속도로 높였다고 말할 수 있다. 해외 많은 나라의 대학에 우후죽순처럼 한국어강좌가 신설되고, 예외도 많지만, 초라했던 기존 프로그램이 활기를 띠게 되었다. 중국과 일본의 폭발적인 한국어교육 붐은 잘 알려져 있다.

왕단(2011)의 보고에 따르면, 과거 60년간 중국의 한국어교육은 놀라운 속도와 엄청난 규모로 세계 어느 지역보다도 큰 발전을 이룩했다고 한다. 중국의 3년제, 4년제 대학 중 한국어학과가 설립된 대학은 2009년 현재 총 약 300개에 달하고 4년제대학 한국어학과의 교수 수는 613명이며 재학생 수는 23,130명이다.

일본의 경우도 여러 논문(예컨대, 오태헌 2006)을 보면, 이미 1995년에도 일본의 565개 4년제 대학중 25.3%에 해당한 143개 대학에 한국어가 개설되었다. 그 8년 후인 2003년에는 전체 대학 702교 중 335교에 한국어가 개설되어 47.7%를 차지하였다. 2004, 2005년에도 최소 10여 개 대학이 추가되었으니 지금은 일본대학의 반수 이상이 한국어를 개설했다고 할 수 있다. 한글능력 검정시험의 연간 수험자 수도 1995년의 3,155명에서 2004년에는 10,000명을 돌파했다는 것이다. 오태헌은 일본인에게는 현재의 한국의 정체성이 "IT국가, 한류"라고 규정하고 이러한 적극적 이미지가 한국어 학습동기로 이어졌고, 2003년도부터 국립대 지망생이 치르는 대학입시센터시험(한국의 수능시험)의 외국어 과목에 한국어가 포함된 것도 학습동기를 유발한 것이라 한다. 나아가 일본에서는 한국어교육을 학문적으로 접근하려는 시도로 넘어서고 있다고 한다.

중국, 일본보다는 못하지만, 미국도 1980년대 초부터 한국어 수강생이 증가하기 시작했다(e.g. Furman et al. 2007). 그리고 30여 년 전에는 한국어를 개설한 대학이 10개교 안팎이었으나 그 후 매년 그 수가 증가하여 현재 북미(미국과 캐나다)에는 140개가량의 대학에 한국어가 개설되어 있다. 미국 현대언어협회(Modern Language

Asociation, MLA)에 의하면, 2009년 학기의 한국어수강 대학생은 총 8,511명으로 나와 있다. 한국어수강생의 증가는 다음과 같은 복합요인의 상호작용의 결실이라고 생각한다. 이러한 요인들은 학생들의 필요를 직접 간접으로 증폭시키기 때문에 학생들이 자발적으로 한국어교실을 찾는 동기가 된다.

(가) 한국기업과 정부 관련 기관의 미국 진출
(나) 각 분야에서 한-미간의 국제교류 증진
(다) 미국정부의 적극적인 외국어교육정책과 각종 지원
(라) 한국정부의 세계화 정책과 각종 지원
(마) 한류
(바) 한국학의 학문적 보급
(사) 한인지역사회의 후세를 위한 한국어 교육열
(아) 각 대학 내의 한국어 교수진의 비전, 지도력, 추진력
(자) 각 대학 당국의 외국어정책과 예산지원
(차) 기타: SAT II실시, 대학 외국어학습의 의무화 등

그리하여 한국어는, 아래 표(MLA자료에 기초)에서 보듯이, 현재 미국대학에서 강의된 200여 개의 외국어 중, 학과목 등록자 수가 13위에 올라 있다. 그러나 일본어와 중국어 등록 수에 비하면 아직 장족의 발전이 요구된다.

Languages in descending order	2002	2006	2009
1. Spanish	746,267	822,985	864,986
2. French	201,979	206,426	216,419
3. German	91,100	94,264	96,349
4. Italian	63,899	78,368	80,752
5. Japanese	**52,238**	**66,605**	**73,434**
6. Chinese	**34,153**	**51,582**	**60,976**
7. Arabic	10,584	23,974	35,083
8. Latin	29,841	32,191	32,606
9. Russian	23,921	24,845	26,883
10. Greek, Ancient	20,376	22,849	20,695
11. Hebrew, Biblical	14,183	14,140	13,807
12. Portuguese	8,385	10,267	11,371
13**.** Korean	**5,211**	**7,145**	**8,511**

5. 하와이대학의 한국어교육과 한국어학 프로그램

한국어교육 발전의 구체적인 실례로 하와이대학의 경우를 본다. 필자가 40년 전 하와이대학의 동아시아어학과 조교수로 처음 임용되었던 당시와 지금을 비교해 보면, 그동안 엄청난 발전이 있었다.

처음(1972년 가을) 3학년급과 4학년급 2반을 맡았는데, 학생 부족으로 암담한 상황이었다. 전 평화봉사단, 군인, 선교사와 한국인과 결혼한 미국인이 주로 수강했는데, 2반을 합해도 학생이 6명이었다. 1, 2학년급은 다른 전임 선생님이 맡으셨는데 모두 합해서 9명이었으니 한 학기 전체 수강생이 15명이었다. 이에 비해서 일본어 수강생은 같은 학기에 1,400여 명이고, 중국어 수강생은 400명 정도였으니 일본어는 우리의 90배 이상이고, 중국어는 25배가량의 비율이었다. 교수진은 일본어가 전임 30여 명이었고 중국어가 10여 명인 반면, 한국어는 조교수인 필자와 전임강사 한 분이 다였다. (그 당시 한국문학은 일본, 중국문학과 더불어 동아시아문학과에 속해 있었고 Peter Lee교수 한 분이 전담했는데, 1983년에 두 학과는 현재의 동아시아 어문학과로 통합되었다.) 그리고 일본어와 중국어는 학사과정과 석사과정이 있었고, 일본어는 박사과정까지 있었는데, 한국어는 아무런 학위과정도 없었고, 대학 내 다른 학과 학생들에게 언어만 교육시키는 봉사 역할을 할 따름이었다.

당시 이러한 고충은 하와이대학만의 일이 아니었다. 그 당시 미국에는 하와이 대 이외에 컬럼비아대, 하버드대, 예일대, 워싱턴대, UC 버클리대, 인디애나대 등 10개 정도의 대학에서 한국어강좌가 개설되어 있었는데, 어려운 여건과 저조한 학생수강 상황은 하와이대학 사정과 비슷하거나 못했다. 이러한 한국어교육의 저조는, 물론, 일본의 식민지, 남북분단과 대치, 한국전쟁, 정치 불안, 빈곤 등으로 인해 아직 한국, 한국인, 한국문화는 세계인의 긍정적인 이목을 끌 만한 입장이 아니었고 한국은 대부분의 미국인의 인식밖에 있었기 때문이다. 학생들은 일본어와 같은 경쟁력이 강한 언어를 제쳐놓고, 힘없는 한국어를 택해야 할 동기나 이유나 용도나 명분이 없었던 것이다. 한국인 교민학생들조차 한국어습득의 필요성을 느끼지 못하고 일부는 일본어를 택했던 것이 사실이었다.

하와이대학 한국어프로그램이 일본어나 중국어와 공존하면서 학생을 유치할 수 있는 경쟁력을 갖추려면, 우선 두 언어처럼 학위과정이 도입되어 한국어를 단순한 언어훈련 단계를 넘어서 학문적으로 발전시켜야 한다고 필자는 판단했다. 그 목적으로 학부 교과과정에 일본어, 중국어처럼 한국어 문법, 작문, 문학작품해독, 신문독해, 언어와 문화, 한자강의 등 내용과목을 신설해서 학생을 유치하고 학사과정의 기반을 구축했다. 나아가 한국어 역사, 방언, 음운론, 통사론, 사회언어학, 교수법 등 대학원 과목도 한국어프로그램에 도입해서 주로 언어학과 대학원생들을 대상으로 이들 과목을 가르치기 시작했다. 이것이 가능했던 것은 필자가 언어학과의 대학원 교수를 겸하고 있었기 때문이었다. 이런 기초준비를 갖춘 뒤에 동아시아 어문학과 통합 후, 1980년대 말에 일본 어문학, 중국어문학과 병행하여 한국 어문학의 석사, 박사 과정을 신설했고, (필자가 동아시아어문학과 학과장으로 있었던) 1995년에 한국어학사 과정을 신설하게 되었다.

더욱이 2007년 미국정부지원으로 유일하게 하와이대학에 신설된 한국어 플래그십 센터에 필자가 소장으로 임명되었다. 최상급 수준 한국어 능력을 갖춘 각자 전공분야(정치학, 경제학, 경영학, 사회학, 역사학, 공학 등)의 한국전문가를 양성하는 것이 이 센터의 목적이었다. 필자는 즉시 한국전문가를 양성하는 소위 플래그십 학위과정, 자격증과정과 그에 따르는 교과과정을 수립해서 동년 가을학기부터 대학원 석사과정을 착수하고 학사과정과 자격증과정은 2008년 가을에 도입했다. 이들 학위나 자격증은 "전문한국어(석사, 학사, 자격증)(MA, BA, or Certificate) in Korean for Professionals"이라고 명명했다. 매년 성적이 우수하고 한국전문가가 되려는 의지가 강하고 한국어 배경이 상당히 있는 학생을 MA, BA 과정에 각각 10명 내외를 입학시켜서 한국어교육, 내용교육, 현지교육, 인턴십 등 집중교육을 시킨다. 자격증과정은 수시로 모집한다.

이렇게 해서 현재 하와이대학 동아시아어문학과의 한국어분과에는 미국에서 가장 규모가 크고 다양한 체계적인 학위과정과 자격증과정을 다음과 같이 설정했다.

일반학위과정	전문(플래그십)학위과정
BA in Korean	BA in Korean for Professionals
Certificate in Korean	Certificate in Korean Professionals
MA in Korean language and linguistics	MA in Korean for Professionals
MA in Korean literature	
PhD in Korean language and linguistics	
PhD in Korean literature	

여기에 따르는 학과목은 학부, 대학원 합해서 총 52과목이다. 추가로 학위과정 학생들은 다른 학과에서 한국학 과목을 선택 수강한다. 이러한 여러 프로그램은 상승, 상호보완하여, 많은 학생을 유치하게 되어 한국어과목 등록학생수는 꾸준히 증가하고 있다.

반면, 일본어와 중국어는 대체로 정체상태에 있다. 아래에서 2011년 봄학기 일본어, 중국어, 한국어과목 등록학생수에서 보듯이 한국어가 중국어를 능가했다.

일본어	중국어	한국어
1,200	397	482

일본어 수강생이 한국어보다 90배, 중국어 수강생이 한국어보다 25배였던 40년 전에 비하면 이것은 기적에 가깝다 할 수 있다.

더욱이 2011년 가을 학기 동아시아 3개 언어의 대학원 전공 학생수를 비교해 보면, 문학은 예나 지금이나 일본, 중국에 뒤지지만, 어학은 일본어나 중국어 프로그램보다 한국어 프로그램에 학생이 월등하게 많음을 볼 수 있다.

	일본어문학	중국어문학	한국어문학
석사과정	20(어학 13; 문학 7)	5(어학 4; 문학 1)	19(전원 어학)
박사과정	17(어학 10; 문학 7)	9(어학 6; 문학 3)	25(어학 23; 문학 2)

그러나 하와이대학의 이런 질적, 양적 발전은 북미의 한국어 교육에서는 예외의 경우이다. 우선 현재 하와이대, UCLA, Brigham Young대, Ohio 주립대, SUNY Binghamton 다섯 대학에만 한국어 학사과정이 있다. 북미에서 한국어학의 석사나 박사과정이 있는 곳도 다섯 대학을 넘지 못한다. 학생등록수를 보더라도 교민학생이 다수 재학 중인 캘리포니아 주립대 등 소수의 대학을 제외하면, 대다수의 기존 프로그램이나 많은 신설 프로그램은 한 학기 등록생 40~50명 정도이고, 북미주 약 140개의 대학한국어 프로그램 중 약 100개 교는 주로 언어교육만 실시하고 있다. 이런 대학들은 필자가 40년 전 하와이대학에서 겪었던 상황과 크게 다르지 않다.

6. 해외 한국어교육의 현안

해외 한국어프로그램의 현황과 문제점에 대한 여러 논문을 읽어보면 많은 공통점과 더불어 나라, 지역, 대학에 따라 특수성을 볼 수 있다. 예를 들면, 오태현(2006)은 모든 면에서 남한이 압도하는 일본의 현 상황에서, 계속 전통적인 북한의 "조선어" 교육과 남한의 "한국어" 교육을 병행하는 교과과정을 바꾸지 못하고 있다는 것이 일본대학의 한국어교육의 심각한 현안이라고 한다.

중국의 경우, 왕단(2011)은 중국의 한국어교육이 이전에 비해 많이 향상되었음을 인정하면서, 현 단계 중국에서의 한국어교육의 문제점을 다음과 같이 지적하였다. 왕단이 포괄적으로 지적한 문제점은 미국 등 세계 많은 대학의 한국어프로그램에도 상당 부분 적용된다고 생각한다.

(가) 한국어학과의 90%가 중국 대도시와 동부 연해 지역 대학에 집중되어 있고 내륙지역은 학과가 있는 대학이 극히 드물 뿐 아니라 교육수준도 낮다.
(나) 한국어교육이 독립된 학문으로서의 정체성 구축을 뒷받침할 만한 연구기반이 아직 충분히 조성되지 못하고 있다(예: 연구 부족, 학술지 결여).
(다) 교수진 규모와 교수 자질이 아직 만족스럽지 않다.
(라) 한국학 연구를 위한 고급인재 양성에 대한 관심이 부족하다.
(마) 지역 내의 협력, 한국과의 협력은 아직 활성화되지 못하고 있다.
(바) 교육과정, 교수법, 평가, 교재 등 한국어 교육의 내적 측면이 미비하고 불충분하다.

왕단의 현안 (가)의 대학의 지역적 분포의 불균형은 미국의 현실이기도 하나, 미국에서는 한국어프로그램 설정은 필요에 따른 해당 대학의 자율적인 결정이기 때문에 현안이 되지 못하고, 또 한국어교육의 질에서 대학 간에 특별한 격차가 없다. 나머지 현안들은 초창기에 미국에서도 많이 고민했던 사안들이었는데, 발전적으로 시정될 문제이다. 미국의 경우, 하와이대학과 같은 일부 대학에서의 대학원과정 신설(1987년), 미국한국어 교육자협회 창설(1994년)을 통한 연례 학술대회와 워크숍, 최신 교수법 이론에 따른 영어권 대학교재 공동개발(총 21권; 2000년부터 출판), 온라인 평가법 개발(2011), 플래그십 학위과정 운영(2007년부터) 등 일련의 노력으로 많은 부분 해결을 보고 있다.

그러나 미국 나름의 몇 가지 미해결의 현안이 있다.

첫째는, 영구교수직(tenured professor)의 부족이다. 북미에 한국어 프로그램이 있는 일반대학 140여 개 중 한국어 영구교수직은 조교수까지 합해도 15명 정도이다. 그중 4명이 하와이대학에 있고[2] 다른 교수들은 소수 대학에 한 명씩 활동하고 있다. 교수직이 있는 대학은 대체로 건전한 프로그램을 개발, 운영하고 있는 반면 교수직이 없는 곳은 대개 전임강사가 프로그램을 담당하고 있다. 어떤 대학은 대학원 조교가 책임을 맡고 있는 곳도 있다. 영구교수직은 학과 내에서 강력한 발언권을 행사하기 때문에 프로그램 발전에 크게 공헌할 수 있다. 그리고 영구교수직이 없는 프로그램은, 많은 실례에서 보듯이, 항상 대학정책이나 예산 변동 앞에 풍전등화격이다. 따라서 중요한 현안은 어떻게 하면 더 많은 영구교수직을 더 많은 대학에 설치하느냐 하는 것이다.

둘째, 언어교육만을 목적으로 하는 프로그램은 단명할 수 있다. 학생의 학술연구를 장려하는 학문 위주의 프로그램으로 개발해야 한다. 위에서 보았듯이 현재 북미주에는 그런 한국어학위과정이 있는 대학은 극히 소수이다. 교수직이 있는 곳도 학위과정이 없는 곳이 많다. 프로그램을 지속적으로 발전시키려면 학위과정으로 발전시키는 것이 최상책이다.

셋째, 대학교과과정에 한국어 최상급 수준까지 도입하는 문제이다. 현재 대부분의 교과과정은 중급이나 상급-하의 수준을 목표로 구성되어 있다. 이 과정을 마치면 생존가능한 의사소통 수준이다. 학생들이 자기 전문 분야의 한국어도 능숙하게 구사하려면 상급-상 내지 최상급 수준까지 도달해야 한다.

넷째, 내용중심교육을 지향하는 문제이다. 언어훈련만을 목적으로 하면 상급-상 또는 최상급 언어능력이 성취되기 어렵다. 학생의 전공분야를 한국어로 습득하게 하고, 한국학 과목을 한국어자료를 사용하여 한국어로 강의하여 학생에게 한국학 내용을 한국어로 습득할 수 있게 한다.

다섯째, 해외 한국어교육의 저변 확대를 위하여, 초-중-고등학생들의 한국어 습득을 장려하는 것이다. 조기 한국어 교육을 통하여 대학에 입학할 때 높은 단계에 배치되도록 한다. 미국의 경우, LA와 New York 등지에 집결된 약 73개의 초, 중, 고교에 한국어가

2 2013년 가을부터 한국어 영구교수직 하나가 추가되었다.

개설되어 있다. 더 많은 학교에 한국어가 도입되도록 한국어교육 관련 기관과 교육자 모두가 협력해야 한다. 한 가지 가능한 방안은 컴퓨터 세대인 초-중-고생을 대상으로 원거리 교육과정의 체계를 구축하여 전국적으로 교육시키는 일이다. 물론 치밀한 기획과 시간과 전문인력과 자금이 필요하다.

여섯째, 한국어교육자 간의 더욱 빈번한 공조, 공동연구, 교육자료 공유, 연구결과 공유, 교육기술공유 등 지속적인 긴밀한 네트워크 체계를 구축한다. 미국한국어교육자협회의 연례학술대회, 워크숍, 학술지 발간 등 활동으로 상당한 효과를 거두고 있다. 2010년부터 미국정부 관계 외국어교육기관들과 하와이대학 플래그십센터 간에 정부 주최로 Korean Language Education and Resources Network (LEARN) Conference를 시작했다. 특히 high-tech교수법을 집중적으로 다루고 있는데 이 대회는 한국어교육의 질 향상에 시사하는 바가 크다.

끝으로, 한국과의 긴밀한 유대는 해외 한국어교육의 근간을 이룬다. 해외한국어교육의 효과적인 운영을 위하여 한국의 정부 관련 기관, 지원기관, 관련 대학 당국, 해당 교수들과 긴밀한 공조가 필요하다. 학생들의 현지교육과 인턴십, 학술교류 등 지속적인 교류가 유지되어야 한다.

7. 해외 한국학 교육과 연구: 현황과 현안

한국학이 이제는 독자적인 지역학으로 확립되어 해외에서 활발히 강의되고 연구되고 있다. 1970-80년대 한국의 급속한 경제발전과 함께 한국학 연구는 활성화되어 왔다. 해외에서 한국학을 비교적 많이 연구하였거나 연구하고 있는 나라는 일본, 소련, 미국, 서유럽의 일부 국가들인데, 현재 한국학이 가장 활발하게 이루어지고 있는 지역은 미국과 캐나다이다(김종명 2006 참조).

해외 한국학이 특히 활기를 띤 것은 국제교류재단이 1991년 창설 이래 12개국의 69대학에 약 100개의 한국학 교수직을 설치했고 교류재단과 한국학중앙연구원의 연구비 지원에 힘입은 바 크다. 교수직은 북미주에 특히 많이 창설되었다. 현재 북미주의 한국어 개설대학 140여 개 중 40여 개 대학에는 언어뿐 아니라 한국과 관련된 인문사회학 과목을 교수하고 있다(2009년 국제교류재단 웹 자료). 그러나 한국학에 관한 학위를 수여하는 대학은 20교를 넘지 못한다.

해외 한국학이라 하면 주로 한국문학, 한국역사, 한국어학이 가장 기본이고 많이 교육되고 연구된다. 그외에 한국의 철학, 불교학, 인류학, 미술사, 영화 연극, 정치학, 사회학, 경제학, 전통 또는 민속음악, 무용 등도 강의되고 대학원 학위과정으로 설정한 대학도 있다. 예를 들면, UCLA는 한국불교학, 한국사, 한국문학, 한국어학 등이, Harvard는 한국사와 한국문학이 활발하다. 하와이대학은 한국어학, 한국사, 한국문학, 아시아학, 한국사회학, 한국민속음악, 도시계획학 등 분야에서 활발하다. 하와이대학은 1972년에 미국최초의 한국학연구소를 창설하여 학회, 세미나, 학술지, 교육과 연구에 전념하고 있다. 지금은 북미에 10여 개의 크고 작은 한국학연구소가 설치되어 있는데 학생 수나 교수진의 규모 면에서 하와이대학이 단연 앞선다. 현재 하와이대학 각 학과에 속해 있는 교수 35명이 한국학연구소 교수진을 이루고 있는데, 이들은 한국학 전문가이거나 한국연구에 관심이 많은 교수들이다.

하와이대학 한국학에서 학생수, 교수진, 교과과정, 명성에서 가장 압도적인 분야는 한국어학이다. 전술한 바와 같이 한국어학 박사학위과정 학생수는 일본, 중국을 무색하게 하고 있다. 동아시아 어문학과의 한국어전공 학생뿐 아니라, 언어학과나 제2언어습득학과 학생들도 한국어학, 한국어습득에 대한 연구를 하기도 한다.

영어권 소수 대학에서 실시 중인 한국어교육과 한국학 교육-연구의 교육프로그램 중 대표적인 두 모델을 소개한다. 하나는 UCLA와 같은 동아시아어문화(East Asian Languages and Cultures) 모델이고 다른 하나는 하와이대학과 같은 동아시아 어문학(East Asian Languages and Literstures) 모델이다.

<table>
<tr><td colspan="5">동아시아어문화과(UCLA 등)</td></tr>
<tr><td>중국어문화
분과</td><td>일본어문화
분과</td><td colspan="3">한국어문화 분과</td></tr>
<tr><td>…</td><td>…</td><td colspan="2">학부과정</td><td>대학원과정</td></tr>
<tr><td>…</td><td>…</td><td>한국어 교육</td><td>한국학 학사
(어학, 역사,
문학 등)</td><td>한국학 석사, 박사
(어학, 역사, 문학,
불교학, 사회학 등)</td></tr>
</table>

<table>
<tr><td colspan="6">동아시아어문학과(하와이대학 등)</td><td>해당 인문 사회
학과</td></tr>
<tr><td>중국
어문학
분과</td><td>일본
어문학
분과</td><td colspan="4">한국어문학분과</td><td>아시아학과, 역사학
과, 사회학과 등</td></tr>
<tr><td>…</td><td>…</td><td colspan="2">학부과정</td><td colspan="2">대학원과정</td><td>학부, 대학원 과정</td></tr>
<tr><td>…</td><td>…</td><td>한국어
교육</td><td>한국어
학사</td><td>한국어학
석사, 박사</td><td>한국문학
석사, 박사</td><td>…</td></tr>
</table>

다른 대학의 통계는 없지만, 하와이 대학의 2011년 현재 한국 어문학 분과 학생은 이미 제시한 대로 다음과 같이 집계된다.

한국어 과목 등록학생: 482
한국어 학사학위과정 전공학생: 49
한국어학 석사학위과정 전공학생: 19
한국어학 박사학위과정전공학생: 23
한국문학 석사학위과정생: 0
한국문학 박사학위과정생: 2

하와이대학의 경우에는, 어학, 문학 이외의 한국학 분야의 교육과 연구는 해당 인문사회학과에서 수강하고 담당 전문교수의 지도하에 학위를 취득하도록 된 다원체제이다. 예를 들면, 한국역사는 역사학과의 한국학 전문교수의 지도하에 학위과정을 밟고 그 과에서 학위를 받는다. 전술한 바와 같이 이들 여러 한국학 교수는 한국학연구소를 통하여 교류하고 상호 협조한다.

이상 미국의 한국학 교육과 연구의 윤곽을 보았는데, 당면한 현안 문제는 어떤 것이 있는지 필자의 좁은 관찰을 기초하여 몇 가지 지적해 보고자 한다.

첫째는, 분야별 한국전문가의 부족과 편재현상이다. 극소수의 특정 분야 전문가가 명문 대학에 편재해 있기 때문에 학생들이 한 군데에 집결되어 한국학의 균형발전을 어렵게 만든다.

둘째, 하와이대학처럼, 한국학연구가 여러 인문사회학과에 산재할 경우 한국학 분야 간의 조정이 어렵고 학생의 학제 간의 균형 있는 발달을 기하기 어렵다.

셋째, 인문사회학과의 한국학 교수들은 한국학강좌 개설을 주저한다. 첫째는 등록학생 미달로 강좌가 취소될 염려가 있고 둘째는 지역학보다는 일반론강의와 연구를 선호하는 학과 분위기에 순응하는 것이 영구직취득과 승급에 유리하기 때문이다.

넷째, 한국학을 전공하는 한국유학생과 일부 교포학생과 비한국계 학생은 한국어가 유창하나, 그 이외의 한국학전공 학생들의 한국어 실력의 부족은 심각하다. 한국학전공 학생들의 한국어능력 향상을 위한 집중훈련이 필요하다.

다섯째, 강의와 연구에서 일본, 중국 등 다른 동아시아 학자들과의 제휴와 교류가 부족하다(손호민 2010 참조). 그리고 한국에 관한 학문 간의 제휴(interdisciplinary)를 표방하는 한국학연구에 실제로는 그런 제휴가 극히 부족하다.

8. 결론

이상에서 살펴본 바와 같이, 해외 한국어교육과 한국학은 한국에 대한 국제적 인식의 변화에 힘입어, 그리고 적극적 지원과 협조로, (내부, 외부의 도전과 시련을 받으면서도) 미증유의 발전을 해 왔다. 비교적 덜 발전한 프로그램과 보다 더 발전한 프로그램 모두 다 유동적인 발전과정의 같은 연속선상에 있다. 아직 모두 미완성 상태이며, 해결해야 할 현안이 산적해 있다. 따라서 개선과 혁신을 위한 무한의 가능성이 열려 있다. 지속적인 발전과 제도화를 위해서는 우리의 지혜와 비전과 리더십과 공조적 실천이 필요한 한편, 지원기관의 계속적인 재정적 뒷받침이 필수조건이다. 인재와 자금이 성공적인 발전의 관건이기 때문이다.

참고 문헌: Chapter 6

김종명. 2006. 「국내의 '해외한국학' 교육: 현황 · 과제 · 방향」. 『아태연구』 제 13권 제1호: 105-28.

손호민. 2009. 「한국어교육의 새 파라다임」. 『국어교육연구』 제24집: 7-36. 서울대학교 국어교육연구소.

손호민. 2010. 「동아시아의 지적 유대의 중요성」 (in Japanese). In *Toyo Bunka Kenkyu* Vol. 13: 1-16. Tokyo: Gakushuin University Press.

吳太憲. 2006. 「일본 대학에서의 한국어 교육 현황과 특징」. 『아태연구』 제13권. 제2호: 105-18.

왕단. 2011. 「중국에서의 한국어교육, 그 현황과 과제」. //yyforum.org/k/kfulpaper/1-2-wangdan%5BK%5D.pdf.

Ebrey, P.B., A. Walthall, & J.B. Palais. 2006. *East Asia: A Cultural, Social, and Political History.* Boston: Houghton Mifflin Co.

Chaika, E. 1982. *Language, The Social Mirror.* Rowley, Mass: Newbury House Publishers, Inc.

Furman, N., D. Goldberg, & N. Lusin. 2007. Enrollments in languages other than English in United States institutions of higher education, Fall 2006. *Modern Language Association Wb publication,* 13 (November 2007): 1-28.

Reischauer, E.O. & J.K. Fairbanks. 1960. *East Asia: The Great Tradition.* Boston: Houghton Mifflin Co.

Reischauer, E.O., J.K. Fairbanks, & A.M. Craig. 1965. *East Asia: The Modern Transformation.* Boston: Houghton Mifflin Co.

Wardhaugh, R. 2010. *In Introduction to Sociolinguistics*, Sixth edition. West Sussex, England: Wiley-Blackwell.

Part II

STRUCTURAL DYNAMISM

7 한국어의 유형적 특징*

1. 들어가는 말[1]

한국어의 유형적 특징을 살피기에 앞서 유형론(typology)의 언어학적 배경과 연구 방법을 잠시 훑어보고자 한다. 유형론은 한편으로는 계통론과 이웃하고 다른 한편으로는 보편론과 이웃한다. 언어의 유형과 계통은 다른 개념인데도 초기 언어학자들은 종종 이를 혼동하여 언어의 유형적 특징을 기준으로 언어의 계통을 분류했었다. 우랄어군, 터키어군, 몽고어군, 퉁구스어군들을 묶어 우랄알타이 어족을 제안한 것도 주로 이 모든 언어에 공유된 구조적 유사성 때문이었다. 즉 단어구조의 교착성, 접미사적 어형 구조, 동사 후행, 부가어 선행, 후치사 구문 등의 유형적 특징을 공유하고 있기 때문이었다. 한국어와 일본어도 같은 특징 때문에 두 언어의 계통적 관계를 주장했을 뿐 아니라 이 두 언어를 알타이 어족에 포함시켰다.

계통이 같은 언어들이 유사한 구조를 갖는 경향이 있지만 그렇다고 유형적인 특징의 공유만으로는 계통적 관계가 입증된 것은 아니고 별도의 이론과 방법을 통해서 계통적 관계를 설정하여야 함은 물론이다. 계통이 분명히 다른 언어들이 같은 유형적 특징을 갖는 경우가 얼마든지 있기 때문이다. 이 글에서는 계통론은 언급하지 않겠다.

2. 유형론과 보편론

유형론은 보편론과 상관 관계에 있다. 유형론은 이미 19세기부터 거론되어 왔으나 특히 최근 거의 40년 동안 언어 보편론과 밀접한 관계를 맺으면서 보편론과 유형론에 대한 관심과 연구와 논란이 유례 없이 활발하다. 이러한 경향은 음성학, 음운론, 형태 통사론, 의미 화용론, 사회언어학, 언어 변화론, 언어 습득론 등 언어 구조와 사용 전반에 걸쳐서 일어나고 있다. 이러한 대세의 효시는 언어 보편성 추구를 위한 두 상반된 주장이 첨예하게 대립되면서부터이다. 그 하나는 노엄 촘스키(Chomsky 1965, 1976, 1981 등)의 주

---

* 이 글은 『**한글**』 282: 61-95(2008.12)에 실려 있다.

1 이 글은 2007년 필자가 호주 멜버른 소재 La Trobe 대학에 distinguished scholar로 초청되어 동대학 Research Centre for Linguistic Typology(RCLT)에 있을 때 쓴 글이다. RCLT의 Director Bob Dixon 교수와 Associate Director Sasha Aikhenvald 교수가 베풀어 준 지성스런 도움에 감사한다.

장으로 언어 보편성의 추구의 최선의 방법은 한 개별 언어의 상세하고도 추상적인 연구라고 하였다. 언어 보편성은 인간 본연의 타고난 특성(innate properties)이기 때문이라고 한다. 촘스키는 아이들이 아무 언어나 쉽사리 습득하는 현상과 언어의 추상적인 심층구조 개념에 입각하여 정연한 논리로 아이들의 선천성을 바탕으로 하는 절대적인 언어보편성 내지 보편문법을 주장하였다. 이에 반해 조셉 그린버그(Greenberg 1960, 1966, 1974 등)의 주장은 언어 보편성의 연구를 위해서는 많은 언어에 대한 자료가 필요하고 보편적 현상은 구체적인 분석을 통해서 설명할 수 있고, 나아가 언어보편성의 설명에는 심리적, 기능적(화용적) 요소들을 고려하여야 한다고 한다. 그린버그는 많은 언어의 표면 구조를 비교하면서 언어현상 간의 시사적 보편성(implicational universals) 의 존재와 보편성의 경향성과 한계성을 주장하고 언어 유형 현상을 논의하였다(Comrie 1981: 1-27; 266-7 참조). 다시 말하면 20세기의 언어 보편성, 유형성 논란의 도화선은 촘스키의 단일 언어(주로 영어) 현상에 근거한 언어보편성 주장과 그린버그의 광범한 복수 언어에 근거한 보편성과 유형성의 주장이 대립되면서 시작되었다고 볼 수 있다.

한국어의 유형적 특징을 살피려는 이 글에서는 촘스키식 관점에 동조하기 어렵다. 첫째는, 아무리 단일 언어를 깊이 연구하여 추상적인 보편성을 제안한다 하더라도 보편적 특성이라고 제안한 사항들이 진정한 보편 사항인지 유형적 특성인지 아니면 그 언어의 고유한 특징인지를 논리만으로는 증명될 수 없다고 생각한다. 구체적으로 계통이나 유형이 다른 여러 언어의 현상을 보지 않고 그러한 제안이 어떻게 보편적 특성이라고 단정할 수 있을 것인가 하는 것이다.

둘째, 아이들의 언어습득의 선천성 또는 선천성 원리를 언어의 절대적 보편성의 근거로 들지만 선천성의 구체적 내용이 무엇인지 그리고 그것이 어떻게 지구에 존재하는 그리고 존재했던 모든 언어의 서로 다른 구조에 통용되는 보편성을 주장할 수 있는 근거가 되는지 아직은 속시원한 해답이 없다.

셋째, 여러 언어의 문법을 비교 연구해 봄으로써 언어 간의 차이의 패턴을 밝혀 낼 수 있고 언어의 다양한 체계적 제약 현상을 찾아내고 탐구할 수 있다. 여러 언어를 비교해 볼 때 그 구조들이 얼마나 풍부하고 다양한가는 아무리 한 언어를 깊게 살펴본들 한 언어만의 연구로는 가히 상상조차 할 수 없는 일이다. 간단한 예로, 대우법 체계가 풍부하게 갖추어진 한국어와 같은 언어와 그런 체계가 전혀 없는 영어와 같은 언어가 어떤 형태의 추상적 절대적 보편성으로 타협이 될 것인지 알 길이 없다. 단일 언어에 기초한 보편성 추구는 분명 극도로 복잡하고 다양한 언어현상을 극도로 단순화하는 연구 태도가 아닐까 한다.

넷째, 모든 언어의 구조가 예외 없이 공유하는 절대적인 보편성은, 극히 추상화되고 관념화된 심층에서가 아닌 한, 드물다는 것은 상당히 입증되고 있다. 실제로 절대적인 보편성이라고 주장된 사항들도 그렇지 않다는 반증들이 여러 현실 언어에서 나오고 있다(Comrie 1981: 7, 20-1등 참조). 예를 들면 "모든 언어에는 명사와 동사의 구별이 있다"는 주장은 지금까지 밝혀진 바로는 절대적 보편성이라고 할 수 있겠지만 한편 "모든 언어에는 동사와 형용사의 구별이 있다"나 "주어-목적어-동사(SOV)의 어순이라면 후치사를 갖는다"라고 주장하기는 그리 쉽지 않다. 오히려 "언어에는 동사와 형용사 구별이 있는 경향이 있다"나 "특정 언어의 기본 어순이 SOV라면 전치사가 아니라 후치사를 사용하는 경향이 있다"라고 하는 상대적(경향적) 보편성이나 유형적 보편성이 더 광범하게 실재하는 언어현상이다. 동사와 형용사를 통사적으로나 어형적으로 구별하기 어려운 언어도 있고, 드물기는 하지만 페샤 언어처럼 SOV언어이면서도 후치사가 아니라 전치사를 사용하는 언어도 있기 때문이다. 따라서 구체적인 언어 자료에 기초한 상대적, 경향적, 유형적 보편성의 추구가 언어 현실에 더 타당하다고 생각한다.

끝으로, 모든 언어가 공유하는 절대적 보편성의 추구는 인간의 두뇌의 연구나 인간의 생득적 언어 능력의 탐구에는 중요하겠지만, 엄연히 존재하는 언어의 광범한 구조적 차이와 언어의 생동성과 체계적인 변화, 언어의 사회적, 문화적, 담화적 기능 등의 추구나 현실적으로 극히 중요한 외국어 습득 문제 등에는 별반 도움이 되지 않는다.

이러한 여러 가지 점에서 볼 때, 단일 언어나 소수의 동일 부류에 속하는 언어에 기초를 두고 연구한 보편성 추구나 주장은 계통이 다르고 지역이 다르고 유형이 다른 여러 언어를 살펴서 탐구하고 검증하여야 한다는 그린버그나 콤리(Comrie 1981) 등의 논리에 동조하고자 한다. 많은 언어를 살펴서 비교해 보지 않고는 보편성이나 유형성에 대한 어떤 논의도 불완전하고 어떠한 신중한 일반성도 찾기가 힘들 것이라고 믿기 때문이다. 여기서 한국어의 유형적 특성을 논의하려는 것도 절대적 보편성과는 무관한 입장에서 언어의 체계적인 차이와 다양성의 중요성을 보고자 하는 것이다.

3. 유형론의 정의와 방법

그러면 언어학에서 유형론이란 무엇인가? 그것은 첫째, 서로 다른 언어들을 비교하여 언어 현상의 구조적 유형들을 찾고 어떤 언어가 어떤 유형에 속하는가를 연구하는 유형적 분류론(typological classification)과 둘째, 언어마다 체계적으로 일어나는 패턴들(cross-linguistic patterns)을 찾고 연구하는 유형적 종합론(typological generalization), 그리고 셋째, 구조주의 언어학, 생성문법 등과 대조되는 하나의 언어 이론 즉 기능적-유형적 설명론(functional-typological approach) 등 이 모두를 망라한다(Croft 2006: 1-2).

콤리(Comrie 1981: 30-2)가 지적하듯이, 많은 언어를 대상으로 보편적 특성을 추구하는 보편론과 언어 사이의 유형적 차이를 추구하는 유형론은 일견 상반되는 분야인 듯 보이나, 실제로는 같은 연구 방법을 사용하고 상보적이다. 흔히 많은 언어에서 어떤 공통성을 찾는 학자는 동시에 언어 유형에도 관심을 갖지 않을 수 없게 되고 또 특정 현상에 대해 유형성 연구를 하려면 그 현상이 모든 언어에 보편적으로 존재할 수 있다는 가정도 하게 된다. 한편, 어떤 연구 작업이 보편성 연구인지 유형성 연구인지 구분하기 어려울 때도 많다. 그리고 언어 유형의 연구 결과가 흔히 경향적 보편성의 발견으로 이어지게 된다. 콤리가 제시한 예로는, 문장 어순에 대한 유형론적 연구를 하다가 SOV, SVO, VSO,

VOS, OVS, OSV의 여섯 가지 순위 중 대부분 언어는 주어가 목적어를 선행하는 처음 세 유형에 속하고 그렇지 않은 나머지 세 유형을 갖는 언어는 극소수에 불과하다는 것을 발견한다. 그러면 경향적 보편성으로 "인간 언어의 기본 어순은 주어가 목적어를 선행하는 것"이라고 규정할 수 있다는 것이다. 따라서 유형론 연구와 보편성 연구는 상반되는 것이 아니고 동일 연구의 다른 측면이고 상호 보완적이라 할 수 있다.

그런데 유형성이나 보편성 추구에서, 세계의 4,000 내지 6,000개의 언어를 모두 다 동원한다는 것은 물론 현실적으로 불가능하다. 그 때문에 대부분의 연구에서는 계통, 지역, 유형을 기준으로 표본한 상당수의 언어를 대상으로 하고 있다.

언어 유형의 효과적인 연구 방법의 실례로 최근 필자가 참여했던 공동 연구 프로젝트를 소개한다. 이것은 호주 멜버른 소재 라트로브 대학교(La Trobe University)의 언어 유형론 연구소(Research Centre for Linguistic Typology)에서 실시하고 있는 방법이다. 이 연구소는 언어 유형론으로 명성 높은 로버트 딕슨(R.M.W. Dixon) 교수가 창설해서 소장직을 맡고 있는데 부소장 알렉산드라 아이켄발드(Alexandra Aikhenvald) 교수와 더불어 끊임없이 새로운 공동 연구 프로젝트를 창안해서 추진시킨다.

공동 연구의 단계를 보면, 우선 딕슨 교수와 아이켄발드 교수의 책임하에 언어학적으로, 유형론적으로 특히 중요하다고 생각하는 논제를 정한다. 그리고 오랜 시일에 걸쳐 거기에 관한 기존 연구 출판 논문들을 탐독한다. 본인들 자신의 현지 조사를 통한 개별 언어 연구 결과는 물론이고 영어 현상을 포함한 일반 이론이나 세계 여러 개별 언어 연구에 대한 철저한 문헌 연구를 실시한다. 이러한 연구를 바탕으로 두 교수 중 한 사람(보통 딕슨 교수)이 공동 프로젝트를 위한 연구 방침서(position paper)를 쓴다. 이 정성스런 연구 방침서에는 프로젝트의 목표, 기존 연구 결과의 총체적 정리와 분류는 물론이고 제안한 공동 연구의 획일적인 연구 방법 등을 자세히 제시한다. 그런 다음, 계통, 지역, 유형을 달리하는 15명에서 20명가량의 개별 언어 전문가를 선정해서 공동 연구의 참여 의사를 타진한다. 초청에 응할 경우 연구 방침서를 보내면서 1년간의 연구 논문 작성 기간을 준다. 그 1년 후 연구팀 전원이 참여하여 각자의 연구 결과에 대한 국제 워크숍을 라트로브 대학에서 일주일 동안 개최한다. 공동 연구에 직접 참여하지 않은 국내 국제 학자들과 대학원 학생들도 다수 참여한다. 일주일 간의 철저한 토론을 통해서 상호 언어의 유형적 특징을 나누고 여러 언어의 유형 패턴을 종합한다. 마지막 날에는 출판 계획을 세운다. 그 후 각 연구 참여자들은 3-4개월간의 여유를 두고 워크숍 결과에 비추어 각자의 논문을 재수정한다. 그런 다음 연구 참여자들의 최종 논문을 모아서 딕슨 교수와 아이켄발드 교수가 공동 편집인이 되어 완전한 단행본으로 구성한 다음 영국 옥스포드 대학 출판부의 언어 유형 연구(Explorations in Linguistic Typology) 총서에 제출한다. 이때 수정된 연구 방침서는 제1장이 되고 나머지 각 언어가 2장, 3장, 4장 등 뒤따르고 마지막 장은 해당 논제의 유형적 분류와 종합론인데 보통 편집 교수 중 한 명이 담당한다. 옥스포드 출판부는 엄격한 심사와 재수정 과정을 거쳐 출판에 이르게 된다.

지금까지 약 10년 간 이 연구소가 추진해 왔던 국제 공동 프로젝트는 "단어"(Word),

"논항수 변화: 타동성의 격 연구"(Changing Valency: Case Studies in Transitivity), "지역적 확산 및 계통적 계승"(Areal Diffusion and Genetic Inheritance), "형용사 범주"(Adjective Classes), "연쇄동사 구문"(Serial Verb Constructions), "이문법 접촉"(Grammars in Contact), "보문화"(Complementation), "절 연결"(Clause Linking), "품사 범주 전환의 파생법"(Word-Class-Changing Derivations) 등이 있었는데 필자가 참여한 공동 프로젝트는 2002년의 "형영사 범주"와 2007년의 "절 연결"과 "품사 전환 파생"이다.[2]

이 연구소가 주관해 온 유형 연구의 방법론은 철저한 자료 분석 중심이고 형태-통사 유형의 경우에는 형태론적, 통사론적 방법과 아울러 가능한 한 의미 범주에도 역점을 두고 실시한다. 연구 방침서에 세부적인 의미 범주를 먼저 제시하고 이 의미 범주를 언어마다 어떤 어휘적, 통사적, 형태적 표식으로 나타내는가를 살핀다. 2002년 "형용사 범주"의 연구에서는 13언어군이 대표되었는데, 의미적 기준으로는 치수(크다-작다, 길다-짧다, 넓다-좁다 등), 연령(젊다 등; '늙다'는 동사), 가치(좋다-나쁘다 등), 색(희다, 검다, 파랗다 등), 물리적 성질(단단하다-부드럽다, 무겁다-가볍다 등), 인간 성향(행복하다-불행하다, 영리하다, 관대하다 등), 속도(빠르다-느리다 등), 난이도(쉽다-어렵다, 복잡하다-간단하다 등), 유사성(같다-다르다, 비슷하다 등), 적격성(맞다-틀리다, 적당하다, 가능하다 등), 양(많다-적다, 충분하다-부족하다 등), 위치(높다-낮다, 멀다-가깝다 등), 기수(하나, 둘, 첫째 등 한국어에는 형용사로는 없음) 등이 제시되었다. 작년의 공동 연구 "절 결합"의 경우에는, 16개의 언어군이 대표되었는데, 연구 대상의 주요 의미 범주와 하위 범주는 다음과 같다: 시간성(계속, 상대성, 조건성); 결과성(원인, 결과, 목적); 결과 가능성; 부가성(무순위 부가, 동일 사항 추가, 부연, 대조); 선택(택일, 거절, 제안); 양태(현실적, 가상적). 그리고 제시된 의미범주에 맞지 않는 표식이나 특이한 범주 표식이 각자의 언어에 있으면 지적하도록 하였다. 여기에 유독 한국어의 경우 양태의 하위범주로 '수단, 방법'을 추가 했다. 접속 어미 '-어서'가 수단, 방법도 나타내기 때문이다.

이러한 철저한 연구 방법으로 각 언어의 특정 현상에 대한 유형적 특징이 밝혀질 뿐 아니라 다른 계통, 다른 지역, 서로 다른 언어 유형에 속한 언어들의 특징이 체계적으로 종합되고 비교되고 분석되어 인간 언어의 유형적 보편성과 특수성을 밝힐 수 있게 된다 (Dixon and Aikhenvald 2004, 2009 참조).

4. 이 논문의 목적

이상과 같은 유형론 연구의 현황을 전제 내지 배경으로 하여 한국어의 형태-통사적 유형 특징을 논의하려 한다. 형태-통사론에만 국한하고 음성-음운론, 어휘론, 담화론 등

---

2 2007년 한 학기 동안 동 연구소의distinguished visiting professor로 초청되어 있으면서 두 프로젝트에 참여하였다.

다른 분야는 논외로 한다.[3]

한국어 유형적 특징을 살피는 데는 두 가지 방법이 있을 수 있다. 하나는 한국어의 여러 구문을 선정해서 각각의 형태적 유형적 특징을 살피는 방법이다. 그런 구문에는 예컨대 서술 구문, 격 구문, 관계절 구문, 보문 구문, 명사화 구문, 접속문 구문, 형용사 구문, 피동-사동 구문, 조동사 구문, 연쇄 동사 구문, 부정 구문, 양화사 구문, 시제-상-양태 구문 등이 있다. 또 하나의 방법은 이들 모든 구문이 공유하는 한국어의 대표적 유형 특징이 무엇인가를 살펴서 종합하는 것이다.

첫째 방법은 방대한 작업이고 심도 있는 연구의 경우 보통 한 구문만 가지고도 한 편의 논문이나 단행본이 될 수 있다. 이런 연구는, 다른 언어와 비교하는 유형론적 관점에서는 아니지만, 지금까지 많은 국어학자, 언어학자들이 해 왔다. 필자의 논문 'The Adjective Class in Korean'(Sohn 2004)이나 'Clause Linking in Korean'(Sohn 2009)도 그런 예인데 단지 유형론적 관점에서 다루었을 뿐이다. 그래서 여기서는 더 손쉬운 두 번째 방법을 따르고자 한다. 즉 한국어의 각종 형태-통사 구문에 두루 내포되어 있는 극히 전형적인 유형 특징을 논하는 방법이다. 이러한 대표적 공시 유형을 종합하는 것이 이 논문의 주된 목적이다. 그리고 부수적인 둘째 목적은 그런 공시적 유형 특징이 한국어의 광범한 문법화 현상과 어떻게 연결되는지를 살핀다. 셋째로는, 한국어의 특징적 유형이 한국어의 형태-통사론적 분석의 방법에 무엇을 시사하는가를 보이며, 더 나아가서, 넷째로는, 한국어의 유형적 특징이 외국어로서의 한국어 교육, 특히 영어 화자의 한국어 습득에, 어떤 영향을 주며 어떤 역할을 하는가에 대해서도 논의하려고 한다. 지면 관계상 이 모든 논의가 극히 개괄적이고 예시적이 될 수밖에 없으나 핵심점은 포함시킨다.

5. 한국어 문법의 유형적 특징

한국어의 모든 종류의 형태-통사 구문에 내재하는 전형적인 공시적 유형 특징은 어떤 것들이 있는가?

5.1. 한국어의 첫 번째 유형적 특징은, 풍부한 교착적, 통합적 어형 구조(agglutinative and polysynthetic morphology)이다.

인간 언어의 총체적 유형 분류(holistic typology)를 위해서 전통적으로 여러 가지 기준을 제안해 왔는데 이미 19세기부터 거론되어 온 것으로 특히 중요한 것은 형태적 유형론과 어순 유형론에 기준을 둔 분류였다. 형태적 유형론에 따라, 언어를 고립어, 교착어, 융합어(또는 굴절어), 통합어 등 4가지 유형으로 분류해 왔다. 고립어는 월남어나 중국어처럼 원칙상 한 단어가 한 형태소로 되어 있고 따라서 형태론의 중요성은 미미하다. 교

3 따라서 이 글은 좁은 의미의 '한국어 문법의 유형적 특징'이라 할 수 있다.

착어는 터키어에서처럼 단어가 하나 이상의 형태소로 구성될 수 있고 형태소 간의 경계가 뚜렷하고 형태소마다 의미와 음운형태가 고정되어 있어서 식별하기 쉽다. 예컨대, 터키어에서는 명사가 수와 격에 따라 일정한 어형 변화를 하는데 수를 나타내는 어미는 항상 격을 나타내는 어미에 선행한다. 융합어는 러시아어에서처럼 형태소 간의 경계가 불분명할 뿐더러 많은 경우 접사들이 쪼갤 수 없이 융합되어 하나의 융합사(portmanteau morph)를 이룬다. 예를 들면 러시아어의 stol-ov '탁자-들의'의 -ov 는 복수의 의미와 소유격의 의미를 동시에 갖지만 이 두 문법 범주를 형태상 분리할 수 없다. 끝으로 통합어는, 축치어나 에스키모어에서처럼 여러 어휘적 또는 문법적 형태소들이 모여서 한 단어를 이루는데, 다음 에스키모어의 예에서 보듯이, 영어 같으면 완전한 문장이 한 단어 속에 들어 있다(Comrie 1981: 39-49).

angya-ghlla-ng-yug-tuq
배-큰-장만하-싶-그이
'그사람은 큰 배를 장만하고 싶어한다.'

그런데, 모든 언어가 이 4대 유형 중 하나에 완벽하게 들지는 않는다. 대체로 한 유형으로 분류될 수 있는 언어도 다른 유형의 특성을 조금씩 지니게 되고 또 끊임없는 언어 변화로 인하여 한 유형에서 다른 유형으로 전환될 수도 있고 현재 옮겨가는 과정에 있을 수도 있다. 영어는 역사적으로 러시아어처럼 융합어였으나 굴절 어미들이 퇴화하고 점점 고립어적인 특성을 지니게 되어 고립어-융합어 중간 단계에 있다고 할 수 있다. 고립어로 분류되는 월남어나 중국어조차도 한 형태소 이상으로 구성된 단어가 얼마든지 있고, 전형적인 통합어로 분류되는 축치어나 에스키모어도 하나의 단어로 문장을 만들 수 없는 제약이 너무 많고 주어가 단어 속에 통합되지 않는 경우가 허다하다. 이런 경우 교착어와의 구별이 어려워진다.

한국어의 경우는 어떠한가? 지금까지 한국어를 교착어로 분류해 왔다. 그러나 한국어도 조사 '에게'가 여격, 정적 처소격, 목표격을 나타내고 '에서'나 '에게서'가 동적 처소격과 근원격을 나타내는 것이나 문장 어미 '요'가 다양한 문장 종류의 표식(평서문, 의문문, 명령문, 제안문)과 상대 대우의 표식을 겸하는 것을 보면 다소 융합어적 성격도 가지고 있다. 그리고 다음 예문에서 보듯이 한 문장이 단어에 내포되어 있는 통합어적 성격도 다분히 지니고 있다.

안녕-하-시-ㅂ-니-까?

이 표현에는 '안녕'(다시 '안'과 '녕'으로 나눔)과 '하'라는 어휘적 형태소가 통합되어 있고 어미 '-시'는 주어가 존경받는 2인칭 내지 3인칭 성인임을나타내고 직설법 어미 '-ㅂ-니'는 청자도 존경의 대상인 성인임을나타낸다. 그리고 문장 어미 '-까'는 화자가 청자에게 상황을 묻는 담화 표현이다. 따라서 이 서술어는 하나의 단어에 완전한 문장의 의미를 내포하고 있어 교착어적이면서 강한 통합어적 성격을 나타낸다. 사실상 통합어에서 흔히 볼 수 있는 목적어와 타동사의 융합은 한국어에서도 '공부를 한다, 결혼을 한다, 선을 본다' 등 수많은 목적어-타동사의 구조가 '공부한다, 결혼한다, 선본다' 등의 자동사로 통합된다. 또한 비대격 자동사(unaccusative verb)가 참여하는 주어-자동사 구조인 '걱정이 된다, 맛이 있다, 재미가 있다, 풀이 죽는다' 등도 '걱정된다, 맛있다, 재미있다, 풀죽는다' 등의 자동사로 통합된다. 이미 수많은 동사나 형용사로 굳어진 '망하다, 토하다, 행복하다, 친구하다, 깨끗하다, 열심이다' 등도 모두 통합어적 성격을 지니고 있다. 네 가지 언어유형에 따른다면, 한국어는 다분히 교착어-통합어의 선상에 있다고 보아야 할 것이다. 즉 형태론과 통사론이 불가분의 관계에 있고 통사 현상이 어형 속에 광범하게 녹아 있다. 몇 가지 친근한 예를 들면 다음과 같다.[4]

첫째, 단어 범주를 바꾸는 어미나 어근의 예는 (가) 명사에서 동사를 파생시키는 '얼룩-지다, 귀-먹다, 잠-들다, 살-찌다, 숨-쉬다, 말-하다, 애-쓰다, 손-보다, 꿈-꾸다'; (나) 명사에서 형용사를 파생시키는 '복-스럽다, 여자-답다, 향기-롭다, 기름-지다; 흉-겹다; 익살-맞다; 귀-엽다; 행복-하다'; (다) 명사에서 부사를 파생시키는 '힘-껏, 끝-내, 마침-내'; (라) 동사에서 명사를 파생시키는 '먹-이,구두-닦-이, 옷-걸-이, 보-기, 모-내-기, 죽-음, 꾸-ㅁ, 어름(〈 얼-음), 집-게, 베-개, 울-보'; (마) 동사에서 형용사를 파생시키는 '그립다(〈 그리-ㅂ), 무럽다(〈 물-업), 우습다(〈 웃-읍), 아프다(〈 앓-브)'; (바) 형용사에서 명사를 파생시키는 '길-이, 키(〈 크-이), 크-기, 기쁘-ㅁ, 가믐(〈 가믈-음), 거름(〈 걸-음), 빨강(〈 빨갛-앙), 미치-광이'; (사) 형용사에서 동사를 파생시키는 '높-이다, 낮-추다, 좋-아-하다, 젊-어-지다, 얕-보다'; (아) 형용사에서 부사를 파생하는 '같-이, 멀-리, 전혀(〈 전하-여)'; (자) 부사에서 명사를 파생시키는 '살살-이, 홀쭉-이'; (차) 부사에서 동사를 파생시키는 '끄덕-이다, 비틀-거리다, 우쭐-대다; 더-하다, 바로-잡다, 가로-막다' 등이다.

둘째, 현대 한국어는 주격, 대격, 여격, 소유격, 구격, 향격, 목표격, 근원격, 자격격, 탈격, 호격 등 다양한 격 표식의 조사가 있고 의미를 한정시키는 보조조사가 풍부하다. 문장에서 이들 조사는 자주 연결되어 나타난다.

> 그 곳-**에서**-**부터**-**만**-**은** 걸-어-야 한다.
> 미국-**의** 태평양-**에서**-**의** 일본-**과**-**의** 전쟁

셋째, 서술 구문에서 서술어에 많은 굴절 어미가 첨가되어 각종 통사, 담화 기능을 수행한다. 동사와 형용사의 구별이 통사적 진행 구문('-고 있다')의 기준으로도 가능하지만 '먹-는다, 좋-다'에서처럼 어미의 차이로 예외 없이 구별된다. 사실상 진행 구문 자체도 '먹고 있다'에서처럼 어미 '-고'가 개입되어야 가능하다. 그리고 접속사 어미는 다른

4 허웅 (1995)은 방대한 한국어 형태론의 집대성이다.

언어에 그 유례를 보기 드물게 많고 다양하다(Sohn 2009 참조). 또한 다양한 서술 어미가 교착성 때문에 융합이 드물고 다음 예에서 보듯이 길게 앞뒤로 연결되는 경우가 많다.

고기가 많이 잡-**히-시-었-겠-어요.**

넷째, 통사론상 종속절은 다음 네 부류로 집약되는데, 이들 각 부류는 각각 부류 특유의 기능을 나타내는 절 어미를 갖는다.

접속절:	'-고, -어서/아서, -(으)면, -어도/아도, -(으)니까, -(으)ㄹ 때, -ㄹ지언정' 등
보문절:	'-어/아, -게, -지, -고, 하고/라고' 등
관계절:	'-(으)ㄴ, -는, -(으)ㄹ, -던' 등
명사화절:	'-(으)ㅁ, -기' 등

다섯째, 형태론 중심의 한국어의 또하나의 특징은 모든 서술어는 구속형이고 단독으로 쓰일 수 없다는 것이다. 절이나 문장 형태를 나타내는 어말 어미가 부착되어야 한다. 즉 '밥을 먹'만으로는 쓰일 수 없고 '밥을 먹는다', '밥을 먹었다', '밥을 먹습니다' 등과 같이 필수적인 어말어미와 수의적인 선어말어미 등과 같이 사용된다.

5.2. 한국어의 두 번째의 유형적 특징은, 문장의 기본 어순이 "주어-목적어-서술어"(SOV)이고 서술어가 문장 말에 놓이는(predicate-final) 원칙은 확고하다.

한 언어의 기본 어순은 그 언어의 통사론의 근간을 이루는 중요하고 기초적인 유형 특징이다. 모든 중요한 통사 구조와 구문이 기본 어순에 좌우되기 때문이다. 그래서 전술한 바와 같이 어순 유형으로 언어를 대별하려는 시도는 19세기부터 시작되었고 그린버그도 일찍부터 어순과 다른 통사 구조(예를 들면 전치사나 후치사)와의 시사적 보편성에 대한 연구를 많이 했다. 예를 들면 영어와 같이 기본 어순이 SVO이면 후치사가 아닌 전치사를 갖고 관계절 등 수식절이 지배사(head)의 뒤에 놓이는 경향이 강하다는 것 등이다.

한국어의 SOV 어순 특히 문말 서술어 원칙은 통사적으로 안정되어 있다고 할 수 있다. 왜냐하면 전술한 바와 같이 SOV어순은 SVO와 VSO언어와 더불어 주어가 동사를 앞서는 유형으로 세계의 대다수 언어의 어순인데다 이 SOV 어순이 주절뿐 아니라 모든 종속절에도 다 같이 적용되고 특히 문말 서술어 원칙은 예외 없이 엄격하기 때문이다. 언어에 따라서는 주절과 종속절의 어순이 달라서 통사적으로 불안전하고 유동적일 수 있지만 한국어의 경우는 서술어 후치 원칙이 어떤 절에서나 예외 없이 적용되기 때문에 극히 조화적이고 안정된 언어인 것이다[5].

5 그린버그(Greenberg 1960)가 쓰기 시작한 '조화'의 개념을 크로프트(Croft 2006: 62; 71-79)가

한국어는 SOV언어인 만큼 SOV언어가 공유하는 시사적 또는 경향적 보편성도 가진다. 예를 들면 아래서 언급할 지배사(head) 후행 원칙에서도 거론하겠지만 '후치사'(전치사가 아닌) 현상은 SOV언어의 경향적 보편성이다.

5.3. 한국어의 세 번째 유형적 특징은, 엄격한 지배사 후행(head-final) 원칙이다.

구절 내에서 제일 중심적인 통사 기능을 담당하거나 통사-의미 범위(scope)가 가장 넓은 어사는 절이나 구나 단어나 조사나 접사나 간에 지배사 역할을 하는데, 이러한 지배사는 지배사를 수식하거나 지배사에 의존하거나 하는 어사의 뒤에 온다. 사실상 서술어가 문장 끝에 항상 와야 하는 것도 이 지배사 후행 원칙에 상응한다. 이 유형적 원칙 때문에 모든 수식어, 예를 들면 지정사, 소유격 구문, 관계절, 접속절, 보문절이 지배사의 역할을 하는 명사, 서술어, 절 등에 선행한다.

또한 엄격한 지배사 후행 원칙 때문에 명사구에서 통사-의미적으로 더 중요한 역할을 담당한 격조사와 한정사가 내용어 뒤에 놓이고 모든 굴절 접사(어미)가 서술어 뒤에 오게 된다. 조동사가 본동사 뒤에 오는 것도 같은 원칙에 따른다고 볼 수 있다. 즉 한국어는 전치사어가 아니고 후치사어 유형에 속한다.

명사화 구문, 관계화 구문, 접속 구문, 보문 구문 등에서 담당 절의 기능을 표식하는 접사들도 모두 이들 구문의 맨 끝에 오게 된다. 접두사는 품사를 바꿀 수 없고 접미사만 이 기능이 가능한 것도 같은 원칙 때문이다. 같은 맥락에서 볼 때, '여기-에서-부터-가, 학교-에-만-은, 학교-로-부터-의, 학교-에-까지-조차-도' 등 구문에서는 격조사와 한정조사의 순서가 대체로 확정되어 있는데, 통사-의미적 범위가 가장 넓은 주격과 목적격과 주제성이 강한 한정사(는, 도, 만)가 맨 뒤에 오고 통사-의미 범위가 적어질수록 더 앞쪽으로 놓이게 된다고 생각된다. 즉 상대적으로 강한 지배사가 더 뒤쪽으로 자리 잡는다. 또 지배사 후행 원칙의 입장에서 볼 때, 다음과 같은 예에서 서술어 뒤에 놓인 어미들 사이의 정착된 순서도 어느 정도 설명할 수 있을 것이다.

들-리-시-었-겠-습-디-다

수동 동사 '들-리'의 어미 '-리'는 영어의 -ed 등과는 달리 통사적 생산성(굴절성)이 없고, 타동사 '듣다'를 어휘적으로 자동사화시킨 파생접미사이다. 통사적 기능이 없고 단어 형성사에 불과하기 때문에 어미 중 가장 앞에 즉 어근에 제일 가까운 자리를 차지한다. 나머지 여섯 어미는 모두 굴절 어미이다. 이들 순서는 우연히 정해진 것은 아니고 지배적 경향을 따른다고 보아야 한다. 더 지배적인 요소가 뒤쪽에 붙는다는 것이다. 여기서 볼 수 있는 현상은 존대어미 '-시'는 주어에 대한 화자의 존대를 나타내고, 어미 '-었'은 주어의 동작이 과거에 일어난 객관적 사실의 표현인데 이 두 어미는 다 문장의 구성 성분인 주

원용하여 다양한 구조의 안정성을 다루고 있다.

어에 관한 것이다. 즉 문장 성분에 관한 사항은 문장 전체에 대한 화자의 판단이나 태도나 주장보다 더 통사-의미적 범위가 좁기 때문에 앞쪽에 놓인 것은 당연하다. 양태 어미 '-겠'은 그 앞까지의 명제에 대한 화자의 의지나 추정의 표현인 만큼 그 앞 문장 내용 전체를 통사-의미적으로 지배한다. 청자 존대사 '-습'은 담화상황의 화자의 태도의 표현, 회상사 '-디'는 '-겠'까지의 명제내용을 화자가 경험했다는 표현인 만큼 그 지배 역할을 한다. 그리고 어말어미 '-다'는 그 앞까지의 명제 전체에 대한 화자의 주장(서술, 단언, 답의 요구, 행동의 요구, 행동의 건의 등)을 표현한다. 통사-의미적 범위나, 의사소통의 역할면에서 가장 핵심적인 어미로 문장의 서법을 결정하는 어말어미(-다, -까, -자, -라, -어, -어요 등)이다. 이들 어말어미만이 필수적 어미로서 전술한 바와 같이 서술어에 이것이 접미되지 않으면 문장이 성립되지 않는다.

따라서 통사-의미의 지배 관계는 '화자의 주장' - '화자의 문장에 대한 태도' - '문장 구성성분에 대한 것'의 순위로 굳어져 있다고 할 수 있다. 이 순위가 한국어의 경우 지배사 후행 원칙에 좇아서 역으로 배열되었다고 볼 수 있다. 그렇다면 주격존대 '-시'와 과거 '-었'은 사실상 어느 순서라도 괜찮을 듯하나 역사상 탄생 위치가 그대로 고정되었다고 할 수 있다. 현대국어의 상대존대 '-습'도 '-디'와 특별히 지배관계가 없다고 생각되나 역사상 객체존대에서 발달된 바 그렇게 고정되었다고 할 수 있다.

5.4. 한국어의 네 번째 유형적 특징은, 주어-술어(subject-predicate) 구조와 주제-해설(topic-comment) 구조를 함께 가지고 있다는 것이다.

예를 들면, 흔히 다주어 구문이라고 불리는 '이 집은 여름이 살기가 좋아요'와 같은 자연스러운 일상 문장에서 '살기가 좋아요'는 주어-술어의 관계이나 '이 집'이나 '여름'은 의미적으로나 통사적으로 '좋아요'와는 직접적인 주-술 관계를 이룰 수 없다. 의미적으로나 통사적으로 가장 적절한 해석은 '이 집'은 뒤따르는 문장을 해설부로 하는 주제이고 '여름'은 또 그 다음에 오는 주-술 문을 해설부로 하는 주제라고 보는 것이다. '꽃은 장미가 향기가 좋아요'나 '선생님이 옷이 소매가 한쪽이 구멍이 났어요'도 같은 계층적 주제-해설 구조이다. 물론 화자가 주제-해설의 개념 없이 주-술 관계로만 표현하려면 '이 집에서는 여름에 살기가 좋아요'나 '꽃 중에서는 장미의 향기가 좋아요'나 '선생님의 옷 소매의 한쪽에 구멍이 났어요'라고 할 수 있다. 그러나 주제-해설 구조로 표현하는 의미와는 다르다.

이러한 주제-해설 관계는 흔히 다목적 구조라고 불리는 '영수가 토끼를 한 마리를 귀를 잡았어요' 나 '사과 큰 것 세 개만 주세요'처럼 목적어에서도 나타난다. 큰 주제에서 작은 주제로 되풀이 일어나는 주제-해설 구조를 통사 구조가 내포하고 있다는 것은 한국어의 유형적 특징으로, 영어를 포함한 많은 언어에서는 찾아볼 수 없다. 이러한 한국어의 특징은 수의적 반복 통사 규칙S → (NP) S와 VP → (NP) VP로 간단히 설명된다. 이러한 반복적 주제-해설 구조는 한국어의 기본 구조로서 다른 어떤 주어-술어 구조에서 변형된 것이 아니다. 변형되었다는 신빙성 있는 증거가 없다.

5.5. 한국어의 다섯 번째 유형적 특징은, 지배사 앞에서 동일 층위의 성분 간의 어순의 치환이다.

지배사 앞의 동일 층위의 성분들은 정보나 주제의 연속성, 강조, 주제화, 스타일 등의 목적으로 치환할 수 있다. 대표적인 예로는 서술어 후행 원칙은 고수하되 주어를 위시한 그 명사구들은, 같은 층위의 성분인 한, 자유로 순서를 바꿀 수 있다. '어제 영수가 집에서 TV를 보았다'를 'TV를 집에서 어제 영수가 보았다'라고 해도 같은 의미의 문법적인 문장이다. 그러나 '꽃은 장미가 예쁘다'를 '장미가 꽃은 예쁘다'로 바꾸거나 '저 소를 꼬리를 잡았다'를 '꼬리를 저 소를 잡았다'로 바꾸면 문법성을 잃는다. 해당 명사구들이 같은 층위에 있지 않기 때문이다.

명사구 안에서 소유격 구문, 관계절 구문, 지정사 등이 그 무게에 따라 비교적 자유로이 치환된다. 대체로 가벼울수록 명사 가까이 놓인다. 의사소통에 더 도움이 되기 때문이다. 소위 양화사 이동도 자유 치환의 예이다. 즉 수량 구조가 주어와 목적어 자리에 오면 다음과 같은 양화사 부동이 허용된다: '두 명의 학생이 어제 왔다', '학생 두 명이 어제 왔다', '학생이 두 명이 어제 왔다', '학생이 어제 두 명이 왔다'. 그러나 '두 명이 학생이 어제 왔다'는 안 된다. 이것은 '학생'이 '두 명' 위에 있어야 하는 한국어의 계층적 주제-해설 구조가 치환을 허용하지 않기 때문이다.

5.6. 한국어의 여섯 번째 유형적 특징은, 대우법의 문법화이다.

체계적인 대우법은 세계의 수많은 기록된 언어 중에서 일본어, 자바어 등 소수의 언어를 제외하면 극히 보기 드문 현상이다. 이 유형 특징에 근거하여 한국어를 (성조 언어 등과 병행하여) 대우법 언어(honorific language)라 할 만하다.

일상 인간 관계의 대화에서 가장 중요한 화자와 청자 간의 관계, 그리고 화자와 주어 지시 인물과의 관계, 화자와 목적어 지시 인물 간의 관계 등을 나타내는 각종 표현들이 언어 구조에 붙박혀 있다. 이것은 단순한 정중(politeness)의 표현이 아니고 규범적이고 문법적인 대우 표현이다. 첫째, '(김) 교수님, 김 여사, 김 교수, 김일호 씨, 김 군, 일호야' 등 일련의 계층적 호칭-지칭 체계가 있다. 둘째, 계층적인 대명사 체계가 있는데 1인칭 '나 - 저, 우리 - 저희', 2인칭 '너-자네-당신-댁-어르신', 3인칭 '그애-그사람-그이-그분-그 어른', 재귀대명사로는 '저-자기-당신' 등의 층위적 표현이 있다. 셋째, 명사는 많지는 않지만 일상생활의 본질적인 '밥-진지; 집-댁; 나이-연세, 이름-성함; 딸-따님, 아내-부인, 이-치아' 등의 구별이 있고, 동사에는 '자다-주무시다; 먹다-잡수시다, 보다-뵙다, 데리고 가다-모시다, 묻다-여쭈다' 등이 있으며, 부사에는 '잘-안녕히' 등 극소수의 구별이 있을 뿐이고, 조사에는 '에게-께; 가-께서'의 두 경우가 있다. 넷째, 주어나 주제가 지칭하는 인물을 대우하기 위해서 그 서술어에 어미 '-(으)시'를 붙인다. 다섯째, 청자 대우법은 존대로 '-습니다; -어요' 등 두 층위가 있고 비존대로는 '-오, -네, -어/아, -(는)다' 등 네 층위가 직설문, 의문문, 명령문, 권유문에서 사용된다. 존대, 비존대는 청자의 연령(아이들은 비대우), 사회적 지위, 직장의 직위, 친족 관계, 내집단, 격식성, 사회 규범 등 복합적이고 상대적인 요소를 기준으로 화자가 선택한다.

5.7. 한국어의 일곱 번째 유형적 특징은 풍부한 생략 현상이다.

문맥이나 담화 상황에서 이해만 되면, 특히 한정사나 격조사가 필요하지 않는 한, 주어, 목적어 등 주요 명사구는 물론이고 서술어도 자유자재로 생략된다. 대명사화 대신 생략을 선호한다. 그리고 '안녕하세요?' '실례합니다", '어디 가세요?' '또 뵙겠어요', '미안해요', '죄송합니다', '용서하세요'처럼 주어나 목적어를 넣으면 오히려 부적절하거나 부자연스런 문장이 되고 만다. 주격조사, 목적격조사, 처소격조사도 회화체에서 자주 생략되고 주절 전체도 화자의 대우 표현 등 상황에 따라 자주 생략된다. 이러한 담화 상황에 민감한 생략 현상 때문에 종종 한국어를 상황 위주의 언어라고도 한다.

6. 한국어 유형론과 문법화

살아 있는 언어는 끊임없이 변한다. 라틴어처럼 변하지 않는다면 그것은 죽은 언어이기 때문이다. 언어는 어휘뿐 아니라 문법 항목도 끊임없이 창조되는데, 어휘나 다른 구문으로부터 문법 사항이 창조되면 이것을 문법화라고 일컫는다. 지금까지의 여러 문법화 연구 학자들(예컨대 Traugott and Heine 1991; Hopper and Traugott 2003; Heine and Kuteva 2007 등)의 주장을 종합해 보면 중요한 문법화 유발 요인은 다음과 같이 요약할 수 있다.

a. 의미의 적절성(semantic suitability)
b. 유형적 타당성(typological salience)
c. 높은 사용 빈도(frequency of use)
d. 인접성(syntagmatic contiguity)
e. 담화(화용) 상황성(locality)

이 중 유형적 타당성을 제외하면 다른 유발 조건은 정도 차이는 있지만 모든 언어에 보편적으로 적용된다. 그러나 유형적 특수성과 문법화의 관계는 언어에 따라 다를 수밖에 없다. 다시 말하면 문법화가 발생할 수 있는 중요한 조건 중 하나는 해당 언어의 유형적 특징에 맞아야 한다는 것이다. 유교사상이 중국의 문화였는데도 중국어에는 체계적인 대우법의 문법화 현상이 발달되지 않았다. 중국어는 고립어 유형이라 형태론이 파고 들어가기 어렵기 때문이었다.

물론 중국어나 영어도 문법화는 계속 일어나지만 그 규모와 유형이 한국어와는 사뭇 다르다.[6] 이미 열거한 한국어의 유형적 특징은 문법화의 온상이 되고 있다. 특히 교착적, 통합적 어형 구조와 지배사 후행 원칙 등은 요소 요소에서 문법화를 자극하고 촉진시킬 여러 가지 여건을 갖추고 있기 때문이다. 지배사가 차지한 어미나 조사의 위치를 문법화가 가장 많이 공략할 것은 당연한 일이고 기타 여러 통사적 위치(slot)도 의미적으로 화용적으로 분화될 수 있거나 생성될 수 있으면 거기는 문법화의 산실이 될 수 있다. 여기서는 지면 관계상 자세히 거론할 수 없고 또 이미 많은 국어학자들이나 언어학자들이 광범하게 다루었기 때문에 다음과 같이 이미 문법화가 굳었거나 진행 과정에 있는 형태나 구문을 예시하는데 그칠까 한다. (괄호 안은 이미 제안되었거나 가능성 있는 출처임).

(가) 격/한정 조사: 에서(〈 에 이시), 부터(〈 붙-어), 보고(〈 보-고), 에게(의 거기-에), 께(〈 ㅅ거기-에), 께서(〈 께-서[〈 이시]: 존대 근원격조사에서 존대 주격조사로 기능 변화), 조차(좇-아), 밖에(〈 밖-에), 보다(〈 보-다가), '인용' 고(〈 하-고), 한테(〈 한 데 '장소'), 이랑, 이나, 이든지(〈 이-랑/나/든지)

(나) 서술어미: -었(〈 -어 이시), -습니다(〈 사옵-나-이-다), -요(〈 이-오), -겠(〈 -게 하-였), -는데!(〈 접속사 -는데 〈 -는 데 '장소'), -ㄹ텐데!(〈 접속사 -ㄹ텐데 〈 -ㄹ 터 '장소' 이-ㄴ 데 '장소'), -다면서? (〈 -다-고 하-면-서), '예측' -을 것이다(〈 -을 것-이다), -거든!(〈 접속사 -거든 + 주절), -더라고!(〈 -더-라고 + 주절), -나보다(〈 -나 보-ㄴ-다) , -ㄹ께요(〈 -ㄹ 것-이-어요), -잖아요(〈 -지 아니 해요), -ㄹ걸!(〈 -ㄹ 것-을 + 주절)

(다) 사동/수동 어미의 기능 분화

(라) 접속 어미: 한국어의 통사 구조 '접속절 + 어미 + 주절'의 '어미' 자리에 무수히 많은 접속 어미가 형성됨: -을 때/무렵/즈음, -기 전에, -는데,-ㄹ텐데, -기 때문에, -기에, -을록, -듯이, -어봤자(〈 -어 보았다 해도), -을까봐(〈 -을-까-보-아), -을까싶어, -을망정, -을지라도

(마) 조동사 구문 탄생: -어 버리다, -어 주다, -어 두다, -어 놓다, -어 가다, -어 보다

(바) 관형사 탄생: 통사구조 '관형사 + 명사구'의 관형사 위치에 새로운 관형사가 명사, 수사, 소유구, 관계절 등에서 도출됨: 외, 새, 별, 헌, 오른, 왼, 한, 두, 웬, 모든

(사) 담화-화행사, 부사: 글쎄요(〈 그럴-싸 해요); 좀(조금), 별로다(〈 별로 좋지 않다), 함께, 정말, 참, 글쎄, 저기, 그런데, 아니!, 뭐

(아) 접속 부사: (〈 그 + 리/러 + 서술구문 + 접속어미) 그리고, 그러나, 그래서, 그래도, 그러므로, 그러니까, 그렇지만, 그래봤자, 그럴까봐; (기타) 또한, 왜냐면, 아니면

---

6 중국어의 '잡다'라는 동사 'ba'(把)가 목적격 조사화하는 것이나 영어의 조동사 'be ~ing', 'be going to', 'used to', 'would', 'keep ~ing', 'have to', 'have ~ed' 등은 모두 문법화 현상이다.

(자) 보문 구문, 보문 동사 탄생: -으면 하다, -게 하다, -는 듯하다 , -어야 하다, -고 싶다, -나 싶다, -ㄹ까 싶다, -ㄹ 것 같다, -ㄹ 성 싶다, -는 법이다, -ㄹ 뻔하다, -음 직하다, -을 만하다, -곤하다(〈 고-는 하다), -어 있다, -고 있다

이와 같은 한국어의 다양한 문법화 현상은 일반 언어변화 연구와 문법화 이론 개발에 크게 공헌하리라 믿는다.

7. 한국어 유형론과 문법 기술

이미 지적한 바와 같이 모든 언어에 공통되는 절대적 보편성을 추구하려면 일단 극단적인 추상화와 고도의 심층구조를 상정하지 않을 수 없다. 더욱이 영어나 동일 계통의 몇몇 언어를 기초로 제안한 심층구조에서 계통이 다르고 유형을 달리하는 언어를 도출하기에는 너무도 어렵고 무리한 과제일 뿐 아니라 원어민의 직관에도 맞지 않는다. 그럼에도 불구하고 지금까지 일반언어학자들은 소위 보편적인 단일 심층구조를 설정하려고 노력했고 개별언어학자들은, 한국어의 경우를 포함해서, 개별언어를 동일 심층구조에서 도출하려고 노력해 왔다. 이와 관련해서 한 가지 당연한 의문은 왜 하필이면 영어 유형을 토대로 설정한 보편 구조가 기본이 되고 여기서 유형을 달리하는 언어의 구조를 도출해야 하는가? 그 반대는 왜 안 되는가? 하는 것이다. 몇 가지 비근한 예를 들어 본다.

(가) 영어의 의문문 형성에서는 의문사를 앞으로 이동하거나 조동사를 도입해서 주어와 도치해서 문두에 놓는다. 한국어에서는 이런 통사적 이동이나 조동사 도입이 없고 대신 문말 어미를 바꾸는 형태적 조작을 한다. 이러한 전혀 다른 두 문법 과정을 보편문법의 심층에서는 어떻게 설정할 것인가?

(나) 수동 구문 형성에서, 영어의 경우 통사적 이동으로 일반화가 가능하나 한국어에서는 제한된 타동사만이 수동 파생어미를 갖기 때문에 통사적 이동이 불가능하고 기저구조에 능동, 수동구문을 함께 상정해야 한다. 이러한 전혀 다른 두 문법 현상을 망라하는 보편문법은 어떤 형태가 되어야 하는가?

(다) 관계절 형성의 경우, 영어에서는 관계화된 명사구를 선행사(지배어) 바로 뒤로 이동시킨 다음 관계대명사화시키는 것으로 설명한다. 한국어에서는 관계화된 명사구가 이동 없이 그 자리에서 삭제되고 그 대신 관계절의 서술어에 시제를 내포한 굴절어미 '-는, -은, -을' 등을 붙여 후행사(지배어)에 연결시킨다. 이러한 전혀 다른 두 문법 과정을 통합하는 보편문법은 어떻게 설정해야 할 것인가?

(라) 영어에서는 '주어-술어' 관계가 기본 통사 구조이고 복수 주어를 허용하지 않는 반면, 한국어는 '주어-술어' 관계뿐 아니라 '주제-해설' 관계도 통사 구조에 내포되어 있는데 이러한 전혀 다른 두 기본 통사 구조를 다 도출할 수 있는 단일 보편 구조는 어떻게 설정할 것인가?

(마) 영어 문법에는 없고 한국어 문법에는 광범하게 존재하는 서술 굴절어미나 존대법은 어떤 보편적 구조에서 도출할 수 있을 것인가?

이런 모든 질문에 명쾌한 해답이 없다면 언어의 절대적 보편성을 무리하게 가정하지 말고 유형적으로 다른 언어군은 아예 서로 다른 통사의 기조구조를 설정하고 각 언어에 타당성 있는 형태-통사론을 마련하는 것이 정도라고 생각한다. 그렇게 함으로써 언어 기술상 많은 무리와 어려움을 피할 수 있고 언어의 본태인 유형성, 이질성, 생동성을 반영하게 된다.

실제로 세계의 다양한 언어를 비교해 볼 때 절대적 보편 현상이라고 할 수 있는 것은 극히 드물고 경향적 보편성이 흔히 있을 따름이다. 보편성이 극소수이고 유형적 특성이 지배적이라면 개별언어 기술에서 군이 확실치 않은 추상적인 보편 구조를 상정하고 거기에서 개별 언어를 도출하려고 애쓸 필요가 없다. 처음부터 개별 언어에 가장 어울리는 즉 그 언어의 표면구조를 가장 잘 반영하고 설명할 수 있는 유형을 기저로 하여 표면 구조를 도출하는 기술, 설명 방법이 경제적이고 철저하고 투명한 방법이라고 생각한다.

한국어를 철저하게 기술하기 위하여 지금까지 제안된 언어의 보편적, 유형적 이론과 방법론을 최대한 이용하는 것은 극히 바람직하다. 일반 이론을 설정하거나 검증하기 위하여 한국어를 도구로 사용하는 것도 또한 바람직하다. 그러나 어떤 가설이나 제안된 이론을 지지하거나 부정하기 위해서 한국어를 왜곡하거나 희생시키는 일은 단연 없어야 한다.

8. 한국어 유형론과 한국어 학습

한국어의 유형적 특징은 외국인의 한국어 습득과 한국어 교육 문제와 직결된다. 이것은 추상적인 보편론 추구로는 될 수 없는 유형론 연구의 실리적이고 응용적인 측면이다. 아이들의 타고난 언어 습득 능력 때문에 어릴 때는 누구나 어느 언어나 그 언어 환경에서 자라면서 쉽게 배운다. 그러나 성인의 경우는 아주 다르다. 아이 때와는 달리 나이가 많아질수록 언어 습득 능력이 대폭 감퇴하기 때문이다. 그런데 같은 성인도 어떤 외국어는 3, 4년 내에도 높은 수준까지 습득할 수 있는가 하면 어떤 다른 외국어는 같은 수준에 오르려면 10년 이상 걸린다.

영어 원어민에게는 한국어가 극히 어려운 언어이다. 미국 국무성의 외국어 교육기관인 해외근무연구원(oreign Service Institute, FSI)이 그 기관에서 배운 미국 학생들의 외국어 능력 인터뷰 자료를 분석했는데, 44개 언어를 통계적으로 비교 분석한 결과, 미국인 성인이 가장 쉽게 배우는 언어(소위 1범주 언어)는 네덜란드어, 불어, 이탈리아어, 포르투갈어, 스페인어 등이었고, 그 다음으로 어려운 2 범주 언어는 독일어, 희랍어, 인도어, 인도네시아어, 우르두어 등이었으며, 그 다음으로 더 어려운 3 범주 언어는 버마어, 핀란드어, 헝가리어, 필리핀어, 노어, 타이어, 터키어, 월남어 등이고, 가장 어려운 4 범주

언어는 아랍어, 중국어, 일본어, 한국어라고 했다(Liskin-Gasparro 1982; Hadley 2001: 25-27). FSI의 분석에 따르면 한국어와 같은 넷째 범주에 드는 언어를 학습하는 학생은 첫째 범주의 언어를 배우는 학생보다 같은 수준에 오르려면 대강 3배의 시간과 노력이 소요된다는 계산이다. 실제로 한국어는 미국 학생들에게는 중국어, 일본어보다도 더 배우기 어려운 언어로 알려져 있다. FSI는 그러한 언어 습득의 난이 문제를 언어의 차이, 문자의 차이, 문화의 차이 등에서 기인하는 것이라고 했다.

그러나 실제로 문자의 차이는 언어습득의 난이에 그리 큰 역할을 하지 못한다고 생각한다. 일본어나 중국어를 로마자로 가르치는 학교에서도 이들 언어를 배우기는 여전히 어렵고 한글을 쓰기 때문에 한국어를 배우기 어렵다는 것을 들은 적이 없다. 한편, 문화가 언어 습득상 중요성이 크다는 것은 잘 알려져 있다. 그러나 문화의 차이도 네 범주의 언어 습득 난이도 등분에 심각한 영향을 준다고는 생각되지 않는다. 범주 2나 3에 속한 언어들도 4에 속한 언어들과 마찬가지로 영어권 문화와는 큰 차이가 있기 때문이다. 그리고 한국에서 중년으로 미국에 와서 수십 년 살면서 미국 문화에 젖을 만큼 젖었는데도 여전히 영어 구사가 힘든 것을 보면 문화 그 자체가 언어 습득의 난이도에 크게는 기여한다고 할 수 없다. 문화 특히 사회 규범이나 가치관은 이미 언어 구조나 담화에 녹아들어 있어서 결국 사회언어적 유형 특징에 포함되어 있다고 할 수 있다. 이렇게 볼 때, 언어습득의 난이도는 두 언어의 유형적 차이가 가장 심각한 원인이라고 할 수 있다. 모국어와는 다른 목표언어의 성음, 어휘, 형태-통사, 사회언어적 용법, 화용적 담화적 패턴 등의 유형적 특징 때문이고 그런 특징이 많고 복잡할수록 습득이 어려워진다. 대개 비슷한 문화권인데도 한국사람이 중국어보다 일본어를 비교적 더 쉽게 배우고, 미국인에게는 그렇게 어려운 한국어를 터키 사람이나 일본사람은 비교적 단시일에 습득하는 사실은 이런 주장을 뒷받침한다.

영어권 성인이 한국어를 가장 배우기 어렵다고 하는 이유는 바로 양 언어의 유형이 극단적으로 다르기 때문이다. 6항에서 제시한 한국어의 일곱 가지 대표적 특징 중 영어와 공유하는 특징은 하나도 없고 오히려 영어는 한국어의 경우와는 정반대되는 특징을 보인다. 비단 언어 구조의 극단적인 차이뿐 아니라 대우법의 존재 때문에 사회언어적 유형의 차이 또한 심하다. 선생님과 고등학생의 취침 전 작별 인사를 예로 든다.

한국인의 경우	학생:	선생님, 안녕히 주무세요.
	선생님:	그래, 너도 잘 자라.
미국인의 경우	학생:	Good night.
	선생님:	Good night.

언어 유형으로 대우법이 없는 영어에서는 학생과 선생님이 같은 표현을 쓰는 데 반하여, 대우 체계를 유형 특징으로 하는 한국어에서는 학생과 선생님은 전혀 다른 표현을 써

야 한다. 다음과 같이 전자는 존대 표현을, 후자는 비존대 표현을 쓴다.

	존대 표현	**비존대 표현**
호칭:	선생님	(학생의 이름)
대명사:	—	너
부사:	안녕히	잘
서술어:	주무-	자
주어 존대:	-세	—
상대 존대 요청:	-요	-아라
담화 표식:	(네)	그래

영어 원어민이 한국어를 배우려면 영어에 없는 또는 영어와는 다른 이러한 세부적인 구조적, 사회언어적 특징을 터득하지 않으면 안 된다. 한국어의 유형적 특징이 외국인의 한국어 습득과 밀접하게 관련되어 있는 만큼 한국어 교육에 시사하는 바가 크다. 특히 한국어 유형과 근본적으로 다른 영어 원어민에 대한 한국어 교육 문제는 심각하고 많은 개선이 요구된다. 해외 대학의 외국어 교과과정은 범주 1에 속하건 4에 속하건 같은 시간을 할애한다. 4년간 공부하면 1범주에 속하는 언어는 상급 수준에 오를 수 있지만 4범주에 속하는 언어는 중급 수준에 그친다. 중급이라면 일상 생활에서 간신이 의사소통이 가능한 '생존 수준'을 의미한다. 그러나 한국에 관한 직업이나 학문이나 교민 자녀의 한국어 보존을 위해서는 중급을 넘어서 상급 수준에 도달할 수 있도록 하는 질 높은 교육을 시도해야 한다. 이를 위한 노력의 일환으로, 학습자의 모국어와 한국어를 면밀히 비교하여, 학습자의 모국어에 없거나 모국어와는 다른 한국어의 세부적인 유형적 특징을 체계적으로 연구하고 밝혀내서 교과과정, 교재, 교수, 평가 등에 반영하여 교육의 질을 높이는 것이 한국어 교육의 중요한 과제이다.

9. 결론

지금까지의 논의를 요약하면, 언어 연구는 단일 언어에 기초한 추상적인 보편성 추구보다도 많은 언어를 대상으로 유형적 차이를 추구하는 것이 더 적절하고 효율적이고 실리적이라는 주장하에, (가) 유형론 연구의 방법을 소개하고, (나) 한국어 문법을 특징짓는 대표적인 유형 패턴을 제시하고, (다) 그러한 패턴과 한국어 문법화 패턴과의 상관 관계를 보았고, (라) 한국어 분석과 기술은 유형론적 바탕 위에서 수행되어야 한다는 것을 역설했으며, (마) 한국어의 유형적 특징은 외국어로서의 한국어 습득과 교육에 지대한 관련이 있다는 것, 그 때문에 학습자의 모국어와 대조하여 철저한 세부적인 연구가 요구된다는 것, 연구 결과를 교과과정, 교재, 교수, 평가 등에 반영하여 한국어 학습에 크게 기여하여야 한다는 것이었다.

한 가지 부언하고 싶은 것은, 한국어는 유형적으로 복잡하고 다양한 구조적 특징을 가진 언어이기 때문에 일반 공시, 통시 언어학에 많은 새로운 구조적 구문적 자료를 제공할 수 있는 언어라는 점이다. 예를 들면, 필자가 참여한 전술한 세 가지 공동 연구에서, 여러 대상 언어 중 한국어만큼 형태론이 다양하게 분화되고 발달한 언어를 찾아볼 수가 없었다. 작년 여름 라트로브 대학 워크숍에서 필자의 '한국어의 절 연결'(Clause Linking in Korean)의 발표가 끝나자 한 참여 교수는 반 농담조로 "유형론 연구를 제대로 하려면 한국어를 알아야 한다"고까지 말했다.

이러한 한국어 구조의 유형적 중요성에도 불구하고 지금까지 한국어에 대한 국제적 인식과 지식의 부족으로 일반언어학, 유형론, 보편론 연구와 저서에서 한국어가 자주 배제되는 경향이 있었고 간혹 인용되더라도 극히 드물었고 때로는 부적절하게 인용되기도 했다.[7] 차세대 한국어 학자들에게 한국어의 학문적 세계화를 적극 추진해 줄 것을 간절히 당부한다.

참고 문헌: Chapter 7

허웅. 1995. 『20세기 우리말의 형태론』. 서울: 샘문화사.

Chomsky, N. 1965. *Aspects of the Theory of Syntax.* Cambridge, Mass.: MIT Press.

Chomsky, N. 1976. *Reflections on Language.* London: Fontana.

Chomsky, N. 1981. *Lectures on Government and Binding.* Dordrecht: Foris Publications.

Comrie, B. 1981. *Language Universals and Linguistic Typology.* Chicago: University of Chicago Press.

Croft, W. 2006. *Typology and Universals,* Second Edition. Cambridge: Cambridge University Press.

Dixon, R.M.W. and A.Y. Aikhenvald (eds.). 2004. *Adjective Classes: A Cross-linguistic Typology.* Oxford, UK: Oxford University Press.

Dixon, R.M.W. and A.Y. Aikhenvald (eds.). 2009. *Clause Linking: A Cross-linguistic Typology.* Oxford, UK: Oxford University Press.

Greenberg, J.H. 1960. A quantitative approach to to the morphological typology of language. *International Journal of American Linguistics* 26: 178-94.

Greenberg, J.H. (ed.). 1966. *Universals of Grammar.* Second Edition. Cambridge, Mass.: MIT Press.

Greenberg, J.H. 1974. *Language Typology: A Historical and Analytical Overview.* The Hague: Mouton.

7 예를 들면, 유형론의 경우 레만(Lehmann 1978)에는 한국어 인용이 한 군데도 없고, 콤리(Comrie 1981)에는 관계 대명사와 관련하여 한 군데 인용되었는데(144쪽) 한글로 옮기면 '현식이 그 래를 때린 막대기'(여기 '래'는 '개'의 잘못)이고, 크로프트(Croft 2006)에도 단 한 군데에 인용되었는데(107쪽) 'in Korean, the conditional copula –*(i)*myen can replace the topic marker –*(n)*un' 이라 했다.

Hadley, A.O. 2001. *Teaching Language in Context*, 3rd Edition. Heinle & Heinle.

Heine, B. and T. Kuteva. 2007. *The Genesis of Grammar: A Reconstruction.* Oxford, England: Oxford University Press.

Hopper, P.J. and E.C. Traugott. 2003. *Grammaticalization.* Second Edition. Cambridge: University Press.

Lehmann, W.P. (ed.). 1978. *Syntactic Typology.* Austin: University of Texas Press.

Liskin-Gasparro, J.E. 1982. *ETS Oral Proficiency Testing Manual.* Princeton, N.J.: Education testing Service.

Sohn, Ho-min. 2004. The Adjective Class in Korean. In Dixon, R. and A. Aikhenvald (2004, 223-241).

Sohn, Ho-min. 2009. Clause Linking in Korean. In Dixon, R. and A. Aikhenvald (2009, 285-317).

Traugott, E.C. and B. Heine (eds.). 1991. *Approaches to Grammaticalization I & II.* Amsterdam: John Benjamins.

8 The Adjective Class in Korean*

1. A typological profile of Korean[1]

With a total of approximately 75 million speakers, Korean is the national and native language of the mono-ethnic Korean people living in North and South Koreas. The current population of South Korea is over 46 million and that of North Korea around 23 million. Some 5.5 million Koreans are estimated to reside outside of the Korean peninsula, the major countries with a large Korean population being USA (2.1 million), China (2 million), Japan (700,000), and the former Soviet Union (500,000).

Typologically, Korean, like Japanese, is a language of head-final AOV- and SV-order syntax. All kinds of modifiers precede their heads. All particles are postpositional, while all inflectional affixes indicating tense, aspect, honorific, modality, and clause type are suffixed to the predicate that occurs at the end of a clause. It is an analytic language with a typical agglutinative morphology, in that a series of suffixes and particles are attached respectively to predicates and nominals in a fixed order with clear-cut meanings and functions. Korean is a 'dependent marking' language, in that the syntactic functions of core constituents are shown mainly by case marking and postpositional particles associated with core NPs.

In Korean, there is a clear syntactic and morphological distinction between nouns and verbs. The major syntactic function of nouns is the head of NP. The order of occurrence among constituents in a noun phrase is (1) relative clause, (2) genitive construction, (3) demonstrative, (4) specifier, (5) the head noun, and (6) case and/or delimiter particles, but the first three elements can be scrambled

* This article was published, as chapter 9, in Dixon, R.M.W and Alexandra Y. Aikhenvald (eds.), *Adjective Classes: A Cross-linguistic Typology* (Oxford University Press, 2004).

1 This is a revised version of the paper I presented at the International Workshop on Adjective Classes held at La Trobe University in Melbourne, Austrailia, in August 2002. I appreciate R.M.W. Dixon and A.Y. Aikhenvald for providing me with valuable comments and suggestions on the earlier version. I take this opportunity to sincerely thank them for inviting me to the impeccably well-organized workshop and giving us generous hospitality.

for stylistic purposes. The major syntactic function of verbs is the head of predicate. All Korean verbs require a clause-type ender. Clause-type enders include sentence-type enders (indicating declarative, interrogative, imperative, propositive, and promissive), conjunctives, relativizers, and complementizers (including the infinitive suffix *-e/-a*). Such enders must always occur at the end of a VP as suffixes.[2]

Korean is often called a free-order language. As long as the predicate-final constraint is maintained, the NPs in a clause can be scrambled rather freely for stylistic purposes. This practice must be due to the fact that Korean has a large number of case-marking particles, including nominative and accusative ones. Other things being equal, however, the most neutral order is subject first, indirect object second to last, and direct object last, with other oblique cases (locative, source, goal, direction, instrument, etc.) in between.

Korean is an honorific language. Sentences can hardly be uttered without the speaker's approximate knowledge of his social relationship with his addressee and human referent in terms of age, social status, kinship, in- or out-groupness, and/or the speech act situation. Honorific forms appear in address-reference terms; human-related nouns and verbs; pronouns; case particles; verbal suffixes, and, above all, six different speech levels (deferential, polite, blunt, intimate, familiar, and plain).

Korean vocabulary consists of native words (approx. 30%), Sino-Korean words (approx. 65%), and loan words (approx. 5%). Some 90% of loan words are from English and the rest are from Japanese, German, Portuguese, Dutch, Italian, and other languages. Except for some adverbs, all SK and loan words have been introduced in the Korean lexicon as nouns regardless of their original word classes in the source languages. Therefore, to function as predicates, the original verbal or adjectival words have gone into compounds, most productively with the native verb/adjective *hata* 'do, be'. Due to the overwhelming number of SK words, there are many native-SK doublets or near-doublets.

2. The adjective class in Korean

While most traditional and contemporary grammarians and lexicographers distinguish between verbs and adjectives in Korean, several linguists including Martin (1992) and Yu (1998) view Korean adjectives as belonging to the class of verbs. Martin (1992: 88-9) assigns all the inflected words (i.e. verbs, adjectives, and copulas) to the class of verbs, dividing it into transitive and intransitive,

2 For this reason, the meaningless citation suffix *-ta* is attached to verb stems in dictionary entries and citation purposes, as we do in this paper, as in *kata* 'go', *cohta* 'good', and *ita* 'be' where *ka-*, *coh-*, and *i-* are respective stems.

including adjectives or 'descriptive verbs' in the intransitive, and assigning the copulas as a subset of descriptive verbs.

Yu (1998) argues that unaccusative verbs are more similar to adjectives than to unergative and transitive verbs in certain morpho-syntactic behaviour and therefore the division between the class of adjectives and that of verbs is not fully justified. There are, however, many significant morpho-syntactic, as well as semantic, features that call for the division between the two classes, as will be elaborated in what follows.

2.1 Identification of the adjective class

Although not as extensive as the noun and verb classes, there is a large class of underived, as well as derived, words in Korean that can be classified as the adjective class as per Dixon's proposal (2004). First, the Korean adjective class is distinct from the noun class in that the former functions as head of VP, inflecting just like the verb class, while the latter is head of NP, inflecting only in number. It is grammatically distinct from the verb class, however, in morphological, syntactic, and semantic functions, as will be seen in detail in §3 and §4.

Second, the adjective class contains a large number of underived, as well as derived, words in all four prototypical adjective semantic types. Underived, monomorphemic native adjectives are illustrated in (1).

(1) 1. DIMENSION

khuta 'big'	*cakta* 'small'
kilta 'long'	*ccalpta* 'short'
nelpta 'wide'	*copta* 'narrow'
kiphta 'deep'	*yathta* 'shallow'
twukkepta 'thick'	*yalpta, yelpta* 'thin'
nophta 'tall'	*nacta* 'low' (as in high-rise, low-rise building)

2. AGE

elita 'infant, young'	*celmta* 'young'
nalkta 'old' (things)	

3. VALUE

cohta 'good'	*napputa* 'bad, wrong'
ssata 'cheap'	*pissata* 'expensive'
kwiyepta 'cute'	*musepta* 'scary'
kopta, yeypputa 'pretty'	*mipta* 'ugly'
nasta 'better, preferable'	*akkapta* 'precious'

4. COLOUR

kemta 'black'	*huyta* 'white'
pulkta 'red'	*phuluta* 'green, blue'
nwuluta 'yellow'	

Third, Korean adjectives function as intransitive predicate of clauses. They cannot function as copula complement within a copula clause. On the other hand, the Korean copula is similar to the English copula in that they function as head of predicate. While adjectives in English and many other languages are used as pre-nominal modifiers without any formal change, Korean pre-nominal adjectives are always in the form of a relative clause, being connected to the head noun by a relativizer suffix such as *-(u)n*, as in *khu-n/cak-un salam* 'big/small person'.[3]

2.2 Membership of the adjective class

Yu (1998: 29) indicates that a dictionary of Korean adjectives has a total of 13,000 entries of which some 2,500 are commonly used. The number of mono-morphemic adjectives, which are all native words, is relatively small and closed. My own count in the 58 page-Korean-English part of the concise Hippocrene Practical Dictionary (New York, 1998) shows that some 100 words are mono-morphemic adjectives out of a total of 335 adjectives (or some 8% of the entire entries, compared to over 50% of nouns and some 25% of verbs).

Where did thousands of poly-morphemic adjectives come from? Some representative derivational sources are illustrated below (for the derivation of nouns, verbs, adjectives, and other word classes, see Sohn 1999: 218–31).

The most productive and open pattern is of the form: adjectival noun + native *-hata* 'be'. Adjectival nouns are nouns morpho-syntactically but adjectives semantically denoting a certain property or a state. They include not only free or bound nouns but also noun-like sound symbolic words (frequently in reduplicated form) most of which are from the native stock. Sino-Korean nouns may be single-syllabic and monomorphemic but much more frequently bi-syllabic and bi-morphemic. When such adjectival nouns compound with the native predicate *hata* 'do, be', the resultant words are regular adjectives both morpho-syntactically and semantically. Adjectival nouns are of three kinds as illustrated in (2):

3 There is a set of adjective-like words that are used only pre-nominally, such as *say* 'new', *oy* 'only', *mat* 'oldest', *oyn* 'left', and all numerals (e.g. *han* 'one', *twu* 'two', *sey* 'three'). These constitute a separate category called specifier or pre-noun, a subset (along with demonstratives) of the determiner class and are not treated as adjectives in Korean grammar in that they do not inflect and are not used as predicate head (e.g. Sohn 1999).

native, Sino-Korean, and loan, with Sino-Korean ones being predominant.

(2) [Native]

kkaykkus-hata (cleanness-) 'clean' *ttak-hata* (pity-) 'pitiful'
ttattus-hata (warmth-) 'warm' *ttokttok-hata* (cleverness-) 'clever'

[SK]

chincel-hata (kindness-) 'kind' *kantan-hata* (simplicity-) 'simple'
phikon-hata (fatigue-) 'tired' *yak-hata* (weakness-) 'weak'

[Loan]

hayphi-hata 'happy' *sumathu-hata* 'smart'
thephu-hata 'tough' *theykhunikhel-hata* 'technical'

Another frequently occurring pattern is of the form: abstract noun + native *-lopta/-sulepta* 'like, characterized by'. In general, the suffix *-lopta* occurs after a vowel and *-sulepta* occurs after a consonant. Loan words do not have this form.

(3) [Native]

oy-lopta (singleness-) 'lonely' *say-lopta* (newness-) 'new'
sulki-lopta (wisdom-) 'wise' *salang-sulepta* (love-) 'lovely'

[SK]

i-lopta (profit-) 'advantageous' *hyangki-lopta* (fragrance-) 'fragrant'
kothong-sulepta (pain-) 'painful' *sang-sulepta* (commonness-) 'vulgar'

Another derivational pattern is of the form: noun + native *-tapta* 'like, worthy of, deserve to be'.

(4) [Native]

kkoch-tapta (flower-) 'flowery' *pom-tapta* (spring-) 'spring-like'
sanay-tapta (man-) 'manly' *sikol-tapta* (country-) 'deserve to be a country'

[SK]

ceng-tapta (affection-) 'friendly' *hakca-tapta* (scholar-) 'deserve to be a scholar'
kwunin-tapta (soldier-) 'soldierly' *yeca-tapta* (woman-) 'ladylike'

In addition, there are a wide variety of adjective compounds consisting of noun + adjective as in *caymi-issta* (interest-exist) 'funny', *him-tulta* (power-enter) 'difficult', and *mas-epsta* (taste-lack) 'tasteless', or adjective + adjective as in *kwut-seyta* (hard-strong) 'strong'.

Many synchronically simple, monomorphemic adjective stems end in a vowel + *p* across many semantic types. Examples are *mukepta* 'heavy', *kakkapta* 'near', *maypta* 'spicy', *mipta* 'hateful', *etwupta* 'dark', *chwupta* 'cold', *ttukepta* 'hot', *swipta* 'easy' (*swita* 'rest'), *wusupta* 'funny' (*wusta* 'laugh'), *akkapta* 'precious' (*akkita* 'value (something)', *mulepta* 'itchy' (*multa* 'bite'), *pankapta* 'glad to see' (*pankita* 'rejoice at'), culkepta 'happy'(culkita 'enjoy'), kulipta 'missed' (kulita 'yearn after'), *maykkulepta* 'smooth' (*maykkul* 'smoothness'), *noyepta* 'offended' (*no* 'anger'), and *kwiyepta* 'cute' (*kwi* 'esteem'). The vowel + *p* or simply *-p* appears to have once been an adjective formative attached to a noun or a verb stem, which is frequently not identifiable at present.

3. Grammatical properties of the adjective class

Dixon (2004) proposes two parameters for recognizing adjective class types. The primary parameter is whether adjectives can fill an intransitive predicate slot (I type: 'verb-like adjectives') or fill a copula complement slot (II type: 'non-verb-like adjectives'). The second parameter is whether adjectives within NP can take some or all of the morphological processes applying to nouns (A type: 'noun-like adjectives') or can take none of them (B type: 'non-noun-like adjectives'). Thus, there are roughly four general adjective types.

(5) Type 1: (I) verb-like and (B) not-noun-like
Type 2: (II) not-verb-like and (A) noun-like
Type 3: (I) verb-like and (A) noun-like
Type 4: (II) not-verb-like and (B) not-noun-like

Korean belongs to Type 1 in that adjectives fill not a copula complement slot but an intransitive predicate slot. When adjectives occur within NP, they take no morpho-syntactic processes applying to nouns, such as definiteness, number, case, possessor, possessed, and NP head. The grammatical properties of the Korean adjective class are similar to those of verbs in functioning as predicate head in both main and embedded clauses, taking similar morphological processes. There are considerable morpho-syntactic differences between verbs and adjectives too, as summarized in Table 1 and elaborated in §3.

Table 1 Grammatical properties of verbs and adjectives

	Morpho-syntactic features	Verbs	Adjectives
1	all bound—requiring a clause-type ender	yes	Yes
2	inflects in all grammatical categories	yes	Yes
3	indicative suffix form within predicate slot	*-nun* after C *-n* after V	ZERO
4	can occur in propositive & imperative	yes	Rare
5	can occur in promissive & admonitive	yes	No
6	function of clause-ender *-ala/-ela*	imperative	Exclamatory
7	indicative suffix form in relative clause	*-nu*	ZERO
8	past relativizer form	*-un* after C *-n* after V	N/A
9	can occur with nominalizers & conjunctive suffixes	yes	yes
10	can take conjunctive suffixes *-(u)lyeko, -(u)le -koca, -nulako, -kose, -nuni*	yes	no
11	can take intensifier *–ti*	no	yes
12	can have derivational affixes *che-, cis-, nay-, pi-,sel-, tes, yes-, -keli, -chi, -coli, -ttuli, -tay*	yes	no
13	can have derivational affixes *-sulep, -lop, -tap, -ah, -tap, -talah, -kyep, -mac*	no	yes
14	can have derivational suffix *–ci*	yes (means process)	yes (means state)
15	can take causative suffixes	yes	yes (derives transitive verbs)
16	meanings of noun + *hata*	activity or process	property or state
17	meanings of reduplication	repeating or continuing action	continuing state
18	can form adverbs	no	yes
19	can form *-ko iss* progressive	yes	no
20	can form *-e/a iss* resultative	yes	no
21	can occur in comparative & superlative	no	yes
22	can occur with phrases *-ki wihaye, -ko siphta*	yes	no
23	can occur with all auxiliary predicates	yes	only some

24	can occur with all thematic roles	yes	only some
25	case marking of object	accusative *(l)ul*	nominative *ka/i*
26	can occur with negative adverbs *an, mos*	both *an* and *mos*	only *an*

3.1 Morphological properties

3.1.1 Within the predicate slot

One feature shared by verbs and adjectives is that all the members of both classes are bound and cannot occur without a clause-type ender. Furthermore, both verbs and adjectives share all the major inflectional categories within the predicate slot: subject honorific, tense/aspect (past/perfect, non-past), modal (volition/conjecture), addressee honorific, mood (indicative, retrospective, requestive), and clause-type (declarative, interrogative, propositive, imperative, promissive, admonitive), as illustrated in (6) where all these categories are manifested.

(6) VERB: ***alh**-usi-ess-keyss-sup-ni-ta*
be.ill-sh-pps-md-ah-in-dc
(a senior person) must have fallen ill

ADJECTIVE: ***coh**-usi-ess-keyss-sup-ni-ta*
happy-sh- pps-md-ah-in-dc
(a senior person) must have been happy

There are, however, morphological criteria by which an adjective can be distinguished from a verb, in that different inflectional allomorphs are attached to them. The most clear-cut difference appears in plain-level non-past indicative forms.[4] If the stem takes the suffix *-nun* (after a consonant-final stem) or *-n* (after a vowel-final stem), it is a verb. If the stem takes a ZERO suffix, it is an adjective.

(7)		plain	subject honorific	
	VERB:	*alh-**nun**-ta* be.ill-in-dc	*alh-usi-**n**-ta* be.ill-sh-in-dc	(someone) is ill

4 The plain-level is the lowest among six speech levels, which is typically used to a child addressee. It is also used to one's own child or grandchild, younger sibling, school junior, and close friend, as well as in general writings such as articles, academic papers, newspapers, and literary works.

	*ka-**n**-ta*	*ka-si-**n**-ta*	(someone) goes
	go-in-dc	go-sh-in-dc	
ADJECTIVE:	*coh-ta*	*coh-usi-ta*	(someone) is good
	good-dc	good-sh-dc	
	khu-ta	*khu-si-ta*	(someone) is big
	big-dc	big-sh-dc	

Notice that extension of the stem to include the subject honorific suffix *-(u)si* does not affect the appearance of the indicative suffix in verbs. This time, *-nun* changes to *-n* because now the stem is vowel-final. All other inflectional suffixes obliterate the verb-adjective distinction, as in *ka-(si-)keyss-ta* 'may go' vs. *khu-(si-)keyss-ta* 'may be big' and *ka-(si-)ni?* 'does (he) go?' vs. *khu-(si-)ni?* 'is (he) big?'

Adjectives are limited mostly to declarative and interrogative sentences, whereas verbs occur in propositive, imperative, promissive, admonitive sentences as well. For example, adjectives with the imperative suffix *-ela/-ala*, the propositive suffix *-ca*, the promissive *-(u)ma/(u)lkkey*, or the admonitive *-(u)lla* in (8a) are not grammatical. There are exceptions, however. Some commonly used human-related adjectives are used in propositive and imperative sentences as well, as in (8b). In general, this subset of adjectives seem to denote daily states that can be changed by human effort.

(8) a. **kipp-ela* 'be happy!' **coh-ala* 'be good!'
**celm-ca* 'let's be young' **nuli-lkkey* 'I promise to be slow'
**sulphu-lla* 'you could be sad'

b. *kenkanghay-la* 'be healthy!' *hayngpokhay-la* 'be happy!'
pucilenha-ca 'let's be diligent' *solcikha-ca* 'let's be frank!'

The plain-level imperative suffix *-ela/-ala* has an exclamatory function only when it occurs with an adjective.

(9)	VERB:	*ikes-ul*	*al-ala!*
		this-ac	know-im
		be aware of this!	
	ADJECTIVE:	*aiko*	*chwuw-ela!*
		oh	cold-exc
			oh, it's so cold!

3.1.2 As modifiers within an NP

Both verbs and adjectives modify a head noun within an NP in the form of relative clause.

(10)	VERB:	*[nay-ka*	*a-**nu**-n]*	*[salam]*
		I sg-nm	know-in-rl	person
		a person I know		
	ADJECTIVE:	*[khi-ka*	*khu-n]*	*[salam]*
		height-nm	big-rl	person
		a tall person (lit. the person whose height is big)		

Notice that, as in *-(nu)n/ZERO* alternation in predicative uses as observed in (7), there is an allomorphic difference in the pre-nominal non-past indicative forms too. That is, *-nu* occurs after a verb stem and ZERO after an adjective stem.

The lack of pre-nominal past forms only in adjectives is another morphological difference. Notice incidentally in (11) that the past relativizer *-(u)n* of verbs is of the same form as the non-past relativizer of adjectives.

(11)	VERB:	(Past)	*alh-**un** salam*	a person who was ill
		(Non-past)	*alh-nun salam*	a person who is ill
	ADJECTIVE:	(Past)	N/A	
		(Non-past)	*coh-**un** salam*	a good person

3.1.3 Nominalizers and conjunctive suffixes

Both verbs and adjectives are essentially the same in nominalization. They are nominalized with a nominalizer such as the factive *-um* or the non-factive *-ki.* While no bare verb or adjective can be head of an NP or make up an NP all by itself, a nominalized verb or adjective functions as head of an NP just like any other noun.

(12)	VERB:	*ka-ss-**um**-ul*	*a-n-ta*
		go-pps-nr-ac	know-in-dc
		(I) know that (he) went	
		*ka-**ki***	*ttaymun-ey*
		go-nom	because-of
		because (he) goes	

	ADJECTIVE:	*coh-ass-**um**-ul*	*a-n-ta*
		good-pst-nom-ac	know-in-dc
		(I) know that (he) was good	
		*coh-**ki***	*ttaymun-ey*
		good- nom	because-of
		because (he) is good	

A morphological difference appears in constructions like *ka-ki-nun ha-**n**-ta* '(he) goes, but' (lit. 'as for going, (he) does' and *coh-ki-nun ha-ta* '(he) is good, but' (lit. 'as for being good, he is'). Notice that the pro-verb *hata* 'do' takes the indicative suffix *-n,* but the pro-adjective *hata* 'be' takes ZERO indicative.

Many conjunctive suffixes are shared by verbs and adjectives, but there are some that are not. While no conjunctive suffixes can occur only with adjectives, only verbs occur with suffixes like *-(u)lyeko* 'intending to', *-(u)le* 'for the purpose of', *-koca* 'wanting to, wishing to', *-nulako* 'while doing (something else)', *-kose* 'and then', and *-nuni* 'instead of doing'.

(13)	VERB:	*sengkongha-lyeko/koca*	*kongpuha-n-ta*
		succeed-intending/wanting.to	study-in-dc
		(I) study in order to succeed	
	ADJECTIVE:	**kippu-lyeko/koca*	*kongpuha-n-ta.*
		happy-intending/wanting to	study-in-dc
		(I) study in order to be happy	

On the other hand, the intensifier suffix *-ti* occurs only with adjectives in the construction of Adjective *x* + *-ti* + Adjective *x*.

(14)	VERB:	**mek-ti*	*mek-nun-ta*	(someone) eats a lot
		eat-*ti*	eat-in-dc	
		**alh-t i*	*alh-nun-ta*	(someone) is very ill
		be.ill-*ti*	be.ill-in-dc	
	ADJECTIVE:	*cha-ti*	*cha-ta*	(something) is very cold
		cold-*ti*	cold- dc	
		tal-ti	*tal-ta*	(something) is very sweet
		sweet-*ti*	sweet- dc	

3.1.4 Derivational affixes

While derivational prefixes do not change word classes, many derivational suffixes do. Most such suffixes are either verb-derivational (e.g. *-keli* 'keep doing'), adjective-derivational (e.g. *-sulep* 'characterized by'), noun-derivational (e.g. *-um* 'fact, thing', *-ki* '~ing'), or adverb-derivational (e.g. *-i* '-ly', *-nay* 'finally').

One prefix shared by verbs, adjectives, and nouns is *es-* 'obliquely', as in verbs *es-kata* (-go) 'go awry', *es-kelta* (-hang) 'stack', adjectives *es-kwuswu-hata* (-tasty) 'rather tasty', *es-pisus-hata* (-similar) 'somewhat similar', and nouns *es-kakey* 'slant-roofed stall', *es-kyel* 'cross-grain' (of timber). On the other hand, prefixes like *che-* 'recklessly', *cis-* 'randomly', *nay-* 'outwardly', *pi-* 'twisted', *sel-* 'insufficiently', *tes-* 'additionally', and *yes-* 'stealthily' occur only with verb stems, whereas prefixes like *ol-* 'early', *say-/si-* 'deep, vivid', *tu-* 'very', and *yal-* 'peevishly' occur only with adjective stems.

Suffixes like *-chi* (intensifier), *-coli* 'gently', *-ttuli* (intensifier), and *-tay* 'do repeatedly' occur only in verbs, whereas suffixes like *-ah* 'give the impression', *-tap* 'like', *-talah* 'rather', *-kyep* 'full', and *-mac* 'characterized by' occur only in adjectives. While no derivational suffix is shared by verbs and nouns or by adjectives and nouns, the suffix *-ci* 'get/be characterized by' is shared by verbs and adjectives. It denotes process in verbs and state in adjectives.

(15) Verb from noun: *kunul-cita* (shade-) 'get shaded'
ellwuk-cita (stain-) 'get stained'

Adjective from noun: *entek-cita* (hill-) 'hilly'
kaps-cita (price-) 'expensive'

Causative suffixes (*-i, -hi, -ki, -li, -wu, -kwu, -chwu, -iwu, -ay*) are also shared by verbs and adjectives. While a causative suffix makes an intransitive verb transitive and a transitive verb ditransitive, it makes an adjective a transitive verb.

(16) Verb → transitive/ditransitive: *wus-kita* (laugh-) 'make (him) laugh'
mek-ita (mek-) 'feed (food) to'

Adjective → transitive verb: *nelp-hita* (wide-) 'widen'
kh-iwuta (big-) 'enlarge, raise'

The most productive way of deriving verbs and adjectives from native or SK verbal and adjectival nouns is to attach the predicate formative *-hata* 'do, be' to them. If a noun denotes an activity or a process, *hata* means 'do' and the resultant word is a verb, as in native *nolay-hata* (song-do) 'sing' and SK *yehayng-hata* (travel-do) 'take a trip'. If a noun denotes a property or a state, *-hata* means 'be' and the resultant word is an adjective, as in native *kkaykkus-hata* (cleanness-be) 'clean' and SK *hayngpok-hata* (happiness-be) 'happy'. The difference shows up when they inflect in the non-past indicative form, as in *yehayng-ha-**n**-ta* 'takes a trip' vs. *hayngpok-ha-ta* 'is happy' and *yehayng-ha-**nu**-n salam* 'a person who travels' and *hayngpok-ha-n salam* a happy person'.

Unlike certain nouns that are reduplicated for plurality (e.g. *cip-cip* houses', *kos-kos* 'places'), verbs and adjectives do not usually participate in reduplication. However, hundreds of verbs and adjectives have derived from reduplicated sound symbolic stems compounded with *-hata.* Most such stems are native, but some SK words are also found. Reduplicated verbs denote repeated or continuing actions or processes, whereas reduplicated adjectives denote continuing state.

(17) VERB: *huntul-huntul-hata* (swing-swing-do) 'swing, rock'
khwung-khwung-hata (bang-bang-do) 'bang'
thwutel-thwutel-hata (grumble-grumble-do) 'grumble'

ADJECTIVE: mikkul-mikkul-hata (slippery-slippery-be) 'slippery'
netel-netel-hata (tatters-tatters-be) 'tattered, ragged'
sayng-sayng-hata (life-life-be) 'lively' (SK)

Difference between adjectives and verbs appears in the former's ability and the latter's inability to form adverbs. A common adverbializer suffix is *-i*, as in *kkaykkus-i* (clean-ly) 'cleanly', *ttattus-i* (warm-ly) 'warmly', *noph-i* (high-ly) 'highly', *manh-i* (much-ly) 'a lot', and *kiph-i* (deep-ly) 'deeply'. Such adverbial derivation is not possible from verbs.

3.2 Syntactic properties

As predicate head, Korean adjectives grammatically function as intransitive verbs in many ways, so much so that Martin (1992) and Martin and Lee (1969) call them 'descriptive verbs' (adjectives) in contrast to their 'processive verbs' (verbs). While adjectives and verbs share a host of syntactic properties, there are characteristic differences too.

First, one surest test that does not allow any exception is that only verbs are made progressive with the construction *-ko issta* (-and exist) 'be ~ing'.

(18) VERB: *nulk-ko* *issta*
get.old-and exist
be getting old

ADJECTIVE: **kippu-ko* *issta*
happy-and exist
being happy

Second, adjectives cannot occur in resultative construction with the phrase *-e/a issta* (-INF exist) 'be in the state of', while intransitive verbs can, as illustrated in (19). (Like adjectives, transitive verbs cannot be used in this construction for different reasons.)

(19) VERB: *hakkyo-ey* *ka-a* *issta*
school-to go-inf exist
went to school and is there now

ADJECTIVE: **acik* *celm-e* *issta*
still young- inf exist
still stay young

Third, only adjectives and adverbs can be compared and thus occur in comparative and superlative constructions as 'gradability' is one of their prototypical semantic properties (Croft 1991). The typical comparative and superlative patterns are given in (20).

(20) a. *A-ka* *B-pota* *te* + *ADJECTIVE*
A-nm B-than more
A is more ADJECTIVE than B

b. *A-ka* *X-cwung-eyse* *kacang/ceyil* + *ADJECTIVE*
A-nm X-among-from most/utmost
A is the most ADJECTIVE among Xs

In casual speech, an adverb can often be omitted in a comparative or superlative construction, as in *A nun B pota te (manh-i) ka-ss-ta* 'A went more than B' and *A-ka X cwung-eyse kacang (manh-i) nol-ass-ta* 'A played most among Xs', where *manh-i* is an adverb meaning 'much'.

Furthermore, the idiomatized superlative phrase *–ki ccak-epsta* 'matchless' occur only with adjectives. Thus, *kippu-ki ccak-epsta* 'happy beyond measure' is natural but **nol-ki ccak-epsta* 'play most' is unacceptable.

Fourth, the 'purposive' phrase *-ki wiha-ye* (NR for) 'in order to, with a view to' and the desiderative phrase *-ko siphta* 'wish to, want to' occur only with verbs before them.

(21)	VERB:	*mek-ki*	*wiha-ye*	*ilha-n-ta*
		eat- nr	for	work-in-dc
		work in order to eat		
		ca-ko	*siph-ta*	
		sleep-to	wish-dc	
		want to sleep		
	ADJECTIVE:	**kippu-ki*	*wiha-ye*	*nolayha-n-ta*
		happy- nr	for	sing-in-dc
		sing in order to be happy		
		**kippu-ko*	*siph-ta*	
		happy-to	wish-dc	
		want to be happy		

Fifth, verbs can take many more auxiliary predicates than adjectives. Auxiliaries like *pelita* 'finish doing', *cwuta* 'do for', *twuta* 'get it done just in case', *nohta* 'do for later', *kata* 'continue', *pota* 'try', and *malta* 'end up' occur only with verbs, whereas *ppacita* 'complete' and *pota* 'appear' can occur with both. The second verb in each example in (22) is auxiliary.

(22)	VERB:	*mek-e*	*pelita*	eat up
		eat-inf	finish	
		wul-ko	*malta*	end up crying
		cry-and	stop	
		talh-a	*ppacita*	completely worn out
		wear-inf	complete	
		o-na	*pota*	appear to come
		come-to	appear	
	ADJECTIVE:	**silh-e*	*pelita*	completely dislike
		dislike-inf	finish	
		**nappu-ko*	*malta*	end up being nasty
		bad-and	stop	
		key.ull-e	*ppacita*	extremely lazy
		lazy-inf	complete	

coh-una *pota* appear to be happy
good-to appear

Sixth, argument structures in terms of thematic roles are different between verbs and adjectives to a great extent. Unlike verbs, adjectives cannot have Agent, Patient, Goal, Source, Direction, and Instrument. They can have Experiencer and Theme as subject.

(23) a. *Mia-nun* *na-lul* *po-ass-ta* <AGT, PAT + VERB>
Mia-tc 1sg-ac see-pst-dc
Mia saw me
Mia-nun *nay-ka* *philyohay-ss-ta* <EXP, TH + ADJECTIVE>
Mia-tc 1sg-nm need-pst-dc
Mia needed me

b. *nalssi-ka* *kay-n-ta* <TH + VERB>
weather-nm clear-in-dc
the weather is clearing
nalssi-ka *coh-ta* <TH + ADJECTIVE>
weather-nm good
the weather is good

Seventh, as observed in (23a), the patient object of a transitive verb takes the accusative particle *(l)ul,* whereas the object (or theme) of an adjective takes the nominative particle *ka/i.* This latter phenomenon is extensively observed in sensory (or psychological) adjectives such as *pulepta* 'envious, envy', *musepta* 'scared, fear', *mipta* 'hateful, hate', *cohta* 'good, like', and *silhta* 'disagreeable, dislike' as in (24) and existential adjectives such as *issta* 'exist/have', *epsta* 'not exist/have', *manhta* 'many, much', and *cekta* 'few, little' as in (25).

(24) a. *na-nun* *ney-ka* *pulep-ta*
1sg-tc 2sg-nm envious-dc
I envy you

b. *ne-nun* *kay-ka* *musep-ni?*
2sg-tc dog-nm scary-q
do you fear a dog?

(25) a. *Mia-ka* *cha-ka* *eps-ta*
Mia-nm car-nm not.have-dc

Mia does not have a car

b. *Yongho-ka* *chayk-i* *manh-ta*
Yongho-nm book-nm many-DC
Yongho has many books

Eighth, while the general negative adverb *an* occurs with both a verb and an adjective, the negative adverb *mos* 'cannot, not' normally occurs only with a verb.

(26) VERB: *hakkyo-ey* *mos* *ka-n-ta*
school-to cannot go-in-dc
(he) cannot go to school

ADJECTIVE: **i* *cha-nun* *mos* *coh-ta*
this car-tc cannot good-dc
this car cannot be good

As observed thus far, adjectives have more limited morphological and syntactic possibilities than verbs do in Korean.

4. Semantics of the adjective class

4.1 Semantic types

The core meaning shared by all adjectives in Korean is 'property' or 'state' as against 'action' or 'process' that characterizes verbs. In addition to the four core semantic types as presented in (1), Dixon's peripheral and other recurrent adjective semantic types include the following. Korean has abundant underived (all native) as well as derived (native, Sino-Korean, and loan) adjectives in each of these types. Synchronically monomorphemic native ones are illustrated in (27). Note that, as in other native lexical items, many adjectives are polysemous and may belong to two or more semantic types. Examples are arranged in antonymic pairs as much as possible.

(27) 5. PHYSICAL PROPERTY

mukepta 'heavy' *kapyepta* 'light'
kechilta 'rough' *putulepta* 'soft, smooth'
kwutta 'hard' *muluta* 'soft'
ccata 'salty' *singkepta* 'not salted'

talta 'sweet'	*ssuta* 'bitter'
maypta 'hot' (taste)	*sita* 'sour'
ttukepta 'hot'	*chata* 'cold, chilly'
palkta 'bright'	*etwupta* 'dark'
malkta 'clear'	*hulita* 'cloudy'
seyta 'strong'	*aphuta* 'sick'
telepta 'dirty'	

6. HUMAN PROPENSITY

cohta 'like'	*silhta* 'dislike'
tepta 'feel warm'	*chwupta* 'feel cold'
kipputa 'happy'	*sulphuta* 'sad'
culkepta 'delightful'	*noyepta* 'indignant'
pankapta 'glad to see'	*cikyepta* 'sick of'
pulepta 'envious'	*twulyepta* 'afraid of'
komapta 'thankful'	*koylopta* 'painful'
kulipta 'beloved'	*pukkulepta* 'ashamed'
aswipta 'feel at a loss'	*kkatalopta* 'fastidious'
puluta 'full' (stomach)	*kophuta* 'hungry'
ecilepta 'dizzy'	*siphta* 'wishful, want'
papputa 'busy'	*key.uluta* 'lazy'

7. SPEED

ppaluta, ssata 'fast, quick'	*nulita* 'slow'
cacta 'frequent'	*tetita* 'tardy, slow'

8. DIFFICULTY

swipta 'easy'	*elyepta* 'difficult'
ikta 'practiced'	*sethwuluta* 'unpracticed'
kkatalopta 'complicated'	*penkelopta* 'intricate'

9. SIMILARITY

kathta 'same'	*taluta* 'unlike, different'

10. QUALIFICATION

paluta 'correct'	*thullita* 'wrong'
olhta 'true'	*kuluta* 'incorrect'
macta 'correct, suitable'	

11. QUANTIFICATION

manhta 'many, much'	*cekta* 'few, little'
tumulta 'rare'	

12. POSITION

nophta 'high'	*nacta* 'low'
kakkapta 'near'	*melta* 'far/distant'

CARDINAL NUMBERS are not adjectives in Korean but form a separate numeral class. Like nouns, they do not inflect and, when used pre-nominally, they behave as specifiers, as in *hana* 'one' vs. *han salam* 'one person'.

There are some lexical or morpho-syntactic characteristics correlated with the above semantic types. For example, in DIMENSION, only the positive terms in antonym pairs have derived nouns with the nominalizer suffix *-i*, as in *kh-i* 'height', *khu-ki* 'size', *kil-i* 'length', *nelp-i* 'width', *kiph-i* 'depth', and *noph-i* 'height'. Also, most monomorphemic adjectives in this semantic type take the suffix *-talah* 'rather, very', as in *noph-talahta* 'lofty', *kheta-lahta* 'very big', and *cop-talahta* 'rather narrow'. In AGE, while the young side of animates is expressed by an adjective, the word for 'old' is expressed only by the verb *nulkta* 'get old' (animate). While inanimate oldness is expressed by an adjective, newness is expressed only by the pre-nominal specifier *say* 'new'. In VALUE, concepts like 'atrocious', 'perfect', 'real', 'odd', 'strange', 'curious', 'necessary', 'crucial', 'important', and 'lucky' are all expressed only in SK-native compounds, as in *wancen-hata* 'perfect', *cwungyo-hata* 'important', and *tahayng-ita* 'lucky'. In COLOUR, there are five monomorphemic native terms: 'blue/green', 'red', 'yellow', 'black', and 'white'. There are, however, a wide variety of derivatives with affixes or partially reduplicated elements, as well as sound symbolic (vowel harmonic) counterparts. For example, *phuluta* 'green, blue' is extended to *phalahta, phelehta* 'green, blue', *say-phalahta, si-phelehta* 'deep green, deep blue', *phulu/phalu-teytey-hata, phulu/phalu-cwukcwuk-hata, phulu/phalu-sulem-hata* 'bluish, greenish', *phulus-phulus-hata, phallus-phalus-hata* 'green/blue here and there'). Here, *a* is a 'bright' vowel, connoting relative brightness, sharpness, lightness, and shallowness, whereas *u* and *e* are 'dark' vowels, connoting relative darkness, heaviness, dullness, and deepness. Partial reduplication like *-teytey* means 'poorly', *-cwukcwuk* 'unevenly', and *phulus-phulus* 'spotted'. There are many finely differentiated SK colour nouns.

As expected, PHYSICAL PROPERTY seems to have the largest class, since the most common function of adjectives in languages is to denote the property of nominal referents. HUMAN PROPENSITY includes sensory adjectives whose morph-syntactic properties were discussed in the previous section. In parallel to

SPEED words such as *ppaluta* 'fast' vs. *nulita* 'slow', there are native pairs that indicate time: *iluta* 'early' vs. *nucta* 'late'.

A syntactic property of DIFFICULTY adjectives is that they take a nominalized clause as a complement in the nominativce case, as in *ku chayk-un* ***ilk-ki-ka*** *elyepta/swipta* 'that book is hard/easy to read'. In SIMILARITY, the meaning 'similar' is expressed either by native *pisus-hata* or SK-native *yusa-hata* or by the past/perfect form of the verb *talmta* 'resemble, look alike'. In QUALIFICATION, there are many poly-morphemic adjectives including SK-native compounds like *kanung-hata* (possibility-be) 'possible' and *cektang-hata* (appropriateness-be) 'appropriate' and native phrases like *swu issta* (way exist) 'possible', *tus hata* (appearance be) 'likely', and *kes kathta* (fact same) 'appear, probable'. In QUANTIFICATION, 'all' and 'some' are expressed only by native noun *motwu* and SK noun *yakkan,* respectively, and 'enough' by SK-native adjectives *chwungpun-hata, cok-hata* and native adjective *neknek-hata* and native verb *calata* 'become enough'. Existential adjectives such as *issta* 'exist', *epsta* 'not exist, absent', and *kyeysita* 'stay' (honorific) may be viewed as forming a subset of this semantic type. In POSITION, 'right', 'left', 'northern', etc. are expressed only by SK nouns or native nominal compounds.

As noticed, antonym pairs are ubiquitous in most semantic types, except perhaps in colour terms. In regard to the syntagmatic order among adjectives, Korean, a relative free-order language, does not seem to have any preferred ordering among different semantic types. In general, individual adjectives with a wider scope tend to occur first.

4.2 Semantic overlap between three major word classes

Lexical items are usually assigned to different word classes based on their morpho-syntactic properties, although meanings are correlated with the grammatical properties to a great extent. For example, Dixon (2004) indicates that the concept of 'beauty' is a noun in some languages (including English) but a verb in others (*totoka* in Fijian). It is an adjective in native Korean (*yeypputa, alumtapta*) and a noun in Sino-Korean (*mi*).

The semantic contents of the adjective classes in Korean and English are very similar in that most adjectives in Korean correspond to adjectives in English, and vice versa. There are, however, some small semantic fields for which Korean has native adjectives while English has verbs, and vice versa.

(28) a.

Verb in English	Adjective in Korean
hate	*mipta*
differ	*taluta*

	miss	*kulipta*
	like	*cohta*
	be	*ita, issta*
b.	Adjective in English	Verb in Korean
	dry	*maluta*
	wet	*cecta*
	old (animate)	*nulkta*
	tired	*cichita*
	dead	*cwukta*

Dixon points out that, in individual languages, a given concept may be coded (1) by both verb and noun; (2) by both adjective and noun; and (3) by both verb and adjective. In English, he finds many instances of (1) and (2), but few of (3), one example being *fear* and *afraid*. He also finds exactly the opposite situation in Dyirbal, in which no overlap is found between verb and noun classes, or between adjective and noun classes, but considerable semantic overlap exists between the classes of verb and adjective. How about Korean? Observe the following pairs, where (a) illustrates non-cognate pairs, (b) cognate pairs, and (c) pairs of no formal difference.

(30)		VERB	NOUN
	(a)	*chita, ttaylita* 'hit'	*tha-kyek* 'blow' (SK)
		ketta 'walk'	*po-hayng* 'walking' (SK)
		tahta 'arrive'	*to-chak* 'arrival' (SK)
		tephta 'cover'	*twukkeng* 'lid'
		elisekta 'stupid'	*papo* 'fool'
	(b)	*elta* 'freeze'	*el-um* 'ice'
		mutta 'bury'	*mut-em* 'grave'
		salta 'live'	*sal-m* 'life'
		sinta 'wear (shoes)'	*sin* 'shoes'
		pista 'comb'	*pis* 'comb'
		payta 'conceive'	*pay* 'stomach'
		ttita 'girdle oneself'	*tti* 'girdle'
		ADJECTIVE	NOUN
	(a)	*etwupta* 'dark'	*am-huk* 'darkness' (SK)
		twulyepta 'afraid'	*kong-pho* 'horror' (SK)
		ppaluta 'fast'	*sok-to* 'speed' (SK)
		pulkta 'red'	*cek-sayk* 'red (colour)' (SK)

(b)	*kilta* 'long'	*kil-i* 'length'
	nophta 'high'	*noph-i* 'height'
	tw*ukkepta* 'thick'	*twukke-y* 'thickness'
(c)	n/a	

	ADJECTIVE	VERB
(a)	*aphuta 'sick'*	*alhta* 'suffer from illness'
	twungkulta 'round'	*tolta* 'turn, go round'
	chata 'cold'	*sikta* 'become cold'
	cekta 'few, little'	*cwulta* 'decrease'
	manhta 'much'	*nulta* 'increase'
	epsta 'empty'	*pita* 'become empty'
(b)	*musepta* 'afraid'	*musewe-hata* 'fear'
	nelpta 'wide'	*nelp-hita* 'widen'
	culk-epta 'happy'	*culk-ita* 'enjoy'
	kuli-pta 'missed'	*kulita* 'yearn after'
	kilta 'long'	*kil-uta* 'bring up, grow'
	calta 'fine, small'	*cal-uta* 'cut (a thing) fine'
(c)	*khuta* 'big'	*khuta* 'grow'
	palkta 'bright'	*palkta* 'brighten'
	hulita 'cloudy'	*hulita* 'get cloudy'
	thullita 'different'	*thullita* 'differ'
	kwutta 'hard'	*kwutta* 'harden'
	nucta 'late'	*nucta* 'get late'

Korean appears to be close to the Dyirbal type as far as the native stock is concerned. When SK words are included, Korean extensively involves both the English and Dyirbal types.

5. Conclusion

Let us sum up the typological characteristics of Korean adjectives. First, Korean is a language with a large adjective class. Monomorphemic adjectives form a close set of native words, while derived adjectives, an open class, are from the native, SK, and loan stocks. Second, the semantic content of Korean adjectives ranges over all the semantic types proposed by Dixon, except the NUMERAL type, which does not share grammatical functions with adjectives and thus constitutes a separate word class. Third, Korean belongs to the type in which adjectives are verb-like, functioning as intransitive predicates, and not-noun-like, not functioning as copula complement. It also belongs to the group in which adjectives function as modifier to the head only through relativization. Fourth, although Korean adjectives are verb-like, there are extensive significant morpho-syntactic differences between the class of adjectives and the class of verbs that significantly warrant the division between the two word classes. Fifth, when an adjective takes a theme object, that object is in the nominative case, generating a double nominative construction. This is particularly the case with sensory adjectives taking an object and existential adjectives denoting possession. Finally, in the native stock, there is considerable semantic overlap between verbs and adjectives but not between nouns and adjectives. If the SK stock is also taken into account, there is great semantic overlap among nouns, verbs, and adjectives.

REFERENCES: Chapter 8

Croft, W. 1991. *Syntactic Categories and Grammatical Relations: The Cognitive Organization of Information.* Chicago: University of Chicago Press.

Dixon, R.M.W. 2004. Adjective classes in typological perspective. In Dixon, R. and A. Aikehenvald (eds.), *Adjective Classes, A Cross-linguistic Typology.* Oxford, UK: Oxford University Press.

Martin, S.E. 1992. *A Reference Grammar of Korean.* Rutland and Tokyo: Tuttle

Martin, S.E. and Y.S. Lee. 1969. *Beginning Korean.* New Haven: Yale University Press.

Sohn, Ho-min. 1999. *The Korean Language.* Cambridge, UK: Cambridge University Press.

Yu, Hyon-Gyong. 1998. *Kwuke Hyengyongsa Yenkwu* (A Study of Korean Adjectives). Seoul: Hankwuk Munhwasa.

9 The Semantics of Clause Linking in Korean*

1. Background and typological profile[1]

Korean is spoken natively by some 80 million Koreans on the Korean peninsula (North and South Korea) and as a second language by many overseas Koreans. Korean is typologically similar to Japanese. This includes similarity in clause linking type. Although some 65 per cent of the Korean vocabulary items are Sino-Korean, there is no genetic or typological relationship between Korean and Chinese.

The most salient typological characteristics of Korean grammar are (i) AOV- (Agent-Object-Verb) and SV- (Subject-Verb) order syntax, (ii) rich agglutinative morphology, and (iii) the intricate honorific system. Due partly to these basic characteristics, Korean manifests many specific features including the following:

(1) (a) Korean allows pre-predicate NP constituents to be scrambled for topic continuity, focus, or stylistic purposes.
(b) Korean is postpositional in the use of nominal particles and inflectional suffixes.
(c) Korean is head final, requiring all modifiers, including adverbials, determiners, and non-main clauses, to precede their heads.
(d) Korean allows for multiple-subject and multiple-object constructions, as in:

* This chapter is a reprint of chapter 12 of Dixon, R.M.W and Alexandra Y. Aikhenvald (eds.), *The Semantics of Clause Linking: A Cross-linguistic Typology* (Oxford University Press, 2009).

1 It is a revised version of the paper I presented at the International Workshop on the Semantics of Clause Linking held at the Research Centre for Linguistic Typology (RCLT) of La Trobe University in Melbourne, Austrailia, in August 2007. I am grateful to Bob Dixon and Sasha Aikhenvald for inviting me as a distinguished scholar to the RCLT to conduct research on Korean and participate in the impeccably well-organized workshop. I appreciate their providing me with valuable comments and suggestions on the earlier version.

John	i	nwun	i	han-ccok	i	ppalkah-ta
John	NM	eye	NM	one-side	NM	red-DC

John's one eye is red.

John	i	thokki	lul	kkoli	lul	kkuth	ul	capp-ass-ta
John	NM	rabbit	AC	tail	AC	end	AC	hold-PST-DC

John grasped the end of the rabbit's tail.

(e) Korean allows major sentential constituents, such as subject and object, to be omitted if recoverable from discourse contexts.
(f) Korean has hundreds of inflectional suffixes that mark grammatical categories, relations, and functions. Frequently suffixes occur one after another in a long sequence.
(g) All Korean predicates (verbs, adjectives, and copulas) are bound in that they cannot be used without a sentence or clause ender.
(h) Korean has a rich set of morphosyntactic and lexical (e.g. nouns, pronouns, verbs, particles, address-reference terms) devices to show social relationships between the speaker and the addressee and between the speaker and the referent(s).

Nine word classes are recognized: Noun, Pronoun, Numeral, Verb, Adjective, Copula, Determiner, Adverb, and Particle. Noun, Verb, Adjective, and Adverb are open classes. Noun, Pronoun, and Numeral function as heads of NPs, whereas Verb, Adjective, and Copula function as heads of predicates, inflecting in terms of tense, aspect, modality, mood, and sentence or clause type. Determiner (including demonstratives and specifiers) modifies nominals, while Adverb modifies predicates, noun phrases, clauses, and sentences. Particle marks case, delimiter, conjunctive, and complement functions.

2. Structures of main and non-main clauses

The basic distinctions between a main and a non-main clause in Korean are whether the clause takes a sentence ender (in a main clause) or a non-main clause ender. Sentence enders occur in a sentence-final position. Canonical sentence enders in their non-past forms are given in Table 1.[2]

2 Note that there are many alternating (slashed or parenthesized) forms in Table 1 and e1sewbere. These are in general due to either vowel harmony (e.g. *-a* or *-ayo* after a syllable with *a* or *o* and -e or *-eyo* otherwise) or the opening or closing of the preceding syllable (the longer form of a pair, such as *-nunta, -supnita, -nun* (-IN), or *-ul* (-PRS), occurs after a closed syllable and the shorter form, such "*as -nta, -pnita, -n,* or *-l*, occurs after an open syllable).

A clause with a sentence ender is still not a main clause if it is followed by the conjunctive particle *man(un)* 'but' or the quotative particle *ko* 'that' (indirect quotation) or *lako/hako* 'saying that' (direct quotation). Thus, the necessary and sufficient condition for a clause to be of main clause type is that it must have a sentence ender without any non-main clause marker following.

TABLE 1. Sentence enders

Sentence type / Speech level	Declarative	Interrogative	Imperative	Propositive
Plain	-(nu)nta [after V]	*-nunya; -ni* [after v]	*-ela/ala;*	*-ca*
	-ta [after ADJ/COP]	*-(u)nya; -ni* [after ADJ/COP]	*-kela*	
Intimate	*-e/a*	*-e/a*	*-e/a*	*-e/a*
Familiar	*-ney*	*-nunka* [after v]	*-key*	*-sey*
		-(u)nka [after ADJ/COP]		
Blunt	*-(u)o* [after v]	*-(u)o* [after v]	*-(u)o*	*-(u)psita*
	-(s)o [after ADJ/COP]	*-(s)o* [after ADJ/COP]		
Polite	*-eyo/ayo*	*-eyo/ayo*	*-eyo/ayo*	*-eyo/ayo*
Deferential	*-(su)pnita*	*-(su)pnikka*	*-(u)sipsio*	*-(u)sipsita*

Non-main clauses in Korean can be classified into the following four types: conjunctive, complement, relative, and nominalized (Sohn 1999: 302-26). These clause types are distinguished by the respective clause enders, as illustrated in (2).

(2) (a) conjunctive clause--its predicate stem is followed by a conjunctive ender: e.g. *-ko* 'and', *-ese/ase* 'and so', *-(u)myen* 'if', *-(u)l ttay* 'when'. Or its finite predicate form (with a sentence ender) is followed by the conjunctive particle *man (un)* 'but'.

(b) complement clause--its predicate stem is followed by a complementizer ender: e.g. causative *-key,* habitual *-kon(un),* infinitive *-e/a.* Or, in indirect quotation, its finite predicate forn (plain-level only) is followed by the indirect quotative particle *ko* 'that'; and in direct quotation, its finite predicate (all levels) is followed by the direct quotative

There are syntactically conditioned alternations, as in the prospective *-(u)l* as a relativizer and *-(u)li* as a pre-ender suffix. Free variants exist too, as in the direct quotative particles *lako* and *hako.*

particle *hako* or *lako* 'saying that'.

(c) relative clause--its predicate stem is followed by a relativizer ender: past or perfective *-(u)n* (after v), non-past *-nun* (after v) and *-(u)n* (after ADJ/COP), prospective *-(u)l,* retrospective *–ten.*

(d) nominalized clause--its predicate stem is followed by a nominalizer ender: non-factive *–ki,* factive *-(u)m,* negative *-ci* (occurs before a negative predicate).

Both main and non-main clauses can take one or more pre-ender suffixes such as (1) subject honorific suffix *-(u)si,* (2) tense-aspect suffix *–ess/ass* (past or perfective) or *–ess/ass-ess* (past-past or past perfective), (3) modal suffix *-keyss* (speaker's volition or conjecture), and (4) mood suffix *-(nu)n/-ni* (indicative), *-te/ti* (retrospective), *-si* (requestive), or *-(u)/l(u)li* (prospective). These suffixes occur in that order.

While the subject honorific suffix *-(u)si* can freely occur in the predicates of both main and non-main clauses, the addressee honorific suffix *-(su)p* occurs only as a component of deferential-level sentence enders. Up until the early twentieth century, however, the addressee honorific suffix *-(sa)o(p)* (equivalent to the current *-(su)p)* was used in conjunctive and nominalized clauses (but not in other types of non-main clauses). Sentence (3a) is an old expression, while (3b) is its contemporary equivalent.

(3) (a) [ce nun cal iss-*sao*-**ni**] ansimha-si-*p*-sio
I TC well stay-AH-**as** rest.assured-SH-AH-IM
I am fine, so please put your mind at rest.
(b) [ce nun cal iss-**uni**] ansimha-si-*p*-sio

The notion of what constitutes a non-main clause is not always straight-forward, because some structures with a non-main clause ender do not appear to be a clause. Auxiliary and serial predicate constructions, which occur productively in Korean, are typical examples, as illustrated in (4).

(4) Mia nun hakkyo lo *kel-e* *ka-a* *peli-ess-eyo*
Mia TC school to walk-INF go-INF finish-PST-POL
Mia walked away to school.

Three verb stems occur in this sentence: *kel, ka,* and *peli.* In Korean grammar, *kel-e ka* 'go on foot' is regarded as a serial verb construction, and *peli* 'finish up' (derived from the verb 'throw away') as an auxiliary verb. The serial construction is similar in form to a conjunctive clause and the auxiliary construction to a main clause. Should we treat sentence (4) as triclausal, biclausal, or monoclausal in terms of clause linking? I will assume that the sentence is monoclausal because there is syntactic and semantic evidence that serial verbs have been lexicalized and auxiliary verbs function as aspectual or modal markers.

As indicated earlier, understood elements are generally omitted in Korean discourse. This also applies to linked clauses. Where pronominalization is appropriate in English, omission usually takes place, as observed in (5).

(5) (a) [(I) *(you)* manna-se] (I) pankap-sup-ni-ta
meet-**so** glad-AH-IN-DC
(I) am glad to see (you).
(b) [*(I)* coysongha-p-ni-ta ***man(un)]*** *(you)* eti lo ka-si-eyo?
sorry-AH-IN-DC **but** where to go-SH-POL
Excuse (me) but where are (you) heading to?

3. Clause linking structures

The present chapter aims to examine the grammatical means that Korean employs to represent the six basic semantic types and subtypes defined in Dixon (2009). It will also be observed how Korean linking markers are related to the Supporting clause [SC] and Focal clause [FC]. As will be examined in detail, linking may be marked by a conjunctive clause ender on the Supporting or Focal clause or by a conjunctive adverbial in the Focal or Supporting clause.[3]

Three English sentences with "Contrast" markers are quoted from Dixon (2009) as in (6-8) for initial typological comparison between English and Korean.[4]

(6) [**Although** John has been studying German for years]$_{SC}$ he does not speak it well.

(7) [John has been studying German for years]$_{SC}$ **but** he does not speak it well.

(8) John does not speak German well, [**although** he has been studying it for years.]$_{SC}$

3 Overall descriptions of Korean conjunctive structure are found in works like Kwon (1985), Nahm (1994), Suh (1996), Sohn (1999), and Yoon (2005).

4 In all sentence examples, Supporting clanses are so marked (with brackets followed by$_{SC}$) wbereas Focal clauses are left unmarked. The bold elements are conjunctive markers (enders or adverbials). A suffix is hyphenated, while a particle is spaced.

All (6), (7), and (S) are rendered in Korean most naturally as (9), where the non-main clause ender *-ciman* 'but; although' is a Supporting clause marker. Instead of *-ciman,* other "contrast" enders such as *–eto/ato* '(even) although' and *-(u)na* 'though; but' can be used.

(9) [John un olay tokile lul paywu-**ciman**]$_{SC}$ cal mos hay-yo
John TC long German AC study-**although/but** well not do-POL

Sentence (7) may be rendered variously as (l0a), (l0b), or (l0c) as well, with a conjunctive adverb such as *kulehㅋciman, haciman, kulayto,* or *kulena,* all meaning 'but; yet; however'.

(10) (a) [John un olay tokile lul payw-eyo.]$_{SC}$ **kulehciman**
John TP long German AC study-POL **however**
cal mos hay-yo
well not do-POL

(b) [John un olay tokile lul paywu-nuntey]$_{SC}$ **kulayt**o
John TP long German AC study-given.that **but.still**
cal mos hay-yo
well not do-POL

Construction (l0a) is considered as two simple sentences, each ending in a sentence ender, each accompanied by an intonation unit of its own. There is a sentence-final pause before the conjunctive adverb. In (l0b), the "background providing" conjunctive ender *-nuntey* 'given that; and; but' is attached to the Supporting clause (hereafter, SC), whereas the Focal clause (hereafter, FC) is preceded by a conjunctive adverb. In (l0C), the SC is followed by a "Contrast" ender and the FC is preceded by a "Contrast" adverb, a strategy to give extra focus on the contrastiveness. In (l0b) and (l0C), one intonation unit encompasses both clauses. In general, native speakers perceive clause linking with a conjunctive adverb or adverbial phrase as slightly more formal, emotive, and/or assertive than the linking with a corresponding clause ender alone. Usages of the two devices are not always the same.

Sentence (8) may also be rendered as (11) in view of the parallel information structure (FC + SC) in both languages.

(11) John un tokile lul cal mos hay-yo. [olay
John TC German AC well cannot do-POL long
paywu-**ciman** (yo)]$_{SC}$
study-**though** POL

Structures like (11), although frequently used in conversation, are viewed intuitively as a reversed sequence with the conjunctive clause supplied as an "afterthought" addition. Notice that the FC is a complete sentence, whereas the detached conjunctive clause lacks a sentence ender. The fact that the detached clause takes an optional polite particle and requires a falling intonation does not justify that it is a complete sentence.

In short, Korean is a typical agglutinative, predicate-final, and head-final language. The main clause follows its non-main clause unless the latter is expressed as an afterthought addition.

(12) (a) canonical order: [non-main clause] + [main clause]
(b) afterthought: [main clause] + [non-main clause]

Clause linking is actualized most naturally and productively by the conjunctive clause type, a prototypical device of linking clauses. This type (type 1) is formed by attaching a conjunctive ender to the predicate of the non-main clause as observed in (2a) and illustrated in (9). There are several structural patterns of conjunctive enders.

(13) (a) predicative suffixes [SUF]: e.g. *-ko* 'and', *-(u)na* 'but', *-(u)nikka* 'because', *-(u)myen* 'if', *-(u)myense* 'while', *-koca* 'in order to', *-telato* 'even though'
(b) conjunctive particle: the only form is *man(un)* 'but', as in (5b). The form *man* is slightly more casual than *manun*
(c) relativized postpostional phrases [-PRS + N + (case particle)]: e.g. *-ul ttay (ey)* (-PRS time at) 'when', *-(n)un tey* (-RL place) 'given that', *-(u)n twi (ey)* (R back at) 'after'
(d) nominalized postpositional phrases [-NOM + (N) + case particle]: e.g. *-ki ttaymwun ey* (-NOM cause for) 'because', *-ki-ey* (-NOM-at) 'as; since; because', *-(u)m-ulo* (-NOM-with) 'as; due to'
(e) conjunctive predicate phrases [NOM/INF/SUF + V/ADJ + SUF]: e.g. *-ki wihay(-se)* (-NOM serve-for) 'for the purpose of; *-e/a po-assca* (-INF try-even.though) 'even though (one) tries to', *-kona-se* (and come.out-and) 'after'
(f) extended conjunctive phrases: e.g. *-(u)l-kka-po-a(se)* (-PRS-whether-think-and) 'for fear that', *-(u)m ey ttal-a(se)* (-NOM at follow-and) 'according to; as (a result of) ', *-(u)l ppun an-i-la* (-PRS being.only not-be-and) 'not only ~ but'

The second productive clause linking type (type 2) is to use conjunctive adverbials (including adverbs and adverb phrases), which precede main clauses. These main clauses are predominantly FCs. That is, two related sentences or clauses can be linked by a conjunctive adverbial, which is a part of the main clause, as illustrated in (10). There are nearly as many conjunctive adverbials as there are conjunctive enders, in that the majority of such adverbials are made up of the anaphoric demonstrative *ku* 'that' or its compound *(ku-li-ha* 'do so' or *ku-le-ha* 'be so') + a relevant conjunctive ender.[5] In addition, there are some other conjunctive adverbials which do not employ the *ku* demonstrative.

Examples of lexicalized conjunctive adverbs with *ku* include: *kuliko (<ku-li-ha-ko* (that-along-do-and)) 'and', *kulayse (< ku-li/le-hay-se* (that-along/like-do/be-as)) 'thus', *kulena (<ku-li/le-ha-na* (that-along/like-do/be-but)) 'but', *kulehciman* (< *ku-li/le-ha-ciman* (that-along/like-do/be-though)) 'however; but', *kulayto* (< *ku-li/le-hay-to* (that-along/like-do/be-even.though)) 'even *so*', *kulenikka* (< *ku-li/le-ha-nikka* (that-along/like-do/be-because)) 'therefore', *kulemyen* (< *ku-li/le-ha-myen* (that-along/like-do/be-if)) 'if so', *kulayya* (< *ku-li/le-hay-ya* (that-along/like-do/be-if.only)) 'if only *so*', *kutaylo* (< *ku-taylo* (that-like/as)) 'like that; *kuttay* (< *ku-ttay* (that-time)) 'then; at that time', *kuhwu* (< *ku-hwu* (that-after)) 'after that; then', *kulentey* (< *ku-le-ha-n tey ey* (that-like-be-R place at) 'at such a place') 'however; but; by the way', and *kukmulo* (< *ku-le-ha-m ulo* (that-like-be-NOM with)) 'therefore'.

Conjunctive adverbs without *ku* include: *tto* 'also; moreover; besides', *tto-nun* (< *tto-nun* (also-TC)) 'or (else)', *hokun* (< *hok-un* (by.any.chance-TC)) 'or (else)', *animyen* (< *ani i-myen* (not be-if) 'if not', *ttalase* (< *ttalu-ese* (follow-and.then)) 'accordingly', *haciman* (< *ha-ciman* (do/be-but)) 'however', *ppun-tele* (<*ku-ppun-tele* (that-being.only-together.with)) ' moreover, not only that', and *tewuki* (< *tewuk-i (more-so.* that)) 'furthermore'.

Simple apposition of two sentences without any clause linking marker (type 3) is not typical in Korean. Rare as they may be, there is one frequently used alternating question pattern. The first clause ends in a rising intonation and the second clause a falling intonation, as in (14). Note that a usual yes-no question ends in a rising intonation.

(14) khephi tu-si-keyss-eyo↑ cha tu-si-keyss-eyo?↓
coffee take-SH-will-POL tea take-SH-will-POL
Would (you) like to have coffee, (or) would (you) like to have tea?

Complement, relative, and nominalized clauses do not have a clause linking

5 There are four deictic demonstratives in Korean, *i* 'this' (near speaker), *ku* 'that' (near hearer), *ce* 'that over there; and *enu* 'which' (indefinite question). Among these, *ku* is used most productively as an anaphoric demonstrative (in the sense of 'that which you and I know).

function. However, these clauses can serve for clause linking by way of clause enders of which they are a part, as observed in (13c, d, e, f) and illustrated in (15). The most frequently used postpositional particle is the locative *ey,* which is frequently omitted.

(15) (a) Relative: [[Kiho ka ka-**n**]$_{RC}$ **twi ey**]$_{SC}$ Mia ka
Kiho NM go-RL **back at** Mia NM
ka-ss-eyo
go-PST-POL
After Kiho went, Mia went.

(b) Nominalized: [[Kiho ka ka-**ki**]$_{NC}$ **cen ey**]$_{SC}$ Mia ka
Kiho NM go-**NOM** **front at** Mia NM
ka-ss-eyo
go-PST-POL
Before Kiho went, Mia went.

In sentence (15a), the relative clause (RC) is embedded in the SC. The combination of the past/perfective relativizer *-(u)n,* temporal/spatial noun *twi* 'back; after', and locative particle *ey* functions as a conjunctive ender with the temporal meaning 'after'. Similarly in sentence (15b), the nominalized clause (NC) is embedded in the SC. The nominalizer suffix *-ki*+temporal/spatial noun *cen* 'front; before' + locative *ey* 'at' has become a conjunctive ender with the temporal meaning of 'before'.

4. Semantic types of clause linking in Korean

Table 2 summarizes the non-main clause enders and main clause adverbials in Korean that are characteristic of the semantic types and subtypes defined in Dixon (2009) in regard to SCs and FCs. The list is not exhaustive.

TABLE 2. Summary of clause linking in Korean

Linking type	§	Markers (conjunctive enders) in non-main clauses			Markers (conjunctive adverbials) in main clauses		
		Form	gloss and example no.	With	Form	gloss and example no.	With
Is, Temporal succession	4.1.1	*-ko*	'and' (16a; 18b; 19b)	SC	*kuliko*	'and'	FC
		-ese/ase	'and then' (17a; 18a; 19a)	SC	*kulayse*	'and then' (21)	FC

		-kose	'and then' (18b; 19b)	SC	*kulikose*	'and then' (21)	FC
		-ko nase	'and then; after' (18b; 19b)	SC	*kuliko nase*	'and then; after that'	FC
		-teni	'and then' (20a)	SC	*kuleteni*	'and then'	FC
		-taka	'and then' (20b)	SC	*kuletaka*	'and then'	FC
Ir, Relative time	4.1.2	*-(u)n hwu/ -twi (ey)*	'after' (15a; 22C)	SC	*ku-hwu; ku twi (ey)*	'after that'	FC
		-(u)n taum (ey)	'after'	SC	*ku taum (ey)*	'after that'	FC
		-ki cen (ey)	'before' (15b; 22a)	SC	*ku-cen (ey)*	'before that'	FC
		-ki ey aphse(se)	'before'	SC	*ku ey aphse(se)*	'before that'	FC
		-(u)l ttay (ey)	'when' (22b)	SC	*ku-ttay*	'then'	FC
		-(u)l mulyep (ey)	'around when'	SC	*ku mulyep (ey)*	'about then'	FC
		-(u)l cek ey	'when'	SC	*kule-l cek ey*	'at that time'	FC
		-(u)l cuum (ey)	'approx. when'	SC	*ku cuum (ey)*	'about then'	FC
		-ese/ase	'when' (44b)	SC	*kulay-se*	'then'	FC
		-ca(maca)	'as soon as'	SC	*kule-ca(maca)*	'thereupon'	FC
		-(u)n/nun cuksi	'as soon as'	SC	*ku cuksi*	'at that moment'	FC
		-(u)n ilay, -(u)n ci	'since'	SC	*kuilay*	'since that time'	FC
		old kkaci	'until'	SC	*kule-n ci*	'since then'	FC
		-(u)l ttay kkaci	'until; by (the time when)'	SC	*kule-ki kkaci*	'until then'	FC
		-tolok	'until the time when'	SC	*ku ttay kkaci*	'until then; by then'	FC
		-(u)n/nul/(u)l	'while; during (the time when)'	SC	*kule-tolok*	'until then'	FC
		tongan (ey)		SC	*ku-tongan (ey)*	'during that time'	FC
		-(u)mye(nse)	'while ~'ing'	SC	*kule-myense*	'while doing/ being so'	FC
Ic, Conditional	4.1.3	*-(u)myen*	'if' (23a, b; 25a, b, c, d)	SC	*kule-myen*	'if *so*'	FC
		-ketun	'if' (23a, b; 25a)	SC	*kule(h)-ketun*	'if so'	FC
		-tamyen/lamyen	'if'	SC	*kuleh-tamyen*	'if so'	FC
		-eya/aya(-man)	'only if' (24)	SC	*kulay-ya(-man)*	'only if so'	FC
		-ess/ass-telamyen (counterfactual)	'if it were the case that'	SC	*kulay-ss-telamyen* (counterfactual)	'if such were the case'	FC
		-takanun	'if (one) keeps doing' (26)	SC	*kule-taka-nun*	'if (one) continues so'	FC

		-(n)un han	'as long as'	SC	*kule-(nu)n han*	'as long as it is so'	FC
		-ci anh(n)un han	'unless'	SC	*kule-ci anh(n) un han*	'unless it is *so'*	FC
		-eto/ato	'even if'	SC	*kulay,to*	'even if it is so'	FC
		-telato	'even if'	SC	*kule-telato*	'even if it is so'	FC
		-(u)lcilato	'even if'	SC	*kele-lcilato*	'even if it is so'	FC
		-(u)lmangceng	'even if'	SC	*kule-lmang-ceng*	'even if it is so'	FC
		-(u)ntul	'even if'	SC	*kule-ntul*	'even if it is so'	FC
		,(u)lcienceng	'even if'	SC	*kule'lcienceng*	'even if it is so'	FC
		-e/a po-assca	'even if (one) tries'	SC	*kulay-po-assca*	'even if one tries so'	FC
					animyen; ani-ketun	'if not'	FC
IIc, Cause	4.2	*-ese/ase*	'as; since' (5a; 17b; 44a, b)	SC	*Waynya-(ha) myen*	*'because'* (28d)	SC
		-(u)nikka	'because; since' (27; 31b)	SC	*Kulayse*	'so; for that'	FC
		-(u)ni	'as; since' (3a,b)	SC	*Kulenikka*	'therefore'	FC
		-nulako	'while doing'	SC	*Kuleni*	'so'	FC
		-ki ttaymull ey	'because' (28a)	SC	*kule-nulako*	'while doing so'	FC
		-(u)mulo	'as; because'	SC	*ku ttamun ey*	'because of that' (28b,c)	FC
		-kiey; -killay	'as; because'	SC	*Kulemulo*	'so; hence; therefore'	FC
		-(u)n/nun thas ulo	'owing to'	SC	*kule-kieylkillay*	'that's why...'	FC
		-(u)n/nun kola	'as; because'	SC	*ku(len) thas ulo*	'owingto that'	FC
		-(u)n/nun kkatalk ey	'for reason that'	SC	*kulen-kolo*	'so; hence; therefore'	FC
		-(u)n/nun mankhum	'now that'	SC	*ku(len) kkatalk ulo*	'for that rea-son'	FC
					kulen mankhum	'that being the case'	FC
IIr, Result	4.2	*-ese/ase*	'since; as' (29; 44a)	SC	*Kulayse*	'thus'	FC
		-(u)n kyelkwa (lo)	'as a result of'	SC	*ku kyelkwa (lo)*	'as a conse-quence'	FC
		-(u)m ey ttala(se)	'according to; as a result of'	SC	*Ttalase*	'accordingly'	FC
		(u)n/null palam ey	'as a result of' (29)	SC	*ku palam ey*	'as a result of that'	FC
IIp, Purpose	4.2	*-(u)le;-(u)ly-eko*	'(in order) to' (30a, b)	FC	*kule-lyeko*	'to do so'	SC

		-koca	'wishing to'	FC	*kule-koca*	'to do so'	SC
		-key(-kkum)	'so that'	FC	*kule-key(-kkum)*	'to do so'	SC
		-tolok	'so that' (31a)	FC	*kule-tolok*	'to do so'	SC
		-(u)lako	'so that'	FC	*kule-lako*	'to do so'	SC
		-ki wihay(se)	'in order to'	FC	*kule-ki wihay(se)*	'to do so'	SC
		-(u)1 mokcek ulo	'in order to'	FC	*ku mokcek ulo*	'for that purpose'	SC
		-(u)1 seym ufo	'with a view to'	FC	*kulel seym ulo*	'intending to do so'	SC
III, Possible Consequence	4.3	*an* ~ *-tolok*	'least' (31a)	SC	*kule(h)-d anhtolok*	'lest it should do/be so' (31b)	FC
		-(u)1 kyengwu (ey)	'in the case that'	SC	*kulel kyengwu (ey)*	'in that case'	FC
		-(u) lkkapoa(se)	'being afraid that' (32)	SC	*kule-lkkapoa(se)*	'fearing it may be so'	FC
		-(u)lkka siph-e(se)	'anticipating'	SC	*kule-lkka siph-e(se)*	'anticipating that'	FC
		-(u)lkka ha-ko	'expecting to do'	SC	*kule-lkka ha-ko*	'expecting that'	FC
IVu,	4.4	*-ko*	'and' (16b,c; 33)	*n/a*	*kuliko*	'and'	*n/a*
Unordered addition		*-(u)mye*	'and' (33)	*n/a*	*ttohan*	'also; and'	*n/a*
IVs,	4.4	*-ko*	'and' (34a)	SC	*kuliko*	'in addition'	FC
Same-event addition		*-keniwa*	'as well as'	SC	*kule(h)-keniwa*	'not only that'	FC
		-(u)1 ppun anila	'not only ~ but'	SC	*ku ppun anila*	'not only that'	FC
		-(u)l ppuntele	'not only ~ but'	SC	*(ku) ppuntele*	'not only that'	FC
		-(u)1 swulok	'the more ~ the more'	SC	*kulel swulok*	'the more it is so ~'	FC
		-nulako	'while doing' (34b)	SC	*kule-nulaka*	'while doing so'	FC
		-(u)myense	'while doing' (34C)	SC	*kule-myense*	'while doing so'	FC
					Tewuki	'moreover'	FC
IVe,		*-(n)untey*	'given that' (l0b; 28c; 35)	SC	*kulentey*	'by the way; yet'	FC
Elaboration	4.4	*-(u)n/nun* cuk	'given that'	SC	*kulencuk*	'therefore; then'	FC
		-(u)n/nun pa	'given that'	SC	*kulen pa*	'therefore'	FC
IVc, Contrast	4.4	*man(un)* [PART]	'but' (5b)	SC	*kulehciman*	'but; however' (l0a)	FC
		-ciman	'but; although' (9; 10c; 11)	SC	*kulena*	'but' (l0c)	FC
		-(u)na	'but; although'	SC	*kulayto*	'but' (l0b)	FC

		-eto/ato	'(even) though; but'	SC	*kule-kenman*	'though'	FC
		-kenman	'though'	SC	*kule-toy*	'but'	FC
		-toy	'but'	SC	*kulentey-to*	'despite that fact'	FC
		-(n)untey-to	'despite the fact that'	SC	*haciman*	'however'	FC
					hena	'but'	FC
					taman	'however'	FC
					tewuki	'furthermore'	FC
Vd, Disjunction	4.5	*-kena*	'or' (36; 39a, b)	*n/a*	*kule-kena*	'or'	*n/a*
		-tunci	'or' (36)	*n/a*	*kule-tunci*	'or'	*n/a*
		two clause apposition only in questions	rising intonation (clause 1) + falling intonation (clause 2) (14; 40)	*n/a*	*hokun; ttonun*	'or; or else' (36)	*n/a*
					animyen	'or; or else'(36;40)	*n/a*
Vr, Rejection	4.5	*-(u)n/nun* tay-sin *(ey)*	'instead of' (37a)	SC	*ku taysin (ey)*	'instead' (37c)	FC
		an ~ ko	'not ~ (but)' (37b, c)	SC	*kule(h)-ci anh-ko*	'not doing/being so'	FC
Vs, Suggestion	4.5	*-nuni (pota)*	'rather than' (38)	SC	*kule-nuni (pota)*	'rather than doing so'	FC
		-nun kes pota	'rather than'	SC	*kule-nun kes pota*	'rather than doing *so*'	FC
VIr, Real manner	4.6	*-(u)n/nun taylo*	'as; according to' (41a)	SC	*kutaylo*	'like that'	FC
		-(u)n/nun kes chelem	'as; like; so ~ as'	SC	*ku chelem*	'like that'	FC
		-(u)n/nun kes kathi	'as; like; so ~ as'	SC	*ku kathi*	'like that'	FC
		(-(u)n/nun)-tusi	'like;as if'(41b)	SC	*kele(h)-tusi*	'like that'	FC
		-tasiphi	'as; in the same way that'	SC	*kule(h)-tasiphi*	'like that'	FC
VIh, Hypothetical manner	4.6	*(machi)* +*-tasiphi*	'as if; like'	SC	*(machi)* + *kule-tasiphi*	'as if doing/being so'	FC
		(-(n)un/(u)l)-tusi	'as if' (42)	SC	*kule-((n)un/l)-tusi*	'as if so'	FC
		-(u)n/nun/(u)l	'as if' (42)	SC	*kule-n/nun/l kes*	'as if (one) would do so	FC
		kes kathi/chelem			*kathi/chelem*		
VIw, Ways/ *means*	4.6	*-ese/ase*	'by' ~ -ing' (43a)	SC	*kulayse*	'by doing so'	FC
		-e/a kaciko	'by' ~ -ing' (43b)	SC	*kulay-kaciko*	'by doing so'	FC

The six semantic types and subtypes will be elaborated one by one in what follows.

4.1. *Temporal (I)*

Temporal linkage of two events, whether it is temporal succession or relative time, is expressed by an SC preceding an FC, with a marker placed in between. Simle apposition is rare in Korean and unnatural if used, except perhaps in a scenario script.

4.1.1. *Temporal succession (Is)* Several conjunctive enders are employed to indicate temporal succession: *-ko* 'and', *-kose* (< *-ko-se* (and-then)) 'and then', *-ko nase(* < *-ko na-se* (and come.out-then)) 'and then', *-ese/ase* 'and then; and so', *-teni* (< *-te-ni* (-RT-as)) 'and then', and *-taka* 'while doing; and then'.[6] The basic function of *-ko* is to connect two independent events or states, which may be pragmatically sequential, simultaneous, or independent. Without pragmatic contexts, (16) can be interpreted as (a), (b), and (c).

(16)	Kiho	ka	nolayha-**ko**	Mia	ka	chwumchw-eyo
	Kiho	NMs	sing-**and**	Mia	NM	dance-POL

(a) Kiho sings and then Mia dances.
(b) Kiho sings and Mia dances. (at the same time)
(c) Kiho sings and Mia dances. (neutral as to temporal order)

Two events in sequential interpretation (16a) follow the iconicity principle, the first clause (SC) denoting the first occurring event and the second clause (FC) the second occurring event. On the other hand, *-kose* and *-ko nase* uniquely denote temporal *sequence.* When either of these replaces *-ko* in (16), only the (16a) reading is obtained.

The ender *-ese/ase* 'and then; and so' denotes sequential occurrence of two "related" events, with the event of the first clause (SC) functioning as a precondition or cause for the event denoted by the second clause (FC). If the subjects of the two clauses are the same, temporal succession interpretation stands out more conspicuously, as in (17a). If the subjects are different, causal meaning stands out, as in (17b).

6 In colloquial speech, *-kose* may be contracted to -ko, *-ese/ase* to *-e/a,* and *-taka* to *-ta.* Thus, the coordinative *-ko* and the subordinative *-ko* contracted from *-kose* are homonymous. The same is true with the mfinitive *-e/a* and the *-e/a* contracted from *-ese/ase.*

(17) (a) [Kiho ka kongwen ey ka-ase]$_{SC}$ nol-ayo
Kiho NM park to go-and.then play-POL
Kiho went to the park and is playing there.
(b) [Kiho ka cha lul phal-**ase**]sc Mia ka wul-ess-eyo
Kiho NM car AC sell-**and.so** Mia NM cry-PST-POL
Kiho sold the car, and Mia cried for that.

The suffix *-ese/ase* cannot be used when its clause does not indicate cause or precondition of the event expressed by the following FC. Sentence (18a) is thus not acceptable because there is no such causal or preconditional relation. A similar meaning is expressed by an SC with *-ko, -kose,* or *-ko nase,* as in (18b).

(18) (a) *[Kiho nun nol-**ase**]$_{SC}$ ca-ss-eyo
Kiho TC play-**and.then** sleep-PST-POL
Kiho played and then slept.
(b) [Kiho nun nol-**ko**; **-kose**; **-ko nase**]$_{SC}$ ca-ss-eyo
Kiho TC play-**and**; **-and.then**; **-and then** sleep-PST-POL
Kiho played and (then) slept.

Similarly, compare the two sentences of a minimal pair in (19). Notice that only (19a) indicates the existence of a cause-effect relation between the two clauses. It presupposes that Kiho and Mia went to the movies together because going to the movies was caused or preconditioned by Kiho's meeting with Mia.

(19) (a) [Kiho nun Mia lul manna-**ase**]$_{SC}$ kukcang ey ka-ss-eyo
Kiho TC Mia AC meet-**and.then** theatre to go-PST-POL
Kiho met Mia and then went to the movies (with her).
(b) [Kiho nun Mia lul manna-**ko**; **-kose**; **-ko nase**]$_{SC}$
Kiho TC Mia AC meet **-and**; **-and. then**; **-and.then**;
Kukcang ey ka-ss-eyo
Theatre to go-PST-POL
Kiho met Mia and (then) went to the movies (by hinrself).

The conjunctive ender *-teni* 'and then'requires a non-speaker subject and a past event, as in (20a), due to the retrospective meaning (the speaker's past observation or experience) in the *-te* part. The "transferentive" conjunctive ender *-taka* 'while' indicates that the event of an SC is interrupted and immediately followed by a different event denoted by an FC, as in (20b).

(20) (a) [pi ka o-**teni**]$_{SC}$ nwun i w-ayo
rain NM come-**and.then** snow NM come-POL
(I saw) it rained and then it (now) snows.

(b) [pi ka o-**taka**]$_{SC}$ nwun i w-ayo
rain NM come-**then** snow NM come-POL
It rained and then (now) it snows.

The second distinct way of expressing temporal succession is by means of conjunctive adverbials such as *kuliko* 'and (then)', *kulikose* 'and then', *kuliko nase* 'and then', *kulayse* 'and then', *kuleteni* 'and then; and *kuletaka* 'and then'. These adverbials precede an FC. In (21), only *kulayse* presupposes that Kiho went to the movies with Mia.

(21) [Kiho nun Mia lul manna-ss-eyo.]$_{SC}$ **kulayse; kulikose**
Kiho NM Mia AC meet-PST-POL **and.so; and.then**
kukcang ey ka-ss-eyo
theatre to go-PST-POL
Kiho met Mia. And then he went to the movies (with her).

4.1.2. *Relative time (Ir)* There are a number of clause enders that mark relative time, as given in Table 3, in which a rough morphemic analysis is made for each ender. All these enders are attached to an SC, which precedes its FC.

TABLE 3. Temporal linking markers (clause enders on SC)

Time of Supporting clause with respect to time of Focal clause			
PAST	FUTURE	SAME TIME	
(u)n twi (ey) (-RL back at) 'after' *-(u)n hwu (ey)* (-RL after at) 'after' *-(u)n taum (ey)* (-RL next at) 'after'	*-ki cen (ey)* (-NOM front at) 'before' *-ki ey aph-se-(se)* (-NOM at front-stand-and) 'before'	*-(u)l ttay (ey)* (-PRS time at) 'when' *-(u)l mulyep (ey)* (-PRS approx. time at) 'around when' *-(u)l cuum (ey)*	POINT IN TIME
		(-PRS approx.time at) 'approx. when' *-(u)l cek ey* (-PRS time at) 'when' *-ese/ase* 'when' *-ca (ma-ca)* (upon stop-upon) 'as soon as' *-(u)n/nun cuksi*	

		(-RL immediate. time) 'as soon as'	
-(u)n ilay (RL since) 'since' *-(u)n* ci (-RL since) 'since' [a duration word required in main clause]	*-ki kkaci* (-NOM until) 'until' *-(u)l ttay kkaci* (-PRS time till) 'until; by (the time when)' *-tolok* 'until the time when'	*-(u)n/nun/(u)l tongan (ey)* (-RL/PRS duration in) 'while; during (the time when)' *-(u)mye(nse)* 'while ~-ing'	LENGTH OF TIME

Notice that a majority of the temporal linking markers have developed from relativized or nominalized postpositional constructions (cf. (13c, d)). In (22), for example, the time/place noun *cen* 'front; before' takes only the non-factive nominalizer *-ki*, the time noun *ttay* 'when' takes only the prospective relativizer *-(u)l*, and the time/place noun *twi* 'back; after' takes only the past/perfective relativizer *-(u)n*.

(22) (a) [sihem kyelkwa ka palphyona-**ki** **cen** (**ey**)]$_{SC}$ Kiho
exam results NM announced-NOM **front at** Kiho
nun kekcenghay-ss-eyo
TC worry-PST-POL
Kiho was worried *before* the exam results were announced.

(b) [sihem kyelkwa ka palphyona-**l** **ttay** (**ey**)]$_{SC}$ Kiho
exam results NM announced-**PRS** **time at** Kiho
nun kippehay-ss-eyo
TC delighted-PST-POL
Kiho was delighted *when* the exam results were announced.

(c) [sihem kyelkwa ka palphyona-**n** **twi** (**ey**)]]$_{SC}$ Kiho
exam results NM announced-**RL** **back at** Kiho
nun hayngpokhay-ss-eyo
TC happy-PST-POL
Kiho was happy *after* the exam results were announced.

The same relative time concepts can be expressed by temporal adverbials, as in Table 4. Notice that the adverbials are anaphoric demonstrative compounds, which mark FCs.

TABLE 4. Temporal linking markers (adverbials on FC)

Time of Supporting clause with respect to time of Focal clause			
PAST	FUTURE	SAME TIME	
ku twi (ey) (that back at) 'after that' *ku-hwu (ey)* (that-after at) 'after that'	*ku-cen (ey)* (that-before at) 'before that' *ku ey aph-s-e(se)* (that at front-stand-and) 'before that'	*ku-ttay (ey)* (that-time at) 'then; at that time' *ku mulyep (ey)* (that about. time at) 'around then' *ku cuum (ey)* (that about. time at) 'about then' *kule-l cek ey* (do/be.so-PRS time at) 'at that time' *kulayse* 'then' *kule-ca (ma-ca)* (do/be.so-upon stop-upon) 'thereupon' *ku cuksi (ey)* (that moment at) 'at that moment'	POINT IN TIME
ku ilay (that since) 'since then' *kule-n ci* (do/be.so-RL since) 'since then'	*kule-ki kkaci* (do/be.so-NOM till) 'until then' *ku-ttay kkaci* (that-time till) 'until then; by that time' *kule-tolok* 'until then'	*ku-tongan (ey)* (that-duration in) 'during that time' *kule-myense* (do/be.so-while ~ -ing) 'while doing/being so'	LENGTH OF TIME

4.1.3. *Conditional (Ic)* Conditional enders are attached to SCs. The generic conditional ender *-(u)myen* may refer to both 'if' and 'when' if not occurring with the modal adverb *manil* 'by any chance' in which case only the conditional meaning is possible. The suffix *-ketun* 'if; in case; provided that' is used only as conditional and only when the FC denotes the speaker's intention, as in an imperative, propositive, or intentive sentence.[7]

(23) (a) [pi ka an o-**myen;-ketun**]$_{SC}$ ka-kela/-ca/-keyss-ta
rain NM not come-**if/when;-if** go-IM/-PR/-intend-DC
Please go!/Let's go/I will go on the off chance that it does not rain.

7 Neither *-(u)myen* nor *-ketun* is inteq>reted exclusively as 'when' or function, as a marker of an interrogative complement clause such as *I don't know if he is coming*. Thus, they are basically conditional markers.

(b) [pi ka o-myen; *-ketun]$_{SC}$ Mia nun aph-ayo
rain NM come-**if/when; -if** Mia TC sick-POL
If/when it rains, Mia gets sick.

Condition is expressed by some other suffixes as well, which do not allow 'when' interpretation. The enders *-tamyen* (after a verb or adjective)/*-lamyen* (after a copula) 'if; provided that' denote a stronger condition than *-(u)myen,* in that they have developed from *-ta/la ko ha-myen* (-DC QT say-if) 'if (someone) says that' with the omission of *ko ha* 'say that'. Exclusive condition is expressed *by* the suffix *-eya/aya(-man)* 'if only'. The full form *-eya/aya-man* conveys stronger exclusiveness than *-eya/aya* does.

(24) [Kiho ka ka-**ya(-man)**]$_{SC}$ Mia to ka-yo
Kiho NM go-**if.only-only** Mia also go-POL
Only if Kiho goes, Mia goes.

There are means to show the distinction between possible and counter-factual conditionals. Compare the possible conditional in (25a), where *-(u)myen* or *-ke-tun* may occur, with the counterfactual conditionals in (25b) and (25c), where only *-(u)myen* can occur.

(25) (a) [nayil Kiho ka o-**myen;** **-ketun**]$_{SC}$ kathi
tomorrow Kiho NM come-if/when; -if together
nol-ayo
play-POL
If Kiho comes tomorrow, (let's) play together.

(b) [nayil Kiho ka o-**myen**]$_{SC}$ kathi nol-**ass-ul**
tomorrow Kiho NM come-**if** together play-**PAST-PRS**
kes i-ntey *yo*
fact be-but POL
If Kiho *were to* come tomorrow, (we) *would* play together.

(c) [nayil Kiho ka w-**ass-umyen**]$_{SC}$ kathi no-l
tomorrow Kiho NM come-**PAST-if** together play-PRS
kes i-ntey *yo*
fact be-but POL
If Kiho *were to* come tomorrow, (we) *would* play together.

(d) [Kiho ka w-**ass-umyen**]sc kathi nol-**ass-ul** **kes**
Kiho NM come-**PST-if** together play-**PST-PRS** **fact**
i-ntey *yo*
be-but POL

If Kiho *had come,* (we) *would have* played together.

Counterfactuality is indicated in both the SC and FC. The SC must have the past or non-past form of the conditional ender *-(u)myen* and the FC must have the past or non-past form of the counterfactual ender-*(u)l kes/the i-ntey* (PRS fact be-but) 'would; could'. For present or future counterfactual, as in (25b, c), either the SC or the FC must be made in the past tense. For past counterfactual, both the SC and FC must be made in the past tense, as in (25d). Counterfactuality may be reinforced by replacing *-ass/ess-umyen* with *-ass/ess-tamyen* or *-ass/ess-telamyen.* The ender *-ass/ess-telamyen,* which has developed from *-ass/ess-te-la ko ha-myen* (-PST-RT-DC QT say-if) 'if (someone) says that it had done/been', is used only as a counterfactual marker for the present, future, or past.

There is a Possible conditional construction which predicts a bad consequence. For this conditional, the suffix *-takanun* (< *taka-nun* (while-TC)) 'if one keeps doing' is used.

(26) [Kiho ka celehkey nol-**takanun**]$_{SC}$ sihem ey
Kiho NM like.that play-**if.keep ~ -ing** exam at
silphayha-keyss-eyo
fail-may-POL
Kiho may fail in the exam, if he keeps playing like that.

The meaning of 'unless' is expressed by the ender *-ci an-h-(n)un han* (-NOM not-do/be-RL limit) 'unless', as in *Kiho ka o-ci anh-nun han* 'unless Kiho comes' and *nalssi ka coh-ci anh-un han* 'unless the weather is good'. Its positive counterpart is *-(n)un han* (RL limit) 'as long as'.

Concessive enders include *-eto/ato, -telato, -(u)lcilato, -ulmangceng, -(u)ntul* and *-(u)lcienceng,* all meaning 'even if', and the recent innovation *-e/a po-assca* (-INF try-even.if) 'even if one tries'. Bak (2007) discusses semantic and pragmatic connection between concessive and conditional enders in Korean.

Conditionals and concessives can also be expressed extensively by conjunctive adverbials in FCs. These adverbials, many of which are in free variation in usage, are listed in Table 2 (Ic).

4.2. *Consequence (II)*

A number of structural patterns mark Cause, Result, and Purpose, as observed in Table 2 (IIe, IIr, and IIp). Table 5 is a morphologically elaborated version. Notice that while Cause and Result enders are attached to SCs, Purpose enders are attached to FCs. On the other hand, Cause and Result adverbials precede

FCs, whereas Purpose adverbials precede SCs. One exception is the adverbial *waynya(ha)myen* 'because', which has recently developed from *way i-nya ko ha-myen* (why is-Q QT ask-if) 'if (someone) asks why (it) is (so)'. This Cause adverbial precedes an SC.

Two semantically close Cause suffixes *-ese/ase* (e.g. (5a), (17b), and (44a, b)) and *-(u)nikka* are most frequently used and linguistically most controversial, as their meanings and usages are hard to define (e.g. Sohn 1992, Nahm 1994, Suh 1996, Cho 2005). In general, *-ese/ase* tends to denote (mild) cause, temporal succession, same time, result, and ways/means, while *-(u)nikka* tends to denote (strong) cause and rarely temporal 'when; while' (along with the speaker's realization of the FC event). When *-ese/ase* in (17b) is replaced with *-nikka,* as in (27), the causal meaning becomes much stronger.

(27) [Kiho ka cha lul pha-**nikka**]$_{SC}$ Mia ka wul-ess-eyo
Kiho NM car AC sell-**because** Mia NM cry-PST-POL
Because Kiho sold the car, Mia cried.

As in other types of clause liking, both suffixal and adverbial markers are used in Cause constructions. This is illustrated in (28).

(28) (a) [Kiho ka o-**ki** **ttaymun ey**]$_{SC}$ Mia to w-ayo
Kiho NM come-**NOM** **cause for** Mia also come-POL
Because Kiho comes, Mia comes too.

(b) [Kiho ka w-ayo.]$_{SC}$ **ku-ttaymun-ey** Mia to w-ayo
Kiho NM come-POL **that-cause-for** Mia also come-POL
Kiho comes. Because of that Mia comes too.

(c) [Kiho ka o-nuntey]$_{SC}$ **ku-ttaymun-ey** Mia to w-ayo
Kiho NM come-and that-cause-for Mia also come-POL
Kiho comes and because of that Mia comes too.

(d) Mia ka w-ayo. [**waynyamyen** Kiho ka o-**ki**
Mia NM come-POL **because** Kiho NM come-NOM
ttaymun i-eyo]$_{SC}$
cause be-POL
Mia comes. Because Kiho comes.

Notice in (28d) that when the adverbial *waynya(ha)myen* is used, its clause must contain a cause-indicating expression such as the phrase *-ki ttaymun* + copula or the clause ender *-nikka* 'as; because', as in *Kiho ka o-ki ttaymun i-eyo* or *Kiho ka o-nikka yo,* both meaning 'because Kiho comes'.

Some complex Cause enders given in Table 2 may be analyzed morphological1y as follows: *-(u)m-ulo* (-NOM-with) 'as; because'; *-ki-ey* (-NOM-at) 'as; because'; *-(u)n/nun thas ulo* (-RL influence with) 'owing to'; *-(u)n/nun ko lo* (-RL cause with) 'as; because'; *-(u)n/nun kkatalk ey* (-RL reason for) 'for the reason that'; and *-(u)n/nun mankhum* (-RL as.much.as) 'now that'.

TABLE 5. Consequence linking markers (clause enders and adverbials)

Conse-quence	Markers with Sup-porting clause Enders	Adverbials	Markers with Focal clause Enders	Adverbials
Cause	*-ese/ase* 'as, since' *-nikka* 'because, since' -ni 'as, since' *-nulako* 'while do-ing' *-ki ttaymun ey* 'be-cause' *-(u)m-ulo* 'as, be-cause' *-ki-ey* 'as, because' *-killay* 'as, because' *-(n)un thas ulo* 'ow-ing to' *-(n)un ko-lo* 'as, be-cause' *-(n)un kkatalk ey* 'for the reason that' *-(n)un mankhum* 'now that'	*waynyamyen* 'because'		*kulayse* 'so' *kulenikka* 'there-fore' *kukeni* 'so' *kuke-nulako* 'while doing so' *ku ttamun ey* 'for that reason' *kulemulo* 'so, hence, therefore' *kule-kiey* 'for that' *kule-killay* 'so' *ku(le-n) thas ulo* 'owing to that' *kule-n ko-lo* 'so, henceefore' *ku(le-n) kkatalk ulo* 'for that rea-son' *kulen mankhum* 'because of that'
Result	*-ese/ase* 'as a result of' *-(u)n kyelkwa (lo)* 'as a result of' *-(u)m ey ttal-a(se)* 'as a result of, ac-cording to' *-(n)un palam ey* (by the wind of) 'as a result of'			*kulayse* 'thus' *ku kyelkwa (lo)* (that result as) 'as a consequence' *ttalase* 'accord-ingly' *ku palam ey* 'as a result of that'
Purpose		---- *kule-lyeko* 'to do so' *kule-koca* 'wishing to do so'	*-(u)le 'to'* (with coming/ going verb) *-(u)lyeko* 'in order to' *-koca* 'wish-ing to'	

kule-key(kkum) 'to be so'	*-key(-kkum)* 'so that'
kule-tolok 'to be so'	*-tolok* 'so that'
kule-lako 'to be so'	*-(u)lako* 'so that'
kule-ki wihay-(se) 'in order to do so'	*-ki wihay-(se)* 'in order to'
ku mokcek ulo 'for that purpose'	*-(u)l mokcek. ulo* 'for the purpose of'
kule-l seym ulo 'thinking to do so'	*-(u)l seym ulo* 'thinking that'

Result is expressed either by enders such as *-ese/ase, -(u)n kyelkwa lo* (-RL result with), *-(u)m ey ttal-ase* (-NOM to follow-and), and *-(u)n/nun palam ey* (-RL wind at), all meaning 'as a result of' on SCs, or by equivalent adverbials on FCs, or by both. The ender *-(u)n/nun palam ey* is a recent metaphorical innovation and is used productively in colloquial speech.

(29) [sensayngnim i aph-usi-**ese;** aph-usi-**n** **palam ey**]$_{SC}$
teacher NM sick-SH-**as.result.of;** sick-SH-**RL** **wind at**
swuep i eps-eyo
class slack-POL
As a result of the teacher's being sick, there is no class.

Purpose is expressed by several clause enders on FCs and corresponding adverbials on FCs. These markers are different from each other in either meanings or in syntactic functions, or in both. For instance, the enders *-(u)le* and *-(u)lyeko* '(in order) to' have similar meanings, but the former occurs only when it is followed by a main clause with a locomotive verb (e.g. 'come'; 'go', 'leave'), whereas the latter does not have such a restriction.

(30) (a) Kiho nun Mia lul manna-**le;** **-lyeko** [kyohoy ey
Kiho TC Mia AC meet-**to;** **-in.order.to** church to
ka-ss-eyo]$_{SC}$
go-PST-POL
Kiho went to the church (in order) to see Mia.

(b) Kiho nun Mia lul manna-***le;** **-lyeko** [ilcik ilena-ss-eyo]$_{SC}$
Kiko TC Mia AC meet-**to**; **-in.order.to** early rise-PST-POL
Kiho woke up early in order to meet Mia.

Some complex Purpose enders are *key(-kkum)* 'so that' where *-kkum* is simply an emphasizer; *-ki wihay-se* (-NOM serve-to) 'in order to'; *-(u)l mokcek ulo* (-PRS purpose with) 'for the purpose of'; and *-(u)l seym ulo* (-PRS account with) 'with a view to; intending to'

4.3. *Possible Consequence (III)*

Possible consequence is expressed by negating a Purpose construction, as in (31).

(31) (a) [kay ka **an** naka-**tolok**]$_{SC}$ mukk-e twu-sey-yo
dog NM **not** go.out-**so.that** bind-INF keep-SH-POL
Keep the dog on a leash, lest it should go out.

(b) [kay ka naka-**nikka**]$_{SC}$ **kule-ci** **anhtolok** mukk-e
dog NM go.out-because **do.so-NOM** **lest** bind-INF
twu-sey-yo
keep-SH-POL
The dog may go out, so keep it on a leash, lest it should do so.

Clause enders like *-(u)l kyengwu (ey)* (-PRS occasion at) 'in the case that', *-(u)l-kka-po-a(se)* (-PRS-whether-think-and) 'being afraid that; for fear that', *-(u)l-kka siph-e(se)* (PRs-whether wonder-and) 'anticipating that; wondering that; in case', and *-(u)l-kka ha-ko* (-PRS-whether expect/do-and) 'expecting to do' are also used for Possible consequence in SCs. Their adverbial counterparts (Table 2: III) occur on FCs.

(32) [pi ka o-**lkkapoa(se)]**$_{SC}$ cip ey iss-ess-eyo
rain NM come-**for.fear.that** home at stay-PST-POL
(I) stayed home for fear that it might rain.

4.4. *Addition (IV)*

The typical ender for Unordered addition (IVu) is *-ko* 'and'. Its formal counterpart is *-(u)mye.* The linked clauses are of equal semantic status, although grammatically the first dause is always subordinate to the second clause. The adverbial equivalents to these enders are *kuliko* 'and' and *ttohan* 'also; and'.

(33) [Kiho nun nolayha-**ko; -mye**] Mia nun chwumchwu-eyo
Kiho TC sing-**and; -and** Mia TC dance-POL
Kiho sings and Mia dances.

Clause enders for Same-event addition (IVs), all marking SCs, indude *-ko* 'and', *-nulako* 'while doing', *-(u)mye(nse)* 'while doing/being; *-keniwa* 'as well as', *-(u)1 ppun an-i-la* (-PRS being.only not-be-and) 'not only ~ but also', *-(u) l ppun-tele* (-PRS being.only-together.with) 'not only ~ but also', and *-(u)l swu-lok* (-PRS the.more) 'the more ~ the more'.

(34) (a) [pang to cop-**ko**]$_{SC}$ cip i pissa-yo.
room also narrow-**and** house NM expensive-POL
The house is expensive, with narrow rooms.
(b) Mia nun [ton pe-**nulako**]$_{SC}$ pappa-ss-eyo
Mia TC money earn-**while** busy-PST-POL
Mia was busy, earning money.
(c) [Kiho nun wus-**umye(nse)**]$_{SC}$ nolayhay-yo
Kiho TC smile-**ing** sing-POL
Kiho is singing, smiling.

The most appropriate and productive ender for Elaboration (IVe) is the background information provider *-(n)untey* 'given that; and; but'. Formal variants are -(u)n/nun cuk (RL when/then) and -(u)n/nun pa (RL fact/place).

(35) [Mia ka san ey ollaka-ss-**nuntey**]$_{SC}$ kkoktayki kkaci
Mia NM mountain to climb-past-**and** top till
ollaka-ss-eyo
climb-PST-POL
Mia climbed the mountain, she climbed right to the top.

Conjunctive enders for Contrast (IVc) include: the particle *man (un)* 'but', which follows a complete sentence, and the suffixal enders such as *-ciman* 'but; although' (colloquial), *-(u)na* 'but; although' (somewhat fonnal), *-eto/ato* 'but; although; even though', *-ken man* 'though', *-toy* 'but' (formal, old style), and *-(n)untey-to* (even though) 'despite the fact that; although; but'. These constructions were illustrated in (9), (10), and (n).

All the above Addition-type clause enders have corresponding adverbials, as listed in Table 2 (IV). Notice that all these adverbials occur on FCs, except those for Unordered addition.

4.5. *Alternatives (V)*

Alternative disjunction (Vd) is expressed by the ender *-kena* 'or' or *-tunci* 'or' in non-main clauses. Or, adverbials like *ttonun* 'or' (formal), *hokum* 'or (else)', or *animyen* 'if not' may be used in main clauses. Or, both an ender and an adverbial can occur together as in (36). There is no SC/FC distinction in alternative disjunction.

(36) Kiho ka chwumchwu-**kena;** **-tunci** **(ttonun; animyen)** Mia ka
Kiho NM dance-**or;** **-or** **or;** **if.not** Mia NM
nolayhay-yo
sing-POL
Kiho will dance or Mia will sing.

Alternative rejection (Vr) is expressed by the ender *-(u)n/-nun taysin (ey)* (RL replacement for) 'instead of; as in (37a), or the phrasal negative ender *an* V/ADJ/COP-*ko* 'not V/ADJ/COP (but)'; as in (37b), both in SCs. The same idea can be expressed by the adverbial *ku taysin (ey)* 'instead (of that)'or *kule(h)-ci anh-ko* 'not doing/being that' in FCs. Both an ender and an adverbial (usually *ku taysin (ey))* may occur together in a sentence for emphasis, as in' (37c).

(37) (a) [Mia ka nolayha-nun **taysin (ey)**]sc Kiho ka
Mia NM sing-RL **instead at** Kiho NM
chwumchwu-eyo
dance-POL
Kiho will dance instead of Mia singing.
(b) [Mia ka nolayha-ci **an-h-ko**]$_{SC}$ Kiho ka chwumchwu-eyo
Mia NM sing-NOM **not-do-and** Kiho NM dance-POL
Mia will not sing, but Kiho will dance.
(c) [Mia ka nolayha-ci **an-h-ko**]$_{SC}$ **ku** **taysin** Kiho ka
Mia NM sing-NOM **not-do-and** **that** **instead** Kiho NM
chwumchwu-eyo
dance-POL
Mia will not sing, but instead, Kiho will dance.

Alternative suggestion (Vs) is expressed in SCs by the ender *-nuni (pota)* (< *-nun i pota* (RL thing/fact than)) or *-nun kes pota* (R thing/fact than), both meaning 'rather than'. The adverbial counterparts, which occur in FCs, are *kule-nuni (pota)* and *kule-nun kes pota,* both meaning 'rather than doing so'. The modal adverb *chalali* 'rather' may be added to the FC for emphasis.

(38) [Kiho ka nolayha-**nuni** **pota**]sc *chalali* Mia ka nolayha-nun
Kiho NM sing-**ing** **than** rather Mia NM sing-RL
phyen i na-ayo
side NM better-POL
Rather than Kiho sings, Mia's singing would be better.

Dixon's distinction in Dixon (2009) between open disjunction (X or Y, but there is a small chance that neither may hold) and closed disjunction (X or Y, with no further alternative possible) is made by syntactic mechanism in Korean, as in (39).

(39) (a) Kiho ka chwumchwu-**kena** Mia ka nolayhay-yo
Kiho NM dance-**or** Mia NM sing-POL
Kiho is dancing or Mia is singing.
(b) Kiho ka chwumchwu-**kena** Mia ka nolayha-**kena** hay-yo
Kiho NM dance-**or** Mia NM sing-**or** do-POL
Kiho is dancing or Mia is singing (or something else).

Sentence (39a) tends to be interpreted as exclusive closed disjunction (X or Y but not both), whereas (39b), in which *-kena is* repeated, a1lows open disjunction or inclusive closed disjunction interpretation (X or Y or both).

As indicated earlier, apposition is used only in questions to indicate closed disjunction. The disjunctive adverbial *animyen* 'if not' can be inserted between the clauses.

(40) ka-si-keyss-eyo↑ (**animyen**) swi-si-keyss-eyo?↓
go-SH-will-POL **if.not** rest-SH-will-POL
Will (you) go or take a rest?

4.6. *Manner (VI)*

Real manner (VIr) is expressed byenders like - *tasiphi* 'as; in the same way that', *-(u)n/nun taylo* (RL as/like) 'as; like; according to', *-(u)n/nun kes chelem/ kathi* (_RL thing/fact like) 'as; like; so ~ as; and *(-(u)n/nun)-tusi* (-RL-as.if) 'like; as if'.

(41) (a) [apeci ka sikhi-si-n **taylo**]$_{SC}$ yelsimhi ilhay-yo
father NM instruct-SH-**RL** **as** hard work-POL
(I) work hard as my father told me to.

(b)

[Mia	ka	nolayha-**tusi**]$_{SC}$	Kiho	ka	nolayhay-yo
Mia	NM	sing-**like**	Kiho	NM	sing-POL

Kiho sings in the same way as Mia does.

Hypothetical manner (VIh) is expressed by the structure consisting of the modal adverb *machi* 'just' and the ender *-tasiphi* 'as; like', *-((u)n/nun/ -(u)l) -tusi* 'as if; like' *or-(u)n/nun/(u)l kes chelemlkathi* 'as if; like' in SCs. The adverb *machi* can be omitted if the content is already hypothetical.

(42)

[(machi)	hanul	i	muneci-**n**	**tusi; -n**	**kes**	**chelem**]$_{SC}$	Kiho
just	sky	NM	fall-**RL**	**as.if; -RL**	**fact**	**like**	Kiho

ka	silmanghay-ss-eyo
NM	disappointed-PST-POL

Kiho was so disappointed, as if the sky had fallen in.

Ways/means (VIw) are expressed by *-ese/ase* 'by ~ -ing' and *-e/a kaciko* (< *-e/a kaci-ko* (-INF hold-and)) 'by (means of) ~ -ing; as illustrated in (43).

(43) (a)

[tol	lo	ttayly-**ese**]$_{SC}$	ku	ciney	ul	cwuki-ess-eyo
stone	with	strike-**by**	the	centipede	AC	kill-PST-POL

(He) knocked the centipede with a stone to death.

(b)

[cha	lul	phal-**a**	**kaciko**]$_{SC}$	chinkwu	lul	tow-ass-eyo
car	AC	sell-INF	**hold.and**	friend	AC	help-PST-POL

(I) helped a friend by selling my car.

All the above Manner enders have corresponding adverbials, which occur in FCs. These are listed in Table 2 (VIr, VIh, VIw).

4.7. *Markers with multiple functions*

Many predicative enders also function as (verbal) complementizers, e.g. *-ko* 'and', *-(u)myen* 'if; wishing', *-key* 'so that', *-tolok* 'so that', *-eya/aya* 'only if', *-(u)lyeko* 'intending to', *-koca* 'wishing to do; *-tusi* 'as if', *-kena* 'or', and *-tunci* 'or'. Some predicative enders have multiple clause linking functions. The ender *-ese/ase* indicates not only Temporal succession (17a), Cause (17b), and Manner (ways/means) (43), but *also* Result and Relative time (same time), as in (44).

(44) (a)

[palam	i	pul-**ese**]$_{SC}$	sakwa	ka	ttelecy-ess-eyo
wind	NM	blow-**so/and**	apple	NM	fall-PST-POL

(i) Apples fell as wind blew. (Cause)

(ii) Wind blew, and apples fell as a result. (Result)

(b) [nal i palk- **ase**]$_{SC}$ ilena-ss-eyo
day NM bright-**as** get.up-PST-POL
(i) Because the day broke, (I) got up. (Cause)
(ii) When the day broke, (I) got up. (Relative time-same time)

The ender *-ko* indicates Temporal succession and Addition, *-(u)myen* Relative time ('when') and Conditional, *-eto/ato* Concession and Contrast, *-nulako* Cause and Same-event addition, *-(u)ni* and *-(u)nikka* Cause and rarely 'when; while', and *-(u)mye/-(u)myense* Same time and Addition. Purposive enders such as *-key(-kkum), -tolok,* and *-(u)lyeko* function as Possible consequence with a negative adverb and *-tolok* marks length of time (future) as well.

Derived enders tend to have their unique conjunctive functions. For instance, *-(u)l ttay (ey)* (PRS time at) 'when', which has developed from a time adjunct, only functions as Relative time and nothing else. The ender *-(n)untey* 'given that; and; but; however, is fully grammaticalized from *-(n)un tey ey* (R place at) and used as a softened version of Contrast, in addition to laboration. None of the conjunctive enders can connect NPs. Only the onjunctive adverbials *kuliko* 'and', *ttonun* 'or', *hokum* 'or', and *animyen* 'if not' can.

5. Clause linking in Korean: summary

As examined thus far, Korean has extensive means of clause linking for all of the major linkage types and subtypes set out in Dixon (2009). Thus, first, the prototypical device is to suffix conjunctive enders to the predicate of the non-main clause. All non-main clauses typically precede their main clauses. Conjunctive expressions by simple apposition are very rare in Korean, the only exception being alternating questions.

Second, as a mirror image of the suffixal device, there is a productive device to use conjunctive adverbials for main clauses. Such adverbials occur in sentence- or clause-initial position. The majority of these adverbials have derived from a combination of the anaphoric *ku* construction and a conjunctive ender.

Third, a clause plus a conjunctive adverbial can stand alone as a complete sentence, while a clause plus a conjunctive ender cannot do so. It is possible to have both a clause ender in the non-main clause and a conjunctive adverbial in the main clause for emphasis or certain rhetorical style.

Fourth, all non-main clauses other than the Purpose, Unordered addition and Disjunction subtypes semantically function as Supporting clauses. All main clauses or sentences with a conjunctive adverbial other than the Purpose, Unordered addition and Disjunction subtypes semantically function as Focal clauses. In the Purpose subtype, non-main clauses with a conjunctive ender function as FCs and main clauses with an adverbial function as SCs.

One exception is a construction with the recently innovated adverb *waynya (ha)myen* 'because', which, as indicated earlier, has developed from *way i-nya ko ha-myen* (why is-Q QT ask-if) 'if (someone) asks why (it) is (so)'. This Cause adverbial marks an SC and this clause follows an FC unlike in other causal expressions. Furthermore, this SC has a vestige of a Cause ender, as we observed in (28d), as if the clause is an "afterthought" addition.

Fifth, major patterns of conjunctive enders are (a) predicative suffixes, simple or complex, (b) a conjunctive particle, (c) relativized postpostional phrases, (d) nominalized postpositional phrases, (e) conjunctive predicate phrases, and (f) extended conjunctive phrases. Many enders such as predicative suffixes are completely morphologized as unanalyzable units, while many derived enders are either in the early stage of grammaticalization and semantic shifts or still somewhat transparent in structure and meanings. The same is true with conjunctive adverbials.

REFERENCES: Chapter 9

Bak, Sung-Yun. 2007. Yangpo wa coken (Concession and condition), *Discourse and Cognition* 14.1: 63-83.

Cho, In-Jung. 2005. Yenghan penyek uy eswun muncey: Iyn-wenin pusacel (Word order problems in English-Korean translation: adverbial clauses of cause), *Bilingual Research* 28: 355-69.

Dixon, R.M.W. and A.Y. Aikhenvald (eds.). 2009. *Clause Linking: A Cross-linguistic Typology*. Oxford, UK: Oxford University Press.

Kwon, Jae-Il. 1985. *Kwuke uy pokhapmun kwuseng yenkwu* (A studyof Korean complex sentence structures). Seoul: Cipmuntang.

Nahm, Ki-Shim. 1994. *Kwuke yenkyel emi uy ssuim* (Usages of clause connectives in Korean). *Seoul:* Sekwan Press.

Sohn, Ho-min. 1999. *The Korean language.* Cambridge: Cambridge University Press.

Sohn, Sung-Ock. 1992. Speaker-oriented and event-oriented causal: a comparative analysis of *-nikka* and *–ese*. *Korean Linguistics* 8: 73-83.

Suh, Chung-Soo. 1996. *Hyentay kwuke mwunpep* (A Contemporary Korean grammar). Seoul: Hanyang University Press.

Yoon, Pyong-Hyon. 2005. *Hyentay kwuke cepsok emi yenkwu* (A study of conjunctive enders in contemporary Korean). Seoul: Pakiceng.

10 Grammaticalization and Semantic Shift*

1. It seems to be a universal phenomenon across languages that morphological elements can be derived historically from originally independent words or a variety of syntactic collocations of words. Talmy Givon's (1971) aphorism that "today's morphology is yesterday's syntax," although apparently an overstatement, is an explicit indication of this universal tendency. It is only recently that Western linguists have become seriously interested in the phenomena of the grammaticalization (or morphologization) of syntactic constructions, the cocommitant development of grammatical meanings, and the reconstruction of earlier syntactic structure based on the morpho-syntactic behavior of existing morpheme sequences.[1]

Albeit tentative, the aim of the present paper is to look into the grammaticalization phenomena of Korean from both syntactico-morphological and semantico-pragmatic perspectives. Specifically, the questions this paper is intended to address are:

(a) What are the typical patterns of grammaticalization in Korean?
(b) How are the syntactic processes of diachronic restructuring effected?
(c) What are the directions, if any, of semantic shift in the course of grammaticalization?

These questions will be elaborated on below. Many grammaticalizations must have taken place such a long time ago that the original forms may not be reconstructable, while others can be associated with their original structure either by means of an analysis of relevant historical records or through internal reconstruction or comparative methods. Let us observe in the following only

---

* This paper is reprinted from *Papers from the 7th International Conference on Korean Linguistics*, ed. by E.J. Baek, pp. 589–603 (1991). Seoul: Hanshin. Note that glosses and some clarifications are added to the reprinted version.

1 The study reported here was made possible by a 1990 International Cultural Society of Korea fellowship. I owe Marshall Pihl not only for the stylistic improvement of the paper but for various linguistic insights that he presented to me from a non-native speaker's point of view.

those examples which are internally reconstructable. Due to time and space constraints, no attempt will be made to detail the procedures of internal reconstruction. Rather, I will simply assume that all the relevant examples to which grammaticalization applies are already internally reconstructed.

2. Let us begin with our first question: What are typical patterns of grammaticalization in Korean? Korean abounds in grammaticalization phenomena. I will survey some of the most salient instances to show what kinds of patterns are available in Korean. First of all, Korean historical linguists seem to agree that the contemporary past/perfective suffix *–ess/ass* is a form derived diachronically from the structure consisting of the infinitive complementizer *–e/a* and the existential predicate *iss*. Similarly, it has been proposed that the subject honorific suffix *–(u)si*, the modal suffix *–keyss* (intentive/presumptive), and the polite sentence-ender *–yo* have derived from complex constructions (e.g. Kown 1988 and elsewhere). Taking only the past/perfective suffix into account, compare the three sentences in (1).

(1) a. Yongho ka hakkyo ey ka-**a** **iss**-ta.
Yongho NM school to go-INF stay-DC
'Yonho went to school and is there.'

b. Yongho ka emeni lul talm-**ass**-ta.
Yongho NM mother AC resemble-PST-DC
'Yongho takes after his mother.'

c. Yongho ka hakkyo ey ka-**ss**-ta.
Yongho NM school to go-PST-DC
'Yongho went to school/Yongho has gone to school.'

(1a) has the original form *–e iss*, with the sense of a past event and its resultative state; (1b) has the grammaticalized form *–ass*, with the resultative state sense; and (1c) has *–(a)ss*, with the past/perfective sense.

A second example may be drawn from the reduction of the defective noun *kes* 'thing, fact, assumed fact', the cooccurring copula *i*, and the infinitive *–e*, as shown in (2) through (4).

(2) a. na nun ka-l kes i-eyyo (prediction/?intention)
I TC go-PRS fact is-POL
'I think I will go.'

b. na nun ka-l ke y-eyyo (prediction/intention)
I TC go-PRS fact is-POL
'I think I will go/I will go.'

c. na nun ka-lkey-yo (speaker's promise)
I TC go-PRM-POL
'I promise to go.'

(3) a. na nun ka-l kes i-p-ni-ta.
I TC go-PRS fact is-AH-IN-DC
'I think I will go.'

b. na nun ka-l ke -p-ni-ta
I TC go-PRS fact -AH-IN-DC
'I think I will go/I will go.'

c. *na nun ka-lkkey-p-ni-ta.
I TC go-PRM-AH-IN-DC
'I promise to go/'

(4) a. Yongho/*you* nun ka-l kes i-eyyo?
Yongho/you TC go-PRS fact is-POL
'Do you think Yongho/you will go?'

b. Yongho/*you* nun ka-l ke -eyyo?
Yongho/you TC go-PRS fact -POL
'Do you think Yongho/you will go?/Will Yongho/you go?'

c. *Yongho/*you* nun ka-lkey-yo?
Yongho/you TC go-PRM-POL
'Do(es) Yongho/you promise to go?'

Notice the gradual formal reduction from (a) to (c) in the sentences in (2), (3) and (4), as in *–l kes i* to *-l ke (y)* to *-lkey*. Notice further that the sentences in (a) and (b) share a parallel syntactic and semantic behavior, as opposed to that in (c), which contains the grammaticalized form *–lkey* (speaker's promise). To those speakers who do not accept intention sense in (a), grammaticalization must have occurred even in (b). Otherwise, (a) and (b) are regarded as synchronically related. The informality connotation accompanying the formal reduction in (b) (*kes* to *ke* and *i* to *y or* zero) may be regarded a pragmatic fact, rather than a semantic content. The fact that (c) is distinct from (a) and (b) in both syntactic structure and semantic content is evidenced in (3) where (c) cannot occur with the deferential sentence ender and in (4) where (c) cannot occur with non-first person subject either in statement or question.

A third example is a set of diachronic main clause deletion phenomena, as illustrated in (5), where [ ] stands for the diachronic trace of deleted main clauses.

(5) a.

apeci	ka	kyey-si-nun	tey [ ]	yo.
father	NM	stay-SH-RL	circumstsnce	POL

'My father is in. (What can I do for you?)'

b.

pi	ka	o-nun	ka [ ]	yo?
rain	NM	come-RL	whether	POL

'Is it raining? (I wonder.)'

c.

ka-po-si-ci [ ]	yo.
go-try-SH-SUG	POL

'Why don't you go?'

d.

kyohoy ey	ka-si-na [ ]	yo?
church to	go-SH-or	POL

'Are you going to church? (May I ask?)'

e.

Yongho ka	aphu-ta-myense [ ]	yo?
Yongho NM	sick-DC-while	POL

'I heard Yongho is sick. Is ittrue?'

f.

ka-ki	silh-ta nikka [ ]	yo?
go-NOM	hateful-DC as	POL

'I told you I don't want to go.'

g.

na	tele	os	ul	pes-ula-ni [ ]	yo?
I	to	dress	AC	take.off-IM-as	POL

'Are you saying I should take off my dress?'

h.

pi	ka	o-te-la	ko [ ]	yo.
rain	NM	come-RT-DC	QT	POL

'I saw it was raining. (You know.)'

i. Yongho ka an o-l ke-l [ ] yo?!
Yongho NM not come-PRS fact-AC POL
'I guess Yongho won't come.'

Native speakers of contemporary Korean conceive and perceive the constructions in (5) as complete independent sentences. Since a separate paper is required to delve into the grammaticalization processes involved in the derivation of the sentences in (5), suffice it here to state my points of speculation that: (a) historical main clause deletion took place in these sentences, (b) this synchronically unrecoverable deletion has been caused probably by both the speaker's intention to economize speech acts and his/her intention to indicate strategic politeness, at first conversationally, but later conventionally, and (c) with conventional main clause deletion, grammaticalization has taken place with semantico-pragmatic change, and the original defective nouns like *tey* 'place, circumstance', *kka/ka*, *ci* 'whether', the original nominalizing suffixes like *ci* 'that' and *–na* 'whether,' the original conjunctive suffixes like *–myense* 'while' and *–nikka* 'because,' the original quotative particle *ko*, and the original defective noun *kes* 'fact' + the accusative particle *ul* are all historically restructured or grammaticalized as part of sentence-final modal elements.

A fourth set of examples includes the deletion of an embedded main clause. Examples are given in (6). Notice the slight meaning difference existing between (a) and (a'), and between (b) and (b').

(6) a. na-n pwuca ka toy-ca [ ] ko il ul sicakhay-ss-ta.
I-TC rich NM become-PR and work AC start-PST-DC
'Intending to get rich, I started a business.'

a′. na-n pwuca ka toy-ca [ ] *ha-ko* il ul sicakhay-ss-ta.
I-TC rich NM become-PR say-and work AC start-PST-DC
i. Thinking about getting rich, I started a business.
ii. Saying "Let's get rich,' I started a business.

b. sicang i panchan i-la ko [ ] wusen mek-ko po-ca.
hunger NM side-dish is-DC and first eat-and see-PR
'Since hunger is a side-dish, let's eat and see.'

b′. sicang i panchan i-la ko *ha-ni* wusen mek-ko po-ca.
hunger NM side-dish is-DC and say-since first eat-and see-PR
'Since it is said that hunger is a side-dish, let's eat and see.'

A fifth set of examples comprises sentences involving diachronic deletion of the quotative particle *ko* and the following information verb *ha* 'say, ask, think, claim, believe'. *Ko ha* deletion is of two general types: synchronic and diachronic. Synchronic *(ko) ha* deletion is very productive and nearly exceptionless, and always recoverable without change in meaning, as illustrated in (7).

(7) a.

nay	ka	encey	ka-n-ta	((ko)	ha)y-ss-e?
I	NM	when	go-IN-DC	QT	say-PST-INT
caki	ka	ka-ca	[(ko)	ha]y	noh-kose.
self	NM	go-PR	QT	say	put-and

'When did I say I would go? You proposed that you and I go.'

b.

na	nun	Yongho	ka	chakha-n	salam	i-la	((ko)	ha)-nun
I	NM	Yongho	NM	good-RL	person	is-DC	QT	say-RL

sayngkak	i	tul-ess-ta.
idea	NM	enter-PST-DC

'It came to my mind that Yongho is a good person.'

Needless to say, deletion of the synchronic *(ko) ha* is accompanied by "informal" or colloquial" connotation. As stated earlier, this is rather a matter of pragmatics than of semantics. On the other hand, there are many sentences where *(ko) ha* deletion is viewed as diachronic. Some are more diachronically fossilized than others. The examples in (8) are ordered roughly from less to more fossilized forms.[2] [ ] marks the place where *ko-ha* is deleted. The meanings of the sentences with *ko-ha* are given in parentheses.

(8) a.

o-nun	salam	i	Yongho	la	[ ]-myen	coh-keyss-ta.
come-RL	person	NM	Yongho	is.DC	-if	good-will-DC

'I wish that the person who is coming is Yongho.'
('If someone says it is Yongho who is coming, I will be happy.')

b.

way-nya	[ ]-myen	nay	ka	silh-ki	ttaymwun	i-ta.
why-is.Q	-if	I	NM	dislike-NOM	because	is-DC

'It is because I don't like it.'
('If someone asks why it is so, it is because I don't like it.')

2 Some idiosyncratic examples include:
i inkan i [-la ko ha-nun kes u]n nwukwu na cwuk-nun-ta.
ii cengchika ka nalttwi-nun ka[ha ko sayngkak]-hamyen paykseng un tothan ey ppaci-ess-ta.

c.

tayk	un	twu	si	ey	ttena-si-n-ta	[ ]-ci	yo?
you	TC	2	o'clock	at	leave-SH-IN-DC	-NOM	POL

'I understand that you are leaving at 2.'
('They say that you are leaving at 2, is that right?')

d. ontol pang i-la [ ]-se patak-man ttattusha-ta.

e. ne pap an mek-ess-ta [ ]-mye(nse)?

f. tto han kaci coken i-la [ ]-ni yo?

g. Yongho nun kitoha-n-ta [ko ha-o]p-si-ko anc-ass-ta.

While synchronic deletion does not affect the syntactico-semantic properties of the sentence, diachronic deletion does in one way or another, as shown in the following sentences.

(9) a. celm-un salam i-la ko hay-se mwusiha-ci ma-la.
a′. *celm-un salam i-la [ ]-se mwusi-ha-ci ma-la.

b. *celm-un salam i-la ko hay-se ha-nun swu eps-kwun.
b′. celm-un salam i-la [ ]-se ha-nun swu eps-kwun.

In many cases, sentences with *(ko) ha* deleted are ambiguous between synchronic and diachronic deletion, as illustrated below.

(10) a. Yongho nun kongpwuha-n-ta [ ]-p-nita.
i. Yongho is studying, you know.
ii. Yongho says (*or* They say) that he is studying.

b. Yongho nun kongpwuha-n-ta [ ]-p-nikka?
i. *Are you saying that Yongho is studying?
ii. Does Yongho say (*or* Do they say) that he is studying?

Notice that (10b) allows only synchronic deletion. That is, diachronic deletion is permitted only in declarative sentences. This type of syntactico-semantic imbalance is usually observed in grammaticalized constructions.

A sixth example is the derivation of the transitive "humble" verb *poypta* 'see (a superior person)'. This verb is assumed to have derived originally from a passive construction, as shown in (11).[3]

(11) a. X(lower person) ka Y(higher person) eykey po-i-op-keyss-ta >
X NM Y to see-PAS-OH-will-DC

b. X ka Y lul poyp-keyss-ta
X NM Y AC see(humble)-will-DC

Notice that the three morphemes *po* 'see' + *-i* (passive suffix) + *-op* (humble suffix: originally object honorific) are coalesced into a single inseparable transitive verb root. Notice further that due to the subcategorial change from intransitive to transitive, the structural rearrangement from the indirect NP to the direct NP also took place.

A seventh example is the derivation of the sentence-ender *–(u)lla* (warning). This morpheme is considered to have derived from *–(u)li-la* (prospective suffix + declarative ender), as illustrated below.

(12) a. tteleci-lla. 'Be careful, you may fall down!'
fall.down-WARNING

b. < tteleci-li-la. 'You may/will (probably) fall down.'
fall down-PRS-DC

Finally, there are many cases where formal reduction is either lacking or optional, but semantic shift occurs. This type may be comparable to the meaning divergence in English *be going to (be gonna),* as in *I am going to (*gonna) school* and *I am going to (gonna) go to school,* or to the idiomatization of *take advantage of,* as in *she was taken advantage of by John*. Some of these phenomena are cases of semi-grammaticalization, in that the grammaticalization is rather weak or in progress. In the following, (a, b, c, d) contain a (semi-)grammaticalized element (*-ki ey* 'because', *-taka nun* 'if', *-ko nun* (habitative aspect), *-l swu eps* 'cannot'), whereas (a', b', c', d') are sentences with ungrammaticalized counterparts. Existence of such unacceptable sentences as (a", d") supports the assumption that sentences (a, d) are grammaticalized. For example, the conjunctive suffix *–ki ey* (the nominalizer *–ki* + the locative case particle *ey)* in the sense of 'because, as' requires that the subject of the main clause be the speaker. Furthermore, the fact that *nun* can be contracted to *n* only in the forms with the semantic change (i.e. 13b, c) seems to indicate that these forms are either grammaticalized or in the process of grammaticalization.

3 Chungmin Lee drew my attention to Korean linguists' interpretation of *–p* as derived from *–op*.

(13) a.

na	nun	pi	ka	o-*ki*	*ey*	cip	ey	iss-ess-ta.
I	TC	rain	NM	come-NOM	at	home	at	stay.PST-DC

'As it rained, I stayed home.'

a′.

sengkong	un	nolyekha-ki	ey	talli-e	iss-ta.
success	TC	make.effort-NOM	on	depend-INF	exist-DC

'One's success depends on one's making efforts.'

a″.

??Yongho	nun	pi	ka	o-ki	ey	cip	ey	iss-ess-ta.
Yongho	TC	rain	NM	come-NOM	at	home	at	stay-PST-DC

'Yongho stayed at home as it was raining.

b.

ileh-key	nol-*taka*	*n(un)*	nakceyha-keyss-ta.
this.way-AD	play-while	TC	fail-may-DC

'You may fail in school if you keep playing like this.'

b′.

aph	ulo	ka-taka	nun	twi	lo	ka-ss-ta.
front	to	go-while	TC	back	to	go-PST-DC

'(He) went forward and then went back.'

c.

nalssi	ka	coh-umyen	nakssicil	ka-*ko*	*n(un)*	hay-ss-ta.
weather	NM	good-if	fishing	go-and	TC	do-PST-DC

'(I/he) habitually went fishing when the weather was fine.'

c′.

Mia	nun	into	ey	ka-ko	nun	tasi	tolao-ci	anh-ass-ta.
Mia	TC	India	to	go-and	TC	again	return-NOM	not.do-PST-DC

'Mia went to India and has never come back.'

d.

tew-ese	ca-*l*	*swu*	*(ka)*	*eps*-ta.
hot-as	sleep-PRS	way	NM	lack-DC

'As it is hot, (I) cannot sleep.'

d′.

coh-un	swu	ka	eps-ta.
Good-RL	way	NM	lack-DC

'There is no good way (solution).'

d″.

*tew-ese	ca-nun	swu	(ka)	eps-ta.
hot-as	sleep-PRS	way	NM	lack-DC

There are many other interesting forms of grammaticalization in all kinds of constructions (including auxiliary/serial verb constructions, conjunctive clauses, complex clauses, particles, and grammatical suffixes), but I think the above eight sets of examples are sufficient to illustrate that Korean, with an SOV agglutinative typology, is abundant in grammaticalization phenomena. To recapitulate, we have seen:

(14) a. complementizer –e + iss > -ess (past/perfective)
b. prospective –l + kes + i + -e > -l kkey (SP's promise)
c. main clause deletion followed by formation of new sentences-enders (-nun tey, -nun ka, -nun ci, -ci, -na, -ta myense, -ta nikka, -ula ni, -ko, etc.)
d. embedded main clause deletion and associated grammaticalization (e.g. ca-ha ko > ca-ko)
e. *(ko) ha* deletion and associated grammaticalization
f. po + passive –i + humble –op > poyp 'see'
g. –uli + la > -ulla (SP's warning)
h. examples of (semi-)grammaticalization

3. Let us consider our second question: How are the syntactic processes of diachronic restructuring effected? From the foregoing observations, it is obvious that grammaticalization in Korean is typically formal and semantic reduction. This is essentially in agreement with some leading proposals that have recently been proposed on the basis of some other world's languages, including English, although the notion of "semantic reduction" is controversial and should be more rigorously defined (e.g. Bybee 1988; Sweetser 1988). Delaying the discussion of semantic aspects to the following section, let us consider the formal reduction side. All the examples given in the previous section manifest formal reduction of one sort or another. Thus, (14a) through (14e) show that, due to grammaticalization, two clauses are reduced to one and three clauses to two. In (14f) and (14g), two morphemes are reduced to one. The stages of the reduction in the course of grammaticalization may be something like those in (15).

(15) complex embedding structure > simplex structure > phrase > stem > root > particle > clitic > affix > zero

A grammaticalization process does not have to go through all the listed stages; nor does one need to start from the beginning.

Let us speculate upon the manner in which such grammaticalization may be effected. It is well known that language changes constantly following the economy principle, that is, the principle of maximum communication with minimum efforts. Thus, according to the economy principle, it is very common for situationally or contextually predictable elements to get deleted in conversation and for neighboring elements with low semantic contents to get contracted or merged with each other. At first, these deletions, contractions, or merges may be conversational or pragmatic, with no semantic change effected. At this stage, the original forms can easily be recovered uniquely from given syntactic or discoursal contexts. For example, native speakers of Korean can recover (16b) if given (16a), because the two sentences are free variants.

(16) a.

Yongho	nun	an	ka-n	tay-yo?
Yongho	TC	not	go-IN	circumstance-POL

'Did Yongho say that he would not go?'

b.

Yongho	nun	an	ka-n-ta	ko	hay-yo?
Yongho	TC	not	go-IN-DC	QT	say-POL

'Did Yongho say that he would not go?'

Similarly, the deleted main clause in (17b) can easily be recovered from (17a).

(17) a.

mwue-la	ha-si-ess-ci	yo?
what-is.DC	say-SH-PST-NOM	POL

'What did you say?'

b.

Mia	ka	wul-te-la	ko	yo.
Mia	NM	cry-RT-DC	QT	POL

'(I said that) Mia was crying.'

If, however, such conversational uses are repeated frequently over a long period of time, new grammatical or lexical meanings (first pragmatic and later semantic) begin to be attached to the new sequence of forms, making the forms fossilized. Some forms are more fossilized than others depending on the length of time and frequency of use. Once fossilization takes place, syntactic irregularities occur, as we have observed. If systematically studied, such syntactic irregularities will provide a firm basis for internal reconstruction. The original meanings are now changed and transparent contexts are replaced by opaque or unpredictable contexts. As a result, original forms cannot easily be recovered but only diachronically reconstructed. The process of syntactic reductions may be illustrated with (2a) and (2c) as shown roughly in the following trees.

(18)

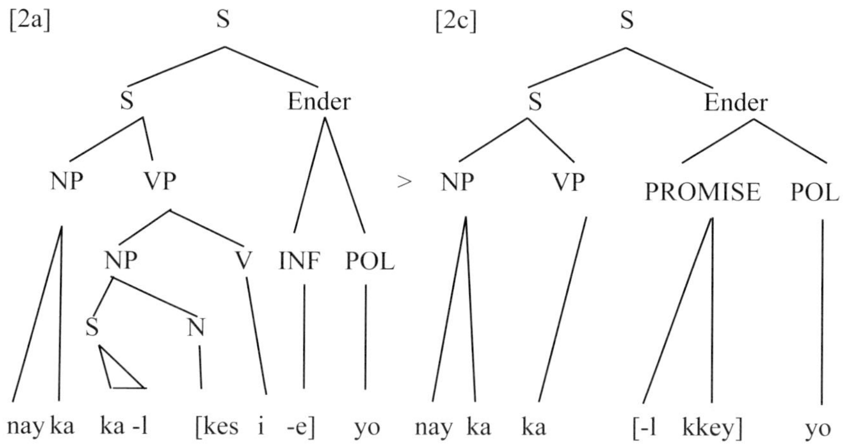

In short, formal reduction tends to occur when the forms are relatively short, their semantic load is light, their occurrence is relatively predictable, causing no synonymity or ambiguity, and they are contiguous on the surface. Main clause deletion is associated not only with the economy principle, but also with politeness.

4. Let us now briefly take up our last question: What are the directions, if any, of semantic shift in grammaticalization? Compared with formal reduction, semantic reduction appears to be multi-dimensional. Furthermore, in my view, this area of linguistic investigation is in its infancy. It is not at all clear as to what parts of original meanings are retained, strengthened, weakened, or lost, and what kinds of grammatical meanings may be added, although some insightful proposals on some limited aspects are available (e.g. Givon 1971, 1980; Sohn 1978; Anderson 1982; Traugott 1982, 1988; Fleischman 1983; Sweetser 1984, 1988; Bybee and Pagliuca 1985; Ransom 1988; Eilfort 1989).

In the remainder of this paper, I will attempt to briefly advance my tentative views in this regard, based on our examples. Let us begin with our first example. The meaning of *cwuk-e iss*, for example, consists of dying and its resultative state. That is, 'dying' denoted by *cwuk-e* precedes the state of existence denoted by *iss* in temporal sequence, hence *cwuk-e* always denotes pastness in relation to the time denoted by *iss*, as discussed in Shin (1988). Now, when two morphemes are coalesced, the two meanings they carried tend to be condensed. One might call this condensation semantic reduction. According to the economy principle, condensation is usually toward a semantic hole and avoids synonymic clash for maximum communication. Sometimes, it occurs even if there is no particular semantic hole, in which case division of semantic scope or morph-syntactic distribution usually occurs. This appears to have been the case with *–e iss > ess*. The earlier past form *–te* has become a past retrospective suffix, while *–ess* denotes general past, present perfective, or resultative state depending on the kinds of co-occurring predicates and syntactic/discourse contexts in which it occurs. Due to the past-oriented suffix *–e* in *-ess,* past and perfective meaning has attached to *–ess* in most of its occurrences. However, due to the vestige of the existence predicate *iss,* the resultative state meaning overrules in such words as *nulk-ess* 'is old', *talm-ass* 'takes after', and *cal saynki-ess* 'is good-looking', where due to the nature of the verb, the resultative state meaning was a semantic hole. Thus, the directions of the semantic condensation may be hypothesized schematically as follows.

(19) V-e iss > -ess

<--------	past
----><----	perfective
-------->	resultative state

That is, I assume that the reduction of *V-e iss* to *–ess* has given past sense when the semantic focus of condensation is toward *V-e*, perfective sense when the focus of condensation is mutual between *–e* and *iss*, and resultative state sense when the focus of condensation is toward *iss*.

The semantic shift in (14b), that is, prediction > intention > speaker's promise, shows that the direction of semantic shift in condensation is from external to internal, objective to subjective, and person-neutral to speaker-centered. This shift is also applicable to (14d), where semantic shift is: saying > thinking > intending, and to (14e) and (14g) which reveal that the shift is from objective to subjective/speaker-centered perception, evaluation or judgment. As for the semantic shift by way of main clause deletion (14c), my earlier study has reached a tentative conclusion given in (20).[4]

(20) The grammatical meaning of a restructured sentence-ender is a complex pragmatico-semantic meaning, composed of (a) the speaker (functioning as the abstract subject), (b) the diluted and generalized sense of possible deleted main predicates (functioning as an abstract verb), (c) the vastly bleached senses of the individual morphemes

4 The recently innovated expression *X nun pyello yey-yo* (< *X nun pyello coh-ci anh-ayo*) 'it's so so' should receive parallel interpretation. However, this is a unique case, in that the original simple sentence lost the whole predicate, and the copula *(y)* is inserted in its place.

constituting the ender, including the sentence-final intonation, and (d) other pragmatically introduced senses.

Thus, for example, in the sentence *pi ka o-te-la ko yo*, the derived grammatical meaning is the speaker's own mild report of his own observation of the propositional content, with some sort of pragmatic casualness. Here, the innovated ender retains the reportive sense, although the main information verb is not expressed. Sentence-enders are the speaker's territory of modality for performative acts of various types. Therefore, it is quite natural for the speaker to be the abstract performative subject in all sentence-enders.

In (14f), the semantic shift is from the speaker's indirectly showing himself to a higher person to his directly seeing him. Thus, indirectness to directness is another pattern of semantic shift. All the examples of semi-grammaticalization essentially follow the patterns discussed above. Thus, for example, the semantic shift in *–ki ey* from 'in doing' to 'because' indicates the shift not only from objective to subjective description but person-neutral to the speaker's own evaluation. Similarly, *taka nun* in the sense of 'if' indicates the speaker's precaution.

It is often proposed that the pattern of meaning reduction is: propositional meaning > idiomatic meaning > lexical meaning > grammatical meaning. Indeed, as evidenced in most of our examples, grammaticalization typically creates morphological or grammatical categories with relevant grammatical meanings. This overall pattern, however, is an over-simplification. In order to understand the deep-rooted courses or directions of semantic shift, semantic exploration into grammaticalization phenomena, as illustrated in this paper, seems to be indispensable. To recapitulate what I have observed with regard to the semantic shift associated with grammaticalization in Korean is summarized in (21).

(21) a. Diachronic structural reduction is often associated with the creation of grammatical categories with grammatical meanings.
b. With structural reduction, meaning becomes condensed.
c. Condensation moves, in principle, toward semantic holes or semantic specification.
d. Condensation avoids creation of synonymy.
e. The direction of semantic shift is from objective to subjective,
f. from person-neutral to speaker-centered,
g. from physical to mental (e.g. saying > thinking > intending > promising),
h. from indirectness to directness, and
i. from concrete to abstract (with semantic dilution or generalization of

existing or deleted elements).

j. Due to deletion, contraction, or merge, pragmatic informality or casualness is created.

Needless to say, there are many loose ends and hasty assumptions in the foregoing discussions. Much further multi-pronged investigation into this interesting area is called for.

REFERENCES: Chapter 10

Anderson, L. 1982. The 'perfect' as a universal and as a language-particular category. In Hopper, P.J. (ed.), *Tense-Aspect: Between Semantics and Pragmatics*, 227-64. Amsterdam: John Benjamins.

Bybee, J.L. 1988. Semantic substance vs. contrast in the development of grammatical meaning. *Proceedings of the 14th Annual Meeting of the Berkeley Linguistics Society*, 247-64.

Bybee, J.L. and W. Pagliuca. 1985. Crosslinguistic comparison and the development of grammatical meaning. In Fisiak, J. (ed.), *Historical Semantics/Historical Word Formation* (Trends in Linguistics: Studies and Monographs 29), 59-84. Berlin: Mouton.

Eilfort, W.H. 1989. The grammar of English *how about* constructions. *Papers from the 25th Annual Regional Meeting of the Chicago Linguistic Society*, 112-22.

Fleischman, S. 1983. From pragmatics to grammar: Diachronic reflections on complex pasts and futures in Romance. *Lingua* 60: 182-214.

Givon, T. 1971. Historical syntax and synchronic morphology: An archeologist's field trip. *Papers from the 7th Regional Meeting of the Chicago Linguistic Society*, 394-415.

Givon, T. 1980. The binding hierarchy ad the typology of complements. *Studies in Language* 4: 333-77.

Kwon, Jae Il. 1988. Cepsokmwun kwuseng uy pyenchen yangsang (Changes in conjunctive constructions). *Linguistic Journal of Korea* 13.2: 493-515.

Ransom, E.N. 1988. The grammaticalization of complementizers. *Proceedings of the 14th Annual Meeting of the Berkeley Linguistics Society*, 364-74.

Shin, Sung-Ock. 1988. *Tense and Aspect in Korean*. Ph. D. dissertation. University of Hawaii.

Sohn, Ho-min. 1978. Contractions as a mechanism of polysemic breeding: A device for speaker involvement in Korean.. Kim, Chin-W (ed.), *Papers in Korean Linguistics*, 185-96.

Sweetser, E.E. 1984. *Semantic Structure and Semantic Change: A Cognitive Linguistic Study of Modality, Perception, Speech Acts, and Logical Relations*. University of Califronia at Berkeley Ph. D. dissertation.

Sweetser, E.E. 1988. Grammaticalization and semantic bleaching. *Proceedings of the 14th Annual Meeting of the Berkeley Linguistics Society*, 389-405.

Traugott, E.C. 1982. From propositional to textual and expressive meanings: Some semantic-pragmatic aspects of grammaticalization. In Lehmann, W.P. and Y. Malkiel (eds.), *Perspectives on Historical Linguistics*, 245-71. Amsterdam: John Benjamins.

Traugott, E.C. 1988. Pragmatic strengthening and grammaticalization. *Proceedings of the 14th Annual Meeting of the Berkeley Linguistics Society*, 406-16.

11 Functional Shift in Case Stacking in Korean

1. The typological characteristic of agglutination in Korean is most distinctly manifested in various syntagmatic sequences of inflectional suffixes in verbals and case or delimiter particles in nominals. This chapter will be concerned only with case-related nominal particles.[1]

As is well known, thematic (theta) roles such as Agent, Patient, Experiencer, Benefactor, Possessor, Location, Source (Inception), Separation from, Goal, Direction, Instrument, and Accompaniment are associated with grammatical relations such as subject, direct object, indirect object, complement, possessive, locative, inceptive/source, ablative, goal, directional, instrumental, and connective. In Korean, such thematic roles and grammatical relations are marked, overtly or covertly, by postpositional case particles such as nominative *ka/i/kkeyse*, accusative *(l)ul*, genitive *uy*, adessive (static) locative-dative-goal *eykey/hantey/kkey* (animate) and *ey* (inanimate), source/inceptive *se*, ablative *pwuthe*, instrumental *(u)lo*, directional *(u)lo*, and comitative or conjunctive *(k)wa/hako/(i)lang*. Semantic delimitations of noun phrases in Korean are also marked by postpositional delimiter particles such as *(n)un* 'as for,' *to* 'also,' *man* 'only,' *cocha* 'even, in addition,' *mace* 'even, also, to the extent of,' *(i)lato* 'as a last recourse,' and *(i)na* 'or something'. Thus, both case and delimiter particles (boldfaced) may occur in sequence after a nominal, as in (1).

(1) *Kim sensayng-nim-**kkey-lo-pwuthe-man-i** hoysin-i w-ass-ta.*
Kim prof.-HT-LC-DR-ABL-only-NM response-NM come-PST-DC
'It is only from Professor Kim that I received a response.'

In the noun phrase in question, three semantic case particles (*kkey, lo, pwuthe*), one syntactic (or structural) case particle (*i*), and one delimiter particle (*man*) occur in sequence with the same nominal argument *Kim sensayng-nim* 'Professor Kim'. As alluded to in (1), syntactic cases such as nominative *ka/i*,

1 Some original ideas of this topic were presented at the 9th International Conference on Korean Linguistics held at the University of London during July 20–22, 1994.

accusative *(l)ul* and genitive *uy* occur in the outer-most morphological layer or slot, in complementary distribution with topic-related delimiters such as *(n)un* 'as for' and *to* 'also', whereas semantic case particles as well as non-topic delimiters occupy inner layers or slots. This generally fixed syntagmatic morphological distribution is further illustrated below.

(2) a. *Kim sensayng-nim-**kkey-lo-pwuthe-man-uy*** *hoysin*
Kim prof.-HT-LC-DR-ABL-only-GN response
'a response only from Prof. Kim'

b. *Kim sensayng-nim-**kkey-lo-man-ul*** *cha-lul* *ponay-ss-ta.*
Kim prof.-HT-LC-DR-only-AC car-AC send-PST-DC
'It is only to Prof. Kim that (I) sent a car.'

Since this paper is concerned with case functions, no further mention will be made regarding delimiters except those which alternate with case functions.

There are many intriguing linguistic issues involved in such case-stacking phenomena as those observed in sentences like (1) and (2).[2] This paper is limited to the observation of the phenomena of what I would call case function privation that takes place in both syntactic and semantic case particles in sentences. That is, one interesting fact observed in such particle sequences in sentences is that one of the case particles, whether overt or omitted, bears a salient syntactic case relation with the predicate (verb, adjective, verbal or adjectival noun), while the rest of them are devoid or deprived of case function but retain only their basic semantic content. I will call such a salient case a 'privileged' case (whose case particles will be underlined hereafter) and the rest 'privative' cases. Thus, the specific questions to be addressed in this paper include the following.

(3) a. Which of the cases is a privileged case and which become privative?
b. What is retained in privative case particles?
c. Can more than one case in case-stacking be privileged? That is, can Korean violate the widely supported case principle of "one-per-sentence"?
d. What determines (or licenses) privileged cases?
e. Do functional shifts in case particles occur in nominal (e.g. genitive) constructions in a way parallel to verbal constructions?

Answers to these and some other relevant issues are addressed in what follows.

2 The term "case-stacking" is borrowed from Gerdts (1991) and Maling (1989).

2. In verbal constructions where a verb or an adjective functions as a head predicate, the privileged case is neither the case in the last slot necessarily, nor a structural case such as nominative or accusative. Let us consider the noun phrase *Kim sensayng-nim-kkey-lo-pwuthe-man-i hoysin-i w-ass-ta* in (1) again. Notice that the nominative particle *i*, the honorific locative/goal particle *kkey*, and the directional particle *lo* are all unable to syntactically relate the nominal argument *Kim sensayng-nim* to the predicate *ota*, because the sentence denotes neither Professor Kim's coming nor the coming of the response to or toward Professor Kim, but the coming of the response *from* him. Thus, none of these case particles can assume a salient case function in this construction.

Although most existing grammar books and dictionaries consider *pwuthe* 'from' as a delimiter and not a case particle (e.g. Yang 1972, Huh 1984, Sung 1978, Tonga Chwulphan-sa 1994), it is the ablative case marked by *pwuthe* that is the privileged case in the given construction. Thus, all the other particles are disqualified as a privileged case marker, although they can be a privileged one in other *ota*-verb constructions like the following.

(4) a. *Kim sensayng-nim-**i*** *o-si-ess-ta.*
(Nominative)
Kim prof.-HT-NM come-SH-PST-DC
'Professor Kim came.'

b. *Minho-nun* *hakkyo-**lo*** *w-ass-ta.*
(Directional)
Minho-TC school-DR come-PST-DC
'Minho came to (the direction of) school.'

c. *Kim sensayng-nim-**kkey*** *sopho-ka* *w-ass-ta.*
(Goal)
Kim prof.-HT-GL parcel-NM come-PST-DC
'A parcel came to Professor Kim.'

Now the question is why, unlike in (4), none of the nominative, directional, and locative/goal cases in the noun phrase *Kim sensayng-nim-kkey-lo-pwuthe-man-i* in (1) can be chosen as a privileged case, despite the fact that the verb *ota* has an argument structure which is compatible with all of them, as alluded to in (4)?

The argument structure of the verb *ota* contains the obligatory <agent> role as the subject and optional roles such as <inception> (marked by the inceptive particle *se*), <source> (marked by the ablative particle *pwuthe*), <goal> (marked by the goal particle *ey*, *eykey*, or *kkey*), and <direction> (marked by the directional particle *(u)lo*). In sentence (1), the obligatory theta role <agent> should be assigned to the pseudo-agentive argument *hoysin* 'response' in order for the sentence to be well-formed and meaningful in the sense that it is Professor Kim's response which came from him. According to the subject choice hierarchy among theta roles, this <agent> argument is chosen as subject and is marked by the nominative *i*. Lack of the subject honorific suffix *–(u)si* in the verb indicates that the inanimate *hoisin* is the subject and *Kim-sensayng-nim* cannot be a subject.

Due to its oblique case particles such as *kkey* and *(u)lo*, whose functions and meanings are incompatible with those of the <agent> role, the argument *Kim sensayng-nim* in (1) cannot function as an agent of the verb *ota* despite its optional co-occurrence with the nominative *i*, disqualifying itself as subject. Thus, the nominative particle *i* whose normal function is to mark the subject cannot function as a subject marker in this construction. It is privative in this case.

As for the three other theta roles <goal>, <direction>, and <source>, all of which are potentially case-relatable to the verb *ota* as observed in (4), only the <source> role is assigned to *Kim sensayng-nim*, making the other roles defunct. Thus, only the <source> role and its ablative case remain privileged. Let us observe why this is so.

All the four theta roles in question and their corresponding cases have dual functions, one privileged and the other privative. Thus, grammatico-semantic contents are different according to this dual function, as shown below with regard to the locomotive verb *ota*.

(5) theta roles/cases

Particles	*Cases*	*privileged* meaning	*privative* meaning
i	*nominative*	subject/complement	exclusive/focus
kkey	*goal/dative/locative*	'to, at'	general location
(u)lo	*directional*	'toward'	general direction
pwuthe	*ablative*	'from'	beginning with

It is obvious that the salient meanings of the three privileged roles/cases of *kkey, (u)lo,* and *pwuthe* are mutually incompatible. On the other hand, the meaning of any one privileged role/case and the meanings of the two privative (defunct) roles/cases are compatible in one way or another. This seems to be the only acceptable combination of functions and meanings if the three roles/cases in question are to coexist grammatically and semantically.

Now, why is only the ablative case privileged in the given construction? The answer seems to be that *pwuthe* occurs last. As a head-final language, a later position has a larger syntactic and semantic scope and privilege than all preceding positions, other things being equal. Thus, in a sequence of case particles all syntactically relatable to the main predicate, the one occurring in the last morphological position is privileged.

Thus, in order for sentence (1) to be grammatical, *Kim sensayng-nim-kkey-lo-pwuthe-man-i* must be interpreted only in the privileged meaning of the ablative case 'from'. In this interpretation, *kkey* provides the meaning of general static location 'at,' devoid of the case meaning 'to', and *lo* provides the meaning of general direction, devoid of the case meaning 'toward'. These privative meanings of *kkey* and *lo* are semantically compatible with the privileged case meaning of *pwuthe* in the literal sense of 'from the direction of the professor's location'.

In contrast, in sentences (6), the noun phrases with an overt or covert nominative case particle function as privileged, per the argument structure of the predicate *ita*, which requires a theme subject. Thus, *i kang-ulo-pwuthe-man-i* functions as the subject, with the nominative *i* as the subject marker, while the ablative role of *pwuthe* becomes defunct and *pwuthe* carries its privative meaning of "beginning with".

(6) a. *i* *kang-**ulo-pwuthe-man-i*** *wuli hakkyo i-ta.*
this river-DR-ABL-only-NM our school is-DC
'Beginning only with this river is our school.'

b. *Kim sensayng-nim-**pwuthe*** *malssumha-si-ess-eyo.*
Kim prof.-HT-ABL talk-SH-PST-POL
'Professor Kim started talking.'

The directional case particle *ulo* in (6a) is privative because it is morphologically followed by another semantic case particle, the ablative *pwuthe*, which happens to be privative. Thus, the following generalization seems to be operative.

(7) In a sequence of case markers which are equally case-relatable to the predicate, the later one acquires priority in case privilege over the preceding one(s).

(7) regulates a privilege hierarchy, and, other things being equal, the last layer (slot) has the highest privilege.

From the foregoing discussions, there seems to be no more than one privileged case in a noun phrase. One might argue, however, that (8a) constitutes an exception. That is, one might suspect that the sentence is not subject to (7), because, at first glance, both the locative/goal *kkey* and the directional *lo* appear to have equal syntactic-semantic relation with the predicate.

(8) a. *Mia-ka Kim sensayng-nim-**kkey-lo** ka-ss-ta.*
(LC/GL-DIRECTIONAL)
Mia-NM Kim prof.-HT-LC/GL-DR go-PST-DC
'Mia went to (the direction of) Professor Kim.'

b. *Mia-ka Kim sensayng-nim-**kkey** ka-ss-ta.* (GOAL)
Mia-NM Kim prof.-HT-GL go-PST-DC
'Mia went to Professor Kim.'

c. *Mia-ka kyohoy-**lo** ka-ss-ta.* (DIRECTIONAL)
Mia-NM church-DR go-PST-DC
'Mia went to (the direction of) church.'

d. *Mia-ka kyohoy-(**ey**) ka-ss-ta.* (GOAL)
Mia-NM church-GL go-PST-DC
'Mia went to church.'

e. **Mia-ka Kim sensayng-**ulo** ka-ss-ta.*
Mia-NM Kim prof.-DR go-PST-DC

f. **Minho-ka kyohoy-ey-**lo** ka-ss-ta.*
Minho-NM church-LC-DR go-PST-DC

Based on (8a), (8b) and (8e), the argument structure of *kata* might be postulated as <agent, goal (directional)> for animates. Based on (8c), (8d) and (8f), it would be <agent, goal OR directional> for inanimates. Notice that (8c) and (8f) indicate that the goal case marker *ey* cannot occur in the expression of DIRECTIONAL for inanimates. This leads us to think that *kkey* before *lo* in (8a) is simply a privative honorific animate locative (not goal) marker, unlike *kkey* in (8b) which functions as a full-fledged goal case marker. It may be comparable to a ZERO marker for privative inanimate locative before the directional marker *lo*. Another reason for considering it an animate locative marker is that *kkey-se* (honorific subject), *eykey-se* 'from' (animate source), *ey-se* 'from' (inanimate source), *kkey-lo-pwuthe* 'from (an honorific person),' and *ey-se-pwuthe* 'from (an object)' all contain a locative/goal particle *kkey*, *eykey*, or *ey* but none of these denotes the goal meaning, only the static locative meaning. Furthermore, observe the following examples and notice that unlike the locomotive verb *kata*, the action verb *tallita* 'run' is unable to activate the goal meaning of the locative/goal particle.

(9) a. *Mia-ka Kim sensayng-nim-**kkey-lo*** *tally-ess-ta.* (LC-DIRECTIONAL)
Mia-NM Kim prof.-HT-LC-DR run-PST-DC
'Mia ran to (the direction of) Professor Kim.'

b. **Mia-ka Kim sensayng-nim-**kkey*** *tally-ess-ta.* (GOAL)
Mia-NM Kim prof.-HT-LC run-PST-DC
'Mia ran to Professor Kim.'

c. *Mia-ka kyohoy-**lo*** *tally-ess-ta.* (DIRECTIONAL)
Mia-NM church-DR run-PST-DC
'Mia ran to (the direction of) church.'

d. **Mia-ka kyohoy-(**ey**)* *tally-ess-ta.* (GOAL)
Mia-NM church-LC run-PST-DC
'Mia ran to church.'

What this implies is that, other things being equal, only the last particle is relevant to privileged case function. That is, (9a) and (9c) are grammatical because the verb *tallita* can take a directional argument, whereas (9b) and (9d) are ungrammatical because the verb cannot take a locative argument. Occurrence of *kkey* in (9a) indicates that it has nothing to do with case relation to *tallita*. It, therefore, is a privative case. Similarly, if *kkey* before *lo* in (8a) is a privative locative (i.e. not a goal) indicating a simple static location, it is incompatible with the argument structure of the predicate *kata* which does not contain a <locative> role. Thus, in (8a), only the directional *lo* is the privileged case particle, directly case-related with the predicate.

Thus, the generally accepted case theoretic principle that only one case in a noun phrase is syntactically related to the predicate is still applicable to Korean despite the widely observable case-stacking phenomena. The foregoing discussions lead us to propose the following generalizations.

(10) a. A noun phrase in a sentence has only one privileged case in relation to its predicate and the rest of the case particles associated with that noun phrase are privative.

b. The privileged case is determined (i.e. licensed) primarily by the argument structure of the predicate and secondarily by the generalization given in (7).

c. The meanings of stacked particles must be semantically compatible. Otherwise, the sentence becomes ungrammatical.

The licensing function that the argument structure of a predicate plays may be more clearly observed by comparing the following two sentences.

(11) a. *tong-ccok-***ulo-man-ul** *ka-ss-ta.*
east-side-DR-only-AC go-PST-DC
'(he) went only to the east side.'

b. *tong-ccok-***ulo-man-ul** *po-ass-ta.*
east-side-DR-only-AC see-PST-DC
'(He) looked only toward the east.'

Notice that in (10a) the directional *ulo* is privileged, whereas in (10b) the accusative *ul* is, both due to the argument structures of the predicates involved. Then, how about the following sentence which is semantically ambiguous?

(12) *Minho-nun* *hakkyo-***ey-se-pwuthe** *tally-ess-ta.*
Minho-TC school-LC-SR-ABL run-PST-DC
a. 'Minho ran from the school.'
b. 'Minho began running at school.'

Obviously, *pwuthe* has two grammatical meanings, one as an ablative case in the sense of '(separation) from' and the other as a delimiter in the sense of 'beginning at/with'. If it is used in the former sense (12a), it is the privileged case, rendering the other cases privative. In contemporary Korean, the sequence *ey-se* (static locative particle+ source/inceptive particle *se*) is grammaticalized as a case marker indicating dynamic location and source, as against static locative *ey,* as in *hakkyo* **ey-se** *no-n-ta* '(He) is playing at school', *hakkyo* **ey-se** *w-ass-ta* '(He) came from school', and *hakkyo* **ey** *iss-ta* '(He) is at school.' Thus, in (12b), we can say that the dynamic locative *ey-se* is the privileged case.[3]

3 Sung (1978:90, 194–5) takes *se* as a delimiter meaning "existence". He suspects that the morpheme developed from the adverbial form (*is-ye*) of the existential adjective *is*. Ko (1989:114-5) maintains that the morpheme is one of the nominative (subjective) case particles as evidenced in such expressions as *twul-i-se w-ass-ta* 'The two persons came.' I treat it as a

3. As already alluded to and partly answered in the preceding discussions, what is left in privative cases/roles when they are deprived of case function is only the delimiter function. All case particles inherently have both case functions, either structural or semantic, and their own semantic content. This semantic content is comparable to the delimiter function. It is this semantic content or delimiter function of one sort or another that is still retained when a case particle is devoid of its case function.

The primary function of the nominative *ka/i* and the accusative *(l)ul* is structural (syntactic) case marking. However, they also denote exclusiveness and focus in the sense of "it is . . . that," in which these particles behave like delimiters. Thus, the privative nominative and accusative case particles lose their structural case marking function, while retaining only their exclusiveness or focus meaning as illustrated in (1). Some more examples follow.

(13) a. *nay syassu-**ey-ka*** *khun kwumeng-i* *na-ss-eyo.*
my shirt-LC-NM big hole-NM appear-PST-POL
'A big hole is on my shirt!'

b. *yeki-**ey-se-ka*** *koki-kwup-ki-ka* *ceyil coh-ta.*
here-LC-SR-NM meat-bake-NOM-NM most good-DC
'Barbecuing is the best at this place.'

c. *san-ey* *ka-ci* *mal-ko* *pata-**ey-l(ul)*** *ka-ca.*
mountain-GL go-NOM stop-and sea-GL-AC go-PR
'Let's go to the beach, not to the mountain.'

Similarly, when occurring alone or after the goal *eykey/hanthey/kkey*, the directional particle *(u)lo* indicates the allative case in the sense of 'toward,' but when it is followed by another case particle such as the ablative *pwuthe* 'from,' or a privileged nominative or accusative case particle, it functions like a delimiter, denoting simply 'the direction of,' as already observed and further illustrated below.

(14) a. *United Airline-i* *hankwuk-**ulo-pwuthe*** *ttena-ss-ta.*
United Airline-NM Korea-DR-ABL depart-PST-DC
'The UA flight departed from Korea.'

---

source/inceptive case particle (H. Sohn 1994, 1999).

b. *tong-ccok-**ulo-ka*** *wuli cip i-ta.*
east-side-DR-NM our house is-DC
'(In) the eastern direction is my house.'

c. *puk-ccok-**ulo-lul*** *po-ala.*
north-side-DR-AC see-IM
'Look at the northern direction.'

When the ablative *pwuthe* becomes privative, it loses its case status, having been demoted to the status of a delimiter, as already observed. Notice that *pwuthe* is followed by the nominative case particle *ka* in (15a) and the whole NP functions as the subject of the sentence. Similarly, in (15b), the whole NP functions as the object of the sentence.

(15) a. *cikum-**ulo-pwuthe-ka*** *muncey i-ta.*
now-DR-ABL-NM problem is-DC
'(lit) From now on is the problem.'

b. *yeksa-**pwuthe-(lul)*** *kongpuhay-la.*
history-ABL-AC study-IM
'Study history first!'

4. Case stacking takes place also in arguments constituting nominal constructions such as genitive and connective structures. Essentially, the same kind of functional shift occurs in such constructions that we have observed in verbal constructions. Thus, for example, the privileged semantic case particle *ey-se* is source or inceptive in *pwusan-**ey-se**-pwuthe-**uy** kongyen* 'performance starting at Pusan,' whereas the privileged semantic case is source represented by the ablative *pwuthe* in *pwusan-ulo-**pwuthe-uy** yehayng* 'travel from Pusan'. These semantic cases, as well as their corresponding theta roles, are assumed to be assigned by the argument structures of the verbal or adjectival nouns involved, such as *kongyen* 'performance' and *yehayng* 'travel'.

One essential difference between verbal and nominal constructions is that in the latter, a privileged structural case must occur in addition to semantic cases. Observe the following examples, where bracketed portions are nominal constructions, with privileged case particles underlined and structural cases boldfaced.

(16) a. [*mikwuk-**uy*** *saiphan-ey-se-**uy*** *ilpon-kwa-**uy***
America-GN Saipan-LC-SR-GN Japan-CM-GN

cencayng]-i *chiyelhay-ss-ta.*
war-NM fierce-PST-DC
'The American war against Japan in Saipan was fierce.'

b. *paywu-ka [hankwuk-ey-se-**wa/na** ilpon-ey-se]* *w-ass-ta.*
actor-NM Korea-LC-SR-CN/DS Japan-LC-SR come-PST-DC
'The actors came from Korea and/or Japan.'

c. [*Kim-sensayng-nim-kkey-lo-pwuthe-man-**uy*** *hoysin*]
Kim-prof.-HT-DR-ABL-only-GN response
'a response only from Professor Kim'

Notice that, unlike in verbal constructions, the privileged structural case in nominal constructions is determined by the last overt or covert case particle. In (16a), the privileged structural case is the genitive in the three noun phrases in question, in that only the genitive case relates all the three arguments syntactically (genitively) to the head nominal *cencayng* 'war'. The dynamic locative *ey-se* and comitative *kwa* manifest their semantic case functions vis-a-vis the head noun *cencayng* 'war', as in the case of verbal constructions. Being a verbal noun with its own argument structure, roughly <agent, dynamic location, accompaniment>, *cencayng* licences the grammaticality of the co-occurring clausemate arguments by assigning the theta roles to them. While the dynamic location and the accompaniment roles are realized as *ey-se* and comitative case *wa*, respectively, the agent role cannot be realized as nominative case unlike in verbal constructions, because this structural case is obligatorily suppressed when the (structural) genitive case which shares the same morphological slot is preemptive. Thus, the genitive construction does not have any nominative case function, either overtly or covertly, although it may have an agent role. The same is true with the accusative case, as in *kyengchal-uy kangto-uy sasal* 'the policeman's killing of the thief' where *kangto* 'thief' is a theme (or patient) of the verbal noun *sasal* 'killing,' yet cannot function as an accusative case.

Notice that the syntactic function of the genitive case is independent of the argument structure of *cencayng*. The genitive case is assigned structurally by the genitive constituent structure of noun phrases, roughly NP → (GN) NP; GN → NP-GN, where GN stands for genitive case, which is marked by an overt or covert genitive particle *uy*.[4]

4 When a nominal construction refers to time-frame such as "before", "after", and "during", genitive case marking may be dispensed with, as in *mikwuk-i saiphan-ey-se ilpon-kwa cencayng tocwung manh-un salam-i cwuk-ess-ta* 'Many people died while America was involved in war with Japan in Saipan.' Notice that in this case the nominative as well

In (16b), the connective particle *wa* 'and,' which is homophonous and partly synonymous with the comitative case particle *wa* 'with' (cf. 16a), is viewed as a privileged structural case in that it marks conjunction in relation to *ilpon* 'Japan.' So does the disjunctive *(i)na* 'or'. Like the genitive *uy*, both the connective *wa* (and its variants *kwa*, *hako*, *(i)lang*, etc.) and the disjunctive *(i)na* occupy the last layer in a noun phrase. Just like the genitive, their presence is licensed not by the following noun or predicate, but by the constituent structure of noun phrases, such as NP → NP-CON NP where CON stands for connective case which is realized as a connective or disjunctive particle. Hence, we may regard them as structural cases despite their rather strong semantic content.

One might argue that the connective and disjunctive cases are not structural on the grounds that, in constructions like [*cencayng-kwa phyenghwa-wa*]-*ka/lul/uy* 'war and peace (nominative/accustive/genitive),' the structural cases *ka/lul/uy* may follow the connective case particle. (Obviously, the second *wa* is simply a meaningless and functionless copy of the preceding particle *kwa*.) However, cases such as genitive and connective/disjunctive are independent of semantic cases in nominal constructions since the two nominal arguments with the semantic cases marked by *ey-se* in (16b), for example, are licensed by the argument structure of the predicate *ota* 'come,' which is roughly <agent, dynamic locative>. That is, the two arguments perform their theta roles and case function vis-a-vis the predicate *ota*. This is not the case with the genitive and connective/disjunctive cases.

As for (16c), one may wonder what the privileged semantic case is and how it is determined or licensed. Semantically, the ablative *pwuthe* is the privileged case, not the locative *kkey* or the directional *lo*, because unlike these two defunct case particles, it retains its privileged case meaning, i.e. 'the response that came from Professor Kim'. Besides, the stipulation in (7) requires us to choose *pwuthe*, other things being equal. But where is the predicate that can assign the ablative role to *pwuthe*? One can speculate that, in a genitive nominal construction whose head is not a predicate noun, the privileged semantic case is determined by the argument structure of an understood abstract predicate. In (16c), the understood abstract predicate may be a deictic motion verb such as COME because the expression presupposes an understood locomotive action from *Kim sensayng-nim* to the current location of his response. Similarly, for example, in *thongil-lo-**uy** kil* 'the road to the national unification,' the understood abstract verb is GO or MOVE, whose argument structure involves the theta role <direc-

as dynamic locative and comitative function as privileged cases. The constituent syntactic structure underlying such constructions must be different from the structure that underlies genitive constructions. Something like NP → S must be postulated for the construction ending in *cencayng*.

tion>.

Alternatively, one may think that, in the lack of a predicate carrying an argument structure (i.e. a verbal noun), (16c) does not have a privileged semantic case; it has only a privileged structural case, i.e. the genitive case marked by *uy*. In this non-abstract account, all the semantic case particles following *Kim sensayng-nim* are considered privative. One unanswered question in this solution is why *pwuthe* retains the semantic content of a privileged case. We may thus draw the following generalizations:

(17) a. In nominal constructions, two privileged cases occur, one structural and the other semantic. The structural case which is assigned syntactically occurs in the last morphological slot. The privileged semantic case is determined by the argument structure of its verbal or adjectival head noun in accordance with (7).

b. When genitive case is present, other structural cases (nominative and accusative) cannot occur.

c. The remaining cases lose their case functions the same way as in verbal constructions.

d. In a genitive construction whose head noun is not a predicate noun, (i) the privileged semantic case is determined by the argument structure of a reconstructed abstract predicate; (ii) (alternatively) there is no privileged semantic case.

5. One question yet to be addressed is: what syntactic-semantic factors are involved in licensing the grammaticality of privative case stacking in given constructions? Although privative cases no longer function as syntactic or semantic cases and behave like delimiters, their occurrences are not always controlled by their inherent delimiting meanings alone. This issue would require too much time and space to be resolved within the scope of this paper. Many interesting proposals are available that provide partial answers to this issue (e.g. Maling 1989; Gerdts 1990, 1991; Kang 1991). Suffice it to present below some illustrative sentences where privative nominative and accusative particles may or may not occur. Some linguists have observed that NM/AC alternations are conditioned largely by the [–/+animacy] feature of the subject (cf. Maling ibid.; Gerdts ibid.).

(18) a. *Mia-nun ilpon-ey ka-key-**lul**/?**ka** toy-ss-eyo.*
Mia-TC Japan-to go-AD-AC/NM become-PST-POL
'Mia is scheduled to go to Japan.'

b. *kyay-ka* *mas-iss-key* *mek-ko-**lul/*ka*** *iss-kwun*!
he-NM taste-exist-AD eat-and-AC/NM stay-AP
'He is eating deliciously.'

c. *cwungkwuk-**ey-lul/ka*** *ka-ko-**lul/ka*** *siph-eyo.*
China-GL-AC/NM go-NOM-AC-AC/NM wishful-POL
'I want to go to China.'

(19) a. *kongpu-ka* *hakkyo-**ey-se-ka/*lul*** *ceyil* *cal* *toy-eyo.*
study-TC school-LC-SR-NM/AC most well done-POL
'(I) can study most efficiently at school.'

d. *Minho-nun* *hakkyo-**ey-se-*ka/*lul*** *nol-ayo.*
Minho-TC school-LC-SR-NM/AC play-POL
'Minho plays at school.'

(20) a. *Minho-ka* *twu-pen(**-i/ul**)* *nemecy-ess-ta.*
Minho-NM 2-time-NM/AC fall-PST-DC
'Minho fell down twice.'

b. *pyek-i* *twu-pen(**-i/*ul**)* *munecy-ess-ta.*
wall-NM 2-time-NM/AC crumble-PST-DC
'The wall crumbled twice.'

REFERENCES: Chapter 11

Gerdts, Donna B. 1990. Relational visibility. In Dziwirek, K. et al. (eds.), *Grammatical Relations*, pp.199–214. The Stanford University Center for the Study of Language and Information.

Gerdts, Donna B. 1991. Case, chomage, and multipredicate domains in Korean. In Kuno, S. et al. (eds.), *Harvard Studies in Korean Linguistics IV*, pp.249–68.

Huh, Woong. 1984. *Kwukehak*. Seoul: Saym Munhwasa.

Kang, Young-Se. 1991. 'Adverbial Nominals' Case is Well Explained by the Generalized Case Marking Principle. In Kuno, S. et al. (eds.), *Harvard Studies in Korean Linguistics*, pp.295–303.

Ko, Young-geun. 1989. *Kwuke Hyengthaylon Yenkwu*. Seoul: Seoul National University Press.

Li, Audrey Yen-hui. 1985. *Abstract Case in Chinese*. Ph.D. dissertation. University of Southern California.

Maling, Joan. 1989. Adverbials and structural case in Korean. In Kuno, S. et al. (eds.), *Harvard Studies in Korean Linguistics* III: 297–308.

Sohn, Ho-min. 1994. *Korean: Descriptive Grammars*. London: Routledge.

Sung, Kwang-soo. 1978. *Kwuke Cosa uy Yenkwu*. Seoul: Hyengsel Publishers.

Tonga Chwulphan-sa. 1994. *Tonga Say Kwuke Sacen*. Seoul: Tonga Publishing & Printing, Co.

Yang, In-Seok. 1972. *Korean Syntax*. Ph.D. dissertation. University of Hawaii.

12 Reanalysis in Korean Complex Predicate Constructions: Causative Derivation*

1. What is variously called reanalysis, restructuring, reformulation, or re-bracketing is the primary diachronic mechanism of morphosyntactic change that frequently leads to grammaticalization (e.g. Langacker 1977; Traugott and Heine 1991; Hopper and Traugott 1993).[1] As Hopper and Traugott (ibid.:32, 56-7) put it, reanalysis, referring to the development of new structures out of old, modifies underlying representations, whether semantic, syntactic, or morphological, and brings about rule change. The secondary mechanism is analogy, the main function of which is to effect not rule change but rule spread (rule generalization or extension). Our main concern here is reanalysis.[2]

Most relevant studies made thus far agree that reanalysis leading to grammaticalization is prototypically unidirectional reduction, forming a cline (e.g. Heine and Reh 1984; Hopper and Traugott 1993). Thus, for instance, Hopper and Traugott (ibid.: 7, 95, 132, 170) propose that a cline of clause combining involves three major cluster points: parataxis (-dependent, -embedded) > hypotaxis (+dependent, -embedded) > subordination (+dependent, +embedded), and a clause-internal cline is of the form: lexical item (used in specific linguistic contexts) > grammatical word > clitic > inflectional affix. As we will see later, Korean data essentially support such a unidirectional cline hypothesis, although more fine-grained cluster points can be established in subordination. This paper will focus mainly on the reanalysis connecting the subordination stage and the stage of derivational and inflectional affixes.

Some reanalyses are more mature or absolute than others in that they have

* This chapter is reprinted from *Japanese/Korean Linguistics* 5: 37–64 (1996), Stanford CSLI Publications. Its original version was presented as a keynote paper at the Japanese/Korean Linguistics Conference held at the University of California at Los Angeles. November 1994.

1 I would like to thank Gerald Mathias and Leon Serafim for several valuable comments and suggestions on an earlier version of this paper.

2 Together with lexicalization and word-order changes, grammaticalization is a major subset of changes involved in reanalysis (Heine and Reh 1984; Heine, Claudi and Hünnemeyer 1991: 215–20; Hopper and Traugott 1993:50).

been completed and historically fossilized in both forms and meanings, whereas premature or ongoing reanalyses manifest morpho-syntactic alternation involving minor semantic shifts. The latter contribute to the opacity of the constructions in question, thus causing synchronic linguists to widely diverge in their attempts at determining the underlying representations of such constructions.[3]

This paper is intended to accomplish two objectives. One is to examine one major type of syntactic reanalysis that involves Korean complex predicate constructions and the associated morpho-phonological reductions and semantic shifts.[4] The other objective is, based in large part on the outcome of the first objective, to specifically advance a hypothesis that the Korean suffixal causative has developed from the periphrastic causative due to syntactic reanalysis, accompanying morpho-phonological reduction, and resultant grammaticalization. In order to place the second objective in a proper perspective, I will first discuss some well attested patterns of reanalysis associated with causative constructions. And then, I will make a proposal on the development of causative suffixes. Finally, through examining more examples of various suffixal derivations, I will provide a broader conceptual perspective in support of my proposal on the development of the suffixal causative from the periphrastic causative.

2. Korean periphrastic causative constructions have developed from the corresponding hypotactic constructions. Thus, for instance, there is no doubt that complex predicate sentences like (1b) have developed from adverbial conjunctive sentences like (1a). X stands for an unspecified subject.

(1) a. *Mia-ka* *chayk-ul* *ilk-key##* *coyonghi* *hay-ss-ta.*
Mia-NM book-AC read-AD quietly do-PST-DC
'X kept quiet, so that Mia could read a book.' (HYPOTAXIS)

b. *Mia-ka* *chayk-ul* *ilk-key#* *hay-ss-ta.*
Mia-NM book-AC read-AD cause-PST-DC
'X caused (for) Mia to read a book.' (SUBORDINATION)

3 This brief study alludes to the significance of the diachronic perspective in many synchronic linguistic descriptions, in that synchronic sections are not as smooth and regular as many tend to assume because many changes are variably ongoing or prematurely stopped. Thus, synchronically puzzling issues may frequently be solved or answered when they are placed in the diachronic plane.

4 There are other types too. For instance, extensive post-complementizer main clause deletions (H. Sohn 1990) and grammaticalization phenomena associated with auxiliary verb constructions (Falsgraf and Park 1994) are some other major types of reanalysis involving Korean complex predicate constructions.

Notice that a clause boundary (##) with a regular phonological pause changes to a word boundary (#) with a minor pause. The meaning of the higher verb *hata* shifts from 'do' to 'cause' and the conjunctive complementizer *-key* with the lexical meaning 'so that' to an infinitive complementizer with the grammatical meaning 'to'. There is little doubt that the first clause of (1a) is hypotactically related to the main clause as a whole, as evidenced by the interpolated *coyonghi*, whereas the first clause of (1b) directly complements the main clause verb.

The above pattern of reanalysis abounds in many other complement verbal constructions in Korean, the typical ones being periphrastic passive, auxiliary verb (*-e* type and *-ko* type), serial verb, and deontic (e.g. (24)) constructions. In all such instances, both hypotactic and corresponding subordinative types of constructions coexist. We may tentatively postulate the surface tree diagrams as in (2) to represent (1a) and (1b), respectively.

(2)

a.

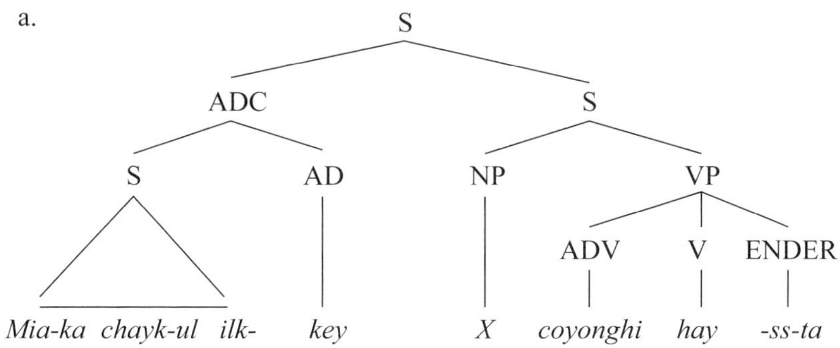

b.

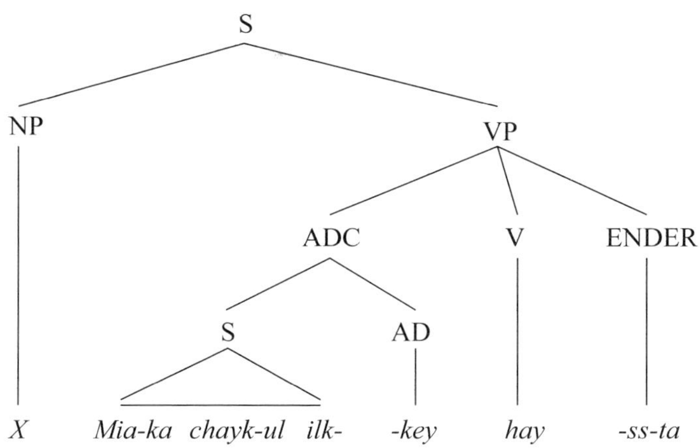

By presenting the trees as in (2a) and (2b), I am proposing that an adverbial clause, represented as ADC in (2), is directly dominated by S in hypotactic constructions and by VP in subordinative constructions.

The primary condition or prerequisite for the type of reanalysis presented in this paper is the contiguity of the upstairs (main clause) predicate with the downstairs adverbializer in the adverbial clause. The second essential condition is structural and semantico-pragmatic reducibility. For instance, syntactically complex and/or semantically heavy conjunctive suffixes are not easily reducible with a following main clause predicate (e.g. *-eto/-ato* 'although', *-ca(maca)* 'as soon as', *-(u)myense* 'simultaneously with', *-(u)nikka* 'because', *-ese/-ase* 'and then, so', the paratactic *-ko* (as against the hypotactic *-e/-a*) 'and', and the nominalizer *-ki* or *-um* (as against the adverbializer *-key*). And the third condition is, as in all grammaticalization phenomena, the productive or frequent use of the pattern in question in certain highly specific discourse contexts.

What constantly operates under such conditions (contiguity, reducibility, and frequency in specific contexts) is gravitation between the embedded clause complementizer and the following main clause predicate, which become bonded to varying degrees both morpho-phonologically and syntactico-semantically as in (1b) and (2b). This bondedness results in various patterns of reanalysis in Korean complex predicate constructions.

3. As observed in (3), case markings alternate in subordinative sentences such as (1b) (unlike in hypotactic ones such as (1a)), rendering the sententiality of the embedded clause somewhat weaker, both semantically and syntactically.

(3) a. *Mia-eykey chayk-ul ilk-key# hay-ss-ta.*
Mia-DT book-AC read-AD cause-PST-DC
'X caused/requested/allowed Mia to read a book.'

b. *Mia-lul chayk-ul ilk-key# hay-ss-ta.*
Mia-AC book-AC read-AD cause-PST-DC
'X caused Mia to read a book.'

The surface structures of the two reanalyzed sentences in (3) may be schematically represented (or rebracketed) as follows.

(4)

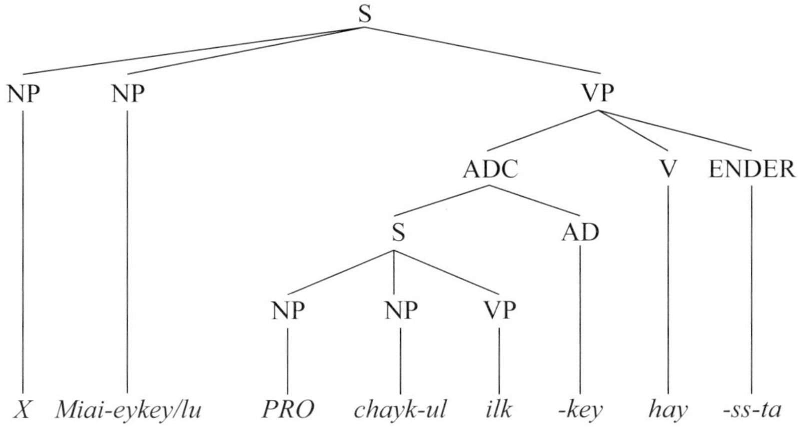

Notice that the original downstairs agent associated only with the downstairs predicate *ilkta* is now associated with the upstairs causative predicate *hata* as its new argument, relegating the downstairs clause to a subjectless surface structure.

While the main clause agent in (1b) causes or arranges the whole embedded clause event to be effected, the main clause agent in (3a) requests, permits or causes the embedded causee to be responsible for the embedded clause event. In (3b), on the other hand, the main clause agent is in total control over not only the causee but also the embedded clause event.

J. Park (1994:100-2) correctly argues that an embedded NP-NM construction indicates biclausal structure more strongly than an embedded NP-DT construction, which is in turn more biclausal than an embedded NP-AC. He provides examples similar to (5) and (6) in support of his claim.

(5) a. *[Mia-ka chayk-ul encey ilk]-key hay-ss-ni?*
Mia-NM book-AC when read-AD cause-PST-Q
'When did X cause Mia to [read a book t]?'

b. *Mia-eykey/lul chayk-ul encey ilk-key hay-ss-ni?*
Mia-DT/AC book-AC when read-AD cause-PST-Q
i. 'When did X cause Mia to [read a book t]?'
ii. '[When did X cause Mia] to read a book?'

As J. Park (ibid.) points out, *encey* modifies only the downstairs verb (ilk) in (5a), as opposed to both up- and downstairs verbs (*ilk* and *hay*) in (5b). When *encey* is interpreted as modifying the upstairs causal verb *hay* (5bii), the upstairs verb is closely bonded with the dowstairs verb, with no phonetic juncture allowed to occur after *ilk-key*. The two verbs behave like a single complex predicate.

In (6), on the other hand, NP-AC is distinguished from NP-NM and NP DT in view of the different behavior of the intransitive goal marker *-ey* and the transitive goal marker *-ey(ta(ka))* (J. Park:113-7; cf. H. Sohn 1977).

(6) a. *Mia-ka/eykey chimtay-ey/*eyta nwup-key hay-ss-e.*
Mia-NM/DT bed-on lie-AD cause-PST-INT
'X caused Mia to lie on the bed.'

b. *Mia-lul chimtay-ey(ta) nwup-key hay-ss-e.*
Mia-AC bed-on lie-AD cause-PST-INT
'X caused Mia to lie on the bed.'

c. *Mia-lul chimtay-ey(ta) nwup-hi-ess-e.*
Mia-AC bed-on lie-CAS-PST-INT
'X put Mia to bed.'

Notice that, unlike sentence (6a) with *Mia-ka/eykey*, sentence (6b) with *Mia-lul* behaves much like the monoclause in (6c).

From a diachronic perspective, two important points can be deduced from these synchronic examples. First, the examples reflect different stages of reanalysis along a diachronic cline. Secondly, such so-called synchronic notions as subject-to-object raising, predicate raising, or predicate incorporation are no more than a diachronic stage of reanalysis. Incidentally, similar 'raising' phenomena are also observed in such other constructions as the following.

(7) a. *na-nun Mia-ka/eykey/lul o-tolok hay-ss-ta.*
I-TC Mia-NM/DT/AC come-so that do-PST-DC
'I had Mia come.'

b. *na-nun Mia-ka/eykey/lul o-la-ko hay-ss-ta.*
I-TC Mia-NM/DT/AC come-IM-QT do-PST-DC
'I told Mia to come.'

c. *na-nun Mia-ka/lul haksayng i-la-ko mit-ess-ta.*
I-TC Mia-NM/AC student is-DC-QT believe-PST-DC
'I believed that Mia is a student.'

d. *na-nun* *Mia-lul/ka* *po-ko* *siph-ess-ta.*
I-TC Mia-AC/NM see-NOM wish-PST-DC
'I wanted to see Mia.'

e. *na-nun* *Mia-lul/ka* *po-ki* *silh-ess-ta.*
I-TC Mia-AC/NM see-NOM dislike-PST-DC
'I disliked seeing Mia.'

4. Let us now consider the derivation of the modal (MOD) inflectional suffix *-keyss* (< *-keys*) from the periphrastic past-tense causative construction *-key h•y-as* (-AD do-PST) 'caused one to (do)'.[5] Diachronic development of this suffix is documented, for instance, in Huh (1972; 1984:459) as shown in (8).

(8) a. *-keys* < *-key hóy-as* [late 18th c. through 19th c.]
-keyss < *-keys* [19th c.]

b. *pyeng-i* *ilehó-ni* *etóy* *sal-key* *hóy-as-nón-ka.*
illness-NM like this-as where live-AD do-PST-IN-Q
'Since the illness is this bad, how could (I, he) possibly live?'
(Hantyung-nok 3, 1795-1805)

c. *amuli* *hóy-eto* *mos* *sal-keys-ta* *hó-si-ko.*
however do-but unable live-MOD-DC say-SH-and
'(He) says he can't live no matter what . . .'
(Hantyung-nok 2, 1795-1805)

As many authors on grammaticalization in other languages assume, the above grammaticalization must have occurred in specific local discourse contexts and then analogically extended to all other similar constructions.[6] Notice in (8b) and (8c) that the speaker-'s presumptive modality meaning appeared in the given discourse context whether or not *-key hóy-as* was reduced morphophonologically to *-keys*. Thus, for instance, the syntactic reanalysis and morphophonological reduction involved in the derivation of the contemporary sentence *Mia-ka chayk-ul ilk-keyss-ta* 'Mia may read the book' are assumed to be schematically as follows.

5 Note that this derivation was antedated by the derivation of the past tense suffix, as will be discussed shortly.

6 Due to the innovation of the semantically quite close suffix *-keyss*, the modal suffix *-(u)li* now occurs largely in complementary distribution with *-keyss*, the former, contracted as *-(u)l*, occurring predominantly in adnominal position, and the latter in finite sentences.

(9) a.

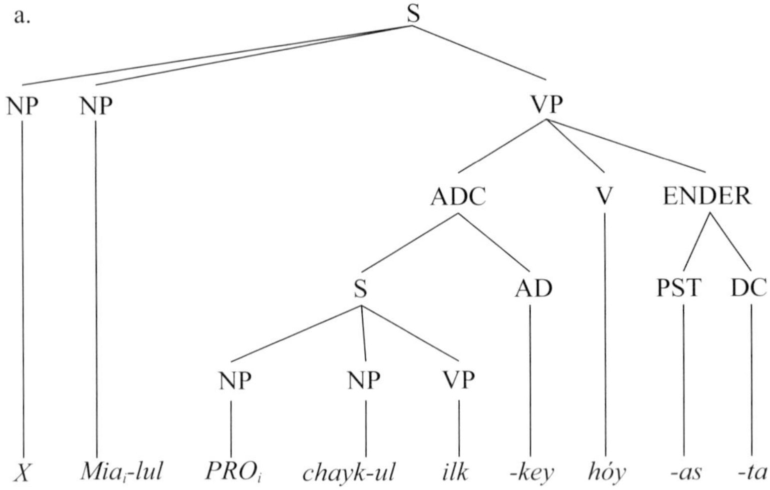

'X allowed Mia to read the book.'

b.

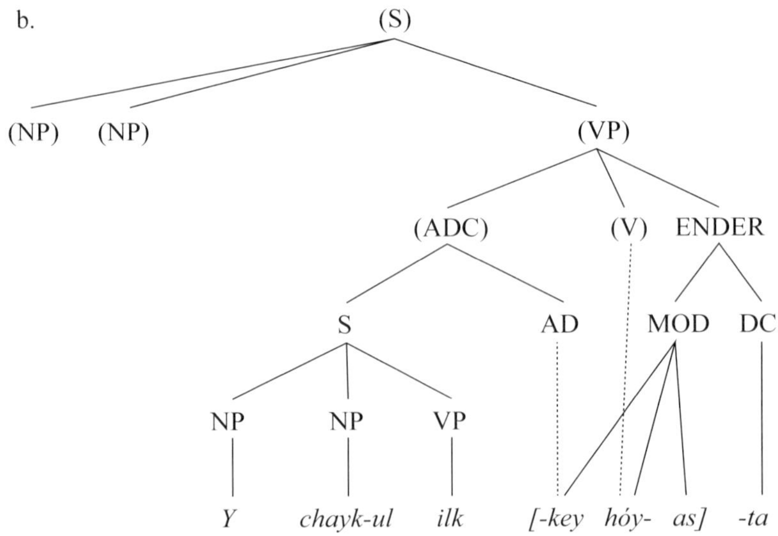

'Y may read the book.'

c.

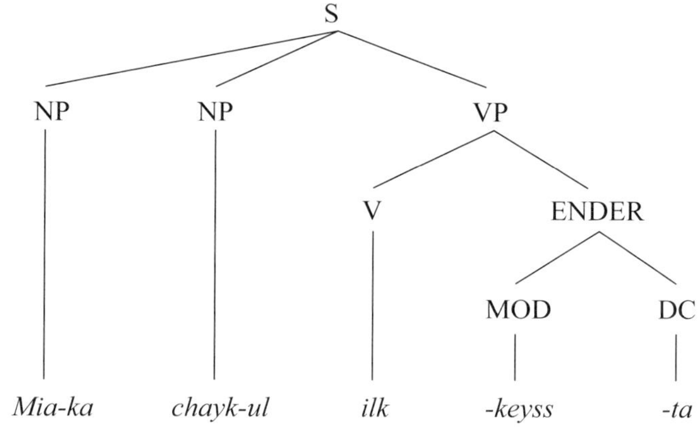

'Mia may read the book.'

Note that with the development of a single grammatical meaning of speaker's presumption from the sequence of three different meanings that the three morphemes *-key* 'so that', *hóy* 'do', and *-as* (past) carried, the former syntactic brackets that existed among the three morphemes were removed and the three defunct morphemes became dominated by the category MOD under ENDER, as indicated in (9b). With the attachment of these three morphemes to MOD as a sister of DC, all the tree nodes which became irrelevant were diachronically pruned, as indicated in parentheses in (9b). For example, the higher VP and V were pruned because the predicate *hóy* became defunct. Similarly, CC and COM were pruned because the suffix -key became defunct as a complementizer. The NP nodes that dominated the unexpressed *X* and *Mia-lul* in (9a) were pruned because their predicate *hóy* no longer functioned as an argument carrier.

Furthermore, the assumed removal of the internal brackets prompted the three defunct morphemes to agglutinate and coalesce into the single inflectional suffix morpheme *-keys* (> *-keyss*) as in (9c). The embedded clause has remained the same, with the verb stem *ilk* still requiring two arguments which are subject and object. The subject position is taken by Mia and the object position by *chayk* in our example. The stranded Ender in (9b) was placed under the remaining VP node. (9c) is the output derived as a result.

In comparison with the above syntactic account, the same phenomena can be accounted for in terms of the following morphological processes:

(a) Due to the strong bondedness among the three morphemes which satisfied the three prerequisites (contiguity, syntactic-semantic reducibility, and textual frequency of occurrence), the original higher predicate *hóy* 'do, cause' lost its

causative meaning together with its predicative function as an argument carrier.
(b) The loss of the semantic and syntactic function of the predicate *hóy* led to its deletion.
(c) As a result, the stranded past tense suffix naturally lost its past tense function because there was no verbal stem whose referent event it could make past. It was doomed to be agglutinated superfluously to the preceding complementizer suffix *-key*.
(d) The newly innovated *-keys* became an inflectional suffix at the position where it was innovated. This position is immediately before the addressee honorific slot, as observed in the contemporary construction *ilk-keyss-sup-ni-ta* '(He) may read it.'
(e) Since the original tense slot in the higher clause is absorbed in the newly innovated suffix -keys, no tense slot was created after the suffix. The original lower clause tense slot before the complementizer *-key*, which allowed only ZERO tense, became a full-fledged main clause tense slot before the new suffix -keys, as seen in the contemporary construction *ilk-ess-keyss-ta* '(He) may have read it' (cf. *ilk-key hay-ss-ta* 'X caused him to read', but **ilk-ess-key hay-ss-ta* '*X caused him to have read.').
(f) As an inflectional suffix, *-keys* needed to have a new function and associated grammatical meanings. It assumed a propositional modality function (speaker/hearer's attitude and mood toward the proposition).

Now, where did the new modal meanings in *-keys* come from? As for the semantic shifts involved, the derived suffix has meanings considerably different from that of its source construction. In addition to some degree of possibility or futurity, the suffix denotes the speaker's volition and circumstantial presumption if the subject is 1st person and the sentence is non-past declarative, and the hearer's volition and circumstantial presumption if the subject is 2nd person and the sentence is non-past interrogative. In all other cases, it only means speaker/hearer's circumstantial presumption, possibility or futurity. Observe the following contemporary expressions.

(10) a. *na-nun* *chayk-ul* *ilk-keyss-ta.*
I-TC book-AC read-MOD-DC
i. I intend to read the book.
ii. I may read the book (judging from the given circumstance).

b. *Mia-nun* *chayk-ul* *ilk-keyss-ta.*
Mia-TC book-AC read-MOD-DC
'Mia may read the book.'

c. *na/Mia-nun* *chayk-ul* *ilk-ess-keyss-ta.*
I/Mia-TC book-AC read-PST-MOD-DC
'I/Mia may have read the book.'

One may naturally wonder how the past causative meaning was replaced by speaker/hearer's present volition and circumstantial presumption, possibility, or futurity. We may think that volition is a root meaning and possibility-futurity or speaker's presumption is an epistemic meaning. Following some relevant proposals of the existing theory of grammaticalization, I assume that semantic shift is effected essentially on the basis of the semantic material of the input elements plus various discoursal and pragmatic inferences. As the data in (8b) show, the semantic shift must have been effected slightly ahead of the formal contractions (cf. coexistence of English *be going to* and *gonna*, both with a prospective aspect meaning). In any case, the morpho-syntactic rebracketing is coterminous with the semantic shift. At least two alternative interpretations may be proposed, one based purely on pragmatic inference and the other from a structural (especially, morph-semantic) perspective.

That is, one way of looking at the meaning shift is in terms of pragmatic inference. Due to the rebracketing of [*-key hóy-as*] as a syntactic unit as a result of the semantic and syntactic weakening of the higher causative verb *hóy* and the past-tense suffix, the original past causative meaning could no longer be sustained. Instead of completely abolishing the former past causative meaning, the newly bracketed form has retained the older meaning in the manner of its pragmatic inference, as hypothesized in (11). ⇒ stands for 'is structurally compressed as' and → 'pragmatically implies'. The cover term ALLOW stands for such causative meanings as 'cause', 'make', 'let', 'have', and 'allow'.

(11) a. *Mia-lul* *chayk-ul ilk-key* *hóy-as-ta*
⇒ *Mia-ka* *chayk-ul* *ilk-keys-ta*

X ALLOWED MIA TO READ BOOK
→ (therefore) Mia may read the book.

b. *na-lul* *chayk-ul ilk-key* *hóy-as-ta*
⇒ *nay-ka* *chayk-ul ilk-keys-ta*

X ALLOWED ME TO READ BOOK
→ (therefore) I may read the book.
→ (therefore) I will read the book.

My second alternative interpretation is that the basic source of volition, presumption and possibility must have been the function of the original *-key* plus the inflectional position in which it was innovated. When *-key* and *hóy-as* were molded into the single morpheme *-keys* to become a new inflectional suffix, the original posteriority meaning denoted by *-key* became predominant. That is, in *V-key hóy-as* 'caused to (do)', the time of the event denoted by V must follow the time of the causation denoted by *hóy*, hence the temporal posteriority meaning of *-key*. This posteriority meaning, plus the speaker/hearer's modality function which developed from the inflectional suffix slot where *keys* was created, evolved into the root meaning of speaker/hearer's volition and the epistemic meaning of presumption, possibility, or futurity. To repeat, as an inflectional suffix, *-keys*, which needed to have a new function and associated grammatical meanings, assumed a propositional modality function (speaker/hearer's attitude and mood toward the proposition) (a) in view of its inflectional position after the tense/aspect suffix and before the addressee honorific position, and (b) in conformity with some universal morpho-semantic principles applicable to SOV languages.

Two things have happened. For one, the speaker got involved in statements and the hearer in questions as abstract performative subject. Apparently, the inflectional position after the tense/aspect slot and before the addressee honorific slot in Korean is associated with speaker/hearer's modality toward the proposition. This position seems to call for speaker/hearer involvement (for such involvement on the performative level, see H. Sohn 1978; Traugott 1988; H. Sohn 1990). Secondly, modality meanings diverged. That is, such modal senses as speaker/hearer's volition developed in addition to the meanings of presumption, possibility and futurity, which are assumed to have appeared first, if anything, due to the temporal posteriority meaning of *-key*.

But how did such meaning divergence take place? My tentative speculation is that the meaning of speaker/hearer's volition is the function of the semantico-pragmatic relatedness between root and epistemic meanings. That is, the root meaning of speaker/hearer's volition in *-keys* seems to have developed side by side with the epistemic sense under specific discourse contexts where speaker and hearer function as sentence subjects HERE and NOW, i.e. when speaker is subject in a present tense declarative sentence or when hearer is subject in a present tense interrogative sentence. In all other environments, only the epistemic sense remains, following the usual grammaticalization process: X > XY under a specific discourse context, where Y is an innovation. The epistemic sense is regarded as X and the root sense as Y.

The suffix *-keys* was created in the same inflectional slot that used to be occupied by the prospective modal suffix *-(u)li*. Due to the innovation of the semantically close suffix *-keys*, the two modal suffixes *-(u)li* and *-keys* are largely in complementary distribution in Contemporary Korean, the former, contracted as *-(u)l*, occurring predominantly in adnominal position, and the latter at sentence-final position.

The root-epistemic distinction observed in *-keys* is also reflected in the prospective suffix *-(u)l(i)* in (12a), which happens to share the same inflectional slot as *-keys*. The English modal auxiliary *will* and the prospective auxiliary *gonna* behave the same way, as in (12b), suggesting the existence of some sort of semantic-pragmatic universality in root-epistemic pairs.[7]

(12) a. *nay-ka ka-li-la; Yongho-ka ka-li-la* (archaic)
nay-ka ka-l ke-ya; Yongho-ka ka-l ke-ya.
'I will go/may go.'; 'Yongho may go.'

b. I will go; Yongho will go.
I'm gonna go; Yongho's gonna go.

Thus, when the subject is the 1st person (speaker) in non-past statements and the 2nd person (addressee) in non-past questions, the root sense may occur, otherwise only the epistemic sense is allowed. This is obviously due to the universal semantico-pragmatic reality that the speaker cannot control somebody else's volition and that the speaker cannot intend to perform a past action or event.[8]

It is not clear at the moment whether the account based purely on pragmatic inference or the morpho-semantic account or some sort of interaction between the two was actually the case. Further study is required in this regard.

5. Having observed the historical development of the inflectional suffix *-keys* (> *-keyss*) from *-key hóy-as*, I cannot resist the temptation to advance a hypothesis which may initially sound far-fetched. That is, I propose that the causative suffixes *-i, -hi, -li*, and *-ki* have been grammaticalized through reanalysis and reduction from the periphrastic causative *-key hóy* 'cause to (do)'. This proposal further leads to another proposal that suffixal passives with *-i, -hi, -li*, and *-ki* have been reanalyzed semantically and functionally from causative suffixes.

---

7 Incidentally, *nay-ka ka-llay* 'I intend to go' denotes the speaker's performative meaning of intention. On the other hand, **Yongho-ka ka-llay* is not possible, in that the speaker cannot intend somebody else's behavior.

8 To prove this theory, authors frequently refer to the development of the prospective temporality marker *gonna* from the progressive *be going to* in such a specific purposive context as *He is going to help Bill* in the sense of 'He is leaving to help Bill' (e.g. Hopper and Traugott 1993).

Time and space do not allow me to delve into the assumed processes of causative-to-passive grammaticalization in this paper. For an extensive discussion on the interrelatedness between middle, passive and causative uses of the suffixes in question, see J. Park (1994), in which all of them are subsumed under the 'causative marker' constructions.[9]

The proposed development of the causative suffixes from the *key hóy* construction is not supported by any historical evidence, because the process is assumed to have taken place before the 15th century when the Korean alphabet was created. Lacking hard historical evidence, this proposal needs to be explored further through much more rigorous internal reconstruction than adumbrated here. In what follows, I will present what has led me to the proposal.

One plausible piece of evidence comes from the phonological material the suffixes have. One important question to address is why the causative suffix has so many phonologically distinct allomorphs. In general but not always, *-hi* appears after a lax stop (e.g. *ilk-hita* 'make read', *cap-hita* 'let hold'), *-ki* after *s* or a nasal (e.g. *ssis-kita* 'make wash', *an-kita* 'make hold in arms'); *-li* after *l* (e.g. *mal-lita* 'dry', *kwul-lita* 'roll'); and *-i* (elsewhere including after a vowel: *po-ita* 'show') (c.f. Y. Kim: 1984). In order to phonologically derive all the different allomorphs synchronically from a single underlying form, many studies have been conducted with various theoretical orientations, but without success (e.g. C. Kim 1973, S. Bak 1982, Y. Kang 1991, Y. Kim 1984, Ahn 1994). This suggests that the allomorphic divergence is amenable to diachronic account. Notice that the suffixes contain the consonants h (as in *hóy*) and *k* (as in *key*). We know that *-li* is a secondary development from *-i*, occurring only after the stem-final *l*, i.e. per the *l*-gemination rule (c.f. Y. Kim 1984).[10] We also know that *k* and *h* easily get deleted both diachronically and synchronically. We also know that *ó* (or *óy* before a consonant) in *hóy* is deleted extensively, as observed in *cen-hy-e* (< *cen-hóy-e*) 'utterly' and *kkaykkus-h-ci an-h-ta* (< *kkaykkus-hóy-ci ani-hóy-ta*) 'is not clean'. Evidence also shows that the current verbal stem *ha(y)* 'do, be' was *hóy*, as reflected in Middle Korean (13a,b) and in Contemporary Korean (13c,d,e). Notice that *y* is deleted before a consonant.

9 Leon Serafim (p.c.) drew my attention to the fact that both causative-like and passive(-like) morphology have been used in Japanese for subject honorification. He also provided me with examples like 'that s.o.b. got his apartment broken into so that he could collect the insurance' and 'oh, woe is me; I got my apartment broken into last night' to illustrate the fact that English uses 'get' (or 'have') as an auxiliary for both causative- and passive-like constructions.

10 L. Serafim (p.c.) believes that historically the *l* gemination rule stems from a syllable-final l followed by a syllable-initial gamma, voiced h, or hiatus (all the same thing, written by Samuel Martin as G), e.g. *kwul-li-ta* < *kwul-Gi-ta?* < **kwulu-khi-ta* < **kwulu-key-hóy-ta* 'make roll'.

(13) a. *li sayng-ul* *po-ti* *mos hóy-an (> ha-n)* *ti* *ola-ni*
Lee Mr.-AC see-NOM not do-RL do-RL since long-so
'Since it is a long time since I saw Mr. Lee,'
(Twusi Enhay (1481) 21:42)

b. *ecul* *kho (< hó-ko)* *atók hóy-a (> hay-e)*
disturbed be-and dazed be-and
'disturbed and dazed' (Sekpo Sangcel (1447) 6:3b)

c. *hay-ela /ha.ye.la/*
do-IM
'Do (it)!'

d. *hay-ese /ha.ye.se/*
do-so
'by doing (it)'

e. *hay-(e)ss-ta /ha.yet.t'a/* or */hayt.t'a/*
do-PST-DC
'did (it)'

The Middle Korean off-glide y may have developed from a full vowel *i*. Even if this was not actually the case, the two off-glide *y*'s in *-key* and *hóy* must have been responsible for the occurrence of the single vowel *i* in the causative suffixes. Then, we can hypothesize, albeit tentatively, that the following diachronic rules applied.

(14) a. i. *-key hóy > -khi*
ii. *-key hóy > -ki*
iii. *-key hóy > -hi*
iv. *-key hóy > -i*

b. *-key hóy > -khi > -ki, -hi > -i*

c. Examples:

-khi: *si-khi* 'make do, order (food)'
pi-khi 'clear, get out of the way ('make empty')'
-ki: *pes-ki* 'undress'
wus-ki 'make laugh'

math-ki 'entrust'
nam-ki 'leave (something)'
sin-ki 'get someone to put on (footwear)'

-hi: *palk-hi* 'brighten'
ilk-hi 'make read'
nelp-hi 'widen'
cop-hi 'make narrow'
anc-hi 'seat'

-i: *po-i* 'show' (dialectally, *pey-ki*)
na-y 'put out'
mek-i 'feed'
cwuk-i 'kill'
kkakk-i 'make cut'
nok-i 'melt (something)'
noph-i 'heighten'

While the assumption underlying (14a) is that the allomorphic causative suffixes derived from the same source independently of each other, that underlying (14b) is that there is a cline of morpho-phonological reduction in the course of grammaticalization. Although it is not immediately obvious whether (14a) or (14b) or an interaction of both was actually the case, let us assume tentatively that the cline in (14b) is what has happened. Occurrence of the suffix *-khi* is extremely rare. Such examples as *si-khi* and *pi-khi* (cf. *pi-wu* 'empty (something)') are perceived by most native speakers as fossilized as single morphemes. Thus, *-khi* was reduced almost obligatorily to *-ki, -hi*, or *-i* depending in large measure on the preceding sound. In general, *-ki* occurs after a stem-final alveo-dental or nasal consonant, whereas *-hi* or *-i* occurs after a non-alveo-dental plosive. In particular, *-i* occurs after a vowel or a tense or aspirate consonant, in that *k* and *h* in *-ki* and *-hi* (or even in *-khi*) weaken in these environements.[11]

There are many exceptions from a synchronic perspective. As in other kinds of diachronic processes that are affected by pressures originating in morphological analogy, many secondary changes must have been made, such as alternations between -hi and -i (e.g. the causative *mek-i* 'feed' vs. the passive *mek-hi* 'be fed') and the development of such causative allomorphs as *-li, -(y)wu, -kwu,* and *-chwu*. Examples of the secondary derivation of causative suffixes are *nal-li* 'fly (something)', *el-li* 'freeze freeze (something)', *kwul-li* 'roll (something)', *il-wu* 'achieve', *ca-ywu* 'make sleep', *tal-kwu* 'make hot', *tot-kwu* 'make higher', and

11 L. Serafim (p.c.) points out that the proposed intervocalic *k/h* weakening strengthens Whitman's (1985:112-23) contention that intervocalic **kh* is what became G: e.g. **pokhi* > **poghi* > **poGi* > *poi* 'show'.

nuc-chwu 'postpone'. Rigorous diachronic analysis of the allomorphic divergence of the causative suffixes is not the concern of this paper.

Several plausible pieces of morphological evidence support the proposed hypothesis on the diachronic derivation of suffixal from periphrastic causatives. There seems to be a morphological parallelism between the derivation of keys in the 18th-19th centuries and the assumed derivation of the causative suffixes before the 15th century:

(15) a. *-key hóy -as > keys*
(absorbing the past tense suffix)

b. *-key hóy > ki/hi/i*
(not absorbing the past tense suffix)

One may wonder why in (15b) it is not *key/hey/ey* which would show complete superficial parallelism. The disparity may be amenable to explanation. When the three-morpheme sequence *key hóy-as* was reduced to the single morpheme *-keys* (pronounced as [ket] or [kes]) from the late 18th century through the 19th century, monophthongization had already occurred by the 16th century and -key [kəy] had been monophthongized as [ke], in which no off-glide appears. On the other hand, the process in (15b) is assumed to have taken place before the 15th century, when the off-glide *y* retained its phonetic quality. Two *y*'s were strong enough to develop into the vowel *i*, as stated above.[12]

Another morphological clue is the slot these suffixes fill. It was stated that the modal *keys* cannot be followed by a past suffix, because it absorbed the past tense suffix in the course of grammaticalization. The causative suffixes behave in an opposite way because they did not absorb the past tense suffix. Furthermore, the fact that the causative suffixes may not be preceded but only followed by the subject honorific suffix *-(u)si* can be attributed to the fact that *hóy* occurred before the honorific slot. The fact that the suffixes are innovated in the position immediately following a verbal stem supports the derivational (rather than inflectional) nature of the suffixes. The grammaticalized causative suffixes are assumed to have spread analogically to many verbal stems, but not to all stems, for various reasons such as avoidance of semantic redundancies or homonymic clashes that would otherwise have occurred.

Syntactically also, there is a close relationship between periphrastic and suf-

12 In parallel with the derivation of *ki/hi/i* from *-key hóy*, the adverbializer *-(h)i* may have developed from *hóy-key* (> *khey*) and analogically generalized as a grammaticalized verbal suffix. Compare *wancen-hi* 'completely' with *wancen-ha-key/wancen-khey* 'completely' and *kkaykkus-i* 'cleanly' with *kkaykkus-ha-key* 'cleanly'.

fixal causatives, suggesting syntactic reduction of the latter from something like the former. Some generative linguists of Korean (Song 1967; Yang 1972, 1976; Patterson 1974; K. Park 1987) even propose the same or an almost identical underlying biclausal structure for the two types of causative, claiming that they are cognitively synonymous. In these proposals, the causative suffix is treated as a higher predicate in the same way as the full-fledged causative verb *hata* is. Thus, for instance, *na-nun Mia-eykey chayk-ul ilk-hi-ess-ta* and *na-nun Mia-eykey chayk-ul ilk-key hay-ss-ta*, both roughly meaning 'I caused Mia to read a book', are viewed as sharing the same underlying structure:

(16)

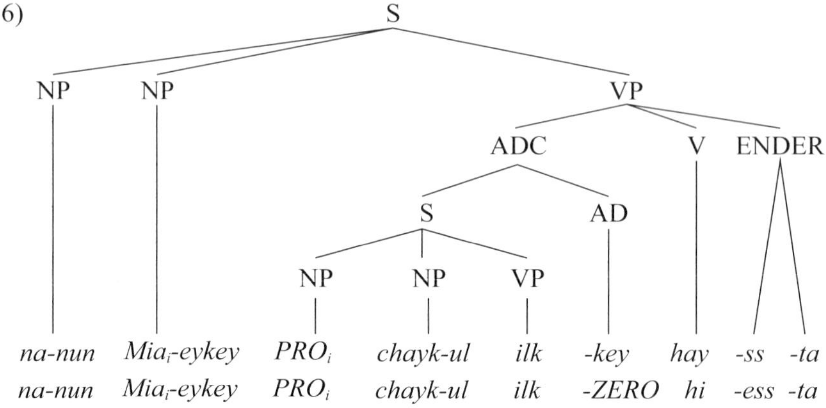

Although I do not subscribe to the biclausal analysis of the suffixal causative, (16) is sufficient to illustrate the historical-syntactic relation between the two types of construction. The diachronic processes involved are assumed to be something like the following.

(17) a.

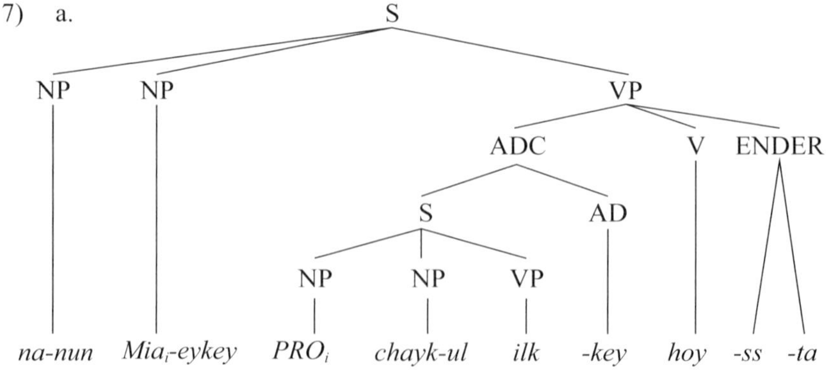

b.

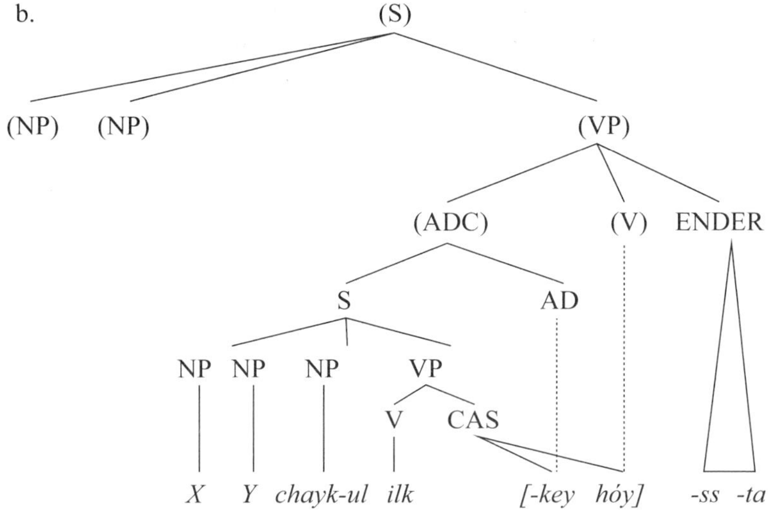

c.

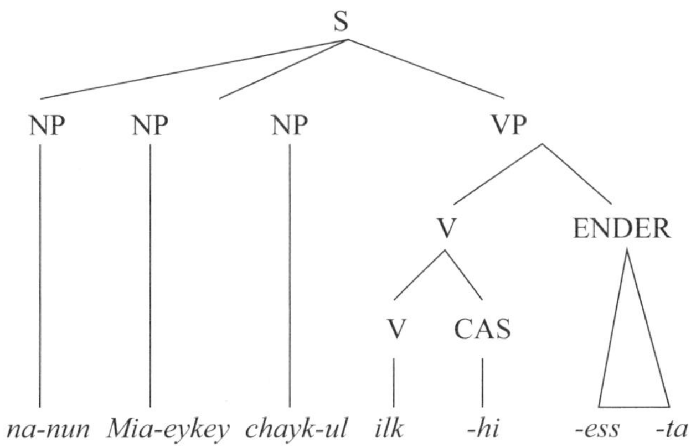

The grammaticalization processes assumed in (17) are similar to those assumed in (9) for the derivation of the inflectional suffix *-keys*. Notice in (17), however, that the innovation took place under the CAS node dominated by V, creating a new derivational suffix. Due to this innovation, the two-argument structure of the predicate *ilk* (agent, theme ___) changed to the three-argument structure of the predicate *ilk-hi* (agent, goal, theme ___).

Several important syntactic differences existing in the two types can be viewed as natural consequences of the reanalysis and reduction processes, because it is a tenet of grammaticalization that reduced structures inevitably lose their independence as sentential structures to a great extent. For instance, in the suffixal causative, occurrence of the nominative case associated with the causee-NP is not allowed to appear, as shown in (18b) and (19b).

(18)	a.	*na-nun*	*Mia-ka/eykey/lul*	*swum-key*	*hay-ss-ta.*
		I-TC	Mia-NM/DT/AC	hide-to	cause-PST-DC
		'I caused Mia to hide.' (SUBORDINATION)			
	b.	*na-nun*	*Mia-*ka/*eykey/lul*	*swum-ki-ess-ta.*	
		I-TC	Mia-NM/DT/AC	hide-CAU-PST-DC	
		'I hid Mia.'			

(19)	a.	*na-nun*	*aitul-u*	*seys-ul/i*	*swum-key*	*hay-ss-ta.*
		I-TC	children-AC	3-AC/NM	hide-AD	cause-PST-DC
		'I caused/made three children hide.'				
	b.	*na-nun*	*aitul-ul*	*seys-ul/*i*	*swum-ki-ess-ta.*	
		I-TC	children-AC	3-AC/NM	hide-CAU-PST-DC	
		'I hid three children.'				

As observed in (18b), even the dative is not allowed if the source predicate (e.g. *swumta* 'hide') is intransitive. This may be because an intransitive verbal is more readily agglutinated to the following higher predicate, thus being reanalyzed faster than a transitive construction (e.g. (16, 17)).

Some semantic evidence can be provided in support of the causative derivation hypothesis. Periphrastic and suffixal causatives denote indirect and direct causation, respectively. This is in accord with the hypothesis of 'diagrammatic iconicity' advanced by grammaticalization theorists (e.g. Haiman 1983). Existence of such syntactico-semantic iconicity between the two types of structure suggests the assumed syntactico-semantic reduction of the suffixal causative from periphrastic constructions.

At this point, one might reasonably ask where we can find temporal posteriority (or futurity) meaning of the reduced 'projective' adverbializer *-key* 'so that, to' similar to that appearing in the derivation of the modal suffix *-keys*. In fact, the suffixal causative does also manifest the posteriority of the event in question, although not as distinctly as in the periphrastic causative, due to its inherent meaning of direct causation. For instance, while *ai-eykey cec-ul mek-i-ess-ta* '(she) fed the baby milk' does not indicate any posteriority of the child's milk-drinking activity in relation to the milk-giving event, *Mia-eykey chayk-ul ilk-hi-ess-ta* '(she) had Mia read a book' indicates that the event of Mia reading would necessarily take place after the causing event.

From a typological perspective, there are reports that periphrastic causatives diachronically change into affixal causatives in such languages as Lahu and Bantu (e.g. Matisoff 1976; Givon 1976). This is in accord with the general diachronic grammaticalization cline (e.g. Givon 1971; Hopper and Traugott 1993). The hypothesized causative reduction agrees with the unidirectional cline hypothesis both morpho-syntactically and semantically. The assumed pattern fits very favorably with other grammaticalization phenomena in Korean, as we will see immediately below.

6. Let us now briefly examine whether the syntactic reanalysis and morpho-phonological reduction deriving grammatical suffixes such as the modal *-keyss* and the causative suffixes are accidental, isolated cases or typical cases. To put it in a nutshell, there are many such examples. Due to space constraints, I will simply enumerate several representative ones with brief notes.

One well documented case is the development of the past/perfective suffix *-ess/-ass* from the resultative complex predicate construction consisting of an intransitive telic verb and the infinitive complementizer *-e/-a* followed by the existential adjective *isi* > *iss* (Huh 1972; 1984:446-461). The past-perfective suffix derived as a result of the fusion of *isi* with the complementizer as shown below.

(20) a. *-es/-as* < *-e/-a isi* [late 15th c. through 16th c.]
-ess/-ass < *-es/-as* [19th c.]
(*-e/-a* 'COM'; *isi* > *iss* 'exist, stay')

b. *Mia-ka w-a isi-ta.* > i) *Mia-ka w-a iss-ta.* 'Mia is here.'
Mia-NM come-COM exist-DC ii) *Mia-ka w-ass-ta.* 'Mia came.'

In contrast to the adverbializer *-key* 'so that, to' which denotes posteriority of an event in relation to the time of causation, the infinitive complementizer *-e/-a*, due to its stative meaning 'in the state of doing or being', indicates the anteriority of the event denoted by the preceding verb in relation to the time of existence denoted by the existential adjective *isi* (> *iss*). It is for this reason that the derived suffix has the pastness or perfective meanings (e.g. S. Sohn 1988; H. Sohn 1990). Just as in the case of causative constructions, the source construction coexists with the derived suffix, as illustrated in (20b).

A second example is the well-known development of the promissive *-lkkey* from the predictive complex construction *-l ke(s) i-e*, as discussed in H. Sohn (1978).

(21) a. *Mia-ka ka-l ke(s) i-e (> i-a).*
Mia-NM go-PRS fact be-INT
'Mia will probably go.'

b. *nay-ka ka-l ke(s) i-e (> i-a).*
i) 'I will probably go.'
ii) 'I intend/will go.'

c. *nay/*Mia-ka ka-lkkey.*
'I/Mia promise(s) to go.'

d. **ney-ka ka-lkkey?*
'Do you promise to go?'

The prospective suffix *-l* and the following defective noun *kes* 'fact' are assumed to have been fused and reanalyzed as a complementizer. Subsequently, this newly innovated complementizer and the following copula *i* and the intimate sentence ender *-e* merged to develop the promissive inflectional suffix *-lkkey*. Notice in (21c) and (21d) that the promissive suffix developed only in the discourse context where subject is the 1st person.

A third example is the construction with the clause-final desiderative suffix *-koca* 'wishing to, wanting to', as illustrated below.

(22) a. *Mia-nun ton-ul pel-ko caw-a saep-ul hay-ss-ta.*
Mia-TC money-AC earn-NOM wish-INF business-AC do-PST-DC
'Mia did business, wishing to earn money.' (HYPOTAXIS)
[Cholla Dialect]

b. *Mia-nun ton-ul pel-ko caw-a hay-ss-ta.*
Mia-TC money-AC earn-NOM wish-INF do-PST-DC
'Mia wanted to earn money.' (SUBORDINATION)
[Cholla Dialect]

c. *Mia-nun ton-ul pel-koca hay-ss-ta.*
Mia-TC money-AC earn-wishing do-PST-DC
'Mia wanted to earn money.' (Standard Speech)

Notice that the contemporary Cholla Dialect gives a clue that the contemporary standard verbal suffix *-koca* has derived from the complex predicate construction *-ko* caw-a. That is, the pre-desiderative complementizer *-ko*, the desiderative adjective cap 'wish' (cf. *siph* in Standard Speech) which is currently used in Cholla and Kyongsang Dialects and the infinitive complementizer *-e/-a* are reduced to a new desiderative suffix *-koca* in Standard Speech. The processes assumed to be involved are given in (23).[13]

(23) a. *pel-ko cap-a* >
  b. *pel-ko caw-a* >
  c. *pel-ko caa* >
  d. *pel-ko ca* >
  e. *pel-koca*

That is, two contiguous complement clauses (. . . *pel-ko* and *caw-a*) are reduced to a single complement construction (. . . *pel-koca*). (23a) is used in Kyongsang Dialect, (23b) in Cholla Dialect, and (23e) in Standard Speech.

A fourth example is the habitual aspect construction with *-kon(un) hata* 'habitually do'. The innovated 'habituality' complementizer *-kon(un)* came from the conjunctive suffix *-ko* 'and' and the topic/contrast particle *-nun*. I speculate that subordinative sentences like (24b) developed from hypotactic sentences like (24a), with the main clause replaced by the so-called light-verb or pro-verb *hata* 'do' construction.

(24) a. *Mia-nun yehayng-ha-ko-nun tto (yehayng)-hay-ss-ta.*
  Mia-TC trip-do-and-TC again trip-do-PST-DC
  'Mia had (already) taken one trip and then took another trip again.' (HYPOTACTIC)

  b. *Mia-nun yehayng-ha-kon(un) hay-ss-ta.*
  Mia-TC trip-do-COM do-PST-DC
  'Mia habitually took trips.'
  (SUBORDINATIVE)

  c. *Mia-nun chayk-ul ilk-kon(nun) hay-ss-ta.*
  Mia-TC book-AC read-COM do-PST-DC
  'Mia habitually read books.'

Once the habituality pattern was established as in (24b), it spread analogically to other similar constructions, as in (24c) where the embedded verb (*ilk*) does

13 Even the standard form *-ko siph-e* 'wish to' was once reduced to *-kopha*, which appears in poems and songs.

not contain the light verb *ha(y)*. The strong structural pressure from pervasive complement constructions that consist of a complement clause followed by the predicate *hata* may have analogically affected the restructuring. For instance, *-kon(un) hata* might have been formed by analogy with the *-ki-n(un) hata* (NOM-TC do) constructions that appears in sentences like *Mia-nun yehayng-ha-ki-n(un) hay-ss-ta* 'Mia did take a trip, but . . .' With the replacement of *tto hata* 'do again' with the pro-verb *hata*, for instance, the meaning carried by *tto* 'also' is taken over by *kon(un)*. Together with the meaning of *ko* 'and', the meaning of repetition or habituality is assumed to have developed.

A fifth example is the development of the clause-final deontic suffix *-eya/-aya* into an incomplete inflectional suffix.

(25) a. *Mia-ka* *w-aya* *nay-ka* *ka-keyss-ta.* (HYPOTAXIS)
Mia-NM come-only if I-NM go-will-DC
'I will go only if Mia comes.'

b. *Mia-ka* *w-ass-eya* *hay-ss-ta.* (SUBORDINATION)
Mia-NM come-PST-only if do-PST-DC
'Mia should have come.'

c. *Mia-ka* *w-(*ass)-aya-(ha)-keyss-ta.*
Mia-NM come-PST-must-do-think-DC
'I think Mia should come.'

In (25c), *-aya-(ha)-keyss* is almost fossilized as a deontic suffix with the meaning of 'must', disallowing the occurrence of a past tense suffix before it.

A sixth example is the innovation of the modal suffix *-na po* 'seem, appear'.

(26) a. *pi-ka* *w-ass-na-po-(*ass)-ayo.*
rain-NM come-PST-seem-PST-POL
'It seems that it rained.'

b. *pi-ka* *w-ass-na po-sey-yo.* (HYPOTAXIS)
rain-NM come-PST-if see-IM
'Please check to see if it rained.'

c. *pi-ka* *w-ass-na po-ass-eyo.*(HYPOTAXIS)
rain-NM come-PST-if see-PST-POL
'(I) checked to see if it rained.'

Notice that unlike in its hypotactic counterparts (26b,c), *-na-po* 'seem, appear' in the subordinative construction (26a) is already fossilized as a modal suffix. Like the modal suffix *-keyss*, it does not permit a past tense suffix to be placed after it.

The seventh example is the innovation of forms with a negative adverb: the modal suffix *-c(i)anh* 'you see!' and the innovated negative verb *-anh* 'not be, not do' (cf. S. Sohn and Kawanishi 1993).

(27) a. *pi-ka* *w-ass-c(i)-an-h-(*ass)-ayo!*
rain-NM come-PST-NOM-not-do-PST-POL
'It rained, you see.'

b. *pi-ka* *o-ci* *an-h-ass-eyo?/*an hay-ss-eyo?*
rain-NM come-NOM not-do-PST-POL/not-do-PST-POL
'Didn't it rain?'

(27a) does not allow a past tense suffix to occur after *-h* since *ci-an-ha* is already fossilized as the inflectional modal suffix *-c(i)anh* 'you see!' in the given discourse context. In (27b), *an hay* 'not do' is not permitted because *anh* is already lexicalized as a single negative verb 'not be, not do'.

Our final example is related to the productive deletion of the quotative *-ko* + *ha* (cf. H. Sohn 1978, 1990). In (28), ( ) indicates the place where *-ko* ha is deleted.

(28) a. *Mia-ka* *cikum* *ca-n-ta-( )-n-ta.*
Mia-NM now sleep-IN-DC-( )-IN-DC
i) 'Somebody says that Mia is sleeping now.'
ii) 'You know, Mia is sleeping now.'

b. *??Minho-ka* *Mia-ka* *cikum* *ca-n-ta-( )-n-ta.*
Minho-NM Mia-NM now sleep-IN-DC-( )-IN-DC
'Minho says that Mia is sleeping now.'

c. *Mia-ka* *cikum* *ca-n-ta-ko* *ha-n-ta.*
Mia-NM now sleep-IN-DC-QT say-IN-DC
'Somebody says that Mia is sleeping now.'

Sentence (28a), with *-ko ha* deleted, has two meanings: speaker's reporting somebody else's assertion and speaker's reporting his own assertion with a subtle modality (i.e. in an indirect way). The first meaning does not involve any grammaticalization because the original quotative meaning is maintained, as in the case of (28c), whereas the second meaning manifests a semantic shift, being different from that of the undeleted construction. This partial grammaticalization in (28a) is reflected in the unnaturalness of (28b) where the partially inflectionalized suffix *ta-n-ta* 'you know' renders the original complex sentence to a simplex sentence and thus does not readily allow two subjects to occur in the sentence.[14]

7. All the above examples illustrate rather clear cases where a complementizer and one or more following elements (mostly a higher predicate) in a complex predicate construction have been reduced to a verbal suffix. To recapitulate the major processes shared by the above examples are:

(i) The basic conditions (or prerequisites) under which reanalysis is triggered are: a) the contiguity of the upstairs predicate (or other elements) with the downstairs complementizer; b) structural, semantic and pragmatic reducibility; and c) productive (frequent) use of the constructions in certain specific discourse contexts in daily interactions.
(ii) Under such conditions, morpho-phonological and semantico-syntactic bonding develops between the complementizer and the following predicate or other elements.
(iii) As a result of the disappearance of internal bracketing in the course of the syntactic and semantic bonding, successive reanalyses and reductions ensue. That is, a phrase boundary changes to a word or morpheme boundary, and some morphemes get formally reduced or lost.
(iv) In the process of grammaticalization, the original lexical meanings and functions of the individual morphemes are compounded, fused or diluted, partially lost or specified, and/or polysemically diversified, while producing new grammatical meanings.
(v) In the course of reanalysis and reduction, many new morpho-syntactic constraints develop.
(vi) Since grammaticalization occurs in a specific local discourse context, as argued for by most theoreticians in this area, the source construction and the derived form usually coexist.
(vii) All the observed cases of reanalysis and reduction reflect a unidirectional

14 The observed patterns of restructuring processes and the accompanying semantic shifts are not unique to the diachronic derivation of the inflectional suffixes observed. They apply not only to other sentence-ending suffixes but also to many other parts of sentence constructions in Korean and other languages (e.g. H. Sohn 1978, 1990; Sweetser 1988; Traugott and Heine 1991; Hopper and Traugott 1993; S. Sohn 1994).

cline of the form: hypotaxis > subordination > compounding > grammatical or lexical word > inflectional or derivational suffix. While some reanalyses such as those that have triggered the derivation of the past tense suffix, causative/passive suffixes, and some modal suffixes have reached the stage of fully grammaticalized suffixes along this cline, others are still progressing along it.

Earlier I proposed that CC is dominated by S if it is hypotactic, as in (2a), and it is dominated by VP if it is subordinative, as in (2b). Our subsequent observations led to the assumption that the cluster points in the cline are further specified, as illustrated in (4), (9c) and (17c). For instance, the cluster represented in (4) may account for the so-called 'subject-to-object raising' in causative and 'believe-think' constructions (e.g. (7c)) and the 'embedded object-to-main object raising' in desiderative constructions (e.g. (7d.e)). The structures illustrated in (9b,c) and (17bc) are the clusters that most of the diachronic suffixal derivations observed above, including the derivation of causative suffixes, end up with.

In short, the hypothesized derivation of the causative suffixes from the periphrasitic causative constructions turns out to fit nicely into all the above grammaticalization processes. This fact, together with the phonological, morphological, syntactic and semantic observations made earlier in regard to causative constructions, renders strong support to the validity of the proposed hypothesis. It appears rather unlikely in view of the theory of grammaticalization and the observed facts that *-key hóy* was not reduced to causative (and then passive) suffixes in the long history of internal development.

REFERENCES: Chapter 12

Ahn, Sang-Cheol. 1994. Phonological Aspects in Causative Suffixation. Presented at the 9th International Conference on Korean Linguistics. London. July 1994.

Bak, Sung-Yun. 1982. Causativization in Korean. *Linguistic Journal of Korea* 7.2: 322–42.

Falsgraf, C., and Insun Park. 1994. Synchronic and Diachronic Aspects of Complex Predicates in Korean and Japanese. *Japanese/Korean Linguistics* 4: 221–37.

Givon, T. 1971. Historical Syntax and Synchronic Morphology. *CLS* 7: 394–415.

Givon, T. 1976. Some Constraints on Bantu Causativization. In Shibatani, M. (ed.), *The Grammar of Causative Constructions, Syntax and Semantics* 6: 321–52. New York: Academic Press.

Haiman, J. 1983. Iconic and Economic Motivation. *Language* 59(4): 781–819.

Heine, B., U. Claudi, and F. Hünnemeyer. 1991. *Grammaticalization: A Conceptual Framework*. Chicago: University of Chicago Press.

Heine, B., and M. Reh. 1984. *Grammaticalization and Reanalysis in African Languages*. Hamburg: Helmut Buske.

Hopper, P.J., and E.C. Traugott. 1993. *Grammaticalization*. Cambridge: Cambridge University Press.

Huh, Woong. 1972. *Cwungsey Kwuke Yenkwu* (A Study on Middle Korean). Seoul: Chongumsa.

Huh, Woong. 1984. *Kwukehak* (Korean Linguistics). Seoul: Saem Munhwasa.

Kang, Yongsoon 1991. Causatives and Passives in Korean. *Harvard Studies in Korean Linguistics* 4: 95–106.

Kim, Chin-W. 1973. Adjustment rules in phonology. In Kenstowicz, M.J. and C.W. Kisseberth (eds.), *Issues in Phonological Theory,* 130–44.

Kim, Young-Seok. 1984. *Aspects of Korean Morphology*. Ph.D. dissertation, University of Texas at Austin.

Langacker, R.W. 1977. Syntactic Reanalysis. In Li, C.N. (ed.), *Mechanisms of Syntactic Change*. Austin, TX: University of Texas Press.

Matisoff, J.A. 1976. Lahu Causative Constructions: Case Hierarchies and the Morphology/Syntax Cycle in a Tibeto-Burman Perspective. In Shibatani, M. (ed.), *The Grammar of Causative Constructions, Syntax and Semantics* 6: 413–42. New York: Academic Press.

Park, Jeong-Woon. 1994. *Morphological Causatives in Korean: Problems in Grammatical Polysemy and Constructional Relations*. Ph.D. dissertation, University of California at Berkeley.

Park, Kabyong. 1987. The Lexical Representation of Korean Causatives and Passives. *Indiana University Linguistics Club*.

Patterson, Betty Soon Ju. 1974. A Study of Korean Causatives. *Working Papers in Linguistics* (University of Hawaii) 6: 1-51.

Sohn, Ho-min. 1977. Goal and Source in Korean Locatives with Reference to Japanese. *Eoneohak* (Seoul National University) 2: 73–98.

Sohn, Ho-min. 1978. Contraction as a mechanism of polysemic breeding: A device for speaker involvement in Korean. In Kim, Chin-W. (ed.), *Papers in Korean Linguistics* (Columbia: Hornbeam Press), 185–96.

Sohn, Ho-min. 1990. Grammaticalization and Semantic Shift. *Papers from the Seventh International Conference on Korean Linguistics*, 425–35.

Sohn, Sung-Ock. 1988. Tense and Aspect in Korean. Ph.D. dissertation, University of Hawaii.

Sohn, Sung-Ock. 1994. Contraction and Semantic Shift in Contemporary Korean". Korean Linguistics. Vol. 8.

Sohn, Sung-Ock, and Y. Kawanishi. 1993. The Grammaticalization of Korean Negation: A Semantic-Pragmatic Analysis of *-canh(a)*. *Harvard Studies in Korean Linguistics* V: 552–61.

Song, Seok Choong. 1967. Some Transformational Rules in Korean. Ph.D. dissertation, Indiana University.

Sweetser, E.E. 1988. Grammaticalization and Semantic Bleaching. *Proceedings of the 14th Annual Meeting of the Berkeley Linguistics Society*, 389-405.

Traugott, E.C. 1988. Pragmatic Strengthening and Grammaticalization. *Proceedings of the 14th Annual Meeting of the Berkeley Linguistics Society*, 406–16.

Traugott, E.C., and B. Heine. 1991. Approaches to Grammaticalization. I & II. Amsterdam: John Benjamins.

Whitman, J.B. 1985. The Phonological Basis for the Comparison of Japanese and Korean. Ph.D. dissertaion, Harvard University.

Yang, In-Seok. 1972. *Korean Syntax: Case Markers, Delimiters, Complementation, and Relativization*. Ph.D. dissertation. University of Hawaii.

Yang, In-Seok. 1976. Semantics of Korean Causation. *Foundations of Language* 14: 55–87.

13 A Grammar of *Po-* 'see' in Korean: A Pan-chronic Approach*

1. Introduction

The aim of this paper is to demonstrate that synchronic properties of language can be better understood if diachronic and variational perspectives are taken into consideration.[1] This will be done by examining the phenomena associated with the native Korean visual perception verb *po-* 'see, look at'. Known cross-linguistically as the most prominent verb of perception among the verbs denoting five senses (e.g. Sweetser 1990:33; Yang 2000; Rhee 2001:130) and, as one of the most frequently used lexical items in Korean, *po-* is synchronically distributed widely over different lexical collocations and morpho-syntactic contexts, performing a variety of polysemic and grammatical functions. It will be shown to what extent *po-* is metaphorically and metonymically extended, grammaticalized, and idiomatized, to what extent it manifests morpho-syntactic irregularities and constraints, and to what extent such irregularities and constraints can be accounted for in terms of evolutionary processes. It will thereby be shown that the panchronic approach will lead to more significant and much-enriched linguistic generalizations and have deeper insight into the nature of language than either a synchronic or diachronic approach alone (cf. Fuss & Trips 2004).

The theoretical and methodological framework of the present analysis is essentially that of grammaticalization, a linguistic area that has made remarkable progress during the past three decades (cf. Hopper & Traugott 2003). Although *po-* is singled out for analysis in this paper, the same approach can apply to other grammaticalization phenomena in Korean. Furthermore, the insights that transpire from the analysis of the Korean visual perception will be useful to the exploration of the genesis and developmental clines of grammatical forms in other

* This is reprinted from *Language Information* (Korea University) 14: 83-117 (2012).

1 This is a revised version of a paper I wrote at La Trobe University in Melbourne, Australia, when I was a distinguished visiting scholar in linguistics at the university's Institute of Advanced Study-Research Centre for Linguistic Typology (RCLT) during the fall semester of 2007. I express my sincere gratitude to Professors Robert Dixon and Alexandra Aikhenvald for inviting me to work with them at RCLT.

languages.

The reason for choosing *po-* for the present analysis is that it manifests extremely versatile semantic and grammatical functions, which can be used as a testing ground for various principles, hypotheses, and claims on grammaticalization that have been advanced based on many languages other than Korean. Interest in *po-* was also stimulated by noticing that *po-* is one of the most frequently used words in Korean, supporting the proposal that frequency, specifically "string frequency", and grammaticalization are closely correlated (e.g. Bybee and Hopper 2002; Krug 1998). A frequency study conducted by the Ministry of Culture and Tourism (2000) shows that the most frequently used verbs are *po-, ka-* 'go', and *cwu-* 'give', in that order (Koo 2003). A similar study by the National Academy of the Korean Language (Academy 2003) reveals that out of 59,000 words, the most frequent verbs and adjectives are *ha-* 'do', *iss-* 'exist', *toy-* 'become', *eps-* 'not exist', *anh-/ani-* 'be not', *po-* 'see', *kath-* 'same', *cwu-* 'give', and *ka-* 'go', in that order.

Available studies on *po-* in English are not many and deal with limited aspects: Park and Strauss (1997) on the semantic scope of *po-* in comparison with Japanese *miru* and English *see*, K. Lee (1993:243–51) on semantics and pragmatics of the auxiliary *po-*, Yang (2000) on *po-ko* as an emergent case marker, Hong & Sohn (2001) on the modal nature of *-na po-*, Rhee (2001) on evidential and comparative functions of *po-* from a typological perspective, and Joo (ms.) on a small-scale corpus study on the functions of *po-*. On the other hand, a large number of studies are available in Korean, dealing with *po-* from either a synchronic or diachronic perspective. Notably, Yun (2002), a work closely related to the present study, touches on most of the earlier studies on *po-* by Korean linguists.

My purpose is to examine a wide range of constructions where *po-* appears from a panchronic perspective. By analyzing the phenomena in a panchronic framework, we can systematically relate the current variations to their developmental sources, mirroring the assumed past with reasonable correctness, as grammaticalization is an everyday fact of language per the "uniformitarian principle" (Labov 1974; Romaine 1982).

2. Synchronic distribution of *po-*

Our first task is to examine how widely the verb *po-* and its grammaticalized forms are distributed on the synchronic plane. At least sixteen lexical, morphosyntactic, and idiomatic categories can be recognized in contemporary Korean.

First of all, the monosyllabic verb *po-* prototypically functions as a transitive verb with two core arguments, a strictly transitive verb in Dixon's (2007) sense.

Basically, it denotes two interlocking visual perceptions: the purposive, intentional *po-,* i.e. 'look at, observe, set eyes on, meet' and the non-purposive, non-intentional, experiential *po-,* i.e. 'see, notice, encounter'. These two semantic properties are reflected in (1a) and (1b), respectively.

(1) *John-un* *Mary-lul* (a)*caseyhi/*(b)*wuyenhi* *po-ass-ta.*
John-TC Mary-AC in.detail/by.chance see-PST-DC
a. 'John had a good look at Mary.'
b. 'John accidentally saw Mary.'

Second, with its basic argument structure intact, *po-* (with its meaning of either intentional or experiential perception) has many metaphorically extended polysemies. Each extended meaning is usually manifest in collocation with the object nouns belonging to a specific semantic class. Korean dictionaries list some ten polysemy classes, each of which consists of one or more sub-polysemies. For example,

(2) a. 'attend to, manage, take charge of, prepare, look after, watch' (e.g. *il-ul po-* 'do one's job', *yeypay-lul po-* 'attend service', *sang-ul po-* 'set the table', *cip-ul po-* 'house-sit')
b. 'examine, inspect' (e.g. *ttang-ul po-* 'examine land to buy')
c. 'read, tell (fortunes)' (e.g. *sinmwun-ul po-* 'read a newspaper', *sacwu-lul po-* 'have one's fortune told')
d. 'recognize, understand, evaluate, judge' (e.g. *sathay-lul palo po-* 'evaluate the situation')
e. 'take (an exam)' (e.g. *sihem-ul po-* 'take an exam')
f. 'buy grocery' (e.g. *cang-ul po-* 'do grocery shopping')
g. 'try (the taste)' (e.g. *mas-ul po-* 'try the taste')
h. 'get (a new relative)' (e.g. *atul-ul po-* 'get a son')
i. 'experience, undergo, result in, encounter' (e.g. *sonhay-lul po-* 'suffer loss')
j. 'relieve nature' (e.g. *sopyen-ul po-* 'urinate')

Notice that visual perception is metaphorically extended to various purposive actions and non-purposive experiences. Collocational restrictions between *po-* and its object are generally so great that only a few specific nouns can occur with each polysemy. For instance, while *po-* occurs with *(si)cang* 'market' to mean 'do grocery shopping', it cannot occur with *kakey* 'store' or *syuphe* 'supermarket' in the same sense. While *po-* combines with *cip* 'house', *kakey* 'store', and *ai* 'child' to mean 'look after' or 'tend', it cannot occur with *paykhwacem* 'department store' and *halapeci* 'grandfather' in the same sense. While *po*- appears with the Sino-Korean *sopyen* 'urine' to mean 'relieve nature', it cannot occur with the native words with the same meaning such as *ocwum* 'urine', which occurs with the verb *nwu* 'let out'. Such fixed collocations are culturally and linguistically conventionalized.

Third, *po*- functions as a cognitive verb meaning 'think, believe'. As a cognitive verb, it can take an NP or clausal complement. The complement usually ends in the particle *(u)lo* 'as' (after an NP complement) or a quotative particle *ko* (after an S complement). In this case, the meaning of *po*- is similar to those of other cognitive verbs such as *sayngkakha*- 'think', *ihayha*- 'understand', and *mit*- 'believe'. However, their meanings and syntactic distributions are not always the same, as shown below.

(3a) *Yongho-ka/lul* *papo* *la-**ko*** ***po**/sayngkakha/mit-(u)sey-yo?*
Yongho-NM/AC fool is.DC-QT see/think/believe-SH-POL
'Do you think/believe Yongho is a fool?'

(3b) *i* *kes-ul* *sako-**lo*** ***po**-l/?sayngkakha-l/*mit-ul* *swu* *eps-eyo.*
this case-AC accident-as see/think/believe-PRS way lack-POL
'We cannot consider this an accident.'

(3c) *na-nun* *ka-lye-ko* *****po**/sayngkakhay/*mit-(a/e)yo.*
I-T go-intend-to see/think/believe-POL
'I am thinking of going.'

Fourth, *po*- functions as the main verb in serial-verb constructions. The preceding verb, followed by a connective suffix, indicates means or manner of the 'seeing' action. Only a limited number of verbs can occur before the main verb *po*- in serial constructions.

(4a) *ku* *yenghwa-lul* *kkok* ***ka-a*** ***po**-sey-yo.*
that movie-AC surely go-and see-SH-POL
'Be sure to go and watch that movie.'

(4b) *sensayng-nim-ul* ***manna-a*** ***poy**-ess-eyo.*
Teacher-AC meet-and see-PST-POL
'I met my teacher.'

Fifth, *po*- is used as an auxiliary verb in the rough meaning of 'try to do (something) to see how it will turn out' or 'do as a try'. It also has the meaning of experiencing an action or state.[2] It shares the same subject with the preceding verb. Unlike in serial verb constructions, not only a verb, as in (5a), but also an adjective, as in (5b), is permitted in the complement clause.

(5a) *na-nun* *i* *os-ul* ***ip**-e* ***pw**-ass-eyo.*
I-T this clothes-AC wear-INF try/experience-PST-P0L
a. 'I have tried to wear this dress.'
b. 'I have once worn this dress.'

(5b) *na-to* *han-ttay* *kananhay* ***pw**-ass-eyo.*
I-too one-time poor.INF experience-PST-POL
'I was once poor, too.'

Often, the auxiliary verb *po-* is used as a hedging device to tone down the illocutionary force expressed by the co-occurring main verb in a face-threatening context. It indicates the speaker's politeness in such a context. Thus, it is used as a kind of politeness marker.

(6a) *icey* *ka* ***po**-si-ci-yo.*
now go try-SH-SUG-POL
'Why don't you go now; How about leaving now.'

(6b) *ney,* *kulem* *ka-a* ***po**-llay-yo.*
yes then go-INT try-intend-POL
'OK, then I better go.'

Sixth, *po-* occurs in complex (cliticized) temporal/causal/conditional connective endings. In these constructions, the literal meaning of *po-* is largely suppressed, while the meaning of the speaker's evaluative modality stands out. No tense-aspect-mood (hereafter TAM) suffixes, including the subject honorific –*(u)si*, can follow *po-*, which means that *po-* no longer functions a regular verb.

(7a) *al-**ko-po-myen*** *motwu* *chakha-n* *salam* *i-eyyo.*
know-and-see-if all good-RL person be-POL
'After all (lit. 'if we see after we knew it'), everybody is good.'

2 It is often proposed that only the attemptive meaning is assigned to the auxiliary *pota* (e.g. Y.J. Ko 1997:62; M. Kim 1998:164; Hong and Sohn 2001). However, it denotes an experiential meaning as well, as in (5a). When an adjective is in the complement clause, only an experiential meaning appears, as in (5b).

(7b) *Mia-ka ttena-**ko-po-ni** na honca nam-ass-eyo.*
Mia-NM leave-and-see-as I alone remain-PST-POL
'Now that Mia has left (lit. as I see after Mia left), I am left behind alone.'

(7c) *nol-**ta-po-myen** kananhay-cy-eyo.*
play-and.then-see-if poor-get-POL
'If you don't work, you will become poor.'

(7d) *nemwu pappu-**ta-po-ni** cenhwaha-l swu eps-ess-eyo.*
too busy-and.then-see-as call-PRS way lack-PST-POL
'Being overly busy, I was not able to call you.'

Seventh, *po-* appears in the complex concessive ending *-e/a po-ass-ca* (pronounced as *–e/a pw-ass-ca* or *–e/a p-ass-ca*)[3] in the senses of 'despite, granted that, even though it is the case that'. Despite the past tense suffix *–ass*, the sequence itself denotes only non-past events. It conventionally implies the speaker's evaluative modality indicating the futility of the event or state expressed by the co-occurring clause.

(8a) *Cia-ka w-**a-pw-ass-ca** towum-i an toy-eyo.*
Cia-NM come-INF-try-PST-though help-NM not become-POL
'Even if Cia comes, she won't be of any help.'

(8b) *Cia-ka yeypp-**e-pw-ass-ca** Miss Korea-nun mos toy-eyo.*
Cia-NM pretty-INF-exp.-PST-though Miss Korea-TC cannot be-POL
'Cia cannot be a Miss Korea no matter how pretty she is.'

Notice that the auxiliary *po-* in such a concessive construction, unlike in a corresponding main clause, does not denote the subject referent's 'attempt' or 'experience' but a part of the speaker's modality. A simple test is to replace *Cia* with the inanimate noun *kkoch* 'flower' in (8b). Then we will have the grammatical expression *kkoch-i yeypp-e-pw-ass-ca* 'even if the flowers are pretty', where *-e-pw-ass-ca* denotes the speaker's modality, but the ungrammatical main clause **kkoch-i yeypp-e-pw-ass-ta* 'the flowers had experience to be pretty', where *–e-pw-ass-ta* denotes the subject referent's past experience.

Eighth, the construction *-(l)ul kka po-* (lit. 'think whether it will') has two evidential usages[4]: one as the anticipatory (or probability à la Rhee 2001:126)

3 A dialectal or idiolectal variant is *–e/a po-ass-tayss-ca* (pronounced as *–e/a p(w)-ass-tayss-ca*).

4 They are evidential in the sense that the meaning has derived from the evaluation of the

connective *–ul kka po-a(se)* 'anticipating that, being afraid that, thinking about' (9a) and the other as the declarative modal sentence ending (in all speech levels) with the meaning of the speaker's half-hearted intention (or non-preferential intentionality à la Rhee ibid.) to take an action (9b) in the sense of 'I might as well; I would rather'. Both verbs and adjectives occur with the anticipatory connective, but only verbs occur with the modal sentence ending. In both usages, *po-* cannot take TAM suffixes or be negated, and the accusative particle cannot be inserted after the defective noun *kka* 'whether, if'.

(9a) *pi-ka* *o-**l*** ***kka*** ***po-a(se)*** *wusan-ul* *kacyew-ass-eyo.*
rain-NM come-PRS if think-so umbrella-AC bring-PST-POL
'I brought an umbrella with me, thinking it might rain.'

(9b) *cwuk-e* *peli-**l*** ***kka*** ***pw-ayo***.
die-INF finish-PRS whether wish-POL
'I wish I would die.'

While any grammatical person can occur as the subject of *-(l)ul kka po-a(se),* only the first person (speaker), whether overt or covert, can occur as the subject in *-(l)ul kka po-ta.* Even if the subject is omitted as in (9b), the understood subject is always the speaker. On the other hand, *po-* cannot have its own subject or object in both structures. The literal meaning in both constructions in the sense of 'see if/whether' is hardly acceptable. For instance, **pi-ka o-l kka po-ase kyelcengha-ca* 'let's decide after we see if it rains or not' and **Mia ka ka-l kka po-ca* 'let's see if Mia will go' are not acceptable. Even **Mia ka ka-l kka po-ta* 'It appears that Mia will go' is hardly acceptable, because the subject of the main verb (*ka* 'go') is not the speaker.

Ninth, *-na po-* or *-(n)un-ka po-* has two distinct usages: the indirect question in the literal meaning of 'see whether' (10a) and the evidential function of the speaker's conjecture in the sense of 'it seems (looks, appears), I guess' (10b).[5] Hong & Sohn (2001) dub the *po-* in the latter use as a "modal functional verb", a one-place predicate requiring a clausal argument. In the evidential usage, *po-* is unable to take TAM suffixes, including honorifics and modal *-keyss* (the speaker's volition/conjecture), nor negation, as in (10 cf.). Only the retrospective evidential in the sense of 'according to what I heard/observed' is allowed, as in (10c). In the evidential usage, no imperative, propositive, or interrogative sentence is allowed. In all speech levels, only the declarative occurs.

situation through visual evidence.

5 For a comprehensive discussion on evidentials or grammatical means of expressing information source, see Aikhenvald (2004).

(10a) *pi-ka* *o-**na**/o-**nun-ka*** ***po**-ass-eyo.*
rain-NM come-whether see-PST-POL
'I checked whether it is raining or not.'

(10b) *pi-ka* *o-**na**/o-**nun-ka*** ***po-ta**.*
rain-NM come-whether appear-DC
'It seems to be raining.'

cf. **pi-ka o-**na**/o-**nun-ka** **po**-ass-ta.*
'It seemed to be raining.'

pi-ka o-na**/o-**nun-ka** an **po**-ta.*
'It does not seem to be raining.'

(10c) *Sewul-ey* *cikum* *pi-ka* *o-**na**/o-**nun-ka*** ***po-te**-la.*
Seoul-in now rain-NM come-whether appear-RT-DC
'According to what I heard, it seems to be raining in Seoul now.'

Tenth, *po-* appears in the complex sentence-ending *–ess-ta pw-a(la)* (-PST-DC see-IMP), which denotes the speaker's warning in a threatening manner. The rough meaning of the ending is '(I will teach someone a lesson; I will do something about it) if someone does . . . !' Although the ending contains a past-tense suffix, it notes a possible future event.

(11) *cwi-ka* *tto* *naw**-ass-ta*** ***pw-ala!***
rat-NM again come.out-PST-DC see-IM
'If a rat comes out again, I will do something about it!'

Eleventh, *(l)ul po-ko* functions as a case marker. In a main sentence, it denotes the direct object (DO), as in (12aii) and (12civ), or indirect object (IO), as in (12bii) and (12ciii). In an embedded sentence, it denotes the subject, as in (8cii). It is attached only to a human noun, used only with a verb of saying or asking, and used only colloquially (H. Lee & C. Lee 1998: 137–9). It literally means 'by looking at', as in (12ai), (12bi), and (12ci), and thus an expression may be ambiguous between this literal meaning and case meanings.

(12a) *na-**l*** ***po-ko** (= na-lul)* *wenmangha-ci* *ma.*
me-AC look.at-and resent-NOM stop
i. 'Don't resent me, looking at me.'
ii. 'Don't resent me.' (direct object)

(12b) *way* *na* ***po-ko*** *(=na eykey)* *mwul-e?*
why me look at-and ask-INT
i. 'Why do you ask, looking at me?'
ii. 'Why do you ask me?' (indirect object)

(12c) *halapeci-ka* *ne-**lul*** ***po****(-si)****-ko*** *papo* *la-ko* *ha-sy-ess-e.*
grandpa-NM you-AC see-SH-and fool be.DC-QT say-PST-INT
i. 'Having seen you, grandpa said you are a fool.' (with *–si*)
ii. 'Grandpa said that **you** are a fool.' (*ne* is embedded subject) (without *–si*)
iii. 'Grandpa said **to you** that you are a fool.' (*ne* is main-clause IO) (without *–si*)
iv. 'Grandpa called **you** a fool.'(*ne* is main-clause DO) (without *–si*)

When *(l)ul po-ko* is used as a case marker, no TAM suffix can follow *po-*. For example, the subject honorific suffix *-(u)si* cannot be attached to *po-* in (12c), despite the fact that the subject ("grandpa") deserves honorification.

Twelfth, the comparative-degree particle *pota* 'than' and the adverb *pota* 'more' contain the form *po* as their phonological component.[6] Although at a glance there does not seem to be any semantic relationship between the *po-* in *pota* and the verb *po-* 'see', historical records indicate that *pota* developed from *(l)ul po-taka* (AC see-while).

(13a) *enni-nun* *na-**pota*** *sey* *sal* *manh-ayo.*
Sister-T me-than 3 age much-POL
'My older sister is three years older than I.'

(13b) *wuli-nun* ***pota*** *na-un* *salm-ul* *chac-aya* *hay-yo.*
We-T more good-RL life-AC search-only.if do-POL
'We have to search for a better life.'

Thirteenth, like many transitive verbs, *po-* can be both passivized and causativized by way of a passive/causative suffix. As in a small number of other verbs such as *cap-hi-* 'be held, cause to hold', *an-ki-* 'be hugged, cause to hug', and *kel-li-* 'be walked, walk someone', *po-* is both passivized (14ai) and causativized (14aii) by the same suffix *–i*, as in *po-i* 'be seen, show'. The passivized *po-* behaves like an auxiliary verb when it follows an infinitive suffix, as in

6 Colloquially, *pota* is often pronounced as *potam,* probably contracted from the topicalized *pota-nun.*

(14b). In this case, *-e po-* 'look, appear' functions as a closely-knit unit with the meaning 'look, appear' and co-occur with visually perceptible adjectives and "ergative"-like verbs (e.g. *cichi-* 'get tired', *nulk-* 'get old', *talm-* 'resemble'). [7]

(14a) *Mia-hanthey* *cha-ka/lul* ***po-y**-ess-ni?*
Mia-to car-NM/AC see-CAS/PAS-PST-Q
i. 'Was the car seen to Mia?' (with *cha ka*)
ii. 'Did (you) show the car to Mia?' (with *cha lul*)

(14b) *onul* *Mia* *nwun* *i* *kh-e* ***po-y**-eyo.*
today Mia eye NM big-INF see-PAS-POL
'Mia's eyes look bigger today.'

Fourteenth, the humble form of *po-* is *poy(p)-* or obsolete *poy.o(p)-*[8] in the sense of 'see, meet (a superior person)'. Korean has developed extensive paradigms of honorifics in both the speaker-addressee perspective (e.g. pronouns, address terms, speech levels) and the speaker-referent perspective (e.g. pronouns, reference terms, subject honorific suffix, object honorific words, honorific subject and dative case particles). The pair *po-* vs. *poyp-/poy-* paradigmatically aligns with several other subject/object honorific words such as *mek-* 'eat' vs. *capswusi-* '(a superior) eats' and *ca-* 'sleep' vs. *cwumwusi-* '(a superior) sleeps', *tayli-* 'accompany' vs. *mosi-* 'accompany (a superior)' and *mwut-* 'ask' vs. *yeccwu(p)-* 'ask/tell (a superior)'.

(15a) *tto* ***poyp**-keyss-supni-ta.*
again see-will-AH-DC
'I will see you again.' (addressed to a superior)

(15b) *sensayngnim-ul* ***poy**-ess-eyo.*
teacher-AC see-PST-POL
'I saw my teacher.'

Fifteenth, there are many conversational formulas and discourse markers that are conventionalized with *po-*. For example, *ye-po-sey-yo* 'hello' (lit. 'look here' [polite level]) is a common usage to answer the telephone. *i-p-a* (< *i-kes p(w)-a*

---

7 An extensive discussion on the syntactic and semantic properties of *–e po-* is made in Yun (2002: 29-39). Yun subscribes to the existing claim that this is an auxiliary verb construction that allows only adjectives to occur as a main predicate.

8 *poypta* and *poy.opta* occur before a consonant, while *poyta* and *poyta* occur before a vowel.

'look this') 'hey, look here' [intimate level] is used to call a child and functions as a discourse marker to explain something in while fighting. Calling one's spouse with *ye-po* (< *yeki po-o* 'look here') 'honey!' is also conventionalized. The expression *han pen man pw-a cwu-sey-yo* (lit. 'please take care of me only once') means 'Please forgive me just once' and the expression *cal pw-a cwu-sey-yo* (lit. 'please take care of me well') 'I count on you'. Phatic expressions include *cheum poyp-keyss-supnita* (lit. 'I intend to see you for the first time') 'Nice to see you', *tto poy-p-keyss-supnita* 'See you again', *tto pw-a* 'Bye', and *ka-po-keyss-eyo* (lit. 'I intend to go') 'See you'.

Finally, there are a large number of words and idioms consisting of *po-* and neighboring elements formed through lexicalization processes (cf. Brinton and Traugott 2006). Some are relatively regular while others are more idiosyncratic. Such lexicalized expressions are too extensive to address in this paper. Suffice it to list some representative patterns with examples below.

(16) *po*-V:
po*-nay-* (see-put.out) 'send, see off'
po*-salphi-* (see-watch) 'take care of'
po*-paywu-* (see-learn) 'learn by seeing'

V/ADJ-*po-*:
*tol-****po****-* (go.round-watch) 'care after'
*nacchwu-****po****-* (lower-see) 'look down upon'
*tot-****po-i****-* (rise-see-PAS) 'be outstanding'
*yath-****po-*** (shallow-see) 'look down upon'

N-*po-*:
*son-****po****-* (hand-see) 'fix'
*pon-****po****-* (model-see) 'model after'
*kkuthcang-****po****-* (end-see) 'put an end to'
*nwunchi-****po****-* (eye.measure-see) 'try to read others' mind'
*ttan-cen-****po****-* (other-shop-see) 'neglect one's main duty'

po-NOM:
po*-ki* (see-NOM) 'example'
po*-m-ay* (see-NOM-at) 'apparently'

Serial:
*al-a-****po****-* (know-INF-see) 'recognize, inquire'
*twu-ko-****po****-* (place-and-see) 'keep a watch over'
*hwulth-e-****po****-* (scrub-INF-see) 'glance over'
*pal-a-****po****-* (wish-INF-see) 'gaze at, look to'
*tol-a-****po****-* (turn-INF-see) 'look back'
*tuly-e-ta-****po****-* (put.in-INF-and-see) 'look into'
*nay-ta-****po****-* (put.out-and-see) 'look up'

po-l-N: ***po**-l-kkol* (see-PRS-look) 'appearance, look'
***po**-l il* (see-PRS work) 'business, errand'

Adverbials: ***po**-la-n tus-i* 'showily'
*ye-**pw**-ala-n tus-i* 'demonstratively'

It is amazing to see how extensively *po-* is distributed across phonology, morphology, lexicon, syntax, semantics, pragmatics, and discourse. Synchronic study alone will be of necessity limited to the analysis of such dynamisms. It will be far more enlightening and linguistically intriguing, therefore, if we take a panchronic approach in order to look into why and how *po* has distributed across different linguistic levels in the way it has, why and how various polysemous meanings have been engendered, why and how many morpho-syntactic irregularities have been formed, and to what extent the different occurrences of *po-* can be accounted for in an integrated manner. This way, we will be able to have deeper insight into the nature and dynamism of language in general and Korean in particular, and obtain linguistically more significant generalizations.

3. Evolutionary clines of *po-*

Now, examination of the synchronic distributions of *po-* given in section 2 from a dynamic, panchronic perspective is in order. In order to explicate the synchronic phenomena of *po-* in this perspective, I would like to employ some useful concepts and putatively universal principles of grammaticalization (Langacker 1977; Givon 1975, 1985; Haiman 1985; Lehmann 1985, 1995; Traugott 1989; 1995; Hopper 1991, 1994; Heine 1992; Hopper 1991; Harris and Campbell 1995; Andersen 2001; Traugott and Dasher 2002; Hopper and Traugott 2003). I subscribe to the definition of grammaticalization as "the change whereby lexical items and constructions come in certain linguistic contexts to serve grammatical functions and, once grammaticalized, continue to develop new grammatical functions". (Hopper & Traugott 2003:xv).

Being extremely prolific, *po-* is one of the fittest for linguistic survival. It has kept breeding its offspring due to the principle of what I would call inertia. In most cases below, we have no way of knowing the relevant contextual data or exact time-depth for individual semantic and structural changes. Such information is immaterial for our purpose, however. We will be concerned only with why and how such changes have come about, not with when. Discussion of lexicalization involving *po-* will be omitted in the following.

3.1 Polysemic diversification

New linguistic forms and meanings are created mostly based on existing material, per the principle of economy (cf. Haspelmath 1999, Brinton and Traugott 2006:69, Hopper & Traugott:72-73). Creation of a new form for each new meaning would be extremely uneconomical not only because of the effort needed to coin new forms but because of human beings' memory and parsing limitations. Thus, existing forms accommodate metaphorically or metonymically extended meanings. These secondary meanings develop in specific contexts (per the locality condition) largely through pragmatic inferencing in accordance with the principle of semantic unidirectionality, from concrete or literal to abstract meanings (e.g. Hopper & Traugott 2003). Such pragmatic meanings become conventionalized as polysemies upon their spread over a speech community (Traugott & Dasher 2002).

As one of the most prolific verbs, *po-* must have followed this general pattern of polysemic breeding. That is, the literal meanings of *po-* illustrated in (1) have been metaphorically extended, frequently without grammatical reanalysis as in (2). I assumed that the purposeful, intentional visual perception has led to various polysemies, such as 'watch, inspect, examine, read, evaluate, look after, attend to, manage, take (charge of), try' through context-induced speakers' pragmatic inferencing conditioned by the frequent use of fixed collocations. Contexts are both linguistic and situational. For example, 'looking at a book' is pragmatically inferred as 'reading a book', because the purpose of looking at a book is to read it. 'Reading books' (not 'reading newspapers') in turn has acquired the pragmatic meaning 'study', because 'studying' and 'reading books' pragmatically denote a more or less coterminous activity. 'Looking at a market place' has developed into 'grocery shopping', because the purpose of going to and looking at a traditional market is typically 'to buy groceries', as in English 'shopping'. Similarly, 'see office work' has purposefully led to 'do office work'; 'did you see an exam?' to 'did you take an exam?'; and 'see the dinner table' to 'set the dinner table" through pragmatic interencing processes, first locally but later through analogical spreading.

I also assume that the non-purposive, experiential visual perception in *po-* has extended to 'encounter, experience, undergo, result in', as in *sonhay (-lul) po-* (loss-undergo) 'incur losses', *taypyen (-ul) po-* (big.comfort-experience) 'have a vowel movement', and *sonca (-ul) po-* (grandson-see) 'get a grandson'.[9]

Frequent omission of the accusative particle *(l)ul* in these collocations is a natural phenomenon due to the principles of economy and unidirectionality, that

9 See Yun (2002: 13-22) for a detailed discussion on this topic.

is, the speaker's tendency to simplify redundant constructions and routinize and conventionalize expressions for the facility of both production and (the hearer's) comprehension. As long as these polysemies have the same basic argument structure, no grammaticalization is involved. An object noun and *po*- may be blended into a compound verb, with change of a word to morpheme boundary, a case of lexicalization which does not concern us here.

3.2 Development of complement construction

As the concrete visual verb *po*- is unidirectionally abstracted or mapped from physical perception to mental perception to cognition, we get polysemies such as "see" (physical seeing) > "regard, view" (mental seeing) > "evaluate, judge" > "believe" > "know", and so on.[10] As a derived cognitive verb, it can now function as the main verb of a complement, typical complement constructions being NP-*(u)lo* and S-*ko,* just like any other cognitive verbs. Thus, its argument structure is shifted from the one with two arguments to the one with one argument and a complement clause. To that extent, it has grammaticalized. The derived cognitive verb *po*- functions like an evidential marker, in that it signals the cognitive source (evaluation of the situation via visual evidence) of the propositional information appearing in the complement. This development took place despite the existence of many other similar cognitive verbs, as per Hopper's principle of layering. Its meaning and collocational usage, however, are minutely distinct from those of the other cognitive verbs such as *sayngkakha*- 'think', *ihayha*- 'understand', *al*- 'know', *mit*- 'believe', *kancwuha*- 'consider, regard', *yeki*- 'consider', and *phantanha*- 'judge', as illustrated in (3). Per Hopper's (1991) principle of persistence, its original semantic features such as 'viewpoint', 'opinion', or 'observation', as well as 'thinking' constrain co-occurrences with certain types of complement constructions, although all the cognitive verbs are allowed to occur in a great majority of contexts. For example, the cognitive verb *po*- is stronger in forces of assertion than *sayngkakha*- 'think', but weaker than *mit*- 'believe' and *al*- 'know'.

3.3 Development of serial verb and auxiliary constructions

Both serial and auxiliary constructions are assumed to have developed from bi-clausal constructions of the kind of sentence in (17).

---

10 This relationship is called the "mind-as-body" metaphor in that bodily experience is a source of vocabulary for psychological states (Sweetser 1990:28–48; Hopper and Traugott 2003:84).

(17) *twi-(lo/*lul)* *tol-a* *na-lul* ***po**-sey-yo.*
back-to/AC turn-and me-AC see-SH-POL
'Please turn back and look at me.'

In this bi-clausal 'hypotaxis' structure, two clauses *twi-lo tolta* 'turn back' and *na-lul po-* 'look at me' are connected by the connector *–a*. If no word, such as *na-lul,* appears between the two verbs, which is usually the case, they become contiguous and tend to stick together (*tol-a po-*). Then, four meanings may transpire depending on the speaker-hearer's communicative intent: (a) literal connective function ('turn around and then see'); (b) serial function with the first verb functioning as a manner adverbial and *po-* remaining as the main verb ('see by turning around'); (c) auxiliary function with the first verb as the main verb and *po-* becoming an auxiliary verb ('try to turn around'); and (d) idiomatized word ('look back').[11]

Both serial and auxiliary constructions are considered 'subordination' structure. In the serial construction, which is loosely grammaticalized in view of the reanalysis involved (bi-clause to mono-clause, i.e. S-*e/a* S > V-*e/a* V), the argument structure of *po-* still remains the same. In this interpretation, (18a) is appropriate in that the object *twi* is the theme of the verb *po-*. Notice that this construction is not acceptable in (17). On the other hand, in the auxiliary construction, which is much more grammaticalized, the reanalysis involved is more complicated. The bi-clause is changed to mono-clause with S-*e/a* S > V-*e/a*-Aux, in that *po-* is de-categorized, having lost its own argument structure to become subordinate to the preceding verb. In this interpretation, (18b) is appropriate.

(18a) *twi-lul tol-a* ***po**-sey-yo.* (where *po* means 'look')
'Please turn back and look.'

(18b) *twi-lo tol-a* ***po**-sey-yo.* (where *po* means 'try')
'Please try to turn back.'

One may wonder how auxiliary meanings came about. Semantic reduction of 'look at, see' to the attemptive 'try' or the experiential 'see' in auxiliary functions can be accounted for in terms of the principles of unidirectionality and persistence. The purposive *po-* takes an agent as the subject and the non-

11 Serial constructions with the connector *-ta* have been fossilized as idiomatic expressions: *neme-ta pota* 'look over'; *nay-ta pota* 'look out'; *chy-e-ta pota* 'look up'; *tuly-e-ta pota* 'look into'; *nayly-e-ta pota* 'look down'; *tol-a-ta pota* 'look back'. Idiomatized auxiliary constructions include *al-a pota* (know-INF try) 'inquire'.

purposive *po-* takes an experiencer as the subject. It is assumed that, in the process of semantic shift toward unidirectional abstraction, the agent meaning gave birth to the meaning of attempt or 'try' as in *mas ul po* 'try the taste', while the experiencer meaning bred the 'experience' meaning as in *sonhay lul po* 'undergo losses'. It is easy to imagine that the purposive meaning indicating 'looking at something' without taking any action yet was reduced to the attemptive meaning, due to the principle of persistence. These meanings are used in the auxiliary function, as well.

The attemptive meaning and the experiential meaning of the auxiliary *po-* may occur together in a sentence. Thus, unless the object noun and/or speech situation is given, *mek-e po-ass-eyo* is ambiguous between 'I have experience of eating' and 'I tried eating'.[12]

In short, the auxiliary *po-* no longer has its own argument structure, but has obtained the status of an independent grammatical unit as an auxiliary, with the speaker's evaluative function in terms of attempt or experience, per Traugott's (1989, 1995) principle of subjectification. Unlike in serial constructions where *po-* occurs only in semantically congruent positions, the auxiliary *po-* has been generalized to occur in all post-verbal positions. It also occurs after an adjective in the 'experience' sense, which is not possible in bi-clausal and serial constructions, as in *aph-a po-sey-yo* 'Why don't you experience being sick?' The 'attempt' and 'experience' meanings have further diverged per the principle of inertia, as will be seen below.

3.4 Development of temporal/causal/conditional connectives

Temporal/causal/conditional connectives, as illustrated in (7), have developed via incipient grammaticalization from the same constructions with literal meanings, as in *–ko po-myen* 'once one does', *-ko po-ni(kka)* 'after one did', *–ta(ka) po-myen* 'while one keeps doing' (lit. 'if one looks while doing . . .') and *–ta(ka) po-ni(kka)* 'since, as . . . , (I realized)' (lit. 'as/when one looks while doing . . .'). Notice that in all these constructions, *po-* is inserted between the two connective suffixes *–ko/ta(ka)* and *–myen/ni(kka)*. Notice further that all these connectives are embedded in tri-clausal constructions like *na-nun il-ul ha-**ta(ka)** **po-ni(kka)** amwu-to eps-ess-ta* 'when I looked around while doing my work, there was nobody'. It is natural that a three-clause sentence can be reduced to two-clause sentence by way of the principles of economy and structural unidi-

12 Note that unlike in English *try to do,* the auxiliary *po* is always "implicative" regardless of experience or attempt. It is more or less like the modal-like use of *try and do,* as in "I will try and get a copy of that to you," although *try and* has some other connotations such as the speaker's lack of confidence in the agent's success (Hopper and Traugott 2003: 50).

rectionality. In the process, *po-* is de-categorized, losing its verb status, having no argument structure of its own, and unable to be made a past tense; and its visual literal meaning was grossly diluted and abstracted. In literal meaning, *po-* is usually preceded only by a verb, as in *ka-taka po-ass-ta* 'see (it) while going' because *–ta(ka)* indicates a shift from one action to another. However, *-taka po-ni(kka)* and *–ta(ka) po-myen* can be preceded by an adjective as well, as in *aphu-ta(ka)/ko po-ni(kka),* suggesting that they are generalized as connective endings (or clitics).[13] Furthermore, in all these derived constructions, the speaker's evaluative viewpoint (the principle of subjectification) is reflected. All this must have been facilitated due to the principle of paradigmatization (per Lehmann 1995:135), in that there is a robust and productive grammatical category, "connective endings", in Korean.

3.5 Development of "futility" concessive connectives

Another complex (cliticized) connective ending we observed in (8) is *-e/a pw-ass-ca.* This is a phenomenon of further grammaticalization of the auxiliary-verb construction per the principle of inertia. In view of its meaning and the morpho-syntactic structure, it must have contracted from the conjunctive clause *-e/a po-ass-ta-ko hay-to* 'even though one says that one tried to do' by way of the well-known *ko ha* deletion and contraction (mono-syllabification) and palatalization of *ta-y-to* to *ca.* Unlike its full source clause, the contracted form denotes much simpler content such as 'even if, granted that . . . , (it will be futile)', suppressing the meaning of *ko ha* 'one says that' per the principle of iconicity (e.g. Givon 1985, Haiman 1985). Here, reanalysis took place so that the auxiliary is no longer a part of the main predicate in the conjunctive clause but a component of the reanalyzed complex connective that denotes the speaker's modality per the principle of subjectification. The derived connective ending has encoded the speaker's casual and negative evaluative viewpoint that devaluates the content of the co-occurring clause. The "futility" meaning is obviously due to the concessive meaning ('even if it is the case that . . .') of the source construction. The "concessive" meaning has obtained "futility" as part of its referential meaning in the process of structural contraction and subjectification. Even in the case of the full source conjunctive clause, "futility" appears as the most salient conversational implicature in its main clause. This conversational implicature is assumed to have transitioned to conventional implicature as a semantic component of the grammaticalized ending.

---

13 This kind of developing endings are treated as clitics, rather than suffixes, in An (1997), M. Kim (1998), and Yun (2002). They are still in the stage of incipient grammaticalization.

Syntactically, unlike its source construction which denotes a real or hypothetical past event, the contracted form *-e/a po-ass-ca* denotes only non-past events and cannot be made a non-past form with the same meaning, as in **-e po-ca.* However, as in other auxiliary constructions, the honorific suffix *–si* can be inserted after *po,* as in *cikum w-a po-**sy**-ess-ca* 'even though you come now (it will be useless)'. Since the honorific suffix can still be inserted, the grammaticalization may be viewed as relatively incipient.

3.6 Development of *–(u)l-kka po-*

The anticipatory evidential connective ending *–(u)l-kka po-a(se)* 'anticipating that; being afraid of' and the "half-hearted intention" sentential ending *–(u) l-kka-po-ta* 'I would rather do', as illustrated in (9), have considerably different semantic contents, depending on whether they appear as a connective or as a sentential ending. The semantic difference between the connective and the sentential ending can be attributed to the different syntactic positions where they appear and the different suffixes used: the non-finite connective *–a(se)* and the finite declarative suffix *–ta*. The degrees of subjectification are considerably different between the two positions. The sentence ending position is much stronger, because that position is the exclusive territory of the speaker's assertive modality in SOV languages. Syntactically, although any person can occur as subject with the connective ending, only the first person (speaker) can occur with the sentential ending.

As a sentential ending, it is a prospective counterpart of the non-prospective *–na-po-/nun-ka-po-* 'seem, appear' (see below) in the same structural paradigm. That is, *-na, -ka,* and *-kka* are allomorphs of the indirect question complementizer 'whether'. The semantic differences that have emerged are due to the prospective suffix *–(u)l*, which is future-oriented, such as "anticipation" and "intention". Since *–(u)l-kka po-* is future-oriented, *po-* functions as a cognitive verb in the sense of 'think'. On the other hand, *–na-po-ta/-nun-ka-po-ta* are present-oriented, and *po-* has a visual perceptual meaning such as 'seem, appear'.

3.7 Development of *na-po/nun-ka-po*

As observed in (10), it is not difficult to see that the sentence-final dubitative evidential marker *na-po-/nun-ka-po-* has developed from the disjunctive suffix *-na/nun-ka* 'whether' followed by the verb *po-*. This dubitative modal sentential ending, which reflects only the speaker's evaluative judgment (per the principle of subjectification), is evidential because it strongly suggests the source of the propositional information, that is, visual evidence, as per the principle of persistence. Namely, the speaker makes an assertion, based on his/her observation of the situation, circumstance, or atmosphere.

This derived evidential modal ending occurs only in a declarative sentence, cannot be negated, and cannot take any TAM suffix except the retrospective suffix (*–te(y)/-ti*). One may wonder why only the visual perceptive verb *po-* has become completely stripped off as an evidential marker. I assume that since *po-* has undergone deeper and wider grammaticalization than most other verbs due partly to its frequency of uses, its inertia and specialization (per Hopper 1991) seem to be more powerful and far-reaching than other verbs. Why then is the retrospective suffix exempted from being lost, as in *caymi-iss-ess-**na-po-te**-la* 'I heard they seemed to have fun'? The retrospective itself is an evidential marker denoting the speaker's own past observation, experience, or hearing (Sohn 1975). It is a necessary grammatical element which cannot easily be eliminated due to its heavy speaker-based semantic content.

3.8 Development of a "threatening" modal ending

A grammaticalized form whose genesis is somewhat similar to the development of *-e/a po-ass-ca* is the 'threatening' expression *V/ADJ–(e/a)ss-ta-p-a(la)* '(I will give someone a lesson) if someone/something does . . .', as illustrated in (11). This form is assumed to have developed from *V/ADJ-(e/a)ss-ta-ko hay po-a(la)* (PST-DC-QT tell.INF try-IMP) 'Try telling (me) that (someone/ something) did/was . . . !'. This source construction does not denote, but may only pragmatically connote, the speaker's "warning" or "threat". It can be used in both past and non-past forms, may take the honorific suffix *si* after *po-,* occurs with all speech level endings, and lacks the speaker's evaluative connotation. Only pragmatically and rhetorically can it imply the speaker's warning or threatening, depending on contexts. This bi-clausal source sentence has grammaticalized into a mono-clause through *ko ha* 'say that' deletion and reanalysis (merging) of the remaining morphemes as a complex modal ending with the meaning of the speaker's warning or threat. That is, the original context-induced pragmatic meaning has become a semantic content of the new decategorized and subjectified ending. The derived ending is used only in a fossilized past form with a non-past hypothetical (conditional) meaning, as if it were a conjunctive clause, in the sense of '(I will do some about it) **if** someone/something does ... !' Although it has an imperative sentence ending, it is no longer a command or request sentence, but a conditional sentence, like the "Suppose…" construction in English. It frequently takes a non-honorific speech-level ending and is used in a self-addressed (monologue) speech act.

3.9 Development of the incipient case marker *((l)ul) poko*

Yang (2000) observes that the sequence of *po-* 'see' and the connective suffix *-ko* 'and' is emerging as a new multi-functional case particle, as illustrated in (12).[14] Again, the principles of economy and unidirectionality that make a complex sentence a simple sentence are responsible to a great extent. As Yang (ibid.) and Rhee (2001) observe, only the visual verb *po-* among all verbs of senses functions this way. We can say that this is due to Hopper's (1991) principle of specialization. Tense, aspect, honorific, and mood suffixes cannot occur after *po-* in the case function. Nor can negation be made. Yet, this is a case of incipient grammaticalization in view of its functional fluidity among three case functions (subject, direct object, and indirect object) each of which has an extremely limited syntactic distribution. Even a cognitive verb like *alli-* 'inform' is not yet accepted as a clause mate of the *((l)ul) poko* case, as in **na-poko ally-e!* 'Please let me know!' Its source meaning ('looking at') is rather vividly reflected in the derived form, per the principle of persistence. Furthermore, the accusative particle *(l)ul* can still appear, albeit rarely.

How have the three case functions become associated with *((l)ul) po-ko*? The indirect object function must have been the first to emerge due to the pragmatic inferencing. That is, the metaphorical-metonymic abstraction involved in the derivation of an incipient goal case marker seems to involve the following process. Saying (something) while looking at a person implicates saying (something) to that person. When physical looking became insignificant, diluted, or redundant between the interlocutors due to frequent conversational uses, especially when the accusative particle *(l)ul* is omitted, "saying (something) while looking at X" is reduced to "saying (something) to X", hence, the genesis of a grammatical case of goal or indirect object. Thus, the indirect object function occurs only when the NP before *((l)ul) poko* is a human noun and the main verb is a verb of saying or asking. In other words, *poko* as a case particle cannot occur without a verb of saying or asking at the present "clitic" stage of morphologization. Now, observe the following three-way ambiguous sentence where *poko* is replaceable by *–ka, -eykey,* and *–lul.* It functions as (i) the embedded subject (*ka*), (ii) the goal of the main verb of saying (*eykey*), and (iii) the object of the main verb of entitling (*lul*).

(19) *Yongho-nun Mia-**poko** (=ka/eykey/lul) papo la-ko hay-ss-eyo.*
Yongho-T Mia-poko NM/IO/AC fool be.DC-QT say-PST-POL

14 Heine and Kuteva (2002:269–70) quote Svorou's (1994) examples of allative cases ('toward,' 'up to,' 'by,' 'for') that have developed from the verb 'to see' in Bihari, Halia, and Tamil.

i. "Yongho said that Mia is a fool.'
ii. "Yongho said to Mia that she is a fool.'
iii. "Yongho called Mia a fool.'

We can speculate that indirect object function (goal case) is extended to subject and direct object function due to syntactic processing. How? Assuming (19ii) is the basic structure which developed from pragmatic inferencing, (19i) must have developed by the hearer's abductive filling of the empty embedded subject position with *Mia-poko* in the course of intake processing during speaker-hearer interactions. Also, *Mia-poko* can easily be interpreted as a direct object, because in that position both the direct and indirect object can appear as free variants, as in *Mia-hanthey* and *Mia-lul.* All this is possible because *poko* is still in fluidity, being not fossilized as a case particle. Notice incidentally that grammaticalization occurs despite the existence of other forms that have the given function, per Hopper's (1991) principle of layering.

3.10 Development of the comparative particle *pota* 'than'

The current comparative particle *pota* 'than' is an unit of fully matured grammaticalization, as illustrated in (13).[15] It has developed from *–(l)ul po-taka* 'while looking at (something)', where *–(l)ul* is an accusative particle and *–taka* 'while, and then' is a transferentive (or interruptive) connective suffix that denotes a change of one action or state to another. It is well known that earlier comparative forms, especially in Middle Korean, were *lawa* and *twu-ko(-n)* (lit. 'place and then') and its allomorphs.[16]

Although in contemporary Korean *pota* is never used as *potaka,* eighteenth and nineteenth century data contain sentences where *potaka* was used instead of *pota* in the contemporary sense of 'than' (e.g. Yun 2002: 50). This attests that *ta* in *pota* is from the transferentive *taka.* In contemporary Korean, *taka* can optionally be contracted in all contexts except in some cases where it is obligatorily deleted, as in *pota.*[17]

15 Heine and Kuteva (2002:269) quote Svorou (1994) as stating that Halia *tara* 'to look, see' has grammaticalized as 'than' in addition to 'to' and 'toward.'

16 Incidentally, it has been attested that *-taka* itself is a suffix that has been grammaticalized from the verb stem *taka* 'approach' and the sequential/infinitive suffix *–a* 'and (then)'. Thus, X *pota* 'than X' is assumed to have developed from X *lul po-taka* 'while looking at X'.

17 Obligatory deletion can also be observed in *nay-ta(*ka) pota* 'look out', *tulye-ta(*ka) pota* 'look into', etc. When it is optionally contractible, transferentive or interruptive meaning (after a verb) and additive meaning (after a noun) is strong, as in *kata(ka) ota* 'come back on the way to go' and *matang ey ta(ka) mwul ul cwuta* 'give water onto the yard', and *pap ey ta(ka) swul kkaci mek-ess-ta* 'ate wine, in addition to meal'.

What are the justifiable processes involved in assuming that *–lul po-taka* 'while seeing' developed into *pota* 'than', whose meanings are so different? As a first approximation, let us observe the following sentences where both *–lul po-taka* and *–pota* can occur as a minimal pair.

(20a) *capci-lul* *po-taka* *sinmwun-ul* *ilk-ess-eyo.*
magazine-AC see-while paper-AC read-PST-POL
'(X) read a newspaper, stopping reading a magazine.'

(20b) *capci-po-ta sinmwun-ul ilk-ess-eyo.*
i. '(X) read a newspaper rather than a magazine.'
ii. '(X) read a newspaper, stopping reading a magazine.'

When the co-occurring verb is in non-past tense, as in *po-taka,* the transferentive suffix *–taka* denotes a short, temporary, and incomplete action. It further implies that the temporary action is followed by a more prominent TAM-marked main verb action as the focus of the utterance. This is particularly the case with head-final languages like Korean. This indicates that the content of the subordinate clause ending in *–taka* received the pragmatic connotation of secondaryness or less preference compared to the content of the main clause if two parallel actions are presented, as implied in (20), where the speaker did newspaper reading, while stopping magazine reading.

Now, with the permanent omission of the accusative particle *–(l)ul,* not only is the length of seeing pragmatically even shorter per the principle of iconicity, but the visual perception meaning of *po-* is also weakened and extremely diluted. The suffix *–taka* was permanently shortened to *-ta*, as in *–(l)ul po-taka* > *po-taka* > *pota.* Although *–(l)ul po-taka* was used usually with a verb in the main clause, once it is fossilized as a comparative-degree particle, it can now be generally used with adjectives as well, as in *X-pota Y-ka yeyppu-ta* 'Y is prettier than X'. Thus, original bi-clausal sentences were changed to mono-clausal comparative sentences, which is a typical case of unidirectionality in grammaticalization. This is not a unique instance of particle development. Similar phenomena of structural reanalysis, semantic shift, and phonological attrition in particle derivation can be observed in (21), whose diachronic rule can be formulated as in (22).

(21) *X-ey/lul pwuth-e(se)* 'being attached to' > *X-pwuthe* 'from X'
X-uy pakk-ey 'at the outside of X' > *X-pakkey* 'except X'
X-lul coch-a(se) 'by following X' > *X-cocha* 'even X '
X-lul machi-e(se) 'by finishing X' > *X-mace* 'so far as X'
X-lul po-ta(ka) 'while seeing X > *X-pota* 'than X'

(22) X-particle$_1$ + V-suffix > X-particle$_3$, where particle$_3$ < V-suffix.
X-particle$_1$ + N-particle$_2$ > X-particle$_3$, where particle$_3$ < N-particle$_2$

The comparative *pota* 'than' has further developed polysemically into an adverb *pota* 'more' as in *wuli-nun pota kh-un huymang-ul kac-ca* 'Let's have a (more) bigger hope'. This cannot be considered a counterexample to the unidirectionality principle, because it must have derived from the construction X (understood element) *pota.* It should be viewed as a lexicalization case of renewal, not a counterexample to unidirectionality.

3.11 Development of passive/causative

In parallel with several hundreds of other transitive verbs, *po-* has undergone causativization and passivization, with the ambivalent derivational suffix *-i*, as observed in (14). By this process, *po-,* like other verbs, has undergone decategorizaion, losing its own original argument structure. Only together with the suffix can it function as a lexical verb—either a three-argument causative verb <agent, goal, theme ___> or a two-argument passive verb <theme, goal ___>. For a proposal that Korean passive suffixes (*-i, -hi, -ki, -li*) developed from the causative suffixes (*-i, -hi, -ki, -li, -wu, -kwu, -chwu*) via functional shift, see Sohn (1996), for example.

The auxiliary-like construction *–e po-i-* 'appear, look' reflects an incipient grammaticalization. Its early stage of reanalysis can be observed in a slight semantic shift in *po-* from 'be seen' to 'look, appear', the constraint in selecting co-occurring predicates, and the lack of a phonological word juncture between –*e* and *–po.*

3.12 Development of the "humble" transitive verb *poyp-*

In regard to the honorific counterpart of *po-*, Yensey (1998: 884) lists all three forms: *poy.op-, poyp-,* and *poy-*. In fact, the first form is extremely formal and used in historical dramas and highly deferential letters, while disappearing in daily usage in contemporary Korean. In view of this usage, as well as the unidirectional principle in phonological attrition, the three forms indicate an evolutionary path in that order, starting with *poy.op-*.

Where did this form come from? It can be analyzed as *po-i-op-* ('see' + passive/causative suffix + Middle Korean object honorific suffix). The contraction of *poi-* to *poy-* is a natural phonological phenomenon. The suffixes *-saop* (after a consonant) and *-op* (after a vowel) were used for object honorification in Middle Korean (e.g. Huh 1984). These suffixes have developed, through functional shift, into present-day addressee honorifics in the form of *-sup* (after a consonant) and *-(u)p* after a vowel (e.g. Sohn 1998). Thus, it is obvious that *poy-op-* was fossilized as an object honorific form of *po-* 'see' before the suffix *–op* underwent a semantic shift and phonological attrition. Our immediate question is whether the suffix *–i* in *po-i-op-* is a passive or causative. That is, which is the source sentence from which *poyp-* has developed?

(23a) *X-nun Y-eykey po-i-ess-ta.* > *X-nun Y-lul poy-ess-ta.*
X-TC Y-to see-PAS-PST-DC X-TC Y-AC see-PST-DC
'X was seen to Y.' > 'X humbly saw Y.'

(23b) *X-nun Y-eykey (caki-lul) po-i-ess-ta.* > *X-nun Y-lul poy-ess-ta.*
X-TC Y-to self-AC see-CAS-PST-DC X-TC Y-AC see-PST-DC
'X showed himself to Y.' > 'X humbly saw Y.'

In both (23a) and (23b), pragmatic inferencing is at work. I propose, however, that the causative construction (23b) is the source. In (23b) X is the agent just as X is in the derived construction, whereas in (23a) X is the theme. In order for the passive sentence to be the source, the theme X must change to the agent which is costly, and the passive (1-place) verb must change to a transitive (2-place) verb, which is also costly, that is, against the principles of economy and unidirectionality. In order for the causative sentence to be the source, only the causative (3-place) verb must change to a transitive (2-place) verb, which is unidirectional. In (23b), 'X shows oneself to Y who is a superior' pragmatically implies 'X sees Y (in a humble manner)', whereas in (23a) 'X is seen to Y who is a superior' does not necessarily imply 'X sees Y (in a humble manner)'.

Our next question is, "Why has lexicalization taken place to derive such an honorific verb?" Korean has long been an honorific language. Various asymmetrical social relations on the speaker-addressee-referent perspectives have been encoded grammatically and lexically. Honorifics are pervasive throughout all levels of the structure and lexicon of the language. Due to this typological salience, words have developed to indicate subject and object honorification. Seeing a superior person is perceived as socially different from seeing a lower person, just like asking a question to a senior person is different from asking a question to a child. Such social need and the lexical lacuna, as well as the principles of politeness and paradigmatization, must have provided pressure for the need to create a new verb.

Due to the principle of economy, the passive/causative form of the existing verb of seeing, *po-,* was utilized. Instead of saying that one will see a superior person directly, it is much politer to say that one will show oneself to a superior person per the principle of politeness.

Along with this argument structure change from a causative to transitive active verb, the intended (or connotative or pragmatic) meaning of politeness or deference has now been built in the word *poy.op-* as a referential (or denotative or semantic) meaning. Change of 3-place predicate to a 2-place predicate is a natural principle of unidirectionality in grammaticalization. Once a new transitive verb is in place with a new transitive argument structure, it is natural that the new verb cannot take a goal case but an accusative case.

3.13 Development of discourse and politeness markers

As illustrated earlier, *po-,* due to its extreme semantic proliferation and frequency in use, participates in creating discourse markers. Auxiliary function has further developed as a hedging device indicating politeness, simply to soften the illocutionary force of the action, as observed in (6). The meanings of experience or attempt ('try') have developed, first pragmatically (conversationally) and then conventionally, into such diminutive use. Space does not allow me to go into this vast area of sociolinguistic interest.

3.14 Phonological attrition

Phonological attrition is not extensive, probably because *po* is already a minimal CV form, which cannot be further reduced without hampering communicative function. In general, ***po**-a* has contracted to ***pw**-a* to *p-a* (as in ***po**-ass-eyo* > ***pw**-ass-eyo* > ***p**-ass*-eyo) in which case the CV syllable *po* is contracted to a consonant phoneme *p.* There are some dialectal peculiarities, as in Kyengsang sentence-final *pey* (Seoul: *pw-a*).

4. Conclusion

In this paper, I have tried to show how extensively and continually one visual perception verb in Korean, the most frequently occurring one, has bred its offspring, showing development along multiple paths or clines. I have also tried to show how extensively the grammaticalization approach can account for the most synchronic irregularities and generalities associated with *po-* in an integrated manner. It has been revealed that various putatively universal conditions and principles are applicable to accounting for the phenomena of polysemic breeding, grammaticalization, and idiomatization associated with *po-* in Korean. Universal conditions cited in this paper include locality, contiguity, frequency of use, and pragmatic inferencing. Relevant universal principles include economy, inertia, unidirectionality, subjectification, iconicity, paradigmatization, layering, persistence, specialization, and decategorization.

Throughout this paper, I have endeavored to demonstrate that, in view of the dynamic and evolutionary nature of language, a panchronic and holistic model of description is more comprehensive, exhaustive, productive, intriguing, and linguistically more generalizable than models based on strict division between synchrony and diachrony on the one hand, and strict division among linguistic levels on the other.

REFERENCES: Chapter 13

Aikhenvald, A.Y. 2004. *Evidentiality.* Oxford, England: Oxford University Press.

Ah, Ju-Ho. 1997. *Hankeuke Muengsa uy Mwunpephwa Hyensang Yenkwu* (A grammaticalization study of Korean nouns). Seoul: Hankwuk Munhwasa.

Brinton, L.J. & E.C. Traugott. 2006. *Lexicalization and Language Change.* Cambridge: Cambridge University Press.

Bybee, J.L. & P. Hopper (eds.). 2002. *Frequency and the Emergence of Linguistic Structure.* Amsterdam: Benjamins.

Dixon, R.M.W. 2007. Explaining transitivity. ms. RCLT. La Trobe University.

Fortson IV, BW. 2002. Review of E.C. Taugott & R.B. Dasher: *Regularity in Semantic Change.* Cambridge University Press (2002). Diachronica, 226–35.

Fuss, E. and C. Trips (eds.). 2004. *Diachronic Clues to Synchronic Grammar.* John Benjamins.

Geis, M.L. & A.M. Zwicky. 1971. On invited inferences. *Linguistic Inquiry* 2: 561–66.

Givon, T. 1975. Serial verbs and syntactic change: Niger-Congo. In Li, C.N. (ed.), *Word Order and Word Order Change,* 47-112. New York: Academic Press.

Givon, T. 1985. Iconicity, isomorphism, and non-arbitray coding. In Haiman, J. (ed.), 187-219.

Haiman, J. (ed.). 1985. *Iconicity in Syntax.* Amsterdam: Benjamins.

Haspelmath, M. 1999. Why is grammaticalization irreversible? *Linguistics* 37: 1043-68.

Heine, B. and T. Kuteva. 2002. *World Lexicon of Grammaticalization.* Cambridge: Cambridge University Press.

Hong, Kyoung-Sun and Young-Sook Sohn. 2001. Syntax and semantics of Korean auxiliary verbs *Po*- in terms of modality. *Harvard Studies in Korean Linguistics IX.*

Hopper, P.J. 1991. On some principles of grammaticalization. In Traugott, E.C. and B. Heine 1991:17–36.

Hopper, P.J. and E.C. Traugott. 2003. *Grammaticalization.* Second Edition. Cambridge, England: Cambridge University Press.

Huh, Woong. 1984. *Kwukehak.* Seoul: Saym Munhwasa.

Joo, H.R. 2006. Corpus analysis of pota (see/look at) for Korean language teachers. In Bley-

Vroman, R. and H. Ko (eds.), Corpus linguistics for Korean language learning and teaching, 63-79. University of Hawaii NFLRC.

Kim, Miyoung. 1998. *Kwuke Yongen uy Cepehwa* (Cliticization of Korean Predicates). Seoul: Hankwuk Munhwasa.

Ko, Yung-Jin. 1997. *Hankwuke uy munpephwa Kwaceng* (Grammaticalization Processes in Korean). Seoul: Kwukhak Calyowen.

Koo, Hyun Jung. 2003. *Hankwuke 'Cwuta'-lyu Tongsa uy Munpephwa Yangsang* (Grammaticalization in Korean verbs of 'giving'). *Eoneohag* (The Journal of the Linguistic Society of Korea), Seoul National University.

Krug, M. 1998. String frequency: a cognitive motivating factor in coalescence, language processing and change. *Journal of English Linguistics* 26: 286-320.

Labov, W. 1974. On the use of the present to explain the past. In Heilman, L. (ed.), *Proceedings of the 11th International Congress of Linguistics,* 825-52.

Lee, Hija and Jonghi Lee. 1988. *Theyksuthu Punsekcek Kwuke Cosa uy Yenkwu* (A Study of Korean Particles through Text Analysis). Seoul: Hankwuk Munhwasa.

Lee, Ki-Gap. 2004. Semantic expansion of the connective ending '-daga' in Korean (in Korean). *Language Research* 40(3):543–72.

Lehmann, C. 1985. Grammaticalization: Synchronic variation and diachronic change. *Lingual e Stile* 20(3): 303–18.

Lehmann, C. 1995. *Thoughts on Grammaticalization.* Munchen and Newcastle: LINCOM EUROPA.

Narrog, H. & B. Heine. 2011. *The Oxford Handbook of Grammaticalization.* Oxford, England: Oxford University Press.

Park, Yong Yae and Strauss, Susan. 1997. How 'seeing' approaches 'knowing' in Korean, Japanese, and English: An analysis of *pota, miru,* and *see.* In Sohn, Ho-min and J. Haig (eds.), *Japanese/Korean Linguistics* 6: 619–38.

Rhee, Seongha. 1996. *Semantics of Verbs and Grammaticalization: The Development in Korean from a Cross-Linguistic Perspective.* Ph.D. dissertation. The University of Texas at Austin.

Rhee, Seongha. 2001. Grammaticalization of verbs of cognition and perception. *Studies in Modern Grammar* 24: 111–35.

Romaine, S. *Socio-Historical Linguistics: its Status and Methodology.* Cambridge: Cambridge University Press.

Sohn, Ho-min. 1975. Retrospection in Korean. *Language Research* (Seoul National University) 11.1: 87-103. Also, in Ho-min Sohn, *Linguistic Expeditions* (Seoul: Hanshin, 1986).

Sohn, Ho-min. 1996. Reanalysis in Korean complex predicate constructions: Causative derivation. *Japanese-Korean Linguistics* 5: 37–64.

Sohn, Ho-min. 1998. Evolution of addressee honorifics. In Lee, Sang-Oak and Duk-Soo Park (eds.), *Perspectives on Korea.* Sydney: Wild Peony.

Sohn, Ho-min. 2001. *The Korean Language.* Cambridge, UK: Cambridge University Press.

Stein, D. and S. Wright (eds.). 1995. *Subjectivity and Subjectivisation—Linguistic Perspectives.* Cambridge: Cambridge University Press.

Svorou, S. 1994. *The Grammar of Space.* Amsterdam and Philadelphia: John Benjamins.

Sweetser, E.E. 1990. *From Etymology to Pragmatics: Metaphorical and Cultural Aspects of Semantic Structure* (Cambridge Studies in Linguistics). Cambridge: Cambridge University Press.

Traugott, E.C. 1989. On the rise of epistemic meanings in English: An example of subjectification in semantic change. *Language* 57: 33–65.

Traugott, E.C. 1995. Subjectification in grammaticalization. In Stein, D. and S. Wright 1995.

Taugott, E.C. and R.B. Dasher. 2002. *Regularity in Semantic Change.* Cambridge, England: Cambridge University Press.

Traugott, E.C. and B. Heine (eds.). 1991. *Approaches to Grammaticalization,* I and II. Amsterdam: John Benjamins.

Van Gelderen, Elly. 2004. *Grammaticalization as Economy.* The Netherlands: John Benjamins.

Yang, In-Seok. 2000. The emerging particle POKO in Korean: A grammaticalization. In De Guzman, V.P. and B.W. Bender (eds), *Grammatical Analysis: Morphology, Syntax, and Semantics. Studies in Honor of Stanley Starosta.* pp. 62-78. Honolulu: University of Hawai'i Press.

Yensey. 1998. *Yensey's Dictionary of the Korean Language.* Seoul: Yonsei University Press.

Yun, Myongsang. 2002. *Tongsa 'pota' uy Mwunpephwa* (Grammaticalization of the verb *pota*). Taycen, Korea: Hannam University Press.

14 An Emergent Category of Interpersonal Modal Endings in Korean*

1. Introduction[1]

In Korean, there are a series of pseudo suffixes that are relatively recent innovations as emergent sentence endings. These endings share many syntactic, semantic-pragmatic, and discourse functions. For example, all of them occur mainly in casual interpersonal speech. All of them denote an intimate speech level (by default) when they occur without being followed by another speech-level element such as the politeness particle 요 *yo*.

Such emergent modal endings are used very productively in daily conversational interaction, more frequently than canonical endings, as observed in the following made-up but natural conversation between two Korean interractants of equal status. A drives the car, guiding B, who looks for a suitable restaurant to have dinner with A. Emergent modal endings (hereafter EMEs) are underlined. Sentence-final boundary tones (or intonation contours) are marked roughly as ~ (rising-falling), ↘ (falling), and ↗ (rising).

(1) A: 이 근방에 괜찮은 인도 음식점이 하나 있는데요. ~

i	kunpang	ey	kwaynchanh-un	Into	umsikcem	i	hana
this	area	at	decent-RL	Indian	restaurant	NM	one

iss-nuntey-yo. ~
exist-EME-POL
'There is a pretty good Indian restaurant in this area NUNTEY-YO.'

* This is reprinted from *the Annual Research Report on Korean Studies*. Vol.13: 1-22 (1913). Kyushyu University, Japan. 2012.

1 The original version of this paper was written at the Research Center of Korean Studies (RCKS) of Kyushu University in Fukuoka, Japan in the summer of 2012 when I was a visiting scholar at Kyushu University for one month. It was presented at an RCKS's colloquium held on June 14, 2012. I extend my heartfelt thanks to Professor Takatoshi Matsubara, RCKS Director, for giving me the golden opportunity to work at the RCKS. Special thanks go to the RCKS staff members (especially Fujita Hanae) for taking care of all necessary procedures and office chores for me prior to and during my stay with the Center.

B: 근데 전 아직 인도 음식은 좀 입에 맞지 않거든요. ~
kuntey ce-n acik Into umsik un com ip ey mac-ci
BTW I-TC yet Indian food TC a.bit mouth to fit-NOM
anh-ketun-yo. ~
not.do-EME-POL
'By the way, somehow Indian food is still not to my liking *ketun-yo.*'

혹 일식집은 없을까요? ↗
hok ilsik cip un eps-ulkka-yo? ↗
by.any.chance Japanese house TC non.exist-EME-POL
'I wonder if by any chance there is a Japanese restaurant *ulkka-yo.*'

전 일식이 괜찮더라구요. ↘
ce-n il-sik i kwaynchanh-te-lakwu-yo. ↘
I-TC Japanese-style NM pretty.good-RT-EME-POL
'I kind of like Japanese food *lakwu-yo*.'

A. 조금 더 나가면 있을걸요. ↗
cokum te naka-myen iss-ulkel-yo. ↗
a.little more go.out-if exist-EME-POL
'If we drive a little further, we will find a few *ulkel-yo*.'

좀 더 나가 볼게요. ↘
com te naka-po-lkey-yo. ↘
a.little more go.out-try-EME-POL
'Let me drive a little further *lkey-yo*.'

B. 번거롭지 않으실른지요. ↘
penkelop-ci anh-usi-llunci-yo. ↘
inconvenient-NOM not.be-SH-may-EME-POL
'I am afraid I am causing inconvenience to you *llunci-yo*.'

A. 번거롭다니요, ~ 전혀요. ↘
penkelop-tani-yo?! ~ cenhye-yo. ↘
inconvenient-EME-POL not.at.all-POL
'Inconvenient *tani-yo*?! Not at all!'

B. 그럼 좀 더 나가 보실래요? ↗
kulem com te naka-po-si-llay-yo. ↗
then a.little more go.out-try-SH-EME-POL
'Then, would you drive a little further *llay-yo*?'

그러죠. ↘
kule-ci-yo. ↘
do.so-EME-POL.
'Certainly I will *ci-yo*.'

All the underlined parts in (1) are EMEs in question. None of them are canonical endings that indicate six speech levels (deferential, polite, blunt, familiar, intimate, plain) in four sentence types (declarative, interrogative, imperative, propositive) (e.g. H. Sohn 1999/2001: 269-71).[2] Furthermore, notice that all EMEs appear in sentence-final positions, immediately before the politeness particle *yo*, if there is one; that their sentence types are generally declarative or interrogative but pragmatically ambiguous among statement, question, suggestion, and request; that their meanings are the speaker's modality toward the addressee; that the modal meanings are largely polysemic, context-sensitive, and not easy to precisely define; and that they do not change the truth value of the propositional contents.

Only some approximate meanings can be given to each EME. Thus, the EME *-(n)untey* is somewhat equivalent to English 'well, you know, I think, what do you think?, what shall we do?, but/and ~, . . .' depending on speech contexts. It contains a trailing note, implicitly inviting the addressee's reaction to the speaker's utterance of the propositional content. The EME *–ketun* refers to the speaker's providing a mild justification, a reason, or a clarification for a past or prospective action, event, or state of affairs, equivalent roughly to English 'that's why, you know what, in fact, truly, just, . . .'. The EME *–ulkka* indicates the speaker's mild question or wondering "I wonder . . ., do you by any chance think whether . . .?, shall we . . .?, would you . . .?'. The EME *–lakwu* or *-lako* roughly means 'I casually report that . . ., I am saying that . . ., I assure you that . . .'. The EME *–ulkkel* refers to the speaker's conjecture 'I guess, I think, I am pretty sure' with a rising intonation and the speaker's regret 'I should have . . .' with a falling intonation. The EME *–ulkey* indicates the speaker' willingness or promise to do an action, 'I will, I am willing to, I promise, I assure you that I will . . .'. The EME *–ullunci* refers to the speaker's mild worry, anxiety, or concern about a future or past action, event or state of affairs, 'I am kind of worried/concerned

2 For example, the canonical ending –다 *-ta* denotes both the plain speech level and the declarative sentence type and the canonical ending –세 *–sey* denotes both the familiar speech level and the propositive sentence type, while the canonical ending –습니까 *–supnikka* denotes both the deferential speech level and the interrogative sentence type. On the other hand, the canonical endings –오 *–o* (blunt speech level), -어/아 *-e/a* (intimate speech level), and –어요/아요 *–e.yo/a.yo* (polite speech level) are used to refer to all sentence types, differentiated by intonation, context, and the speaker's intent.

that . . ., I am afraid that . . .'. The EME *–tani* indicates the speaker's denial of what the interlocutor has just said, 'I don't think so, quite the contrary, far from it, not at all, what you said is not true'. The EME *–ullay* refers to the speaker's (in statement) or hearer's (in question) determination or intention to do an action ('I'm willing to . . ., I am going to . . ., I would like to . . ., I intend to . . ., would you like to . . .'). Finally, the EME *–ci* refers to the speaker's suggestion, assurance, belief, or commitment with a falling or rising-falling intonation and the speaker's supposition or suspicion with a rising intonation.

There are a number of questions regarding why EMEs appear so productively in coversation, what their syntactic, semantic, and pragmatic functions are, where they came from and how, what kinds of underlying universal principles there are to explicate all their occurrences and functions, and what kind of grammatical category or paradigm can be established to embrace such EMEs in Korean. The aim of this paper is to address all these questions, with the objective to provide a unified account of the linguistic properties of all Korean EMEs.

The overall descriptive framework on which my proposals and arguments are based is grammaticalization theories that have transpired during the past forty years (e.g. Traugott 1982; Lehmann 1985, 1995; Hopper 1991; Traugott & Heine 1991; Bybee, J.L. & P. Hopper 2002; Traugott, E.C. and R.B. Dasher. 2002; Hopper & Traugott 2003; Davidse, Vandelanotte & Cuyckens 2010; Narrog & Heine 2011). This paper refers to a number of universal concepts, principles, and hypotheses that have been proposed to explicate the genesis of new grammatical forms and categories from existing elements and constructions. One proposal particularly relevant to the present discussion is in regard to (inter)subjectivity and (inter)subjectification, as quoted below:

> One branch of my own work over the twenty-five years since the publication of Traugott (1982) has been to study the semanticization over time of subjectivity, understood as relationship to the speaker and the speaker's beliefs and attitudes, and of intersubjectivity, understood as relationship to the addressee and addressee's face. I have called the diachronic process of semanticization "(inter)subjectification", . . . (Traugott 2010: 29-30)

There are a large number of works by Korean linguists that deal with various aspects of individual EME items. Some representative works are listed in (2).

(2) -(ㄴ)은데(요): 이기동 (1979), 이은경 (1999), Y Park (1999, 2006), 하치근 (2003), 조민하 (2011)
-거든(요): 구현정 (1989), 이해영 (1996), 채영희 (1998), Y Park (1998), 신지연 (2000), 구현정 • 이성하 (2001), M Park & S Sohn (2011)

-다고(요): 방운규 (1995), 유현경 (2002), 김홍범 (1987), 방성원 (2004), S Rhee (2007)
-다니(요), -다면서(요), -단다, -다니까(요): H Sohn (1978), 김홍범(1987), S Sohn (2003), 이금희 (2006)
-더라고(요): H Sohn (1999), Yuen (2003)
-지(요), -(ㄴ)은지(요): 서정수 (1994), H Lee (1999), 허웅 (2000), 하치근 (2006)
-을걸(요): 강현화 (2008), 권영은(2008), 최동주 (2009)
-잖아(요): Kawanishi (1993), Kawanishi & S Sohn (1993), Ju & S Sohn (2011)

Since my main objective is to present a unified account of the genesis of EMEs and linguistic and discourse functions common to all EMEs, discussions on individual items are only illustrative. Readers are referred to the above and other works for detailed studies of individual EME items.

2. Discourse function of EMEs

As observed in (1), all EMEs occur mainly in casual conversational interactions which call for effective sustenance of interpersonal relations. EMEs are instrumental in effectively performing the interactional function, and not the transactional function of language. For this reason, EMEs are predominantly used in the interpersonal mode of communication such as daily interactions, telephone, on-line, and face-to-face conversations, and rarely in the presentational mode of communication such as news reports, lectures, scholarly books and journals, and newspaper articles where interpersonal relations between the speaker/writer and the general public are marginal. In formal letters, which are more or less of the presentational mode, use of EMEs is minimal, as illustrated in the e-mail message in (3), which I received from a professor in Korea when I was in Fukuoka, Japan in May, 2012. Only one EME (underlined) appears, while the deferential canonical ending (bold-faced) is predominant.

(3) 손호민 선생님께,

두 분께서 큐슈에 계신지는 몰랐**습니다**. 저도 몇 일 전에 도쿄에 볼 일이 있어서 잠시 다녀왔**습니다**. 큐슈에서 사모님과 편안하고 즐거운 시간 보내시다가 서울에 무사히 오시길 기원 드**립니다**. 마침 집사람도 6월 중순 경 서울에 잠시 오게 되어 있으니 함께 뵈러 가도록 하겠**습니다**. 집사람도 선생님과 사모님을 서울에서 뵐 수 있게 되었다고 아주 기뻐하고 있**습니다**. 그럼 21일 목요일 저녁 6:00 경 숙소로 모시러 가겠**습니다**. 그런데 서울에는 어느 호텔에 머무실 예정이<u>신</u>

지요? 감사**합니다**.
YKW 올림

'Dear Professor Ho-min Sohn,

I was not aware that you and Mrs. Sohn are in Kyusu SUPNITA. I myself made a short business trip to Tokyo a few days ago SUPNITA. I pray that you and Mrs. Sohn make a safe trip to Seoul after having an enjoyable time in Kyushu PNITA. As it so happened that my wife is scheduled to come back to Seoul for a while in the middle of June, we will visit you in Seoul SUPNITA. My wife was very happy to hear that she could see you two in Seoul SUPNITA. We will pick you up at your hotel on Thursday, the 21st, at 6:00 p.m. SUPNITA. By the way, may I ask which hotel you plan to stay at in Seoul NCIYO?
Thank you PNITA.
Respectfully, YKW'

Notice in (2) that all sentence endings used are the canonical declarative ending in the deferential speech level, except one in the last part of the letter. This exceptional ending is the EME –는지요 *–(n)unciyo* 'I wonder . . ., may I ask . . .', which is used to convey a polite indirect question. This ending is pronounced with only a falling intonation in spoken communication, indicating that it is not a straightforward question which might impair the addressee's negative face (Goffman 1967, Brown and Levinson 1987). Asking for information indirectly using an EME in the polite speech level sounds politer than the direct canonical question ending in the deferential speech level, such as 어느 호텔에 머므실 예정이십니까? *enu hothel ey memu-si-l yeyceng i-si-pnikka?* 'Which hotel would you plan to stay at?' Since the indirect speech act asking for information invites the addressee's answer albeit indirectly, the sentence is regarded as an interpersonal mode of communication. All the other sentences in the letter are essentially presentational in that the writer reports what he feels, felt, thinks, thought, does, did, or will do.

Thus, I propose that the major discourse function of Korean EMEs is to effectively carry on interactional discourse in casual contexts. EMEs mitigate illocutionary force, contributing to politeness and solidarity building to a great extent in casual interaction. In an asymmetrical interaction and/or in formal conversations, as between a company employee and his president, a social superior is relatively free to use EMEs but a lower person must be careful about choosing appropriate EMEs toward his or her superior, as some EMEs connote a high level of casualness and informality.

3. Genesis of EMEs

Contemporary EMEs are rarely found in Middle Korean data. On the other hand, there is ample evidence that they are relatively recent innovations. Then, where did they come from? There are many pieces of morpho-syntactic evidence that all EMEs have diachronically developed from complex sentence constructions. I propose that, essentially, two basic types of evolution are operative: (a) main-clause omission and (b) smain clause compression, the former being more productive in Korean. Let us examine the first type in 3.1 – 3.3 and the second type in 3.4.

3.1 Evidence of diachronic main-clause omission

A large number of EMEs are assumed to have developed from subordinate clauses with the unrecoverable omission of the co-occurring main clauses. One may wonder what kinds of solid evidence there are to claim that EMEs originated from subordinate clause constructions following diachronic main clause omission. I would like to advance the following several pieces of evidence in support of this claim.

First, all the EMEs of the main-clause omission type have their counterparts in subordinate clauses in contemporary Korean. Notice in (4) that the counterparts (bold-faced) in subordinate clauses have meanings similar or related to those of the corresponding EMEs in (1).

(4) a. 비가 오**는데** 갈까요? ↗

pi	*ka*	*o-**nuntey***	*ka-l*	*kka*	*yo?* ↗
rain	NM	come-while	go-PRS	Q	POL

‘Shall we/I go despite the rain?’

b. 비가 안 오**거든** 오세요. ↘

pi	*ka*	*an*	*o-**ketun***	*o-sey-yo.* ↘
rain	NM	not	come-if	come-SH-POL

‘Please come provided that it does not rain.’

c. 비가 **올까** 싶어요. ↘

pi	*ka*	*o-**l-kka***	*siph-eyo.* ↘
rain	NM	come-PRS-whether	think-POL

‘I am afraid it may rain.’

d. 비가 오더**라고** 했어요. ↘

pi	*ka*	*o-te-**la***	***ko***	*hay-ss-eyo.* ↘
rain	NM	come-RT-DC	QT	say-PST-POL

'(I/Somebody) said he/she saw it raining.'

e. 비가 **올걸** 몰랐어요?↗

pi	*ka*	*o-**l***	***ke***	***l***	*moll-ass-eyo?* ↗
rain	NM	come-PRS	fact	AC	not.know-PST-POL

'Didn't you know that it would rain?'

f. 비가 **올지** 누가 알아요. ↘

pi	*ka*	*o-**l-ci***	*nwu*	*ka*	*al-ayo.* ↘
rain	NM	come-PRS-if	who	NM	know-POL

'Who would know whether it will rain?'

g. 비가 온**다(고하)니** 안 가겠어요. ↘

pi	*ka*	*o-n-**ta***	***(ko***	***ha)-ni***	*an*	*ka-keyss-eyo.* ↘
rain	NM	come-IN-DC	QT	say-because	not	go-will-POL

'Because (they) say it is raining, I won't go.'

h. 비가 오**지** 않아요? ↗

pi	*ka*	*o-**ci***	*an*	*h-ayo?* ↗
rain	NM	come-NOM	not	do-POL

'Isn't it raining?'

The coexistence of the identical or similar forms with similar meanings in two different syntactic functions is strong evidence that both derived from the same source (A > B, C) or one diverged from the other, as per Hopper's (1991) principle of "divergence" (A > A, B). The direction in the case of divergence must have been from subordinate elements to EME's as per the principle of unidirectionality in grammaticalization. Subordinate elements generally have referential or textual meanings, whereas EMEs, as sentence endings, have subjectified and intersubjectified meanings that are abstract and expressive, indicating the speaker's modality toward the addressee. It is a generally accepted thesis among grammaticalization scholars that semantic and pragmatic changes are unidirectional from basic, usually concrete, literal and objective meanings to gradually more metaphorically and metonymically extended abstract, subjective meanings. EMEs are typical cases of subjectification and intersubjectification (e.g. Traugott 1982, 2010; Hopper and Traugott 2003; Davidse, Vandelanotte & Cuyckens 2010).

A second piece of evidence is that, while none of the EMEs in question developed prior to the corresponding subordinate-clause elements, there are ample research findings indicating that EMEs appeared later (e.g. 이현희 1982; 고영진 1997; 김태엽 1998, 2000; 구현정 • 이성하 2001; 안주호 2003; 하치근 2003, 2006). This suggests that, due to the unrecoverable omission of main clauses, the ending parts of subordinate clauses were grammaticalized and upgraded to main clause endings as EMEs.

A third piece of evidence that the innovated EMEs have developed from subordinate clause elements is that EMEs and the corresponding subordinate elements share some morpho-syntactic constraints. For example, both the EMEs and subordinate clause elements can take only the polite-level particle 요 *yo*. Note that the particle *yo* can occur after all major constituents, if politeness is intended. No other speech-level endings can come after the EMEs of the main-clause omission type, in the same way as after subordinate clause elements. Observe the examples in (5).

(5) a. 비가 오는데(**요**) 배가 떠날까**요**? ↗

pi	*ka*	*o-nuntey(-**yo**)*	*pay*	*ka*	*ttena-lkka-**yo**?* ↗
rain	NM	come-while-POL	boat	NM	depart-EME-POL

b. *비가 오는**뎁니다** 배가 떠날**깝니까**? ↗

**pi*	*ka*	*o-nuntey(-**p-ni-ta**)*	*pay*	*ka*	*ttena-lkka-**p-ni-kka**?* ↗
rain	NM	come-while-POL	boat	NM	depart-EME-AH-IN-Q

Shared syntactic constraints indicate that EMEs are recent innovations which still retain their original syntactic, semantic, and morphological properties, as per Hopper's (1991) principle of "persistence" in incipient grammaticalization.

One final piece of evidence is that all EMEs of the main clause omission type are used only as an intimate-level ending when they are not followed by the politeness particle *yo*. When they are followed by *yo*, their intimate speech level becomes defunct and, together with *yo*, they function as polite-level endings. This behavior is the same as the canonical intimate ending –어/아 *–e/a*, in that this ending also becomes defunct in terms of speech level before *yo*, becoming no more than a phonological fragment (as the first vowel) of the polite-level ending –어요/아요 *–e.yo/a.yo*. For example, 이 그림 좋아(요) *i kulim coh-**a(-yo)*** 'this picture is good' and 이 그림 좋은데(요) *i kulim coh-**untey(-yo)*** 'I think this picture is good, (I wonder what you think?)' are equivalent in terms of speech levels. Utterances with an intimate level ending is popularly called "half-talk" (반말 *pan mal*) in Korean, in that the utterance is understood as incomplete as to speech levels, as it is neither a deferential (e.g. *-supnita*) or polite (e.g. *-e.yo/*

a.yo) level, nor a plain (e.g. *-ta*) or familiar (e.g. *-ney*) level. The fact that EMEs are incomplete 'half talk' endings suggest that they were originally not sentence-final elements but developed from non-final positions. As an SOV, head-final, honorific language, Korean indexes speech levels in sentence-final positions. But EMEs do not inherently mark a fixed speech level but are contextually determined, suggesting that they diverged from subordinate clause sources. Notice in (6) that B's response only with a subordinate clause is perceived as an intimate level without *yo* and as a polite level with *yo*.

(6) A: 언제 미아를 봤니? ↗
encey Mia lul po-ass-ni
when Mia AC see-PST-Q
'When did you see Mia?'

B: 학교에 가면서(요). ↘
hakkyo ey ka-myense(-yo)
school to go-while-POL
'(I saw her) on the way to school.'

The canonical intimate ending *–e/a* also originated from the conjunctive suffix (often called an infinitive suffix) whose basic function is to connect two predicates, as in 걸**어**가다 *kel-**e** kata* (walk-*e* go) 'go walking' and 잡**아**기다 *cap-**a** mekta* (catch-*a* eat) 'catch and eat'. Like an EME, the canonical intimate ending *-e/a* came into being with the deletion of the second predicate. This fact further supports the thesis that the sources of the EMEs of the main clause omission type were subordinate clauses.

3.2 Grammaticalization processes

In contemporary Korean, main clauses, as well as other major constituents, are extensively omitted in conversation when they are uniquely recoverable from the given discourse contexts or speech situations. For example, observe the dialogue in (7).

(7) A: 일하러 안 가니? ↗
ilha-le an ka-ni? ↗
work-to not go-Q
'Aren't (you) going to work?'

B: 비가 개면요. ↘
pi *ka* *kay-myen* *yo.* ↘
rain NM clear.up-if POL
'(I will) when it stops raining.'

A can easily recover B's omitted main clause content as 가요 *ka-yo*. The main clause omission, which is recoverable from contexts in this way, is a synchronic process. In this case, no grammaticalization is involved. The (B) construction is still perceived as a conjunctive clause, with the unexpressed main clause content understood. Thus, no structural or meaning change has taken place in the conjunctive suffix –면 *–myen* 'if'.

Grammaticalization processes such as structural reanalysis, semantic-pragmatic shift, phonological attrition, and analogical spread are activated when repeated omission of unrecoverable main clauses is conventionalized, leaving no syntactic trace. For example, observe (8).

(8) A: 일하러 안 가니? ↗
ilha-le an ka-ni? ↗
'Aren't you going to work?'

B: 비가 많이 오는데요. ~
pi *ka* *manhi* *o-nuntey-yo.* ~
rain NM much come-EME-POL
'Well, it's raining a lot, so . . .' (I won't go; I may not go; I will go later; how can I go?; what shall I do? . . .)

Notice in (8B) that no main clause is uniquely recoverable. The omitted main clause can have various pragmatic meanings, as illustrated in the parentheses. The speech situation might give some hints as to the exact content of the omitted main clause that the speaker may have intended, but syntactically such a clause cannot be uniquely recoverable due to the opacity. If native speakers intentionally or habitually continue to omit a certain type of main clause in certain local contexts for some reason, then language-internal grammaticalization processes tend to be activated to upgrade the subordinate clause to the status of a main clause. Grammaticalization, including structural reanalysis and semantic-pragmatic shift, takes place in the clause-final position to generate an EME, because a main clause or an independent sentence in Korean requires a sentence ending. As an agglutinative, SOV order, and head-final language, Korean requires utterance-final positions to be the speaker's territory of TAMs (tense-aspect-modality). Grammaticalization in that position involves subjectification and/

or intersubjectification, with the speaker's stance as the core. Let us observe the EME –는데 *–(n)untey* as an example. It was created via the following simplified grammatical processes:

Stage 1: relative clause construction -(ㄴ)은 데에 *–(n) tey ey* (R place in/at/to) 'in/at/to the place where . . .'
Stage 2: conjunctive suffix -(ㄴ)은데 *–(n)untey* [occurs in a subordinate clause] 'while, in the circumstance that . . ., given that . . .'
Stage 3: EME –(ㄴ)은데 *-(n)untey* [occurs in a main clause]

All three stages coexist in contemporary Korean, which indicates that the stage 2 form diverged (or split) from the stage 1 construction, and the stage 3 form diverged from the stage 2 form. This phenomenon is in accord with the principle of morpho-syntactic and semantic unidirectionality (e.g. Hopper & Traugott 2003) and the principle of divergence (Hopper 1991): A > A/B; B > B/C. It is also in accord with Traugott's (1982) proposed formula of semantic change: propositional > textual > expressive.

데 *tey* is a bound place noun requiring a relative clause. This place noun underwent a metonymic extension to mean time or circumstance 'while, as, circumstance' per the principle of unidirectional semantic abstraction or pragmatic inferencing (e.g. place > circumstance/time > quality). Thus, expressions like (9) illustrate where stage 2 (textual meaning) could diverge from stage 1 (referential meaning) through frequent omission of main clauses after *–(n)untey* (cf. Bybee & Hopper 2002 for the frequency principle).

(9) 비 오는 데(에) 가지 마. ↘
pi *o-nun* *tey* *(ey)* *ka-ci* *ma.* ↘
rain come-R place to go-NOM stop.IMP
i. 'Don't go to the place where it rains.'
ii. 'Don't go while/as it is raining.'

Stage 2 developed from stage 1 through (a) loss of word boundary between -(ㄴ)은 and 데, (b) deletion of the place particle 에, (c) decategorization of the relativizer -(ㄴ)은 and the noun 데 to become a conjunctive suffix with the meaning of 'given that, while, in the circumstance that' per the principle of decategorization (Hopper 1991). Stage 3 developed from stage 2, motivated by massive main clause omission. In this stage, the EME coded the speaker's subjectivity and intersubjectivity, with various connotative or pragmatic meanings such as 'I wonder what to do, what shall we do?, what would you like me to do'. Thus, the sentence in stage 3 may be schematically shown in (10).

(10)

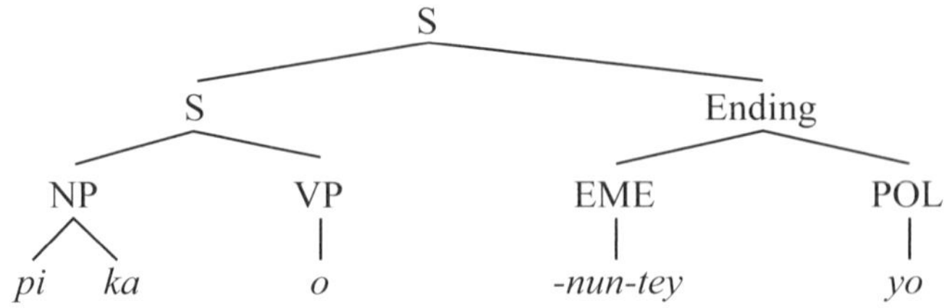

Let us examine another set of EMEs consisting of a canonical sentence-type ending (declarative *-ta, -la,* interrogative *–(nu)nya,* propositive *-ca,* or imperative *-ula*) and the quotative particle (QT) *ko/kwu.* In contemporary Korean, the bare quotative particle *ko* is widely used in two contexts, one in response to an echo-question, as in (10a), and the other as an EME with a sentence type ending, as in (11b).

(11) a. A: 용호가 뭐라고 했어요? ↘

Yongho	*ka*	*mwue-la*	***ko***	*hay-ss-eyo?* ↘
Yongho	NM	what-be.DC	QT	say-PST-POL

'What did Yongho say?'

B: 비가 오더라고요. ↘

pi	*ka*	*o-te-la*	***ko***	*yo.* ↘
rain	NM	come-IN-DC	QT	POL

'(He said) he saw it raining.'

b. A: 하와이 날씨는 어땠어요? ↘

Hawaii	*nalssi*	*nun*	*ettay-ss-eyo?* ↘
Hawaii	weather	TC	be.how-PST-POL

'How was the weather in Hawaii?'

B. 비가 오더라고요. ↘

pi	*ka*	*o-te-**lako-**yo.* ↘
rain	NM	come-QT-EME-POL

'I saw it raining, you know.'

In (11aB), the main clause verb of saying (*hay-ss* 'said') is understood and thus *ko* functions as an indirect quotative particle, whereas in (11bB), no such a uniquely recoverable verb can be posited. Sentences with –더라고 *–te-lako* are frequently used in casual interpersonal discourse to narrate or report the speaker's own personal experience and observation in a casual and polite way.

It is assumed that, due to the repeated main clause omission in *ko* constructions in conversation, the omission became gradually conventionalized, making the main clause unrecoverable and orphaning the quotative particle *ko* in the utterance-final position. Thus, the orphaned *ko* gradually coalesced with the preceding sentence-type ending, as per Lehmann's (1985) principle of "coalescence", to become an EME through structural reanalysis (e.g. changing a word boundary to a morpheme boundary, decategorizing a quotative particle to a modal suffix) and semantic-pragmatic shift (e.g. subjectification and intersubjectification). Thus, while the main clause predicate (e.g. 하- *ha-* 'say') after *–la ko* (DC QT) can take any person, the grammaticalized EME *–lako* has encoded only the speaker as an abstract subject in the sense of 'I REPORT THAT'. Furthermore, due to the frequent use of *-lako* with the preceding retrospective suffix *–te,* the sequence *–te-lako* behaves like an extended EME to refer to the speaker's mild narration or report of his or her own experience or observation. Notice that the innovated EME retains the reportive meaning inherited from the omitted predicate, as per Hopper's (1991) principle of persistence.

Naturally, we have no way of knowing who originated such innovations, where and when. We also do not know exactly what specific subordinate and main clauses were actually involved in initiating the innovations. All we know is that most of them are relatively recent innovations in varying degrees of maturity. Based on the above-mentioned assumptions, I propose the formula (12) to account for the unrecoverable main clause omission that triggers the genesis of EMEs.

(12) [SCx + MCy] → [SCx] > [MCx (-yo)]
Where SC = subordinate clause; MC = main clause

The formula (11) states that a main clause (MC) in a complex sentence construction is synchronically and recoverably omitted in discourse. If main clause omission becomes habitual and conventional after a certain type of subordinate construction, and thus no main clause is synchronically recoverable, the subordinate clause construction involved becomes gradually restructured as a main clause. In this gradual diachronic process that changes a subordinate construction to a main one, various single or complex elements that end the subordinate construction become an EME through grammatical reanalysis and semantic-pragmatic shifts, optionally followed by phonological attrition. Once reanalyzed as a new grammatical morpheme, the generated EME spreads analogically and is suffixed productively to various sentences as endings, as illustrated in (1). The innovated EME may be optionally followed by the politeness particle *–yo* if the addressee deserves the speaker's normative or strategic politeness.

3.3 Subclasses of the main clause omission type

In (1), all but –을게 *–ulkey* and –을래 *–ullay* are EMEs of the main clause omission type. Although all EMEs have similar grammatical and discourse functions in present-day Korean, they have developed from multiple structural sources, as reflected in their morphological structures. Based on the structural features of their source constructions, I propose the following three subclasses of the main clause omission type. Some additional EMEs are introduced in the list as well. Yet, the list is not exhaustive.

(a) Relative-head type: the EMEs that have developed from relative clause constructions consisting of a relativiser and a noun phrase. The head of a noun phrase is usually a bound noun:

- -을지↘ *-ulci* < *-ul ci* (PRS assumed.fact) 'whether one will . . .'
- -(ㄴ)은지↘ *-(n)unci* <*-(n)un ci* (IN assumed.fact) '(I wonder) whether/what/who/where/. . .'
- -(ㄴ)은가↗ *-(n)unka* < *-(n)un ka* (IN whether) '(may I ask) *WH-word* one does/is . . .'
- -을까↗ *-ulkka* < *-ul kka* (PRS whether) '(may I ask) *WH-word* one will . . .'
- -을걸↗ 'I think . . .'; *-ulkel* < *-ul kes ul* (PRS fact AC) 'the fact that will . . .'
- -을걸/을것을↘ *-ulke(su)l* 'I should have . . .' < *-ul kes ul* (PRS fact AC) 'the fact that will . . .'

(b) Conjunctive type: the EMEs that have developed from conjunctive suffixes with semantic shift, usually without formal change:

- -거든~ *-ketun* < *-ketun* 'provided that, if, while, given that, on the condition that . . .'
- -고/구↘ *–ko/kwu* 'by the way, as well, also, . . .' < *-ko/kwu* 'and'
- -나↗ *–na* 'I wonder . . .' < *-na* 'whether, or'
- -으려고↗ *–lyeko* 'would you like to . . .?' < *-lye ha-ko* (intend do-and) 'intending to . . .'
- -을라(고)↘ *–ulla(ko)* 'I am afraid, be careful . . .' < *-lye ha-ko* (will do-and) 'be about to . . .'
- -다니~ *-tani* < *-ta ko ha-ni* (DEC QT say-as) 'as one says that . . .'
- -다면서↗ *–tamyense?* 'I heard ~ is that true?' < *-ta ko ha-myense* (DC QT say-while) 'saying that . . .'
- -다니까↗ *–tanikka* 'I told you that . . .' < *-ta ko ha-nikka* (DC QT say-because) 'because one says that . . .'

–(ㄴ)은데~ *-(n)untey* <-*(n)untey* 'given that' < *-(n)un tey ey* (R place at) 'at/in/to the place where'

(c) Nominalizer type: the EMEs that have developed from a nominalizer:

–지↘ *-ci* < *-ci* (NOM) '(not) that, (not) to' (requires a negative word (*ani* 'not', *mos* 'unable', *ma(l)* 'don't')
–기는↘ *–kinun* 'indeed, . . ., not at all' < *-ki nun* (NOM TC) 'regarding that . . .'

(d) Quotative type: EMEs that have developed from quotative constructions:

–더라고↘ *–te-lako* < *-te-la ko* (-RT-DC QT) '(say) that one saw/experienced that . . .'
–(ㄴ/는) 다고/라고↘ *–(n/nun)tako/lako* 'I assure you' < *-(n/nun)-ta/la ko* (-IN-DC QT) '(say) that . . .'

3.4 Main clause compression

The second basic type of EME genesis is diachronic reanalysis via the syntactic and semantic compression or contraction of a main clause construction (e.g. H Sohn 1978; S Sohn 1996). The EMEs illustrated in (13) belong to this type.

(13) a. Promissive –을게 *-ulkey* 'I promise that . . ., I am willing to . . .'
Intentive –을래 *–ullay* 'I am gonna . . ., I will . . .'

b. Affective reportive –대 *-ta-y* '. . . you know'
Tag question (agreement-seeking) -잖아 *–canh-a* 'isn't it right!, . . . you know'

We can intuitively know that the promissive EME –을게 *–ulkey* is a more grammaticalized form of the "predictive" modal construction –을 거야 *-ul ke-y-a* (PRS fact-be-INT) 'will probably be/do'. Due to the loss of syntactic boundaries and semantic/pragmatic shift toward intersubjectification, the predictive meaning has shifted to the speaker's promise or assurance towards the addressee for the benefit of the latter. The predictive modal suffix itself is a grammaticalized and subjectified form of the originally complex (bi-clausal) construction –을 것이아/것이어 *–ul kes i-a/e* (PRS fact be INT) 'it may be a fact that . . .'. Notice that *–ulkey*, an intersubjectified EME, is an intimate-level ending as it has absorbed the canonical intimate speech level ending –어/아 *–e/a* in the process of grammaticalization. Syntactic and semantic differences between the promissive EME and the predictive suffix are observed in (14).

(14) a. 영수가/내가 갈거야/갈겁니다. ↘
Yengswu/nay ka ka-lke.y-a/ka-lke-p-ni-ta. ↘
Yengswu/I NM go-will.probably-INT/go-will-AH-IN-DC
'Yengswu/I will probably go.'

b. 내가/*영수가 갈게/*갈겝니다. ↘
*nay/*Yengswu ka ka-lkey/*ka-lkey-p-ni-ta.* ↘
I/Yengswu NM go-EME.INT/go-EME-AH-IN-DC
'I promise/will go.'

Notice that in (14a) the subject can be any person and any speech-level ending can occur, but in (14b) the subject must be the speaker (1st person) and only the intimate or polite ending can occur. This indicates that *–ulkey* is intersubjectified as a promissive ending ('I promise to you that') from the subjectified predictive ending ('I predict that'). Promise or assurance can be made only about one's own action or dynamic state. Thus, *-ulkey* requires that the proposition contain an action verb (not stative verb like 알다 *alta* 'know', 모르다 *moluta* 'not know') or a dynamic adjective (e.g. 건강하다 *kenkanghata* 'healthy') but not a static adjective (e.g. 젊다 *celmta* 'young', 기쁘다 *kipputa* 'happy'), as shown in (15).

(15) a. 나는 모를거야 / 건강할거야 / 기쁠거야. ↘
na nun molu-lke.y-a / kekangha-lke.y-a / kipp-ulke.y-a. ↘
I TC not.know-will-INT / be.healty-will-INT/be.happy-will-INT
'I may not know / I will be healthy / I will be happy.'

b. 나는 *모를게 / 건강할게 / *기쁠게 ↘
*na nun *molu-lkey / kekangha-lkey / *kipp-ulkey* ↘
I TC be.healty-will-INT/be.happy-will-INT
'I promise that I will not know / I will be healthy / I will be glad.'

Thus, *-ulkey* inherently contains the following semantic { }, syntactic [ ], and pragmatic < > features: {speaker's promise, assurance}, [+INT], [+1st person subject], [+action verb, +dynamic adjective ___], <benefit to hearer>.

The intentive EME –을래 *-ullay* has developed from the bi-clausal intentive construction –으려고/을려고 *–ul(l)yeko ha-y* (intending do-INT) 'I intend to do, plan to do, think about doing' with the very general *–ko ha* deletion. Compare the EME construction (16b) with its source construction (16a).

(16) a. 영수가/내가 가려/갈려(고) 해. ↘
Yengswu/nay ka ka-l(l)yeko ha-y. ↘
Yengswu/I NM go-intend do-INT
'Yengswu is/I am willing to go.'

b. 내가/*영수가 갈래. ↘
*nay/*Yengswu ka ka-llay.* ↘
I/*Yengswu NM go-EME.INT
'I am gonna go/*Yengswu is gonna go.'

Notice again that unlike its source construction, the EME sentence does not allow any person except the 1st person in statement and the 2nd person in question. In addition to structural compression, the EME is a result of semantic subjectification and pragmatic intersubjectification. One major pragmatic difference between *–ilkey* and *–ullay* is that the former is used when the proposition is uttered majorly for the benefit of the hearer and the latter is used when the proposition is uttered majorly for the benefit of the speaker, expecting the addressee's approval or agreement. In casual conversation among younger generation speakers, the volitive modal suffix *–keyss-* is hardly used, being replaced by the EME *–ullay*. The EME *-ullay* has not absorbed the canonical intimate ending *–e/a* completely. Thus, the plain level *-ulla-nta* and the deferential level *-ulla-pnita* may occur along with the polite *–ullay-yo.*

While the EMEs in (13a) require the speaker (1st person) subject, those in (13b) allow the subject to be of any person. Yet, all of them are results of structural and semantic reduction plus subjectification and intersubjectification. The affective reportive EME –대 *–ta-y* has developed from –다고 해 *-ta ko ha-y* (DC QT say-INT) 'say that . . .' as a result of 고 하 *ko ha* 'say that' deletion. Since the EME has not absorbed the intimate ending, the plain *–ta-nta,* the familiar *-ta-ney,* and the deferential *–ta-pnita* occur, in addition to the intimate/polite –*ta-y(-yo).* This EME indicates the speaker's informing the addressee of the propositional content with a casual and affective stance (cf. H Sohn 1978). Thus, for example, Mia's mother may tell Mia's friend, 우리 미아는 지금 잔단다 *wuli Mia nun ca-ntanta* 'I am sorry but my daughter Mia is sleeping now, (so she cannot play with you)'. This expression does not convey somebody else's report but the speaker's own with a casual and solitarity-laden stance.

The tag-question EME *–canh-a* 'is that right?, you know' has contracted and grammaticalized from the complex negative construction *-ci ani ha-ye* (NOM not-do/be-INT) 'it is not that . . .' through compression (e.g. boundary loss, contraction, and inter-subjectification). It indicates the speaker's seeking an agreement from the addressee (e.g. Kawanishi & S Sohn 1993; Ju & S Sohn 2011). As no canonical ending is incorporated, the EME can occur in all speech levels.

3.5 Common properties

As has been observed thus far, all EMEs, whether they are of the main clause omission type or of the main clause compression type, are results of essentially the same unidirectional grammatical reanalysis and analogical spread, along with unidirectional semantic-pragmaitic shift and optional phonological attrition. Reanalysis includes splitting, boundary reduction or loss, decategorization, and recategorization, among others.

All EMEs have developed in complex sentences, reducing complex sentences to simple sentences for which they serve as endings. I tentatively propose that the grammatical meanings of all EMEs be generalized as in (17).

(17) An EME has complex semantic-pragmatic meanings, composed of (a) the speaker as abstract subject, (b) addressee as abstract (direct or indirect) object, (c) the speaker's subjective and intersubjective modal meanings (functioning as abstract predicate), which have abstracted from the meanings of the original morphemes constituting the ending and omitted elements, (d) casualness and informality, (e) interactive solidarity with reduced illocution, and (f) other contextually induced meanings.

For example, the extended EME *-te-lako* is interpreted as having an abstract semantic-pragmatic meaning like "I CASUALLY AND ON FRIENDLY AND POLITE TERMS INFORM YOU THAT I WITNESSED THAT…" The speaker functions as the abstract subject. The statement meaning comes from the original declarative sentence ending *-la* and the falling intonation. The reportive meaning is abstracted from a typical omitted predicate, that is, a verb of saying. The complement meaning of "THAT" is from the quotative particle *ko*. The meaning of "I OBSERVED" comes from the retrospective suffix *-te*. The casualness, solidarity, and relative politeness in reportive illocution all appear to be due to the omission of an explicit main-clause verb of reporting.[3]

---

3 My analysis of the reinterpreted grammatical meaning is partly in agreement with Bybee's (1988) proposal that the lexical meaning of a morpheme or construction serves as the basis for semantic substance in grammaticalization, and with Sweetser's (1988) proposal that the aspect of meaning which is preserved in grammaticalization is the (metaphorically structured) image-schematic referential structure, as well as with Hopper's (1991) principle of persis-

4. Causes and motivations

We have thus far observed the two interrelated types of grammaticalization involved in the genesis of EMEs: main-clause omission and main-clause compression. As we have observed, all EMEs of both types have developed from a complex construction, changing a multi-clausal construction to a mono-clausal one following similar grammaticalization (reanalysis) processes. Once generated this way, all EMEs can be attached to any sentence for various semantic, pragmatic and strategic purposes, as long as syntactic, semantic, and sociolinguistic constraints are not violated. One question in regard to the main clause omission type is: what has motivated or caused native speakers to frequently or conventionally omit a certain type of main clause even when it was not uniquely recoverable?

Needless to say, the principle of minimum effort in linguistic change underlies the extensive omissions, compressions, and contractions in all parts of Korean complex or simplex sentences in daily conversation. Various major syntactic constituents and units are omitted in conversation whenever they are understood. Thus, Korean is often called a discourse-oriented language. Omitted structure and content are easily recoverable contextually or situationally. Native speakers' frequent synchronic omissions per the principle of minimum effort must have led to structural reanalyses and genesis of EMEs.

As I extensively discussed in H. Sohn (1997), if we assume that minimum effort is the only motivating factor for main clause omission, however, some questions may arise. For one, the economy principle in communication normally applies to the extent that no communicative ambiguity thereby results. Non-recoverable omissions go against this principle. It violates Grice's (1975) Cooperative maxims, especially, that of quantity and manner and Lakoff's (1973) rule of clarity (i.e. "Be clear"). Furthermore, conversation is carried out not only by omitting contextually recoverable elements but also by adding many illocution reducing or illocution strengthening elements, violating the principle of minimum effort. For instance, in addition to the direct speech in (18a), native speakers of Korean use nominalized expressions as in (18b) and clauses equivalent to English 'it seems *or* it appears that', as in (18c) simply out of courtesy or humility.

(18) a. 저 안 가요.↘

ce *an* *ka-yo.*↘

I not go-POL

'I am not going.'

---

tence. See also Hopper and Traugott (2003).

b. 저 안 갈 거예요.↘

ce	an	ka-l	ke	yey-yo.↘
I	not	go-PRS	fact	be-POL

'I am probably not going.'

c. 저 안 갈 것 같아요.↘

ce	an	ka-l	ke	kath-ayo.↘
I	not	go-PRS	fact	same-POL

'It appears that I am not going.'

Finally, extensive daily uses of the innovated EMEs illustrated in (1) are also against the minimum-effort principle, because sentences with EMEs usually are heavier and longer than those with canonical endings.

All this suggests that the economy principle is not sufficient to explicate the phenomena of unrecoverable main-clause omission and that native speakers habitually make purposive omissions as well. I would like to propose that the politeness principle also underlies unrecoverable main-clause omission in Korean. As alluded to in the discussion of the EMEs *–(n)untey* and *-lako*, I would like to propose that unrecoverable main clause omission is also motivated by native speakers' intent to mitigate, dilute, or tone down the illocutionary force contained in main clauses in conversational interaction. We may say that native speakers of Korean flout or violate, for instance, Lakoff's rule of clarity or Grice's Cooperative maxims to express strategic linguistic politeness, in order to avoid coerciveness or imposition toward their interlocutors in face-threatening speech acts. That is, strategic linguistic politeness for smooth interpersonal communication appears to have been one of the main causes for repeated main clause omission, which triggered structure-internal grammaticalization. I will elaborate this proposal in terms of politeness theory in what follows.

It has been known that language has two interrelated functions: (a) a transactional function which purports to establish an optimally efficient transmission of information, and (b) an interactional function which purports to establish and maintain interpersonal relationships. In speech acts, principles such as Grice's (1975) Cooperative maxims (quality, quantity, manner, relevance) and Lakoff's (1973) rule of clarity (i.e. "Be clear") are to be observed in order to maximize the transactional function of language. The interactional function of language, on the other hand, is performed by native speakers via a variety of putatively universal politeness principles and strategies, as well as culture-specific norms and values and language-specific politeness devices. Several insightful proposals have been advanced for universal politeness principles and strategies (Goffman 1967; Lakoff 1973; Leech 1983; Fraser 1980, 1990; Brown and Levinson

1987, Watts, et al. 2005). For example, Lakoff's (1973) rules of politeness consist of (a) Don't impose, (b) Give options, and (c) Make addressee feel good. Fraser (1980, 1990) advances a so-called conversational-contract view. He suggests that politeness operates within the current terms and conditions of the conversational contract entered into by the participants in an interaction in an effort to maintain the interaction conflict-free. Fraser (1980) associates politeness with his notion of mitigation, defining mitigation as a strategy for reducing the force of a speech act whose effects are unwelcome to the addressee.

Goffman (1967) and Brown and Levinson (1987) have advanced the face-saving view. In particular, Brown and Levinson maintain that linguistic strategies are means of satisfying both communicative and face-oriented ends, and describe linguistic politeness in terms of face maintenance. They establish five levels of linguistic strategies for politeness, as (a) direct strategy, (b) positive politeness strategies, (c) negative politeness strategies, (d) off-record strategies, and (e) no speech act. These five levels of strategies are to be employed in that order when the risk of face loss increases. I am particularly interested in their negative politeness and off-record strategies here. While Brown and Levinson's positive politeness strategies essentially boost the addressee's positive face or self-image, their negative politeness strategies are oriented toward partially satisfying the addressee's negative face, that is, his basic desire to maintain his freedom of action, his freedom from imposition, his territory, and his self-determination. Brown and Levinson propose ten negative politeness strategies, some of which are: Be conventionally indirect; Give deference; Question, hedge; and Nominalize. Brown and Levinson's off-record communicative acts are those which the speaker performs when he wishes to avoid responsibility for his acts, leaving it up to the addressee to decide how to interpret them. Some of the fifteen off-record strategies they propose are: Give hints; Give association clues; Presuppose; Understate; Be ironic; Use metaphors; Use rhetorical questions; Be ambiguous; and Be incomplete, use ellipsis. Thus, linguistic politeness is, in one way or another, closely related to indirect speech acts, unless the speech acts are performed for the interest of the addressee or for great urgency. For example, Lakoff's rules of politeness, Don't impose and Give options, may best be observed when the speech acts are performed indirectly, mitigating the speaker's assertive illocution in statement, question, proposal, and command. As we have examined, Brown and Levinson's negative politeness strategies and off-record strategies focus essentially on indirect speech acts of various types.[4]

4 In fact, the mitigating strategy is employed when the speech act in question is some sort of a face-threatening act. Reinforcement of illocutionary force may occasionally be used when a speech act is in the interest of the addressee. In actual speech acts, however, mitigation is much more common than reinforcement, since an absolute majority of our conversational interac-

With the above theoretical background, let us observe the Korean data in (1) again. Obviously, the most distinct pragmatic function of a main clause is to perform the speaker's speech act with appropriate illocutionary force by means of the propositional content and the typical sentence-type enders in which six different speech levels are incorporated. If the main clause is declarative, the speaker asserts the propositional content. If it is interrogative, the speaker requests the addressee to respond verbally. If it is imperative or propositive, the speaker asks the addressee to respond with some kind of action. In all these speech acts, the speaker imposes his views on the addressee to varying degrees. If the speech acts are not particularly in the interest of the addressee, they frequently constitute face-threatening acts toward the addressee.

With the main clause content unexpressed, therefore, the speaker may be able to avoid or weaken such imposition or responsibility for his acts. Since the sentence ending particle *yo* (polite) or zero (intimate) is present with appropriate intonation contours, relevant speech acts have been performed, but the lack of the expressed propositional content significantly weakens the illocutionary force, giving the addressee extensive options. Indeed, the innovated grammatical categories function as illocution-diluting devices, with their still surviving lexical meanings. The enders *-nun-tey*, *-nun-ka*, and *–nun-ci* and *–(u)l-ke-l* all contain a bound noun, which functions as a hedge that mitigates illocutionary force. One of Brown and Levinson's negative politeness strategies is Nominalize. Similarly, the quotative particle *ko* and the conjunctive suffixes *–na, -ketun,* and *-nikka* function as hedges, even though they are reanalyzed as sentence endings. This is because they still carry the bleached version of the original semantic content as a quotative particle or a conjunctive suffix.

As already alluded to, the original semantic contents of the omitted main clauses are superimposed with great dilution on the newly developed grammatical categories. Thus, the weakened meanings, together with the hedging functions of the innovated categories, have become conventionalized as devices of politeness in Korean. Due to the omission of a main clause, some connotation of informality is also attached to the innovated meanings. For example, compare the three sentences in (19), one a complex sentence (a), one a direct simplex sentence (b), and one a sentence with an innovated EME (c).

(19) a. 비가 오는데 어떻게 하시겠어요? ↘

pi	*ka*	*o-nun-tey*	*ettehkey*	*ha-si-keyss-eyo?* ↘
rain	NM	come-given.that	how	do-SH-will-POL

'It's raining; what are you going to do?'

tions are face-threatening acts. Main clause deletion is by and large associated with mitigation, and therefore, this paper is concerned mainly with mitigation.

b. 비가 와요.↘
pi *ka* *w-ayo.*↘
rain NM come-POL
'It's raining.'

c. 비가 오는데요. ~
pi ka o-nun tey yo. ~
'It's raining ...'

Native speakers would easily judge that the innovated form (19c) is politer and sounds somewhat more informal than the other two expressions in interaction. Similarly, compare the two sentences in (20). Notice that they have the same truth value, but are different in connotative meanings.

(20) a. 비가 오더라고요.↘
pi *ka* *o-te-la* *ko* *yo.*↘
'It was raining, you know.'

b. 비가 옵디다.↘
pi *ka* *o-p-ti-ta.*↘
rain NM come-AH-RT-DC
'I saw it raining.'

Again, native speakers would agree that (20a) has softer illocution and is more casual than its counterpart in (20b), which is more blunt and assertive despite the use of the deferential ender *-p-ti-ta*. Brown and Levinson's two off-record strategies are Be ambiguous and Be incomplete, use ellipsis. These are precisely what Koreans have done to attain politeness in their language use. This has led me to propose that strategic politeness is one of the two main causes (along with the economy principle) for native speakers to omit unrecoverable main clauses.

5. Grammatical category

No doubt, all the sentences with an innovated EME are now perceived and used as complete simple sentences by contemporary Koreans. Then, what grammatical category can we assign to the innovated EMEs? Many Korean dictionaries and grammar books term EMEs as "exclamatory" sentence endings.

Since all EMEs occur in sentence-final position and indicate the speaker's stance in discourse, it is obvious that they are a kind of modal elements. They do not seem to be epistemic or deontic modals, as the basic semantic-pragmatic function is to indicate neither the speaker's degree of commitment to the truth of the propositional content, nor the speaker's ability, permission, or obligation in regard to the propositional content. The primary function of EMEs is not in the speaker-proposition perspective but in the speaker-addressee perspective, indicating the speaker's modal stance toward the addressee in conversational interaction. Let us examine (20) for illustration.

(20) 비가 왔겠는데요. ~
pi *ka* *w-ass-keyss-nuntey-yo.* ~
rain NM come-PST-may-EME-POL
'It may have rained, (what shall we do?)'

In this utterance, 비가 오 *pi ka o* is the proposition, -았 *–ass* is a tense/aspect (past/perfective) suffix indicating the anteriority of the propositional content to the utterance time, –겠 *-keyss* is an epistemic modal indicating the speaker's degree of certainty about the proposition, and –는데 *–nuntey* is an EME that indicates the speaker's stance toward the addressee. Notice that an EME occurs after an epistemic or deontic modal in a sentence.[5]

In view of the distinct morpho-syntactic, semantico-pragmatic, discourse properties that all EMEs have, I propose to assign a separate grammatical category or paradigm. In morpho-syntax, they occupy a TAM position between the slot of epistemic/deontic modal suffixes and the slot of sentence-type endings. In semantic-pragmatics, they express the speaker's intersubjectivity. In discourse, they are used as casual, interactive, interpersonal, and solidarity-building mode of communication. In view of these characteristic linguistic properties, I would like to propose, tentative as it may be, that this EME category be termed "interpersonal modal endings".

6. Conclusion

In this paper, I have endeavored to give an integrated account of the genesis and morpho-syntactic and discourse functions of EMEs in Korean. Specifically, I have argued or proposed that in Korean (a) a number of modal sentence endings (termed emergent modal endings or EMEs) have recently been innovated as a new grammatical paradigm, to which new members are constantly being

5 EMEs share the same morphological slot and syntactic behavior with the "exclamatory" endings like –네(요) *–ney(-yo)* and -군(요) *–kwun(-yo)*. I assume that the productive genesis of new EMEs was motivated by the pre-existence of such a limited functional set, per the principle of paradigmatization (Lehmann 1985).

added; (b) all EMEs have an interactional (not transactional) discourse function and are used for a casual interpersonal mode of communication; (c) all these EMEs have developed from a wide variety of complex constructions following universal grammaticalization principles and processes; (d) EMEs have developed via one of the two developmental patterns: main-clause omission and main-clause compression; (e) all EMEs denote subjectivity and intersubjectivity in their coded and/or pragmatic meanings of the speaker's modality; (f) the economy principle and the politeness principle are assumed to be two major factors that motivate unrecoverable main clause omissions; and (g) the new innovated paradigm be termed "interpersonal modal endings", as their modal functions are interpersonal in the speaker-addressee perspective.

Finally, one may wonder what has caused the recent proliferation of EMEs in Korean. I propose that the typological properties of Korean and recent radical change in Korean social structure are jointly responsible for the massive genesis of EMEs in relatively recent times.

First of all, typologically, Korean is an SOV order language with rigid head-final syntax. It is also a language of typical agglutinative morphology with a rich set of grammatical morphemes (particles and suffixes) attached to content words such as nouns, verbs, and adjectives to indicate their grammatical functions and relations in sentence. Another typological feature of Korean is its strong discourse-orientation. One manifestation of the discourse-orientation is the free omission of syntactic constituents, including main clauses, whenever they are understood from discourse contexts. Anaphoric reference is frequently made in the discourse level than in the sentence level. The above typological features of Korean are partly responsible for the genesis of the emerging paradigm of a productive set of interpersonal EMEs.

Secondly, since the end of the World War II in 1945, Korea has undergone progressively rapid transformation in all walks of life. First, Korean society has transformed from the former rigidly closed and hierarchical feudal society to an open, democratic, globalizing, capitalistic society. Second, mass media has developed to an unprecedented extent. Third, the opportunities of daily interpersonal communication have enormously increased. Fourth, Koreans' cultural values have shifted from the traditional rigid hierarchism toward egalitarianism to a great extent, with their strong traditional collectivism retained. Thus, Koreans' overall pattern of interpersonal communication has shifted from the earlier power-based to the casual, solidarity-based one. In a hierarchical feudal society, social interactions were generally static, with interpersonal communication largely normative. The contemporary Korean society, on the other hand, is based on free market economy and thus calls for constant communicative interactions. Interpersonal communication has become much more strategic for smooth day-to-day social interaction. Strategic communication requires omission of illocution-laden expressions via contraction and deletion of forms and constructions, which have contributed to the genesis of EMEs in contemporary Korean.

REFERENCES: Chapter 14

강현화. 2008.「'-을걸'의 특성과 후회표현의 양상」.『이중언어학』38:43-68.

구현정. 1989.『현대국어의 조건월 연구』. 건국대학교 박사학위 논문.

구현정•이성하. 2001.「조건 표지에서 문장종결 표지로의 문법화」.『담화와 인지』8.1: 1-19.

권영은. 2008.『한국어교육에서의 후회표현 연구』. 한국외국어대학교 석사학위논문.

김태엽. 1998.「국어 비종결어미의 종격어미화에 대하여」.『언어학』22. 한국언어학회.

김태엽. 2000.「국어종결어미화의 문법화 양상」.『어문연구』33.

김흥범. 1987.「'-다면서', '-다고', '-다니'의 구조와 의미」.『말』12: 83-87. 연세대학교 언어연구교육원.

방성원. 2004.「한국어 문법화 형태의 교육 방안: '-다고'관련 형태의 문법 항목 선정과 배열을 중심으로」.『한국어교육』15.1: 93-110.

방운규. 1995.「간접인용마디의 '고 하-'구성에 대하여」.『한말연구』한말연구모임.

서정수. 1994.『국어문법』서울: 뿌리 깊은 나무.

신지연. 2000.「텍스트언어학의 이론과 응용: 어말어미 '-거든-'에 대한 연구」.『텍스트엉어학』8. 한국텍스트언어학회.

안주호. 2003.「인용문과 인용표지의 문법화에 대한 연구」.『담화와 인지』10.1.

유현경. 2002.「어미 '-다고'의 의미와 용법」.『배달말』31: 101-4. 배달말학회.

이기동. 1979.「연결어미 '-는데-'의 화용상의 기능」.『인문과학』40/41 합집. 연세대학교 국학연구소.

이은경. 1999.「구어체 택스트에서의 한국어 연결어미의 기능」.『국어학』34. 국어학회.

이해영. 1996.『현대 한국어의 활용어미의 의미와 부담줄이기의 상관성』. 이화여자대학교 박사학위논문.

채영희. 1998.「담화에 쓰이는 '-거든'의 화용적 기능」.『한국어 의미학』3:159-177.

이금희. 2006.「인용문 형식의 문법화: 문법화 과정과 문법화 정도에 대하여」.『국어학』48. 국어학회.

이현희. 1982.「국어종결어미의 발달에 대한 관견」.『국어학』11.

조민하. 2011.「'-는데-'의 종결기능과 억양의 역할」.『우리어문연구』4. 우리어문학회.

최동주. 2009.「종결어미 '-ㄹ걸'의 기능과 문법적 특성」.『국어학』54: 226-50.

하치근. 2003.「'데' 짜임월의 문법화 과정」.『한글』216: 97-121

하치근. 2006.「'지'짜임월의 문법화 현상 연구」.『우리말 연구』18: 27-55.

허웅. 2000.『20세기 우리말의 형태론』. 서울: 샘문화사.

Brown, P. and S. Levinson. 1987. *Politeness*. Cambridge, England: University Press.

Bybee, J.L. 1988. Semantic substance vs. contrast in the development of grammatical meaning. *Proceedings of the 14th Annual Meeting of the Berkeley Linguistics Society*, 247–64.

Bybee, J.L. and P. Hopper (eds.). 2002. *Frequency and the Emergence of Linguistic Structure.*

Amsterdam: Benjamins.

Davidse, K., L. Vandelanotte, and H. Cuyckens (eds.). 2010. *Subjectification. Intersubjectification and Grammaticalization.* Berlin/New York: De Gruyter Mouton.

Fraser, B. 1980. Conversational mitigation. *Journal of Pragmatics,* 4: 341–50.

Fraser, B. 1990. Perspectives on politeness. *Journal of Pragmatics,* 14: 219–36.

Goffman, E. 1967. *Interaction Ritual: Essays on Face-to-Face Behavior*. New York: Anchor Books.

Grice, H.P. 1975. Logic and conversation. In Cole, P. and J. Morgan (eds.), *Syntax and Semantics* 3: Speech Acts. New York: Academic Press. Pp. 41-58.

Hopper, P.J. 1991. On some principles of grammaticalization. In Traugott, E.C. and B. Heine (eds.), *Approaches to Grammaticalization,* I and II. Amsterdam: Benjamins. Pp. 17–36.

Hopper, P.J. and Traugott, E. C. 2003. *Grammaticalization (2nd Edition).* Cambridge, England: University Press.

Ju, Hee and Sung-Ock Sohn. 2011. Sequential context of *–canh-a(yo): hearers' perspective. Japanese/Korean Linguistics* 20: 1-15.

Kawanishi, Y. 1933. An analysis of non-challengeable modals: Korean *–canha(yo)* and Japanese *-janai*. *Japanese/Korean Linguistics* 3: 95-111.

Kawanishi, Y. and Sung-Ock Sohn. 1993. The Grammaticalization of Korean Negation: A Semantic-Pragmatic Analysis of *-canh-*. *Harvard Studies in Korean Linguistics V*: 552–61.

Lakoff, R. 1973. The logic of politeness: Or, minding your p's and q's. *Proceedings of the 9th Regional Meeting of the Chicago Linguistic Society*, 292–305.

Lee, Hyo Sang. 1999. A discourse-pragmatic analysis of the committal *–ci* in Korean: A synthetic approach to the form-meaning relation. *Journal of Pragmatics* 31: 243–75.

Leech, G.N. 1983. *Principles of Pragmatics*. London/New York: Longman.

Lehmann, C. 1985. Grammaticalization: Synchronic variation and diachronic change. *Lingual e Stile* 20(3): 303–18.

Lehmann, C. 1995. *Thoughts on Grammaticalization.* Munchen and Newcastle: LINCOM EUROPA.

Lehmann, W.P. and Y. Malkiel (eds.). 1982. *Perspectives on Historical Linguistics.* Amsterdam: Benjamins.

Narrog, H. and B. Heine. 2011. *The Oxford Handbook of Grammaticalization.* Oxford, England: University Press.

Park, Mee-Jeong and Sung-Ock Sohn. 2002. Discourse, Grammaticalization, & Intonation: An analysis of *–ketun* in Korean. *Japanese/Korean Linguistics* 10: 306-19.

Park, Yong Yae. 1998. A discourse analysis of the Korean connective *-ketun* in conversation. *Crossroods of Language, Interaction, and Culture* 1: 71-89.

Park, Yong Yae. 1999. The Korean connective *–nŭnde* in conversational discourse. *Journal of Pragmatics* 31: 191-218.

Park, Yong Yae. 2006. Politeness in conversation in Korean: The use of *–nŭnde.* In Sohn, Homin (2006, pp.164-73).

Rhee, S. 2007. Subjectification of Reported Speech in Grammaticalization and Lexicalization. *Harvard Studies in Korean Linguistics* 12: 590-603.

Sohn, Ho-min. 1978. Contractions as a mechanism of polysemic breeding: A device for speaker involvement in Korean. In Kim, Chin-W. (ed.), *Papers in Korean Linguistics,* 197-205. Columbia: Hornbeam Press.

Sohn, Ho-min. 1997. Politeness as a cause of linguistic change. Invited paper presented at the 2007 colloquium of the Institute for Advanced Study of La Trobe University, Melbourne, Australia on November 19, 2007. ms. Also in this volume.

Sohn, Ho-min. 1999/2001. *The Korean Language.* Cambridge: Cambridge University Press.

Sohn, Ho-min. 1999. Functional Transfer in Sentence-final Positions in Korean and Japanese. *Language Information* 3: 145–85. Seoul: Korea University Press.

Sohn, Ho-min (ed.). 2006. *Korean Language in Culture and Society.* Honolulu: University of Hawaii Press.

Sohn, Sung-Ock. 1996. Contraction and restructuring in modern Korean: A case of incipient grammaticalization. *Chicago Linguistics Society.* 30: 391-403.

Sohn, Sung-Ock. 2003. On the emergence of intersubjectivity: An analysis of the sentence-final *nikka* in Korean. *Japanese/Korean Linguistics* 12: 52-63.

Sweetser, E.E. 1988. Grammaticalization and semantic bleaching. *Proceedings of the 14th Annual Meeting of the Berkeley Linguistics Society*, 389–405.

Traugott, E.C. 1982. From propositional to textual and expressive meanings: Some semantic-pragmatic aspects of grammaticalization. In Lehmann, W.P. and Y. Malkiel (1982, 245–71).

Traugott, E.C. 2010. (Inter)subjectivity and (inter)subjectification: A reassessment. In Davidse, K., et al. (2010, pp. 29-71).

Traugott, E.C. and R.B. Dasher. 2002. *Regularity in Semantic Change.* Cambridge, England: University Press.

Traugott, E.C. and B. Heine (eds.). 1991. *Approaches to Grammaticalization I & II.* Amsterdam: Benjamins.

Watts, R.J., S. Ide, and K. Ehlich (eds.). 2005. *Politeness in Language.* Berlin: Mouton de Gruyter.

Yuen, S.A. 2001. *Socio-pragmatic functions of Korean interactive sentence enders from politeness perspective.* Ph.D. dissertation. University of Hawaii at Manoa.

15 Evolution of Addressee Honorifics in Korean*

1. Introduction[1]

Recent linguistic theories on grammaticalization (e.g. Traugott and Heine 1991; Hopper and Traugott 1993) have opened a new horizon for more systematic analysis of the phenomena of grammaticalization in Korean. Putatively universal principles and mechanisms that have been found to be applicable across different languages may serve as useful means to account, in a principled manner, for many hitherto mystified or controversial developments of grammatical elements (especially affixes and particles) in Korean.

This paper is aimed to analyze, within the framework of such putatively universal principles and mechanisms, the morpho-syntactic, semantic, and phonological evolution of the addressee honorific inflectional suffix *-(su)p* in relation to the immediately following mood suffixes such as indicative *-ni*, retrospective *-ti*, and requestive *-si*. These addressee and mood suffixes appear in contemporary sentence enders such as the following.

(1)	declarative indicative:	*-(su)p-ni-ta*
	interrogative indicative:	*-(su)p-ni-kka*
	declarative retrospective:	*-(su)p-ti-ta*
	interrogative retrospective:	*-(su)p-ti-kka*
	propositive:	*-(su)p-si-ta*
	imperative:	*-(su)p-si-o*

Long-standing controversies have centered around (a) the meaning of the morpheme *-sôp* (> current *-(su)p*) in the 15th century and its subsequent semantic shift, (b) the function of the former putatively addressee honorific (AH) suf-

* This is reprinted from Lee, S.O. and D.S. Park (eds.), *Perspectives on Korea,* 480–90. Sydney: Wild Peony, Ltd. (1998).

1 This paper was presented at the 3rd Pacific and Asia Conference on Korean Studies. The University of Sydney. Sydney. Australia. July 1–4, 1996.

fix *-(ng)i*, and (c) the relation between *-sôp* and its later variants with the current blunt sentence ender *-so/-o* (e.g. Ogura 1938; Kim 1960, 1962; An 1961, 1982, 1992; Lee 1962; Huh 1972, 1975, 1984; Im 1985; Martin 1996). The issue that has attracted the most heated arguments among scholars is the first half of the first issue, that is, over the meaning of the suffix *-sóp* in Middle Korean, especially in the 15th century. The present paper concerns the first issue, focusing on the dynamic evolution of the suffix from its source verb.

Based on the literature of the 15th century and earlier, Huh (1972) assumes that the contemporary addressee honorific suffix *-(su)p* evolved from the verb *sólp* 'tell, inform (a senior)' which was widely used as an independent verb in the 15th century and earlier, side by side with the use of the same form as an object (or non-subject) honorific suffix. I will argue in this paper that five evolutionary stages (or clusters) are involved in the morpho-semantic development of *-(su)p* from its source verb *sólp*. The approximate periods given in brackets are based partly on Huh's descriptions and partly on speculation.

(2) a. Stage I.

sólp was used only as a ditransitive main verb, in the sense that "SUBJECT tells/informs respectable OBJECT"; No syntactic restriction occurred. [until early Old Korean].

b. Stage II.

An auxiliary verb *sólp* was split (diverged) from the main verb *sólp,* in the sense that "SUBJECT shows respect/humility to OBJECT in doing..."; Occurs only after another "main" predicate. [during Old Korean period]

c. Stage III.

Evolution of the auxiliary verb into the object honorific suffix *-só(l)p*, in the sense that:

(i) "SUBJECT/SPEAKER shows respect/humility to OBJECT"
(ii) "SPEAKER shows respect/humility to OBJECT";

Occurs in both embedded and finitive predicates, usually in the morphological slot before the subject honorific suffix *-(ó)si.* [during Old or Early Middle Korean period until the 16th century]

d. Stage IV.

-sóp as an addressee honorific suffix, co-existing with the original addressee honorific suffix *-(ng)i,* in the sense that "SPEAKER shows respect/humility to ADDRESSEE"; Occurs in both finitive and nonfinitive predicates, in the morphological slot after the subject honorific as it does now. [during Early Modern Korean period--from around the 17th century]

e. Stage V.

-(su)p as the only AH suffix, in the sense that "SPEAKER shows respect/humility to ADDRESSEE"; Occurs only in finitive predicates. [during Modern and Contemporary Korean period]

This overview is further elaborated in what follows.

2. Structural and Formal Evolution of *-(su)p*

Observing the coexistence of the verb *sólp* 'tell, inform (a respectable person)' and the identically spelled object-honorific "suffix" *-sólp* in the *hankul* and *Itwu* literature of the 15th century and earlier, Huh (1972: 53, 57-58) claims that the suffix *-sôlp* developed from the verb *sólp*. I support Huh's claim as undoubtedly valid from the following universal theoretical points of view.

First, the claim is in accord with the universal thesis that grammatical elements prototypically develop from full words or complex constructions. Meillet (1912), a pioneer in the field, viewed grammaticalization as the evolution of grammatical forms out of earlier ordinary lexical forms. Thus, it is entirely natural that the suffix *-sólp* had the main verb *sólp* as its historical source.

Second, authors on grammaticalization have revealed that only a very limited set of lexical items function as sources for grammaticalization (e.g. Traugott 1982; Bybee and Pagliuca 1985; Traugott and Heine 1991; Hopper 1991; Heine, et al. 1991). According to these theorists, source concepts for grammaticalization refer to some of the most elementary human experiences, such as concrete objects, processes, behaviors, locations or immediate environment of man. With regard to processes and behaviors, source concepts refer to some of the most basic human activities, like 'do/make', 'take/hold', 'say', 'finish', 'go', 'come', 'leave', 'arrive', 'be/exist', 'be at', 'sit', 'stand', 'lie (down)', and 'stay/live'. Thus, as a basic human activity, the 'saying' verb *sôlp* most qualified as a source (input) for the derivation of the suffix (output).

Third, as extensively discussed in Heine, et al. (1991a) and Traugott and König (1991), grammaticalization is essentially a unidirectional process of semantic abstraction, metaphorical, metonymic or otherwise. Thus, it is natural and semantically justified that concrete activity such as speaking to a respectable person in a deferential manner can be abstracted as a grammatical marker of respect in the course of grammaticalization.

Finally, the formal identity between the input and output at the initial stage of grammaticalization is widely attested to across languages. For example, the same English form *be going to* was split into the original progressive meaning of "be going to someone or some place" and the grammaticalized modal auxiliary meaning of purpose or intention. The phonological reduction to *be gonna* is a later development.

Stage II is still a hypothetical one, pending empirical evidence. Many languages have shown, however, that grammaticalization is a gradual, step-by-step process without any radical jumps (cf. Lichtenberk 1991; Heine, et al. 1991a). This may be called the principle of gradualness. In Korean also, inflectional suffixes such as the past tense suffix *-ess* is derived from the existential phrase *V-e isi* and the modal *-keyss* from the past periphrastic causative phrase *V-key hay-ess* (Sohn 1995). Notice that in these cases, the phrase *-e isi* and the phrase *-key hay-ess* are auxiliary constructions occurring after their respective main verbs. Furthermore, Korean auxiliary verbs like *cwuta* 'give the benefit of, do/be for', *hata* 'shows the sign of', *pelita* 'finish up', and *pota* 'try' are derived from their main verbs through semantic abstraction and syntactic dependency. These auxiliary verbs have not become affixes yet, except perhaps in such constructions as *-canha* 'surely, indeed' (< *ci ani ha?* 'isn't it the case?') and *-na pota* 'it appears to' which are suffix-like (Sohn, 1996). It is reasonable therefore to postulate Stage II with the abstract meaning "SHOWS RESPECT TO SOMEONE in doing..." given to the hypothetical modal auxiliary verb.

The evolution of the auxiliary into the suffix is assumed to have taken place before the Middle Korean literature became available. Or, the case might be that scholars have not been able to locate the evidence of Stage II in the literature, because, first, the morphological position of the hypothetical auxiliary verb and that of the suffix would have been the same, i.e. right after the cooccurring main verb; second, the two forms would have been identical; and third, the meanings of the two would have been quite similar.

Stage III has been abundantly attested to in the literature of Middle Korean. The auxiliary verb *sólp* had already developed into the inflectional suffix in the 15th century literature, as shown in many works. For example, Huh (1972) presents the allomorphic alternations as follows.

(3) a. 15th c. allomorphs of *-sóp* (Huh, ibid.: 30, 58)

	before consonant	before vowel
after k, p, (ph), s, (h):	*sóp*	*sób*
after t (c, ch, th):	*cóp*	*cób*
after vowel, n, m, (l):	*zóp*	*zób*

b. later developments (Huh, ibid.: 62-63)

sóp > sap, sup, saop
sób > sóo > sao
cóp > cap, caop
cób > cóo >cao
zóp > óp > ap, op, p, up, uap, uop
zób > zóo > óo, oo > o, io

This stage may be subdivided into (i) and (ii) in view of the degree of speaker involvement which will be discussed under the section of semantic-functional shift. As mentioned earlier, the major issue with regard to this stage which has been addressed by many linguists is how to determine the meaning of the suffix as used in the 15th century. This issue will be taken up in a later section.

One morphological characteristic of the suffix at this stage is that it occurred before the subject honorific suffix *-ósi* (> *-usi*) as illustrated from the 15th century literature by Huh (1972).

(4) *et-cóp-no-ngi-ta* [Worin 2:69] (Huh, ibid.: 29)
top-sóp-koce [Sangwonsa] (Huh, ibid.: 32)
kilu-zób-ósi-ni-ngi-ta [Worin 10:19] (Huh, ibid.: 34)
mut-cób-ósi-te-ni [Worin 21:9] (Huh, ibid.:4 8)
nas-sób-ósi-ni-ngi-sko [Sokpo 11:24] (Huh, ibid.: 49)

The appearance of the suffix *-sóp* before the subject honorific suffix implies that it still retained its vestige as a verb stem which occurs before a subject honorific suffix then and now.

Stage IV is also amply attested to in the literature. Beginning around the 17th century, this suffix took the morphological slot after the subject honorific as it does today. At the same time, it denoted speaker's respect, deference, or humility toward addressee as it does today. Together with the older addressee honorific suffix *-ngi*, it functioned as an additional addressee honorific suffix. This is well illustrated by Huh (ibid.: 67–75) as follows.

(5) a. *musaha-ni-ngi-ta*
wenha-no-ngi-ta
munanha-si-te-ngi-ta

b. *cyoyonghi swi-óp-so*
unca lól nip-sóo-la

c. *neki-óp-ni-ngi-ta*
kiskehó-óp-ni-ngi-ta

While the suffix *-ngi* did not occur in embedded clauses, *-sóp* occurred in both finitive and nonfinitive positions, as in the 15th c. and in contemporary writings. Huh (ibid.) indicates that when both *-sóp* and *-ngi* were used, the highest degree of deference was shown. Huh further observes that the addressee honorific suffix *-ngi* began to lose the nasal phoneme *ng* from the 16th century.

(6) *nyemnyeha-nó-i-ta*
mek-sóp-nó-i-ta
kuli hó-óp-ssa-i-ta

This honorific usage of *-sóp* and *-i* still holds in deferential letters and religious practices.

(7) a. *ka-op-na-i-ta.* 'I humbly say that I am going.'
b. *ka-op-na-i-kka?* 'I humbly ask if you are going.'
c. *cec-uop-ko* 'I humbly say that it gets wet, and'

Notice in (7c) that only the newly developed addressee honorific suffix may occur in an embedded clause.

Stage V is a contemporary one in which the old addressee honorific *-(ng)i* disappeared from spoken Korean and the new addressee honorific suffix *-sóp* diverged into two phonologically conditioned allomorphs only in finitive enders: *-sup* (after a consonant) and *-p* (after a vowel). This new suffix is used only in finitive enders. The embedded *-sóp* which does not show up in spoken Korean did not undergo the same allomorphic alternation.

The diachronic processes of the grammaticalization involved in the five stages may be schematized as follows.

(8) a. *sólp (main) > saloy (main) > archaic*
b. *sólp (main) > sólp (auxiliary) > -só(l)p (suffix) > -(su)p*

Notice that, as Huh also points out, the source verb *sólp* independently evolved to *saloy*, which is now an archaic verb with the same meaning.

(8) illustrates an essential universal principle that a grammatical form diverges or splits from the original form and co-exists with the latter for a considerable period of time (cf. Lichtenberk 1991; Hopper 1991). Hopper (ibid.: 22) terms this phenomenon the principle of divergence which states "When a lexical form undergoes grammaticalization to a clitic or affix, the original lexical form may remain as an autonomous element and undergo the same changes as ordinary lexical items." Thus, the main verb *sôlp* developed independently to *saloy*, while the diverged auxiliary verb *sólp* evolved, also independently, into the current addressee honorific suffix.

(8) also supports the thesis that grammatical forms may also arise out of other grammatical forms, advancing usually from a less grammatical to a more grammatical status (Kurylowicz 1965; Lehmann 1985; Heine and Reh 1984).

Furthermore, (8) demonstrates the current thesis that mature grammaticalization is frequently accompanied by phonological attrition or reduction: *sólp* > *-sóp* with many allomorphs > *-(su)p*.

3. Functional and Semantic-pragmatic Evolution

As for the semantic-functional shift, I will attempt to account for the gap between the source or input concept of a junior's telling or informing a respectable senior and the output concept of speaker's deference toward addressee, by postulating several intermediate stages of development.

First, in view of the gradualness principle of grammaticalization and semantic abstraction (e.g. Lichtenberk 1991; Heine, at al. 1991a), one can easily assume the presence of an active stage when "tell a respectful person" (as a full verb) was diverged to "show respect to a person in doing..." (as an auxiliary verb). Subsequently, the auxiliary verbal meaning must have abstracted to the meaning of subject referent's deference, first, to the indirect object referent, and then, to direct object referent. The stage (Stage III) of subject's deference to object is attested to by the fossilized indirect object honorific *yeccwu-p* 'inform, ask' and direct object honorific *poy-op* 'see (a senior)'. The current direct object form *(lul) poy-op* must have derived from the indirect object *(eykey) po-i-op* 'show oneself to (a senior)' through minor grammaticalization.

(9) a. subject "tells" a respectful object (main verb: *sólp*)

b. subject "shows" respect to indirect object (auxiliary verb: *sólp*)

c. subject's respect to indirect/direct object (suffix: *-só(l)p*)

I argue that at the stage of grammaticalization into a suffix (Stage III), speaker must have begun to become a part of the meaning of the suffix, first as a pragmatic or conversational meaning, and later as a conventionalized and denotative meaning. I base this argument not only on the principle of subjectification proposed in such works as Traugott and Heine (1991), but also on my own earlier analysis of Korean (Sohn 1978). That is, grammaticalization is a unidirectional process of subjectification toward the speaker-involvement. As grammaticalization becomes mature, speaker gets involved as part of the meaning of the developed grammatical element. Earlier, I (Sohn ibid.) illustrated speaker involvement with such examples as *-ul kes i-eyo* > *-ul kkey-yo* 'I promise' and *-n ta-ko hanta* 'they say . . .' > *-ntanta* 'I assume/say that . . .' Thus, once the verb became grammaticalized as an inflectional suffix, speaker began to get involved in the order of (i) and (ii) under Stage III in (2) in view of the gradualness principle (e.g. Lichtenberk 1991; Heine, at al. 1991).

Thus in this Stage, as Huh (1972: 95) describes, the suffix in (i) was used when three conditions were met: (a) subject's action was directed toward the object ("non-subject" in Huh's claim), (b) subject was lower than the object, and (c) speaker intended to verbally honorify the object. It may be assumed that this speaker involvement was reinforced in a later stage as indicated in the sub-stage (ii).

In view of the iconicity principle (cf. Haiman 1983, 1985; Givon 1990) and the mechanisms of reanalysis and analogical spread, the semantico-functional shift from (9a) through (9c) must have caused syntactic reanalysis from a full sentence to auxiliary construction to a verbal inflectional morpheme. (9c) must have resulted in something similar to (10).

(10) SUBJECT OBJECT Verbal Stem-*só(l)p-si-nó-ngi-ta*
OH-SH-IN-AH-DC

Now, we are yet to account for the disappearance of the OH meaning from *-só(l)p* and its replacement with the AH (addressee honorific) meaning despite the existence of a separate addressee honorific suffix *-(ng)i*.

There seem to be several forces which "conspired" to push the meaning of OH out of the newly developed suffix *-sóp* and replace it with the meaning of AH. First, as Huh (1972) also points out, when the referent of OBJECT is a respectable addressee, *-sóp* necessarily shows respect to addressee, thus obtaining an addressee honorific sense pragmatically (i.e. conversationally). Second, a distinct unidirectional semantic shift as grammaticalization becomes mature is subjectification or speaker involvement as stated above. This is attested to universally by many languages, including Korean (Sohn 1978), and is particularly the case with inflectional suffixes. Third, syntactically and pragmatically, object is much less important in terms of deference than addressee in interactive communication. Obviously, addressee honorifics is the most significant of all honorific expressions in Korean in social interactions. This strong sociolinguistic pressure must have been instrumental in the replacement of the OH meaning with the AH meaning. Furthermore, development of the productive benefactive honorific auxiliary *tulita* (from 'give') and the honorific case particle *kkey* for object honorification must have obliterated suffixal object honorification. All these and other factors must have made speaker's deference toward object an unstable stage and replace it with speaker's deference to addressee in the grammaticalization cline.

According to the regular formula of semantic shift, A > A,B > B (Heine, et al. 1991b: 166), OH and AH must have co-existed for a while before AH took over the suffix completely. Morphologically, the new suffix *-sóp* moved from the pre-SH position toward the end of the suffixal slots. Also, as is common in grammaticalization, significant phonological attrition occurred as dictated by the principle of iconicity. Since the new suffix took over the addressee honorific, the old addressee honorific suffix *-(ng)i* became weakened phonologically and semantically. It merged with the preceding mood suffixes, with the deletion of the initial consonant *ng* in *-ngi* and the final vowel in *-nó/-te/-só*, resulting in *-ni/-ti/-si*. Now, due to the principle of iconicity, these one-syllable portmanteau morphemes have lost the addressee honorific meaning to a great extent, taking on only the mood meanings. The following shows the three stages of development.

(11) a. SUBJECT OBJECT Verbal Stem-*sóp-nó/te/só-ngi-ta*
OH/AH-IN/RT/RQ-AH-DC

b. SUBJECT OBJECT Verbal Stem-*sóp-nó/te/sa-ngi-ta*
AH-IN/RT/RQ-AH-DC

c. SUBJECT OBJECT Verbal Stem-*(su)p-ni/ti/si-ta*
AH-IN/RT/RQ-DC

All the foregoing discussion essentially supports the most fundamental principle of grammaticalization: the principle of unidirectionality. All structural changes, semantic shifts and phonological attritions are toward one direction, with no reversals: full verb > auxiliary > suffix; subjectification cline; and morpho-phonological reduction.

4. Controversies over the Interpretation of the Middle Korean -*sóp*

An (1992:89) summarizes the four distinct sets of views in the interpretation of what he calls Middle Korean "Humilitive" Suffix -*sóp* as follows, supports his earlier view again:

(12) a. speaker's humility toward addressee (Ogura 1938; Kim 1962)
b. speaker's deference toward non-subject referent (Huh 1954, 1975)
c. lower subject referent's relation to higher non-subject referent (Jun 1958)
d. combination of b and c (An 1961; Huh 1962=1972)

Since all of the above interpretations are based on empirical data, I simply assume that they are valid in different respects. Still one unanswered question is what made the authors so divergent in their views. They may have looked at different stages (or clusters) of evolution which frequently co-exist in a grammaticalization cline. If so, the order of semantic shifts would be (12c) > (12d) > (12b) > (12a). At the initial stages when the main verb *sólp* meant 'tell higher indirect object referent' and the auxiliary verb *sólp* meant 'show deference to indirect object referent', the speaker may have simply reported the fact objectively with the least evaluative judgement. If this situation or interpretation sustained at the initial stage when the auxiliary verb began to function as a suffix, (12c) would have resulted. However, due to the principle of speaker involvement in affixal grammaticalization, the next stage should have been (12d). Then, in order to reach the contemporary stage where the suffix denotes speaker's deference toward addressee, the intermediate stage must have been (12b) where subject/speaker's relation to object (or non-subject) referent was replaced primarily by speaker's relation to object referent. The last stage (since around the 17th century) is where the speaker-object perspective was replaced by the speaker-addressee perspective. Thus the following subjectification (speaker involvement) stages can be assumed. Note that object is both direct and indirect.

(13) a. subject-object perspective (12c)

b. subject/speaker-object perspective (12d)

c. speaker-object perspective (12b)

d. speaker-addressee perspective (12a)

As mentioned earlier, a typical structure of grammaticalization allows a prolonged co-existence at the initial stage of source forms/meanings and diverged forms/meanings (A > A,B > B). Such may have been the case with the suffix -*sóp* until it became fixed as an addressee-honorific suffix.

The following diagram shows the grammaticalization processes involved in the evolution of the contemporary addressee honorific -*(su)p*.

(14)

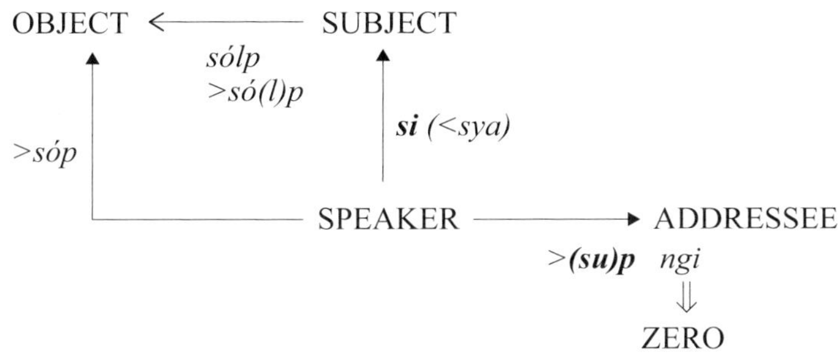

REFERENCES: Chapter 15

An, Pyong-hi. 1961. Cwuchey kyem.yang-pep uy cepmisa '-sôp' ey tayha.ye. *Cintan Hakpo* (Seoul) 22: 103–66.

An, Pyong-hi. 1982. Cwungsey kwuk.e uy kyem.yang-pep yenkwu ey tayhan panseng. *Kwukehak* 11: 1–24.

An, Pyong-hi. 1992. *Kwuk.esa Yenkwu*. Seoul: Munhak-kwa Ciseng-sa.

Bybee, J.L. and W. Pagliuca. 1985. Cross Linguistic Comparison and the Development of Grammatical Meaning. In Fisiak, J. (1985)

Fisiak, J. (ed.). 1985. *Historical Semantics and Historical Word Formation*. Berlin: De Gruyter.

Givon, T. 1990. *Syntax: A Functional-Typological Introduction*, Vol. 2. Amsterdam: John Benjamins.

Haiman, J. 1983. Iconic and Economic Motivation. *Language* 59(4): 781–819.

Haiman, J. (ed.). 1985. *Iconicity in Syntax*. Amsterdam: John Benjamins.

Heine, B., U. Claudi, and F. Hünnemeyer. 1991a. *Grammaticalization: A Conceptual Framework*. Chicago: University of Chicago Press.

Heine, B., U. Claudi, and F. Hünnemeyer. 1991b. From Cognition to Grammar—Evidence from African Languages. In Traugott and Heine (1991).

Heine, B., and M. Reh. 1984. *Grammaticalization and Reanalysis in African Languages*. Hamburg: Helmut Buske.

Hopper, P.J. 1991. On Some Principles of Grammaticalization. In Traugott and Heine (1991).

Hopper, P.J. and E.C. Traugott. 1993. *Grammaticalization*. Cambridge: University Press.

Huh, Woong. 1954. Contaypep-sa. *Sengkyun Hakpo* 1.

Huh, Woong. 1961(=1972). *Cwungsey Kwuke Yenkwu*. Seoul: Cengum-sa.

Huh, Woong. 1975. *Wuli Yeys Malpon*. Seoul: Saym Munhwa-sa.

Huh, Woong. 1984. *Kwukehak*. Seoul: Saym Munhwa-sa.

Im, Hong-bin. 1985. Hyentay uy {-sap-} kwa yeysa nophim uy "-o" ey tayhaye. In To, Suhi & Chin-W. Kim (eds.), *Papers in Korean Linguistics Commemorating the Eightieth Birthday of Profession Hyonggi Kim*. Taejon: Changhak-sa.

Jun, Jaegwan. 1958. *sóp* ttawi kyem.yangsa sanko. *Kyengpuk tayhakkyo nonmuncip* 2.

Kim Hyong Kyu. 1962. Kyengyangsa muncey uy caylon. *Han-Geul* (Seoul) 129.

Ko, Young-geun. 1989. *Kwuke Hyengthaylon Yenkwu*. Seoul: Seoul National University Press.

Kurylowicz, J. 1965. The Evolution of Grammatical Categories. *Esquisses Linguistiques* 2:38–54.

Lee, Sung Nyong. 1962. Kyem.yangpep yenkwu. *Asey.a Yenkwu* 5.2.

Lehmann, C. 1985. Grammaticalization: Synchronic Variation and Diachronic Change. *Lingua e Stile* 20(3): 303–18.

Lehmann, W.P. and Y. Malkiel (eds.). 1982. *Perspectives in Historical Linguistics*. Amsterdam: John Benjamins.

Lichtenberk, F. 1991. On the Gradualness of Grammaticalization. In Traugott and Heine (1991).

Martin, S.E. 1996. The Middle Korean Marker of Politeness *-ngi*. Festschrift fot Professor Kimoon Lee, 1011–22. Seoul: Sin.gu Munhwa-sa.

Meillet, A. 1912. L'évolution des formes grammaticales. *Scientia* 12.

Ogura, Simpei. 1938. *Joosengo ni okeru keyyoo-hoo, sonkei-hoo no jodoosi*. Tokyo: Doyoo Bungo.

Sohn, Ho-min. 1978. Contraction as a mechanism of polysemic breeding: A device for speaker involvement in Korean. In Kim, Chin-W. (ed.), *Papers in Korean Linguistics* (Columbia: Hornbeam Press), 197–205.

Sohn, Ho-min. 1996. Reanalysis in Korean Complex Predicate Constructions: Causative Derivation. *Japanese/Korean Linguistics* 5: 37–64.

Traugott, E.C. 1982. From Propositional to Textual and Expressive Meanings: Some Semantic-Pragmatic Aspects of Grammaticalization. In Lehmann and Makiel (1982).

Traugott, E.C. and B. Heine (eds.). 1991. *Approaches to Grammaticalization I & II*. Amsterdam: John Benjamins.

Traugott, E.C. and E. König. 1991. The semantics-pragmatics of grammaticalization revisited. In Traugott, E. and B. Heine (1991).

Part III

SOCIOLINGUISTIC AND PRAGMATIC ISSUES

16 Korean in Culture and Society: An Introduction*

1. General remarks

A widely accepted thesis is that language and communication represent and reflect the culture and society of native speakers; hence a popular metaphor is that language is a mirror of culture and society.[1] For instance, Sapir (1921, 1961) indicates that language, as a social behavior, can be seen as a way to describe and represent human experience and understand the world; that is, as a way to reflect the underlying cultural patterns.[2] The interrelationship among language, culture, and society is vivid in the structure and function of discourse, because no discourse can be meaningfully conducted without language material, cultural background, and social context.

In regard to language and culture, it is frequently claimed by anthropological linguists that language not only reflects culture but also shapes culture to a certain degree. This concept of mutual influence is known as linguistic relativity. For instance, Whorf (1956) holds that grammatical and lexical categories are a key to understanding the basis of human behavior, since these categories divide and then organize nature into concepts in our minds, and ascribe significances as we do. This view, widely known as the Whorfian hypothesis (of linguistic relativity), claims that language not only reflects culture but also considerably colors or shapes cognitive culture, including speakers' thought patterns. A corollary is that different degrees of linguistic difference are associated with different degrees of cultural difference.

---

* This chapter is a reprint of chapter 1 (Introduction) of Sohn, Ho-min (ed.), *The Korean Language in Culture and Society* (University of Hawaii Press 2006).

1 The relations among language, culture, and society are expressed variously as "language in culture and society", "language in relation to culture and society", "language in social and cultural context", "language as a cultural manifestation of a society", and "the cultural and social nature of language".

2 For more discussions on this issue, see Hymes (1974); Chaika (1982); Fasold (1991); Blount (1995); Shaul and Furbee (1998); Hinkel (1999); Foley (1999), Trudgill (2000), and Hadley (2001), among many other works.

In regard to language and society, Hymes (1974) and other sociolinguists emphasize the importance of the social functions of language and the close relation between language and social context, because social interaction is carried out through language.[3] Hymes argues that language has both referential and social meaning, the latter including social and contextual factors such as the relationship between the participants in terms of role, power (e.g. age, kinship, status, gender) and solidarity (e.g. intimacy-distance), speech settings or scenes, the purpose of interaction, and so on. For instance, forms and uses of address terms are almost totally directed by such social and contextual factors, the patterns of which differ considerably from one cultural setting to another. Also, people say the same thing in different ways, as the ways of speaking reflect different social functions (e.g. "Who's calling?" vs. "May I ask who's calling?"; "I'm sorry" vs. "I apologize"). A person prefers "I apologize" in a formal setting but usually does not say it when talking to a friend or family member. While social contexts, norms, and conventions mandate the appropriate uses of language in a society, the way people talk also influences or colors social contexts to a certain extent. For instance, contexts can be manipulated when speakers use slang, in-group terms, swear words, lower or higher speech levels, or yell or scold.

By examining a language system and its communicative use, we can discover the socio-cultural nature of that language. Socio-cultural nature includes not only lexical and sentential meanings but also native speakers' underlying values, attitudes, behavioral patterns, ways of thinking, and the patterns of the social structure.

What then is language? As a self-contained system, language, whether spoken or written, has two major sides: the linguistic system and its use. The linguistic system of a language includes sound patterns; a lexicon consisting of idioms, words, stems, roots and affixes; word structure; phrase and sentence structure; semantic, pragmatic and discourse patterns; and the writing system (in societies that have graphic means to represent speech). The use of a language refers to communication by means of the linguistic system. When people use language, they do more than just convey information, knowledge, thoughts, and feelings. At the same time, people use language in subtle ways to define and/or maintain their relationship to the interlocutor, to identify themselves as part of a social group, and to establish the kind of speech event they are in (Fasold 1991: 1). That is, language is used for establishment, maintenance, and enhancement of human relationships. Also, as knowledge and a tool for thought, language may be used for problem solving or in formulating new concepts (Shaul and

3 Other sociolinguistic works include Chaika (1982); Fasold (1991); Blount (1995); McKay and Hornberger (1996); Coulmas (1997); and Trudgill (2000).

Furbee 1998: 42–3). These functions of language are well expressed in Sapir's (1921) views that language has referential function (what is said), expressive function (how it is said), and socialization function (a unifying function among special interest groups and a rapport function at social gatherings).

Next, what is culture? Different anthropologists offer different definitions, and no precise common denominator can be found. Brooks (1975) classifies culture into two major types: "Olympian culture" or "culture MLA" (meaning the great **m**usic, **l**iterature, and **a**rt achieved by the people of a society) on the one hand and "Hearthstone culture" or "culture BBV" (meaning the **b**eliefs, **b**ehavior, and **v**alues of the people of a society). Brooks' Olympian culture was often called "Big-C" (formal) and his Hearthstone culture "little-c" (daily life) by foreign language professionals in the last few decades. The "Big C" culture included the formal institutions (social, political, and economic), the great figures of history, and those products of literature, fine arts, and the sciences that were traditionally considered elite culture. The "little c" culture included those aspects of daily living studied by the sociologist and the anthropologist: housing, clothing, food, tools, transportation, and all the patterns of behavior that members of the culture regard as necessary and appropriate.

Seelye (1994: 23) defines culture broadly as embracing "all aspects of human life, from folktales to carved whales", encompassing everything that people learn to do. This involves Brooks' both Olympian and hearthstone culture, the patterns of everyday life, the "do's" and "don'ts" of personal behavior, and all the points of interaction between the individual and the society.[4] In this broad definition of culture, language, as learned behavior, may be regarded as a part of culture. However, many linguists, ethnolinguists, sociolinguists, and foreign language specialists view culture in a narrower sense and deal with language as a self-contained entity more or less distinct from other types of culture.

National Standards (1996: 43–6) defines culture in terms of three components: philosophical perspectives, behavioral practices, and products of a society (i.e. the 3 P's). Philosophical perspectives refer to the traditional and contemporary values, norms, beliefs, assumptions, cultural meanings, etc. held by the people of a society, all of which combine to form the cultural group's "worldview". Behavioral practices, defined as "patterns of social interactions" and viewed as having derived from philosophical perspectives, refer to patterns of behavior accepted by a society. In short, they represent the knowledge of "what to do, when, and where". The products include all kinds of tangible

4 From this perspective, Korean culture is everything Koreans have learned, including the Korean lifestyle. Due to this popular concept of culture, we frequently hear expressions such as *kyothong munhwa* 'traffic culture', *uncen munhwa* 'driving culture', *umsik munhwa* 'food culture', *umcwu munhwa* 'drinking culture', and so on.

and intangible cultural items. Examples of tangible products are books, paintings, cathedrals, chopsticks, toys, clothing, dwellings, foods, crafts, and tools, while examples of intangible products are oral tales, music, dances, dramas, games, rites, sacred rituals, and systems of education. Whatever the form of the product, its presence within the culture is required or justified by the underlying *perspectives* of that culture and the cultural *practices* that involve the use of that *product*. The interrelations of the three components of culture are schematized as follows.

(1)

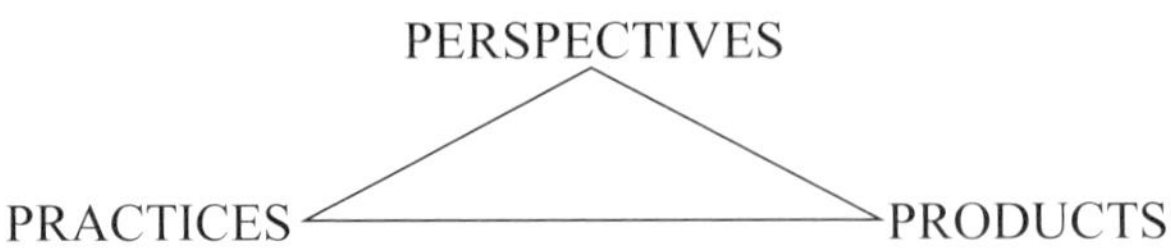

The intimate connection between language and culture derives from the fact that language is the primary vehicle for expressing cultural perspectives as well as products and for participating in social practices and interactions, and that all aspects of culture including all walks of life are inextricably woven into the language of those who live in the culture.[5]

Lastly, what is society? Society is defined in dictionaries as a community, nation, or broad grouping of people with common traditions, institutions, and collective activities and interests. Shaul and Furbee (ibid.: 7, 17) define a society as the actual grouping or array of humans that has its own language and its own sets of art, music, ideology, values, beliefs, social norms of conduct, technologies and so on which we usually call the culture of that society. This appears to mean that a society is simply a community with its own language and culture.

Nostrand (1978) subclassifies society into smaller units as various organized institutions: familial, religious, economic-occupational, political, judicial, educational, intellectual-aesthetic, recreational, the mass media, age or gender groups, ethnic, religious and other minorities, etc. In addition, society may further be viewed from a micro perspective in terms of various concrete social contexts in which human interactions take place, such as a classroom setting, a church service, a weather forecast, a dinner reception, a club meeting, an infor-

5 For instance, members of Korean and Japanese cultures are status-conscious (a perspective) in terms of a hierarchical scale based on age, social status, education, or similar variables. In these cultures, the exchange of business cards (a product) that provides key information is a helpful *practice*. Because these cards facilitate social interaction and are treated with respect, one should not scribble someone else's name or telephone number on the business card (taboo *practice*). The information on the card also directly affects the adequate nonverbal behavior (practice) of those involved in the communicative interaction, as well as the choice of proper linguistic forms that indicate status.

mal interaction between a teacher and a student or between a senior and a junior in a school setting, between a husband and a wife at home, a shop owner and a customer, and between a supervisor and his subordinates in a company. These micro social contexts are significantly related to and interact with language uses, especially in terms of various social factors such as age, social status, rank, gender, kinship, solidarity-distance dimension, and degrees of imposition. Thus, a society consists of various institutions, social contexts, and social factors, as well as one or more languages and cultures.

Language, culture, and society are inseparably interwoven, in that the existence of each is conditioned by the existence of the others. Through its multi-faceted structure and a wide variety of communicative uses, language, both spoken and written, represents, reflects, and frequently even shapes or organizes cultural perspectives, practices and products on the one hand and social activities, patterns, systems and institutions on the other. Thus, for example, it is through language that the native speakers' cultural values and related behaviors are formulated and expressed; and it is through language that social relationships with others are practiced or negotiated and social identities constructed.[6]

2. Evolution of the Korean language in relation to culture and society

Korea has maintained a unique dynamic trio of language, culture, and society for thousands of years. Just as Korean culture and society have not developed monolithically without any outside influence, neither has the language. Language has always interacted with culture and society, both reflecting and influencing the latter. During their long history, Koreans have been in constant contact with the people of other countries, notably China, Japan, and the United States. These contacts have had tremendous impact on the process of molding the culture and society of Korea. As a result, the Korean language, with its allegedly Altaic linguistic skeleton (grammatical structure, sound patterns, and basic vocabulary), has borrowed (either from sheer necessity or from prestige motivation), absorbed, and nativized a large number of words, expressions, and other linguistic features that are associated with imported socio-cultural items, concepts, patterns, and systems. Korean culture and society are reflected most

6 In parallel to the term ethnography or anthropology, which is the description of cultures, and the term sociology, which is the description of societies, we have ethnolinguistics or anthropological linguistics to refer to the study of the systematic relations between language and cultural phenomena and sociolinguistics to refer to the study of the systematic relations between language and social groups and social contexts. In particular, the study of the appropriate use of language in actual socio-cultural, as well as linguistic, contexts according to such factors as politeness, gender, and age is called the ethnography of speaking or communication (e.g. Labov 1973; Hymes 1974; Saville-Troike 1982; Fasold 1991; Shaul and Furbee 1998).

productively and distinctly in the vocabulary, but also in the linguistic structure and contextual use of the language. The following discussion will be limited to overviewing the Korean vocabulary, illustrating metaphorical expressions, and briefly touching on communication patterns. For other linguistic and socio-cultural features, see the relevant chapters throughout this volume.

2.1 Vocabulary

Currently, the Korean vocabulary consists of approximately 30% native, 65% Sino-Korean (Chinese character based; hereafter SK), and 5% loan words. The inherited culture and society of Korea are most distinctively reflected in the native stock of the vocabulary. Native words refer to concepts essential to the maintenance of basic human life and indicative of the time-honored culture of traditional Korea. Thus, not only body parts, natural objects, flora and fauna, core kinship terms, personal pronouns, low-level numerals, times of the day, seasons, basic actions of all sorts, physical and psychological states, culinary actions, and items relating to essential food, clothing, and shelter but also terms for agriculture and fishery, honorific expressions, ideophones or mimeses, and grammatical relations are all symbolized by native words, although many of these coexist with synonymous or similar SK words as doublets. For instance, Korea has been agricultural, and native vocabulary retains many diversified terms related to agriculture. Thus, rice, a Korean staple food, is represented by many native words: *mo* 'rice seedling', *pye/nalak* 'rice plant, unhusked rice', *ssal* 'husked rice', *ssalaki* 'broken bits of husked rice', *pap* 'cooked rice', *nwi* 'unhusked rice mixed with husked rice', *olpye* 'early ripening rice plant or its unhusked rice', *ipssal* 'white husked rice', *ch'ap-ssal* 'glutinous husked rice', *meypssal* 'nonglutinous husked rice', *swungnywung* 'scorched-rice tea', *ttek* 'rice cake', and *yes* 'rice candy'.

Kinship terms of the native stock are limited (SK words are predominant as will be seen in chapter 9). Native kinship terms cover two generations up and one generation down, as well as ego's siblings, as in *apeci* 'father', *emeni* 'mother', *halapeci* 'grandfather', *halmeni* 'grandmother', *acessi* 'uncle', *acwu-meni* 'aunt', *oppa, olapeni* 'older brother (of a female)', *nwuna* 'older sister (of a male)', *enni* 'older sister (of a female)', *awu* 'younger sibling (of the same sex)', *nwui* 'sister', *atul* 'son', *ttal* 'daughter', *chokha* 'nephew, niece', *sawi* 'son-in-law', and *myenuli* 'daughter-in-law'.

A noteworthy class of native actions is reflected in the verbs of 'wearing' and 'carrying' which are differentiated depending on what parts of the body are involved. These include *chata* 'wear (a watch, a sword, a decoration)', *chita* 'carry an inanimate object on the back', *epta* 'carry an animate object on the back', *ita* 'carry on the head', *ipta* 'wear (a dress)', *twuluta* 'drape around (a shawl)', *kelchita* 'throw on', *kkita* 'wear (gloves, a ring, glasses)', *mayta* 'wear (a tie)', *meyta* 'carry on the shoulder', *sinta* 'wear (footwear)', *ssuta* 'wear (headgear, an umbrella, glasses)', and *talta* 'wear (a decoration, a nametag)'.[7]

The native stock is characterized by the proliferation of several thousand sound symbolic or ideophonic words. Examples are *phatak* vs. *petek* 'flapping, flopping, splashing', *panccak* vs. *penccek* 'glittering', and *callang* vs. *challang* vs. *ccallang* 'jingling', *nolahta* vs. *nwulehta* 'be yellow', *kosohata* vs. *kwuswuhata* 'taste or smell like sesame or rice tea', and *tongkulhata* vs. *twungkulehta* 'be round'. As observed in these examples, connotational differences in sound symbolism are reflected in both vowels and consonants. In view of their providing the feelings of vividness, expressiveness, and vitality, they are widely employed for their effect in literary works of all genres, as well as in daily communication.

The most extensive contribution to the maturation of the Korean vocabulary came from some two thousand years (beginning as early as the first century B.C.) of contact with the Chinese language (a non-Altaic language), culture, and society, especially the written Chinese through which traditional Chinese culture and civilization were propagated into Korea.[8] China had long been the center of East Asian civilization before the nineteenth century when Western cultures began to penetrate East Asia. Many written Chinese words flooded into Korea, enriching the Korean vocabulary, especially during the periods of the Three Kingdoms (57 B.C.–935 A.D.), Kolye (918 A.D.–1392 A.D.), and Cosen (1392 A.D.–1910 A.D.). Thus, the Chinese influence on the Korean language, as well as on traditional Korean culture and society, is great indeed.

Koreans and the Japanese are considered (though not uncontroversially) to have descended from the same Altaic ancestors, and thus Korean and Japanese are the closest Altaic languages, sharing a great many genetic and typological features. For instance, the basic Subject-Object-Verb order is shared and some three hundred basic vocabulary items are cognates (e.g. K *pyel* vs. J *hosi* 'star'; K *sem* vs. J *sima* 'island'; K *kom* vs. J *kuma* 'bear'; K *tal* vs. J *tsuki* 'moon'). Furthermore, through close contact with the Japanese people, especially during the thirty-five years of Japanese colonization of Korea until the end of the

7 A somewhat similar distinction is made in Japanese.

8 Although the Chinese influence ceased over a century ago, the Chinese characters, due to their ideographic and monosyllabic nature, have been used extensively for the coinage of thousands of new words in Korea and Japan as well as in China, to express constantly emerging new concepts and products. In fact, the Chinese script has long been an integral part of the writing systems of Koreans, and was the only system before the creation of Hankul by King Seycong in 1446.

World War Two in 1945, Korean language, culture, and society have undergone considerable influence from Japan, and vice versa. The most distinct Japanese influence on the Korean language in modern times is the all-out importation of thousands of Sino-Japanese (SJ) words that the Japanese created by translating all kinds of Western words and other modern concepts using Chinese characters. SJ words are pronounced either in sound-based reading (e.g. *gak-ko2* 'school'; *an-nai* 'guidance'; *gen-kin* 'cash') or in meaning-based reading (*iri-guchi* 'entrance'; *ko-uri* 'retail'), but they are borrowed into Korean only in sound-based reading (*hak-kyo* 'school'; *an-nay* 'guidance'; *hyen-kum* 'cash'; *ip-kwu* 'entrance'; *so-may* 'retail'). In general, only SJ words lacking SK counterparts have been imported. For instance, SJ *hon* 'book', *te-gami* 'letter', *ten-ki* 'weather', and *tomo-dachi* 'friend' were not borrowed into Korean because there exist corresponding SK *chayk, phyen-ci, il-ki*, and *chin-kwu*, respectively.

Up until 1945 when Korea was liberated from thirty-five years of Japanese colonization, loan words from Europe and America were introduced into Korean exclusively through Japanese. Only since 1945 has direct importation from English been prevalent, due to both need-based and prestige-based motivation. A large number of English words have been introduced together with American socio-cultural concepts, products, and institutions. Many existing loan words from other languages, as well as many SK words, have been replaced by English loans. As a result, English appears to comprise over 90% of some 20,000 loan words currently used in Korean. New loan words are constantly imported from English on a daily basis due to global communication in the current Internet era. In fact, most borrowings after 1945, especially in South Korea, are words from English, which range over all aspects of life including clothing, food and drink, automobiles, fashion, advertisements, sports, arts, social activities, politics, and economy, as well as in all areas of science and technology. Random examples are *aisu-khulim* 'ice-cream', *allipai* 'alibi', *hinthu* 'hint', *kolphu* 'golf', *kulwup* 'group', *khakteyil* 'cocktail', *khalla* 'collar', *khalloli* 'calorie', *khaseys* 'cassette', *khatheykoli* 'category', *khaymphesu* 'campus', *khemphyuthe* 'computer', *khephi* 'coffee', *khuleytis khatu* 'credit card', *nyusu* 'news', *phathi* 'party', *pica* 'visa', *picyen* 'vision', *pesu* 'bus', *puliphing* 'briefing', *liphothu* 'report', *seymina* 'seminar', *sepisu* 'service', *seyil* 'sale', *syophing* 'shopping', and *s(y)wuphe* 'supermarket'. Indeed, Korean language, culture, and society are heavily influenced by American counterparts, in the same way as they were influenced by everything Chinese or Japanese in the past.

Both SK and loan words are an integral part of the Korean vocabulary. Their impact on the Korean language is great, enriching the Korean vocabulary. When synonyms exist, native words usually represent somewhat unsophisticated traditional culture, both mental and physical, whereas SK words, conveying more formality, tend to denote higher quality objects and more formal, abstract, and sometimes more socially prestigious concepts than their native counterparts do. Loan words are, in general, associated with modern and stylish objects and concepts. For instance, the native word *karak* for 'rhythm' is usually used with reference to traditional Korean folk songs, the SK word *un-yul* in formal or academic situations, and the loan word *litum* for some sort of Western flavor.

2.2 Metaphorical expressions

The socio-cultural nature of the Korean language is also observed in various metaphorical expressions, such as maxims, proverbs, idioms, and slang (see chapters 7 and 10; H.S. Kim 2000). For instance, K.M. Lee's (1980) dictionary of Korean proverbs contains some 7,000 entries. Worded in the form of a phrase or a clause, these expressions reflect many aspects of the traditional culture and society of Korea. The majority of them are in native words, occasionally mixed with SK words, as illustrated below.

(2) a. *chennyang pic-to mal-lo kaph-nunta.*
'A million-dollar debt can be repaid by words.'
[Used to encourage polite and strategic language use.]

b. *pyelwuk-to nachccak-i iss-ta.*
'Even a flea has a face.'
[Refers to a shameless person—stressing the importance of social face.]

c. *amthalk-i wul-myen cip-an-i mangha-nta.*
'If a hen cackles, the house will be ruined.'
[Used to indicate that a woman should be quiet, i.e. obey her husband.]

Native idioms and idiomatic expressions are innumerable. Some examples are *kim-sayta* (steam-leak) 'fail', *maum-mekta* (mind-eat) 'make up one's mind', *nwun-melta* (eye-far) 'be blind', *kkoli-chita* (tail-wiggle) 'seduce', *nach epsta* (face lack) 'be ashamed', *palam-phiwuta* (wind-kindle) 'have a secret love affair', *tola-kasita* (turn-go) 'die' (honorific), *khongpap mekta* (bean-rice eat) 'serve a penal sentence', *maum-e tulta* (mind-into enter) 'like', *mok caluta* (neck cut-off) 'fire', *son-pota* (hand-see) 'fix, teach a lesson', *palmok-capta* (ankle-hold) 'block, interfere', and *miyek-kwuk mekta* (seaweed-soup eat) 'fail an exam'. Native-SK idioms include *sathang-pallim* (sugar-coating) 'flattery, cajolery', *pihaengki thaywuta* (plane-give ride) 'flatter', *hon-nayta* (soul-take out) 'scold', *yakpang-uy kamcho* (herb pharmacy-of licorice) 'person active in everything', and *sik-un cwuk mek-ki* (cooled gruel eating) 'very easy'. Native-loan idioms include *puleikhu kelta* (break-operate) 'block', *ppayk cohta* (back good) 'have a powerful supporter', *opa-hata* (over-do) 'over-react, overdo', and *hithu chita* (hit hit) 'score a success'. Purely SK idioms also occur extensively. Some examples are *chwun-chwu* (spring-fall) 'age' (honorific), *nay-oy* (inside-outside) 'husband and wife', *phung-wel* (wind-moon) 'poem'; *sik-en* (eat-word) 'breaking a promise'; *sam-chon* (3-node) 'uncle', *sa-chon* (4-node) 'first cousin', *tong-mun-se-tap* (east-question-west-answer) 'irrelevant answer'; and *il-sek-i-co* (1-stone-2-birds) 'killing two birds with one stone'.

2.3 Communication patterns

Use of language for communication is largely conventional in accordance with various socio-cultural rules and norms, as well as linguistic rules. The most salient communicative feature reflecting the culture and society of Korea is the well-developed pattern of honorifics and their appropriate uses. While there is little power distinction in Western languages such as English, socio-cultural stratification is reflected in Korean sentence structure. Sentences can hardly be uttered without the speaker's proper knowledge of his or her social relationship with the addressee and referent in terms of age category, social status, kinship, and in- and out-groupness. The intricate social stratification between the speaker and addressee and between the speaker and third-person human referents are encoded in the linguistic structure of the language. There are several levels of sentence endings indicating distinct speech levels in terms of the speaker-addressee relation (e.g. statement endings *-supnita, -eyo/ayo, -(s)o, -e/a, -ney, -ta*); hierarchical sets of addressee-reference terms (e.g. *Kim-sensayng-nim, Kim-sensayng, Kim-Yongho-ssi, Kim-kwun, Yongho, Yongho-ya*), kinship terms (e.g. *apenim, apeci, appa* 'father, dad'; *hyeng-nim, hyeng* '(male's) older brother'; *nwunim, nwuna* '(male's) older sister'; *tongsaeng* 'younger sibling'); subject-honorific suffix *-(u)si,* subject case particles (neutral *ka* vs. honorific *kkeyse*) and dative case particles (neutral *ekey/hanthey* vs. honorific *kkey*); and some honorific verbs (e.g. plain *mekta* vs. honorific *capswusita* 'eat'; *cata* vs. *cwumusita* 'sleep'; *pota* vs. *poypta* 'see'; *cwuta* vs. *tulita* 'give'), nouns (e.g. plain *pap* vs. honorific *cinci* 'meal'; *i vs. chia* 'teeth'; *ilum* vs. *sengham* 'name'; and *nai* vs. *yensey* 'age'. Also, the honorific system contains a hierarchical set of pronouns. Compare the Korean singular pattern with that of English below. D refers to demonstrative: *i* 'this', *ku* 'that near you or we know', and *ce* 'that over there'.

(3) **English** **Korean**

I: *na* (plain; addressed to lower adult, intimate equal, child)
ce (humble; addressed to equal or higher adult)

you: *tayk* (polite; to equal or lower stranger adult)
tangsin (blunt; to lower adult, old-generation spouse)
caney (familiar; to adolescent [rarely], one's wife [rarely], son-in-law, younger brother-in-law)
caki (intimate; to young spouse, boy/girl-friend)
ne (plain; to child, one's own child)

he/she/it: D-*pun* (deferential; refers to distant adult equal, superior)
D-*i* (familiar; refers to familiar adult, one's husband)
D-*salam* (intimate; refers to intimate adult, one's wife)
D-*ay* (plain; refers to child, childhood friend)
D-*kes* (thing)

Notice that the Korean pronoun system has the following features not shared by English: (a) plain/humble distinction in first person; (b) five-way hierarchical distinction in second person, yet (c) no second person pronoun for higher adult addressees (noun substitutes such as *apeci* 'father' and *sensayng-nim* 'teacher' must be used); (d) five-way hierarchical distinction in third person; (e) no gender distinction, and (f) social distance-solidarity is relevant to a certain degree.

Honorific and non-honorific expressions are used in communication either symmetrically (between power equals) or asymmetrically (between power non-equals), depending on social factors indicating power and solidarity. Asymmetrical use of honorifics and non-honorifics is illustrated in (4).

(4) Daughter-in law: *ape-nim cinci capswu-sey-yo.*
'(*lit.,*) Father, please have your meal.'

Father-in-law: *kulay, ne-to pap mek-ela.*
'(*lit.,*) OK, you have your meal too.'

Both utterances in (4) are used naturally, normatively, and appropriately. The daughter-in-law's utterance is honorific and the father-in-law's response is non-honorific. Notice the asymmetrical uses of the words which are referentially the same, *ape-nim* vs. *ne* 'you'; *cinci* vs. *pap* 'meal', *capswu-* vs. *mek-* 'eat', subject honorific *-sey* vs. zero, and polite ender *-yo* vs. plain ender *-ela.*

In contemporary Korea, age- and kinship-based asymmetries are most prominent. While age categories such as child, adolescent, and adult are significant to generate asymmetrical language use among out-group people, even a few years of age difference become significant among close in-group members. Asymmetrical use of honorifics is often observed in rank differences in job situations, but when age and rank conflict, mutual deference is usually observed. Gender-based asymmetry tends to disappear among younger generation speakers, while it is still considerably persistent among older speakers.

Major underlying differences in cultural perspectives and practices between Koreans and Americans, for example, as they appear in verbal and non-verbal communication seem to be that while Americans generally hold egalitarian and individualistic consciousness, highly valuing personal autonomy (Wierzbicka 2002), Korean interpersonal relations are, in general, still strongly tied to social hierarchism and collectivistic ideals, highly valuing interpersonal dependency (Sohn 1986).

(5) Value orientations

Americans:	personal autonomy	a. Egalitarian b. Individualistic
Koreans:	interpersonal dependency	a. Hierarchical b. Collectivistic

Asymmetry in communicative uses of honorifics is indicative of the value of relative hierarchism that Koreans still cherish. Compared to Korean, English has hardly any hierarchical honorific forms. There is no asymmetrical use of pronouns. Pairs like 'dine' versus 'eat', 'care for' versus 'like', and 'Good Morning' versus 'Hi' may be viewed more as a matter of formality than of hierarchy. At most, we can observe an asymmetrical use of the title and last name (e.g. *Mr. Smith*) and the first name (e.g. *John*). Even here, the asymmetry tends to lead easily to mutual use of the first name as the relation becomes closer. Thus, a strong value orientation of Americans is egalitarian, which is manifest not only in communicative patterns but also in all aspects of social life.

There are many indications in communicative patterns that Koreans are relatively collectivistic as compared to Americans' individualistic value orientation. For instance, as mentioned above, only two or three years of age difference between in-group members may be significant enough to call for asymmetrical address terms and speech levels, which is not the case with out-group members. Many verbal expressions are allowed only to in-group members (e.g. the address term *senpay* 'senior') and kinship terms are extensively used to non-kin in Korean (terms like 'grandfather', 'grandmother', 'uncle', 'aunt', 'older sister', 'older brother'). The extensive and obligatory use of "I" in English and the extensive omission of "I" in Korean suggest that *I* exists independently of others in American culture but is not outstanding in Korean communication. Koreans usually use a plural possessive form (neutral *wuli* or humble *cehuy* 'our'), where English speakers would use a singular form (*my*), as in *wuli nala* 'our country' vs. *my country*; *cehuy cip* 'our house' vs. *my house*; and *wuli tongsayng* 'our younger sibling' vs. *my younger sibling.*

There are many other verbal and non-verbal communicative patterns reflecting the individualism of Americans and the collectivism of Koreans. Whereas Americans are willing to talk to strangers or people they don't know well and smile and offer greetings to anybody who passes by, Koreans usually don't smile or offer greetings to strangers, tending to avoid talking to strangers or out-group members, while eager to talk to in-group members, acquaintances, and interested parties such as one's clientele. Honoring others' privacy is valued as polite in the United States, whereas verbal and non-verbal expressions for involvement and concern with others' lives are frequently regarded as much politer than not in Korea. Tied to this absence of privacy is a tendency for Koreans to ask questions about things that Americans would consider personal and rude, such as marriage, salary, age, and the price paid for the addressee's belongings. Americans express their individual opinions and exert fair influence, usually adopting the majority rule, whereas, due to strong ties to one's immediate family, organization, or community, Koreans are generally less assertive, and decisions are frequently made by the head of the group or reached by consensus.

Koreans' communication patterns can also be observed in the use of politeness routines such as requests, apologies, refusals, compliments, compliment responding, expressions of gratitude, congratulations, welcomes, greetings, leave-takings, inquiries, promises, arguments, claims, and complaints. While Americans make compliments, gratitude, and apologies very often, Koreans are generally parsimonious in expressing them.[9] For instance, Byon (2001) has observed that his American subjects used English compliments about thirty-three times more often than Koreans used Korean compliments and that Americans used gratitude expressions about four times more often than Koreans did. Byon's study also shows that, in requests, Americans normally use indirect speech, regardless of any power differences, while Koreans use indirect speech when speaking to someone in authority, and direct speech when speaking to someone with a lower status. I recently received a copy of the following e-mail message from one University of Hawaii professor to another.

9 Wolfson (1989) points out that the high frequency with which Americans compliment is often perceived by members of many other cultures as effusive, insincere, and possibly motivated by ulterior considerations.

(6) Dick, Would it be out of line for me to ask what an average start up cost for Natural Sciences would be? John

This kind of elaborate indirect speech between colleagues is not common between two Korean colleagues. In fact, Americans' elaborate indirect speech reflects Americans' culture valuing negative face (the desire for privacy). In fact, Americans value both negative face and positive face (the desire for social endorsement), and to satisfy these two kinds of face in interaction, extensively use a wide variety of strategic politeness devices, such as well-developed politeness routines and indirect speech-act patterns.[10] This communicative pattern of Americans may be attributed to their underlying values of personal autonomy that underlies egalitarianism and individualism.

On the other hand, due to the social stress on vertical and horizontal relations among individuals, saving social face is very important to Koreans. It is well known that Koreans are extremely concerned with how others (usually in-group people and acquaintances) think of them, reflecting the social orientations of communicative patterns. Because of the emphasis on relations among individuals rather than on the individual him- or herself, inter-dependency has often been regarded as a virtue for many Koreans.

3. Socio-cultural dynamism in the Korean language

All living languages fluctuate and change due not only to external influences such as borrowings of linguistic and socio-cultural elements from other societies but also to their internal dynamism—spontaneous linguistic evolution and socio-cultural shifts. Changes and variations are extensive in the Korean language in relation to culture and society. For instance, NLRI (2000) is a collection and explanation of 235 basic words covering fourteen areas of indigenous Korean culture and society: food, clothing, dwelling, holidays, beliefs, play and games, music, fine arts, literature, dance, cultural assets, social systems, indigenous products, and symbolism. Many of these are SK words such as *so-cwu* 'Korean hard liquor', *kwi-sin* 'spirit, ghost', *hoe* 'sliced raw fish or meat', and *mu-tang* 'shaman'. It seems that some forty of these words are associated with traditional items or customs that are no longer generally used or practiced by contemporary Koreans. Words of this category include *kama* 'palanquin', *kas* 'traditional cylindrical Korean hat made of bamboo or horsehair', *namak-sin* 'wooden shoes', *tatumi-cil* 'smoothing cloth by pounding', *tayngki* 'pigtail ribbon', *mays-tol*

10 For an extensive discussion of positive and negative politeness in relation to positive face and negative face, see Brown and Levinson (1987).

'hand mill', and *sang-thwu* 'topknot of hair'. Words denoting still partially used items or practices include *cikey* 'A-frame carrier', *kama-soth* 'big kettle', *ko-sa* 'offering a sacrifice to spirits', *kwus* 'exorcism', *kangkang-swullay* 'Korean circle dance', *kangceng* 'glutinous rice cracker fried in oil', *koc-kam* 'dried persimmons', *tok* 'earthenware jar', *pinye* 'ornamental hairpin', *kuney* 'swing', *nel-ttwiki* 'seesaw', and *pesen* 'Korean socks'. On the other hand, words of common use include *pap* 'cooked rice', *kwuk* 'soup', *kochwu-cang* 'red-pepper paste', *kwukswu* 'noodles', *kimchi* 'kimchee', *kimcang* 'preparing kimchee for the winter', *ccikay* 'Korean pot stew', *ttek* 'rice cake', *song-phyen* 'pine-needle rice cake', *in-sam* 'ginseng', *namul* 'cooked vegetables', *chima* 'skirt', *cekoli* 'Korean jacket', *sey-pay* 'New Year's bow', *seng-myo* 'visit to one's ancestral graves', *ssilum* 'Korean wrestling', *alilang* 'Arirang folk song', *tol* 'one's first birthday', *swuce* 'spoon', *thay-kuk-ki* 'South Korean flag', *mu-kwung-hwa* 'rose of Sharon (South Korean national flower)', and *sa-cwu* '"Four Pillars" for the year, month, day and hour of one's birth; one's birth date which is believed to influence one's fortune'. See the appendix for annotations of selected terms.

With the demise of the feudal and aristocratic culture and society of Korea where ascribed social classes prevailed, all linguistic patterns, forms, and meanings of aristocratic, feudal elements have either fallen out of use or undergone semantic change in one way or another. According to C.Y. Kim (1976: 57–8), the societies of the Three Kingdoms were characterized by caste system (in which positions are defined by pedigree, religion, etc.), those of Korye and Cosen dynasties were estate systems (in which ascribed social ranks are defined by law), and that of the last part of the Cosen dynasty was a class system in which superior/inferior status is determined by individuals' abilities and achievements. In particular, Cosen society had a system of four strictly hierarchical estates: *yangpan* or aristocrats, *cwungin* or Middle estate, *sangmin* or commoners, and *chenmin* or lowlies. Furthermore, minutely divided social strata were also based on the newly introduced Confucian ideology, which placed unprecedented emphasis on extensive discriminations among people in all spheres of life. Confucianism, which provided the ideology for the foundation of the Cosen dynasty, stipulated an ethical code that categorized and regulated five basic types of interpersonal behaviors, four of which are based on hierarchical human relations that stress the subordinate's unilateral obedience to the superior. That is, Confucianism required human relationships to be based strictly on the principle of *sam-kang-o-lyun* (3-bonds-5-principles) 'the three bonds and five relationships'. The five relationships of Confucianism are loyalty of subject to sovereign, filial piety of child to parent, distinction between husband and wife, precedence of senior over junior (in terms of age, kinship, social status), and fidelity between friends. The 'three bonds' are the first three and the most important of the five.

The intricate structure of the Korean honorific system germinated in such traditional culture and society. Reflecting the earlier caste and estate systems, the honorific patterns and usages were much more complex and stratified than those we have now. As the estate social system has evolved into a more democratic class system with prevailing Western ideologies while the Confucian ideology has been greatly diluted in modern and contemporary Korea, the honorific system has been considerably simplified accordingly. Further changes and variations probably due to the ongoing globalization, especially through the Internet, of American culture and society such as egalitarian and individualistic values and democratic social institutions can be observed on a daily basis. There are many linguistic aspects demonstrating this dynamism, of which the following are noteworthy.

The highest speech level that existed until the early modern period, represented by the verbal ending *-naita* (statement), has been obliterated with the demise of feudal aristocratic society.[11] As a result, the second highest level up until the early modern period, represented by *-supnita* (statement), now functions as the highest level in contemporary Korean. The current polite ending *-eyo/ayo*, which used to be a feminine variant of the third-level ending *-(s)o,* has become a higher speech level and now is used by both males and females extensively as an informal counterpart of the *–supnita* level. On the other hand, the *-(s)o* ending level, due to its blunt connotation, has been gradually disappearing, together with the familiar level represented by the endings *-ney* (statement). Thus, the six-level system of the older generation has been reduced to a four-level one in the standard speech of the younger generation (deferential, polite, intimate, and plain), as illustrated by *ka-pnita, ka-yo, ka,* and *ka-nta* 'goes', respectively. See chapter 11 for an extensive discussion on this topic.

In addition to the changes in honorifics, terms like *paykceng* 'butcher', *mesum* 'farm servant', *cong* 'servant', *taykam* 'His Excellency', *nali* 'your honor, sir', *satto* 'lord', and *manim* 'My Lady, My Lord' are referred to only as historical facts. Terms like *yangpan* 'two highest social classes', *yengkam* 'lord', *tolyennim* 'young master', *sangnom* 'commoner', and *tepusali* 'resident servant' have survived but undergone semantic change to 'gentleman, one's husband', 'elderly man, one's husband', 'husband's younger brother', 'bastard', and 'free-ride living with another family', respectively. Feudalistic terms like *senpi* 'classical scholar', *setang* 'village school', *kwake* 'traditional civil service examination', and *pusa* 'county head' have been replaced, with considerable functional shift, with modern terms like *hakca* 'scholar', *hakwen* 'cram school', *kosi* 'civil service examination', and *sicang* 'mayor' or *kwunswu* 'county chief', respec-

11 This speech level is used now only in historical dramas and novels and religious players.

tively.

A conspicuous sociolinguistic change concerns *ap-con-pep* (*lit.,* 'rules for honorific suppression'). This traditional rule regulates that a speaker cannot use honorific forms to talk about a superior referent, if the addressee is higher than that referent. While high school educators and conservative speakers still insist that the rule be observed, the majority of people ignore it in actual language use (e.g. H.S. Kim 2000). Indeed, the Korean language is in transition in this and many other respects. In recognition of both the tradition and actual usage, the NLRI (1992: 95–7) interpreted the following sentence in which the subject ('father') honorific suffix *–sy* may appear as socially appropriate.

(7) *halapeci, apeci-ka cinci capswu-si-la-ko ha(-**sy**)-ess-supni-ta.*
'Grandfather, father asked you to eat.'

Disappearance of *ap-con-pep* may be accounted for in terms of the mitigation of the speaker's traditional high regard for the addressee. Nowadays, younger generation speakers no longer feel obligated to lower their usual regard toward the referent no matter how much more superior the addressee may be. The socio-cultural and psychological change involved is diagrammed as follows, where the speaker is no longer seriously conscious of the hierarchical relationship between the addressee and the referent. Notice that the earlier small humble ego has now become a big self-asserting EGO.

(8)

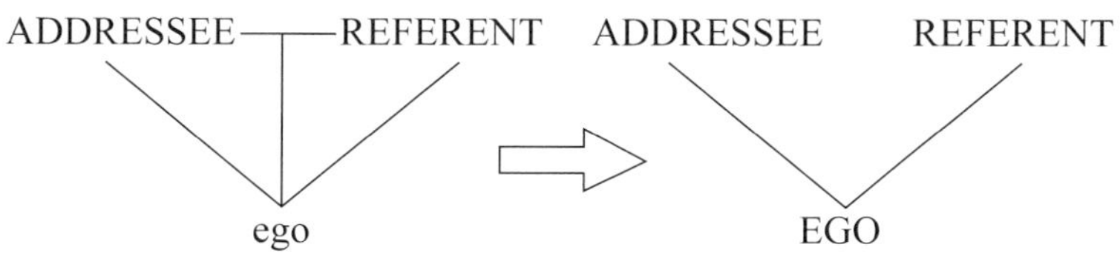

It seems obvious that the most essential socio-cultural correlate with the honorific dynamism is a gradual shift in Koreans' value orientation from strong traditional hierarchism and collectivism to weaker forms, moving toward relatively egalitarian and individualistic consciousness. With the collapse of the feudal social order and introduction of democracy in the Korean constitution since the liberation from the Japanese colonization in 1945 and with the country open to all western, especially American, culture and society where egalitarianism and individualism are highly valued, the new western influence has slowly but steadily permeated all walks of Korean life, diluting traditional values even in the psychology of older generation speakers. Daily contacts with such societies in this age of information, the Internet, and globalization have contributed to the shift of the psychological pattern of Koreans, particularly the younger generation. Furthermore, with extensive college education of women and females' large-scale advancement in society, women's rights have been enhanced. Other things being equal, little significant gender-based inequality is observed in the younger generation, although some inequality still persists, especially among older generation speakers. As the service industry has become important in contemporary profit-seeking Korean society, personal respect for others' characters or deference based only on age have become significantly diluted. Instead, dynamic use of honorifics for strategic purposes is pervasive in interpersonal interaction. For instance, sales people use deferential forms as well as high address terms toward much younger customers, frequently with a deep bow.

Family structure has also changed. The extended family where strict collectivistic and hierarchical relations were held among three or more generations has been reduced to the nuclear family consisting of two generations. Due to economic affluence and parents' high expectations of children, children are most cherished and coddled in a nuclear family, where egalitarianism and individualism are considerably cultivated.

The rigid forms, meanings, and usage of honorifics of the traditional society have relaxed considerably due to the changing values of Korean society. Symmetrical language use is often heard between young siblings and even between a mother and a daughter in casual contexts. Recent innovations include the equalization of the title *ssi* 'Mr., Ms.', which was earlier used to address one's juniors but now is used to address one's colleagues; reciprocal use of *caki* 'you' (*lit.,* 'self') between young couples; and the use of the kin term *enni* '(female's) older sister' to address female clerks, restaurant waitresses, or customers, regardless of the addressee's age and the addresser's age or gender. Frequently, *enni* is used strategically to show intimacy, in replacement of the usual term *akassi* 'young lady, Miss'. Another phenomenon of leveling off is upgrading of certain occupational titles.

(9) *kanho-pu* → *kanho-wen* → *kanho-sa* → *kanho-sa-nim* 'nurse'
wuncen-su → *wuncen-sa* → *ki-sa* → *kisa-nim* 'driver'
chengso-pu → *chengso-wen* → *mihwa-wen* 'cleaner'

All the above socio-cultural and psychological shifts and the corresponding sociolinguistic reflexes may be diagrammed as shortening of the axis of power and the lengthening of the axis of individual solidarity, as schematized in (10).

(10)

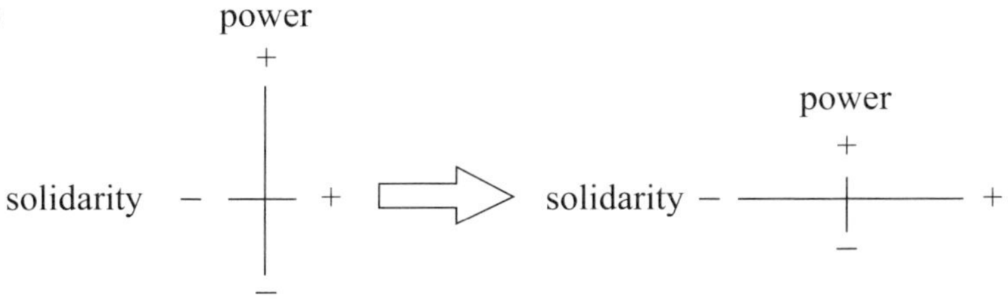

Various works cited thus far and other valuable works such as NLRI's *Say Kwuke Saynghwal* series, the journal *Sahoy Enehak*, Lee et al. (1999), and Y. Park (2001, 2002), will provide the reader with a broader spectrum and deeper knowledge about the Korean language in relation to culture and society.

REFERENCES: Chapter 16

Blount, B.G. (ed.) 1995. *Language, Culture and Society: A Book of Readings.* 2nd edition. Prospect Heights, IL: Waveland Press.

Brooks, N. 1975. The analysis of language and familiar cultures. In R.C. Lafayette (ed.), *The Cultural Revolution.* Lincolnwood, IL: National Textbook Company.

Brown, P. and S. Levinson. 1987. *Politeness: Some Universals in Language Usage.* Cambridge, UK: Cambridge University Press.

Byon, Andrew. 2001. *The Communicative Act of Requests: Interlanguage Features of American KFL Learners.* Ph.D. dissertation. University of Hawaii.

Chaika, E. 1982. *Language: The Social Mirror.* Rowley, Mass.: Newbury House.

Coulmas, F. (ed.) 1997. *The Handbook of Sociolinguistics.* Oxford: Blackwell.

Fasold, R. 1991. *Sociolinguistics of Language.* Oxford: Basil Blackwell.

Foley, W.A. 1999. *Anthropological Linguistics.* Oxford: Blackwell.

Hadley, A.O. 2001. *Teaching Language in Context* (third edition). Boston: Heinle & Heinle.

Hinkel, E. (ed.). 1999. *Culture in Second Language Teaching and Learning.* Cambridge, UK: Cambridge University Press.

Hymes, D. 1974. *Foundations in Sociolinguistics: An Ethnographic Approach.* Philadelphia: University of Pennsylvania Press.

Kim, Chae-Yun. 1976. Social strata. In Chun, Shin-Yong (ed.), *Korean Society. Korean Cultural Series* 6. Seoul: International Cultural Foundation.

Kim, Hye-Sook. 2000. *Hyentay Kwuke-uy Sahoycek Mosup-kwa Ssuim* (Social Aspects and Usage of Contemporary Korean). Seoul: Welin.

Labov, W. 1973. *Sociolinguistic Patterns*. Philadelphia: University of Pennsylvania Press.

Lee, Ki-Moon. 1980. *Soktam Sacen* (A Dictionary of Proverbs). Seoul: Ilcokak.

Lee, Seung-Jae et al. 1999. *Hankwuke-wa Hankwuk Munhwa* (Korean and Korean Culture).

Seoul: Saymun-sa.

McKay, S.L. and N.H. Hornberger (eds.). 1996. *Sociolinguistics and Language Teaching.* Cambridge, UK: Cambridge University Press.

NLRI (National Language Research Institute). 1992. *Phyocwun Hwapep Haysel* (Explanations on Standard Ways of Speaking). Seoul: Kwuklip Kwuke Yenkwuwen.

NLRI (National Language Research Institute). 2000. *Hankwuk Munhwa Kicho Yonge* (Basic Terms of Korean Culture). Seoul: Kwuklip Kwuge Yenkwuwen.

National Standards. 1996. *Standards for Foreign Language Learning: Preparing for the 21st Century.* National Standards in Foreign Language Education Project. Lawrence, KS: Allen Press.

Nostrand, H.L. 1978. The 'Emergent Model' applied to contemporary France. *Contemporary French Civilization* 2. 2: 277–94.

Park, Young-Soon. 2001. *Hankwue-uy Sahoy Enehak.* Seoul: Hankwuk Munhwasa.

Park, Young-Soon. 2002. *Hankwuk Munhwalon* (A Study of Korean Culture). Seoul: Hankwuk Munhwasa.

Sapir, E. 1921. *Language: an Introduction to the Study of Speech.* New York: Harcourt, Brace and World.

Sapir, E. 1961. *Culture, Language, and Personality.* Berkeley: University of California Press.

Saville-Troike, M. 1982. *The Ethnography of Speaking: An Introduction.* Oxford, England: Basil Blackwell.

Seelye, H.N. 1994. *Teaching Culture: Strategies for Intercultural Communication.* Lincolnwood, Ill.: National Textbook Company.

Shaul, D.L. and N.L. Furbee. 1998. *Language and Culture.* Prospect Heights, Ill.: Waveland Press.

Sohn, Ho-min. 1986. Intercultural communication in cognitive values: Americans and Koreans. In Sohn, H.M., *Linguistic Expeditions,* 438–71. Seoul: Hansin.

Trudgill, P. 2000. *Sociolinguistics: an Introduction to Language and Society.* London: Penguin Books.

Wierzbicka, Anne. 2002. The theory of cultural scripts as a tool of cross-cultural communication. In *Korean Linguistics Today and Tomorrow.* Proceedings of the 2002 International Conference on Korean Linguistics. Seoul, Korea.

Whorf, B.L. 1956. *Language, Thought, and Reality: Selected Writings of Benjamin Lee Whorf.* (Carroll, J., ed.). Cambridge: The MIT Press.

17 Language Purification Movements in the Two Koreas*

1. Introduction

The term "purification" encompasses the notions of 純化 (*swunhwa*) 'purification', 浄化 (*cenghwa*) 'cleansing', and 醇化 (*swunhwa*) 'refinement'. The last concept is in common use when talking about *Kwuke Swunhwa Wuntong* in South Korea, which is equivalent to North Korea's *Mal Tatumki Wuntong.* [1] Thus, purification movements refer to the governmental and non-governmental activities aimed at eliminating undesirable elements and replacing them with more desirable elements and maintaining the refined language. The activities having to do with language purification can be described as instances of language planning and language policies as well as their implementation.

As soon as Korea was liberated from Japan in 1945, use of the Korean language and *hankul* was restored and became a symbol of liberation and independence. Thus, the two separated Koreas independently launched extensive crusades against illiteracy based on *hankul*, demanding a national language free from foreign elements such as Chinese characters and Japanese words and expressions. In South Korea, Hankul Hakhoy took the lead in this campaign, whereas in North Korea, Kim Il Song's 1946 Teachings (*kyosi*) on the purge of

---

* This papers is reprinted from Kim-Renaud, Y.K. (ed.), *Korean Linguistics* (Journal of the International Circle of Korean Linguistics) 12: 141–60. The original version was presented at the 2002 Annual Meeting of the American Association of Asian Studies, Washington, D.C. April 4–7, 2000.

1 Even before and during the Japanese occupation of Korea (1910–45), there were notable Korean language purification movements. For instance, Cwu Si-kyeng's founding of Kwuke Yenkwuhoy in 1908, his students' organization of Cosene Yenkwuhoy in 1921 (later changed to Cosene Hakhoy and to Hankul Hakhoy), the latter's legislation of *Hankul Macchwumpep Thongilan* in 1933 and establishment of *Phyocwun mal* in 1936 were early language purification movements. The use of the Korean language, including its writing system, *Hankul*, however, was suppressed, and the Korean people were forced to use Japanese as the sole means of communication. By 1942, Korean was phased out as a subject in school curricula. Nevertheless, the Korean language and *Hankul* were used at home, and *Hankul* was refined by patriotic scholars.

Japanese remnants in education and the fight against illiteracy kindled a widespread movement.

Although the two Koreas' purification movements started with essentially the same nationalistic spirit, the subsequent developments have led to markedly different consequences, mainly due to (a) complete physical separation for over half a century, (b) polarized political, social, and ideological divergence, and (c) the distinct language standardization policies implemented by the two governments, culminating in North Korea's institution of "Cultured Speech" (*munhwa-e*) as their standard language as against South Korea's traditional "Standard Speech" (*phyocwun-mal*). Since language purification movements in Korea diverged only after the end of World War 2, our discussion will focus on the period since 1945.

Language purification movements in the two Koreas have centered on (a) the exclusive use of *hankul*, (b) language standardization, (c) lexical refinement, and (d) *hankul* orthographic conventions, romanization of Korean, grammar, and usage. Our discussion will be limited to the issues of exclusive use of *hankul*, language standardization, and lexical refinement, the three areas considered to have the most significant and far-reaching impact on language use in the two Koreas.[2]

Numerous studies are available in South Korea on the North Korean language, the two Koreas' language policies and linguistic divergence between the two Koreas.[3] According to Choy (2001: 63), there are over 450 such studies, most of which have been conducted since M. Kim (1985), who first made extensive North Korean data available to the general public. There have also been numerous scholarly gatherings to discuss the issues related to linguistic divergence between the two Koreas and the search for ways to narrow the gap.[4]

Based on many previous studies, the present paper aims to: identify and discuss the major conceptual goals that have motivated various purification movements (section 2); compare the two Koreas' policies and practices relating to the *hankul*-only policy vis-à-vis the mixed use with characters and argue for the importance of character education (section 3); observe the emergence and nature of Cultured Speech vis-à-vis Standard Speech (section 4); overview the extent of lexical refinements and the degree of divergence (section 5); and conclude the

2 For divergent practices relating to orthographies, grammars, and usages, see M. Kim (1985), Sohn (1997), Yi et al. (1988), and Y. Ko (2001), among other works.

3 For an overview of language policies in the two Koreas, see, for instance, M. Kim (1985), C.W. Kim (1977), Sasse (1979), Cen and Choy (1989), Sohn (1997, 1999), King (1996), Y. Ko (1999), and Co and Kim (2002).

4 It is remarkable that many recently published South Korean dictionaries have entries of North Korean words.

paper with some general suggestions for linguistic unification (section 6).

2. Why purification movements?

There are numerous forces promoting linguistic admixture, such as need-based or prestige-based borrowing; acculturation; globalism and globalization; convenience; attraction to newness, creativity, and foreignism; search for diversity; international competitiveness; and netizenship. Trudgill (2000: 44) indicates that ideas about the possibility and desirability of preserving 'linguistic purity' (i.e. defending a language against 'contamination' by loanwords from other languages) are false. This implies that it is neither possible nor desirable to preserve linguistic purity by blocking off incoming foreign elements. Yet, both Koreas have been spending enormous amount of time, money, energy, manpower, and collective wisdom for perennial purification movements. Why? The answer seems to be essentially three-fold: nationalism, ideology, and utilitarianism.

As in many other nations in the world, nationalism is the key philosophical underpinning that motivates language purification movements in both Koreas. The connection between nationalism and language has long been argued for, and the national unit is most commonly defined in terms of language (e.g. Safran 1999). Both Koreas share strong nationalism, although the North appears to be relatively more nationalistic in terms of language policies and purification movements. Koreans in both Koreas belong to one and the same ethnic unit, speaking one and the same language and using one and the same indigenous writing system, *hankul*. Koreans in the divided Koreas endeavor to maintain and express ethnic identity, pride, unique characteristics, sentiment, traditions, and cultural values by means of the 'uncontaminated' language. As a result, they have conducted intensive purification movements with the nationalistic spirit and with the eventual unification of the two Koreas in mind. With this shared idea of preserving the purity of and refining the ethnic language, efforts have been made in both Koreas to eradicate illiteracy, eliminate existing undesirable foreign elements such as Chinese characters and Japanese loans, uphold the *hankul*-only policy, refine existing words (*kwuke swunhwa* or *mal-tatumki*), and block the massive inflow of unwieldy foreign words as much as possible by replacing them with native words or commonly used (or nativized) Sino-Korean elements, although to different degrees and extents. Thus, despite the independently conducted movements, nationalism has recently been functioning as a centripetal force to converge respective purification activities toward unifying the language.

The diametrically opposing socio-economic and political ideologies have also motivated directly or indirectly the respective purification efforts. The ideological orientation of the South is free, open democracy and capitalism, whereas that of the North is based on rigid, closed authoritarianism and socialism, which are responsible for the development of different world views and different socio-economic and political systems. The views of language are also different. In the South, language is viewed as a means of communication, as based on Western linguistic theory and practice, whereas in the North it is a powerful tool or "weapon" for establishing socialism, as based on the materialistic linguistic theory from the former Soviet Union (e.g. Y. Ko 1999). Different language policies and movements have ensued as a result. Influenced by Western capitalism, South Korea is more generous in accepting English terms as loanwords, whereas the North has coined new words for socialistic ideas, given new metaphorical meanings to existing words and expressions, and imported many socialistic terms from Russia and China, either as they are or by translation.[5]

The ideological differences have also produced different degrees of success in purification movements and in the resultant impact on the general public. In South Korea, currently Kwuklip Kwuke Yenkwuwen, under the Ministry of Culture and Tourism is in charge of the tasks of refining the vocabulary. Also, several non-governmental organizations such as Hankul Hakhoy have continued to carry on purification movements and many individual scholars make a host of constructive proposals. As a result, pluralistic sets of refined words have been published.[6] Despite all the efforts of the government, scholars, and academic associations, South Korea, a free, open democratic and capitalistic nation, has achieved only limited success because, above all, the general public is free to use their preferred forms, whether they are Japanese loans, English words, or slang.

North Korea's language policy is not only for purification but also for indoctrination and spreading party ideology (e.g. Coulmas 1999: 411). Since North Korea has forcefully and systematically conducted purification movements under the strong leadership of the government, the monolithic activities of the government are bound to be highly successful and the impact of the results on the general public is necessarily great. Thus, although the two Koreas equally endeavor to purify and refine the ethnic language by eliminating foreign elements, the outcomes and the impact on the people are considerably different. As

5 For instance, both Koreas avoid using each other's ideology-laden words, as in S *chinkwu* vs. N *tongmu* 'friend/comrade' and S *kwukmin* vs. N *inmin* 'people'.

6 For instance, Hankul Hakhoy's *Swiwun Mal Sacen* (1984) and *Wuli Thopakimal Sacen* (2002), the Ministry of Culture and Sports' *Kwuke Swunhwa Yonge Calyocip* (1996), and Kwuklip Kwuke Yenkwuwen's *Kwuke Swunhwa Calyocip* (1992, 1993, 1999, 2000) are some of the representative collections.

T. Kim (2000) indicates, the language policies of the North are controlled by 'the power of authority' while those of the South are controlled by 'the power of the market' to a large extent.

Both Koreas implement purification for utilitarian purposes to a great extent. Language purification is needed to: (a) enhance standardized national education of high quality; (b) promote efficient, effective, and smooth communication; and (c) encourage the people to use correct and refined language. Language standardization is essential in this regard. Issues on Chinese character education are also motivated by utilitarianism. Since 1945, development of all aspects of life, including scientific, technological, political, economic, social, and cultural advancements, has constantly required the two Koreas to coin or borrow new words corresponding to new concepts. Utilitarianism, including communicative efficiency, seems to be an important criterion in choosing proper forms. A general tendency appears to be that the North tends to depend more on native elements and the South more on Sino-Korean and loan elements.

3. Exclusive use of *hankul*

3.1. South Korea

As already indicated, exclusive use of *hankul* was the most intense movement in both Koreas upon the liberation of Korea from Japan. Since 1948, however, the South Korean government has implemented notoriously fluctuating and inconsistent policies because of the opposing movements of the *hankul*-only scholars (Hankul Hakhoy scholars) and pro-character scholars. The government's unprincipled policies since 1948 are summarized below (cf. Sohn 1999; C.S. Song 1999):

(1) South Korean policies on the exclusive use of *hankul*

- 1948: Proclamation of the law of exclusive use of *hankul*
- 1949: Permission to use necessary Chinese characters alongside *hankul*
- 1950: Decision to use Chinese characters mixed with *hankul*
- 1955: Announcement of the law of exclusive use of *hankul*
- 1964: Pronouncement of the revised law on the exclusive use of *hankul*, permitting the use of 1,300 characters in textbooks of elementary and secondary schools
- 1968: The Presidential decree for the exclusive use of *hankul*
- 1970: Enforcement of the *hankul*-only policy, removing all Chinese characters from the textbooks of elementary and secondary schools

1972: Reinstatement of the education of 1,800 characters at secondary schools
1975: Inclusion of characters side by side with hankul in secondary school textbooks

Although at present 900 characters are taught at intermediate and 900 at high schools as per the 1972 decision, current practices of character education are extremely unsatisfactory in terms of teaching methods, class time, and emphasis (M. Kim 1999; C.S. Song 1999). M. Kim cites *Cosen Ilpo* articles (1997 & 1998), in which only 46% of the surveyed college graduates knew how to write the names of their alma maters in characters; and only 45.7% could write their fathers' names and only 30.7% could write their mothers' names in characters. In short, the current generation in the South is nearly character-illiterate.

3.2. North Korea

From 1945 to the early 1960s, North Korean language policies were aimed at eradicating illiteracy, eliminating the use of Chinese characters, and promoting intensive Korean language education. Success of these policies was due to Kim Il Song's 1946 Teachings on the *hankul*-only policy and the North Korean government's initiation in 1949 of compulsory elementary education.

Through his 1964 and 1966 Teachings, however, Kim Il Song revived character education for reading purposes only, so that the people could read South Korean publications as well as the books and records of the past. Based on pertinent reports in 1956 issues of the North Korean journal, *Cosen Emun,* M. Kim (1999) claims that character education had already begun in 1953 with three purposes: (a) to comprehend the books and materials of the past, (b) to understand the etymology and roots of Sino-Korean words, and (c) to facilitate the study of Chinese culture. He argues that Kim Il Song's Teachings officially confirmed what had already been practiced in North Korea.

Currently in North Korea, a total of 3,000 Chinese characters are taught from the fifth grade of elementary schools to college (2,000 characters before college and 1,000 characters in college) and North Korean students' character knowledge is remarkable (e.g. M. Kim 1999).

3.3. Arguments for character education

Superiority of *hankul* for Koreans to any other writing system on earth is widely recognized beyond any doubt.[7] I maintain, however, that knowing Chi-

7 Thus, I am sympathetic with the nationalistic and other cogent arguments of Hankul Hak-

nese characters is important for utilitarian purposes.[8] In addition to the need for character education in South Korea on a par with North Korea for linguistic unification, the following points justify the importance of character education.

a. Through the use of characters for some two thousand years, Koreans have imported all aspects of advanced Chinese, Japanese, and even western culture and civilization and developed and recorded their own culture and scholarships. Knowledge of characters is indispensable to understand, preserve, and further develop traditional culture.[9]
b. Chinese characters are, as P. Nam (1999) argues, the common property and heritage of the cultural sphere of Chinese characters.[10] With character knowledge, it is easy for Koreans, Chinese, and Japanese to communicate in writing and learn mutual languages, cultures, and societies. Koreans should have character knowledge in order to remain in that cultural sphere, since writing and culture are inseparable to a great extent.
c. Some 65% to 70% of the Korean vocabulary items are character-based Sino-Korean words. Character study is necessary in order to grasp accurate meanings of Sino-Korean words through correct understanding of the meanings of the constituent morphemes. This will enormously enhance the speaker's vocabulary power.
d. Characters have enormous word-formational power. While the native stock is not flexible enough to coin new words, mono-morphemic and monosyllabic Chinese characters can easily be used to form an infinite number of new words. Lack of character knowledge leads to the extreme decline of word-formational power and will inevitably contribute to flooding of foreign words into Korean.[11]
e. Without characters, it is difficult to distinguish a great many homonyms, although context helps to a certain extent. Thus, characters function as units of morphological analysis in Sino-Korean homonyms. According to my count based on the 1,800-character set of the South and 3,000 character set of the North, on an average, a single Hankul syllable is 4.5-way ambiguous in the

hoy (as presented in *Hankul Say Sosik* series and many other works) in support of exclusive use of *hankul*.

8 Recent works in favor of character education include K. Song (1999), M. Kim (1999), C.S. Song (1999), P. Nam (1999), Y. Park (2001), and Sohn (2002).

9 The Chinese script was the only official script available to Koreans before the fifteenth century when the Korean alphabet was created, which became an official writing system only since the *Kapo* Reform at the end of the 19th century.

10 Similarly, Coulmas (1999: 399) indicates that the Far East has been defined as the domain of chopsticks and Chinese characters.

11 It is often claimed that word formational power contributes to the enhancement of thinking power and application power.

South set and 6.8-way ambiguous in the North set in terms of corresponding characters. The most ambiguous one is *sa*, which corresponds to 32 characters in the 1,800 set and 44 characters in the 3,000 set. The 32 characters are given in (2i). The 44 characters of the North include all the South Korean characters except one (賜 'give'), plus the 13 characters as given in (2ii).

(2) Characters representing *sa*:

i. 司私斜社寫詐事蛇辭史詞射士思沙巳死賜仕謝絲使斯四祀舍寺邪師似捨查
ii. 些唆奢徙瀉獅砂篩紗肆赦飼麝

It seems that exclusion of 賜 was ideologically motivated, in that the character has a feudalistic and class connotation, as it is used in *hasa* (下賜) 'give to a subordinate'. In short, characters are the most convenient units and tools for morphemic analysis.[12]

f. In the reality of population supremacy of the character cultural sphere over the English speaking world and rapidly developing economy in East Asia, neglect of Chinese character study will result in the loss of international competitiveness.

g. In the face of accepting English words as loans rather indiscriminately, character study will awaken the Korean people to identify themselves as Asians, rather than being assimilated to Western culture and values.

h. P. Nam (1999) argues that Korean Studies is facing a peril in that scholarly manpower with sufficient character knowledge is short.

i. From the perspective of cost effectiveness, once a limited number of characters are learned, such knowledge can be extensively utilized throughout all disciplinary fields. As P. Nam notes, compared to learning 22,000 English words over some ten years of study to take the TOEFL exam, learning 1,800 characters is practically nothing, especially because students are already familiar with associated Sino-Korean words.

In the course of controversy between pros and cons over character education, the use of characters by the general public and mass media has dwindled to an extreme degree. Moreover, the character courses at schools have degraded from required to elective, and college examinations have stopped including character tests.

Although North Korea requires 2,000 characters to be learned before college, it will not be necessary in South Korea to increase the number. According to Y.

12 To solve the ambiguity problem, the South Korean government, in 1988, allowed all public documents to include necessary characters side by side with *Hankul*.

Nam's (1999) count, a total of 7,310 characters are used in the entire 316,721 Sino-Korean entries in the *Phyocwun Kwuke Taysacen* (by Kwuklip Kwuke Yenkwuwen), but only 1,589 characters are used in 90% of all Sino-Korean entries and 2,256 characters in 95% of them. Although it is important to review and revise the existing 1,800-character set (for instance, as suggested by H. Kim 1999), approximately 1,800 characters for secondary education appears to be on the right track.

What I am advocating is not the all-out mixed use (i.e. writing) of *hankul* and characters as widely practiced in the past, but character education for acquiring knowledge as well as utilitarian purposes as indicated above. For instance, character education is needed for efficient learning and quick recognition of Sino-Korean expressions, for grasping their precise meanings, for coinage of new words and phrases, for clarifying ambiguous expressions (by providing characters in parentheses), and for reading of traditional books and documents of all kinds as well as various scholarly books and articles.

A crucial task to be implemented especially in South Korea, therefore, is to reinforce Chinese character education in secondary schools, making it required. It is also essential for college entrance examinations to reintroduce characters in tests of the Korean language. Unlike learning a spoken second language, which is most effective during the critical period (before 12 years of age), elementary education in Chinese characters does not seem to be necessary. Secondary schools are good enough because at that stage, students have already mastered a sufficient number of Sino-Korean words that are associated with characters.

4. Language standardization

The standard speech (or language) must be legislated and refined as a means of common use for public education, textbook and dictionary compilation, standard communication, mass media, and so on.[13] Hankul Hakhoy's legislation, under the Japanese colonial government, of *Hankul Macchwumpep Thongilan* in 1933 and *Phyocwunmal Moum* in 1936 were the earliest systematic standardization movements. In the former, the Standard Speech of Korea is simply defined as "the contemporary Seoul speech of educated middle-class Koreans", and in the latter, standard vocabulary headings are listed followed by nonstandard variants.

In South Korea, the 1936 definition of Standard Speech was observed until

13 A very general definition of the term *standard* is that "a standard variety is generally one which is written, and which has undergone some degree of regularization or codification (for example, in a grammar and a dictionary); it is recognized as a prestigious variety by a community." (Holms 2001:76).

1988, when the Ministry of Education proclaimed the new Regulations of Standard Speech. In the Regulations, Standard Speech is defined as, in principle, the contemporary Seoul speech widely used by educated citizens. The Regulations consist of two parts: (1) the principles of assessing the words of Standard Speech (26 clauses) and (2) standard pronunciations (30 clauses). In the former, standard forms and dialectal forms are distinguished, while in the latter, correct pronunciations of standard forms are regulated.

In North Korea, Kim Il Song initiated the policy of Cultured Speech (*munhwa-e*) to standardize Korean based essentially on the Pyongyang dialect and Kim Il Song's self-reliance (*cwuche*) ideology (1964–present). This was done through two sets of his language-related Teachings (via dialogues with linguists), one in 1964 and the other in 1966. The former presented the basic directions and the latter substantiated them. Kim's major directives in the former are: (a) coinage of new words and recovery of old words be based on native elements; (b) use of loanwords be limited; (c) Chinese characters be abolished in writing but taught for reading purposes only; (d) unnecessary Sino-Korean words be removed from dictionaries; (e) a nationwide campaign be undertaken for the correct use of the language; and (f) Korean language education be improved and strengthened at all levels of education. In the 1966 Teachings, Kim elaborated on detailed procedures of refining vocabulary, while directing the linguists to preserve and develop the national characteristics of the Korean language based on the speech of Pyongyang. This is the notion of Kim's Cultured Speech. Kim denounced Seoul-based Standard Speech as having lost its legitimacy as a national language because 'it is deprived of national characteristics and popular elements and has become the speech of bourgeoisie, a jumble filled with Western, Japanese, and Chinese elements…' An unprecedented linguistic reform has thereby resulted, aiming at realizing Kim's Teachings for 'Cultured Speech'.

Although Kim Il Song's Teachings and North Korea's *Cosenmal Taysacen* (1992) define Cultured Speech as a speech culturally refined with Pyongyang speech as the basis, it is well known that Cultured Speech is, in fact, based much more on Standard Speech than on Pyongyang dialect (e.g. Kwak 2001). Except for spelling and pronunciation of word-initial *l* and *n* (before *i/y*), the Cultured Speech is similar to Seoul-based Standard Speech. Thus, for example, despite the Pyongyang dialect's prevalent un-palatalized forms such as *thenti* (S *chenci*) 'heaven and earth'', kinship terms like *apaci* 'father', *omani* 'mother', many particles (e.g. subject *-lay* [standard: *ka/i*]), and sentence endings (*-summey, -weyta* [standard: *-eyo/ayo*]), Cultured Speech includes only the corresponding Seoul-based standard forms. Similarly, compare the following.

(3)

	'cat'	'scissors'	'pepper'	'dragonfly'	'earthworm'	'bat'
Standard:	*koyang*	*kawi*	*kochwu*	*camcal*	*cilengi*	*pakcwi*
Cultured:	same as above					
Pyongyang:	*konayng*	*kawu*	*tangchwu*	*chayncali*	*tileyi*	*ppalcwi*

All this indicates that Cultured Speech is closer to Standard Speech than to Pyongyang dialect. One important difference, however, is that while South Korea has never upgraded dialectal forms as standard, North Korea has incorporated some 4,000 North Korean dialectal forms in Cultured Speech as per Kim Il Song's Teachings (Pak 1999: 225–6). According to Kwak (2000: 9, 12), acceptance of dialectal forms as standard is based on the principles in (4).

(4) North Korean principles accepting dialect forms as standard

a. Refuting the legitimacy of the South Korean Standard Speech
b. Supplementing the paucity of standard native words with dialectal elements
c. Utilizing dialectal elements as data for refining words
d. Standardizing the language with words that are agreeable to the feelings of the general public

North Korea's dialectal policy seems to be an excellent one, in that it salvages many endangered dialectal elements, while enriching the impoverished standard native vocabulary for general use. One side effect may be that it has contributed to lexical divergence between the two Koreas. However, as Pak (ibid.) and Kwak (ibid.) point out, it is rare that Standard Speech forms were replaced with dialectal forms, because the general public of the North have long been using Standard Speech forms. In principle, dialectal forms are introduced only when Standard Speech forms are not used by North Koreans (5a) or Standard Speech forms are not available (5b). Otherwise, dialectal forms (some 1,000) are standardized together with South Korean standard forms as doublets or triplets (5c).

(5)

	South	**North**	
a.	*kewi*	*keysani*	'goose'
	sangchi	*pulwu*	'lettuce'
	kwukmul	*maluk*	'soup'
b.	—	*tupey*	'seeding instrument'
	—	*aswuhata*	'regrettable'
	—	*coylopta*	'very pitiful'
c.	*komul*	*komul/muchikey/poswungi*	'powdered bean'

nay	*nay/naykwul*	'smoke'
ppalli	*ppalli/nallay*	'quickly'
cangin	*cangin/kasi-apeci*	'wife's ather'
taynim	*taynim/komayki*	'ankle bands'
ka	*ka/kasayngi*	'edge'
kaywul	*kaywul/kaykol*	'brook'
keycipai	*keycipai/eymina*	'girl'

Thus, Cultured Speech consists of the following.

(6) Cultured Speech = Standard Speech as basis + selected North Korean dialectal elements (frequently along with Standard Speech forms) + independently refined or coined words (frequently along with Standard Speech forms).

5. Lexical refinement

As many authors have observed, the most significant linguistic divergence is in the lexicon, in that independent refinement movements in the two Koreas have targeted lexical items primarily and most extensively. The targets are mainly Sino-Korean words and loan/foreign words.

In South Korea, for instance, in 1992 the Korean government's Department of General Affairs published a list of 8,673 refined legal and administrative terms; and in 1996, the Department of Culture and Sports (present Department of Culture and Tourism) issued a collection of 5,575 refined words from Japanese loans, Japanese-style Sino-Korean words, and English and other loanwords in the following cultural areas (S.C. Yi et al. 1999 ; Park 2001), where Jp stands for Japanese, SK Sino-Korean, and NT native. Examples are given in each category.

(7) Construction: *kali-kwumitatey* (Jp) > *imsi-colip* (SK) 'temporary setup'
ssumi (Jp) > *pyektol-ssaki* (NT) 'brick piling'
Arts: *kakwupucci* (Jp) > *thul* (NT), *aykca* (SK) 'frame'
teysayng (dessin) > *somyo* (SK) 'rough drawing'
Sewing: *kasaney-nwui* (Jp) > *kyepchye pakki* (NT) 'overlap sewing'
nochi (notch) > *kawi-cip* (NT) 'notch'
Daily life: *teping* (dubbing) > *cay-nokum/nokhwa* (SK) 're-recording'
kongnan (SK) > *pin-khan* (NT) 'blank, empty space'
tantoli (Jp) > *chaypi* (NT-SK), *tansok* (SK) 'preparation'
Politics: *mathatoo* (matador) > *huksayk sencen* (SK)

	ciltha (SK) > *kkwucicum* (NT) 'scolding'
Dietary:	*oteyn* (Jp) > *kkochi* (NT) 'skewered stuff'
	walipasi (Jp) > *namu ceskalak* (NT) 'chopsticks'
Newspaper:	*keylasuli* (Jp) > *kyocengsoy* (SK) 'proof sheet'
	kositkwu (Jp from 'gothic') > *kotikchey* (loan-SK) 'gothic'
Forestry:	*cihakyeng* (SK) > *ttangsok cwulki* (NT) 'underground root'
	chwukceykong (SK) > *twuk-ssaki* (NT) 'building a bank'
Computer:	*puuthing* > *ttuywuki* (NT) 'booting'
	pechwuel > *kasang* (SK) 'virtual'
	tholelensu > *heyong hankyey* (SK) 'tolerance'
	piteyotheyksu > *yengsang chengpo* (SK) 'videotex'

In North Korea, lexical purification movements started since 1946 with the goals of making words easy, simple, concise, clear, and accurate, eliminating Japanese loans and Japanese-style words, and refine wrong or undesirable expressions (cf. Cen and Choy 1989: 45; Y. Park 2001: 138). The movements have involved (a) refining existing words, (b) activating dialectal and obsolete native elements, and (c) coining new words based on native elements as much as possible. In particular, since the 1960s, North Korea has carried out an all-out campaign to artificially reform the language through *mal tatumki* as part of the Cultured Speech movement in accordance with Kim Il Song's Teachings. As a result, in 1982, the North announced a total of approximately 50,000 words as refined and, in 1986, established approximately 25,000 refined words (*tatumun mal*) as standard, by abandoning about half of the 1982 list probably to avoid a radical impact on the people's language use (e.g. Pak 1999: 226; Kwak 2001: 8–10).

Kwak quotes statistics indicating that some 63,000 North Korean words are different from the corresponding South Korean words. Does this mean that the languages of the two Koreas have diverged to an extent that may hamper mutual communication to a significant degree? The answer is no. Why?

a. A major portion of the lexical differences is in spellings and pronunciations, not in meanings, as in S *ilon* vs. N *lilon* 'theory' (e.g. Cen and Choy 1989; Sohn 1997; Y. Ko 1999). Such differences rarely hamper communication between the two Koreas.
b. Many refined words in both Koreas are similar or identical (Pak: 1999: 221). Based on the South Korean Ministry of Culture and Tourism's recent *Dictionary of Comparative North-South Languages*, Kwak (2001) claims that high-frequency daily words in the two Koreas manifest a high level of homogeneity in lexical meanings.

c. South Koreans need little effort to understand many North Korean refined words due to easiness and popularity, as in *tosilak* vs. *pap-kwak* 'lunch box', *hwamulsen* vs. *cim-pay* 'cargo ship', *sikto* vs. *pap-kil* 'esophagus'; *kwukmin* vs. *inmin* 'people', *sanpha* vs. *cosanwen* 'midwife', *phama* vs. *pokkum meli* 'perm', and *nokku* vs. *son-kichek* 'knock'.

d. As discussed in the previous section (SEE examples in (5)), North Korea's adoption of the plural standard contributes not only to the unification of the language but also to the facility with which North Koreans understand Standard Speech. More examples are in (8).

(8)	**South**	**North**	
	kwunto	*kwunto, muli sem*	'archipelago'
	kisengpok	*kisengpok, ciun os*	'ready-made clothes'
	naiphu, khal	*naiphu, papsang khal*	'knife'
	neythu ope	*neythu ope, kumul nemki*	'going over the net'
	lotheli, neykeli	*lothali*	'rotary'

Thus, it may be safe to say that, in general, the differences between Cultured Speech and Standard Speech are at the level of dialectal differences, as between the Standard Language and the Cenla or Kyengsang dialect, as indicated in Kwak (ibid.), Choy (2001), and T. Kim (2001).

Major lexical divergence is due to the use of an enormous quantity of English loanwords in South Korea and the great disparity in the use of technical terms in the two Koreas. While North Korea has refined the existing loanwords and suppressed incoming foreign words as much as possible, changing them into appropriate native or common Sino-Korean words, South Korea, despite purification efforts, has been unable to block the massive, forceful, and ever-increasing infiltration of English words into all areas of Korean life since the 1960s (S. Kim 1998: 16). Some examples are given below (cf. Pak 1999: 227):

(9)	**South**	**North**	
	tones	*kalakci-ppang*	'dough-nut'
	palkheni	*naymin-tay*	'balcony'
	khethun	*changmun-po*	'curtain'
	aisukhulim	*elum-poswungi*	'ice cream'
	nokum theyip	*lokum-tti*	'audio-tape'
	wenphisu	*tallin-os*	'one-piece dress'
	thwuphisu	*nanwin-os*	'two-piece dress'

The extent to which younger generation South Koreans use and abuse English loanwords is great indeed, as discussed in C.U. Song (1998), U. Yi (1998), C. Yi (1998), S.H. Ko (1998), S.Yi (1998), and Pak (1999) and many other works. For instance, C.U. Song (ibid.: 29) shows that 63.2% of all the titles of T.V. programs are wholly or partly in English loanwords; 47% of the menus of computer communication are wholly or partly in English loanwords; and 96% of the names of beauty shops are in English and other loanwords. Loanwords used in South Korea are not necessarily need-based, but also prestige-based to a great extent. It is said that the main culprits who indiscreetly introduce English loanwords and spread them to the general public on a daily basis are mass media and the market (T. Kim 2001).

Based on a 1999 joint survey conducted by the Kwuklip Kwuke Yenkwuwen and Hankwuk Emun Cinhunghoy, T. Kim (ibid.: 93) states that North Korean residents are totally unaware of 8,284 loanwords commonly used in South Korea, including such simple terms as *nyusu* 'news'. This may be an inevitable consequence of globalization, openness, and industrialization in South Korea, yet it is an astonishing number.

C.U. Song (1998) proposes some useful ways to systematically conduct loanword purification in South Korea. For instance, his suggestions include that widely used loanwords should not be refined; that refined words should reflect the general feelings of the people; and that refinement should begin with high-frequency loanwords that are not assimilated to Korean yet. He further urges that the government reinforce the laws and regulations related to loanwords and establish an organization in charge exclusively of loanword matters, that mass media and intellectuals refrain from indiscreet use of loanwords and take the lead in promoting refined loanwords, and that scholars do intensive research on loanwords and publish a standard loanword dictionary.

I propose one step further from the perspective of linguistic unification. That is, loanword purification activities in both Koreas should be conducted in light of what the other side has done and is doing. It is indeed preferable for scholars from both Koreas to seriously cooperate to produce a unified set of refined loanwords.

The second distinct and treacherous area of lexical divergence that calls for immediate attention is related to all kinds of technical terms, such as political, military, economic, legal, medical, mass media, and information technology terms. These terms are mostly related to loanwords and Sino-Korean words. Efforts should be made for scholars, specialists, administrators, and practitioners in respective areas from both Koreas to come up with unified terms, as in the case of the compilation of the unified *Kwukcey Phyocwun Cengpo Kiswul Yonge Sacen* (1997). As discussed in detail in P. Kim (2001), the joint North-South publication of the dictionary of information technology terms is a remarkable event. This is a result of three meetings of the International Conference for Computerization of Korean Language held in Yanbien, China, from 1994 to 1996. This conference was sponsored by South Korea's Kwuke Cengpo Hakhoy, North Korea's Cosen Kwahak Kiswul Chong Yenmayng, and China's Yenpyen Kwahak Kiswul Hyephoy. Through its third conference in 1996, South and North Korea agreed on the standardized terms. A total of 2,109 terms covering some thirty areas were standardized for use in both Koreas and China. Approximately 80% of them are single terms, and the remaining 20% are plural terms that incorporate suggestions from both Koreas. Even the terms 'computer' and 'calculator' have plural entries, as observed below.

(10)		**South**	**North**
	'computer'	*censanki*	*kyeysanki*
	'calculator'	*kyeysanki*	*swusanki*

P. Kim states that this dictionary is widely utilized in the North, whereas it is merely a recommended book in the South, again because of the power of the market where many loan words are preferred. This event may serve as a model for future cooperation between the two Koreas toward linguistic unification.

6. Conclusion

Albeit somewhat sketchily, I have overviewed what the two Koreas have done for language purification in regard to Chinese characters, language standardization, and lexical refinement, and in what areas and to what extent the separate purification movements have contributed to both linguistic homogeneity and divergence. I have advanced some evaluations and suggestions as relevant.

The enormous results achieved by the continued language purification and refinement efforts in both Koreas are of paramount value to Koreans' quality of linguistic life. When separately refined sets of words are combined into a unified whole, the impoverished native vocabulary will be greatly enriched in terms of not only the quantity but also semantic refinement and specification. Furthermore, with ample refined Sino-Korean words and useful need-based loanwords, the Korean vocabulary will be exceedingly enriched. For instance, the native *chwum*, the Sino-Korean *muyong*, and the English loan *taynsu* all mean 'dance'', but their semantic, cultural, and contextual nuances are significant.

Since the two Koreas have now opened their doors to each other, it is opportune for linguists, specialists, practitioners, and administrators from both Koreas to jointly implement resolute and forceful purification movements to achieve linguistic unification. Linguistic unification is an important strategy in implementing political unification (Trudgill 2000: 80, 130). Unlike many multilingual, multi-cultural, multi-ethnic nations in the world, the Korean people in both Koreas are homogeneous, being monolingual, mono-cultural, and mono-ethnic. Therefore, the Korean language is a signal of the identity of the Korean people, and linguistic unification is one of the crucial tasks before and after the unification.

While there is still a huge amount of divergence yet to be bridged, we have observed that there is great homogeneity also, in that: divergence is very minor in high-frequency vocabulary; Cultured Speech is based on Standard Speech; Standard Speech elements and North Korean dialectal elements are frequently entered into Cultured Speech as doublets or triplets; both Koreas have refined most Japanese loans; and both Koreas have similar sets of Chinese characters for educational purposes. All these facts will facilitate linguistic unification.

Many constructive suggestions have been made to homogenize or unify the language (e.g. Y. Ko 1996, 1999, 2001; Sohn 1997; Pae 1999; Y. Park 2001; P. Kim 2001; Choy 2001; T. Kim 2001; Kwak 2001; Cen 2001). Time and space do not allow me to go into details here. Basically, close cooperation between the two Koreas is essential so that various issues involved in linguistic divergence and unification may be jointly resolved with mutual trust, respect, and patience and with the sole goal of enhancing the linguistic life of all the Korean people.[14]

REFERENCES: Chapter 17

Co, Ohyen and Kim Yongkyeng. 2002. *Nampukhan Ene uy Ihay* (Understanding of South and North Korean Languages). Seoul: Yeklak.

Cen, Swuthay. 2001. Selo talun phyokipep uy thongil pangan (A proposal to unify the different spelling conventions). *Say Kwuke Saynghwal* 11.1.

Cen, Swuthay and Choy Hochel. 1989. *Nampukhan Ene Pikyo* (A Comparative Study of South and North Korean Languages). Seoul: Tosechwulphan.

Choy, Hochel. 2001. Selo talun ehwi uy tongcilseng ul wihan pangan (A proposal to homogenize the different lexicons). *Say Kwuke Saynghwal* 11.1.

Coulmas, F. 1999. The Far East. In Fishman (1999). In Fishman, J.A. (ed.), *Handbook of Language and Ethnic Identity.* Oxford: Oxford University Press.

Holmes, Janet. 2001. *An Introduction to Sociolinguistics.* Essex, England: Pearson Education Limited.

Kim, Cengsep. 2003. Wuli mal cengchayk uy panghyang (Proposed directions of Korean lan-

14 As discussed above, the efforts and achievements made by the people engaged in information technology are very suggestive in this regard (P. Kim 2001).

guage policies. *Hankul Say Sosik* 374 (October 2003): 8-11.

Kim, Chin-W. 1977. Divergence in language policies in Korea. In Kim, C.-W. (ed.), *Papers in Korean Linguistics*. Columbus, SC: Horn Beam Press.

Kim, Hungkyu. 1999. Kwuke saynghwal uy hanca sayong pinto yenkwu (A frequency study of character uses in Korea). *Say Kwuke Saynghwal* 9.1.

Kim, Minswu. 1985. *Pukhan uy Kwuke Yenkwu* (A Study of Korean in North Korea). Seoul: Korea University.

Kim, Minswu. 1999. Pukhan uy hanca kyoyuk (Character studies in North Korea), *Say Kwuke Saynghwal* 9.2.

Kim, Pyengsen. 2001. Solo talun cengpo kiswul yonge uy tongcilseng hoypok pangan (A proposal to recover the homogeneity in information technology terms). *Say Kwuke Saynghwal* 11.1.

Kim, Seycong. 1998. Oylay-e uy kaynyem kwa pyenchensa (Concept and development of loanwords). *Say Kwuke Saynghwal* 8.2.

Kim, Thaysik. 2001. Enlon uy nampukhan ene tongcilseng hoypok pangan (A proposal to recover the homogeneous mass media language in the South and North). *Say Kwuke Saynghwal* 11.1.

King, R. 1996. Language, politics and ideology in the post-war Koreas. In McCann, D. (ed.), *Korea Briefing*, 109–44. Asia Society.

Ko, Senghwan. 1998. Sinmun capci punya uy oylay-e sayong silthay (Use of loanwords in newspapers and magazines). *Say Kwuke Saynghwal* 8.2.

Ko, Yengkun. 1996. *Wuli ene Munhwa uy Ppuli lul Chacase* (In Search of the Roots of Our Language and Culture). Seoul: Hansin.

Ko, Yengkun. 1999. *Pukhan uy ene-munhwa* (Linguistic Culture of North Korea). Seoul: Seoul National University Press.

Ko, Yengkun. 2001. Nampuk kyupem munpep uy thongil pangan (A proposal to unify the normative grammars of the South and North). *Say Kwuke Saynghwal* 11.1.

Kwak, Chungkwu. 2001. Nampukhan ene icilhwa wa ku ey kwanlyen toyn myech muncey (Linguistic divergence between the South and North Korea and some related issues). *Say Kwuke Saynghwal* 11.1.

Nam, Phunghyen. 1999. Hanca-e wa hanca honyong. *Say Kwuke Saynghwal* 9.2.

Nam, Yunjin. 1999. Kwuke sacen phyocey-e uy hanca pinto (Frequency of Chinese characters in the Korean Language Dictionary). *Say Kwuke Saynghwal* 9.1.

Pay, Cwuchey. 1999. Kwuke swunhwa. In Yi Sungcay et al. (1999, 169–78).

Pak, Kapswu. 1999. *Arumtawun Wulimal Kakkwuki* (Cultivation of Beautiful Korean). Seoul: Cipmun-tang.

Park, Young-soon. 2001. *Hankwuke uy Sahoy-enehak* (Korean Sociolinguistics). Seoul: Hankwuk Munhwasae.

Safran, W. 1999. Nationalism. In Fishman, J.A. (ed.), *Handbook of Language and Ethnic Identity.* Oxford: Oxford University Press.

Sasse, W. 1979. Cultured Language: Implementation of a policy in North Korea. *Korean Linguistics* 2.

Sohn, Ho-min. 1997. Orthographic divergence in South and North Korea: Toward a unified spelling system. In Kim-Renuad, Young-Key (ed.), *The Korean Alphabet.* Honolulu: University of Hawaii Press.

Sohn, Ho-min. 1999. *The Korean Language*. Cambridge: Cambridge University Press.

Sohn, Ho-min. 2002. Preface. Choon-Hak Cho et al. *Chinese Characters in Korean.* Honolulu: University of Hawaii Press.

Song, Cay-Se. 1999. Hankwuk uy hanca kyoyuk. *Say Kwuke Saynghwal* 9.2.

Song, Chel-Ui. 1998. Woylay-e uy swunhwa pangan kwa swuyong taychayk (Proposed plans to refine and accept loanwords). *Say Kwuke Saynghwal* 8.2.

Song, Kijung. 1999. Hanca munhwakwen. *Say Kwuke Saynghwal* 9.2.

Trudgill, P. 2000. *Sociolinguistics.* London: the Penguin Group.

Yi, Cengpok. 1998. khemphyuthe thongsin punya uy oylay-e sayong (Use of loanwords in computer communication). *Say Kwuke Saynghwal* 8.2.

Yi, Oklyen, Kim Huycin, Kim Yengca, and Kim Cengun. 1998. *Nampukhan ene Yenkwu* (Studies on South and North Korean Languages). Seoul: Pakiceng.

Yi, Senyeng. 1998. Sangho sangphyo punya uy oylay-e sayong (Use of loanwords in trade names and trade marks). *Say Kwuke Saynghwal* 8.2.

Yi, Unkyeng. 1998. Pangsong punya uy oylay-e sayong (Use of loanwords in broadcasting). *Say Kwuke Saynghwal* 8.2.

Yi, Sungcay et al. 1999. *Hankwuke wa Hankwuk Munhwa.* Seoul: Saymun-sa.

18 Orthographic Divergence in South and North Korea: Toward a Unified Spelling System*

1. Introduction

Linguistic divergence between South and North Korea since 1945 has been accelerated mainly by three interrelated factors: complete physical insulation between the two Koreas; polarized political, ideological, and social distinctions; and the different language policies implemented by the two governments.[1] As a result, a thick socio-political dialectical division, with two standards of speech, has been superimposed on the long existing historical-geographical dialects. The two standards of speech are Seoul-based P'yojunmal (Standard Speech) in the South and P'yŏngyang-based Munhwaŏ (Cultured Speech) in the North. Linguistic divergence is found not only in the lexicon, phonology, grammar, and usage, but also in orthography. The aim of the present chapter is to examine the extent to which *han'gŭl* spelling divergence exists, to investigate what has caused the divergence, and to suggest some directions leading to a unified spelling system.[2] Disparities will be observed in two current systems: South

---

* This is reprinted from Kim-Renaud, Y.K. (ed.), *The Korean Alphabet: Its History and Structure*, pp. 193–218. University of Hawaii Press. 1997. The McCune-Reischauer Romanization system is followed in transcribing Korean expressions.

1 Ideological distinctions are reflected in respective educational goals. South Korea aims to develop the nation and the national culture through recognition, development, and fulfillment of each individual's fullest potentialities (National Education Charter). North Korea's goal is to bring up the rising generation as revolutionaries who will fight for a socialist society and the masses (the Constitution). Thus, language is regarded as a means of communication in South Korea, but as a means of thought reform and of strengthening the people's "revolutionary consciousness for the continual class struggle" in North Korea. The language policies of the two Koreas are surveyed in Sohn 1991. See also LIASS 1976; C. Kim 1978; Sasse 1980; M. Kim 1985; Chon and Choy 1989; COH 1990; Ko 1990; and Park 1991).

2 In a broad sense, Korean orthography includes Chinese characters and Romanization as well. There are still pros and cons regarding the use of Chinese characters in South Korea. The South Korean government repeatedly adopted and abolished the policy of the exclusive use of *han'gŭl* until 1972, when it fixed the current practice that 1,800 basic characters be taught for reading and writing at intermediate (900) and high (900) schools. This policy does not mean

Korea's *Han'gŭl match'umpŏp* (MOE 1988a) and North Korea's *Kaejŏnghan Chosŏnmal kyubŏmjip* (KLAC 1988). Extensive reference will be made to such previous works by M. Kim (1985), E. Lee (1989), and Lee and Ahn (1991).

Both *Hang'ŭl match'umpŏp* and *Kaejŏnghan Chosŏnmal kyubŏmjip* were derived from *Han'gŭl match'umpŏp t'ong'ilan* (KLA 1933) through repeated revisions. While only minor modifications were made in South Korea before *Han'gŭl match'umpŏp*, two major revisions were made in North Korea before *Kaejŏnghan Chosŏnmal kyubŏmjip*: *Chosŏnŏ ch'ŏlchapŏp* in 1954 and *Chosŏnmal kyubŏmjip* in 1966. The sharing of the source system and the fact that both systems follow two basic spelling principles stipulated in 1933, however, have prevented extreme diversification. One of the basic principles is the principle of morphophonemic spelling. This principle specifies that the original forms of the roots and affixes in compounds and derivatives should be identified as much as possible and spelled accordingly; but if the etymology is not clear, or if the original sounds are unpredictably changed or fossilized, they should be spelled as they are pronounced (MOE 1988a: 1.1; KLAC 1988, *Match'umpŏp*-General Rule). The other basic principle that North and South Korea share is that of word-based spacing (MOE 1988a: 1.2; KLAC 1988, *Ttŭiŏssŭgi*-General Rule). An external deterrent against radical divergence seems to be the fact that the governments and scholars of both Koreas are keenly cognizant of the adverse effect of linguistic diversification on their reunification efforts. For instance, Kim Il Sung's 1964 and 1966 language-related Teachings (*kyosi*) via dialogues with linguists called for the implementation of Chuch'e-oriented linguistic reforms but warned against radical changes (in regard to a proposed script reform, the teaching of Chinese characters, and spacing conventions) in preparation for national reunification.[3] Such activating and deterring forces

that society (the general public, newspapers, books) is bound by this set of characters. In North Korea, Kim Il Sung's 1946 Teachings and the initiation in 1949 of compulsory education launched, with complete success, the *han'gŭl*-based literary movement, abolishing Chinese characters altogether. Kim Il Sung's 1964 and 1966 Teachings, however, reinstated character teaching for reading only, to enable students to understand South Korean publications. The major issue in Romanization is what sort of alphabetic symbols are to be used for individual sounds and how they are to be spelled. This has been a longstanding question in South Korea until 1984, when the Ministry of Education abolished its 1959 system and enacted a revised system based essentially on the McCune-Reischauer system. It is reported that a recent tentative agreement between South Korea and North Korea is that South Korea's vowel symbols and North Korea's consonant symbols will be used.

3 Kim's 1964 Teachings present the basic directions of his language policies and his 1966 Teachings substantiate them. The areas covered are script reform, Sino-Korean words, loanwords, Chinese characters, spacing and word forms, vocabulary refinement, the campaign for proper language use, and Korean language education, as well as the concept of Cultured Speech (see Sohn 1991 and other works for details).

have affected spelling differences between the two Koreas, but not to an extreme degree.

The existing differences seem to have been created by three partly interrelated causes: (a) the emergence of two standards of speech, (b) different linguistic analyses of similar or identical phenomena, and (c) different conventions followed in breaking with tradition for the sake of regularization. Two standards of speech have emerged because North Korea has legislated Cultured Speech as standard in pronunciation and spelling, in accordance with Kim Il Sung's 1966 Chuch'e-oriented Teachings.[4] Kim called for preserving and developing the national characteristics of Korean based on the speech of P'yŏngyang, suggesting the term Munhwaŏ (Cultured Speech) rather than P'yojunmal (Standard Speech). Munhwaŏ is defined as "the richly developed national language that is formed centering on the revolutionary capital under the leadership of the proletarian party that holds sovereignty during the socialism-constructing period, and that all people hold as a standard because it has been refined revolutionarily and polished culturally to fit the proletariat's goals and lifestyle" (LIASS 1973). North Korea denounces P'yojunmal, claiming that "it has lost its legitimacy as a national language because it is deprived of national characteristics and popular elements and has become the speech of the bourgeoisie, a jumble filled with Western, Japanese, and Chinese elements owing to American imperialists and their followers' national language erasure policy" (Chong et al. 1981; KISU 1983).[5] In South Korea, P'yojunmal is defined as "the contemporary Seoul speech used by educated people" (MOE 1988b), modified from the definition in KLA (1933, 1936), which read "the contemporary Seoul speech used by middle-class people."

Different linguistic analyses are observed, among other things, in the determination of morphemic fossilization in compounds and derivatives. Although both spelling systems share the morphophonemic principle, the CV principle that requires, for example, the syllable division of V.CV and not of VC.V within a morpheme (e.g. 사람 sa.ram, not 살암 sar.am 'person'), and word-based spac-

4 Some historical justification for the establishment of Cultured Speech is found in Y. Kim 1978. Cultured Speech is also claimed to be the model for the national language that is formed with Kim Il Sung and Kim Chong Il's speech as the nucleus (Chong and Lee 1984). Ki-moon Lee (personal communication) points out that despite North Korea's assertion to the contrary, Cultured Speech is based essentially on Standard Speech, not on the P'yŏng'yang dialect. One example is that Cultured Speech includes patalized Sino-Korean forms, such as *chŏnggŏjang* 'station' and *ch'onji* 'heaven and earth' rather than the P'yŏng'yang forms *tŏnggŏdang* and *t'yŏndi*. It is premature, however, to subscribe to this view, since Cultured Speech is based on the P'yŏng'yang dialect in many other respects, such as the word-initial *l* and *n*.

5 This definition of North Korea's is unwarranted because so-called polluted expressions are excluded from Standard Speech (MOE 1988b; Huh 1991).

ing, the question often arises whether an element should be interpreted as a single fossilized morpheme or as a composite of two or more morphemes, whether a speech sound is morphophonemically significant, or whether a sequence of words is to be analyzed as a compound.

The two systems adopt different conventions in regularizing forms and concepts, breaking with tradition to different degrees, as in the names of letters, treatment of the epenthetic *s* (*sai-siot*), treatment of some Sino-Korean diphthongs, and spacing. It appears that North Korea's system has broken with tradition more frequently, pursuing more formal uniformity. This may be due partly to Kim Il Song's Chuch'e language theory, which is closely tied to Kim's "Anti-Japanese Struggle" during World War II, Marxist-Leninist language theory, and North Korea's Cultured Speech Movement, which has prevailed since Kim's 1966 Teachings (Ko 1990). It has been observed by Ko (1990) and others that North Korea has ceased to applaud KLA (1933) since the late 1960s.

2. Extra-spelling Conventions

In addition to spelling and spacing disparities, the two Koreas disagree on three other conventions, direction of writing, names of *han'gŭl* letters, and alphabetic order for dictionaries and other purposes.

As for the direction of writing, South Korea follows the tradition allowing both horizontal and vertical writing, whereas North Korea stipulates that horizontal writing be used in principle (KLAC 1988). In South Korea, most newspapers use vertical writing, whereas a recent trend in other publications is to favor horizontal writing, owing to typewriter and computer practices, visual expediency, and Western influence.

Disparity also appears in the names of three consonant letters (ㄱ *k*, ㄷ *t*, ㅅ *s*) and geminate consonant letters (MOE 1988a: 2.4; KLAC 1988: 1.1). In the following, romanized equivalents are given under corresponding *han'gŭl* expressions as needed.

(1) Names of *han'gŭl* letters

	ㄱ	ㄷ	ㅅ	ㄲ	ㅃ
SK:	기역 ki.yŏk	디귿 ti.gŭt	시옷 si.ot	쌍기역 ssang.gi.yŏk	쌍비읍 ssang.bi.ŭp
NK:	기윽 ki.ŭk	디읃 ti.ŭt	시읏 si.ŭt	된기윽 toen.gi.ŭk	된비읍 toen.bi.ŭp

North Korea changed the traditional names of the three letters to conform to the other consonant terms. Whereas South Korea's traditional Sino-Korean term *ssang* 'twin' is a purely letter-based term (for example, twin letters in South Korea), North Korea's newly introduced native term *toen* 'hard, tense' is a sound-based term (for example, tensed sound quality in North Korea). North Korea's use of *toen* might have been urged by Kim Il Sung's 1964 and 1966 Teachings that call for maximum use of native terms.

The alphabetic orders used for dictionary entries and so forth do not agree, as shown below (MOE 1988a: 2.4; KLAC 1988: 1.1).

(2) Syllable-onset consonants

SK:

ㄱ	ㄲ	ㄴ	ㄷ	ㄸ	ㄹ	ㅁ	ㅂ	ㅃ	ㅅ	ㅆ	ㅇ
k/g	kk	n	t/ d	Tt	l/r	m	p/b	pp	s	ss	ng

ㅈ	ㅉ	ㅊ	ㅋ	ㅌ	ㅍ	ㅎ
ch/j	tch	ch'	k'	t'	p'	h

NK:

ㄱ	ㄴ	ㄷ	ㄹ	ㅁ	ㅂ	ㅅ	ㅇ	ㅈ	ㅊ	ㅋ	ㅌ
k/g	n	t/d	l/r	M	p/b	s	ng	ch/j	ch'	k'	t'

ㅍ	ㅎ	ㄲ	ㄸ	ㅃ	ㅆ	ㅉ
p'	h	kk	tt	pp	ss	tch

(3) Syllable-nuclear vowels and diphthongs

SK:

ㅏ	ㅐ	ㅑ	ㅒ	ㅓ	ㅔ	ㅕ	ㅖ	ㅗ	ㅘ	ㅙ	ㅚ	ㅛ
a	ae	ya	yae	ŏ	e	yŏ	ye	o	wa	wae	oe	yo

ㅜ	ㅝ	ㅟ	ㅞ	ㅠ	ㅡ	ㅢ	ㅣ
u	wŏ	wi	we	yu	ŭ	ŭi	i

NK:

ㅏ	ㅑ	ㅓ	ㅕ	ㅗ	ㅛ	ㅜ	ㅠ	ㅡ	ㅣ	ㅐ	ㅒ	ㅔ
a	ya	ŏ	yŏ	o	yo	U	yu	ŭ	i	ae	yae	e

ㅖ	ㅚ	ㅟ	ㅢ	ㅘ	ㅝ	ㅙ	ㅞ
ye	oe	wi	ŭi	wa	wŏ	wae	we

(4) Syllable-coda consonants (*patch'im*)

SK:

ㄱ	ㄲ	ㄳ	ㄴ	ㄵ	ㄶ	ㄷ	ㄹ	ㄺ	ㄻ	ㄼ	ㄽ	ㄾ	ㄿ
k/g	kk	ks	n	nj	nh	t/d	l/r	lk/lg	lm	lp/lb	ls	lt'	lp'

ㅀ	ㅁ	ㅂ	ㅄ	ㅅ	ㅆ	ㅇ	ㅈ	ㅊ	ㅋ	ㅌ	ㅍ	ㅎ
lh	m	p/b	ps	s	ss	ng	ch/j	ch'	k'	t'	p'	h

NK:

ㄱ	ㄳ	ㄴ	ㄵ	ㄶ	ㄷ	ㄹ	ㄺ	ㄻ	ㄼ	ㄽ	ㄾ	ㄿ	ㅀ
k/g	ks	n	nj	nh	t/d	l/r	lk/lg	lm	lp/lb	ls	lt'	lp'	lh

ㅁ	ㅂ	ㅄ	ㅇ	ㅈ	ㅊ	ㅋ	ㅌ	ㅍ	ㅎ	ㄲ	ㅆ
m	p/b	ps	ng	ch/j	ch'	k'	t'	p'	h	kk	ss

Notice in (2) and (3) that complex letters immediately follow each corresponding basic letter in South Korea but are grouped after all basic letters in North Korea. North Korea's onset consonant order agrees with *Han'gŭl match'umpŏp t'ong'ilan* (KLA 1933), but its diphthongal order does not. Thus, for example, the triple letter ㅞ *we* (i.e. ㅜ *u* + ㅓ *ŏ* + ㅣ *i*) is placed at the end in North Korea, whereas it is placed before the double letter ㅟ *wi* in South Korea (in the sequence ㅜ *u*, ㅝ *wŏ*, ㅞ *we*, ㅟ *wi*). Further notice the North Korean order among double letters, placing ㅘ *wa* and ㅝ *wŏ* after ㅚ *oe*, ㅟ *wi*, and ㅢ *ŭi*. E. Lee (1989: 155) states that whereas in *Han'gŭl match'umpŏp t'ong'ilan* the order among complex letters is determined on the basis of the first letter of a complex, in the North Korean system the complex letters are arranged on the basis of the added (second) letter, thus in the order ㅣ *i* (ㅐ *ae*, ㅒ *yae*, ㅔ *e*, ㅖ *ye*, ㅚ *oe*, ㅟ *wi*, ㅢ *ŭi*), ㅏ (ㅘ *wa*), ㅓ *ŏ* (ㅝ *wŏ*), ㅐ *ae* (ㅙ *wae*), and ㅔ *e* (ㅞ *we*). A partially sound-based approach in North Korea is observed in (2) and (4). The letter ㄲ *kk*, for example is regarded simply as the doubling of the ㄱ *k* in South Korea, whereas it is treated as an independent entity that has nothing phonemically to do with ㄱ *k* in North Korea. Thus, the only difference between the two systems in (4) is that ㄲ kk and ㅆ ss are placed at the end in North Korea. North Korea's order of coda consonants deviates not only from South Korea's system but also from *Han'gŭl match'umpŏp t'ong'il-an*, whose order is ㄱ *k*...ㅎ *h*, ㄲ *kk*, ㄳ *ks*, ㄵ *nj*...ㅄ *ps*, ㅆ *ss*.

Let me make a few comments on the above North-South disparities. With regard to the direction of writing, although North Korea hardly practices any vertical writing in publications, its use is allowed in exceptional cases. Since a definite trend in South Korea is to prefer horizontal writing, this divergence is not a major issue. As for the names of the letters ㄱ *k/g*, ㄷ *t/d*, and ㅅ *s*, North Korea's regulation, which is a deviation from tradition, is preferred for its simplicity. Between South Korea's letter-based term *ssang* and North Korea's sound-based term *toen*, the latter is preferable in that all the simple letters describe respective sound qualities in word-initial and word-final positions. Compared to *ssang*, which does not provide any phonological information, *toen* not only implies the independent phonemic status of geminate letters, but also gives information on the tenseness feature of the sounds.

With regard to alphabetic order, later versions of *Han'gŭl match'umpŏp t'ong'il-an* regulated the order of the twenty-four basic letters without specifying where complex letters were to be placed in relation to the basic letters. As a result, there have been inconsistent dictionary entry orderings in South Korea, as illustrated below:

(5) a. Martin et al.: A Korean-English Dictionary (1967)

가	까까머리	가까이	까까중
ka	*kkakkamŏri*	*kakkai*	*kkakkajung*
가가호호	가깝다	가건물	가격
kagahoho	*kakkapta*	*kagŏnmul*	*kagyŏk*
가난	까마귀	굴뚝	
kanan	*kkamagwi*	*kulttuk*	

b. Hyŏnmunsa (현문사): *Han'gugŏ taesajŏn* (1976)

가	가가호호	가건물	가격
ka	*kagahoho*	*kagŏnmul*	*kagyŏk*
가까이	가깝다	가난	굴뚝
kakkai	*kakkapta*	*kanan*	*kulttuk*
까까머리	까까중	까마귀	
kkamagui	*kkakkajung*	*kkamagwi*	

Martin et al. (1967) and several other well-known dictionaries belong to the first type, where tensed consonant letters are not given independent status but are considered ancillary to their corresponding basic letters.[6] Hyŏnmunsa (1976) and many other recently edited dictionaries are of the second type, where all the words with an initial tense consonant are entered only after all the corresponding lax-consonant initial words. The Ministry of Education (MOE 1988a) has declared the second type to be the standard, as in (a) above. As for vowels and diphthongs, almost all existing dictionaries in South Korea follow the order given in (b).

Although North Korea's order is to some extent phonologically motivated, South Korea's purely graphically oriented order is preferable. In South Korea, for example, ㅐ *ae* is regarded as a combination of the letters ㅏ *a* and ㅣ *i* irrespective of its phonological value; hence it is placed right after ㅏ *a*. In North Korea, it is viewed as a single phonemic unit /ɛ/, which has nothing to do with the phoneme /a/; hence it is placed after all the basic vowel and related diphthong letters. For one thing, the general public perceives ㄲ *kk*, ㅃ *pp*, ㅐ *ae*, ㅔ *e*, and so on, to be related to ㄱ *k/g*, ㅂ *p/b*, ㅏ *a*, and ㅓ *ŏ*, respectively. They are linguistically naïve, being concerned more with letters than with the sounds represented by the letters. Graphic orientation of dictionary users and compilers is also observed in English, where words like *philosophy* and *pneumonia* are entered under P, and not under F and N, respectively. Second, South Korea's order is easy to remember, because the ordering rule involved is simply that all the complex letters with arbitrary initial X must follow the basic X in the alphabetic order of the component noninitial letters, as in ㅓ *ŏ*, ㅔ *e*; ㅜ *u*, ㅝ *wŏ*, ㅞ *we*, ㅟ *wi*; and ㄱ *k*, ㄲ *kk*, ㄳ *ks*. Thus, mnemonically, South Korea's system is superior to North Korea's. The mnemonic complexity of North Korea's order of vowel and diphthong letters is reflected in C. Kim's (1991) statement that simple letters come before double letters, which in turn come before triple letters, and that among double letters, complex letters ending in ㅣ *i* precede complex letters beginning with ㅗ *o* and ㅜ *u*. Third, North Korea's order among vowel and diphthong letters appears to be based on quite an unmotivated principle. Why should the added letter, rather than the first letter, be given the head status? Why the unusual order of the ㅣ *i* followed by ㅏ *a*, ㅓ *ŏ*, ㅐ *ae*, and ㅔ *e*? Finally, other things being equal, tradition is to be followed. As pointed out in Nam (1987), in *Hunmin chŏng'ŭm* ㄲ *kk*, ㄸ *tt*, and so forth, are explained immediately after their corresponding simple letters. Also, it is well known that in Middle Korean, ㅐ /*ay*/, ㅔ /*ŏy*/, and ㅚ /*oy*/, for example, were phonemic diphthongs composed of ㅏ *a*, ㅓ *ŏ*, ㅗ *o*, and ㅣ *i*. *Han'gŭl match'umpŏp t'ong'ilan* (KLA 1933) and its later versions also implied that ㅐ *ae* and ㅒ *yae*, for example, are combinations of ㅏ *a* + ㅣ *i* and ㅑ *ya* + ㅣ *i*.

Like South Korea's tradition, North Korea's current system also treats the letter ㅇ occurring in a vowel-initial syllable as a consonant letter, despite its silent

6 Nam (1987) illustrates another differently ordered set of this type.

quality, and orders it after ㅅ *s*. *Han'gŭl match'umpŏp* (MOE 1988a) gives all complex letters independent status, stipulating that, for example, words with the initial ㄲ *kk* be entered only after all the words with the initial ㄱ *k*. This is a step toward North Korea's system, where ㄲ *kk* and so forth are given independent status. Dictionary users in the two systems need only be aware of the locational difference of the geminate consonant letters as far as the onset and coda consonants are concerned. However, the serious fact remains that the divergent orders of syllable nuclear vowels and diphthongs cause great confusion to dictionary users.

3. Spelling Divergence and Standards of Speech

The following sets of examples of spelling divergence are essentially the result of phonological differences existing between Standard Speech and Cultured Speech.

Sino-Korean ㄹ *l/r*

In Standard Speech, Sino-Korean word-initial ㄹ is not pronounced before the vowel sound [i] and the semivowel sound [y] and is pronounced as [n] elsewhere (6a). Word-medial (but morpheme-initial) Sino-Korean ㄹ also frequently becomes silent before [i] and [y] (6b). In Cultured Speech, this ㄹ is pronounced and is spelled as such. Sino-Korean words with ㄹ that are phonetically identical in Standard and Cultured speech are spelled identically (6c).

(6)	a.	SK:	이발,	역사,	노동,	내일,	누누이
			ibal,	*yŏksa,*	*nodong,*	*naeil,*	*nunui*
		NK:	리발,	력사,	로동,	래일,	루루이
			ribal,	*ryŏksa,*	*rodong,*	*raeil,*	*rurui*
	b.	SK:	나열,	비율,	역이용		
			nayŏl,	*piyul,*	*yŏngniyong*		
		NK:	라열,	비률,	역리용		
			rayŏl,	*piryul,*	*yŏngriyong*		
	c.	SK:	분리,	인류,	실례		
			pulli,	*illyu,*	*sillye*		
		NK:	분리,	인류,	실례		
			pulli,	*illyu,*	*sillye*		

Sino-Korean ㄴ *n*

In Standard Speech, all word-initial and some definable word-medial (but morpheme-initial) Sino-Korean ㄴ's become silent before [i] and [y] and thus are not spelled, whereas Cultured Speech requires them to be pronounced and spelled.

(7)	SK:	이탄,	여성,	요소,	영령,	신여성
		it'an,	*yŏsŏng,*	*yoso,*	*yŏllyŏng,*	*sinnyŏsŏng*
	NK:	니탄,	녀성,	뇨소,	년령,	신녀성
		nit'an,	*nyŏsong,*	*nyoso,*	*nyŏllyŏng,*	*sinnyŏsŏng*

Vowel Harmony

While vowel harmony is strictly onserved in Cultured Speech, there is silght deviation from it in Standard Speech. The deviation is in polysyllabic ㅂ *p/b* irregular predicates followed by an infinitive suffix, in which *w* (from ㅂ *p/b*) and the suffix are pronounced as ㅝ *wŏ*, regardless of the bright/dark quality of the preceding vowel, as in (8). Monosyllabic ㅂ irregular predicates in Standard Speech observe vowel harmony, as in 도와 *towa* (help-INF).

(8)	SK:	아름다워,	고마워,	가까워서,	괴로웠다
		arŭmdawŏ,	*komawŏ,*	*kakkawŏsŏ,*	*koerowŏtta*
	NK:	아름다와,	고마와,	가까와서,	괴로왔다
		arŭmdawa,	*komawa,*	*kakkawasŏ,*	*koerowatta*

Sporadic Lexical Disparities

Only Cultured Speech shows umlauting in certain words (9a), whereas only Standard Speech shows vowel fronting in certain other words (9b).

(9)	a.	SK:	지푸라기,	부스러기,	호루라기	
			chip'uragi,	*pusŭrŏgi,*	*horuragi*	
		NK:	지푸래기,	부스레기,	호루래기	
			hip'uraegi,	*pusŭregi,*	*horuraegi*	
	b.	SK:	뼉다귀,	귀절,	쇠고기,	외양간
			ppyŏktagwi,	*kwijŏl,*	*soegogi,*	*oeyangkan*
		NK:	뼉다구,	구절,	소고기,	오양간
			ppyŏktagu,	*kujŏl,*	*sogogi,*	*oyangkan*

Only Cultured Speech has aspiration in words like those below.

(10) SK: 수범, 수곰, 아내, 갈치,
subŏm, *sugom*, *anae*, *kalch'i*,
가뜩이, 축축이, 똑똑지, 거북지
kattŭgi, *ch'ukch'ugi*, *ttokttokchi*, *kŏbukchi*

NK: 수펌, 수콤, 안해, 칼치,
sup'ŏm, *suk'om*, *anhae*, *k'alch'i*,
가뜩히, 축축히, 똑똑치, 거북치
kattŭk'i, *ch'ukch'uk'i*, *ttokttokch'i*, *kŏbukch'i*

Numerous other native words are pronounced differently in Standard and Cultured speech:

(11) SK: 우뢰, 긁어모아, 퍽이나, 달걀,
uroe, *kŭlgŏmoa*, *p'ŏgina*, *talgyal*,
원수, 햅쌀, 크낙새, 네째
wŏnsu, *haepssal*, *k'ŭnaksae*, *netchae*

NK: 우레, 그러모아, 퍼그나, 닭알,
ure, *kŭrŏmoa*, *p'ŏgŭna*, *talgal*,
원쑤, 햇쌀, 클락새, 넷째
wŏnssu, *haetssal*, *k'ŭllaksae*, *nettchae*

Sino-Korean Words with Popular Pronunciation (俗音 Sogŭm)

Both systems stipulate that Sino-Korean words with popular pronunciation (as distinct from their regular pronunciation) are to be spelled as they are pronounced. Thus, many such words are spelled identically in South Korea and North korea, such as 나팔 *nap'al* (from 라팔 喇叭 *rap'al*) 'bugle', 남색 *namsaek* (from 람색 藍色 *ramsaek*) 'indigo', 요기 *yogi* (from 료기 療飢 *ryogi*) 'relieving hunger', and 희로애락 *hiroaerak* (from 희노애락 喜怒哀樂 *hinoaerak*) 'joy, anger, sorrow, and pleasure'. There is, however, phonetic/spelling divergence in some words:

(12) SK: 곤란, 논란, 한라산, 유월, 폐렴
kollan, *nollan*, *hallasan*, *yuwŏl*, *p'yeryŏm*

NK: 곤난, 론난, 한나산, 류월, 페염
konnan, *ronnan*, *hannasan*, *ryuwŏl*, *p'eyŏm*

Loanword Spelling

Spellings of loanwords are considerably different in South Korea and North Korea. The following examples are from Chong et al. (1981), Chon and Choy (1989: 258-270), and Lee and Ahn (1991). North Korea's spellings of terms for general objects are influenced by Russian and Japanese, whereas South Korea's spellings reflect English pronunciations.

(13)		'balance'	'cover'	'dilemma'	'cup'	'dance'	'minus'
	SK:	밸런스,	커버,	딜레마,	컵,	댄스,	마이너스
		paellŏnsŭ,	*k'ŏbŏ,*	*tillema,*	*k'ŏp,*	*taensŭ,*	*mainŏsŭ*
	NK:	바란스,	카바,	지렌마,	고뿌,	딴스,	미누스
		paransŭ,	*k'aba,*	*chirenma,*	*koppu,*	*ttansŭ,*	*minusŭ*
		'missile'	'candle'	'jack'	'jelly'	'studio'	'radio'
	SK:	미사일,	캔들,	잭,	젤리	스튜디오,	라디오
		misail,	*k'aendŭl,*	*chaek,*	*chelli,*	*sŭt'yudio,*	*radio*
	NK:	미싸일,	간데라,	쟈끼,	쩰리	스타지오,	라지오
		missail,	*kandera,*	*chyakki,*	*tchelli,*	*sŭt'ajio,*	*rajio*

As for place names, North Korea's spellings follow the pronunciations used in the respective countries, apparently in accordance with Kim Il Sung's suggestion in his 1964 Teachings. South Korean spellings follow the English tradition.

(14)		'Jakarta'	'Congo'	'Hungary'	'Cairo'	'Vatican'
	SK:	자카르타,	콩고,	헝가리,	카이로,	바티칸
		chak'arŭt'a,	*k'onggo,*	*hŏnggari,*	*k'airo*	*pat'ik'an*
	NK:	쟈까르따,	꽁고	웽그리아,	까히라,	바띠까노
		chyakkarŭtta,	*kkonggo,*	*wenggŭria,*	*kkahira,*	*pattikkano*
		'Sweden'	'Mexico'	'Canada'		
	SK:	스웨덴,	멕시코,	캐나다		
		sŭweden,	*meksik'o,*	*k'aenada*		
	NK:	스웨리예,	메히꼬,	카나다		
		sŭweriye,	*mehikko,*	*k'anada*		

Spelling Divergence and Linguistic Analysis

The following contrastive sets are the result of different linguistic analyses of similar or identical phenomena. Although South Korea and North Korea share the morphophonemic spelling principle, there are numerous cases there phonetically similar or identical compounds and derivatives receive different morphemic analyses in terms of phonological, morphological, or semantic fossilization, and hence spelling divergence occurs. In some cases, South Korea's spellings are more faithful to morphemic etymology; in others, North Korea's are.

ㅗ/ㅛ o/yo, ㅓ/ㅕ ŏ/yŏ

After ㅣ *i*, ㅐ *ae*, ㅔ *e*, ㅚ *oe*, ㅟ *wi*, ㅢ *ŭi*, or after the verb 하 *ha* 'do', South Korea's ㅗ *o* and ㅓ *ŏ* frequently contrast graphically with North Korea's ㅛ *yo* and ㅕ *yŏ*, respectively, as manifested in the spellings of the blunt level suffix (15a), the infinitive suffix (15b), and the adverbial suffix (15c).

(15)	a.	SK:	아니오,	가시오,	학생이오	
			anio,	*kasio,*	*haksaeng'io*	
		NK:	아니요,	가시요,	학생이요	
			aniyo,	*kasiyo,*	*haksaeng'iyo*	
	b.	SK:	되어,	띄어쓰기,	비었다,	하였다
			toeŏ,	*ttŭiŏssŭgi,*	*piŏtta,*	*hayŏtta*
		NK:	되여,	띄여쓰기,	비였다,	하였다
			toeyŏ,	*ttŭiyŏssŭgi,*	*piyŏtta,*	*hayŏtta*
	c.	SK:	드디어,	도리어,	구태여	
			tŭdiŏ,	*toriŏ,*	*kut'aeyŏ*	
		NK:	드디여,	도리여,	구태여	
			tŭdiyŏ,	*toriyŏ,*	*kut'aeyŏ*	

The above words are usually pronounced with the semivowel [y] inserted in both Standard and Cultured speech. South Korea treats this semivowel as phonologically predictable, whereas North Korea treats it as a part of restructures morphemes. South Korea's practice seems to be preferable in (a) and (b) above in view of native speakers' psychology and the morphemic regularity involved in the blunt level suffix and the infinitive suffix. North Korea's practice appears favorable in (c), however, in that, for instance, 어/여 in the adverb 드디어/드디여 *tŭdiyŏ* 'finally' is not different in pronunciation from 여 *yŏ* in the adverb 구태여 *kut'aeyŏ* 'deliberately', and native speakers no longer perceive 어/여 ŏ/*yŏ* and 드디 *tŭdi* as two separate morphemes.

Tensing

After the prospective suffix ㄹ/을 *l/ŭl*, lax stops (ㄱ *k/g*, ㅂ *p/b*, ㄷ *t/d*, ㅈ *ch/j*, ㅅ *s*) become tensed stops in both Standard and Cultured speech. In both South Korea and North Korea, these lax stops were spelled in single (lax) stops until

1957, when in South Korea a decision was made at a Korean Language Society general meeting to spell certain fossilized suffixes with geminate letters, as shown below. North Korea's practice is to follow tradition and spell them consistently as single letters.

(16)	SK:	−을까,	−을꼬,	−을쏘냐,	−을지라도,	−을수록
		-ŭlkka,	*-ŭlkko*,	*-ŭlssonya*,	*-ŭlchirado*,	*-ŭlsurok*
	NK:	−을가,	−을고,	−을소냐,	−을지라도,	−을수록
		-ŭlka,	*-ŭlko*,	*-ŭlsonya*,	*-ŭlchirado*,	*-ŭlsurok*

It is important to consider grammaticalization phenomena in legislating spelling conventions. Frequently, however, it is not easy to determine to what extent forms need to be grammaticalized in order to be considered morphological units for spelling. We need to take into account such criteria as psychological reality, phonological and grammatical regularity, simplicity, naturalness, and tradition. For example, spelling the simple ㄱ *k* in ㄹ/을게 *l/ŭlkke* 'I promise' in South and North Korea can not be sufficiently justified despite its diachronic grammaticalization from ㄹ/을 것이어 *l/ŭl kŏsiŏ*, in view of its complete structural, formal, and semantic restructuring. South Korea's spelling change of ㄹ/을가 *l/ŭlkka* to ㄹ/을까 *l/ŭlkka*, in contrast, might be somewhat premature in that it is still in the process of restructuring, manifesting the regular sense "whether," the partly restructured sense "I wonder," and the fully restructured sense "shall I/we?" In the first two senses, the spelling of ㄹ/을까 *l/ŭlkka* loses parallelism not only with 은/는가 *ŭn/nŭn ka* but also with ㄹ/을지 *l/ŭlchi*.

Compounds

Different etymological considerations are given to certain compounds. Below, (17a) illustrates the cases where South Korea is more faithful to etymology and (17b) the cases where North Korea is more faithful.

(17)	a.	SK:	넋두리,	넓적코,	넓죽한,	몸닦달,
			nŏkturi,	*nŏpchŏkk'o*,	*nŏpchukhan*,	*momdaktal*,
			가죽나무,	벗나무		
			kajungnamu,	*pŏnnamu*		
		NK:	넉두리,	넙적코,	넙죽한,	몸닥달,
			nŏkturi,	*nŏpchŏkk'o*,	*nŏpchukhan*,	*momdaktal*,
			가중나무,	벗나무		
			kajungnamu,	*pŏnnamu*		

where 넋 means 'soul, spirit', 넓 'wide', 닦 'polish, clean', 가죽 'tree-of-heaven', and 벚 'cherry'.

b. SK: 앎니, *amni*, 잠깐, *chamkkan*, 닭조림, *takchorim*, 손뼉, *sonppyŏk*, 돌맞이, *tolmaji*, 눈썹 *nunssŏp* 멋쩍다, *muŏtchŏkta*,

NK: 앎이, *amni*, 잠간, *chamkan*, 닭졸임, *takchorim*, 손벽, *sonpyŏk*, 돐맞이, *tolmaji*, 눈섭 *nunsŏp* 멋적다, *muŏtchŏkta*,

where 이 means 'tooth', 졸 'get boiled down', 돐 'one full year', 적 'small, little', 간 'space', 벽 'wall', and 섭 'brow.

If no regular phonological pattern is violated, it may be preferable to retain generally known etymological information as much as possible, as in South Korean 넋두리 *nŏkturi* 'speaking on behalf of the dead, a complaint', because such spellings have an ideographic function and thus facilitate morpheme recognition, not to mention their compliance with tradition. Between South Korean 넓적코 and North Korean 넙적코 'flat nose', both pronounced *nŏpchŏkk'o*, however, the latter is preferable, because the consonant cluster *lp* in 넓 *nŏlp* is usually simplified to *l* in pronunciation before a consonant.

Derivatives

Different morphemic interpretations of phonetically identical derivatives are illustrated below.

(18) a. SK: 널따랗다, *nŏlttarat'a*, 일꾼, *ilkkun*, 걸쭉하다, *kŏltchuk'ada*, 떠버리, *ttŏbŏri*, 좁다랗다, *choptarat'a*, 각성바지 *kaksŏngbaji* 빛깔, *pitkkal*,

NK: 널다랗다, *nŏltarat'a*, 일군, *ilkun*, 걸죽하다, *kŏlchuk'ada*, 떠벌이, *ttŏbŏri*, 좁다랗다, *choptarat'a*, 각성받이 *kaksŏngbaji* 빛갈, *pitkal*,

b. SK: 쌕쌕이, *ssaekssaegi*, 오뚝이, *ottugi*, 홀쭉이, *holtchugi*, 개구리, *kaeguri*,

		일찍이,	더욱이,	생긋이	
		iltchigi,	*tŏugi,*	*saenggŭsi*	
	NK:	씩씨기,	오뚜기,	홀쭈기,	개구리,
		ssaekssaegi,	*ottugi,*	*holtchugi,*	*kaeguri,*
		일찌기,	더우기,	생그시	
		iltchigi,	*tŏugi,*	*saenggŭsi*	

c.	SK:	스무남은,	그렇지,	어떻지,	한사코,	아무튼
		sŭmunamŭn,	*kŭrŏch'i,*	*ŏttŏch'i,*	*hansak'o,*	*amut'ŭn*
	NK:	스무나믄,	그러치,	어떠치,	한사코,	아무튼
		sŭmunamŭn,	*kŭrŏch'i,*	*ŏttŏch'i,*	*hansak'o,*	*amut'ŭn*

Let us take two examples of divergent stipulations on the matter of fossilization. According to South Korea's system, when a root in question (e.g. 씩씩 *ssaekssaek* 'hissing') occurs with either the verb 하 *ha* 'do' or the derivational suffix 거리 *kŏri* 'keep doing', it must be spelled in its original morphemic form. Thus, although this morpheme does not occur with *ha*, it does occur with *kŏri*; hence 씩씩이 *ssaek.ssaeg.i* 'a jet plane'. North Korea's system regulates that only when a root in question occurs with the *ha* verb must it follow morphemic spelling. Since 씩씩 *ssaekssaek* cannot occur with the *ha* verb, 씩씨기 *ssaek.ssae.gi* is chosen.

In pairs like South Korean 이렇지 *irŏch'I* versus North Korean 이러치 *irŏch'I* 'to be like this', South Korea interprets the stranded ㅎ *h* (from 하 *ha*) as belonging to the preceding syllable as a coda, apparently in view of its important morphosemantic independence, whereas North Korea imposes it on the onset consonant of the following syllable, probably in view of its phonetic blending with the following consonant. Like North Korea, however, South Korea spells 한사코 *hansak'o* 'persistently', 기필코 *kip'ilk'o* 'by all means', 여하튼 *yŏhat'ŭn* 'at any rate', 아무튼 *amut'ŭn* 'anyhow', and 예컨대 *yek'ŏndae* 'for example' instead of 한샇고 *hansak'o*, 기픯고 *kip'ilk'o*, 여핳든 *yŏhat'ŭn*, 아뭏든 *amut'ŭn*, and 옣건대 *yek'ŏndae*. Thus, North Korea's practice attains more formal uniformity, if not functional generality.

Divergence and Conventions

Orthographic divergence may occur when the same or similar pronunciations that receive identical linguistic analysis are still spelled differently, owing to the different conventions followed in South Korea and North Korea.

Epenthetic ㅅ *s* (sai-siot)

It is well known that the so-called epenthetic *s* has been spelled variously in both North and South Korea. It is spelled in South Korea only when the preceding noun root ends in a vowel (a) in native and a small number of Sino-Korean compounds and is left out otherwise (b). In North Korea (since 1966), it is left out everywhere, except when the preceding root is interpreted as a prefix (c).

(19)	a.	SK:	냇가,	빗물,	숫자,	셋집,	나뭇잎	
			naekka,	*pinmul*,	*sutcha*,	*setchip*,	*namunnip*	
		NK:	내가,	비물,	수자,	세집,	나무잎	
			naekka,	*pinmul*,	*sutcha*,	*setchip*,	*namunnip*	
	b.	SK:	강가,	길가,	논일,	안고,	감소,	굶지
			kangka,	*kilka*,	*nonnil*,	*anko*,	*kamso*,	*kumchi*
		NK:	강가,	길가,	논일,	안고,	감소,	굶지
			kangka,	*kilka*,	*nonnil*,	*anko*,	*kamso*,	*kumchi*
	c.	SK:	뒷일,	웃집,	샛별			
			twinnil,	*utchip*,	*saetpyŏl*			
		NK:	뒷일,	웃집,	샛별			
			twinnil,	*utchip*,	*saetpyŏl*			

Sino-Korean Diphthong C-ye

Both South Korea and North Korea spell 계 *kye*, 례 *rye*, 혜 *hye* in relevant Sino-Korean words, despite their having been phonetically monophthongized as [ke], [re], and [he], respectively (a). Only South Korea allows two more consonant-initial diphthong letters, 몌 *mye* and 폐 *p'ye*, in Sino-Korean words (b). The original monophthongs are not affected in South or North Korea (c).

(20)	a.	SK:	계산,	의례,	은혜	
			kesan,	*ŭrye*,	*ŭnhe*	
		NK:	계산,	의례,	은혜	
			kesan,	*ŭrye*,	*ŭnhe*	
	b.	SK:	몌별,	연몌,	폐쇄,	화폐
			myebyŏl,	*yŏnmye*,	*p'eswae*,	*hwap'e*
		NK:	메별,	연메,	페쇄,	화페
			mebyŏl,	*yŏnme*,	*p'eswae*,	*hwap'e*
	c.	SK:	게시판,	휴게실		
			kesip'an,	*hyugesil*		
		NK:	게시판,	휴게실		
			kesip'an,	*hyugesil*		

Spacing

While morphophonemic spellings have a degree of ideographic function, facilitating morpheme and word recognition, spacing contributes to the recognition of syntactic units. As stated earlier, South Korea and North Korea share the basic principle that spaces be placed between words. While South Korea observes this principle rather narrowly, North Korea's convention is, in many cases, to spell two or more words without spacing, giving them compound status. North Korea's practice may partly result from Kim Il Sung's 1964 and 1966 Teachings, in which Kim indicated that the practice of the time allowed too many spaces. In the examples below (for details, see M. Kim 1985; E. Lee 1989; Lee and Ahn 1991), ^ stands for optional spacing.

(21) a. bound nouns

SK:	아는 이,	뜻한 바,	놀 수,	그 밖의,	세 개
	anŭn i,	*ttŭt'an pa,*	*nol su,*	*kŭ pakkŭi,*	*se gae*
NK:	아는이,	뜻한바,	놀수,	그밖의,	세개
	anŭni,	*ttŭt'anpa,*	*nolsu,*	*kŭbakkŭi,*	*segae*

b. Sino-Korean proper nouns and technical terms

	'Mr.Yi Kisŏn'	'Dr. Lee'	'6.25 Incident'	'vowel harmony'
SK:	이기선 씨,	이 박사,	6.25사변,	모음 조화
	igisŏn ssi,	*Yi paksa,*	*yugio sabyŏn,*	*moŭm johwa*
NK:	이기선씨,	이박사,	6.25사변,	모음조화
	igisŏnssi,	*Yibaksa,*	*yugiosabyŏn,*	*moŭmjohwa*

c. common noun sequences

	'many yrs'	'all citizens'	'school front'	'students themselves'
SK:	여러 해,	시민 모두,	학교 앞,	학생 자신
	yŏrŏ hae,	*simin modu,*	*hakkyo ap,*	*haksaeng chasin*
NK:	여러해,	시민모두,	학교앞,	학생자신
	yŏrŏhae,	*siminmodu,*	*hakkyoap,*	*haksaengjasin*

d. proverbs and idiomatic expressions

SK:	수박 겉 핥기;	꿩 구워 먹은 자리
	subak kŏt halki;	*kkwŏng gwŏmŏgŭn chari*
NK:	수박겉핥기;	꿩구워먹은 자리
	subakkŏthalki;	*kkwŏnggwŏmŏgŭn chari*
	'*licking the watermelon surface*' *(superficiality)*	'*the place where people ate a broiled pheasant*' *(no trace)*

e. numerals (spacing units: 만 *man*, 억 *ŏk*, in South Korea; 백 *paek*, 천 *chon*, 만 *man*, 억 *ŏk*, 조 *cho* in North Korea)
SK: 이억 오천삼백오십이만 오천이백이십사
iŏk och'ŏnsambaegosibiman och'ŏnibaegisip'sa
NK: 이억 오천 삼백 오십이만 오천 이백 이십사
iŏkoch'ŏnsambaek osibiman och'ŏn ibaek isip'sa
'253,525,224'

f. auxiliary predicates

SK:	보여 주다,	주고 싶다,	집어먹어 보아라
	poyŏ chuda,	*chukko sipta,*	*chibŏmŏgŏ poara*
NK:	보여주다,	주고싶다,	집어먹어보아라
	poyŏjuda,	*chukkosipta,*	*chibŏmŏgŏboara*

g. verbal and adverbial compounding

SK:	꽃 같다,	하늘 높이,	용서 못 한다
	kkot kata,	*hanŭl nop'i,*	*yongsŏ mot handa*
NK:	꽃같다,	하늘높이,	용서 못한다
	kkotkata,	*hanŭlnop'i,*	*yongsŏ mot'anda*

4. Conclusion

Let me conclude with some suggestions. Linguistic unification is a key to the recovery of national identity and the reunification of Korea. As an immediate step, it is imperative that Korean linguists from South Korea and North Korea, preferably joined by overseas scholars, get together to discuss the issues involved in containing this ever-growing linguistic diversity and recovering linguistic homogeneity. One general issue is the impact of the ongoing Chuch'e-based language purification movement in North Korea and the more or less laissez-faire policy toward the influx of foreign elements in South Korea.[7] North Korea has been nativizing thousands of Sino-Korean words used by the South Korean public. South Korea, in contrast, has already admitted into its lexicon over ten thousand loanwords from English, while coining numerous Sino-Korean words or introducing Sino-Japanese terms as needs arise.

I have examined the major aspects of orthographic divergence and the relevant issues involved, suggesting solutions in certain cases. Many of them are linguistically intriguing and deserve joint scholarly discussion for resolution.

7 While North Korea has been successfully conducting Chuch'e-based language purification, South Korea is achieving only limited success in the ongoing purification efforts of its government, scholars, and language associations.

There is no reason why a unified spelling system cannot be legislated. Not only do North and South Korea have nearly the same phonological data, but they also follow the same principles of morphophonemic spelling and word-based spacing. The provisions of *Han'gŭl match'umpŏp* (MOE 1988a) and *Kaejŏng Chosŏnmal kyubŏmjip* (KLAC 1988) are largely terminological variations. For example the same morphophonemic principle may be defined in different terms. *Han'gŭl match'umpŏp* states, "In principle, *han'gŭl* spellings follow Standard Speech pronounciations in accordance with grammatical structure" (MOE 1988a: 1.1), whereas *Kaejŏng Chosŏnmal kyubŏmjip* states, "Korean spellings are based on the principle that each meaningful unit in words is spelled the same way wherever it occurs, but in certain cases, spelling words as pronounced or following tradition is permitted" (KLAC 1988, General Rule). An extensive number of such terminological variations can easily be combined into a unified system through joint scholarly deliberations. Furthermore, the most desirable area in which to begin linguistic unification efforts appears to be orthographic divergence, in that the problems involved are relatively free from political and ideological sensitivity.

According to Chon and Choy's (1989) count based on Chong et al. (1981) and H. Lee (1982), (a) 1,400 words have identical pronunciations but different spellings, and (b) 3,130 words have different pronunciations and different spellings. Interestingly, (c) 930 words have different pronunciations but identical spellings, as illustrated in 정열 (SK *chŏng.nyŏl*; NK *chŏng.yŏl*), 창고 (SK *ch'ang.go*; NK *ch'ang.ko*), 넓다 (SK *nŏl.ta*; NK *nŏp.ta*), and 돌배 (SK *tol.bae*; NK *tol.pae*).

With enough scholarly cooperation, there will be no serious problem in unifying the spellings of the (a) group, in view of their phonetic identity. This is a group whose disparities are caused by different linguistic analyses or different conventions. As for the (b) group, which are due to different standards of speech, the majority are Sino-Korean words such as those with the initial ㄹ *l* or ㄴ *n*. In view of the fact that we have many identically spelled words with different pronunciations that belong to the (c) group, some (b) group words may also be unified in spelling without much difficulty.

In general, North Korea's system is oriented toward formal uniformity, as observed in examples such as SK 드디어 versus NK 드디여 *tŭdiyŏ* (cf. SK/NK 구태여 *ku.t'ae.yŏ*); SK 괴로워 *koerowŏ* versus NK 괴로와 *koerowa* (cf. SK/NK 고와 *kowa*); SK 거북지 *kŏbukchi* versus NK 거북치 *kŏbukch'i* (SK/NK 행복치 *haengbokch'i*); SK 바닷가 *padatka* versus NK 바다가 *pada.ka* (cf. SK/NK 바다에 *padae,* 강가 *kang.ka*); SK 일꾼 *ilkkun* versus NK 일군 *ilkun* (cf. SK/NK 농군 *nonggun*); and SK –을까 –ŭlkka versus NK –을가 *–ulka* (cf. SK/NK –는가 –*nŭn'ga*, -을 것 *–ŭl kŏt*). In all these cases, South Korean linguists have taken different criteria.[8] Joint research is essential to narrow down such numerous discrepancies through intensive linguistic analysis from synchronic and diachronic perspectives, on the other hand, and structural and sociolinguistic perspectives, on the other. Recourse to such criteria as simplicity, generality, naturalness, psychological reality, and tradition, as well as to restructuring and grammaticalzation theory, will lead to eliminating many of the disparities.

Until the reunification of Korea is realized, a unified spelling system will have no recourse but to accommodate both standards of speech and treat unresolved disparaties as doublets applicable either to both Koreas (e.g. SK 수범 *subŏm* versus NK 수펌 *sup'ŏm*; SK 갈치 *kalch'i* versus NK 칼치 *k'alch'i*) or only to the relevant areas (e.g. SK 이론 *iron* versus NK 리론 *riron*; SK 여자 *yŏja* versus NK 녀자 *nyŏja*). As an alternative way of unifying the spelling systems, Huh (1991) proposes that both South Korea and North Korea adopt the 1948 version of *Han'gŭl match'umpŏp t'ong'ilan*, in that this version, written purely in *han'gŭl*, was shared by the two Koreas. Simple and ideal as it may be, this solution may not be easily acceptable to North Korea, in that adopting the 1948 version presupposes North Korea's abolishment of Cultured Speech and acceptance of Standard Speech.

Fortunately, there are some indications that both Koreas are endeavoring to approach the other's system. For example, South Korea has changed C-읍니다 *-ŭmnida* to C-습니다 *–sŭmnida*, given independent status to complex letters, and introduced optionality in many spacing rules. North Korea has abolished the earlier distinction between the velar and nasal coda consonant letter ㅇ and the syllable-initial letter ㅇ and become more generous in using spacing than in the 1971 *Kyubŏmjip*.

REFERENCES: Chapter 18

Chon, Su-tae, and Ho-chol Choy. 1989. *Nambukhan ŏnŏ pigyo* (A linguistic comparison between South and North Korea). Seoul: Tosŏch'ulp'an nokchin.

Chong, Sun-Ki et al. 1981. *Hyŏndae chosŏnmal sajŏ* (A modern Korean dictionary). 2nd edition. P'yŏng'yang: Kwahak Paekkwasajŏn Ch'ulp'ansa.

Chong, Sun-Ki, and Ki-Won Lee. 1984. *Sajŏnp'yŏnch'an riron yŏn'gu* (A study of lexicography). P'yŏng'yang: Sahoegwahak Ch'ulp'ansa.

Choy, Ki-Ho. 1990. "Hyŏndae Chosŏnmal sajŏn" kwa pukhan ŏnŏjŏngch'aek (A dictionary of Modern Korean and North Korean language policies). *COH* 1990: 277-89.

8 Ko states that South Korea's orthography is "excessively grammatical" compared with North Korea's system and that compromise is needed for a unified orthography (1990:20).

COH (Chaha ŏmun hakhoe). 1990. *Pukhan ŭi Chosŏnŏhak* (Korean linguistics in North Korea). Seoul: Hanshin Co.

Huh, Woong. 1991. Nam-buk ŭi mal kwa kŭl (Speech and writing in South and North). *Han'gŭl saesosik* (*Han'gŭl* news) 229: 4-6.

Kim, Chin-W. 1978. Linguistics and language policies in North Korea. *Korean Studies* 2: 159-175.

Kim, Chin-W. 1991. Han'gungmal kwa Chosŏnmal (The South and North Korean languages). *Mal* (language), 15: 35-47.

Kim, Min-su. 1985. *Pukhan ŭi kugŏ yŏn'gu* (Studies of Korean in North Korea). Seoul: Korea University Press.

Kim, Young Hwang. 1978. *Chosŏn minjogŏ palchŏn ryŏksa yŏn'gu* (A study of the development of the national language). P'yŏng'yang: Kwahak Paekkwasajŏn Ch'ulp'ansa.

KISU (Kim Il Sung University). 1983. *Ŏŭm mit muncharon* (A theory of speech sounds and letters). P'yŏng'yang: Kim Il Sung University Press.

KLA (Chosŏnŏ Hakhoe: Korean Language Association). 1933. *Han'gŭl match'umpŏp t'ong'il-an* (A proposition for unified h*an'gŭl* spelling conventions). Seoul: Chosŏnŏ Hakhoe.

KLA. 1936. *Chosŏnŏ p'yojunmal moŭm* (A collection of Korean standard words). Seoul: Chosŏnŏ Hakhoe.

KLAC (Kugŏ sajŏng wiwŏnhoe: Korean Language Assessment Committee). 1988. *Kaejŏnghan Chosŏnmal kyubŏmjip* (A revised collection of Korean language norms). P'yŏng'yang: Sahoegwahak Ch'ulp'ansa.

Ko, Young-geun. 1990. Chuch'e language theory and North Korean linguistics. *Seoul Journal of Korean Studies* (Seoul National University), 3: 2-20.

Lee, Eun-jong. 1989. Nambukhan ŭi match'umpŏp pigyo yŏn'gu (A comparative study of South-North Korean spelling conventions). *Han-geul* 205: 151-77.

Lee, Huy-sung. 1982. *Kugŏ taesajŏn* (A great dictionary of Korean). Seoul: Minjung Sŏrim.

Lee, Huy-sung, and Pyong-hi Ahn. 1991. *Han'gŭl match'umpŏp kang'ŭi* (Lectures on the *han'gŭl* spelling system). Seoul: Sin'gu-munhwasa.

LIASS (Sahoe kwahagwŏn ŏnŏhak yŏn'guso: Linguistic Institute, Academy of Social Sciences). 1973. *Chosŏn munhwaŏ sajŏn* (A dictionary of Korean cultured speech). P'yŏng'yang.

LIASS. 1976. *Uri tang ŭi ŏnŏjŏnch'aek* (The language policies of our party). P'yŏng'yang: Sahoegwahak Ch'ulp'ansa.

MOE (Ministry of Education). 1988a. *Han'gŭl match'umpŏp* (The *han'gŭl* spelling conventions). Seoul: Mun'gyobu.

MOE. 1988b. *P'yojunŏ kyujŏng* (Standard speech regulations). Seoul: Mun'gyobu.

Nam, Ki-Shim. 1987. Kugŏ sajŏn ŭi chamo ŭi ch'arye wa p'yojeŏ ŭi paeyŏsun e kwanhayŏ (On ordering the alphabetic letters and entries in a Korean dictionary). *Inmun kwahak* (Yonsei University), 57: 1-18.

Park, Youngsoon. 1991. Language policy and language education in North Korea. *Korea Journal* 31.1: 28-40.

Sasse, Werner. 1980. The "cultured language": Implementation of a policy in North Korea. *Korean Linguistics* 2: 67-76.

Sohn, Ho-min. 1991. Language policies and linguistic divergence in the two Koreas. *Sino-Platonic Papers* (University of Pennsylvania), 27: 95-102

19 Korean in Contact with Chinese*

1. Introduction

The Korean lexicon is characterized by many foreign elements which have become integral and indispensable components.[1] The traditional borrowing was mainly from Chinese, whereas the modern pattern is predominantly from Japanese, English, and other European languages, of which borrowings from English occupy approximately 90 percent. Although borrowings from Chinese ceased long ago, Chinese characters have been used to coin thousands of new words as needs arose. All Koreanized words based on Chinese characters, whether they are ancient borrowings directly from China or re-borrowings indirectly from Sino-Japanese (hereafter SJ), or new coinages in Korea, are commonly called *hancha-ŏ* (한자어) 'Chinese character words' or Sino-Korean (hereafter SK) words. Only those borrowings which are not SK are called *oerae-ŏ* (외래어) 'loanwords' (literally 'words from abroad'). The remainder of the Korean lexicon consists of *koyu-ŏ* (고유어) 'inherited words' or native Korean words. Roughly, the ratios of these three stocks in the Korean lexicon are: 30 percent inherited (or native) Korean words, 65 percent SK words, and 5 percent loanwords.

Statistics indicate that SK words are particularly predominant in science magazines and scholarly journals and books, as well as in political, economic, and financial columns of newspapers, whereas native words prevail in novels and domestic and women's magazines as well as in the social columns of newspapers. Loanwords are widespread in magazines and newspapers on sports, cooking, fashion, technology, and other aspects of recently imported culture.

In general, SK words are considered much more "native-like" than loanwords, in that they have a much longer history. Thus, many native speakers mistakenly consider SK words like *pang* 'room', *mun* 'door, gate', *chuk* 'porridge',

* This is a reprint of chapter 4 in Sohn, Ho-min (ed.), *Korean Language in Culture and Society* (University of Hawaii Press, 2006). A great portion of the content of this chapter is extracted from Sohn (1999/2001). The McCune-Reischauer Romanization system is followed in transcribing Korean expressions.

1 See chapters 1, 2, and 3 in Part I of this volume for more discussions on the Korean lexicon.

suyŏm 'beard', *tongsaeng* 'younger sibling', and *yo* 'blanket' as native words and native words like *tongan* 'during', and *ai* 'child' as SK words.

The SK origin of more than half of the total Korean vocabulary can be attributed to two facts: (a) that Chinese culture and learning deeply permeated all facets of Korean life in the past, as historically Korea had been long subordinated to the political and cultural influence of China; and (b) that, due to their ideographic and monosyllabic nature, Chinese characters facilitate the creation of new words to represent the new concepts and products that continuously appear as civilization progresses. Thus, as will be seen, nearly all terms in academic fields, politics, occupations, economy, law, society, and other cultural aspects, as well as personal, place, and institutional names, and numerals, numeral counters, months, days of the week, color terms, and kinship terms are SK. The difference between SK and SJ words is primarily in pronunciation.

2. The origin of Sino-Korean words

Before the nineteenth century, when Western cultures began to penetrate East Asia, China had long been the center of East Asian culture and civilization. Chinese culture and civilization were propagated to neighboring countries mainly through written Chinese based on Chinese characters. However, due to the lack of historical data, it is not known exactly how and when Chinese and Chinese characters were first introduced into Korea. The only deduction we can make is that practical knowledge of Chinese and the Chinese script in Korea dates back to 194 B.C., when Wiman, from Yen in China, founded a primitive Korean state in the northwestern part of the peninsula. Subsequently, the establishment by China's Han dynasty of their four commanderies on the soil of Wiman's Ancient Chosŏn in 108 B.C. must have familiarized the resident Koreans with Chinese and the Chinese script. According to *Samguk Sagi* (Historical Records of the Three Kingdoms [1145]), the Koguryŏ people had the Chinese script from the very beginning of their existence as a state in 37 B.C. *Samguk Sagi* also records that history books written in Chinese characters were compiled in the Paekche dynasty in A.D. 375 and in the Silla dynasty in A.D. 545. A historical record also shows that a Paekchean named Wang In went to Japna with many Chinese books around A.D. 400. Furthermore, one stele that was erected in A.D. 414 in honor of King Kwanggaet'o of Koguryŏ contains over 1,800 Chinese characters. All these suggest that Chinese culture and characters had achieved considerable popularity in the Korea of the Three Kingdoms period. With the unification of the Korean peninsula by the Silla dynasty in A.D. 677, the use of Chinese characters in Korea gained even more popularity since Silla's unification was achieved with Tang China's military support. Subsequently, contact between the two countries increased.

Until the time of Soji-maruhan, the twenty-first king of the Silla dynasty, the names of the state and of the king were in native words. Words like *maruhan* and *niskŭm* meant 'king'. During the reign of King Chijŭng (A.D. 503), the term for 'king' was changed to the Chinese word *wang* and the name of the country to Silla, a two-syllable SK word which is assumed to have sounded close to the native term. Personal names of Silla male aristocrats were also changed in accordance with the Chinese pattern (consisting usually of a one-character family name followed by a two-character given name, as in Kim Yusin), although commoners and women retained their native names up until recent years.

In the second year of King Sinmun (A.D. 682) of Unified Silla, *Kukhak* (*lit.*, national studies), a government agency in charge of national education, was established, and many Chinese classics began to be taught. In the sixteenth year of King Kyŏngdŏk (A.D. 757), native place names were changed to two-character SK, and in his eighteenth year, all official titles were also made SK. Although all place names in the country were changed to SK, some native names still survive alongside them. For example, the city of Taejŏn (consisting of the characters *tae* meaning 'big' and *jŏn* meaning 'field) is still also called (but not written) *Hanbat*, *han* meaning 'big' and *bat* 'field' in native words, although the practice is disappearing among the young generation.

SK words began to overtake native words in the Koryŏ dynasty. This was particularly the case after King Kwangjo adopted, in 958, the Chinese system of civil service examinations based on Chinese classics. The Chosŏn dynasty saw the all-out infiltration of Chinese characters into every facet of Korean culture and society, chiefly because of the dynasty's adoption of Confucianism as a national ideology, and, as a result, the popular admiration of everything Chinese. Thus, the ruling classes of Korea devoted their entire lives to the study of classical Chinese, written in characters, because it was the main goal of education, the official means of conducting government affairs and documenting public and private records, and the medium of civil service examinations. Children of the ruling classes started learning written Chinese around the age of five, whereas most common people remained completely illiterate before the creation and promulgation of the Korean alphabet *han'gŭl* by King Sejong of the Chosŏn dynasty in 1446.

3. The three layers of SK words

There are three layers of SK words: (a) those introduced from China, (b) those introduced from SJ, and (c) those coined in Korea, as illustrated respectively in (1).

(1) Three layers of SK words

a. SK words from Chinese

cha-yŏn (self-so) 'nature'
ch'ŏn-ji 'heaven and earth'
hak-saeng (study-student) 'student'
pyŏn-hwa (change-change) 'change'
sin-ch'e (body-body) 'body'
ŭi-bok (wear-clothes) 'clothes'
chil-mun (essence-ask) 'question'
hak-kyo (study-house) 'school'
hyo-ja (filial-son) 'filial son'
pu-mo (father-mother) 'parents'
t'ae-yang (grand-sun light) 'sun'

b. SK words from SJ

ip-ku (enter-mouth) 'entrance'
kong-jang (work-place) 'factory'
mun-pŏp (sentence-rule) 'grammar'
pi-haeng-gi (fly-go-machine) 'plane'
ch'uk-ku (kick-ball) 'football'
kwa-hak (science-study) 'science'
yak-sok (agree-bind) 'promise'
yŏng-hwa (shine-picture) 'movie'

c. SK words coined in Korea

ch'aek-po (book-wrapper) 'wrapping cloth for books'
ch'ong-gak (all-horn) 'bachelor'
il-gi (day-energy) 'weather'
oe-sang (outside-upside) 'on credit'
pok-tŏk-pang (blessing-virtue-room) 'real estate agency'
p'yŏn-ji (comfortable-paper) 'letter'
sa-ju (4-pillar) 'destiny' (year, month, day, and hour of one's birth)
sam-ch'on (three-node) 'uncle'
sik-ku (eating-mouth) 'family member'
so-sik (termination-breathing) 'news'

The first layer has the largest number of members. The SK words in this layer were introduced mainly through Confucian classics, historical and literary works, and Chinese works written in colloquial Chinese. Some SK words were introduced from spoken Chinese after the current SK pronunciations were fixed around the eighth century, as in *pae-ch'u* (cf. SK *paek-ch'ae*) 'Chinese cabbage', *si-wŏl* (cf. SK *sip-wŏl*) 'October', and *yu-wŏl* (cf. SK *yuk-wŏl*) 'June', where *pae* 'white', *si* 'ten', and *yu* 'six' are from later spoken Chinese *bai*, *si*, and *ryu*, respectively.

Many words which came from Chinese have undergone semantic change, as in *mi-ŭm* 'thin gruel' (originally 'rice-drink'), *nae-oe* 'husband and wife' (originally 'inside and outside'), *sam-si* 'three meals' (originally 'three times'), and *yuk-ch'on* 'second cousin' (originally 'six nodes', i.e. nodes of kinship in a family tree). Similarly, SK *yang-ban* used to refer to the two (civilian and military) highest social classes, but is now used roughly in the sense of 'gentleman'; and SK *yŏng-gam*, which was used to denote a high-ranking government official, is now used to refer to any elderly man. Certain other SK words came from Chinese in ancient times and have behaved as if they were native words. Still other SK words have undergone drastic change, either in form alone or in both form and meaning, as illustrated in (2).

(2) Ancient borrowing

ch'o 'candle' (SK *ch'ok* 'candle')
huch'u 'black pepper' (SK *ho-ch'o* 'barbarian pepper')
kaji 'eggplant' (SK *ka-ja* 'eggplant')
kage 'store' (SK *ka-ga* 'false house')
kanan 'poverty' (SK *kan-nan* 'hardship')
pobae 'treasure' (SK *po-p'ae* 'treasure shell')
puch'ŏ 'Buddha' (SK *pul-ch'e* 'Buddha's body')
put 'calligraphy brush' (SK *p'il* 'brush, pen', ancient Chinese *piet*)
sarang 'love' (SK *sa-ryang* 'consideration')
sanyang 'hunting' (SK *san-haeng* 'mountain going')
sŏngnyang 'matches' (SK *sŏk-ryu-hwang* 'sulfur')
ssŏlmae 'sled' (SK *sŏl-ma* 'snow horse')
ssŭ 'write' (SK *sŏ* 'write', ancient Chinese *siwo*)
t-okki 'rabbit' (SK *t'o* 'rabbit', proto-Chinese **t'ogs*)

While early SK words coined in Korea are not many, a great many SJ words were coined in Japan during the Meiji Restoration, as English and other Western cultural and scientific terms had to be translated into Japanese. These and many other SJ words coined in Japan have been introduced into the Korean lexicon with the pronunciation modified, as in SK *ŏn-ŏ-hak* (SJ *gen-go-gaku*) 'linguistics' and SK *pi-haeng-gi* (SJ *hi-ko-ki*) 'airplane'.

4. Sino-Korean pronunciation

Scholars do not agree on the details of the origin of SK sounds. It is generally assumed, however, that the pronunciations of Chinese characters used in the northern part of China during the Sui and Tang dynasties around the seventh and eighth centuries constituted the basis of SK sounds. This was during the Unified Silla period, when massive amounts of written materials about Chinese civilization were imported from China. Thus, pronunciations of contemporary Chinese-character words in Korean are similar to those of Late Middle Chinese, although some independent vowel and consonant changes as well as the loss of tones have occurred in Korean. For instance, compare the pronunciations of contemporary Korean and Mandarin with Late Middle Chinese (cf. Pulleyblank 1991).

(3)	Korean	Mandarin	Late Middle Chinese
'one'	*il*	*yi*	*jit*
'three'	*sam*	*san*	*sam*
'six'	*(r)yuk*	*liu*	*liwk*
'eight'	*p'al*	*ba*	*pa:t*
'nine'	*ku*	*jiu*	*kuw*
'north'	*puk*	*bei*	*puôk*

Notice the similarities between Korean forms and the corresponding Late Middle Chinese forms and the differences between Korean and Mandarin forms. A superficially irregular pattern is that Middle Chinese *jit* and *pa:t* correspond to Korean *il* and *p'al*, respectively. This is partly because SK words have followed the Korean pattern of sound changes since they were introduced into Korea. Middle Chinese initial *j* has been deleted in Korean where it appears before the vowel *i*, compared to the deletion of SK word-initial *n* and *l/r* before the vowel *i*. Thus, the variant forms *i/li* 'reason' and *ron/nol* 'discuss' in South Korean SK *i-ron* (reason-discuss) 'theory' and *nol-li* (discuss-reason) 'logic', and the variant forms *nyŏ/yŏ* 'female' in *nam-nyŏ* 'male and female' and *yŏ-nam* 'female and male', are due to their undergoing the native pattern of sound changes. As for the productive correspondence between Korean word-final *l* and Middle Chinese word-final *t*, it is still controversial whether Middle Chinese *t* changed to *l* before or after it entered Korean.

There are other phonological rules that apply to both native and SK words. The rule changing *n* to *l* before or after *l* applies to both native and SK, as in native *sŏl-lal* (from *sŏl* + *nal*) 'New Year's Day' and SK *sil-la* (from *sin* + *la*) 'Silla dynasty'. Palatalization has also applied to both native and SK words, as in native *chida* (from *tida*) 'lose in a game' and SK *ch'ŏn-ji* (from *t'yŏn-di*) 'heaven and earth'. Both native and SK words contract *ai* to *ae*, as in native *sae* (from *sai*) 'bird' and SK *nae-il* (from *rai-il* 'come-day') 'tomorrow'.

SK words have many unique phonological characteristics too (cf. K.-J. Song 1986). First, the three tense consonants *pp*, *tt*, and *tch* do not occur at all in SK roots, and even *kk* and *ss* are limited to one or two roots, for example, in *kkik* 'smoke, drink', *ssang* 'pair', and *ssi* 'Mr., Mrs., Miss.' Second, *p', t', ch, ch', s,* and *k',* as well as all tense consonants, do not occur in syllable-final position in SK roots. Third, consonant clusters (e.g. *ps*) do not occur in SK roots. Fourth, the most productive diphthong is *yŏ*, which follows the widest variety of consonants, as in *yŏn-* 'research', *pyŏng* 'bottle', *(r)yŏl* 'row', *p'yŏn-* 'side', *kyŏn-* 'see', *nyŏ-* 'female', and *hyŏng* 'older brother'. Finally, phonological contraction is very rare in SK words.

5. The enrichment of the Korean vocabulary

The impact of SK and loanwords on all aspects of the Korean language is great. Besides the addition of new lexical items representing new concepts, the most significant effect is the proliferation of a large number of partly or wholly synonymous expressions. Synonymous words, however, have been associated with different shades of meaning, stylistic nuances, or social values, enriching the Korean vocabulary. When native-SK or SK-loan doublets or native-SK-loan triplets exist, native words usually represent unsophisticated traditional culture, both mental and physical, and SK words, conveying more formality, tend to denote higher, quality objects and more formal, abstract, and sometimes more socially prestigious concepts than their native counterparts. Loanwords are, in general, associated with modern, stylish and technological objects and concepts. For example, the native word *karak* 'rhythm' is usually with reference to traditional Korean folk songs, the SK word *un-yul* (rhyme-law) in formal or academic situations, and the loanword *ridŭm* for some sort of Western flavor. The phenomenon of native-SK doublets is widespread, particularly in non-scientific and non-academic areas as in (4).

(4)	Native	SK	
	ch'an-mul	*naeng-su*	'cold water'
	il-chari	*chik-chang*	'job'
	kap	*ka-gyŏk*	'price'
	kil	*to-ro*	'road'
	korŭda	*sŏn-t'aek-(hada)*	'choose'
	kot	*chang-so*	'place'
	nara	*kuk-ka*	'country'
	ot	*ŭi-bok*	'clothes'
	pap	*sik-sa*	'meal'
	saram	*in-gan*	'human'
	son-bal	*su-jok*	'hands and feet'
	sum-swida	*ho-hŭp-(hada)*	'breather'
	talgyal	*kye-ran*	'egg'
	yŏl	*sip*	'ten'

The two members of each doublet set may not mean exactly the same thing and frequently have different usages. Even when they share the same meaning, SK words tend to be more formal and abstract (detached from vivid reality), and thus can sound more prestigious, and sometimes even pedantic. Native words generally belong to colloquial speech, while their SK counterparts tend to be found in literary language, academic vocabulary, and formal speech. For example, using *nara* manifests more emotional attachment than *kuk-ka* (*lit.,* country-house). Thus, *uri nara*, not *uri kuk-ka*, is used to refer to 'our country'. The native word *il-chari* (*lit.,* work-place) refers usually to a low-paying and/or part-time job such as blue color work, whereas SK *chik-chang* generally implies a professional white-color job. SK counterparts are also frequently used for deferential objects.

(5)	Native (plain)	SK (deferential)	
	anae	*pu-in*	'wife'
	abŏji	*pu-ch'in*	'father'
	chal	*an-nyŏng-hi*	'safely'
	chip	*taek*	'house'
	i	*ch'i-a*	'tooth'
	irŭm	*sŏng-ham*	'name'
	nai	*yŏn-se*	'age'

Thus, for instance, the native word *chip* is used when referring to one's own house, but the corresponding SK word *taek* is used when referring to the house of a socially distant equal or higher adult.

In addition, native-SK hybrids have also been coined with a redundant native element, as in *sae sil-lang* 'bridegroom' (*lit.,* new bridegroom), *ch'o-ga chip* 'thatched house' (*lit.,* thatched house house), *ch'ŏga chip* 'wife's house' (*lit.,* wife's house house), *mok sugŏn* 'muffler' (*lit.,* neck handkerchief), *sok naeŭi* 'undergarment' (*lit.,* inside undergarment), and *morae sajang* 'sandy beach' (*lit.,* sand sandy beach).

In the battle for survival with those loanwords which have been introduced since the end of World War II, some SK words have given in to loanwords. For example, the SK word *sŭng-gang-gi* (move up-move down-machine) had long been used to denote 'elevator', but has been gradually replaced by the loanword *ellibeit'ŏ;* and the loanword *k'ŏmp'yut'ŏ* is more frequently used than SK *chŏn-san-gi* (electronic-calculate-machine) for 'computer'. The SK word *t'a-ja-gi* (hit-letter-machine) and the loanword *t'aip'ŭrait'ŏ* for 'typewriter' and the SK word *chŏn-ch'a* (war-vehicle) and the loanword *t'aengk'ŭ'* 'tank' seem to be used with about equal frequency. Many SK words are still used exclusively, as in *sŏn-p'ung-gi* (fan-wind-machine) 'electric fan', *cha-dong-ch'a* (self-move-vehicle) 'car', *chŏn-hwa* (electric-talk) 'telephone', *ch'ong* 'gun', and *naeng-jang-go* (cold-store-storehouse) 'refrigerator'.

6. The obliteration of native words

While unprecedentedly enriching the Korean vocabulary with new lexical items, the predominance of SK words has resulted in the deplorable consequence of many native words' having been lost in the battle with SK words and, as a result, having disappeared from usage long ago, frequently irrecoverably. While Chinese characters in Japanese are read with both SJ pronunciation and the pronunciation of corresponding native words, thereby contributing to the maintenance of native words, Chinese characters in Korea are read only in SK pronunciation, which has contributed to the disuse of native words. Many native words have been either completely wiped out by Chinese words or, at best, have passed to an archaic status. Some of these unfortunate native words that were common in the writings of the Chosŏn dynasty period are given below, together with the SK replacements:

(6)	Native	SK	
	ae	*chang*	'intestine'
	chŏja	*si-jang*	'market'
	chŭmŭn	*ch'ŏn*	'thousand'
	ŏbŏi	*pu-mo*	'parents'
	karam	*kang*	'river'
	moe	*san*	'mountain'
	mut	*yuk-chi*	'land'
	nuri	*se-sang*	'world'
	on	*paek*	'hundred'
	pŏt	*ch'in'gu*	'friend'
	pua	*p'ye*	'lung'
	yang	*wi*	'stomach'

7. Structure of SK words

SK words are more analytic and therefore semantically more transparent than native words. SK words are composed, by and large, of two or more roots, with each root consisting of a single syllable, as in *hak-kyo* (study-house) 'school', *kyo-hoe* (teaching-meeting) 'church', *in-gan* (human-relation) 'human', *sŏn-saeng* (preceding-birth) 'teacher', and *tae-hak-kyo* (big-study-house) 'university'. The last root in a SK word frequently indicates a semantic category. For instance, the terms for different branches of learning all contain the root *hak* 'study, learning'.

(7)	*ŏn-ŏ* (speech-word) 'language'	*ŏn-ŏ-hak* 'linguistics'
	mun- 'letters, sentence, literature'	*mun-hak* 'literature
	saeng-mul (live-thing) 'living creature'	*saeng-mul-hak* 'biology'
	su 'number'	*su-hak* 'mathematics'
	ŭi- 'medicine'	*ŭi-hak* 'medical science'

The order of the roots in SK compounds usually follows that of Chinese. For instance, in the SK-native compound *sig-ŏn-hada* (eat-word-do) 'break a promise', SK *sig-ŏn* 'eat-word' follows the verb-object order, not the Korean object-verb order. Similarly, the SK compound *yu-bi-mu-hwan* (have-preparation-not have-trouble) 'To be prepared is to have no anxiety' follows the Chinese order. The Korean order produces an unacceptable word, *pi-yu-hwan-mu*.

8. Semantic classes

SK words tend to express objects, institutions, and concepts of modern civilization. Representative semantic classes in SK are listed below.

- All contemporary Korean surnames and most given names are in SK. Two hundred seventy-four surnames are in current use, most of which consist of one Chinese character, the exceptions including *Che-gal*, *Hwang-bo*, *Nam-gung*, *Sa-gong*, *Sŏ-mun*, *Sŏn-u*, *Tok-ko*, and *Tong-bang*, which have two characters. The ten most common surnames, which account for 65.4 percent of the whole population, are *Kim* (Kim), *I* (Lee), *Pak* (Park), *Ch'oe* (Choe), *Chŏng* (Chung, Jung), *Kang* (Kang), *Cho* (Cho), *Yun* (Yoon), *Chang* (Chang, Jang), and *Im* (Lim), in that order of frequency. The three surnames *Kim*, *I*, and *Pak* are held by 45 percent of the population, with *Kim* alone accounting for 21.7 percent. The typical form of a given name consists of two characters, while only a very few are single-character. Given names follow the surname, as in I Sun-sin, Kim Suk-hŭi, Pak In, Nam-gung Ok-pun, and Sŏn-u Hwi.
- Most place names are in SK. Except for the name of the capital city, *Sŏul* 'Seoul', which is a native word, all administrative districts and units are in SK: *Kyŏng-gi-do* 'Kyonggi Province', *Pu-san* 'Pusan', *Chong-no-gu* 'Chongno Ward', and *Myŏng-dong* 'Myeong Block'. Names of islands, lakes, mountains, rivers, parks, and various other scenic spots and places

of historic interest are mostly in SK, as in *Paek-tu-san* 'Mt. Paektu', *Han-gang* 'Hang River', *Pul-guk-sa* 'Pulkuk Temple', and *Kyŏng-bok-kung* 'Kyongbok Palace'. Names of oceans, countries, and continents are also in SK, as in *T'ae-p'yŏng-yang* (great-peace-ocean) 'Pacific', *Il-bon* 'Japan', *Mi-guk* 'America', (guk 'country'), *Yŏng-guk* 'England', *Tog-il* 'Germany', *Chung-guk* 'China', *Ho-ju* 'Australia' (*ju* 'continent'), and *Mi-ju* 'American continent(s)'.

- Many other proper names, including those of institutions, firms, restaurants, stores, hotels, tearooms, books, newspapers, and transportation means are in SK: *Yŏn-se tae-hak* 'Yonsei University', *Hyŏn-dae* 'Hyundae', *Ho-ban sik-tang* 'Hoban Restaurant', *Han-yang ap'at'ŭ* 'Hangyang Apartment', *Ch'un-hyang-jŏn* 'Story of Chunhyang', *T'ong-il-ho* 'T'ongil Train', and *Tong-a il-bo* 'Tonga Daily'.
- Academic, technical, and occupational terms are in SK: *kyo-yuk* 'education', *su-sul* 'surgery', *se-p'o* 'cell', *san-ŏp* 'industry', *nong-ŏp* 'agriculture', *kyo-su* 'professor', *ŭi-sa* 'medical doctor', *pak-sa* 'Ph.D.', *chang-gwan* 'government minister', *mok-sa* 'pastor', *ki-sa* 'driver', *chang-gun* 'general', and *si-jang* 'mayor'.
- Names of institutions and organizations are in SK: *hoe-sa* 'company', *ŭn-haeng* 'bank', *chŏng-bu* 'government', *kuk-hoe* 'National Assembly', *pŏb-wŏn* 'court', *kyo-yuk-pu* 'Ministry of Education', *yu-ch'i-wŏn* 'kindergarten', *tae-han-min-guk* 'Republic of Korea', and *tae-t'ong-nyŏng* 'president (of a nation)'.
- Various cultural products and concepts are in SK, including *ch'a* 'car', *kwa-ja* 'candy, cookie', *ŭi-ja* 'chair', *ch'aek-sang* 'desk', *ch'im-dae* 'bed', *cha-jŏn-gŏ* 'bicycle', *chang-hwa* 'boot', *chŏn-hwa* 'telephone', *sin-mun* 'newspaper', *kŏn-mul* 'building', *man-nyŏn-p'il* 'fountain pen', *kyŏng-je* 'economy', *min-ju-ju-ŭi* 'democracy', and *mu-yŏk* 'trade'.
- Days of the week, folk festivals, national holidays, and seasonal divisions are in SK. Days of the week are: *ir-yo-il* (sun-shine-day) 'Sunday', *wŏr-yo-il* (moon) 'Monday', *hwa-yo-il* (fire-) 'Tuesday', *su-yo-il* (water-) 'Wednesday', *mog-yo-il* (wood-) 'Thursday', *kŭm-yo-il* (metal-) 'Friday', and *t'o-yo-il* (soil-) 'Saturday'. Some of the SK national holidays are *sin-nyŏn* (new-year) 'New Year's Day', *sing-mog-il* (plant-tree-day) 'Arbor day [April 5]', *ch'u-sŏk* (autumn-evening) 'Thanksgiving Day [August 15 in the lunar calendar]', and *sŏng-t'an-jŏl* (holy-birth-day) 'Christmas Day'.
- SK numerals are extensively used, since native ones are not available for 100 and above: *il* '1', *i* '2', *sam* '3', *sa* '4', *o* '5', *yuk* '6', *ch'il* '7', *p'al* '8', *ku* '9', *sip* '10', *sib-il* '11', *p'al-sip* '80', *ku-sip-ku* '99', *paek* '100', *ch'ŏn* '1,000', *man* '10,000', *sim-man* '100,000', *paeng-man* '1,000,000', *ch'ŏn-man* '10

million', *ŏk* '100 million', *paeg-ŏk* '1 billion', *ch'ŏn-ŏk* '10 billion', and *cho* '100 billion'.

- There are many SK numeral counters that either coexist with synonymous native counterparts or are complementary to the native stock. Examples are *chang* 'sheet' (e.g. paper), *kap* 'case' (e.g. cigarettes, matches), *kae* 'item' (e.g. desk, stone, clock, watch), *kwŏn* 'volume' (e.g. books, notebooks), *myŏng* 'person' (any category of person), *ssang* 'pair' (any animate couples), *tae* 'equipment' (e.g. cars, typewriters, pianos, TV sets, machines), and *yŏl* 'row' (any objects). Examples of measurement counters are *kwan* (3.75 kg), *kŭn* (600 g), *wŏn* (unit of Korean currency), *to* 'degree', *nyŏn* 'year', *wŏl* 'month', *il* 'day', *si* 'o'clock', *pun* 'minute', *ch'o* 'second' (e.g. 2000 *nyŏn* 6 *wŏl* 15 *il* 2 *si* 30 *pun* 15 *ch'o*).
- Color terms are finely segmented by combining different basic color-terms. Each color term is usually followed by the SK word *saek* 'color', as in *hwang-saek* 'yellow (color)'. Examples are *chŏk* 'dark red', *hong* 'red', *hŭk* 'black', *nok* 'green', *paek* 'white', *hwang* 'yellow', *ch'ŏng* 'blue', *kal* 'brown', *nam* 'indigo, dark blue', *hoe* 'grey', *cha* 'purple', *chu* 'vermilion', *cha-ju* 'maroon', *chu-hwang* 'orange', *ch'ŏng-nok* 'bluish green', *pun-hong* (powder-red) 'pink', and *hŭk-kal* 'dark brown'.
- The system of SK kinship terms is very complex, building on [male vs. female], [husband vs. wife], [elder vs. younger], [consanguinity vs. in-law], [mother's side vs. father's side], and [generations up vs. generations down]. The combination of roots representing various semantic components is systematic. For instance, from the SK roots in (8a) have derived various kinship terms such as those in (8b, c, d).

(8)

a.

pu-/bu- 'father'	*mo-* 'mother'	*pu-/bu-* 'husband'
pu-/bu- 'wife, lady'	*ch'ŏ* 'wife'	*cho-/jo-* 'grandparent'
cha-/ja- 'son'	*nyŏ-/yŏ* 'daughter'	*son-* 'grandchild'
si- 'husband's side'	*nam* 'male	*mae-* 'younger sister'
oe- 'mother's side'	*suk-* 'uncle'	*chang-* 'wife's side'
cha- 'older sister'	*che-/je-*'younger sibling'	*i-* 'maternal aunt/uncle'
hyŏng 'older brother'	*ko-*'paternal aunt/uncle'	

b. Ascending generations

pu-mo 'parents'	*si-bu-mo* 'husband's parents'
cho-bu 'grandfather'	*cho-bu-mo* 'grandparents'
chang-in 'wife's father'	*chang-mo* 'wife's mother'

suk-pu 'paternal uncle'	*sung-mo* '*suk-pu*'s wife'
ko-mo 'paternal aunt'	*ko-mo-bu* '*ko-mo*'s husband'
i-mo 'maternal aunt'	*i-mo-bu* '*i-mo*'s husband'
oe-suk-pu 'mother's brother'	*oe-jo-mo* 'maternal grandmother'

c. Ego's generation

cha-mae 'sisters'	*ch'ŏ-je* 'wife's younger sister'
ch'ŏ-hyŏng 'wife's older sister'	*ch'ŏ-nam* 'wife's brother'

d. Descending generations

cha-nyŏ 'son and daughter'	'*cha-bu* 'daughter-in-law
son-ja 'grandson'	*son-nyŏ* 'granddaughter'

- SK metaphorical expressions, such as idioms, maxims, and proverbs, are abundant. These expressions reflect traditional culture (cf. Grant 1982). The literal meanings of many idiomatic SK expressions have been obliterated, and their implied meanings (indicated in brackets below) have become idioms in their place.

(9) *cha-hwa-ja-ch'an* (self-picture-self-praise) 'praising one's own drawing' [self-laudation]
ŏ-bu-ji-ri (fish-man-'s-advantage) 'fisherman's advantages' [winning advantage from a disturbed state of affairs (from an old story that when a clam and a snipe fought, a fisherman caught both of them)]
il-sŏk-i-jo (1-stone-2-bird) 'one stone, two birds' [killing two birds with one stone]
tong-mun-sŏ-dap (east-ask-west-answer) 'east question and west answer' [irrelevant answer]
yong-du-sa-mi (dragon-head-snake-tail) 'head of dragon and tail of snake' [bright beginning and dull finish]

9. Conclusions

Despite the fact that Korea (together with China, Japan, Vietnam, etc.) has long been known as a country belonging to the cultural sphere of Chinese characters, both South and North Korean governments have attempted to eliminate Chinese characters from practical use, so that the Korean alphabet *han'gŭl* can be exclusively used. This effort has not been successful in South Korea. The current practice of the general public is the mixed use of characters and *han'gŭl*, and the Ministry of Education has allowed 1,800 characters to be taught at secondary schools. In North Korea, however, the *han'gŭl*-only policy has been enormously successful. While Chinese characters have been abolished from everyday use, a limited number of characters are taught in schools for reading purposes only. For more on these issues, see Sohn (2004).

The South Korean government has attempted but failed to place any particular restrictions on the use of difficult SK words. In view of the power and efficiency of Chinese characters in forming words, the creating and use of SK words are expected to continue in South Korea. On the other hand, the North Korean government, while emphasizing the preservation of native-like SK words, has been discouraging the popular use of unnecessary SK words. It has removed many SK words from dictionaries, replacing them with new words coined from native elements. Such restrictions in North Korea notwithstanding, SK words will remain an integral part of the Korean vocabulary in both Koreas.

REFERENCES: Chapter 19

Cho, Choon-Hak, Yeon-ja Sohn, and Heisoon Yang. 2002. *Korean Reader for Chinese Characters*. Honolulu: University of Hawaii Press.

Grant, B. K. 1982. *Korean Proverbs*. Salt Lake City: Moth House Publications.

Martin, S. E. 1992. *A Reference Grammar of Korean*. Rutland, Vermont: Charles E. Tuttle.

Pulleyblank, E. 1991. *Lexicon of Reconstructed Pronunciation in Early Middle Chinese, Late Middle Chinese, and Early Mandarin*. Vancouver: University of British Columbia Press.

Sae Kugŏ Saenghwal 9.1/9.2. 1999. National Academy of Korean Language Research, Seoul.

Sohn, Ho-min. 1999/2001. *The Korean Language*. Cambridge, UK: Cambridge University Press.

Sohn, Ho-min. 2004. Language purification movements in North and South Korea. *Korean Linguistics* 12: 141-60. Also in this volume (chapter 17).

Song, Ki-joong. 1986. Remarks on modern Sino-Korean. *Language Research* 22.4: 469-501.

20 Politeness Strategies in Korean*

1. As is widely known, human language has two interrelated and mutually complementary functions: the function of transmitting meanings and the function of establishing interpersonal relationships.[1] Politeness is related essentially to the second function of language, that is, the function of opening, maintaining, or reinforcing smooth interpersonal relationships. If an utterance is not structured and expressed in a polite way, not only is the human relationship impaired, but also the intended meaning may not be conveyed in the speaker's intended way. When we express such phatic expressions as *Annyeng-ha-sey-yo*? 'How are you?' in Korean or "Good Morning" in English, for example, our intention is not to convey such meanings as asking about the addressee's well-being or stating the condition of the morning weather, but simply to maintain a smooth and polite human relationship with the addressee.

The notion of politeness is characterized popularly by correct social usage and marked by consideration, tact, deference, or courtesy (Webster's Seventh New Collegiate Dictionary 1965). From the linguistic perspective, a number of linguists have recently endeavored to define politeness in terms of universal rules, strategies, principles, or maxims. Let me briefly review some representative proposals below.

2. One very frequently quoted proposal is Lakoff's (1973). She suggests three rules of politeness, as given in (1).

(1) a. Do not impose on the addressee;
b. Give the addressee his options; and
c. Make the addressee feel warm and friendly.

* This is reprinted from Baek, E.J. (ed.), *Papers from the Sixth International Conference on Korean Linguistics*, pp. 655–60 (1989). Seoul: Hanshin Publishing Co.

1 A preliminary version of this paper was presented under the title of "Politeness in Korean" at the 40th Association for Asian Studies Annual Meeting in San Francisco in March 1988. This is a revised and expanded version.

These putatively universal rules of politeness are only partially true, when we take the Korean language into account. For one thing, all three rules are relevant only to the addressee. As reflected in Korean honorifics, politeness is relevant not only to the addressee, but also to other relevant human referents, as observed in (2).

(2) A STUDENT TO ANOTHER STUDENT

a. kyoswu-nim i o-si-n-ta.
professor-HT NM come-SH-IN-DC
'The professor is coming.'

b. *kyoswu ka o-n-ta.
Professor NM come-IN-DC

Lakoff's rules are unable to predict the impoliteness of (2b), because *kyoswu* here is not an addressee but a third person referent. Secondly, Lakoff's rules do not mention anything about the speaker's humbleness, which is very important in Korean sociolinguistic reality. For example, consider the dialogue in (3).

(3) HOST: pang i nemwu tew-usi-ci-yo?
room NM too warm-SH-SUP-POL
'The room is too warm, isn't it?'

GUEST: a. tep-ci anh-ayo.
warm-NOM not.be-POL
'No, it's not.'
b. *tew-usi-ci anh-ayo.
Warm-SH-NOM not.be-POL

The host used the honorific suffix *–usi* to indicate his deference to the understood subject that denotes his guest. On the other hand, the guest should not use the honorific suffix to describe his own state of mind or feeling. One plausible cross-cultural universal is that the speaker cannot exalt himself, his action or state, or possessions in linguistic terms.

Third, in Korean culture, imposing on or not giving option to the addressee is frequently very natural and generally polite, when the speech act is in the interest of the addressee, or when the addressee is an in-group inferior person. For example, imposing upon the addressee to eat more by means of the repeated imperative expression *Te tu-sey-yo* 'Have more' is considered more polite than the "Would you care for some more?" type of question. Similarly, the imperative

Cenhwa pat-ala 'Answer the phone!" in Korean is as polite as "Can you answer the phone?" in English when uttered to one's child.

In their monumental study on universal politeness, Brown and Levinson (1978, 1987; henceforth B&L) rebut the doctrine of cultural relativity in interaction, and claim that superficial cross-cultural diversities can emerge from underlying universal pragmatic principles. Maintaining correctly that linguistic strategies are means satisfying both communicative and face-oriented ends, and describing linguistic politeness in terms of face maintenance, they establish five levels of linguistic strategies for politeness, as shown roughly in (4).

(4) a. direct strategy
  b. positive politeness strategies
  c. negative politeness strategies
  d. off-record strategies
  e. no speech act

B&L's direct strategy involves performing a speech act in the most direct, clear, unambiguous, and concise way possible, as stated in Grice's (1975) maxims of conversational cooperation (quality, quantity, relevance, and manner). The circumstances for this strategy include cases when the speech act is used for great urgency, desperation, or efficiency; or in the addressee's interest; or where the speaker is vastly superior in power to the addressee.

B&L's second level of strategies is for positive politeness, which is oriented toward the addressee's positive face or self-image. These strategies are all intended essentially to indicate that the speaker is a cooperator or seeks common ground with the addressee. Fifteen positive politeness strategies are proposed, some of which are as follows: *Notice, attend to hearer's wants, needs, interests, goods; Use in-group identity markers; Include both speaker and hearer in the activity; Exaggerate interest, approval, sympathy with hearer; Seek agreement; Avoid disagreement; Joke; and Give reasons.* Utterances like "Your watch is very nice, where did you buy it?" or its Korean counterpart *Sikey cham coh-ney-yo, eti se sa-sy-ess-eyo?* may belong to the strategy of noticing/ attending the addressee. In-group identity markers may include jargon or slang, contraction and ellipsis, and such in-group address forms as 'darling', 'honey', *yepo* 'honey', *Ilmin-a* 'Ilmin!', and *Kim-hyeng* 'Mr. Kim!' (lit. 'Brother Kim'). The strategy of including both the speaker and addressee may be illustrated by "Let's have a cookie" instead of "Let me have a cookie", and *Nay ka ka-ca* 'Let me go' instead of *Nay ka ka-keyss-ta* 'I will go.'[2]

---

2 The propositive sentence ender *–ca* in Korean agrees, in principle, with the first person

B&L's negative politeness is oriented toward partially satisfying the addressee's negative face, that is, his basic desire to maintain his freedom of action, his freedom from imposition, his territory, and his self-determination. It is often pointed out that negative politeness is the most important and sensitive in English-speaking society. I ascribe this situation primarily to English-speakers' strong value orientation toward egalitarianism and individualism (Sohn 1986). B&L propose ten negative politeness strategies, some of which are: *Be conventionally indirect; Give deference; Question, hedge; Apologize; Impersonalize speaker and hearer; Nominalize; and Go on record as incurring a debt.* For example, polite utterances like "Can you pass the salt?" (instead of "Pass the salt") or its Korean counterpart *Sokum com cwu-si-keyss-eyo?* (instead of *Sokum cwu-sey-yo*) may belong to the conventional indirect strategy.

According to B&L, an off-record communicative act is an act that cannot be interpreted as expressing one clear communicative intention. The speaker performs this speech act when he wishes to avoid responsibility for his act, leaving it up to the addressee to decide how to interpret it. Fifteen off-record strategies are proposed, which include, among others, *Give hints; Give association clues; Presuppose; Understate; Be ironic; Use metaphors; Use rhetorical questions; Be ambiguous; and Be incomplete, use ellipsis.* Thus, for example, saying "It's cold in here" or its Korean counterpart *Pang i chwup-kwun-yo* hints to the addressee to shut the window, or turn on the heater, or for them to move to another room, etc. depending on the speech situation.

B&L's last level of strategy is just to keep silent, without performing any speech act. They assert that the more a speech act threatens the speaker's or the addressee's face, the more the speaker will wish to choose a strategy on a higher level. A great majority of B&L's politeness strategies are also applicable, in general, to the parallel speech acts of Korean. Again, however, they hardly touch on politeness toward third person referents. Nowhere in their system can Korean honorifics be properly placed. As we have seen above, one of their negative politeness strategies is *Give deference*, with an example like "Excuse me, sir, but would you mind if I close the window?" Korean honorifics or deference patterns are based on such sociocultural variables as age and social status, and not triggered by the need of negative politeness.

Another influential proposal is made by Leech (1983), who relates the Gricean Cooperative Principle and his Politeness Principle. Defining polite and impolite beliefs as beliefs which respectively are favorable and unfavorable to the addressee or a third party, Leech formulates the Politeness Principle as

---

plural subject, including the speaker and addressee. Only in exceptional cases, such as in an entreaty, is the first person singular allowed.

"Minimize (other things being equal) the expression of impolite beliefs." Under this politeness principle, he presents seven maxims, as shown in (5).

(5) a. tact
b. generosity
c. approbation
d. modesty
e. agreement
f. sympathy
g. phatic

Of primary interest in Leech's maxims is tact, to the discussion of which he devotes much space. He points out that the most important kind of politeness in English-speaking society is that which is covered by the operation of the Tact Maxim. This maxim reads "Minimize cost to other; Maximize benefit to other." Leech proposes three scales where his Tact Maxim is relevant: the cost-benefit scale that concerns the propositional content of an utterance, the indirectness (optionality) scale that concerns the illocutionary force of an utterance, and the social distance scale that concerns the vertical (power) and horizontal (solidarity) relationship between the speaker and addressee or a third party. Thus, for example, the greater the cost of a speech act to the addressee, the greater the horizontal social distance of the hearer from the speaker; and the greater the authoritative status of the addressee with respect to the speaker, the greater will be the need for indirectness in the expression of an utterance, if the speaker is to observe the Tact Maxim. As conceived in this way, the Tact Maxim can explain, for example, why the indirect utterance "Would you mind answering the phone?" or its Korean counterpart *Cenhwa com pat-a cwu-si-kyess-eyo?* is more polite than the direct utterance "Answer the phone" or *Cenhwa pat-usey-yo*, and why the direct utterance "Have another sandwich" or its Korean counterpart *Sayntuwichi hana te tu-sey-yo* is more polite than the indirect utterance "Would you mind having another sandwich?" or *Sayntuwichi hana te tu-si-keyss-eyo?*

The comments I have addressed to the other proposals are also applicable to Leech's characterization of politeness maxims. His proposal is only partially true of Korean, in the dimension of pragmatic usage of utterances. Even here, culture-specific value orientations constrain utterance usages to a great extent. Strong culture-bound politeness is encoded structurally in the honorifics of Korean, whose use are socially constrained and by and large obligatory, and are much more crucial than the use of the expressions, such as indirect speech acts, that are governed by Leech's politeness maxims.

Largely in the same vein as the above three proposals, other authors have related politeness to various ways of modifying the illocutionary force of speech acts. For example, Searle (1975) acknowledges the importance of politeness for issuing indirect directives. Fraser (1978, 1980; Fraser and Nolan 1981) associates politeness with his notion of mitigation, defining mitigation as a strategy for reducing the force of a speech act whose effects are unwelcome to the addressee. Holmes (1984) proposes on the one hand the notion of attenuation vs. boosting of illocution, and on the other the notion of positively affective vs. negatively affective speech acts. Attenuation of a negatively affective speech act or boosting of a positively affective speech act contributes to politeness, an approach essentially similar to the operation of the Tact Maxim proposed by Leech (1983).

What I regard as major drawbacks of the various proposed universal accounts of linguistic politeness discussed thus far may be summarized as follows. First of all, none of them touches on honorifics, either addressee or referent honorifics, in any systematic way.[3] Second, most of the proposals (except perhaps for Leech 1983) are concerned only with the speaker-addressee perspective. That is, the speaker-referent perspective is generally ignored. Third, most of the proposals are concerned only with the pragmatic uses of sentential expressions, and do not clearly distinguish between systematic linguistic devices and universal pragmatic uses of them. Fourth, all of the proposals are overly concerned with universal aspects. That is, sociocultural differences are slighted. It seems to me that all the aforementioned proposals are, by and large, oriented toward horizontal societies, where egalitarianism and individualism are dominant. As we have observed, such proposals fail to describe in any satisfactory way linguistic politeness prevailing in vertical societies, especially in those societies where relative social stratification and collectivistic values are systematically encoded in linguistic structure and patterned in pragmatic usages.[4]

Korean society still manifests considerably strong hierarchism and collectiv-

---

3 B&L (1978, 1987) bring up honorifics here and there (e.g. 1987:22-25, 179-187, 276-280), but fail to incorporate them as an integral part of their politeness strategies. For example, they (1987:23) argue that "honorifics are frozen conversational implicatures, constituting some of the best examples of Grice's category of *conventional implicature*." Korean honorifics, which are based largely on such power-oriented variables as age, kinship, and social status, are far from being "frozen" implicatures.

4 An honorifics-related observation from the evolutional perspective that covers both horizontal and vertical societies is made by Brown and Gilman (1960), who distinguish between power and solidarity as two basic dimensions underlying the usage in many languages of Europe and India of the familiar pronoun T (e.g. French *tu*, German *du*, Italian *tu*, and 13th-18th c. English *thou*) and the polite pronoun V (e.g. French *vous*, German *Sie*, Italian *Lei*, and 13th-18th c. English *ye*). Brown and Gilman observe that T was originally associated with condescension and intimacy and V with deference and distance, and that, since the last century, solidarity has largely won over power and thus T is now associated generally with intimacy and V with distance.

ism, as these are reflected in their contemporary linguistic behavior. For example, the rules, strategies, and maxims discussed thus far do not explain why Koreans must know and use extremely intricate patterns of addressee and referent honorifics for effective and polite communication; why Koreans are so sensitive to age in performing speech acts; why Koreans are overly courteous to some people but act with no regard for others; why an angry Korean tends to downgrade address terms and speech levels; why Koreans cannot use a second person pronoun when addressing a social superior; why Korean adults most frequently use the deferential speech style for smooth daily social interaction; and why a Korean finds it impolite to say "Thank you" immediately after someone praises his family member or possession or when someone gives him a gift or invites him for dinner. These and many other politeness phenomena are regarded not as random, unrelated facts, but as arising from the systematic patterns of Koreans' holistic cultural values, clustered around time-honored hierarchism and collectivism.

3. Let me present some concrete linguistic examples that are indicative of Korean's holistic value orientations, as opposed to Americans' generally atomistic-mechanistic culture.[5] For one thing, in English, such titles are *Professor, Father, Reverend, Dr., Mr., Mrs., and Miss* have hardly any hierarchical connotation, but simply indicate professional role, marital status, or sex differences. In Korean, however, titles like *kyoswu-nim* 'Mr. professor', *sinpwu-nim* 'Mr. Father', *paksa-nim* 'Mr. Ph.D.', *sensayng-nim* 'Mr., Mrs., Miss (teacher)', *yesa* 'Madam', *paksa* 'Dr.', *sensayng* 'Mr., Mrs., Miss', *ssi* 'Mr., Mrs., Miss', *kwun* 'Mr.', *yang* 'Miss', as well as the vocative particles *I* (addressed to a preadult) and *a* (addressed to a child), are strongly hierarchical. For example, a man named *Ilmin Kim* may be addressed with a variety of different address terms, which are given in (6) in the decreasing order of deference.

(6) Kim-paksa-nim 'Mr. Dr. Kim' > Kim sensayng-nim 'Mr. Kim' > Kim-paksa 'Dr. Kim' > Kim sensayng 'Mr. Kim' > Kim ssi 'Mr. Kim' > Kim kwun 'Mr. Kim' > Ilmin i > Ilmin a

One can never address a social superior without such an honorific suffix as –*nim*. Thus, for example, *Kim-paksa* 'Dr. Kim', *Kim-sensayng* 'Mr., Mrs., Miss', *Kim-ssi* 'Mr., Mrs., Miss', *Kim-kwun* 'Mr. Kim', as well as English loan terms like *Dr. Kim, Mr. Kim,* and *Miss Kim*, are used only to a social equal or inferior.

5 Yoshikawa (1982) makes a comparative study of the Japanese people's so-called 'holistic' communication patterns and Americans' 'atomistic-mechanistic' patterns.

Second, while there are essentially no speech levels in English, six distinct speech styles (or levels) are used in Korean to indicate the speaker's different regards toward the addressee: deferential, polite, blunt, familiar, intimate, and plain. These speech styles are reflected in sentence enders and again are strongly hierarchical.[6] The most important factor that triggers the use of these different styles is age category: adult, pre-adult, and child (e.g. Sohn 1986: Ch. 4). The other factors involved are social status, intimacy, formality, kinship, and sex.

Third, observe the different degrees of politeness associated with the expressions in (7), which all correspond to English "that person".

(7) ku elusin > ku elun > ku pwun > ku i > ku salam > ku ca
'that person'

These different expressions refer to an adult, but notice the decreasing degree of deference. One cannot refer to a social superior with *ku salam* or *ku ca*. Lexical differentiation of this sort and its association with social stratification indicates that Koreans are still hierarchy-oriented in their cultural values.

Fourth, observe the dialogue between a school teacher and his student in (8).

(8)	STUDENT:	sensayng-nim,	annyenghi			cwumwu-sey-yo.
		teacher-HT	peacefully			sleep-SH-POL
		'Good night.'				
		(lit. 'Mr. teacher, sleep peacefully!')				
	TEACHER:	kulay,	ne	to	cal	ca-la.
		right	you	also	well	sleep-IM
		'Good night.'				
		(lit. 'Right, you also, sleep well!')				

Notice that, unlike in English, the student and teacher are using two entirely different forms of utterance: *sensayng-nim* vs. *ne*, *annyenghi* vs. *cal*, *cwumwu-sey* vs. *ca*, and *–yo* vs. *–la*. Due to hierarchy-oriented consciousness, Korean adults want to be treated with deference from outgroup members. For this reason, the principle of mutual deference is the most favorable mode of communication between equal adults, Thus, address terms like *kisa-nim* 'Mr. Driver', *son-nim* 'Mr./Mrs./Miss guest', *uysa-sensayng-nim* 'Mr. teacher doctor', and

6 The six speech styles are conflated in form with the four major sentence types (declarative, interrogative, imperative, propositive) in Korean. Thus, in declarative sentences, the deferential ender is *–sup-ni-ta*, the polite ender *–eyo*, the blunt ender *–so/-uo*, the familiar ender *–ney*, the intimate ender *–e*, and the plain ender *–ta*.

samo-nim 'Mrs. teacher's wife', as well as the deference or polite speech level and the subject honorific suffix, are of common daily use in Korea.

Fifth, when two unequal adults meet, the person who is socially inferior (usually in terms of age) often asks the superior to lower the speech level, by saying *malssum nacchwu-sey-yo* 'Please lower your words'. This situation occurs when the superior has turned out to be much older than oneself, a friend of one's father or older brother, a former senior in high school, and so on.

Sixth, in (9) through (11) observe some frequently encountered dialogues between two Korean adults, and notice the way utterances are made indirectly. Speaker A and Speaker B in the following examples may be adult equals.

(9) A: te tu-sey-yo!
more take-SH-POL
'Please eat some more.'

B: kwaynchanha-yo.
O.K.-POL
'It's O.K.'

A: te tu-si-la-nikka-yo!
more take-SH-IM-I.insist-POL
'I insist, have some more!'

B: kulay po-lkka-yo?
do.so try-shall.I-POL
'Then, shall I try?'

A: os i cham yepp-eyo.
dress NM very pretty-POL
'Your dress is really pretty.'

B: mwuel-yo, ssakwulye y-eyyo.
not.at.all-POL cheap.stuff is-POL
'Not at all. It's a cheap stuff.'

A: sensayng-nim sengham i ettehkey toy-si-p-ni-kka?
teaher-HT name NM how become-SH-AH-IN-Q
'What is your name?'
(lit. 'What does your honorable name become?')

B:	Kim Ilmin	i-lako	ha-p-ni-ta.
	Kim Ilmin	is-that	call-AH-IN-DC
	'I am called Kim Ilmin.' (lit. 'people call (me) Kim Ilmin')		

Due probably to strong collectivism, Koreans' communicative patterns are allusive in many speech situations. Modesty, *cheymyen* 'face or self image in relation to others', and *nwunchi* 'reading other's mind' are highly valued. For this reason, a host of conversational implicatures are employed in daily conversations. It is considered generally impolite to immediately accept someone's offer to eat more food or to say "Thank you" immediately after someone praises your possessions. Notice in (11) how indirectly the speech act is made. Indirect speech acts of this kind are frequently used to indicate politeness in Korean.

Seventh, notice in (12) how English sentences with 'I' as subject can be translated naturally in Korean without 'I' as an overt or covert subject.

(12)	a.	Can I get a shave?			
	a′.	myento	com	hay	cwu-si-keyss-eyo?
		shave	just	do	for.me-SH-intend-POL
		'Can you give me a shave?'			
	b.	Can I see your driver's license?			
	b′.	myenhecung	com	poy-e	cwu-sey-yo.
		License	just	show-INF	for me-SH-POL
		'Please show me your license.'			
	c.	I'd like an American breakfast.			
	c′.	yangsik	ulo	cwu-sey-yo.	
		Western	with	give-SH-POL	
		'Please give me a Western-style (breakfast).'			
	d.	I have a son.			
	d′.	atul	i	hana	iss-eyo.
		Son	NM	one	exist-POL
		'I have a son. (lit. 'A son exists')'			
	e.	I beg your pardon?			
	e′.	tasi	malssumhay	cwu-si-keyss-eyo?	
		Again	say	for.me-SH-intend-POL	
		'Can you say it again?'			

e″. cal an tulli-nun tey-yo.
well not be.heard-RL-circumstance-POL
'It is not heard clearly.'

f. May I speak to Mr. Smith?
f′. Smith-ssi kyesey-yo?
Smith-HT stay-POL
'Is Mr. Smith at home?' (lit. 'Does Mr. Smith exist?')

g. May I help you?
g′. ettehkey o-si-ess-eyo?
how come-SH-PST-POL
'May I help you? (lit. 'How did (you) come?')

Use of overt 'I' (and 'you') as a sentential subject is suppressed in many speech situations. This situation-orientation in communication appears to be due partly to the expression of politeness and partly to the collectivistic value of traditional and contemporary Korean culture.

4. In short, the notion of politeness is both universal and culture-bound, in that its reflection in linguistic structures and pragmatic usages manifests two-sidedness. In order to deal with linguistic politeness in truly universal and language-specific terms, covering all ranges of human societies, I propose to recognize two interrelated dimensions: that of linguistic devices and that of sociolinguistic rules of language use, as schematized in (13a) and (13b). Needless to say, many of the insights that are contained in other authors' works are incorporated in the proposed scheme. (13a) consists of four major sets of politeness-indicating devices: honorifics, illocution-modifying devices, expressive devices, and figurative devices. Each major set is subclassified along various dimensions. In (13a), ISAs stands for indirect speech acts and EPs stands for explicit performatives. In a broad sense of the term, ISAs (indirect speech acts) may include most of the other mitigating devices, such as hedges, tags, downtoners, passivization, nominalization, and ellipsis (e.g. Sohn 1986: ch.2). In a narrow sense as adopted here, however, ISAs cover only those cases in which one illocutionary type, such as declarative, is changed into another illocutionary type, such as an interrogative (e.g. Searle 1975).

I presume that under this overall framework, individual languages employ different linguistic strategies and forms. I would claim that the scheme is universal because even the languages of the most egalitarian societies, such as English-speaking societies, also have some honorifics. Address terms like *Mr.*

President, *Dr. Smith*, and *Sir* and such lexical items as *gentleman* (vs. *man*), *lady* (vs. *woman*), and *dine* (vs. *eat*) may be regarded as belonging to honorifics in English. Which devices are given particular importance depend on the specific languages and culture. In Korean, honorifics are the most crucial devices of politeness, although the other sets of devices are also extensively used (cf. Sohn 1986: ch. 4). In America, honorifics are of minimal significance, while illocutionary and expressive devices receive great importance. For example, in polite directive acts, Americans hardly use direct speech acts, but almost always use such indirect speech acts as "Can you open the door, please" (e.g. Wierzbicka 1985).

The various universal proposals discussed earlier are relevant, in general, only to illocutionary and expressive devices. For example, Lakoff's rules of politeness, Searle's indirect directives for politeness, and Fraser's notion of politeness are related in general only to mitigation devices. Holmes's proposal is related in general only to mitigation and reinforcement. B&L's proposals are relevant mainly to illocutionary and expressive devices. Many of B&L's positive politeness strategies belong to the expressive devices in my framework, their direct strategy and many of the negative politeness strategies to my conventional mitigation, and many of their off-record strategies to me allusive mitigation. Leech's tact maxim is covered essentially by illocutionary devices in my framework and his other maxims by my expressive devices.

(13) a. Devices of Linguistic Politeness

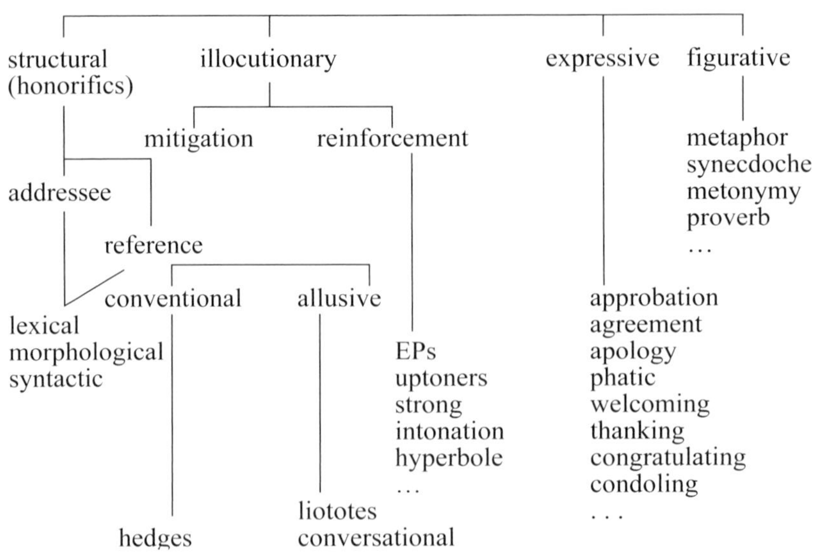

ISAs	implicatures
tags	. . .
ellipsis	
downtoners	
passivization	
nominalization	
disclaimers	
softening intonation	
use of modal elements	
cogitatives	
. . .	

b. Pragmatic and sociolinguistic rules of polite language use that are based on (1) universal pragmatic principles and (2) culture-specific norms, values, and assumptions

As indicated in (13b), I propose that various linguistic devices are put to actual use in accordance with universal pragmatic rules and language-specific sociolinguistic rules that are appropriate to each linguistic community. These rules are based on universal pragmatic such as those proposed by the authors reviewed above, and on culture-specific norms, values, and assumptions. As we observed earlier, cultural differences are great and, accordingly, sociolinguistic rules of language use are diverse. For example, Americans do not generally respect age, but Koreans strongly do so. In particular, such power-based variables as relative age, kinship, social status, occupational rank, sex, and interest relationship, and such solidarity-based variables as intimacy, groupness, and formality are essential in the formulation of the rules for the use of polite expressions in Korean (Sohn 1986: Ch. 4). Americans seem to place greater emphasis on expressiveness than on modesty, while the reverse seems to be generally true among Koreans. All these will explain, for example, why Koreans must use honorifics in the way they do, and why they should not utter the phatic expression "Thank you" immediately after someone praises their wife. As mentioned earlier, B&L propose "Give deference" as a negative politeness strategy. This strategy is far from being universal, but is a rule of honorific usage applicable to English or some other related languages, but not to Korean.

5. In what follows, I will present some Korean expressions illustrating the different linguistic devices that are listed in (13a). As for the dimension of pragmatic and sociolinguistic rules, sporadic allusions have been made thus far, but lack of space does not allow me to go into details here. For proposals regarding pragmatic rules, which are largely of universal nature, see Brown and Gilman (1960), Lakoff (1967), Fraser (1980), Cho (1982), Leech (1983), Holmes (1984), B&L

(1987), and Sohn (1986, 1987). For some proposals regarding sociolinguistic rules of language use, especially on the use of honorifics, see Hwang (1975), D. Lee (1975), Park-Choi (1976, 1978), Wang (1979), Cho (1982), Dredge (1983), Suh (1984), and Sohn (1986), among other works.

As for the structural devices of politeness, Korean has probably the most intricate and systematic patterns of honorifics in the world.[7] As has been alluded to in many previous examples, honorifics are associated with both the speaker-addressee perspective (addressee honorifics) and the speaker-referent perspective (referent honorifics such as subject, dative, and object honorifics). Honorifics are observed in address-reference terms, honorific titles, personal pronouns, case particles (subject, dative, and vocative), euphemistic words, and verbal suffixes. Between addressee and referent honorifics, the former is more significant in view of the importance of face-to-face interaction (e.g. Sohn 1988). Among referent honorifics, subject is more important, thus structurally and lexically more diversified, than dative, which is in turn more important than object. Thus, for example, subject honorification is expressed by the presence of the single suffix *–(u)si*, whereas addressee honorifics are stratified as six different hierarchical sentence-enders. Observe the sentence in (14), in which both the addressee and referent (subject and dative) honorifics are illustrated. A daughter-in-law would use such a polite language.

(14) apenim, emenim kkeyse halmenim kkey ton ul
father mother NM grandmother to money AC
tuli-si-ess-up-ni-ta
give-SH PST AH IN-DC
'Father, mother gave money to grandmother.'

In (14), the deferential address term *apenim* (neutral form: *apeci*), the addressee honorific suffix *–(s)up*, and the deferential indicative declarative suffixes *–ni-ta* conspire to indicate addressee honorification. Similarly, the deferential reference term *emenim* (neutral form: *emeni*), the deferential subject case particle *kkeyse* (neutral form: *ka/i*), and the subject honorific suffix *–(u)si* constitute subject referent honorification. The deferential reference term *halmenim* (neutral form: *halmeni*), the deferential dative case particle *kkey* (neutral form: *eykey/hanthey*), and the dative honorific verb *tuli* (plain form: *cwu*) are used to indicate dative referent honorification. Notice that the speaker uses the def-

7 At the conference on honorifics sponsored jointly by Portland State University and Reed College in April 1988, I discovered that among the many languages whose honorifics were discussed, Korean honorific patterns were the most extensive and systematic, rating over lexical, morphological, and syntactic areas.

erential verb *tuli*, because he perceives that his grandmother is higher than his mother. Notice further that there is a syntactic agreement among the addressee honorifics, among the subject honorifics, and among the dative honorifics.

The subsets of illocutionary devices in Korean are illustrated in (15). (15a) is a case of conventional mitigation: (15b) a case of allusive mitigation, and (15c) a case of reinforcement.

(15) a. ssuleyki com chiwe cwu-si-keyss-eyo?
garbage just take for me-SH-intend-POL
'Can you take out the garbage for me?'

b. ssuleyki cha ka w-ass-eyo.
garbage truck NM come-PST-POL
'The garbage truck is here.'

c. ese tule o-sey-yo.
quickly enter come-SH-POL
'Please come in. (lit. 'Come in quickly.')

As observed in (15a), use of the hedge word *com* 'just, a little bit', the benefactive auxiliary verb *cwu* 'give, for me', the volition/presumption modal suffix *–keyss*, and the interrogative indirect speech act is a conventional formula for indirect directives in Korean. On the other hand, allusive devices like the conversational implicature in (15b) are open-ended, being partly universal and partly culture-bound. Mitigation is used not only to soften the speaker's illocutionary force, but also to give options for the addressee to choose from in making a decision. Illocutionary reinforcement, as shown in (15c), is used when the intended act is strongly in the interest of the addressee. Thus, one pragmatic rule for politeness may be that the more the intended act is disadvantageous to the addressee, the more the utterance must be mitigating, while the more the intended act is in the interest of the addressee, the more the utterance must be direct or even reinforcing.

Expressive devices include both conventional and non-conventional expressions. Like many other languages, Korean has many conventional forms, as illustrated below.

(16) a. chwukhaha-p-ni-ta.
congratulate-AH-IN-DC
'Congratulations to you!'

b. sillyeyha-p-ni-ta.
be.rude-AH-IN-DC
'Excuse me.'

c. komap-sup-ni-ta.
thankful-AH-IN-DC
'Thank you.'

d. chenmaney-yo.
not.at.all-POL
'Not at all; You are welcome.'

e. annyengha-sey-yo.
peaceful-SH-POL
'How are you?'

f. annyenghi ka-sey-yo.
peacefully go-SH-POL
'Good-bye.'

g. tto poyp-keyss-up-ni-ta.
again see-intend-AH-IND-DEC
'See you again.'

h. pangkap-sup-ni-ta.
glad-AH-IN-DC
'Welcome.'

i. coysongha-p-ni-ta.
guilty-AH-IN-DC
'I am sorry.'

Figurative devices include not only such lexical items as *hwacangsil* (vs. *pyenso*) 'toilet (lit. 'make-up room')' and *chwunchwu* (vs. *yensey*) 'age (lit. 'spring and autumn')' but also sentential expressions, as illustrated by the use of a proverb in (17).

(17) onun ceng i kow-aya kanun ceng i kop-ci-yo.
Coming love NM good-if.only going love NM good-SUP-POL
'I am sorry I cannot help you (as love should be mutual).'

Interaction of linguistic devices belonging to different sets is ubiquitous, as has been observed in many examples given thus far. To give another example, the two utterances in (18) mean the same thing, but (18a) is less polite than (18b), despite the fact that the former is in the deferential speech level and the latter in the polite speech level. Notice that (18a) is a direct speech act, whereas (18b) is a mitigated speech act (with the ellipsis of a main predicate). Other things being generally equal, mitigated expressions are more polite than direct expressions.

(18) a. pi ka o-p-ti-ta.
rain NM come-AH-RT-DC
'I saw it raining.'
b. pi ka o-te-n tey-yo.
rain NM come-RT-RL circumstance-POL
'I saw it raining. (What would you like to do?)'

As Hwang (1975:151) points out, it is true that one can be deferential without necessarily being polite, or condescending without necessarily being impolite. This is precisely because different devices interact. Screaming to an adult stranger, for example, saying *Naka-si-p-si-o* 'Get out!' is impolite in a usual sense of the term, if the act of going out would not be in the interest of the addressee, because the imperative form with loud voice contributes to impoliteness. However, notice that the speaker used the deferential speech level, at least showing his socially appropriate regard to the addressee. If the speaker used a blunt or lower speech level, impoliteness would be multiplied.

REFERENCES: Chapter 20

Brown, P., and S. Levinson. 1978. Universals in language usage: Politeness phenomena. In Goody, E. (1978, 56-289).

Brown, P., and S. Levinson. 1987. *Politeness*. Cambridge, UK: University Press.

Brown, R.W., and A. Gilman. 1960. The pronouns of power and solidarity. In Sebeok, T.A. (1960, 253-76).

Cho, Choon-Hak. 1982. *A Study of Korean Pragmatics: Deixis and Politeness*. Ph.D. dissertation. University of Hawaii.

Cole, P., and J. Morgan (eds.) 1975. *Syntax and Semantics 3: Speech Acts*. New York: Academic Press.

Dredge, C.P. 1983. What is politeness in Korean speech? *Korean Linguistics* 3: 21-32.

Fraser, B. 1978. Acquiring social competence in a second language. *RELC Journal* 9.2: 1-21.

Fraser, B. 1980. Conversational mitigation. *Journal of Pragmatics* 4: 341-50.

Fraser, B., and W. Nolan. 1981. The association of deference with linguistic form. *International Journal of the Sociology of Language* 27: 93-109.

Goody, E. (ed.) 1978. *Question and politeness: Strategies in social interaction*. Cambridge, UK: University Press.

Grice, H.P. 1975. Logic and conversation. In Cole and Morgan 1975: 41-58.

Holmes, J. 1984. Modifying illocutionary force. Journal of Pragmatics 8: 345-65.

Hwang, Juck-Ryoon. 1975. *Role of Sociolinguistics in Foreign Language Education with Reference to Korean and English Terms of Address and Levels of Deference*. Ph.D. dissertation. University of Texas, Austin. Seoul: Kwangmoon-sa.

Lakoff, R. 1973. The logic of politeness: Or, minding your p's and q's. *Proceedings of the Ninth Regional Meeting of the Chicago Linguistic Society*, 292-305.

Lee, Dong-Jae. 1975. Some problems in learning Korean second person pronouns. In Sohn, H. (1975, 19-32).

Leech, G.N. 1983. Principles of pragmatics. London/New York: Longman.

Linguistic Society of Korea. (ed.) 1987. *Linguistics in the Morning Calm II*. Seoul: Hanshin Publishing Co.

Park-Choi, Young-Soon. 1976. Kwukekyengepep uy sahoyenehakcek yenkwu. Kwuke Kwukmwunhak 72/73: 47-65.

Park-Choi, Young-Soon. 1978. Aspects in the Development of Communicative Competence with Reference to the Korean Deference System. Ph.D. dissertation. University of Illinois, Urbana.

Searle, J. 1975. Indirect speech acts. In Cole, P. and J. Morgan (1975, 59-82).

Sebeok, T.A. (ed.) 1960. *Style in Language*. Cambridge, Mass: MIT Press.

Sohn, Ho-min (ed.) 1975. *The Korean Language: Its Structure and Social Projection*. Honolulu: University of Hawaii Center for Korean Studies.

Sohn, Ho-min. 1986. *Linguistic Expeditions*. Seoul: Hanshin Publishing Co.

Sohn, Ho-min. 1987. Strategies of indirection in language. In Linguistic Society of Korea (1987, 167-96).

Sohn, Ho-min. 1988. Typological characteristics of Korean honorifics. Paper presented at the conference on honorifics, Portland, Oregon. April.

Suh, Cheong-Soo. 1984. *Contaypep uy Yenkwu* (A Study of Honorifics). Seoul: Hanshin Publishing Co.

Wang, Hahn-Sok. 1979. Sociolinguistic rules of Korean honorifics. *Inlywuhak Noncip* 5: 91-118.

Wierzbicka, A. 1985. Different cultures, different languages, different speech acts. *Journal of Pragmatics* 9: 145-78.

Yoshikawa, Muneo. 1982. Japanese and American modes of communication and implications for managerial and organizational behavior. Paper presented at the 2nd International Conference on Communication Theory: Eastern and Western Perspectives. Yokohama, Japan, July.

21 Honorific Patterns in Korean

1. Linguistic politeness

Language has essentially two functions: the function of transmitting information and knowledge and the function of maintaining human relationships. The former is often called 'transactional function', and the latter 'interactional function'.[1] It is the interactional function that is relevant to linguistic politeness. Although linguistic expressions of politeness are ubiquitous across all languages, their forms and functions are different from language to language, being conditioned by respective linguistic structures and usage, and patterns of underlying socio-cultural values of the speakers. The socio-cultural values that are relevant to linguistic politeness are related to not only power variables such as age, kinship, gender, social status, and occupational rank, and solidarity (or familiarity) variables such as the in- and outgroupness scale, the intimacy and distance scale, and the formality scale, but also different degrees of face threat associated with various speech acts.

As I argued in Sohn (1989), most putatively universal proposals by Western scholars (e.g. Lakoff 1973, Brown and Levinson 1987) are only partially valid, in that linguistic politeness is viewed only as a feature of *strategic* language *use* in social interaction. Specifically, first, hardly any Western scholars touches on honorifics, either addressee or referent honorifics, in any systematic way. This is serious deficiency in that in languages like Korean and Japanese, utterances cannot be made without the speaker's determination of his/her speech levels during social interactions with the addressee. Second, proposals by Western scholars are concerned only with the speaker-addressee perspective, while the speaker-referent perspective is generally ignored. Third, none of them brings up normative politeness use, in addition to strategic politeness use. Fourth, no proposal

---

1 This paper was prepared for the conference on Properties of the Korean Language hosted by the University of Texas at Austin on March 27, 1999. I thank Miho Choo, conferene organizer, for inviting me to this important conference. I appreciate Haejin Koh for providing me with valuable comments on the original version of this paper.

takes into account vertically oriented and/or collectivistically oriented societies in any explicit or implicit manner. In fact, very few proposals have discussed cultural perspectives in any significant way. In Chinese, Japanese, and Korean cultures, for example, imposing on or not giving options to the addressee is very natural and generally polite when the speech act is in the interest of the addressee, as when imposing upon the addressee to eat more.

In short, I argue that linguistic politeness is a significant feature of both language *structure* and *use* on the one hand and is used both *normatively* (obligatorily per discernment) and *strategically* (optionally and volitionally) on the other. I further argue that language-specific politeness devices and normative and strategic uses are crucially based on time-honored cultural perspectives. In addition, as an important social phenomenon and a facet of communicative competence and performance, linguistic politeness is both universal and culture-bound in that its reflection in linguistic patterns and pragmatic usages manifests two-sidedness.

That is, I assume that there are universal linguistic devices for politeness from which individual languages and cultures choose from (cf. Sohn 1989). Also, the sociolinguistic rules and conventions of politeness language use in a linguistic community are based in large measure on universal pragmatic principles in language use, filtered by the underlying cultural perspectives such as social norms of behavior, value orientations, and cultural assumptions. For instance, a putatively universal principle is that indirect speech acts are appropriate in requests or refusals in order to mitigate or soften the act to some degree. For example, it is common in English to use a question form for a request, as in (1).

(1) Would you be kind enough to move your car so I can get out?

The above kind of indirect speech act would be very frequent in Korean between distant adult equals or to a social superior. However, mismatches appear in several respects. First, the corresponding Korean forms are marked by appropriate social indexing for normative politeness. Second, when the same kind of request is made to an in-group junior or child, the speech act usually is relatively more direct. Third, first name basis between colleagues is an aspect of typical solidarity-based American culture, which is never shared by either Koreans or Japanese. This kind of mismatch is due to the difference in cultural perspectives.

Another example is that, some time ago, a U.S. military officer left a note in Korean as in (2a) on the door of my office. An adult Korean native speaker would have said (2b) instead.

(2) a. "... *nay ka tangsin ul encey po-l swu iss-sup-nikka? ...*"
'(lit.) When can I see you?'

b. "... *(cey ka) kyoswu-nim ul encey poy-l swu iss-keyss-sup-nikka? ...*"
'(lit.) When do you think I can see you?'

Native speakers of Korean immediately know that this grammatically correct expression, with the deferential sentence ender, is nevertheless socially inappropriate and impolite. First, the first pronoun *na(y)* should not be used toward a social superior; the humble form *ce(y)* must be used instead, but, in this case, the pronoun is usually omitted because it is contextually understood. Second, the pronoun *tangsin*, though it is higher than the plain form *ne* and the familiar form *caney*, still cannot be used to an adult social superior or equal because it is not high enough to be used so. The person used it apparently because he thought this high-level second person pronoun is appropriate in such a context. He was not aware of the sociolinguistic rule that no regular Korean second-person pronoun should be used toward a social superior or adult equal (except to one's spouse) in Korean and an appropriate third-person nominal such as *kyoswu-nim* 'professor" or *sensayng-nim* 'teacher' or a recently innovated pronoun *elusin* (used only to an aged social superior) must be substituted for the pronoun. Third, the person used the plain verb *pota* 'to see' as in English, not knowing that the humble counterpart *poypta* 'to see (a higher person)' is appropriate in such a context. Fourth, for further politeness, it is a conventional strategy to add the modal suffix *–keyss* to the main verb, which denotes the speaker/hearer conjecture. Thus, (2b) is a corresponding polite expression.

Why is (2b) conceived and perceived as appropriate and polite by native speakers of Korean, while (2a) is not? It is because the relevant sociolinguistic forms, rules, and conventions are crucially correlated with the cultural perspectives of Koreans' relative hierarchism that senior persons should be treated appropriately with proper honorific forms.

As alluded to in the above examples, linguistic politeness is expressed in a wide variety of devices in all cultures and societies. In Sohn (1989), I proposed a universal framework of linguistic politeness devices that human languages utilize. The scheme I proposed consists of four major sets (structural, illocutionary, expressive, and figurative) and many sub-sets of politeness-indicating devices. Which devices are given particular importance depends on the specific languages and cultures involved. In Korean, Japanese, and Javanese, for instance, structural devices including extensively hierarchical address/reference terms and honorifics are the most crucial devices of politeness, although other sets of devices are also extensively used. In the United States, honorifics are of minimal significance, while illocutionary and expressive devices receive greater importance. The various putatively universal proposals advanced by Western scholars on politeness are relevant, in general, only to illocutionary and expressive devices. The politeness devices are realized as linguistic patterns and forms in each linguistic community.

Use of such politeness patterns and forms in socio-culturally appropriate ways is controlled by various sociolinguistic rules and conventions of language use, both normative and strategic. Such rules and conventions are in accordance with the interactants' relative power and solidarity, speech context, the nature of imposition, and universal pragmatic principles such as those proposed by Lakoff, Brown and Levinson, and some others, filtered by cultural perspectives such as culturally-bound norms of behavior, value orientations, and commonly-shared cultural assumptions.

The aim of this paper is to examine how politeness is expressed in the structure and use of the Korean language in comparison to the expression of politeness in English. It will be observed that Korean patterns are vastly different from English patterns, reflecting the different underlying socio-cultural values held respectively by Koreans and English-speaking people.

2. Normative and strategic politeness

In their monumental work entitled *Politeness: Some Universals in Language Usage* (1987), Brown and Levinson assume that all competent adult members of a society value face.[2] Face is of two kinds, positive and negative. Positive face is people's want to be approved of, such as the want to be praised, while negative face is people's want not to be impeded or imposed by others, such as the want not to be ordered to do something. All acts that threaten face are termed face threatening acts (FTAs). Brown and Levinson view linguistic politeness as the strategic use of linguistic devices to redress the addressee's potential loss of face. This strategy-oriented definition of politeness may be sufficient to a great extent in societies such as the English-speaking world where hierarchical social stratification is not encoded systematically in the linguistic structure. For instance, in (3), compare English and Korean in expressing 'Good night' by son and father.

(3) a. English Son: *Good night, Dad.*
Father: *Good night, John.*

2 Face is defined as the positive public self-image people want to claim for themselves.

b.	Korean	Son:	*Apeci,*	*annyenghi*	*cwumu-sey-yo.*
			father	peacefully	sleep
		Father:	*ne to*	*cal ca-la.*	
			you also	well sleep	

Notice in English that son and father use the same expression except for the address terms, a kinship term by the son and a given name by the father. In Korean, on the other hand, they use entirely different utterances. Not a single element is shared. Under no circumstances can the son use any part of his father's utterance in expressing 'Good night' to his father, and vice versa. Both the son's and the father's utterances are appropriate and polite. They must always be used in that way. Use of them is by no means strategic, but is socially and culturally normative.

Thus, some recent studies on linguistic politeness in languages like Japanese have identified two types of politeness, normative (or discernment) and strategic (or volitional), claiming that Brown and Levinson's definition of politeness covers only strategic politeness (cf. Hill et al. 1986; Matsumoto 1988, 1989; Gu 1990; Ide 1989; Kasper 1990; Sohn 1990; J. Koo 1995). The function of normative politeness is social indexing, while that of strategic politeness is face-saving. In general, expression of normative politeness is bound by cultural norms of a society, while expression of strategic politeness is controlled by interlocutors in interactive speech act situations in performing their communicative goals. Thus, while the former is largely culture-bound, the latter is universal to a great extent. Both types of politeness expressions normally occur together in the same discourse.

By and large, normative politeness is expressed by time-honored grammatical forms of politeness, which are popularly called honorifics, whereas strategic politeness is expressed by various assertion-softening or assertion-reinforcing measures, such as phatic expressions, conversational formulae, hedges, intonation, direct and indirect speech acts, and silence, as well as praises, approval, sympathy, seeking agreement, and giving options to the addressee (see Brown and Levinson 1987 for several dozens of politeness strategies).

3. Lexico-suffixal patterns of honorifics

Honorifics (indexical politeness forms) are a set of linguistic forms in which interpersonal relationships are systematically encoded. Unlike English, Korean is a language with an elaborate system of honorifics. Sentences cannot be uttered without the speaker's approximate knowledge of his social relationship with the addressee and/or referent in terms of age category (adult, adolescent, or child), social status, kinship, and/or in- and outgroupness. The honorific system of Korean is the most systematic among all known languages, followed perhaps by Japanese and Javanese. In this respect, Korean may be called an honorific language. The patterns of Korean honorifics include the structure and use of speech levels, personal pronouns, address-reference terms, some content words and particles, and subject- and addressee-honorific suffixes.

3.1. Speech levels

As alluded to in (3), English does not have any distinct speech levels. Korean, on the other hand, has six speech levels (styles, or 'registers') represented by sentence enders. Different speech levels are used by the speaker based on whom he is talking to. The speech levels are interwoven with the four major sentence-types in suffixal realizations, as in (4).

(4)

	Declarative	**Interrogative**	**Imperative**	**Propositive**
plain	*-ta*	*-ni?/-nu-nya?*	*-kela* or *-e/ala*	*-ca*
intimate	*-e/a*	*-e/a?*	*-e/a*	*-e/a*
familiar	*-ney*	*-na?/-nun-ka?*	*-key*	*-sey*
blunt	*-(s)o/-(s)wu*	*-(s)o?/-(s)wu?*	*-(u)o/-wu*	*-(u)p-si-ta*
polite	*-(e/a)yo*	*-(e/a)yo?*	*-(e/a)yo*	*-(e/a)yo*
deferential	*-(su)p-ni-ta*	*-(su)p-ni-kka?*	*-si-p-si-o*	*-si-p-si-ta*

The plain level is used by any speaker to any child, to one's own siblings, children, or grandchildren regardless of age, to one's daughter-in-law, or between intimate adult friends whose friendship started in childhood, etc.[3]

The intimate level (polite-level form minus *-yo*), also called a half-talk style, is used by an adult to an adult junior such as a student, by a child of pre-school age to his or her family members including parents, or between close friends whose friendship began in childhood or adolescence. This level is frequently intermixed with the plain or familiar level in the same discourse with the same person

The familiar level, typically used by a male adult to an adult inferior or adolescent such as a high school or college student or to one's son-in-law or to an

3 One noteworthy fact is that use of propositive sentence enders is generally avoided if the addressee is the speaker's senior adult. This is because the speaker cannot request a social superior to take an action together with himself. Thus, the utterance *sensayng-nim, ce wa ham-kkey ttena-si-p-si-ta* 'Professor, let's leave together' sounds very rude when uttered to one's senior. Indirect speech strategies must be employed.

old friend, is becoming obsolete (cf. Sohn 1986). The blunt level (especially *-(s)o* and *-(u)o*), which is sometimes used by a boss to his subordinates, tends to disappear from daily usage probably due to its blunt connotation. Most younger generation speakers use only the plain, intimate, polite, and deferential levels.

The most popular level towards an adult is the polite one, which is an informal counterpart of the deferential level. This level is widely used by both males and females in daily conversations. While females predominantly use this level in all conversations, males use both the polite and deferential levels to address an equal or superior adult. Even in a formal conversational situation, the deferential and polite levels are intermixed by the same interlocutors in the same discourse. In formal situations such as news reports and public lectures, only the deferential style is used.

3.2. Personal pronouns

While English personal pronouns have person, number, and gender distinctions as in *I, you, he, she, it, we,* and *they*, Korean personal pronouns have person, number, and speech level distinctions.

(5)

		Singular	Plural
First person:	Plain	*na*	*wuli(-tul)*
	Humble	*ce*	*ce-huy(-tul)*
Second person	Plain	*ne*	*ne-huy(-tul)*
	Familiar	*caney*	*caney-tul*
	Intimate	*caki*	*caki-tul*
	Blunt	*tangsin*	*tangsin-tul*
		tayk	*tayk-tul*
Third person (*D* stands for a demonstrative)			
	Thing	*D-kes*	*D-kes-tul*
	Child	*D-ay*	*D-ay-tul*
	Adult-familiar	*D-salam*	*D-salam-tul*
	Adult-blunt	*D-i*	*D-i-tul*
	Adult-polite	*D-pun*	*D-pun-tul*
Reflexive pronouns 'self'			
	Plain	*ce(-casin)*	*ce(-casin)-tul*
	Neutral	*caki(-casin)*	*caki(-casin)-tul*
	Deferential	*tangsin(-casin)*	*tangsin(-casin)-tul*

In general, the first person plain form *na* is used when talking to a child or a younger adult, the humble form *ce* is used when talking to a senior or an adult equal.

The second person plain form *ne* is used to address or refer to a child or equivalent (e.g. one's own child or grandchild). The familiar form *caney* is used by a superior to a much younger adult or adolescent inferior (e.g. one's adult student), or by a parent-in-law to a son-in-law, etc. Use of the reflexive pronoun *caki* as a second person 'you' is a recent innovation which is used to one's spouse or boyfriend or girlfriend. The blunt form *tangsin* is used to refer to an adult inferior, e.g. by a boss to his subordinate. It is also used between husband and wife in which case the form carries an affectionate connotation. The form *tayk* (lit. '(your) honorable house') is used to refer to an adult stranger and cannot be used to an ingroup member or a social superior. Thus, even though there are many second person pronouns, Korean does not have a pronoun to refer to a socially superior person. Consequently, Koreans make an extensive use of nouns for pronominal substitution, as in *sensayng-nim* 'you' (lit. 'esteemed teacher') and *sacang-nim* 'you' (lit. 'esteemed company president').

For third person pronouns, demonstrative compounds are used, which consist of hierarchical nouns *kes* 'thing', *ai*/*ay* 'child', *salam* 'person', *i* 'person', and *pun* 'esteemed person'. Between *i* and *salam*, the former is considered relatively higher. In general, a husband refers to his wife with *ce salam* 'that person', whereas a wife refers to her husband with *ce i* 'that person'. There are also three kinds of reflexive pronouns which are sensitive to speech levels. The form *ce* is used to refer to a child or a lower person, *caki* is used for children and equal adults, and *tangsin* is used to refer to a respected person.

3.3. Address-reference terms

The pattern of English address-reference terms is relatively simple, as shown in (6).

(6) Address-reference terms in English

title sequence	*Mr. President*, *Mr. Chairman*
title alone	*Professor, Sir, Doctor, General, Madam*
title + last name	*Professor Smith*, *Mr. Haig, Dr. Ing*
full given name	*James*, *Christine, Samuel*
nickname	*Jim, Chris, Sam*
affectionate nickname	*Jimmy, Chrissy, Sammy*

Notice that the first three kinds of terms indicate professional roles. They are used when no solidarity is involved. The second three kinds are essentially based on different degrees of solidarity. Thus, a title and last name can easily be changed to a nickname when the interlocutors become closer.

Compared to this relatively simple and flexible English pattern, an extensive set of highly stratified address-reference terms are used in Korean. There seem to be at least ten levels as given in (7), which are ordered roughly in decreasing deference and/or distance.

(7) Address-reference terms in Korean

i.	*taythonglyeng-kak.ha*	'His Excellency President'
ii.	*ape-nim*	'hon. father'
	Kim-paksa-nim	'hon. Dr. Kim'
iii.	*Kim sensayng*	'Mr./Mrs./Ms. Kim' (lit. 'teacher Kim')
	apeci	'father'
	Kim kwacang	'Division Chief Kim'
	Kim paksa	'Dr. Kim'
	takthe Kim	'Dr. Kim'
	misisu Kim	'Mrs. Kim'
	Kim Mia-ssi	'Ms. Mia Kim'
iv.	*misuthe Kim*	'Mr. Kim'
	misu Kim	'Miss Kim'
v.	*Minho-ssi*	'Mr. Minho'
vi.	*Kim-ssi*	'Mr. Kim'
vii.	*Kim (Minho)-kwun*	'Mr. (Minho) Kim'
	Kim (Mia)-yang	'Miss (Mia) Kim'
viii.	*Minho-kwun*	'Mr. Minho'
	Mia-yang	'Miss Mia'
ix.	*Kihan i*	'Kihan!'
x.	*Mia ya*	'Mia!'

While English honorific titles such as *Mr., Mrs., Miss,* and *Ms.* are used primarily to indicate gender roles and marital status and are not hierarchical, Korean honorific titles are definitely hierarchical. For instance, *kak.ha* is limited to the President of a nation (this usage is becoming obsolete in favor of *-nim*), while *-nim* is widely used for one's superiors or distant adult equals, *-ssi* for colleagues or subordinates, and *-kwun/-yang* for much younger inferiors or subordinates.

The most frequently used title for a social superior or a distant adult equal is

-nim. In Korean, all kinds of professional titles (including section chief, division chief, company president, nurse, and taxi or bus driver) plus the honorific title *-nim* are used, as in *kwacang-nim* 'Section Chief', *kanhosa-nim* (lit. 'Ms. nurse'), and *kisa-nim* (lit. 'Mr./Ms. driver'). This indicates that unlike Americans, Koreans are very status conscious in all walks of life.

When *-nim* is removed, no deference is shown. Thus, address-reference terms without *-nim* are used to address or refer to a close colleague or an adult social inferior. Noteworthy is the fact that, in speech, a married woman uses *ape-nim* 'father' and *eme-nim* 'mother' to address or refer to her parents-in-law and *apeci* and *emeni* or *appa* and *emma* for her own parents.

The title suffixes such as the Sino-Korean *-ssi*, *-kwun*, *-yang*, and loan *misuthe*, *misisu*, *misu*, *takthe* do not convey deference. Unlike in English, the loan titles *Dr.* and *Mrs.* are used to an adult equal or junior adult and never to a senior person. *Mr.* and *Miss* are usually used to a junior adult. A family name + *-ssi* is used by an adult to an adult male whose occupation is socially low, such as an adult janitor or a delivery person, as in *Kim-ssi*. This may be because a family name without a given name does not carry any solidarity and *-ssi* does not carry deference. Thus, a preferred recent practice is to add *acessi* (lit. 'uncle') or *acwumeni/acwuma* (lit. 'aunt') after *-ssi* as in *Kim-ssi acessi* and *Kim-ssi acwuma.* A similar case is that *hyeng* 'older brother' is used to address or refer to one's (usually male's) male senior but family name + *hyeng* (e.g. *Kim hyeng*) is used for one's equal or junior.

Personal names with the vocative particle (*i*) are used for addressing one's intimate adult friends or one's adult or adolescent students, as in *Kihan-i* 'Kihan!' Personal names or other nouns with the particle *(y)a* are for addressing children, as in *Yongho ya* 'Yongho!' and *papo ya* 'You fool!' Sometimes, *(y)a* is used to family members as a diminutive marker without lowering the honorific level, as in *apem a* '(child's) Dad!' (addressing one's adult son), *enni ya* 'Sis!' (female speaker), and *nwuna ya* 'Sis!' (male speaker).

In English, the difference between a title and family name like *Mr. Smith* and first name like *John* are dependent not so much on the power dimension as on the solidarity dimension. In Korean, on the other hand, solidarity functions little in the use of address-reference terms in a power-laden relationship such as between a professor and a student. No matter how close a person is to his senior in the workplace, he cannot use an address term without a professional title and the honorific title *-nim*. Thus, he must use *Kim Minho kwacang-nim, Kim kwacang-nim,* or *kwacang-nim,* but never *Kim Minho kwacang, Kim kwacang,* or *kwacang,* let alone *Kim Minho, Minho* or *Minho-ya.*

Unlike in English, kinship terms used as address-reference terms are highly diversified in Korean, including terms for older siblings such as *oppa, hyeng, nwunim,* and *enni.* Furthermore, kinship terms are extensively used to non-kin. Among ingroup members, terms like *hyeng* and *enni* are commonly used.

3.4. Content words and particles

English distinguishes between "like" and "care for", between "eat" and "dine", between "give" and "bestow", between "Hi" and "Good Morning", etc. Again, this distinction does not seem to imply social stratification. As observed in (6), Korean has a limited set of nouns and predicates to refer to a superior or distant adult's family member, possession, and action, as well as some humble predicates to refer to one's own or an inferior person's action in reference to a superior person. Humble predicates are transitive, and their direct or indirect object is a superior person. In addition, two particles, nominative and dative-locative-goal, have corresponding honorific forms. (There is no honorific form for the accusative particle.) While the neutral particles *i/ka* and *eykey/hanthey* are used for both children and adults without any particular deference, the honorific ones are used only for adults to indicate special deference.

(8)		**Honorific**	**Plain**	**Gloss**
	noun	*puin/samo-nim*	*che/anay/manwula*	'wife'
		tayk	*cip*	'house'
		atu-nim	*atul*	'son'
		olapeni(m)	*oppa*	'(female's) older brother'
		cinci	*pap*	'meal'
		sengham	*ilum*	'name'
		yensey	*nai*	'age'
	predicate	*kyeysita*	*issta*	'stay'
		capswusita	*mekta*	'eat'
		cwumusita	*cata*	'sleep'
		tolaka-sita	*cwukta*	'die'
		annyengha-sita	*cal issta*	'be well'
		Humble	**Plain**	**Gloss**
	predicate	*tulita*	*cwuta*	'give'
		mosita	*teylita*	'accompany'
		poypta	*pota*	'see'
		aloyta	*allita*	'inform'
		yeccwuta	*mutta*	'ask'

	Honorific	Neutral Case	
particle	*kkeyse*	*ka/i*	subject
	kkey	*eykey/hanthey*	dative/locative/goal

3.6. Subject- and addressee-honorific suffixes

Unlike English, Korean has a productive suffixal device for subject honorification, employing the inflectional suffix *-(u)si/-(u)sey* (from *-(u)si* + *-e* in *-e.yo*) immediately after a predicate stem when the subject referent deserves the speaker's deference, as in *kyoswu-nim i ka-si-n-ta* 'The professor is going.'

Korean also has a suffix for addressee honorification (in addition to the polite-level sentence ender *-eyo*). The addressee honorific suffix *-(su)p* (*-sup* after a consonant; *-p* after a vowel) appears only with the deferential speech level, as in *i kulim un coh-**sup**-ni-ta* 'This picture is good' and *ce nun ka-**p**-ni-ta* 'I am going.' In sentences like *Kim-sensayng-nim un ka-**si**-ess-**sup**-ni-kka?* 'Did Professor Kim go?', both the subject referent and the addressee are referred to using honorifics.[4]

4. Syntactic patterns of honorifics

The various honorific forms given above co-occur in sentences. In order to see how, it is essential to distinguish two main dimensions: the dimension of referent honorifics (speaker–referent perspective) and that of addressee honorifics (speaker–addressee perspective). The former concerns the speaker's regard for a referent appearing overtly or covertly in a sentence, whereas the latter is associated with the speaker's regard for the addressee in a speech situation. In actual speech situations, addressee honorifics are more important and thus more finely segmented than referent honorifics in view of the subtlety of interpersonal feelings and 'face' involved in face-to-face interactions. The dimension of referent honorifics may be subclassified into subject, object, and oblique (e.g. dative, locative, goal, source) honorifics, in that the nominals in these grammatical functions may have deferential forms that trigger deferential or humble predicates. Among referent honorifics, subject honorifics are the most significant and therefore occur most productively. Many deferential predicates as well as the honorific suffix *-(u)si* are associated with the subject. The syntactic distribution

4 The distinction between the perspectives of speaker–addressee and speaker–referent is structurally so tenacious that even when the addressee is coreferential to the subject referent, the two are grammatically differentiated, as in ***sensayng-nim kkeyse*** *encey ttena-**si**-keyss-**sup**-ni-kka?* 'When are you going to leave, Professor?', where both the subject honorific suffix and addressee honorific suffix occur.

of the two perspectives is illustrated in (9) and (10).

(9) A daughter-in-law to her father-in-law

ape-nim, *eme-nim kkeyse* *halme-nim kkey yak ul tuli* *-si-ess* *-sup-ni-ta*

DATIVE REFERENT HONORIFICATION

SUBJECT REFERENT HONORIFICATION

ADDRESSEE HONORIFICATION

'Father, mother gave medicine to grandmother.'

In (9), object honorification is irrelevant because *yak* 'medicine' is non-human. Dative honorification is expressed by the honorific forms *halme-nim* 'grandmother' (cf. neutral *halmeni*) and *kkey* 'to' (cf. neutral *eykey*/*hanthey*) as well as by the humble verb *tulita* 'give (to a superior)' (cf. plain *cwuta*). Subject honorification is reflected in the honorific noun *eme-nim* 'mother' (cf. neutral *emeni*), honorific subject particle *kkeyse* (cf. neutral *ka*/*i*), and the subject honorific suffix *-si.* Addressee honorification is expressed by the honorific address term *ape-nim* 'father' (cf. neutral *apeci*), the addressee honorific suffix *-sup,* and the deferential sentence-type ender *-ni-ta* (indicative–declarative). Compared to the expression in (9), the sentence in (10) is a non-honorific expression, uttered typically to a child about another child.

(10) A girl to her friend

Milan a, *Minho ka* *Mia hanthey yak ul cwu* *ess* *-e*

DATIVE REFERENT NON-HONORIFICATION

SUBJECT REFERENT NON-HONORIFICATION

ADDRESSEE NON-HONORIFICATION

'Milan, Minho gave medicine to Mia.'

Notice in (9) and (10) that honorific forms manifest agreement, spreading throughout a sentence.[5] Thus, an honorific sentence looks markedly different from its plain counterpart. An honorific expression and its non-honorific counterpart may have the same truth values, but very distinct socio-cultural meanings and connotations. Further notice that addressee (non-) honorifics appear in the outermost layer of a sentence and referent honorifics in the inner layer, with subject honorifics taking a more outside position than dative and object honorifics. Since the addressee is a discoursal element and has no place in the sentential proposition, its honorific or non-honorific expression may occur as a vocative or address term preceding the main sentence, with its syntactic reflexes limited to the last part of the predicate (e.g. *-sup-ni-ta*).

5. Strategic politeness expressions

In addition to the use of honorifics which are generally normative, linguistic coding of politeness appears in many strategically conventionalized ways both in Korean and English, as we observed in (1) and (2). If a speech act is performed for the benefit of the addressee, the utterance is usually direct, often utilizing the imperative sentence type, as strong assertion is frequently needed for politeness. Examples are *ese o-si-p-si-o* 'Welcome' (lit. 'Come quickly') and *annyenghi cwumu-sey-yo* 'Good night' (lit. 'Sleep peacefully').

If a speech act is not for the benefit of the addressee but for the speaker or somebody else, indirect speech acts are felicitous because direct speech acts are often 'face-threatening' to the addressee's positive self-esteem or to his freedom from imposition. Indirect utterances are used especially when the addressee is a senior or a distant equal or the utterances in question are made for the benefit of the speaker. Observe in (11) the decreasing degrees of indirectness which in turn denote decreasing degrees of politeness in both Korean and English. English translations are approximate.

(11) a. *sillyeyha-p-ni-ta man, mun com yel-e cwu-si-keyss-e.yo?*
'Excuse me, but would you please open the door for me?'
b. *mun com yel-e cwu-si-keyss-e.yo?*
'Would you please open the door for me?'

5 Honorific agreement is particularly intriguing regarding the use of the suffix *-(u)si* in relation to its trigger. In general, this suffix is attached to the predicate if the subject of the predicate denotes an adult who deserves the speaker's deference. However, this suffix is also triggered by a nominal which is not the subject of a predicate, as in *ce uy **apeci** nun khi ka cak-**usey**-yo* 'My father is short' and ***apeci** uy somay ka ccalp-**usey**-yo* 'The sleeves of your clothes are short, Dad', where ***apeci***, rather than the subjects of the predicates (i.e. *khi*, *somay*), triggers the honorific suffix (cf. Sohn 1992 and Yun 1993).

c. *mun yel-e cwu-si-keyss-e.yo?*
'Would you open the door for me?'

d. *mun com yel-e cwu-sey-yo.*
'Please open the door for me.'

e. *mun yel-e cwu-sey-yo.*
'Open the door for me.'

f. *mun ye-sey-yo.*
'Open the door.'

All these sentences are in the polite speech level, and thus may be uttered to an adult. However, (9f) is a sheer command in both Korean and English and thus impolite unless the act of opening the door is for the sake of the addressee. In general, the longer a sentence is, the more indirect and therefore the more polite it is, since more hedges are included. In (9a), several hedging devices are involved: the request-introducing formula *sillyeyha-p-ni-ta man* 'excuse me but'; the diminutive *com* 'just, a little, please'; the benefactive auxiliary verb *cwuta* 'do for'; the modal (conjectural) suffix *-keyss* 'would'; and the interrogative sentence type with rising intonation. Use of interrogative sentences for requests has become quite popular recently.

Omission of main clauses is a productive mechanism for performing indirect speech acts. By omitting a main clause which usually carries the speaker's assertion, the speaker can give the addressee the option of making the final decision (H.M. Sohn 1990). Examples are given in (12).

(12)	a. *pi ka o-nun tey [ ] yo.*	'It's raining.'
	b. *pi ka o-te-la ko [ ] yo.*	'I saw it raining.'
	c. *pi ka o-na [ ] yo?*	'Is it raining?'
	d. *pi ka o-n-ta-myense [ ] yo?!*	'I heard that it is raining. Is that true?'
	e. *pi ka o-ci [ ] yo?*	'It's raining, isn't it?'

Notice that all these sentences do not end in a regular sentence ender but in an element which normally occurs in a subordinate clause. These clause-final elements have come to be grammaticalized as sentence-final enders due to the habitual omission of main clauses out of strategic politeness.

There are many indirect speech acts which are idiomatized. One such case is to pose a question to a social superior about his or her name, age, and other things. The formula is *etteh-key toy-sey-yo?* 'What is ...?' (lit. 'How does it become?'), as in (13).

(13) a. *ilum i mwe yey-yo?*'What is you name?' (to a child or junior adult)
a′. *sengham i etteh-key toy-sey-yo?* (to a senior or distant adult)
'May I ask your name?' (lit. 'How does your name become?')

b. *nai ka myech i-sey-yo?* 'How old are you?' (to a child or junior adult)
b′. *yensey ka etteh-key toy-sey-yo?* (to a senior or distant adult).
'May I ask your age?' (lit. 'How does your age become?')

6. Conclusion

Thus far, I have made sketchy observations of the linguistic expressions of normative and strategic politeness in Korean in brief comparison to English. One major difference between Korean and English politeness expressions is the presence in Korean and the absence in English of an extensive system of honorifics. Hence, Korean is a typical honorific language. As has been observed, Korean honorifics are essentially hierarchical, from plain at the bottom to deferential at the top, and their uses are generally normative. In contemporary Korea, the primary socio-cultural variable in using honorifics appears to be the addressee's age categories such as adult, adolescent, and child. Then come such other variables as in-/out-groupness, occupational rank, kinship, and formality. In English, on the other hand, the system of honorifics is negligible. At most, English has several kinds of address-reference terms. Unlike in Korean, however, these terms carry little hierarchical connotation. Rather, their uses are governed by professional roles and the degree of solidarity.

These differences between Korean and English can be ascribed to different underlying socio-cultural values. Koreans still value traditional hierarchism to a considerable extent in interpersonal interactions, whereas English-speaking people generally hold egalitarian value orientations. In addition, as alluded to here and there in the above, use of Korean honorifics and politeness strategies is also governed by the collectivistic value of Koreans. Extensive use of kinship terms to non-kin is an example. In short, the structure and use of politeness expressions in Korean cannot be properly grasped without understanding Korean people's deep-rooted hierarchical and collectivistic consciousness as opposed to English-speaking people's egalitarian and individualistic consciousness.

It has been well documented that Korean, together with Chinese, Japanese, and Arabic, is one of the most difficult languages for Americans to learn. It takes about three times more for a native English speaker to learn Korean than to learn a European language such as French, Spanish, or German in order to attain the same level of proficiency. The reason is obvious in view of the preceding discussions. In linguistic structure, usage, and underlying socio-cultural values,

Korean is extremely different from English. Awareness of such differences will greatly facilitate the study of the Korean language.[6]

REFERENCES: Chapter 21

Brown, P. and S. Levinson. 1987. *Politeness.* Cambridge, UK: Cambridge University Press.

Cho, Choon-Hak. 1982. *A Study of Korean Pragmatics: Deixis and Politeness*. Seoul: Hanshin.

Fraser, B. 1980. Conversational mitigation. *Journal of Pragmatics* 4: 341–50.

Fraser, B. 1990. Perspectives on politeness. *Journal of Pragmatics* 14: 219–36.

Hwang, Juck-Ryoon. 1975. Role of sociolinguistics in foreign language education with reference to Korean and English: terms of address and levels of deference. Ph.D. dissertation. University of Texas at Austin.

Gu, Yueguo. 1990 Politeness phenomenain Modern Chinese. *Journal of Pragmatics* 14: 237-57.

Hill, B. et al. 1986. Universals of linguistic politeness: Quantitative evidence from Japanese and American English. *Journal of Pragmatics* 10: 347-71.

Ide, S. 1989. Formal forms and discernment: two neglected aspects of linguistic politeness. *Multilingua.* 8: 223-48.

Kasper, G. 1990. Linguistic politeness: current research issues. *Journal of Pragmatics.* 14(2): 193-218.

Kim, Hyey-Suk. 1991. *Hyentay Kwuk.e uy Sahoy.en.ehakcek Yenkwu* (A Sociolinguistic Study of Contemporary Korean). Seoul: Thayhaksa.

Koo, Jasook. 1995. Politeness theory: Universality and specificity. Ph.D. dissertation. Harvard University.

Lakoff, R. 1973. The logic of politeness: or minding your p's and q's. *Papers from the Ninth Regional Meeting of the Chicago Linguistic Society.* Chicago: Chicago Linguistic Society, 292–305.

Leech, G.N. 1983. *Principles of Pragmatics*. London/New York: Longman.

Lee, Woo-Kyu. 1991. Honorifics and Politeness in Korean. Ph.D. dissertation. University of Wisconsin at Madison.

Matsumoto, Y. 1988. Reexamination of the universality of face: politeness phenomena in Japanese. *Journal of Pragmatics* 12: 403-26.

Matsumoto, Y. 1989. Politeness and conversational universals: Observations from Japanese. *Multilingua* 8: 121-37.

Mun, Mae-Ran Park. 1991. Social Variation and Change in Honorific Usage among Korean

6 Recent studies on Korean honorifics and politeness include Hwang 1975; Cho 1982; Wang 1984; Suh 1984, 1996; Sung 1985; Lee 1991; Mun 1991; Yun 1993; and Koo 1995, among many other works.

Adults in an Urban Setting. Ph.D. dissertation. University of Illinois at Urbana-Champaign.

Sohn, Ho-min. 1986. *Linguistic Expeditions.* Seoul: Hanshin.

Sohn, Ho-min. 1989. Politeness strategies in Korean. *Papers from the Sixth International Conference on Korean Linguistics,* 655-69. Also in this volume.

Sohn, Ho-min. 1990. Main clause deletion in Korean: politeness as a cause of linguistic change. ms. Presented at the 1990 Association for Asian Studies Meeting. Chicago.

Sohn, Ho-min. 1992. Honorific agreement in Korean. In Cho, S.W. and H.H. Lee (eds.). *A Festschrift for Tae-ok Kim*, 604-33. Seoul: Hankwuk Munhwasa. Also in this volume.

Suh, Cheong-Soo. 1984. *Contaypep uy Yenkwu* (A Study of Korean Honorifics). Seoul: Hanshin.

Suh, Cheong-Soo. 1996. *Kwuk.e Munpep* (A Korean Grammar). Seoul: Hanyang University Press.

Sung, Kychul. 1985. *Hyentay Kwuke Taywupep Yenkwu* (A Study of Korean Honorifics). Seoul: Kaymunsa.

Wang, Hahn-Sok. 1984. *Honorific Speech Behavior in a Rural Korean Village: Structure and Use*. Ph.D. dissertation. University of California at Los Angeles.

Yun, Sung-Kyu. 1993. *Honorific Agreement.* Ph.D. dissertation. University of Hawaii.

22 Honorific Agreement in Korean*

Numerous attempts have revealed interesting linguistic properties associated with the honorific inflectional suffix *-(u)si* (e.g. Song 1967, H. Lee 1970, C. Lee 1973, Chang 1973, Park 1975, Im 1976, Shibatani 1976, Park-Choi 1978, Lukoff 1978a, 1978b, C. Cho 1982, Suh 1984, Sung 1985, Kuno and Kim 1985, Sohn 1986, Y. Kim 1987, E. Cho 1988, Shin 1989, H. Kim 1990, and Yun 1991).[1] Syntactically, the suffix requires an agreement with a cooccurring NP; semantically, it bears the content of speaker's deference toward the referent of that NP; sociolinguistically, its appearance is constrained by various sociocultural norms; and pragmatically, its use is sensitive to speech act situations and speaker's psychological attitude. There are problems, however, which are yet to be resolved. In this paper, an alternative proposal will be made, based on a wide variety of data, regarding what syntactic, semantic, and pragmatic conditions are responsible for triggering so-called direct or indirect honorification.[2]

It is widely held that the suffix *-(u)si* is attached to the predicate if the subject of the predicate denotes an adult who deserves the speaker's deference, hence such terms as "subject honorification" and "honorific agreement".[3] For example, the subject noun phrase (NP) in the sentences in (1) obligatorily triggers the honorific suffix in the predicate without any doubt, when the honorifically neutral noun *sensayng* 'teacher' is provided with the honorific title *-nim* and the

* This is reprinted from Cho, S.W. and H.H. Lee (eds.), *A Festschrift for Tae-ok Kim*, 604-633. Seoul: Hankwuk Mwunhwasa (1992).

1 This paper was written for Professor Tae OK Kim, my special colleague, in commemoration of her sixtieth birthday (*hoykap*).

2 Subject honorification in complex sentences is studied in Kuno and Kim (1985), Y. Kim (1987), and Shin (1989). Sociolinguistic aspects are not considered in this paper, but some representative works are listed in the references.

3 The speaker's deference toward the referent is conditioned not only by objective such as socio-cultural variables as relative age, social status, kinship, and sex but by such subjective variables as the degree of solidarity and the speaker's psychological attitude. Compared with addressee honorifics whose use is largely obligatory, the use or non-use of the subject honorific suffix is controlled by the speaker to a great extent, without rendering the sentence in question socially unacceptable.

honorific nominative subject/topic particle *kkeyse*.[4] Hereafter, I will call an NP responsible for the presence or absence of the honorific suffix an honorific antecedent (HA).

(1) a. ***Kim sensayng-nim*** ***kkeyse*** *phikonha-**si**-ess-eyo.*
Kim teacher-HT HSM tired-SH-PST-POL
'Professor Kim was tired.'

b. ***Kim sensayng-nim*** ***kkeyse*** *o-**si**-ess-eyo.*
Kim teacher-HT HSM come-SH-PST-POL
'Professor Kim has come.'

The appearance of *-(u)si* becomes syntactically optional in the following sentences, in which both *-nim* and *kkeyse* are lacking. Since *sensayng* alone is honorifically neutral, despite its having an adultness feature, use or non-use of the honorific suffix hinges on the speaker's pragmatic attitude toward or sociolinguistic relationship with the referent of *sensayng*. With the suffix, deference is paid to the referent, whereas no deference is shown without it, evidencing that the suffix has its own semantic content.

(2) a. *Kim sensayng* *i* *phikonha-(si)-ess-eyo.*
Kim teacher NM tired-SH-PST-POL
'Professor Kim was tired.'

b. *Kim sensayng* *i* *o-(si)-ess-eyo.*
Kim teacher NM come-SH-PST-POL
'Professor Kim came.'

There are cases, however, which defy the simple generalization that only the subject functions as an HA. One serious problem with this traditional generalization is related to the identification of subject. The claim that the element triggering the honorific suffix is the subject is circular at best. A related problem is that some obvious subjects do not function as an HA, but the cooccurring topic (or higher subject), locative, or possessive NP does, as illustrated respectively

4 Y. Kim (1987) claims that some nouns should be specified as containing inherent features in the lexical entry, as in *apeci*(1) [+HON], *apeci*(2) [-HON], *apenim* [+HON] 'father'; *atul* [-HON], *atunim* [+HON] 'son', etc. This way, he argues, not only is the speaker's interpretation dispensed with in the otherwise purely syntactic description, but also is a biimplicational agreement principle maintained in his GPSG analysis. Interesting as it may be, this topic will not be considered here.

in (3a), (3b), and (3c). Can we claim that these topic, locative or possessive NPs are subjects simply because they trigger the honorific suffix?

(3) a.

apeci nun	*os*	*i*	*somay*	*ka*	*ki-si-eyo*
father TC	clothes	NM	sleeve	NM	long-SH-POL

'As for father, the sleeves of his clothes are long.'

b.

i	*os*	*i*	*halmeni*	*kkey*	*mac-usi-eyo?*
this	clothes	NM	grandmother	HLOC	fit-SH-POL

'Do these clothes fit you, grandmother?'

c.

Kim sensayng-nim	*tayk*	*ey*	*chayk*	*i*	*manh-usi-eyo?*
Kim teacher-HT	home	LOC	book	NM	many-SH-POL

'Does Professor Kim have many books at home?'

Let us observe some less problematic sets of sentences first. Examine the copulative sentences in (4).

(4) a.

Kim sensayng-nim	*kkeyse*	*hwanca*	*ka*	*an*	*i-si-eyo.*
Kim teacher-HT	HSM	patient	NM	not	be-SH-POL

'Professor Kim is not a patient.'

b.

Kim sensayng-nim	*kkeyse*	*hwanca*	*ka*	*toy-si-ess-eyo.*
Kim teacher-HT	HSM	patient	NM	become-SH-PST-POL

'Professor Kim has become a patient.'

Notice that the two NPs in each of these sentences are in the nominative case and the HA in each honorific agreement is the first NP. There is no doubt that this HA, which is Theme, is the subject in view of its carrying the "aboutness" sense and occupying the sentence initial position, in addition to its honorific triggering function. That the second NP is not a subject is evidenced by its lack of the "aboutness" sense, rare movement to sentence initial position (e.g. 5a,a'), inability to trigger honorification (e.g. 5b,b'), and impossibility of being followed by the honorific subject/topic particle *kkeyse* (e.g. 5c,c'). The second NP may be termed the complement in the traditional sense.

(5) a.

**hwanca*	*ka*	*Kim sensayng-nim*	*i*	*an*	*i-si-eyo.*
patient	NM	Kim teacher-HT	NM	not	be-SH-POL

'Professor Kim is not a patient.'

a′. **hwanca ka Kim sensayng-nim i toy-si-ess-eyo.*
patient NM Kim teacher-HT NM become-SH-PST-POL
'Professor Kim has become a patient.'

b. *cey atul i moksa-nim i an i-(*si)-eyo.*
my son NM priest-HT NM not be-SH-POL
'My son is not a priest.'

b′. *cey atul i moksa-nim i an toy-(*si)-ess-eyo.*
my son NM priest-HT NM not become-SH-POL
'My son did not become a priest.'

c. *I sensayng-nim i hakcang i/*kkeyse an i-si-eyo.*
Yi teacher-HT NM dean NM/HSM not be-SH-POL
'Professor Lee is not the dean.'

c′. *I sensayng-nim i hakcang i/*kkeyse toy-si-ess-eyo.*
Yi teacher-HT NM dean NM/HSM become-SH-PST-POL
'Professor Lee became the dean.'

Observe another type of double nominative construction in which "psychological" adjectives occur.

(6) a. *apenim i kay ka pwulew-usi-ess-eyo.*
father NM dog NM envy-SH-PST-POL
'Father envied the dog.'

b. *apenim i Mia ka kuliw-usi-ess-eyo.*
Father NM Mia NM miss-SH-PST-POL
'Father missed Mia.'

There is ample evidence that the first NP in these sentences is Experiencer subject and the second one is a non-subject Theme. For one thing, positional switching of the two NPs results in the concomitant switching of the thematic roles. Second, only the first NP allows the occurrence of the honorific subject/topic particle *kkeyse*, in addition to the honorific triggering function. Furthermore, as some linguists may have observed, only the first NP triggers reflexivization, as shown in (7), where the reflexive *caki* 'self' refers to Mia, and not *Yongho*.

(7)

Mia nun	*Yongho*	*ka*	*caki cokha*	*pota te*	*miw-ess-eyo.*
Mia TC	Yongho	NM	self niece	than more	hate-PST-POL

'Mia hated Yongho more than her niece.'

The second nominative NP in psychological constructions may be termed ergative for the present purpose. For one thing, it indicates a Theme relation to the cooccurring Experiencer subject, and yet takes a nominative case. Secondly, as in (8a), free nominative-accusative alternation occurs before the psychological adjective *-siphta* 'wish'. Third, as in (8b), the accusative particle must occur when the predicate is a transitive psychological verb. Finally, as in (8c), there is a set of psychological adjectives, such as *sulphuta* 'sad', *koylopta* 'distressing', and *kipputa* 'happy', which are one-place predicates in contrast to the two-place psychological adjectives illustrated above.

(8) a.

Mia ka	*mikwuk*	*ey*	*ka-ko*	*ka/lul*	*siph-ess-eyo.*
Mia NM	America	to	go-CM	NM/AC	wish-PST-POL

'Mia wanted to go to America.'

b.

apenim	*i*	*kay*	*lul*	*pwuleweha-si-ess-eyo.*
father	NM	dog	AC	envy-SH-PST-POL

'Father envied the dog.'

c.

apenim	*i*	*sulph-usi-ess-eyo.*
father	NM	sad-SH-PST-POL

'Father was sad.'

The class of psychological constructions seems to include sentences like the following, where a non-psychological predicate and the immediately preceding "psychological" noun are compounded to behave as a complex psychological predicate.

(9) a.

apenim	*i*	*ku*	*chayk*	*i*	*[caymi*	*ka*	*iss]-usi-ess-eyo.*
Father	NM	the	book	NM	interest	NM	exist-SH-PST-POL

'Father was interested in the book.'

b.

apenim	*i*	*Nami*	*ka*	*[maum*	*ey*	*tu]-si-ess-eyo.*
father	NM	Nami	NM	mind	to	enter-SH-PST-POL

'Father liked Nami.'

c. *apenim i yehayng i [kep i na]-si-ess-eyo.*
father NM trip NM fear NM appear-SH-PST-POL
'Father was scared of the trip.'

d. *apenim i ku il i [sok i sangha]-si-ess-eyo.*
father NM the event NM mind NM hurt-SH-PST-POL
'Father was distressed by the event.'

The syntactic and semantic unity between the parenthesized elements in each sentence in (9) is observed in their transitivized counterparts, as in (10).

(10) a. *apenim i ku chayk ul [caymi (ka) iss]-e ha-si-ess-eyo.*
father nm the book AC interest NM exist-CM do-SH-PST-POL
'Father was interested in the book.'

b. *apenim i Nami lul [maum ey tul]-e ha-si-ess-eyo.*
father NM Nami AC mind to enter-SH-CM do-SH-PST-POL
'Father liked Nami.'

c. *apenim i yehayng ul [kep (i) na]-a ha-si-ess-eyo.*
Father NM trip AC fear NM appear-CM do-SH-PST-POL
'Father was scared of the trip.'

d. *apenim i ku il ul [sok (i) sangha]-y ha-si-ess-eyo.*
father NM the event AC mind NM hurt-CM do-SH-PST-POL
'Father was distressed by the event.'

The parenthesized elements remain as a coherent unit in (10) with the emotive sense intact. The first NP is viewed as Experiencer subject in both (9) and (10) and the second NP as Theme ergative in (9) and Theme object in (10). The complex psychological predicate is viewed as having been restructured from an NP + VP. Examine another set of multiple nominative sentences.

(11) a. *apenim i kamki ka tu-si-ess-eyo.*
Father NM cold NM enter-SH-PST-POL
'Father has caught a cold.'

b. *halapeci kkeyse pyenghwan i na-si-ess-eyo.*
Grandfather HSM sickness NM occur-SH-PST-POL
'Grandfather got sick.'

c.	*wuli*	*moksa-nim*	*i*	*caymi*	*ka*	*iss-usi-eyo.*
	Our	priest-HT	NM	fun	NM	exist-SH-POL

'Our priest is funny.'

Here again, restructuring seems to have taken place. Notice that the first NP is the HA in each sentence. In view of the typical thematic properties of the predicates *tulta* 'enter', *nata* 'appear, occur', and *issta* 'exist' which require Goal or Location, *kamki, pyenghwan*, and *caymi* must originally be Theme subjects, as schematized in (12a). However, with the idiomatization of *kamki ka tulta, pyenghwan i nata*, and *caymi ka issta* in the sense of 'catch a cold', 'get sick', and 'be interesting', respectively, the original topic has now become restructured as the sole subject, as in (12b).[5]

(12) a.

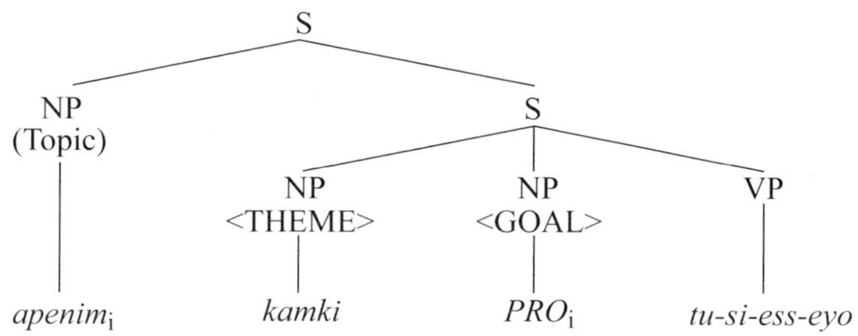

b.

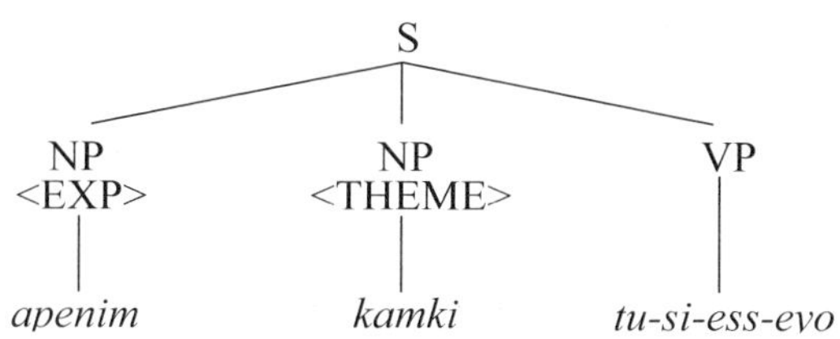

Semantically, apenim, halapeci, and *wuli moksa-nim* in (11) are Experiencers. Syntactically, unlike the "locative-topic" constructions to be discussed shortly, the sentences in (11) do not allow its locative counterpart. *Apenim eykey kamki ka tu-si-ess-eyo* ((lit.) 'A cold entered my father'), *halapeci kkey pyenghwan i na-si-ess-eyo* ((lit.) 'Sickness appeared in grandfather'), and *wuli moksa-nim eykey caymi ka iss-usi-eyo* ((lit.) 'A fun exists at our priest') are extremely awkward. That is, only the subjectivized structure is allowed, in which the first

5 Idiomatization here is a matter of degree. For example, the fact that *apenim kkeyse tu-si-n kamki* 'the cold father caught' is acceptable but **apenim kkeyse iss-usi-n caymi* 'the interest father is in' is not suggests that *kamki-tulta* 'catch a cold' is less idiomatized than *caymi-issta* 'interesting'.

NP is Experiencer subject and the second NP is Theme ergative.

The term "direct honorification" is often used to refer to those phenomena in which the predicate agrees in honorification with its immediate subject. Thus, all the aforementioned sentences are cases of direct honorification, in that each predicate requires two arguments for its case frame, as in [NP1 + NP2 ___], where the nominative NP1 is the subject and the HA. In these constructions, subject honorification is generally obligatory.[6]

Up to this point, HAs are uniquely predictable by the syntactic structure alone. That is, the subject is the HA in such simple sentences, whether they are single or multiple nominative constructions. This unique predictability does not hold in locative, possessive, and topic constructions.

Let us observe locative and corresponding topic constructions first. These sentences are characterized by the existence of both the locative and topicalized forms of an NP. This NP occurs with a nominative Theme subject. The thematic role of the locative NP may be either Experiencer or Location, but its topicalized counterpart functions only as Experiencer. In such sentences, the Experiencer (not Location) locative or topic, not the subject, may function as the HA, hence a case of indirect honorification. Examine the sentences in (13–15), which illustrate both adjectives and process (or non-controllable) verbs.

(13) a.

apenim	*eykey/i*	*kay*	*ka*	*iss-usi-eyo.*
father	LOC/NM	dog	NM	exist-SH-POL

'Father has a dog.'

b.

apenim	*eykey/i*	*ton*	*i*	*chwungpwunha-si-eyo.*
father	LOC/NM	money	NM	enough-SH-POL

'Father has enough money.'

(14)

apenim	*eykey/i*	*wuhwan*	*i*	*sayngki-si-ess-eyo.*
father	LOC/NM	trouble	NM	occur-SH-PST-POL

'Father is grief-stricken.'

(15) a.

apenim	*kkey/kkeyse*	*koki*	*ka*	*cal*	*caphi-si-eyo.*
father	HLOC/HSM	fish	NM	well	catch-SH-POL

'Father is catching many fish.'

---

6 I will follow Lukoff (1978b:547) in using the terms "obligatory" and "optional". Lukoff means obligatory or optional not by grammar but by social convention, i.e. by the etiquette of speech. Thus, failure to use the honorific suffix indicates the speaker's "disrespect" for the referent in obligatory cases, but not in optional cases.

b. *apenim kkey/kkeyse cey nolay ka tulli-si-ess-eyo.*
father HLOC/HSM my song NM heard-SH-PST-POL
'Father could hear my song.'

All the above predicates share affectiveness.[7] Here I am proposing to make a distinction between "affective" and "descriptive" with regard to predicates, although the term "affective" does not appear to be an optimal one. A predicate is affective (as against descriptive), if its thematic structure is of the form [Experiencer + Theme ___], that is, if its referent affects the referent of the Experiencer NP, whether the Experiencer is a syntactic subject, locative, or topic and the Theme is a syntactic subject, object, or ergative. Psychological predicates that we have discussed earlier are affective. For example, *pwulepta* 'enviable' is only affective, whereas *cohta* is affective in the sense of 'like' and descriptive in the sense of 'good'. Many non-psychological predicates may be affective too. For example, the adjective *philyohata* is affective when it means "need" but descriptive when it means "necessary" or "be needed". The existential predicates *issta, epta, chwungpwunhata*, and *manhta* are affective when they denote possession, but descriptive if they denote location. *Sayngkita* is affective in the sense of 'come to have' and descriptive in the sense of 'appear'. Similarly, the passive intransitives *caphita* 'catch, be caught', *mekhita* 'have appetite, be eaten', etc. are both affective and descriptive, although sense-related passive verbs like *tullita* 'hear, be heard' are used usually as affective. In general, controllable verbs, whether intransitive or transitive, are hardly affective.

The sentences in (13) through (15) all share the two interrelated syntactic structures schematized in (16). For example, (13a) is appropriate for the locative and (13b) for the corresponding topic constructions.

(16) a.

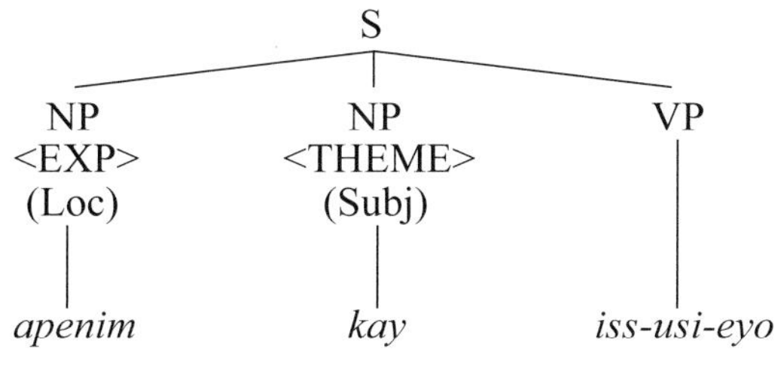

7 Lukoff (1978) introduces the notion of "pertinence" in order to deal with the phenomena under discussion. It is yet to be determined whether the syntactico-semantic notion of affectiveness introduced in this paper is indeed preferred to Lukoff's pragmatic notion of pertinence. I will not go into the discussion of this problem here.

b.

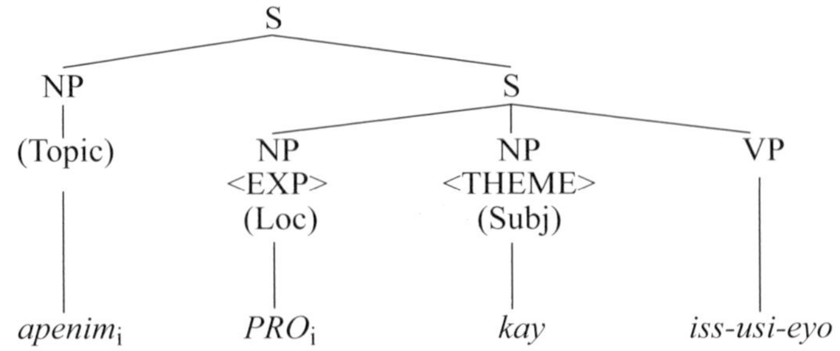

Indirect honorification in locative-topic constructions is obligatory, as far as the predicates involved are used as affective. A fronted locative NP (as in 16a), to a lesser degree, and a topicalized NP (as in 16b), to a greater degree, tend to function as Experiencer by forcing an ambivalent (descriptive/affective) predicate to be interpreted as affective. (Incidentally, the locative NP in (3b) is not fronted.) Conversely, a purely descriptive predicate does not normally allow a non-Experiencer locative NP to be topicalized, as we will see shortly.

There are, on the other hand, sentences of the locative-topic type in which direct honorification is permitted, with the Theme subject NP as the HA. This is when this NP denotes animateness. Examine sentences (17).

(17) a. *Mia eykey/ka coh-un sensayng-nim i kyeysi-eyo.*
Mia LOC/NM good-MD teacher-HT NM exist-SH-POL
'Mia has a good professor.'

b. *Mia eykey/ka swukpwu-nim tul i manh-(usi)-eyo.*
Mia LOC/NM uncle-HT PL NM many-SH-POL
'Mia has many uncles.'

c. *wuli hakkyo ey/ka apenim i philyoha-(si)-eyo.*
our school LOC/NM father NM necessary-SH-POL
'My father is needed at our school.'

d. *na(y) eykey/ka sensayng-nim i sayngki-(si)-ess-eyo.*
me/I LOC/NM teacher-HT NM appear-SH-PST-POL
'I have got a teacher.'

e. *ce(y) eykey/ka sensayng-nim i poi-(si)-eyo.*
I/me LOC/NM teach-HT NM be seen-SH-POL
'I can see the professor.'

Notice in (17) that the subjects (Themes) are deferential nouns. A deferential subject must be predicated by an euphemistic word, if such a word is available, as in (17a). Since *-(u)si* is historically built into such euphemistic words, no addition or deletion of it is possible regardless of affective or descriptive use of the predicate. In (17a), *kyeysita* may denote both existence, i.e. affective (with *eykey* and *ka*) and location, i.e. descriptive (with *eykey*). As indicated above, the adjectives *manhta* 'have many, be many' and *philyohata* 'need, be needed', the process verb *sayngkita* 'come to have, appear', and the passive verb *poita* 'see, be seen' each have two meanings, affective and descriptive. In the affective sense, the honorific suffix cannot be used, because in this case, the HA (Experiencer) does not denote a deferential person. Only in the descriptive sense does the suffix appear, being obligatorily associated with the subject (Theme) NP. Here again, the topicalized version usually goes with the affective sense of the predicate. Observe the following set of examples, where the subject NP is animate. When we interpret the predicate only as descriptive, the subject is the only HA, and the locative NP cannot be topicalized, in that it cannot function as Experiencer but only as Location.

(18) a. *halapeci* *eykey/*i/*nun* *Mia ka* *iss-(*usi)-eyo.*
grandfather LOC/NM/TC Mia NM stay-SH-POL
'Mia is staying with grandfather.'

b. *Mia eykey/*i/*nun* *sensayng-nim* *i* *kyey-si-eyo.*
Mia LOC/NM/TC teacher-HT NM stay-SH-POL
'The professor is staying with Mia.'

c. *swunkyeng* *eykey/*i/*un* *apenim* *i* *caphi-si-ess-eyo.*
police LOC/NM/TC father NM caught-SH-PST-POL
'My father was arrested by the police.'

What we have observed with regard to locative-topic constructions may be summarized as follows.

(19) a. When the predicate is descriptive (i.e. [LOCATION THEME ___]), Theme is the HA; and when the predicate is affective (i.e. [EXPERIENCER THEME ___]), Experiencer is the HA.

b. When the predicate is an euphemistic word, the honorific triggering function becomes neutralized.

c. A topic construction forces the descriptive-affective predicate to be interpreted as affective. Thus, a purely descriptive predicate does not allow a non-Experiencer locative NP to be topicalized.

Another productive type of indirect honorification may be called possessive-topic, in that both a possessive and its corresponding topic NP may function as an HA under certain conditions. One basic condition is that the possessee NP must be subject or locative. Other conditions to be met will be discussed shortly. Let us first consider constructions where the possessee NP is subject.

(20) a. *sensayng-nim uy/i sayngkak i olh-usi-eyo.*
teacher-HT GN/NM idea NM right-SH-POL
'The professor's idea is right.'

b. *sensayng-nim uy/kkeyse phal i pwuleci-si-ess-eyo.*
teacher-HT GN/HSM arm NM broken-SH-PST-POL
'The professor's arm is broken.'

c. *sensayng-nim uy/kkeyse kasum i ttwi-si-ess-eyo?*
teacher-HT GN/HSM heart NM jump-SH-PST-POL
'Did the professor's heart palpitate?'

d. *sensayng-nim uy/kkeyse yenkwu ka cal an toy-si-eyo.*
teacher-HT GN/HSM research NM well not do-SH-POL
'The professor's research is not going well.'

The possessive and the corresponding topic constructions are viewed as having (21a) and (21b), respectively. Notice that, as in locative-topic pairs, (21a) is structurally embedded in (21b).

(21) a.

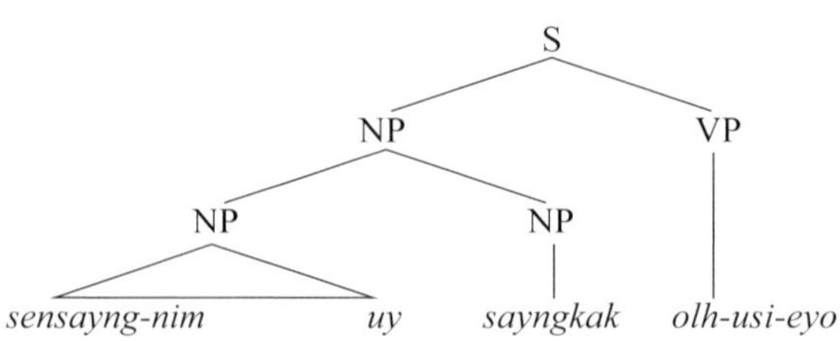

b.

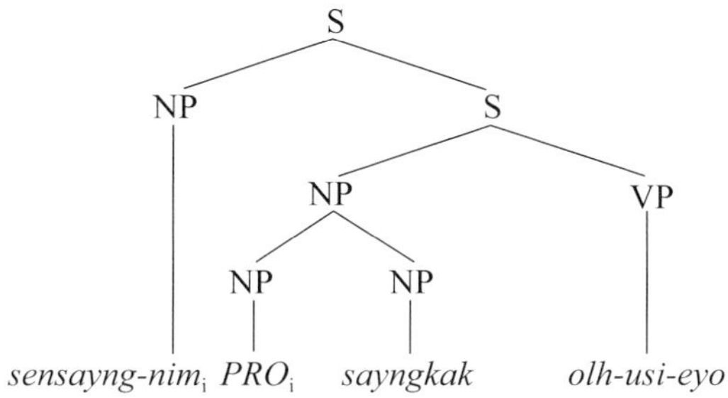

While honorification is obligatory in sentences (20), the appearance of *-(u)si* is either optional or dispensed with in constructions like those in (22).

(22) a.

sensayng-nim	*uy/i*	*tayk*	*i*	*i*	*kunche*	*i-(si)-eyo.*
teacher-HT	GN/NM	home	NM	this	near	be-SH-POL

'The professor's home is in this vicinity.

b.

apenim	*uy/i*	*cikcang*	*i*	*me(l)-(si)-eyo.*
father	GN/NM	job place	NM	far-SH-POL

'Father's working place is far.'

c.

apenim	*uy/i*	*saep*	*i*	*penchangha-(si)-eyo.*
father	GN/NM	business	NM	thrive-SH-POL

'My father's business thrives.'

d.

sensayng-nim	*uy/i*	*cha*	*ka*	*kkaykkusha-((?)si)-eyo.*
teacher-HT	GN/NM	car	NM	clean-SH-POL

'The professor's car is clean.'

e.

sensayng-nim	*uy/i*	*cha*	*ka*	*kocangna-(?si)-ess-eyo.*
teacher-HT	GN/NM	car	NM	break-SH-PST-POL

'The professor's car is broken down.'

Notice that there are degrees of optionality. It will be hardly justifiable to claim that sentences (22) have underlying structures different from the ones for sentences (20). That is, it is not due to syntactic structure which causes the obligatoriness in (20) and different degrees of optionality in (22). Before exploring this matter, observe the following set of sentences, which demonstrate that the subject, not the possessor or its corresponding topic NP, may function as the HA, a case of direct honorification. These sentences are in contrast with those illustrated in (20) and (22), which require obligatory and optional indirect honorification, respectively.

(23) a. *Mia uy/ka apeci ka mwusew-usi-eyo.*[8]
Mia GN/NM father NM scary-SH-POL
'Mia's father is scary.'

a′. *sensayng-nim uy/i kay ka mwusew-(*usi)-eyo.*
teacher-HT GN/NM dog NM scary-POL
'The professor's dog is scary.'

b. *Mia uy/ka emeni ka cip ul naka-si-ess-eyo.*
Mia GN/NM mother NM home AC go out-SH-POL
'Mia's mother went out of the house.'

b′. *sensayng-nim uy/i sonca ka cip ul naka-(*si)-ess-eyo.*
teacher-SH GN/NM grandson NM home AC goout-SH-PST-POL
'The professor's grandson went out of the house.'

Now the question to address is: what factors are responsible for the different patterns of honorific agreement that are illustrated in (20), (22), and (23)? The appearance of *-(u)si* seems to depend on three factors: (a) the degree of cohesion between the possessor and the possessee, (b) the animacy scale of the possessee NP, and (c) the stativity/activity scale of the predicate.

Different degrees of semantico-pragmatic cohesion between the referents of the possessor NP and and the possessee NP are correlated with the different degrees of optionality in honorific agreement between the possessor NP and the predicate. As some linguists have already observed (e.g. Lukoff 1978b), sentences (20) reveal that the semantic inalienable whole-part relationship obtains between the possessor and its possessee. Inalienable items include not only body parts, but words, claims, songs, concepts, emotion, actions, age, personal name, etc. Since the possessee is an inalienable part of its human possessor, the possessee is necessarily inanimate. This inalienable relationship causes the possessor or its corresponding topic NP (i.e. the first NP) to be the obligatory HA. This generalization applies regardless of whether the possessor is in the genitive case or in the topic position. If the "inalienable part" condition is not met, indi-

8 Adjectives like *mwusepta* 'be afraid of, scary', *chwupta* 'feel cold, cold', and *cohta* 'like, good' are used as both affective and descriptive. When used as affective, they agree in honorification with the Experiencer NP, as already observed. When they are descriptive, they always agree with Theme subject.

rect honorification is either optional as in (22) or not preferable in favor of direct honorification as in (23).

It is generally recognized in Korean culture that *tayk* 'home', *cikcang* 'working place', *os* 'clothes', *saep* 'business', *cangsa* 'business', etc., as well as personal belongings such as cha 'car', *sikyey* 'watch', and *moca* 'hat', are essential elements for the possessor to maintain his daily living, and the description of such items affects directly to the welfare or interest of the possessor. These items are considered pseudo-inalienable parts of the possessors, and many native speakers opt, albeit optionally, to have the predicate agree in honorification with the possessor, rather than the possessee NP. This is the situation in (22). On the other hand, there is no such inalienability relationship between the possessor NP and the animate possessee NP in (23). Here, the possessee NP tends to function as the HA, as discussed immediately below.

As for the animacy scale of the possessee NP, when this NP denotes an animate, the predicate is usually associated with that NP in honorific agreement. Animacy is stronger if the NP denotes an adult than a child. Thus, for example, a deferential possessee NP must trigger the honorific suffix. An animal possessee NP also functions as an HA, requiring the absence of *-(u)si*, even if the possessor NP refers to a deferential person. All this is illustrated in (23) in the above.

As for the stativity/activity scale, adjectives are more vulnerable to indirect honorification than process or non-controllable intransitive verbs, which are in turn more susceptible of indirect honorification than action verbs, in that controllable action tends to be related more directly to the immediate actor or Agent than to the possessor of the actor. This means that the more active or controllable a predicate is, the stronger is the subjecthood of the immediate subject of the predicate. Conversely, the more stative or non-controllable a predicate is, the weaker is the subjecthood, allowing greater empathy toward the possessor, locative, or topic. Thus, for example, *tayk i i kunche i-si-ta* '(his) home is near by' and *tayk i me-si-ta* '(his) home is far away' are more acceptable than *tayk i tha-si-n-ta* '(his) home is burned down' and *tayk i mwuneci-si-n-ta* '(his) home collapses'. Such degree is observed even when the subject is animate. Assuming that the professor's grandson is a five year old boy, observe sentences (24).

(24) a. *sensayng-nim uy sonca ka kwiyew-(?usi)-eyo.*
teacher-HT GN grandson NM cute-SH-POL
'The professor's grandson is cute.'

b. *sensayng-nim uy sonca ka aphu-(??si)-eyo.*
teacher-HT GN grandson NM sick-SH-POL
'The professor's grandson is sick.'

c. *sensayng-nim uy sonca ka ilena-(*si)-eyo.*
teacher-HT GN grandson NM get up-SH-POL
'The professor's grandson is getting up.'

d. *sensayng-nim uy sonca ka thipi lul po-(*si)-eyo.*
teacher-HT GN grandson NM T.V. AC see-SH-POL
'The professor's grandson watches the T.V.'

The honorific suffix is slightly more tolerable in (24a) than in (24b). This may be because *kwiyepta* denotes a state of the speaker's subjective evaluation of Theme (*sonca*) and thus somewhat weakens Theme's animacy, whereas *aphuta* denotes an objective state of Theme. A controllable action verb, whether it is intransitive or transitive, does not allow indirect honorification. The subject of a controllable action is Agent. Thus, the stativity/activity scale is coterminous with the Theme/Agent scale of the subject. What we have said thus far with regard to possessive-topic constructions may be summarized as follows.

(25) a. If subject is animate, no indirect honorification is allowed.

b. If subject is inanimate, its possessor NP functions as the HA in the following ways:

i. If the possessee is a physically or mentally inalienable part of the the possessor, then the possessor NP functions as an obligatory HA.

ii. If the semantic relation between the possessor and possessee is of a pseudo-inalienable whole-part, the possessor NP functions as an optional HA. There are degrees of optionality depending on the nature of predicates, significant divisions being stative > uncontrollable process > intransitive controllable action > transitive controllable action, where X > Y indicates that X tolerates indirect honorification more than Y, other things being equal.

Consider now constructions in (26) where the possessee NP occurs as locative.

(26) a. *sensayng-nim uy/i sayngkak ey calmos i iss-usi-eyo.*
teacher-HT GN/NM idea LOC mistake NM exist-SH-POL
'The professor has a mistaken idea.'

b.

apenim	*uy/i*	*tali*	*ey*	*congki*	*ka*	*na-si-ess-eyo.*
father-HT	GN/NM	leg	LOC	boil	NM	appear-SH-PST-POL

'Father has a boil on his leg.'

c.

apenim	*uy/i*	*son*	*ey*	*kasi*	*ka*	*pakhi-(si)-ess-eyo.*
father-HT	GN/NM	hand	LOC	thorn	NM	stuck-SH-PST-POL

'A thorn is stuck in father's hand.'

d.

sensayng-nim	*uy/i*	*pang*	*ey*	*chayk*	*i*	*manh-(usi)-eyo.*
teacher-HT	GN/NM	room	LOC	book	NM	many-SH-POL

'The professor has many books in his room.'

e.

sensayng-nim	*uy/i*	*cha*	*ey*	*pwul*	*i*	*na-(?si)-ess-eyo.*
teacher-HT	GN/NM	home	LOC	fire	NM	occur-PST-POL

'The professor's car caught a fire.'

f.

sensayng-nim	*uy/i*	*pang*	*ey*	*cwi*	*ka*	*iss-(*usi)-eyo.*
teacher-HT	GN/NM	room	LOC	rat	NM	stay-SH-POL

'The professor's room has a rat.'

g.

Mi	*uy/ka*	*cip*	*ey*	*noin*	*i*	*manh-usi-eyo.*
Mia	GN/NM	home	LOC	elder	NM	many-SH-POL

'There are many aged people at Mia's.'

Each of these sentences is composed of a possessive NP embedded in a locative NP. As will be seen shortly, the loctives themselves can also be topicalized. Therefore, what we have observed previously with regard to locative-topic and possessive-topic constructions are generally applicable to sentences (26). For example, (25a) applies to sentences (26f,g) where the animate subject is an obligatory HA. Notice that in an inalienable possessor-possessee locative NP (e.g. 26a,b,c), the possessor NP behaves as the head in honorific agreement, with its animate feature being percolated up to the higher NP. In the case of pseudo-inalienable constructions, such percolation appears to be optional. The difference in the acceptability of *-(u)si* in (26d,e) is due to the stativity/activity scale.

Similarly, the various generalizations made earlier may account for the different degrees of acceptability of the honorific suffix in the following possessive-locative sentences. Despite the fact that the identical locative NP is given in all the sentences, the honorific suffix is the most obligatory in (27a) and the least acceptable in (27e).

(27) a.

apenim	*uy*	*elkwul*	*ey*	*cem*	*i*	*iss-usi-eyo.*
father	GN	face	LOC	mole	NM	exist-SH-POL

'There is a mole on father's face.'

b.

apenim	*uy*	*elkwul*	*ey*	*congki*	*ka*	*na-si-ess-eyo.*
father	GN	face	LOC	boil	NM	appear-SH-PST-POL

'A swelling came out on father's face.'

c.

apenim	*uy*	*elkwul*	*ey*	*ingkhu*	*ka*	*mwut-(usi)-ess-eyo.*
father	GN	face	LOC	ink	NM	stick-SH-PST-POL

'Father's face is smeared with ink.'

d.

apenim	*uy*	*elkwul*	*ey*	*phalli*	*ka*	*anc-(?usi)-ess-eyo.*
father	GN	face	LOC	fly	NM	sit-SH-PST-POL

'A fly is sitting on father's face.'

e.

apenim	*uy*	*elkwul*	*ey*	*phalli*	*ka*	*ttong*	*ssa-(*si)-eyo.*
father	GN	face	LOC	fly	NM	feces	excret-SH-POL

'A fly is excreting on father's face.'

In (27a) the subject is an inalienable body part (Theme) and the existential predicate is used as possessive (thus, affective); in (27b) an inalienable subject (Theme) occurs with a non-controllable verb; in (27c) an alienable subject (Theme) occurs with a non-controllable verb; in (27d) the subject is animate (Agent) and the verb controllable; and in (27e) the subject is animate (Agent) and the verb controllable and transitive.

At this point, it needs to be pointed out that one of the syntactic characteristics of Korean is its proliferation of multiple topic (or nominative) construction, as can be represented below.[9]

(28) $S \rightarrow (NP)\ S$

This rule allows recursiveness of NP, with one topic stacked on top of another. Sentences (29) are multiple possessive-topic constructions, and (30) illustrates cases with both possessive-topic and locative-topic constructions.

9 In the rule $S \rightarrow (NP)\ S$, NP is a topic with the following S as its comment (Sohn 1986). This NP shares many features with subject, hence the traditional term "multiple subject" constructions. For example, the honorific subject particle *kkeyse* can be attached to both deferential topic and subject.

(29) a. *apenim uy/kkeyse meli uy/ka twi uy/ka pan i*
father GN/HSM head GN/NM back GN/NM half NM
aphu-si-ess-eyo.
hurt-SH-PST-POL
'Father had an ache in the back half of his head.'

b. *apenim uy/i meli ka aph i peskieci-si-ess-eyo.*
father GN/NM head NM front NM peeled-SH-PST-POL
'The front of father's head became bald.'

c. *apenim uy/kkeyse os uy/i somay ka ki-(si)-eyo.*
father GN-HSM dress GN/NM sleeve NM long-SH-POL
'The sleeve of my father's clothing is long.'

d. *sensayng-nim uy/kkeyse apenim uy/kkeyse phal i*
teacher-HT GN/HSM father GN/HSM arm NM
pwuleci-si-ess-eyo.
broken-SH-PST-POL
'The professor's father got his arm broken.'

(30) a. *apenim uy/i nwun ey/i nwun-kop i kki-si-eyo.*
father GN/NM eye LOC/NM eye-wax NM stained-SH-POL
'Father's eyes are gummy.'

b. *apenim uy/i son ey/i kasi ka pakhi-(si)-ess-eyo.*
father GN/NM hand LOC/NM thorn NM stuck-SH-PST-POL
'A thorn is stuck in my father's hand.'

c. *apenim uy/i cha ey/i pwul i na-(?si)-ess-eyo.*
father GN/NM car LOC/NM fire NM occur-SH-PST-POL
'Father's car caught fire.'

Due to the multiplicity of NPs, the distance between the honorific trigger and the verb becomes greater and accordingly the indirectness in honorification becomes greater. As a result, honorific agreement may sometimes be slightly diluted, although not to a significant degree. Time and space do not allow us to go into the discussion of these constructions. Simply stated, the generalizations regarding honorific agreement that have been made thus far, together with the notion of percolation, will account for indirect honorification in multiple possessive-topic and locative-topic constructions.

It seems that there is a hierarchy among different types of HAs in terms of honorific triggering power. For one thing, a hierarchy exists among the three major thematic roles that function as an HA: Agent, Experiencer, and Theme in that order. Examine the following sentences.

(31) a.	*sensayng-nim*	*un*	*awunim*	*i*	*cakkoha-si-ess-eyo.*
	teacher-HT	TC	brother	NM	pass away-SH-PST-POL

'As for the professor, his younger brother passed away.'

b.	*apenim*	*kkey/kkeyse*	*sensayng-nim*	*i*	*poi-si-ess-eyo.*
	father	HLOC/HSM	teacher-HT	NM	be seen-SH-PST-POL

'Father saw the professor.'

c.	*sensayng-nim*	*eykey/i*	*cey*	*apenim*	*i*	*philyoha-si-eyo.*
	teacher-HT	LOC/NM	my	father	NM	need-SH-POL

'The professor needs my father.'

d.	*halapenim*	*kkey*	*apenim*	*i*	*telmi*	*lul*	*caphi-si-ess-eyo.*
	grandfather	HLOC	father	NM	nape	AC	caught-SH-PST-POL

'Grandfather seized father by the nape of the neck.'

(31a) illustrates that only Agent is an HA. (31b) suggests that an Experiencer Locative NP has a stronger honorific triggering function than the Theme subject NP. (31c) indicates that if a locative NP is interpreted as Experiencer with the verb interpreted as affective, it is the HA, otherwise the Theme subject NP is the triggerer. When there is no Experiencer Locative, as in (31d), the Theme subject NP always functions as the HA, whether there is an honorific NP elsewhere or not.

In each Topic and non-Topic pair, the Topic NP triggers honorification more strongly than the corresponding (Experiencer) Locative or Possessive NP, as shown in (32).

(32) a.	*sensayng-nim*	*uy*	*tayk*	*i*	*me(l)-(si)-eyo.*
	teacher-HT	GN	home	NM	far-SH-POL

'The professor's home is far away.'

a′.	*sensayng-nim*	*i*	*tayk*	*i*	*me-si-eyo.*
	teacher-HT	NM	home	NM	far-SH-POL

'As for the professor, his home is far away.'

b. *emeni eykey cha ka iss-(usi)-eyo.*
mother LOC car NM exist-SH-POL
'Mother has a car.'

b′. *emeni ka cha ka iss-usi-eyo.*
mother NM car NM exist-SH-POL
'Mother has a car.'

As alluded to earlier, a possessee NP is stronger than a possessor NP, as shown in sentences (33) where the predicate agrees with the possessee NP in honorification.

(33) a. *sensayng-nim uy/i apenim i aphu-si-eyo.*
teacher-HT GN/NM father NM sick-SH-POL
'The professor's father is sick.'

b. *sensayng-nim uy/i apenim i mikwuk ey ka-si-eyo.*
teacher-HT GN/NM father NM America to go-SH-POL
'The professor's father is going to America.'

Thus, the hierarchy is assumed to be: Agent> Experiencer Topic > Experiencer Locative > Theme Subject > Possessor Topic > Possessor Genitive. Non-Experiencer Locative, Theme Object, Goal, etc. have no place in this hierarchy, in that they never trigger the honorific suffix.

Pragmatic dimensions also come into the picture. In particular, there are many ways for the addressee to affect the speaker's use of the honorific suffix, mainly because of the importance of face-to-face interpersonal interaction. For example, as Lukoff (1978b) also observes, when the deferential addressee himself is the subject, possessor, or locative, the otherwise optional honorific marker *-(u)si* becomes obligatory and the otherwise less acceptable or unacceptable *-(u)si* tends to become optional, a case of hyper-deference. Compare the paired sentences below.

(34) a. *Kim sensayng-nim uy/i tayk i i kunche i-(si)-eyo?*
Kim teacher-HT GN/NM home NM this near be-SH-POL
'Is Professor Kim's home near here?'

a′. *sensayng-nim uy/i tayk i i kunche i-si-eyo?*
teacher-ST GN/NM home NM this near be-SH-POL
'Is your home near here, Professor?'

b. *Kim sensayng-nim uy/i samwusil i tew-(?usi)-eyo.*
Kim teacher-HT GN/NM office NM hot-SH-POL
'Professor Kim's office is hot.'

b′. *sensayng-nim uy/i samwusil i tew-(usi)-eyo.*
teacher-HT GN/NM office NM hot-SH-POL
'Your office is hot.'

c. *wuli apeci uy/ka cha ka kocang i na-(*si)-ess-eyo?*
our father GN/NM car NM hitch NM appear-SH-PST-POL
'Is my father's car out of order?'

c′. *apeci uy/ka cha ka kocang i na-(si)-ess-eyo?*
father GN/NM car NM hitch NM appear-SH-PST-POL
'Is your car out of order, father?'

The same effect is generally observed when the speaker talks about the addressee's ingroup people and when a third person referent is within the ear-shot.

In addition to the addressee involvement, the speaker's own personal feeling toward the referent is often functional in the use or nonuse of the honorific suffix.[10] As a matter of fact, in obligatory cases, the speaker may show intentional disrespect toward a socially superior referent by not using the honorific suffix, as in (35a). On the other hand, one may show excessive politeness by using it, as in (35b). Although the suffix is generally omitted in referring to a public person, one may express particular personal regard to the referent by using the suffix, as in (35c).

(35) a. *sensanyng-nim o-ass-ta.*
teacher-HT come-PST-DC
'The professor came.'

b. *sensayng-nim koyangi ka ippu-si-eyo.*
teacher-HT cat NM pretty-SH-POL
'Your cat is pretty.'

10 To account for the optional occurrence of the honorific suffix, as in *sensanyng-nim tayk i khu-(si)-ta* 'the professor's house is big', Lukoff (1978:555) proposes to distinguish between the "generality" and "specificity" of reference. When the speaker's remark is taken as a general, objective comment, the suffix is generally omitted, whereas when the remark is to be taken as pertaining specifically to the honorific referent, conveying the speaker's personal interest toward the referent, the suffix usually appears.

c. * *taythonglyeng i mikwuk ulo ttena-(si)-ess-eyo.*
President NM America to leave-SH-PST-POL
'The President left for America.'

Furthermore, there is considerable individual variation in perceiving such pseudo-inalienability. This is compounded with individual variation in the speaker's empathy and expression of politeness. That is, some people use the honorific suffix more lavishly than others.

REFERENCES: Chapter 22

Chang, Suk-Jin. 1973. *A Generative Study of Discourse. Language Research* 9.2. Supplement.

Cho, Choon-Hak. 1982. *A Study of Korean Pragmatics: Deixis and Politeness.* Ph.D. dissertation. University of Hawaii.

Cho, Euiyon. 1988. *Some Interactions of Grammar and Pragmatics in Korean.* Ph.D. dissertation. University of Illinois at Urbana-Champaign.

Im, Hong-bin. 1976. Contay, kyemyang uy thongsa celcha ey tayhaye. *Mwunpep Yenkwu* 3. Seoul.

Kim, Hui-sook. 1990. *Hyentay kwuke uy kongson phyohyen yenkwu.* Ph.D. dissertation. Sukmyong University.

Kim, Yong-Bum. 1987. A GPSG approach to Korean honorifics. In Kuno, S. et al. (eds.), *Harvard Studies in Korean Linguistics.* Seoul: Hanshin.

Kuno, S. and Young-Joo Kim. 1985. The honorific forms of compound verbals in Korean. In Kuno, S. et al. (eds.), *Harvard Studies in Korean Linguistics.* Seoul: Hanshin.

Lee, Chungmin. 1973. *Abstract Syntax and Korean with Reference to English.* Ph.D. dissertation. Indiana University.

Lee, Hong-Bae. 1970. *A Study of Korean Syntax.* Ph.D. dissertation. Brown University.

Lukoff, F. 1978a. Ceremonial and expressive uses of the styles of address of Korean. In Kim, Chin-W. (ed.), *Papers in Korean Linguistics.* Columbia: Hornbeam Press.

Lukoff, F. 1978b. On honorific reference. *Festschrift for Prof. Woong Huh.* Seoul: Seoul National University Press.

Park, Yangkyu. 1975. Conching cheyen uy thongsacek thukcing. *Cintan Hakpo* 40.

Park-Choi, Young-Soon. 1978. *Aspects in the Development of Communicative Competence with Reference to the Korean Deference System.* Ph.D. dissertation. University of Illinois, Urbana.

Shibatani, Masayoshi. 1976. Relational grammar and Korean syntax. *Language Research* 12.2.

Shin, Sung-Ock. 1989. Honorifics in complex sentences. *Korean Language Education* 1.

Sohn, Ho-min. 1986. *Linguistic Expeditions.* Seoul: Hanshin.

Song, Seok-Choong. 1967. *Some Transformational Rules in Korean*. Ph.D. dissertation. Indiana University.

Suh, Cheong-Soo. 1984. *Contaypep uy Yenkwu* (A Study on Honorifics). Seoul: Hanshin.

Sung, Kychul. 1985. *Hyentay Kwuke Taywupep Yenkwu* (A Study of Contemporary Korean Honorifics). Seoul: Kaymwunsa.

Yun, Sung-Kyu. 1991. Topic-oriented *si* Honorifics in Korean. Presented at the 1991 Harvard Workshop in Korean Linguistics.

23 Politeness Formulas in L2 Acquisition: An Intercultural Perspective*

1. Introduction[1]

Language is not only a communicative tool but also an interactive tool. That is, it has essentially two interrelated functions—transmission or sharing of information, knowledge, and feelings, on the one hand, and establishment, maintenance, and enhancement of human (social and interpersonal) relationships on the other. This distinction between transactional and affective or attitudinal functions is particularly clear and important in interpersonal communication where both functions of language are conspicuous and interact delicately. The distinction is even more significant in intercultural communication because different languages and different cultures are involved.

The transactional function of language can be performed most effectively in terms of economy and clarity, as suggested, for example, by Lakoff's (1973) rule of clarity ("be clear") and Grice's (1975) Cooperative Principle (CP) and its four maxims of quality, quantity, relevance, and manner. Thus, this function calls for, among others, linguistic competence including phonetic, phonological, lexical, morph-syntactic, semantic, and sociolinguistic accuracies as well as communicative fluency.

On the other hand, the affective or attitudinal function of language can be attained best in terms of pragmatic (pragmalinguistic and sociopragmatic) competence including linguistic politeness. For instance, when we meet a colleague in the morning, we utter *annyeng-ha-sey-yo* "How are you?" in Korean, *ohayoo-*

---

* This is reprinted from *the Proceedings of the 2007 Annual Conference the Pan-Pacific Associate for Applied Linguistics,* pp. 51–76. This paper was presented for a keynote speech at the Annual Conference of the Pan-Pacific Association for Applied Linguistics held in Bangkok, Thailand. December 19-21, 2007.

1 This paper was prepared in Melbourne, Australia, at the La Trobe University Research Center for Linguistic Typology (RCLT) when I was at RCLT for a semester in the fall of 2007. I am grateful to Bob Dixon and Sasha Aikhenvald for inviting me as a distinguished scholar to the RCLT.

gozai-masu "Good morning" in Japanese, and *Good morning* or *Hi* in English. Through such politeness rituals, our intention in these utterances is not to convey such literal meanings as asking about the addressee's well-being or being early or stating the condition of the morning weather, but simply to maintain a smooth and polite human relationship with the addressee. Thus, it is the function of establishing, maintaining, and enhancing human relationships that is relevant to linguistic politeness, among other things.

"Politeness formulas" refers to the formulas of linguistic politeness. Thus, it is necessary at the outset to examine how concepts like linguistic politeness, linguistic formulas, and politeness formulas have been defined and dealt with in the literature. Then, we will take up the roles and functions politeness formulas play in second language acquisition and the issue of how to have learners efficiently acquire them.

2. Linguistic politeness

Linguistic politeness of one way or another exists in all cultures. Let us first dwell on what linguistic politeness is and how it is treated by linguists. There is no doubt that the position of linguistic politeness is an integral part of pragmatics, in that pragmatics is the study of communicative action in its socio-cultural context or the study of the use of language in human communication as determined by the conditions of society (e.g. Mey 2001: 6; Kasper & Rose 2001: 2; Swann et al. 2004: 248). Although how to precisely define linguistic politeness has been extremely controversial, it may be generally viewed as language use whose purpose is to establish harmony and mutual comfort and promote rapport by considering others' feelings (e.g. Hill et al. 1986) or as forms of friction-reducing behaviour in personal interaction (Lakoff 1973) and thus relates to the linguistic expression of concern for others (e.g. courtesy, deference) (Swann et al. ibid.).

A number of linguists have endeavoured to precisely define linguistic politeness in terms of universal rules, strategies, principles, or maxims. For instance, Lakoff (ibid.) proposes three rules of politeness: Don't impose on the addressee; Give the addressee options; and Make the addressee feel good.

Brown and Levinson (1978, 1987; henceforth B&L) rebut the doctrine of cultural relativity in interaction and claim that superficial cross-cultural diversities can emerge from underlying universal pragmatic principles. Building on the notion of face, which refers to a person's public self-image, B&L distinguish two aspects of face: 'positive face', the desire for appreciation and approval by others, and 'negative face', the desire not to be imposed on by others. In their theory, positive or negative politeness operates only when positive or negative face needs are at risk. These strategic options of handling face-threats are called politeness.

B&L established five levels of linguistic strategies for politeness—Direct strategy; Positive politeness strategies; Negative politeness strategies; Off-record strategies; and No speech act—and provided a number of concrete strategies for each level.[2] Politeness strategies are the resources available to interlocutors to balance their own face needs against those of others. Interlocutors' moment-to-moment choices of strategies are based on their intuitive calculation of the relative closeness or distance of their relations with their interlocutor(s), the relative difference in their status, and how much of an imposition they are making.

Leech's (1983: 81) "politeness principle" model states that people need to minimise the expression of impolite beliefs or, in its positive form, maximise the expression of polite beliefs. Under this principle, he presents six maxims of politeness: Tact; Generosity; Approbation; Modesty; Agreement; and Sympathy. He points out that the most important kind of politeness in English-speaking society is that which is covered by the operation of the Tact Maxim. This maxim reads "Minimize cost to other; Maximize benefit to other" in terms of three scales: the cost-benefit scale that concerns the propositional content of an utterance, the indirectness scale that concerns the illocutionary force of an utterance, and the social distance scale that concerns the vertical (power) and horizontal (solidarity) relationship between the speaker and addressee or a third party.

Fraser (1980, 1990) advances a so-called conversational-contract view. This suggests that politeness operates within the current terms and conditions of the conversational contract entered into by the participants in an interaction in an effort to maintain conflict-free interaction. Fraser (1980) associates politeness with his notion of mitigation, defining mitigation as a strategy for reducing the force of a speech act whose effects are unwelcome to the addressee.

Of all the politeness theories advanced thus far, B&L's (ibid.) is the most elaborate and extensive, attracting the most attention from linguists, especially in regard to their claim that there are culturally universal principles underlying politeness. Many subsequent linguists (e.g. Watts, Ide, & Ehlich 2005; Locher & Watts 2005; Holtgraves 2005a; and several papers in Lakoff & Ide 2005)

---

2 For instance, under the Positive politeness strategies, B&L propose fifteen concrete strategies including "Notice, attend to hearer's wants, needs, interests, goods"; "Exaggerate interest, approval, sympathy with hearer", "Seek agreement", "Avoid disagreement", and "Give reasons". Under the Negative politeness strategies, they propose ten strategies including "Be conventionally indirect"; "Give deference"; "Question, hedge"; "Apologize"; "Go on record as incurring a debt". Under the Off-record strategies, fifteen strategies are listed including "Give hints"; "Give association clues"; "Presuppose"; "Understate"; "Use metaphors"; "Use rhetorical questions"; "Be ambiguous"; "Be incomplete"; and "Use ellipsis".

argue against the universality thesis propounded by B&L. Those anti-universal arguments are based on diverse language-use data from different cultures. For instance, in the introductory chapter of Watts, Ide, & Ehlich (2005), Watts claims that "politeness will always be a slippery, ultimately indefinable quality of interaction which is subject to change through time and across cultural space" and the pursuit of both an a priori predictive theory of politeness and a post-facto descriptive theory of politeness should be abandoned. Instead, he argues that analysts need to "pay closer attention to how participants in social interaction perceive politeness," a move toward discursive approaches to politeness. Several papers in Watts, Ide, & Ehlich (ibid.) and Lakoff & Ide (2005) deal with non-Western languages such as Hebrew, Japanese, and Thai. The key point of these papers is that politeness cannot be defined in the same way across cultural spaces.

Similarly, I argued earlier in Sohn (1989) that all the earlier universality proposals are only partially valid, in that linguistic politeness is viewed only as a feature of strategic language use in social interaction. For instance, Lakoff's and Leech's conversational maxims of politeness, B&L's face-oriented politeness strategies, and Fraser's contractual politeness are all pertinent only to strategic language use, hardly to language structure on the one hand and normative use on the other. The fact of the matter is that linguistic structure also strongly manifests linguistic politeness, as observed more distinctly in honorific languages such as Korean, Japanese, and Javanese, and many politeness expressions are used dictated by socio-cultural norms and values.

As reflected in extensive misperceptions or misunderstandings in spoken and written intercultural communications (e.g. Moeschler 2004; Watts, Ide, & Ehlich ibid.; Lakoff & Ide ibid.), there is tremendous socio-cultural (norms and values) variability in terms of what constitutes politeness, how politeness is expressed or conveyed, who is polite to whom, and so on. Besides, each culture has its commonly accepted verbal conventions and usages. In Korean, Chinese, Japanese, and Russian cultures, for example, imposing on or not giving options to the addressee is often very natural and generally polite when the speech act is in the interest of the addressee, as when "imposing" upon the addressee to eat more in casual contexts. The concept of "face" itself, B&L's central universal notion, is thus considerably culture-bound and is perceived and conceived quite differently from culture to culture. As a result, sensitivity to B&L's strategies is not equal in all cultures. For example, while the imperative forms are rarely used to issue requests (for speaker's benefit) in favour of indirect speech acts in English, this is not necessarily the case with many other cultures such as Chinese (Tsuzuki et al. 2005), Russian (Larina 2007), and also Japanese and Korean. Kallia (2005) reveals the differences in the uses of imperatives among English,

German, and Greek.

Furthermore, linguistic politeness is expressed with a wide variety of linguistic devices such as address/reference terms, honorifics, politeness formulas, indirect speech act forms, various hedging devices, polite auxiliaries, sentence enders with appropriate intonation contours, hesitation, and so forth. Such politeness devices are picked up by interlocutors in accordance with established sociolinguistic rules and culture-bound conventions, norms, and values. Thus, different cultures may choose different kinds of devices for the same speech acts. One additional point is that linguistic politeness in any culture is not static but dynamic reflecting socio-cultural dynamism.

Despite all of the theoretical differences in defining the nature of linguistic politeness, there is no question that it is associated with harmonious interpersonal relations. In short, linguistic politeness is an essential aspect of human interactive behaviour, an important socio-cultural phenomenon, and a facet of communicative competence and performance. It is both universal and culture-specific, having both universal aspects and culture-bound manifestations, as reflected in linguistic patterns and pragmatic usages of each language. That is, languages share many universal components of politeness especially in higher abstract and principled levels, but also differ in unpredictable ways, especially in lower, specific manifestation levels. Both sides are significantly relevant to L2 acquisition because many problems and misunderstandings in intercultural communication arise from the difficulty of finding appropriate linguistic means to signal harmonious attitudes to interlocutors in given speech act contexts. This difficulty is by and large due to the different social organizations and norms and cultural values underlying L1 and L2.

3. Linguistic formulas and politeness formulas

Language is basically conventional. Otherwise, the members of the linguistic community would have great difficulty in producing, processing, and comprehending sentences and discourses. In the same vein, formulaic expressions, which are highly conventionalized, facilitate communication by providing ready-made expressions.

Linguistic formulas are also variously called *formulaic languages, formulaic sequences, chunks, prefabs (prefabricated speech), (interactional) routines, formulaic routines,* and *routine formulae*. According to Swann et al. (2004), formulaic language refers to set phrases or expressions such as idioms (e.g. *to all intents and purposes*), metaphorical uses (e.g. *kick the bucket* 'die', *piece of cake* 'easy', and *get out of here* 'don't fool me'), and greetings formulae (e.g. *pleased to meet you*). Bardovi-Harlig (2006: 4) quotes several definitions as they are used in language acquisition research and sociolinguistic perspective: "Routines are whole utterances that are unusually error-free and show no transitional states of development or systematic order of acquisition. They are learned as unanalyzed wholes, much as one learns a single word" (Dulay et al. 1982: 232–3); "Routine formulae are highly conventionalized prepatterned expressions whose occurrence is tied to more or less standardized communication situations... In embodying social knowledge they are essential in the handling of day-to-day transactions" (Coulmas 1981: 3–4). "A formula is a sequence, continuous or discontinuous, of words or other meaning elements, which is, or appears to be, prefabricated, that is, stored and retrieved whole from memory at the time of use, rather than being subject to generation or analysis by the language grammar" (Wray 2000: 465).

In pragmatics, terms like "semantic formulas" and "pragmatic strategies" are employed to refer to conventionalized expressions associated with various speech acts. For instance, in regard to the speech act of apology, the perpetrator uses semantic formulas such as an expression of apology, a statement of responsibility, an offer of repair, and/or a promise of forbearance (Olshtain and Cohen 1991; Bardovi-Harlig ibid.). Semantic formulas are usually conventional but need not be formulaic.

I will take all the above definitions into account as appropriate. Although many formulas may be learned as unanalysed wholes, they can be and, in fact, should be analysed for L2 instructional purposes. Needless to say, formulas occupy certain syntactic and discourse positions, and thus they are analysable in relation to other grammatical functions and categories; their morpho-syntactic compositions, semantic, pragmalinguistic, sociopragmatic, and discourse properties, and cross-cultural differences must be studied and revealed. Unlike some arguments to the contrary, I maintain that teaching and learning of L2 formulas contribute to language acquisition to a great extent through developing the pragmatic and sociolinguistic competence of the learners.

Politeness formulas constitute a subset of linguistic formulas. They are conventionalized polite expressions used in various speech acts in interactive contexts. They are formulaic expressions that maintain, promote, or boost smooth interpersonal relations, while conveying transactional content in speech acts, written or spoken. Thus, non-interactive idioms or expressions and non-polite metaphorical formulas are not politeness formulas. Politeness formulas are culturally and interpersonally so sensitive and context-bound that improper use or non-use of politeness formulas in given contexts can immediately lead to impoliteness and can be detrimental to carrying on smooth conversation. It is well known that people easily forgive foreigners' grammatical or lexical mistakes, but are very sensitive to an inappropriate or non-use of politeness formulas as they tend to be attributed to intentional cause.

Unlike idioms and other non-polite formulas whose meanings are by and large given in dictionaries, the pragmalinguistic and sociopragmatic meanings of politeness formulas are generally not readily available in dictionaries and grammar books and are hard to grasp and pin down without interactive contexts. This is particularly the case with L2 language learners whose socio-cultural and pragmatic backgrounds are distinct from those of L2. All this suggests the importance of politeness formulas for second language teaching, learning, and research.

Politeness formulas involve two kinds, relatively more ritualized ones (such as "Good Morning") and relatively more strategic ones (such as "Would you do me a favor?"), although borderline cases are numerous. Both kinds of expressions are politeness devices in that non-use of them immediately leads to impoliteness. These two kinds correspond to Janney and Arndt's (1992) social politeness and interpersonal politeness (or tact), respectively. Janney and Arndt regard politeness not as a static logical concept but as a dynamic interpersonal activity that can be observed, described, and explained in functional interactional terms. They distinguish between social politeness and interpersonal politeness (or tact), saying that both types of politeness are culturally acquired and are interrelated in speech. The function of social politeness is essentially to coordinate social interaction—to regulate the mechanical exchange of roles and activities—whereas the function of interactional politeness is to preserve face and regulate interpersonal relationships. One main means for social politeness is to follow conventions of social politeness, often termed "conversational routines", "politeness formulas", "politeness conventions", or "formulaic expressions". One main means for interpersonal politeness is to be tactful, i.e. behaving in an interpersonally supportive way and empathizing with others, and not saying or doing things that threaten or offend them or injure their feelings. While Janney and Arndt limit "politeness formulas" to their social politeness, I will use the term more broadly to cover both their social and interpersonal politeness as long as the linguistic forms are conventionalized.

4. Importance of politeness formulas in L2 acquisition

Early research in second language acquisition included empirical studies of formulas used by adult learners, but the Universal Grammar (UG) emphasized the rule-governed nature of language production, maintaining that knowledge of formulas did not contribute to syntactic development (e.g. Bardovi-Harlig 2006: 1–2). There has recently been a renewed interest in formulas in the second language studies literature (e.g. Kasper & Rose 2001; N. Schmitt 2004). In particular, the focus of recent research is the function of formulas in language acquisition and language use, whether among native speakers or learners. Advantages of learners' knowledge and use of L2 politeness formulas in L2 acquisition may be summarized as follows:

(a) Pragmatic or pragmalinguistic competence is an indispensable component of language learning. Interactive speech acts, such as request, suggestion, invitation, promise, offer, refusal, agreement, introduction, excuse, thanking, apology, complaining, congratulating, complimenting, condoling, and greeting, are required to be conducted in a polite manner. Such speech acts are by and large through exchanges of politeness formulas. Learning of politeness formulas and storing them in the learners' repertoires are, therefore, an essential requirement for attaining interactive pragmatic competence, as politeness formulas constitute a substantial part of adult native speakers' pragmatic competence. For example, if a learner of English has acquired and naturally and productively used conventionalized politeness expressions such as those in (1) in interactive situations (data from Holtgraves 2005b: 2029), there is no doubt that he or she has achieved a considerable level of pragmalinguistic competence in English.

(1) *Be careful. There is a cop near.*
(Warn: imperative plus assert negative state)
Keep at it. You'll do fine. (Encourage: imperative plus optimism)
Please, please, please. I've got to see this movie.
(Beg: assert strong desire plus humble mode of achievement)
Do you know the time? (Ask: indirect request for information)
Would you like to come for dinner tomorrow?
(Invite: request hearer's presence with low degree of strength)
I swear I will be neater after this weekend.
(Promise: strongly obligate speaker to perform possible future action)
If you need some help then give me a call. (Offer: conditional promise)
You're right. It is wrong to do that.
(Agree: assert previous proposition and/or correctness of proposition)
I haven't been feeling well. (Excuse: assert reason for negative situation)
I appreciate your help. I couldn't have done it without you.
(Thanks: express gratitude for event benefiting speaker)
I'm sorry that I ruined your shirt. (Apology: express regret for negative act for which speaker irresponsible)
That's awesome. I'm so happy for you. (Congratulate: express pleasure at hearer's outcome–high degree of strength)
I like your new coat. (Compliment: express approval of hearer's object/event– low degree of strength)

(b) The knowledge and use of politeness formulas contribute to sociolinguistic or sociopragmatic competence, which involves appropriate language use in social and interactive contexts or situations. In this connection, Coulmas (1981) indicates that language learners need to acquire a sizable repertoire of formulas in order to cope efficiently with recurrent and expanding social situations and discourse requirements. Similarly, House (1996: 227–8) emphasizes the importance of learning formulas at any learning stage because formulas embody the given community's common societal knowledge and thus are essential in the verbal handling of everyday life.

For instance, the English casual acceptance formula *Sure, no problem* is appropriate for request contexts but not for offer contexts. This sociopragmatic knowledge can prevent the overgeneralization observed in Kecskes' (2000) example in (2), where one learner used the same response *Sure, no problem* in requests and offers.

(2) a. Can I borrow your pen? — *Sure, no problem.*
  b. Can I talk to you after class? — *Sure, no problem.*
  c. Would you like some candy? — **Sure, no problem.*

Thus, felicitous use of politeness formulas in correct socio-cultural and discourse contexts or situations enhances the learner's sociolinguistic competence.

(c) The knowledge and use of politeness formulas contribute to cross-cultural awareness and thus to intercultural communicative competence, as users of formulas are communicating across cultures. Intercultural communication is communication between members of different cultural groups, who may bring different language practices or ways of speaking and different expectations, social norms, and cultural values as well as different discourse conventions and usages (e.g. Swann et al. 2004: 149). Being polite in intercultural communication is a very complicated and sensitive skill, as politeness formulas are usually not translatable, being used in different situations, and can be easily misunderstood. Encapsulating cultural elements, L2 politeness formulas reflect intercultural differences between L1 and L2 speakers, which are responsible for communication difficulties such as misinterpretations and misconceptions (e.g. Clyne 1996; Moeschler 2004). Being polite in another culture requires skills of using culturally specific strategies and modifying verbal and non-verbal behaviour (Larina 2007).

For instance, the concept of congratulation applies to birthdays and Christmas in Korea and many other societies in the same way as it is used in such achievement situations as promotion and graduation, which is not the case in

English (Happy Birthday! Merry Christmas!). Thus, such societies' expressions can be rendered as "Congratulations on your birthday!" and "Congratulations on Christmas!" Another example is that English speakers find it difficult to understand why Japanese and Koreans say "I'm sorry" in situations when a more appropriate response is actually "thank you".

In Korean society, asking a senior addressee's age is culturally accepted. There is a politeness formula to do this, as in (3), where NM = nominative; SH = subject honorific; AH = addressee honorific; HQ = honorific question ender.

(3) *yensey ka etthehkey toy-si-p-nikka?*
age NM how become-SH-AH-HQ
'How old are you? (lit. what does your age become?)

This indirect speech formula is used to ask about a senior person's name, address, hometown, family, and even the time. Examples (4) and (5) are recent email exchanges between two senior faculty members in an American university setting. X is a Japanese female (complainant) and Y is an American male (perpetrator).

(4) Email to Y (with copies to other members)

ミーティングの部屋をどこにするかというだけのメッセージに、何故個人情報、身体的情報が公表されたのでしょうか。アメリカという国は個人情報を大切にする国だと思っていましたが、このようにコミッティーに全く関係のない人々にまで個人情報をもらすとは、余りにも無神経で、常識ある者のするべきことではないと思います。正式に謝っていただきたいと思います。. . . X

(5) Email to X (with copies to other members)[3]

I apologize for the error. I thought I was sending the message to the office staff, but I sent it by mistake to everybody. That certainly was not my intention. At the time, I THOUGHT the correct address for the staff was 000, since I use the same kind of addresses for groups. Once again, I make this apology publicly and hope that you will accept it. Y

3 Incidentally, these apology strategies essentially conform to Olshtain and Cohen's (1991) five strategies or patterns in the apology speech act set: two general strategies which depend less on contextual constraints and three situation-specific strategies: General strategies (i. formulaic expression or explicit expression of apology; ii. acknowledgment of responsibility) and Situation-specific strategies (i. explanation; ii. offer of repair; iii. promise of nonrecurrence).

Notice the different communicative styles. In (4), the main complaint in the first sentence is expressed in the passive construction, nominalised form using *no,* and the polite conjectural question, a typical formula of an indirect speech act. The request for formal apology is another carefully worded indirect speech act, using the hedge "I think", the desiderative "wish", and the humble auxiliary verb "humbly receive". The pronoun "I" does not appear at all. All these represent a typical Japanese indirect communicative style to express negative politeness. Example (5), on the other hand, expresses a sincere apology, another negative politeness strategy in B&L's terms. All the semantic formulas are assertive, worded straightforwardly and explicitly, with "I" appearing seven times and no indirect speech or hedging device appearing. This may be considered a typical American communicative style of apology.

(d) Does learning of formulas contribute to grammatical development? A series of studies in L2 acquisition indicate that there is little evidence that the use of formulas resulted in syntactic development (e.g. Bardovi-Harlig 2006: 1). For instance, Schmidt's (1983) well-known three-year longitudinal study shows that his subject Wes's grammar did not catch up with the apparent structure of his formulas. Wes's data demonstrated no subject-verb inversion in questions, except in formulaic utterances. Thus, formulaic expressions like *Shall we go, Do you have time,* and *Are you busy* were correctly uttered, whereas *Ah, you has keys?* and *When Tim is coming?* were not.

It seems to me, however, that the data does not serve as evidence for the lack of the formulas' contribution to grammatical development, because the structure of the learned formulas could slowly affect Wes's non-formulaic constructions by analogy and generalization. Indeed, the given data for Wes includes *Shall we maybe go out coffee now, or you want later?,* which gives this developmental hint. As Bardovi-Harlig (2006: 7–8) indicates, the acquisition of pragmatics by the lowest level learners has not been well documented in interlanguage pragmatics. She further mentions that R. Ellis (1984) does provide information of the development of grammar.

In view of the nature of language learning through generalization and analogy, it is legitimate to assume that repeated and frequent uses of ample formulas and conventionalized expressions in discourse frames will lead to the learner' lexical, morpho-syntactic, and semantic development, as language ability tends to develop holistically. Indeed, generalization is an essential component of human cognition, especially language. It allows people to use language in new ways they have not been directly exposed to.

(e) The use of politeness formulas allows learners early entry into communication even when there is lack of competence in target language rules. This contributes to improving the learners' discourse and conversational competence. Politeness formulas are relevant not so much to syntax but more to the discourse level in that they appear in interactive situations. Their key roles and functions are the appropriate uses of them in interactive situations in discourse situations. Thus, frequent and fluent use of politeness formulas will necessarily contribute to smooth discourse operations.

(f) Finally, the knowledge and frequent use of formulas allow for fluency in production and faster processing and comprehension, while saving the speaker planning time that can be used where it is needed more urgently. Psychologically, all this will boost the learner's courage, self-confidence, and interest in the learning and use of the target language.

5. Teaching of politeness formulas

Now, should politeness formulas be explicitly taught? As indicated in Chick (1996: 344), sociolinguists generally agree that sociolinguistic conventions and rules of different social groups can be learnt through awareness raising of one type or another and not through explicit teaching. For instance, Gumperz and Roberts (1980) suggest involving both learners and native speakers in evaluative discussion of their interethnic encounters to raise their awareness of their own contributions to miscommunication. Wolfson (1989) argues that learners' acquisition of sociolinguistic rules can be facilitated by teachers who have the necessary information and knowledge about speech acts, values, and patterns at their command.

While accepting fostering learners' awareness as a useful approach, I nevertheless subscribe to explicit teaching of politeness formulas to adult learners. First, learning of politeness formulas through awareness raising alone is insufficient and time-consuming and can be fragmentary. How can we expect a learner who is not in the L2 emersion situation to internalize the culture-bound usages of all such formulas by him- or herself from scratch within a limited time frame?

Second, politeness formulas are predictable to the native language users. Such conventionalized expressions are "situation-bound utterances" (Kecskes 2000), which constitutes a closed set. The context or situation enables the understanding of the words spoken or written, as in "Help yourself!", which is typical of a "hospitality" situation, and "Let's get together some time", which is a typical parting reply (Mey 2004: 38). In view of their relatively manageable quantity and the definable contexts in which they occur, politeness formulas are amenable to efficient curriculum design, materials development, classroom teaching, and testing. Once they are taught and learned, learners can practice and use them with native speakers in real communicative situations because such formulas are context bound, frequently occur in daily interactions, and are in immediate need. Therefore, they must be taught systematically and intensively in various contexts lest the learners use the forms inappropriately.

Third, as already indicated, language is and has to be essentially conventional in order for the speakers to mutually understand without much effort. Thus, in second language acquisition, such convention building is important for learners to communicate with native speakers with facility. Otherwise, communication will be greatly hampered, broken down, with misunderstandings resulting. One cannot expect to achieve this competence through fostering of awareness alone. Words and phrases and many grammar points can be self studied. The classroom should be used for more pragmatic training.

Fourth, in learning politeness formulas, a common source of miscommunication is pragmatic transfer, that is, the use of the rules of speaking of one's native language when interacting with members of another community. While there are ample universality-based positive transfers, there are also a host of negative transfers as well. Without contextualised culture-bound acquisition, formula use can exhibit over-generalization, under-generalization, or misuse. Using *mianhayyo* 'I'm sorry' even to one's senior by an American learner of Korean is over-generalization, because there is a separate form, *coysonghayyo,* for a senior (Sohn 2001). In cases of under-generalization, learners do not use formulas where they are expected. A formula may be misused as in the case of using *I'm sorry* by Japanese and Korean learners of English, where *Excuse me* or *Thank you* is more appropriate. Explicit contextualized teaching will contribute to keeping learners from falling into such pitfalls. Indeed, learners need the instructor's explanations of the forms and their felicitous usages but also must receive subsequent reinforcing practice for notice and intake and then take verbal and written post tests to check their learning.

Fifth, there are some experimental studies on successful explicit teaching. Olshtain and Cohen (1991) propose the following five steps for teaching speech acts.

(6) a. Diagnostic assessment
b. Model dialogue
c. The evaluation of a situation
d. Role-play activities
e. Feedback and discussion

Dunham (1992) describes ten techniques for teaching complimenting behaviour.

(7) a. Reviewing how it is done in the native culture
b. Reviewing how it is done in the United States
c. Vocabulary phrase list
d. Student practice
e. Role playing in pairs
f. Teacher role play with students in front of the class
g. Projects in which learners must compliment native speakers
h. Students' oral reports to the class following their field experiences with native speakers
i. Connecting techniques to lengthen conversation
j. Paired interaction with complimenting and connecting techniques

Sixth, some recent data-based research results also indicate that explicit instruction of L2 pragmatics is more effective for L2 acquisition than implicit instruction. For example, Kasper & Rose (2001) maintain that, although some universal pragmatic knowledge can be positively transferred from L1 to L2, adult L2 learners do not always use such information. The implication is that learners need instruction – pedagogic intervention for pragmatic development – so that they might be aware of such L1-transferable pragmatic knowledge and use it in L2 contexts (cf. Yanagisawa 2007). The studies on Japanese as a Foreign Language (JFL) classroom in this volume offer valuable insights in respect to which components could or should be taught and what kind of instructional approaches are available. Three studies are introduced below.

Tateyama (2001) reports on her investigation on the effects of explicit and implicit instruction in the use of a Japanese routine formula, *sumimasen,* on beginning JFL learners. This commonly used Japanese phrase has three different functions, i.e. getting attention ("Excuse me"), apologizing ("I'm sorry"), and expressing gratitude ("Thank you"). Both explicit and implicit groups were given four treatments over an eight-week period. The explicit group received explanations on the use of *sumimasen* and watched the same video clips, which included this routine. The implicit group received no explanations but only watched the same clips. Multiple-choice test results reveal that the explicit group performed better in items which involved higher formality, indebtedness, and severity of offence. On the other hand, the explicit group became overly polite, which suggests that the explicit instruction resulted in teaching-induced hyper-correction. The author suggests that interactional routines seem to be teachable even to beginners before they develop analysed second language knowledge.

Yoshimi (2001) examines the effects of explicit instruction on JFL learners in the use of Japanese discourse markers in narratives, such as *n desu, n desu kedo,* and *ndesu*[4] which have organizational and interactional functions. The participants were divided into experimental and control groups. The experimental group received explicit instruction which consisted of (a) the explanatory handout, (2) the native speaker (NS) model, (3) the planning session (composing their stories with NSs), (4) communicative practice (perform their planned telling to an NS), and (5) feedback (given by NSs). The experimental group received such explicit instruction three times per week over 16 weeks, which was withheld from the control group except for regular, in-class small group interaction with NSs. The quantitative analysis reveals that in the post-treatment storytelling, the experimental group made significant gains in both frequency and accuracy (i.e. not producing errors), while no discourse markers were produced by the control group, which indicates the beneficial effects of explicit instruction combined with communicative practice and feedback.

Cook (2001) investigates JFL learners' pragmatic awareness of a Japanese polite speech style. The three conventionalized expressions like those in (8) share the same referential content, but have different linguistic features denoting different levels of politeness or humbleness.

(8) a. *Doozo yoroshiku*
b. *Doozo yoroshiku onegai shimasu*
c. *Doozo yoroshiku onegai itashimasu*
Lit. 'I humbly request you to treat me well.'

Cook reports that 80 percent of the 120 JFL experimental learners, who were asked to listen to three job applicants with expressions like (8), focused only on the referential content and were unable to recognize the polite versus impolite speech styles indexed by linguistic features (e.g. plain verb form or *-masu*). They were unable to recognize polite hedges such as to *omoimasu* 'I think' either.

Through interviews with instructors, Cook found that except for the difference between the formal *masu* and informal plain verb forms, the instructors were not aware of the co-occurring features that contributed to the polite versus impolite speech styles. Accordingly, no explicit instruction was given in respect to the pragmatic meaning indexed by these features. Based on the findings, Cook suggests that it is necessary to teach a range of co-occurring linguistic features that constitute a particular speech style and that it is important for these features, especially the relationship between a linguistic form and its social meaning, to be brought to learners' attention so that they will become more noticeable.

4 Korean equivalents would be *ketunyo, nunteyyo, nun ke yeyeyo*, etc.

There are two important implications in Cook's findings. First, instructors should be trained in both the pragmatic awareness of politeness formulas and effective instructional methods so that they may effectively teach formulas to students. Second, extensive pragmatic and pedagogical research should be conducted from a cross-cultural perspective to prepare for such teacher training (see next section).

All the above research results can be applied to learners of Korean, English, and other languages. For instance, rough Korean equivalents of (8) are like (9).

(9) a. *cal pwuthakha-nta*
b. *cal pwuthakha-y*
c. *ca pwuthakha-ney*
d. *cal pwuthakha-yyo*
e. *cal puthakha-pnita*
f. *cal puthak tuli-keyss-sumnita*
Lit. 'I humbly request your favour to treat me well.'

Roughly speaking, the formulas in (9) are typically used when the speaker is introduced to a social equal for the first time or when the speaker sincerely asks a favour of the addressee. In the former case, their function is more or less ritualistic and usually the interactants exchange the same formula. In the latter case, the speech act is somehow not considered imposition on the addressee, but rather tends to enhance the addressee's face by recognizing the his/her ability or power to handle the requested matter. It is up to the addressee whether to comply with the request or not. Different speech levels are involved from 'plain' in (9a) to 'deferential' in (9e), appropriate use of which is essential. In (9f), features such as *tuli* 'give to a higher person' and *–keyss* '(I) will' are added to *pwuthak* 'asking favor'. Contextualized acquisition of the formulas cannot be expected without elaborate explicit instruction.

Thus, in order for politeness formulas to take meaningful roles and functions in L2 pragmatics and second language acquisition, they must be captured, taught, and learned systematically. It must be emphasized that formulas must be taught with appropriate contexts (or situations) given, not at the syntactic but at the discourse level of speech acts. Well-organized explicit classroom instruction should at least include the following items:

(10) a. presentation of natural syntactic collocations in which the formula occurs and natural discourse frames in which those sentences occur
b. succinct explanations of semantic-pragmatic meanings of the formula
c. explicit account of the contexts where it can and cannot occur

d. cross-cultural comparison
e. context-based interactive practices
f. recognition and production tests (e.g. multiple-choice identification tests, role plays)

In addition, various instructional strategies proposed by many researchers should be taken into account to design the best classroom models possible.

6. Research on acquisition of L2 politeness formulas

In view of the significant roles they play in intercultural pragmatics and second language acquisition, more extensive data-based pragmatic and pedagogical research covering a wide range of politeness formulas is required from a L1/L2 comparative perspective. The role and function of formulas and the learning of formulas and formulaic sequences have only just begun to be described through empirical research for adult learners in the area of second language pragmatics. The fact that Kasper & Rose (2001) is the first edited volume devoted solely to data-based classroom research on general L2 pragmatics eloquently indicates that the research in the field is still in the fledgling stage.

So far, research on politeness formulas appears to have heavily concentrated on requests and apologies.[5] Regarding apologies, for example, more than a dozen research papers focus on the Japanese apology act *sumimasen* alone in regard to cross-cultural misunderstanding between Americans and Japanese. These studies include Coulmas (1981), Kimura (1994), Ide (1998), Kumatoridani (1999), and Tateyama (2001).

Several studies on apologies in English have been conducted from a cross-cultural perspective, usually employing a discourse completion test as their analytic tool (e.g. Cohen & Olshtain 1981; Trosborg 1987; Blum-Kulka et al. 1989; Olshtain 1989). Larina's quantitative study on English and Russian politeness strategies for requests and invitations reveals a clear cross-cultural difference. Eighty English and eighty Russian native speakers were used for the study. To social inferiors, English speakers predominantly used indirect formulas such as "I'd like to ~", "Can I ~", "Will you kindly ~", "Would you (kindly) ~", "Would you like to ~", "Would you mind ~", "Could I ~", and "Could you possibly ~". On the other hand, Russians predominantly used imperatives in the same contexts. Larina indicates that Russians regard indirect speech acts in such contexts are insincere and ambiguous and thus inappropriate. She attributes the distinct

5 For Korean, 'requests' are dealt with in Byun (2006) and others and "apologies" in Sohn (2001).

linguistic phenomena to English-speakers' culture valuing "personal autonomy/privacy" and "equality" and Russians' culture valuing "collectivism" and "power distance". Thus, unlike in English communication, indirect strategies are less typical and direct style prevails for Russian communication, because of the traditional short social distance between individuals and relatively high power distance.

Apologies, requests, and invitations are only a tip of the iceberg in the vast areas of speech acts. There is a rich vein yet to be explored. Typically, politeness formulas include speech act patterns where strong face-oriented linguistic politeness is called for. Searle's (1969, 1979) classification of speech acts and Holtgraves's (2005b) work based on Searle's show an extensive list of interactive speech acts. These include (a) Directives: request, recommend, suggest, forbid, advise, claim, warn, encourage, beg, demand, ask, invite; (b) Commissives: refuse, consent, accept an offer, accept an apology, reject an offer, threaten, promise, offer, reassure; (c) Assertives: accuse, argue, predict, admit, criticize, agree, blame, remind, guess, deny, correct, introduce, excuse; and (d) Expressives: praise, condole, disapprove, approve, greet, welcome, sympathy, thanks, apology, complain, brag, congratulate, compliment.

Every one of these speech acts deserves exploration from data-based pragmalinguistic, sociopragmatic, discoursal, cross-cultural, and/or pedagogical perspectives. In particular, results of research on politeness formulas in these perspectives will be of enormous significance to L2 acquisition.

REFERENCES: Chapter 23

Bardovi-Harlig, K. 2006. On the role of formulas in the acquisition of L2 pragmatics. In Bardovi-Harlig, K., J.C. Felix-Brasdefer, and A.S. Omar (eds.), *Pragmatics & Language Learning* 11: 1–28 (2006). NFLRC, University of Hawaii at Manoa.

Blum-Kulka, S., J. House, and G. Kasper (eds.). 1989. *Cross-cultural Pragmatics: Requests and Apologies*. Norwood, NJ: Ablex.

Brown, P. and S. Levinson. 1978. Universals in language usage: In Goody, E. (ed.), *Questions and Politeness. Strategies in Social Interaction*, 56–289. Cambridge, UK: Cambridge University Press,

Brown, P. and S. Levinson. 1987. *Politeness. Some Universals in Language Usage*. Cambridge, UK: Cambridge University Press.

Byon, S.P. 2006. Korean cultural values in request behaviors. In Sohn, H.M. (ed.), *Korean Language in Culture and Society*. Honolulu: University of Hawaii Press. 2006.

Chick, J.K. 1996. Intercultural communication. In Mckay, S.L. and N.H. Hornberger (eds.), *Sociolinguistics and Language Teaching*, 329–48. Cambridge, UK: Cambridge University Press.

Clyne, M. 1996. *Inter-cultural Communication at Work: Cultural Values in Discourse.* Cambridge, UK: Cambridge University Press.

Cohen, A.and E. Olshtain. 1981. Developing a measure of socio-cultural competence: The case of apology. *Language Learning* 31(1): 113–34.

Cook, Haruko M. 2001. Why can't learners of JFL distinguish polite from impolite speech styles? In Kasper, G. and K.R. Rose (2001): chapter 5.

Coulmas, F. 1981. Introduction: Conversational routine. In Coulmas, F. (ed.), *Conversational Routine. Explorations in Standardized Communications Situations and Pre-patterned Speech* 2:1–18. The Hague: Mouton.

Dulay, H., M. Burt, and S. Krashen. 1982. *Language Two.* Oxford: Oxford University Press.

Dunham, P. 1992. Using compliments in the ESL classroom: an analysis of culture and gender. *Minne TESOL Journal* 10: 75–85.

Ellis, R. 1984. *Classroom Second Language Development.* Oxford: Pergamon.

Fraser, B. 1980. Conversational mitigation. *Journal of Pragmatics,* 4: 341–50.

Fraser, B. 1990. Perspectives on politeness. *Journal of Pragmatics,* 14: 219–36.

Grice, H.P. 1975. Logic and conversation. In Cole, P. and J. Morgan (eds.), *Syntax and Semantics, Vol. 3: Speech Acts*, 41–58. New York: Academic Press.

Gumperz, J. and C. Roberts. 1980. Developing Awareness Skills for Interethnic Communication. *Occasional Papers* No. 12. Singapore: SEAMEO Regional Language Centre.

Hill, B. et al. 1986. Universal of linguistic politeness: quantitative evidence
from Japanese and American English. *Journal of Pragmatics*, 10: 347–71.

Holtgraves, T. 2005a. Social psychology, cognitive psychology, and linguistic politeness. *Journal of Politeness Research* 1.1: 73–93.

Holtgraves, T. 2005b. The production and perception of implicit performatives. *Journal of Pragmatics* 37: 2024–43.

House, J. 1996. Developing pragmatic fluency in English as a foreign language: Routines and metapragmatic awareness. *Studies in Second Language Acquisition* 17: 225–52.

Ide, R. 1998. 'Sorry for your kindness': Japanese interactional ritual in public discourse. *Journal of Pragmatics.* 29: 509–29.

Janney, R.W. and H. Arndt. 1992. Intra-cultural tact versus intercultural tact. In Watts, R.J. et al. (eds.), *Politeness in Language.* Berlin: Mouton.

Kallia, A. 2005. Directness as a source of misunderstanding: The case of requests and suggestions. In Lakoff, R. & S. Ide (eds.) 2005.

Kasper G. and K.R. Rose (eds.). 2001. *Pragmatics in Language Teaching.* Cambridge, UK: Cambridge University Press.

Kecskes, I. 2000. A cognitive-pragmatic approach to situation-bound utterances. *Journal of Pragmatics* 32: 605–25.

Kimura, Ki. 1994. Multiple functions of *Sumimasen. Issues in Applied Linguistics* (Regents of the University of California) 5.2: 279–302.

Kumatoridani, T. 1999. Alternation and co-occurrence in Japanese thanks. *Journal of Pragmatics,* 31: 623–42.

Lakoff, R. 1973. The logic of politeness: or minding your p's and q's. *Papers from the Ninth Regional Meeting of the Chicago Linguistic Society.* Chicago: Chicago Linguistic Society, 292–305.

Lakoff, R. and S. Ide (eds.). 2005. *Broadening the Horizons of Linguistic Politeness.* Amsterdam: John Benjamins.

Larina, T. 2007. Cultural values and negative politeness in English and Russian. Linguistic List. E-mail: larinat@list.ru.

Leech, G.N. 1983. *Principles of Pragmatics*. London/New York: Longman.

Locher, M.A. and R.J. Watts. 2005. Politeness theory and relational work. *Journal of Politeness Research* 1.1: 9–33.

Mey, J.L. 2001. *Pragmatics: An Introduction.* Boston & Oxford: Blackwell.

Mey, J.L. 2004. Between culture and pragmatics: Scylla and Charlbdis? The precarious condition of intercultural pragmatics. *Intercultural Pragmatics* 1.1: 27–48.

Moeschler, J. 2004. Intercultural pragmatics: A cognitive approach. *Intercultural Pragmatics* 1.1: 49–70.

Olshtain, E. 1989. Apologies across languages. In Blum-Kulka, S. et al. (1989).

Olshtain, E. and A.D. Cohen. 1990. Thee learning of complex speech act behavior. *TESL Canada Journal,* 7(2): 45–65.

Olshtain, E. and A.D. Cohen. 1991. Teaching speech act behavior to nonnative speakers. In Celce-Murcia, M. (ed.) *Teaching English as a Second or Foreign Language.* New York: Newbury House.

Schmidt, R. 1983. Interaction, acculturation, and the acquisition of communicative competence: A case study of an adult. In Judd, E. & N. Wolfson (eds.), *Sociolinguistics and Language Acquisition.* Rowley, MA: Newbury House.

Schmitt, N. (ed.). 2004. *Formulaic Sequences: Acquisition, Processing and Use.* Amsterdam: John Benjamins.

Searle, J. 1969. *Speech Acts.* Cambridge: Cambridge University Press.

Searle, J. 1979. *Expression and Meaning.* Cambridge, UK: Cambridge University Press.

Sohn, Ho-min. 1989. Linguistic devices of Korean politeness. *Papers from the Sixth International Conference on Korean Linguistics,* 655–69.

Sohn, H.M. 2001. "Teaching Politeness Routines in Korean." *The Korean Language in America* 6: 25–35.

Swann, J., A. Deumert, T. Lillis, and R. Mesthrie. 2004. *A Dictionary of Sociolinguisitcs*. Edinburgh: Edinburgh University Press.

Tateyama, Y. 2001. Explicit and implicit teaching of pragmatic routines: Japanese *sumimasen.* In Kasper, G. and K.R. Rose (2001): chapter 10.

Trosborg, A. 1987. Apology strategies in natives/non-natives. *Journal of Pragmatics* 11: 147–67.

Tsuzuki, M., K. Takahashi, C. Patschke, and Qin Zhang. 2005. Selection of linguistic forms for requests and offers: Comparison between English and Chinese. In Lakoff, R. and S. Ide (2005).

Watts, R.J., S. Ide, and K. Ehlich (eds.). 2005. *Politeness in Language.* Berlin: Mouton de Gruyter.

Wolfson, N. 1989. *Perspectives: Sociolinguistics and TESOL.* New York: Newbury House.

Wray, A. 2000. Formulaic sequences in second language teaching: Principle and practice. *Applied Linguistics* 21: 463–89.

Yanagisawa, M. 2007. Review of Kasper, G. and K.R. Rose (eds.), 2001. Electronic Journal of Foreign Language Teaching Vol. 4, Suppl. 1: 73–7. (Centre for Language Studies, National University of Singapore)

Yoshimi, D. 2001. Explicit instruction and JFL learner's use of interactional discourse markers. In Kasper, G. and K.R. Rose (2001): chapter 11.

24 Politeness as a Cause of Linguistic Change in Korean*

1. In Korean, a series of recently innovated sentence enders are used very productively in daily conversation, more frequently than the canonical sentence-type enders that incorporate six speech levels. These new interactive enders occur in only two speech levels, polite (marked) and intimate (unmarked), take only one sentence type, declarative or interrogative, and share a common pragmatic feature of "mitigated illocutionary force."

The aim of this presentation is to observe what these new enders are and what kind of semantic-pragmatic functions they perform, to speculate on how they came into being, and to propose that strategic politeness was a main cause for triggering such rather radical grammatical innovations.

2. Let us first examine the data in (1) through (6).[1] Korean sentences are given in the polite ender *yo,* followed by a rough terminal intonation contour.

(1) a. *pi* *ka* *o-**nun-tey*** *yo* ~
rain NM come-RL-place POL
'It's raining. [What shall we/I do?]'

b. *pi* *ka* *o-**nun-ka*** *yo?* /
rain NM come-RL-whether POL
'[Do you think] it's raining?'

c. *pi* *ka* *o-**nun-ci*** *yo?* \
rain NM come-RL-if POL
'[I wonder if] it's raining.'

* This paper was presented at the 2007 colloquium of the Institute for Advanced Study of La Trobe University, Melbourne, Australia on November 19. An original related idea was presented at the 1990 Association for Asian Studies Meeting in Chicago.

1 This paper was finalized when I was staying at La Trobe University Research Center for Linguistic Typology (RCLT). I am grateful to Bob Dixon and Sasha Aikhenvald for inviting me as a distinguished scholar to the RCLT.

(2) a. *pi* *ka* *o-**ketun*** *yo~*
Rain NM come-since/if POL
'It's raining, [that's why.]'

b. *pi* *ka* *o-**na*** *yo?/*
rain NM come-or POL
'Is it raining? [I wonder.]'

(3) *pi* *ka* *o-n-**ta-nikka*** *yo/*
rain NM come-IN-DC-because POL
'[I told you that] it's raining.'

(4) *pi* *ka* *o-**te-la-ko*** *yo*
rain NM come-RT-DC-QT POL
'It was raining, [you know.]'

(5) *pi* *ka* *o-**ci*** *yo?~*
rain NM come-NOM POL
'It's raining, [isn't it?]'

(6) *pi* *ka* *o-**l-ke-l*** *yo/*
rain NM come-PRS-fact-AC POL
'It will probably rain, [I suppose.]'

All the bold-faced parts are innovated enders whose exact meanings are hard to define. Only the approximate meanings are given in brackets under each sentence. The three forms in (1), *-nun-tey, -nun-ka,* and *-nun-ci,* are also used as conjunctive enders with slightly different meanings. The conjunctive –*nun-tey* is a background information provider, meaning 'given that', and *-nun-ka* 'whether' and *-nun-ci* 'if, whether' denote indirect questions. These enders developed originally from the relative clause construction, consisting of the indicative relativizer *–nun* and its bound head noun, *tey* 'place', *ka* 'whether', or *ci* 'if'.

The forms *–ketun* and *–na* in (2) are inherent conjunctive enders with the meanings respectively of the conditional or mild reason 'since, (even) if, provided that, given that'[2] and the alternative question 'or, whether…or'. When the form *–ketun* is used as a conjunctive ender, it usually means condition and rarely

2 As conditional, the suffix *–ketun* is used only when the following main clause denotes the speaker's intention (e.g. imperative, propositive, and intentive).

reason. As a sentence ender, it does not carry a conditional sense but the sense of mild justification. The form *–ta-nikka* 'I told you' in (3) developed from *–ta ko ha-nikka* 'because (I) told you that' where *–ta* is a declarative ender, *ko* is a quotative particle, *ha* is the verb of saying, and *–nikka* 'because, as' is a conjunctive ender denoting strong reason.

The form *te-la-ko* in (4) is a quotative construction in which the quotative particle *ko* 'that' is preceded by the retrospective suffix *–te* (speaker's own observation or experience) and the declarative ender *la* (a variant of *ta*). The form *–ci* in (5) is a nominalizer which typically occurs before a negative verb or adjective (as in *pi ka o-ci anh-ayo* 'it is not raining'). The sequence *–(u)l-ke-l* in (6) consists of a prospective relativizer *–(u)l* and its bound head noun *ke(s)* 'thing, fact' followed by the accusative particle *–(u)l.*

Thus, none of the innovated sentence enders in (1) through (6) are canonical sentence enders and none of the sentences in which the enders occur is a typical sentence. Furthermore, none of the enders carries their denotative or referential meanings but only the speaker's modality meaning of one sort or another.

3. Based on the above observations, we may hypothesize that all sentence enders in (1) through (6) have developed from subordinate clauses with the unrecoverable omission of relevant main clauses. Naturally, we have no way of knowing exactly who originated the innovations, where and when. We also do not know what specific subordinate and main clauses were actually involved in generating the innovations. I assume, however, that the structural change was of the pattern given in (7).

(7) [Subordinate Clause X + Main Clause Y]S > [Main Clause X]S

The pattern (7) states that the Main Clauses (Ys) in complex sentences were diachronically deleted; and the original subordinate Clauses (Xs) were restructured as main clauses. During this process, the elements that ended the subordinate Clauses became Main Clause enders through grammatical reanalysis and semantic-pragmatic shifts. Once generated as new grammatical morphemes in this way, the enders must have spread analogically and were used productively as they are now.

No doubt, all of the sentences with the innovated sentence enders are perceived and used as complete simple sentences by contemporary Koreans, although dictionaries rarely contain the enders. Even if some dictionaries include a few of them, their functions are not defined properly. Thus, for example, Martin, et al.'s (1967: 369) Korean-English Dictionary includes the ender *–nun-tey* as a sentence-final exclamatory that shows surprise or interest, similar to 'You see it's a case of doing...' Some other dictionaries define the sentence ender –*ketun* as an exclamatory, meaning 'surely, indeed'.

One may wonder what kinds of solid evidence there are for the proposal that the sentence enders in question developed from subordinate clauses by way of diachronic main clause omission. The following pieces of evidence may be advanced.

First, as indicated in the above, all the innovated enders are also used as subordinate clause elements in Contemporary Korean, as illustrated in (8) through (13).

(8) a. *pi ka o-**nun-tey** ka-l kka yo?* /
rain NM come-RL-place go-PRS Q POL
'Shall we/I go despite the rain?'

b. *pi ka o-**nun-ka** po-sey-yo* \
rain NM come-RL-whether see-SH-POL
'Please see whether it's raining.'

c. *pi ka o-**nun-ci** a-sey-eyo?* /
rain NM come-RL-if know-SH-POL
'Do you know if it's raining?'

(9) a. *pi ka o-**ketun** o-sey-yo* \
Rain NM come-since/if come-SH-POL
'Please come if it's raining.'

b. *pi ka o-**na** alapo-sey-yo* \
rain NM come-or check-SH-POL
'Please check to see if it's raining.'

(10) *pi ka o-n-**ta** **(ko ha)-nikka** an w-ayo*
rain NM come-IN-DC QT say-because not come-POL
'Because (I) said it was raining, (he) does not come.'

(11) *pi ka o-**te-la** **ko** hay-ss-eyo* \
rain NM come-RT-DC QT say-PST-POL
'(Somebody) said he/she saw it raining.'

(12) *pi ka o-**ci** an h-ayo?* /
rain NM come-NOM not do-POL
'Isn't it raining?'

(13) *pi* *ka* *o-**l*** ***ke*** ***l*** *moll-ass-eyo?* /
rain NM come-PRS fact AC not.know-PST-POL
'Didn't you know that it would rain?'

The coexistence of the same or similar forms with similar meanings in two different syntactic functions is a strong piece of evidence that one diverged from the other, as per Hopper's (1991) principle of "divergence" (A > A, B) in incipient grammaticalization. The direction of divergence must have been from subordinate to main, because, as subordinate elements, they generally have referential meanings, whereas, as sentence enders, their meanings are abstract, indicating the speaker's modality. It is a generally accepted thesis among grammaticalization scholars that semantic and pragmatic changes are from basic, usually concrete, literal and objective meanings to gradually more metaphorically and metonymically extended, abstract, and (the speaker's) subjective meanings. Historically also, none of the subordinate-clause elements in question appeared in sentence-final positions in Middle Korean, which indicates that the innovations occurred relatively in recent times.

Secondly, all innovated sentence enders show a variety of morpho-syntactic limitations. This fact also indicates that they are recent innovations which still retain their original syntactic and morphological properties, as per Hopper's (ibid.) principle of "persistence" in incipient grammaticalization. For one, all of them can take only the polite-level particle *yo,* otherwise they are in the intimate level. The attachment of polite *yo* to the innovated enders is not a newly developed process, because *yo* can be attached to any type of sentence and any major constituent of a sentence if politeness is intended. The fact that no other speech-level enders can come after the innovated enders are illustrated in (14).

(14) a. **pi* *ka* *o-nun-tey-**p-ni-ta***
rain NM come-RL-place-AH-IN-DC
'It's raining. [what shall we do?]' (deferential declarative)

b. **pi* *ka* *o-ci-**ni**?*
rain NM come-NOM-Q
'It's raining, [isn't it?]' (plain interrogative)

Furthermore, the innovated sentence enders must be interpreted either only as declarative or only as interrogative. In (1) through (6), the sentences marked by a question mark must be used only as questions, otherwise always as declarative. For instance, *-nun-tey* cannot be used in other sentence types than the declarative. Moreover, all enders must be followed by their unique intonation contours, as marked in (1) through (6).

Third, the innovated sentence enders do not fit in any traditional canonical paradigms of enders. They indeed form a new paradigm or grammatical category with a new set of morphological enders. This may be viewed as conforming to Lehmann's (1985) principle of "paradigmatization" (the tendency for grammaticalized forms to be arranged into paradigms). We are yet to devise a proper term to designate this paradigm or category. In Korean, we already have categories like mood, modal, addressee honorific, and sentence type.

One last piece of evidence to justify the diachronic main clause omission is that the newly developed sentence enders tend to retain some of the essential semantic material of the putatively omitted main clauses, as per Hopper's principle of persistence. In particular, as will be seen in more detail later, the new enders incorporate certain generalized meanings of the putatively omitted main clause predicates. For example, the innovated ender *–nun-tey* in (1a) contains such implied meanings as 'what are you going to do?' or 'what shall we/I do?', although these implied meanings are far weaker than the meanings given by the explicit main clause predicate such as in (15).

(15) *pi* *ka* *o-nun-tey* ***ettehkey*** ***ha-si-keyss**-eyo?*
rain NM come-RL-place how do-SH-will-POL
'It's raining, what will you do?'

In short, all the above observations support the proposal that there was diachronic main clause deletion for the genesis of the new grammatical paradigm.

4. Let us now speculate on how grammaticalization followed non-recoverable main clause deletion. In Contemporary Korean, main clauses, as well as other major constituents, are extensively omitted in conversation when they are uniquely recoverable from the given discourse contexts or speech situations. For example, observe the dialogue in (16).

(16) a. Father: *ilha-le* *an* *ka-ni?*
work-to not go-Q
'Aren't (you) going to work?'

b. Son: *pi* *ka* *an* *o-myen* *yo.*
rain NM not come-if POL
'If it does not rain.'

The omitted main clause in (16b) is easily recoverable from (16a). The main clause deletion which is uniquely recoverable from contexts is a synchronic process. In this case, no grammaticalization takes place because there is a synchronic discourse trace of the omitted clause. Grammaticalization processes such as grammatical reanalysis and semantic-pragmatic shift must have been activated only after an omitted main clause was no longer uniquely recoverable from the discourse context. Such an unrecoverable omission is possible when the speaker omits his or her own main clause in the discourse. For example, observe (17).

(17) a. Father: *ilha-le an ka-ni?*
'Aren't you going to work?'

b. Son: i. *pi ka o-nun-tey ettehkey ka-yo?*
'How can I go in the rain?!'

ii. *pi ka o-nun-tey yo.* ~
'It's raining.
(I cannot go; how can I go?; what shall I do?...)'

Notice that *–nun-tey* is used as a conjunctive ender in (17bi) and as a main clause ender in (17bii). In the latter case, no main clause is uniquely recoverable. The speech situation might give some hints as to the omitted main clause that the speaker may have intended, but syntactically such a clause cannot be recovered due to the opacity. If native speakers intentionally or habitually continue to omit a certain type of main clause in certain local situations for one reason or another, then language-internal grammaticalization processes tend to be activated. Such processes are semantic-pragmatic shifts accompanied by grammatical reanalysis that may involve decategorization, recategorization, agglutination, contraction, fusion, deletion, and so on. Since the sentence-final position in predicate-final languages like Korean is the speaker's territory of modality, it is natural that grammaticalization in that position takes place with the speaker as the center. This kind of situation must have happened when the sentence ender –*nun-tey* developed from the conjunctive ender. The form *–nun-tey* in (17bii) is an innovated sentence ender, which can be schematically shown in (18).

(18)

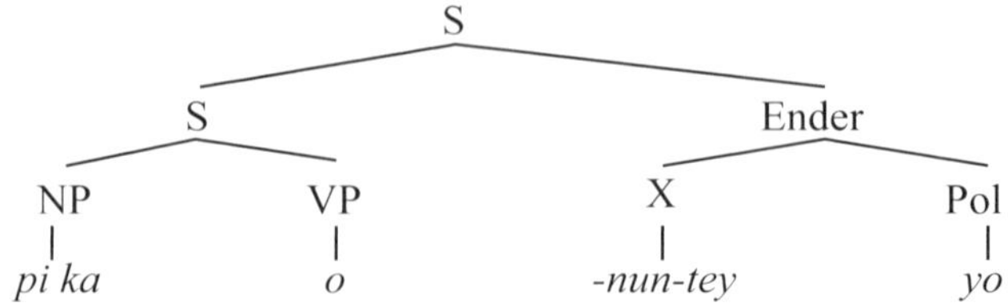

Thus, it is assumed that the direction of development of *–nun-tey* is from the relative clause head with its referential meaning (Relativizer + Noun in the sense of 'the place where...'), to a conjunctive ender for background provision (in the sense of 'given that…'), and then to the sentence ender with the modal meaning of softening illocutionary force (in the sense of 'what shall we/I do'). This directional assumption is supported by the current theory that the direction of grammaticalization is toward gradual semantic-pragmatic abstraction, as already indicated. This supports Traugott's (1982) proposed formula: propositional > textual > expressive.

All the other sentence enders in (1) through (6) are considered as results of essentially the same grammaticalization that took place following native speakers' frequent main clause omissions. There are some individual differences too. One intriguing ender is *–te-la-ko* in (4), which is repeated in (19).

(19) *pi* *ka* *o-**te-la-ko*** *yo*
rain NM come-RT-DC-QT POL
'It was raining, you know.'

Sentences with *–te-la-ko* are very frequently used in conversation to narrate or report the speaker's own personal experience and observation. It appears that this innovated sentence ender developed through two stages: first, genesis of the sentence ender *ko* and, second, coalescence of this *ko* with the retrospective sentence ender *–te-la.*

In Contemporary Korean, the bare quotative particle *ko* is widely used in two contexts, one in a response to an echo-question, as in (20b), and the other as an illocutionary force mitigating device, as in (21b).

(20) a. Father: *mwue-la* *ko* *(hay-ss-ni)?*
What-be.DC QT say-PST-Q
'What did you say?'

b. Son: *pi* *ka* *o-n-ta* ***ko*** *yo*
rain NM come-IN-DC QT POL
'(I said) it's raining.'

(21) a. Father: *ilha-le* *an* *ka-ni?*
'Aren't you going to work?'

b. Son: *pi* *ka* *o-n-ta* ***ko*** *yo*
rain NM come-IN-DC QT POL
'It's raining, you see.'

In (20b), the main clause verb of saying (*hay-ss* 'said') is understood and thus *ko* functions as an indirect quotative particle, whereas in (21b), no such uniquely recoverable verb can be posited. One may think of many possible main clauses such as "Didn't I tell you it's raining?" and "Should I tell you it's raining?" In order to avoid expressing such blunt remarks, the speaker (the son) simply omits the entire main clause, leaving behind the quotative particle *ko* alone. As a result of the frequent uses of this kind of indirect strategy, the bare or orphanated quotative particle is assumed to have grammaticalized as a sentence ender that denotes the speaker's mild assertion of the propositional content of the new main clause, together with allusion to omitted main clause predicates.

This innovated *ko* obviously coalesced with the retrospective sentence ender *–te-la* to generate the extended ender *te-la-ko,* as per Lehmann's (1985) principle of "coalescence" in grammaticalization. The derived grammatical meaning is the speaker's narration or report of his or her own experience or observation. Notice that the innovated ender retains the reportive meaning, although the main verb of saying is not expressed.

Now, we can tentatively generalize the derivations of the grammatical meanings of innovated sentence enders roughly as in (22).

(22) A grammaticalized sentence ender has complex semantic-pragmatic meanings, composed of (a) the speaker (functioning as an abstract subject), (b) the diluted and generalized meaning of omitted main predicates (functioning as an abstract predicate), (c) the more or less bleached meanings of the individual morphemes constituting the ender, including the sentence-final intonation, and (d) other pragmatically introduced meanings.

The semantic and pragmatic analysis of the innovated sentence enders summarized in (22) is essentially applicable to all the enders in (1) through (6). For example, the innovated ender *-te-la-ko* is interpreted as having the semantic-pragmatic meaning of something like "I MILDLY AND CASUALLY INFORM YOU THAT I OBSERVED (it raining)." As already indicated, sentence enders in Korean are the speaker's territory for his performative acts of various types. Thus, the speaker functions naturally as the abstract performative subject in all enders. The statement meaning comes from the original declarative sentence ender *-la* and the falling intonation. The reportive meaning is abstracted from a typical deleted predicate, that is, a verb of saying. The complement meaning of "THAT" is from the quotative particle *ko*. The meaning of "I OBSERVED" comes from the retrospective suffix *-te*. The mildness in reportive illocution is due to the absence of an explicit reportive verb. Some pragmatic meaning of casualness seems to be due to the omission of the main clause.[3]

5. We have thus far observed that repeated non-recoverable main clause omissions have triggered grammaticalization. Our next question is: Why did speakers repeatedly omit a certain type of main clause even when it could not be uniquely recoverable? In other words, what caused the frequent non-recoverable omission? One possible answer may be that it is due to the minimum effort principle, that is, to minimize speech production effort, as in the case of recoverable omissions. If this answer is correct, the semantic-pragmatic meaning of illocutionary force mitigation is simply the effect of grammaticalization, and not the cause or motivation. In this interpretation, however, a number of questions come to mind. For one, the economy principle in communication normally applies only to the extent that no communicative ambiguity thereby results. Non-recoverable omissions go against this principle. It would violate, for example, Grice's (1975) Cooperative maxims, especially, that of quantity and manner and Lakoff's (1973) rule of clarity (i.e. "Be clear"). Also, there are a large number of conjunctive enders, relative heads, nominalized constructions, and other subordinate elements which have not diverged to become sentence enders. One would naturally wonder why they have not undergone the minimum-effort principle. Furthermore, conversation is carried out not only by omitting contextually recoverable elements but also by adding many illocution reducing or illocution strengthening elements including clauses, violating the principle of minimum effort. For instance, in addition to the direct speech in (22a), native speakers of Korean use nominalized expressions as in (22b) and clauses equivalent to English 'it seems *or* it appears that', as in (22c) out of courtesy or humility, even if the speaker is sure of the propositional content.

(22) a. *e* *an* *ka-yo*
I not go-POL
'I am not going.'

b. *ce* *an* *ka-l* *ke* *yey-yo*
I not go-PRS fact be-POL
'I am probably not going.'

3 My analysis of the reinterpreted grammatical meaning is partly in agreement with Bybee's (1988) proposal that the lexical meaning of a morpheme or construction serves as the basis for semantic substance in grammaticalization, and with Sweetser's (1988) proposal that the aspect of meaning which is preserved in grammaticalization is the (metaphorically structured) image-schematic referential structure, as well as with Hopper's (1991) principle of persistence. See also Hopper and Traugott (2003).

c. *ce* *an* *ka-l* *ke* *kath-ayo*
I not go-PRS fact same-POL
'It appears that I am not going.'

Finally, extensive daily uses of the innovated sentence enders illustrated in (1) through (6) are also against the minimum effort principle.

One might propose the frequency of use of certain subordinate elements or enders as the cause of unrecoverable main clause omission and subsequent grammaticalization. Indeed, frequency of use is one of the major causes of grammaticalization, but the issue here is what caused frequent main clause omission which activated grammaticalization. The most frequently used conjunctive enders like *–ko* 'and', *-ese* 'and (then), as', and *–umyen* 'if' and nominalizers like *-ki* and *–um* have not been grammaticalized as sentence enders, precisely because main clause deletion did not and do not productively occur in complex sentences with such enders.

Then, what is it that motivated unrecoverable main clause omission that led to the genesis of a new paradigm of grammatical morphemes in question? As was alluded to in connection with the grammaticalization involved in *–nun-tey* and *ko*, I would like to propose that main clause omission was motivated by native speakers to mitigate, dilute, or tone down the illocutionary force contained in main clauses in their own speech acts. We may say that native speakers flouted or violated, for instance, Lakoff's rule of clarity or Grice's Cooperative maxims to express strategic linguistic politeness. That is, native speakers of Korean deliberately omitted (and still do) main clauses of certain complex sentences to avoid coerciveness or imposition toward their interlocutors in face-threatening speech acts. In other words, strategic linguistic politeness for smooth interpersonal communication appears to have been the main cause for repeated main clause omission, which triggered structure-internal grammaticalization. Grammaticalization processes may have originated synchronically and conversationally at first, but as time passed with repeated usage, the forms involved must have become conventionalized and diachronically reanalyzed and fossilized as grammatical elements. This is somewhat parallel to English speakers' use of such conventionalized interrogative forms as "**Can you/would you** pass the salt?" and "**May I** borrow your pen?" for polite requests, although these expressions are not yet crystallized as grammatical morphemes as in Korean. I will elaborate this proposal in terms of politeness theory in what follows.

6. It has been known that language has two interrelated functions: (a) a transactional function which purports to establish an optimally efficient transmission of information, and (b) an interactional function which purports to establish and maintain interpersonal relationships. In speech acts, principles such as Grice's (1975) Cooperative maxims (quality, quantity, manner, relevance) and Lakoff's (1973) rule of clarity (i.e. "Be clear") are to be observed in order to maximize the transactional function of language. The interactional function of language, on the other hand, is performed by native speakers via a variety of putatively universal politeness principles and strategies, as well as culture-specific norms and values and language-specific politeness devices. Several insightful proposals have been advanced for universal politeness principles and strategies. For example, Lakoff's (1973) rules of politeness consist of (a) Don't impose, (b) Give options, and (c) Make addressee feel good. Leech's (1983) Politeness Principle, Maximize polite beliefs; minimize impolite beliefs, include the maxims of tact, generosity, approbation, modesty, agreement, and sympathy. For example, Leech's maxim of tact (i.e. strategic conflict avoidance) reads "Minimize cost to other and maximize benefit to other."

Fraser (1980, 1990) advances a so-called conversational-contract view. He suggests that politeness operates within the current terms and conditions of the conversational contract entered into by the participants in an interaction in an effort to maintain a conflict-free interaction. Fraser (1980) associates politeness with his notion of mitigation, defining mitigation as a strategy for reducing the force of a speech act whose effects are unwelcome to the addressee.

Goffman (1967) and Brown and Levinson (1987) have advanced the face-saving view. In particular, Brown and Levinson maintain that linguistic strategies are means of satisfying both communicative and face-oriented ends, and describe linguistic politeness in terms of face maintenance. They establish five levels of linguistic strategies for politeness, as (a) **direct strategy**, (b) **positive politeness strategies**, (c) **negative politeness strategies**, (d) **off-record strategies**, and (e) **no speech act**. These five levels of strategies are to be employed in that order when the risk of face loss increases. For example, the direct strategy involves performing a speech act in the most direct, clear, unambiguous, and concise way possible. This strategy is used when the speech act is used for great urgency, desperation, or efficiency; or in the addressee's interest; or where the speaker is vastly superior in power to the addressee. The strategy of no speech act or keeping silent is exercised when the face-threatening risk is the greatest. I am particularly interested in their negative politeness and off-record strategies here.

While Brown and Levinson's positive politeness strategies essentially boost the addressee's positive face or self-image, their negative politeness strategies are oriented toward partially satisfying the addressee's negative face, that is, his basic desire to maintain his freedom of action, his freedom from imposition, his territory, and his self-determination. Brown and Levinson propose ten negative politeness strategies, some of which are: **Be conventionally indirect**; **Give deference**; **Question, hedge**; **Apologize**; **Impersonalize speaker and hearer**; and **Nominalize**. For example, "Can you pass the salt?" instead of "Pass the salt," belongs to the conventional indirect strategy.

Brown and Levinson's off-record communicative acts are those which the speaker performs when he wishes to avoid responsibility for his acts, leaving it up to the addressee to decide how to interpret them. Some of the fifteen off-record strategies they propose are: **Give hints**; **Give association clues**; **Presuppose**; **Understate**; **Be ironic**; **Use metaphors**; **Use rhetorical questions**; **Be ambiguous**; and **Be incomplete, use ellipsis**.

Thus, linguistic politeness is, in one way or another, closely related to indirect speech acts, unless the speech acts are performed for the interest of the addressee or for great urgency. For example, Lakoff's rules of politeness, **Don't impose** and **Give options**, may best be observed when the speech acts are performed indirectly, mitigating the speaker's assertive illocution in statement, question, proposal, and command. As we have examined, Brown and Levinson's negative politeness strategies and off-record strategies focus essentially on indirect speech acts of various types.[4]

7. With the above theoretical background, let us observe the Korean data in (1) through (6) again. Obviously, the most distinct pragmatic function of a main clause is to perform the speaker's speech act with appropriate illocutionary force by means of the propositional content and the typical sentence-type enders in which six different speech levels are incorporated. If the main clause is declarative, the speaker asserts the propositional content. If it is interrogative, the speaker requests the addressee to respond verbally. If it is imperative or propositive, the speaker asks the addressee to respond with some kind of action. In all these speech acts, the speaker imposes his views on the addressee to varying degrees. If the speech acts are not particularly in the interest of the addressee, they frequently constitute face-threatening acts toward the addressee.

With the main clause content unexpressed, therefore, the speaker may be able to avoid or weaken such imposition or responsibility for his acts. Since the

4 In fact, the mitigating strategy is employed when the speech act in question is some sort of a face-threatening act. Reinforcement of illocutionary force may occasionally be used when a speech act is in the interest of the addressee. One case of reinforcement may be the restructured derivation of the promissive *-l kkey yo* 'I promise' through contraction (rather than deletion) from *-l kes i-eyo* 'will probably be or do'. Promise presupposes benefit or advantage to the addressee. In actual speech acts, however, mitigation is much more common than reinforcement, since an absolute majority of our conversational interactions are face-threatening acts. Main clause deletion is by and large associated with mitigation, and therefore, this paper is concerned mainly with mitigation.

sentence ender *yo* (polite) or zero (intimate) is present with appropriate intonation contours, relevant speech acts have been performed, but the lack of the expressed propositional content significantly weakens the illocutionary force, giving the addressee extensive options. Indeed, the innovated grammatical categories function as illocution-diluting devices, with their still surviving lexical meanings. The enders *-nun-tey*, *-nun-ka*, and *–nun-ci* and *–(u)l-ke-l* all contain a bound noun, which functions as a hedge that mitigates illocutionary force. One of Brown and Levinson's negative politeness strategies is **Nominalize**. Similarly, the quotative particle *ko* and the conjunctive suffixes *–na, -ketun,* and *-nikka* function as hedges, even though they are reanalyzed as sentence enders. This is because they still carry the bleached version of the original semantic content as a quotative particle or a conjunctive ender.

As already alluded to, the original semantic contents of the omitted main clauses are superimposed with great dilution on the newly developed grammatical categories. Thus, the weakened meanings, together with the hedging functions of the innovated categories, have become conventionalized as devices of politeness in Korean. As indicated earlier, due to the omission of a main clause, some connotation of informality is also attached to the innovated meanings. For example, compare the three sentences in (23), one a complex sentence (a), one a direct simplex sentence (b), and one an innovated sentence (c).

(23) a. *pi* *ka* *o-nun-tey* *ettehkey* *ha-si-keyss-eyo?*
rain NM come-given.that how do-SH-will-POL
'It's raining; what are you going to do?'

b. *pi* *ka* *w-ayo.*
rain NM come-POL
'It's raining.'

c. *pi ka o-nun tey yo.* ~
'It's raining...'

Native speakers would easily judge that the innovated form (23c) is politer and sounds somewhat more informal than the other two expressions in interaction. Similarly, compare the two sentences in (24). Notice that they have the same truth value, but are different in connotative meanings.

(24) a. *pi* *ka* *o-te-la* *ko* *yo.*
'It was raining, you know.'

b. *Pi* *ka* *o-p-ti-ta.*
Rain NM come-AH-RT-DC
'I saw it raining.'

Again, native speakers would agree that (24a) has softer illocution and is more casual than its counterpart in (24b), which is more blunt and assertive despite the use of the deferential ender *-p-ti-ta*.

Brown and Levinson's two off-record strategies are **Be ambiguous** and **Be incomplete, use ellipsis**. These are precisely what Koreans have done to attain politeness in their language use. This has led me to propose that strategic politeness is one of the main causes of grammatical change.

8. Now, in addition to the strategic politeness discussed thus far, there is another major type of politeness in Korean, which may be called normative politeness because the uses of politeness forms are largely mandatory in terms of socio-cultural norms and values. The factors involved in the expressions of normative politeness include power variables such as relative age, kinship, rank, and school grade, and solidarity variables such as ingroup versus outgroup, intimacy, and formality. Normative politeness is expressed largely by honorifics and address-reference terms in Korean.

None of the above quoted Western linguists who proposed the universality of politeness made the distinction between the two important types of politeness.[5] They treated only strategic politeness as if it was the only politeness and lumped power, distance (solidarity), and imposition together to define their strategic politeness (e.g. Brown and Levinson 1987; Leech 1983). In Korean, however, power and solidarity variables are expressed largely by honorifics and address-reference terms and the degrees of impositions are expressed largely by various indirect speech acts. Needless to say, rise and fall of address-reference terms and honorifics, including speech levels, have been caused by Koreans' power- and solidarity-based normative politeness. I will not go into this issue here. All I would like to argue in conclusion is that politeness, both strategic and normative, is an important cause of grammatical change in Korean, a language with rich morphological dynamism.

5 Some of the problems in the universal proposals regarding politeness principles and strategies are discussed in a number of works (e.g. Hill et al. 1986; Blum-Kulka 1987; Sohn 1987, 1988; Jucker 1988; Matsumoto 1988, 1989; Ide 1989; Watts, Ide, & Ehlich 2005).

REFERENCES: Chapter 24

Blum-Kulka, S. 1987. Indirectness and politeness in requests: Same or different? *Journal of Pragmatics* 11: 131–46.

Brown, P. and S. Levinson. 1987. *Politeness*. Cambridge, UK: Cambridge University Press.

Bybee, J.L. 1988. Semantic substance vs. contrast in the development of grammatical meaning. *Proceedings of the 14th Annual Meeting of the Berkeley Linguistics Society*, 247–64.

Fraser, B. (1980). Conversational mitigation. *Journal of Pragmatics,* 4: 341–50.

Fraser, B. (1990). Perspectives on politeness. *Journal of Pragmatics,* 14: 219–36.

Goffman, E. 1967. *Interaction Ritual: Essays on Face-to-Face Behavior*. New York: Anchor Books.

Grice, H.P. 1975. Logic and conversation. In Cole, P. and J. Morgan (1975, 41–58).

Hill, B. et al. (1986). Universal of linguistic politeness: quantitative evidence from Japanese and American English. *Journal of Pragmatics*, 10: 347–71.

Hopper, P.J. 1991. On some principles of grammaticalization. In Traugott, E.C. and B. Heine 1991: 17–36.

Hopper, P.J. and E.C. Traugott. 2003. *Grammaticalization.* Second Edition. Cambridge, England: Cambridge University Press.

Ide, S. 1989. Formal forms and discernment: Two neglected aspects of universals of linguistic politeness. *Multilingua* 8.2/3:223–48.

Jucker, A.H. 1988. The relevance of politeness. *Multilingua* 7.4:375–84.

Lakoff, R. 1973. The logic of politeness: Or, minding your p's and q's. *Proceedings of the 9th Regional Meeting of the Chicago Linguistic Society*, 292–305.

Leech, G.N. 1983. *Principles of Pragmatics*. London/New York: Longman.

Lehmann, C. 1985. Grammaticalization: Synchronic variation and diachronic change. *Lingua e Stile* 20:303–18.

Lehmann, W.P. and Y. Malkiel (eds.). 1982. *Perspectives on Historical Linguistics*. Amsterdam: John Benjamins.

Matsumoto, Y. 1988. Reexamination of the universality of face: Politeness phenomena in Japanese. *Journal of Pragmatics* 12:403–26.

Matsumoto, Y. 1989. Politeness and conversational universals—observations from Japanese. *Multilingua* 8-2/3:207–21.

Sohn, Ho-min. 1987. Strategies of indirection in language. In Linguistic Society of Korea (ed.), *Linguistics in the Morning Calm* II, 167–96. Also in this volume.

Sohn, Ho-min. 1989. Politeness strategies in Korean. In Baek, Eung-Jin (ed.), *Papers from the Sixth International Conference on Korean Linguistics*, 655–69. Also in this volume.

Sweetser, E.E. 1988. Grammaticalization and semantic bleaching. *Proceedings of the 14th Annual Meeting of the Berkeley Linguistics Society*, 389–405.

Traugott, E.C. 1982. From propositional to textual and expressive meanings: Some semantic-pragmatic aspects of grammaticalization. In Lehmann, W.P. and Y. Malkiel (1982, 245–

71).

Traugott, E.C. and B. Heine (eds.). 1991. *Approaches to Grammaticalization I & II.* Amsterdam: John Benjamins.

Watts, R.J., S. Ide, & K. Ehlich (eds.). 2005. *Politeness in Language.* Berlin: Mouton de Gruyter.

25 Strategies of Indirection in Language*

1. Introduction[1]

The goals of this lecture are to clarify what indirection in language (what Heringer (1972) and others call indirect speech acts) means and where it stands in the classification of speech acts, and discuss some major problems and issues that are associated with the research on indirect speech acts.[2]

The term 'strategies' in this lecture is a pragmatic notion, taken simply to mean more or less conventionalized regular practices of producing and understanding linguistic expressions (cf. Geukens 1978, Parret 1984). The term 'indirection' or 'indirect' is a vague notion which has multi-uses and usually refers to a matter of degree. Its use here will be limited to the cases of indirectly performed illocutionary speech acts or 'indirect speech acts' (ISAs for short). The term ISAs, in turn, has been used in various senses, some being overly broad and some extremely narrow in their coverage. For example, on the one extreme, one may call an ISA any speech act which is not literal, including all varieties of euphemistic expressions; and, on the other extreme, one may regard ISAs as those non-direct speech acts which can be explained only in terms of felicity conditions on the secondary illocutions or by the so-called conversational postulates. My position is somewhere in between and will essentially follow Searle and others who use the label ISA for an illocutionary act that is indirectly performed through speaking literally in saying something (e.g. Searle 1975:60).[3] Fraser

---

* This is reprinted from Linguistic Society of Korea (ed.), *Linguistics in the Morning Calm* II, pp. 167–96. (1988).

1 This is a forum lecture delivered at the 1986 Seoul International Conference on Linguistics sponsored by the Linguistic Society of Korea, held at Yonsei University, July 29 – August 1. I am grateful to the Linguistic Society of Korea for inviting me to deliver this lecture. The research for this lecture was supported by grants from the Office of Research Administration and the Center for Korean Studies of the University of Hawaii.

2 As I discussed indirect speech acts in Korean in Sohn (1986: 266-80), Korean data are minimally included in this paper.

3 Many taxonomies have been proposed for illocutionary acts, e.g. Austin (1962), Searle (1976), Bach and Harnish (1979), Hancher (1979), and Stiles (1981), among others. For

(1980:345fn) similarly states that "an act is performed indirectly if the speaker intends the hearer to infer his intention from the recognition first of some more direct act." A question posed by Davison (1975:157) is whether ISAs are two simultaneous illocutionary acts or whether they are primarily one illocutionary act, and secondarily some other speech act. A majority of ISA researches seem to believe the latter, and talk about ISAs when a primarily intended illocutionary act is performed by a secondary illocutionary act.

As Searle (1975) puts it, the main problem posed by ISAs is "how it is possible for the speaker to say one thing and mean that but also to mean something else… and how it is possible for the hearer to understand the indirect speech act when the sentence he hears and understands means something else." Accounting for ISAs is one of the central concerns of many recent scholars working on pragmatics, in that one of the main topics speech act theory deals with I the formulation of general rules for inferring non-literal from literal meaning (e.g. Wunderlich 1980:291).

As an initial approximation to ISA phenomena, let us examine the example in (1), which is not an invented data but a note I found inserted under the window-shield wiper of my car when I came out of church service one recent Sunday in Honolulu.

---

example, Searle's (ibid.) five types of illocutionary acts are directives, commissives, representatives, expressives, and declaratives. Bach and Harnish (ibid.: 40-1) divide illocutionary acts into communicative and conventional ones, the former further into constatives, directives, commissives, and acknowledgements and the latter into effectives and verdictives. The division between communicative and conventional illocutionary speech acts is based on the former's succeeding by means of the hearer's recognition of the speaker's intention and the latter's succeeding by satisfying a convention. According to Bach and Harnish (ibid.), "*constatives* express the speaker's belief and his intention or desire that the hearer have or form a like belief. *Directives* express the speaker's attitude toward some prospective action by the hearer and his intention that his utterance, or the attitude it expresses, be taken as a reason for the hearer's action. *Commissives* express the speaker's intention and belief that his utterance obligates him to do something (perhaps under certain conditions). And *acknowledgements* express feelings regarding the hearer or, in cases where the utterance is clearly perfunctory or formal, the speaker's intention that his utterance satisfy a social expectation to express certain feelings and his belief that it does." Each of the four main kinds of communicative acts is classified into a number of subtypes. Thus, assertives, predictives, confirmatives, concessives, suggestives, etc. are contstative acts; requestives, questions, prohibitives, permissives, and advisories are directive acts; promises and offers are commissive acts; and apologize, condole, congratulate, greet, thank, and bid are acknowledgement acts. Bach and Harnish (ibid.: 110-111) state that effectives effect changes in institutional states of affairs by means of mutually believed conventions, as in vetoing a bill and consecrating a site and *verdictives* are judgments that have official and binding import by convention, as in calling a runner out and finding a defendant guilty.

(1) Please could you be more thoughtful in parking and leave an access for others to get out? Thank you!

The note, although written, should certainly be considered a speech act performed to me. If it were regarded simply as consisting of two sentences, all I would have done was read it and get the semantic literal content; however, I was quite embarrassed to see the note and felt in the wording some kind of politeness toward me, since, albeit conventional, it was phrased carefully in an indirect way. That is, the note brought about what Austin (1962) called perlocutionary effects on me by means of the locutionary act of uttering the sentences-in this case, among other things, embarrassment on my part and politeness on the writer's part. The note also performed a requestive illocutionary act, i.e. requesting me to be more thoughtful in parking. This request was not made directly, by using an imperative form such as " Be more thoughtful...," but indirectly through a syntactically interrogative form, hence an ISA. In other words, the writer of the note employed a strategy of indirection in order to mitigate or soften his intended illocutionary force of request, apparently out of politeness.[4]

As anybody would do, I immediately perceived in the note the act of request, without consciously going through inferential steps from the literal question to the request. That is, the inference was 'short-circuited'. This intuitive perception of request may have been due to the presence of the adverbial *please* that occurs only in requests or directives and never in questions, the use of the standardized indirect request formula *Could you ...?*, and the appending of *Thank you*, which may follow one's own request but never one's own question.[5]

Now, observe the dialogue in (2), which is from Coulthard (1977:65).

(2) Linus: Do you want to play with me, Violet?
Violet: You are younger than me. (Shuts the door)
Linus: (Puzzled) She didn't answer my question.

As Dolitsky (1983:44) observes, the humor involved in this dialogue is that the rational reader shares the unsaid assumption that Violet has made, i.e. that children only play with children their own age, but poor Linus does not share

4 All this reminds us that speech act theory maintains that the sentence level and the speech act level have to be distinguished, that the same sentence can serve to express different sorts of speech acts, ans that semantics studies aspects of the literal meaning of sentences and other expressions, whereas pragmatics is concerned with the conditions and principles according to which the speaker and the hearer determine the context- and use-dependent utterance meanings.

5 For example, we don't say "Are you a student? Thank you" to anybody, but we can say "Please type this letter for me. Thank you" to our secretary.

this assumption and is unable to infer Violet's intended rejection expressed though an ISA in an allusive way. Unlike (1), this dialogue does not give any special linguistic cues that the utterances is indirect in the given discourse context. In such a case, the hearer should get to the 'primary' illocutionary meaning (rejection in the given case) from the 'secondary' illocutionary act (statement in the given case) through a number of inferential steps on the basis of the literal meaning, the context given, and general conversational principles, as we will see later. That is, when the hearer decides that the literal illocution is irrelevant in the given context, he assumes that the speaker is cooperating and his utterance must have some relevance, and that therefore the speaker must have meant something else, which is retrievable because it must be related to the literal meaning in a certain way. In (2) also, the main motivation of the use of the allusive ISA by Violet may be attributed to politeness.

It is due to the sensitive human emotions involved in communication in interpersonal encounters that ISAs are called for and may be performed universally across cultures, as part of the strategies used to tone down or sometimes even strengthen utterance forces, i.e. strategies of indirection.[6] For example, one cannot perform such a blunt 'face-threatening' act (á la Brown and Levinson 1978) as "Close the door," or the Korean equivalent "*mwun tat-useyyo*," to a distant equal or to a social superior when the act of closing the door is definitely in the interest of the speaker. Hence there is a necessity for an ISA to attain the communicatively intended goal while saving the addressee's face. This is why ISAs are particularly significant in face-to-face, subjective interpersonal encounters, where evoking of emotions is keen and direct, but are not as important and performed much less, in such objective speech acts directed to a broad audience as writings in books, public lectures, announcements, academic discussions, and news reports. In the same vein, performance of direct speech acts is generally called for in such circumstances as the neutral description of an event or information provision; or when there is great urgency or desperation; or in the interests of efficiency; or in the hearer's interest; or where the speaker is vastly superior in power to the hearer. All this is precisely because language has two basic communicative functions: (a) transmission of meanings and (b) evoking of emotions. That is, language is not only a means of transmitting knowledge, information, and other various meanings, mainly through the propositional content, but also a means of regulating interpersonal relations, mainly through performing various types of illocutionary acts. The former communicative function, regarded usually as objective, rational, and speaker-oriented, affects the

6 Needless to say, different cultures manifest different sensitivities to the use of ISAs. For example, English speakers tend to use indirect directives much more frequently than Korean speakers do. See section 9.

beliefs and/or intentions of the hearer, whereas the latter function, usually called subjective, emotional and hearer-oriented, affects the hearer's feelings and/or attitudes (e.g. Lee 1983:20). In order for the former function to be performed effectively, language must be used explicitly, logically, and straightforwardly without redundancy, in accordance, for example, with Grice's (1975) Cooperative Principle and the associated Maxims.[7] For the latter function, this is not always the case. Rather, strategies of indirection used to evoke emotions flout Grice's Maxims by providing seemingly ambiguous, redundant, irrelevant, or even contradictory information that, from a pragmatic point of view, serves an affective function, invoking a perlocutionary effect by expressing the speaker's polite, or other, attitude toward the hearer.

In short, as Lee (1983) and others observe, illocutionary acts are governed by four factors: (a) propositional content, (b) illocutionary force, (c) communicative function, and (d) context. The first two factors are expressed by Searle (1969) as *F(P)*, where *F* stands for illocutionary force (i.e. the strength with which the purpose of a speech act is presented) and *P* the propositional content. ISAs are related mainly to *F*, which, in turn, is determined by or derives from the varied interaction or combination of the other three factors.

Of the various types of illocutionary acts, the category of directives is the most sensitive to the performance of ISAs, due mainly to the fact that in directives, which are by and large face-threatening acts, the second (hearer-oriented) communicative function frequently plays a major role in making the act effective. For example, by performing a directive act indirectly, the speaker can make the hearer feel good by allowing him options (cf. Lakoff 1974). Thus, directives take many different linguistic forms in ISAs, which receiving the most attention in the linguistic literature, as is the case with Searle (1975).

2. ISA research and speech act classification

Before we take up some particular questions and issues, let us briefly look at the history of ISA research and where ISAs stand in relation to other speech acts. The history of ISA research is very brief. It is still a fledgling field where many problems are yet to be solved and a large number of areas yet to be explored. Stimulated at first by Sadock's (1970, 1971) notions like 'whimperative' and 'queclarative' and Gordon and Laoff's (!971) 'conversational postulates',

7 Grice's cooperative principle is: Make your contribution such as required by the accepted purpose or direction of the talk exchange. Grice's four maxims: Quality maxim (Try to make your contribution one that is true); Quantity maxim (Make your contribution as informative as is required); Relevance maxim (Make your contribution relevant); and manner maxim (Be perspicuous)

linguists and linguistic philosophers such as Heringer (1972), Sadock (1974), Searle (1975), Davison (1975), Lee (1976), Bach and Harnish (1979), Fraser (1980), Van der Auwera (1980), Leech (1983), and many others have further developed the notion of indirection in language under the rubric of ISAs or strategies of indirection. For example, Sadock deals with sentences similar to example (1) as syntactic phenomena, i.e. as underlyingly request sentences; Gordon and Lakoff's conversational postulates include, for example, you can convey a request by saying that you want the hearer to do something, which is to deal with such indirectly directive sentences as "I want you to leave right away"; Heringer began to use the term 'indirect speech acts'; and Searle realized that Gordon and Lakoff's conversational postulates are not really 'postulates', because ISAs can be better explained in terms of Gricean conversational principles and other speech act theory that Grice and he had developed.

ISA researchers are not in agreement regarding the classification of speech acts, but based on various authors' competing proposals (e.g. Anscombre 1977, Diller 1978, Searle 1969, 1975, Bach and Harnish 1979), as well as my own view, the following tentative classification can be reconstructed, where numerals in parentheses refer to the relevant examples.

(3)

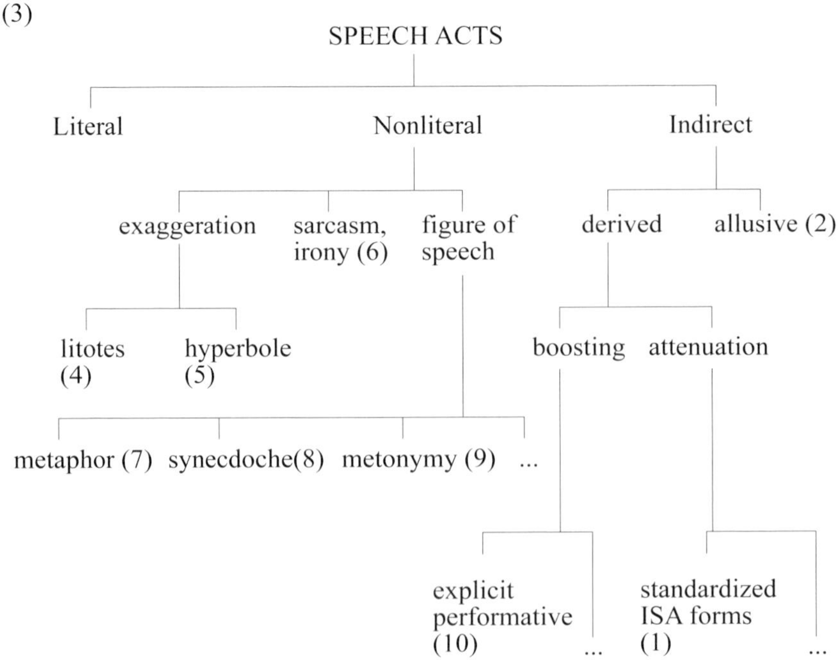

When the speaker utters a sentence and means exactly and literally what he says, it is a case of a literal illocutionary speech act. Nonliteral acts are those in which the literal meaning is not intended (i.e. the literal claims is false) in the given circumstance, although what is said and what is meant are related in a certain way, and usually only the propositional content, rather than the illocutionary force, is affected by nonliterality. In understatement (litotes) and overstatement (hyperbole), for example, we claim respectively less and more than we intend to claim, as illustrated in (4) and (5).[8]

(4) a. Not bad! (Very good!, Great!
b. It's OK. (Good!)

(5) a. No one understands me. (Not enough people understand me.)
b. That was the worst book I've ever read. (it was very bad.)

In sarcasm and irony, one means roughly the opposite of what is said, as in (6).

(6) Boy, this car is terrific! (terrible)

Based on the types of connection between what is said and what is meant, metaphors (sharing of certain associated semantic components) as in (7), synecdoche (part-whole relation) as in (8), and metonymy (close association) as in (9) are distinguished. For the discussion of metaphors as a case of maxim exploitation, see Levinson (1983: 147-162).

(7) The ship plows the sea.
(8) We need two warm bodies (persons).
(9) Washington (the United States Government) announced that.

As for ISAs, they are indirect in the sense that their success is tied to the success of the literal act. Unlike in nonliteral acts, mainly the illocutionary force, rather than the prepositional content, is affected in ISAs. An ISA is either derived conventionally from a certain syntactic formula, or is derived allusively entirely from the speech context and situation. A derived ISA is either a case of boosting as in (10), or a case of attenuation as in (1).[9] In section 3 I will explain

8 It is often pointed out that advertisers make a systematic use of overstatement in slogans, as in: "When you say "Bud", you've said it all' (all that needs to be said about beer) (Bach and Harnish 1979: 67).

9 The terms 'boosting' and 'attenuation' are borrowed from Holmes (1984); who uses them to refer to illocutionary force modifying strategies in general, rather than ISAs per

why I make explicit performatives a proper subset of ISAs despite the widely held view to the contrary.

(10) a. I order you to leave the room.
b. I apologize for the mistake.

The three major sets of illocutionary speech acts given in (3) may, in general, be characterized as in (11), where *S* is what is said, *M* is what is meant, *F* and *G* are illocutionary forces, and *p* and *q* are prepositional contents.

(11) a. S(Fp) = M(Fp) in literal acts
b. S(Fp) = M(Fq) in nonliteral acts
c. S(Fp) = M(Gp) in indirect acts

3. Explicit performatives

How to handle explicit performatives is one of the current issues in speech act research. A commonly held view, since Austin (1962), is that performative utterances, despite their declarative grammatical form, do not describe, report or constate anything at all, i.e. are not statements but are performative acts or doings and hence not true or false. Rather, the job of the performative formula is that of "making explicit (which is not the same as stating or describing) what precise action it is that is being performed by the issuing of the utterance" (Austin ibid.:61). Thus, explicit performative utterances have been considered the most direct, explicit, and literal speech acts. For example, "I promise to be there by 10" is regarded as a 'direct and explicit' act, whose 'direct and non-explicit' counterpart is "I'll be there by 10" (Lee 1983:24).

This widely held view has been challenged by some philosophers (e.g. Lemmon 1962, Lewis 1970, Aqvist 1972) and linguists (e.g. Cornulier 1975, Allwood 1976:207-8, Anscombre 1977, Kempson 1977:64ff., Fodor 1977, Bach and Harnish 1979), whose various claims, some competing and others complementing with one another, may be summarized as in (12).

(12) a. Explicit performatives comprise two illocutionary acts-a doing and a stating.
b. Performatives have the sole peculiarity of being verified by their very

---

se. Thus, she includes as boosting devices strong stress, high volume, rhetorical questions, exclamations, and various lexical boosters, in addition to explicit performatives. As devices for attenuating strategies, she presents high pitch, low volume, tag questions, some form of double negative, lexical downtoners, and digression signals.

use. To utter a performative is what makes the statement true.

c. As an order, a promise, or an apology per se, performative utterances are neither true nor false. As statements, however, they are true or false.

d. Since an explicit performative utterance is the statement of what one is doing, it is an indirect or at least nondirect speech act.

My view of explicit performatives as ISAs is based on the following observations. First of all, it is illogical to say that the use of a performative verb in an explicit performative utterance is not a statement while the use of the same verb in a non-explicit performative utterance is a statement, simply because the former use involves something other than a statement. Observe the examples in (13).

(13) a. I order you to leave the room.
b. I ordered you to leave the room.

A more reasonable account will be to say that (13a) is a statement of an act of order at the utterance time and place (i.e. here/now), whereas (13b) is a statement of a past act of order. There is yet another type of order, which is not performative but generic, as illustrated in (14b), i.e. a statement of a generic act of order.

(14) a. Speaker A: What is your normal reaction when I make too much noise?
b. Speaker B: I order you to leave the room.

The two homonymous forms (13a) and (14b) are disambiguated if we use words like *hereby* and some sort of performative gesture which are acceptable only in (13a).

Second, it has frequently been claimed by linguists that sentences like (13a) are explicit performatives of order and those like (13b) implicit performatives of statement. If (13b) is an implicit performative statement superimposing the whole sentence, there is no reason not to view (13a) as an implicit performative statement superimposing the explicit performative sentence. This is particularly the case because the notion of embedded performatives is widely accepted.

Third, the claim that there are two illocutionary acts in a performative sentence may be supported by languages like Korean. Observe the sentence in (15a) and (15b), which are Korean renderings of (13a) and (13b), respectively.

(15) a.	*pang-ul*	*ttena-l*	*kes-ul*	*myenglyengha-n-ta.*
	Room-AC	leave-will	fact-AC	order

b. *pang - ul* *ttena-l* *kes-ul* *myenglyenghay-ss-ta.*
ordered

(where AC = accusative particle)

One may say, as in the English counterparts, that (15a) is an explicit performative of order and (15b) an implicit performative statement. Notice, however, that both (15a) and (15b) have the 'statement' suffix *–ta*, evidencing that (15a) is the statement of a performative act of order, whereas (15b) is the statement of a past event of ordering.

Fourth, the two-act hypothesis will allow syntactico-semantic description of a language to be made more economically and elegantly than the Austinian view will, because a one-to-one relationship between sentence-type (e.g. declarative) and basic illocutionary type (e.g. statement) can be established. We can say, for example, that English utterances always indicate their speech act types. That is, whether the utterances are context-dependent or context-free, the three major sentence-types in English, i.e. the imperative, interrogative and declarative, have the illocutionary forces traditionally associated with them, i.e. directing, questioning, and stating, respectively.

Fifth, Bach and Harnish (1979) suggest that in utterances like (13a), statement is also intended, albeit not as a primary intention, in that the speaker succeeds in the ordering by virtue of the statement, and that utterances like "Leave; that's an order", where the acts of doing and stating are kept distinct, correspond to explicit performatives of order which perform both acts at once.

Finally, an argument for the ISA status of explicit performatives is in order. As already stated, the definition that I subscribe to is that ISAs are those cases in which one illocutionary act that is primary is performed indirectly by way pf performing another act that is secondary. If we apply this definition to explicit performatives, we can say that a performative act, which is primary, is performed indirectly by way of a statement, which is secondary. Thus, explicit performative utterances are indirect, and literally are statements (constatives or representatives). This claim is supported by the parallelisms existing between explicit performatives (e.g. 16a) and standardized indirect formulae (e.g. 16b), which are obviously ISAs, as distinct from the corresponding literal speech acts (e.g. 16c).

(16) a. I order you to go out.
b. I want you to go out.
c. Go out.

Notice that (16a) and (16b) have the same syntactic structure, with order and want as main verbs and to go out as complements; both are pragmatically directive despite the declarative forms they have; and both have a similar "short-circuited" inference pattern in that the hearer immediately perceives them as directive. The only salient pragmatic difference seems to be that (16a) is a case of boosting illocutionary force and (16b) a case of attenuating it.

Fraser (1980) maintains that a performative structure such as "I hereby request that you leave" is the most direct means of performing a speech act, whereas embedded performatives such as "I must request that you leave" are indirect ways of requesting. I would rather view both unembedded and embedded performatives as ISAs, the difference being that the former are illocutionary force boosting and the latter illocutionary force attenuating devices.

4. Inference strategies

How does the hearer understand the indirect primary illocutionary act from understanding the literal secondary illocutionary act? The related question is: How is it possible for the speaker to mean the primary illocution when he only utters a sentence that means the secondary illocution.

According to Searle (1975), the hearer gets to the 'primary' illocutionary meaning through a number of inferential steps on the basis of the literal meaning, the context, the general pattern of speech act performance (á la Serlian speech act theory contingent upon felicity and other conditions), and conversational principles (á la Grice 1975). That is, when the hearer decides that the literal illocution is irrelevant in the given context, he assumes that the speaker is cooperating and his utterance must have some relevance, i.e. the speaker must have meant something else which is retrievable because it must be related to the literal meaning in certain ways. Searle (ibid.) presents two examples of inferential stops, one related to allusive utterances like our example (2) and the other to more standardized utterances like our example (1). Both sets of his inferential steps are very similar and of the same general pattern. Let us roughly follow Searle's line of inferential steps with our example (2), assuming that I am Linus.

Step 1. I made a proposal to Violet, and in response she has made a statement to the effect that I am younger than she is (facts about the conversation).

Step 2. I assume that Violet is cooperating in the conversation and that therefore her remark is intended to be relevant to our talk exchange (relevance principle of conversational cooperation).

Step 3. A relevant response must be one of acceptance, rejection, counterproposal, further discussion, etc. (theory of speech acts).

Step 4. But her literal utterance was not one of these, and so was not a relevant response (inference from Steps 1 and 3).

Step 5. Therefore, she probably means more than she says. Assuming that her remark is relevant, her primary illocutionary point must differ from her literal one (inference from Steps 2 and 4).

As Searle points out, this step is a crucial one, because unless a hearer has some inferential strategy for finding out when primary illocutionary points differ from literal illocutionary points, he has no way of understanding indirect illocutionary acts. Poor Linus went successfully through Step 4, but failed to go into Step 5. Assuming that I am a mature and more rational Linus, let us move onto the next steps.

Step 6. Violet's statement that I am younger than she is probably her acceptance or rejection, counterproposal, etc. (theory of speech acts).

Step 7. Violet's pointing out of our age differences cannot be associated with her acceptance of my proposal, because if acceptance were intended, she would have directly and clearly said so (quantity and manner principles of conversational cooperation); and it cannot be associated with her counterproposal, since she shut the door and disappeared (inference from Step 6 and facts about the conversation).

Step 8. Violet's statement probably is her rejection, because children usually and *more comfortably play with children their own age, and her assertion of* age difference therefore implies her distancing me (inference from Steps 6 and 7).

Step 9. Felicity conditions on the acceptance of a proposal are the hearer's ability and intention to perform the act predicated in the proposaitional content condition (theory of speech acts). Violet probably has given her statement as a reason for her being unable or not intending to play with me.

Step 10. Violet probably wants to be polite; she does not want to hurt me by flatly saying "no"; and she has said something that has a consequence that she probably cannot accept my proposal (inference from Step 8 and 9).

Step 11. Therefore, her primary illocutionary point is to reject the proposal (inference from 10).

I have added here a few points, such as those described in Steps 7, 8, 9, and 10, to Searle's inferential framework. In particular, I have included the hearer's intention as a felicity condition in Step 9. I have also included politeness in Step 10, although Searle has not in his sample inferential steps.

Bach and Harnish (1979) have proposed what thy term the Speech Act Schema, which is essentially if the same nature as Searle's, but is a more elaborated general pattern of the hearer's inference.

In normal conversation, the hearer goes through the steps involved in the above reasoning subconsciously. There are various degrees of inferential complexity, depending not only on such elements as conventionality of the expressions and mutual contextual beliefs. Thus, for example, certain types of expression in a culture are especially suited to the indirect performance of certain types of illocutionary acts. As we have seen, standardized indirect expressions like our example (1) allow us to short-circuit inference steps to get to the indirect illocutionary intent of the speaker.

5. Conventionality

Searle (1975:75) sees conventionality as the biggest problem posed by his analysis; why, if the mechanisms by which ISAs are meant and understood are perfectively general, do some syntactic forms such as the (a) sentences in (17) through (19) work better than others, such as the (b) sentences.

(17) a. Can you hand me that book on the top shelf?
b. Is it the case that you at present have the ability to hand me that book on the top shelf?

(18) a. Do you want to open the window?
b. Do you desire to open the window?

(19) a. Can you open the window?
b. Are you able to open the window?

The fact that the first member of each pair has stronger ISA potential is observed by its taking *please* more naturally than the second member. To this problem, Searle (ibid.:77) answers as follows: "In order to be plausible candidate at all for use as an indirect speech act, a sentence has to be idiomatic. But within the class of idiomatic sentences, some forms tend to become entrenched as conventional devices for indirect speech acts. In the cases of directives, in which politeness is the chief motivation for the indirect forms, certain forms are conventionally used as polite requests. Which kinds of forms are selected will, in all likelihood, vary from one language to another."

Searle does not attempt to explain why certain forms are more idiomatic and tend to be more conventionalized than others. Let us speculate some linguistic causes for the relative degrees of conventionality, while admitting that there must be some other cases as well, such as socio-cultural aspects and arbitrary linguistic habits. Compare the verbs *can* and *be able to* in (19), for example. These two verbs share the concept 'ability' and in many contexts they are free variants (e.g. "He can do the job" vs. "He is able to do the job"), although, as Sadock (1974:78) puts it, for making a request the *can* construction is rather straightforward and the *be able to* construction sneaky.

Geukens's (1978:266ff.) observations seem to be very relevant for our purpose, although they are intended to refute Sadock's "idiom" thesis and not to account for conventionality. That is, *can* is an auxiliary verb and is only a subpart of the verb phrase, whereas *be able to* is the main verb of the whole sentence. *Can* is phonetically reducible to *kn*, whereas *be able to* cannot be so reduced. *Can* is normally not stressed, whereas *be able to* is always stressed. The meaning of *can* is much less specific than the meaning of *able*, which normally denotes physical capacity. As a result, the relative communicative load and the topicality that an auxiliary verb carries in a sentence are likely to be small compared with those that a main verb carries, hence the information conveyed by *can* is easier to overlook than that conveyed by *be able to*. All this may have led to the different degrees of conventionality in the pragmatic behavior of the two sentences in (19). If we add a stress on *can* in (19a), making it s so-called tonic syllable (Halliday 1970), the request interpretation becomes as "sneaky" as (19b).

Another related question concerns explicit performatives. Why is (20a) an order, whereas (20b) and (20c) are more statements?

(20) a. I order you to leave the room.
b. It is the case that I order you to leave the room.
c. I state that I order you to leave the room.

Again, the reason seems to be that all the three main verbs receive primary inferential prominence, but only the one in (20a) is the performative verb of order, while the other two are simply statement or descriptive verbs. Then, one might ask why (20a) is to be construed as a statement of a performative order, as we proposed earlier, while (20c) is not. My answer would be that an implicit performative like the statement underlying (20a) and an explicit performative like the statement verb of (20c) carry different communicative loads and that (20c) actually contains another implicit performative statement. An implicit performative is usually realized as ZERO in English but as a verbal suffix in Korean, as previously observed.

Further observe the sentences in (21), where (21a) lacks the main auxiliary verb and (21b) the main verb phrase (*do you think*).

(21) a. Why not stop here.
b. How about stopping here.

Some authors point out these two so-called whimperative utterances are nearly idiomatized as requestive suggestions, (21b) being more so (e.g. Searle 1975). We can speculate that there is an order among different types of linguistic elements appearing in the verb phrase which is correlated with different degrees of communicative load, which are in turn correlated, other things being equal, with conventionality for indirect illocution. The order of the verbal elements from heavy to light communicative load seems to be: main verb—main auxiliary verb—main verb suffix (as in Korean)—dropping of auxiliary verb—dropping of main verb. The different degrees of conventionality for indirect illocution seem to apply in reverse. There may also be some other factors involved, such as relative semantic heaviness, relative length, frequency of usage, etc. of the competing lexical items, which may cause, for example, *want* to be more readily conventionalized than *desire*.

6. Standardized indirect formulae

It seems that almost all ISA researchers agree that most ISAs should be analyzed (a) inferentially and (b) conversationally, as outlined thus far, except for standardized or conventionalized indirect act formulae. Here scholars diverge. Thus, our question is how the literal meaning and the speaker's intended meaning are interrelated in standardized indirect formulae, such as our example (1). There are two general lines of thinking in this regard that may be termed the idiom hypothesis (e.g. Sadock 1974, Green 1975) and convention (or inference- or implicature-convention) hypothesis (e.g. Searle 1975, Morgan 1978). Sadock (ibid.), for example, thinks that sentences like those in (22) are ambiguous as to their force, with one meaning being interrogative and the other "idiomatically" imperative.

(22) a. Can you pass the salt? (Pass the salt!)
b. Will you be quiet? (Be quiet!)
c. Why don't you shut up! (Shut up!)

Sadock (chs. 4-6) presents half a dozen arguments against any theory that claims standardized indirect forms are inferential and for the existence of idiomatic readings in standardized forms. Sadock's proposal is that the request reading of sentences like (22) comes through "whimperative formation" from a semantic structure like that in (23), which is also thought to underlie imperatives.

(23)

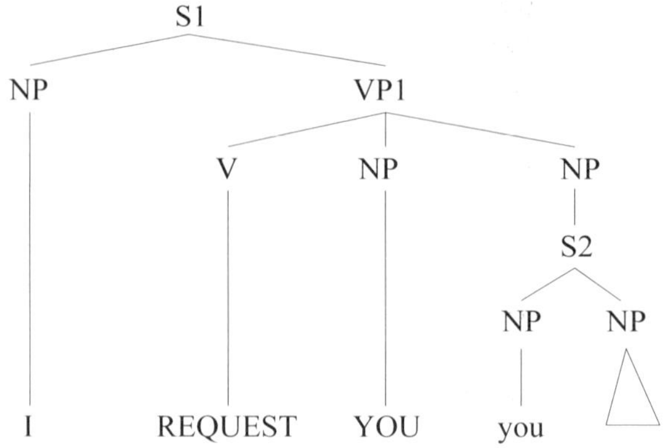

Sadock's first sort of evidence is related to the distribution of words like please, which occur either preverbally or postsententially when the verb denotes a requested action.

(24) a. (Please) Close the door (please).
  b. Passengers will (please) not lean out the windows (please)!
  c. I (*please) enjoy (*please) playing tennis (*please).
  d. When will you (*please) keep score (*please)?

Whimperatives in (22) follow the imperative pattern (e.g. 24a, b) rather than statement (e.g. 24c) or question (e.g. 24d). Sadock also points out that certain expressions cooccur with clear cases of imperatives and standardized ISA forms, but do not co-occur with interrogatives.

(25) a. Wash the car, someone!
  b. *When will you wash the car, someone?
  c. Will you wash the car, someone?

(26) a. Buzz off!
  b. *When will you buzz off?
  c. Will you buzz off?

Sadock advances similar arguments for various other cases such as tag-imperative *(VP, will you?)*, impositives *(Why don't you VP?; Shouldn't you/we VP?)*, queclaratives *(Does anyone VP anymore?* = [I declare that] no one VPs any more), pseudo-imperatives *(Move and I'll shoot)*, requestions *(Columbus discovered America in?)* and tag-questions.

The main strength of the idiom hypothesis is often said to be that it has outlined how certain syntactic relations might be formalized, although no actual derivations using motivated rules are provided. As Searle (1975) and Bach and Harnish (1979) point out, the main weakness include its multiplying of meanings beyond necessity and its failure to show how, in general, ISAs are related to direct speech acts.

The convention hypothesis claims that the indirect use relies on illocutionary conventions, i.e. on the notion of convention of use as against convention of language. According to this thesis, the speaker's being able to produce and to perceive standardized illocutions is due to the knowledge that the utterance of a sentence literally used to perform one sort of illocutionary act also counts as the indirect but immediately identifiable performance of some other sort of illocutionary act. These conventions serve to bypass or short-circuit the inferences used to arrive at indirect illocutions. Searle (1975:64ff.), for example, while presenting six standard groups of sentences that could regularly be used to make indirect requests and other directives such as orders, observed several facts in support of his 'conventionality' thesis. For one thing, standardized indirect directives do not have an imperative force as part of their meaning, as in (27).

(27) *I'd like you to do this for me, Bill, but I am not asking you to do it or requesting that you do it or ordering you to do it or telling you to do it.*

Another way of putting what Searle maintains is that, since the request force in (27) can be cancelled with subsequent descriptions, it is to be construed as a conversational implicature that is associated not with the sentence meaning but with the speaker meaning.

A second fact Searle observes is that there is a systematic 'conventional' relation between standardized directive ISA forms and directive illocutions in a way that there is no systematic relation between allusive ISA forms and illocutions. Still another fact is that standardized ISA forms are not idioms like *kick the bucket*, and admit of literal responses as in (28).

(28) a. Sally: Why don't you be quiet, Henry?
Henry: Well, Sally, there are several reasons for not being quiet.

b. A: Can you pass the salt?
B': No, sorry, I can't, it's down there at the end of the table.
B": Yes. I can. (Here it is).

c. [in a recent movie]
kidnapped police (referring to the dynamite the robber had):
May I ask what that's for?
robber: Certainly you may.

A related fact is that standardized ISA forms can also be used as literal utterances, as in the use of (28bA) by a doctor wishing to know the medical progress of a patient's arm injury. In the same vein, Bach and Harnish (1979) provide evidence that whimperatives (in their direct use) function like interrogatives. For example, responses to whimperatives are patterned like responses to interrogatives, not like those to imperatives, as observed in (29).

(29) A: Do you have the ability to pass the salt?
A': Can you pass the salt?
B: [*salt-passing]

(30) A: Pass the salt!
B: (Sure!) [salt-passing]

Note that the whimperative in (29A') requires a verbal response whether the request is combined with or not, but imperatives like (30A) require verbal response only if they are not complied with.

As a further piece of evidence that indirect formulae are not idioms, Searle (1975:68) observes that word-for-word translation across cultures often produces expressions with the same ISA potential, as can be illustrated in (31). This is generally not the case with most idioms.

(31) a. Could you give me the salt?
b. Pourriez-vous me donner le sel?
c. *sokum com cwu-si-l swu iss-usey-yo*? [Korean]
salt just give-SH-PRS way exist-SH-POL
(lit. 'Is there any way that you will give me the salt?')

A final piece of evidence for the inference/implicature-convention thesis is that, as mentioned elsewhere, if we give a strong stress to the auxiliary verb, as in "CAN you pass the salt?", then the sentence changes to the literal meaning only. This fact also seriously weakness the idiom theory.

Admitting that Sadock (1974) and Green's (1975) idiom hypothesis is less convincing than Seaerle (1975) and Morgam's (1975) hypothesis of convention of use, how should we account for the coocurrrence of the sentence adverbial *please* and interrogative sentences from the perspective of the non-idiom thesis. Searle does not take up this problem. I have noted at least three different proposals in this regard.

Gordon and Lakoff (1971) claim that since all questions are to be represented as requests for information on the semantic level, they, as requests, naturally allow the sentence adverbial *please*. This claim, however, does not account for the occurrence of *please* in declarative sentences like (32a), and its non-occurrence in interrogative sentences like (32b,c), all of which are used as indirect request utterances.

(32) a. I'd like a case of Budweiser, please.
     b. *Must you make such big noises, please?
     c. *isn't this room stuffy, please?

Secondly, Geukens (1978) proposes to consider please as a lexicalization of a conditional sentence comparable to such expressions as if you don't mind, if you like, if it please you, and if you please. He adds that if the semantic structure of please is construed this way, surface questions with please can be considered as semantic questions, and that non-occurrence of the sentences like those in (33) is a matter of pragmatically and culturally defined restrictions.

(33) a. *Take one more step, please, and I'll shoot.
     b. *Have a Merry Christmas, please.

This semantic approach, although somewhat loose and circular, may be able to deal with sentences like those in (32).

A third proposal is made by Bach and Harnish (1979), who are more sympathetic with Searle's position than with Sadock's, although they are not completely satisfied with the former either. Arguing that ISA formulae are not even completely conventionalized but more or less standardized to varying degrees due to repeated uses, they suggest that interrogative sentences in which please occurs are not fully grammatical, although their recurrent use makes them seem perfectly acceptable. That is, they are not really grammatical interrogatives and cannot be used as literal questions. They maintain that please is to be construed as an illocutionary modifier and that it occurs paragrammatically, as do illocutionary modifiers in general, modifying what the speaker is doing indirectly and not what he is saying.

7. Felicity conditions

From the inception of ISA research, felicity conditions (FCs for short) have been referred to in relation to ISAs. FCs are so named because they are regarded as conditions of or specifications for the appropriate performance of speech acts. For example, we cannot request our hearer to do something when we know that he is completely unable to do it. In a request, therefore, the hearer's having the ability to perform the act is a preparatory FC, the speaker's wanting the hearer to do the act is a sincerity FC, the speaker's predicating a future act of the hearer is a prepositional content FC, etc. Heringer (1972), Searle (1975), and other ISA researchers describe the relation between primary and secondary meaning in terms of FCs, claiming that the speaker uses such FCs in performing his ISAs and the hearer infers the speaker's indirect illocutionary intent based on FCs. Heringer (ibid.), for example, claims that only those non-direct speech acts which are accounted for in terms of FCs are ISAs. The ISA status of our example (1) is thus confirmed by its being a question about the ability of the hearer to perform the action requested in the speech act, because this ability is a preparatory FC for a request. Similarly, the following ISAs all relate to and can be accounted for in terms of the FCs of requests, in that they can be performed by asserting or questioning an FC (the examples are from Dillion 1977:109-111):

(34) I want you to take out the garbage.
Can you take out the garbage?
Are you willing to take out the garbage?
Are you planning to take out the garbage today?
Do you intend to take out the garbage today?
Are you going to take out the garbage today?
Will you take out the garbage today?[10]

On the other hand, a non-conventionalized form like our example (2) bears no relation to an FC, but expounds a reason for the action (i.e. rejection) performed by the speech act. Heringer would not consider allusive indirect expressions like (2) as ISAs, although Searle (1975) would.

The fact that not all ISAs can be explained in terms of the usual FCs on speech acts has been notices by many. Not only allusive ISAs but many standardized ISA formulae cannot be associated with FCs. Searle (1975:71-72) recognizes three types of standardized directive ISA forms: those having to do with

10 Although Dillon (1977) states that the last utterance in the examples is not an indirect or "softened" request, I include it here because it is a request through a question and can be relatable to GCs in one way or another.

FCs, those having to do with reasons for doing the act, and those embedding one element inside another. These are illustrated respectively in (35a), (35b), and (35c).[11]

(35) a. Could you be a little more quiet?
I would like you to go now.
Officers will henceforth wear ties at dinner.
b. Would you mind not making so much noise?
You should leave immediately.
It would be a good idea if you left town.
c. Might I ask you to take off your hat?
I would appreciate it if you could make less noise.

According to Searle, the sentences in (35a) concern, respectively, a preparatory FC (the ability of the hearer to perform the act), a sincerity FC (the desire of the speaker that the hearer perform the act), and a prepositional content FC (the predication of the act of the hearer); and (35c) is a special class only by courtesy. Although there is some doubt about recognizing the (35c) type as distinct from the other two (FCs and reasons), an abundance of sentences of types (35b) and (35c) suggest that a traditional analysis in terms of FCs does not cover all ISAs. Gordon and Lakoff (1971) and Garvey (1975) also follow this line of argument. On the other hand, one could argue for setting up new FCs in order to generalize the FC-based account of ISAs (e.g. Green 1975, Heringer 1976). For example, Heringer (ibid.:18ff.), in dealing with utterances like "You may go," introduces a new type of FC involving *permission*. As proposed earlier, the hearer's intention to do the act has to be postulated as another FC, in addition to those that Searle (1969, 1975), for example, already proposed. For example, Korean request speech acts like (36) are due to the questioning of the hearer's intention to do the act.[12]

(36) *sokum com cwu-si-keyss-eyo*?
salt just give-SH-intend-POL

11 As regards indirect directives, the first three of Searle's (1975:72-74) four strategies ('generalizations'), by means of which the speaker makes an indirect directive and the hearer finds out how a primary illocutionary point differs from a secondary illocutionary point are FC-related ones and the fourth one reads: S [speaker] can make an indirect directive by either stating that or asking whether there are good or overriding reasons for doing A [future action], except where the reason is that H [hearer] wants or wishes, etc., to do A, in which case he can only ask whether H wants, wishes, etc., to do A.

12 One might also propose to include *reason* for doing an act as some sort of FC.

'Could you give me the salt, please?'
(lit. 'Would you intend to give me the salt?')

8. ISAs and politeness

Our last major question concerns the relation between ISAs and politeness, in that politeness is an essential condition for both effective communication and smooth interpersonal relationships, while perhaps the strongest motivation for the use of ISAs is the need for politeness.

As Van der Auwera (1980:48) notes, Grice (1975:47) introduced the idea that politeness can be used to explain the comprehension of certain implicatures, but unfortunately, he did not elaborate on this theme. Lakoff (1973, 1974), Mohan (1974), Aijmer (1977) and others hold that the politeness principle is something of the same type as Grice's conversational cooperative principle, but they do not seriously relate this idea to their accounts of ISAs.[13] Brown and Levinson's (1978) extensive work on putatively universal politeness strategies based on the notion of face-threatening acts also does not deal with the problem of ISAs in any significant manner. As already briefly touched upon, Searle acknowledges the importance of politeness for issuing indirect directives in various places, but does not assign politeness any role in the explanation of how people comprehend ISAs.

Three works are particularly noteworthy in this connection: Fraser's notion of mitigation, Holmes's concepts of attenuation and boosting of illocutionary force, and Leech's explication of how the Cooperative Principle (CP for short) and the Politeness Principle (PP for short) interact in the interpretation of indirectness.

Defining mitigation as a strategy for reducing the strength or force of a speech act whose effects are unwelcome to the hearer, Fraser (1978, 1980; Fraser and Nolan 1981) proposes that use of indirectness, or ISAs, is one of the strategies used to mitigate a speech act, e.g. to soften the effects of an order, ease the blow of bad news, make a criticism more palatable, etc. Since Fraser's concept of mitigation is that it is a modification of only those effects which are unwelcome to the hearer, we do not, for example, speak of mitigating the force of our praise. Fraser also maintains that mitigation in his sense occurs only if the speaker is also being polite. Fraser proposes six ways, which he calls strategies, for the

13 Lakoff (1973), for example, subsumes Grice's principle and maxims under her rules of clarity, while proposing rules of politeness as another set of rules of pragmatic competence, as summarized in the following.

Lakoff's rules of pragmatic competence: 1. Be clear; 2. Be polite

Lakoff's rules of politeness: 1. Don't impose; 2. Give option; 3. Be friendly

speaker to express his intention of mitigation, admitting that there these are not exhaustive. The most obvious one is to perform ISAs, and the others include use of distancing techniques like passivization as in (37a), disclaimers as in (37b), parenthetical verbs as in (37c), tag questions as in (37d), and hedges as in (37e).

(37) a. All passengers are required by FAA regulation to
fasten their seat belts.
(cf. I hereby request that you fasten your seat belts.)
b. I hate to do this, but …
If I'm not wrong …
If you wouldn't mind…
c. This is the right road, I guess.
We can, I think, do it over again.
d. You were there, weren't you?
e. Technically speaking, …

Thus, for example, the use of the passive brings the hearer into focus, thereby moving the speaker and his involvement more into the distance, and parenthetical verbs weaken the claim of truth which would be implied by a single assertion.

Dissatisfied with Fraser's narrow concept of mitigation, Holmes (1984) introduces the notions of attenuation and boosting, and of positively affective as well as negatively affective speech acts. Speculating that the notion of mitigation must have attracted particular attention because researchers are most familiar with the so-called negative-politeness cultures (Brown and Levinson 1978:250), she maintains that mitigation in Fraser's sense is only one of the strategies available for modifying the illocutionary force of one particular group of speech acts. Observe the figure and the resultant affective meanings in (38) (adapted from Holmes 1984), where attenuation and boosting interact with positively and negatively affective speech acts.

(38)

Strategies	*Speech acts (SAs)*	*Affective meanings*
Boosting	Positively affective SAs	Increase solidarity
	Negatively affective SAs	increase social distance
Attenuation	Positively affective SAs	increase social distance
	Negatively affective SAs (= Mitigation)	increase solidarity

Notice in this framework that Fraser's mitigation is nothing but the attenuation of negatively affective speech acts, only one of the four communicative strategies for modifying illocutionary forces. Notice further that an analysis of the affective meaning of attenuating and boosting illocutionary forces is presented in terms of the speaker-hearer relationship. This is because one of the basic reasons why a speaker might wish to modify an illocutionary force is to express his attitude to the hearer in the utterance context (Kennedy 1979, Holmes 1982).[14] Boosting the force of a positively affective SA can be interpreted as an expression of politeness, as in (39a), and boosting the force of a negative affective SA can be seen as an expression of impoliteness, as in (39b). On the other hand, attenuating a positively affective SA can be interpreted as a strategy likely to increase the social distance between the interlocutors, and hence impolite, as in (39c), and attenuating a negatively affective SA can be seen as a strategy likely to contribute to the development or maintenance of the speaker-hearer relationship, as in (39d).

(39) a. *Really* you are *amazingly* pretty.
b. *My god* you are *such* a fool.
I will *bloody well* murder that dog of yours.
c. I *must* welcome you.
You are *kind of* pretty *in a way*.
d. I *must* warn you…
(cf. I warn you…)
You are *a bit of* a fool you *know*.
(cf. You are a fool.)

Holmes's analysis does not indicate where ISAs in our sense fit in, since nowhere does she mention them. Since, however, she includes IFIDs (illocutionary force indicating devices) as a case of boosting the negatively affective SA, ISAs (both derived and allusive) should also be included in her framework as a case of attenuation. As has been alluded to, strategies of indirection should cover both boosting and attenuation. Needless to say, Holmes's analysis is far from being complete, but, compared with Fraser's, it shows a better picture of the general communicative strategies for modifying the force of speech acts. If, for one thing, we consider such pragmatic parameters holding between the speaker

14 For example, an adult Korean may use the following ISA to a senior person, even though he/she knows that his/her teacher is definitely leaving the school.

sensaying-nim i hakkyo lul ttena-si-nun kes kath-supnita.
(direct speech: *sensaying-nim i hakkyo lul ttena-si-pnita.*)
'It appears that the professor is leaving tomorrow.'

and hearer as power and solidarity, role relationships, relative rights and obligations, size of imposition, etc., the generalizations she proposes must be modified accordingly. For example, a student's using an expression like "Would it be too much if I asked you to please pass the salt?" to a close friend would, contrary to what Holmes predicts, increase social distance rather than solidarity, despite its attenuation of a negatively affective speech act. It would sound sarcastic at best.

Finally, Leech (1983) presents a much more elaborate model, relating the CP (Cooperative Principle) and the PP (Politeness Principle) on the one hand, and politeness and indirectness on the other. Devoting three chapters to politeness and other conversational principles, and concerned mainly with so-called interpersonal rhetoric, i.e. realistic and 'effective' talk exchanges in conversation, Leech begins his discussion by saying that Gricean CP is necessary but not sufficient, and that indirect illocutions and politeness must be dealt with in terms of scales. He maintains that the CP in itself cannot explain (a) why people are often so indirect in conveying what they mean, or (b) what the relation is between literal and intended meaning (his sense and force, respectively). Recognizing the importance of politeness in these respects, he proposes the PP as a first order concept, of the same rank as the CP. He also introduces other less important principles such as the Irony Principle, Banter Principle, Interest Principle, and Pollyanna Principle in order to account for irony, exaggerations, metaphors, and other nonliteral illocutions such as euphemisms.

Leech formulates the PP as: *minimize (other things being equal) the expression of impolite beliefs*. Defining polite and impolite beliefs as beliefs which respectively are favorable and unfavorable to the hearer or a third party, Leech points out that the most important kind of politeness in English-speaking society is that which is covered by the operation of the Tact maxim, which reads *Minimize cost to other; Maximize benefit to other*. Leech proposes three scales where the Tact maxim is relevant: The cost-benefit scale, optionality/indirectness scale, and social distance scale. The cost–benefit scale concerns the propositional content of an utterance, and thus is not directly related to the working of ISAs. For example, in normal situations, saying "Peel these potatoes" is costly to the hearer and thus much less polite than saying "Enjoy your holiday," which is less beneficial to the hearer than saying "Have another sandwich." The optionality/indirectness scale concerns illocutionary forces, and hence is relevant to ISAs. Leech states that indirect illocutions tend to be more polite because they increase the degree of optionaity, and because the more indirect an illocution is, the more diminished and tentative its illocutionary force tends to be. Leech presents (40) as an example of this scale.

(40)		indirectness	less polite
Answer the phone.	↓	↑
I want you to answer the phone.	
Will you answer the phone?	
Can you answer the phone?	
Would you mind answering the phone?	
Could you possibly answer the phone?		↓
Etc.		more polite

Notice in (40) that the degree of indirectness correlates with the degree to which the hearer is allowed the option of not performing the intended action, so that it becomes progressively easier for the hearer to say no. Although Leech does not seem to take boosting acts as ISAs, he notes that there is close interaction between this scales and the cost-benefit scale, saying that utterances whose prepositional content is beneficial to the hearer become less polite with increasing indirectness in his sense, as in "You must have another sandwich", "have another sandwich", and "Would you mind having another sandwich?". Notice that utterances like "You must have another sandwich" are a case of indirectness of a boosting type in our sense, as compared with indirectness of an attenuation type, such as "Would you mind…?"

The third scale Leech proposes is that of social distance. It consists of vertical and horizontal subscales which are reminiscent respectively of power and solidarity in sociolinguistics (e.g. Brown and Gilman 1960, Sohn 1986: 389-410). These subscales are interrelated with the other two scales previously mentioned. For example, between two close friends, who occupy equal status in the vertical scales and close relationship in the horizontal scale, such indirect utterances as "Could you possibly answer the phone?" increase social distance and are construed as an insult or a joke at best. Leech (ibid.:127) summarize the way these various parameters influence tact as in (41).

(41) a. the greater the cost of A to H,
b. the greater the horizontal social distance of H from S,
c. the greater the authoritative status of H with respect to S,
d. the greater will be the need for optionality, and correspondingly for indirectness, in the expression of an impositive, if S is to observe the Tact Maxim.

Time and space do not allow me to discuss the other PP maxims (generosity, approbation, modesty, agreement, sympathy, phatic) and other Principles that Leech proposes, which are not directly related to ISAs. Suffice it here to point out that the maxims and principles will not all apply to all cultures equally. Some cultures may give politeness a higher rating than cooperation in certain situations or give precedence to one maxim rather than another. For example, some cultures, such as that of Korea, may value the Modesty Maxim more highly than the Approbation Maxim; the reverse appears to be true with other cultures, like America.

9. Future topics of interest

Time and space constraints prevent us from discussing many other interesting aspects of ISAs. One such topic is the relation between ISAs and conversational implicatures. Are the two concepts the same or different, or is one a subset of the other? This question is extensively addressed in Van der Auwera (1980) and in some other works cited there.

Another topic that deserves attention is whether the presence of both literal force and derived force are absolutely required for an utterance to be classed an ISA. This so-called literal force hypothesis (LFH) is discussed in such works as Van der Auwera (1980), Gazdar (1981), and Levinson (1983).

A third topic that merits exploration is the range of putatively universal linguistic, kinesic, and paralinguistic devices available for strategies of indirection. Devices for indirection in some individual languages have been observed (e.g. Searle 1975, Fraser 1980, and Holmes 1984 for English, and Sohn 1986:266-280 for Korean), but I have failed to see any significant study done from a universal perspective except perhaps for Brown and Levinson (1978). However, they are concerned more with universal politeness strategies than with systematic indirect illocutionary force indicating devices.

A fourth topic that will be of great interest is the sociolinguistic or ethnographic approach to the study of ISAs. I agree with Stubbs (1983), for example, who points out that, due to its focus on single utterances of the invented nature, current speech act theory tends to neglect the importance of the social contexts in which an act is performed, of the negotiable nature of speech acts that is usually observable only in connected discourse, and of the diversity of forms by which various illocutionary forces are conveyed and the associated stylistic implications. Further noting that speech act theory has tended to study the formulation of such trivial speech acts as salt passing and taking out the garbage, Stubbs calls for the study of more socially significant acts such as sending people to prison, fining people money, offering or declining marriage, and making contracts.

One final important topic is the cross-cultural analysis of ISAs. Speech act theory is often criticized for its ethnocentricity, in that it tends not only to neglect cultural differences but to propose various universal hypotheses based on an Anglo-Saxon bias. While there are many putatively universal features that appear to be shared by different societies, there is also a variation in the degree to which different cultures are sensitive to the need for ISAs, since different cultural variables such as norms, values, and assumptions are tied up with the performance of speech acts. There are some contrastive studies on the topic, devoted mainly to comparing English and another language. Wierzbicka (1985), for example, observes that English, as compared with Polish, places heavy restrictions on the use of imperative sentences and instead makes extensive use of interrogative and conditional forms as directive acts, and that linguistic differences are associated with cultural differences such as spontaneity, directness, intimacy, and affection (in Polish society) vs. indirectness, distance, tolerance, and anti-dogmaticism (in Anglo-Saxon society). Cho (1982) and Sohn (1986: 438-71) compare English and Korean in terms of cross-cultural differences.

REFERENCES: Chapter 25

Ajimer, K. 1977. *Acts of Deference and Authority*. Gothenburg Papers in Theoretical Linguistics 34. Gothenburg: Linguistic Department.

Allwood, J. 1976. *Linguistic Communication as Action and Coopertaion*. Gothenburg Monographs in Linguistics 2. Gothenburg: Linguistics Department.

Anscombre, J. 1977. La problématique de I'illocutoire derive. *Language et Société* 2: 17-41.

Aqvist, L. 1972. *performatives and verifiability by the use of Language*. Uppsala: Philosophical Studies.

Austin, J. L. 1962. *How to do things with words*. Cambridge, Mass.: Harvard University press.

Austin, J. L. 1970. *Philosophical Papers*. Oxford: oxford University Press.

Bach, K. and R. M. Harnish. 1979 *Linguistic Communication and Speech acts*. Cambridge, Mass.: MIT Press.

Brown, P. and S. Levinson. 1978. Universals in language usage: Politeness phenomena. In Goody, E. (1978, 56-289).

Brown, R. and A. Gilman. 1960. The pronouns of power and solidarity. In Sebeok, T.A. (1960, 253-76).

Cho, Choon-Hak. 1982. *A Study of Korean Pragmatics: Deixis and Politeness*. Seoul: Hanshin.

Cole, P. (ed.). 1978. *Syntax and Semantics 9: Pragmatics*. New York: Academic Press.

Cole, P. and J. L. Morgan (eds.). 1975. *Syntax and Semantics 3: Speech Acts*. New York: Academic Press.

Cornulier, B. D. 1975. La notion d'auto-interprétatopn. *Étedes de Linguistique Appliquée* 19: 52-82.

Coulthard, M. 1977. *An introduction to Discourse Analysis*. London/HongKong: Longman.

Davison, A. 1975. Indirect speech acts and what to do with them. In Cole, P. and J. Morgan (1975, 143-85).

Diller, A. 1978. La forme en-rais dans les actes indirectes de langage. *Actes de la Session de Linguistique de Bourg-Saint Maurice*. Paris: Sonseil Sceientifique de la Sorbonne Nouvelle.

Dillon, G. L. 1977. *Introduction to Contemporary Linguistic Semantics*. Engle wood Cliffs, N.J.: Prentice-Hall.

Dolitsky, M. 1983. Humor and unsaid. *Journal of Pragmatics* 7: 39-48.

Fodor, J. D. 1977. *Semantics*. New York: Crowell.

Fraser, B. 1978. Acquiring social competence in a second language. *RELC Journal* 9. 2: 1-21.

Fraser, B. 1980. Conversational mitigation. *Journal of Pragmatics,* 4: 341-50.

Fraser, B. and W. Nolan. 1981. The association of deference with linguistic form. *International Journal of the Sociology of Language* 27: 93-109.

Garvey, C. 1975. Requests and responses in children's speech. *Journal of Child Language* 2: 41-63.

Gazdar, G. 1981 Speech act assignment. In Joshi, A.K., B.L. Webber, and I.A. Sag (1981, 64-83).

Geukens, S.K.J. 1978. The distinction between direct and indirect speech acts: Towards a surface approach. *Journal of Pragmatics* 2: 261-76.

Goody, E.N. (ed.). 1978. *Questions and Politeness*. Cambridge, UK: Cambridge University Press.

Gordon, D. and G. Lakoff 1971. Conversational postulates. *Papers from the Seventh Regional Meeting of the Chicago Linguistic Society*.

Green, G.M. 1975. How to get people to do things with words: The whimperative question. In Cole and Morgan (1975, pp. 107-141)

Grice, H.P. 1975. Logic and conversation. In Cole, P. and J. Morgan (1975, 41-58).

Halliday, M.A.K. 1970. *A Course in Spoken English: Intonation*. London: Oxford University Press.

Hancher, M. 1979. The classification of cooperative illocutionary acts. *Language in Society* 8: 1-14.

Heringer, J.T. 1972. *Some Grammatical Correlates of Felicity Conditions and Presuppositions. Ohio State University Working Papers in Linguistics* 11: iv-110. Formerly reprinted and distributed by the Indiana University Linguistics Club.

Holmes, J. 1984. Modifying illocutionary force. *Journal of Pragmatics*, 8, 345-365.

Joshi, A.K., B.L. Webber, and I.A. Sag (eds.). 1981. *Elements of Discourse Understanding*. Cambridge, UK: Cambridge University Press.

Kempson, R. M. 1977. *Semantic Theory*. Cambridge, UK: Cambridge University Press.

Kennedy, G. D. 1979. Semantic Priorities in English language teaching. RELC Journal 10.2: 14-35.

Lakoff, R. 1973. The logic of politeness: Or, minding your p's and q's. In Corum, C., T.C. Smith-Startk, and A. Weiser (eds.), *Papers from the Ninth Regional Meeting of the Chicago Linguistic Society*.

Lakoff, R. 1974. What you can do with words: Politeness, pragmatics and performatives. *Berkeley Studies in Syntax and Semantics* 1. XVI-1-XVI-55.

Lee, P.A. 1976. Impositive speech acts. *Ohio State University Working Papers in Linguistics* 21: 98-144.

Lee, P.A. 1983. Form and function in illocutionary acts. *University of Hawaii Working Papers in Linguistics* 15.2: 19-38.

Leech, G. 1983. *Principles of Pragmatics.* London: Longman.

Lemmon, E.J. 1962. On sentences verifiable by their use. *Analysis* 22: 86-9.

Levinson, S.C. 1983. *Pragmatics.* Cambridge, UK: Cambridge University Press.

Lewis, D.K. 1970. General semantics. *Synthese* 22: 18-67.

Mohan, B.A. 1974. Principles, postulates, politeness. In *Papers from the Tenth Regional Meeting of the Chicago Linguistic Society*.

Morgan, J. 1978. Two types of convention in indirect speech acts. In Cole, P. (1978, 261-80).

Parret, H. 1984. Regularities, rules and strategies. *Journal of Pragmatics* 8: 569-92.

Sadock, J.M. 1970. Whimperatives. In Sadock and Vanek 1970.

Sadock, J.M. 1971. Queclaratives. *Papers from the Seventh Regional Meeting of the Chicago Linguistic Society*.

Sadock, J.M. 1974. *Toward a Linguistic Theory of Speech Acts*. New York: Academic Press.

Sadock, J.M. and A. L. Vanek (eds.). 1970. *Studies Presented to Robert B. Lees by His Students.* Edmonton: Linguistic Research Inc.

Searle, J. 1969. *Speech Acts: An Essay in the Philosophy of Language*. Cambridge: Cambridge University Press.

Searle, J. 1975. Indirect speech acts. In Cole, P. and J. Morgan (1975, 59-82).

Searle, J. 1976. The classification of illocutionary acts. *Language in Society* 5: 1-24.

Searle, J., F. Kiefer, and M. Bierwisch (eds.). 1980. *Speech Act Theory and Pragmatics.* Synthese Language Library. Dordrecht, Holland: D. Reidel Publishing Co.

Sebeok, T.A. (ed.). 1960. *Style in Language*. Cambridge, Mass.: MIT Press.

Sohn, Ho-min. 1986. *Linguistic Expeditions.* Seoul: Hanshin.

Stiles, W.B. 1981. Classification of intersubjective illocutionary acts. *Language in Society* 10: 227-50.

Stubbs, M. 1983. Can I have that in writing, please? Some neglected topics in speech act theory. *Journal of Pragmatics* 7: 479-94.

Van der Auwera, J. 1980. *Indirect Speech Acts Revisited.* Bloomington: Indiana University Linguistics Club.

Part IV

TEACHING KOREAN AS A FOREIGN LANGUAGE

26 Sociolinguistic and Pragmatic Appropriateness in Proficiency-oriented Korean Language Instruction*

1. How to deal with sociolinguistic problems, as related to social contexts and cultural norms, and pragmatic problems, as related to speech participants and speech acts, has been a major issue in foreign language education in recent years.[1] This is not only because one of the main goals of foreign language learning is cross-cultural communication, and human communication necessarily involves the psychological attitudes of the participants, but because grammatical sentences frequently become inappropriate in specific contexts and speech situations. Such problems are particularly sensitive in the functional use of spoken language which involves face-to-face human interaction.[2]

The sociolinguistic and pragmatic issue is of paramount significance in Korean language education in the United Stated for the following reasons among others. First, such cognitive cultural aspects of the two societies as values, world views, ideas, assumptions, and expectations differ immensely, and these differences are mirrored in the linguistic structure, language use, and non-verbal behavior of the two peoples. Second, Korean is an honorific language and its complex registers reflect intricate and delicate interpersonal relationships to the extent that a Korean may not speak without his knowledge of his relative status in relation to the person addressed. Third, Korean vocabulary contains a large number of culturally unique words and phrases, as well as doublets of native and Sino-Korean origins whose cultural connotations are divergent. Fourth, Korean is a so-called situation-oriented language which, among other things, forces situationally understood elements to be omitted in utterances under certain structural and pragmatic conditions. The Defense Language Institute's rating of Korean as the most difficult language for Americans to learn can be attributed

* This paper is reprinted from *Bilingual Education for Overseas Koreans* 8: 461–90 (1991).

1 The present proposal has derived from a research in developing the oral component of Korean Proficiency Guidelines as a University of Hawaii National Resource Center project.

2 I began this study in Korea during the summer of 1990 under an International Cultural Society of Korea grant. I completed it for publication in 1991 while I was a Fullbright fellow in Korea.

to the sociolinguistic and pragmatic, as well as structural, disparity existing between English and Korean.

In this paper, I will discuss (a) what kind of sociolinguistic and pragmatic variables in Korean should be taught, and (b) when and (c) how. Throughout my discussion, I will refer to relevant insights advanced by the ongoing push for proficiency-oriented language instruction. That is, the focus of foreign language education in the United States has recently shifted from the knowledge of a language to "proficiency" in the language, with speaking proficiency stressed from the very beginning of the language learning stage (e.g. Omaggio 1984, 1986). Thus, the concept of proficiency-based or functionally-based language education is becoming the guiding principle around which foreign language curricula, teaching, and testing are designed and developed. I propose in this paper that Korean language teaching, especially for oral proficiency, be redirected and reorganized along the proficiency-oriented approach.

In the proficiency-oriented framework, not only the pronunciation, grammar, vocabulary and fluency, but also pragmatic and sociolinguistic competences are a part and parcel of proficiency requirements. For example, Canale (1983) and Canale and Swain's (1980) integrative model of communicative competence include four components: grammatical, sociolinguistic, discourse, and strategic. Grammatical competence is no doubt the most basic extensive and essential, because it includes knowledge of vocabulary, pronunciation, spelling, word formation, and sentence structure. However, sociolinguistic competence is another indispensable component in language learning in that it is the ability to use grammatical forms and meanings appropriately in sociocultural contexts that determines the successful transmission of such communicative functions as greeting, statement, apology, question, answer, direction, request, ordering, and suggestion. For example, a register that is appropriate to a child or close friend is totally inappropriate to a socially distant adult in Korean.

Canale and Swain's discourse competence refers to the ability to use cohesive linguistic devices, such as pronominals, adverbials, conjunctions, and transitional expressions, to achieve unity of thought and continuity in a text. Strategic competence refers to the ability to use verbal and nonverbal communicative strategies to compensate for communicative breakdowns or to enhance communicative effectiveness. These two competences partly intersect with what is called pragmatic competence in this paper.

The push for "language teaching for proficiency" is based on the "functional trisection" consisting of communicative function, content, and accuracy and the assessment of different kinds of skills (speaking, listening, reading, writing, pragmatic and sociocultural awareness) at different proficiency levels (novice [0], intermediate [1], advanced [2], superior [3 and above] and their subdivisions). The proficiency movement is not promoting or advocating any particular single method of instruction. It attempts to accommodate an eclectic approach called "the relative contribution model". That is, every new proficiency level represents a new constellation of the factors of function, content, and accuracy, and the relative contribution of specific language subskills-pronunciation, vocabulary, grammar, fluency, and sociolinguistic and pragmatic appropriateness-changes from level to level (Higgs 1984:5).

In order to get a glimpse of American students' strengths and weaknesses in Korean oral proficiency and to gain a preliminary insight into what, when and how to teach with regard to sociolinguistic and pragmatic variables, I have examined some twenty interview tapes of the Korean Oral Proficiency Interviews (OPIs) that we had conducted.[3] Thirteen of them are representative as summarized below. N stands for Novice, I for Intermediate, A for Advanced, and S for Superior (level of a near native speaker).

(1)

Prof. level	Interviewee	Interviewer	Ethnicity	Classroom learning	Residence in Korea
N-low	Ba (f)	(Sohn)	Caucasian	100 hrs (UH)	0
N-mid	Ca (f)	(Sohn)	Caucasian	100 hrs (UH)	0
N-mid	Or (f)	(Sohn)	Malaysian	100 hrs (UH)	0
N-mid	Ol (f)	(Yuen)	Caucasian	100 hrs (UH)	0
N-high	Iv (f)	(Sohn)	Italian	300 hrs (UH)	0
N-high	Su (f)	(Yang)	Korean	100 hrs (UH)	Came to US at 3
I-low	Ly (f)	(Shulz)	Caucasian	600 hrs (DLI, UH)	2 months
I-mid	Je (f)	(Yang)	Korean	300 hrs (UH)	Came to US at 1
I-mid	Ka (m)	(Yuen)	Korean	100 hrs (UH)	Came to US at 3
I-high	Mo (f)	(Yuen)	Korean	100 hrs (UH)	Came to US at 6
A	Hi (f)	(Yang)	Korean	100 hrs (UH)	Came to US at 8
S	Yu (m)	(Yuen)	Japanese	A few yrs	6 yrs
S	Ti (m)	(Yang)	Caucasian	A few yrs	8 yrs

The proficiency ratings shown in (1) and my analysis of interview data have

3 The OPI's were conducted by Heisoon Yang (Ehwa Womans University), Carol Shultz (Columbia University), Su-Ah Yuen (University of Hawaii) and myself before and during a Korean oral proficiency workshop at the University of Hawaii in January 19-21, 1991. The ACTFL (the America Council on the Teaching of Foreign Language) procedures were followed in the Korean OPI's. The interview tapes were rated at the workshop consisting of the interviewers, D. Hiple (ACTFL), and Dong Jae Lee (University of Hawaii) according to the ACTFL Proficiency Guidelines.

led to the following generalizations: other things being equal, (a) the proficiency levels of students are proportionate to the length of their residence in Korea (b) Korean-Americans living with their monolingual parents have received higher ratings than others due to constant exposure to Korean language and culture, (c) Japanese students are rated higher than Western students due obviously to their linguistic and cultural similarity with Koreans, (d) pattern-oriented students have received lower ratings than those who are more situation-oriented, and (e) non-Koreans are much weaker in sociolinguistic, pragmatic, and listening competence than Korean Americans. All this suggests the significance of sociolinguistic and pragmatic aspects in Korean language education.

2. Let us first take up the question of what kind of sociolinguistic and pragmatic variables should be taught to the students of Korean. I propose six sociolinguistic and pragmatic categories for overseas Korean language education, as shown in (2).[4] This does not mean that they should be taught in a certain order, independently of each other. They are largely interrelated in utterances. In particular, the rules, norms, and principles in category VI underlie the components of the other categories to teach in each proficiency level. How to effectively, efficiently, and systematically teach them is one of the major tasks Korean language professionals are yet to work out.

(2) Six categories to teach
- I. Culture-sensitive vocabulary
- II. Conventionalized expressions
- III. Honorific patterns
  - a. Hearer honorifics and speech levels
  - b. Referent honorifics
- IV. Strategic speech acts
- V. Nonverbal behavior
- VI. Underlying sociolinguistic rules, cultural norms, and pragmatic principles

As for culture-sensitive vocabulary, Park (1989) proposed sixteen classes as very relevant, which include terms symbolizing Korea, terms for food, clothing, shelter, cultural assets, literature, music, arts, dance, sports and games, trademarks, flowers, personalities, tradition, etiquettes, tourist resorts, etc. To this list we can add classifiers, terms for holidays, color terms, terms for body parts, names of representative mountains, rivers, cities, expressways, and institutions,

4 Park (1989) classifies cultural elements in Korean into (a) honorifics, (b) idioms and proverbs, (c) general vocabulary, and (d) linguistic changes and innovated terms.

family names, emotive words, basic sound symbolic words, and pragmatically sensitive words (e.g. *tanita* 'go and come', *kata* 'go', *ota* 'come', *cwuta* 'give', and demonstratives), as well as a large variety of expressions with unique cultural connotation. For example, the kinship term *oppa* is different from English older brother in two ways. First, it has a narrower semantic scope, in that it refers only to female's older brother. Second, it is used as not only a reference term but also an address term, in that in Korean culture, siblings are hierarchical, using unequal terms of address (e.g. *oppa* vs. given name). Cultural connotation refers roughly to those aspects of the meaning of an expression within a cohesive culture which are only implied, not explicit or denotative, yet reflect native speakers' shared value judgments, perceptions and reactions.

Cultural connotations are so strongly shared by the members of the ethnolinguistic community that violation of connotational norms meets immediate negative reactions from the members. For example, Koreans use *noin* and *mom pwulphyenhan i* with favorable connotation, and *nulkun i* and *pyngsin* with pejorative connotation, although they have the same denotative meanings "aged person" and "crippled person," respectively. Kinds of cultural connotation that expressions may carry include the speaker's social standing, localism, archaism, technicality, learnedness, foreignism, slangyness, taboo, intensity, pejorativeness, euphemism, and formality (Bloomfield 1933: 151-7 and Kwon 1986: 38-40).

As indicated earlier, one vexing problem for the learners of Korean is the abundance of doublets of native and Sino-Korean origins, whose syntactico-morphological distributions are not always the same and whose sociocultural connotations are vastly different. When doublets occur in the same linguistic or social context, Sino-Korean forms frequently gives more prestigious or deferential connotation, as *pwuchin* vs. *apeci* 'father', *canye* vs. *aitul* 'children', *sengham* vs. *ilum* 'name', and *yensey* vs. *nai* 'age'. Correct use of numerals alone gives American learners enough trouble, in that use of two sets of numerals, native (N) and Sino-Korean (SK), is often irregular. For example, hours must be expressed with native numerals, whereas minutes and seconds in Sino-Korean, as in *yeltwu* (N) *si* (SK) *sip i* (SK) *pwun* (SK) 'twelve o'clock twelve minutes'. Although a general rule is that a native element occurs with a native element and a Sino-Korean with a Sino-Korean in word or phrase formation, this is not always the case. Thus, *yel twu* (N) *pwun* (N) vs. *sip-i* (SK) *myeng* (SK) '12 persons' and *yel twu* (N) *sal* (N) vs. *sip-i* (SK) *sey* (SK) '12 years old' follow this general rule but classifier sequences like *yel* (N) *kwen* (SK) '10 volumes', *cha* (SK) *twu* (N) /**i* (SK) *tay* (SK) 'two cars), *cha* (SK) *sumwu* (N) *tay* (N) / *i sip* (SK) *tay* (SK) '20 cars', etc. show irregularity.

Lexical misuse in our sample data is illustrated in (3). Notice that many of the errors are made in culture-sensitive words. Hereafter, A stands for the interviewer and B the interviewee. Correct forms of the intended meanings are given in brackets. Parenthesized forms in brackets are grammatical but redundant.

(3) a. A: 하와이는 언제 오셨어요?
*Hawaii nun **encey o-syesse.yo**?*
'When did you come to Hawaii?'

B: 하와이는 **두** 년 전에 **갔**어요. (N-mid; Ol)
Hawaii nun ***twu*** *nyen cen ey* ***ka-****sse.yo*.
[(하와이는) **이** 년 전에 **왔**어요.]
'I came to Hawaii two years ago.'

b. A: 한국친구하고 한국말 해봤어요?
hankwuk chinkwu hako hankwuk-mal hay pw-asse.yo?
'Have you tries speaking Korean with your Korean friends?'

B: 아니요, 한국친구하고 한국말 **말씀**하지 않**아요**. (N-mid; Ca)
anio, hankwuk chinkwu hako hankwukmal ***malssum****ha-ci an-a.yo*.
[아니요, 한국친구하고 한국말 해보지 않았어요.]
'No, I haven't tried to speaker in Korean with my Korean friends.'

c. A: 아, 자동차로 날마다 오세요?
a, catongcha lo nal-mata o-seyyo?
'Oh, are you coming to school by car every day?'

B: 아니요. 일 주 **두** 일이 있는데요, **두개** 번 **합**니다. (I-low; Ly)
anio, ilcwu ***twu*** *il -i iss-un tey yo*. ***twu-kay*** *pen* ***ha-pnita***.
[아니요. 일주에 두번 수업이 있는데, 두번 옵니다.]
'No, I come twice a week, as I have two classes.'

d. A: 형제가 있습니까? 형이나 동생?
hyengcey ka iss-supnikka? hyeng ina tongsayng?
'Do you have siblings-brothers or sisters?'

B: 지금요, 여동생 두 **개**하고 남동생하고, (I-low; Ly)
cikum yo, yetongsayng ***twu kay*** [*twul*] *hako namtongsayng hako*.
[지금 여동생 둘하고 남동생 하나 있어요.]
'Now I have two younger sisters and one younger brothers.'

e. A: 더운 날씨 안 좋아하세요?
tewun nalssi an coh-a ha-seyyo?
'Don't you like hot weather?'

B: **아니요.** (I-mid; Je)
Ani-yo.
[예.].
'No.'

f. A: 동생 있어요?
tongsayng iss-e.yo?
'Do you have younger siblings?'

B: 네, **여자** 누나하고 **큰 오빠**있어요 하나. (I-mid; Ka)
ney. ***yeca*** *nwuna hako* ***kwun oppa*** *iss-e.yo hana.*
[네, 누나 하나하고 형 하나 있어요.]
'I have an older sister and an older brother.'

g. A: 아버지는 무엇을 하시는 분이세요?
*apeci nun mwue*s ul *ha-si-nun pwun* ***i-seyyo***?
'What is your father doing?'

B: 아버지는 차 고쳐요. 차 몸 고쳐요. (I-mid; Ka)
apeci nun cha kochy-e.yo. ***cha mom*** *kochy-e.yo.*
[아버지는 차 고치세요. 차체 수리하세요.]
'My father fixes cars. He runs a body shop.'

Language use is conventional to a great extent. This is particularly the case with the spoken language used in daily encounters. Conventionality of language use explains why many grammatical expressions are appropriate in certain contexts and become inappropriate in many other contexts. Thus, it is essential for learners to master culturally sensitive and pragmatically conventionalized expressions, together with not only the contexts but also the speaker-hearer relations in which they are used appropriately. A typical case is the use of a wide variety of phatic expressions, as illustrated in (4), where only the deferential or polite ending is used. These expressions are sensitive to contexts and interpersonal power and solidarity.

(4) 안녕하세요? *Anneyngha-seyyo*? 'Hi!; How are you?; Good morning; Good afternoon; Good evening.'

안녕히 가세요/계세요. *Annyenghi ka-seyyo/kyey-seyyo*. 'Good-bye.'
안녕히 주무세요; 잘 자요. *Annyenghi cwumwu-seyyo*; *cal ca-yo*. 'Good night!'
고맙습니다; 감사합니다. *Komap-supnita*; *kamsaha-pnita*. 'Thank you.'
천만에요; 별말씀을요. *Chenman ey-yo; pyel malssum ul-yo*. 'Not at all.'
실례합니다. *Sillyeyha-pnita*. 'Excuse me.'
미안해요. M*ianhay-yo*. 'I am sorry; Thank you.'
죄송합니다. *Coysongha-pnita*. 'I am awfully sorry; I am grateful.'
글세요. *Kulssey-yo*. 'Well.'
또 뵙겠어요. *Tto poy-pkeysse.yo*. 'See you again.'
어디 가세요? *Eti ka-seyyo*? 'Where are you going?'
어떻게 오셨어요? *Ettehkey o-syesse.yo*? 'May I help you?'
수고하세요. S*wuko ha-seyyo*. 'Good-bye.'
잘 자녀오세요. *Cal tanye o-seyyo*. 'Good-bye.'
처음 뵙겠어요. *Cheum poyp-keysse.yo*. 'Hi!; Nice to see you.'
잘 부탁합니다. *Cal pwuthakha-pnita*' (lit. I count on you.')
만나서 반갑습니다. *Manna-se pankap-supnita*. 'I am glad to see you.'
말씀 좀 묻겠어요. *Malssum com mwut-keysse.yo*. 'May I ask a favor of you?'
잠깐만 기다려 주세요. *Camkkan man kitalye cwu-seyyo*. 'Wait a minute please.'

In addition to phatic expressions, there are a great many culture-bound idioms and proverbs that must be used appropriately in conversations. For example, the term for 'eye' alone appears in such expressions as *nwun i nophta* 'fastidious, have high standards' (lit. 'eyes are high'), *nwun i melta* 'blind' (lit. 'eyes are far'), *nwun i maypta* 'have dexterous eyes' (lit. 'eyes are hot (taste)'), *nwun yoki hata* 'delight (feast) one's eyes' (lit. 'appease one's eye hunger with'), *nwun ey kesullita* 'offend the eye' (lit. 'be opposed to eyes'), *nwun ul sokita* 'cheat' (lit. 'cheat eyes'), and *ton ey nwun i etwuecita* 'be covetous of money' (lit. 'eyes become dark to money'). Similary, *maum ey tulta* 'like' (lit. 'come into mind'), *meli ka tolta* 'be crazy' (lit. 'head turns around'), *meli ka cal tolta* 'be smart' (lit. 'head turns well'), *meli ka tolci anhnunta* 'be stupid' (lit. head does not turn'), *ephchin tey tepchinulako* 'to make matters worse' (lit. 'to attack the turned over'), *cwi cwukun tusi co.yonghata* 'quiet like a dea rat', *kemun meli ka phappwuli toy-l ttay kkaci* 'throughout one's life' (lit. 'until dark hair becomes (white) onion roots') and thousands of other metaphorical expressions and proverbs are culture-bound idiomatic expressions with varying degrees of difficulty and frequency usage. In our sample data, (5a) is a case of an unnecessary use of the formula *mianha-pnita* 'I am sorry' when she could not understand the interviewer's question immediately. This is obviously due to an interference from English. (5b) is a case of the use of a grammatical but pragmatically less acceptable form.

(5) a. A: *ettehkey hakkyo ey wa.yo? pessu lo wa.yo*?
B: *a, o! mianhapnita. catongcha ey kapnita* [*lo opnita*]. (I-low; Ly)

b. A: *elmana kelly-e.yo*?
B: *cha lo hakkyo ey o-myen isip pwun man kelly-e.yo*
[*pakkey an kelly-e.yo*]. (I-mid; Je)

Korean may be termed an honorific language, in that linguistic communication is impossible without using hierarchically structured honorifics which are built in all utterances. Knowledge and appropriate use of honorific patterns in contexts, therefore, constitute the most important sociolinguistic and pragmatic requirement in Korean language education. Honorifics are viewed from the speaker-hearer perspective, in which case we may talk about addressee honorifics, and from the speaker-referent perspective, in which case we may talk about referent honorifics which comprise subject, object, and dative honorifics. Use of honorifics is contingent upon the relative age, kinship, social or occupational status, degree of formality or intimacy, in- or out-groupness, etc. between the speaker and a referent appearing in a given speech utterance on the other. For example, Korean has six different speech levels or registers that reflect addressee honorifics. Since there are many studies on Korean honorifics, I will not take up the details here. The example in (6) which illustrates the expression of "good night" between an elementary intermediate (not college) student and his/her teacher may be sufficient to indicate the complexity and significance of honorific patterns in Korean.

(6) student: *sensayngnim annyenghi cwumwyseyyo*.
'Good night, teacher.'
(lit. Mr. Teacher, sleep peacefully)

teacher: *kulay, ne to cal cala*.
'Good night.'
(lit. Yes, you too, sleep well.)

Notice that unlike in English, the interlocuters must use entirely different registers. Compare *sensayngnim* with *ne* 'you', *annyenghi* with cal 'well', *cwumwusey* with *ca* 'sleep', *-yo* with *–la* (imperative sentence ender), and (*ney*) with *kulay* 'yes'. Use of asymmetrical speech acts are ubiquitous. Even between adult equals, the speech forms are not the same when in/out-groupness is involved, as shown below:

(7) A: *samonim un myech si ey cinci capswuseyyo*?
'What time does your wife eat?'
B: *cip salam un yelsi ey pap mekeyo*.
'My wife eats at 10.'

In our sample data, the polite addressee honorific ender (-*yo* form) is used quite appropriately by students in all levels. However, one recurrent error pattern is the frequent omission of –*yo* (often replacing it with the intimate form) when a word or phrase, instead of a sentence, is called for as an answer.

(8) a. A: *ilponmal etise paywesseyo*?
B: *Hawaii tayhakkyo ey*. (N-mid; Or)

b. A: *hakkyo ey ol ttay ettehkey oseyyo*?
B: *cha wuncen hay*.

c. A: *cha iyaki com hay cwuseyyo. etten cha yeyyo*?
B: "Blue Honda". *ccokuman cha. say keya. say ke cha. cekum hayse ton* "pay" *hayko*. (N-high; Su)

d. A: *mikwuk cha yeyyo*?
B: *anya. ilpon cha yeeyo*. (I-mid; Je)

The most frequent error pattern is the misuse of the subject honorific suffix –*usi*.

(9) a. A: *hankwuk ey ka pwasseyo*?
B: *anio, hankwuk ey* ***ka posici anayo*** [*ka poci anasseyo*]. (N-mid; Ca)

b. A: *Hawaii tayhakkyo tahyhak wen haksaying iyeyyo*?
B: *anio, Hawaii tayhakkyo man* ***taniseyyo*** [*tanyeyo*]. (N-mid; Ol)

c. A: *kongpwu haci anhko mwues ul haseyyo*?
B: *TV* ***poseyyo*** [*pwayo*]. *poko* "music" *to tuleyo. cenhwa keleyo*. (N-mid; Iv)

d. A: *hankwuk ey ka pon cek issuseyyo*?
B: ***epssuseyyo*** [*epsseyo*]. (N-high; Su)

e. A: *mwel hasysseyo*?
B: *wuli khun emeni ey* [*eykey*] *cey ka* ***poysile*** [*poyle*] *kasseyo*. (I-mid; Ka)

f. B: *encey Hawaii ey wasseyo* [osyesseyo]? (N-mid; Ca)
B: *Sewul [lo] pwuthe Hawaii ey* ***kasseyo*** *[*osyesseyo]? (N-mid; Or)
B: ***kalswu isseyo*** [*osil swu issuseyyo*]? (I-low; Ly)
B: "shopping" ***haysseyo*** [*hasyesseyo*]? (I-mid; Je)

Lower interviewees have difficulty in correctly using the other speech level enders (e.g. *–supnita* and *–ta*), deferential words (e.g. *kyeysita* 'stay', *cwumwusita* 'sleep' and *tulita* 'give'), and personal pronouns. Observe the following examples.

(10) a. A: *Hawaii ey kacok i isseseyyo*?
B: ….
A: "kacok" is "family".
B: *ah, emeni Pennsylvania* ***isseyo*** [*kyeyseyyo*]. (N-low; Ba)

b. A: *myechsi ey cip ey kaseyyo*?
B: *History swuep i* ***kyeyseyyo*** [*isseyo*]. (N-mid; Ol)

c. A: *mwues towa tulil kkayo*?
B: "ticket" *towa* ***tulil*** [*cwusil*] *swu* ***isseyo*** [*issuseyyo*]? (I-mid; Ka)

d. B: *pwuin to Hawaii ey* ***isseyo*** [*kyeyseyyo*]? (N-mid; Or)
B: ***tangsin*** [*sensayngnim*] *to kulehkey* ***ilhapnikka*** [*il hasipnikka*]? (I-low; Ly)
B: *ce nun han sikan* [*hwu*] *ey* "interview" *isski ttaymwun ey ce uy cakheys ul* "clean" *hay* ***tulikeysseyo*** [*cwusikeysseyo*]? (I-mid; Je)

While use of honorifics is socially normative and structurally encoded, there are many strategically oriented speech acts whose goals is to either tone down or boost the illocutionary force of the utterances for politeness (cf. Sohn 1986). A typical set consists of indirect speech acts which use interrogatives for a request downtoners, euphemistic phrases, passivization, hedges, vagueness, ellipsis or incomplete sentences, metaphors, hints, rhetorical questions, allusions, etc. to tone down assertive force (cf. Sohn ibid.). For example, expressions like *yensey ka ettekey toyseyyo*? 'How old are you/is he?'; *ettehkey osyessna yo*? 'May I help you?'; *cal molukeyssnun tey yo* 'I am not sure'; *malssum com yeccwue pwato toyl ci molukeyssupnita* 'May I ask you a question?'; and *Smith ssi lako hanun pwun kyeysimyen com pakkwe cwusikeysseyo*? 'Can I talk to Mr. Smith if he is available? belong here. Furthermore, indirect speech acts include such strategic expressions as those filling in communicative gaps which otherwise lead to communication breakdowns. Inappropriate use or nonuse of indirect speech acts are ubiquitous in our sample data, some of which are illustrated below.

(11) a. A: "English" *lul hankwukmal lo mwe lako hayyo*?
B: ***mollayo*** [*molukeyssnun teyyo*]. (N-mid; Or)

b. A: *kalpi elma cengto hayyo?*
B: ***mollayo. an pissa*** [*molukeysseyo. pyello an pissayo*] (I-low; Su)

c. A: *mwues ul kongpwu haseyyo?*
B: *cikum* "Liberal Arts" *kongpwu hanun* ***ke yeyyo*** [*teyyo*]. (I-mid; Je)

d. A: *halmeni yensey ka enu cengto toyseyyo?*
B: ……
A: *nai ka myech sal icyo? halmeni.*
B: *phalsip sal ieyyo.* (I-mid; Je)
A: *Kangyep ssi nun hakkyo onun kes oy ey talun hasinun kes isse.yo?*
B: *tasi hanpen* ***mal haseyyo*** [*malssumhay cwuseyyo*]. (I-mid; Ka)

In our sample data, only those at advanced or superir levels know how to use strategic speech acts in a relatively proper way. Observe the following interviews with students rated advanced or superior. Bold-faced forms are considered strategic speech acts.

(12) (A; Hi)
a. A: *chinkwu to yeca chinkwu ka te coha.yo*?
B: ***ku ken salam nalum i yeyyo***.

b. A: *namphyen kam ulo sayngkak hal swu issnun kulen isangcek in namca nun etten salam i yeyyo*?
B: *namca ka chakhayya toyko yeca ipcang kathun kes cal* ***ala cwunun*** *salam*.

(13) (S; Yu)
a. A: *cey ilum un S ipnita.* ***sengham i ettehkey toyseyyo***?
B: *satto lako hapnita.*
A: *onul nalssi ka ettehseyyo*?
B: *com siwenhan* ***kes kathun*** *tey yo*.

b. A: *taykang com selmyenghay* ***cwul swu issusikeysseyo****?*
B: *ney, ku kes un ile hako hankwuke uy ku hancae* ***isscanhayo****? thukhi ku tongsa lose nun "kongpwu hata" kulen kes i ettehkey pwunsek toyya hanun ci. Kulen kes ul, ney.*

(14) (S; Ti)
a. A: *mwe lul cenkong haseyyo?*
B: *ney, hankwuk mwunhak cenkong hako isssupnita. thukhi sico tayhayse kwansim i* ***manhketun yo****. hyentay sico.*

b. A: *keki se mwuel hasyesseyo?*
B: *ku ttay phyenghwa pongsatan ulo kasssupnita. nahwanca chon ey issesse.yo. cengchakchon ey. cenla namto issnun* ***ku*** *kwangcwu issci* ***anhsupnikka****? Kwangcwu eyes ttelecin keki acwu ccokkuman maul issnun tey, hohyeywen ilako issnun tey, nahwanca chon ipnita.*

Nonverbal behavior, such as gestures, facial expressions, eye contacts, and silence, is an integral component of sociolinguistic and pragmatic competences. For example, Koreans have many hierarchy-sensitive gestures. At a dinner table, a socially inferior person must wait until a social superior sits down and starts eating; one does not smoke in the presence of a social superior; (though not an inferior) a Korean must bow; and a Korean must rise when an obvious social superior appears on the scene, and he cannot pass in front of an obvious social superior (for more discussion on Korean's nonverbal behavior, see Sohn 1986). Thus, nonverbal behavior includes proper etiquettes not only in a variety of interpersonal encounters, such as conversations between unequals, between distant or intimate equals, but also in many conventional situations, such as family life, shopping, table manners, business life, wedding, funeral, exchange of gifts, greetings, sports, amusements, etc. All these should be part of culture learning in foreign language classrooms.

The last category of sociolinguistic and pragmatic aspects is sociolinguistic rules, cultural norms, and pragmatic principles. Culture learning is a process of acculturation into a foreign culture, developing favorable attitudes toward that culture. Its objectives in foreign language education intercultural communication and intercultural understanding, as well as better appreciation of the learner's own culture from a comparative perspective. Thus, for example, rules like "one cannot use honorific to a child unless for educational purposes," "a child cannot use a plain or familiar speech level ender to an adult," "one should use the honorific ender *–nim* after a professional title when addressing to a distant equal or superior," "one cannot use loan terms Mr. X or Dr. X addressing one's seniors" are sociolinguistic rules.

Cultural norms of Koreans range over their interpersonal value orientations, ideas, assumptions, world views, and expectations. For example, Koreans' values for relative hierarchism, collectivism, emotionalism, and formalism as against Americans' egalitarianism, individualism, rationalism, and pragmatism, underlie Koreans' verbal and nonverbal behavior (cf. Sohn 1986 for details). Pragmatic principles include cooperative and politeness principles (or rules or strategies) in interpersonal encounters, as discussed in such works as lakoff (1973), Grice (1975), Searle (1975), Cho (1982), Leech (1983), Brown and Levinson (1987), and Sohn (1986, 1988, 1989). For example, Lakoff's rules of politeness (a. Don't impose on the addressee, b. Give him his options, c. Make him feel warm and friendly) and Brown and Levinson's extensively politeness strategies are partly applicable to the pragmatic usage of Korean.

Such partly universal and partly Korean-specific principles underlie conventionalized expressions, honorifics, strategic speech acts, and nonverbal behavior to a great extent. Thus, a systematic instruction of the Korean language and its sociocultural variables, cultural connotations of words, phrases, sentences, and discourse utterances, as well as culture-bound nonverbal behavior.

3. Let me turn to a brief discussion of the question of when to teach those sociolinguistic and pragmatic variables in Korean which have been illustrated thus far. Contrary to the widely held proficiency-oriented claim that sociolinguistic variables play a minimal role at the initial stage of language learning, I propose on empirical grounds that in Korean they play a major role from the beginning of language learning. For example, according to Higgs and Clifford's (1982) putatively universal relative contribution model, sociolinguistic variables play a minimal role at the low end of the rating scale but are crucial to attaining superior level ratings. Even minimum communication is impossible in Korean without considerable familiarity with sociolinguistic aspects, however, in that such aspects are built in the structure of the language in the form of honorifics. Hence, many of these aspects should be introduced from the very beginning of language instruction. One of the important tasks of Korean language professionals is to design graded curriculum and instruction, that is, to determine what elements and information are to be introduced in what levels. One recommendable approach is to make us of the ACTFL guidelines as the organizing principle for such a design. ACTFL Proficiency Guidelines (and Interagency Language Roundtable (ILR) Scales as well for that matter) represent a progressive and well-graduated sequence of levels of linguistic and communicative development, outlining general performance criteria and specifying contexts and situations appropriate to each level. These experientially-based descriptions can effectively be used, with relevant modification, to structure the Korean language program, in that they enable us to identify what students have to know in order to function at a given level of competence, thus making us know what to teach.

Because of the different requirements at different oral proficiency levels of function, content, and accuracy, not only pronunciation, vocabulary, grammar, and fluency, but also pragmatic and sociolinguistic aspects must be focused differently at different levels. The Oral Novice Level (ACTFL 0) requires "enumeration of memorized material" to be the primary function that can be expressed; common, isolable semantic groups of lexical items to be the content; and simple intelligibility to be the accuracy. Thus, the basic vocabulary of daily usage including culture-sensitive words, pronunciation, idiomatized phatic expressions, and basic honorific elements such as the polite level ender must be given primary focus in developing teaching materials and syllabuses for the Novice level.

The Oral Intermediate Level (ACTFL 1) requires the student to create with language, asking and answering basic, concrete questions in areas of immediate personal need and initiating, minimally sustaining, and closing basic communicative tasks in a simple way. Together with vocabulary (including more cultural terms), pronunciation, and grammar, many basic sociolinguistic rules and cultural norms and associated linguistic expressions need to be introduced at this level, such as the Korean value orientations regarding age, kinship, and status-based hierarchical interpersonal relationships and collectivistic mentality, as well as essential linguistic honorifics and speech levels. For pragmatic proficiency appropriate for this level, students need to be trained in the conversational use of a wide variety of conventionalized speech acts and the underlying sociocultural assumptions.

The Oral Advanced level (ACTFL 2) is characterized by the speaker's ability to initiate, sustain, and bring to closure a wide variety of communicative tasks, including school and work situations, and narrate and describe with paragraph-length connected discourse. At this level, therefore, pragmatic and sociolinguistic competence as well as nonverbal behavior, along with grammatical accuracy, are particularly important. All the different speech-levels, euphemistic expressions (e.g. *issta* vs. *kyeysita* 'stay'), essential strategies, as well as associated linguistic rules and cultural norms must be introduced to classroom instruction for students aiming this level.

The Oral Superior Level (ACTFL 3 & ILR 3-5) is characterized by the speaker's native-like ability to participate in formal and informal conversations on practical, social, professional, and abstract topics, and support opinions and hypothesize, using native-like discourse strategies. Thus, the speakers at this level are expected to be familiar with most of the components of the six sociolinguistic and pragmatic categories discussed earlier, as well as the other accuracy areas (vocabulary, pronunciation, grammar, and fluency). Therefore, instructional materials and activities for students aiming this level must be designed accordingly.

4. My last question is *how* to teach sociolinguistic and pragmatic variables. This question is closely related to foreign language teaching methodology in general. A number of significant methods for foreign-language instruction have been proposed and practiced in America. The grammar-translation method dominated for more than a century, before the audiolongual method began to prevail in postwar America. The former method has been considered inappropriate because other important needs (such as speaking and listening) have remained unsatisfied. The audiolingual method, backed by structural linguistics and behaviorist leaning theory, is based on the assumption that a language is a system of speech habits. Learning was viewed by behaviorists as systems of habits acquired and strengthened through repetition and positive reinforcement. Audiolingual pattern practices were emphasized accordingly. This method didn't work satisfactorily, however, in that, after mastering the patterns of a foreign language, students could not use the language as they had expected to.

Influenced in large part by the diverse linguistic and learning theories that have appeared after the fall of structuralism and behaviorism, many post-audiolingual methods or approaches have appeared. These include cognitive code learning, the Natural Approach, Silent Way, Suggestopedia, Total Physical Response, counseling-learning, and so on (e.g. Higgs 1984: 4). Krashen's (1982) Monitor Model is particularly interesting in view of its insights in the acquisition-learning distinction, natural order hypothesis, the monitor hypothesis, the input hypothesis, and affective filter hypothesis (cf. Omaggio 1986: 29-34). Most of these methods are self-limiting. However, in that each method has its merits and demerits. Indeed, there is no one right way to teach languages, hence the rise of the so-called eclectic approach, which is advocated by the proficiency-oriented movement.

As indicated earlier, grammatical pattern-oriented instruction which is followed by many American classrooms is inefficient from the functional perspective. This is evidenced in our pattern-oriented interviewees, with whom communication was nearly non-existent, because they do not know even the most basic vocabulary items such as body parts. Observe the following dialogue with a pattern-oriented student.

(16) (N-low; Ba; Completed Korean 101)
A: *encey Hawaii tayhakkyo ey tule osyesseyo*?
B: *aniyeyyo. Michigan tolayeyyo.*

A: *onul i myechil i yeyyo*?
B: "*onul*" *i mwue mal i yeyyo*?
A: *nwuka kaluchiseyyo*?
B: "*nwuka*"?
A: *ikes un mwe yeyyo*? (pointing to "eye")
B: We didn't learn body parts. We learn more grammatical patterns.
A: *mwusun grammatical pattern ul paywesseyo*?
B: *oh! ulkkayo; ulkes kathayo; ki ttaymwuney; pakkey. ton i epsesski ttaymwun ey saci anhayo; pi ka omyen phathi ey kaci anhkeysseyo.*

Learning process must be interesting, and it is well known that rote memorization of patterns is boring. Communication breakdowns due to the lack of the knowledge of essential lexical items cause frustration to students. All this is detrimental to students' affective domain of language learning. More importantly, grammar-pattern orientation is far from real-life situation which is indispensable to proficiency oriented instruction.

As a framework for a proficiency-oriented approach to formal language instruction, Omaggio (1986: 34-6) advances the following five hypotheses, around which classroom instruction, activities, and materials may best be organized when the students' long-range goal is Superior proficiency.

(17) *Hypothesis 1.*
Opportunities must be provided for students to practice using language in a range of contexts likely to be encountered in the target culture.

Corollary 1. Students should be encouraged to express their own meaning as early as possible after productive skills have been introduced in the course of instruction.
Corollary 2. A proficiency-oriented approach promotes active communicative interaction among students.
Corollary 3. Creative language practice (as opposed to exclusively manipulative or convergent practice) must be encouraged in the proficiency-oriented classroom.
Corollary 4. Authentic language should be used in instruction wherever and whenever possible.

Hypothesis 2.
Opportunities should be provided for students to practice carrying out a range of functions (task universals) likely to be necessary in dealing with others in the target culture.

Hypothesis 3.
There should be concern for the development of linguistic accuracy from the beginning of instruction in a proficiency-oriented approach.

Hypothesis 4.
Proficiency-oriented approaches should respond to the affective needs of students as well as to their cognitive needs. Students should feel motivated to learn and must be given opportunities to express their own meanings in a non-threatening environment.

Hypothesis 5.
Cultural understanding must be promoted in various ways so that students are prepared to live more harmoniously in the target-language community.

Except perhaps for Hypothesis 4, all the other hypotheses are relevant directly or indirectly to sociolinguistic/pragmatic competency, suggesting the significance of this component in language instruction. Under the above five working hypotheses, Omaggio (ibid.: 357-432) presents many useful suggestions and concrete samples of proficiency-oriented instructional activities, including those for teaching for cultural understanding.

Language learners' sociolinguistic and pragmatic competence can be developed most efficiently through optimal interactions with the native speakers of the target language. This obvious fact is also evidenced in our interview data. Thus, the native contexts and speech situations should be simulated in classrooms, especially in the elementary and intermediate level instruction. This is a training in acculturation, because the learning of sociolinguistic and pragmatic variables is by and large coterminous with the degree of acculturation. In addition to well-organized lecturers and frequent tests, therefore, vocabulary, conventionalized expressions, honorifics, strategic speech acts, nonverbal behavior, and underlying rules, norms, and principles may best be trained in terms of contextualization, through such means as short dialogue forms, role plays, minidramas, audiotapes, and videos, covering a wide variety of real world contexts. I propose therefore that our low-level Korean skill classes (e.g. Korean 101-2, 201-2) and conversation classes be designed taking the above proficiency-oriented insights into account. I further propose that in lectures, the sociolinguistic and pragmatic patterns of the two languages (e.g. English and Korean) should be compared explicitly.

5. Conclusion

In this paper, I proposed six categories of sociolinguistic and pragmatic aspects to be trained in Korean language education; suggested that sociolinguistic and pragmatic variables must be introduced from the very beginning of the Korean language instruction; found that the pattern practice approach is inefficient; and proposed to adopt the methods of proficiency-oriented instruction for oral proficiency in Korean.

Despite the rapid increase in student population and opening of new programs in recent years, Korean language education in American universities is still in its fledgling stage, especially compared with such well-established programs as Spanish, French, German, Japanese, and Chinese. The existing texts, syllabuses, teaching, and testing for the Korean language skill courses (KOR 101-402) at the University of Hawaii, as well as in many other universities in the United States, are still based essentially on the grammatical pattern approach and the grammar translation method, and thus are far from being able to effectively develop students' oral proficiency, in that sociolinguistic, pragmatic, and cultural problems cannot be given systematic attention in such an approach. The pattern approach must be replaced with the proficiency approach for oral proficiency and the grammar-translation method should be limited to advanced reading levels. I believe that proficiency-oriented texts, syllabus design, lesson planning, instruction, and testing will not only improve overall Korean language education to a great extent but also students' sociolinguistic, pragmatic, and cultural awareness and proficiency. Extensive and detailed research is yet to be done toward this goal.[5]

REFERENCES: Chapter 26

ACTFL. 1986 & 1987. *Japanese* and *Chinese Proficiency Guidelines.*

ACTFL. 1989. *Oral Proficiency Interview.* ACTFL.

Bloomfield, L. 1933. *Language*. New York: Henry Holt & Co.

Brown, P. and S. C. Levinson. 1987. *Politeness.* Cambridge, UK: Cambridge University Press.

Canale, M. 1983. From communicative competence to communicative language pedagogy. In Richards, J. and R. Schmidt (1983).

Canale, M. and M. Swain. 1980. Theoretical bases of communicative approaches to second language teaching and testing. *Applied Linguistics* 1: 1–47.

---

5 A set of Korean language proficiency guidelines are being developed at the University of Hawaii. The aforementioned workshop (see note 2) is a part of this endeavor.

Cho, Choon-Hak. 1982. A Study of Korean Pragmatics: Deixis and Politeness. Ph.D. dissertation, University of Hawaii.

Cole, P. and J. Morgan (eds.). 1975. *Syntax and Semantics 3*. New York: Academic Press.

ETS (Educational Testing Serive). 1982. *Oral Proficiency Testing Manual.*

Grice, H. P. 1975. Logic and conversation. In Cole, P. and J. Morgan (1975, 41–58)

Higgs, T.V. (ed.). 1982. *Curriculum, Competence, and the Foreign Language Teacher.* ACTFL Foreign Language Education Series, vol. 13. Lincolnwood, Ill.: National Textbook.

Higgs, T.V. (ed.). 1984. *Teaching for Proficiency, the Organizing Principle.* Lincolnwood, Ill.: National Textbook.

Higgs, T.V. and R. Clifford. 1982. The *push toward* communication. In Higgs, T.V. (1982).

Krashen, S. 1982. *Principles and Practice in Second Language Acquisition.* New York: Pergamon Press.

Kwon, Oryang. 1986. *Cultural Connotations of English forKoreans.* Seoul: Hanshin Co.

Lakoff, R. 1973. The logic of politeness: Or, minding your p's and q's. *Papsers from the Ninth Regional Meeting of the Chicago Linguistic Society.* Chicago: University of Chicago.

Leech, G. N. 1983. *Principles of Pragmatics.* London: Longman.

Omaggio, A.C. 1984. The proficiency-oriented classroom. In Higgs, T.V. (1984).

Omaggio, A.C. 1986. *Teaching Language in Context: Proficiency-Oriented Instruction.* Boston, Mass.: Heinle & Heinle Publishers.

Park, Young Soon. 1989. Ceyi ene kyoyuk ulose uy mwunhwa kyoyuk (Cultural instruction as a second language education). *Bilingual Education for the Overseas Koreans* 5: 43–60.

Rambert, R.D. 1985. Foreign language instruction: A national agenda. *Foreign Language Annals* 18.5: 379-83.

Richards, J. and R. Schmidt (eds.). 1983. *Language and Communication.* London: Longman.

Searle, J. R. 1975. Indirect speech acts. In Cole, P. and J. Morgan (1975, 59–82)

Sohn, Ho-min. 1986. *Linguistic Expeditions.* Seoul: Hanshin.

Sohn, Ho-min. 1988. Strategies of indirection in language. *Linguistic in the Morning Calm* II, 167–96. Seoul: Linguistic Society of Korea. Also in this volume.

Sohn, Ho-min. 1989. Politeness strategies in Korean. *Papers in the Sixth International Conference on Korean Linguistics*, 655–60. Seoul: Hanshin. Also in this volume.

27 Korean Proficiency Guidelines: Needs, Procedures, Principles and Implications*

1. The Korean language faculty of the University of Hawaii (UH), in cooperation with a specialist from the American Council on the Teaching of Foreign Languages (ACTFL) and two faculty members from Columbia University and Ewha Women's University, have developed a set of draft Korean Language Proficiency Guidelines (KPGs) as appended to this paper (APPENDIX I).[1] The aim of this paper is to present the needs, procedures, principles and implications involved in developing the Guidelines. This paper is organized as follows. The rest of this section will be devoted to the discussion of needs for KPGs. The procedures followed in developing KPGs, together with a brief history of UH's KPGs project, are given in section 2. Some basic principles and pedagogical implications underlying KPGs are taken up respectively in sections 3 and 4. Section 5 concludes the paper, projecting some future action.

Let me begin by briefly dwelling on the need for a set of standardized KPGs from national and international perspectives. Undeniably, the language-teaching profession in the academic sector of the United States up until the 1970s suffered from the lack of a generally accepted sequence of measurable learning objectives. No standardized academic criteria or procedures were available for testing proficiency levels. Language study was limited, in general, to a classroom activity with little application to practical contexts. Curriculum, texts, instruction, and achievement tests hardly brought up the question of probable success or failure with the language in real world situations. On the practical side, it was widely observed that American students lacked functional foreign language ability, especially in the area of speaking, to a deplorable extent. On the other hand, the nation was in urgent need of many Americans who have functional foreign-language skills and understand other cultures, in view of the

* This paper is reprinted from *Korean Language Education* 4: 191–230 (1993).

1 The original version of this paper was presented at a conference on Korean language education, held at the University of California at Berkeley in June, 1992. I take this opportunity to thank the UC Berkeley Center for Korean Studies for the invitation.

rapidly expanding global politics, diplomacy, finance, commerce, defense, cultural interchange, and other international affairs in which America was engaged.

It was in such circumstances that President Carter's Commission on Foreign Language and International Studies was established in 1978. In 1979, the Commission recommended, among other things, that the academic language teaching community adopt standardized performance or proficiency standards. In response to this recommendation, ACTFL, with assistance from the Educational Testing Service (ETS) and Federal Interagency Language Roundtable (ILR), launched in 1981 an academic project entitled "A Design for Measuring and Communicating Foreign Language Proficiency," funded by the U.S. Department of Education. The goal of the project was to establish language proficiency achievement goals at all levels of proficiency, with special attention to establishing standards and procedures to measure speaking proficiency. As a result, ACTFL published in November 1982 the ACTFL Provisional Proficiency Guidelines, a series of descriptions of proficiency levels for speaking, listening, reading, writing, and culture in a foreign language. This 1982 version was since revised as ACTFL Proficiency Guidelines in 1986 (appendix II). ACTFL also devised the procedures of the Oral Proficiency Interview (OP1) in conformity with their Proficiency Guidelines. The OP I is a test of an individual's functional speaking ability in a foreign language through a face-to-face conversation with a trained tester for a period of 10 to 30 minutes. The resulting tape-recorded speech sample is then rated on a hierarchical scale from no practical ability to function in the language (novice-low) to the ability equivalent to that of an educated native speaker (superior). The need for OPIs is great because the traditional paper-and-pencil tests arc unable to assess a speaker's current foreign language speaking proficiency in various practical situations.

The ACTFL Guidelines, as well as the OPI procedures, were developed based on their antecedents, such as the 1979 President's Commission report, various government agencies' efforts to teach and test functional language ability, the academic work in communicative syllabuses, and the theory and practice related to communicative function A direct forerunner on whose language skill level descriptions ACTFL depended heavily is the Foreign Service Institute (FSl) of the U.S. Department of State. During World War II, FSI already established language level standards covering all four language skills. In the 1950s, FSI started to assess the oral proficiency of its personnel through an OPI in accordance with their skill level descriptions. Use of the FSI's level descriptions and OPI became widespread across government agencies, and these were standardized by ILR (Federal Interagency Language Roundtable), a consortium of government language training agencies. These level descriptions and the OPI remained largely in the government domain until the aforementioned recommendation by the President's Commission opened a way to the academic sector. The ILR government institutions not only assisted ACTFL in establishing academic standards and procedures but also endorsed the program. One important difference between ILR and ACTFL guidelines lies in the rating scale. As shown in Table 1 (Buck 1989), the ACTFL scale represents four of the six major levels (0-5) of the original ILR scale. The four major levels are SUPERIOR (Can support opinion, hypothesize, discuss abstract topics, and handle a linguistically unfamiliar situation), ADVANCED (Can narrate and describe in past, present and future time/aspect, and handle a complicated situation or transaction), INTERMEDIATE (Can create with language, ask and answer simple questions on familiar topics, and handle a simple situation or transaction), and NOVICE (No functional ability; speech limited to memorized material).

TABLE 1. Comparison between ACTFL Scale & ILR Scale

ACTFL SCALE	ILR SCALE
Superior	5 (Native or bilingual proficiency)
	4+
	4 (Distinguished proficiency)
	3+
	3 (Professional or working proficiency)
Advanced High	2+
Advanced	2 (Limited working proficiency)
Intermediate High	1+
Intermediate Mid	1 (Survival Proficiency)
Intermediate Low	
Novice High	0+
Novice Mid	0 (No practical proficiency)
Novice Low	

Notice in the table that the ILR scale has more subdivisions in the upper side whereas the ACTFL counterpart shows more subdivisions in the lower side. For example, the ACTFL Superior Level rating corresponds to performance profiles which comprise ILR Levels 3-5. This disparity is due to the academic setting where proficiency of non-native language students is more differentiated at the lower side, and rarely go beyond the advanced level even after they have completed four years of language skill courses.

Along with the Generic Guidelines, ACTFL has also established language-specific descriptions of graduated proficiency, producing sets of Proficiency Guidelines for such languages as French, German, Spanish, Arabic, Chinese, Japanese, Russian, and Hebrew. It was in this context that the UH Korean language faculty implemented the KPGs project with assistance from ACTFL.

Needs for KPGs are augmented by the following realities First, in terms of the number of speakers, Korean ranks the 11th among some 3,000 languages spoken in the world. Some 5 million Koreans are residing outside of Korea. The current Korean-American population in the United States is over 1,100,000, the third among Asian ethnic groups, following Chinese and Philipinos, but preceding 800,000 Japanese-Americans.

Second, Korea's visibility is growing fast on the international horizon, due to her miraculous economic and political development, as well as cultural, military and geopolitical significance. For example, Korea has developed into the world's tenth leading country in trade.

Third, together with Arabic, Chinese and Japanese, Korean belongs to the category of the most difficult languages for English speakers to learn, according to studies done by FSI and Defense Language Institute. As observed in Table 2 (Lisbn-Gasparro 1982), it roughly takes 720 hours of instruction (equivalent to 3 years at the University of Hawaii-KOREAN 101-2, 201-2, 301-2) under ideal conditions to enable a student with an average aptitude for languages to reach Level 1+ or Intermediate High.

TABLE 2: Expected levels of speaking proficiency in languages taught at FSI.

Group I: Afrikaans, Danish, Dutch, French, Haitian Creole, Italian, Norwegian, Portuguese, Romanian, Spanish, Swahili, Swedish

Length of Training	Aptitude for Language Learning		
	minimum	average	superior
8 weeks (240 hours)	1	1/1+	1+
16 weeks (480 hours)	1+	2	2+
24 weeks (720 hours)	2	2+	3

Group II: Bulgarian, Dari, Farsi, German, Greek, Hindi, Indonesian, Malay, Urdu

Length of Training	Aptitude for Language Learning		
	minimum	average	superior
16 weeks (480 hours)	1	1/2+	1+/2
24 weeks (720 hours)	1+	2	2+/3
44 weeks (1320 hours)	2/2	2+/3	3/3+

Group III: Amharic, Bengali, Burmese, Czech, Finnish, Hebrew, Hungarian, Khmer, Lao, Nepali, Filipino, Polish, Russian, Serbo-Croatian, Sinhala, Thai, Tamil, Turkish, Vietnamese

Length of Training	Aptitude for Language Learning		
	minimum	average	superior
16 weeks (480 hours)	0+	1	1/1+
24 weeks (720 hours)	1+	2	2/2+
44 weeks (1320 hours)	2	2+	3

Group IV: Arabic, Chinese, Japanese, Korean

Length of Training	Aptitude for Language Learning		
	minimum	average	superior
16 weeks (480 hours)	0+	1	1
24 weeks (720 hours)	1	1+	1+
44 weeks (1320 hours)	1+	2	2+
80-92 weeks (2400-2760 hours)	2+	3	3+

While ACTFL Guidelines for Arabic, Chinese and Japanese are available, no Korean Guidelines have been established.

Fourth, Korean is currently taught at some forty major universities in the United States alone. As needs for communicative function in Korean grow all over the world, Korean language programs for non-Koreans continue to be either newly established or expanded both in and out of Korea, with the number of students rapidly increasing (e.g. Sohn 1990).

2. It was due to the aforementioned needs for KPGs in the national and international context that the KPGs project was initiated at UH in January 1990.[2] Initiation of the KPCs project was farther expedited by the need to maintain the complementality with the other UH East Asian languages (Chinese and Japanese), both of which have respective sets of ACTFL-endorsed Proficiency Guidelines, as indicated earlier.

The KPGs project team produced a set of draft Guidelines in the middle of 1990, on the basis essentially of the ACTFL Generic Guidelines and modeled after ACTFL's Japanese and Chinese Guidelines.[3] The draft Guidelines were

2 The University of Hawaii faculty members are Dong Jae Lee and me, and Heisoon Yang (Ewha Women's University) was invited for that purpose.

3 A major portion of the draft was contributed by H. Yang.

partially tested for their validity with different levels of students in Korean at UH in the fall of 1990. Furthermore, testing materials for reading and writing were prepared in large quantities with the help of two research assistants.

As a first step toward obtaining ACTFL's eventual approval and adoption of the draft KPGs as their Guidelines, we contacted David Hiple, then ACTFL OPI Director, for advice regarding further actions. Dr. Hiple was willing to assist us in developing Korean-specific Guidelines through ACTFL's usual experientially-based procedures and by collecting authentic materials. It is widely assumed and generally recognized that oral proficiency is the most significant and basic among the four skills. Therefore, it was agreed that we concentrate ourselves on speaking guidelines first. Korean speaking guidelines had to be based not only on the descriptions of the ACTFL Generic Guidelines but also on the specific data to be obtained through Korean OPIs. Moreover, it is known that an efficient method of developing a set of speaking proficiency guidelines is to constantly check, test and revise earlier drafts through OPIs. Thus, it was agreed that the KPGs team receive OPI training first In January 1991, a three-day OPI workshop was conducted at UH, where the project members received intensive training from David Hiple in Korean OPIs.[4] Lee (UH), Schulz (Columbia) Yang (Ewha), Sua Yuen (then UH graduate student in Korean) and myself were trained in ACTFL OPI procedure including OPI skills and rating methods, with the ACTFL Generic Guidelines as the basis. Tables 3 and 4 show ACTFL's Guideline-based OPI assessment criteria for speaking proficiency (Buck 1989).

TABLE 3. Assessment Criteria: Speaking Proficiency

Global Tasks/ Functions	Context	Content	Accuracy	Text Type
Superior				
Can discuss extensively by supporting opinions, abstracting and hypothesizing	Most formal and informal settings	Wide range of general interest topics and some special fields of interest and expertise; concrete, abstract and unfamiliar topics	Errors virtually never interfere with communication or disturb the native speaker	Extended discourse

4 At the request of David Hiple, Carol Schulz at Columbia University was invited to join the project. She had some previous experience in Korean OPIs.

Advanced				
Can describe and narrate in major time/ aspect frames	Most formal and informal settings	Concrete and factual topics of personal and public interest	Can be understood without difficulty by speakers unaccustomed to non-native speakers	Paragraph discourse
Intermediate				
Can maintain simple face-to-face conversation by asking and responding to simple questions	Some informal settings and a limited number of transactional situations	Topics related primarily to self and immediate environment	Can be understood, with some repetition, by speakers accustomed to non-native speakers	Discrete sentences and strings of sentences
Novice				
Can produce only formulaic utterances, lists and enumerations	Highly predictable common daily settings	Common discrete elements of daily life	May be difficult to understand, even for those accustomed to non-native speakers	Discrete words and phrases

TABLE 4. Accuracy Assessment

Superior: Errors virtually never interfere with communication or disturb the native speaker

Fluency: smooth flow of speech with little or no overt evidence of search for appropriate language forms; ability to use some rhetorical devices to mark emphases in discourse and a variety of organizational patterns to link paragraphs into extended discourse

Grammar: occasional, unpatterned deviations from the native norm in some complex and low-frequency constructions

Pragmatic Competence: confident use of various conversation management devices to get the message across effectively and to compensate for remaining gaps in control of the language

Pronunciation: some influence of native language phonological features may still be detectable

Sociolinguistic Competence: appropriate use of the major registers and ability to use some cultural references and idioms
Vocabulary: broad general vocabulary enabling circumlocution, with refinement in special areas of interest or expertise

---

Advanced: Can be understood without difficulty by speakers unaccustomed to dealing with non-native speakers

Fluency: occasional groping for words and suitable language forms; ability to use some cohesive devices for linking sentences into paragraph-length discourse
Grammar: good control of frequent simple constructions and some complex constructions
Pragmatic Competence: largely successful use of various devices to get the message across and to compensate for imperfect control of the language
Pronunciation: some influence of native language phonological features is likely
Sociolinguistic Competence: ability to use some major registers and a few common cultural references and idioms
Vocabulary: good control of the most common genera! vocabulary

---

Intermediate: Can be understood, with some repetition by speakers accustomed to dealing wtih non-native speakers

Fluency: speech halting with frequent groping for words and appropriate language forms; little or no use of cohesive devices to link sentences
Grammar: partial control of only the most frequent constructions
Pragmatic Competence: use of various devices to get meaning across and to compensate for limited control of the language only occasionally successful
Pronunciation: influence of native language phonology may be strong
Sociolinguistic Competence: ability to use a few of the most frequent markers of social relations
Vocabulary: limited to high-frequency, concrete, personal lexical items

---

Novice: May be difficult to understand, even for speakers accustomed to dealing with non-native speakers

Fluency: constant groping for words and suitable language forms with frequent unfilled pauses

Grammar: except for memorized material, minimal control of even the most frequent constructions
Pragmatic Competence: attempts to participate in a conversation unsuccessful; unable to adapt memorized forms to express personal meanings
Pronunciation: influence of native language phonology may be very-strong
Sociolinguistic Competence: markers of social relations limited to a few memorized formulae
Vocabulary: limited to common elements of everyday life

Table 5 represents ACTFL's general OPI structure that we had to follow in OPIs in Korean (Buck 1989).

TABLE 5. General OPI Structure; Phases and Planes of the OPI

Four phases: WARM-UP → LEVEL CHECKS ↔ PROBES → WIND-DOWN				
Three planes	ITERATIVE PROCESS			
Psycho-logical	Puts interviewee at ease	Shows interviewee what s/he can do	Shows interviewee what s/he cannot do	Return interviewee to level at which s/he functions most accurately; gives interviewee feeling of accomplishment
Linguistic	Reacquaint a interviewee with language, if necessary	Checks for functions & content handled with greatest accuracy	Checks for functions & content handled with least accuracy	Gives interviewer chance to check that iterative process is complete
Evaluative	Gives tester preliminary indication of skill level	Finds highest level of sustained performance (floor)	Finds first level at which performance can no longer be sustained (ceiling)	

We interviewed some thirty UH students of Korean before and during this workshop (cf. Sohn 1991a and 1991b). During the summer and fall of 1991 (while I was taking a sabbatical leave in Korea), Dr. Hiple was invited as a fellow of the federally funded UH National Foreign Language Research Center (NFLRC) and trained Ms. Yuen (then NFLRC intern) in more Korean OPIs, while revising the earlier draft Korean speaking guidelines quite extensively based on the new OPI data. On December 3, 1991, Dr. Hiple conducted a teleconference on Korean OPIs with 17 Korean language departments in the United States joining, where OPI concepts and procedures were presented and Korean OPIs were demonstrated by Yuen.[5] In the spring of 1992, Hiple and Yuen, with assistance from the other project team members, were engaged in revising previously drafted listening, reading, and writing guidelines, introducing a variety of authentic materials. Listening examples were taken from OPIs; reading examples from student feedback via "talk-alouds" and recall protocol exercises; and writing examples from students' responses to writing tasks.

In May 1992, a project committee was convened, with Hiple, Lee, Schulz, Sohn, Yang, and Yuen participating, to finalize the draft Guidelines and complete the project through a clause-by-clause discussion and final testings by several OPIs. The outcome of this final meeting is in APPENDIX I of this paper, with task examples for reading and writing guidelines omitted. In a nutshell, the overriding goal in developing KPGs was to encourage in the Korean language teaching community performance-based instruction and assessment by providing sample descriptions of functional linguistic behaviors in Korean ranging from total beginner to full professional (UH SLTCC 1992:i).

3. KPGs are modeled par excellence after the ACTFL Generic Guidelines and Japanese, Chinese and Hebrew Guidelines. Thus, as in the ACTFL Generic and language-specific Guidelines, KPGs are organized not only for the assessment of different kinds of skills (speaking, listening, reading, and writing) at different proficiency levels, but also in such a way that they represent a graduated sequence of steps that can be used to structure a proficiency-based Korean language program. They are intended, so to speak, to provide a "common yardstick" for the proficiency-based Korean language profession (cf. Liskin-Gasparro 1989:13). Thus, in the ACTFL Guidelines and KPGs, the concept of language proficiency is the guiding or organizing principle by which language curricula, teaching, and testing are to be designed around well-defined levels of language skills (cf, Omaggio 1986:42). The language proficiency here means "the ability to function effectively in the language in real-life contexts". It is for this reason that proficiency-oriented instruction and testing have become a catch phrase in foreign language education, especially since the publication and dissemination of the ACTFL Guidelines. In fact, Stansfield and Kenyon (1992) point out that the ACTFL Guidelines were the subject of over 400 articles in professional journals by 1988, and that as a method of assessing global oral proficiency, the OPI

5 I participated in the teleconference from Seoul.

has also been widely disseminated.[6] This eloquently represents the current trend that the focus of foreign language education in the United States has shifted from the "knowledge" of a language to "functional proficiency" in the language, with particular emphasis on speaking proficiency from the very beginning of the language learning stage.

Related to the proficiency principle is the globality principle underlying both ACTFL Guidelines and KPGs. That is, as observed in the ACTFL assessment criteria in speaking proficiency in Table 3, "global communicative task/function" is a key criterion for proficiency testing, along with the criteria of "context", "content", "accuracy", and "text types". Furthermore, proficiency is measured globally based on all these criteria, and not individually.

Another pedagogical principle implied in the ACTFL Guidelines and KPGs is that there is no one definitive approach to language teaching. The push for proficiency is not promoting or advocating any particular single method of instruction. It attempts to accommodate an eclectic approach called "the relative contribution model". That is, every new proficiency level represents a new constellation of the factors of global tasks/functions, context, content, accuracy, and text-type. Thus, for example, the relative contribution of accuracy subskills (pronunciation, vocabulary, grammar, fluency, and sociolinguistic and pragmatic appropriateness) changes from level to level (e.g. Higgs 1989:5).

4. As mentioned thus far, KPGs are expected to provide the Korean language teaching community with standards for the assessment of learners' proficiency levels in different language skills. Such assessments may serve for various instructional and practical purposes, including placement tests and employment or promotion. KPGs are also expected to allow us to set up standardized proficiency goals in the instructional setting. In addition to such obvious objectives, KPGs have other significant pedagogical implications for Korean language education. For one thing, KPGs can function as guidelines for the preparation of functional syllabuses for the instruction of Korean. As Makino (1991) points out, a functional syllabus as implied in ACTFL Guidelines and KPGs emphasizes communicative function, and thus is directly tied up with proficiency testings. It is an ideal combination of a structural syllabus emphasizing vocabulary and grammar and a situational syllabus emphasizing speech contexts and situations. Textbooks and learning processes can also be reoriented toward proficiency in natural communication in real-life contexts and activities, covering all

6 According to Standfield and Kenyon (1992), during the 1980s, ACTFL trained approximately 2,000 oral proficiency testers in Spanish, French, German, and Russian alone. Kyoko Hijirada (personal communication) informed me that eleven Japanese instructors in Hawaii have been certified as Japanese testers.

speaking, listening, reading and writing in different levels (e.g. Omaggio 1986; Hijirida 1990; Hijirida and Uyetake 1991).

5. The draft KPGs have been sent to ACTFL for acceptance as their Guidelines. As in the case of ACTFL's Generic and existing language-specific Guidelines, the KPGs, if approved, will be subject to periodic revision for improvement.

At present, there are no Korean OPI testers. Schulz and Yuen who have done extensive OPIs with students in Korean have been recommended to ACTFL for certification as Korean OPI testers. If they are so certified, they will be in an excellent position to demonstrate OPIs in Korean and train prospective testers in a variety of Korean OPI workshops. Such workshops will provide the participants not only with the training in OPI procedures but with many interesting facts, principles, methods and implications regarding proficiency-oriented Korean language education.

REFERENCES: Chapter 27

Buck, Kathryn. 1989. The ACTFL *Oral Proficiency Interview*. ACTFL, Inc.

Higgs, Theodore V. 1989. *Teaching for Proficiency, the Organizing Principle*. Lincolnwood, Illinois: National Textbook Co.

Hijirida, Kyoko, 1990. How to improve ACTFL-aiming proficiency (written in Japanese). *Nihongo Monthly* June: 100-2.

Hijirida, Kyoko and Diane Uyetake. 1991. Techniques and strategies for teaching culture in Japanese classrooms (in Japanese). *Japanese-Language Education around the Globe* 1: 201-9.

Liskin-Gasparro, Judith E. 1982. ETS *Oral Proficiency Testing Manual*. Princeton, N.J.: Educational Testing Service.

Liskin-Gasparro, Judith E. 1989. The ACTFL Proficiency Guidelines: A historical perspective. In Higgs, T.V. (1989, 11-42).

Makino, Seiichi. 1991. Issues in ACTFL Proficiency Guidelines and Oral Proficiency Interview (written in Japanese). *Japanese-Language Education around the Globe* 1: 15-32.

Omaggio, Alice C. 1986. *Teaching Language in Context: Proficiency-Oriented Instruction.* Boston, Mass.: Heinle & Heinle Publishers, Inc.

Sohn, Ho-min. 1990. Korean language education in the United States. *Bilingual Education for the Overseas Koreans* 7: 19-80.

Sohn, Ho-min. 1991a. Sociolinguistic and pragmatic appropriateness in proficiency-oriented Korean language instruction. *Bilingual Education for the Overseas Koreans* 8: 461-90.

Sohn, Ho-min. 1991b. Patterned weaknesses in OPI interviewees in Korean. *Korean Lan-*

guage Education 3: 197-220.

Stansfield, Charles W. and Dorry M. Kenyon. 1992. The development and validation of a simulated oral proficiency interview. *The Modern Language Journal* 76.2: 129-41.

UH SLTCC (University of Hawaii Second Language Teaching & Curriculum Center). 1992. *Korean Proficiency Guidelines*. NFLRC Research Notes #5.

28 Performance-based Principles and Proficiency Criteria for KFL Textbook Development*

1. KFL Textbook Development Project: Background

In view of the educational, cultural, academic, and strategic significance of the role that the Korean language has begun to play in English-speaking countries such as Australia, Canada, England, New Zealand, and the United States, as well as in the non-English speaking world such as China and Japan, quality education of Korean as a foreign language (KFL) is much needed.[1]

Instruction of KFL is making an unprecedentedly rapid growth both overseas and in Korea (e.g. Sohn and Lee 1995). For example, over sixty universities, some 700 weekend Korean community schools, and a dozen high schools in the United States currently offer Korean language courses. Eight universities and several high schools in Australia have Korean language programs. This growing interest in Korean is due mainly to the near-miraculous development of the Korean economy, the marked increase in the overseas Korean population, overseas Korean parents' aspiration fur their children's bilingualism, and the firm commitment and sincere efforts of various Korean and foreign educational, government, research and funding organizations to enhance the quantity and quality of KFL education, promote Korean culture, and encourage Korean studies. The leading of Korean has thus been greatly promoted since the language is the foundation on which all areas of Korean studies are built; it is not only the means by which non-Koreans conduct cross-cultural communication with Koreans but also the basis through which overseas Koreans maintain their national heritage, identity and pride.

---

* This was a keynote paper presented at the 6th International Conference of the International Association for Korean Language Education, held in Seoul in August 1995. It appeared in *Korean Language Education* 6: 67–98 (1995).

1 The original version of this paper was written at the National Foreign Language Center in Washington, D.C, in June 1994 under an Andrew Mellon collaborative fellowship. I am indeed grateful to NFLC for the golden opportunity to work with other fellows on Korean language textbook development guidelines for one month.

At present, KFL programs in English-speaking countries serve the following student needs:

(1) a. satisfying one- or two-year language requirement
b. communicating with Koreans in the business or tourism field
c. achieving a level of Korean to enhance their employment opportunities
d. reading and speaking their ethnic language and communicating with their parents and fellow Koreans
e. developing full proficiency in Korean for teaching, missionary diplomatic, military or other professional purposes
f. conducting research and writing in their areas of specialization in Korean studies including Korean language and literature.

Unfortunately, KFL instruction in English-speaking countries, is inadequate to meet the above needs. The answer lies in the effective teaching of KFL supplemented with superior textbooks and other teaching or learning aids. Undeniably, most Korean language Professionals overseas, especially college level teachers, are dissatisfied with existing beginning-level instructional materials and suffer from a lack of adequate advanced level textbooks. Although elementary and second-level Korean level textbooks are abundant, each with its own characteristic strengths, many of them are either unsatisfactory or inadequate for classroom use by English-speaking students (e.g. Lee 1993; Sohn and Lee 1995). The inferiority of these textbooks is characterized by an abundance of significant errors, insufficient or inadequate explanations of grammar and culture points, paucity of adequate exercises, drills and tests, lack of methodological sophistication, and a lack of proficiency goals, criteria or principles. There are very few useful drill and resting books, teacher's manuals, and visual leaching or learning aids. There are even fewer choices for advanced levels; the few available texts are generally poor in sequencing vis-a-vis proficiency levels, grammatical and cultural annotation, and skill-integration exercises and task-based drills. Manuals or books on systematic Chinese character learning or integrating the1 Korean language and culture are scarce. There is no dictionary of a Korean reference grammar, nor usage dictionary, for English-speaking students of KFL. Nor is there any useful manual on KFL composition.

Keenly cognizant of this situation, the participants (approximately fifty) of the three-day conference for KFL textbook development planning (sponsored by The Korea Foundation and the University of Hawaii) held in Seoul in January 1994 agreed that a long-term collaborative endeavor was urgently needed in order to develop a series of KFL textbooks and other instructional aids for English speaking college students. This plan, fully endorsed by The Korea Foundation (KF), led to the launching in July 1904 of a monumental KF-supported six-year collaborative project to develop the following materials. These materials arc regarded as integral components essential to comprehensive and successful KFL education for English speaking students (see Sohn and Lee 1995 for details).[2]

(2) a. *KOREAN I*: main text, workbook, teacher's manual, audio & video tapes, CAI software
b. *KOREAN II*: main text, workbook, teacher's manual, audio & video tapes, CAI software
c. *KOREAN III*: main text, audio & video tapes, CAI software
d. *KOREAN IV*: main text, audio & video tapes, CAI software
e. a volume of *CHINESE CHARACTER STUDIES*
f. a volume of *KOREAN COMPOSITION*
g. a volume of *MODERN KOREAN LITERARY READER*
h. two volumes of *ADVANCED READINGS IN KOREAN*
i. a volume on *KOREAN LANGUAGE IN CULTURE AND SOCIETY*
j. *TEACHER'S MANUAL*
k. *A DICTIONARY OF KOREAN GRAMMAR AND USAGE*

The set of proposed textbooks and learning aids are intended and will be designed to serve the diverse student constituency described in (1) above. The KFL instructional materials will be developed collaboratively by approximately fifty university faculty teaching Korean to English-speaking students throughout the world.

2. Proficiency-oriented Approach

Formulating a set of pedagogical principles for the development of the projected textbooks and other learning aids especially for KOREAN I-IV and a set of objective criteria for each level (KOREAN I-IV and above) in terms of proficiency goals, contents and functions are essential for the success of the collaborative textbook development project. A major reason that many previous textbook writers failed is the lack of such principles and criteria. This is particularly a vital requirement if a project is to be carried out collaboratively since such a project will be conducted by geographically scattered researchers with different disciplinary backgrounds, diverse methodological orientations, and varying degrees of pedagogical experience. Moreover, not all participating researchers

2 Video tapes and computer-assisted instruction (CAI) software for KOREAN I-IV will be developed later when sufficient funds and relevant personnel are available.

are well versed in the recent concepts and methodologies for effective foreign language instruction.

Foreign language curricula, textbooks and other teaching materials, and classroom instruction in the United States and elsewhere are being reorganized and redirected toward a performance-based, proficiency-oriented approach, frequently with ACTFL (American Council on the Teaching of Foreign Languages) Proficiency Guidelines serving as a common yardstick. With ACTFL Guidelines' concept of proficiency levels as the basic organizing principle, the performance-based approach incorporates eclectically various strengths existing in such available foreign language instructional methodologies as the grammar translation method, direct methods, audiolingual methodology, cognitive approaches, and communicative approaches.

What then is *proficiency* as understood in performance-based language teaching and learning in contemporary foreign language education? It is far from Chomsky's (1965) notion of competence plus performance, which is devoid of any reference to situational or sociocultural appropriateness. Rather, it is somewhat similar to the communicative competence, as advocated by Campbell and Wales (1970), Hymes (1972), Savignon (1972, 1983), Munby (1978), and Canale and Swain (1980), among many others. These authors' notion of communicative competence includes the knowledge of the rules of language use, including sociolinguistic, pragmatic and contextual competence, in addition to grammatical competence. In particular, the co0pntemporary concept of proficiency is very close to Canale's (1983) concept of communicative competence, which refers to both (a) an individual's underlying *knowledge* about language and communicative language use and (b) his *skill* to perform with this knowledge base in actual communication situations. Simply stated, this notion of proficiency means the ability to function effectively in the language in real life contexts.

Then, one might ask how the proficiency conceived by the so-called communicative approach and that upheld by the performance-based approach are different, if any. The current conceptualization of the term *proficiency* in the performance based language education includes specifications about the levels of competence attained in terms of the *tasks or functions* performed, the contexts and content areas in which the language user can function, the *accuracy* with which the language is used, and the text types (word, phrase, sentence, paragraph, and discourse) that can be bundled (cf. Higgs and Clifford 1982; Omaggio 1986). This refined concept of proficiency is reflected precisely in the ACTFL Proficiency Guidelines.[3] Thus the most essential difference between the

3 Although teaching for proficiency has always been the central issue in second-language

communicative approach and the performance-based approach in foreign language education is that the former is not backed by explicit proficiency guidelines and the latter is anchored to them (cf. Makino 1991). Other differences are that grammar is explicitly localized as a subclass of the accuracy component only in the latter and that more elaborate pedagogical principles and instructional techniques and methods are being formulated or developed centering around the performance- based approach. In this respect, performance-based language education can be defined as proficiency guidelines-based communicative instruction. Since ACTFL's Generic Proficiency Guidelines and the ACTFL-approved Korean Proficiency Guidelines (appended in Sohn 1993) will serve our purpose most directly and effectively, it is proposed that these Guidelines be followed in developing and organizing our textbooks.

3. Proposed Performance-based Principles

The performance-based approach subscribes to a set of pedagogical principles such as contextualization, personalization, student-centeredness and task/function orientedness (to be elaborated below). A 1904 *Newsletter* (No. 36) published by the American Northeast Conference of Foreign Language Teaching reports a set of valuable guidelines for effective foreign language instruction that the National Association of District Supervisors of Foreign Languages had identified. These guidelines are based essentially on the performance-based principles and practices that are observed widely in the United States, as quoted below:

(3) Characteristics of Effective Foreign Language Instruction
  a. The teacher uses the target language extensively and encourages the students to do so.
  b. The teacher provides opportunities to communicate in the target language in meaningful and purposeful activities that simulate real-life situations.
  c. Skill-getting activities enable students to participate successfully in skill-using activities. Skill-using activities predominate.
  d. Time devoted to listening, speaking, reading and writing is appropriate to course objectives and to the language skills of students.

---

education, the concept of proficiency or proficiency-oriented language instruction was vague until ACTFL, in cooperation with the Education Testing Service (ETS) and Federal Interagency Roundtable (FIR), developed a set of Generic Proficiency Guidelines in 1982 and revised them in 1986 and, as a method of assessing global oral proficiency, devised the procedures of the Oral Proficiency Interview (OPI) in conformity with the Guidelines.

e. Culture is systematically incorporated into instruction.
f. The teacher uses a variety of student groupings.
g. Most activities are student-centered.
h. The teacher uses explicit error correction in activities that focus on accuracy and implicit or no error correction in activities which focus on communication.
i. Assessment, both formal and informal, reflects the way students are taught.
j. Student tasks and teacher questions reflect a range of thinking skills.
k. Instruction addresses student learning styles.
l. Students are explicitly taught foreign language learning strategies and are encouraged to assess their own progress.
m. The teacher enables all students to be successful.
n. The teacher establishes an affective climate in which the students fed comfortable taking risks.
o. Students are enabled to develop positive attitudes toward cultural diversity.
p. The physical environment reflects the target language and culture.
q. The teacher uses the textbook as a tool, not as a curriculum.
r. The teacher uses a variety of print and non-print materials including authentic materials.
s. The teacher engages in continued professional development in the areas of language skills, cultural knowledge, and current methodology.

It is proposed that our forthcoming Teacher's Manuals include such instructional guidelines as above, since many of our current and prospective KFL teachers may not be familiar with the principles and practices of (performance-based foreign language instruction. Our textbook developers are also recommended to refer to the above guidelines in developing performance-based materials.

As for desirable textbooks, Bragger (1985) and Omaggio (1986: 410) illustrate a good proficiency-oriented textbook as one including the following:

(4) a. contextualized language-practice activities
b. personalized and creative practice activities
c. suggestions for group work and active communicative interaction among students
d. authentic language in exercises, readings, and dialogues, as well as abundant realia throughout the text, integrated with language-practice activities

e. functional/notional concepts, together with ample opportunities to practice a range of tasks using these concepts
f. clear and concise grammatical explanations that enable students to work toward accuracy goals from the beginning of instruction
g. appealing topics, themes, readings, and activities that respond to the needs and interests of students
h. cultural material integrated with language-practice activities, selected to reflect both deep and surface culture phenomena, and incorporating both "hearthstone" and "Olympian" culture in «i balanced fashion that will appeal to student's interests.

Our textbook developers are recommended to follow a set of performance-based principles which underlie various practical suggestions illustrated above. We therefore propose the following unordered set of methodological principles as the overarching conceptual framework in Preparing the Main Texts (KOREAN I-IV), Activity Workbooks (KOREAN I & II), Teacher's Manuals (KOREAN I & II), and the accompanying audio-visual and CAI materials. It is also recommended that such other textbooks as *Selected Reading in Korean, Chinese Charter Studies. Korean Composition,* and *Korean Language in Culture and Society* be developed under the same principles as much us possible. These principles are derived or formulated from (a) current theories and methodologies on performance-based foreign language instruction; (b) various performance-based practices, such as those presented above; (c) ACTFL and Korean Proficiency Guidelines; (d) reviews of many existing textbooks of Korean and other languages (e.g. Tsukuba Language Group 1991; Tohsaku 1994; Sohn and Lee 1995); (e) discussions in National Foreign Language Center (NFLC) seminars held in Washington, D.C. in June 1994; and (f) our long teaching experiences. Inevitably, some of these principles are cross-dimensional and thus partly interlocking. However, such partial overlappings simply reinforce the importance of the principles involved.

PRINCIPLE 1: STUDENT-CENTEREDNESS

Traditional teacher-centered, lecture based classroom instructional settings tend to limit the role of the student to that of responder in which students are most often asked to answer questions. In student-centered approaches, students are asked to make inquiries, act out simulated survival situations, narrate or describe events, hypothesize, argue, persuade, provide opinion, or carry out many other language functions that are necessary in everyday encounters with others in the target language. Students are held responsible for their own learning.

For instance, the use of small-group and paired communicative activities that allow students to practice language in context for some simulated or real communicative purpose should lead more readily to the development of oral proficiency than do methods that are primarily teacher-centered or that focus mainly on language forms and convergent answers. In the early levels of instruction, it is probably best that such activities lie carefully structured and monitored to encourage the development of linguistic accuracy.

PRINCIPLE 2: PERSONALIZATION

Creative language practice, as well as adaptive and interactive practice, (as opposed to exclusively manipulative or convergent practice) must be encouraged in performance-based instruction. That is, language practice must be personalized. Thus, students should be given ample opportunities to express their own meanings as early as possible after productive skills have been introduced in the course of instruction, apply their knowledge to coping with real-life situations, and participate in active communicative interaction among them. To reach the Intermediate Level of proficiency, learners need to be able to create with the language.

PRINCIPLE 3: CONTEXTUALIZATION

Learning a language is much more than learning its grammar and vocabulary out of context. Students must acquire communicative competence and peformative skills. To achieve this, they should be able to use the target language in proper communicative contexts. This is particularly the case for English speakers learning Korean in that Korean is very different from English not only in structure but also in sociolinguistic and cultural aspects. From the very beginning of instruction, therefore, students should be given ample opportunities to learn language in a range of contexts likely to be encountered in the target culture. Accordingly, the success of a KFI textbook depends on how well the textbook is designed to naturally contextualize Korean conversations, grammar and cultural expressions.

Some of the situational contexts likely to he included at the Novice and Intermediate Low/Mid Levels (i.e. KOREAN I & II) are basic travel and survival needs (food, clothing, hotel accommodations, transportation, and the like), appropriately handling daily social encounters, and coping with school or work related situations. Students should also be taught to handle simple question-and-answer situations and discuss or write about concrete topics such MS their own background, family, and interests.

PRINCIPLE 4: USING AUTHENTIC MATERIALS

Performance-based methodology emphasizes the use of authentic language in instructional materials wherever and whenever possible (Omaggio 1986: 47). Authentic materials are those language materials which are written or spoken for native speakers. The contexts for language practice should he devised, as much as possible, from culturally authentic sources or contexts. The use of real or simulated travel documents, hotel registration forms, biographical data sheets, train and plane schedules, authentic restaurant menus, labels, business cards, receipts, warrantee papers, advertisements of all sorts, city maps, photo pictures, signs, newspapers, and magazines will acquaint the students more directly with real language than will exclusive use of any set of artificially contrived materials. Videotapes authentic or simulated exchanges between native speakers, radio and television broadcasts, films, songs, and the like at all levels have long been advocated by foreign language educators as stimulating pedagogical aids.

Authenticity is especially important in developing task oriented listening and speaking skills (see Principle 5 below). The task that students are asked to perform with authentic material must be geared to their proficiency level.

The main reason for using authentic materials as the foundation of curriculum preparation is that students will thereby be able to gain global proficiency to perform their language tasks in the target language and cultural environment. The use of authentic texts docs not imply, however, that we should abandon the use of materials created for instructional purposes. Rather, an efficient blend of the two seems more appropriate.

PRINCIPLE 5: FUNCTION/TASK ORIENTATION

Opportunities should he provided for students to practice a range of functions/tasks likely to be necessary in dealing with others in the target culture (e.g. Omaggio ibid: 48). Students should he introduced, through a variety of strategies and techniques including role-plays, to a variety of functional tasks that have been carefully sequenced to help them cope with the real world communication demands they will face.

The list of possible tasks that individuals should be able to handle at each level of proficiency is given in the ACTFL Proficiency Guidelines and ACTFL-approved Korean Proficiency Guidelines (see Section 4 below). These lists may be useful in designing a sequence of functional language practice activities that will build towards those competences at higher levels of proficiency.

PRINCIPLE 6: SEQUENCING

Seamless progression from relative easiness to relative difficulty throughout all proficiency levels covering all language skills is essential in materials development. Krashen (1982) asserts that language learners/acquirers acquire language that is directed at their current level of competence (comprehensible input), but will understand structures that are beyond the level from contextual cues in the message or from extralinguistic cues. Both teachers and students frequently experience extreme frustration when they encounter an abrupt transition from the second-level Korean to the third level, especially when the latter textbook contains a host of materials which have not been covered previously.

Sequencing strictly in accordance with global proficiency levels and criteria is essential in presenting conversational, grammatical and cultural materials. It is proposed that in general, sequencing be in conformity with the four skill proficiency levels, as described in the ACTFL and Korean Proficiency Guidelines. The descriptions in the Guidelines are useful in designing the KFL textbooks in that they outline general performance criteria and specify the kinds of contexts and situations handled with reasonable ease at each proficiency level. The Guidelines are progressive in nature. Knowing what kinds of competences lie at the next level will help us sequence materials and choose activities that will enable learners to make appropriate progress towards the goals identified at the beginning of the instruction process.

Frequency and utility should also be taken into account in ordering the presentation of materials. In preparing activity materials, elementary practices such as substitution come first, followed by semantic cognitive drills, which are in turn followed by communicative task activities.

PRINCIPLE 7: ACCURACY CONCERN

Despite some arguments to the contrary (e.g. Krashen 1982), emphasis on accuracy in phonology, morphology, lexicon, syntax, semantics, socio-linguistics, and pragmatics by providing various natural activities is essential from the beginning of instruction. Attention to accuracy is fundamental in early language learning situations if one is to attain more than a minimal competence in a foreign language, for incorrect forms and inappropriate communication strategies tend to be fossilized. Thus, accuracy is particularly essential to those learners who want to function eventually beyond Advanced Level.

As Higgs and Clifford (1982) and Omaggio (ibid: 50) stress, the decision to strive for linguistic accuracy from the beginning of instruction does not imply a de-emphasis of communicative language use in the classroom, Canale and

Swain (1980) echo this point of view, suggesting that the best approach might be one which begins with a combination of emphasis on grammatical accuracy and on meaningful communication.

In grammar instruction, the formal grammar lesson should he kept as brief and as uncomplicated as possible, at least in lower-level language courses, to ensure that most of the class hour can be spent on active, creative language practice. One important approach that allows the teacher to focus on particular structures in a lesson, while encouraging active communication, is, to ask students lo read grammatical explanations and other lesson content before coining to class. The teacher then uses class time for verifying, through active practice, that the material has been understood. Another approach may be by means of contextually designed audio-visual devices. In any case, grammar rules must be acquired through a learner-centered approach.

PRINCIPLE 8: CULTURE LEARNING

For many years, foreign language educators have been emphasizing the need to incorporate culture learning into the curriculum and to promote global awareness and cross-cultural understanding (e.g. Stern 1981). Many language courses today, however, do not include the systematic study of culture vis-à-vis language for various reasons. For one, textbooks have often been inefficient in the r treatment of cultural themes and thus have provided little help in identifying appropriate sequences of cultural instruction. For another, as Crawford-Lange and Lange (1981) assert, teachers may not have been adequately trained in the teaching of culture and therefore do not have strategies for integrating culture study with language or for creating a viable framework for organizing instruction around cultural themes.[4] The existing Korean language textbooks, curriculum and instruction practices are no exception.

Extensive sociolinguistic and socio-cultural information should be incorporated in our forthcoming textbooks, so that students may learn to use Korean appropriately and live harmoniously in the Korean community. One indispensable sociolinguistic and pragmatic aspect is the extensive discussion of the appropriate uses of Korean honorifics and politeness strategies, which are markedly different from English.[5]

The culture learning to be incorporated in our textbooks will encompass not

4 Hooper Rasberry (1994) states that "culture as the broader context in which language develops, culture as intimately linked with language, and language as a reflection of culture are not regularly and consistently taught in the majority of our classrooms."

5 For suggested sociolinguistic items to be included in Korean language instruction, see Sohn (1991a).

only Brooks's (1975) so-called Olympian culture or Audio-lingual Method's big-C culture (e.g. art, literature, music, history, and geography) but also, more importantly in lower levels, Brooks's so-called Hearthstone culture or Audio-lingual Method's little-c culture (patterns for living, beliefs, behavior, and values). No doubt, students who are able to deal with cultural differences communicate better in the language and study the language for a longer time. They are likely to survive and function better in the global village.

PRINCIPLE 9: MOTIVATING

Language instruction and instructional materials should respond to the student's affective, as well as cognitive, needs. Students should continue to be motivated to stay in class and attain their desired proficiency levels. Hooper-Hasberry (1994) points out that students tend to be motivated to learn a language and continue that study when they find the study interesting, relevant and utilitarian. Instructional materials, as well as teaching methods, must be geared toward these motivating factors: interesting content and enjoyable learning processes and environments, direct relevance to their needs, and immediate practical utility. In this regard, conversations, reading materials, cultural notes, visual presentations, task activities, and multimedia technology materials may be designed to provide greater interest, relevance, and utility to students. For instance, various aspects of the life of overseas Koreans may constitute some relevant topics.

Several recent methodological developments put great emphasis on the affective aspects of learning and acquisition (e.g. the Counseling-Learning Approach, Confluent Education, the Natural Approach, and Suggestopedia). Stevick (1980) and Krashen (1982) emphasize the close relationship between poor performance and anxiety and tension in the learning environment. Thus, students should not only feel motivated to learn but also be given opportunities to express their own meanings in a non-threatening environment.

PRINCIPLE 10: SKILL INTEGRATION

It is proposed that the performance-based approach's principle of skill integration be subscribed to for the development of KOREAN I-IV. That is, skills in speaking, listening, reading, and writing will be integrated appropriately in each lesson. This approach has many advantages.

First, although the needs of students are varied, devising a multiple tract curriculum may not tie practicable in the current state of Korean language education in the academic sector. The four-skill approach is a practical way to meet different needs.

Second, over 80% of the students learning Korean in the United Stales and Canada and a considerable portion of students of Korean in Australia are ethnic Koreans who have long been exposed to their parents' spoken Korean to a great extent, although their reading and writing competence is virtually nill. The four-skill approach in textbook development is ideal for such students because they can concentrate relatively more on reading and writing while non-Korean learners may devote themselves relatively more to shaking and listening.

Third, four skills in the same lesson will greatly facilitate learning the language because the different skills for the same topic, situation, task or function will reinforce each other.

Fourth, it is possible to present authentic casual speech and formal written language on the same topic in the same lesson and have students learn the differences through phonological, grammatical, semantic and pragmatic explanations given on the relations between casual, contracted forms vs. corresponding deliberate, full forms.

PR1NCIPLE 11: COMPETENCE-PERFORMANCE BALANCING

One of the principles that performance based theoreticians advance is the balance between skill getting and skill using. This concept may lie rephrased as the balanced training in communicative competence and communicative performance. This is essentially equivalent to the concept of the so-called *fact* and *act*, respectively. This distinction is reflected in our plan to develop separate textbooks for KOREAN I & II: Main Text for communicative competence and Activity Workbook for communicative performance.

PRINCIPLE 12: SPIRALING

To help the learning process, all the lessons in the textbooks are to be designed and organized to maintain what has been covered in previous lessons. Topics, vocabulary items, grammatical patterns, and cultural aspects should be reintroduced repeatedly for reinforcement, frequently with added or expanded notes or information.

Thorough indexing of phonological, lexical, grammatical and cultural items at the end of each volume is an excellent device not only for easy reference but also for checking whether the spiralings are properly introduced.

PRINCIPLE 13: GOAL-OR1ENTRDNISSS

All instructional materials should he developed with explicit statements of proficiency goals. In the development of the proposed textbooks for KOREAN I-IV and above, the proficiency goal to be achieved for each textbook level must be determined and stated in terms of ACTFL's and Korean Proficiency Guidelines' proficiency level. None of the existing Korean language textbooks sets learners' proficiency goals in any of the four language skills. ACTFL's and Korean Proficiency Guidelines establish nine levels (Novice low, Novice-mid, Novice-high; Intermediate-low, Intermediate-mid, Intermediate-high; Advanced, Advanced high; Superior) for speaking, listening, reading, and writing. It is essential to establish proficiency goals for the different levels of the textbooks to be developed. Section 4 below presents the proficiency levels to be achieved for the different levels.

Each lesson of each main text must begin with stated objectives in terms of the communicative function/task, structural aspects and cultural points to be learned and end with appropriate measures to assess students' achievement of the goals. Activity workbooks should be designed with stared goals and objectives.

PRINCIPLE 14: SCHEMATIZING

Various research indicates that adult learners bring past experience into the learning situation, Adults learn more effectively if the learning processes take place through analysis, synthesis, and evaluation. Cognitive psychology, as Ausubel (1978) puts it, stipulates that learning must be meaningful to be effective and permanent, involving active mental processes (perception, acquisition, organization, and storage of knowledge) and being relatable to existing knowledge (i.e. cognitive structure) the learner already possesses. New knowledge is constructed by comparison with and evaluation of the learner's previously acquired knowledge base (or knowledge schemata). That is, intended or desired language learning can be achieved effectively and efficiently through a variety of such previously acquired knowledge schemata. Intensive visualization, contextualization of the text, brainstorming, prediction, and having students recall what is known about the topic and react to visual clues, etc. arc essential for textbook development as well as for-classroom activities.

As for visual presentation, extensive inclusion of illustrations, graphics, and picture-oriented exercises is extremely important, as are video materials. Seeing is believing and learning--a picture is worth a thousand words, so is a gesture.

PRINCIPLE 15: CONTRASTIVE EXPLANATION

While Korean shares many universal linguistic and cultural features with English, it is radically different in a host of specifics. Since adult learners use their cognitive power for language learning, contrastively explaining partly overlapping phenomena between Korean and English languages and between Korean culture and the culture of the English-speaking world is effective. Results of error analysis of phonological, morphological, syntactic or sociolinguistic aspects between Korean and English will be useful in presenting contrastive accounts (e.g. Sohn 1986, 1991a, 1991b).

PRINCIPLE 16: EXPERIENTALISM

Any textbook developer, no matter how well he or she is equipped theoretically and methodologically, would not be able to produce excellent materials if (s)he does not have serious and sufficient classroom teaching experience in the courses for which textbooks will be developed. Thus, when decisions must be made between alternative approaches, the developer's own experience in teaching, as well as in previous materials development, will frequently function as a guide.

Experienced classroom teachers know what students want to learn, where students have great difficulty in learning, how much materials should be covered in a week, in what order grammar points are presented and trained, what motivate students to learn, etc. Expert Language instructors are thus walking guidelines for textbook development.

4. Proficiency Criteria for KOREAN I-IV: Goals, Contents and Functions[6]

4.1. Proficiency Goals

The four-level KFL textbooks (KOREAN I-IV) and other higher-level textbooks such as a literary reader, a volume on selected readings, and a composition manual should be developed with clear proficiency goals set. The nine proficiency levels that ACTFL's Generic Proficiency Guidelines and the Korean Language Proficiency Guidelines describe are recommended to be used as a common yardstick in designing the Korean Language textbooks.[7]

6 For details on the proficiency levels, contents, and functions/tasks for speaking, reading, writing and listening, refer to the ACTFL's Generic Proficiency Guidelines and Korean Language Proficiency Guidelines appended in Sohn (1993).

7 The Korean Proficiency Guidelines were formulated within the framework of ACTFL's

In connection with curricular sequencing (e.g. KOREAN I-IV and above), one important question to address is: what level of proficiency can students expect to reach at the end of a given course of study? How long does it take to reach, say, the Intermediate-high Level of oral proficiency in Korean? The United States Foreign Service Institute's (FSI) analysis of oral proficiency interview data collected from its own students in forty-four languages has revealed that, for American students, the easiest languages include Afrikaans, Danish, Dutch, French, Italian, Haitian, Portuguese, Spanish, Swahili, etc., the next group in difficulty includes Bulgarian, German, Greek, Hindi, Indonesian, etc., the third most difficult language includes Burmese, Finnish, Hebrew, Lao, Pilipino, Russian, Tamil, Turkish, Vietnamese, etc., and the most difficult languages (Category 4 languages) are Arabic, Chinese, Japanese, and Korean (Liskin-Gasparro 1982). The expected levels of speaking proficiency in these most difficult languages taught at FSI are as follows.

(5) LENGTH OF TRAINING APTITIDE FOR LANGUAGE LEARNING

	Minimum	Average	Superior
16 weeks (480 hours)	0+	1	1
24 weeks (720 hours)	1	1+	1+
44 weeks (1320 hours)	1+	2	2+
80-92 weeks (2400-2760 hours)	2+	3	3+

According to the above data, it takes 720 hours of intensive instruction under ideal conditions to enable an average student to reach Intermediate-High Level (1+) in oral skills in Korean. 720 hours is roughly equivalent to three years of language study, including lab hours, at the University of Hawaii (UH): Korean 101-2 (first year), 201-2 (second year), and 301-2 (third year). The data further suggests that at end of first year Korean at UH (300 hours) an average student may attain Novice-High (0+) or Intermediate-Low (1-) and at the end of the second year (600 hours) he may be rated as Intermediate-Mid (higher side of 1). Including the other language skills as suggested for Chinese by the National Foreign Language Resource Center (NFLRC) of the University of Hawaii, the following proficiency goals may be established.

(6) KOREAN I: Intermediate-low in all four skills
KOREAN II: Intermediate-mid in all four skills

Generic Guidelines. The ACTFL Generic Guidelines are intended to be universal, in that they are experientially designed based on actual testing data from scores of unrelated languages, including Korean, and based on most of the influential language teaching theories and practices currently available.

KOREAN III: Intermediate-high in listening, speaking, and reading; Intermediate-mid-high in writing
KOREAN IV: Advanced in listening, speaking, and reading; Intermediate-high in writing

Thus, it is proposed that the Main Texts, workbooks and audio-visual aids for the four levels in KOREAN be developed according to the proficiency goals set in (6).

4.2. Contents by Levels

NFLRC has recently defined contents for four years of Chinese (based on 5 class-hours a week and lab). With a few modifications, we may use the same guidelines for KOREAN I-IV, as follows.

KOREAN I (Goal: Intermediate-low)

a. Basic topics such as: classroom objects, colors, numbers, clothing, telling time, dates (month/day/current year), weather/seasons, family members, self-identification (nationality and profession), courtesy expressions (*please, thank you*, etc.), and money denominations.
b. Such survival topics as personal/biographical information, restaurant/foods, directions around town, activities/hobbies, daily routine, transportation, talking on phone, living quarters, health matters, post office, shopping, and purchases. (Some of these survival topics may be assigned to KOREAN II.)

KOREAN II (Goal: Intermediate-mid)

a. Some of the survival topics illustrated under KOREAN I.
b. Courtesy requirements such as: greetings, introductions, making appointments, accepting, refusing, invitations, and polite formulaic expressions.
c. Concrete topic such as: current events, past experiences, and future plans.
d. Face-to-face conversations including description, narration, statement of opinions on topics of a general, factual nature, such as: current events, past events, and future events. (Some of these may be assigned to Korean III.)

KOREAN III (Goal: Intermediate-high)

a. Some of the face-to-face conversations illustrated under KOREAN II.

b. Audio and written one-way communications on factual matters, including broadcast news, announcements, instructions and directions, newspaper and magazine articles, popular movies and television shows, and detailed correspondence.

KOREAN IV: (Goal: Advanced)

a. Discussion and one-way communications on factual and abstract issues in areas such as: politics and political systems, economic and financial systems, history, customs and mores, press and media, education and educational systems, philosophical and religious systems, literature and literary text arts, science and technology, medicine and health, and law and enforcement.

4.3. Functions by Levels and Skills

NFLRC has defined the functions that average students are expected to perform at the end of each level as follows.

4.3.1. Speaking Functions

KOREAN I (Goal: Intermediate-Low)

a. Use limited memorized material in simple statement or question from.
b. Name and identify objects, people, places.
c. Giving name, place of origin, simple personal information.
d. Express membership in organization, family, institution.
e. Express agreement and disagreement.
f. Ask and answer questions.
g. Participate in short conversations.

KOREAN II (Goal: Intermediate-Mid)

a. Express own meaning using recombinations of known materials in simple sentences.
b. Get into, through, and out of simple survival situations.
c. Transfer current learned material to new situations and contexts.
d. Produce strings of linger sentences relating to one topic.
e. Participate fully in casual conversations.
f. Give instructions, simple reports.
g. Make simple comparisons.

KOREAN III (Goal: Intermediate-High)

a. Give simple narration and description in past, present, and future modes.
b. Make simple comparisons.
c. Deal with complications in such situations as may be encountered in the target culture.
d. Give instructions and simple reports.

KOREAN IV (Goal: Advanced)

a. Hypothesize.
b. Support opinions.
c. Persuade others of one's point of view.
d. Describe in detail with precision.
e. Narrate in detail with precision.

4.3.2. Reading Functions

KOREAN I (Goal: Intermediate-Low)

a. Recognize the Korean spellings for memorized material.
b. Read for directional purposes standardized messages, such as menu items, prices, time/date.
c. Puzzle out pieces of selected authentic material relating to survival needs.
d. Puzzle out very simple hand-printed messages by native writers to foreigners.
e. Interpret set expressions in areas of immediate need.

KOREAN II (Goal: Intermediate-Mid)

a. Identify key facts and some details in descriptive material on daily life and news events.
b. Identify key facts and some details in carefully written personal communication.
c. Discern linkages among sentences in simple connected texts.

KOREAN III (Goal: Intermediate-High)

a. Read and understand a limited number of basic Chinese characters.
b. Understand main ideas and most supporting details of factual narrations and descriptions.
c. Understand abstract topics in a familiar context.
d. Understand description and narrations of factual material and non-technical prose.

KOREAN IV: (Goal: Advanced)

a. Read and understand a reasonable number of Chinese characters and write many of them.
b. Understand most material on both concrete and abstract topics.
c. Understand new vocabulary in context through contextual guessing strategies.

4.3.3. Writing Functions

KOREAN I (Goal: Intermediate-Low)

a. Prose correctly the basic spellings of the Korean alphabet.
b. Reproduce from memory some familiar words or phrases and recombinations of these.
c. Supply information on simple forms and documents.
d. Able to write memorized sentences.

KOREAN II (Goal: Intermediate-Mid)

c. Write short messages, postcards.
b. Take down simple notes, such as telephone messages.
c. Take notes in some detail.
d. Write simple letters, brief synopses, summaries of biographical data, work and school experience.

KOREAN III (Goal: Intermediate-High)

a. Write social and more formal correspondence.
b. Write summaries, descriptions, narrations of several paragraphs.
c. Take notes in some detail.

KOREAN IV: (Goal: Advanced)

a. Hypothesize and conjecture in writing.
b. Write short research papers.
c. Defend point of view, support hypotheses in writing.

4.3.4. Listening Functions

KOREAN I (Goal: Intermediate-Low)

a. Interactive listening skill necessary for the Intermediate-low speaking functions plus the following:
b. Identify some high-frequency words and phrases in broadcast-recorded materials.

c. Identify the main idea of broadcast materials in areas of immediate need, including advertising, public announcements, warning, instructions, weather and news reports, telephone messages.

KOREAN II (Goal: Intermediate-Mid)

a. Identify key facts and some details of broadcasts or recordings in descriptive material on daily life and news events.
b. Understand outline of plot in episodes from soap operas and popular movies.

KOREAN III (Goal: Intermediate-High)

a. Understand majority of face-to-face speech in standard dialect at normal rate.
b. Get main ideas and most supporting details of reports on factual material and non-technical prose.

KOREAN IV: (Goal: Advanced)

a. Understand main themes and most supporting detail in television shows and movies for a general audience.
b. Understand most content (factual and abstract) of one-way communications.
c. Understand new vocabulary in context through guessing strategies.

5. Conclusion

The foregoing performance-based principles and proficiency criteria are proposed to apply to not only the ongoing KFL textbook development but also KFL instruction in general. The proposals essentially represent what have recently been advocated strongly and practiced widely in foreign language education in the United States and elsewhere. The proposals are also intended to effectively achieve such goals for foreign language learning as those proposed in ACTFL (1995). Still unofficial as they may be, ACTFL's (ibid.) five proposed goals, as given below, adequately summarize what ought to be pursued through foreign language learning in the twenty-first century.

(7) a. Communication in languages other than own language.
b. Gain knowledge and understanding of other cultures.
c. Connect with other disciplines and acquire information through the foreign language.
d. Develop insight into own language and culture.

e. Participate in multilingual communities and global society.

ACTFL (ibid.) presents required learner's standards under each goal as follows. The standards of the first goal (5a) are that, through the foreign language, students (i) engage in conversations, provide and obtain information, express feelings and emotions, and exchange opinions; (ii) understand and interpret written and spoken language on a variety of topics; and (iii) present information, concepts, and ideas to an audience of listeners or readers on a variety of topics. The standard of the second goal (5b) is that, through learning the foreign language, students demonstrate knowledge and understanding of the traditions, ideas and perspectives, the literary and artistic expressions, and other components of the cultures being studied. The standards of the third goal (5c) are that students (i) reinforce and further their knowledge of other disciplines through the foreign language; and (ii) gain access to information and perspectives that are only available through the foreign language and within culture. The standards of the fourth goal (5d) are that students (i) recognize that different languages use different patterns to communicate; and (ii) recognize that cultures view situation. Finally, the standards of the fifth goal (5e) are that students (i) use the language both within and beyond the school setting; and (ii) use the language for leisure and personal enrichment. Although ACTFL (1995) indicates that these goals and standards are still unofficial and may further be refined, I take the liberty of quoting them here in view of their significant relevance to KFL instruction and textbook development.

REFERENCES: Chapter 28

ACTFL (American Council on the Teaching of Foreign Languages, Inc.). 1995. *Standards for Foreign Language Learning: Goals for the 21st Century* (unofficial draft).

Ausubel, D. 1978. *Educational Psychology: A Cognitive View*. New York: Holt, Rinehart and Winson.

Bragger, J.D. 1985. The development of oral proficiency. In Omaggio, A.C. (1985).

Brooks, N. 1975. The analysis of language and familiar cultures. In. Lafayette, R.C (1975).

Campbell, R. and R. Wales. 1970. The study of language acquisition. In Lyons, J. (1970).

Canale, M. 1983. From communicative competence to communicative language pedagogy. In Richards, J. and R. Schmidt (1983).

Canale, M. and M. Swain. 1980. Theoretical bases of communicative approaches to second language teaching and testing. *Applied Linguistics* 1: 1-47.

Chomsky, N. 1965. *Aspects of the Theory of Syntax*. Cambridge, Mass.: MIT Press.

Crawford-Lange, L. and D. Lange. 1984. Doing the unthinkable in the second-language classroom. In Higgs, T.V. (1984).

Higgs, T.V. (ed.). 1982. *Curriculum, Competence, and the Foreign Language Teacher*. ACTFL Foreign Language Education Series, vol. 13. Lincolnwood, III.: National Textbook Co.

Higgs, T.V. (ed.). 1984. *Teaching for Proficiency, the Organizing Principle*. Lincolnwood, III.: National Textbook Co.

Hooper-Rasberry, G. 1994. Presenting cultural links for language learners using multimedia. Mellon Fellowship Final Report—A Sketch presented at a National Foreign Language Center Seminar. June.

Hymes, D. 1972. On communicative competence. In Pride, J.B. and J. Holmes (1972).

Krashen, S. 1982. *Principles and Practice in Second Language Acquisition*. New York: Pergamon Press.

Larsen-Freeman, D. and M.H. Long. 1992. *An Introduction to Second Language Acquisition Research*. London and New York: Longman.

Lafayette, R.C. (ed.). 1975. *The Cultural Revolution*. Lincolnwood, III.: National Textbook Co.

Lee, Dong Jae. 1993. A review of recently published Korean textbooks. *Korean Language Education* 4: 249-81.

Liskin-Gasparro, J.E. 1982. *ETS Oral Proficiency Testing Manual*. Princeton, N.J.: Educational Testing Service.

Long, M.H. and G. Crookes. 1992. Three approaches to task-based syllabus design. *TESOL Quarterly* 26.1: 27-56.

Lyons, J. (ed). 1970. *New Horizons in Linguistics*. Harmondsworth, UK: Penguin Books.

Makino, S. 1991. Issues in ACTFL Proficiency Guidelines and Oral Proficiency Interview (written in Japanese). *Japanese-Language Education around the Globe* 1: 15-32.

Munby, J. 1978. *Communicative Syllabus Design*. Cambridge, UK: Cambridge University Press.

Nagara, S., et al. 1990. *Japanese for Everyone: A Functional Approach to Daily Communication*. Tokyo: Gakken Co.

Omaggio, A.C. (ed.). 1985. *Proficiency, Curriculum, Articulation: The Ties That Bind*. Middleburry, Vt.: Northeast Conference.

Omaggio, A.C. 1986. *Teaching Language in Context: Proficiency-Oriented Instruction*. Boston, Mass.: Heinle & Heinle Publishers, Inc.

Pride, J.B. and J. Homes (eds.). 1972. *Sociolinguistics*. Harmondsworth, England: Penguin Books.

Richards, J. and R. Schmidt. (eds.). 1983. *Language and Communication*. London: Longman.

Rivers, Wilga (ed.). 1992. *Teaching Language in College: Curriculum and Content*. Lincolnwood, III.: National Textbook Co.

Savignon, S.J. 1972. *Communicative Competence: An Experiment in Foreign Language Teaching*. Philadelphia: Center for Curriculum Development.

Savignon, S.J. 1983. *Communicative Competence: Theory and Practice*. Reading, Mass.: Addison-Wesley.

Sohn, Ho-min. 1986. *Linguistic Expeditions*. Seoul: Hanshin.

Sohn, Ho-min. 1991a. Sociolinguistic and pragmatic appropriateness in proficiency-oriented Korean language instruction. *Bilingual Education for Overseas Koreans* 8: 461-90. Also in this volume.

Sohn, Ho-min. 1991b. Patterned weaknesses in OPI interviewees in Korean. *Korean Language Education* 3: 197-220. Also in this volume.

Sohn, Ho-min. 1993. Korean proficiency guidelines: Needs, procedures, principles, and implications. *Korean Language Education* 4: 191-230. Also in this volume.

Sohn, Ho-min and Dong Jae Lee (eds.). 1995. *A New Frontier in Korean as a Foreign Language*, Proceedings of the KFL Textbook Development Planning Conference. Honolulu: KLEAR.

Stern, H.H. 1981. Directions in foreign language curriculum development. In *Proceedings of the National Conference on Professional Priorities*. Hastings-on-Hudson: ACTFL.

Stevick, E. 1980. *Teaching Languages: A Way and Ways*. Rowley, Mass.: Newburry House.

Tohsaku, Yasu-Hoko. 1994. *Yookoso: An Invitation to Contemporary Japanese*. New York: McGraw-Hill, Inc.

Tsukuba Language Group. 1991. *Situational Functional Japanese*. 8 volumes. Tokyo: Bonjinsha Co.

29 Curricular Goals and Content Standards for K-16 Korean Language Learning*

1. Introduction

One of the most important tasks facing Korean language educators in the United Stales is strengthening and articulating Korean language instruction from elementary to college levels (K-16: from Kindergarten to the 16th grade) in terms of curriculum, teaching materials, instruction, and assessment.[1] Significant results in the acquisition of language and culture can be obtained only through extended, well-articulated sequences.

In order to strengthen and articulate Korean language instruction, meet diverse student needs effectively, and perform our mission 10 globalize Korean language study, it is essential, among other things, for Korean language educators at all instructional levels in the United States to adopt and implement the curricular goals and content standards specified in the national standards for foreign language learning (NSFLEP 1996).

The primary aim of (his presentation is, therefore, to review and discuss (a) what the national standards are (the philosophy, five curricular goals, and eleven content standards) and (b) how they can be integrated in Korean language education in order to strengthen and articulate K-16 instruction. The presentation will conclude with a 15-minutc video "Integration of National Standards in a Japanese Language Classroom" (developed by the National Foreign Language Resource Center at the University of Hawaii at Manoa, 1999).

2. National Standards

The development of national content standards across disciplines for K-12

* This paper is reprinted from *Korean Language in America* Vol 5: 3–16 (2000).

1 The original version of this paper was presented at the 5th Annual Conference on Korean Language Education of the American Association of Teachers of Korean, held in Los Angeles in August, 2000.

was triggered in 1989 with the approval of the nation's governors and President George Bush and continued under the Clinton administration. In 1993, foreign language education became the seventh and last subject area to receive federal funding for developing national standards whose purpose was to establish curricular goals, standardize content, and improve the quality of foreign language education for students in kindergarten through twelfth grade. Needless to say, such impetus or change in foreign language teaching grew out of the reality that programs across levels simply were not preparing learners to function as educated citizens in a multilingual and multicultural society (cf. James 1998; Glisan 1999; Watzke 2000).

During the three-year period from 1993, an eleven-member task force, representing a variety of languages, levels of instruction, program models, and geographical regions formulated and developed the philosophy, five broad curricular goals, and eleven content standards for foreign language education in 21st century America. The content standards define what all students in the United Stales should know and be able to do as a result of lengthened foreign language instruction (Lafayette and Draper 1996). These standards are intended to serve as a gauge for excellence, as states and local districts carry out their responsibilities for curriculum in the schools (NSFLEP: 13). Under each standard axe provided sample progress indicators for grades four, eight, and twelve.

The draft document was pilot-tested at six sites and reviewed by thousands of teachers, specialists, and administrators. The finalized 109-page document, entitled the Standards for Foreign Language Learning: Preparing for the 21st Century (hereafter *Standards*) (NSFLEP 1996). was adopted by the U.S. Department of Education as national standards and endorsed by most major foreign language associations in the United States, and many states have already modeled their own standards after the *Standards* document (James ibid.).

Let me quote the philosophy, curricular goals, and content standards specified in the *Standards* as summarized in ACTFL (1997).

Philosophy:

> Language and communication are at the heart of the human experience. The United States must educate students who are linguistically and culturally equipped to communicate successfully in a pluralistic American society and abroad. This imperative envisions a future in which ALL students will develop and maintain proficiency in English and ax least one other language, modem or classical. Children who come to school from non-English backgrounds should also have opportunities to develop further proficiencies in their first language.

Several essential points are contained or assumed in this philosophy (cf. NSFLEP; 7). First, competence in more than one language and culture enables Americans to communicate with other people in other cultures in a variety of settings, participate more fully in the global community and marketplace, and gain direct access to additional bodies of knowledge. Second, all levels of American schools must have effective foreign language programs as part of the core curriculum to educate all students in foreign languages and cultures. Third, all American students must study foreign language and culture continuously over a long period of time in order to "develop and maintain proficiency". Fourth, immigrant students should be educated in their mother tongue.

One particular strength of the *Standards* document is the recognition that teaming a language takes time, far more lime than the average two-year sequence of courses at either the secondary or post-secondary levels (Wells 199B; Watzke 2000). Because foreign language study in America customarily begins late in the educational sequence and because our educational system has institutionally compartmentalized levels, mastering a second language has come to be seen as an extraordinary challenge for many American students even in "easy" languages such as Spanish, French, and German. The *Standards* make it clear that only extended, well articulated sequences produce significant results.

In order to accomplish the above-mentioned basic philosophy, five broad curricular goals have been identified by the task force. These goals are known as the five C's in that all the five goals begin with the letter C: Communication, Cultures. Connections. Comparisons, and Communities. Under each goal area, rationale, discussion, and two or three content standards are presented. The standards are the essential skills, knowledge, and understanding that students need to have in order to achieve each goal. All foreign language educators, curriculum developers, and others are urged to use these goals and standards as a gauge for curriculum, textbook and other teaching materials development, instruction, and assessment.

Five C's and Content Standards:

(1) Communication: *Communicate in languages other than English.*

Standards: Students (a) engage in conversations, provide and obtain information, express feelings and emotions, and exchange opinions; (b) understand and interpret written and spoken language on a variety of topics; and (c) present information. concepts, and ideas to an audience of listeners or readers on a variety of topics.

(2) Cultures: *Gain knowledge & understanding of other cultures.*

Standards: Students demonstrate an understanding of (a) the relationship between the practices (patterns of verbal and non-verbal behavior) and perspectives (traditional ideas, attitudes, beliefs and values) of the culture studied: and (b) the relationship betweentangible or intangible products (e.g. a painting, a piece of literature, an oral tale, a dance, an educational system) and perspectives of the culture studied.

(3) Connections: *Connect with other disciplines and acquire information.*

Standards: Students (a) reinforce and further their knowledge of other disciplines through the foreign language; and (b) acquire information and recognize distinctive viewpoints that are only available through the foreign language and its culture.

(4) Comparisons: *Develop insight into the nature of language and culture.*

Standards: Students (a) demonstrate understanding of the nature of language through comparisons of the language studied and their own; and (b) recognize that cultures use different patterns of interaction and can apply this knowledge to their own culture.

(5) Communities: *Participate in multilingual communities at home and around the world.*

Standards: Students (a) use the language both within and beyond the school setting; and (b) show evidence of becoming life-long learners by using the language for personal enjoyment and enrichment.

As is apparent, none of the five C's can be isolated from another. All of them are closely interwoven. Needless to say, the most important C is communication. Communication is at the heart of second language study, whether it takes place face-to-face, in writing, or across centuries through the reading of literature (NSFLEP: 27). That is, communication involves (la) interpersonal, (1b) interpretive, and (1c) presentational modes, Glisan (1999) points out that these three communicative modes emphasize the context and purpose of the communication and depict the four language skills as working in an integrated fashion. She also points out (hat being engaged in interpersonal communication (e.g. face-to-face conversation) means a change from the teacher as the center to the students' accepting greater responsibility for interacting with others and making themselves understood in the process of "negotiation of meaning". She further indicates that the interpretive mode of the *Standards* goes beyond the traditional idea of comprehension, since interpretation also involves the listener's or reader's ability to glean meaning "between the lines" and bring his or her background knowledge and ideas to the task ((NSPLEP: 22-33).

Culture is indispensably tied with communication. Students cannot truly master the language until they have also mastered the cultural contexts in which the language occurs (NSFLEP: 27). According to NSFLEP (43), the term "culture" is understood to include the philosophical perspectives (traditional ideas, attitudes, values, etc.), the behavioral practices (patterns of social interactions, etc.), and the products—both tangible and intangible—(books, tools, foods, laws, music, games, etc.) of a society. The products and practices are derived from the philosophical perspectives that form the world view of a cultural group. These three components of culture are closely interrelated among themselves as well as with language use. The Cultures Standards offer a framework for enabling students to explore ways in which the products and practices of people both reflect and are reflected by their perspectives. An educated individual needs to develop an awareness of other people's patterns of behavior, world views, and unique way of life, and learn about contributions to other cultures to the world at large.

Learning languages provides connections to additional bodies of knowledge (NSFLEP: 27). Connecting the foreign language curriculum with students' other academic subjects opens doors to information and experiences which enrich the students' entire school and life experience. Through the Connections Standards, learners have the opportunity to develop their intellect by learning new information in fields of study in which (hey are interested (e.g. history, music, literature, computer science, international relations, education, economy).

Watzke (2000) argues that the diversity of occupational interests of college students who study foreign language supports the proposal for connecting language learning experiences to multiple content areas, and that integrating occupational interests with work or study-abroad experiences, or even with international business or service organizations in the Untied Steles, would appeal to the broader body of students studying foreign languages. Watzke points out that language across the curriculum initiatives at several colleges and universities provide examples and resources for bridging foreign language study with other disciplines and the skills necessary for various occupations.

Through the study of a new language system and the way such a system expresses meanings in culturally appropriate ways, students gain insights into the nature of language, linguistic and grammatical concepts, and the communicative functions of language in society, as well as the complexity of the interaction between language and culture. As students expand their knowledge of cultures, they continually discover perspectives, practices, and products that are similar to as well as different from those in their own culture. Through comparisons and contrasts with the language and culture studied, students develop greater insight into their own language and culture and realize that numerous ways of viewing the world exist (NSFLEP: 27). In addition, by comparing both cultural and linguistic systems, students develop critical thinking abilities.

A changing American society and a world of instant global communication require American citizens to be proficient not only in English but also other languages. With these skills, Americans can directly access knowledge and information generated by other countries. These skills enable language students 10 participate in multilingual communities at home and around the world in a variety of contexts and in culturally appropriate ways. This proficiency is developed and sustained by learning and using a language over a long period of time. Moreover, students find that their ability to communicate in other languages enables them to expand their employment opportunities both at home and abroad, and allows (hem to pursue their own interests for personal rewards. That is, the Communities Standards make it clear that knowledge of and experience with another language, culture, and content help prepare an educated member of a society to function effectively with members of other communities.

The *Standards* presents a framework for a lengthened learning sequence (K-12) by presenting three sample progress indicators for grades 4, 8, and 12 under each standard. These indicators illustrate what students should know and be able to do at the end of years of language and culture study. For instance, by the end of Grade 8, die progress indicator for Standard (1b) (interpretive mode of communication) reads as follows: Students (i) comprehend information and messages related to other school subjects, (ii) understand announcements and messages connected to daily activities in the target culture, (iii) understand the main themes and significant details on topics from other subjects and products of me cultures as presented on TV. radio, video, or live presentations, (iv) understand the main themes and significant details on topics from other subjects and products of the cultures as found in newspapers, magazines, e-mail, or other printed sources used by speakers of the target language, (v) identify the principal characters and comprehend the main ideas and themes in selected literary texts, and (vi) use knowledge acquired in other settings and from other subject areas to comprehend spoken and written messages in the target languages (NSFLEP: 40).

Following the descriptions of the content standards is a 28-page section of *learning scenarios* to assist teachers in making the transition to standards-oriented instruction. Most of the scenarios are based on actual classroom activities submitted by teachers participating in a nine-month pilot study. Bach scenario includes a list of the targeted standards, a brief description of the activity and the type of classroom in which it was used, and a reflection of how the scenario addresses the standards.

In short, the *Standards* offers a vision of what students should know and be able to do with another language. In order to attain these standards, students require a foreign language program that provides rich curricular experiences. The *Standards* stipulate that students should be given ample opportunities to explore, develop, and use communication strategies, learning strategies, critical thinking skills, and skills in technology, as well as the appropriate elements of the language system and culture (NSFLEP: 28-32).

Since its publication in 1996, the *Standards* has been extended to the university level. Many language groups are developing their own language standards within the framework of the *Standards*, exemplifying language-specific learning scenarios and expanding the *Standards* to include the four years of college language study for continuity and coherence of *Standards*-based instruction. Thus. *Standards*-based foreign language education is the most powerful movement in contemporary foreign language education in the United States. As Long (1999), Sharpley-Whiting (1999). Brager and Rice (1999), and others argue, what is needed now is genuine dialogue between K-12 foreign language educators and university/college specialists. The goals and outcomes in college and university instruction, assessment, and curricula must be calibrated to build on and expand the elementary and high school foreign language experience to effectively transition students. The *Standards* provides an opportunity to improve and make invaluable foreign language education nationally and as an effective pedagogical mechanism for articulation between and within elementary, secondary, and postsecondary educational levels. This extension to college is not only essential, because the *Standards* specifies a set of sound and desirable national curricular standards for foreign language education for the first time in history, but also inevitable because college and university foreign language programs will receive *Standards*-based students from high schools (cf. James 1998).

3. Strengthening and Articulation for K-16 Korean Language Learning

Now, what should we as Korean language educators do with the *Standards*? I propose that the *Standards* be used as a "springboard" to improve Korean language teaching at all levels. That is, I propose that the same philosophy, curricular goals and content standards be observed, as the organizing principles, in Korean language curriculum development, textbooks, internet and other instructional materials development, classroom instruction, and development of assessment tools. This is because they are the nationally accepted curricular goals and standards; offer a clear vision for the future and a rationale for inclusion of all students in language study; provides new ways of looking at instructional resources; establish a model for accountability across levels; provide cognitive and pedagogical continuity for students, thus linking content to language use; etc. (cf. James 1998; Swaffar 1999; Tohsaku 1999). Adherence to the above goals and standards in Korean language education will be conducive to students' learning a high level of communicative and cultural skills and having a sounder foundation for all areas of Korean studies.

(1) Philosophy

First of all, in accordance with the essential points presented in the philosophy, our mandate is to endeavor, by all means, first, to assist as many schools as possible to establish, maintain, and/or enhance a well-articulated Korean language curriculum; second, to promote Korean language widely through well-articulated and high quality curriculum, instructional materials, leaching, and assessments, so that as many students as possible may take Korean courses over an extended period of time; and third, to have all Korean heritage students study Korean to attain a superior level of proficiency and use it throughout their lives. In these respects, we should arduously compete with over 100 other foreign languages being taught in the American educational system.

(2) Curricular goals and standards

In order to strengthen and articulate K-16 Korean language education, both educators and students need to have firm curricular goals and content standards in Korean language study. Students learn Korean for vastly diverse needs. A majority of students indicate that they are learning Korean in order to communicate with Koreans for various practical purposes. Also, many students learn Korean to understand Korean people, literature, culture and society better. Some learn Korean for professional purposes such as business, law and medicine practices, as well as Korean language teaching. Others study Korean as (he means or goals of their academic research. Many high school students study Korean for the SAT II Korean exam. A large portion of the students study Korean as part of their graduation language requirement. In order to accommodate these diverse student needs most effectively and perform our missions to globalize Korean language study, we should conduct Korean language education in accordance with the five curricular goals and eleven content standards specified in the *Standards*.

The *Standards* task force identified the five goal areas incorporating all the various reasons for foreign language study. Thai is, foreign language instruction covering all five goal areas will be beneficial to all students.

(3) Articulation

On the basis of the classification issued by the U.S. Foreign Service Institute in 1973. Korean is known as a group 4 language. Their findings show that it lakes roughly three times as long for an average native speaker of English to reach the same proficiency level in Korean as in a group 1 language such as Spanish. This has led Jorden and Walton to classify Korean among the world's "truly foreign languages". The implication is that, just to get through (he basics in Korean, students need two solid years, especially if they are serious about the acquisition of all language skills and not just exposure. Thus, one of the most important tasks in the 21st century is to strengthen and articulate Korean language instruction in grades K-16. NSFLEP (18) indicates that since (he time of study required for proficiency in "difficult" less-commonly taught languages is longer than for other modern languages, it is important to encourage long-sequence programs which begin at the pro-college level. Earlier starts with language instruction assure greater success for more students (NSFLEP; 19).

Currently, Korean is hardly taught at regular elementary schools (K-6) in the United Slates. Only popular languages such as Spanish. French, German, Italian. Japanese, Latin, and Russian are currently offered in varying degrees For instance, during 1998-99 academic year, Japanese was taught as a regular foreign language course at 75 elementary schools around the country to some 28.000 students, with an average class time of 120 minutes per week, all the way from kindergarten (Kataoka and Furuyama 1999). Korean was offered only al some 30 secondary schools (grades 7-12) to some 2,000 students, whereas Japanese was taught at several hundred secondary schools to nearly 50.000 students.

Under these circumstances, every possible effort must be exerted by Korean language educators and the Korean-American community to introduce Korean into grades K-12, so that Korean can be permanently built into the academic system of the United States. There is no reason why elementary and secondary schools in large cities such as Los Angeles. New York, Chicago, and Philadelphia where a large number of Korean Americans are heavily concentrated cannot offer Korean language courses, if strong and continued public opinions are expressed through American mass media.

Fortunately, over 800 heritage schools offer Korean language (2 hours per week) and culture (1 hour per week) instruction to elementary and even some secondary school students. Heritage school curricula must be reinforced and maximally utilized so that students who have learned Korean at heritage schools can start at higher-level Korean courses in secondary and post-secondary schools.

Also, short- or long-term field study (in-country study) in Korea must be an important part to be integrated into students' on-campus academic programs for the twin benefits of immediacy and constant exposure. It is very difficult for speakers of English to reach a functional ability solely through academic programs in the United States. They need extensive immersion study This demand on tune and resources is best accommodated by placing students in Korea, a total immersion situation (cf. W.P. Rivers 1998 and Larson 1999 for effective study abroad). Furthermore, cultural contexts are critical in language training, especially for cultures as radically different as America and Korea It is strongly recommended that students in East Asian languages go abroad at the end of the second year of language study, that is, after completing two years of basics (cf. Larson ibid.).

Thus, lengthened learning should include both K-12 and higher education. The expanded effort to link language education across K-16 instructional levels involves attention 10 numerous tasks: creating continuity of learning; linking the goals, content, instruction, and assessment of curricula; integrating the language with other academic disciplines; and focusing on the individual learner within an educational development framework (Lange 1997). I propose that articulating Korean language learning must be done with the *Standards* as the organizing principles. It must be emphasized that articulation requires professional involvement at all levels of instruction.

In discussing the issue of articulation based on the *Standards*, Brager and Rice (1999) argue that now is the time for university faculty to collaborate with colleagues in K-i2 so that extended foreign language study, as advocated by the framers of the *Standards*, will indeed span from K through 16. They envisage the "new" *Standards*-educated student who will arrive in college in a few years, as follows. Among other things, he/she:

- is less likely to view the teacher as the sole or even primary source of knowledge
- is used to making connections among academic disciplines and is accustomed to interdisciplinary ways of thinking
- is used to interpretation
- is used to presentational modes of displaying knowledge and skills (poster sessions, portfolios, video creation, etc.) rather than evaluations based primarily on written and oral tests
- is likely to have more highly developed critical thinking skills

- has a more integrative view of language (as opposed to the more traditional separations among language components such as grammar, vocabulary, communicative functions)
- is used to guessing and taking chances with (he language
- knows how to retrieve information from a variety of authentic sources (Internet, target language textbooks, magazines, newspapers, keypals, films)
- has learned how to distinguish between what is important and what is not important to the understanding of a particular topic
- is a better reader, both in terms of reading strategies for dealing with unfamiliar material and in terms of different text types
- is better able to discuss and debate about topics

Their argument is that university-level faculty need to rethink our traditional ideas of courses and classes, materials, classrooms, and majors in order to make them more flexible and therefore better able to attract and retain this new generation of students.

a. Structurally, classes are not the only answer.

Individualization and customization may be introduced at the beginning and intermediate levels to ensure flexivity. For example, small groups of students (similar language backgrounds, similar goals and interests) can proceed through the courses at their own speed: accelerated learners can finish a course in the middle of a term and immediately begin the next level; those who need extra time may take a term and a half to complete a course. At more advanced levels, where students' goals and interests diverge more widely, we need to multiply the available options, expanding language-across-the-curriculum opportunities.

b. Pedagogically, traditional materials are no longer sufficient.

Flexible classes will require flexible materials. If textbooks are to remain viable options for courses where students work at individual paces, they will need 10 provide multiple points of access (text, computer, CD. video) as well as a broader range of topical material, including multiple types of activities and assessment instruments, to accommodate students with diverse learning styles and objectives. It is clear that *Standards*-educated students accustomed to working with a variety of authentic materials (films. TV and radio broadcasts, popular literature and school textbooks from the target cultures. Internet sites, etc.) will not be content to rely exclusively on pedagogically altered, semi-authentic materials.

c. Physically, traditional classrooms need to be redesigned.

We have to design integrated learning spaces (technology-supported classrooms) that allow students to move smoothly and quickly from a small-group practice session to an individual work session at a computer or a VCR to an assessment conference with the instructor to a large-group discussion or a lecture or film presentation. At the same time, we will need to encourage students to use the language beyond the school setting by engaging directly (in nearby multilingual communities) or indirectly (letters, keypals. Internet chat groups) with speakers of the target language. In addition, we will have to continue to increase opportunities for study abroad (not just in language-based programs), internships, and other types of experiential education.

d. Administratively, the ten-course or thirty-two credit major may no longer be relevant.

To accommodate the "new" generation student, we must accept the idea that students do not all need to take the same courses and also that students do not all need to take the same number of courses. One possible way of rethinking a language major is in terms of a combination of competencies and experiences.

(4) Korean-specific Standards

Although the descriptions of the philosophy, curricular goals, and content standards are applicable to Korean language education as the organizing principles, the *Standards* is generic and thus not a curriculum guide. We will therefore need to develop Korean-specific content standards in the near future based on the *Standards*. These will maintain the format, philosophy, 5 C's, and content standards of the *Standards*, but offer Korean-specific progress indicators and learning scenarios.

We will need to develop Korean-specific performance standards. ACTFL has developed generic Performance Guidelines (Swender and Duncan 1998) which comprehensively describe the language performance levels (novice, intermediate, pro-advanced, advanced) students are expected to gain following specific durations of classroom instruction. Each performance level consists of six performance areas: (a) comprehensibility (how well are they understood?), (b) comprehension (how well do they understand?), (c) language control (how accurate is their language), (d) vocabulary use (how extensive and applicable is their vocabulary?), (e) communication strategies (how do they maintain communication?), and (f) cultural awareness (how is their cultural understanding reflected in their communication?); and each performance area covers the three modes of communication (Interpersonal, Interpretive, Presentational). While the *Standards* provides content standards that define the "what" of foreign language learning in American classrooms, the ACTFL Performance Guidelines are the performance standards that define "how well" students should be expected to do the "what". It is recommended that Korean-specific performance standards be modeled after these ACTFL Guidelines.

As Falsgraf (to appear) points out, a complete set of standards must have standards of not only content (what students need to know and do) and performance (how welt students need lo perform) but also assessment (how accurately and fluently students perform). With all three, the standards can serve maximally as a basis of instruction, curriculum, and evaluation, and thus function as a vehicle for improving performance. We should develop performance assessment tools in which reliable and valid samples of student performances (oral interviews, written notes, reading-based tasks, etc.) are collected to make consistent judgments of whether or not those samples meet a standard. Assessment tasks are to be created directly from the content and performance standards covering all interpersonal, interpretive, and presentational modes. For instance, Oregon Japanese teachers have created approximately 25 oral performance assessment tasks at each Benchmark (specific functional criteria which students must meet), which is regularly updated and revised to ensure reliability, validity and fairness (Falsgraf ibid.).

4. Conclusion

I propose that a collaborative task force with qualified representatives from all levels of schools collaborate to develop the documents of Korean language standards, performance guidelines, and assessment tools covering K-16. Also we should design and formulate detailed articulation strategies nationwide, including an educational framework, curriculum (courses and lesson plans), appropriate materials, good practice in technology, and critical issues of assessment and placement. Language, literature, linguistics, pedagogy, culture, and other disciplinary studies roust be integrated in all levels of Ac curriculum. The draft document must be reviewed by interested parties at all levels and (lie final version should be made available via the Internet. These measures should reflect the coherence of the curriculum and should be transparent to learners and their teachers at all levels (cf. Wells 1988). We have a long way to go before we reach the goal of a multi-year language-learning continuum for K-16, but we must set out as soon as possible.

REFERENCES: Chapter 29

ACTFL (American Council of Teachers of Foreign Languages), 1997. *Standards for Foreign Language learning—Preparing for the 21st Century*: Executive summary.

Brager, J.D. and D.B. Rice. 1999. The implications of the Standards for higher education. *ADFL Bulletin* 31.1: 70-2.

Falsgraf, C. To appear. Pedagogic implications of standards-based education. Nara, Hirosihi (ed.), *Advances in Japanese Pedagogy*. Columbus: Ohio State University Press.

Glisan, E.W. 1999. The impact of Standards on higher education, for more than just the sake of "continuity", *ADFL* Bulletin 31.1: 75-8.

James, D. 1998. The impact on higher education of Standards for foreign language learning: Preparing for the 21st Century. An ACTFL White Paper.

Kataoka, Hiroko and Hiroko Furuyama. 1999. A study of Japanese FLES programs in the United States. Breeze (The Japan Foundation & Language Center in Los Angeles) 19: l-6.

Lafayette, R.C. (ed.). 1996. *National Standards—A Catalyst for Reform*. Lincolnwood, ILL: National Textbook Company.

Lafayette, R.C. and J.B. Draper. 1996. Introduction 10 National Standards—A Catalyst for reform. In Lafayette, R.C. (1996, 1-8).

Lange, Dale L. 1997. Models of articulation: struggles and successes. *ADFL Bulletin* 28.2: 31-42.

Larson, P. 1999. "Doing" language: making new links. *ADFL Bulletin* 30.3: 28-31.

Long, D.R. 1999. Breaking down the barriers: implications of Standards for foreign language learning for United States universities. *ADFL Bulletin* 31.1: 78-9.

NSFLEP (National Standards in Foreign Language Education Project). 1996. *Standards for Foreign Language Learning: preparing for the 21st Century*. Lawrence, KS: Allen Press. Inc.

Rivers, W.P. 1998. Is being there enough? The effects of homestay placements on language gain during study abroad. *Foreign Language Annals* 31.1: 492-500.

Sharpley-Whiting. T.D. 1999. Postsecondary education and implications and uses of Standards for foreign language learning. *ADFL Bulletin* 31.1: 84-9.

Swaffar. J. 1999. The case for foreign languages as a discipline. *ADFL Bulletin* 30.3: 6-12.

Swender, E. and G. Duncan. 1998. ACTFL Performance Guidelines for K-12 Learners. *Foreign Language Annals*. 31.4: 479-91.

Tohsaku, Y.-H. 1999. National Standards in Japanese Language Classrooms. ms. for Standards Familiarization Workshop at the University of Hawaii. May 27-28.

Watzke. J. 2000. Student transitions from the high school classroom to the college major: implications for reform. *ADFL Bulletin* 31.3: 45-52.

Wells, E. 1998. Standards for foreign language learning: implications and perceptions. An ACTFL White Paper.

30 Korean Flagship: A New Frontier for Advanced Language Study*

1. A brief history

The Korean Flagship education is implemented as an integral component of the Language Flagship initiative, which was conceived, created, and implemented by the National Security Education Program (NSEP) at the U.S. Department of Defense.[1] NSEP was established by the *David L. Boren* National Security Education Act of 1991 as an important investment in vital expertise in languages and cultures critical to U.S. national security and international competitiveness. The program was mandated to award the following:

(a) Scholarships to U.S. undergraduate students to study abroad in areas critical to U.S. national security.
(b) Fellowships to U.S. graduate students to study languages and world regions critical to U.S. national security.
(c) Grants to U.S. institutions of higher education to develop programs of study in and about countries, languages and international fields critical to national security and under-represented in U.S. study.

As an initiative of NSEP, the Language Flagship began in 2000 as a small pilot project to challenge a few U.S. universities to establish non-degree post-BA programs for advanced language education to produce graduates with a profes-

* This paper appeared in Sohn, H.., S. Cheon, and H. Koh (eds.), *Innovations in Teaching Advanced Korean*, 2012 Special Issue of *The Korean Language in America*, pp. 3-17. The original version was a keynote paper titled "Korean Flagship at UHM: Past, Present, and Future", which was presented at the National Conference on the Korean Flagship Initiative: Toward Creating Global Professionals, hosted by the Korean Language Flagship Center, University of Hawaii at Manoa, Honolulu, HI. May 2010.

1 In February 2012, NSEP officially merged with the Defense Language Office (DLO) to create a new office, the Defense Language and National Security Education Office (DLNSEO), with Michael Nugent as its first director.

sional level of language proficiency. The first Flagship grants were awarded in 2002 for Korean, Arabic, Russian and Chinese. The University of Hawai'i at Mānoa (UHM) was selected for Korean.

Since then, NSEP has rapidly expanded the number of Flagship programs, growing from four to nine critical languages: Arabic, Chinese, Hindi Urdu, Korean, Persian, Portuguese, Russian, Swahili, and Turkish/Uzbek. Based on the initial four-year experience with various Flagship programs, NSEP announced a major transition plan in 2006, shifting the focus from post-B.A. to undergraduate programs and from non-degree to degree programs. Only three post-B.A. programs remained as M.A. programs: Ohio State University for Chinese, the University of Maryland for Arabic, and the UHM for Korean. At the same time, most of the earlier Flagship programs at individual universities were promoted to Flagship Centers, while several others were designated as Flagship Partner Programs. As of now, the Flagship community is comprised of 26 Flagship Programs (including Centers and Partner Programs) at domestic institutions of higher education and 10 overseas centers for nine critical languages, and three K-12 pilot programs, one for Arabic and two for Chinese. For Korean, only one domestic center (UHM Korean Language Flagship Center) and one overseas program (at Korea University in Seoul) are available.

The initial Korean Flagship program at UHM recruited the first cohort of students in 2003. This two-year program was a non-degree, non-certificate program, including intensive one-year domestic training at UHM and one-year overseas training at Korea University in Seoul. This initial Korean Flagship program at UHM was promoted to the Korean Language Flagship Center as of the summer of 2007.

2. The Language Flagship overview

Now, let us briefly overview what the Language Flagship initiative is. The website of the Language Flagship (www.thelanguageflagship.gov) provides its mission statement as follows:

> "The Language Flagship is a national initiative to change the way Americans learn languages through a groundbreaking approach to language education for students from kindergarten through college and graduate school. The program leads the nation in designing, supporting, and implementing a new paradigm for advanced language education. Through an innovative partnership among the federal government, education, and business, The Language Flagship seeks to graduate students who will take their place among the next generation of global professionals, commanding a supe-

rior level of proficiency in languages critical to U.S. competitiveness and security."

In order to fulfill the above mission, The Language Flagship has set its current objectives as follows:

- Establish programs for undergraduate students in all majors and disciplines that teach critical languages to the professional level (ILR 3, ACTFL Superior) and beyond during their course of study.
- Re-engineer existing language programs at all levels to provide students with opportunities and additional support for advanced language learning leading to professional level proficiency.
- Promote and improve on teaching excellence in the target language.
- Stimulate institutional support and long-term commitment to reforming language learning.
- Articulate domestic programs with high-quality overseas study centers; Improve national capacity in critical languages.

The gist of the Flagship initiative is "creating global professionals commanding a superior-level of proficiency in a critical language." Flagship programs are unique in that they offer the following benefits:

- Intensive language and culture instruction, including group training and individual tutoring, in a U.S. university setting
- Advanced language and long-term cultural immersion overseas where students enroll in foreign universities
- Language immersion internships through our public-private partnership with international organizations and corporations
- The opportunity to attain professional-level language proficiency, including in a non-language academic major of students' choosing

3. Innovations by the UHM Korean Language Flagship Center

In order to fulfill the Flagship mission and objectives as presented above, the Korean Language Flagship Center (KLFC), built on the previous non-degree post-B.A. program, has been implementing the following six major expanded tasks in cooperation with the UHM Department of East Asian Languages and Literatures (EALL):

(a) Introduction of new Flagship degree programs
(b) Program revamping for superior-level language and culture training
(c) Intensive and innovative instruction
(d) Overseas immersion education
(e) Content-based, domain-based instruction
(f) Outreach to pre-college students

Let us briefly discuss each of these tasks. First, creation of degree and certificate programs:

(a) Introduction of new Flagship degree programs

The earlier non-degree post-B.A. Flagship program was transitioned into a program of M.A. in Korean for Professionals as of the fall of 2007. This transition was motivated, in large measure, by students' serious dissatisfaction with a program that provides them with no formal credential of any sort after two years of intensive domestic and overseas immersion training. Thus, the new Flagship M.A. track was created and added, as a third track, to the existing M.A. tracks in Korean language and Korean literature in the EALL department.[2]

As of the fall of 2008, a new undergraduate degree track, titled B.A. in Korean for Professionals, was created as an additional track to the existing B.A. in Korean program. Subsequently, we have added Certificate and pre-college programs as well. Thus, the Korean Section of the department of EALL consists of the academic programs in Table 1:

TABLE 1. Academic programs of EALL Korean Section

Regular Programs	*Flagship Programs*
—	Pre-college program
B.A. in Korean	B.A. in Korean for Professionals
Minor in Korean	—
Certificate in Korean	Certificate in Korean for Professionals
M.A. in Korean Language & Linguistics	M.A. in Korean for Professionals
M.A. in Korean Literature	—
Ph.D. in Korean Language & Linguistics	—
Ph.D. in Korean Literature	—

Compare the expected student learning outcomes between the regular and Flagship programs below in Table 2 (pre-college program is not included):

2 As of the fall of 2012, NSEP has suspended its support to the three remaining MA programs.

TABLE 2. Student learning outcomes[3]

Programs	*Student Learning Outcomes*
B.A. in Korean	ILR2; specialized knowledge in Korean language, literature, and culture
B.A. in Korean for Professionals (dual degrees encouraged)	**ILR 3; competence in Korean in students' major areas and occupational culture**
Minor in Korean	ILR 1 or above; basic knowledge in Korean language & linguistics, literature, and culture
Certificate in Korean	ILR 1 or above; basic knowledge in Korean language, literature, and culture
Certificate in Korean for Professionals	**ILR 3; competence in Korean in students' major areas and occupational culture**
M.A. in Korean language/linguistics	ILR 3; specialized knowledge and competence in Korean linguistics, sociolinguistics, and language pedagogy; language teaching ability
Ph.D. in Korean language/linguistics	ILR 3; specialized knowledge and competence in Korean linguistics, sociolinguistics, and language pedagogy; university language teaching ability; ability for scholarly contribution
M.A. in Korean literature	ILR 3; specialized knowledge in various literary genres
Ph.D. in Korean literature	ILR 3; specialized knowledge in different literary genres; ability for scholarly contribution; university-level teaching ability
M.A. in Korean for Professionals	**ILR 3; competence in professional Korean in students' major areas and occupational culture**

Regular programs are designed to essentially develop students' disciplinary expertise in language/linguistics and/or literature through training in language history, linguistic structure, sociolinguistics, language acquisition, language pedagogy, literary history, criticism, and cultural studies. On the other hand, the new Flagship programs, except for the pre-college program which is intended to build a college-bound pipeline in Korean language and culture, are professionally oriented to develop students' superior-level proficiency in Korean in all four communicative skills and culture and in their non-language fields of study. Thus, for example, graduates with the highest degree in regular programs aspire to become university faculty in Korean language/linguistics or literature,

3 Interagency Language Roundtable (ILR) is a federal interagency organization established for the coordination and sharing of information about language-related activities at the federal level. ILR proficiency-level scale is a set of descriptions of abilities to communicate in a language: ILR level 1 = elementary proficiency; ILR level 2 = limited working proficiency; ILR level 3 = professional working proficiency; ILR level 4 = full professional working proficiency; and ILR level 5 = native or bilingual proficiency.

whereas graduates of the Flagship program aspire to function as a global Korea specialist. Accordingly, the two series of programs differ from each other in terms of academic missions and objectives, students' orientations and motivations, curriculum and instruction, intensity in language and culture training, instructional materials, and expected student learning outcomes. The two programs are mutually synergetic and complementary, however.

New Flagship curricula for M.A., B.A., and Certificate programs were introduced to meet the relevant degree and Certificate requirements, as indicated in regard to the program revamping below. While the M.A. program is a single degree program for students with diverse non-language undergraduate majors, B.A. students are encouraged to pursue the Flagship B.A. degree simultaneously with another Bachelor's degree. At present, all B.A. students are in dual degree programs.

(b) Program revamping for superior-level language and culture training

Unlike government institutions such as the Defense Language Institute (DLI), most American universities tend to slight the serious differences among foreign languages, standardizing curriculum and instruction, class size, and contact hours. However, the fact is that learning a so-called Category 4 language such as Korean, Chinese, Japanese, or Arabic requires three times more time than learning a Category 1 language such as Spanish or French in order to reach the same level of proficiency.[4]

A student who begins Korean from the novice level and takes all core skill courses all the way to the fourth level over four years, will learn Korean through approximately 500 contact hours. Expected levels of speaking proficiency in Category 4 languages (Arabic, Chinese, Japanese, and Korean) are given in Table 3, as per the Foreign Service Institute's experientially-based study (Liskin-Gasparro 1982; Hadley 2001: 25-27). Five hundred contact hours places the student of Korean at only ILR 1 (ACTFL Intermediate-Low).[5]

---

4 A reviewer points out that the four-level categorization was originally formed in relation to the abilities of monolingual English native speakers and wonders how this applies to heritage learners. This is an interesting issue that calls for serious research.

5 ACTFL stands for the American Council on the Teaching of Foreign Languages. ILR level 0 is equivalent to ACTFL Novice level, ILR level 1 to ACTFL Intermediate level, ILR level 2 to ACTFL Advanced level, and ILR levels 3, 4, 5 to ACTFL Superior level.

TABLE 3. Expected levels of speaking proficiency in category 4 languages

Length of Training	Aptitude for Language Learning		
	Minimum	Average	Superior
16 weeks (480 hours)	0+	1	1
24 weeks (720 hours)	1	1+	1+
44 weeks (1320 hours)	1+	2	2+
80–92 weeks (2400–2760 hours)	2+	3	3+

With the addition of high-level reading, composition, and culture courses, the Korean language curriculum of the four-year system in the United States is generally designed so that the highest level is ILR 1+ (ACTFL Intermediate-High) or ILR 2 (ACTFL Advanced-Low). Textbooks and other instructional materials are developed accordingly. This means that the existing programs cannot accommodate students, such as Flagship students, who enter college with an Advanced-Low or above level and aspire to raise their level to Advanced-High (ILR 2+) or Superior (ILR 3 or 3+).

This situation mandated us to revamp the existing program to accommodate students seeking the ILR 3 or 3+ (ACTFL Superior level). Thus, we created many higher level language and content courses, as listed below. We plan to add more courses as needed. All of these courses are taught only in Korean. The Flagship curriculum (*existing courses; 600+ levels are graduate courses) is as follows:

- Individual Feedback (individualized instruction for lower levels of Korean proficiency (KOR 399)
- Advanced Korean 1, 2 (KOR 401-402)*
- High Advanced Korean 1, 2 (KOR 403-404)
- Korean Proficiency through Film (KOR 480)*
- Readings in Chinese Characters (KOR 307/308)*
- Media Analysis in Korean, 1, 2 (KOR 421-422)
- Language and Culture of Korean (KOR 470)
- Selected Readings in Korean (Regular course) (KOR 425)
- Selected Readings in Korean (Flagship course) (KOR 425)
- Korean for Career Professionals (students' respective areas) (KOR 485)
- Korean for Academic Purposes (students' respective areas) (KOR 486)
- Korean Abroad (KOR 496: 8 credits for MA students, 12 credits for BA students upon successful completion of one-year study in Korea)
- Enhanced Readings (in students' respective areas) (KOR 499)
- Advanced Vocabulary (KOR 499)
- Individual Feedback (KOR 499)

- Media Research in Korean (KOR 621)
- Comparative Studies of North and South Korean Languages (KOR 622)
- Interdisciplinary Research in Korean (KOR 623)
- Analysis of Korean Academic Discourse (KOR 624)
- Directed Research in Korean (individualized instruction) (KOR 699)
- Research Seminar in Korean Language (KOR 730)

Notice that many new Flagship courses have been added to the existing programs, while also taking advantage of existing courses.

(c) Intensive and innovative instruction

Strengthening the curriculum was not enough to meet the needs of advanced-level students. As indicated above, the greatest weakness in the existing Korean programs is the shortage of classroom contact hours and of the opportunity to use the language. Three to five hours a week is not enough for any significant Korean language learning. The Flagship model is to train students for twenty contact hours a week, including 16 classroom hours and four individual tutoring hours. Tutors are selected from UHM graduate students from Korea in diverse disciplinary fields. Thus, students are trained through a total of 1,500 contact hours during the domestic and overseas immersion training.

Not only is training very rigorous, but various pedagogical innovations are designed, introduced, or accommodated, applying current developments in acquisition theories and instructional practices to classroom instruction and instructional materials development. We strive to raise instructional quality and efficiency to meet the diverse needs of the students. In addition to the content-based instructional methodology, the Task Based Language Teaching (TBLT) method is employed for graduate students, for example. Weekly or bi-weekly public presentations are required for students in both graduate and undergraduate programs. Graduating MA students are required to write a publishable scholarly paper in Korean, while undergraduate students are required to write a capstone paper in Korean upon completion of their one-year overseas immersion program. Innovative materials are being developed according to student needs. Students' language development in skills in four modalities, translation, and culture are constantly monitored and regularly assessed from pre-admission to graduation.[6]

One recent innovation is the development of online assessment tools. Exist-

6 We consider incorporating high-level technology, for which various presentations at the Department of Defense-supported annual Korean LEARN (Language Education and Resources Network) conference series will provide valuable resources.

ing Korean language testing tools are inadequate in assessing high-advanced and superior level proficiency in Korean. With grants received from NSEP and with the help of a specialist from the Defense Language Institute, the Korean Flagship faculty (led by Dong-Kwan Kong and Hye Ri Joo) have completed developing on-line assessment tools, which are being uploaded on-line shortly. On-line assessment tools are aimed at assessing students' fine-grained upper level reading, listening, and writing proficiency.

Another project we are currently working on is the transcription and analysis of the extensive Oral Proficiency Interview (OPI) data from Flagship students' entry and exit exams. Our research results will reveal persistent errors, as well as improvements, in lexical, collocational, structural, sociolinguistic, discourse, and cultural aspects. The results will be employed for improved instruction and materials development.

(d) Overseas immersion education

One of the most significant requirements is the one-year overseas immersion training. In addition to the complete socio-cultural immersion, both graduate and undergraduate students are required to (a) take superior-level language classes at Korea University (KU)'s Korean Language and Culture Center, (b) take two content courses in their major fields at regular classes along with KU students, and (c) receive year-round professional internship training (two days a week) in various organizations and institutions in students' areas of study. Through internship training, students will learn professional vocabulary and language use as well as Korean professional culture, let alone building human relationships.

(e) Content-based, domain-based instruction

As the mission of The Language Flagship is to cultivate global professionals with a Superior-level proficiency in the language, the Korean Flagship curriculum in both domestic and overseas programs is essentially content-based and students' domain-based. It is also modularized and individualized to a great extent. All students come to the Korean Flagship programs with a diverse background in their disciplinary fields, ranging over humanities, social sciences, and professional areas. We are trying to satisfy the needs of all students with such diverse disciplinary background, in order to train them to become a global professional. We regularly invite Korean faculty in diverse disciplines to lecture in Korean for our students. We endeavor to employ tutors in students' non-language major areas for assistance in both language and content.

One recent innovation we have made in the curriculum, textbook development, and instruction is integration of Korean language and culture with Korean studies. This new course covers a comprehensive survey of the key disciplinary areas of Korean studies (mainly in humanities and social sciences but also in education and science as well as popular culture). This innovation was motivated by the dire needs repeatedly expressed by Korean Flagship students conducting overseas studies at Korea University in Seoul. Our students indicated that, despite their advanced-level proficiency in Korean, they were constantly troubled by the inability to follow educated dialogues as well as academic discussions, let alone class lecturers, due to the lack of a solid foundation in Korean history, tradition, culture, and society. Indeed, at the advanced level, background knowledge plays a crucial role in comprehension. Our students suffered from the lack of such knowledge due to the lack of K-12 educational experience in Korean contexts. In order to fill this knowledge vacuum of Flagship students, we introduced a new foundational interdisciplinary content course two years ago, for which we collaboratively developed a textbook, titled *Essentials of Korean Culture* (edited by Ho-min Sohn and Sang Yee Cheon), covering Korean history, religion and philosophy, education, language, literature, politics and government, economics, society, family and gender, visual and performing arts, science and technology, and food and sports. This textbook is written in authentic Korean for content training as well as language improvement.

(f) Outreach to pre-college students

As indicated in the mission statement, The Language Flagship emphasizes integration of language skills into K-12 education, so that high school graduates may enter college with an established and measurable skill in the language. Korean is taught at only about 130 universities and only 73 K-12 schools in the United States. While the universities teaching Korean are widely distributed across the nation, the 73 schools are mostly located in Los Angeles and New York areas where Korean-American populations are concentrated, as shown (Sohn, Jeong, & Park 2009) in Table 4.

TABLE 4. Schools offering Korean courses

Levels of Schools	*No.*	*Notes*
High schools	42	
Intermediate schools	10	1 is a dual language program.
Elementary schools	8	6 are dual language programs.
K-12 schools	10	
Others (3-12 or 4-12)	3	1 is a dual language program.
TOTAL	73	

No K-12 school regularly offers Korean in the state of Hawaii and most other states. In these circumstances, KLFC faculty has initiated a number of projects and programs. First, KLFC introduced a pre-college summer intensive program in 2009 in collaboration with the UHM Outreach College. Second, Haejin E. Koh and Hee-Jeong Jeong established and taught a temporary afternoon Korean program at Moanaula High School in 2010. Third, Haejin Koh and Hee-Jeong Jeong received a State Department NSLI-Y grant in 2010 and took a group of 18 nationally-selected high school students to Korea for six weeks of language and culture study. Fourth, since 2010, Haejin Koh has initiated a Korean language program at Roosevelt High School with funds cost-shared by the UHM NRC-East Asia.

In the lack of enough Korean language programs in K-12 schools, some 1,000 Korean community schools are available nationwide. Each school usually offers three contact hours of instruction (mostly on Saturdays): two hours for language and one hour for cultural activities. A majority of the students are elementary school students, followed by intermediate school students. High school students are relatively very small in number. There are some 35 community schools in Hawaii. KLFC faculty has initiated two projects related to community schools. First, needs assessment of the Korean community schools in Hawaii was conducted to identify what issues and challenges these schools were confronted with (Sohn, Huh, and Choi 2007). It was revealed that the following aspects should be improved in most community schools, which is assumed to be the case in most other community schools in the nation.

a) Shortage of high-quality instructional materials
b) Generally low teacher quality
c) Shortage of classroom hours
d) Insufficient culture learning
e) Weak curriculum
f) Unsatisfactory learning environment (facilities, etc.)
g) Poor operation of schools
h) Financial difficulty
i) General lack of parental concern and cooperation
j) General lack of student motivation
k) Lack of networking among heritage schools

Second, since 2009, Sang Yee Cheon has been coordinating bi-annual teacher training workshops for Korean community school teachers in Hawaii. Each workshop lasts for either seven (in 2009) or five weeks (in 2011), covering what to teach and how to teach. Instructional technology is incorporated as well.

All the above pre-college outreach efforts are intended to eventually develop a viable model for pre-college Korean language training and K-16 articulation in curriculum and instruction.

4. Current and future challenges

The Korean Language Flagship Center is still in its infancy, and its challenges are multi-faceted. The most serious challenge is how to sustain and institutionalize the Flagship programs when federal funding is drastically reduced or terminated.

As we have observed in the above, almost all academic affairs such as degree programs, course requirements, curricula, students, and scholarship awards for Flagship education have been integrated with those of the regular programs of the department as the third M.A. track, along with the tracks of language and literature and as the second undergraduate track, along with regular BA/Certificate track. Regular and Flagship programs are synergic and complement each other. Flagship students can take regular advanced courses, and advanced regular students can take Flagship courses. Part of the faculty members are shared between regular and Flagship programs.

Then, why are sustainability and institutionalization a challenge? The major issue is faculty lines. Currently, 4.5 full time equivalents are Flagship faculty paid fully by the federal grants. The issue is who will teach Flagship courses if the federal grants are either radically reduced or terminated. NSEP requests the universities involved to take over faculty lines, preferably one full-time position per year, so that NSEP may increase student fellowships and scholarships instead. This NSEP request has not been satisfactorily complied with at UHM due to internal budgetary constraints. NSEP has supported UHM for the past ten years to build the Flagship programs as they are now. NSEP has gradually, but steadily, reduced funding in recent years. In order to keep up with this reduction in federal funding as much as we can, we have taken action to merge certain domestic (UHM) Flagship courses with advanced regular courses, while increasing class sizes.

One sudden decision NSEP made at the end of 2011 was to terminate funding to all three existing M.A. programs (Arabic, Chinese, and Korean) as of the fall semester of 2012. This decision was due mainly to the budget cut of the Department of Defense, but also partly to comply more strictly with the Language Flagship's 2006 transition plan to transition post-BA programs to undergraduate programs. In preparation for the expected termination of two federally-funded faculty members as of June 30, 2012, we are endeavoring to merge all domestic (UHM) undergraduate-level (400 level and below) Flagship courses with regular program courses, leaving six graduate (600+ level) courses per year intact. An issue at present is who will teach these graduate courses, if the UHM administration does not come to aid by providing a regular position. The last resort is that the three existing faculty members teach the six courses and the language courses they would be assigned be taught by lecturers. Our overseas program at Korea University will be adjusted without suffering much blow. In short, we are forced to sustain and institutionalize the M.A. program much earlier than expected.

Another challenge related to sustainability is how to recruit more students. Student recruitment is a perennial issue. We admit students into Flagship programs only when they are (a) academically outstanding, (b) highly motivated to become Korea specialists in their fields, and have (c) Korean proficiency levels of ACTFL Intermediate-High through Advanced-High. (Superior-level and native speakers are not accepted). A major problem is how many students in the United States meet all three minimum qualifications and how we can identify and recruit them. The Language Flagship encourages each Flagship Center to recruit about 20 undergraduate students per year. Through various recruitment strategies and rigorous screening, KFLC usually admits a dozen BA and a dozen MA students per year, far shorter than the national goal.

A related issue we face is that, while we are endeavoring to make balanced recruitment between heritage and non-heritage students, the majority of the students with the required upper-level proficiency in Korean are heritage students. Thus, we are compelled to slightly relax the minimum entry level proficiency for non-heritage students, from Intermediate-High to Intermediate-Mid or -Low. As a result, we are endeavoring to revise the curriculum and adjust instructional methods and materials to deal with the widened entry levels of students. Furthermore, the goal of producing only Superior-level students has to be somewhat mitigated.

A third challenge is how to effectively build up the K-12 pipeline and integrate and articulate K-16 Korean language education, which can be attained best through standards-driven program development, curriculum, instruction, and assessment (e.g. ACTFL Proficiency Guidelines, National Standards for Foreign Language Learning, ACTFL Performance Guidelines for K-12 Learners, ACTFL Integrated Performance Assessment, and KLFC-developed online assessment tools).

Our immediate task is, thus, how to develop Korean programs in K-12 schools. This is indeed a tough issue to resolve, as Korean has to compete with commonly taught languages such as Spanish and French as well as other popular Asian languages such as Chinese and Japanese. While Korean is an SAT II language which more than 4,000 high school students take the exam each year, it is not an AP exam language yet, since not enough high schools offer Korean.

Our small-scale projects and programs toward this goal are merely experimental in nature. In fact, establishing sound institutional K-12 pipelines requires cooperative efforts of all involved at national, state, school, and community levels, as well as parents and students.

In the meantime, what KLFC can do is to continue to try to build high school programs one at a time, while training pre-college students at UHM and conducting teacher training workshops for community schools. Development and delivery of an online distance learning network covering well-articulated K-16 curriculum, instruction, instructional materials, and assessment tools will be a viable option, much faster, more economical, and more effective way of reaching K-12 students nation-wide than establishing costly institutional Korean language programs. This is a hopeful challenge ahead, although funds and expert personnel are required.

Our fourth challenge is the issue of innovation and diffusion. Innovation and diffusion are a Flagship motto as implied in the wording "groundbreaking approach to language education" in the mission statement. While various innovations have been made at KFLC on the curriculum, materials development, instruction, and assessment, there is a great limitation that the small number of Flagship faculty can do. We will need stronger partnership with outside faculty and experts in government language institutions as well as in other academic departments and institutions and language-related academic associations, such as the American Association of Teachers of Korean (AATK) and ACTFL. In particular, we will need assistance from the Defense Language Institute for effective use of technology to enhance instruction and facilitate learning. Inter-institutional cooperation and networking is essential for further innovative language education.

Diffusion is another challenge. Although we have presented at various conferences what we have innovated, the impact still appears to be minimal. Practically, introduction of a Flagship-level program in the Korean language programs of most academic institutions may not be ready yet and still remains as an ideal, as more instructional faculty, more funds, and more students are needed. This issue will remain a challenge ahead.

One last challenge is how to efficiently partner with the business sector and funding and other internship organizations in Korea. As the three diamonds in the Flagship logo symbolize, creating a solid partnership among education, government and business to advance language education in the United States is a foundational mission of the Language Flagship. The basic idea is that the government and business function as supporters of Flagship education and, at the same time, beneficiaries to receive well-trained global professionals with superior language proficiency. At the national level, the Language Flagship endeavors to partner with the business sector, undertaking, for example, to assess and understand the needs for global skills in business, as continued input from the business sector will sharpen our insights into language and cultural factors that affect business' success. At the local level, we, the KLFC, are required to develop partnerships with the local and Korean business sectors for internship and funding. On the other hand, we have secured enough organizations and institutions in Korea where our students conduct job-related internship. We are, however, are still endeavoring to secure scholarships for students and project funds from funding organizations in Korea. All this constitutes a challenge we are currently facing.

5. Conclusion

In this paper, I have summarized what The Language Flagship is all about, what KLFC has been doing, and what challenges it is facing. I have tried to point out that the Korean Language Flagship Center presents a new paradigm of advanced Korean language teaching and learning in the academic sector. It is a new, innovative model constructed based as much as possible on various strengths of language training systems and approaches available in both government and academic institutions. In this sense, KLFC performs the function of a bridge in Korean language pedagogy between the government and academic sectors on the one hand, and between the Flagship program and regular programs, with the eventual goal to "re-engineer" all Korean language programs in academic institutions to incorporate the Flagship model for advanced language training.

REFERENCES: Chapter 30

손호민, 허소린, 최윤화. 2007. 「하와이주 한인사회학교의 실태분석」 (Needs assessment of the Korean community schools in Hawaii). *Proceedings* of the 7th International Association for Korean Language Education Annual Conference, pp. 587-603.

Hadley, A. O. 2001. *Teaching Language in Context.* 3rd Edition. Boston: Heinle & Heinle.

Liskin-Gasparro, J. E. 1982. *ETS Oral Proficiency Testing Manual.* Princeton, N.J.: Education Testing Service.

Sohn, Ho-min, Hee-Jeong Jeong, and Miyung Park 2009. Toward K-16 articulation for advanced Korean language learning: A survey report on the U.S. K-12 Korean language program. Ms. University of Hawaii Korean Language Flagship Center. In this volume.

31 미국 내 한국어교육의 현안과 주도적, 혁신적 대처*

1. 서론

각종 통계와 필자 자신의 40년간의 관찰과 경험에 의하면, 미국의 각급학교 한국어 수강생의 수는 과거 30년 동안 꾸준한 증가세를 보이고 있다.[1] 예를 들면, Modern Language Association Wb에 실린 Furman, Goldberg, and Lusin (2007)의 논문에 따르면, 미국대학에서 가르치는 200 남짓의 외국어 중 한국어는 2006년 현재 수강생 순위가 14위이고, 학생수는 7,145명이다. 과거 30년간의 대학 한국어 수강생의 꾸준한 증가 상황을 보면 다음과 같다.

연도:	1960	1970	1980	1990	1995	1998	2002	2006
수강생수:	168	101	374	2,286	3,343	4,479	5,211	7,145

한국어수강생의 증가는, 재미 한인인구의 증가, 한국의 경제발전, 미국정부의 적극적인 외국어교육정책과 국책언어(critical languages) 정책, 한국정부의 세계화 정책, 한류, 한국학의 학문적 보급, 한인사회의 2세를 위한 한국어 교육열, 한국어 교육자들의 활동, 각급 교육기관의 협조 등 많은 외적, 내적 요인의 상호작용의 결실임은 물론이다.

그러나, 한국어 수강생수를 다른 주요 언어의 수강생수와 비교해 보면, 현격한 차이를 보인다. 표 1에서 보듯이 2006년 14위를 점한 한국어는, 수강생 66,605명으로 5위를 점한 일본어나 수강생 51,582 명으로 6위를 점한 중국어와는 필적할 수 없는 열세에 있다. 더욱이 1위인 스페인어(822,985명)나 2위인 불어(206,426명)와는 비교도 할 수 없는 "less commonly taught language"이다. 현재, 미국의 140여 개의 일반 대학에 한국어가 개설되어 있는데, 이 수는 미국 전체에 있는 약 7,000개의 대학의 50분의 1에 해당한다. 후술하는 바와 같이 정규 K-12학교의 한국어교육은 더욱 빈약하다.

---

* 이 글은 2010년 제1차 한국어 Language Education and Resource Network (LEARN) Conference의 기조강연 자료로 작성한 것이다. 한국어를 모르는 청중이 많아서 실제 발표는 Issues, Initiatives, and Innovations in Korean Language Pedagogy라는 제목으로 영어로 진행했다.

1 This is a keynote paper presented at the inaugural Korean LEARN conference at the DLI, Monterey, California. April 27-30, 2010.

TABLE 1. Fall 2002 & 2006 language course enrollments in US institutions of higher education (Furman, Goldberg & Lusin 2007:13)

Languages in descending order	2002	2006	% Change
1. Spanish	746,267	822,985	10.3
2. French	201,979	206,426	2.2
3. German	91,100	94,264	3.5
4. Italian	63,899	78,368	22.6
5. Japanese	52,238	66,605	27.5
6. Chinese	34,153	51,582	51.0
7. Latin	29,841	32,191	7.9
8. Russian	23,921	24,845	3.9
9. Arabic	10,584	23,974	126.5
10. Greek, Ancient	20,376	22,849	12.1
11. Hebrew, Biblical	14,183	14,140	-0.3
12. Portuguese	8,385	10,267	22.4
13. Hebrew, Modern	8,619	9,612	11.5
14. Korean	**5,211**	**7,145**	**37.1**

2. 현안문제

이러한 상황에서 한국어 학습은 양적으로나 질적으로 대폭 강화되어야 한다. 간혹 한국어 습득의 필요성(need) 또는 수요(demand) 문제가 거론된다(예컨대 Silva 2007). 어려운 한국어를 왜 배워야 하는가의 문제이다. 다 아는 사실이지만 간단히 한국어학습의 필요성(need, demand)과 중요성에 대해서 정리하고 현재 공급량(supply, capacity)의 극단적인 부족을 논의해 본다.

우선, 한국어를 모국어로 사용하는 한인 인구가 세계 12위 안팎인데다, 현재 6백만의 한국계 인구가 미국, 중국, 일본, 구 소련을 포함한 세계 도처에 이주해서 살고 있다. 한국은 세계 12위로 알려진 동아시아의 주요 경제강국이다. 다수의 한국인구의 미국 진출과 한국경제의 지속적 성장만으로도 한국어 습득의 수요가 된다.

한국학을 위시한 학문적 수요도 크다. 한국은 오랜 역사상 중국과 일본 간의 교량적 역활을 하면서, 여러 가지 독창적인 문화를 창조해 왔다. 따라서 동아시아를 논하면서 한국을 제외하고 중국과 일본만을 논할 수 없게 되었다. 언어, 문학, 역사를 포함한 인문사회과학 전반에서 볼 수 있듯이, 역사적으로나 현실적으로 한국학을 중국학이나 일본학의 일부로 다룬다는 것은 불가능하다. 모든 분야에서 양자의 중간에서, 어느쪽으로도 속하지 않는 독자성과 특수성과 발전상을 지니고 있기 때문이다. 또한, 남북의 분단은 인문사회과학의 시험대가 되어 한국에 관심 있는 많은 학자, 학생들의 연구대상이 되고, 한국어의 언어유형적 특성 때문에 언어학자들의 관심도 크다. 이러한 모든 학문을 위해서는 상급 수준의 한국어 습득이 필수요건이다.

더욱이 현실적인 국제교류 측면에서, 한국은 외교, 통상, 재정, 학술, 과학기술, 환경, 군사, 문화 등 모든 분야에서 미국과는 불가분의 관계에 있는 나라이다. 이러한 관계는 언어를 통해서 이루어지고 지속되고 발전한다. 영어가 모국어가 아닌 한국과의 원활한 관계와 교류를 적극적으로 유지하기 위해서는 미국민이 한국어, 한국문화의 능력을 갖추어야 한다. 영어가 유창하고 미국문화를 잘 아는 한국인은 극소수이기 때문이다. 따라서 한국어와 한국문화 교육은 미국의 국가경쟁력과 안보 그리고 한국과의 우호적인 관계의 증진을 위해서 필수요건이다.

사회적 차원에서도, 200만이 넘는 한국계 인구가 미국에서 건실한 한국계 지역사회를 형성하고 지역문화를 발전시키고 있다. 특히 한국인의 교회 문화는 날로 성장, 팽창해 간다. 이러한 지역사회에 참여하고, 이들과의 원활한 교류를 위해서는 한국어 구사가 필수이다. 한국어능력은, 일반 한국인들과의 교류는 물론, 미국에서 한국이나 한국인에 관련되는 다양한 직종에 극히 도움된다.

그리고 한국계 후예의 한국어와 한국문화의 습득과 보존은 개인의 학업, 직업, 가족과의 관계, 지역사회의 참여, 한국과의 유대, 정체성유지 등에 극히 중요하다. 특히 한국어, 한국문화는 한국계-미국인이라는 이중정체성 확보의 필수요건이다.

다시 말하면, 미국의 경쟁력, 안보, 국제교류의 증진 등 국가정책적 목적과, 학문적, 교육적, 사회적, 개인적 목적을 위한 한국어능력의 수요는 크다. 여기에 가세하여, 한류의 전파, 고급 한국제품의 대량의 보급과 가시화, 한국 정부의 한국어, 한국학의 세계화 정책에 따른 각종 지원, 미국정부의 국책언어정책에 따른 각종 연구비와 장학금 지원 등은 학생들의 한국어 학습을 크게 자극한다. 이러한 여러 수요를 충족시키기 위해서는, 한국어교육의 대폭적인 질적, 양적 향상이 시급하다. 이러한 질적, 양적 향상을 도모하기 위하여, 적어도 다음 여섯 가지의 상호 연관된 현안을 시급히 해결하여야 한다고 굳게 믿고 있다.

(1) 대체로 ILR 1+나 ILR 2(ACTFL Intermediate-high or Advanced-Low) 수준을 목표로 한 기존 한국어교육 프로그램을 ILR 2+ 또는 3 (ACTFL Advanced-High또는 Superior)까지 훈련시킬 수 있는 프로그램으로 개편하는 문제
(2) 학생의 전문분야를 포함하여 최상급 한국어능력(ILR 3)을 갖춘 (한국학이나 전문직종에서) 한국전문가를 양성하는 문제
(3) 더 많은 초등학교와 중고등학교에 한국어프로그램을 개설하여 한국어교육의 저변을 확대시키는 문제
(4) 교과과정, 교과서 등의 교육자료, 교수법, 평가법 등에서, 초-중-고-대(K-16)의 한국어 교육을 체계적으로 연계시키는 문제
(5) 한글학교의 한국어교육의 질을 향상시키는 문제
(6) 한국어 프로그램이 없는 학교의 K-16학생들에게 K-16 한국어 교육을 제공하는 원거리 교육체제를 구축하는 문제

현재 미국의 모든 한국어교육의 여건하에서, 이러한 중요한 현안문제를 효과적으로 해결하려면, 필요한 인적, 물적자원과 지속적인 프로그램과 전문성이 갖추어진 대학에서 주도적으로 계획하고 실험하고 실천해야 효과적이라고 생각한다. K-12의 프로그램 개발에서도 주정부 교육부와 학교 당사자는 대학 한국어담당 교수진의 경험과 전문성을 구하고 그들과 긴밀한 공조하에 실행하여야 성공을 거둘 수 있다고 생각한다. 공조의 필요성은 결국 K-12과정을 마친 학생들이 대학 프로그램으로 진학하기 때문이기도 하다. 우선, 위에 든 현안문제의 해결을 위해서 하와이대학에서 그동안 어떤 주도적이고 창의적인 활동을 시도해 왔는지를 간단히 소개하고, 나아가서 앞으로의 과제는 무엇인지를 제안하고자 한다.

3. 현안문제 해결을 위한 주도적, 창의적 시도

하와이대학에서는 2002년부터 National Security Education Program(NSEP)의 지원하에 최상급 수준을 목표로한 한국어플래그십 교육을 실시해 왔다. 처음 5년간은 대학졸업생을 상대로 비학위과정으로 운영했다. 그러나, 이 시범기간 동안 비학위과정으로 인한 학생의 동기 부족, 정규 한국어 학위과정과의 유리, 플래그십 학부과정의 결여 등 여러 가지 약점이 노출되어, 2007년부터는 종전 비학위프로그램을 한국어플래그십 센터로 승격시키고, 동시에 전문한국어 석사과정, 학사과정, 자격증과정을 신설하게 되었다. 플래그십언어교육의 미션과 이니셔티브에 따라, 한국어플래그십센터에서는 주로 위의 현안문제 (1)과 (2)의 해결을 위해 노력했다. 그리고 부분적이고 불완전하지만, (3), (4), (5), (6)의 문제도 시범적인 차원에서 조금씩 시도하고 있다.

이러는 과정에서, 창의적인 국내·해외의 정규·하기 프로그램의 개발, 내용중심의 교과과정과 교수안 개발, 내용중심의 교재개발, TBLT(task-based language teaching) 등 교수법 도입, 최상급 독해와 청취를 포함한 online 평가도구 개발 등 일련의 교육프로그램과 프로젝트를 실시하고 있다. 현안문제 (6)의 원거리교육 체계는 아직 요원하지만 앞으로 여러 전문가와의 긴밀한 협조하에 이룩되어야 할 사안이다. 이하 현안문제에 관해 하와이 대학이 시도해 온 활동을 부연하면 다음과 같다.

(1) 최상급지향을 위한 교육체제의 개편(program revamping)

우리가 잘 알듯이, 한국어는 영어권 성인에게는 습득하기 가장 어려운 소위 4범주의 언어이다. Mark Petersen이 한국어만을 유독 5범주로 규정하려는 데는 나도 동조한다. 영어와는 음성·음운·음절·어형·문장의 유형구조가 완전히 양극을 이루고, (소수의 외래어 외에는) 공통어휘(cognates)가 없고, 문자가 전혀 다르고, 사회언어적 차이, 담화형태의 차이가 극히 다르다. 이러한 언어적 차이뿐 아니다. 가치관 등 정신문화의 차이, 행동문화나 문화유산의 차이, 미국학과 한국학의 학문적 차이까지도 극심하다.

현재 미국대학의 정규 한국어 핵심과목(core course)의 교과과정은 2년제, 3년제, 4년제가 있는 것이 보통인데, 4년제의 경우, 1급, 2급, 3급, 4급으로 나누어 각급을 일년간(두 학기 또는 3분기) 수학하고, 수업시간 수는 일주일에 5시간(1, 2급) 내지 3시간(3, 4급)을 할애하는 것이 보통이다. 그 외에 드물게는 (하와이대학처럼) 독해, 작문, 문학, 문화교육, 한자교육도 곁들인 학교도 있다. 1급에서 시작하여 4급까지 4년간 핵심과목만을 택한다면 총 약 500시간을 공부하게 된다. 우리가 흔히 참고로 사용하는 FSI 의 보수적 언어습득통계인 표 4에서 보듯이, 500시간으로는 겨우 ILR 1의 수준에 도달한다(Liskin-Gasparro 1982; Hadley 2001: 25 - 27). 한편, 스페인어, 독일어, 불어 등 영어와 동족언어의 경우는 같은 시간 안에 한국어보다 3배나 빨리 습득할 수 있기 때문에 4학년급을 마치면 ILR 2(ACTFL Advanced) 수준에 도달할 수 있다.

TABLE 2. Expected levels of speaking proficiency: Arabic, Chinese, Japanese, Korean (Liskin-Gasparro 1982; Hadley 2001: 25–27)

Length of Training	Aptitude for Language Learning		
	Minimum	Average	Superior
16 weeks (480 hours)	0+	1	1
24 weeks (720 hours)	1	1+	1+
44 weeks (1320 hours)	1+	2	2+
80–92 weeks (2400–2760 hours)	2+	3	3+

ILR 1의 수준이면 일상생활의 survival level은 유지되나 그 이상의 언어기능은 수행할 수 없다. 대학입학 전에 한국어를 배웠거나 가정이나 한글학교나 한국에서 장기간 한국어에 접한 학생은 대학에서 보통 2학년급 또는 3학년급부터 시작하기 때문에 4년간 배우면 ILR 1+까지도 도달할 수 있다. 이런 점을 감안하여 현존 대학의 한국어프로그램과 교재, 교수법은 대체로 ILR 2를 최고한으로 편성된다. 그러나 플래그십 학생들처럼 그 이상 수준을 목표로하는 학생들을 훈련시키는 교과과정은 되어 있지 않다.

따라서 최상급을 지향하는 교육을 위해서는, ILR 3을 목표로 하는 교과과정, 교재, 학생지도, 평가도구를 개발해서 도입해야 한다. 이 문제를 타결하기 위해서 하와이대학에서는 다음과 같은 조치를 취했다.

첫째, 종전의 교과과정의 보강(curriculum reinforcement)이다. 다음 목록에서 보듯이, 하와이대학의 기존 상위급과목 위에 더 높은 수준의 과목을 추가 신설했다(*는 기존 상급과목이고 나머지는 신규과목; 600 단위는 대학원 과목). 이 모든 과목은 한국어로만 수업이 진행된다. 즉 기존 한국어 프로그램에 덧붙여 ILR 2+와 그 이상을 목표로 하는 교육과정으로 개편하였다. 앞으로도 시행착오를 거쳐가면서 가일층 향상된 교육과정과 교재 개발, 평가도구 개발에 진력할 것이다.

Curriculum (*existing courses; **600+** levels are graduate courses)

- Advanced Korean 1, 2 (KOR 401-402)*
- High Advanced Korean 1, 2 (KOR 403-404)
- Korean Proficiency through Film (KOR 480)*
- Readings in Chinese Characters (KOR 307/308)*
- Essentials of Korean Culture for Advanced Language Learners (KOR 470)
- Selected Readings in Korean (media search) (KOR 425)
- Korean for Career Professionals (students' respective areas) (KOR 485)
- Korean Abroad (KOR 496: 8 credits for MA students, 12 credits for BA students upon successful completion of 1-year study in Korea)
- Enhanced Readings (in students' respective areas) (KOR 499)
- Advanced Vocabulary (KOR 499)
- Individual Feedback (KOR 499)
- Media Research in Korean (KOR 621)
- Comparative Studies of North and South Korean Languages (KOR 622)
- Interdisciplinary Research in Korean (KOR 623)
- Analysis of Korean Academic Discourse (KOR 624)
- Directed Research in Korean (individualized instruction) (KOR 699)
- Research Seminar in Korean Language (KOR 730)

둘째, 집중교육모델(intensive training model)이다. 현존하는 한국어 프로그램의 가장 큰 약점은 언어접촉시간과 언어사용기회가 너무도 부족한데 있다. 집중 몰입 교육을 통하여 이러한 난관을 돌파하고자 하는 것이다. 즉 최상급의 한국어를 추구하는 학생들에게 프로그램 재학 중 가능한 최대한의 언어접촉 시간과 가능한 최대한의 언어사용 기회를 부여한다. 한국어 플래그십 교육의 경우, 2년제의 석사과정을 예로 들면, 1년간의 국내 집중 교육은 일주일에 20시간의 언어접촉 교육(16시간의 교실 교육과 4시간의 개인교사 교육) 을 실시한다. 두 학기면 700시간 가까이 학습하는 셈이다. 그러고 나서 후술하는 바와 같이, 한국에 가서 여름부터 1년간의 현지 몰입 교육을 받는다. 국내와 현지 교육을 합하면 대략 1,500시간의 언어접촉 교육을 받게 된다. 이 시간에는 교육과정 밖의 일반 언어, 문화 몰입 시간은 가산되지 않았다. 2년간 1,500시간가량의 교육을 감안할 경우, 표 3에서 보았듯이 FSI의 보수적인 기준에 따르더라도 ILR 1+나 2부터 시작한 학생은 ILR 3에 오를 수 있다.

학부과정은 보통 국내 집중교육이 3년 내지 4년이고 여기에 1년간의 현지 몰입교육(언어훈련, 전공수업, 인턴십)이 추가되기 때문에 보통 ILR 0+나 1 정도부터 입학시킨다.

셋째, 위에서 언급한 현지 몰입교육(In-country training in language, major areas, and occupational internship)이다. 플래그십 학부 과정과 대학원 과정(그리고 앞으로 실

시될 자격증과정)이 국내 집중프로그램과 1년간의 해외 현지몰입프로그램으로 이루어져 있다. 현지 몰입교육 프로그램은 고려대학 언어교육원 한국어 언어 문화센터에 위촉하여 실시하고 있다. 몰입교육은 (a) 국내 집중교육에 연계된 철저한 현지 언어, 문화 훈련, (b) 전공과목 수강, (c) 학생들 전공에 맞는 인턴십과 인턴십과 관련된 한글로 쓴 졸업논문 작성으로 구성된다. 국내 대학의 프로그램과 해외 현지 몰입교육 프로그램은 교과과정, 교육자료, 교수법, 평가법, 학생의 능력 수준, 학생 지도 등 모든 면에서 치밀하게 연계된다.

넷째, 교육의 질과 효율성(Instructional quality and efficiency)이다. 같은 기간이라도 회전속도가 빠르고 효율적으로 일할수록 기업이윤이 많아지듯이, 교육에서도 같은 시간 내에 교육의 질과 강도를 높이면 습득이 상대적으로 더 빨라짐은 물론이다. 학생 중심의 교육, 한국어 전용 수업, 창의적 교수법, 최상급 수준의 교재개발, 모국어 화자의 활용, 학생 전공에 맞는 개인교사 활용, 풍부한 미디어 및 기타 자료 활용, 캠퍼스 내 몰입환경 조성 등을 통해서 교육의 질과 강도를 높인다.

학생이 한국어의 4기능과 문화를 가장 효율적으로 배울 수 있도록 우수한 교사진을 양성, 개발, 확보한다. 교사의 빈번한 평가와 피드백, 상호 수업 참관 등으로 계속적인 질적 향상을 도모한다.

다섯째, 평가제도도 대폭 개선해야 한다(improvement of testing processes). 학생의 4기능 언어능력의 향상도를 입학부터 졸업 때까지 구두입학시험, 진단시험, 배치시험, 주기적 능력향상도 측정시험, 졸업 시의 언어능력시험, 졸업발표시험을 통하여 학생 개개인의 강점과 약점을 평가 파악하여 한국어와 전공분야에서 ILR 3으로 졸업하도록 철저히 지도한다. 그리고 각 프로그램의 운영도 자체적으로나 peer review를 통해서 계속 평가한다. 현존하는 한국어 평가도구에는, 최상급의 독해와 청취능력의 평가기준이 세분화되어 있지 않다. 이 때문에 DLI의 평가전문가 Dr. James Dergen을 두 차례 초청하여 workshop을 실시했고, 금년 여름까지 한국어플래그십팀에 의한 online 평가도구가 완성될 예정이다.

하와이대학에서는 교육의 질을 높이고 학습의 능률을 올리기 위한 이상 열거한 일련의 방책을 강구하고 실시하고 있다. 교수법의 향상, 상호 수업참관, 내용중심의 교과과정과 교재개발, 새로운 평가도구 개발 등 온갖 노력을 경주한다. 그리고 모든 수업은 한국어로만 진행된다. 학급당 학생 수는 6명 내지 7명이고 학생들의 수업은 학생들의 많은 토론과 발표를 요구한다. 대학원에서는 철저한 과제 중심 교육(TBLT)을 위주로 한다. 하와이대 플래그십교육 철학은 그저 가르쳐서 내보내는 교육이 아니라 학생 개개인에 각별한 주의를 기울여 손색없는 한국전문가가 되도록 최선을 다하는 것이다. 학생 개개인의 진도를 계속 평가하고 강점, 약점을 철저히 가려내서 강점을 장려하고 약점을 시정하고 언어능력의 부족한 학생은 개인 지도, 개인 교사, 하기 집중교육, 하기 현지교육 등을 통해서 보강한다.

(2) 한국전문가 양성(Cultivation of Korea Specialists with Superior or ILR 3 Proficiency)

2002년 플래그십언어교육이 창안되기 전에는, 항국어교사 양성을 제외하면, 미국이나 한국의 일반대학에는 최상급 한국어를 구사할 수 있는 한국전문가를 양성하는 한국어교육프로그램이 전혀 없었다. 미국정부 관련 교육기관에만 있었다. 일반대학에는 직업상의 한국전문가는 물론 한국학을 연구하는 학생들을 위한 체계적인 전문 수준의 한국어교육 프로그램도 없었다.

2002년 플래그십프로그램의 창설로 처음으로 한국전문가 양성을 위한 언어훈련이 시작되었다. 이미 언급했듯이 처음은 비학위과정으로 운영해 오다가 보다 효과적인 운영을 위해서 2007년부터 전문한국어 석사과정, 학사과정, 자격증과정을 신설하였다. 석사과정은 단일 학위과정인데, 이미 학부나 대학원에서 각자 자기 전공(예건대 국제정치학, 외교학, 경제학, 경영학, 역사, 사회학, 인류학, 공학 등)의 학사학위나 석사학위가 있는 학생들이 수학한다. 학사과정은 복수전공을 장려하여 현재 모든 학생이 자기의 전공분야와 전문한국어를 복수전공으로 하고 있다. 석사과정과 학사과정에는 각각 전국적인 모집공고를 통해서 매년 우수한 학생 12명(각각 2개반) 내외를 입학시키고 있다. 그외에도 이미 다른 분야에서 학사나 석사학위를 취득한 학생을 수용하여, 비교적 단기(하기집중교육 + 1년간의 현지교육) 훈련을 통해서 전문한국어자격증을 주는 과정은 1, 2년후부터 실시할 예정이다. 기존프로그램과 플래그십프로그램이 목표로한 학생학습성과(student learning outcome)를 종합하면 다음과 같다.

TABLE 3. Korean language and literature programs at UHM

Certificate programs	Student learning outcomes
Certificate in Korean	ILR 1 or above; basic knowledge in Korean language, literature, and culture
Certificate in Korean for Professionals	ILR **3;** competence in Korean in students' major areas and occupational culture

Undergraduate programs	Student learning outcomes
BA in Korean	ILR 2; specialized knowledge in Korean language, literature, and culture
BA in Korean for Professionals **(**dual degree encouraged**)**	ILR **3;** competence in Korean in students' major areas and occupational culture

이러한 전문한국어 교과과정은 이미 (1)항에서 언급한 바와 같이 많은 새로운 상급, 최상급의 과목을 기존 상급과목 위에 추가하였다. 이들 교과과정은 고정된 것이 아니라, 다양한 학생들의 다양한 요구(need)를 최대한 반영하도록 해마다 내용을 검토하고 조정한다.

그리고 전술한 바와 같이 고려대학에서 1년간의 집중 언어문화교육(여름, 가을, 겨울, 봄), 전문학과 과목 취득, 전문직업 인턴을 받는다. 석사과정은 졸업논문을 한글로 작성하여 논문심사를 통하여 학위를 받는다.

교육은 철저한 내용중심(content-based) 교과과정, 학생의 전공분야 위주(domain-based)로 실시한다. 즉 한국어의 어형구조, 통사구조, 의미구조, 어휘, 담화체계 자체를 훈련시키는 것이 아니라 한국의 역사, 종교철학, 언어, 문학, 예술, 정치, 경제, 사회, 등의 내용과 학생 전공분야의 내용을 전적으로 한국어로 교수하고 이러한 내용교육을 통해서 최상급 한국어를 자연스럽게 습득하도록 한다. 이 목적을 위해서 전공분야에서 원어민 개인교사를 채용 보강한다. 그리고 전공분야의 프로그램과 협조하고 전공분야를 담당하는 교사가 언어교사가 아니면 코스 개발, 언어지도법 등 언어교육에 대한 사전 훈련을 요한다.

개별화 교과과정(modularized curriculum), 개별 학점제도, 개별 독해/연구 지도, 개인 지도, 하기 집중교육, 개별 평가, 컴퓨터 on-line 학습 등 주문식 개별화 학습법을 언어교육에 포함시킨다. 개별 지도를 통하여 학생들의 다양한 언어습득 배경, 다양한 능력 수준, 다양한 전공 분야, 다양한 학습 속도, 다양한 약점과 강점, 교포학생과 비교포학생의 차이 등을 극복한다.

현지 한국학생들과 더불어 전공과목을 수강함으므로서 전공과목의 한국어를 향상시키고, 현지 전공분야의 인턴십을 통하여 전문직종언어와 직업문화를 터득하도록 한다.

(3) K-12의 한국어프로그램 개발

L2는 나이가 어려서 시작할수록 더 잘 습득한다는 "critical period"의 개념(Eric Lennerberg 1967)은 정설로 받아들여져 있다. 또 이중언어의 습득은 단일 언어 사용에 비해 모국어 구사 능력뿐 아니라 지능발달에 더 유리하다는 많은 연구 결과가 있다. 그리고 SAT Korean 시험성적은 학생들의 English, 수학, 과학 등의 SAT 성적과 비례한다는 최근 보고도 있다. 그리고 대학의 외국어교육만으로는 가장 배우기 쉬운 전통언어(독어, 불어, 스페인어)조차도 잘 해야 ILR 2 수준밖에 성취하지 못한다는 것도 잘 알려져 있다. 따라서 미국정부와 외국어 교육계에서는 K-12의 외국어 교육을 의무화하였다.[2]

정희정, 고혜진이 발표한 바와 같이 미국의 10만 개 이상의 K-12 학교 중 총 73개에 불과한 학교에서 정규 한국어과목의 교육을 실시하고 있다. 그것도 정규학교는 한국인 인구가 집중되어 있는 LA 중심의 캘리포니아 주와 뉴욕 주, 뉴저지 주에 집결되어 있고 기타 극소수만이 워싱턴 주와 일리노이 주에 있다(손호민, 정희정, 박미영 2009). 한국계 인구가 4만5천 인 하와이주를 포함해서, 한국계가 상당히 많이 거주하는 여러 주에 한국어를 정규과목으로 개설한 K-12학교가 하나도 없다.

2 조기 한국어 교육의 절실함과 초-중-고-대의 한국어 교육의 연계의 중요성에 대해서는 필자가 이전의 발표에서 충분히 논한바 있다(손호민 2000, 2008).

TABLE 4. Current status (Sohn, Jeong & Park 2009; Jeong 2010)

High School	42
Middle School	10
Elementary School	8
K-12 (including Preschool-12)	10
Others (3-12 and 4-12)	3
TOTAL	73*

* Includes 8 (ES 6, MS 1, Other1) Korean-English Dual Language Programs

더 많은 K-12학교에 한국어를 도입하도록 하는 문제는 과거 20년간 미국의 한국인 사회(예컨대 SAT장학재단)와 한국어교육계(예컨대 AATK)에서 강연, 토론, 언론(신문, 방송, TV), 학술대회, 지원 등을 통해서 지속적으로 거론하고 장려하고 시도하고 실천해 온 중대한 현안문제이다. 그런데도 불구하고 그 결과는 기대에는 미치지 못하는 것이 현실이다. 한국어가 SAT II과목으로 채택되고 현재 연 4천 명 이상의 고등학생이 응시하는데도 K-12의 학교수는 그리 큰 변동이 없다. 아직 AP프로그램이 없다는 점, 스페인어나 중국어나 일본어와의 경쟁에서 밀린다는 점, 자금 부족, 교사 부족 등 여러 가지 심각한 이유가 있다(손호민·정희정·박미영 2009).

그렇다고 자생적인 발전을 기대하면서, 속수방관하고 있을 수도 없는 일이다. 과거 2, 3년 사이에 새로 생긴 프로그램도 있지만 폐쇄하는 프로그램이 20개교가량 된다는 것으로 미루어보아 사정이 더욱 악화될 수도 있다. 이러한 불균형한 한국어교육의 현실에서 한국어플래그십센터는 K-12생을 대상으로 몇 가지 시범사업을 실시했다.

첫째, 대학에 pre-college summer intensive program을 설치하는 방법이다. 2009년 여름부터 우선 중고등학생을 대상으로 하기집중한국어교육 프로그램을 개설했다. 중학생들은 학점 없는 수업이었고 고등학생은 하와이대학의 중급수준(201-2이나 301-2)의 학점(1년분에 해당)을 취득했다. 처음 실시한 이 두 프로그램은 29명의 참가 학생들(미국 본토에서 온 4명 포함)과 교사들과 학부모의 호평을 받았다. 이 프로그램을 통해서 (1) 학생이 대학에 들어와서 보다 상위 수준의 한국어부터 시작할 수 있고, (2) 중고등학교 당국과 학부모를 자극하여 중고등학교에 한국어프로그램을 개발하도록 유도할 수 있고, (3) 대학 한국어교육에 체계적으로 연계되는 파이프라인 과정의 구축에 도움이 된다. 당초에는 초등학생 대상의 프로그램도 계획했으나, 실행을 미루었다.

둘째, 한국 학생이 비교적 많은 중고교 하나(Moanalua High School)를 시범적으로 선정하여, 플래그십센터의 두 교수(정희정, 고혜진)가 학생들을 대상으로 요구조사를 실시한 결과, 많은 학생들(특히 비한국계)이 한국어교육을 희망함을 발견했다. 이 두 교수는 현재 이 학교에서 비학점과정으로 일주일 2시간씩 시범적으로 출장강의를 한다.

셋째, 플래그십센터에서는 하와이의 2개 대표적 K-12 학교(Moanalua 포함)에 한국어프로그램을 시범적으로 개설하기 위하여 주 정부, 학교 당국과 공조하여 연방정부 DOE에 5년간(2011~2016)의 지원신청을 제출한 상태이다. 이 지원을 받게 되면, 하와이대학 플래그십 측은 교육구와 해당 학교의 긴밀한 공조하에, 교과과정과 교수요목 개발, 교재개발, 교육방법 개발, 평가도구 개발, 교사연수프로그램 개발, 그리고 실제 수업 등이 실시될 것이고, 가능하면 교사자격증제도도 하와이대학 사범대학과 공조하에 설립할 계획이다. 이 모든 것이 성공하면 이러한 창의적인 모델은 하와이 내의 다른 학교뿐 아니라 미국 여러 주의 학교에도 보급될 것이다.

(4) **K-16**교육의 연계**(K-16** articulation**)**

외국어교육은 단시일에 이루어지지 않는다. National Standards가 지적하듯이, 최상급 수준에 도달하기 위해서는 16년 이상의 장기간의 지속적인 학습이 필요하고, 그 수준을 유지 내지 향상시키기 위해서는 평생 동안 계속 사용해야 한다.

외국어교육의 효율성을 높이기 위해서 이음매 없는 K-16의 종적 연계의 문제는 그 필요성과 방법논에 대한 논의나 실천노력이 오랫동안 지속되어 왔다. 연계 없는 교육은 한국어, 일본어와 같이 영어와는 언어구조가 전혀 다른 외국어에서 흔히 볼 수 있듯이, 12년간의 초중고의 교육에도 불구하고 대학에서 초급이나 잘 해야 중급을 되풀이해야 하는 결과가 된다. 한국어의 경우도 필자는 여러 기회에서 체계적인 연계의 필요성을 강조해 왔다(Sohn 2000, 2005, 손호민 2008).

미국 한국어교육의 K-16간의 교원들 간의 유대는, 제한적으로 AATK와 ACTFL Korean SIG 를 통한 다소의 인적, 학술적 교류, 최근 ACTFL 주최의 Korean National Standards(2010) 편찬을 통한 공동노력과 SAT II 시험문제 출제위원회, SAT II재단을 통한 협조 등이 있다. 이는 아직 제한적이기는 하지만 국가적이고 정책적인 차원의 노력이기 때문에 앞으로의 세부적 연계의 반석이 된다고 생각한다. 세부적인 연계란, 회의, 워크숍 등을 통한 교사들 간의 인적 연계는 물론이고, 교과과정, 교수요목, 교재, 교수법, 평가법 등의 연계를 말한다. 다시 말하면, 학생이 무엇을 알아서 활용해야 하는가의 교육내용(content)과 학생이 어떻게 언어를 효과적으로 구사할 수 있는가의 수행능력(performance)과 학생이 얼마나 잘 수행하는지를 평가할 수 있는 평가법(assessment)에 관한 연계이다. 이미 다른 기회에도 여러 차례 주장했듯이(e.g. Sohn 2000), 이러한 세부적인 분야에서 K-16을 연계시키기 위해서는 가장 객관적이고 포괄적이고 현실적이며 치밀하게 제정된 National Standards와 ACTFL의 평가지침(정부의 ILR에 상당함)을 기준으로 삼아야 한다는 것이다. 이미 K-12의 외국어 교육은 전국적으로 이들 기준에 바탕을 두고 시행하고 있고, 결국 K-12에 있는 학생이 대학교육의 파이프라인이기 때문이다.

실로 K-16의 한국어교육의 프로그램은 정규과정이나 여름 단기 집중과정이나 현지교육과정이나 교사양성과정이나 모두 National Standards를 직접, 간접으로 적용해서 개발 내지 수정할 것을 주장하는 바이다. 이는 단순히 국가적 표준에 입각한 체계적인 연계만을 위하는 것이 아니라, 5C의 교과내용기준에 따라 교육의 질을 향상시키는데도 극히 도움이 될 것이기 때문이다.

이제 각급 학교 대표로 구성된 위원회에서 한국어의 National Standards 초안도 완성되었으니, 이 Standards에 따른 구체적인 교과과정의 연계 프로젝트를 구상하고 개발해야 할 것이다.

하와이대학 한국어플래그십센터에서는, 체계적인 연계는 아니지만, 기술한 바와 같이, 한국어교육연계의 일환으로 중고등학생의 하기 집중 교육을 시작했고, 출장강의를 시도하고, 주 교육부와 해당 학교와 공조하여 연방교육부에 지원신청을 하였다. 또 후술하는 바와 같이 한글학교 교사훈련도 착수하였다. 이러한 일련의 시도에는 직접, 간접으로National Standards와 ACTFL의 Prificiency Guidelines를 기준으로 삼고 있다.

(5) 한글학교의 질적 향상

이미 본 바와 같이, 미국의 K-12의 한국어교육프로그램, 특히 K-9의 정규 한국어교육프로그램은 극히 열악하다. 이들 초중학생이 한국어를 배울 수 있는 곳은 교포 1세 가정이거나 전국적으로 1000개가량 되는 한글학교이다. 많은 1세 가정에서 부모가 자식에게 자연스런 한국어를 사용하여 생활하면, 학생의 일상한국어가 향상된다. 아울러 한국 TV나 책을 일상적으로 즐기게 되면 상당히 높은 수준의 한국어를 배워서 사용할 수 있게 된다. 그러나 가정교육은 이민 1세가 생존할 경우에만 가능하다. 대체로 이민 2세부터는 한국어를 잃게 되고 가정에서 사용하지 않기 때문이다.

한편, 전국적으로 일시에 약 50,000명가량의 초중등학생이 한글학교에 다니는데, 열악한 교육환경에서 통상 매주 토요일 3시간(한국어 2시간, 한국문화체험 1시간)을 배운다. 한인 인구 45,000의 하와이 주에도 한국어를 정규로 가르치는 K-12학교는 하나도 없지만 한글학교는 25~30개가량 있다. 재미 한국인이 현재 200만 명이 넘고 교회가 수천에 이르고 이들 숫자는 계속 증가하는 한편, 한국어를 가르치는 K-9학교는 극소수임을 감안하여, 한글학교는 계속 존속할 것이다.

한글학교에서는 일주일 2시간의 한국어교육인 만치 10주(한 분기)를 해도 20시간밖에 되지 않는다. 일년(2~4분기) 내내 4분기를 다녀도 겨우 80시간의 수업을 하게 되어, 언어능력의 향상은 크게 기대할 수 없다. 그러나 한글학교에 다님으로써, (1) 발음, 한글, 일상적 표현 등 한국어의 기초를 습득하게 되는 것 이외에, (2) 학생들이 미국시민~한국민족이라는 확연한 이중적 동질성을 터득하게 되고, (3) 한국문화와 한국인사회를 어려서부터 접촉하여, 장차 이중언어인, 이중문화인으로 자랄 수 있고, (4) 한국사람들과의 우호적인 관계를 어려서부터 개발할 수 있게 되고, (5) 한국어와 문화를 계속 습득하려는 동기를 개발할 수 있다. (2) ~ (5)와 같은 이점은 정규학교에서는 경험하기 어려운 장점이다.

불완전하고 열악한 상황인데다 정규교육기관도 아니지만, 현재로서는 그리고 앞으로도 오랫동안, 한글학교가 초중등생을 담당하는 한국어 교육기관으로 기능할 수밖에 없다는 것은 부인할 수 없다. 그러나 현존 한글학교 운영에는 여러 가지 애로사항이 많다. 플래그십팀의 하와이 한글학교 실태조사(손호민, 허소린, 최윤화 2007)에 의하면, 다음과 같은 문제점을 안고 있다.

- 교재 부족
- 교사자질 부족
- 수업시간 부족
- 한국문화교육 부족
- 교과과정 및 학기구성 취약
- 학교운영의 체계성 부족
- 열악한 수업환경 (시설)
- 재정 및 정부지원 부족
- 학부모의 노력/관심/ 학생의 동기 부족
- 한글학교 간 정보공유 부족

이러한 상황은 다른 주에서도 공통된 현상임에 틀림 없다. 초중등학생을 조금이라도 더 어려서부터 한국어교육을 시작하게 하려면, 그리고 그들에게 조금이라도 나은 조건의 교육을 제공하려면, 위에 열거한 약점을 제거하여 한글학교의 질을 향상시키지 않으면 안 된다. 그러나 이들 여러 문제와 취약점은 일조일석에 시정되기 어렵고, 한국정부정책과 지원기관, 미국한국학교연합회(NAKS), 미국한국어교육자 협회(AATK), 대학의 한국어 프로그램, 후원종교단체, 교민사회, 학부모, 학생 등 관련된 모든 기관과 단체와 개인의 다방면의 헌신적인 노력이 있어야 해결될 것이다. 결국 많은 한글학교 출신이 대학에서 한국어를 계속하게 되므로 이들에 대한 교육을 소홀히 해서는 안 된다.

전국의 한글학교는 현재 전국규모의 협회인 NAKS와 남가주의 한글학교 연합회와 각지역의 지역협의회의 산하에 있는 상황에서 대학에서 주도적으로 할 수 있는 일이 제한되어 있다.

하와이대학에서는, 한글학교의 질 향상과 학생의 동기부여를 위하여 우선 가능한 세 가지 일을 시작했다. 하나는 모든 한글학교를 대표하는 교사들을 대상으로 한 1년 1회의 5주간의 집중 교사훈련이고, 둘째는 한국일보와의 공조로 한글 글짓기와 한국어 연설 대회의 개최이다. 셋째는 전술한 바와 같이 중학생반의 하기 non-credit 집중교육이다. 한글학교에서 상급반을 마친 초등학생들을 위한 하기 집중교육도 계획하고 있으나 실시는 유보하고 있다.

(6) 원거리 교육체계

전술한 바와 같이, 미국의 대다수 주의 K-12 학교에 한국어프로그램이 없다. 주로 교회에 부설된 한글학교만 산재해 있을 따름이다. 또한 전국 소재 3,000여 개 대학 중 겨우 100여 대학에서만 한국어가 개설되어 있는데, AATK의 Website에 의하면, 이들 대학 중 약 3분의 1은 2학년급까지만 있고, 3분의 1은 3학년급까지, 그리고 나머지 3분의 1은 4학년급까지 있다. DLI 등 정부관계 교육기관에서는 군인, 정부공무원들이 습득한 한국어를 잃지 않도록, maintenance 또는 remedial 프로그램이 마련되어 있다(하와이에도 하나 있다). 또 군인들을 하와이대학 같은 일반대학에 의뢰하여 하기 집중교육을 실시하기도 한다. 그러나 일반 K-16의 학교는 졸업 후 한국어를 계속 유지할 수 있는 체계적인 프로그램이 마련되어 있지 않다. 그리고 일반인이 한국어를 배울 수 있는 기회는 많지 않다. 간혹 대학이나 주정부나 지역사회에서 야간의 초급한국어를 개설하는 정도이다.

이런 상황에서 컴퓨터를 이용하는 원거리교육체제의 구축은 중요하고 시급하다. 한국어교육의 혜택을 받지 못하는 K-16학생, 졸업생, 군인, 공무원, 일반인 등을 위해서 그리고 학습한 한국어의 유지, 재활을 위해서, 정규K-16 한국어교육을 원거리교육체제로도 개발하여야 한다. 현재, 한글교육 등 기초한국어교육을 위한 각종 컴퓨터 프로그램이 상품화되어 있다. 그리고 Vassar College, Trinity College, University of Arizona, 호주의 Monash University 등에서 시행하는 다양한 형태의 online 자습언어프로그램(Self-instructional Language Program—SLIP)도 있다.[3] K-16 각급학교의 교실교육에 상응하는 체계적인 online 한국어교육체계의 개발과 구축은 한국어교육계의 공동과제이다.

교사와 대면해서 학습하고 다른 학생들과 상호작용하면서 언어와 문화를 배우는 교실교육보다 원거리교육이 갖는 약점도 있지만, 한편 더 유리한 점도 적지 않다. K-16의 교과과정, 교재, 평가의 연계교육의 개발과 실시가 용이하고, 학생의 통학시간의 절약, 공평한 학습, 각자의 편리한 시간 이용, 학습속도 조절의 가능 등이다. 무엇보다도 근처에 한국어교육기관이나 교사가 없을 때, 원거리교육은 선택을 불허하는 교육수단이 된다. 다른 대학도 그렇겠지만, 하와이 대학 한국어 프로그램에서는 매년 수차례씩 개인이나 기관으로부터 원거리교육 프로그램이 있는지 문의받는다. 최근 본토 어느 교육감이 AATK에 초등학교 한국어 원거리 프로그램이 있는지 문의해 온 것을 읽은 적이 있다.

DLI에서는 많이 연구하고 시도하는 것으로 알지만, 일반 K-16학교에서 현재 적극적으로 시도하는 데가 있다는 말은 듣지 못했다. 하와이대학에서는 오래전부터 중국어, 일본어, 한국어 등 상급반을 대상으로 원거리교육을 개발해 오고 있는데, 7, 8년 전에 3학년급 한국어수업을 원거리수업으로 수년간 시범적으로 실시한 적이 있었는데, 개발

3 현재 National Association of Self-Instructional Language Programs에 등록되어 있는 약 50개의 SLIP 언어 중 한국어는 아랍어, 일본어, 중국어, 러시아어, 포르투갈어, 인도어, 스와힐리어, 월남어에 이어, 아홉 번째로 많이 이용된다고 한다(Silva 2007:112-3).

한 교재가 적절하지 않았고 이용하는 학생이 많지 않았으며, 관리하는 조교선생에게 지급할 자금이 부족해서 중단했다. 박미정 교수가 개발해서 실시 중인 hybrid 원거리수업(주당 2시간의 online수업과 1시간의 교실수업) KOR 380(드라마를 통한 한국어)를 성공적으로 실시하고 있다. 박미정 교수가 지금 개발중인 KOR 480(영화를 통한 한국어)와 KOR 425(단편소설, 수필을 통한 한국어) 등은 곧 완성될 것이다. 한편, 플래그십팀이 최상급까지의 online을 통한 assessment tools for reading and listening을 개발 중이며, 플래그십학생의 교육을 위한 하와이대-고려대 간의 상설화상회의장치를 설치 중에 있다.

4. 과제와 결론

한국어 학습 인원수의 확대, 최상급 한국어 구사자의 최대한의 배출, 한국전문가를 가능한 한 많이 양성하려면, 적어도 위에 든 6가지 현안의 해결에 비례한다고 생각한다. 6가지 현안을 다 만족스럽게 해결한다는 것은 쉬운 일이 아니다. 실로 K-16의 한국어교육은 아직 넘어야 할 산이 너무도 많다. 관련된 모든 사람과 기관이 심혈을 기울여야 한다. 6가지 현안을 조금이라도 더 경제적이고 효율적으로 극복하기 위해서는 다음과 같은 교육적, 정책적 조치도 필요하다.

(1) 국가적으로 개발되고 승인된 각종 외국어교육 기준을 익히고 준수해야 한다. 이러한 기준들은 6가지 현안을 타결하는 조직원칙(organizing principles)을 제공하고, 한국어교육을 담당하는 모든 인사와 학습자의 시간과 돈과 노력의 중복을 막아주고 체계적이고 효율적인 교수와 학습이 가능하도록 한다. 현재 그러한 기준의 대표적인 것은, ILR(Inter-Language Roundtable) 기준이나 ACTFL(American Council on Teachers of Foreign Languages) Proficiency Guidelines를 전폭 병행 수용하여 플래그십 평가 기준으로 삼는다. 둘째, K-16의 연계적 언어습득 기준과 5C(Communications, Cultures, Contact, Comparison, Community)를 규정하는 미국정부의 "21세기 미국 외국어 교육 기준"의 원리와 5C와 3 modes 그리고 11 기준 을 플래그십 교육에 참고하고 원용한다.
(2) 컴퓨터를 끼고 사는 현세대나 차세대 학습자를 위하여, 컴퓨터를 이용한 교육능률의 향상은 필수불가결의 사안이다. 이번 회의에서도 압도적인 발표가 컴퓨터를 이용한 창의적인 교수방법, 학습법의 개발이다. 컴퓨터 자체의 hardware, software의 발전과 병행하여, 보다 세련되고 보다 경제적이고 효율적인 교수법, 학습법의 개발이 계속 이루어지기 바란다.
(3) 효과적인 언어습득은, 말이나 글을 통한 대인간 교제(interpersonal mode)이거나, 말이나 글을 통한 발표(presentational mode)이거나, 말이나 글을 통한 담화나 담론을 이해하는 해석(interpretive mode)이거나 간에 실제 사용을 통해서 가장 잘 이루어진다는 것은 상식화되어 있다. 따라서, 각급의 한국어교육은 모두 discourse-pragmatic uses

를 중심으로 이루어져야 한다는 것이다. 음성음운, 단어, 관용어, 연어, 문법 모두 담화상황과 문맥 안에서 교수되고 배우도록 하여야 한다.

(4) 언어습득이론과 실제를 수용하여 더 짧은 기간에 더 많은 실효를 거둔다. 한국어교육의 창의적인 프로그램 설계, 교과과정 설계, 교재 개발, 교수법 개발, 평가법 개발, 교육제도의 개선을 위하여, 제2 언어 습득에 관한 확고한 이론과 실제, 주도적이고 창의적인 연구결과, 성공적 학습사례 등을 도입하고 수용하고 응용할 것을 강조한다.

(5) 일반 대학과 정부 관련 학교와의 돈독한 networking이 절실하다. 특히 압도적으로 많은 우수한 교수들이 계속 새로운 교수법, 학습법을 개발하는 DLI교수진과의 공조와 협력이 요구된다. 지금도 부분적으로 AATK, ACTFL, 국제한국어교육학회(IAKLE) 등 학회를 통한 교수간의 학술교류가 이루어지고 있으며, DLI의 Dr. Dergen을 초청한 assessment workshop, Dean Sahi Kang을 초청한 OPI workshop 등은 하와이대학과 같은 일반대학에 큰 도움이 되고 있다. 한편, 하와이대학에서 석사, 박사 학위를 취득하고 DLI에서 근무하는 분도 상당히 많다. 그리고, 하와이대학에서는 금년부터 군인들을 위한 하기 집중 한국어교육을 통한 한국어 Certificate프로그램을 실시한다. 군인들은 15학점의 하와이대학 학점과 Certificate를 받게 된다. 이 회의의 주제인 정부 관련 교육기관 간의 언어교육과 교육자원의 networking뿐 아니라, 정부관련학교와 일반대학 간의 networking뿐 아니라 공동연구 프로젝트도 개발했으면 한다. 이러한 일련의 지속적인 공조는 한국어교육에 전반적인 상승효과를 가져온다. 해당 교육기관의 발전뿐 아니라, 앞서 말한 한국어교육의 여섯 가지 중대 현안의 효과적인 타결에도 많은 도움이 되리라 생각한다.

참고 문헌: Chapter 31

손호민. 2008.「초-중-고-대 한국어교육의 연계와 교육기관의 공조」.『범세계 한국어교육기관 간의 교류와 협력』, 3-12. (제2회 범세계 한국어교육단체, 지역대표자 세미나). 한국국제교류재단· 국제한국어 교육학회.

손호민, 허소린, 최윤화. 2007.「하와이 한인사회학교 실태분석」.『국제한국어 교육학회 17차 국제학술대회 자료집』, 587-603.

Cho, Sungdai, Insook Chung, & Mark Peterson. 2006. Korean as a world language. *The Korean Language in America* 11: 1-16.

Furman, N., D. Goldberg, & N. Lusin (2007). Enrollments in languages other than English in United States institutions of higher education. Fall 2006. *Modern Language Association Wb publication*, 1-28. 13 November 2007.

Hadley, A.O. 2001. *Teaching Language in Context*, 3rd Edition. Heinle & Heinle.

Lennerberg, E. 1967. *Biological Foundations of Language*. New York: John Wiley & Sons, Inc.

Liskin-Gasparro, J.E. 1982. *ETS Oral Proficiency Testing Manual.* Princeton, N.J.: Education testing Service.

Silva, D.J. 2007. Issues in Korean Language Teaching in the United States: Recent Facts and Figures. *The Korean Language in America* 12: 106-25.

Sohn, Ho-min. 2000. Curricular Goals and Content Standards for K-16 Korean Language Learning. *Korean Language Learning in America* 5: 3-16. Also in this volume.

Sohn, Ho-min, Hee-Jeong Jeong, and Miyung Park. 2009. Toward K-16 articulation for advanced Korean language learning. ms. University of Hawaii Korean Language Flagship Center. Also in this volume.

32 하와이주 한인사회학교 실태 분석*

1. 서론[1]

현재, 미국에서는 148개 대학, 50개가량의 중고등학교, 6개가량의 초등학교에서 한국어교육을 실시하고 있다. 대학의 경우는 전국에 산재한 주요 대학에 크고 작은 한국어 프로그램이 있는 반면, 초 · 중 · 고등학교는 한국사람이 많은 캘리포니아, 뉴욕 등에 몰려 있다. 한인 인구가 220만 명으로 알려진 미국에서 정규 초 · 중 · 고등학교의 한국어교육은 극히 열악한 실정이다. 예를 들면 한인 인구 5만(전체 인구의 4%)의 하와이주에는 초 · 중 · 고교 어느 곳에서도 단 한 학급의 한국어도 개설되어 있지 않다.

그러나 강력한 영어를 모국어로 하는 미국에서 한국어교육의 이러한 열악성은 불가항력이라 볼 수도 있다. 따라서 앞으로 빠른 시일 내에 정규 초, 중, 고교에 광범위하게 한국어를 도입한다는 것은 많은 현실적인 상황과 이유와 사정을 고려할 때 그리 쉽게 이룰 수 있는 일은 아니다. 그러나 앞으로 한국의 국제 위상과 경쟁력을 더 고취시키고 재미 한인과 교육자 그리고 한국 정부가 혼연 일체가 되어 체계적인 기획과 꾸준한 공동 노력과 재정 지원을 아끼지 않으면 점차 상당히 개선시킬 수 있을 것으로 기대된다.

한국어를 고급 수준까지 습득해서 자유롭게 구사할 수 있으려면 어려서부터 체계적으로 배워야 함은 물론이다. 특히 성인 미국인에게는 한국어가 가장 배우기 힘든 언어로, 불어나 독일어를 배우는 것보다 3배의 시간과 정력을 쏟아야 같은 수준으로 올라갈 수 있는 언어이다(cf. Liskin-Gasparro 1982; Hadley 2001: 26). 성인과는 달리 어려서는 충분한 시간을 들여 교육시키면 어느 언어이고 비교적 쉽게 배울 수 있기 때문에 한국어야말로 초등학교에서부터 기초를 다져 나가야 대학에서 고급 수준을 터득하게 된다.

다행한 일은, 초 · 중 · 고의 이러한 심각한 교육상의 공백을 메우고 한인 2세에게 민족언어 문화를 교육시키기 위하여 1970년도 후반부터 하와이를 효시로 점차 미국 곳곳에 주로 종교단체를 중심으로 한인지역사회학교(Korean community schools)가 설립되기

---

* 손호민 · 허소린 · 최윤화 공동 집필. 이 보고서의 축약된 글은 2007 IAKLE(International Association for Korean Language Education)의 17회 국제한국어교육대회에서 발표했고, 그 회의자료집(587–603쪽)에 게재되어 있다.

1 이 실태분석은 하와이대의 National Resource Center-East Asia의 지원을 받아 2006-7 동안 실시했다.

시작했다. 현재 거의 1,000개가량의 크고 작은 한인 학교(통상 한글학교라 함)가 미국 방방곡곡에 산재해 있는데 학생 20여 명의 작은 학교로부터 500명에 이르는 큰 학교도 있다. 이들 학교는 한인 교회나 사찰이라는 한국언어 문화에 둘러싸여, 한인 후세에게 민족 유산인 언어와 문화를 전수하고 한민족의 동질성을 교육한다는 점에서, 외국어로서의 한국어를 가르치는 정규 학교보다 어느 면에서는 더 의미있고 더 효율적인 교육이 될 수도 있을 것이다.

이렇듯 한인지역사회학교(이하 한글학교)의 역할과 기능의 중요성에 비추어, 이들 학교의 교과과정, 교과서, 다매체 교육자료, 교사, 학생지도 방법, 시설, 재정문제 등을 향상시켜야 함은 물론이고 학생들의 학습 동기, 교사들의 가르치려는 열정, 자녀의 한국어 교육의 필요성에 대한 학부모들의 인식 등을 높이는 일은 가장 중요한 당면 과제이다. 그러려면 우선 이 모든 면의 현 실태를 정확히 수집하고 분석해서 파악하는 일이 선행되어야 함은 물론이다.

지금까지 여기저기에서 한글학교에서의 학생들 언어습득 목표와 현황, 교육자료, 시험자료, 동기 등에 대한 실태조사를 실시한 바 있고 부분적인 통계자료도 나와 있다(일반 외국어습득 실태조사 방법과 한글학교 조사 결과에 대해서는 첨부 문헌 참고). 그러나 한글학교 안팎의 여러 모순을 정확히 파악하고 시정책을 모색해서 한글학교가 지향하는 근본 목표(예를 들면, 한국어와 한국문화의 지식과 능력의 향상)를 만족하게 수행하게 하려면, 일단 한 지역의 모든 한글학교를 망라하여 보다 근본 문제에 대한 체계적인 면담과 조직적 설문을 통한 철저한 실태조사가 절실히 필요하다.

이러한 목적으로 본 연구팀은 2006년 중순부터 2007년 중순까지 일 년간 하와이주에 소속된 총 24개 한글학교가 고질적으로 안고 있는 제반 문제를 체계적인 면담과 설문을 통해서 조사하고 분석했다. 물론 근본적인 목적은 이러한 각종 문제를 어떻게 해결해서 한글학교의 질을 향상시켜서 초 · 중 · 고등학생들의 한국어교육에 기여할 것인가로 귀착된다. 그리고 하와이의 문제는 곧 미국 전체의 문제이기 때문에 하와이의 문제에 대한 해결책은 곧 미국 전체의 문제에 대한 해결책의 일환으로 볼 수 있다.

이번 실태조사 분석은 다음 다섯 단계로 진행했다. 첫 단계는 한글학교 현황 파악을 위한 교장 대상의 설문조사이고, 둘째 단계는 학부모, 학생, 교사 등 한글학교 관련자에 대한 면담조사이며, 셋째 단계는 학부모, 교사, 학생을 대상으로 한 설문지 조사이고, 넷째 단계는 설문지 분석이며, 마지막 결론 단계는 앞으로의 대책과 해결의 실마리를 제안하는 것이다. 이러한 여러 과정을 간략하게 논의하고자 하는 것이 이 논문의 취지이다.

2. 학교현황 및 주요 현안(1, 2, 3 단계 조사)

기술한 바와 같이, 제 1단계에서는 하와이주의 한글학교 현황을 파악하기 위하여 24개교의 교장에게 설문지를 배부하였는데, 그중 15개교(오아후섬 13개교, 힐로시 1개교, 사모아 1개교) 교장만이 설문에 응답했다. 설문 내용은 학기구성(연간 학기 수, 매학기

기간, 여름학기 기간), 등록금, 교사 및 교감 수, 학생 수, 학급 수, 반편성 기준, 분반 시험, 학생 성취도 측정 방법, 교재 지원 현황, 문화 학습 시간, SAT II Korean 준비반 유무, 멀티미디어 활용 유무, 재정적 보조 유무 등 16개 항목을 포함했다.

제2단계에서는 이러한 교장 설문지 답변 결과를 참조하여 자세한 질문서를 준비하고 두 명의 연구원(허소린과 최윤화)이 한글학교에 직접 간접으로 관련된 33명을 대상으로 면접을 실시하였다. 이들 33명은 (a) 소규모, 중규모, 대규모 학교를 대표하는 교장 3명, 교사 5명, 학부모 8명, 학생 9명, (b) 한글학교와 관련된 대학 전임 2명, (c) 하와이 한글학교 협의회 대표 1명, (d) 전학생 2명, (e) 자녀를 한글학교에 보내지 않는 부모 3명 등이다. 면담 전체를 녹음했고 이 녹음자료는 전부 전사했다. 그리고 면담에서 제기된 모든 주요 문제점과 현안을 자세히 검토하여 통계적으로 분류했다.

제3단계의 설문지 조사 단계에서는, 상술한 면담자료 분석 결과에 기초하여, 많은 사람들이 지적한 특히 중요한 문제들을 체계적으로 정리하여 설문지 조사에 포함시켰다. 설문지는 학생, 학부모, 교사 각각을 대상으로 따로따로 소책자를 작성했다(책자 첨부 생략). 즉 6, 7개 항의 큰 설문 분야를 설정하고 이중 5, 6개 분야는 각 분야마다 많은 소항목의 설문 내용을 제시하여 1(찬성 안함)에서 5(가장 찬성함)의 등급에 따라 평가하도록 했다. 그리고 마지막 한 두 분야는 서술식 개방 질문의 형식을 취했다.

학생, 학부모, 교사에 대한 큰 설문 분야는 주로 (a) 한글학교에 다니는 또는 (학부모의 경우는) 보내는 이유, (b) 한글학교에서 배우고자 하는 분야, (c) 한글학교에서 학생들이 특히 좋아하는 사항들, (d) 한글학교의 문제점들, (e) 문제에 대한 해결책, (f) 교사 연수, (g) 기타 한글학교에 바라는 것 등이다.

이들 책자는 20개 한글학교에 속하는 학생 508명, 학부모 508명, 교사 117명 등 총 1,133명에게 배부하였다. 이들 설문책자 중 완성되어 돌아온 수는 16개 학교에서 학생 73명(14.37%), 학부모 87명(17.13%), 교사 40명(34.19%) 등 총 200권(17.65%)이었다.

3. 설문지 분석 (제4 단계)

이들 모든 설문 결과에 대한 분석을 요약하면 다음과 같다.

3.1.한글학교에 다니는 이유

우선 한글학교에 다니는 또는 보내는 이유로 학생들, 학부모, 교사가 각각 매긴 순위는 다음과 같이 대동소이하다. 단지 학생들과 교사는 부모의 권유 때문에 다닌다는 데 비중을 두는 데 비해 학부모는 자녀의 장래 직장 때문에 보낸다는 이유가 부각된다.

〈표1〉 한글학교에 다니는 이유—학생 응답

한글학교에 다니는 이유	참여자수	평균치	표준편차	최소치	최고치
To learn the Korean language	69	4.26	1.01	1	5
Because my parents want me to attend	67	3.90	1.26	1	5
To communicate with my parents in Korean	67	3.78	1.08	1	5
To learn more about Korean culture	65	3.52	1.09	1	5
To maintain my identity as a Korean	66	3.44	1.19	1	5
To better my chances of finding a good job	67	3.19	1.47	1	5
To meet Korean friends	68	3.10	1.35	1	5
To prepare for the SAT II Korean	64	2.47	1.36	1	5

〈표2〉 한글학교에 다니는 이유—학부모 응답

한글학교에 보내는 이유	참여자수	평균치	표준편차	최소치	최고치
To help them learn the Korean language	82	4.90	0.30	4	5
To better their chances of finding a good job	83	4.67	0.63	2	5
To help them learn about Korean culture	80	4.64	0.73	2	5
To help them maintain their identity as Korean	80	4.61	0.83	1	5
To communicate with them in Korean	77	4.36	1.06	1	5
To help them meet Korean friends	74	3.42	1.16	1	5
To help them prepare for the SAT II Korean	72	3.06	1.51	1	5

기타: "한인사회에 도움이 되기 위하여" (1), "아이들이 한국에 사는 사촌들과 커서까지도 친근한 관계를 위해서" (1)

〈표3〉 한글학교에 다니는 이유—교사 응답

학생이 한글학교에 온다고 생각하는 이유	참여자수	평균치	표준편차	최소치	최고치
To learn the Korean language	38	4.18	0.87	3	5
Because their parents want them to go	38	4.18	1.14	1	5
To communicate with their parents in Korean	37	3.97	1.12	1	5
To better their chances of finding a good job	36	3.61	1.20	1	5

To maintain their identity as a Korean	36	3.50	1.13	1	5
To learn more about Korean culture	36	3.39	1.02	1	5
To meet Korean friends	36	2.86	1.13	1	5
To prepare for the SAT II Korean	36	2.42	0.94	1	4

기타: "친척들과의 의사소통" (1)

3.2. 한글학교에서 배우고자 하는 분야

한글학교에서 배우기를 원하는 것은 학생, 부모, 교사 모두 첫째는 한국어이고 둘째는 한국문화, 그리고 그 다음이 SAT II Korean이다.

3.3. 한글학교에서 학생들이 좋아하는 사항들

학생들이 한글학교에서 특히 좋아하는 항목으로는 다음과 같다. 선생님에 대한 관심이 가장 많다는 것을 보여준다. 학생들에게 한국어 교육에 대한 동기를 부여하는 데 교사의 자질과 역할이 가장 중요하다는 것을 시사한다.

〈표4〉 한글학교에서 학생들이 좋아하는 사항

한글학교에서 학생들이 좋아하는 사항	참여자수	평균치	표준편차	최소치	최고치
Teacher	67	3.99	1.05	1	5
Listening	69	3.72	1.08	1	5
Speaking	69	3.59	1.13	1	5
Reading	69	3.57	1.33	1	5
Meeting new Korean friends	67	3.54	1.18	1	5
Field trips	67	3.48	1.43	1	5
Playing sports	65	3.42	1.47	1	5
Learning Korean arts	67	3.41	1.38	1	5
Textbooks	68	3.34	1.36	1	5
Writing	69	3.29	1.28	1	5
Watching K-dramas	65	3.29	1.62	1	5
Listening to K-music	66	3.23	1.36	1	5
Watching K-movies	65	3.05	1.56	1	5
Grammar	67	2.99	1.25	1	5
Contests (writing, speech, etc.)	66	2.32	1.24	1	5

기타: "Singing Korean songs, dancing in Korean dresses (Hanbok), playing K-games" (1)

3.4. 한글학교의 문제점

한글학교의 문제점에 대한 학부모와 교사의 의견은 다음과 같다. 학부모와 교사의 문제점 인식이 크게 다르지 않고 학생들의 동기 부족, 정부 보조의 결여, 교재 등이 심각한 사항으로 인식되고 있다.

〈표5〉 한글학교의 문제점—학부모 응답

한글학교의 문제점	참여자수	평균치	표준편차	최소치	최고치
Lack of government support	77	3.90	1.30	1	5
Lack of students' motivation	79	3.48	1.19	1	5
Lack of parents' concern and participation	79	3.46	1.22	1	5
Learning materials	58	3.45	1.19	1	5
Financial difficulties	78	3.44	1.25	1	5
Lack of systematic management	79	3.43	1.14	1	5
Short instruction hours (3 hours per a week)	77	3.27	1.17	1	5
Poor facilities	80	3.24	1.15	1	5
Curriculum	78	3.22	1.18	1	5
Teacher	53	3.21	1.35	1	5
Lack of culture instruction	79	3.16	1.04	1	5
Placement	78	2.92	1.31	1	5
Lack of other activities	80	2.76	1.13	1	5
Semester organization	62	2.56	1.17	1	5

〈표6〉 한글학교의 문제점—교사 응답

한글학교의 문제점	참여자수	평균치	표준편차	최소치	최고치
Lack of students' motivation	40	3.80	1.02	1	5
Lack of info exchange among different schools	8	3.75	0.71	3	5
Lack of government support	40	3.70	1.20	1	5
Learning materials	28	3.57	1.32	1	5
Financial difficulties	40	3.50	1.24	1	5
Curriculum	40	3.43	1.11	1	5
Short instruction hours (3 hours per a week)	40	3.43	1.28	1	5

Lack of parents' concern and participation	40	3.38	1.25	1	5
Lack of info exchange among teachers	39	3.33	1.15	1	5
Lack of teacher training	40	3.28	1.26	1	5
Lack of systematic management	40	3.25	1.30	1	5
Lack of culture instruction	39	3.21	1.15	1	5
Placement	39	3.08	1.20	1	5
Teacher	26	3.00	1.10	1	5
Poor facilities	39	2.95	1.28	1	5
Lack of other activities	40	2.80	1.16	1	5
Semester organization	34	2.44	1.19	1	5

학기 구성(semester organization)이 문제가 되는 이유로는: "교사 부족" (1); "공립학교의 일정에 어느 정도 맞추어야 하니까" (1); "이 부분은 학생들의 방학에 맞춰서 하는 문제라 flexible하기 때문" (1) 등을 들고 있다.

특히 교재 문제에 대해서는 다음과 같이 응답하고 있다. 다매체 자료의 결여, 교재의 다양성 부족, 학생의 흥미를 유발할 수 있는 교재의 결여, 문화 차이가 반영된 교재의 부족 등의 순서로 지적되고 있다.

〈표7〉 교재에 대한 문제점—학부모 응답

교재에 대한 문제점	참여자수	평균치	표준편차	최소치	최고치
Lack of multimedia materials	75	3.67	1.13	1	5
Not arousing students' interest	77	3.60	1.23	1	5
Lack of various materials	75	3.59	1.24	1	5
Not reflecting cultural differences between Korea & U.S.	76	3.49	1.06	1	5
Not reflecting students' proficiency level	75	3.39	1.18	1	5
No textbook	66	3.32	1.27	1	5

기타: "쓰고 읽는 위주로 되어 말을 하는 데 별 도움이 못됨" (1)

〈표8〉 교재에 대한 문제점—교사 응답

교재에 대한 문제점	참여자수	평균치	표준편차	최소치	최고치
Lack of multimedia materials	40	3.68	1.31	1	5
Lack of various materials	40	3.65	1.21	1	5

Not arousing students' interest	39	3.54	1.12	1	5
Not reflecting cultural differences between Korea & U.S.	39	3.53	1.28	1	5
Not reflecting students' proficiency level	38	3.24	1.26	1	5
No textbook	32	3.09	1.33	1	5

기타: "흥미있는 교육방식이 더 필요하다(음악, 연극, 창극 등등)"; "아직도 가르쳐야 하는 부분이 너무 많이 필요"

교사 문제에 대해서 학부모와 교사들이 평가하는 바는 다음과 같다. 교사의 자격 문제, 교수법 문제, 미국 교육에 대한 인식 부족 등이 지적되고 있다.

〈표9〉 교사에 대한 문제점—학부모 응답

교사에 대한 문제점	참여자수	평균치	표준편차	최소치	최고치
Teacher qualifications	76	3.21	1.36	1	5
Teaching methodology	79	3.20	1.39	1	5
Lack of understanding of U.S. education	77	3.08	1.31	1	5
Lack of student discipline plan	76	3.04	1.35	1	5
Teachers studying in the U.S. as students	66	2.74	1.21	1	5
Local teachers	51	2.73	1.20	1	5

〈표10〉 교사에 대한 문제점—교사 응답

교사에 대한 문제점	참여자수	평균치	표준편차	최소치	최고치
Teaching methodology	40	3.15	1.00	1	5
Lack of understanding of U.S. education	40	3.10	0.96	1	5
Teacher qualifications	40	2.98	1.07	1	5
Lack of English proficiency	40	2.68	1.14	1	5
Lack of Korean proficiency	40	2.10	1.03	1	4

학부모의 경우, "아무나 교사하는 것이 아니라 교사의 능력과 자질을 평가했으면 좋겠고 한글학교 협의회에서 심사하여 채용하였으면 좋겠다"는 의견도 있다. 유학생 교사와 현지인 교사의 장단점에 대해서도 학부모들은 다음과 같은 다양한 평을 제시하고 있다.

〈표11〉 유학생 교사와 현지인 교사의 장단점—학부모 응답

(a) 유학생 교사의 경우	응답수
Lack of eagerness and responsibility	2
Frequent turn over	2
"They seem to be preoccupied with their school tasks"	1
Lack of English proficiency	1
"유학생 교사일지라도 능력에 따라서 다르다."	1

(b) 현지인 교사의 경우	응답수
Lack of Korean language proficiency	1
"교사들이 책임감을 가지고 한 학기 동안 책임감을 느꼈으면 합니다. 가끔은 중간에 그만둔 분이 계시거든요."	1

(c) 기타 의견	응답수
"(현지인 교사는) 책임감은 더 우월한 것 같음 (compared to 유학생 교사)."	1
"(현지인 교사는) 한국문화와 미국문화를 동시에 학생들에게 전달하여 보다 쉽게 이중 문화를 배울 수 있도록 하기 때문에."	1
"현지인 교사, 유학생 교사 누구나 교사라는 능력을 갖추고 있으면 된다고 생각한다. 누구도 그런 것으로 문제가 될 수는 없다고 생각한다. 아이들이 잘 따르고 잘 배우면 된다고 생각한다."	1
"선생님이 반말을 한다, 집에서도 안 하는…"	1
"교사들의 전문성 부족"	1

3.5. 문제에 대한 해결책

한글학교가 당면한 여러가지 현안 문제에 대해서 학부모와 교사가 제시하는 해결책은 다음과 같은 순위이다.

〈표12〉 문제에 대한 해결책—학부모 응답

한글학교의 각종 문제에 대한 해결책	참여자수	평균치	표준편차	최소치	최고치
Developing & providing multimedia materials	74	4.15	1.11	1	5
Developing various Korean materials	78	4.12	1.13	1	5
Establishing overall plans and strategies for systematic Korean language education	76	4.12	1.01	1	5
Developing materials based on students' needs	78	4.09	1.08	1	5

Giving foreign language credits	78	4.09	1.12	1	5
Systematic education according to students' level	75	4.05	1.04	1	5
Offering various classes	75	4.03	0.91	2	5
Raising awareness of the importance of Korean language education among community people	75	4.03	1.20	1	5
Curriculum improvement	75	4.00	1.00	1	5
Offering various teacher training	74	3.96	1.21	1	5
Giving teachers better treatment	78	3.96	1.20	1	5
Integration of Korean community schools	82	3.85	1.45	1	5
Designating a model community school	78	3.49	1.57	1	5
Tuition increase	77	2.97	1.51	1	5

〈표13〉 문제에 대한 해결책—교사 응답

한글학교의 각종 문제에 대한 해결책	참여자수	평균치	표준편차	최소치	최고치
Developing various Korean materials	40	4.20	0.88	2	5
Raising awareness of the importance of Korean language education among community people	39	4.15	0.96	2	5
Establishing overall plans and strategies for systematic Korean language education	37	4.14	0.92	2	5
Systematic education according to students' level	39	4.13	0.83	2	5
Developing materials based on students' needs	40	4.10	0.98	2	5
Developing & providing multimedia materials	40	4.03	1.07	1	5
Offering various teacher training	40	3.98	1.03	1	5
Offering various classes	40	3.90	0.90	2	5
Giving foreign language credits:	39	3.79	1.15	1	5
Curriculum improvement	40	3.78	0.89	2	5
Giving teachers better treatment	40	3.73	1.01	1	5
Integration of Korean community schools	36	3.42	1.32	1	5
Tuition increase	39	2.92	1.24	1	5
Designating a model community school	39	2.82	1.23	1	5

이상 한글학교의 각종 문제에 대한 해결책과 관련하여, 몇 가지 문제에 대한 학부모와 교사의 서술적 의견을 살펴본다.

첫째, 한글학교 통합(Integration of Korean community schools) 문제에 대한 학부모와 교사의 반응은 다음과 같다. 전반적으로 유보적인 견해를 보여 준다.

학부모 반응

—찬성론:
- "한글학교가 하나로 통합되어 정부 차원에서 아니면 교포 전체적인 차원에서 운영이 된다면 질적으로 그리고 더 나아가서는 한국 정부에도 국위를 선양하는 역할을 담당하리라고 기대함. 미래를 바라보는 정부가 되길 바라며."
- "전문적인 학교 설립"
- "하루빨리 통합되었으면 좋겠다."
- "한글학교가 보다 많이 발전해서 자라나는 아이들이 우리나라 말을 잃지 않고 잘할 수 있도록 보다 더 큰 한글학교가 생겼으면 하는 바람이다."

—반대론:
- "지리적인 문제, 사는 지역과 너무 먼 지역으로 가야 하며 그에 따른 pick up drop off 문제" ; "자기 지역에 있기를 희망" (응답수: 9)
- "너무 복잡할 것 같다" (3)
- Lack of individual care (2):
- 기타 의견: "많은 인원으로 인한 개별적인 관심 부족이 생길 것 같음"; "possible tuition increase"; "학원화가 되질 않을까?"; "각 교회나 사찰 등에 부속된 한글학교의 자유스러운 학습 분위기에 비해 기존 학교다운 딱딱함 유발"; "많은 아이들을 수용할 장소와 교사들의 능력이 있는지"; "정부 지원과 한글학교 간의 단합이 힘들 듯"; "통합은 무리인 것 같다"; "책임감 회피"; "의견충돌"; "기득권?"

교사 반응

- "한글학교가 대부분 교회나 성당 같은 종교단체에 기반하고 있기 때문에 현실상 통합에 어려움이 많을 것으로 생각됨" (3명)
- Resources 문제에 대한 다양한 의견: "협조가 되어야 하고 시설과 자원이 구비되어야"; "통합할 시에 장소 제공과 교사 선정 등 모든 세부 시스템을 재정비하는 데 걸리는 시간. 통합하지 않아도 작은 그룹 안에서도 얼마든지 정비될 수 있다고 본다"
- 기타 의견: "건물, 시간(집이 멀 경우)"; "상당한 재정과 시간 소요 예상, 개별 한글학교의 특성이 발휘되지 못함"; "현재 운영 중인 한글학교 교장들의 통합 의지 정도"; "학교대로 교육하던 방침을 서로 반영하려고 하다가 의견 다툼이 나지 않을까 염려됨"; "복잡하겠고 진짜 학교도 아닌데 제대로 운영을 못 하니까"; "불가능할 것이다. 교사 교육 등의 백업 위주의 개선 필요"; "누가, 무엇을 하느냐 보다 필요의 인식 부족이 더 문제"; "monopoly! No!"

둘째, 모범학교 지정(designating a model community school) 문제에 대한 학부모와 교사의 반응은 전반적으로 찬성보다는 부정적 견해를 보여 준다.

학부모 반응

- "모범학교 선정 기준의 보편성, 객관성 우려" (4)
- "부모들이 모범 한글학교에만 입학시키려고 할 것이다"; "모범으로 하는 학교로 가려는 한국인 부모들의 치맛바람 등등. 이에 따른 다른 한글학교의 운영이 힘들어질 것이며, 모범 한국학교를 보내려면 시험도 pass해야 하는 방침이 생길 수도 있다" (6)
- Only small number of students would benefit from it. (2)
- 기타 의견: financial burden"; "타학교 학생들의 자격지심이 생길 수 있지 않을까?"; "평등한 기회제공의 결여"; "지역별로 몇 학교를 지정했으면 좋겠습니다"; "질투심, 질타, 경쟁심 악화"

교사 반응

- "지나친 경쟁을 유도할 수 있다" (3)
- "한 학교를 지정하는 것은 타학교의 사기 저하 원인"; "모범학교의 지원에 질투심을 유발" (2)
- "불공평할지 모른다. 오직 한 학교에 혜택이 돌아가니까" (2)
- 기타 의견: "학교 선정의 어려움"; "참여와 협조 부족"; "Politics"

셋째, 일반 초 · 중 · 고에서 한글학교 학점을 인정토록 추진하는 문제에 대해서는 학부모와 교사의 반응이 찬반 양론인데 "필요하지만 시기상조"라는 의견이 지배적이다. 다소 부정적인 의견으로는 다음과 같은 것들이 있다.

학부모 반응

- "학점 인정 문제"
- "너무 부담이 될 것 같습니다."
- "강제성으로 자율분위기 저해"
- "공부 안 하는 애들 부모의 반대가 예상됨"
- "Location and facility issue"
- "학생들의 stress, 교사들의 전문성 자질 수준"
- "너무 공부 위주로 갈 수 있음"
- "체계적이며 객관적인 평가 체제의 공통된 커리큘럼의 개발이 있어야 함"
- "그것에 대한 생각은 해보지 않았음. 시일이 걸릴 것 같음."
- "비교적 다른 외국어에 비해 한국 어린이들에겐 한국어가 접할 기회가 많이 쉬우

므로 다른 외국어 공부 등한시."

- "그럼 좋겠지만 이민을 금방 온 학생들에게는 이익이겠지만 여기서 오래 살고 있고 한글을 잘 모르는 애들은 좀 문제가 될 것 같다."
- "아이들 공부해야 하는 어려움! 하지만 장점이 더 많아 OK!"
- "중간에 낙오됨. 영어냐, 한글이냐 선택으로 인해 선택의 폭이 좁아질 것 같음. 그냥 걸치고 있으면 안 될 것 같음"
- "교포 사회의 관심과 정부의 충분한 지원이 필요"
- "현지인식부족"

교사 반응

- "학생들의 참여를 유발시키겠지만 한글학교의 순수한 목적과 동기를 훼손할 수 있음"; "동기부여에 그리 도움이 되지 않을 것 같음"
- "시험 준비 위주의 교육이 될 수 있음"
- "교육이 체계적이지 못한 상황에서 점수 내기가 어려울 것임"
- "현실성 부족"
- "대부분의 한글학교 학생은 유치원 초등학교 정도의 학생들이고 한국어만을 배우는 것이 아니라 한국인 혹은 다른 곳에서 온 친구들과 교류하는 곳이므로 일반학교와는 다른 의미의 커뮤니티라고 생각함"
- 기타 의견: "필요성 및 동기 부여가 될 것이다."; "더 열심히 하겠죠!"; "커리큘럼과 교육내용이 같아야 하고 평가기준도 같아야 할 것"; "될 수만 있다면, 그러나 굳이 필요할까요? 이른 감이 있음"; "제도적 장치가 필요성을 더욱 인식시킬 수 있지 않을까?"

넷째, 수업료 인상 문제에 대해서도 학부모와 교사의 반응이 다양하다. 전반적으로 인상에 부정적인 태도가 많다.

학부모 반응

- 학부모의 재정부담 (7): "자녀가 많을 경우 더욱 가중"; "빈민자의 교육기회 상실 우려"; "학부모들은 영어 수학 피아노 기타 등등을 우선시하기 때문에 비싸지면 한국어교육을 미루다가 시기를 놓칠 수 있음"
- "많은 학생들이 학교에 등록을 거부할 것 같음" (3)
- "등록금 인상보다는 정부 지원 또는 한인사회기관의 지원이 필요" (2)
- 기타 의견: "학생들이 얼마만큼 변화가 있느냐에 따라 달라질 것임"; "등록금을 인상해 보다 나은 환경에서 공부할 수 있다면 찬성합니다"; "교육 시설과 교재 개발, 선생님들의 자질에 따라 인상해도 될 것이라 생각한다"

교사 반응

- 등록수가 줄 것임 (5)
- "학부모의 재정적 부담" (1): "학생들은 주 3시간 교육에 적당한 등록금을 내고 있다고 생각함. 인상이 학부모의 반발 예상 우려"
- 기타 의견: "등록금 인상보다 재정을 잘 활용할 수 있는 체계적인 커리큘럼과 운영진 정비가 더 시급함"; "등록금 인상을 한다고 해서 양질의 한국어 교육을 바로 기대할 수는 없을 것 같음. 이것보단 한국어 교재의 개발과 교사연수가 더 효과적일 것임"; "인상하는 만큼 효과가 있을지 의문이다"
- "요사이 한글학교가 많이 세워져 좋은 현상이지만 너무나 등록금을 인하하여 질적으로 떨어지는 경향이 있으므로 등록금을 평준화하여 질적으로 좋은 학교를 만들어야 한다"

3.6. 교사 연수

교사들에게 보낸 설문지에 교사연수에 관한 질문이 있는데 교사들이 연수를 통해서 배우고 싶어하는 사항은 다음과 같다.

〈표14〉 연수 희망 사항

연수 희망 사항	교사수
Student discipline plan	30
Practical use of multimedia	25
Korean teaching methodology	24
Material development	24
Understanding of U.S. education	20
Korean spelling system	13
Korean spacing system	13
Korean grammar	12

기타: "유아, 초등, 중등별에 따른 교육 방법 – 동일한 내용이지만학생 연령별에 따라 다른 접근 방법이 요구되는 것 등" (1) / "문법보다는 관심 유발 방법이 더 필요치 않을까?" (1) / "한국어 문법. 맞춤법, 띄어쓰기, 교수법은 교사 스스로 공부할 수 있음" (1)

〈표15〉 연수 방법

연수 방법	교사수
Workshop을 통해서	31
Conference를 통해서	15
On-line education을 통해서	16

〈표16〉 연수 횟수

연간 횟수	1	**2**	3	4	6	Total
교사수	5	**23**	3	6	1	38

3.7. 한글학교에 바라는 것

설문지의 마지막 개방적 질문인 "한글학교에 바라는 것"에 대해서는 학부모와 교사와 학생들에 의해 다양한 의견들이 제시되고 있다. 많은 경우 전술한 통계적 자료분석과 중복되는 의견이지만 참고로 인용한다.

학부모의 경우:

- "기존의 교회 산하 운영이 아니라 단독 한글학교 운영(기구 보완) 등을 고려해서 각 지역별로 지원할 수 있었으면 좋겠다"
- "More accurate assessments for individual children needed"
- "한글 능력 test의 기회가 많았으면 (level test) 좋겠다"
- Support for students from lower income families: 한국어 가르치고 싶으나 등록금을 낼 형편이 안 돼서 한글학교에 보내지 않는 가정을 볼 수 있다. 소득에 따라 지원하는 방침이 있으면 모두에게 기회가 주어지지 않을까 싶다"
- More events: "웅변대회 등 발표회 기회가 많았으면 좋겠다"
- 학생 수준에 맞는 체계적인 교육: "한국어 수준과 학생의 연령에 따른 반편성이 필요하고 그에 맞는 교재 및 다른 소재 선정이 필요하다"; "학생들 수준에 어려운 교육은 흥미를 잃을 수 있다고 생각함"
- 수업 방법 개선: "빠른 진도보다는 반복의 학습효과와 학생들 스스로 한국어에 대한 흥미와 관심을 갖고 수업에 임할 수 있는 분위기의 수업 방식이 이루어졌으면 한다"; "한국문화를 학생들에게 소개할 때 시간을 좀더 늘려서 학생들이 즐겁고 이해할 수 있게 하기 바람"; "너무 한국적인 것만 추구하지 말고 아이들이 재미와 흥미를 느끼는 프로그램도 겸하였으면 좋겠다"; "다양한 한국어 교육과 다양한 문화를 접할 수 있도록 그래서 아이들이 한국어에 대해서 흥미를 느낄 수 있게 했으면 좋겠다"
- 교사와 학생 간의 유대: "교사와 학생간의 교통이 있어야 한다. 결석을 하면 왜 했나, 주중에 전화 한 통 하는 것도 아이들에겐 소속감도 주고 잊고 있던 숙제도 할 수 있는 계기가 되지 않을까. 적어도 선생님들은 10분 전엔 와서 준비하고 있어야 한다고 생각한다"
- 한국어만 사용할 것: "한글학교에 와 있는 일주일 중 3시간은 완전한 한국말 시간이었으면 하며 한국에서 학교를 다니는 아이들이 배우는 국어 산수 자연 과학 음악 등등 모든 것을 한국 교재로 학습한다면 지식도 습득해 가면서 그에 따라 자연스러

운 한국어 학생이 될 듯싶다"; "이해를 하든지 못하든지 한글학교에서는 한국말만 해야 함(이해를 못하면 질문은 영어로)"; "한글학교에 오면 한국말로 말할 수 있도록 해주고 한국말로 말하면 무엇이 좋다는 것을 인식시켜주면 감사하겠다(한국인으로서의 정체성 확립)"

- "하와이대학 한국학 연구소, 영사관을 통하여: 1. 교육방식의 통일 2. 해외동포 자녀 교육을 위한 특별예산법 발의 요청(시급한 문제임) 3. 해외동포 자녀를 위한 한국어교육 모델 개발하여 시범학교 지정 교육"
- "고정된 선생님이 지속적으로 지도 바람. 매번 다른 선생님으로 바뀌기 때문에 학생들의 진도를 확인할 수 없다"
- "저학년 학생일수록 한글학교에 다니는 것이 친구들 만나고 노는 재미이지만 고학년이 될수록 한글학교에 다니는 것이 시간 낭비라는 생각을 하고 있는 것 같다. 한글학교 측에서 고학년생에 맞게 특별활동 시간을 마련해 주기 바람"

교사의 경우:

- 교사의 자질 향상: "교사들의 자기 개발, 교습법 연구, 또한 학부모들의 교사에 대한 인식 변화와 그들을 존중하는 자세가 선행되어야 함"; "교사들의 사명의식과 끊임없는 자기 개발을 통해 학생들에게 언제나 신선한 느낌을 주는 교사들이 많아지길 소원한다. 많은 학부모들의 지혜로운 관심이 있었으면 한다"; "좀더 열정적으로 선생님께서 가르친다면 한국인과 한국어를 배워야 한다는 데 자긍심이 생길 것 같다. 그 후에 다른 방법이 개선된다면 효과적이지 않을까"; "한국어 교육에 대한 전문인의 부족, 전문인 양성에 힘써야……"
- "한국말, 문화, 역사의 중요성에 대하여 교포사회에 대한 전반적인 계몽이 필요함"
- "하와이대학 한국학연구소가 좀더 열림으로 인하여 다양한 행사, 연극, 음악회 등등이 있으니 학생들을 참가시켜 한국말을 배우고자 하는 의욕이 생기도록 하면 좋겠다"
- "한 학기에 한 번 정도 한글학교 페스티벌을 연합으로 개최하여 학생들이 다양한 한국문화를 체험하고 새로운 친구들과 함께 즐거운 시간을 보내도록 하여 한국과 한국에 대한 관심과 흥미를 유발시킨다"
- "한국학교 등록금을 단일화해야 한다. 새로 세우는 학교는 너무나 낮추어 받기 때문에 기존의 학교가 힘들다"; "요사이 한글학교가 많이 세워져 좋은 현상이지만 너무나 등록금을 인하하여 질적으로 떨어지는 경향이 있으므로 등록금을 평준화하여 질적으로 좋은 학교를 만들어야 한다"; "현행 등록금 정도를 유지하고 정부기관이나 한인회의 협조 요청"
- 교재 개발: "흥미롭고 재미있는 교재가 알선되길"; "동화책 등 아이들이 흥미를 가지고 동기를 부여받을 자료가 부족함"; "한국에 재미있게 배우고 있는 교재를 수집해서 각 한글학교에서 사용되기를"; "전문적인 자료나 종합센터가 절실히 필요"

- 학습시간 부족: "1주일에 1회 하루에 소요시간이 너무 적다고 생각한다. 적어도 1주일에 2~3회 정도면 배운 것을 사용하고 잊어버리지 않겠지만 1주일에 2시간 배운 것이 크게 향상된다고 생각지는 않는다. 허락된다면 2~3회 정도"

학생의 경우:

- Better snacks
- More fun activities
- "Breaks in the middle of class"
- More speaking, more reading, more writing, more culture
- More contact/class hours
- Higher level Korean classes
- No English in class
- Scholarships
- More field trips
- More explanation and conversation, speaking Korean to me more
- More songs

4. 결론과 건의

이상 분석에서 보듯이 학부모와 교사와 학생은 한글학교 발전을 저해하는 여러가지 문제점을 제시했고 나아가 많은 해결책들을 제안했다. 즉 앞으로 한글학교를 개선하려면 무엇을 어떻게 해야 할 것인가, 어떤 것을 우선적으로 해야 하는가, 무엇을 피해야 하는가 등의 자세한 지침이 마련되었다고 할 수 있다. 그러나 해결책으로 제안된 다매체 자료의 개발, 다양한 교재의 개발, 학생의 요구를 만족시키는 교재, 체계적인 교육 방법 수립과 교과과정 개발, 교사훈련, 다양한 학급 설치, 한글학교의 중요성 선양, 학습동기 증진 등 이 어느 것 하나도 손쉽게 이루어질 수는 없고 NAKS의 연례회의에서 보듯이 많은 인력과 노력과 시간과 자금이 소요된다. 즉 각종 필요사항과 현안과 문제점은 충분히 그리고 샅샅이 밝혀졌지만 이를 광범위하게 해결하는 일은 엄청난 일이다. 가능한 것부터 점진적으로 해결하고 개선해 나가야 할 것이다.

그리고 우리가 당면한 근본적인 문제는 한글학교 운영 자체라기보다 많은 초 · 중 · 고등학생들에게 어떻게 학습동기를 강하게 부여해서 질 높은 한국어 교육을 시키느냐에 있다. 그렇게 함으로써 대학에서는 중상급이나 상급반부터 한국어 학습을 시작하게 되고 졸업 때까지는 최상급 수준의 한국어를 지향하게 된다.

여기에 초 · 중 · 고생들의 한국어 교육과 한글학교 개선책을 위한 한 가지 시범프로그램을 제안하고자 한다. 좀 급진적인 제안이지만, 대학의 한국어교육 전문 교수, 강사, 조교들이 개입해서 주도적인 역할을 하자는 것이다. 즉 이 시범프로그램을 하와이대학과 같은 데에서 우선 실시해 보자는 것이다.

하와이대학에는 미국에서 가장 규모가 큰 한국학 센터(Center for Korean Studies)와 신설된 미국 유일의 한국어 플래그십 센터(Korean Flagship Center)가 있다. 한국어교육의 연구와 실천의 차원에서 그리고 지역사회 봉사 차원에서 Korean Flagship Center가 주축이 되고 Center for Korean Studies 가 장소와 기타 협조를 제공하면 시범프로그램의 운영이 큰 부담 없이 수행될 수 있을 것이다. 수업 담당 인적자원은 Flagship Center와 동아시아 어문학과의 한국어 교수, 강사, 조교들로 충분하다.

여기서 제의하는 시범프로그램은 매년 단기(6주) 여름집중(immersion) 프로그램으로 하루에 5시간(오전 3시간은 집중언어; 오후 2시간은 한국어를 통한 문화활동)으로 구성되기 때문에 매 여름 동안 총 150시간의 집중 훈련이 실시된다. 이것은 대학의 3학기(1.5년) 한국어 교육의 분량에 해당한다.

우선 첫해에는 시범적으로 1급, 2급, 3급 각 반에 10명씩 30명만 선발한다. 이들 30명은 모두(최상급을 지향하는 Flagship의 방침에 따라) 이미 한국어 학습 동기가 강한 한국어 중급 수준(Intermediate-low, -mid, -high)에 있는 학생들만 선발한다. 가급적 언어적으로나 문화적으로나 지능적으로 동질성을 유지하기 위하여 원칙상 1급에는 초등학생, 2급에는 중학생, 3급에는 고등학생을 수용한다. 한편 매년 여름 한글학교 교사를 위한 교사 연수 워크숍을 실시한다. 이들 교사들은 수업 참관도 하면서 실제 교수법을 습득한다.

여름 첫 수업 시작 전에 2년에 걸쳐 필요한 자금확보, 철저한 교과과정 수립, 다매체 자료를 포함한 광범한 교재 준비, 필요한 행정절차 완료, 학생 모집, 시범프로그램 교사 훈련, 한글학교 교사 워크숍 준비 등을 실시한다. 이 모든 계획수립과 준비 과정에서 본 논문에 제시된 모든 문제점, 개선책 등을 기본지침으로 삼는다.

이러한 시범프로그램은 한글학교 통합 방안도 아니고 모범 한글학교 개발도 아니다. 기존 한글학교의 질을 향상시키는 데 자극과 도움을 주고 일반 정규학교로 하여금 한국어 과목을 도입하도록 간접적으로 유도하는 효과 이외에도, 우수한 최상급 수준의 한국어 학생을 길러 내는 pipeline 구실을 하자는 것이다. 즉 한국어 교육을 위한 다목적 프로그램인 것이다. 그리고 한글학교 기준으로는 거의 최고급 수준에 해당하는 소수의 우수한 Intermediate 수준의 학생만 수용하기 때문에 한글학교의 학생 수에 하등 영향이 없고 또 대부분의 한글학교가 휴교인 여름학기를 이용하기 때문에 더욱 아무런 상충도 일어나지 않는다. 여름 시범프로그램이 끝나면 가을 학기에 각자의 한글학교로 돌아가서 가일층 높은 수준의 한국어를 배우게 된다.

그외에도 이 시범프로그램의 장점은 첫째, 일단 프로그램이 실시되면 수업료를 받기 때문에 자급자족으로 운영된다. 둘째, 모든 교육, 학사 문제를 대학 교수 주도하에 조직적이고 체계적이고 책임있게 다루게 된다. 셋째, 이 프로그램에서 한국어과 석·박사 학생들이 교생실습을 할 수 있다. 넷째, 모든 학생들이 동기가 강하고 언어 능력, 연령, 지능, 문화에서 대체로 동질적이기 때문에 학습활동이 효율적이다. 다섯째, 이 프로그램을 거친 학생들은 대학에서 계속 상급, 최상급을 추구할 가능성이 크다. 여섯째, 이 프로그램은 한인 지역사회 발전에 크게 기여할 수 있다. 마지막으로, 이런 시범프로그램이 성공적으로 실시되면 하와이의 모든 한글학교와 초 · 중 · 고교에뿐 아니라 미국 본토에도 파급효과가 일어날 것이 기대된다.

참고 문헌: Chapter 32

손호민. 2004.「재외동포 한국어 교육의 현황과 미래」.『제5차 한국어 교사 학술대회 자료집』, 10–22. 미주한국학교연합회 주최. Los Angeles. 2004년 8월 28일. Also in this volume (chapter 5).

이동재· 조수근·이미선·송민선·William O'Grady (공편). 2000. *Studies on Korean in Community Schools.*『한인학교의 한국어 교육 연구』. Second Language Teaching & Curriculum Center. University of Hawaii at Manoa.

이정은. 2005.「재외동포의 이중언어상용 상황과 한국어 학습 양상의 특이성—질적 연구 방법을 통한 교육 현장 사례 분석을 중심으로」.『사회언어학』13.2: 193–217.

Berwick, R. 1989. Needs analysis in language programming: from theory to practice. In Johnson, R.K. (ed.) *The Second Language Curriculum*. Cambridge: Cambridge University Press.

Brindley, G. 1989. The role of needs analysis in adult ESL programme design. In Johnson, R. K. (ed.) *The Second language Curriculum*. Cambridge: Cambridge University Press.

Brown, J. D. 1995. *The elements of language curriculum: A systematic approach to program development*. Boston, MA: Heinle & Heinle.

Hadley, A.O. 2001. *Teaching Language in Context, 3rd Edition*, Heinle & Heinle.

Lee, Dong-Jae, Jin-hwa Lee and Si-Won Park. Needs analysis of the Korean Community Schools in Hawaii (a Center for Korean Studies project). Ms.

Seedhouse, P. 1995. Needs analysis in the general English classroom. *ELT Journal* 49: 59-65.

33 Toward K-16 Articulation for Advanced Korean Language Learning*

1. Background

Current initiatives in foreign language education in the United States are geared toward building solid national resources of advanced-level foreign language experts in a wide variety of professional domains. The most powerful federal-level initiative in this regard is that of the Language Flagship of the National Security Education Program (NSEP) in Washington, D.C., as alluded to in its mission statement:

> "The Language Flagship leads the nation in designing, supporting, and implementing a new paradigm for advanced language education. Through an innovative partnership among the federal government, education, and business, The Language Flagship seeks to graduate students who will take their place among the next generation of global professionals, commanding a superior level of fluency in one of many languages critical to U.S. competitiveness and security." (http://www.thelanguageflagship.org/)

Korean is one of the critical foreign languages designated by U.S. government agencies such as the Department of Defense (to which NSEP belongs), Department of Education, and State Department.[1] The Language Flagship established the Korean Language Flagship Center (KLFC) at the University

* Ho-min Sohn, Hee-Jeong Jeong, and Miyung Park. This report has resulted from a preliminary survey and needs assessment of the K-12 schools offering Korean in the U.S. This project was conducted in 2008-9 with a small grant that Ho-min Sohn received from the National Resouce Center-East Asia at the University of Hawaii at Manoa.

1 Other than Korean, NSEP has designated Arabic, Chinese, Russian, Turkish, Hindi-Urdu, Persian, Portuguese, Swahili, and Portugese as critical languages. Since 2007, The Language Flagship of NSEP has established one or more federally-funded Flagship centers for each critical language to design, develop, implement, and disseminate advanced-level language programs. The Korean Language Flagship Center is housed in the University of Hawaii at Manoa under the directorship of Ho-min Sohn.

of Hawaii at Manoa in 2007 to design, develop, and implement an educational model to cultivate global professionals commanding a superior-level fluency in Korean.

Korean is one of the most difficult languages (so-called Category 4 languages) for American adults to learn. A novice-level student with an average learning aptitude can attain a (ACTFL-based) superior level in spoken Korean through a total of approximately 2,500 hours of contact hours (Liskin-Gasparro 1982; Hadley 2001: 25–27). This means that a novice-level American student has no way to attain a superior level in Korean through regular American college education alone, which usually provides no more than 500 classroom contact hours per student over four years. Even KLFC provides a total of approximately 1,500 ~ 1,700 contact hours covering both domestic and overseas training. Thus, in general, those who have extensive pre-college exposure to Korean during the K-12 period can expect to attain a superior level at the end of college education.

Under these circumstances, it is essential for Korean language educators and administrators to develop, expand, and enhance K-12 programs that will function as efficiently articulated pipelines to college education. In regard to KLFC's endeavors, Sohn (2009) has delineated a comprehensive model to enhance the quantity and quality of Korean language education in the United States, as outlined below.

(1) Revamp the existing programs and curriculum to accommodate students aspiring to attain superior-level proficiency in Korean language and culture, including the language and culture of students' major areas,
(2) Implement intensive quality language/culture training,
(3) Domain-specific content-based language training,
(4) Incorporate at least one-year of overseas immersion training (language & culture, domain, professional internship),
(5) Assist more and more elementary and secondary schools to begin a standard-based Korean language program,
(6) Articulate K-16 language pedagogy in terms of curriculum, instructional materials, teaching methods, and assessment, with the National Standards as the guiding and organizing principle,
(7) Improve the quality of community school education, and
(8) Develop effective distance learning to reach K-16 students without a Korean language program in their institutions.

Of these, items (1) through (4) are successfully implemented through the KLFC's newly established MA and BA programs in Korean for Professionals at the University of Hawaii at Manoa and the overseas Flagship field program at Korea University in Seoul. These programs admit students usually at an intermediate-high to advanced-high level and train them to move up a superior (professional) level, through the processes outlined in items (1) through (4). Students in a lower level than the Intermediate-High are trained intensively in the Flagship-bound program before they are advanced to the Flagship program.

Items (5) through (8) involve the Korean language education for K-12 students and seamless articulation of K-12 KFL education with that of college education. As indicated above, K-12 students should learn Korean extensively in order to attain superior-level proficiency at college. Thus, building a solid K-12 pipeline is a crucial issue in overall Korean language education in the United States. Though still in the experimental stage, KLFC has recently initiated some preliminary projects to address (5) through (8). In particular, with small grants received from the National Resource Center--East Asia at the University of Hawaii at Manoa, KLFC has conducted two survey projects: (a) a needs assessment of Hawaii community schools in 2007 (reported in Sohn, Huh, and Choi 2007: reprinted in this volume) and a preliminary survey and needs assessment of the K-12 schools offering Korean classes in America in 2008-9 (conducted by the present authors). The aim of the present paper is to present the results of the second project and some additional endeavors we have made in regard to the training of K-12 students and K-16 articulation.

2. K-12 Programs Survey Project

Although there has been a notable growth in KFL education in the United States since the early 1990s, KFL education is more concentrated in colleges and universities than in primary and secondary schools, a phenomenon of a reverse pyramid with the primary schools numbering the least. Moreover, articulation between the secondary level and the post-secondary level has been minimal. How to help develop or enhance Korean programs in K-12 schools and how to articulate K-16 KFL education are indeed tough perennial issues yet to resolve. This is particularly the case because, in K-12 schools, Korean has to compete with commonly taught languages such as Spanish, French, and German as well as other popular Asian languages such as Chinese and Japanese.

Before planning any worthy measures to assist K-12 education and K-16 articulation, it is essential to grasp first hand what the state-of-the-art is. Thus, we conducted a survey of K-12 Korean language programs at primary and secondary schools nationwide. The survey was carried out with the following objectives in mind: (i) to help increase the number of K-12 schools with KFL programs; (ii) to create a solid K-16 articulation in terns of language curricula, instructional materials, teaching methods, and assessment tools; (iii) to build and sustain a network of K-12 teachers and college teachers; and (iv) to enhance professional development and support for K-12 Korean language teachers.

We began this project with a list of schools compiled by the Foundation for Korean Language and Culture in USA (www.klacusa.org) in 2008. According to the Foundation's list, sixty-six schools were offering Korean language programs (KLPs) as of 2008. By 2009, nineteen of the sixty-six schools closed their KLPs due to a lack of funding and low enrollments, while four new programs were added. While we were analyzing the collected data, twenty-two additional schools with KLPs were identified. Thus, it turned out that as of December 2009, seventy-three schools were offering KLPs, as shown in Table 1. Notice that more than half of the seventy-three schools with a KLP are high schools.

TABLE 1. Number of K-12 Korean language programs by level of school

School	Number
High School	42
Middle School	10
Elementary School	8
K-12 (including preschool – 12th grade)	10
Others (Centers, grade 3rd or 4th-12th)	3
Total	73*

* Includes 8 (ES 6, MS 1, Other S1) Korean-English dual language programs.

The vast majority of schools offering KLPs are located in New York and California, as shown in Table 1. Thirty-one states, including Hawaii, do not have any school offering Korean.

TABLE 2. Number of K-12 Korean language programs by state

State	Number	State	Number
CA	37	AZ	1
NY	10	CT	1
IL	3	FL	1
NJ	3	IN	1
AL	2	MA	1
GA	2	MD	1
OR	2	NM	1
VA	2	PA	1

WA	2	TN	1
TX	1	**Total**	**73**

Significance of Korean language study in elementary and middle schools is not easily justifiable to parents and students unless a language sequence is already in place in high schools. When high school curricula do not exist, Korean language classes in elementary and middle schools function only to introduce students to a new language and culture, rather than to equip them with meaningful and relevant foreign language abilities. An exception to this pattern is the dual language programs, in which the elementary school curriculum is designed to produce students who are bilingual in Korean and English.

Out of 73 schools, 50 schools cooperated with our project. We telephone-interviewed with a teacher at each of these schools, the results of which are summarized in the following.

2.1. Korean program administration

Most Korean programs began with courses only at the elementary level in the 1990s. Since 2000, many programs have expanded their curriculum to aim at higher proficiency levels. This can be attributed, by and large, to the growing visibility of Korea due to the popularity of South Korean pop culture and South Korea's increased global competitiveness. At present, ninety-eight percent of the schools with a KLP offer Korean as a foreign language as elective within the regular curriculum. Some ninety percent of the existing programs teach Korean offer elementary-, intermediate-, and advanced-level courses, teaching four to five hours per level per week.

2.2. Students

More than eighty percent of the students enrolled in Korean classes are Korean heritage students or recent Korean immigrant students with a high level of oral-aural fluency. There are, however, a few schools where over ninety-five percent of the students are non-Korean students; these include religious schools and schools in which Korean is the only Asian language offered. Ninety percent of the schools reported a rise or no significant change in student enrollment before 2009, while the rest suffer from declining enrollments. With the exception of religious schools and the dual language programs, teachers generally have great difficulty in recruiting many students due to the keen competition with Spanish, Chinese, and/or Japanese on one hand and the lack of Korean AP (Advanced Placement) and IB (International Baccalaureate) courses. Thus, a KLP is a less appealing option due to the general perception that the Korean language does not offer as great a competitive edge to students' academic and professional careers as proficiency in Spanish, Chinese, or Japanese does.

2.3. Motivation

Korean language courses at all levels cater to two student constituencies: Korean heritage students and non-Korean heritage students. These two groups of students usually arrive in class with different sets of interests and motivations to learn the Korean language. They usually have disparate levels of knowledge and exposure to Korean history and culture as well. The reasons for learning Korean that the two sets of students provide can roughly be summarized as follows:

Korean heritage students provide the following reasons: (1) to maintain their heritage language, (2) to explore and understand Korean culture and Korea, (3) to obtain a good grade (SAT II and university foreign language credits), and (4) to fulfill parents' expectation. In contrast, non-Korean students provide the following reasons: (1) interests in Korea and Korean culture, (2) Hallyu (the Korean Wave), (3) teacher's recommendation o encouragement, and/or (4) religious reasons.

2.4. Teaching

Our survey identified two particular aspects in regard to the use of teaching materials. First, because no standardized textbook exists, in some ninety percent of the schools surveyed, teachers create and compile their own teaching materials. These materials are based on various existing textbooks, other written sources, and various multi-media resources that teachers have obtained from Korean consulates and cultural centers. Consequently, second, instructional materials are different from school to school. It may be no exaggeration to say that, in the fifty schools with a KLP, fifty different materials are used. Examples of various textbooks in use include various college texts developed by the University of Hawaii at Manoa, Yonsei University, Ehwa Woman's University, Korea University, and Sogang University and *Step by Step* and *Alive Korean Language* published by commercial publishers. In addition to the four core language skills, all schools incorporate Korean culture, literature, and history content by using multimedia, literature, drama/films, and Internet resources. Also, depending on students' language and cognitive levels, teachers also employ various activities such as role plays, skits, games, movie making, projects, and presentations.

3. Challenges and needs related to K-12 Korean programs

Throughout this project, we have observed that despite the K-12 Korean language teachers' individual efforts to promote Korean language and culture, KLPs face various institutional challenges, as the stability of a program depends upon several institutional factors: (i) the type of school and its commitment to a Korean language curriculum; (ii) availability of secure, long-term funding; and (iii) KLPs' levels of competitiveness with other courses and other languages, which negatively affects enrollments in Korean language classes.

These challenges generate several needs within KLPs, which must be addressed through the development and implementation of curricular and organizational support mechanisms at the national level: (i) methods for the placement of students into the levels best suited to their current comprehension and fluency levels; (ii) greater opportunities for teacher development and training, and venues through which teachers can share information about teaching materials and methods; (iii) the development of a standardized curriculum; (iv) the development of standardized proficiency levels; and (v) the creation of a network for teachers to provide support and maintain connections with one another.

4. Proposal

Based on this survey, we offer our proposal, albeit tentatively, for implementing K-16 articulation for Korean language instruction as summarized in Table 3.

TABLE 3. Proposal for K-16 articulation

<table>
<tr><th>Textbooks</th><th>Teachers</th><th>Curriculum and program</th><th>Competitiveness</th><th>Motivation</th><th>Funding</th></tr>
<tr><td colspan="2">Exchange system for teachers</td><td>Model program</td><td colspan="2">Maintenance of SAT II Korean and development of AP courses</td><td>Support from the Korean government and business</td></tr>
<tr><td colspan="2">Sharing of materials and resources</td><td>Standardized assessment tools</td><td></td><td>PR efforts</td><td></td></tr>
<tr><td colspan="2" rowspan="2">Multi-media materials development</td><td></td><td></td><td colspan="2">PTA</td></tr>
<tr><td></td><td colspan="2">College credits</td><td></td></tr>
<tr><td rowspan="2">Textbooks designed for K-12</td><td>Professional development</td><td rowspan="2"></td><td colspan="2" rowspan="2">Korean language program
→ pre-college program
→ intensive summer program in Korea</td><td rowspan="2"></td></tr>
<tr><td>Teacher license</td></tr>
</table>

Some issues related to the effective implementation of the proposed articulation are briefly discussed in what follows.

4.1. Standards

Sohn (2000) has proposed that the *Standards* be adopted as a model for nationally accepted curricular goals and standards that address the following four objectives: (i) a clear vision for the future of language study; (ii) new ways of looking at instructional resources; (iii) a model for accountability across levels; and (iv) cognitive and pedagogical continuity for students. Sohn has also proposed that the *Standards for Foreign Language Learning* (1996) be observed as the organizing principles in K-16 Korean language articulation, for the following: (i) curriculum, (ii) textbook and other instructional materials, (iii) classroom instruction, and (iv) assessment tools. For this matter, the immediate need, according to Sohn, is for Korean language educators to collaboratively develop supplements to the *National Standards* such as Korean-specific content standards (what students need to know and do) based on the generic *Standards* and Korean-specific performance standards (how well students need to perform) based on ACTFL generic Performance Guidelines.

4.2. Educational needs

During the last twenty years, a strong suggestion for improving foreign language education has emerged from recognizing the educational needs of less commonly taught languages, which had been overlooked in the U.S. language policies. From 1982 to 1994, for example, French, German, Latin, and Spanish accounted for more than 95.5 percent of all total language enrollments, according to a 2001 U.S. Department of Education report. Due to the rapidly growing number of Asian immigrants, however, there has been an increase in the number of students learning minority languages such as Korean, Japanese, Chinese and Vietnamese. Many K-12 schools use the term "world language" in place of "foreign language" to emphasize that no language is foreign in the U.S. (Watzke 2003).

However, our survey findings indicate that only 73 out of over K-12 130,000 schools chose to offer Korean classes and the majority of them are in Califirnia and New York. In order for K-16 articulation to be meaningfully implemented, many more schools should offer Korean. Thus, it is essential for policy makers and educators to pay more attention to less commonly taught languages such as Korean and the state governments should encourage and financially support more schools to offer the minority languages that students are eager to learn such as Korean.

However, the predominant selection of modern languages for K-12 foreign language instruction does not capture the inclusive nature of multiple languages spoken in every community around us. The addition of minority languages will contribute to the growth of foreign language enrollments since students have more chances to learn the languages they are personally interested in.

According to our survey, over 80 % of the students enrolled in Korean classes are Korean heritage students. Our survey results suggest that the effort to maintain and develop Korean language has been attributed to the resources and desires of heritage language communities (Wiley, 2003). That is, there is a rising interest among Korean heritage learners in learning their mother tongue. The survey we conducted, as well as many previous studies (e.g. Cho 2000; Lee 2002; Lee and Kim 2008), suggests that Korean heritage language learners want to learn Korean in order to explore their heritage and to better connect with their family and community members. Due to their pre-existing knowledge in the language, heritage language speakers can serve as a valuable national resource for strengthening proficiency in less commonly taught languages, including critical languages (O'Connell and Norwood 2007). Utilizing heritage language speakers has "clear potential to help address shortages in foreign language and area experts" by training them in advanced academic levels for their language and an understanding of their cultural heritage and communities (O'Connell and Norwood 2007: 133).

In the U.S., there are currently more than 1,000 Korean community schools most of which are affiliated with Korean churches, with no financial assistance from the U.S. government (Shin 2005. These community schools face many problems such as absence of standardized curriculum, lack of appropriate textbooks, and shortage of qualified teachers. We can accommodate the needs of foreign language speakers and content area experts only by mandating foreign language coursework in the K-12 curriculum. We are in dire need of state government's positive support not only for couese offerings but also for K-16 articulation.

4.3. Level-to-level articulation

The best way to meet the language expertise needs of the country is to build a broad base of American citizens who have received an effective education in one or more languages for longer periods of time in consecutive semesters. In order to achieve this, we need to have a smooth and efficient transition from one level of language study to the next. After all, K-12 students are the pipeline of university programs. Without proper articulation across the K-16 spectrum for consistent and rational progression of instruction with respect to content standards and instructional approaches, it is usually the case that students are placed in lower level classes when they enter a university.

A foreign language education policy cannot provide students with extended learning sequences by simply taking a segment from the K-12 sequence. For elementary school students, language study cannot be continued unless a language sequence is already in place for middle and high schools in the same school district. According to our survey results, students typically start learning Korean as a foreign language elective in ninth grade and continue for only two years. Out of 73 schools, most of the schools that offer Korean are limited to high schools. This means that the study of the Korean language is generally delayed until the final stage in the K-12 sequence. Also, according to the teachers interviewed, most Korean classes are restricted to beginning-level Korean classes, and consequently, the traditional two year sequence produces "learners with skills limited to learned expressions and restrained interactions (NSFLEP, 1999, p.14, as cited in Watzke, 2003). For this reason, learning opportunities resulting in greater proficiency in the Korean language are very rare.

According to the ETS Oral Proficiency Testing Manual, nearly 2,760 hours of study is required to achieve an advanced level of competency in Korean (Liskin-Gasparro, 1982). Therefore, we should introduce Korean language study in a child's early education to help students reach advanced levels later in life. This should be a long-term initiative with carefully staged sequences to support student progression that is measured and documented. We should be sure to require a minimum of four to six years of study in a language as a prerequisite for high school graduation. This would allow students to enter college already fairly fluent and literate in a language, and students can prepare for the job market with usable language skills. Also, university students can enhance their professional-level language ability and area study by taking more advanced language and content courses at the university.

In order to increase enrollments in KLPs and their competitiveness with other languages, we have to promote the Korean language subject test in the SAT II. Since Korean was first introduced as one of the SAT subject tests in 1997, the number of students taking Korean language courses has shown a surprising increase. The addition of Korean in the SAT subject tests has inspired Korean-American students to learn Korean (Lee, 2002). It has also contributed to an increase in the number of schools offering Korean language courses and the number of students studying Korean. To further motivate students to study Korean and encourage instructors to promote Korean courses, schools must begin offering AP classes in the Korean language and to encourage the ETS and U.S. Department of Education to continue administering the Korean language subject test in the SAT II.[2]

4.4. Model program implementation

In order to ensure that Korean as a foreign language will be taught at all K-12 schools successfully, a model program must be implemented at all levels of instruction. The KDLP model, which is currently limited to elementary schools, should be expanded. Model programs should introduce Korean language in children's early years and then build upon acquired skills through well-designed instruction in the higher grades. This will help other teachers and school administrators within each school district follow the pioneer groups' example. Hawai'i is the ideal place to implement Korean language instruction in the K-12 system due to its large Korean-American community, multicultural diversity, and rigorous Korean language programs at the university.

While designing this articulation, teachers, administrators, and curriculum developers should keep in mind that the ultimate advantage of the study of a foreign language should go beyond college preparation or high school graduation. It should extend to the use for professional and vocational purposes, participation in local communities, and contribution to society at large. In the process of pilot school implementation, the following questions should be answered for students to develop higher levels of Korean language proficiency: (1) What are the skills that all students should learn upon completion of a learning sequence?; (2) Do these skills provide a base for those students who will continue their studies in the foreign language?; (3) What are the clear missions and objectives for beginning, intermediate, and advanced level studies?; and (4) Do these skills prepare all students for using the language in their professional domains after graduation?

4.5. Assessment

Another important issue mentioned by our respondents is assessment. Many teachers are dissatisfied with placement. Most of the programs have neither standardized placement tests nor exit exams appropriate for K-12 students. It is necessary to create a general proficiency standard so that meaningful assessments of student progress can be made. Our survey findings show that more than 90% of the schools create their own placement test combining a written test and a simple interview, and over the course of the year, student learning is assessed using written midterm and final exams. It is urgent to develop valid and reliable standardized placement tests and exit exams to monitor students'

2 While Korean is an SAT II language which more than 4,000 high school students take each year, it is not an Advanced Placement exam language yet, since not enough high schools offer Korean.

exiting knowledge and progression at the end of each unit of instruction. The tests should incorporate not only reading and grammar but also the productive skills, that is, speaking and writing. The exit exams are especially crucial at each instructional level to make sure that students master the necessary skills when moving to the next level of foreign language study. Educators from all levels of instruction should communicate and collaborate with one another in order to develop common principles and goals that facilitate the transition of language students through various stages of study. Many articulation efforts have to resolve issues of student learning outcomes and standardized tools to measure students' knowledge of the Korean language.

4.6. Distance learning

Our final major issue is how to develop a well-articulated K-16 distance education network in the academic sector. While government institutions including FSI and DLI are delivering online instruction extensively, hardly any systematic attempt has been made in the academic sector, despite the fact that distance learning will be much advantageous. A K-16 distance learning system is not only necessary but also feasible. For example, several universities such as Vassar College, Trinity College, University of Arizona, and Monash University have uploaded self-instructional Korean language programs on their websites to a limited scope. Moreover, we can articulate K-16 curricula, instruction, and assessments most efficiently via online distance education.

5. Conclusion and directions for further study

Our survey results imply wide-ranging directions for further research. First of all, to have a better understanding of the current status of Korean programs in U.S. K-12 schools, we should carefully examine the relationship between existing language policies and actual educational practices through an ethnographic field study. Research methods such as participant observations and in-depth insite interviews will enable us to uncover the internal and external factors that promote or inhibit Korean language education. Also, observing classes closely and looking at the interactions between the teacher and students will provide insight into the K-12 Korean teacher's teaching practices, language learning activities and the materials used, students' interests, and student performance, all of which are beneficial to improving Korean language instruction.

Second, an urgent need exists to develop textbooks for K-12 Korean learners. Teachers are using different and disparate self-made materials, which perpetuates inconsistencies within curricula among Korean language programs and schools across the U.S. In addition, many textbooks currently used in K-12 schools are designed for college students. Thus, textbooks should be developed that are appropriate to the cognitive levels and language abilities of K-12 students. Designing the textbooks and curriculums should reflect the emerging interests of heritage language learners and foreign language learners in learning Korean for different purposes. Needs analysis is a fundamental component of systematic curriculum development (Iwai et al. 1999). Few studies have been conducted to determine precisely what the Korean language learners' current and future communicative needs are and what types of tasks and materials may help them achieve the objectives of their foreign language study. Research should be conducted to grasp an in-depth understanding of the real-world conditions and environments that are closely associated with the learners' Korean language practices and the specific tasks that they want to accomplish in their own communities. Based on these needs and domains of the language use outside the classroom, teachers and textbook developers can select and identify pedagogic tasks and learning objectives.

Third, along with a pilot program implementation, Korean language teacher training programs must be developed at the university level to facilitate the production of highly qualified Korean language teachers at the K-12 level. Our survey findings show that over 95% of the schools have at least one Korean full-time teacher. However, few teachers (mostly in California) have credentials in Korean language teaching; very few universities in the U.S. offer teacher certification programs for prospective Korean language teachers. Full-time teachers often teach Korean in addition to other subjects such as ESL or mathematics. Only Korean dual language program teachers are required to have a Korean language teaching license. Implementing Korean language teacher certification programs at institutions such as the University of Hawaii at Manoa (UHM) will help to produce highly qualified Korean language teachers at the K-12 level. UHM's program can provide prospective Korean language teachers with specialized training in Korean linguistics, pedagogy, and curriculum development.

Last but not least, one of the most fundamental aspects of ensuring a successful Korean language program is to develop positive pubic relations and to promote community awareness of this critical-need language. Informational sessions, workshops, and open-house sessions with parents, community members, and teachers need to be held on a regular basis.

References: Chapter 33

Cho, G. 2000. The role of heritage language in social interactions and relationships: Reflections from a language minority group. *Bilingual Research Journal* 24.4: 369-84.

Cho, H.-Y. 2000. Heritage' language learning and ethnic identity: Korean Americans' struggle with language authorities. *Language, Culture, and Curriculum* 14.2: 26-41.

Christian, D. 1999. Looking at federal education legislation from a language epolicy/planning perspective. In Huebner, T. and K. A. Davis (eds.), *Sociopolitical Perspectives on Language Policy and Planning in the U.S.A.* Amsterdam/Philadelphia: John Benjamins Publishing Company.

Hadley, A.O. 2001. *Teaching Language in Context*, 3rd Edition. Heinle & Heinle.

Iwai, T., K. Kondo, D.S.J. Lim, G.E. Ray, H. Shimizu, and J.D. Brown. 1999. *Japanese language needs assessment 1998-1999* (NFLRC Network #13). University of Hawaii Second Language Teaching and Curriculum Center. http://www.nflrc.hawaii.edu/NetWorks/NW13/.

Kirsch, C. 2008. *Teaching Foreign Languages in the Primary School: Principles and Practice.* London: Continuum.

Lally, C.G. 2001. *Foreign language program articulation: Current practice and future prospects.* Westport, CT: Bergin & Garvey.

Lee, J.S. 2002. The Korean Language in America: The role of cultural identity and heritage language. *Language, Culture, and Curriculum* 15.2: 117-33.

Lee, J.S. and H. Kim. 2007. Attitudes, motivation and instructional needs of heritage language Learners. In Kondo-Brown, K. and J.D. Brown (eds.), *Teaching Chinese, Japanese, and Korean heritage students: Curriculum, needs, materials, and assessment.* Mahwah, NJ: Lawrence Erlbaum.

Liskin-Gasparro, J.E. 1982. *ETS Oral Proficiency Testing Manual.* Princeton, N.J.: Educational Testing Service.

O' Connell, M.E. and J.L. Norwood (eds.). 2007. *International education and foreign languages: Keys to securing America's future.* Washington, DC: National Academies Press.

Osborn, T.A. 2002. *The future of foreign language education in the United States.* Westport, CT: Bergin & Garvey.

Shin, S.J. 2005. *Developing in Two Languages: Korean Children in America.* Clevedon, UK: Multilingual Matters.

Sohn, H.-M. 2000. Curricular Goals and Content Standards for K-16 Korean Language Learning. *Korean Language in America* 5: 3-16.

Sohn, H.-M. 2009. The Language Flagship paradigm and Korean language education (in Korean). *Research in Korean Language Pedagogy* (Seoul National University Press). Vol. 24: 21-45.

Watzke, J.L. 2003. *Lasting Change in Foreign Language Education: A Historical Case for Change in National Policy.* Westport, CT: Praeger.

Wiley, T. 2001. Policy formation and implementation. In J. K. Peyton, D. Ranard, & S. McGinnis (eds.), *Heritage Languages in America. Preserving a National Resource*, 99-108 (2001). Washington, DC: Center for Applied Linguistics and Delta Systems.

34 Evolution of the Korean Program at the University of Hawaii at Manoa: A Narrative History*

1. Overview[1]

The Korean Program at the University of Hawaii (UH) has 65 years (1946–present) of thorny history of evolution.[2] Roughly speaking, the first twenty-five years (up to about 1970) was a long, tough struggle for survival of both the program and faculty.[3] During this "stage 1" period, the Korean program was deplorably shaky. Not many students wanted to take Korean classes, preferring Japanese, Chinese, Hawaiian, or European languages instead. After all, at that time, most Americans had a negative image of Korea: a former colonial territory of Japan, a poverty-stricken country, a country devastated by the Korean War, and (after the Korean War) a country constantly vigilant against North Korea. As sociolinguists (e.g. Chaika 1982, Wardhaugh 2010) would say, the Korean language had no competitive power, no market value, and no brand. The Korean language was not particularly valued as part of Korean studies either, since Korean studies itself had not yet become an established field. This remained true even after the establishment of the Center for Korean Studies at UH in 1972. In their seminal book, titled *East Asia: The Great Tradition* (1960), Reischauer and Fairbanks treated Korea as a variant of the Chinese cultural pattern, allotting

---

* This paper is included in Hye-Sook Wang's (ed.) forthcoming monograph titled *Narrative Hitory of Korean Programs in U.S. Colleges and Universities* (publisher: TBA).

1 This paper was completed at the Research Center of Korean Studies (RCKS) of Kyushu University in Fukuoka, Japan in the summer of 2012 when I was invited as a visiting scholar for one month. I am most grateful to Professor Takatoshi Matsubara, RCKS Director, for giving me the golden opportunity to work at RCKS. Special thanks go to the RCKS staff members (especially Fujita Hanae) for taking care of all procedural matters and office chores for me prior to and during my stay with the Center.

2 I am grateful to Haejin E. Koh for her meticulous editing of this paper.

3 The various statistical data in this paper are culled from old hand-written records and printed documents stored in the Department of East Asian Languages and Literatures facilities. I am indebted to Evelyn Nakanishi, who assisted me in uncovering the relevant data for this study.

only 9% of the entire book to the discussion of Korea vis-à-vis China and Japan. In AY 1960-61, the Korean enrollments at UH plunged to an embarrassingly all-time low of 6 (3 in Fall 1960 and 3 in Spring 1961), threatening the very existence of the feeble Korean program. UH was not the only university with this deplorable state of affairs. None of the Mainland universities with a Korean program were faring any better.

Yet, fortunately, the UH administration and the department endeavored to save the Korean Program amidst the thriving Japanese and Chinese programs. Two tenure-track faculty positions in Korean were created in 1962 and 1968. With the establishment of the Center for Korean Studies on campus, another tenure-track faculty position in Korean language was added in 1972, resulting in a solid three-member faculty line-up.

Gradually, fortune began to smile. The Korean program slowly came out of the long hopeless, dark tunnel and saw a ray of hope, although not a brilliant one. Some 17 years (roughly 1970–1987), which I would call "stage 2", following the initial long "stage 1" period of stagnation saw a slowly but steadily growing stage, parallel to the national trend in Korean enrollments (Furman, Goldberg & Lusin, 2007). This period reflected Korea's economic development, which began to change Americans' negative image of war-torn Korea to a positive image of a country of hope. At the same time, due to the U.S. government's policy to open doors to Asian immigration as of 1965, Korean immigrants flooded into all states of the U.S., including Hawaii. Korea, Korean people, Korean language, and Korean culture began to gain visibility in multi-ethnic American society. Korean heritage students began to register for Korean classes in record numbers. The enrollment peak of this period was AY 1985-86, when the annual enrollments reached 118 (57 in Fall 1985 and 61 in Spring 1986).

The next fifteen years (roughly 1987–2003), which I would term "stage 3", represents a stage of rapid growth due to Korea's distinct visibility worldwide mostly as a result of Korea's hosting the 1988 Summer Olympic Games and continued economic growth. More and more American students, including heritage students, took Korean classes. Institutionally also, in 1987, the department established both MA and PhD degrees programs in Korean. Furthermore, the establishment of the BA in Korean program in 1995 completed the Korean Program, making it parallel to the Japanese and Chinese programs for the first time. The annual enrollments rose as high as 343 in AY 2002-03 (187 in Fall 2002 and 156 in 2003).

Finally, the current stage (2003–present), i.e. "stage 4", has seen a further great leap forward in the Korean program, especially with the introduction of the federally-funded Korean language Flagship program. Moreover, the so-called Korean wave, including K-drama and K-pop, has continued to attract a large number of students to Korean classes.

In AY 2011-12, for the first time in the history of the Korean program at UH, the annual enrollments passed 1,000 (586 in Fall 2011 and 465 in Spring 2012). This number places Korean second to Japanese (2,459) and ahead of Chinese (855). The PhD program in Korean language and linguistics attracts more students than those of Japanese and Chinese.

Korean Studies gradually became recognized as an established field of area studies worldwide. Ebrey, Walthall, and Palais's *East Asia: A Cultural, Social, and Political History* (2006), another seminal work on East Asia, allots 50% of the book to China, 30% to Japan, and 20% to Korea, describing Korea as an independent process of development in East Asia. The Korean language is no longer a valueless, powerless language; it carries brand power with considerable market value worldwide.

As a reference point for subsequent discussion of the evolution of the Korean Program, a bird's eye-view of the major milestones is given in Table 1.

TABLE 1. Major events related to the Korean Program

Stage	Dates	Major Events	Remarks
Stage 1: 1946-70	Fall 1946	First instruction of Korean began in the Department of Asian and Pacific Languages, UH.	by Kwandu Park, a part-time lecturer.
	Fall 1962	The first regular tenure-track position in Korean was created. New literature courses were added to the language curriculum, beginning Fall 1963.	Peter H. Lee was hired as assistant professor.
	Fall 1968	The second regular tenure-track position in Korean language was created.	Dong-Jae Lee was hired as instructor.
Stage 2: 1970-87	Fall 1971	The Department of Asian and Pacific Languages was split into three departments: East Asian Languages, East Asian Literatures, and Hawaii and Indo-Pacific Languages and Literatures.	
	1972	The Center for Korean Studies was established as the first area center at UH and as the first of its kind in the U.S.	Dae Sook Suh was appointed as Director.
	Fall 1972	A third regular tenure-track faculty position in Korean language was created.	Ho-min Sohn was hired as assistant professor.
	Fall 1983	Merging of Department of East Asian Languages and Department of East Asian Literatures into the current Department of East Asian Languages and Literatures (EALL)	

Stage	Dates	Major Events	Remarks
Stage 3: 1987-03	Fall 1987	MA & PhD programs in Korean language and Korean literature were established, with relevant curricula and graduate courses developed and introduced.	
	Fall 1995	BA in Korean was launched. Previously, only Minor and Certificate in Korean had been in existence.	Ho-min Sohn was EALL department chair.
	Fall 2002	The federally-funded Korean Flagship program was established as a non-degree post-baccalaureate program. The National Security Education Program (NSEP) was the federal sponsor.	Michael Long was appointed as Program Director.
Stage 4: 2003-present	Fall 2003	A fourth regular tenure-track position in Korean language was created.	Ji-Ha Hwang was hired as assistant professor.
	Fall 2007	The Korean Flagship program was promoted to the Korean Language Flagship Center (KLFC). KLFC established MA in Korean for Professionals in the Department of EALL as a third track of the Korean Program along with Language/linguistics and Literature.	Ho-min Sohn was appointed as Center Director.
	Fall 2008	KLFC established new BA and Certificate programs in Korean for Professionals in the department of EALL as a second track along with the regular BA and Certificate program in Korean.	
	Fall 2010	A fifth regular tenure-track position in Korean language was created.	Sang Yee Cheon was hired as assistant professor.
	Fall 2012	Federal funding to the Flagship MA program was discontinued, resulting in complete institutionalization of the MA program.	The BA program is still funded by NSEP.
	Fall 2013	A sixth regular tenure-track position in Korean language was created to sustain the Flagship MA program.	Dong Kwan Kong was hired as assistant professor.

Table 2 gives the years of the inceptions of Korean, Japanese, and Chinese instruction and degree programs.

TABLE 2. Years of launching language instruction and degree programs

Languages	First language course offered in	BA program started in	MA program started in	PhD program started in
Japanese	1921	1942	Lang: 1968 Lit: 1968	Lit: 1969 Lang: 1987
Chinese	1922	1942	Lang: 1968 Lit: 1968	Lang: 1987 Lit: 1987
Korean	1946	1995	Lang: 1987 Lit: 1987	Lang: 1987 Lit: 1987

2. Data and information source

I am one of only a handful of surviving witnesses to the history of the Korean Program at UH. At first, I was simply a bystander, superficially observing the fledgling program from outside as an East-West Center supported PhD student in linguistics in 1965-69 and then as a linguistic researcher at the UH Pacific and Asian Linguistic Institute in 1971-72 Then, in the fall of 1972, I joined the Korean Program, as I was employed as a tenure-track assistant professor of Korean by the Department of East Asian Languages. At the time of my hire, the Chair was John DeFrancis, a Chinese language specialist.

I can comfortably narrate the history of the past forty years of the Korean program, as I have personally observed, experienced, and collaboratively led the program through both the initial dark period of struggle for survival and the bright period of growth. I am particularly in an excellent position to talk about the program development, as I served as Korean Section Head for many years, Acting/Interim Chair of the Department of East Asian Languages for two and a half years, Chair of the Department of East Asian Languages and Literatures for seven years (1993-2000), and Director of the Korean Language Flagship Center for six years (2007- present). I also served as a faculty member of the Center for Korean Studies since its inception in 1972 and as its Director for six years (2004-2010), and thus, I am familiar with the close interaction between the Center and Korean Program activities.

I am fortunate to be able to access the department's detailed records on enrollments, teaching faculty, and other relevant information. These records were carefully documented by office secretaries and Evelyn Nakanishi, a long-time department student services specialist and graduate student advisor. Like me, Ms. Nakanishi, a "walking history" of the department, has served the department for more than forty years, including seven years as Assistant to the Chair when I was Chair of the department.

3. A brief narrative history

As in most other minority foreign language programs around the world, Korean language instruction at UH started with the poorest state of affairs. Instruction first took place in the fall of 1946. This was one year after World War II ended on August 15th of 1945, which liberated Korea from 35 years of Japanese colonial rule. The instruction took place in the Department of Asian and Pacific Languages, with Kwandu Park, an architect (with no training in language pedagogy), employed as a part-time lecturer.[4] K. Park started with only one basic-level general course, numbered KOR 100, with 10 enrollments in Fall 1946 and 6 in Spring 1947. Two years later, in the fall of 1948, the department added the first-year (or elementary-level) course, numbered KOR 101, and in the fall of 1951, the second-year course, numbered KOR 200. K. Park taught these courses as a lecturer for five years until the spring of 1951. It is not clear who succeeded K. Park from 1952 to 1961. The department record shows that a person named K. Kim taught in AY 1961-62, and then Peter H. Lee was hired in 1962 as a tenure-track assistant professor.

From 1960 to 1968, the department made a number of curricular changes:

(a) Abolishment of KOR 100 and KOR 200
(b) Splitting of KOR 101 into 101 (Fall) and 102 (Spring)
(c) Addition of KOR 151-2 as second-year Korean
(d) Addition of KOR 201-2 as third-year Korean
(e) Addition of KOR 401-2 (Korean literature in English)
(f) Addition of KOR 415-6 (Korean grammar)
(g) Addition of KOR 417-8 as fourth-year Korean
(h) Addition of KOR 491 (Contemporary Korean literature)
(i) Addition of KOR 499 (Advanced study essay) & KOR 699 (Directed research)
(j) Addition of KOR 750 (Research seminar in Korean)

The above curricular changes are indicated in Table 3, along with enrollments in Korean courses. Japanese and Chinese annual enrollment totals are given for comparison. Table 3 includes enrollments for the academic year only, not for the summer sessions.

4 In addition to Korean, the department also taught Chinese, Hawaiian, Hindi, Indonesian, Japanese, Sanskrit, Tagalog, Thai, and Vietnamese.

TABLE 3. Korean Course Enrollments for Fall 1946 – Spring 1968

AY	F46-S47	F47-S48	F48-S49	F49-S50	F50-S51	F51-S52	F52-S53	F53-S54	F54-S55	F55-S56	F56-S57
100	10-7	?-?	17-15	17-?	11-21	10-8	9-4	7-3	9-5	12-8	7-2
101			7-6	10-?	9-24	5-5	5-6	3-3	2-1	1-2	5-7
200						4-5	1-1	4-3	0-4	1-0	1-1
Semester total	10-7	?-?	24-21	27-?	20-45	19-18	15-11	14-9	11-10	14-10	13-10
KOR AY total	17	?	45	?	65	37	26	23	21	24	23
JPN AY total	583	762	815	602	1009	526	614	521	446	452	512
CHN AY total	135	143	98	90	101	54	37	63	37	50	40

AY	F57-S58	F58-S59	F59-S60	F60-S61	F61-S62	F62-S63	F63-S64	F64-S65	F65-S66	F66-S67	F67-S68
100	2-2	4-?	2-2								
101-2	1-3	2-?	- -	3-3	6-5	10-6	13-8	12-8	4-2	5-4	5-6
151-2					6-5	1-1	6-5	5-5	5-4	1-2	3-5
200	- -	- -	2-2								
211-2						1-1	1-1	5-5	5-2	5-3	7-5
401-2							3-2	6-4	2-1	1-1	1-
415-6								1-	2-	3-3	- -
417-8							1-1	- -	2-3	1-1	3-4
491-2									1-	1-1	1-1
499									1-1	- -	- -
699							1-	- -	- -	- -	- -
750											-1
Semester total	3-5	6-?	4-4	3-3	12-10	12-8	25-17	28-23	22-15	17-15	20-22
KOR AY total	8	?	8	6	22	20	41	51	37	32	42
JPN AY total	466	538	836	965	1264	1677	1908	1911	2247	2427	2668
CHN AY total	47	56	96	172	323	371	416	426	438	608	547

Notes: - : existing course not offered in that semester.
blank : non-existent or abolished course.
? = no record available.

Notice that the annual enrollments in Korean classes fluctuated from a low of 6 (in AY 1960-61) to a high of 65 (in AY 1950-51). In contrast, the Japanese academic year totals were between 446 and 2,668; while the Chinese totals were between 56 and 608.

In the fall of 1968, the language skill courses were renumbered based on the system still in place today: KOR 101-2 (Elementary), KOR 201-2 (Intermediate), KOR 301-2 (Third-level), and KOR 401-2 (Advanced). In the fall of 1969, more literature courses were added: KOR 361-2 (Literature in translation-Poetry), KOR 461-2 (Contemporary literature), KOR 490 (Reference material-Korean studies), and KOR 495 (Advanced study senior essay). Except for KOR 361-2, these new courses failed to attract any students until 1971.

In 1971, the Department split into three departments: (a) Department of East Asian Languages (EALA), (b) Department of East Asian Literatures (EALI), and (c) Department of Hawaiian and Indo-Pacific Languages and Literatures (HIPLL)[5] Thus, the Korean language program belonged to EALA and the Korean literature program to EALI. Due to this split, only the three East Asian languages (Japanese, Chinese, and Korean), along with their faculty, curricula, and students, constituted the Department of EALA, while the literatures of the three languages, along with the relevant faculty, curricula, and students, formed a separate department of EALI. As a result, the two full-time faculty in Korean, one in language (Dong Jae Lee, Instructor) and one in literature (Peter Lee, Professor), were separated, with two part-time language lecturers remaining in EALA. The Korean language skill courses (KOR 101-2, KOR 201-2, 301-2, 401-2) and the newly added KOR 431-2 (Selected readings in Korean) constituted the entire curriculum of the Korean language program at EALA, while all literature courses moved to EALI.

Table 4 indicates the above curriculum and program changes. The double lines before the fall of 1971 represent the separation of EALI and EALA. From this point forward, only EALA courses and enrollments are discussed in this paper.

TABLE 4. Korean Course Enrollments for Fall 1968–Spring 1977

AY	F68-S69	F69-S70	F70-S71	F71-S72	F72-S73	F73-S74	F74-S75	F75-S76	F76-S77
101-2	9-6	8-4	11-9	15-8	7-3	16-13	15-8	16-8	18-12
201-2	2-2	4-4	3-3	5-5	2-2	2-4	6-8	4-3	1-1
301-2	4-5	5-6	4-3	5-4	4-4	3-5	4-4	4-5	2-5
361-2		- -	4-3						
401-2	2-2	2-2	8-10	5-5	2-2	3-3	-2	3-	9-8
431-2				7-6	- -	5-3	2-2	7-9	9-10

5 HIPLL was recently disbanded with the creation of the Department of Indo-Pacific Languages and Literatures (IPLL), as it is now, when Hawaiian language and literature moved under the newly launched School of Hawaiian Knowledge in 2007.

AY	F68-S69	F69-S70	F70-S71		F71-S72	F72-S73	F73-S74	F74-S75	F75-S76	F76-S77
461-2		- -	- -							
490		- -	- -							
495		- -	- -							
Total	17-15	19-18	30-28		37-28	15-11	29-28	27-24	34-25	39-36
KOR AY total	32	37	58		65	26	57	51	59	75
JPN AY total	2062	2344	2271		2524	2739	3152	3177	3162	2967
CHN AY total	860	611	627		617	774	854	663	539	525

I joined the EALA Department in the fall of 1972. As I was still committed to the UH Pacific and Asian Linguistics Institute, I had to split my time and worked for EALA on a half-time basis for a year. Due to my limited service, the Department was not able to offer KOR 431-2 and, as a result, the annual enrollments were only 26. From the following year, I worked as a full-timer for EALA, and enrollments gradually rose.

One conspicuous fact in Table 4 is that, after the division of the languages and literatures in the three East Asian programs, student enrollments showed little change in EALA compared to the previous unified department. This means that enrollments were predominantly on the language side. This further suggests that the separate literature department would not be able to sustain itself without the cooperation and the synergy of the language programs.

Indeed, twelve years later in the fall of 1983, university budgetary constraints and low enrollments in literature compelled the two East Asian departments to reunite into the single Department of East Asian Languages and Literatures (EALL), as it is now. Today, the Department of EALL is the largest of its kind in the world outside of East Asia, in terms of the number of faculty, curricular diversity, student enrollments, and degree programs. In particular, the Japanese program has always been predominant among all foreign language programs offered at UH, due partly to the overwhelming Japanese heritage population that occupies nearly 24% of the entire population of the multi-ethnic state of Hawaii.[6]

In discussing the aspects of Korean language instruction at UH in the following, only these three East Asian languages are compared, disregarding the other Asian and Pacific languages, let alone European languages, taught at the UH.

6 The Korean heritage population is only about 4% of the entire population of Hawaii, and the Chinese heritage population is about 6%.

With the merger of the East Asian languages and literatures departments, the literature side added (or reintroduced) KOR 261-2 (Literary translation: poetry), KOR 461-2 (Introduction to Korean Literature: Traditional-Modern), and KOR 610 (Korean Poetry) to the curriculum of the Korean Program. On the language side, existing KOR 431-2 (Selected Readings in Korean) were renumbered as KOR 481-repeatable once. New upper-division content courses KOR 470 (Korean language and Culture), KOR 420 (Korean Composition), and KOR 451-2 (Structure of Korean: Sounds and Grammar) were added, which drew many advanced students, including linguistics graduate students. Table 5 indicates this program reunion with double lines before the fall of 1983, as well as additions of new language and literature courses and enrollments.

TABLE 5. Korean Course Enrollments for Fall 1968–Spring 1977

AY	F77-S78	F78-S79	F79-S80	F80-S81	F81-S82	F82-S83	F83-S84	F84-S85	F85-S86	F86-S87
101-2	14-12	12-6	13-7	7-5	8-9	7-6	10-8	7-7	9-5	11-10
201-2	4-5	5-5	5-5	10-7	5-4	7-5	7-5	5-5	7-6	8-5
301-2	5-7	3-4	5-4	6-4	3-3	5-5	4-6	3-3	5-5	7-6
401-2	7-4	4-5	4-6	6-7	4-6	4-4	3-8	5-5	4-6	5-5
420								6-	11-18	7-
431-2	5-5	-3	7-7	9-12	16-14	18-18	11-12			
451-2								5-	- -	4-5
470									-19	-8
481								8-10	20-2	3-
499			-2	1-1	1-	- -	- -	- -	1-	- -
261-2							3-2	- -	- -	- -
461-2							1-	- -	- -	- -
610										3-
Semester total	34-33	24-23	34-31	39-36	36-37	41-38	39-42	39-30	57-61	45-42
KOR AY total	67	47	65	75	73	79	81	69	118	87
JPN AY total	2893	2490	2127	2007	2000	1971	2142	1901	1867	1833
CHN AY total	432	408	401	410	454	503	667	564	537	479

In the meantime, UH was reorganized as the UH system, absorbing all seven community colleges and two four-year colleges spread across four islands within the state of Hawaii. The original UH was renamed as the University of Hawaii at Manoa (UHM), which is the flagship campus, where the Department of EALL and other language departments continued to be housed.[7]

In the fall of 1987, the Department of EALL launched the MA and PhD degree programs in Korean language/linguistics and in Korean literature. For this purpose, a set of new graduate courses had been developed and added to the curriculum. On the language/linguistics side, I developed courses such as KOR 631 (History and Dialects of Korean), 632 (Korean Phonology and Morphology), 633 (Korean Syntax and Semantics), 634 (Korean Sociolinguistics), 635 (Introduction to Korean Language Pedagogy), and 730 (Seminar in Korean Language). More graduate courses have subsequently been added.

The graduate degree programs started to attract graduate students into the Korean Program, slowly at first but in larger numbers as years went by. Moreover, the 1988 Summer Olympic Games had portrayed a brighter image of Korea and Korean people to the world. Thus, not only have the Korean course enrollments grown, but perhaps more importantly, the rate of growth has grown and even surpassed those of Japanese and Chinese, as shown in Table 6.

TABLE 6. Korean course enrollments for Fall 1987 - Spring 2003 in comparison with those of Japanese and Chinese

AY	F87-S88	F88-S089	F89-S90	F90-S91	F91-S92	F92-S93	F93-S94	F94-S95	F95-S96
Semester total	43-53	60-65	65-71	73-74	93-93	111-102	120-102	116-135	118-110
KOR AY total	96	125	136	147	186	213	222	251	228
JPN AY total	2213	2361	2516	2828	2815	2594	2656	2728	2740
CHN AY total	442	409	465	542	565	523	561	639	635

AY	F96-S97	F97-S98	F98-S99	F99-S00	F00-S01	F01-S02	F02-S03
Semester total	130-138	105-129	132-128	128-99	145-112	114-111	187-156
KOR AY total	268	234	260	227	257	225	343
JPN AY total	2774	2570	2255	1994	2001	2028	2305
CHN AY total	521	584	583	553	497	553	580

7 At present, Korean is taught at three community colleges of the UH system: Kapiolani Community College, Honolulu Community College and Leeward Community College. Of these three, Kapiolani has the largest program with a tenured Korean language faculty and two part-time lecturers. The Korean programs of Honolulu and Leeward are of a smaller scale, each taught by a single part-time lecturer.

For seven years from 1993 to 2000, I served as EALL Department Chair. Internally, I succeeded in establishing the Board of Regents-approved B.A. in Korean program. Externally, I was instrumental in launching the American Association of Teachers of Korean (AATK) in 1994 and became the inaugural president. Another major achievement was the successful implementation of an international collaborative project for college-level Korean language textbook development with a million-dollar grant from the Korea Foundation. This project was implemented by the then newly-established Korean Language Education & Research Center (KLEAR), incorporated with the State of Hawaii in 1994. Since its founding, I have been serving as President of KLEAR. Since 2000, a total of twenty KLEAR textbooks have been published, covering both language skills and cultural contents.

4. Recent Developments

The Korean Program has expanded and grown even more with the introduction of the Korean Flagship program in the fall of 2002. The Korean Flagship is implemented as an integral component of The Language Flagship initiative created by the National Security Education Program (NSEP) at the U.S. Department of Defense.[8] In 2002, NSEP awarded the first Flagship grants for Korean, Arabic, Russian and Chinese, and UHM was selected for Korean.[9] During a year of preparation, the Korean Flagship program recruited the first cohort of students for 2003-04. The two-year Flagship program was a non-degree, non-certificate program, including intensive one-year domestic training at UHM and one-year overseas training at Korea University in Seoul.

After four years of experience with post-baccalaureate training, NSEP transitioned all post- baccalaureate programs to undergraduate programs in 2007, with three exceptions: Korean at UHM, Chinese at Ohio State University, and Arabic at University of Maryland. UHM received an additional NSEP grant to implement the undergraduate Flagship program in Korean. At the same time, at NSEP's request, the Korean Language Flagship Center (KLFC) was established at UHM, with me as Director, replacing the former Flagship program, to operate all Korean-related Flagship education.[10] KFLC endeavors to faithfully fulfill the

8 NSEP was established in 1991 to cultivate vital expertise in languages and cultures critical to U.S. national security and international competitiveness. Currently nine languages are designated as critical, including Arabic, Chinese, Hindi/Urdu, Korean, Persian, Portuguese, Russian, Swahili, and Turkish.

9 The grant proposal was prepared by Michael Long (at Department of Second Language Studies, SLA), Dong Jae Lee, and me. Michael Long assumed the directorship of the approved program.

10 Currently, a total of 26 such Centers have been established, covering the nine critical

Flagship mission to create "global professionals commanding a superior-level of proficiency in a critical language." Flagship programs, including the KLFC programs, are unique in that they offer the following features:

- Intensive language and culture instruction, including group training and individual tutoring, in a U.S. university setting
- Advanced language and long-term cultural immersion overseas where students enroll in foreign universities
- Language immersion internships through our public-private partnership with international organizations and corporations
- The opportunity to attain professional-level language proficiency, including in a non-language academic major of students' choosing

Upon its inception, KLFC established an MA (2007) and BA and Certificate (2008) in Korean for Professionals, as additional tracks to the existing regular MA, BA, and Certificate tracks in EALL. In 2009, we launched a pre-college program in an effort to articulate K-16 Korean language education. For a detailed account of the Flagship initiatives, see Sohn (2009). Students in the regular tracks are more academically oriented, whereas those in Flagship programs are more professionally oriented. However, many undergraduate courses, such as Advanced Korean, Korean language and culture, selected readings in Korean, Korean proficiency through film or drama, are taken by both student groups. At present, the Korean Section of the Department of EALL has about forty Flagship track B.A. students (compared to some 25 regular track B.A. students) and seventeen Flagship track M.A. students (compared to one in the regular track M.A. language/linguistics program). One distinctive effect of the addition of Flagship education is the enrollment increase since 2003, with another major jump in 2007, as indicated in Table 7. In addition, it is undeniable that the Korean Wave with popular K-drama and K-Pop attracts many students, particularly non-heritage students, to Korean classes. Korean enrollments have been surpassing Chinese enrollments since the fall of 2007, a miraculous phenomenon that nobody had ever dreamed of. In AY 2011-12, Korean annual enrollments passed the 1,000 mark.

languages. UHM is the only center for Korean.

TABLE 7. Course enrollment trend since 2003

AY	F03-S04	F04-S05	F05-S06	F06-S07	F07-S08	F08-S09	F09-S10	F10-S11	F11-S12
Total	198-170	268-249	228-288	306-326	369-388	432-393	430-390	468-482	586-465
KOR AY total	368	517	516	632	757	825	820	950	1051
JPN AY total	2531	2652	2813	2731	2687	2774	2535	2527	2459
CHN AY total	641	630	693	734	663	778	717	845	855

5. State-of-the-Art of the present UHM Korean Program

5.1. Organizational structure

Along with the Korean literature program, the Korean language and linguistics program constitutes the Korean Section of the Department of East Asian Languages and Literatures (EALL). The EALL Department, together with the Departments of English and History, is one of the three largest departments in UHM. The sister sections of EALL are those of Chinese and Japanese, each of which consists of language and literature programs. Only the Korean language/linguistics program is further sub-divided into the regular program and Flagship program. The Department of EALL, together with five other departments (English, European-American, Indo-Pacific, Linguistics, and Second Language Studies) constitutes the College of Languages, Linguistics, and Literature (LLL), the only college of its kind at an American university.

TABLE 8. Organization structure of the Korean program

<table>
<tr><td>UHM college</td><td colspan="12">LLL</td></tr>
<tr><td>Depart- ments</td><td colspan="7">EALL</td><td rowspan="4">ENG</td><td rowspan="4">EUR</td><td rowspan="4">INDOPAC</td><td rowspan="4">LING</td><td rowspan="4">SLS</td></tr>
<tr><td>Sections</td><td colspan="2">Chinese</td><td colspan="2">Japanese</td><td colspan="3">Korean</td></tr>
<tr><td>Programs</td><td>Lang</td><td>Lit</td><td>Lang</td><td>Lit</td><td colspan="2">Lang</td><td>Lit</td></tr>
<tr><td>Sub-tracks</td><td></td><td></td><td></td><td></td><td>Reg</td><td>Flag</td><td></td></tr>
</table>

All three East Asian languages and literatures have BA, MA, and PhD programs both in language/linguistics and in literature. Only Korean has additional tracks called BA and MA in Korean for Professionals (Flagship BA and MA). Thus, at present, the Korean Section of the Department of EALL consists of the academic programs presented in Table 9.

TABLE 9. Academic programs of EALL Korean Section

Program	*Regular Programs*	*Flagship Programs*
Pre-college	---	Pre-College Honors Program
BA	BA in Korean	BA in Korean forProfessionals
Minor	Minor in Korean	---
Certificate	Certificate in Korean	Certificate in Korean for Professionals
MA	MA in Korean Language & Linguistics MA in Korean Literature	MA in Korean for Professionals
PhD	PhD in Korean Language & Linguistics PhD in Korean Literature	---

5.2. Graduate programs

Since their inception in 1987, the regular-track MA and PhD programs in Korean have cultivated a number of fine MAs and PhDs. Many graduates and ABD's are currently working as full-time university faculty. Thus far, three PhDs and six MAs in literature have graduated. The three PhDs are professorial faculty at Ohio State University, SUNY-Binghamton, and University of Auckland in New Zealand. On the other hand, as of Spring 2013, twenty PhDs have been produced and 13 are still ABDs in language and linguistics, all under my supervision. A total of fourteen MAs in language and linguistics have also graduated. Among these, a total of twenty-five PhDs, ABDs, and MAs are working at the following institutions of higher education as full-time faculty: Harvard (2), Georgetown, Notre Dame, Emory, Pittsburgh, Penn State, SUNY-Albany, SUNY-Binghamton, Iowa, Rice, Arizona State, UC Berkeley, UCLA, UC San Diego, Defense Language Institute (5), Chicago, UHM (2), UH-Kapiolani, and Hankuk University of Foreign Studies in Seoul.Since its inception in 2002, the Flagship graduate program has graduated a total of 100 students. Under a non-degree post-baccalaureate program (2002-2007), a total of 44 graduated from the program. Under the MA program (2007-present), a total of 56 students in MA in Korean for Professionals have graduated.

The statistics of the current graduate students are given in Table 10, in comparison with the Chinese and Japanese programs. Of the 18 MA students in Korean language and linguistics, 17 are Flagship MA students while only 1 is in the regular program.

TABLE 10. Graduate Students enrolled in EALL as of Fall 2012

Degree	Japanese		Chinese		Korean		Total
	Lang/Ling	Literature	Lang/Ling	Literature	Lang/Ling	Literature	
MA	13	7	2	2	**18**	**1**	43
PhD	14	8	6	2	**25**	**4**	59
Total	27	15	8	4	**43**	**5**	102

5.3. Faculty

As indicated in Section 3, Korean language instruction started with one part-time lecturer in 1946, who taught for five years. A large number of temporary part-time lecturers have been employed as needs arose on a semester basis. Some UH faculty members in other programs were occasionally assigned to teach Korean language classes (e.g. W. Henthorn, Z. Song, Y.S. Kubota). A number of visiting professors and scholars have been invited from Seoul National, Yonsei, Ewha, Korea, Catholic, Sogang, Kyung-Hee, Donga, and Sangmyung. Some stayed only one semester while others stayed for several years (e.g. Y.S. Lee, C. H. Park, S. Koo, S.J. Kim, T.O. Kim, J.D. Park, H.S. Yang, C.H. Cho, S.K. Seo, J.H. Eom, H.S. Shin, K.H. In, and S. Suh).

Thus far, the Korean Program has been allotted six regular tenure-track positions, one in literature and five in language/linguistics. The six positions have been maintained as follows:

TABLE 11. Hiring of tenure-track positions

Faculty	*Disciplinary area*	*Year hired*	*Remarks*
Peter H. Lee	Korean literature	1962	Moved to UCLA in 1987. Retired.
Dong Jae Lee	Korean language & linguistics	1968	Retired in 2010.
Ho-min Sohn	Korean language & linguistics	1972	Current professor
Marshall Phil	Korean literature	1989	Passed away in 1996.
Yung-Hee Kim	Korean literature	1997	Current professor
Ji-Ha Hwang	Korean language & linguistics	2003	Passed away in 2005.

Faculty	***Disciplinary area***	***Year hired***	***Remarks***
Mee-Jeong Park	Korean language & linguistics	2006	Current associate professor
Sang Yee Cheon	Korean language & linguistics	2010	Current assistant professor
Mary S. Kim	Korean language & linguistics	2010	Current assistant professor
Dong Kwan Kong	Korean language & linguistics	2013	Current assistant professor

Thus, the six regular positions have been filled as follows. Italicized faculty members are current occupants of the positions:

(1) Peter H. Lee > Marshall Phil > *Yung-Hee Kim*
(2) Dong Jae Lee > *Mary S. Kim*
(3) *Ho-min Sohn*
(4) Ji-Ha Hwang > *Mee-Jeong Park*
(5) *Sang Yee Cheon*
(6) *Dong Kwan Kong*

From the program inception until 2009, Flagship faculty members have been hired with federal funding. For example, in 2009, three faculty in the MA program, two faculty in the BA program, and one program officer were fully supported by federal funds provided by NSEP. Due to the gradual reduction in federal funding in subsequent years, UHM has absorbed two faculty lines (one in 2010 and the other in 2013), while integrating certain language and culture courses offered by the regular and Flagship programs. The two tenure-track positions have been filled by Flagship faculty Sang Yee Cheon and Dong Kwan Kong, respectively. At present, only two Flagship faculty (full-time instructor Sumi Chang and program officer Lydia Chung) are fully funded by NSEP.

A full-time instructor position was created in the fall of 1993, and Seok-Hoon You (currently professor of linguistics at Korea University) was hired to fill the position. When he moved to Harvard in 1996, the position was closed and two Graduate Assistant positions were created instead. As of Fall 2013, the Korean Section of EALL is provided with a total of seven Graduate Assistants (GAs), who independently teach (mainly lower-level) language courses. At present, five of these GA positions are held by the language/linguistics program, one by the literature program, and one by the Flagship (Korean for professionals) program.

In addition, usually a dozen part-time lecturers are employed per semester to teach undergraduate language and literature courses. These lecturers are hired mostly from among current Ph.D. students in Korean language-linguistics and literature.

5.4. Course offerings

A wide variety of undergraduate and graduate courses in Korean language/linguistics and literature are offered every semester. While most language courses are offered every year, most of the graduate courses (600 level and above) are offered once every two years. The Korean courses offered at present by the Korean Section of the department are presented in Table 12.

TABLE 12. Current Course offerings (as of AY 2013-14)

Course number	*Course title*	*# of credits*	*# of sections*	*Frequency of offering*
KOR 101	Elementary Korean 1	4	6	fall & spring
KOR 102	Elementary Korean 2	4	3	fall & spring
KOR 105	Accelerated Elementary Korean	8	1	fall
KOR 111	Elementary conversational Korean 1	3	1	fall
KOR 112	Elementary conversational Korean 2	3	1	spring
KOR 201	Intermediate Korean 1	4	4	fall & spring
KOR 202	Intermediate Korean 2`	4	2	fall & spring
KOR 205	Accelerated Intermediate Korean	8	1	spring
KOR 301	Advanced intermediate Korean 1	3	2	fall
KOR 302	Advanced intermediate Korean 2	3	2	spring
KOR 307	Readings in Chinese characters 1	3	1	fall
KOR 308	Readings in Chinese characters 2	3	1	spring
KOR 380	Korean proficiency through TV drama	3	1	fall or spring
KOR 399	Directed reading in advanced intermediate Korean	variable	1	spring & fall
KOR 401	Advanced Korean 1	3	1	fall
KOR 402	Advanced Korean 2	3	1	spring
KOR 403	High-advanced Korean 1	3	2	fall
KOR 404	High-advanced Korean 2	3	2	spring
KOR 420	Korean composition	3	1	spring or fall
KOR 421	Media analysis in Korean 1	3	2	fall
KOR 422	Media analysis in Korean 2	3	2	spring
KOR 425	Selected readings in Korean	3	2: regular & flagship	fall & spring
KOR 451	Structure of Korean 1	3	1	fall
KOR 452	Structure of Korean 2	3	1	spring

Course number	*Course title*	*# of credits*	*# of sections*	*Frequency of offering*
KOR 470	Language and culture of Korea	3	1	fall or spring
KOR 480	Korean proficiency through film	3	1	fall or spring
KOR 485K	Korean for career professionals	3	1	Fall
KOR 486K	Korean for academic purposes	3	1	Spring
KOR 493	Introduction to traditional Korean literature	3	1	Fall
KOR 494	Introduction to modern Korean literature	3	1	Spring
KOR 496	Korean abroad	variable	1	fall & spring
KOR 499	Directed reading in advanced Korean	variable	2	fall & spring
KOR 613	Korean verse	3	1	as needed
KOR 614	Korean narrative	3	1	as needed
KOR 615	Korea Drama	3	1	as needed
KOR 621	Media Research in Korean	3	1	Fall
KOR 622	Comparative studies of contemporary South and North Korea	3	1	Spring
KOR 623	Interdisciplinary research in Korean	3	1	fall
KOR 624	Analysis of Korean academic discourse	3	1	spring
KOR 631	History and dialects of Korean language	3	1	as needed
KOR 632	Korean phonology and morphology	3	1	as needed
KOR 633	Korean syntax and semantics	3	1	as needed
KOR 634	Korean sociolinguistics	3	1	as needed
KOR 635	Pedagogy of teaching Korean as a second language	3	1	as needed
KOR 636	Korean conversation analysis	3	1	as needed
KOR 640	Literary translation of Korean	3	1	as needed
KOR 645	Research in Korean language acquisition	3	1	as needed
KOR 652	Major authors in modern Korean literature	3	1	as needed
KOR 655	Practicum: Teaching Korean as a second language	3	1	as needed
KOR 664	Topics and issues in modern Korean literature	3	1	as needed
KOR 699	Directed research	variable	1	as needed
KOR 720	Research seminar in Korean literature	3	1	as needed
KOR 730	Research seminar in Korean language	3	2: regular & flagship	fall & spring
EALL 281	Korean literature in translation: traditional	3	1	fall

Course number	*Course title*	*# of credits*	*# of sections*	*Frequency of offering*
EALL 282	Korean literature in translation: modern	3	1	spring
EALL 360	Literary traditions of East Asia	3	1	as needed
EALL 472	East-West cultural encounters	3	1	as needed
EALL 601	Current issues in East Asian languages	3	1	as needed
EALL 602	Introduction to East Asian linguistics	3	1	as needed
EALL 603K	Bibliographical and research methodology	3	1	as needed
EALL 700	Thesis research	variable	1	as needed
EALL 800	Dissertation research	1	1	as needed

5.5. The Center for Korean Studies (CKS)

Established in 1972, the CKS coordinates and develops resources for the study of Korea at the University of Hawaii. The Center seeks to promote interdisciplinary and intercultural approaches to Korean studies by drawing on its faculty members in disciplines as diverse as anthropology, architecture, art, Asian studies, communication, creative writing, economics, ethnomusicology, education, geography, history, language, linguistics, literature, management, political science, sociology, law, and urban and regional planning. (http://www.hawaii.edu/korea/pages/about/mission.html)

The Center was created by the University of Hawaii Board of Regents as the first of its kind in the nation and the first area center at the university. Before 1972, a group of several UH faculty in areas such as Korean history, literature, and political science initiated and developed the idea of establishing the CKS on campus. To my recollection, the main arguments advanced for creating a center for Korean studies at the UH were that at least one U.S. campus of higher education should have a center to study Korea (a) as a historical and cultural bridge between China and Japan and (b) as a politically, ideologically, and physically divided country, that is, as a social science laboratory, and that the University of Hawaii is the most suitable and ideal venue for such a center in view of the facts that the UH was equipped with a concentration of the most Korea specialists among U.S. institutions; Hawaii was the first America soil where Korean immigrants settled and had a large Korean community; Hawaii was a geographical center connecting Korea and the U.S. Mainland; and Hawaii was a multicultural society. The Center, whose aim is to promote Korean studies worldwide as well as within the UH system through instruction, research, publication, support for faculty and students, and community outreach, interacts closely with the Korean language and literature programs in many ways. All the faculty members in

Korean language and literature are regular faculty of the CKS. Student scholarships, faculty research, and conference management are generously supported by the CKS. Many academic, cultural, and community-related events and activities are implemented jointly by CKS and the Korean Section of the Department of East Asian Languages and Literatures.

The CKS started in 1972 with ten Korea-related faculty, including myself. In 40 years, it has evolved to comprise thirty-nine faculty at present, covering many colleges and departments. The first Director was Dae Sook Suh (1972-95), during whose term the CKS building was completed in 1980 with funds contributed by the Korean government, the State of Hawaii, and the Korean-American community in Hawaii. The succeeding directors are Chung H. Lee (Economics, 1995-98), Edward Shultz (History, 1998-04), Ho-min Sohn (Language/Linguistics, 2004-10), Yung-Hee Kim (Literature, 2010-13), and Sang-Hyop Lee (Economics, 2013-16). Up to now, from the Korea Foundation and other sources, the CKS has received about six million dollars in endowed funds for Korea-related activities, including a two-million dollar endowment for faculty recruitment.[11]

6. Prospect and conclusion

At present, the Korean language and linguistics program at UHM is recognized as one of the largest and most well-established and productive academic programs of its kind in the world outside of Korea. As observed thus far, the Korean Program, especially language instruction and linguistics research, has made enormous progress from its long faltering inception. As I have mentioned here and there in the above, the underlying external and internal factors that jointly and in synergy motivated and propelled such a rapid development may be summarized as follows roughly in the order of importance:

External factors:

(a) Korea's rapid economic growth and effect in global economy
(b) Rapid increase in Korean immigrant population (more than two million Koreans in the U.S. at present)
(c) The Korean Wave
(d) Introduction of SAT II Korean
(e) Korean-American community's efforts to promote Korean among heritage children
(f) Korean government's globalization policy and investment to promote

11 I was instrumental in establishing this endowment when I was CKS Director, receiving a one-million dollar grant from the Korea Foundation and raising a significant portion of the required matching funds.

Korean language education and Korean studies overseas (e.g. Korea Foundation and Academy of Korean Studies)

(g) Increase in close interactions between Korea and the U.S. in all areas

(h) Presence of Korean businesses and government agencies in the U.S.

(i) U.S. government's critical language policy

(j) U.S. government's policy to promote foreign languages and area studies

(k) National-level Korean language associations' initiatives and activities

Institutional factors:

(a) UH's strategic, financial, and moral support to promote Korean language and Korean studies

(b) Korean Program faculty's vision, initiative, leadership, and dedication

(c) Institutionalization of foreign language requirement (UHM has long established two years of foreign language study as a graduation requirement for most majors.)

(d) Academic diffusion of Korean studies

All the above factors have favorably interacted in creating the Korean Program as it is today. As long as the above factors continue to sustain synergic interaction, the Korean program will continue to grow and flourish.

Needless to say, there are many areas yet to be improved, such as curriculum innovation, development of innovative instructional methods, improvement of assessment tools, and online distance learning. Indeed, the tasks yet to be performed are endless.

While instruction and research in Korean language and linguistics have made a great leap forward, Korean literature has long suffered from a shortage of degree students. This trend generally applies to other languages as well. Furthermore, cooperation between Korean language and Korean studies is essential, but, unfortunately, this has not been satisfactorily implemented, as not many American students study Korean studies and not many Korean studies courses are offered. Strengthening this link is an important area to be pursued (for a detailed discussion of this issue, see Sohn 2011).

REFERENCES: Chapter 34

Chaika, E. 1982. *Language the Social Mirror.* Rowley, Mass: Newbury House Publishers, Inc.

Ebrey, P.B., A. Walthall, and J.B. Palais. 2006. *East Asia: A Cultural, Social, and Political History.* Boston: Houghton Mifflin Co.

Furman, N., D. Goldberg, and N. Lusin. 2007. Enrollments in languages other than English in

United States institutions of higher education, fall 2006. *Modern Language Association Wb publication* 13: 1-28 (November 2007).

Reischauer, E.O. and J.K. Fairbanks. 1960. *East Asia: The Great Tradition.* Boston: Houghton Mifflin Co.

Sohn, Ho-min. 2009. Han'gugŏ kyoyuk ui sae p'aradaim (A new paradigm of Korean language education). *Kugŏ Kyoyuk Yŏn'gu* 24: 7-36.

Sohn, Ho-min. 2011. Haeoe taehak ui han'gugŏ kyoyuk kwa han'gukhak ui hyŏnan (Issues in overseas college-level korean language education and korean studies). In *Korean Studies Education for Intercultural Communication,* 11-52. Academy of Korean Studies, Korea.

Wardhaugh, R. 2010. *Introduction to Sociolinguistics,* Sixth Edition. West Sussex, UK: Wiley-Blackwell.

INDEX